William Man...
Paul Reid

"MAJESTIC."
—*The Washington Post*

"BREATHTAKING."
—*The Boston Globe*

THE
LAST LION

WINSTON SPENCER CHURCHILL

DEFENDER OF THE REALM, 1940–1965

Praise for *The Last Lion*

"[Reid's] palpable enthusiasm at thinking about Churchill demonstrates once again . . . the grip this iconic figure can still exercise on the imagination. . . . Reid [uses] his journalist's eye to pick up on small details or points of color that illustrate a wider truth."

—RICHARD ALDOUS, *The New York Times Book Review*

"Masterful . . . It was worth the wait. . . . The collaboration completes the Churchill portrait in a seamless manner, combining the detailed research, sharp analysis and sparkling prose that readers of the first two volumes have come to expect."

—*Associated Press*

"Following Manchester's lead . . . [Reid] dutifully includes both the admiring and disparaging remarks of Churchill's colleagues and contemporaries, presenting everyone's take with equanimity."

—*The Wall Street Journal*

"This book is superb. It has tremendous pace, rich detail and immense drama."

—*The Washington Post*

"Reid has produced a third *Last Lion* that is both magisterial and humane. Cue the trumpets."

—*Vanity Fair*

"It's a must-read finale for those who loved Manchester's first two books."

—*USA Today*

"The final volume of Manchester's life of Winston Churchill is majestic and inspiring."

—*People*

"Masterful . . . [and] breathtaking . . . [Reid] finished the race with agility, grace, and skill. . . . This is a book that is brilliant and beautiful, evocative."

—*The Boston Globe*

"Reid has produced a volume about the climax of Churchill's career which ably captures the fullness of the story. . . . Straightforward, well written, and compelling."

—*The Weekly Standard*

"The long-delayed majestic account of Winston Churchill's last twenty-five years is worth the wait. . . . Manchester (and Reid) matches the outstanding quality of biographers such as Robert Caro and Edmund Morris, joining this elite bank of writers who devote their lives to one subject."
—*Publishers Weekly* (starred review)

"Those who want a detailed account of Churchill's two terms as prime minister and leadership during World War II will find this book a literary feast. . . . It's a worthy finale to an exhaustive portrait of one of the last century's true titans."
—*The Washington Times*

"This is surely the best installment of the [series]. . . . Reid has written a winning, full-blooded biography."
—*Newsday*

"Reid has written a thorough and complete analysis of these years, and it is a worthy finale to the first two volumes."
—*The Christian Science Monitor*

"Reid learned well from Manchester, and the finished book is a worthy conclusion to what must be considered one of the most thorough treatments of Churchill so far produced. An essential conclusion to Manchester's magnum opus."
—*Library Journal* (starred review)

"[Reid] keeps the 1,000-plus pages turning. . . . [He] has heeded the words of his subject, and brought the decades-long project begun by his mentor to a dignified conclusion."
—*The Philadelphia Inquirer*

"Magnificently delineated . . . The story of Churchill and Britain in the Second World War . . . is vividly evoked by Manchester and Reid."
—*Winnipeg Free Press*

DEFENDER OF THE REALM
1940–1965

Books by William Manchester

Disturber of the Peace (1951)

The City of Anger (1953)

Shadow of the Monsoon (1956)

Beard the Lion (1958)

A Rockefeller Family Portrait (1959)

The Long Gainer (1961)

Portrait of a President (1962)

The Death of a President (1967)

The Arms of Krupp (1968)

The Glory and the Dream (1974)

Controversy (1976)

American Caesar (1978)

Goodbye, Darkness (1980)

The Last Lion: Visions of Glory (1983)

One Brief Shining Moment (1983)

In Our Time (1985)

The Last Lion: Alone (1988)

A World Lit Only by Fire (1992)

The Last Lion: Defender of the Realm (co-author Paul Reid) *(2012)*

THE LAST LION

Winston Spencer Churchill:
Defender of the Realm,
1940–1965

William Manchester and Paul Reid

BANTAM BOOKS TRADE PAPERBACKS
NEW YORK

2013 Bantam Books Trade Paperback Edition

Published in the United States by Bantam Books,
an imprint of The Random House Publishing Group,
a division of Random House LLC,
a Penguin Random House Company, New York.

BANTAM BOOKS and the HOUSE colophon are registered trademarks of
Random House LLC.

Originally published in hardcover in the United States by Little, Brown
and Company, a division of Hachette Book Group, in 2012, and is
reprinted by arrangement with the publisher.

Library of Congress Cataloging-in-Publication Data (revised for vol. 3)

Manchester, William Raymond.
    The last lion, Winston Spencer Churchill./William Raymond
Manchester and Paul Reid.
    Includes index
    Contents: v.1. Visions of glory, 1874–1932—v.2. Alone, 1932–1940—
v.3. Defender of the realm, 1950–1965.
    I. Churchill, Winston, Sir, 1874–1965. 2. Great Britain—Politics
and government—20th Century. 3. Great Britain—Foreign relations—
20th century. 4. Prime ministers—Great Britain—Biography.
I. Paul Reid. II. Title.
DA566.9.C5M26 1983 941.087'092'4[B] 82-42972
ISBN 978-0-345-54863-4

Printed in the United States of America on acid-free paper

www.bantamdell.com

9 8 7 6 5 4 3

To the memory of

JOHN COLVILLE, C.B., C.V.O.

1915–1987

Harrovian, Civil Servant, Fighter, Pilot, Scholar

(William Manchester, August 1994)

FOR BARBARA

(Paul Reid, August 2012)

In freta dum fluvii current, dum montibus umbrae
Lustrabunt convexa, polus dum sidera pascet;
semper honos nomenque tuum laudesque manebunt.

As long as rivers shall run down to the sea,
or shadows touch the mountain slopes,
or stars graze in the vault of heaven,
so long shall your honor, your name,
your praises, endure.

VIRGIL, *AENEID*, 1:607–9

ARRAY

MAPS

AUTHOR'S NOTE

In 1988, William Manchester began writing *The Last Lion: Defender of the Realm,* the third and final volume of his biography of Winston Churchill. Bill's research was complete. He had assembled his notes in fifty-page bound 8½ × 21-inch paper tablets, which he called his long notes, or "clumps." More than forty such tablets were dedicated to the war years 1940–1945, and a few addressed the postwar years 1946–1965.

His notes consisted of photocopied extracts from myriad sources, including Churchill's speeches, wartime memoirs, letters and telegrams Churchill sent and received, diary entries of contemporaries, official documents, newspaper clippings, and numerous secondary sources. They also included excerpts from transcripts of more than fifty interviews Bill conducted in the early 1980s with Churchill's friends, family, and colleagues.

Between 1988 and 1998, Bill, in increasingly poor health, wrote about one hundred pages of *Defender of the Realm,* a first draft covering the German invasion of France and the Low Countries in May 1940, and the beginning of the Battle of Britain in July 1940. Then, in 1998, he suffered two strokes that left his speech slightly slurred and his left leg partially paralyzed. Although the strokes did not steal his memory or his ability to formulate complex thoughts, Bill could no longer connect those thoughts on paper. He could no longer write.

My first encounter with Bill was on the page, when I read his account of the assassination of President Kennedy, *The Death of a President.* By the time I met Bill in person, I had read all of his nonfiction works. Like so many readers, I thought the first two books of *The Last Lion* were magnificent, and like so many, I eagerly awaited the final volume.

In 1996, I covered a reunion in West Palm Beach of Bill's World War Two Marine buddies for the *Palm Beach Post,* where I worked as a reporter. Bill, ill with pneumonia, could not attend. Two years later, in 1998, I accompanied five of those old Marines to Bill's home in Middletown, Connecticut, for a reunion designed to raise his spirits after his strokes and the death earlier in the year of his wife of fifty years, Judy. The Marines had all achieved success in life—an industrialist, a petroleum engineer, an oceanographer and Magellan biographer, and a Baptist minister with a doctorate in divinity—and they were proud of their service as enlisted men. By the end of the weekend, I felt as if all these Marines were my good friends, including Bill.

Our friendship deepened in the years that followed. I visited Bill often, sometimes in the company of the old Marines, who gathered at Bill's house once a year. Bill and I chatted by phone regularly. We talked history, politics, and, always, baseball, specifically the annual autumn demise of our Boston Red Sox. He asked for, and I sent him, copies of my stories. I felt certain that he would never finish *Defender of the Realm,* but when I suggested that he find someone to complete the book, he would shake his head no. He and his publisher, Little, Brown, regularly received calls and letters—even surprise office visits—from fans around the world asking when the book would be finished. In 2001 Bill told the *New York Times* that he could no longer put words to paper. Eventually, he agreed to consider a collaborator, but none proposed worked out. My surprise, therefore, was total when, late one evening in early October 2003, during one of my visits to Middletown, Bill asked me to finish *Defender of the Realm.* "You write," he said, "I'll edit. My red pencils are sharpened and ready."

He sent me home that weekend with about a dozen of his clumps and several books having to do with the Battle of Britain. My mission was to write sixty pages on the Blitz. Based on their impressions of my sample chapter, Bill, Don Congdon, Bill's agent of fifty years, and Little, Brown decided I should proceed. Our collaboration began.

But it would not last long. By early 2004 Bill was very ill. He died on June 1. By then I had realized that his clumps were not intended for literal transcription, but had served Bill as a narrative catalyst. The notes were arranged neither strictly chronologically nor by topic or character. Bill had inked into the margins numerous shorthand reminders and color-coded references to topics and sources only he could decipher. Some he had explained to me, others he had not. The notes had helped guide Bill toward a form—a portrait of Churchill—that he had already envisioned, much as an architect's rough line drawings can conjure in his mind an image of his finished building. The notes contained enormous amounts of information, but they had no outline and no sense of narrative structure. Bill's notes spoke to him in ways they could not speak to me.

Over the course of several months, I assembled much of the original source material Bill had used, including the full transcripts of the interviews he had excerpted in his notes. To this I added a digital edition of *Winston S. Churchill: His Complete Speeches 1897–1963,* edited by Robert Rhodes James, along with new editions of memoirs and diaries of Churchill's contemporaries. I perused official British government documents that had not been released when Bill was assembling his notes. I reread Bill's earlier biographies and histories for insight into his approach to narrative pace and cadence. Only then could I begin to write the book.

Bill spent many years on the Wesleyan University campus as an adjunct professor of history and writer in residence, but he was not an academic. He was a storyteller who made history accessible by masterful use of the dramatist's tools—plot, setting, and character. He and I often discussed his approach, and agreed that the biographer must get out of the way of his subject, who should be placed squarely within his times and be allowed to speak and act for himself. In the case of the greatest Englishman of the twentieth century, the importance of doing this is obvious.

At the start of the project, I spoke at length with the eminent British historian Sir John Keegan, who offered encouragement and guidance. Churchill's namesake grandson, Winston S. Churchill, gave generously of his time, up to his death in 2010, answering yet more questions on the subject of Sir Winston, as did Churchill's daughter, Lady Soames.

I thank the following friends and colleagues who offered wise counsel as the years went by; many read and commented on the manuscript in its various stages: Sanford Kaye, Jim Case, Rich Cooper, Jane Deering, Tess Van Dyke-Gillespie, Bill Gillespie, David Rising, Jeff Baker, Albin Irzyk (Brigadier General, U.S. Army, ret.), John Newton, Craig Horn, Howard Bursen, Dr. Porter Crow, Virginia Creeden, and Alex and Joan Balas. Thanks also to my former editors at the *Palm Beach Post*—Tom O'Hara, Jan Tuckwood, and Melissa Segrest—whose journalistic standards are in the highest and best tradition of American newspapering. Alan White (British Foreign Office, ret.) offered vital insight into the workings of the British government. Journalist John Murawski examined the manuscript with a reporter's eye. Doctors Audrey Tomlinson, Ron Pies, David Armitage, and Michael First brought their vast clinical expertise to bear on matters of Churchill's mental and physical health. My thanks also go to Maggi LeDuc, a recent graduate of American University, who spent many long hours in a successful search for photographs that captured the spirit of Churchill and his times.

Historian Lynne Olson, author of *Citizens of London,* gave sound advice over the years when asked, and I asked often. Roosevelt scholar Warren Kimball provided invaluable guidance on the Churchill-Roosevelt relationship.

Lee Pollock, executive director of the Churchill Centre, put the resources of that organization at my disposal. Those who seek to learn more about the extraordinary life of Sir Winston Churchill are well advised to begin their search by contacting Lee at www.winstonchurchill.org. Richard Langworth, editor of the Churchill Centre quarterly, *Finest Hour,* combed the manuscript for historical accuracy, as he had done for volume two, *Alone.*

Over the past eight years, Little, Brown publisher Michael Pietsch and editorial director Geoff Shandler have given this project their full support. I thank them and assistant editor Liese Mayer and editorial assistant Brandon Coward, who, with constant good cheer, helped guide the project through its final stages.

I owe my editor, William D. Phillips, an immeasurable debt of gratitude. Six times the manuscript passed between us, and six times Bill wrought improvements. This is his book, too. And after Bill finished his perusals of the work, Pamela Marshall took up her copyediting task, from the first word to the last, twice. It has been a pleasure to work with Bill and Pamela, but foremost, it has been an honor.

I am profoundly grateful to Bob Kopf, Ken Linge, and Jim Miller; Ray Foster, my neighbor from Lynn, North Carolina; my brother, Jim Reid; and my good and true friends Marcello and Diane Fiorentino. Without them, this project could not have come to fruition.

My agent Don Congdon did not live to see the finished manuscript. Don's son and partner, Michael, stepped in and, like so many who had a hand in this project, did so with enthusiasm.

In 2003 Bill Manchester, with one simple declarative sentence, changed my life: "I'd like you to finish the book." Bill died years before he could hold in his hand a complete manuscript of *Defender of the Realm*. But even though he was not here to discuss the project, or to review my pages or help me decipher his cryptic notations, our partnership remained intact. Bill trusted me to tell this story, and for that I thank him.

Five others, who long ago set in motion my role in this story, also did not live to see the completed manuscript: John and Eleanor Reppucci, my childhood neighbors in Winchester, Massachusetts; my sister Kathy; and my parents, Mary and Sam Reid, he a son of South Boston and the United States Naval Academy. They all loved a good tale, and all could spin one. My introduction to Churchill came almost six decades ago. On Saturday mornings I stood next to the stove as my father, attired in his old Annapolis bathrobe and a seaman's cap, flipped pancakes and fried eggs while reciting along to Churchill's wartime speeches, which played on our old RCA Victrola. "Listen to Winston," my father commanded, stabbing the air with the spatula in syncopation with Churchill's words. I listened.

One year my father put the six volumes of Churchill's *The Second World War* under the Christmas tree. Quoting Churchill, he summed up the moral of the story thus: Never give in.

I offer those words to a new generation of readers, including my son, Patrick, who enthusiastically critiqued every permutation of the manuscript, my daughters, Georgia and Mary, and my stepsons, August and Alex. Never Give In.

Paul Reid
August 2012
Tryon, North Carolina

Preamble
The Lion Hunted

On June 21, 1940, the first day of summer, Winston Churchill was the most visible man in England. France accepted Hitler's surrender terms that day and, with virtually all of Europe now under the swastika, with the Soviet Union a Nazi accomplice, and the United States isolationist, Britain and the Dominions confronted the Third Reich alone. Prime minister for only six weeks, Churchill was defending more than his island home. As first minister of the Crown he was also the central figure of the British Empire, then extant, comprising almost one-quarter of Earth's landmass and almost a quarter of its population. The gravity of his role was obvious. Yet though all saw him, all did not see him alike. He was a multifarious individual, including within one man a whole troupe of characters, some of them subversive of one another and none feigned.

At No. 10 Downing Street everyone referred to the newly appointed sixty-five-year-old P.M. as "the Old Man." In many ways he was an alarming master. He worked outrageous hours. He was self-centered and could be shockingly inconsiderate. Because of his lisp, and because he growled so often, his speech was often hard to follow, and aides had to learn what he meant when he referred to "that moon-faced man in the Foreign Office" or "Lord Left-leg-limps." Although he never actually overruled his military advisers, he refused to delegate any of the prime minister's powers to his staff. He wanted to make all decisions because, Sir Ian Jacob recalled, "he was determined to be Number One." Jacob served as military assistant secretary to the War Cabinet during the war, and came to know Churchill's obstinacy well.[1]

Not only did Churchill insist on oversight of strategic matters, he mired himself in the details as well. Because the noise of modern warfare was appalling, he decided soldiers would be issued earplugs. It occurred to him that World War One weapons, taken as trophies, could be made fit for action. A survey was launched. And what would be done, he demanded to know, to safeguard the animals at the zoo if German bombs blew open the cages? Some of his musings on the finer points of warfare were prescient. He asked his liaison to the Chiefs of Staff, Major General Hastings ("Pug") Ismay, to expedite the development of "some projectile which can be fired from a rifle at a tank like a rifle grenade, or from an anti-Tank [sic] rifle, like a trench-mortar bomb."

Yet woe unto the underling who brought to Churchill's attention details he considered petty. When King George's minister in Reykjavík suggested that Icelandic civilians be evacuated before the expected German invasion of that country, Churchill shot back, "Surely this is great nonsense." The dangers faced by Icelanders were "trifling" and "anyhow they have a large island and plenty of places to run into." He thoroughly enjoyed his meanderings in the thickets of details. One day that spring, while fiddling with an operational model of a mine intended to be deployed in the Rhine basin, he turned to an aide and said, "This is one of those rare and happy occasions when respectable people like you and me can enjoy pleasures normally reserved to the Irish Republican Army."[2]

This small pleasantry exchanged with a subordinate was not a rare behavior, yet neither was it a regular occurrence. Underlings were more likely to experience his wrath. His pale-blue eyes telegraphed his moods, and when his gaze—"as warm as summer sunshine" when he was pleased—turned ice-cold, his staff knew an eruption was forthcoming. Certainly his roar was awesome—he terrorized his admirals, his generals, and, daily, his staff. "God's teeth, girl, can't you even do it right the second time, I said ripe, ripe, ripe—P P P," he bellowed to Elizabeth Layton, a new typist at No. 10 who had the misfortune to interpret a mumbled "ripe" as "right." Yet, as usual after his outbursts, Churchill uttered his version of an apology—he "forgave" Layton—and "was very amiable for the rest of the day." Actually, his nature was informed by humane sympathy for all troubled men, including those Englishmen (he always preferred English and Englishmen to British and Britons) he held responsible for England's present plight. Learning that a mob had stoned Stanley Baldwin's car, he immediately invited the former prime minister to No. 10 for a two-hour lunch (at a time when every minute was precious to him), and when he was told that Neville Chamberlain was dying of cancer—Chamberlain would not survive 1940—Churchill instructed his staff to telephone all good news to the disgraced former prime minister.[3]

Baldwin later told Harold Nicolson* of his lunch with Churchill, adding that he left Downing Street "a happy man" while feeling "a patriotic joy that my country at such a time should have found such a leader." Of Churchill, Baldwin offered, "The furnace of war had smelted out all of the base metals from him." Not all. In private he relished skewering his fallen enemies. He and his wife, Clementine, once recounted for luncheon guests the rumor emanating from Baldwin's household that Baldwin was a

---

* Harold Nicolson (1886–1968), biographer, historian, diarist, member of Parliament from 1935 to 1945. From May 1940 to June 1941 he served under Duff Cooper as parliamentary secretary in the Ministry of Information. He later moved to the BBC. He was married to the writer Vita Sackville-West. Their sons, Nigel and Ben, served in the British armed forces during the war.

"haunted man." The former P.M. was so disrespected by his family and household staff, so the story went, that when he complained that the wireless was playing too loud, somebody turned it up even *louder*. And when the Baldwin family cupboard went bare, it was Baldwin who was dispatched by his relatives to the grocer to restock the larder. When asked by friends of Baldwin to submit a testimonial for the former prime minister's eightieth birthday tribute, Churchill, through an intermediary (and thinking his remark private), gave them: "I wish Stanley Baldwin no ill, but it would have been much better if he had never lived." And in his most famous cut of Baldwin, he said, "Occasionally he stumbled over the truth, but hastily picked himself up and hurried on as if nothing had happened." As for Chamberlain, Churchill told his new private secretary and a junior member of his staff, Jock Colville, that the former prime minister was "the narrowest, the most ignorant, most ungenerous of men." On one occasion, Churchill managed to denigrate both Chamberlain and Baldwin in one breath, when he offered to his doctor, "Baldwin thought Europe was a bore, and Chamberlain thought it was greater Birmingham." His pettiness was as unfeigned as his generosity, his sentimentality, and his love of England.[4]

Members of the Private Office (private secretaries, orderlies, typists) were expected to be obedient and uncritical; in effect the prime minister said, "Thou shalt have no other god but me." His temper was fearful. When he lost it, he would turn on whoever happened to be nearby, and, like other men of his class and generation, he never apologized or explained, though later he would go out of his way to mollify the injured party by, say, complimenting him on his handwriting, or by murmuring, "You know, I may seem to be very fierce, but I am fierce with only one man, Hitler." On June 27, the week of the French surrender, Clementine wrote him the lone truly personal letter that passed between them that year. She directed his attention to a potentially disastrous state of affairs in immediate need of prime ministerial intervention: his behavior toward his staff. "There is a danger," she wrote, "of your being generally disliked by your colleagues and subordinates because of your rough sarcastic & overbearing manner." No doubt it was the strain, she wrote. Yet, she too had noted deterioration in his manner: "You are not as kind as you used to be." She advised him that he would not get the best results from irascibility and rudeness, which would "only breed either dislike or a slave mentality." She signed the missive, "Please forgive your loving and watchful Clemmie." Beneath her signature she sketched a cat (Winston had called her "Kat" for almost three decades). There is no record of Churchill's response. None would have been necessary. That the letter survived, their daughter Mary later wrote, indicates a temperate reaction.[5]

There would be no long absences from each other in 1940, as there had been in all the previous years of their marriage, when work or war or holidays took one or the other abroad. Proximity, usually in the dank confines of the subterranean No. 10 Annexe, would be the byword in coming months, during which time his ferocity toward his staff diminished not a whit.

All who were with him then agree that the Old Man had more important matters on his mind than the sensitive feelings of subordinates. In any event, in time they came to adore him. Jock Colville later recalled, "Churchill had a natural sympathy for simple people, because he himself took a simple view of what was required; and he hated casuistry. That was no doubt why the man-in-the-street loved him and the intellectuals did not." Churchill, for his part, considered those on the left who anointed themselves the arbiters of right and wrong to be arrogant, "a fault," Colville recalled, Churchill "detested in others, particularly in its intellectual form." For that reason, Churchill "had dislike and contempt, of a kind which transcended politics, of the intellectual wing of the Labour party," which in turn despised Churchill. In 1940 the intellectualism of the left was inimical to Churchill and to Britain's cause, which was simplicity itself: defeat Hitler.[6]

Churchill cared little for obtuse political or social theories; he was a man of action: state the problem, find a solution, and solve the problem. For a man of action, however, he was exceptionally thoughtful and well read. When serving as a young subaltern in India, he amassed a private library that included Aristotle's *Ethics* and *Politics,* Plato's *Republic,* Schopenhauer on pessimism, Malthus on population, and Darwin's *Origin of Species.* Reading, for Churchill, was a form of action. After a lifetime of reading—from the sea-adventuring Hornblower novels to the complete Shakespeare and Macaulay—he possessed the acumen to reduce complex intellectual systems and constructs and theories to their most basic essences. He once brought a wartime dinner conversation on socialism to an abrupt end by recommending that those present read Maurice Maeterlinck's entomological study, *The Life of the White Ant.* "Socialism," Churchill declared, "would make our society comparable to that of the white ant." Case closed. Almost a decade later, when the Labour Party, then in power, nationalized British industries one by one, and when paper, meat, gasoline, and even wood for furniture were still rationed, Churchill commented: "The Socialist dream is no longer Utopia but Queuetopia."[7]

Late in June, Eric Seal, his senior private secretary, remarked upon how much Churchill had "changed since becoming P.M.," how he had "sobered down, become less violent, less wild, less impetuous." That was untrue. It was Seal's view of him that had altered. Churchill himself had not changed at all. His character had been fully formed at the turn of the century, as an officer in Victoria's imperial army, as a war correspondent, and as a young MP under the Old Queen. And he knew it. Listening to recordings of *The Mikado* one evening, he said they brought back his youth and the Victorian era, "eighty years which will rank in our island history with the Age of the Antonines." Upper-class Englishmen who had come of age then, when the empire stood at flood tide, possessed a certitude, an indomitable faith in England, confidence in their own judgment, and an indubitable conviction that they understood the world and were its masters.[8]

In many ways Churchill remained a nineteenth-century man, and by no means a common man. He fit the mold of what Henry James called in *English Hours* "persons for whom the private machinery of ease has been made to work with extraordinary smoothness." His valet warmed his brandy snifter over a neatly trimmed candle; his typists and secretaries kept more candles at the ready in order to light his cigars (Cuban *Romeo y Julieta* were his favorites). He had never ridden a bus. The only time he availed himself of the London Underground was during the general strike in 1926. Clementine dropped him off at South Kensington but Winston did not know how to navigate the system, with the result that "he went round and round not knowing where to get off, and eventually had to be rescued." He never carried cash, except to casinos and the occasional derby, where an aide would take care of the business of procuring chips or placing bets on worthy steeds.[9]

Clementine, ten years Winston's junior and far more versed in domestic economics, kept the household books; she and the staff did the purchasing. Churchill did not (directly) "bestow his custom" upon local merchants. This man who embodied the English spirit never attended a jumble sale or, readying himself for the day's labors, tucked a wrapped pasty into the pocket of his cardigan, or queued in a bakery for a bag of warm, fresh scones. In the years before he became prime minister, even his train tickets were bought for him. As befitted a man of his class and stature, he never prepared a meal in his life. Once, having announced his desire to spend a weekend at his country home, Chartwell, rather than in London, Clementine reminded him that the kitchen staff there was not in residence. "I shall cook for myself," Winston replied. "I can boil an egg. I've seen it done." When he was ready to leave on a trip, he would ask, not whether the chauffeur was behind the wheel but, "Is the coachman on his box?" His bodyguard, Scotland Yard detective inspector Walter Thompson, recalled that on the rare occasions when Churchill drove his own automobile, "he was forever just missing things, or not quite missing them and denting cars, his own and others. People shouldn't be in his way, was his theory."[10]

To drive with Churchill, recalled Thompson, "was to take your life into your hands." On one journey Churchill, then Chancellor of the Exchequer, turned into a narrow lane in Croydon only to encounter a construction project in the road and a long line of backed-up automobiles. A policeman signaled Churchill to stop, but Churchill ignored the constable and instead drove up onto the sidewalk in order to bypass the scene. Many were the occasions when Thompson, to avert disaster, had to reach over and yank the wheel from Churchill's hands. When Churchill actually collided with some hapless Londoner's automobile, he did not believe that any damage could possibly be of his doing, a mind-set he also applied to his frequent collisions with subordinates, parliamentary colleagues, and foreign poten-tates. Robert Boothby, one of Churchill's most loyal supporters during the Wilderness Years when he was out of office and without influence, recalled that Churchill simply did not much care for what other people thought, and cared not at all about how they might *feel*. "It was this curious absence of interest or affection that may have helped make him a great leader." Churchill "was often callous," Boothby recalled, but then, "he had a war to fight" and little time for social niceties.[11]

Churchill refused to accept changes in geographical names; Istanbul remained Constantinople ("though for stupid people Istanbul may be writ-ten in brackets after it"). Ankara remained Angora (he told the Foreign Office he would refuse to call Angora cats by any other name). Peking remained Peiping, Sebastopol, Sevastopol, and Iran, Persia. Likewise, he preferred traditional military terms to the modern—"cannon" for artil-lery, "muskets" for rifles, and "frigates" for destroyers. When he drafted a cable to Franklin Roosevelt requesting a gift or loan of fifty old frigates, Jock Colville suggested he substitute "destroyers," since the president might not know what the prime minister was referring to. It was in youth and early manhood, especially in the company of the officers of the 4th Hussars, resplendent in their blue and gold, impeccable in manners at the table, that he had acquired his lifelong love of tradition, ceremony, color, gaiety, pageantry, and formality. Protocol was important to him. He told his cabinet: "Gentlemen, we are engaged in a very serious business. We must conduct it in a serious way." In correspondence he expected them to address him as "Dear Prime Minister," and his replies opened "Dear For-eign Secretary," "Dear Chancellor of the Exchequer," "Dear Minister of Aircraft Production," etc. Letters for his signature were not to end with "sincerely" unless he determined that he was, indeed, sincere.[12]

The romantic glow of Victorian militarism, when casualties were few and victories enormous, accounted for his ambivalent view of warfare. He said, "War, which was cruel and glorious, has become cruel and squalid."

But the glory was still there for him. No other British prime minister, not even Wellington, had donned a uniform while in office. Churchill wore the light blue livery of an (honorary) RAF commodore and regretted that British soldiers no longer wore red coats.[13]

Afterward everyone who had been around him in 1940 remembered the Old Man's astonishing, unflagging energy. He was overweight and fifteen years older than Hitler; he never exercised, yet "he was working," Kathleen Hill, one of Churchill's typists, recalled, "all the time, every waking moment." His old friend from the First World War, Edward Spears, who had not seen him in many years before that spring, felt "an astonishment such as I had never felt before at his strength and vitality. I had known he possessed these qualities in lavish measure, but now he exuded power and confidence, radiating them as if he were their very fountain-head." Young Jock Colville marveled at "Winston's ceaseless industry," and wrote that it was "refreshing to work with somebody who refuses to be depressed even by the most formidable danger that has ever threatened this country...he seems to be the man for the occasion. His spirit is indomitable and even if France and England should be lost, I feel he would carry on the crusade himself with a band of privateers."[14]

To the British public he had become the ultimate Englishman, an embodiment of the bulldog breed, with the pugnacious set of his jaw, the challenging tilt of his cigar, his stovepipe hat, his pronouncement that "foreign names were made for Englishmen, not Englishmen for foreign names" (he always sounded the final "s" in Calais), and his fondness for red meat. In a letter to his Minister of Food he wrote, "Almost all the food faddists I have ever known, nut eaters and the like, have died young after a long period of senile decay. The British soldier is far more likely to be right than the scientists. All he cares about is beef.... The way to lose the war is to try to force the British public into a diet of milk, oatmeal, potatoes, etc., washed down, on gala occasions, with a little lime juice."[15]

He himself had always ignored dietary rules and rarely paid a penalty for it, and he drank whatever he wanted, usually alcohol, whenever he wanted it, which was often. Harry Hopkins (Franklin Roosevelt's most trusted adviser and go-to man) entered Churchill's bedroom one morning to find the prime minister in bed, wrapped in his pink robe, "and having of all things a bottle of wine for breakfast." When Hopkins commented on his breakfast beverage, Churchill replied that he despised canned milk, but had no "deep rooted prejudice about wine, and that he had resolved the conflict in favor of the latter." Furthermore, the Old Man told Hopkins, he ignored the advice of doctors because they were usually wrong, that he had lived almost seven decades and was in perfect health, and that "he had no intention of giving up alcoholic drink, mild or strong, now or later."[16]

His normal wartime regimen included a glass of white wine at breakfast (taken as a substitute for tea during the war, when only canned milk was available). Then, a weak scotch and soda, refreshed with soda throughout the morning. At lunch, perhaps a port, always Pol Roger champagne, a brandy or two (likely Hine, and bottled in the previous century), sometimes a beer. After his nap and before dinner he'd nurse another whisky* (Johnnie Walker Red Label was his favorite brand). At dinner, more champagne during the meal, followed often by "several doses of brandy" in the latter stages. He loved his meals as much as the libations that accompanied them. As recalled by his grandson, Winston S. Churchill, his favorite dinner began with *madrilène* (chilled, almost jellied consommé), followed by *goujons* (small filets of North Sea sole), then roast beef, thin-sliced, with Yorkshire pudding and roasted potatoes, followed by his favorite sweet, *bombe glacée* (puffs of ice cream cocooned within ice cream). Before retiring for the evening, his valet (Frank Sawyers, during the war) would pour another port or two, perhaps a final weak whisky while Churchill worked in his study. Another such drinker would recoil from food, but Churchill's appetite was unaffected, and he rarely lost possession of his remarkable faculties.[17]

Clearly he was blessed with a remarkable constitution, one which disposed of alcohol with exceptional efficiency. His detractors and enemies either implied he was a drunk or, in the case of Hitler and Goebbels, denounced him outright as a "twaddler and a drunkard." Yet Robert E. Sherwood, Franklin Roosevelt's speechwriter and biographer, wrote that although Churchill's "consumption of alcohol...continued at quite regular intervals through most of his waking hours," it did so "without visible effect on his health or mental processes. Anyone who suggested he became befuddled with drink obviously never had to become involved in an argument with him on some factual problem late at night...." Churchill's drinking habits, Sherwood wrote, were "unique" and his capacity "Olympian."[18]

Despite his prolonged, consistent, and prodigious consumption of alcohol, Churchill was not a drunk. But neither was he a moderate social drinker, as some of the memoirs and protestations of his close friends and private secretaries maintain. His former staff spin a consistent tale, that Churchill nursed a lone weak whisky and soda all day, replenished and diluted by splashes of soda, which is true but overlooks the daylong augmentation with other spirits. On occasion he would go too far, such as described in Jock Colville's account of taking the Old Man up to bed at around 3:00 A.M. after a brandy-fueled evening. Both Colville and Churchill thought it hilarious when Churchill, attempting to settle into an

---

* In Britain, Scotch whisky; in the U.S., rye whiskey.

armchair in order to remove his shoes, missed the chair entirely and fell onto the floor in a jumble of legs and arms. "A regular Charlie Chaplin," Churchill offered as he struggled to regain his footing. Later in the war, Field Marshal Sir Alan Brooke, Chief of the Imperial General Staff, was summoned by Churchill in the middle of the day. Brooke, who often noted Churchill's prodigious intake of alcohol, that night told his diary, "I found him very much worse for wear for evidently having consumed several glasses of brandy at lunch." Such slides into outright drunkenness were exceedingly rare for Churchill, but they occurred.[19]

He went nowhere without his supply of whisky close at hand, kept at the ready by his bodyguard or his valet. When he visited the United States during Prohibition, he secreted his whisky (and his Webley service revolver) past U.S. Customs, making him a violator of the Volstead Act, indeed, given his thirst, a habitual violator. When he was struck and severely injured by a car in New York City, he finagled a prescription for alcohol from his attending physician, Otto C. Pickardt. The injury, Pickardt wrote, "necessitates the use of alcoholic spirits, especially at meal times." The quantity was "indefinite" but at a minimum was to be about eight fluid ounces. The British essayist C. P. Snow encapsulated the paradox of Churchill's drinking when he remarked, "Churchill cannot be an alcoholic because no alcoholic could drink that much." It could of course be argued that had he exemplified the ideal of moderation—more exercise, less drink, less reckless behavior, fewer cigars—he might well have lived a full and rich life for many years beyond the ninety he was granted.[20]

Churchill once summed up his relationship with drink thus: "I have taken more out of alcohol than alcohol has taken out of me."[21]

He kept hours that would stagger a young man. Late each evening, at midnight or shortly thereafter, a courier arrived in Downing Street with the first editions of the morning newspapers, eight or nine in all. The Old Man skimmed them before retiring, and sometimes, Kathleen Hill later recalled, he would telephone the *Daily Mail* to inquire about new developments in a running story. On June 18 Colville noted: "Winston was furious because the morning papers, which he likes to see before going to bed, had not arrived. In his emotion he upset his whisky and soda over all his papers."[22]

The prime minister's day began at eight o'clock in the morning, when he woke after five or six hours' sleep and rang a bell summoning his usual breakfast: an egg, bacon or ham or chipped beef (when meat was available), sometimes a piece of sole, all washed down by his glass of white wine, or a pot of tea, a black Indian blend. Then a typewriter arrived, accompanied by a stenographer—usually Mrs. Hill or Miss Watson—to whom he would dictate a stream of memos as she rapidly hammered them out and he worked his way through a large black dispatch box. The typewriters were advertised as "silent." They were not. The Great Man resented every click of the keys, and made his displeasure known to the typists. He hated any noise (including ticking clocks, which he banned from his room) that intruded upon his equilibrium, and his business with the box.[23]

The box, which he had organized, was the absolute center of Britain's war against the Third Reich. Inside were numbered folders containing papers approximately 16" x 13." The first one, the "top of the box," as it was called, dealt with matters considered "really urgent" by his secretaries, according to one of them, John Peck, "not only by objective standards of importance, deadlines, and so on, but in part subjectively by the degree of the Prime Minister's personal interest at the time. So we had to see and understand what was in his mind, and he relied on us to do this." Below the top were folders containing military and foreign office telegrams, reports from the Chiefs of Staff (after screening by Churchill's military liaison Pug Ismay), answers to questions he had raised concerning every aspect of British life—food supplies, crop yields, railroad capacity, coal production. Nothing escaped his attention.[24]

Churchill's private secretaries, John Peck, Eric Seal, John Colville, and John Martin, carried keys to this box. There was another, buff-colored box. Only Churchill had the key to that one. Inside were German military orders—at first from the Luftwaffe, later from the Wehrmacht and the SS, and much later from Admiral Dönitz's U-boats—all decoded and translated for him. In the first days of the war, Polish intelligence officers had captured a German electromagnetic cipher machine; Polish mathematicians subsequently examined the machine and smuggled a replica to the British. The British cryptographers, stationed at Bletchley Park, a Victorian redbrick, white-trimmed, and copper-roofed complex north of London, called the machine "Enigma." Each day the enemy reset the code and each day the men at Bletchley tried to break it, often without complete success. But the Bletchley crowd decrypted enough messages often enough to give Churchill an over-the-shoulder look at German plans (except U-boat plans, for which a slightly different and more complex encoding machine was used). The Bletchley wizards tended to be young and bearded, with long hair, dirty fingernails, and disheveled clothing. When the prime minister first saw them, he remarked to their chief, "Menzies, when I told you to leave no stone unturned, I didn't mean you to take me quite so literally."[25]

At the outset, he told the War Cabinet secretary that "all directions emanating from me are made in writing, or should be immediately afterwards confirmed in writing." Any instruction not in writing was invalid. The edict seems petty at first glance, but it precluded any subordinate from mucking up the works by misinterpreting and passing on down the line a prime ministerial command. The sheer volume of paperwork confirmed the wisdom of Churchill's edict that nothing submitted to him, not even a technical account of changes in the manufacture of tanks, could be longer than a single sheet of paper. During a meeting at Admiralty House, he lifted one that wasn't, and said: "This report, by its very length, defends itself against scrutiny." But Churchill, in turn, contributed to the lengthening paper trail with his river of memos marked "Action This Day" and "Report in 3 Days." Many began, "Pray tell me...," or "Pray explain...," which earned his memos the moniker "Winston's prayers."[26]

When reading and signing his missives at his desk, he often wore special sleeves over the cuffs of his jacket in order to protect them from any graphite or ink that might conspire to besmirch his outerwear. The sleeves, together with the occasional green eyeshade, lent to him the air of a plump typesetter. A perusal of the objects on his desk and side table, however—paperweights fashioned from gold medals, crystal inkstands with sterling lids, numerous bottles of pills and powders, and cut-crystal decanters of whisky—identified the owner as a Victorian gentleman of no small means.[27]

There were snarls, and he was responsible for some of them. Churchill's many gifts did not include the administrative. He had little understanding of organization. When a major issue arose, he gave it his full attention, ignoring his other responsibilities, which, because he had taken personal charge of everything affecting the strategic direction of the war, were many. He procrastinated. In his autobiography, *My Early Life,* he wrote: "I do think unpunctuality is a vile habit, and all my life I have tried to break myself of it." He never succeeded. He was always late for trains, although as P.M. he could demand that the trains wait for him. "Winston is a sporting man," Clementine once told his bodyguard. "He likes to give the train a chance to get away." In crises, he fell hopelessly behind on the box. He avoided dull topics, and boring papers lay unread weekend after weekend, until, gritting his teeth, he waded through them. He would make plans, Jock Colville recalled, but was "inclined to forget to tell any of us and then to forget himself." He once called his military chiefs to No. 10 for a 4:00 P.M. meeting. They arrived at the appointed hour; Churchill did not. Aides were sent off to locate the prime minister. They found him "enjoying a whisky and soda in the smoking room at the House."[28]

Some of his problems emanated from men he himself had selected. His staff believed that he was a poor judge of character and that he sometimes insisted upon unsuitable appointments. Men who had fought valiantly won his uncritical admiration. He wanted to give high office to Admiral Sir Roger Keyes of Zeebrugge, a hero of the First World War, though the admiral's mental powers were clearly failing. Orde Wingate, who would win fame as a daring commander of Burmese guerrillas, also caught his eye, though Wingate, who Churchill's doctor, Charles Wilson (made Lord Moran in 1943), thought was quite possibly insane, proved hopeless when given other responsibilities. Of course, those who had stood with Churchill against Munich always found favor with him. In his eyes Anthony Eden, who had quit the Chamberlain government in protest, could do no wrong. That was not a unanimous feeling; P. J. Grigg, permanent under secretary at the War Office, said of Eden, "The man is complete junk."[29]

Only up to a point did Churchill accept Ben Franklin's maxim that *well done is better than well said*. He liked things well done *and* well said. Perhaps because Churchill himself was so articulate, he sometimes misjudged those who were not. The Middle East commander Lieutenant General Sir Archibald Wavell, though a published poet and fluent in Russian, was shy and unforthcoming—attributes that to Churchill implied Wavell was almost dumb—and he remained tongue-tied when the P.M. tried to elicit his views about the war. His fellow generals thought Wavell a magnificent commander. Thus, the prime minister withdrew his objections to him with great reluctance and later wished he hadn't. He never appreciated the gifts of Air Chief Marshal Sir Hugh Dowding, the greatest RAF hero of the war, because of Dowding's reticence. Ironically, the Old Man's extraordinary fluency in discussion was sometimes a handicap. He could out-argue anyone, even when he was wrong. All who were close to him remember what Sir Ian Jacob (then a colonel, later promoted to lieutenant general)calls his "most devastating method of argument." Jacob recalled how he would "debate, browbeat, badger, and cajole those who were opposed to him, or whose work was under discussion." Churchill did not thrust and parry in such duels; he knew only how to thrust. Only later did it become clear that those who vehemently disagreed with him, and stated their case clearly, were those who won his respect. They survived to fight another day, which given Churchill's temperament was likely the next day. He was hard on those he called on the carpet, but he was harder on himself. "Every night," he told Colville, "I try myself by court martial to see if I have done anything effective during the day. I don't mean just pawing the ground—anyone can go through the motions—but something really effective."[30]

"Idleness was a concept unknown to him," recalled his daughter Mary. Idleness was the handmaiden to boredom, and boredom was an enemy to be vanquished. When Churchill found himself bored, recalled Scotland Yard's Inspector Thompson, he became "a kicker of waste baskets, with an unbelievably ungoverned bundle of bad temper." At such times, Thompson wrote, it is best to stay away from him "and this his family seeks to do." The Old Man's foul mood persisted until—the sooner the better for all concerned—he distanced himself from the agent of boredom. Such was the case one evening later in the war when Churchill, Colville, and several American guests viewed *Citizen Kane*. Colville termed it "a deplorable American film.... The P.M. was so bored that he walked out before the end." He did so again during a White House viewing of *Oliver Twist,* leaving the president and Mrs. Roosevelt sitting alone. Boredom, for the Old Man, was an assault on his equilibrium, inflicted in these cases by movies that failed to engage him but usually by a droning bureaucrat or a dinner guest in whom he had scant interest. He would at first put on an air of civility in such circumstances, his doctor recalled. "Then, as if exhausted by his act of civility, he would make no further attempt at conversation, sitting all hunched up and scowling at his plate." Finally, he would *har-rumph* and walk off. Churchill "found it difficult to put on an act of affability even when circumstances positively demanded it," Colville wrote. "He drew a conscious distinction between those with whom it was agreeable to have dinner and those who...were part of the scene."[31]

When boredom struck, he could be depended upon to make a "ruthless break" in pursuit of a more enjoyable source of entertainment. The balm might take the form of dictating a letter, singing off-key renditions of Gilbert and Sullivan, perhaps wielding his trowel to lay bricks in the gardens at Chartwell. (Chartwell was soon closed for the duration of the war, the furniture draped in sheets. Most of the staff of gardeners, kitchen maids, the chauffeur, and housemaids were furloughed. Only a caretaker remained.) He always kept his quiver full of possible activities: read a novel, feed his goldfish, address his black swans, parse the newspapers, declaim on England's glorious past. Painting had long afforded Churchill the happy combination of quietude and a focus for his restless mental energy, but during the war, he would unpack his easel, brushes, and oils only once: at Marrakech after the Casablanca Conference. Gambling had always been another option, but the war had put an end to those pleasures, at least in casinos. He soon was gambling with his armies, tanks, and ships. Whether aboard a train, tucked under his bedclothes with his newspapers strewn about, or presiding at the dinner table, he was "absolutely incapable" of doing nothing, recalled his literary assistant Sir William Deakin: "He could switch off in a marvelously tidy way."

Once years before, recalled Inspector Thompson, during a train journey in North Africa, Churchill (then a cabinet member) decided he wanted a bath. He ordered the train stopped. Then he ordered a tub he had spotted in the baggage car removed and set out in the sands. It was filled to brimming with hot water siphoned from the locomotive's boiler. And there, as the train let off steam, Churchill "bathed with half of Africa agape." It fell to Thompson to shadow Churchill when he made his ruthless breaks. "He will move at a moment's notice. He will move without notice. He is an animal. In war he is particularly feral."[32]

In relief of boredom, almost any action—short of the wicked—would do, with one prerequisite: it had to possess value, and Churchill was the arbiter of the value. There simply was none to be had by sitting through *Citizen Kane* or lingering in reception lines where strangers grabbed for his hand as if they owned it. No value accrued from entertaining humorless dinner guests. In the end, when boredom struck, his most reliable source of relief—the only source of relief he never tired of—was himself. He once told a friend that his idea of a delightful evening was to enjoy fine food in the company of friends, to then discuss the fine food, and then to move on to a good discussion "with myself as chief conversationalist." What could be more stimulating than to listen to the sound of his own voice while declaiming on some topic of abiding interest, such as the Boer War or, in 1940, the need to kill Huns?[33]

He was his own favorite audience. He regularly quoted at great length from Macaulay's *Lays of Ancient Rome,* and Walter Scott's "Marmion," feats of memory Colville found to be "remarkable" yet sometimes "rather boring." Boring for Colville perhaps, but not for Churchill. His old friend Violet Bonham Carter recalled that if a long recitation of Macaulay's verse did not suffice to keep his gears meshed, he would revert to another favorite subject: himself. Lord Moran wrote, "Winston is so taken up with his own ideas he is not interested in what other people think." That was partially true; he was more interested in what other people *did*. Herbert Samuel, Lloyd George's successor as head of the old Liberal Party, believed Churchill was not interested in reasoned arguments, but rather, asked, "Will it work in practice?" One of Moran's observations, however, doesn't pass muster: "He [Churchill] must lose a chunk of his life this way, and must often be lonely, cut off from people." In fact, Churchill found real joy in the company of his friends and family. He loved being with small children; "wollygogs" he called them, and wollygogs were always granted immunity from his growls and snarls. He surrounded himself with people who cared for him, people who hung on his every word. And why should they not; he was Winston Churchill. If he chose not to take an interest in someone, that person remained invisible. Years later, Frank Sinatra, by then the most famous crooner on the planet, rushed up to Churchill, grabbed his hand, and exclaimed, "I've wanted to do that for twenty years." Churchill, not at all happy with being touched by a stranger, turned to a private secretary and demanded, "Who the hell was that?"[34]

*   *   *

He once complained to Lord Moran of a loss of feeling in his shoulder, apparently caused by a pinched nerve. Should he be concerned about this? Churchill asked. "Sensation doesn't matter," replied the doctor. "No," Churchill shot back, "life is sensation; sensation is life." In this need for stimulation he was one with fellow wit and fellow Tory Dr. Samuel Johnson, who considered *action* the necessary prerequisite for a well-lived life. Churchill needed to complete the circuit between the goings-on in his mind and the external world. Once he generated an idea, he felt compelled to actualize it. When he pledged that RAF bombs would consume Nazi Germany, he did so not simply to hear himself speak — that was a delightful collateral benefit — but because he intended to deliver on his promise. "The only guide to a man is his conscience," he once told the Commons, "the only shield to his memory is the rectitude and sincerity of his actions."[35]

Descartes believed the wellspring of human essence could be expressed thus: *Cogito, ergo sum.* But Churchill was not a man of philosophical bent, and, like most Englishmen, he held continental rationalism in low regard. Empiricism — Locke and Hume — was the English way. Churchill saw things more along the lines of *I act, therefore I am.* Lord Samuel once offered to Lord Moran that Churchill "has never ever taken any interest in speculative thought, in philosophy and religion." That was only partially true. He loved to engage in scientific and technological speculation, intellectual realms where the imagination could soar and where ideas were tested, results obtained, and improvements made in the lives of people. In 1932 he published *Thoughts and Adventures,* a collection of essays in which he predicted the atomic bomb and atomic-powered electrification (and the risks to humanity); bioengineering of crops and animals (and perhaps people); and television (which, when it became a reality, he detested). "Projects undreamed-of by past generations will absorb our immediate descendants," he wrote, "comforts, activities, amenities, pleasures will crowd upon them, but their hearts will ache, and their lives will be barren, if they have not a vision above material things."[36]

On the day France fell, Churchill summoned Dr. R. V. Jones, just twenty-eight and a junior scientist working in RAF Intelligence, to No. 10 to argue his hypothesis (heretical to more senior scientists) that the Germans were using radio beams to target Britain. The raids, infrequent and usually directed at northern ports, had begun the previous October. Churchill expected them to increase in frequency and deadliness now that Hitler had control of the airfields of the Low Countries and France. Backed by Churchill, Jones in the coming months figured out how to jam the German beams and delivered one of the most important victories of the war. Jones later wrote of Churchill: "He understood the essence of supreme decisions: yea or nay, right or left, advance or retreat....He knew the strengths and weaknesses of experts....He knew how easy it is for the man at the summit to receive too rosy a picture from his Intelligence advisors....Alone among politicians he valued science and technology at something approaching their true worth, at least in the military application."[37]

Churchill's embrace of the new did not extend to the art and science of governing. The Oxford philosopher and Latvian Jewish émigré Sir Isaiah Berlin later proposed in his essay *Churchill and Roosevelt* that Churchill remained politically a European man of the nineteenth century, despite his embrace of modern technologies and his belief in their promise, despite his insatiable curiosity and his appetite for new knowledge. Britain's glorious *imperial* past informed Churchill, who presumed it would likewise inform the future. But Franklin Roosevelt, Berlin argues, saw — and Churchill did not — that the past and all of its traditions could be jettisoned in order to produce a new political order from whole cloth. Where Roosevelt was an imaginative though cautious political visionary, Churchill was an imaginative and incautious preservationist. "Churchill...looks within," Berlin wrote, "and his strongest sense is the sense of the past."

After reading Plato and Aristotle as a young man, Churchill declared for agnosticism. Although he embraced the Greek philosophical antecedents of Christianity, he found no intellectual reward in theological exercises. He subscribed to the Christian values of mercy and forgiveness, but his beliefs were not dictated by doctrine, and certainly not by clerics. He had been informed by his experiences as a soldier and journalist, and he rejected the carrot and stick of heaven and hell. The idea of an afterlife was not much more than an afterthought for Churchill, and one he considered equivalent to a belief in ghosts and goblins. He claimed he "did not much believe in personal survival after death, at least not of the memory." The thought of oblivion did not vex him. Where others found only terror in the prospect of the negation of self, Churchill found sanguineness, and fodder for irreverent asides. He did not believe in another world after death, he told his doctor, but "only in 'black velvet' — eternal sleep," which did not stop him from playing whimsically with other possibilities in painterly terms: "When I get to Heaven I mean to spend a considerable portion of my five million years in painting, and so get to the bottom of the subject. But then I shall require a still gayer palette than I get here. There will be a whole range of wonderful new colours which will delight the celestial eye." Churchill's fanciful heaven was also a distinctly pluralistic place where the full spectrum of humanity would mingle forever (although the membership list would never do for Churchill's earthly private dining society, the

Other Club): "Indians and Chinese and people like that. Everyone will have equal rights in Heaven...that will be the real welfare state.... Of course, I admit I may be wrong. It is conceivable that I might well be reborn as a Chinese coolie. In such case I should lodge a protest." In a similar impish vein, he once proclaimed a proof for God's existence "is the existence of Lenin and Trotsky, for whom a hell is needed."[38]

As for the act of dying, the transition from consciousness to nothingness or to some manner of *somethingness,* Churchill would have agreed with Dr. Johnson, who said dying "lasts so short a time," and it does a man "no good to whine.... It matters not how a man dies, but how he lives."[39]

Such were Churchill's sentiments exactly. In 1915, before departing on a planned journey to Turkey (he never made the trip), he entrusted his lawyer with a letter he wrote to Clementine, to be delivered in the event of his death: "Death is only an incident, & not the most important that happens to us.... If there is anywhere else, I shall be on the lookout for you." He believed that were his final moment on earth to arrive via a German bomb, it would be due to chance. To Jock Colville, he quoted the French mathematician Henri Poincaré: "I take refuge beneath the impenetrable arch of probability." Fate, not the Lord, would call Churchill home, although he once told Colville whimsically that were heaven ordered on the model of a constitutional monarchy, "there was always a possibility that the Almighty might have occasion to 'send for him.' "[40]

He detested superstition. A court case being prosecuted by His Majesty's Government caught his attention. He demanded of the home secretary "why the Witchcraft Act, 1735, was used in a modern court of justice?" It was all "obsolete tomfoolery" that inhibited the court's ability to function. He thought much the same of churchgoing. He was at best an infrequent visitor to God's house. His private secretary Anthony Montague Browne recalled that Churchill claimed he "rarely went to church. When approached about this, he [Churchill] said he was not a pillar of the church but a buttress—he supported it from the outside." If he had to sit through a sermon on national days of prayer or state occasions, Jock Colville later wrote, he preferred that the pastor speak to politics or war, "but no Christianity." His visits to church were so rare that Colville was shocked one Sunday late in the war when Churchill attended a service. It was the first time in almost four years that Colville had seen him do so. Only toward the end of the service did Colville grasp Churchill's real motive for attending. After the minister delivered his sermon, the Old Man walked up to the pulpit and delivered one himself. He loved the glory and pageantry of christenings, funerals, and coronations performed within the mossy precincts of Britain's ancient village churches or within the silent grandeur of its great cathedrals, not for any proximity to the divine but because such rituals offered proximity to England's storied past. Churchill was deeply moved by the melodic grace of hymns, by the power of voices uplifted in song. He loved the rolling peal of village church bells calling the faithful to worship, but, writes the British historian Roy Jenkins, there is no record of Churchill ever having left Chartwell in response to the summons. A Bible rests to this day on his bedside table at Chartwell, a sight that moves many visitors to conclude he sought guidance in Scripture. He did not. When Lord Moran, spying the Bible, asked Churchill if he read it, he replied, "Yes, I read it; but only out of curiosity."[41]

Jock Colville thought it the "supreme blasphemy" when, over lunch one day, Churchill said, "Every nation creates god in its own image." Yet history lent credence to that judgment; even Hitler claimed that god was on his side.[42]

He disliked holy men in general: "the old humbug Gandhi," Greek Archbishop Damaskinos ("a pernicious priest"). Church of England prelates did not adorn Churchill's dinner table. He considered the Anglican clergy to be a priggish and hypocritical lot. Why dine with those who would take moral umbrage to his ending an evening singing lustily and dancing about to Viennese waltzes while attired in an outrageous red dressing gown, a warmed snifter of brandy in one hand, and a cigar (or rifle) in the other? The death later in the war of William Temple, the archbishop of Canterbury, "caused the P.M. no sorrow," Colville wrote. "In fact he was quite ribald about it." Temple was a scholar and philosopher, but Churchill "who as far as the English clergy was concerned had a touch of King Henry II about him, disliked Temple's left-wing tendencies and his outspoken political comments." Churchill was a Cavalier, the clergy were Puritans—worse, Puritans with a leftward list. This, for Churchill, made them and their brand of Christianity suspect.

Churchill squeezed the present for all it was worth. He believed meaning is found only in the present, for the past is gone and the future looms indeterminate if it arrives at all. Churchill was an old trooper who, whether at his easel, speaking in the Commons, or dining with his cronies, manifested the soldier's creed: savor the moment, for it may be the last. Yet for Churchill, if there were to be tomorrows, they would arrive on *his* terms. He was an optimist, not a determinist; the world was indeed often cruel, but it need not remain so. He subscribed to a variation of the Nietzschean, monumental view of history that he had arrived at from his youthful reading of Gibbon (*all* of Gibbon) and Winwood Reade's *The Martyrdom of Man,* a must-read for young thinkers in the late nineteenth century. In his book Reade attributed to history a Darwinian, a survival of the fittest, continuum. Churchill, paraphrasing Reade in a letter to his mother, wrote, "If the human race ever reaches a stage of development—when religion will cease to assist and comfort mankind—Christianity will be put aside as a crutch which is no longer needed, and man will stand erect on the firm legs of reason."[43]

He synthesized his Gibbon and Reade and concluded that the greatness and goodness of the past could be recaptured through the exercise of will. God would play no part in the saga, because God, if indeed there was a God, was unwilling or unable to intervene. Yet that paradigm left open the possibility that a force of evil—such as Hitler—might well impose his will on the future. Churchill employed his present moments to plan his—and the world's—better tomorrows through the exercise of *his* will. By doing so he intended to deny Hitler his supposed destiny. Churchill, not God, would safeguard the future of Europe and the British Empire, and he would do so by the vigorous exercise of his imagination and the imposition of his will by the only means he knew—action, action this day, action every day.

He saw communism not as the atheistic negation of Christian ideals (as did Franklin Roosevelt) but as the twisted fulfillment of those ideals. At dinner one evening later in the war he recited to his guests a Soviet creed:

"I love Lenin,
Lenin was poor, and therefore I love poverty,
Lenin was hungry, therefore I can go hungry..."

"Communism," Churchill declared when he finished, was "Christianity with a tomahawk."[44]

Traditional religions at least held out the hope of mercy, love, and a forgiving deity. Not so the "non-God" religions that had overtaken Germany and Russia (although Churchill muted his criticism of Bolshevism after his alliance with Stalin). Three years before war came, during the early months of the Spanish Civil War, Churchill warned Britons of the "war between the Nazis and the Communists: the war of the non-God religions, waged with the weapons of the twentieth century. The most striking fact about the new religions is their similarity. They substitute the devil for God and hatred for love. They are at each other's throats wherever they exist all over the world...." Britons, he warned, "must not blind their eyes to the power which these new religions exercise in the modern world. They are equipped with powerful agencies of destruction, and they do not lack their champions, their devotees, and even their martyrs."[45]

Chamberlain—and France—had blinded his eyes to the threat, with the result that Hitler and his apostles brought their gospel first to Poland,

and now to Holland, Belgium, and France. Churchill intended that it not
be brought to England.

He believed in Virtue and Right, not as matters of dogma, but as objective realities. Virtue was manifested in action. It took the form of the Aristotelian mean. Courage, the supreme virtue, could be found somewhere
between cowardice and foolhardiness. Paraphrasing Samuel Johnson,
Churchill wrote in *Great Contemporaries:* "Courage is rightly esteemed
the first of human qualities because ... it is the quality which guarantees all
others." Among the others was magnanimity. *In Victory: Magnanimity,*
Churchill chimed, never revenge fueled by hatred. This was a virtue first
expressed by Aristotle and most recently ignored by Hitler in Poland and,
a generation earlier, by the good Christians who drafted the Carthaginian
terms (Churchill believed) of surrender imposed upon Germany and Austria after the Great War. The argument put forth then that Germany had
behaved like a mad dog since the Franco-Prussian War and deserved to
wear the shortest possible leash was, for Churchill, flawed. It violated
another of his maxims, *In Peace: Goodwill.* He believed that an economically healthy Germany was necessary for European stability.

Yet here now came the Hun again, waging a war that might soon result
in the extermination of England. In fighting his battle to preserve liberty in
England and restore it in Europe, there could be no middle path, no mean,
and Churchill acknowledged none. Weapons and strategies that showed
promise — special operations, assassination, sabotage, bacterial "spore"
bombs, atomic fission bombs, aerial obliteration of German cities — were
justified by the ends. Any weapon, especially one deployed often, accurately, and ruthlessly, was a fine weapon. His was a distinctly Old Testament approach to rendering justice. As much as he admired the merciful
and demanded that generosity follow victory, *In War, Fury** formed his
philosophy of battle.[46]

In his youthful readings of Aristotle and Plato he discovered the pre-
Christian philosophical antecedents that the Catholic Church later appro-

---

* For an inscription on a monument to the Great War to be erected at Versailles,
Churchill had suggested "In war fury; in defeat defiance, in victory magnanimity, in
peace goodwill." The suggestion was rejected (Colville diary, Jan. 24, 1941). Ever
willing to rework a phrase with an eye toward future historical considerations,
Churchill replaced "fury" with the more temperate "resolution" on the frontispiece of
his six-volume war memoir.

priated and folded into its doctrine. He taught himself well and created a code he could live by. He was seduced by the powerful simplicity of Aristotle's mean and Plato's analogy of the charioteer, who in order to successfully navigate his way must keep a tight rein on his brace of winged horses.

Churchill had as much difficulty riding smoothly in double harness as he did in keeping his car on the road, but in the end, he achieved his mean. It was a moral journey of many twists and turns, of chutes and ladders. Images of him in his dressing gown, rifle at his shoulder, marching about late of an evening hardly conjure an image of the Aristotelian mean. He possessed, John Martin recalled, a "zigzag streak of lightning on the brain." The Old Man zigged and zagged in many of his strategic decisions as war leader when, literally and metaphorically, he was all over the map. For every diarist who notes his exuberance, fairness, geniality, or generosity, there is to be found another who alludes to his roughness, his sarcasm, his low moods, and his bellicosity—sometimes the same observer on the same day. Yet Churchill's journey toward the mean could unfold in no other way. "If he hadn't been this sort of bundle of energy that he was," recalled Martin, "he would never have carried the whole machine, civil and military, right through to the end of the war."[47]

Endowed with a prodigious memory, Churchill seemed to remember every poem he had ever read, the lyrics of every song, and the chapter and verse of vast numbers of biblical passages, and he would recite them almost anywhere. Embarrassed once years earlier by not having heard of Keats's "Ode to a Nightingale," he set himself to memorizing all of Keats's odes, and enjoyed reciting them "mercilessly," in the estimation of Violet Bonham Carter. He could endlessly quote Dr. Johnson, and freely appropriated and paraphrased the doctor's witticisms. Byron's *Childe Harold's Pilgrimage* was a Churchill favorite, although he did not share Byron's melancholic view that man's greatest tragedy is his ability to conceive a perfection that he cannot attain. Rather, Churchill told his countrymen in the battle against Hitler, "If we can stand up to him, all Europe may be free and the life of the world may move forward into broad, sunlit uplands." "Invictus," a nineteenth-century ode to willpower by William Ernest Henley, was another Churchill favorite.

> *It matters not how strait the gate,*
> *How charged with punishments the scroll,*
> *I am the master of my fate:*
> *I am the captain of my soul.*[48]

He reserved a special affection for American writers, particularly Twain, Melville, and Emerson. As with the English canon, his knowledge was broad. Once, motoring though Frederick, Maryland, with Franklin and Eleanor Roosevelt and FDR's close adviser Harry Hopkins, Churchill saw a road sign for candy named for Barbara Frietchie, the Union patriot who flew her Stars and Stripes in defiance of Rebel troops marching past her house. Roosevelt, noting the sign, recited two lines of John Greenleaf Whittier's poem about Frietchie:

"Shoot, if you must, this old gray head,
But spare your country's flag, she said."

When Roosevelt allowed that those were the only lines he knew, Churchill weighed in by reciting the entire poem, sixty lines. Then, he began a long monologue on the strategic genius of Stonewall Jackson and Robert E. Lee. He continued on as the miles sped past, oblivious to the effect on his companions. "After a while," he later wrote, "silence and slumber descended upon the company."[49]

Churchill's love of history was abiding and his knowledge profound. Memorizing dates and place-names has always been the bane of schoolchildren. Yet for a few, Churchill assuredly among them, history is more than a time line, more than the sequencing and parsing of collective memory. In those such as Churchill, history, by way of imagination and discipline, becomes part of personal memory, no less so than childhood recollections of the first swim in the ocean or the first day of school. Churchill did not simply observe the historical continuum; he made himself part of it. Classical venues, and Churchill's "memory" of them—from the Pillars of Hercules and on around the Mediterranean to Syracuse, Rome, Sparta, Alexandria, and Carthage—informed his identity in much the same way his memories of his family's ancestral home, Blenheim Palace, did, or his father's London house, where as a boy he charged his toy soldiers across Persian carpets. He may have been born a Victorian, but he had turned himself into a Classical man. He did not live in the past; the past lived on in him. Harry Hopkins, who came to know Churchill well, noted the mystical relationship he had with the past, especially the military past: "He was involved not only in the battles of the current war, but of the whole past from Cannae to Gallipoli." Alexander the Great, Boudicca, Hadrian, King Harold, Prince Hal, Pitt, and of course his luminous ancestor Marlborough had all played their parts in earlier scenes of the same play and upon the same stage that Churchill and his enemies now played their parts.[50]

All who knew him had heard him recite, at one time or another, Macaulay's *Lays of Ancient Rome:*

Then out spake brave Horatius,
The Captain of the gate:
"To every man upon this earth
Death cometh soon or late.
And how can man die better
Than facing fearful odds,
For the ashes of his fathers,
And the temples of his gods."

All who knew him came to know that in Churchill such sentiments were intrinsic.

Churchill's most endearing trait was also his most remarkable. He was probably the most amusing warlord in history. His very appearance could endlessly entertain his family and staff. On June 16, Colville took urgent dispatches to the P.M.'s room and "found him lying in bed, looking just like a rather nice pig, clad in a silk vest." Smoking a long cigar and stroking his cat, Nelson, he prowled the corridors of No. 10 wearing a soldier's steel helmet (called by all a "tin hat"), a crimson dressing gown adorned by a golden dragon, and monogrammed slippers complete with pom-poms. Sometimes he carried on anthropomorphic conversations with Nelson (including an admonition to be more stouthearted after the cat flinched during an air raid). Anticipating the need to move with dispatch during air raids, Churchill designed a one-piece suit with many zippers, permitting him to don it quickly. All members of his staff, including the stenographers, called the suit his "rompers." Churchill called the outfit his "siren suit," because he jumped into it at the first howl of the air-raid sirens. He designed the rompers; Henry Poole & Co. of Savile Row crafted them and delivered them.[51]

Any circumstance might trigger Churchill's humor reflex. Once, after delivering a speech in Parliament on American aid, he rode home to Downing Street in the back of a limousine, belting out "Old Man River." When his doctor once recited lines from John Milton's *Lycidas*— "While the still morn went out with sandals grey..."—Churchill countered, "He was on the wrong side on the Civil War." During a visit to Rome, he was introduced to the leaders of various Italian political factions. Greeting one group, he asked, "What party are you?" "We are the Christian Communists," came the reply. Churchill could not contain himself: "It must be very inspiring to your party, having the Catacombs so handy." One day in the House, he was forced to sit through the delivery of a long and tedious report rife with statistics. He noticed an elderly MP leaning forward with an antique ear trumpet pressed to his ear, struggling to hear the report.

Churchill turned to a colleague and asked, "Who is that idiot denying himself his natural advantages?"[52]

Chequers—the ancient Buckinghamshire country house that had been the country retreat of prime ministers since 1917—was guarded by vigilant sentries and could be approached only by those who knew that day's password. One night during that first week of summer it was "Tofrek," site of an 1855 battle in the Sudan. That evening, excited by the sound of a plane overhead, Churchill ran out, shouting, "Friend! Tofrek! Prime minister!" There, late at night, he would recite lines from *Hamlet*, or Byron, or sing music hall ballads he had not heard since the 1890s. Sometimes, when a recording of *The Blue Danube* was playing, he would waltz around the room alone, his right hand flat against his shirt and his left arm extended as though he were supporting the hand of a partner. Clementine, if present, would likely not join her husband. She understood that he often played and worked simultaneously. While gliding around the room, he very often crafted phrases to deploy in upcoming speeches, and to interrupt him was out of the question. However, on one occasion (years later), two cabinet ministers considered their business more important than Churchill's speech preparation. They bounded up the stairs, headed for his bedroom, where he was dictating his notes. As they waited outside, a secretary announced their presence to the Old Man. "Tell them to go and bugger themselves," came the volcanic response. Then a pause, and, "Tell them there is no need for them to carry out that instruction literally."[53]

The prelude to a speech in the House of Commons was *opéra bouffe*. He would craft it, not in the calm of a study surrounded by reference books but while on the telephone, or prancing around the Great Hall at Chequers, or propped up in bed, or bowed over a map, waging war. He composed every word of every speech; no committee of speechwriters toiled at No. 10. His bath was a favorite venue for speech preparation (he was proud of being able to control the taps with his toes while he dictated). In the midst of other tasks, he would start muttering phrases to himself: "To the gates of India"; "this bloodthirsty guttersnipe"; "this star of England." When a cabinet minister called Germans "sheep," Churchill snarled, "*Carnivorous* sheep." In two words he captured the essence of his foes better than Baldwin or Chamberlain could in two hours of speechifying. When Hitler was the subject, Churchill struck and struck again, each cut more ferocious than the one before: "This wicked man, the repository and embodiment of many forms of soul-destroying hatred, this monstrous product of former wrongs and shame, has now resolved to try to break our famous Island race by a process of indiscriminate slaughter and destruction." He fertilized every phrase with imagery, and weeded them of any word that could choke his message. He tried them out over dinner with colleagues, with different adjectives, different emphasis, to measure their rhythms and to hear how they sounded. He might pause to pluck a pinch of snuff from his gold snuffbox (it had once belonged to Admiral Nelson), pop it into a nostril, and emit a sneeze with robust delight. He sometimes offered a pinch to his young, female typists, who politely declined. The creative process so absorbed him that he often became oblivious to events unfolding in the room, as on the day his cigar ash ignited his bed jacket. One of his private secretaries, noting the rising smoke, offered, "You're on fire, sir. May I put you out?" The P.M., not looking up, responded with nonchalance, "Yes, please do." And kept right at his work.[54]

The climax of his ruminations would come on the day of delivery. Always at least fifteen minutes late, he might still be in bed, dictating the final draft to a typist, or inking in changes, when he should have been on his way to Parliament. Anxious whips would be telephoning from the House, his staff would be begging him to hurry, his valet would be dressing him and flicking cigar ash from his shirt (always a delicate task, for Churchill did not like to be touched). Meanwhile, messengers held the elevator, and his chauffeur, outside, gunned the engine. Finally he would totter out, still dressing, tucking his spectacles and cigar case and loose cigars and his little snuffbox into sundry jacket pockets, checking the numbered pages to be sure they were in the right order.[55]

Moments later, when he rose from the front bench to address the House, he would be greeted by a respectful hush from members and from the galleries, where journalists and foreign ambassadors leaned forward in anticipation. If his words were to be given in secret session, the cue to clear visitors from the Strangers' Gallery would come when he gazed upward and declared, "I espy strangers." Secret sessions of the House therefore posed a small problem for Churchill; his most delightful phrases would be lost to the press and diplomatic pouches, and therefore lost to the outside world. Churchill's solution was simplicity itself; he simply repeated the favored phrases over dinner or in the House smoking room, thus assuring that they would appear in Max Beaverbrook's newspapers the *Daily Express* and the *Evening Standard*. Or, if Churchill wanted the Duke of Alba's daily secret report to Franco to contain a nugget of misinformation from the Old Man himself, he might repeat a phrase to some Foreign Office minion who was known to dine with the Spaniard. Thus, secret session or no, if Churchill wanted to say something, he said it. Only words can live forever, he liked to say; it would simply not do for his words to die on the floor of the House.

Churchill, like Samuel Johnson and Shakespeare, could string together phrases that resonated with Glasgow pub patrons, Welsh coal miners, and Cockney laundresses, as well as with the Harold Nicolsons and Lady Astors. At his dinner table or in the Commons during Questions, he sprayed the room with fusillades of bons mots. But his broadcasts and speeches were strategic assaults, not tactical, and were crafted with infinite care. His broadcasts sound so English, but in fact their structural foundations date to Cicero. Gibbon and Shakespeare, and Churchill's reading of them, had a hand in that. Gibbon, when read aloud, is a slow burn, more fuse than fireworks, yet the prose is perfectly balanced and perfectly ordered; each point meticulously advanced until in the climactic resolution only one inescapable conclusion can be reached. Gibbon's cadence permeates Churchill's speeches, which in structure and delivery were like a trebuchet, its mechanism slowly and steadily wound by Churchill until the maximum tension was reached, at which point he launched his verbal missile. Then, beginning with his next breath, he re-armed his siege engine and prepared for the next shot.

Although Shakespeare's name does not appear in the index of his four-volume *History of the English-Speaking Peoples,* Churchill read and memorized Shakespeare his whole life, and imbued his speeches with metrical tributes to the Bard. He embodied the Shakespearean notion that a man's essence is to be found in his actions, and his words, the authenticity and value of which would be confirmed or debunked by the actions that followed. He did not so much speak to Englishmen (as Franklin Roosevelt did to Americans in his homespun fireside chats), as for them. In doing so he represented their destiny and their role in the current struggle, which could only end in either national survival or national annihilation. Hitler, an opportunist and nihilist romantic, told his people much the same.

Churchill dictated all speeches, memos, and letters to his typists, usually young and female, who typed away while he paced about the room, fetched his thoughts, and put them into words. When he dictated directly to the typewriter, the typists found themselves in peril, for to change flimsies in the middle of a long dictation would produce a "primitive wrath." "Come on, come *on!*" he'd growl. "What are you waiting for!" "Don't fidget so with that paper! *Stop it!*" He was personally insulted by any pause necessitated by the mechanics of the infernal machine. He displayed, wrote his bodyguard, an "appalling, almost childish" unwillingness to learn the mechanics of typing or of typewriters. None of his staff recollect ever seeing Churchill put a finger to a typewriter keyboard. Nor did he ever write his own memos. Other than signing them, recalled William Deakin, Churchill "never wrote a line in his life. I have never seen him put pen to paper." Actually, Churchill had written his early books in longhand, and of course his dispatches from Cuba and the veldt. But once elected to the Commons, and forever after, he indulged his love of dictation.[56]

He disliked the taking of dictation by shorthand, which would have kept the stenographers in the chase and allowed them to type in peace outside his presence. He believed shorthand only added one more step to the process of setting his thoughts down on paper. He allowed an exception to the ban when he was on the move—in a car, onboard a rolling ship, or strutting through the halls of Chequers or Parliament, conditions which even he understood were not conducive to wielding a typewriter. Not a moment was to be wasted by the typists, as young Patrick Kinna, a lance corporal and trained stenographer who had worked for the Duke of Windsor, learned the first time he entered the prime minister's room to take a letter. Without looking up or acknowledging Kinna, Churchill, pacing, intoned, "This is a melancholy story...." Kinna, thinking Churchill was about to tell a tale, set down his pencil and notepad, and said, "Oh dear! How unfortunate." "*Well*," Churchill grumbled, "*take it down.*" It was a memo to the Admiralty, ruing the paucity of aircraft carriers. Kinna survived the day and served Churchill for the rest of the war as a member of the team.[57]

Woe unto the typist who had to ask the Great Man to repeat a phrase. His staff knew that to guess at what he said was far preferable to asking him to repeat it. The typists had to engage in a fair amount of guessing (as Elizabeth Layton had learned) because Churchill often mumbled and, to make matters worse, often while pacing about far across the room, his back to the typist. When he didn't mumble, he rumbled, strings of phrases all but indecipherable to the struggling scribes. When he dictated while in bed, propped up on his pillows, words were lost as newspapers fluttered to the floor, or the telephone rang, or he summoned his valet to refresh his refreshment. As with the collecting of his thoughts in preparation for a speech, he liked to dictate letters and memos while a gramophone played his favorite recordings of old music hall standbys—"After the Ball," "Goodbye, My Love," perhaps Harry Lauder belting out "Keep Right On Till the End of the Road." The typists had to blot out the background noise in order to parse his phrases, a supremely difficult task when Churchill instructed his valet to turn the volume higher. Finally, when the typist finished, and before she could pull the paper from the typewriter, Churchill would thrust out a hand and utter a curt "*Gimme.*"[58]

Typists earned about two pounds per week, about forty dollars a month, less than the wages of a corporal in the U.S. Army. As well, they were expected to remain at their post even as German bombs fell into nearby courtyards.[59]

Churchill had been a professional writer before he became a statesman; he had supported his family with a tremendous stream of books and articles.

His love of the language was deep and abiding, he had mastered it as few men have, and he was quick to correct anyone who abused it, especially those who tried to camouflage sloppy thinking with the flapdoodle of verbose military jargon or bureaucratese. He believed, with F. G. Fowler, that big words should not be used when small words will do, and that English words were always preferable to foreign words. He said: "Not compressing thought into a reasonable space is sheer laziness." On his orders "Communal Feeding Centres" were renamed "British Restaurants," as "Local Defense Volunteers" had become "Home Guard." And why not "ready-made" rather than "prefabricated"? "Appreciate that" was a red flag for him; he always crossed it out and substituted "recognize that." Another was "intensive" when "intense" was required. Once John Martin, driving along the Embankment with him, described the winding of the Thames as "extraordinary." Churchill corrected him: "Not 'extraordinary.' All rivers wind. Rather, 'remarkable.'" In the margins of official documents, he often quoted *Fowler's Modern English Usage,* a copy of which he sent to Buckingham Palace on his first Christmas as prime minister.[60]

John Martin believed that the P.M.'s "interest in basic English was inspired by politics rather than linguistics: it was a means of promoting 'the English-speaking club.'" Certainly that was one reason. He believed that all countries where English was spoken, including America, should merge. Here lay a profound contrast with the foreign policies of his predecessors at Downing Street. They had focused upon the Continent and the various combinations of the great powers there. Neville Chamberlain had referred to the United States with amusement and contempt, and called Americans "creatures." But Churchill, though a European patriot, looked westward, and not only because he knew Hitler could not be crushed without American troops. British to the bone, he was nevertheless the son of an American mother, and long before the war, he had envisaged a union of the world's English-speaking peoples: the United Kingdom, the United States, Canada, Australia, South Africa, and the far-flung colonies of the British Empire.[61]

In his parliamentary speeches, and particularly in his broadcasts to his besieged island, his genius for the language fused with his idealized image of England and Englishmen, or the "British race," formed in the last quarter of the nineteenth century — a people endowed with fearlessness, gallantry, nobility, a unique sense of honor, and invincibility. He still exulted in the memory of colonial conquests, when the Enfield rifles and Maxim guns of the Queen's armies were challenged only by primitive weapons, imperial flags flew proudly, and British casualties, even in the Indian Mutiny, were always light. The slaughter of the 1914–1918 war had appalled Britons, including Churchill, and had exhausted and disillusioned many, but not Churchill. Now, drawing fire from the terrible red glow across the Channel, he was exhilarated. His first four hundred days in office — from early May 1940 to mid-June 1941, a ghastly time for millions of Europeans — were, for him, the supreme chapter in his life. Later he wrote that it was "the most splendid, as it was the most deadly year in our long British and English story." He believed that 1940 was a time when "it was equally good to live or die." Years after the war, John Martin remarked to him that life was not as exciting as it had been. Churchill replied jovially, "You can't expect to have a war all the time."[62]

Based on his reading of Lord Moran's memoirs, Anthony Storr, the eminent British psychiatrist, believed that the source of Churchill's strength lay in his "inner world of make-believe," the sort of fantasies imaginative men call up from time to time when bored or disappointed. For most of the 1930s, Churchill had been both. After June 1940, Storr believed, that world of imagination "coincided with the facts of external reality in a way that rarely happens to any man." After the fall of France, Churchill became the hero he had always dreamed of being. Storr compares this to passionate love, "when, for a time, the object of a man's desire seems to coincide exactly with the image of a woman he carries within him." In that dark time, Storr argues, what England needed was not a shrewd, composed, balanced leader, but a prophet, a heroic visionary, a man who could dream dreams of victory when all seemed lost — a man who could inspire not only Britons but also Americans. "Had Churchill been a stable and equable man," Storr writes, "he could never have inspired the nation. In 1940, when all the odds were against Britain, a leader of sober judgment might well have concluded that we were finished."[63]

And yet, despite the fact that Churchill was prone to sentimentality, was mercurial, and at times lacked strategic military sense, he had, through intuitive leaps and careful analysis during the 1930s, arrived at an astonishingly accurate forecast of the calamity that had since befallen Europe and England. The events of September 1939 had proven him England's *most* sober statesman, as well as its most prophetic. Other sober and equable men, who lacked his imagination and penetrating vision, had allowed Britain to stumble unprepared into this war.

Storr's Churchill is complex, which Churchill certainly was, and a lifelong depressive, which he likely was not. The widely held belief that Churchill fought depression throughout his adult life stems in large part from Storr's musings and Lord Moran's memoir, in which he recounts his service as Churchill's personal physician. Moran probed Churchill during his last decade with leading questions about his "black dog" of depression and painted the octogenarian statesman in hues of decrepitude and despondency. Based on the writings of Moran and Storr, the idea that Churchill was a lifelong depressive and probably bipolar took hold in mental health circles, and it lingers still in the popular imagination (but not in the minds of Churchill's family, friends, and his official biographer, Sir Martin Gilbert). Yet Churchill likely did not suffer from mental illness. The story of the "black dog" begins in 1911, when, in a letter to Clementine, Winston enthused over a German doctor who was said to be able to cure depression: "I think this man might be useful to me—if my black dog returns." (Samuel Johnson called his bouts with melancholia his "black dog.") Churchill went on to tell Clementine that when the dog departed, "All the colors came back into the picture." His letter describes what modern psychiatrists call a moderate adult depressive episode. The "light faded out of the picture," Churchill wrote. When prompted by Moran in 1944, Churchill recounted the episode, as well as the sensations of vertigo that had long ago troubled him—feeling unease while standing at a ship's railing or on a railroad platform, where he liked to put a pillar between himself and the approaching train. To this, Churchill added a vital conclusion: "And yet I don't want to go out of the world at all in such moments." Despondency or thoughts of self-obliteration never attached to Churchill's low moods. After 1911 he never again wrote of the black dog.[64]

Storr's diagnosis of Churchill has since been supplanted by more exact psychiatric diagnostic protocols. Churchill could indeed be moved to gloom and long silences by events great and small—a crushing naval loss, the death of a much-loved pet, the mention of the name of a long-dead comrade-in-arms. He was easily moved to tears. "I blub an awful lot," he once told a private secretary, and he never apologized for his blubbing. He became quite irritable over unnecessary delays or secretarial foul-ups or generals who proved unwilling or unable to fight. He just as readily could turn off his temper, and his worries. He did not exhibit what are now considered to be the symptoms of major adult depression: prolonged (two weeks or more) and regular (at least yearly) periods of loss of interest in work and family, lack of interest in socializing, difficulty in making decisions, sleep loss, feelings of low self-esteem, and feelings of being unloved or not worthy of being loved, sometimes accompanied by spells of inconsolability. Nor did he show symptoms associated with the mania end of the manic-depressive spectrum: *decreased* need for sleep, rapid speech, racing thoughts, euphoria or extreme optimism, increased sexual drive, spending sprees, and inability to concentrate.[65]

It is true that as an adult Churchill took wildly unnecessary risks at the gaming tables and on the battlefield (which London itself was for much of

1940) and drank heavily—symptoms of depression when accompanied by several others—but he never lost his ability to function. He worried, he fretted, he grew weary at times, but he never despaired. In fact, it is part of the contradictory nature of the man that he manifested various symptoms of depression—risk taking, excessive drinking, mood swings—not intermittently, but regularly, even daily, and for his whole life.

Although psychiatrists caution against trying to prove a negative in the case of Churchill's "black dog," they also caution against any retroactive diagnosis such as Storr's. Jock Colville and one of Churchill's military liaisons, Fitzroy Maclean, recalled rare occasions when Churchill claimed "he had the black dog on his back." He did not mean that he was depressed in a clinical sense, but only that he was having a bad day. Both Colville and Maclean recalled from their own upbringings that English nannies used the term "black dog" to describe the moods and emotional outbursts of young children. Throughout the war, Churchill, knowing that a dark and defeatist exterior inspired no confidence in those he needed by his side in order to win the war, did not indulge gloom but exorcised it. When visitors to Chequers or the underground No. 10 Annexe marveled at Churchill's good cheer, he voiced a variation on a theme he had once voiced to Colville: he took his strength from the "splendid *sangfroid* and morale of the British people." When Pug Ismay, strolling one day with Churchill in the garden at Chequers, offered, "whatever the future held, nothing could rob him of credit for having inspired the country....," Churchill replied, "It was given to me to express what is in the hearts of the British people. If I had said anything else, they would have hurled me from office."[66]

Nothing—not his moods, not Britain's defeats, not the slow strangulation of the U-boat blockade, not his reluctant generals—impeded Churchill's capacity to inspire his countrymen and to fight for their salvation. Nothing diminished his love for his family. Nothing undercut his love of life. If one accepts Freud's dictum that mental health is the ability to love and work, Churchill possessed his full mental health.

If anything, Churchill had attained what the American humanist psychologist Abraham Maslow called "self-actualization," the condition at the top of Maslow's "hierarchy of needs," where is found creativity, morality, spontaneity, and the ability to parse problems, accept facts, and refute prejudices.

Churchill was never modest, yet he bridled at the suggestion that he had transformed Britons. He believed the British race had "the lion heart"; he only supplied the roar. He believed they had always been heroic. Afterward, much as in his response to Pug Ismay, he said: "It fell to me to express the sentiments and resolves of the British nation in that supreme crisis of its life. That to me was an honor far beyond any dreams or ambitions I have ever nursed, and it was one that cannot be taken away." At the time, however, he said, "It is destiny. Destiny has put me here, now, for this purpose." Yet, "destiny" for Churchill meant only that he had arrived at this place and time; destiny did not guarantee the success of his mission. Only his actions, freely taken, could do that. He acknowledged the possibility that human affairs may be watched over and guided, as part of "the Almighty's Great Design into which all our human actions fit if we do our duty." His abiding agnosticism precluded certainty in the matter of divine influence, but not in the matter of doing his duty. Destiny, like fate, is all things to all men. Here it may be seen as that dynamic force within Churchill that, in combination with his will, altered history during the summer of 1940. Europe lay under Hitler's boot, from the Pyrenees to the Arctic Circle, from beyond the Vistula to the English Channel, across which three weeks earlier the British army had fled, leaving French beaches strewn with abandoned tanks, trucks, cannons, rifles, rations, and the bodies of those Tommies who had not made it out. The Führer's victorious generals now paced the French shore and gazed toward England's white-chalk cliffs, just visible across the narrow waters of the Dover Strait.[67]

It would be a mistake to imagine Hitler in 1940 as a deranged Charlie Chaplinesque buffoon given to spewing spittle on the uniforms of dumbfounded Prussian subordinates during purple-faced tirades. The Führer was quite in command of his faculties that spring, at the top of his game. He had served five years with honor in the trenches during the Great War and been awarded the Iron Cross for bravery. He had been wounded three times—twice by shrapnel and once by gas, which temporarily blinded him. He had fought in twelve battles. Hitler anointed himself, the military historian Sir John Keegan wrote, "first soldier of the Reich," yet he had earned that title by virtue of his courage during the Great War. His regiment—the 16th Bavarian Reserve—had suffered more than 100 percent casualties (military statisticians compute casualties based on the ratio of the original number of men in any unit to the number of replacements). Hitler in 1940 knew the inhuman hardships of war better than many of his generals, yet he also found the Great War to be "the greatest of all experiences." Only the final result had proved unsatisfactory, a defeat inflicted as much by Germany's national loss of will as by the Entente armies. Germany, then, had not deserved victory. This time would be different. This time already was different. Hitler was winning.[68]

Adolf Hitler was now the greatest conqueror in German history, his destiny fulfilled, by the exercise of *his* will. The war, such as it was, was just about over. The British must surely sue for peace, and Hitler was prepared to offer generous terms, for he respected the English race. "He liked the Englanders," recalled one of his SS bodyguards years later, adding, "except for Churchill." The Führer's Reich now basked in a splendorous Alpine dawn born of barbarity, deceit, and sheer Teutonic will. Britain stood alone in twilight, awaiting the seemingly inevitable descent of darkness. Were Churchill to prove himself a dangerous fool by rejecting Hitler's peace terms, one final task would remain before the former corporal, the failed artist—the "housepainter" as Churchill called Hitler—could assume his place as master of his new European order: the severing of the British Empire's head from its body.[69]

This was the status of Churchill, of London, of Britain and the British Empire, on the longest day of that year.

Hitler and his generals knew that they could crush the remnants of Britain's army in a matter of days if they could only reach them, there, across the narrows and beyond the cliffs. But the cold Channel waters lapping at the conquerors' boots only underscored an ancient and elemental truth; they were land warriors. Unlike English general officers, they were not "salt water generals." They had no plans in place to cross the sea, did not understand the sea, and in fact, they and Hitler feared it. Churchill did not. The Channel was his moat, England his bailey; he intended to fight from his battlements until he could muster the men and arms necessary to strike out, across the Channel and into Europe, and finally someday, however long it took, across the Rhine and into Germany, to Berlin, where he would achieve his stated objective: final and absolute victory over Hitlerism. Were Hitler or destiny to deny him that, he told his cabinet, he fully expected each of them, himself included, to die "choking on his own blood upon the ground."[70]

THE STORY THUS FAR, SEPTEMBER 1939–MAY 1940

Churchill's nemesis, Adolf Hitler, was a wicked political genius who rose to power by finding, and then occupying, the dark places in the German mind. The Führer's gifts were not confined to his Reich, however. Although he spoke no foreign tongues and had never been overseas, he possessed an intuitive gift for exploiting weaknesses in what Germans call *das Ausland,* that revealing Teutonic word that welds together all nations outside the Reich into a single collective noun. Again and again in the 1930s, he had dared the allied governments of Britain and France to stand up to his acts of aggression. Aghast at the prospect of another European war, they had turned away again and again, sacrificing their pride, their honor; even their prospects of national survival. In the meantime, his armed strength multiplied. Finally, at the end of the decade, after six years of preparation, he was ready. At dawn on Friday, September 1, 1939, he sent fifty-six Wehrmacht divisions roaring eastward into Poland. Now London and Paris had no choice. They were bound to Warsaw by military alliances. They had to declare war, and, reluctantly, they did.

In the Berlin suburb of Zossen, headquarters of the Führer's *Oberkommando der Wehrmacht* (Supreme Command of the Armed Forces, OKW), his field commanders were, in their turn, aghast. By turning to the east, ignoring the armies of England and France, he had defied OKW's basic strategic principle, and invited a two-front war. Worse, he had stripped the defenses on the Reich's Western Front, leaving a thin force of twenty-three second-rate divisions to face eighty-five heavily armed enemy divisions. It was a historic opportunity for Généralissime Gustav-Maurice Gamelin of France, who commanded the Allied troops. The German Supreme Command chief, *Generalfeldmarschall* Wilhelm Keitel, later testified that "a French attack would have encountered only a German military screen (*militärischen Schleier*), not a real defense." To win the war, Gamelin had but to issue one command: *"En avant!"* His troops could have marched into the *Ruhrgebiet*, the heartland of German industry, and the war would have been over.

But he didn't do it. Except for a token sortie in the direction of the Saar and its coal mines and steel furnaces—a meaningless gesture meant to encourage the Poles, yet one from which the Nazis fled—Allied troops remained where they were. Then, in five weeks of blitzkrieg, or lightning warfare, the Nazi juggernaut crushed Poland, freeing the Wehrmacht to turn westward. The moment had passed. French and British troops steeled themselves for the shock of a German offensive, but none came. They waited. And waited. By May of 1940 all had remained quiet on the Western Front for eight months. What fighting there was had been largely confined to the open seas, the realm of the Royal Navy, and the barren coast of Norway. On land, the great armies squatted idly opposite one another week after week in an unnatural silence.

Berliners called this extraordinary hush, unique in the history of modern warfare, *der Sitzkrieg.* In Paris it was *la drôle de guerre* (the amusing war), in London the Bore War. Churchill called it the Twilight War; America's Senator William Borah, the Phony War. In England and France, the public, feeling emotionally ruptured after bracing themselves for the worst, returned instead to the pleasures of peace. But as the conflict entered its ninth sterile month, life was about to stir within in it. The greatest of all wars was about to erupt at last in a convulsion of violence, slaughter, and terror.

Afterward everyone remembered the weather. The winter of 1939–1940 had been a white horror, Europe's cruelest since 1895 (and, though neither Paris nor London knew it, the only reason Hitler hadn't attacked), but spring was coming at last, and coming fast. Though March was its usual mottled mess, temperatures were exceptionally mild. Then, across the Continent, primroses were out, fruit trees were budding, crocuses teeming. As early as April 3, Sir Alexander Cadogan, a British diplomat with a green thumb, noted in his diary: "The herbaceous plants seem all alive-oh" and "Meadows are greening up nicely and copses purpling."[71]

Within a fortnight the season had acquired a radiant, crystalline tone. So pure was the air that vision seemed enhanced, objects being perceived with a cameo-like clarity as sharp and well defined as a fine etching. Magnolias, snowdrops, and bright azaleas rioted in Kensington and Whitechapel alike. Mollie Panter-Downes wrote in *The New Yorker* that the floral displays in London parks "have been so magnificent that it's a pity that the garden-loving Britons haven't had more heart to go and see them," adding that the season ahead "looks as though it were going to be the best, as far as weather and growing things go, that England has had in years." Then she noted: "The tulips in the big beds outside Buckingham Palace are exactly the color of blood."[72]

In the Low Countries across the Channel, cultivating garden tulips had been a major Dutch industry since the eighteenth century, selling the world triumph tulips, breeder's tulips, and Darwin, parrot, cottage, and Mendel tulips. These were approaching their peak in late April and would soon to be joined by graceful white tulips, always the loveliest. In tiny Luxembourg, the beauty of the gladioli was unprecedented. Belgium's spring had always been announced by the tall, graceful plane and poplar trees elegantly lining Brussels' wide gray streets, and now they, too, wore veils of pale green.

It was that rarity, a genuine idyll, a blessed time of crystal-clear air, of radiant mornings, of gentle twilights, and of soft, balmy evenings, when a delicate, bluish moisture fell on orchards and gardens. In late April, whipped-cream clouds hung motionless overhead; then the sky cleared. For six weeks not one drop of rain fell. Clothed in sunlight, their spirits soaring, people found pleasure in just lifting their faces to an immaculate heaven that seemed wider and higher and of a deeper blue than any before.

Alec Cadogan was rapturous: "It's a lovely spring with sparkling air and wonderful blossoms and the whole world looking like paradise." The same enraptured theme ran through other diaries, journals, and letters. Anthony Eden noted the "unbroken sunshine." At No. 10 Downing Street, Jock Colville rose early each morning to ride in Richmond Park, rejoicing in the "warm and summery weather." General Sir Edmund Ironside, Chief of His Majesty's Imperial General Staff and thus England's top soldier, wrote of "the most gorgeous weather," and noted a week later that it was "still the most gorgeous weather." In the rue de la Paix in Paris, the Duchess of Windsor, smartly dressed in a *Union des Femmes de France* uniform, supervised a soldiers' canteen, and wrote her Aunt Bessie, "We have never had such a beautiful spring." That spring was, the American war correspondent Vincent Sheean later wrote, "the loveliest Paris had ever known." Then, remembering its climax, he added, "the weather itself formed part of the human drama." In the Reich, some were reminded of August 1914, when German infantrymen in spiked helmets had written home of *Kaiserwetter*. Now their sons called it *Hitlerwetter*. General Heinz Guderian, the Nazi tank commander, was more specific. In his diary he called it *"völlig Panzerwetter."*[73]

Paris, always Europe's most colorful city, had joined the dazzling spectacle with cannas, dahlias, daffodils, and freesias — seen at their best advantage in the gardens of the Tuileries — while along the Seine and the capital's broad boulevards, the trees beloved by Parisians approached the height of their vernal flowering, their blossoms standing like small pink candles, and their dark green lapping leaves so delicately tarnished, in places so exquisite, that *Paris Soir* compared them to Renoir. Clare Boothe, touring Western Europe in that fourth month of 1940, wrote, "Now, in April, chestnuts burst into leaf on the lovely avenues of Paris, sunlight danced off the opalescent gray buildings, and the gold and gray sunsets, glimpsed through the soaring Arc de Triomphe at the end of the long splendid vista of the Champs-Élysées, brought a catch of pain and pleasure in your throat. Paris was Paris in April!"[74]

Paris was *gai* — a gaiety which, in retrospect, seems cruelly ironic. Immediately after the declaration of war, all theaters had closed, but now they reopened and were packed. So were the opera houses, cinemas, restaurants, and nightclubs; the stands at the Auteuil Hippodrome; the flower market at the Madeleine; the spring art exhibition at the Grand Palais; the *Concours d'Élégance* automobile race in the Bois de Boulogne sponsored by Renault and Citroën — even the Left Bank hall where the five academies gathered to hear Paul Valéry deliver his *Pensée de l'art française,* a lecture more widely covered by the Paris dailies that week than the war on all its fronts.

This year French fields had been plowed by troops. It was strange duty for soldiers in wartime, but thus far it had been a strange war; in isolated skirmishes the French arms had suffered only two thousand casualties, a third of the Royal Navy's losses in sea actions. Even so, the *Conseil Supérieur de la Guerre* (Supreme War Council) had bridled at the idea of soldiers manning plows and planting potatoes, arguing that such work was demeaning to their profession. However, the government, at the insistence of deputies with agricultural constituencies, pointed out that although career officers were professional soldiers, their troops were not; the men they commanded were peacetime civilians, many of them farmers, and if someone didn't turn the earth and sow it, France would lose the war by starvation.

Some officers, among them Colonel Charles de Gaulle, were relieved when the generals were forced to back down. France's army had a great reputation, even in Berlin, but idle troops are worrisome. The British Expeditionary Force, or BEF, had dealt with the problem of inactivity during the winter. Although there were still fewer than four hundred thousand British soldiers on the Continent—only 18 percent of the Allied ground forces—their quality was high, in part because officers kept spirits up with programs of vigorous exercise. The French did not. As the war entered its third season, the armies of France were stagnating, even rotting.

Every allowance must be made for the French, and the French soldier of 1940 must be regarded with great compassion. With the exception of Serbia, no nation had suffered so terribly in the Great War. Because their fathers had been bled white, the World War II generation, unlike that of 1914, simply wanted to be left alone.

At the time, this atrophy of spirit was imperfectly understood. In 1938, Churchill had called the French army "the most perfectly trained and faithful mobile force in Europe." In January 1940, to his dismay, he found that the French did not view the war "with uprising spirit or even with much confidence." He blamed the long months of waiting that had followed the collapse of Poland. This hiatus, he believed, had given "time and opportunity" for the "poisons" of communism and fascism to be established. It was certain, he wrote, that the quality of the French army was being "allowed to deteriorate during the winter."[75]

The eight-month lull at the front was seen variously. Vincent Sheean wrote that there was "no possible doubt that a dawn must come, one day or the next, when the gray rivers of the German flood would begin to roll westward over Holland, Belgium and France... and yet, in the way people have, I think we only half believed the inevitable until it had taken place."[76]

Since the expected curtain-raiser would have brought vast bloodshed, others were optimistic, including some who should have known better. General André Beaufre saw it as "a giant charade acted out by mutual consent" that would lead to nothing serious "if we play our part right." Alfred Duff Cooper, who had resigned from Chamberlain's cabinet to protest the Munich sellout, fatuously told an American audience in Paris that the Allies had "found a new way to make war, without sacrificing human lives."[77]

Many argued that it must stop, that it couldn't go on this way, that there was no point to it. Prime Minister Neville Chamberlain privately said he had "a hunch" that the war would be over by summer. Others felt otherwise; eminent men in Paris and London were persuaded that the war would continue as it was, with the naval blockade slowly strangling the Führer's Reich. That would take a year or two, of course, but by then the British would have fifty divisions in the field, and doubtless the Americans would sail over with a hundred more to deliver the coup de grâce. (It was the sort of showy thing they liked to do.)

The arguments of the distinguished scholar Alfred Sauvy to the contrary, the French masses had accepted the war, however reluctantly. They believed France would win it. They felt "sure," William L. Shirer, the CBS radio correspondent in Berlin, observed, "that all a democracy had to do to win a war was to declare it, that if a 'free nation' was united in its desire to win, no 'slave-driven force' like Hitler's could defeat it...they talked to you about the gigantic War Effort, and explained to you how, because this was a democracy, the War Effort was certainly greater than in Germany, because it was voluntary." Shirer noted a growing conviction that "in this peculiar war there was no need to suffer, to deprive oneself of the good, easy life. Sacrifice was not this time needed."

The French government encouraged such lullabies. Its deputies had invested Premier Édouard Daladier with dictatorial powers over French industry, including the right to conscript labor, but he had not used them. Factories that could have been converted to munitions manufacture were still turning out civilian goods. The Parisian firms of Lelong, Balenciaga, and Molyneux were exporting silks that Frenchmen would next see in German parachutes. Food was unrationed; so was gasoline, despite the fact that every gallon had to be imported. A subcommittee of *députés* had recommended that ski slopes and the Côte d'Azur resorts be reopened.

De Gaulle, the lonely Cassandra, wrote to Paul Reynaud, then still French Minister of Finance: "Now, as I see it, the enemy will not attack us for some time.... Then, when he thinks we are weary, confused, and dissatisfied with our own inertia, he will finally take the offensive against us, possessing completely different cards in the psychological and material line from those he holds at present." He was right, but when the upstart colonel told Pierre Brisson, editor of *Le Figaro,* that he felt uneasy over the French enemy's passivity, Brisson ridiculed him: "Don't you see that we have already won a bloodless Marne?"[78]

The British, possessing on the whole a better record on European battlefields, ought to have been more realistic. They weren't. Instead, they were
complacent. The Isle looked fine; ergo, the Isle *was* fine. In the autumn, the
Times had proclaimed Britain's "grim determination" to see it all through,
but nine months after the outbreak, English life had returned to normal.
Idle men dozed on Hyde Park "deck chairs"; the sheep lazed away the days
in London's park enclosures, and admiring crowds gathered by the nearby
duck ponds. In 1940, the city's skyline was still dominated by St. Paul's, by
the steeples of Wren's fifty other baroque churches, by the neo-Gothic
Houses of Parliament and Big Ben. Blacked out now, it loomed serenely on
moonlit nights, invoking in some memories of the imperial capital before
the arrival of electricity. Nightlife was as innocent and diverting as ever;
John Gielgud was King Lear; Emlyn Williams's *Light of Heart* played to
busy houses; elsewhere in the West End the most popular dance tunes were
the American "Deep Purple" and "Somewhere over the Rainbow." Clearly
Londoners were less interested in the war than in the rituals of peace. The
Times, ever the vigilant recorder of multifarious ornithological sightings,
reported the return of swallows, cuckoos, and even nightingales.

Churchill tried to wake the nation. Speaking that March on the BBC,
HMG's first lord of the Admiralty warned his countrymen that "more
than a million German soldiers, including all their active and armored
divisions, are drawn up ready to attack, on a few hours' notice, all along
the frontiers of Luxembourg, of Belgium and of Holland. At any moment
these neutral countries may be subjected to an avalanche of steel and fire,
and the decision rests in the hands of a haunted, morbid being who, to
their eternal shame, the German people have worshipped as a god." He
observed that in Britain "there are thoughtless dilettanti or purblind
worldlings who sometimes ask us: 'What is it that Britain and France are
fighting for?' To this I answer: 'If we left off fighting you would soon find
out.' "[79]

Nevertheless Lord Haw-Haw, a pseudonym for William Joyce, the English traitor who broadcast Nazi propaganda to Britain from Berlin—for
which he would later hang—was not yet resented; most Britons considered him merely amusing. At No. 10 Downing Street, the young diarist
Jock Colville noted: "The war looks like being an immobile affair on the
Western Front." After an evening in town, Colville wrote of seeing "a
group of bespectacled intellectuals remain firmly seated while God Save
the King was played." He commented: "Everybody looked but nobody did

anything, which shows that the war has not yet made us lose our sense of proportion or become noisily jingoistic." He had yet to learn that tolerance is a weakness in a nation at war, and that in wartime, jingoism becomes patriotism. The Germans already knew it. Had Berliners snubbed *"Deutschland Über Alles"* or sat through the *"Horst Wessel Lied,"* they would have been fortunate to lose only their freedom.[80]

The burgeoning spring revealed a minor scandal. The sandbags piled high around entrances to Whitehall government buildings split open and sprouted green weeds, clear evidence that they had been filled, not with sand, as stipulated in contracts, but with cheaper earth. Inevitably a question was raised in the House of Commons, though it was never really answered, largely because no one much cared. Sandbags and the other impedimenta of war—the barrage balloons, the air-raid trenches in the city's parks, the air-raid wardens, and the gas masks, which, as *Punch* pointed out, were carried only by officers and high civil servants—like stories of the evacuated children and jokes about women in uniform—had become banal. Indeed, the war itself had turned into a tiresome commitment to be grudgingly met.

That mood began to shift in the first week of May. The public, misled by the press, which had been misled by the government, had been under the impression that their troops were driving the Germans out of Norway. In fact it was the other way around. The fiasco ended on Thursday, May 2, when Prime Minister Neville Chamberlain rose in the House of Commons to announce that the British troops, having suffered a stunning defeat, were being evacuated. That weekend a Gallup poll revealed the public's disillusionment: fewer than a third now supported Chamberlain.

Parliament debated the Scandinavian losses on the following Tuesday. On Wednesday the Labour Party forced a division—a vote of confidence—and more than one hundred members of Chamberlain's own party deserted him. So stinging a rebuke should have led to the immediate fall of the prime minister's government. Clinging to office, the P.M. spent that evening trying every conceivable political maneuver to stay in office. All failed.

In Berlin that same day—Wednesday, May 8, 1940—William L. Shirer noted "a feeling of tension in the Wilhelmstrasse today." He added, "I hear the Dutch and Belgians are nervous. They ought to be." The Associated Press reported that two German armies, one from Bremen and the other from Düsseldorf, were moving toward the Dutch frontier. That angered the Germans; nevertheless, Shirer wrote that his censors "let me hint very broadly that the next German blow would fall in the west—Holland, Belgium, the Maginot Line, Switzerland."[81]

In Brussels the papal nuncio requested an audience with King Leopold to relay a warning from the Vatican. The pope had learned that a German invasion of Belgium was "imminent." Two coded dispatches to Brussels from the Belgian embassy in Berlin confirmed it. The Hague was alerted by the Dutch military attaché in Berlin.

Hitler was in a state of high excitement. In *Mein Kampf* he had sworn to destroy France in "a final, decisive battle (*Entscheibungskampf*)." Now the hour was at hand. General Jodl noted in his diary: "The Führer does not want to wait any longer....He is very agitated. Then he consents to postponement until May 10, which he says is against his intuition. But [he will wait] not one day longer."[82]

In the Château de Vincennes, Généralissime Gustav-Maurice Gamelin announced the restoration of normal peacetime leave in the French army. Four days earlier General André-Georges Corap, commander of the French Ninth Army, had told his men: "Nothing will happen until 1941." A Paris headline, welcoming the coming weekend, read: DÉTENTE AU HOLLANDE (Relaxation in Holland).

Because Britannia ruled the waves, the Admiralty in Whitehall determined overall naval policy for the war, but with the 400,000 troops of the British Expeditionary Force outnumbered by over 2,100,000 French, the disposition of troops was fixed by the short, courtly Gamelin. The *généralissime* was confident he could stop the enemy because he believed he knew exactly where they were going to attack. It would be through Belgium, precisely where they had come in August of 1914, when, achieving complete strategic surprise, the gray tide of the Reich's huge right wing, a million strong, had swept down and cut a swath seventy-five miles wide, enveloping France's left flank. That had been among the last imaginative maneuvers on the Western Front in 1914–1918. The French had avoided immediate disaster by falling back and rallying on the Marne. Then the sidestepping had begun as each army tried to outflank the other. Neither could. The result was a stalemate. The Allies found themselves defending for more than four years a snakelike chain of trenches that began on the Swiss border and ended 566 miles away on the English Channel. Breakthroughs were impossible, because whenever a position was in peril it could be swiftly reinforced; troop trains packed with defending troops could rocket to the tottering sector before the attacking infantrymen, plodding ahead at the three-miles-an-hour pace of Napoleonic foot soldiers, could reach their objective.

Gamelin foresaw a precise encore. But this time, he assured his countrymen, the war would not be fought on "the sacred soil" of France. Under his

Plan D, he would send his armies into the great northern plain of eastern Belgium and meet the enemy there on the line of the Dyle River. Where else, he asked, could the Nazis come? It was everyone's opinion that a German invasion through Switzerland was inconceivable, and France's perimeter comprised the Belgian plain (Flanders) on the left, the great Ardennes forest in the center, sprawling across Luxembourg, Belgium, and northern France, and the eighty-seven-mile Franco-German border, where the two hostile powers confronted one another directly.

This last location held no threat. Every inch of it was now defended by the most expensive system of fixed fortifications in history, the mighty steel-and-concrete Maginot Line, manned by forty-one divisions. When Lord Gort, commander of the British Expeditionary Forces, and a group of British generals toured the fortifications, they asked their French guide, René de Chambrun,* how much it had all cost. Fifty-five billion francs, Chambrun replied, over ten years. Then, realizing his English guests were of a seafaring nation and calculated in pounds sterling, Chambrun put the numbers into a nautical perspective: Had France spent the same amount of money building the biggest and fastest of battleships, of which there were about twenty-five in all the navies of the world, the French fleet would now consist of *fifty* such behemoths. Thus, Chambrun explained, the interconnected forts and artillery batteries of Maginot could be thought of as a great line of "land battleships," an analogy the British appeared to grasp. Gort, Chambrun wrote, "could not conceal his astonishment." Chambrun did not disclose to his guests that the cost of the line had precluded investments in tanks and mechanized units. Nor did he and his guests take the naval analogy far enough, for battleships are mobile and can react to changing tactical conditions. Forts—"land battleships"—are not and cannot.

Le Maginot, as the line was known to all Frenchmen, was named for André Maginot, a politician who, like Premier Édouard Daladier, had spent four years suffering in the trenches of the first war and vowed: never again. To be sure, the line ended at the Belgian border. Consideration was given to building it up to the northern French coast but the French believed that would send the wrong signal to Belgium, that their troops wouldn't even bother to fight until the Germans got to the French border. Some members of the *Conseil Supérieur de la Guerre* had urged that the line be extended to the Meuse River, within Belgium, but that was vetoed by

---

* Chambrun, a descendant of Lafayette, was a lawyer before he was mobilized, and served as a liaison to the British. Following the fall of France, he was a guest of Franklin Roosevelt aboard the presidential yacht *Sequoia,* where he gave the president a briefing on the battle.

Maréchal Henri-Philippe Pétain, the French commander of the army in 1918. To reach the Meuse, the Germans would have to pass through the Ardennes—a thickly wooded Hans Christian Andersen forest, slashed with deep ravines, and fogged with mist rising from peat bogs—*"impénétrable,"* Pétain declared, thus ruling it out as a channel of invasion. By the process of elimination, Gamelin reasoned, that left the Belgian plain as the only possible battlefield.[83]

Although he did not see them, he faced grave problems. Napoleon had warned his commanders against forming a picture—deciding in advance what the enemy was going to do. That is precisely what Gamelin had done. It never occurred to him that the Germans, having watched one great plan fail in 1914, might have formed another. Gamelin had also overlooked an ominous change in Belgium's rulers. In the last war King Albert had been a mighty ally, but in 1936, his son, Leopold III, had astonished Europe by renouncing his country's military alliance with France and Britain. In any new war between Germany and France, he declared, Belgium would be neutral—as though such an absurdity were possible. He had actually gone so far as to fortify his border with France, and had told the French that an extension of *Le Maginot* to the North Sea would be looked upon in Belgium as an unfriendly gesture.[84]

But Gamelin's greatest error was his assumption that warfare had not changed since the Armistice in 1918. His *Conseil Supérieur* took the same view, although there were a few vigorous dissenters, among them Colonel de Gaulle. De Gaulle was making a pest of himself, insisting that the French must study the swift Nazi conquest of Poland with tanks. Tanks, he said, had revolutionized battle; new strategies were needed to turn them back. As early as November 11, 1939, he had sent General Headquarters an aide-mémoire on the lessons of the Polish campaign, chiefly the need for fluidity on the battlefield, specifically the formation of a mechanized shock corps (*armée de métier*), soldiers specially selected and trained to lead an attack. Unless France followed the German example, he predicted, the gasoline engine would demolish French military doctrines even as it demolished fortifications.

But his superiors thought him absurd. One of them asked the others, Suppose the Boche panzers did burst through the lines. Where would they refuel? None of them reflected on the fact that since 1918, thousands of filling stations had appeared in northern France. To them they were irrelevant. After all, these petrol stations—which, like 91 percent of the automobiles in the country, had not existed in 1918—were there to serve civilian automobiles, not German panzers. The fact that both cars and tanks used the same fuel was disregarded.

Some war correspondents, haunted by the spectacle of the Führer's armored columns crushing the gallant Poles, remained troubled, but at Gamelin's *grand quartier général* they were told sharply that a replay of the blitzkrieg here was impossible. General Dufieux, the army's retired commander of tanks, declared that Nazi armored units could not "hurl themselves unsupported against our lines and penetrate deeply without facing complete destruction." Another senior officer chided the foreign press for its doubts: "Ah, my fellows, how naive you are!" A war of movement across the dry Polish plains, yes. But through the Ardennes, through the Dutch floods, through the Belgian defenses, through the Maginot—through the tank-traps and barbed wire and casemates, in the face of our powerful air force—that was absurd."[85]

In adopting the strategic defensive, the French high command was expressing the caution of a France whose World War I wounds were still unhealed. All the great battles had been fought on French or Belgian soil, and 1,315,000 *poilus* ("hairy," "virile") had been killed in action—27 percent of all men between the ages of eighteen and twenty-seven, a figure that does not include the wounded: those left blind, or legless, or armless, or with no limbs at all. The survivors lacked the strength or the will to lift the tricolor again. Unlike generations of Frenchmen gone before them, they understandably felt no craving for grandeur, no desire for Gallic supremacy in Europe. They did not want to lose this war, but neither did they much crave victory. In fact, they did not even *want* victory. France had no war aims. Everything desirable, as they saw it, was already French. They asked for nothing from the Germans but peace.

   Thus the decision to leave the initiative to the Nazis was more political than military. *Le Maginot* was as much a state of mind as a fortified line; when Daladier's government fell that March, conduct of the war was entrusted to Paul Reynaud only after he promised to undertake no offensive against the enemy. The idea of attacking Germany was, the deputies agreed, preposterous. After the Polish collapse, the most bellicose had lost heart. In the *Chambre des Députés,* all political parties became defeatist. Even before Hitler could deliver another *Friedensrede,* a peace speech calling on the Western allies to end the war now that he had enslaved another country—he had been posing as a prince of peace for seven years—the Communist delegation in the *Chambre* demanded that the deputies debate the "proposals for peace which are going to be made." Alexis Léger, the secretary-general of the Foreign Office, told the American ambassador William Bullitt: "The game is lost. France stands alone against the three dictatorships. Great Britain is not ready. The United States has not even changed the neutrality act. The democracies are again too late." Alfred

Sauvy concluded simply that the country had "refused the war" ("*on refusait la guerre*").[86]

But this was not a chess match, where a gambit could be refused. And Hitler would deliver no proposals of peace on the upcoming weekend of May 10. He intended to deliver something else entirely.

The timidity of the French high command had exasperated Churchill ever since the war's outbreak. They had rejected every initiative suggested by him—bombing the Ruhr, for example, or mining the Rhine—on the grounds that it might invite Nazi reprisals. "This idea of not irritating the enemy," he later wrote, "did not commend itself to me.... Good, decent, civilized people, it appeared, must never themselves strike until after they have been struck dead." This Gallic trepidation even ruled out air reconnaissance, which defies understanding because the Luftwaffe was overflying French lines every day. Had Allied planes done the same in early May, they would have been astonished at enemy preparations below. Eight military bridges had been thrown across the Rhine, and three armored columns stretched back from the river for one hundred miles.[87]

In fact, one French pilot did see the buildup on the evening of the eighth of May. He was over the Ruhr, returning from a propaganda mission, dropping leaflets urging the German people to overthrow Hitler and thus bring peace. Above Düsseldorf he looked down and saw a sixty-mile line of tanks and trucks headed for the Ardennes. They were driving with their lights on. He reported his discovery. It was dismissed as not credible.

This was not the first time such intelligence had been dismissed, but it would be the last. Five months earlier, as Europe slept away the winter, a German airplane carrying two staff officers was blown off course and forced to land in Belgium. The officers tried, and failed, to burn the papers they carried, which happened to contain OKW's revised operation orders for the invasion of the Low Countries, including a thrust through the Ardennes. British intelligence perused the captured papers. The high arts of deception and double-cross being well practiced by both the Germans and the British, it was concluded that the papers were a plant, a ruse, and therefore, unbelievable.[88]

On Thursday morning, May 9, the 250th day of the war, Chamberlain faced the bitter truth: he was through. The debacle in Norway had finished him. It had become obvious that Britain needed an all-party national government, and Labour refused to serve under him. Given the huge Tory majority in the House, a legacy of the general election of 1935, the new prime minister would have to be a Conservative. The party's leadership wanted Lord Halifax, the foreign secretary. So did Chamberlain. So did the King. However, Tory backbenchers and Labour MPs leaned toward the first lord of the Admiralty, Winston Churchill. Halifax bowed out. Telephoning London from his battalion, Randolph Churchill asked for news. His father told him: "I think I shall be Prime Minister tomorrow."[89]

At 9:00 P.M. that night Hitler issued the code word "Danzig."

The mightiest army in history was ready, and at 4:19 A.M. on Friday, May 10, 1940, more than two million German soldiers in coalscuttle helmets surged forward. The Wehrmacht was crossing the frontiers of Belgium, Holland, and Luxembourg, attacking on a front extending from the North Sea to the Swiss frontier. Hitler had repeatedly sworn never to violate their neutrality, but he meant to conquer France, and the Low Countries were in his way.[90]

At 5:30 A.M. Belgium asked the Allies for help. Gamelin phoned General Alphonse Georges, his field commander in the northeast.

Georges asked: "Well, General, is it the Dyle operation?"

Gamelin said: "Since the Belgians are calling on us, do you see what else we can do?" (*"Que nous puissons faire autre chose?"*) Georges replied: "Obviously not."

Gamelin sealed it: "We must go into Belgium!" (*"Nous devons entrer en Belgique"*). Five minutes later Georges ordered five French armies and the British Expeditionary Force across the frontier. There was some unpleasantness with the Belgian border guards, who hadn't been told of the decision in Brussels. One official demanded visas from the British 3rd Division—the divisional commander, Major General Bernard Montgomery, put him under arrest—and on several roads Belgian obstacles, erected to block a French invasion, still barred the way. None slowed the Allied troops, now plunging ahead.[91]

The BEF was in high spirits. Tommies blew kisses as they passed smiling women and, wrote Clare Boothe, who was there, "stuck up their thumbs in the new gesture they had, which meant 'O.K., everything's fine.'" They were singing "Roll Out the Barrel," a Czech drinking song that had been popular since Munich, nineteen months earlier, and a ballad based on an Australian folk song:

Run, Adolf, run Adolf, run, run, run!
Here comes a Tommy with his gun, gun, gun!

They also sang songs their fathers had sung a generation ago: "Tipperary," "Keep the Home Fires Burning," and "Pack Up Your Troubles in Your Old Kit Bag." Among older officers there was a remarkable mood of déjà vu. In the *New York Times,* Drew Middleton wrote: "It was almost as if they were retracing steps taken in a dream, they saw again faces of friends long dead and heard the half-remembered names of towns and villages."[92]

By evening the best trained of the Allied troops were deep in both Belgium and Holland. Here, Gamelin assured everyone, was the German *schwerpunkt*—the strategic center of effort as defined by Prussian staff doctrine.

His blunder was fatal.

At Hitler's eyrie at Bad Münstereifel, twenty-five miles southwest of Bonn, the Führer danced with joy. His generals could scarcely believe their luck. General Adolf Heusinger excitedly scrawled in his diary: "They have poured into Belgium and fallen into the trap!"[93]

The upcoming Sabbath was Whitsuntide, traditionally part of a long holiday weekend for Englishmen, and celebrated by Christians as the day the Holy Spirit descended upon Christ's disciples. Londoners were impressed when, on Friday, having learned of the attack upon the Low Countries, their government canceled the bank holiday; it meant, wrote Mollie Panter-Downes for *The New Yorker,* "The government is really getting a move on." No reliable news was coming out of the Low Countries, and that was bad. Yet Britons were calm; no excited crowds took to the streets. Panter-Downes wrote: "It takes a good, stiff dose of adversity to release the formidable strength in what Harold Nicolson called 'the slow grinding will power of the British people.' To that has been added the quickening realization that they are fighting for their lives."[94]

For almost a decade Churchill had drummed warnings to his countrymen that this day would come. Three hundred years earlier, during the English Civil War, both the Royalist and Parliamentary armies introduced drummers into their ranks. They went into battle unarmed and beat out coded orders that could be heard over the crash of muskets and cannon: *form up, face right, left, volley.* The drummers were not meant to inspire or comfort their comrades, or to introduce confusion and fear into enemy ranks, yet within the blinding stinking smoke and bloody mayhem of combat, their relentless, rhythmic, *tap* and *thrum* did just that. Where the drummers of England went, Empire followed. Rudyard Kipling glorified them in "The Drums of the Fore and Aft," in which the courage of two young regimental drummers inspires the regiment, which, on the verge of annihilation at the hands of Afghan tribesmen, regroups, attacks, and at the end of the slaughter claims victory.

Churchill's heroes—Pitt, Marlborough, Nelson—had not only led, they had inspired. Winston Churchill was prepared now to step forward as England's master and commander, and its drummer. But were his King and countrymen ready for him? Would Britons join him when the Hun arrived, and fight alongside him to the end? Were they prepared, each and all, to die in defense of family, home, King, and country? Churchill was. He had readied himself for this moment during every hour of every day for six decades, when he first sent his toy armies charging across the floors of his father's London town house.

The glorious weather held. Lilacs—in English folklore the harbingers of springtime rebirth—bloomed across the land. "Lovely day," Alexander Cadogan noted in his diary hours before Hitler gave his order to attack. "Tulips almost at their best and everything smiling, except human affairs."

Cadogan, a Chamberlain loyalist, by then knew that the Chamberlain government was finished. "But *what*," he asked his diary, "are we going to put in its place?" Who would lead? "Attlee? Sinclair? Sam Hoare?"

He eliminated one candidate out of hand: "Winston useless."[95]

Cyclone

Shortly after tea on Friday, May 10, fifteen hours after Hitler drove his steel into the Low Countries, Neville Chamberlain reluctantly returned the seals of his office to King George VI, who received them with equal reluctance: "I accepted his resignation," the sovereign wrote in his diary that evening, "& told him how grossly, unfairly I thought he had been treated." Shortly after six o'clock, the King anointed as prime minister the massive, stooped, sixty-five-year-old first lord of the Admiralty, Winston Leonard Spencer Churchill. Later King George became one of Churchill's most ardent admirers, but his feelings were mixed at the time. In his diary that day Jock Colville wrote that the King "(remembering perhaps the abdication, which Churchill had opposed) is understood not to wish to send for Winston." Nevertheless, an all-party government was essential, and Labour had been adamant: they would not serve under Chamberlain.[1]

Defending Britain and her Empire would be the new prime minister's responsibility for the next five years, or until he was hurled from office by Parliament or Hitler. Yet, as he rode back from Buckingham Palace, neither he nor anyone else in London felt unduly alarmed over the course of the war. Little was known that evening about the day's developments across the Channel. The Luftwaffe had bombed airfields in Belgium and Holland; parachute troops had landed among the Belgians, who were said to be fighting well; Dutch resistance was reportedly "stubborn"; and the Allies were taking up strong positions on the Antwerp-Namur Line, preparing to defend the Albert Kanaal. Everything was going as expected, or so it seemed at that hour.[2]

When the BBC announced Churchill's appointment that night, his daughter Mary, seventeen, listened to the broadcast in the small cottage at Chartwell where her governess lived. When it finished she switched off the wireless and said a prayer for her father.[3]

Churchill was surrounded by his family, whether at No. 10 or in the underground Annexe. Of the older Churchill children, only Sarah, the actress, was still a civilian, living with her husband in a Westminster Gardens flat, and soon she too would be commissioned in the Women's Auxiliary Air Force (WAAF). Sarah's husband, Vic Oliver, Austrian by birth, the son of Baron Viktor Oliver von Samek, had renounced his barony, changed the "k" in Viktor to "c," and was now an American citizen. Churchill, upon first meeting Oliver in 1936, took an immediate dislike to the man, and in a letter to Clementine cut loose. Oliver was "common as dirt," possessed "a horrible mouth," and spoke with "an Austro-Yankee drawl." Yet no mention was made of the one trait which many in the English aristocracy would have found sufficient to dismiss Vic Oliver outright: his family was Jewish. It would not have occurred to Churchill to do so. He measured the man.[4]

Of the other children, Diana and Randolph were already officers, she in the Women's Royal Naval Service (WRNS, or Wrens in naval slang), Randolph in his father's old regiment, the 4th Hussars. Mary worked in a canteen and for the Red Cross and lived with her parents. So did Randolph's twenty-year-old wife, Pamela, who was expecting their first child in October. When the air raids began with June's full moon, Pamela and her father-in-law shared bunk beds in the basement of No. 10. Because she was pregnant, hers was the bottom bunk, and in the early hours of each morning she woke to hear Churchill laboriously climb the short ladder to his. Clementine slept in another basement bedroom.[5]

As prime minister, Churchill was also surrounded by a large official family, "The Secret Circle," as he called them. Always at his elbow were his three private secretaries, John ("Jock") Colville, who remained at No. 10 after Chamberlain's departure, and Eric Seal and John Martin, whom Churchill had brought over from the Admiralty. Also within earshot were his typists, Kathleen Hill, Grace Hamblin, and Edith Watson, who had aided every P.M. since Lloyd George. Pug Ismay served as his liaison with His Majesty's Chiefs of Staff, whose offices were in Richmond Terrace: the chiefs were Admiral Sir Alfred Dudley Pound, General Sir John Dill, and Air Marshal Sir Cyril Newall. Colville told his diary that Churchill considered the three chiefs to be "sound, but old and slow." Air Marshal Sir Charles Portal replaced Newall in October.[6]

A recent arrival at No. 10 was Dr. Charles Wilson, the P.M.'s personal physician, who kept a diary from the day of his appointment. On first meeting the doctor, Churchill treated him as he did all underlings, with a mixture of curtness and impatience. Dr. Wilson had found Churchill in bed, at noon, reading papers, which he continued to peruse as Wilson stood nearby, waiting for some acknowledgment. Finally, from Churchill: "I don't know why they're making such a fuss." Churchill snarled, "There's nothing wrong with me." That was true enough, for the doctor makes no further diary entries for the remainder of the year.[7]

Churchill hadn't wanted a doctor; he claimed that there was nothing wrong with him. Churchill's old friend Max Beaverbrook insisted, however, and no one could insist more strenuously than "the Beaver," as everyone called him. That was why Churchill had named him chief of aircraft production. England had to have planes for the coming air battle. In pursuit of a vital goal, the Beaver was ruthless, unscrupulous, even piratical. He seized factories, broke into warehouses, and imprisoned those who tried to stop him. None of this was against the law. On May 22, Parliament had passed an Emergency Powers (Defence) Act giving His Majesty's Government sweeping prerogatives. One section, 18B, effectively removed the *habeas* from *habeas corpus*. HMG held absolute power over all British citizens, requiring them "to place themselves, their services, and their property at the disposal of His Majesty," specifically of the minister of defence, who happened also to be the prime minister. Churchill could have become a dictator had he so chosen. Instead he became almost obsessive in his belief that the House should be fully informed of all developments.[8]

Among the other newcomers to HMG were three Churchill votaries—"the fearsome triumvirate," Colville called them—whom the civil servants had awaited with dread: Brendan Bracken, MP; Frederick Lindemann ("the Prof"); and Major Desmond Morton, a Westerham neighbor of Churchill who had played a vital role in Churchill's prewar intelligence net, assembling proof of England's military unpreparedness. But Morton lacked access to the most vital intelligence, from Bletchley. Within a year Morton's star began to set, since Churchill, informed by Bletchley, no longer needed his own private secret service, and Morton apparently did not provide enough panache at the dinner table to rate a regular weekend dinner invitation. Churchill's friendships admitted to a certain degree of utilitarian relativity, though for the time being Morton's past loyalty trumped his diminishing utility. Bracken had long been Churchill's most devout supporter in the House of Commons. He was also a very odd young man who, to Clementine's annoyance, had in the 1920s encouraged rumors that he was Churchill's natural son (he ceased doing so at Churchill's request). The Prof was even odder. German born, educated at Berlin University, a bachelor and vegetarian, he believed that all women looked upon him as a sex object. But he was a brilliant physicist and a consummate interpreter of science for laymen. He was to become the strongest advocate for the unrestricted bombing and burning of the cities of his homeland.[9]

Churchill, his family, his colleagues, and his cronies were prepared to meet whatever came their way via Berlin. If Britons were not yet prepared, Churchill intended that they soon would be.

It is impossible to exaggerate the influence of World War I on the opening battles of World War II. Afterward, Churchill wrote that it was "a joke in

Britain to say that the War Office is always preparing for the last war." That was also true of soldiers, and it was equally true of statesmen—even the Führer was preoccupied with the trench fighting of 1914–1918. Churchill was no exception. During the Great War he had learned certain precepts of modern warfare, including one of immense significance: tactical breakthroughs were impossible, because whenever a position was in peril, it could be swiftly reinforced. The continuous front had never broken. And another lesson learned: nothing in that war had happened quickly.[10]

In the current war, *everything* was happening quickly—too quickly—and none of it good. German panzers were smashing all the old strategic and tactical paradigms. Britain's survival depended upon finding the weaknesses in the Nazi strategy, and then exploiting them. This would be Churchill's ultimate problem. His immediate problem was political: Conservative MPs, who held 432 of the 607 seats in the House, dominated Parliament. The source of this problem lay in the country's last general election, five years earlier. Misled by Prime Minister Stanley Baldwin, who had assured Parliament that England's defenses were more than adequate, Britain had elected a House of Commons top-heavy with irreconcilable pacifists and die-hard appeasers. Since then, the country's mood had turned 180 degrees, but in their hearts, the Conservative majority remained loyal to the memory of Baldwin and the disastrous policies of Neville Chamberlain, even though they had led England to this fearful pass.

The new P.M., though a Tory himself, had been their gadfly throughout the 1930s, a vehement opponent of their "Splendid Isolation," which they defined as "a plea for the detachment of Britain from Continental quarrels." Again and again he had warned of the Nazi menace, demanding larger defense budgets. The fact that subsequent events had proven him right and them wrong did not endear him to them. An embittered R. A. ("Rab") Butler (an appeaser and Chamberlain loyalist) called Churchill "a half-breed American" and "the greatest adventurer in modern political history." That Friday, the tenth, Butler denounced "this sudden coup of Winston and his rabble." Another Conservative MP wrote Stanley Baldwin—who had described Churchill as part of "the flotsam and jetsam of political drift thrown up on the beach"—that "the Tories don't trust Winston. After the first clash of war is over it may well be that a sounder Government may emerge." A civil servant noted, "There seems to be some inclination in Whitehall to believe that Winston will be a complete failure and that Neville will return." The pacifist editor Max Plowman wrote: "Perhaps Winston will win the war. Perhaps he won't. How anybody could *expect* him to, I don't know, in view of his unparalleled record in losing everything he puts his hand to."[11]

The permanent secretariat at No. 10 Downing Street, who knew Churchill only as a critic of his predecessors, despaired. For as long as the private secretaries there could remember, Baldwin or Chamberlain had been in power. They were mostly Tories themselves, young gentlemen working in what had been, until then, a comfortable private home, where everything went smoothly and quietly, with messengers summoned at the tinkle of a bell, clean towels and ivory brushes in the cloakroom, and everything, as one of them put it, "reminding the inhabitants that they were working at the very heart of a great empire, in which haste was undignified and any quiver of the upper lip unacceptable." Everything about Churchill's reputation horrified them. Jock Colville wrote in his diary that Churchill's rise "is a terrible risk, and I cannot help feeling that this country may be manoeuvred into the most dangerous position it has ever been in." Later Colville recalled that "in May 1940 the mere thought of Churchill as Prime Minister sends a cold chill down the spines of the staff at No. 10 Downing Street.... Seldom can a Prime Minister have taken office with the Establishment so dubious of the choice & so prepared to have its doubts justified." Quite apart from the fortunes of war, already darkening England's prospects for survival, Churchill's government was being launched in very rough political waters.[12]

They swiftly calmed. "Within a fortnight," Colville wrote, "all was changed." Churchill arrived on the scene like a summer squall at a sailboat regatta. Whitehall was galvanized, and the office at No. 10 was pandemonium. Bells were ringing constantly, telephones of various colors were being installed in every nook at No. 10, and the new prime minister was attaching maroon labels demanding "Action This Day" or green ones saying "Report in Three Days" to an endless stream of directives that were being dictated to typists in the Cabinet Room, the P.M.'s bedroom, and even his bathroom, with replies expected within minutes. Ministers, generals, and senior civil servants appeared and departed within minutes. Working hours began early each morning and ended after midnight. "The pace became frantic," another private secretary, John Martin, recalled. "We realized we were at war."[13]

Chamberlain had been cold and orderly; Churchill, John Martin recalled, was "a human dynamo." In the words of Sir Ian Jacob: "His pugnacious spirit demanded constant action. The enemy must be assailed continuously: the Germans must be made to 'bleed and burn.'" Churchill appointed himself his own minister of defence, thereby assuring that he himself, working through Major General Ismay, would manage the Chiefs of Staff, conducting the war day by day, even hour by hour. Yet Churchill always took care to pass his wishes to the generals through Ismay, whose "loyalty to his seniors and juniors was absolute" such that, in turn, he was never shy about telling Churchill just what the generals and their Joint Planning Staff thought of his suggestions—often, not much, which led Churchill to call the JPS "the whole machinery of negation." Ismay's loyalty to Churchill did not insulate him from prime ministerial outbursts any more than did the allegiance of others on the Old Man's staff. After one contentious meeting with the Chiefs of Staff, he let loose on the "pusillanimity and negative attitude" displayed by the chiefs, "and you are one of the worst," he declared to the indignant Ismay. After another unsatisfactory meeting with his COS and Ismay, Churchill told Colville, "I am obliged to wage modern warfare with ancient weapons."[14]

Sir Ian Jacob recalled that as deferential as Ismay was to his boss and the Chiefs of Staff, Churchill learned quickly that Ismay never allowed the usual feelings of protocol to stand in the way of speed and efficiency of work. "He was without vanity," Jacob later recalled, "and inspired in all those who worked with him the same spirit of loyalty he in such great measure possessed." At about 9:30 each morning (if Churchill hadn't kept Ismay up most of the night), Ismay and Churchill met, the Old Man usually in bed, the early editions of the newspapers strewn hither and yon, the air saturated with the stale aroma of cigars. At these briefings Churchill passed along any memos he had dictated the night before. Most were brief queries or suggestions; some were strongly worded opinions. A memo signed in red ink meant Churchill wanted action. A memo signed in red ink, and affixed with the slip "Action This Day," was the prime ministerial equivalent of a five-alarm fire.[15]

As Ian Jacob later observed, Churchill was "determined to be No. 1 and to use all the political powers of a No. 1 directly." In front of his place at the cabinet table he placed a square of cardboard bearing a quotation from Queen Victoria during the Boer War: "Please understand that we are not interested in the possibilities of defeat. They do not exist."[16]

The impact of all of this on his civil service secretariat was enormous. The journalist Virginia Cowles wrote: "The whole of 10 Downing Street throbbed with an energy it had not seen since the days of Lloyd George."[17]

Parliament was another matter. On his third day in office, Churchill rose in the House of Commons for the first time as prime minister and invited the members to affirm his new government. Harold Nicolson wrote in his diary: "When Chamberlain enters the House he gets a terrific reception, and when Churchill comes in the applause is less." The P.M.'s statement was brief but eloquent; it was then that he said, "I have nothing to offer but blood, toil, tears, and sweat." His peroration was, as usual, a taking of the ramparts by words alone, and, as usual, it was dismissed by his detractors in the Commons and by his enemies in Berlin as typically Churchillian hyperbole, misplaced given unfolding events in France, and perhaps delusional. It was in fact a solemn oath, a statement of literal intent, which admitted to no ambiguity: "You ask, what is our aim? I answer in one word: It is victory, victory at all costs, victory in spite of all terror, victory, however long and hard the road may be, for without victory, there is no survival. Let that be realized; no survival for the British Empire" and all it has stood for, "no survival for the urge and impulse of the ages, that mankind will move forward toward its goal." Labour and Liberal MPs cheered. Many Tories sat silent; they were still fuming over Churchill's ascendancy to No. 10. The historian Laurence Thompson noted: "Conservative anger that the wrong man had been shot over Norway continued for many months."[18]

The campaign for Norway had lasted two months, from early April until early June. By late May, southern and central Norway had been abandoned by British and Norwegian forces, although Narvik, Norway's northernmost ice-free port, had been cleared of Germans by British troops, who, if reinforced, were poised to strike toward the Swedish iron-ore fields so critical to Hitler. Thus to interdict Swedish war shipments had been the objective of the March plan (code-named Wilfred) to lay mines in Norwegian waters. But Wilfred was scotched by Chamberlain and Halifax for fear of offending Norway and Sweden. Narvik (and the million tons of iron ore stored there) had been Churchill's main objective from the start, but by early June, events in France dictated that the cause be abandoned. The evacuation did not go well. On the afternoon of the eighth of June, 1940, the aircraft carrier HMS *Glorious*—fleeing Norway with as many aircraft and men as she could carry—was intercepted in the Norwegian Sea by the German battle cruisers *Gneisenau* and *Scharnhorst*. *Glorious,* and two escorting destroyers, were sunk by gunfire in just over two hours, with the loss of more than 1,500 officers and men of the Royal Navy, Royal Marines, and Royal Air Force. Churchill, first lord of the Admiralty when the Norwegian adventure began, and prime minister when it ended, had already taken responsibility for the disastrous outcome. For much of the remainder of the war, the loss of *Glorious* and the specter of *Gneisenau* and *Scharnhorst* moved Churchill at times to dubious naval strategy. He was still coming to terms with modern naval warfare, and not entirely successfully; the success of the German battle cruisers and the vulnerability of *Glorious* seemed to imply that fast, heavy ships still ruled the waves. In fact, aircraft carriers, if deployed properly, posed a mortal threat to battle cruisers. Hitler, meanwhile, pocketed the Norwegian and Swedish ore, but would pay heavily for those prizes; during the next four years, more than 160,000 of his best troops remained in Norway awaiting the return of the English. Other than shooting Norwegian patriots and chasing down the occasional British commando, more than twelve priceless Wehrmacht divisions would miss the war. Churchill, in turn, became obsessed with returning to Norway, and during the next four years drove his military chiefs to distraction with what Sir Alan Brooke called "his mad Norwegian plans." Hitler, in fact, read Churchill's ambitions exactly.[19]

Because Churchill well understood that criticism of his career centered on his history of questionable strategic judgments and his notoriety for being willing to change sides, his chief political concern was reconciliation with the House, and he made a major effort to do so. He invited Chamberlain into his government both as lord president of the council and leader of the House, and sent him a note: "No one changes houses for a month." Beginning on May 13, his third day in office, he began working at No. 10 afternoons while his predecessor leisurely moved out upstairs, but during those early weeks, he conducted most of HMG's business from Admiralty House, using its drawing room, with its furniture carved with dolphins ("the fish room," he called it), for cabinet meetings. He could scarcely ignore the issues that had divided him and the appeasers for seven years, but his references to them were light, even bantering; introducing one appeaser to his wife, he beamed as he said, "Oh, yes, my dear, he has the Munich medal with bar." He would have been happy to see the last of his foreign secretary and a major appeaser, Lord Halifax, but he kept him in the Foreign Office for the present. This put Churchill in an awkward position with those who had backed him during the lean years and now wanted all "the old crowd" thrown out, but he was adamant. "If we open a quarrel between the past and the present, we shall find that we have lost the future," he said, and, later, "No one had more right than I to pass a sponge across the past. I therefore resisted these disruptive tendencies."[20]

Inevitably politics determined his cabinet choices. He had to form a government with all parties represented, and he hadn't much time. Most senior posts were filled by May 13. Clement Attlee (lord privy seal), Arthur Greenwood (cabinet minister without portfolio), and Ernest Bevin (minister of labour) came from the Labour benches. Bevin's inclusion testified to the true nature of the coalition; he was a former teamster, the son of a domestic servant and unknown father, and most assuredly not one of Churchill's crowd. From the Liberals, Archibald Sinclair, Churchill's longtime friend and second in command of Churchill's battalion in the trenches, went to the Air Ministry. From Churchill's own camp, Sir John

Anderson, a Chamberlain appointee, stayed on as Home Secretary. Leo Amery, Churchill's old friend from Harrow (and sometimes his critic) as well as a pugnacious anti-Chamberlain rebel, was given the India secretariat. Anthony Eden went to the War Office. Only one appointment hit a snag. The problem wasn't political. Churchill wanted Lord Beaverbrook as minister of aircraft production. The King objected. That was understandable: Beaverbrook was a highly controversial figure, objectionable in many ways. However, Churchill was going to need a lot of airplanes soon, and he knew this man had the drive and the ruthlessness to get them one way or another. Beaverbrook, he told Jock Colville, was "twenty-five percent thug, fifteen percent crook and the remainder a combination of genius and real goodness of heart."[21]

The King bowed to his judgment. Churchill did settle one score. Sir John Reith, minister of information and creator of the modern BBC, had barred him from the BBC during the 1930s and, after the war's outbreak, intrigued against him. Churchill fired Reith on May 12 and replaced him with Alfred Duff Cooper, who had quit Chamberlain's government in protest against the Munich Agreement. Churchill soon found new duties for the appeaser Reith, at the Transport Ministry. The War Cabinet—"the only ones," he said, "who had the right to have their heads cut off on Tower Hill if we did not win"—comprised five men: himself, Chamberlain, Attlee, Halifax, and Greenwood.[22]

In the country, where his popularity was soaring, his conciliatory manner toward those who had scorned him was remarked upon and widely praised. Few noticed how he quietly put the greatest possible distance between himself and the most objectionable of them. Sir Samuel Hoare was sent as ambassador to Spain, Lord Harlech to South Africa, Lord Swinton to the African Gold Coast, Malcolm MacDonald to Canada, and, before the year was out, Halifax to the United States. Presently he would use this very effective maneuver to banish the Duke of Windsor, a sometime admirer of the Third Reich, an admiration as narrow and shallow as he was. But Churchill could not banish their abiding doubts of his abilities. On the day Churchill told Halifax he would remain at the Foreign Office, Halifax wrote in his diary, "I have seldom met anyone with stranger gaps of knowledge, or whose mind worked in greater jerks. Will it be possible to make it work in orderly fashion?" Then Halifax answered his own question with such profound understatement as to call into question whether he truly grasped Britain's plight: "On this much depends."[23]

At the outset, Churchill later wrote, "no fresh decision was required from me or my colleagues." Plan D was in operation, British troops had reached the Dyle River, and so, the new prime minister wrote, he did not "in the slightest degree wish to interfere with the military plans"; instead, he merely "awaited with hope the impending shock." The War Cabinet authorized the detention of enemy aliens living in Britain, debated the wisdom and morality of bombing German territory, and approved messages from the P.M. to President Roosevelt and Mussolini. Roosevelt's answer was cordial but disappointing. Churchill had asked for the "loan of 40 or 50 old" U.S. destroyers; the President explained that to honor the request would violate Congress's Neutrality Acts. Il Duce, in reply to Churchill's suggestion to stay out of the fray, was rude. Italy, he bluntly replied, was an ally of Nazi Germany.[24]

The world's eyes were on the Low Countries across the Channel. The British were following this front with special anxiety, aware of the threat to England should the Nazis establish bases that close to Britain. Enemy successes there were spectacular but not really alarming. In the Netherlands 4,000 Nazi parachutists and German infantrymen captured key bridges over the Meuse River and forced a Dutch surrender after the Luftwaffe's terror bombing of Rotterdam, which destroyed 25,000 homes and massacred more than 1,000 (not the 30,000 claimed by the Dutch government, a figure that terrified Britons). Meantime, in Belgium, German airborne troops and specially picked paratroopers had crossed the Albert Kanaal and seized the country's mighty Fort Eben-Emael. Nazi infantry then turned southward to take Liège from the rear.[25]

But the Belgian, French, and British troops were fighting well. Despite furious German assaults, the Dyle Line had not been breached. Two enemy divisions briefly penetrated it in a tangled railroad yard near Louvain, but the Tommies of General Bernard Montgomery's 3rd Division swiftly routed them.

South of Louvain two panzer divisions, supported by waves of Junkers Ju 87s — "Stuka" dive-bombers — mounted an even stronger attack on the grounds of an agricultural school at Gembloux. Instantly General Jean-Georges-Maurice Blanchard ordered a counterattack by the French First Army. These were crack troops, descendants of the poilus whose valor, inspired by the tricolor and their fierce national anthem, had awed Europe in the century and a half since the French Revolution.

They drove the Germans back and back, and Gamelin felt vindicated. This, he said, proved that he had anticipated the German *schwerpunkt;* the Nazis had come where he expected them to come, and the Allied Line was unbroken. The British were less sure. The RAF had not been caught on the ground, but it had been battered in the air. On Sunday, May 12, Air Chief Marshal Sir Cyril Newall reported "undue losses of medium bombers in relation to the results attained," and on Monday, when the Chiefs of Staff committee met in Admiralty House, with Churchill in the chair for the first time as minister of defence, the consensus was that "it was not yet certain" where the enemy's main effort was to be made. General Ironside, Chief of the Imperial Staff, believed the Germans might be consolidating their position on this front before mounting an offense elsewhere, possibly "an intensive air attack in Great Britain." Churchill thought the situation "far from satisfactory." One officer noticed an ominous sign. The Luftwaffe bombers, he pointed out, had achieved air superiority over the northern battlefield, yet they were leaving columns of French reinforcements marching to the front unmolested. Why should the Germans want more Allied troops on this front?[26]

No one, not even Pétain, had declared the Ardennes Forest to be *absolutely* impenetrable, though his error was equally egregious. What he had said was that the Ardennes was "impassable to strong forces." In fact it was good tank country, with many fields and trails. The French should have known that—they had held maneuvers there in 1939. The forest's trees were actually an asset, serving to camouflage armor and troop movements from aerial surveillance.

The German strategy in 1940 could be summed up in the code word by which the Wehrmacht general staff in Zossen anointed the operation: "*Sichelschnitt,*" or "scythe cut." Here, as in Poland, the scythe would exploit the Reich's new concept of warfare: deep penetration of enemy territory by mobile armored forces, with infantry following. In planning his drive, Hitler had divided his forces into three army groups. The one that had struck in the Low Countries comprised thirty divisions, including three panzer divisions. A second, tying down the Maginot Line, in the west, was given nineteen divisions. The great blow would be delivered in the center by the third: forty-five divisions, including seven panzer divisions, commanded by Gerd von Rundstedt. This juggernaut would plunge through Luxembourg and the Ardennes, and vault over the Meuse River north and south of Sedan, some 70 miles southwest of Liège, on the east bank of the Meuse and a dozen miles inside France. That would put the main German force at a point roughly 125 miles from Paris and 175 miles from the Channel ports of Calais, Gravelines, and Dunkirk. The German high command knew the Allies were vulnerable in the Sedan sector; the line was thinly held by two French armies of older, poorly trained, and ill-equipped married men.

The French high command had estimated that it would take at least fifteen days for any strong enemy force to negotiate the thickets and deep wooded ravines of the Ardennes. The Germans, who had rehearsed elaborately in the Black Forest, did it in two, sweeping Belgian infantry-men before them. To the horror of the unprepared French defenders in the vicinity of Sedan, on Sunday the twelfth, the mechanized spearhead of Rundstedt's seven panzer divisions — 1,800 tanks, 17,000 other vehicles, and 98,000 men — appeared on the east bank of the Meuse. The answer to the question of why the Luftwaffe had allowed French reinforcements to drift northward toward Holland had arrived with terrible certainty: the real *schwerpunkt* was at Sedan.

The Meuse, the Nazis had known, would be their most forbidding obstacle. It was narrow and swift at this point; confronting the attackers on the far bank were well-placed batteries of heavy artillery. That would have sufficed in 1918, but this was a different war. On Monday, Rundstedt silenced every French field piece, every howitzer, by skillful use of tactical air — Stukas and other low-level bombers — which so terrorized the gun-ners that they abandoned their cannons. Nazi rubber boats reached the opposite shore unmolested; beachheads were established north and south of Sedan; pontoon bridges spanned the Meuse, then heavy bridges, and, finally, on Tuesday morning, lumbering and growling, came the Nazi tanks. By noon on Tuesday, May 14, the Germans had established a formi-dable pocket on French soil, three miles wide and two miles deep.

It was time, and past time, for a French counterattack. At 5:30 P.M. on the thirteenth, orders were issued, and a strong force of French tanks advanced, backed by the infantry of the 55th Division. History's first great battle of mechanized armor seemed imminent. The French position was far from hopeless. The German flank was exposed to the French tanks, and not all the panzers, artillery, and infantry were across the Meuse and in position. French tanks were well armored; many carried 75mm cannon, heavier than the guns on many German tanks. Unfortunately, the French chose not to mass their tanks for a steel-fisted assault, instead dispersing them along too broad a front. More unfortunately, the *Conseil Supérieur de la Guerre,* having determined that armor was to be used only in support of infantry, had forbidden the installation of radios in their turrets. The French drivers, unable to communicate with one another, could not coor-dinate an assault. The consequence was disastrous. Within two hours of the battle opening on the fourteenth, the panzers had destroyed fifty French tanks; the rest, a few dozen, fled.

That was the small disaster. The great disaster began sometime between 6:00 and 7:00 P.M., when, according to the French corps commander, "the situation evolved with a disconcerting rapidity toward catastrophe." Bluntly put, the defenders panicked. Men threw down their rifles and ran, crowding the roads, and they did not stop until they had reached Reims, sixty miles away. Few officers tried to discourage them. One who did later recalled their response. "Colonel," they said, "we want to go home, back to our little jobs (*nos petit boulots*). There's no use trying to fight. There's nothing we can do. We're lost! We've been betrayed!"[27]

In a well-disciplined army they would have been shot on the spot. But everyone, officers and men, seemed infected with the fear, which spread. "The roof fell in," wrote William L. Shirer. One regiment after another broke, until the entire Ninth Army—some two hundred thousand men—ceased to exist. A dazed divisional commander wandered into the army's headquarters to report: "Of my division I fear I am the only one left." The Second Army, on the right flank of the Ninth, fell back. Meantime the Germans, who were arriving in great numbers, began to capture them. Charles de Gaulle, moving up to take command of a brigade, was shocked to see "many soldiers who had lost their weapons.... Caught up, as they fled, by the enemy's mechanized detachments, they had been ordered to throw away their arms and make off to the south so as not to clutter up the roads. 'We haven't time,' they had been told, 'to take you prisoners!' "[28]

The French defensive line was now breached by a hole sixty miles wide, and German armor, followed by infantry, was streaming through it. Incredibly, no one in Paris knew what was happening. Field commanders, ashamed to report the truth, played down the debacle, assuring General Georges' headquarters that everything was under control, and hour by hour Georges relayed their optimism to Gamelin in Vincennes. As late as Wednesday, when the Battle of the Meuse was over and the French hopelessly routed, Gamelin's communiqué reported: "To sum up, the day of May 15 seems to show a lessening in the intensity of enemy action.... Our front, which was 'shaken' (*'ébranlé'*) between Namur and the region west of Montmédy, is reestablishing itself little by little."

One man knew better. It says much about France's military establishment that the first Parisian to learn the truth was a civilian: Paul Reynaud. The premier had studied the possibilities of tank warfare, and he had spies in the army, informers who sent him word of what was actually happening. At 5:45 P.M. on Tuesday, May 14, the fifth day of the enemy offensive, he wired Churchill: "The situation is indeed very serious. Germany is trying to deal us a fatal blow in the direction of Paris. The German army has broken through our fortified lines south of Sedan.... Between Sedan and Paris there are no defenses comparable with those in the line, which we must restore at almost any cost." He then asked for ten more Royal Air Force squadrons "immediately."[29]

The prime minister told Ironside to check this; the CIGS (Chief of the Imperial General Staff) sent a liaison officer "to find out what the real situation is." Later in the day Ironside told Churchill, "We could get nothing out of" either Gamelin or Georges. Ironside suggested that perhaps Reynaud was being "a little hysterical." But the French premier knew he was right. At seven o'clock the next morning he woke Churchill with an anguished telephone call. "We have been defeated!" he cried in English. "We are beaten! We have lost the battle!" The P.M., his mind still mired in the trenches of 1914–1918, said, "Surely it can't have happened so soon!" As Churchill recalled afterward, Reynaud replied, "The front is broken near Sedan; they are pouring through in great numbers with tanks and armored cars." Churchill told him, "All experience shows that the offensive will come to an end after a while." Within five or six days, he said, the enemy would have to halt for supplies; that would be the moment for a counterattack. But the premier repeated, "We are defeated; we have lost the battle." Churchill said he was willing to come over "and have a talk."[30]

Ringing up Ironside, the prime minister repeated the conversation, commenting that Reynaud had seemed "thoroughly demoralized." Ironside told him that "we have no extra demands from Gamelin or Georges, both of whom are calm, though they both consider the situation serious." The P.M. then called Georges, an old friend. Georges, quite cool, reported that the breach at Sedan was "being plugged." But late that afternoon Reynaud sent another message: "Last week we lost the battle. The way to Paris lies open. Send all the troops and planes you can." Churchill sent four squadrons of fighters, then decided it was "imperative to go to Paris." At 3:00 P.M. on May 16 he took off in an unarmed Flamingo, a civilian passenger plane, accompanied by General Ismay, General Sir John Dill, and Inspector Walter Thompson of Scotland Yard, a fifty-year-old ex-copper who had served as Churchill's bodyguard a decade earlier and had been called out of retirement to again protect the Great Man.

Over the French coast the prime minister peered down, and Thompson saw his face go gray. Churchill was looking, for the first time, at the war's refugees. There were now over seven million of them fleeing from the Germans, swarming down the highways, shuffling, exhausted, aching from the strain of heavy loads on their backs. No one had told them to evacuate the battlefields; they were evacuating themselves. Barns, sheds, and garages had disgorged into throughways an extraordinary collection of vehicles: farm carts, trucks, horse-drawn carts, hay wagons, and ancient automobiles saddled with sagging loads of mattresses, kitchen utensils, family treasures, and bric-a-brac. Cars bombed by the Luftwaffe stood in flames, and here and there among straggling vagabonds lay corpses of children and the very old, who, unable to keep up, had been machine-gunned by Nazi pilots who saw panic as an ally of their comrades in the Wehrmacht.[31]

In their memoirs the generals on both sides would complain about the obstacles these people created, but the refugees looked at it differently, and

Churchill saw it their way. The great tragedy was coming into focus for Churchill. He was also beginning to understand Reynaud's alarm. He later wrote: "Not having had access to official information for so many years, I did not comprehend the revolution effected since the last war by the incursion of a mass of fast-moving heavy armour." This Nazi drive would not have to pause for supplies; as de Gaulle had foreseen, the panzers were filling their tanks at the filling stations of northern France.[32]

The prime minister's Flamingo landed at Le Bourget, and as they alighted, Ismay felt "an unmistakable atmosphere of depression." Events were moving swiftly in Paris. Gamelin foresaw the end. William Bullitt, the American ambassador, had been with Daladier when the *généralissime* called to break the news. He had told them: "It means the destruction of the French army. Between Laon and Paris I do not have a single corps at my disposal." The panic had reached the French capital. Parisians realized that there were an extraordinary number of automobiles with Belgian license plates on the streets "just passing through," the drivers told them; "the Boche is right behind us." Everyone seemed to know that Gamelin had told the highest officials of the republic, *"Je ne répons plus de rien"* ("I am no longer responsible for anything").[33]

At the Quai d'Orsay Reynaud, Daladier, and Gamelin awaited the British in a large room looking out on a garden "which," Ismay wrote, "had appeared so lovely and well-kept on my last visit, but which was now disfigured with clusters of bonfires." The French were burning their official papers. This was Churchill's first meeting as a member of the Allied Supreme War Council, and Ismay was "interested to see how he handled the situation."

He dominated the proceedings from the moment he entered the room. There was no interpreter, and he spoke throughout in French. His idiom was not always correct, and his vocabulary was not equal to translating with exactitude all the words that he required. But no one could have been in any doubt as to his meaning.[34]

He began by telling them that although their plight was grave, this was not the first time they had been in a crisis together; the Ludendorff offensives of early 1918 had nearly destroyed them and their ally, the United States. He was confident that they would survive this one. Then he asked for a briefing. Gamelin gave it. Stepping up to a map on an easel, he talked for five minutes, describing the Germans' breakthrough. He said they were advancing with unprecedented speed. Their intentions were unknown; they could reach the coast or turn on Paris. At the end Churchill slapped him heartily on the shoulder — the general winced — and told him that this would become known as "the Battle of the Bulge." ("Boogle" was the closest he could come to this.) Then he asked him where his strategic reserve was: *"Où est la masse de manoeuvre?"* Gamelin shook his head and replied: *"Aucune."* He had none.

There was a long pause while Churchill, speechless, stared absently at the elderly men carrying wheelbarrows of documents to the fires. *No strategic reserve.* It had never occurred to him that commanders defending five hundred miles of engaged front would have left themselves without reserves; no one could defend with certainty so wide a front, but when the enemy broke the line, the defenders should have a mass of divisions ready to counterattack. He was, he wrote, "dumbfounded."[35]

After the war it was Churchill's recollection, confirmed by Ismay, that he did not argue strategy with Reynaud, Daladier, and Gamelin. "There couldn't have been a disagreement," he said. "We didn't know enough about the situation to disagree." However, the French notes on this point are quite detailed. According to them, Churchill vigorously opposed ordering a general retreat by the Allied troops in Belgium. This, the P.M. said, was a time to "hold fast." He did not believe the panzer breakthrough was "a real invasion." As long as the tanks were "not supported by infantry units," they were merely "little flags stuck on the map," because they would be "unable to support themselves or to refuel." The French records quote him as telling them, "I refuse to see in this spectacular raid of the German tanks a real invasion."[36]

Churchill may not have *argued* strategy that day, but he proposed one—to hold fast—and it was unrealistic. It was characteristic of him that he always approved of attacks, and seldom retreats, even when, as here, failure to withdraw would mean encirclement and annihilation. Reynaud silenced him by pointing out that all the field commanders, including Lord Gort, believed the French should fall back.[37]

Churchill was, however, thoroughly justified in asking Gamelin when and where he proposed to attack the flanks of the German bulge. The *généralissime*'s dismaying, unresponsive reply was "inferiority of numbers, inferiority of equipment, inferiority of method," followed by a hopeless shrug of the shoulders. The *généralissime* saw only one hope of salvation: the commitment of six more RAF squadrons to the battle. It was, he said, the only way to stop the panzers.

Churchill vigorously replied that tanks should be the target of artillery, not of fighter planes; fighters should "cleanse the skies" (*"nett le ciel"*) over the battle. Bombing the Meuse bridges was not a proper job for the RAF; nevertheless they had attempted to do it, at great risk, and had lost thirty-six aircraft. "You can replace bridges," he said, "but not fighters." He had just sent four more squadrons, forty-eight planes, and it was vital that Britain's metropolitan air force be available to command the air over

Britain in order to protect defense factories from the Luftwaffe. Britain had only a limited number of squadrons in England, and, he said, "We must conserve them." He did not think another six squadrons would "make the difference."

Daladier replied, "The French believe the contrary." The discussion became acrimonious. Gamelin had touched a vital nerve. Both sides were, to a degree, disingenuous. What the French really believed was that the British should throw everything they had into the struggle for France, and that if the Allied cause were to lose, both countries should go down together. The British believed that if France went down—and they were beginning to contemplate that possibility—Britain and the Empire should go on alone. That was why Air Chief Marshal Sir Hugh Dowding had put himself on record as "absolutely opposed to parting with a single additional Hurricane."

At the British embassy that evening, the prime minister weighed the French appeal. He should have rejected it, but his sympathy for them outweighed his reason, and he wired the War Cabinet that they should give this "last chance to the French Army to rally its bravery and strength. It would not be good historically if their requests were denied and their ruin resulted." The War Cabinet was apprehensive, but it was difficult to say no to the P.M. They reluctantly agreed, provided the Hurricanes returned to English bases each night. In the interests of security this decision was sent to Ismay, a veteran of the Indian army, in Hindi— *"Han,"* for "yes."[38]

In Paris the embassy staff assumed that the good news would be telephoned to the French. Churchill insisted upon delivering it in person. "This," Ismay comments, "was in character." Churchill reminded him of someone giving children presents and wanting to see the expressions on their faces as they opened their gifts: "He was about to give Reynaud a pearl beyond price, and he wanted to watch his expression as he received it." To the P.M.'s surprise, the premier had left his office—it was midnight—so he sought directions to his home. That was awkward. Reynaud and his mistress, Mme la Comtesse de Portes, were living in a small apartment on the Place du Palais-Bourbon, hiding from his wife. Nevertheless Churchill and Ismay eventually found him there. Receiving them in his bathrobe, he thanked them profusely. Then Churchill insisted that he summon Daladier, with whom the premier was barely on speaking terms. The war minister left *his* mistress, Mme la Marquise de Crussol, to come and wring their hands in silent gratitude.[39]

Back in London, the prime minister found nothing but problems defying solution. Another one hundred thousand Belgians had arrived in Britain, begging for shelter, and every report from the Continent told of a continuing

German advance. The P.M.'s mood was defiant. Roosevelt reaffirmed the impossibility of loaning Britain U.S. destroyers. As well, a strict reading of the Neutrality Act of 1939 forced Roosevelt to deny Churchill's request to send an aircraft carrier to America to pick up some of the more than three hundred Curtiss P-40 fighter planes awaiting shipment. During these months American aircraft purchased by Britain had to be flown to the Canadian border, where, in order to abide by U.S. laws preventing trans-shipment, they were pushed or towed (often by horse) across the border before continuing on, by ship, to England. The P-40s, Churchill was told, would be ready for delivery in two or three months. After digesting Roosevelt's decisions, he wrote a cordial reply and then growled to Colville: "Here's a telegram for those bloody Yankees. Send it off tonight." It was Trinity Sunday. Clementine attended services at St. Martin-in-the-Fields and returned indignant. The rector had preached a pacifist sermon and Clementine had walked out. Churchill said: "You ought to have cried 'Shame,' desecrating the house of God with lies!"[40]

That evening—May 19—he was to address the nation over the radio. He was driven to Chartwell, soon to be closed for the war's duration. There he could visit his goldfish, sit in the sun, and reflect, but he found no peace there. He wanted to feed his black swans, but to his consternation he found that foxes had eaten all but one. Then Anthony Eden called. The matter was urgent, and would become more so in the days ahead. Lord Gort had just called. The French army south of the BEF had melted away, leaving a vast gap on the British right. He was in a dilemma. He could leave the Belgians to their fate and fight southward to rejoin the French, or he could fall back on the Channel ports and fight it out with his back to the sea. His preference was to withdraw toward Dunkirk. Ironside had told him that "this proposal could not be accepted at all." Churchill, always against retreat, agreed. In Dunkirk, he said, the BEF would be "closely invested in a bomb-trap, and its total loss would be only a matter of time."[41]

After forty years in the House of Commons, Churchill instinctively swung his head from left to right. That would not do on the BBC, so Tyrone Guthrie of the Old Vic stood behind him and held his ears firmly as he spoke at a desk in a small room, his text illuminated by a green lamp. Addressing the country, he began:

> I speak to you for the first time as Prime Minister in a solemn hour for the life of our country, of our Empire, of our Allies, and above all of the cause of Freedom. A tremendous battle is raging in France and Flanders. The Germans, by a remarkable combination of air bombing and heavily armored tanks, have broken through the French defenses north of the Maginot Line, and strong columns of their armored vehi-

cles are ravaging the open country, which for the first day or two was without defenders.... Side by side, the British and French peoples have advanced to rescue not only Europe but mankind from the foulest and most soul-destroying tyranny which has ever darkened and stained the pages of history. Behind them, behind the Armies and Fleets of Britain and France, gather a group of shattered states and bludgeoned races: the Czechs, the Poles, the Norwegians, the Danes, the Dutch, the Belgians upon all of whom the long night of barbarism will descend, unbroken even by a star of hope, unless we conquer, as conquer we must; as conquer we shall.[42]

"At last the country is awake and working," wrote the diehard Tory Tom Jones.

"The hour has struck," wrote the commander of the Portsmouth Naval Base, Admiral Sir William Milbourne James, "and the man has appeared."[43]

Churchill had spoken of the French "genius for recovery and counterattack, for which they have long been famous," adding, "I have invincible confidence in the French army." He may have believed it. He had always been an arch-Francophile; in 1916, commanding a British battalion in the trenches, he had worn a poilu's helmet to show his confidence in England's ally. Thus far, Fleet Street had supported this view: "One hears," Mollie Panter-Downes reported in *The New Yorker,* "nothing but admiration for the heroic French resistance." But Gamelin was no Foch, and his troops were not the soldiers of 1914–1918. After the men on both sides had laid down their arms, a group of American war correspondents toured the scenes of struggle and concluded, in the words of William L. Shirer, that "France did not fight.... None of us saw evidence of serious fighting. The fields of France are undisturbed. There was no fighting on any sustained line... no attempt to come to a halt on a line and strike back in a well-organized counter-attack."[44]

The Führer's *Panzergruppen* had roared down unmined roads, passed unmolested under overlooking heights unsited with artillery. Strategic bridges had been unblown. French prisoners said they had seen no combat; whenever battle seemed imminent, they were ordered to retreat. The Channel ports, notably Boulogne and Calais, had been defended mostly by the British. Shirer thought the defending armies seemed to have been "paralyzed as soon as the Germans made their first break-through. The French, as though drugged, had no will to fight, even when their soil was invaded by their most hated enemy. It was a complete collapse of French society and of the French soul."[45]

Even Churchill had begun to have doubts about the French. The day before his Sunday broadcast, debating whether to send Britain's 1st Armored Division to Gamelin, he had told Ismay: "One must always be prepared for the fact that the French may be offered very advantageous terms of peace, and the whole weight be thrown on us." Gamelin himself had all but abandoned hope. Saturday evening he had calmly explained "the causes of our defeat" to Reynaud. It was the ninth day of the battle, and the *généralissime* was ready to quit. Even the hopelessly overmatched Poles had held out for three weeks.[46]

On Monday, May 20, the 2nd Panzer Division reached Abbéville, at the mouth of the Somme, and Noyelles on the coast. The Germans had cut France in half, thereby trapping a million Allied soldiers in the north, including the Belgian army, more than half the BEF, and the First and Seventh French Armies—France's best troops. It was a stunning triumph. But it was also the hour of the Nazis' maximum danger. Their tanks had created a corridor almost two hundred miles long and twenty miles wide, from the Ardennes to the Channel, but they had outdistanced the Wehrmacht's foot soldiers, and tanks alone could not hold the German gains against determined counterattacks. They would be vulnerable until their infantry arrived in strength.

Hitler knew it and was frightened. In his aerie he envisaged a second Marne, with the French rallying and striking back with a deadly blow. Jodl noted: "The Führer is terribly nervous. He is worried over his own success, will risk nothing and insists on restraining us....He rages and screams that we are on the way to ruining the whole operation and that we are in danger of a defeat."

This was, in fact, the critical moment; everything that followed turned upon it. As a disillusioned Churchill told the House of Commons four weeks later:

> The colossal military disaster...occurred when the French High Command failed to withdraw the northern armies from Belgium at the moment when they knew that the French front was decisively broken at Sedan and on the Meuse. This delay entailed the loss of fifteen or sixteen French divisions and threw out of action for the critical period the whole of the British Expeditionary Force, a total of twenty-five divisions of the best-trained and best equipped troops [which] may have turned the scale.[47]

Gamelin finally saw it. On Sunday he drew up "Instruction No. 12," ordering two offensives: the troops in the north were to fight south across the tank corridor while French troops on the Somme drove northward, cutting off the 2nd Panzer Division. But on Monday, before he could issue the orders, Reynaud sacked him and chose seventy-three-year-old General Maxime Weygand as his successor, a short, spruce, fox-faced officer who, as one Englishman said, resembled an "aged jockey." Weygand had never before commanded troops in battle; he had made his reputation as a staff officer. He was a political general, a monarchist, a hero of the militantly conservative Croix de Feu, and an Anglophobe. Despite his age he was exceptionally vigorous, but he had arrived in Paris exhausted, recalled from Syria; immediately after assuming command he went to bed. Before retiring he canceled Gamelin's Instruction No. 12.

The situation in the corridor was fluid. Every hour was critical now. The gap between the German armor and its supporting formations was closing. Yet when the new *généralissime* woke, he announced that he would tour the front before making a decision. By the time he returned and reissued the order, the corridor was thick with defenders. After four strenuous days the enemy had strengthened it by rushing infantry and motorized artillery to beef up both sides of it. The chance had passed.

At 6:30 P.M. Monday, a British officer had wired London that Luftwaffe bombers had severed rail service between Amiens and Abbéville, and that night, panzers at Abbéville cut off the British army's supply bases and the French armies in the south. Ironside, returning from France Tuesday morning, reported that another enemy tank column had been sighted passing Frévent, "probably making for Boulogne." There was "nothing wrong with the French troops themselves," he said, but the commanders seemed "paralyzed." In his diary he wrote, "Personally I think we cannot extricate the B.E.F....God help the B.E.F., brought to this state by the incompetence of the French command." Dill, who was with Georges, telegraphed that a northward drive by the French was "improbable."[48]

"In London," Ismay wrote, "we felt we were being harshly treated by the French High Command...they had told us nothing, and we were completely in the dark." Aware of the constantly shifting face of the battle, Churchill tried again and again to reach Reynaud by telephone. It was impossible. All lines between Paris and London had been cut. He told Colville, "In all the history of war I have never known such mismanagement." In his diary Colville commented: "I have not seen Winston so depressed." Desperate for information, the prime minister, against the advice of the Chiefs of Staff, decided to fly to Paris the following morning, Wednesday, May 22.[49]

The Flamingo landed at Le Bourget shortly before noon; the P.M. and his party went straight to the *généralissime*'s GHQ in the Château de Vincennes, an old fort suggestive of *Beau Geste,* guarded by Algerian troops dressed in white cloaks and bearing long curved swords. Weygand, greeting them, "was brisk, buoyant, and incisive," Churchill wrote. "He made an excellent impression on us all." Telling them that the panzers "must not be allowed to keep the initiative, he gave them a detailed description of what instantly became known as the Weygand Plan. It was Gamelin's Instruction No. 12, too late, though the British had no way of knowing that then. Churchill put it in writing "to make sure there was no mistake about what was settled." After the *généralissime* and Reynaud approved the text, it was telegraphed to the War Cabinet in London.

Specifically, the plan provided for an attack southward "at the earliest moment, certainly tomorrow," by eight divisions of the BEF and the French First Army. Simultaneously, a "new French Army Group" of between eighteen and twenty divisions, after forming a line upon the Somme, would "strike northward and join hands with the British divisions who are attacking southward in the general direction of Bapaume." The more Churchill thought about it, the better he liked it. That evening, Ironside noted, "Winston came back from Paris about 6:30 P.M. and we had a Cabinet at 7:30 P.M. He was almost in buoyant spirits, having been impressed by Weygand."[50]

The plan was impossible—all of it. The Allied forces in the north could not drive southward; all were heavily engaged with the enemy. And Weygand's own orders to his divisions in the south merely directed them to recapture local objectives. "The Weygand plan," as William L. Shirer later wrote, "existed only in the General's mind." It may not have existed even there. As Shirer noted, "no French troops ever moved up from the Somme."[51]

And Gort received no instructions from Vincennes. Indeed, he had heard nothing from GHQ for four days. Learning of this at 4:50 the following afternoon, Churchill called Reynaud—the lines were open again—to ask why. The voices on the other end were incoherent. At 6:00 P.M. he called again. This time he reached Weygand, who had thrilling news: his new French army in the south had already thrown the Germans back and retaken Amiens, Albert, and Péronne. In Admiralty House, Colville noted that this reversal of fortunes was greeted as "stupendous"; "gloom gave way to elation."[52]

It was a lie. Weygand had known from the beginning that the Allied cause was doomed. His only hope, he had told Georges on May 20, was *"sauver l'honneur des armées françaises"* ("save the honor of the French armies"), whatever that meant. His distrust of England and Englishmen was profound, though not unusual among Frenchmen with his convictions. Reviewing his deception, Colville later concluded that "Weygand was determined...that *we* should go under if *he* did." It is also possible that he was looking for a scapegoat. If so, he found one, and found him quickly. On Tuesday, the day before Churchill's flight to Vincennes, Gort had attempted to break the enemy's encircling line with an attack on the

German flank. He set his sights on Arras and went after it with two British divisions, supported by sixty light French tanks. The enemy commander, then unknown, was Erwin Rommel. The action was unexpected; Rommel reported a "heavy British counterattack with armour." On Wednesday Gort saw that a heavy German force was preparing to move against both his flanks, and he withdrew.[53]

Weygand heard about this Thursday morning. He angrily demanded that Reynaud protest, and the premier sent Churchill—who didn't even know of Gort's attack—two reproachful telegrams, which concluded: "General Weygand's orders must be obeyed." The *généralissime* put his protest in writing, declaring that "as a result of the British retreat" the drive southward had to be abandoned. It was at this point that Churchill assigned Edward Spears* the delicate task of improving relations between the two allies. Spears was half French and completely bilingual, a Conservative MP who had been a friend of Churchill's since the Edwardian era. They had been fellow officers in World War I, in which Spears had been wounded four times. He left a striking description of Churchill at the height of the war's first crisis. Summoned to Admiralty House in the middle of the night he found Churchill:

> . . . sitting relaxed and rotund in an arm-chair at his desk. He offered me a cigar, looked at me a moment as if I were a lens through which he was gazing at something beyond, then the kindliest, friendliest expression spread over his face as he focused me, his face puckered in a lovable baby-like grin, then he was grave again. "I have decided," he said, "to send you as my personal representative to Paul Reynaud. You will have the rank of a Major General. See Pug.† He will brief you. The situation is very grave."[54]

It was more than grave. It was catastrophic. Now all France, like ancient Gaul, was divided into three parts:

In the south, below the Somme—where Weygand actually planned to make his stand—lay 90 percent of France, including Paris. It was no longer the serene France of those early spring days, however. Spears reported that the roads were choked with refugees, top-heavy wagons, and

---

* He appears in volume 1 of this work as Edward Spiers. He changed the spelling of his name in 1918.
† Ismay, who looked like one.

"cars with boiling radiators." Over three hundred thousand poilus, members of military formations which no longer existed, were roaming the countryside; some, he reported, had shot their officers and were "robbing passers-by in the forests near Paris." French officers, captured by the Germans but given their parole, had returned to their homes, seemed to be enjoying their families, and weren't even interested in news of the fighting.

In the north, a desperate amalgam of Allied forces—more than half the BEF, the Belgians, and three French armies—was fighting for survival.

Between the two, a broadening, solidifying belt of enemy territory stretched across France from the Sedan, in the east, to Abbéville on the coast. Capturing Paris was every German's dream, and the panzers could have turned that way.

Instead they had wheeled northward and were driving toward the Channel ports, historically England's last line against invasion.

Churchill was aware of the danger. On the Sunday before his flight to Vincennes, Ironside had warned him that the BEF might soon be cut off from the French, in which case they could only be supplied through Boulogne, Calais, and Dunkirk. Now all three had been heavily bombed by the Luftwaffe the previous night. Dunkirk could not be used; ships sunk by the Nazis blocked its entrance. On Tuesday, Boulogne, directly in the path of the panzers, was reinforced by the 20th Guards Brigade and the Irish and Welsh Guards, the last available army units still in England. It was in vain; the German armored columns were irresistible; on Wednesday, while Churchill was being introduced to Weygand, evacuations were under way there. In his diary, Ironside wrote: "*4 p.m.* Boulogne was definitely gone....So goes all the people in Boulogne, including the two Guards battalions. A rotten ending indeed." He added: "Gort is very nearly surrounded....I don't see that we have much hope of getting the B.E.F. out." But the following evening he noted: "The German mobile columns have definitely been halted for some reason or other."[55]

Although no one realized it at the time, this was one of the turning points in the war. The "Halt Order" (*Haltordnung*), as it came to be known, has been endlessly debated. Had the panzers continued to advance, evacuation of the BEF would have been impossible. Yet the reasons for the pause seem clear. Rundstedt needed time for the German infantry to catch up with his tanks. Moreover, after fourteen days of offensive action, the men were exhausted and their machines badly in need of repairs.

Hitler lengthened the halt. Two days of downpours had made the Flanders swamps virtually impassable for armored vehicles. General Heinz Guderian, the panzer leader, who had first opposed the halt, conceded that "a tank attack is pointless in the marshy country which has been completely soaked by the rain....The infantry forces of this army are more suitable than tanks for fighting in this kind of country."[56]

Moreover, the Nazis' chief enemy continued to be France, and they did not believe they had already defeated what was considered the best army in Europe. Their push toward Paris, they believed, would be long and bloody. They needed to refit for that. Finally, they did not know that they had trapped 400,000 French, Belgian, and British men in the north. Afterward, Luftwaffe general Albert Kesselring said: "Even 100,000 would have struck us as greatly exaggerated."[57]

Leaders in both Paris and London continued to debate impractical plans. On Friday, May 24, Weygand bitterly complained that "the British Army has carried out, on its own initiative, a retreat of forty kilometers towards the ports when our troops moving up from the south are gaining ground towards the north, where they were to meet their allies." In another sharp telegram to London, Reynaud commented that the British action "has naturally compelled General Weygand to modify his arrangements" and that he has been forced to abandon "any idea" of uniting the Allied armies. His Majesty's Government was disconcerted. Ironside wrote: "Why Gort has done this I don't know. He has never told us what he was going to do or even when he had done it." In his reply to Reynaud, Churchill said that "no doubt the action was forced on Lord Gort." This was "no time for recriminations," he said, though he conceded that Gort should have kept him informed and that he did not doubt that the French "had grounds for complaint."[58]

They had none. Weygand's troops still weren't advancing, and Gort had not retreated. However, with each passing hour the commander of the BEF realized that he would have to do something, and soon. His army—the only army Britain had—was in mortal danger, nearly encircled, trapped in a pocket seventy miles from the sea and only fifteen to twenty-five miles across. Their lines of communications had been cut. Their only allies were the Belgians and the remnants of the First French Army. The ports through which the BEF's two hundred thousand men were supplied were either bombed out or already in enemy hands. The Tommies were down to a four-day supply of ammunition and rations. Panzers were in Gravelines, barely ten miles from Dunkirk, the BEF's last remaining port of escape. The panzers were closing in, and the Belgians were on the verge of surrender; already their last link with General Alan Brooke's corps, northeast of Menin, had been broken, creating a breach between which the Nazis would pour once they found it.

Of the Channel ports, only Calais and Dunkirk were still free. The army might be cut off from them at any time. In his diary Brooke wrote: "Nothing but a miracle can save the B.E.F. now, and the end cannot be far off." The British had lost all confidence in General G. H. Billotte, the

French commander in the north. Ironside, calling at Billotte's command post on May 20, had been horrified. He wrote of him: "No plan, no thought of a plan. Ready to be slaughtered. Defeated at the head without casualties. *Très fatigué* and nothing doing. I lost my temper and shook Billotte by the button of his tunic. The man is completely beaten."[59]

John Standish, the 6th Viscount Gort of Limerick—"Jack" to his fellow generals—was not greatly admired by them. At best, the French said, he would be a good battalion commander. He lacked intellect, said the British staff officers (Gamelin's intellect had been much admired in London, and even in Berlin). But Gort's courage was extraordinary. As a Guards officer in the last war, he had won the Victoria Cross, three Distinguished Service Orders, and the Military Cross. He was, if anything, an overdisciplined soldier, and now he faced an excruciating decision. He had heard nothing from Weygand for four days. Ironside had brought him orders from the War Cabinet, specifically forbidding a withdrawal to the sea, telling him, instead, to attack southward. But now he knew that only annihilation awaited him there. In Berlin, Germany's foreign minister Ribbentrop had already told the press: "The French army will be destroyed and the English on the Continent will be made prisoners of war." Rommel wrote in his diary: "Now the hunt is up against sixty encircled British, French and Belgian divisions."

During the afternoon of Saturday, May 25, Gort received a distress signal from Brooke: "I am convinced that the Belgian army is closing down and will have stopped fighting by this time tomorrow. This, of course, entirely exposes our left flank." Lieutenant General Sir Ronald Adam, the army's other corps commander, confirmed Brooke. Gort's reserves were gone. The only British soldiers not engaged with the enemy were two divisions, the 5th and the 50th, which were awaiting orders to open the southern attack the next day. In his command post at Prémesques, he spent most of that afternoon staring at wall maps of northern France and the Channel ports. At 6:30 P.M. he canceled the offensive and dispatched the 5th Division to plug the gap on Brooke's flank. Then he wired Eden, telling him what he had done and why he had done it.

The telegram was delayed. At 10:30 that evening, before it could arrive, Churchill independently reached the same conclusion. After consulting Reynaud, he instructed Eden to telegraph Gort: "It is clear...that it will not be possible for French to deliver attack in the south.... You are now authorized to operate towards coast forthwith in conjunction with the French and Belgian armies." The formal evacuation order reached Prémesques the next day, Monday, May 27.

A week earlier, King Leopold had informed the British through Admiral of the Fleet Sir Roger Keyes that should his troops lose contact with the French and British, "capitulation would be inevitable." Leopold also per-

sonally warned his fellow monarch George VI of Belgium's "imminent surrender" the same day Brooke wrote to Gort. Still, the shock was great in
Paris and London when, on Tuesday afternoon, the twenty-eighth, King
Leopold, without informing his allies or consulting his advisers, surrendered the entire 274,000-man Belgian army, opening a twenty-mile gap
between Brooke's corps and the coast near Nieuport.[60]

Lord Halifax, HMG's tall, ectomorphic foreign secretary, thought this
was an excellent time to negotiate a peace with Hitler. On the twenty-
seventh, Halifax—the last of the major appeasers to fall from favor (if not
from office)—told the War Cabinet that "it is not so much now a question
of imposing a complete defeat upon Germany, but of safeguarding the
independence of our own Empire." The Italian ambassador to Britain, he
reported, had approached him with "fresh proposals" for a peace conference, and he thought they should seize this opportunity. Churchill replied
that, yes, peace could be achieved "under a German domination of
Europe," but, no, that was a condition "we could never accept."[61]

Exasperated, Halifax argued that if Il Duce offered terms "which do not
postulate the destruction of our independence, we should be foolish if we
did not accept them." Provided Britain's independence were not in jeopardy, he held, it would be proper for Britain, confronted with two or three
months of air raids, "to accept an offer which would save the country from
avoidable disaster." Sir Alexander Cadogan, permanent under secretary in
the Foreign Office and a minor appeaser, thought the prime minister's defiant reply "too rambling and romantic and sentimental and temperamental. Old Neville still the best of the lot." To Halifax's horror, Churchill
said that if France surrendered, Britain would go it alone. The foreign secretary persisted. The following day he dominated the War Cabinet's afternoon meeting, proposing an Anglo-French approach to Mussolini,
suggesting that he "might be persuaded to act as mediator." Attlee replied
sharply, pointing out that this would amount to asking Il Duce "to intercede to obtain peace terms for us." Churchill, jaw outthrust, growled that
it would "ruin the integrity of our fighting position in this country.... Let
us therefore avoid being dragged down the slippery slope with France."[62]

As the meeting broke up, Halifax told Cadogan he was going to resign,
saying, "I can't work with Winston any longer." That evening he wrote in
his diary: "I thought Winston talked the most frightful rot.... It does drive
one to despair when he works himself up into a passion of emotion when
he ought to make his brain think and reason." However, the foreign

secretary changed his mind after Cadogan, a Foreign Office mandarin of the first order, replied: "Nonsense: his rodomontades probably bore me as much as they do you, but don't do anything silly under the stress of that."[63]

But patriotic ardor was stirring in England. In the 1930s, Churchill had been denounced as a "warmonger." Now his critics were branded "defeatists." A short service of intercession and prayer was held in Westminster Abbey; it was crowded with men who had cheered Munich only twenty months ago. Churchill wrote: "The English are loth [sic] to expose their feelings, but in my stall in the choir I could feel the pent-up, passionate emotion, and also the fear of the congregation, not of death or wounds or material loss, but of defeat and the final ruin of Britain."[64]

Now that the war edged closer to their homes and hearths, the British public began to learn the truth. Until the final week of May, Britons had been largely optimistic. The wakening came slowly because they had been told so little. As late as May 24, the *Times* asked, in a headline, ARE WE REALLY AT WAR? Hotels and theaters were crowded, the story reported; idle young men cloistered around amusement parks; holidays were being observed; in London's West End unemployed miners sang for coppers as though Britain and her empire were still at peace.[65]

The press, aided and abetted by military censors, bore much responsibility for this tranquillity. On May 13, a *Times* headline announced, BEF SWEEPS ON. On Tuesday, May 14, the day after Guderian's panzers began pouring across the Meuse, a *Times* analyst told readers: "In general, it may be said that the Germans have not made contact with the bulk of the French and Belgian forces." Other newspapers followed the same line. War news was reaching Englishmen in a promiscuous rush. Vital information was there, if you knew where to look, but it was buried beneath dispatches claiming RAF victories, accounts of French troops forming for a mighty counteroffensive, denials of German communiqués, and such predictions of enemy defeats as "GERMAN MOTORISED UNITS DRIVING INTO FRANCE BELIEVED TO FACE DESTRUCTION." Suddenly on May 22, Britons were told that the Nazis were at Abbéville, 140 miles *behind* the Allied lines in Belgium and heading for the Channel ports. For the next week the papers were full of contradictory stories about fighting in Flanders. Finally, on May 30, the British public were told: "ALLIES TRYING TO FIGHT WAY TO FRENCH COAST IN DIRECTION OF DUNKERQUE." Harold Nicolson wrote Vita Sackville-West, "Oh my dear, my dearest, that we should come to this!" Stanley Baldwin's wife wrote the *Times,* urging churches to fly the Cross of St. George as a sign that England was fighting for Christianity against evil. "It is a daily inspiration to myself," she wrote, "to look out of my window and see that our parish church is bearing the Red Cross of St. George on its tower night and day." The piety of Lady Baldwin was unsurprising. But the crisis brought the war effort some unlikely converts. Bertrand Russell wrote Kingsley Martin that he had renounced pacifism, declaring that if he were young enough to fight, he would enlist. On that desperate Tuesday when the Belgian king surrendered, George Orwell wrote in his diary: "Horrible as it is, I hope the B.E.F. is cut to pieces rather than capitulate."[66]

Gort, having withdrawn his 5th Division from the impossible southern adventure and flung it into the gap left by the Belgians, felt the full fury of the Nazi attack. A vanguard of 85,000 Germans, supported by reserves and, now, by refitted tanks, fell upon famed regiments: the 3rd Grenadiers, the 2nd North Staffordshire, the 2nd Sherwood Foresters, the Royal Inskilling Fusiliers, the Royal Scots Fusiliers, the 6th Seaforth Highlanders, and the Duke of Cornwall's light infantry. They held until the 42nd and 50th Divisions could move up to the line. The battle there, between Warneton and Ypres, raged throughout the withdrawal, with very heavy losses.

The greatest sacrifice was made by the Calais garrison: the 229th Anti-tank Battery; battalions from the King's Royal Rifle Corps, the Rifle Brigade, the Royal Tank Regiment, and the Queen Victoria's Rifles, supported by a thousand brave French soldiers. British destroyers lay off Calais, ready to save the men. Instead, Churchill decided, they must be abandoned. It was essential, he told Ironside, that they fight to the last man, holding the enemy in check; otherwise, Ironside wrote, "it would have been impossible to have used Dunkirk as a point from which to evacuate the B.E.F. and the 1st French Army," because the vast German divisions would have reached the beach and cut them off. The "grim decision," Ismay called it, was made on the night of May 26. Ironside, Ismay, and Eden were with the prime minister at the time.[67]

It was Eden's lot to telegraph this order to Brigadier C. N. Nicholson, commanding the Rifle Brigade that he must fight to the destruction of his command: "The eyes of the Empire are upon the defence of Calais, and H.M. Government are confident that you and your gallant regiments will perform an exploit worthy of the British name." Shortly before midnight, he again wired him: "Every hour you continue to fight is of greatest help to the B.E.F.... Have greatest admiration for your splendid stand." Churchill was uncharacteristically mute during dinner. Later he wrote, "One has to eat and drink in war, but I could not help feeling sick as we afterwards sat silent eating at the table."[68]

Now the two hundred thousand men of the BEF cut off in the north and the remnants of the First French Army, outnumbered three or four to one, fell back down the narrow corridor leading to the sea, fighting by day and retreating at night, with every step contested by the Germans. The 1st Coldstream Guards held the line for thirty hours before disengaging. The 2nd Gloucestershire and the 4th Royal Sussex regiments outflanked a German column. The 2nd Buffs broke the momentum of a German wheeling movement. The 1st Cameroons, reduced to forty survivors, nevertheless counterattacked and drove the enemy back across the Canal de la Lawe. Surrounded, a battalion of the Welch Fusiliers fought their way back to the Lys. Strung out between Ypres and the Warneton-Comines Canal for nine miles, the 6th Black Watch, the 13/18th Hussars, the 3rd Grenadier Guards, the 2nd North Staffordshire, and the 2nd Sherwood Foresters counter-attacked, flinging back the claw of a German pincer movement. The 2nd Buffs were reduced to the strength of a weak company but blocked a penetration near Godewaersvelde.

Like all soldiers, they fought best when they had learned to hate, and the enemy they faced, which prided itself on its use of terrorism, gave them strong reasons for rage. After the SS *Totenkopf* division had captured a hundred men of the 2nd Royal Norfolk, many of them wounded, the SS lined their prisoners up against a barn wall and machine-gunned them, shooting or bayoneting those who still showed signs of life. Two Tommies, hidden by the bodies, crawled away to tell the tale. Alan Brooke was deeply shocked. In the first war he had fought Germans, but these were *Nazis*.

Late on May 26, Brooke himself narrowly escaped capture. Sleepless, he was driven from one command post to another, his driver honking his way through demoralized refugees, including the inmates from an insane asylum, who stood by the side of the road wearing inane smiles and waving at the mass of troops and refugees. Brooke commanded by word of mouth—the army's signals communications had broken down—issuing fresh orders to commanders as the situation changed, transferring battalions to other divisions, directing Montgomery to make a dangerous night flank march across the front of the attack. Immediately after he had crossed one bridge over the canal, it blew up behind him. Near Ypres he lay under a cottage fence, having hastily abandoned his car at the approach of thirty-six Luftwaffe bombers. When he tried to take a two-hour nap in a stone hut, he was blown out of bed.[69]

There are a thousand reasons why the withdrawal to the coast shouldn't have worked, but it did. To be sure, the cut-off army paid a dreadful price—68,710 casualties, nearly a third of its strength—but the majority of these were wounded who would fight again. Much of the achievement may be credited to the military traditions of the Empire, which gave Britain skilled professional officers and highly disciplined regular soldiers, the grandsons of Kipling's red-coated Mulvaneys. The very names of their regiments and battalions evoke ghosts of past glory, infantry of the line and cavalry troopers loyal to King and Country, the legacy of imperial armies that had given Britain's soldiers a small island for their birth and the whole world for their grave, regiments in one of which, the 4th Hussars, handsome young Winston Churchill had served as a lieutenant.[70]

A week before the Belgian surrender, and after almost two weeks of crushing defeats on the Continent, Churchill asked Chamberlain to study "the problems which would arise if it were necessary to withdraw the BEF from France." On Monday, May 20, staff officers went through the motions of outlining a tentative plan. Assuming that Calais, Boulogne, and Dunkirk would be available, low-level planners believed they could evacuate two thousand men a day. The "hazardous evacuation of very large forces" was briefly mentioned, then relegated to the bottom of the agenda; its possibility seemed very remote. That changed in less than twenty-four hours. Tuesday morning, "the emergency evacuation across the Channel of very large forces" led the agenda, and Churchill ordered steps to "assemble a large number of small vessels in readiness to proceed to ports and inlets on the French coast." Transport officers from Harwich to Weymouth were directed to list all ships up to a thousand tons. The Admiralty appointed Vice-Admiral Bertram Ramsay to command the operation. It was codenamed Dynamo. He was immediately given thirty-six ships, most of them cross-Channel ferries. His headquarters, hacked out of Dover's white cliffs, overlooked the troubled waters.

By the twenty-sixth, London was in despair. At seven o'clock that evening the Admiralty, on Churchill's instructions, sent out the message: "Operation Dynamo is to commence." On the twenty-eighth, with the evacuation from Dunkirk under way for almost twenty-four hours, Churchill warned the House of Commons to "prepare itself for hard and heavy tidings." Privately he feared that "the whole root and core and brain of the British army" was "about to perish upon the field or be led into an ignominious and starving captivity." The Chiefs of the Imperial General Staff informed him that, in their view, a full-scale attack on England was "imminent." Yet, each of the three service chiefs—army, navy, and RAF—parsed the data at hand after his own fashion; none was reading the same tea leaves as the others.[71]

The diary of the CIGS reflects Britain's grim mood. On the twenty-third, Ironside had written, "I cannot see that we have much hope of getting any of the B.E.F. out." Two days later he predicted, "We shall have lost all our trained soldiers by the next few days unless a miracle appears to help us." Two days later his entry read: "The news in the morning is bad.... I met Eastwood [the commander of the 4th Division in France] on the steps of the War Office. He had come over last night and described things as very bad. He did not expect any of the B.E.F. to get off at all." The following evening Ismay wrote, "The Prime Minister asked me how I would feel if I were told that a total of 50,000 could be saved. I replied without hesitation that I would be absolutely delighted, and Churchill did not upbraid me for pessimism." As late as May 30, with the Luftwaffe swarming over the Dunkirk beaches, the King was told that they would be lucky to save 17,000. Ironside wrote: "Very little chance of the real B.E.F. coming off. They have now sunk three ships in Dunkirk harbour and so there is very little chance of getting any units off."[72]

Eight months earlier the Poles had lost all hope; the French were losing theirs; but with few exceptions the morale of Englishmen was actually rising. Blessed with that great moat between them and the Continent, they were defiant. On the afternoon of May 28, Churchill assembled the full cabinet — some twenty ministers — in his room in Parliament to tell them everything he knew about the fighting and what lay in the balance. Then he said, "I have thought carefully in these last days whether it was part of my duty to consider entering in negotiations with That Man.* And I am convinced that every man of you would rise up and tear me down from my place if I were for one moment to contemplate parley or surrender. If this long island story of ours is to end at last, let it end only when each of us lies choking in his own blood upon the ground."

To his surprise, several men jumped up, ran to his chair, shouting, and clapped him on the back. Afterward he wrote: "I was sure that every Minister was ready to be killed quite soon, and have all his family and possessions destroyed rather than give in. In this they represented the House of Commons and almost all the people. It fell to me in those coming days and months to express their sentiments on suitable occasions. This I was able to do, because they were mine also."

Hugh Dalton, long his opponent in the House, wrote: "He was quite magnificent. [He is] the man, and the only man we have, for this hour."[73]

In 1940 Dunkirk was an ancient seaport; many of the buildings facing the shore dated from the sixteenth century. Before the war, its ten miles of empty sand had attracted thousands of vacationing French and Englishmen, but when Lord Gort's gaunt, exhausted, unshaven soldiers fell back

---

* "That Man" to Churchill was always Hitler.

upon it in those last days of May, the Luftwaffe had transformed it into a battered ruin. All the houses had been abandoned. The only sound came from crackling, exploding fires in the city. Buoys had been blasted from the water. Sunken ships blocked entrances to the harbor, which, by all the canons of seamen, had become a shattered, useless port. The wide beaches were within range of Calais-based Krupp artillery, which never let up. Tommies were also vulnerable to shrieking, dive-bombing Stukas and strafing Messerschmitt Bf 109s that were using as their beacon a billowing column of smoke from bombed oil tanks near the west pier. These tanks were to burn throughout the crisis, tainting the air with their foul stench. It was from this cauldron that the Royal Navy, all the available merchant ships, and British yachtsmen in private boats intended to rescue a quarter-million exhausted, bleeding men.

Nor was that all. Apart from the sunken hulks and smashed docks, the harbor confronted mariners with other challenges. Fifteen-foot low tides left a long, shallow foreshore bare for a half mile to seaward, which meant that no vessel could approach closer than that. Neither could Dunkirk be approached directly from the Straits of Dover. Instead, seamen had to navigate an 800-yard-wide deepwater channel that ran parallel to the coast for many miles. The only ameliorating feature of the port, and it was a frail one, was a mole, or breakwater, that sprang in a great curve from an eleventh-century fortress and extended 1,400 yards seaward. This jetty was the East Mole. Most breakwaters are made of stone. This one was a narrow wooden structure barely wide enough to accommodate three men walking abreast. Bringing craft alongside it would be both difficult and, because of the tides, hazardous. Moreover, the East Mole had not been built to survive the stresses of berthing ships alongside it. No one knew whether it could survive the strain.

By the morning of May 26, the navy had assembled a ragtag armada of 860 vessels in Dover. Of Britain's 160 destroyers, almost half were attached to the Home Fleet, and only forty-one were available. These had been augmented by appealing to all yacht clubs along the coast and by commandeering everything afloat in English waters. In addition, French, Belgian, and Dutch skippers had volunteered, bringing the argosy total to 900 boats. On May 26, they were anchored three-deep along the Dover quays: trawlers, river barges, schooners, minesweepers, fireboats, corvettes, hospital ships, fishing sloops, launches, paddle wheelers, smacks, coasters, lifeboats, scows, tugs, the London fire float *Massey Shaw,* the ferries *Brighton Queen* and *Gracie Fields,* Channel packets such as the *Princess Maud,* and every variety of pleasure craft. Tom Sopwith's America's Cup challenger *Endeavour* was there, with him at the helm. So were the launch *Count Dracula;* the yacht *Sundowner,* piloted by Commander Charles H. Lightoller, the senior surviving officer of the *Titanic;* and the Yangtze gunboat *Mosquito.* The Earl of Craven was going to sea as third engineer on a tug. The Honorable Lionel Lambert had armed his yacht and was sailing with his chef. And Captain Sir Richard Pim of the Royal Navy, the commander of the prime minister's map room, was commanding a Dutch *schuit.* Churchill looked around, demanded, "Where's Pim?" and was elated when told.[74]

Just crossing the Channel, forty miles wide at this point, was harrowing for amateurs. The sea was choppy, and since the outbreak of the war, light-ships and lighted buoys had been blacked out, and the enemy was continually mining these waters. The navy swept three narrow lanes; vessels that strayed from them, and some did, went down. Lying off the French coast between shoals, awaiting their turn to go in, helmsmen tried desperately, in narrow waters, to take evasive action against the German aircraft, which seemed to be everywhere. Then, when they went in, or as far in as they could get, they saw the long serpentine lines of Tommies stretching over the dunes. To the crews of boats entering after sunset, weaving between the sunken hulks, the beaches seemed to be swarming with fire-flies. These were the lighted cigarettes of infantrymen awaiting a ride home. Some men stood waist-deep in water for hours, praying for rescue, but though bombed and machine-gunned, none broke.

During the first day of evacuation—Monday, May 27—small craft dodged in, picked up as many men as they could, and ran them out to the destroyers and Channel ferries, which formed the backbone of the fleet. This continued throughout the nine days and nights of Dunkirk, but only eight thousand soldiers were evacuated that Monday. Clearly the little craft could not do the job alone. The beach master decided to bring the ships in and test the flimsy East Mole. It held. It wasn't the best of moorings; at low tide, men had to jump to decks, and when a rough sea rushed against the pilings, sucking, swirling, and widening the distance to be covered, each leap became a gamble. Some Tommies lost and sank to their death. The Germans bombed the jetty again and again. One morning it took a direct hit from a low-flying bomber. Ships' carpenters patched it. Another bomb hit the hull of the paddle wheel steamer *Fenella* below the waterline just after she had been boarded by six hundred troops. She sank immediately, taking them with her. Nevertheless, the mole did all that could have reasonably been asked of it.

As did the little boats. Repeatedly they ran aground; soldiers would push them off and vault aboard. Sometimes overloaded craft capsized, drowning the heavily laden Tommies. Some crewmen brought collapsible boats; soldiers tried to paddle with their gun butts; it didn't work; they tried their luck elsewhere. Makeshift piers were put together with trucks, wreckage, and driftwood. The skipper of a minesweeper raised his bow as high as possible, came in at twelve knots, and dropped two stern anchors as he beached. Nearly three thousand men used the ship as a bridge to deeper water, where other vessels awaited them. As the Luftwaffe found more victims, oil slicks made rescue filthy work, and flames from burning ships illumined the harbor from sundown to dawn. German bombers also littered the harbor with more sunken hulks. One destroyer was hit while waiting at the mole. She caught fire and drifted out, blocking the harbor entrance until a trawler towed her aside.[75]

Ashore, there was some concern about the French soldiers. Those on the perimeter were fighting magnificently, but idle poilus had become a problem. "French Army now a rabble," Brooke wrote in his diary on May 29, "and complete loss of discipline. Troops dejected and surly, refusing to clear road and panicking every time German planes come over." That, he believed, was one reason the evacuation was slow. Another was an insufficient number of small boats. He asked Gort to pressure the Admiralty. Instead Gort sent two emissaries to the prime minister: Lord Munster, his aide-de-camp, and a junior officer, John Churchill, the prime minister's nephew. Young Churchill arrived at Admiralty House that same evening, "soaking wet," as he later recalled, "and still in full battle kit." Winston and Clementine, both in dressing gowns, greeted him fervently. "Johnny!" his uncle said delightedly. "I see you have come straight from battle!"[76]

Churchill wanted to know why his nephew was so wet: "Have you come straight out of the sea?" Johnny said that he had, and would be returning immediately. Lord Munster, immaculately attired in staff dress and jackboots appropriate to the function, received less attention, though Churchill agreed to prod the Admiralty. All who recall the incident remember not the message but Churchill's enthusiasm for the war. "We felt," recalled General Sir Ian Jacob, "that he would have liked to be fighting on the beaches himself."[77]

Altogether six destroyers were sunk and twenty-six damaged during the ten days of Dunkirk. Another 112 vessels went down, including the *Mosquito* and the *Gracie Fields,* lost on her way home with 300 Tommies. At times men on boats crossing to Dover had to make their way through the floating corpses of their comrades. The progress, or lack of it, was discouraging; by the night of May 28, only about 25,000 soldiers had been evacuated, and on June 2, the heavy air attacks forced suspension of daylight action. Nevertheless, the operation continued, favored by fair weather, and now they had the hang of it. Operation Dynamo, conceived in despair, with faint hope that a small fraction of the army could be saved, was astonishing the world.

On May 28, the number of evacuees was low: 17,800. "All this day of the 28th," Churchill wrote afterward, "the escape of the British army hung in the balance." On May 29, however, the figure was 47,310; on May 30, 53,823; on May 31, 68,014; on June 1, 64,429; and on June 2, 26,256. That

was supposed to be the end of it, but Admiral Ramsay made one last perilous attempt to lift off the gallant French rearguard, and he returned with
26,175 polius. Altogether, Dynamo had rescued 338,226 Allied soldiers,
112,000 of them French, although a greater number of French troops
turned and went home, to take their chances.

Behind them they had "left their luggage," as Churchill put it: 2,540
artillery pieces, 90,000 rifles, 11,000 machine guns, nearly 700 tanks,
6,400 anti-tank rifles, 20,000 motorcycles, 45,000 trucks and other vehicles, and vast ammunition dumps.[78]

But the great thing, for the English public, was that the men were back.
They had heard stories of the heroic rearguard action. "Then," Mollie
Panter-Downes told readers of *The New Yorker* on June 2, "it was learned
that the first war-stained, exhausted contingent had arrived on British
shores, and the relief and enthusiasm were terrific." Churchill never much
liked *The New Yorker,* deriding it as *The New Porker* (he had a moniker
for everyone), but here came Panter-Downes with journalistic testimony to
the heroics in England. He could not have bought more favorable press.[79]

Still, the news added up to disaster. On June 4 Churchill told the House
the story of Dunkirk. "Wars," he told them bluntly, "are not won by evacuations" and "what has happened in France and Belgium is a colossal military disaster." Nevertheless, he said, Dunkirk was "a miracle of deliverance,
achieved by valor, by perseverance, by perfect discipline, by faultless service, by recourse, by skill, by unconquerable fidelity." Britain would "out-
live the menace of tyranny, if necessary for years, if necessary alone."

Even though large tracts of Europe and many old and famous states
have fallen or may fall into the grip of the Gestapo and all the odious
apparatus of Nazi rule, we shall not flag or fail.... We shall go on to
the end, we shall fight in France, we shall fight on the seas and oceans,
we shall fight with growing confidence and growing strength in the
air, we shall defend our island, whatever the cost may be, we shall
fight on the beaches, we shall fight on the landing grounds, we shall
fight in the fields and in the streets, we shall never surrender.

And even if, which I do not for a moment believe, this island or a
large part of it were subjugated and starving, then our empire beyond
the seas, armed and guarded by the British Fleet, would carry on the
struggle, until, in God's good time, the New World, with all its power
and might, steps forward to the rescue and the liberation of the old.[80]

In his diary Jock Colville wrote: "Went down to the House to hear the
P.M.'s statement on the evacuation of Dunkirk. It was a magnificent oration which obviously moved the House." Next day the *News Chronicle*

called the address "a speech of matchless oratory, uncompromising candour, and indomitable courage." Harold Nicolson wrote his wife, Vita Sackville-West: "This afternoon Winston made the finest speech that I have ever heard." She wrote back: "I wish I had heard Winston make that magnificent speech! Even repeated by the announcer it sent shivers (not of fear) down my spine. I think one of the reasons why one is stirred by his Elizabethan phrases is that one feels the whole massive backing of power and resolve behind them, like a great fortress; they are never words for words' sake." That evening, in a broadcast to the United States, a constituency that Churchill desperately needed to reach, Edward R. Murrow, the CBS man in London, said: "He spoke the language of Shakespeare with a direct urgency which I have never before heard in that House." Later, the historian Brian Gardner wrote of the address that it had "electrified not only his own country, but the world. With it, Churchill won the complete confidence of the British people, which he had never before enjoyed. Whatever was to happen, Churchill's place in the national life was assured; he would never be in the wilderness again."[81]

Churchill also worked a challenge to Hitler into his address: "When Napoleon lay at Boulogne for a year with his flat-bottomed boats and his Grand Army, he was told by someone, 'There are bitter weeds in England.' There are certainly a great many more of them since the British Expeditionary Force returned."[82]

None were more bitter than Churchill.

Charles Corbin, the French ambassador, was alarmed. He called at the Foreign Office to ask what the prime minister had meant by declaring that Britain would, if it came to that, carry on alone. He was told that he had meant "exactly what he had said." That, members of Corbin's staff told diplomatic correspondents, was "not exactly encouraging the French to fight on against fearful odds."[83]

The French were getting nervous. As they saw it, the British army had bolted, leaving them to the enemy's mercies. Of course, the evacuation would have been unnecessary if the French strategy had not been hopelessly wrong or if Weygand had not been a liar. Moreover, the original intent of the operation, as seen by Gort, Churchill, and Ironside, had been to extricate the BEF and then land it in the south, rejoining their allies. The loss of their equipment meant they had to be refitted, but Churchill intended to then send the troops back, and Reynaud, Weygand, and the French high command knew it. Even as Dunkirk wound down, Churchill had landed two fresh British divisions below the Somme. Nevertheless, he had been aware of the uneasiness across the Channel. On May 30, he had decided to convene a meeting of the *Conseil Supérieur de la Guerre* in Paris the following day. With him he would take Clement Attlee, Pug Ismay, and Sir John Dill, the new Chief of the Imperial General Staff, Ironside staying behind as the new commander in chief of Home Forces, to organize English defenses against the invasion threat. Spears would meet them at Villacoublay Airport.[84]

Flying over France had become more hazardous since Churchill's last flight to the theater. Although the Flamingo was escorted by nine Spitfires, north of Paris the sky was swarming with Nazi fighters. Churchill's pilot detoured and they arrived late. Spears saw the hunched but resilient figure of the prime minister emerge, "obviously in grand form. He might not have had a care in the world.... Danger, the evocation of battle, invariably acted as a tonic and a stimulant to Winston Churchill."[85]

The *Conseil* met at 2:00 P.M. on May 31, in a large first-floor room, giving out on a garden, in the Ministry of War in the rue Saint-Dominique, with the conferees sitting at an immense green-baize-covered oval table, the visitors on one side and, facing them, their hosts: Reynaud, Admiral Jean Darlan; Paul Baudouin, a protégé of Reynaud's mistress and an admirer of the defeatist Pétain; Weygand, booted and spurred; and, finally, a newcomer to the war council: eighty-four-year-old Maréchal Henri-Philippe Pétain, in mufti.

Reynaud had appointed Pétain his deputy premier, hoping to increase the public's confidence in the government. In France the old marshal was regarded as a hero of the last war, *le vainqueur de Verdun* (the conqueror of Verdun). The British saw him differently. In 1917 he had suppressed a mutiny in the French army by promising his soldiers that the British and the Americans would do most of the future fighting. He was, moreover, an impassioned Anglophobe who despised democracy; the responsibility for France's present plight, he believed, lay with the leftist Popular Front of 1935. "Now," Ismay thought, Pétain "looked senile, uninspiring, and defeatist."[86]

Churchill opened by suggesting that they consider three questions: the Allied force still in Norway, the fighting in Flanders, and the strong likelihood that Mussolini would soon enter the war at Hitler's side. First, however, he thought the French would be interested in a piece of good news. The Dunkirk evacuation was succeeding beyond all expectations: 165,000 men had been taken off, including 10,000 wounded. It was then that Weygand sounded the first dissonant note. In an aggressive, querulous voice, he interrupted to ask, "But how many French? The French are being left behind?"[87]

The Englishmen present expected a Churchillian outburst. All the signs were there: the light had died out of his face, he was drumming his fingers on the table, and his lower lip jutted out like the prow of a dreadnought. Clearly he was angry, and with reason. Weygand had known of Operation Dynamo for six days, but had neglected to tell his commander in the north and had issued no orders authorizing French participation in the evacuations. Indeed, that was one of the reasons the prime minister had flown over. However, he controlled himself; his expression became sad; he said quietly, "We are companions in misfortune. There is nothing to be gained from recrimination over our common miseries."[88]

Baudouin wrote that there were "tears in his eyes," that he was obviously moved by "the common sufferings of England and France." Spears felt that "a stillness fell over the room." They then proceeded with the agenda, agreeing, first, to reinforce the Allied armies in France by withdrawing their forces from Norway. Briefly they discussed fortifying a redoubt in Brittany, into which they might withdraw if France fell. The RAF would bomb Italian targets if Mussolini entered the war. At that point the French translator, misunderstanding the P.M., said it was understood that British soldiers at Dunkirk would embark before the French. Churchill interrupted him; waving his arms, he roared in his extraordinary accent: *"Non! Partage bras dessous, bras dessous"*—the soldiers from both countries would leave together, arm in arm.[89]

The French wanted more RAF squadrons. Churchill pointed out that His Majesty's Government had already given ten additional squadrons, needed for the defense of Great Britain. If they lost the rest, the Luftwaffe could, with impunity, attack "the most dangerous targets of all, the factories producing new aircraft." It was, he said, "impossible to run further risks" with British aircraft.

What concerned him most was the flagging spirit of all Frenchmen—soldiers, civilians, and, except for Reynaud, members of the government. He could not say that there, of course, but he wanted them to know that England meant to crush Nazi Germany, whatever the cost. "I am absolutely convinced," he said, his voice rolling with oratorical cadences, "that we have only to fight on to conquer. If Germany defeats either ally or both, she will give no mercy. We should be reduced to the status of slaves forever. Even if one of us is struck down, the other must not abandon the struggle. Should one comrade fall in battle, the other must not put down his arms until his wounded friend is on his feet again."[90]

Attlee endorsed every word the prime minister had said, adding: "Every Englishman knows that the very basis of civilization common to both France and Britain is at stake. The Germans kill not only men, but ideas." Reynaud was pleased; that was the line he had been taking with his ministers. They, however, were divided. Spears thought that Baudouin had been swept away by Churchill's fire. Not so; in his diary he wrote that he had been "deeply troubled" by Churchill's vow and asked, "Does he consider that France must continue the struggle, cost what it may, even if it is useless? We must clear that up."

Beaming, Churchill said merrily: *"Fini l'agenda!"*

But he himself was not finished. As they rose from the table, gathering in groups to discuss this or that, Churchill headed for Pétain, followed by Spears. The old man had not said a word. His voice would carry great weight with the people of France, and the P.M. thought he looked "detached and sombre, giving me the feeling that he would face a separate peace." One of the Frenchman said that if events continued on their present course, France might have to reappraise its foreign policy, including ties to Britain, and "modify its position." Pétain nodded. Spears told them in perfect French that such a change would result in a British blockade of French ports. Then, looking directly into Pétain's eyes, Spears said, "That would not only mean blockade but bombardment of all French ports in German hands." Afterward Churchill wrote, "I was glad to have this said. I sang my usual song: we would fight on whatever happened or whoever fell out."[91]

No one had mentioned the Anglo-French *accord* signed by both governments nine weeks earlier—they had solemnly agreed to "neither negotiate nor conclude an armistice or treaty of peace except by mutual agreement." In March, when the pledge was signed, the strength of the opposing forces on the Western Front had been roughly equal, but by May 31, when the *Conseil* was meeting in Paris, the Nazi edge was enormous. The Germans had taken almost 500,000 prisoners at a cost of 60,000 casualties. Unaccountably, Weygand issued no orders to move the seventeen divisions manning the Maginot Line. As a consequence he had to face the coming onslaught with forty-nine divisions. The Germans attacked with 130 infantry and ten panzer divisions—almost three thousand tanks.

On June 5 the Germans launched their offensive against the Somme. The French, fighting desperately, held their line for two days and thwarted a pincer movement toward Creil from Amiens and Péronne, but on June 7, the 7th Panzer Division, led by Erwin Rommel, broke through toward Rouen, and on Sunday, June 9, they were over the Seine. That day they lunged across the Aisne, took Dieppe and Compiègne; then tanks drove through the breach toward Châlons-sur-Marne before turning eastward toward the Swiss frontier, to cut off the huge garrison in *le Maginot*. Rommel drove his tanks so far and so fast that the English called the 7th Panzers the Ghost Division. Nobody—including the German high command—knew where it was until it appeared someplace where it was not expected.

On Monday, June 10, Italy declared war on Britain and France. Franklin Roosevelt declared in a radio broadcast, "The hand that held the dagger has plunged it into the back of its neighbor." Churchill merely muttered, "People who go to Italy to look at ruins won't have to go as far as Naples and Pompeii in the future." He ordered that all male Italian citizens be rounded up and interned. A few hours after Mussolini's declaration of war, mobs smashed the windows of Soho's spaghetti joints, but in London, unlike in Rome, there were no organized demonstrations against the new enemy. Mussolini's dagger was very small. Almost immediately the French hurled back Il Duce's badly led, dreadfully equipped army. Churchill wired Roosevelt: "If we go down Hitler has a very good chance of conquering the world." In that case, small dagger or no, Mussolini would get his share.[92]

That night, as German armies advanced toward Paris, the prime minister decided to fly to Paris once more, hoping to persuade the French to defend their capital. Then a message arrived, telling him the government was leaving it. "What the hell," he growled, fuming until a second telegram told him they could meet at Briare, on the Loire, eighty miles south of Paris. Tuesday morning—the eleventh—he took off with Ismay, Eden, and Spears, escorted by twelve Hawker Hurricanes. He wanted to fly over the battlefields, but the pilot told him that the flight plan made that impossible; he and the Hurricanes were following precise instructions from the Air Ministry.

Briare airfield was deserted. Churchill, massive in black, leaning on his stick, looked around, beaming, as though this airstrip were the place he had sought all his life and finally found. Several cars drove up, the first driven by a sullen colonel "who, from his expression," Spears wrote, "might have been welcoming poor relatives at a funeral procession." The ambiance was equally unpleasant when they arrived at the red-brick Château du Muguet. Spears felt that "our presence was not really desired."

They were shown into a large dining room. There the Frenchmen—with one exception, Charles de Gaulle, whom Reynaud had made a general, serving as the premier's under secretary of state for defense and war—sat with hung heads, staring at the table, like prisoners awaiting sentencing. To Ismay, Pétain seemed "more woebegone than ever," while Weygand appeared "to have abandoned all hope."[93]

Churchill tried to cheer them up by revealing that a Canadian division would be landed in France that night, joining the three British divisions already in the line, and another division would arrive within nine days.

They remained glum. Weygand said that the army's plight was hopeless. The Allies had lost thirty-five divisions—over half a million soldiers. He said: "There is nothing to prevent the enemy reaching Paris. We are fighting on our last line and it has been breached. I am helpless. I cannot intervene, for I have no reserves. It was the break-up of the army (*"C'est la dislocation"*).Then he went too far. He was asked what would happen if another breach were made and replied: "No further military action will be possible." Eden noted that Reynaud immediately intervened sharply: "That would be a political decision, Monsieur le Général." Weygand bowed and said, "Certainly," but then he struck again, blaming "those responsible"—the French politicians—"for entering the war with no conception of Nazi power."[94]

Churchill couldn't, or wouldn't, believe that France was in extremis. In the beginning he had hunched over the table, his face flushed, following the *généralissime*'s every word, but at the end he looked away, said nothing, stared at the ceiling, ignoring Weygand but glancing quizzically at de Gaulle several times. He asked to see his old friend General Georges. Georges appeared and confirmed everything Weygand had said. Even as they spoke, he said, the enemy was only sixty miles away. The P.M., though visibly shaken, sought to revive the willpower of the French. His mouth was working; he searched for the words, found them, and spoke warmly and deeply. He wished, he said, to express his admiration for the gallant resistance of the French and Britain's deep sorrow that her contribution had been so slight. "Every Englishman," he told them, "is profoundly grieved that further military help cannot be given to France in this grave hour." Had the BEF not returned from Dunkirk naked, nine divisions of Britons would now be fighting alongside the poilus. As it was, England was sending all she had left, leaving her island virtually defenseless. Then he reminded them of 1918, when the Allies had been so close to defeat, and said that might be true now; all intelligence reports agreed that the Germans were exhausted, at the end of their tether. The cloud might lift in forty-eight hours. Weygand broke in to say they hadn't that much time; they were down to "the last quarter of an hour."[95]

Churchill wouldn't quit. He wanted to set the French afire with the flame of Britain's defiance. His words, Spears wrote, "came in torrents, French and English phrases tumbling over each other like waves rushing for the shore when driven by a storm. No matter what happened, he told them, England would fight—on and on and on, *toujours*, all the time, everywhere, *partout, pas de grâce*, no mercy. *Puis la victoire!*" He offered all the British support he could muster, including troops on their way from Britain's Dominions and colonies, and suggested alternatives to a French defeat, raising again the possibility of a Breton redoubt, into which the troops could withdraw, supplied by the Royal Navy. He wanted Weygand's army to fight in Paris, telling them how a great city, if valiantly defended, could absorb immense enemy armies. He suggested that the French government retreat to North Africa. If all else failed, he proposed guerrilla warfare.[96]

The French were hostile, Weygand scornful, and Pétain, who had sat silent until now, incredulous, mocking, and, finally, angry. The old *maréchal* dismissed the prime minister's vow that the British would fight on alone as absurd: "Since France cannot continue the struggle, wisdom dictates that England should seek peace, for certainly she cannot carry on alone." To make Paris "a city of ruins," he said, would not affect the issue. As for guerrillas, he said: "That would mean the destruction of the country."[97]

The most protracted discussion arose from the French demand that every plane left in the Royal Air Force be committed to the battle now raging. The appeal was unanimous: Pétain, Weygand, Georges, and Reynaud agreed that the RAF was their last hope, and that it could turn back the German tide. If the aircraft were withheld, Reynaud predicted, "Without doubt history will say that the battle of France was lost for lack of planes." "Here," said Weygand, "is the decisive point. Now is the decisive moment. The British ought not to keep a single fighter in England. They should all be sent to France." Ismay, Eden, and Spears were holding their breaths. Air Chief Marshal Dowding, chief of Britain's Fighter Command, had warned the prime minister and the War Cabinet that if any more fighter squadrons were sent to France, he could not guarantee the defense of England, and they were afraid that the prime minister's generosity, his love of France, his impulsiveness, and his innate optimism would prompt him to make a disastrous commitment of further air support.[98]

He didn't. According to Ismay, after a long pause he said very slowly, "This is *not* the decisive point. This is not the decisive moment. The decisive moment will come when Hitler hurls his Luftwaffe against Britain. If we can keep command of the air over our own island—that is all I ask—we will win it all back for you."[99]

Reynaud, Ismay noted, was "obviously moved." The premier asked, "If we capitulate, all the great might of Germany will be concentrated upon invading England. And then what will you do?" Thrusting his jaw forward, the P.M. replied that he hadn't thought about it carefully, but that broadly speaking, he would propose to drown as many of them as possible and then to *"frapper sur la tête"* ("hit on the head") any of them who managed to crawl ashore.[100]

It is odd that none of the Englishmen raised the question of the *French* air force. France had one, commanded by General Joseph Vuillemin, a daring

pilot in the last war but now obese and incompetent. Vuillemin had angered
the British by commenting that RAF support in the opening days of the German offense had arrived "tardily and in insufficient numbers." In fact, Britain had sent a hundred bombers, all the RAF had then, to bomb the Meuse
bridges and had lost forty-five of them. On May 28 Vuillemin had also said
the RAF had three hundred planes in England and had sent only thirty to
France—this at a time when eight to ten frontline British squadrons—96 to
120 aircraft—were in action every day supporting the French. Indeed, during the fall of France all but ten of the RAF's fifty-three fighter squadrons
saw action over France and the Low Countries, and of those ten, three were
night fighters, two were in Norway, and one was nonoperational.

During the fall of France the British lost 959 aircraft and nearly 300
pilots.* The French lost 560 planes, 235 of them destroyed on the ground.
The performance of the French air force was baffling, even to its leaders
and even after the war. At the outset, Vuillemin had more than 3,287 planes.
(The Germans had 2,670.) Yet only a third of French aircraft saw action.
Furthermore, between May 10 and June 12, French factories delivered 1,131
new airplanes, 688 of them fighters. Indeed, when France dropped out of
the war, Vuillemin found that he actually had more first-line aircraft than
he had had when the great Nazi offensive began. "What is this mystery
about our planes?" General Gamelin asked afterward, testifying before a
Parliamentary Investigating Committee. "Why out of 2,000 fighters on
hand at the beginning of May 1940 were fewer than 500 used on the Northeast Front? I humbly confess to you that I do not know." Commenting on
the confusing figures, he said, "We have a right to be astonished." Certainly
it is astonishing that the *généralissime* was astonished.[101]

At 10:00 P.M. the conferees dined. Weygand invited de Gaulle to sit
beside him and flushed when the new general chose the chair beside
Churchill instead. Already there was an unspoken bond between Churchill
and Reynaud's protégé. The formation of that bond was probably the
only accomplishment of the Briare meeting. For Churchill the last straw
came at bedtime. Before retiring, the prime minister and the premier had
coffee and brandy together. Reynaud said Weygand had told him, "In
three weeks Britain would have her neck wrung like a chicken." Then Rey-

---

* Reliable figures are difficult, and often impossible, to find. However, the French
official history, *Histoire de l'Aviation Militaire Française* (Paris, 1980), puts the British sacrifice much higher: "The losses suffered by the RAF in France are enough in
themselves to demonstrate its effective participation in the battle of May–June 1940.
More than 1,500 flyers were killed, wounded, or missing, and more than 1,500 planes
of all types were destroyed."

naud revealed that Pétain had told him that "it will be necessary to seek an armistice." Once the *"vainqueur de Verdun"* had been considered the guardian of French honor. Now, the premier said, the marshal "has written a paper on the subject which he wishes me to read. He has not handed it to me yet. He is still ashamed to do it." Churchill, appalled, thought Pétain should have been even more ashamed to have supported, "even tacitly, Weygand's demand for our last twenty-five squadrons of fighters when he has made up his mind that all is lost and that France should give in."[102]

Inspector Thompson, who prepared the prime minister's bath on these trips, had been billeted in another building and was without transportation. Thus Churchill awoke alone the next morning. Two French officers were finishing their café au lait in the conference room, which was the château's dining room, when a big double door burst open, confronting them with what one later described as "an apparition resembling an angry Japanese genie"—an irate, plump Churchill with sparse, mussed hair, dressed in a flowing crimson dressing gown belted with silk, and angrily demanding: *"Uh ay ma bain* [where's my bath]?"[103]

His frustration mounted after a telephone call from a furious air marshal, Sir Arthur Barratt, stationed in Salon. Barratt reported that local authorities, fearful of reprisals, had not permitted RAF bombers to take off for targets in Italy. They had dragged farm carts on the runway, forcing him to cancel the mission. Others in the British party thought that was the last straw. However, the P.M. did not reproach his hosts. Tormented by the martyrdom of the French and by England's niggardly contribution to the Allied cause here, he disregarded the incident.[104]

The next morning, the twelfth, after Churchill had exacted a promise from Admiral Darlan never to surrender the French fleet, the British party left. Near tragedy brushed them on the way home. Unescorted by Hurricanes—an overcast sky had grounded them—they were flying over Le Havre when the sky cleared and the pilot saw two Heinkel bombers below, firing at fishing boats. The unarmed Flamingo dived to a hundred feet above the sea and raced for home. According to Inspector Thompson, one of the Nazi fighters fired a burst at them, but then they were gone, and the prime minister landed safely at Hendon.[105]

In parting, Churchill had told Reynaud that in the event of any "change in the situation," the French premier must let His Majesty's Government know "at once" so that the British could return "at any convenient spot" to discuss the situation before the French took any irrevocable step "which would govern their action in the second phase of the war." Clearly England's allies were at the end of their tether. Late that evening, HMG learned that the British 51st Division had surrendered to the Germans in the fishing port of St-Valéry-en-Caux, a loss of more than 12,000 men. In his diary Jock Colville wrote: "Speaking of the surrender of the 51st Division, W. said it was the most 'brutal disaster' we had yet suffered."[106]

Early on the thirteenth, when Churchill was donning his sleeping smock, Reynaud phoned. The connection was bad. Eventually Colville got through to one of the premier's aides. The message was grim: the premier and his advisers had moved from Briare to Tours; he wanted Churchill to meet him at the Préfecture there that same afternoon. This would be the P.M.'s fifth flight to France in less than four weeks. At 11:00 A.M. he and his party gathered at Hendon—Ismay, Eden, Beaverbrook, Halifax, and Cadogan. Escorted by eight Spitfires, the Flamingo detoured around the Channel Islands and entered French air space over Saint-Malo.

Lashed by a thunderstorm, they landed on an airstrip pitted with bomb craters. The field was deserted. No one was there to meet them. They taxied around the craters, looking for someone, and found a group of French airmen lounging outside a hangar. Churchill disembarked and told them, in his appalling French, that his name was Churchill, that he was the prime minister of Great Britain, and that he would be grateful if they could provide him with *"une voiture"* to carry him and his small staff to the town's Préfecture de Police. The airmen loaned them a small touring car, into which they crammed themselves with great difficulty and much discomfort. Halifax's long legs were a problem; so was the P.M.'s bulk. No one at the Préfecture knew who they were or had time for them. Luckily an officer appeared, recognized them, and led them to a small restaurant, where they lunched on cold chicken, cheese, and Vouvray wine.[107]

It was there that they were found by Paul Baudouin. In what Churchill called "his soft, silky manner," Baudouin lectured them on the hopelessness of French resistance. No one knew when Reynaud would appear, or even where he was. At length the premier arrived, followed by General Spears and Sir Ronald Campbell, the British ambassador. The meeting—destined to be the last of the *Conseil supérieur de la guerre*—was to be held in the *Préfet*'s study, a small, shabby room looking out on an unkempt garden. The study was furnished with a desk, behind which Reynaud presided, and assorted unmatched chairs. Churchill took a leather chair and eyed his French hosts warily. He was confronting France's split personality. Reynaud—still backed by a majority of the Chamber and the Senate—stood for a never-say-die, death-before-dishonor last stand against Nazi barbarism, with which Churchill agreed. Baudouin, Churchill knew, represented the defeatists; in his final report to Whitehall, Campbell would describe Baudouin as a man whose "dominating motives were fear and the desire to stand in well with the conqueror after the inevitable defeat." Even now Churchill had not grasped how eager for peace such men were. U.S. ambassador to France William Bullitt, no admirer of the British, told Washington that "to have as many companions in misery as possible, they hoped England would be rapidly and completely defeated by Germany and [that] the Italians would suffer the same fate." As for their own country, Bullitt reported, they hoped France would become "Hitler's favorite province."[108]

Reynaud told the British that Weygand had declared Paris an open city; panzers were in Reims; Nazi troops were below the Seine and the Marne. It was too late to withdraw into a *rédout Breton*. He himself wanted to "retreat and carry on, but the people would remain; France would cease to exist." Therefore the alternative was "armistice or peace." He asked what the British position would be "should the worst come" and raised the issue of the pledge—made at France's insistence and signed by him—that neither ally would made a separate peace. The French wanted to be left off the hook. They had, he said, "already sacrificed everything in the common cause," had "nothing left," and would be shocked if the English failed to understand that they were "physically incapable of carrying on." Would Britain face the hard facts now confronting France?

Spears quietly pointed out that capitulation was not the only alternative to war. Norway had not surrendered; neither had Holland. In the meantime, Churchill scowled, weighing his words. Britain, he replied at last, knew what France had endured and was still suffering. If the BEF had not been cut off in the north, they would be fighting beside the French now. They could not be there "owing to our having accepted the strategy of the army in the north." The other Englishmen sat up. They had long hoped he would say that. The reason for the present crisis was not a lack of fighter planes. It was GHQ's decision to ignore the Ardennes threat and send the best Allied troops into Belgium. The British had not yet "felt the German lash" but knew its force, the prime minister rasped. "England will fight on. She has not and will not alter her resolve: no terms, no surrender." He hoped France would carry on, fighting south of Paris and, if it came to that, in North Africa. Time was of the essence. It would not be "limitless: a pledge from the United States would make it quite short." A "firm promise from America," he said, "would introduce a tremendous new factor for France."

He was grasping at straws. Churchill knew that Roosevelt's hands were tied by the U.S. Constitution. As well, if Roosevelt announced his intention to seek an unprecedented third term in office, he surely would not do so on an interventionist platform. Indeed, Roosevelt made no announcement that June, telling Americans only that he would abide by the decision of the July Democratic convention. The P.M. also knew that Washington then had no arms to give. So did Reynaud. Although unschooled in American politics, the premier had served as France's *ministre de finance* for the first six months of the war, had bought some arms from the United States, and knew how little matériel was there. Nevertheless he accepted the possibility of American intervention. It was a delusion. Churchill was wrong to have encouraged it, though much of the blame was Ambassador Bullitt's. Alistair Horne points out that "through him [Bullitt] the French government was led to expect far greater aid than could possibly have been forthcoming at that time."[109]

Briefly stirred, the premier agreed to appeal to Roosevelt. Nevertheless he again asked that Britain agree to "a separate peace." The prime minister replied that although Britain would not "waste time in reproaches and recriminations," that was "a very different thing from becoming a consenting party to a peace made in contravention of the agreement so recently concluded." Then he reported that the Royal Navy was fast approaching a tight blockade of the Continent, which could lead to famine, from which an occupied France could not be spared. The French could not withdraw from the war and remain on good terms with the British. Reynaud, disturbed, darkly remarked: "This might result in a new and very grave situation in Europe."[110]

They had reached an impasse. Spears scribbled a note to Churchill suggesting a pause. Churchill told Reynaud he must confer with his colleagues "dans le jardin [in the garden]." The Englishmen withdrew to pace around the garden, "a hideous rectangle," in Spears's words, surrounded by a muddy path. After twenty minutes Beaverbrook spoke up: "There is nothing to do but repeat what you have said, Winston. Telegraph to Roosevelt and await the answer." He added: "We are doing no good here"; therefore, "Let's get along home."

And so they did. Everything now depended upon the reply from Washington. Reynaud, who had been joined by Charles de Gaulle, seemed confident that the Americans would save his country. As they prepared to leave, Churchill noted that among the Allied prisoners in France were 400 Luftwaffe pilots. He asked that they be sent to England, and the premier immediately agreed. As the P.M. passed de Gaulle, he said in a low tone, "L'homme du destin [the man of destiny]." The general remained impassive, but he understood: The French troops who had escaped from Dunkirk to Britain formed an army in waiting, but were without a leader. Large French forces in Brittany, who might fight on, likewise were in need of leadership. "There is apparently a young French general named de Gaulle," Colville told his diary the day before, "of whom Winston thinks a great deal." He did, and his statement to de Gaulle amounted to both a challenge and a promise of support were de Gaulle to lead a resistance in Brittany. On some level everyone knew that the alliance was finished, and it was in keeping with its last five ragged weeks that it should end in a grotesque scene. Outside the Préfecture, the Comtesse de Portes accosted Churchill, crying: "Mr. Churchill, my country is bleeding to death. I have a story to tell and you *must* hear me. You must hear my side of it. You must!" He ignored her and entered his car. Later he remarked: "She had comfort to give him. I had none."[111]

What Baudouin did was less forgivable. From time to time in the *Préfet*'s study, when Reynaud was speaking, Churchill had nodded or said, "*Je comprends,*" indicating his comprehension of words before they were translated. After Churchill's car had left, de Gaulle called Spears aside to tell him that Baudouin was "putting it about, to all and sundry, notably to the journalists," that Churchill had shown "complete understanding of the French situation and would understand if France concluded an armistice and a separate peace." De Gaulle asked, "Did Churchill really say that?" If he had, it would sway those not prepared to break France's pledge and permit defeatists to argue that there was no point in fighting on when even the English didn't expect it.

Spears replied that Churchill had said no such thing, and decided to race to the bomb-pitted runway before the prime minister's Flamingo took off. He arrived in time and his view was confirmed. Churchill told him, "When I said '*Je comprends,*' that meant I understood. *Comprendre* means understand in French, doesn't it? Well, when for once I use the right word in their own language, it is going rather far to assume that I intended it to mean something quite different. Tell them my French is not so bad as that." Spears did, but few listened, perhaps because Baudouin was telling them what they wanted to hear. The lie found its way into official French records and was even used against Churchill when he tried to remind them of the accord. During the armistice negotiations, Admiral Darlan declared that "the British Prime Minister, informed on June 11 [*sic*] of the necessity in which France found herself of bringing the struggle to an end, said that he understood that necessity and accepted it without withdrawing his sympathy from our country. He is therefore not qualified to speak otherwise."[112]

Reynaud's appeal, cabled to Washington the next morning, June 14, declared that unless the president gave "France in the coming days a positive assurance that the United States will come into the struggle in a short space of time...you will see France go under like a drowning man after having thrown a last look toward the land of liberty from which she was expecting salvation." In Washington, Secretary of State Cordell Hull called the plea "extraordinary, almost hysterical." Nevertheless, the president's reply went further than Hull and his other advisers wished. He assured the premier that Americans were doing everything in their power to send all the matériel they could and were redoubling their efforts because of their "faith and support of" the democratic ideals for which the French were fighting. Roosevelt encouraged the embattled French to fight on even in North Africa.

Although Roosevelt had pointed out that he could not make military commitments on his own authority, Churchill told his War Cabinet that Roosevelt's message came "as near as possible to a declaration of war and probably as much as the President could do without Congress." Beaverbrook thought an American declaration of war was now inevitable, but this was just more straw grasping. Significantly, the president had not made his cable public, and when the prime minister asked for permission to do this, it was denied. On June 14—the day Paris fell and the French government headed for Bordeaux—Colville noted: "It seems that the P.M.'s expectations last night of immediate American help were exaggerated. Roosevelt has got to proceed cautiously, but the plain truth is that America has been caught napping, militarily and industrially. She may be really useful to us in a year; but we are living from hour to hour." That day, the order went out to bring the rest of the BEF home from south of the Seine.[113]

De Gaulle, who had been commuting between London and France as a liaison officer, now proposed a measure born of desperation. On June 16, lunching at the Carleton Club with Churchill and the French ambassador, he argued that "some dramatic move" was essential to keep France in the war. He advanced the idea of a joint Allied declaration. The British and French governments would declare the formation of an Anglo-French Union, the two nations uniting as one. Churchill liked it; so did the War Cabinet, and de Gaulle immediately took off for Bordeaux to submit the proposal. Spears wrote that after reading a draft of the declaration, Reynaud was "transfigured with joy." It came, he said, at the best possible time. The council of ministers was meeting at 5:00 P.M. "to decide whether further resistance is possible," and the premier told Spears that he believed the vision of union would thwart an armistice. However, the premier's mistress Hélène de Portes was with them—she knew every state secret; one vital document, missing for hours, was found in her bed—and she read the draft over a secretary's shoulder. Everything she knew, she shared with Baudouin. Before Reynaud could tell his ministers the news, they already knew it and had been told all the arguments against it.

Meantime Churchill was preparing to cross the Channel once again, this time aboard a warship just after midnight on the seventeenth. At 9:30 P.M. he boarded a special train at Waterloo Station, prepared to leave for Southampton. Clementine had come to see him off. Kathleen Hill, who was also on board, recalled: "We had taken our seats on the train and were waiting. There was a delay. There had been some hitch." Indeed there had. Ambassador Campbell had phoned No. 10 to report that a "ministerial crisis" in Bordeaux made the meeting impossible. Churchill disembarked "with a heavy heart," as he later wrote. He knew what was coming next, and Colville set it down: "Reynaud has resigned, unable to stand the pressure.... Pétain has formed a Government of Quislings, including [Pierre] Laval, and France will now certainly ask for an armistice in spite of her pledge to us." Later he added: "The Cabinet met at 11.00 and shortly afterwards we heard that Pétain had ordered the French army to lay down its arms." Churchill growled, "Another bloody country gone west."[114]

Colville wrote: "After the Cabinet the P.M. paced backwards and forwards in the garden, alone, his head bowed, his hands behind his back. He was doubtless considering how best the French fleet, the air force and the colonies could be saved. He, I am sure, will remain undaunted."[115]

De Gaulle was trapped in Bordeaux. The men now forming a new French government believed him to be—as he was—their enemy. They represented one France, he another; if left free, they knew, he would divide the country and offend the Nazis, whose servants they now were. To him their separate peace was shameful. Because he was determined to carry on the war, the British were still his allies. They were also his best hope of escaping from here and forming a new army on free soil, but the British were leaving the new France, which, they knew, did not wish either them or him well.

The issue had already been decided. The French defeatists were preparing to move to Vichy—an appropriate seat for Pétain's new government, the *Times* acidly commented, Vichy being a favorite resort of invalids. They were already drawing up legislation to abolish the republic and set up a dictatorship—the État Français—when General Spears and Ambassador Campbell arrived at Bordeaux's Quartier Général, the premier's temporary office in the rue Vital-Carles. They hoped to persuade him to stay in office. It was a doomed call—he had lost control of his cabinet and had submitted his resignation—which led to unexpected consequences. At 10:00 P.M. they had entered the building's huge, darkened hall. As they were approaching its wide staircase, Spears had noticed a tall figure standing bolt upright behind one of the columns, "shrouded," as he recalled afterward, "by shadow." It was de Gaulle, who had called him in a loud whisper. He said, "I must speak to you. It is extremely urgent." After the general explained that Reynaud awaited them, de Gaulle whispered, "I have very good reason to believe Weygand intends arresting me." Spears told him to stay "exactly where you are," and, after the brief, sad appointment with Reynaud, suggested they meet within the hour at the nearby Grand Hôtel Montré.[116]

De Gaulle explained a plan to encourage a French *Résistance* movement, using London as his base. Spears approved; he phoned Churchill, who agreed. Spears had a plane at the Bordeaux airport. They would fly out at 7:00 A.M. the next morning, the seventeenth. He never knew where de Gaulle spent that night—the hotel was too dangerous—but in the morning the self-appointed leader of the Free French (as those poilus who fled to Britain called themselves) appeared with an aide and an immense amount of baggage. Because there were French authorities at the field—the hunt for de Gaulle had already begun—it was decided that he and his aide-de-camp would behave as though they had come to see Spears off. In Spears's words, "We had begun to move when with hooked hands I hoisted de Gaulle on board"; the aide followed "in a trice." The baggage was tossed on board. De Gaulle arrived at No. 10 Downing Street in time for lunch. Pétain, upon learning what had happened, convened a military court. The expatriated general was found guilty of treason and sentenced to death in absentia. Churchill, of course, took another view. He wrote that de Gaulle had "carried with him, in this small aeroplane, the honour of France."[117]

De Gaulle was one of countless thousands of others escaping Vichy's État Français that week. When the armies ceased fire at 12:40 P.M. on Monday, June 17—Britain's first day alone—French ports and airfields were enveloped in chaos. Escapees from Austria, Czechoslovakia, Poland, and Scandinavia, many of them Jews, had found refuge in France. Their names were on Gestapo lists, they knew it, and they were frantic. RAF fields on French soil were closing down; pilots and ground crews were taking off for home. Forty thousand British fighting men, together with Belgian and Polish soldiers, were being evacuated from Brest, Cherbourg, St-Nazaire, Bordeaux, and Saint-Malo. It was a time of appalling tragedies, unnoted at the time and forgotten in the next five years of struggle for mastery of the Continent. One, which would have shocked the world even in wartime, was the loss of the liner *Lancastria,* just as she was leaving St-Nazaire with five thousand troops and civilian refugees aboard. Nazi bombers sank her, and three thousand drowned. Churchill forbade publication of this, saying, "The newspapers have got quite enough disaster for today, at least." Among the uprooted were Queen Wilhelmina of Holland, a fugitive from her own homeland granted asylum by King George; Somerset Maugham, who had fled his Cannes villa in a boat packed with fellow refugees, in which he spent three weeks without changing clothes; and, most remarkably, the Duke of Windsor, the former King Edward VIII, accompanied by his Baltimore duchess.

On the sixteenth, when de Gaulle was describing his mission to General Spears in a Bordeaux hotel suite, the telephone there had rung. Henry Mack, Ambassador Sir Ronald Campbell's first secretary, answered it and, to his astonishment, found himself talking to the Duke, who was calling from Nice. He and the Duchess were marooned there, he explained. Could a destroyer be sent to pick them up? Mack, shocked, told him there was only one British ship in Bordeaux's harbor, and that was a collier. He suggested that the Windsors drive to Spain. They did. They were staying with Sir Samuel Hoare, Britain's ambassador in Madrid, when the Duke decided to lean on Winston Churchill. After all, they were old friends. Churchill had nearly destroyed his own career trying to keep the Duke, then King, on his throne. Now Windsor wanted to return to England. He also insisted that he be appointed to an official position. And: "In the light of past experience, my wife and myself must not risk finding ourselves once more regarded by the British public as in a different status to other members of my family." All of this he sent Churchill in a telegram. In a separate message, Hoare reported that they wanted to be briefly received by the King and Queen, and that news of the meeting appear in the Court Circular.[118]

Apart from the fact that Churchill was busier than any other prime minister in the history of England, meeting any of these demands was impossible. The Duchess was anathema to the royal family, particularly Mary, the Queen Mother, and their opinion of her husband had plummeted upon learning that he and his wife admired Hitler. The Windsors had since the war's outbreak muted their former openly pro-Nazi rhetoric, but remained vehemently anti-Semitic, and moved comfortably in circles sharing their views. Also, although the Duke may have forgotten it, he was in uniform. At the war's outbreak, he had been commissioned a major general and appointed a liaison officer with the French. After the Germans entered Paris, he had been assigned to the *Armée des Alpes,* then to military headquarters in Nice. Although Ambassador Campbell's private secretary had suggested he go to Spain, no one had authorized him to do so. What to do with him?[119]

King George VI told Churchill: "Keep him out of England *at all costs.*" Churchill wired the Duke, curtly reminding him that he had "taken active military rank," and "refusal to obey orders" would create a grave situation. He added, but then cut: "Already there is a great deal of doubt as to the circumstances in which Your Royal Highness left Paris." The King's private secretary suggested the Duke be appointed to the army staff in Cairo; Churchill vetoed that. By now the Windsors were in Lisbon, where a British agent sent back word that the Duchess's activities were alarming; she was reported to have said that she and her husband could accept the possibility of German victory. The King's private secretary wrote No. 10 that "this is not the first time that this lady has come under suspicion for her anti-British activities, and as long as we never forget the power she can exert over him in her efforts to avenge herself on this country we shall be all right."

It was the King who proposed that his brother be appointed governor and commander in chief of the Bahamas. This was a royal comedown; the Bahamas was down there with the Falkland Islands and Ghana—the Gold Coast—in lack of imperial importance. Nevertheless, Churchill, who had better things to do, offered the Bahamian post to Windsor, adding, "Personally, I feel sure it is the best option in the grievous situation in which we all stand. At any rate, I have done my best." Later that day he asked Beaverbrook, "Max, do you think he'll take it?" According to Colville, who was present, Beaverbrook said, "He'll find it a great relief," and Churchill said, "Not half as much as his brother will."[120]

Windsor accepted it, though noting that he did not "consider my appointment as one of first class importance," and observing that it was "evident that the King and Queen do not wish to put our family differences to an end." But there was more. The prime minister told him there were conditions. His two British servants, being of military age, would have to serve in the army, and neither the Duke nor his Duchess would be permitted to visit the United States. The P.M. further warned that "sharp and unfriendly ears will be picked up to catch any suggestion that your Royal Highness takes a view about the war, or about the Germans, or about Hitlerism, which is different from that adopted by the British nation and Parliament.... Even while you have been staying in Lisbon, conversations have been reported by telegraph through various channels which might have been used to your Royal Highness's disadvantage." Warning Roosevelt that the Duke was on his way, he explained that he had been "causing His Majesty and His Majesty's Government some embarrassment," and that "Nazi intrigue seeks, now that the greater part of the Continent is in enemy hands, to make trouble about him."[121]

Churchill had ended his message to Windsor with "I thought your Royal Highness would not mind these words of caution." Of course the Duke minded, and he flouted them. Interviewed by the American magazine *Liberty,* he encouraged isolationists to leave no stone unturned in their campaign to keep the United States out of the war, this at a time when Churchill was toiling to get the U.S. *into* it. American guests were told by both the Duke and Duchess that their country would be foolish to fight at England's side. It was too late, they said; Britain was finished.[122]

On June 18 the moon was full—a bomber's moon. Colville noted the moon's phase in his diary, adding: "The air raids will now begin. They were bigger last night than hitherto, and Cambridge was hit, a row of houses being destroyed." Colville was correct. The Germans had been sending, intermittently, small forces of bombers in search of industrial and military targets since the previous autumn. Now they began to visit regularly.[123]

—

The June 22 surrender of the French, beside whom Britons had been prepared to fight to the bitter end, staggered all of Britain. Britons began to realize that the way of life they had known and loved was vanishing. People walked about as though in a daze. Bus conductors punched tickets in silence; Cockney newsboys, usually irrepressibly cheerful, mutely handed out papers. No one could remember when London had been so quiet. "At places where normally there is a noisy bustle of comings and goings," wrote an American observer, there was "the same extraordinary preoccupied silence." Mollie Panter-Downes reported in *The New Yorker* on June 28:

> The French acceptance of the crushing armistice terms came as a profound shock to the public, which had been simple enough to believe Marshal Pétain when he declared that France would make no shameful surrender.... The average uninformed citizen found it difficult to believe that anything could be more shameful than an agreement which handed over weapons of war, airfields, munition works, and industrial areas to be used unconditionally."[124]

It is in this context of anger and bitterness that Churchill's action against the French fleet must be seen. To put it in the best possible light, the behavior of Admiral Jean Louis Xavier François Darlan was duplicitous. As France's naval chief of staff he had given his solemn word to everyone around him that if events led to an armistice with the Nazis, he would order all French warships to take refuge in British ports. To a French general he said that, if necessary, he would place every vessel under the Union Jack. He told a member of the *Chambre des Députés* who was also on his staff: "If an armistice is signed for one day, I shall round off my career with an act of glorious indiscipline; I shall sail with the Fleet." As late as the evening of June 16, with the cease-fire only hours away, he assured Sir Ronald Campbell: "So long as I can issue orders to it [the fleet] you have nothing to fear." Even de Gaulle believed him. "A feudal lord," he said, "does not surrender his fief."[125]

Suddenly Darlan was the most important man in the war. Weygand's army was a shattered hulk, but the French navy—the fourth-largest in the world, after Britain, the United States, and Japan—included some of the fastest, most modern ships afloat: three modern and five older battleships, eighteen heavy cruisers, twenty-seven light cruisers, sixty submarines (twenty-four had been sunk), and more than fifty destroyers. All were important. Were Hitler to grab just one-third of the French navy, he'd almost double the size of the German navy overnight. Britain's army was small and weaponless; her air force was outnumbered by the Luftwaffe. Sea power was vital to the nation's survival, but if the French, German, and Italian navies were combined, the Royal Navy would be overwhelmed. As Churchill saw it, "Admiral Darlan had but to sail one of his ships to any port outside France to become master of all French interests beyond German control"—in short, the entire French colonial empire.[126]

Why did he stay? He appears to have had several motives. His hatred of the British lay deep; he believed that for Frenchmen, there was no difference between England (as the French always called Britain) and Germany; Pétain was offering him power; and he was convinced that the Nazis would win the war. He told Ambassador Bullitt that he was "certain that Great Britain would be conquered by Germany within five weeks unless Great Britain should surrender sooner." When Bullitt remarked that Darlan seemed pleased by that prospect, he smiled and nodded in agreement. As for his promises, he preserved honor, at least in his own eyes, by resigning his commission and taking office as Pétain's minister of marine. It was now his duty to enforce the policies of the new government whether he approved of them or not.[127]

As late as June 22, first sea lord Admiral Dudley Pound told the War Cabinet that Darlan was taking "all possible steps" to prevent his ships from falling into Nazi hands. Churchill believed that they could not rely on one man's word, because the issue was "so vital to the safety of the whole British Empire." Within hours he was vindicated. At 6:50 P.M. they learned the terms of the armistice on June 22. The French had signed it without consulting their ally. Article VIII stipulated that the "French war fleet . . . will be assembled in ports to be specified and then demobilized and disarmed under German or Italian control."

The British had been betrayed. The ships would be delivered into enemy hands while still fully armed. Hitler declared that Germany did not intend to use them during the war, but as the prime minister rhetorically asked Parliament: "What is the value of that? Ask half a dozen countries, what is the value of such a solemn assurance? Furthermore, the armistice could be voided at any time on any pretext of 'non-observance.'"[128]

The French fleet formed but one part of a much larger story. With the French surrender, the British naval blockade of the Baltic—the closing of the Skagerrak and Kattegat Straits to German ships—was broken. The Germans now held European ports from Norway through Denmark, Holland, Belgium, and France to the Bay of Biscay. The German capture of the Channel ports—Dieppe, Cherbourg, Brest, St-Nazaire, La Rochelle,

Le Havre, and Lorient—had changed the entire dynamic of the war. Operating from these ports the Reich's submariners had to sail for only a day or two in order to reach British shipping lanes. Immediately the British ceased merchant sailings into or out of the Southwest Approaches, the sea-lanes that ran south of Ireland and into the Irish Sea, to Bristol and Liverpool. That left the Northwest Approaches—the sea-lanes between Northern Ireland and Scotland—as the only route into Britain.

Peril also loomed in the Mediterranean, where the French navy had been charged with securing the western part of that sea. The French navy was no longer a factor, unless it fell into the hands of the Germans and Italians, and that, Churchill later wrote, would confront "Great Britain with mortal danger." To fill the void left by the French in the western Mediterranean, the British drew heavily from the Home Fleet—itself preparing against possible invasion—to create Force H at Gibraltar, a powerful fleet of battleships, an aircraft carrier, and numerous cruisers, destroyers, and submarines. The commander of Force H, Vice Admiral James Somerville, was given three objectives: keep the Germans out of the Mediterranean, keep the Italians in, and impose a naval blockade on Vichy France and its northwest African dominions. But how to remove the French fleet from the equation?[129]

Churchill found himself confronted, he later wrote, with "a hateful decision, the most unnatural and painful in which I have ever been concerned." There was no easy solution, although some thought so; on June 25, George Bernard Shaw wrote to him: "Why not declare war on France and capture her fleet (which would gladly strike its colors to us) before A.H. recovers his breath? Surely that is the logic of the situation?" Churchill knew the French fleet would gladly do no such thing, and any use of force to cripple it would enrage Vichy. Yet as the British blockade of Vichy tightened, French hostility would become inevitable anyway. Therefore the War Cabinet, with Churchill the apostle of force majeure, approved an operation that, in his words, would comprise "the simultaneous seizure, control, or effective disablement of all the accessible French fleet." Accessible were ships now in English waters and those anchored at Alexandria, the Algerian city of Oran, and Dakar, in West Africa.[130]

The first phase of the British action was code-named Operation Grasp. In the early hours of July 3, armed boarding parties took over all French vessels in the ports of Portsmouth, Plymouth, Falmouth, Southampton, and Sheerness. There was virtually no resistance; one French and one English sailor were killed when the crew of the French submarine *Surcouf* disputed the issue. Surprise was complete, and the ease with which the French ships were taken demonstrated, as the prime minister pointed out, "how easily the Germans could have taken possession of any French ships lying in ports which they controlled."[131]

The second phase, Operation Catapult, was more difficult. The P.M. called it "the deadly stroke...in the western Mediterranean." In the eastern Mediterranean, at Alexandria, they were lucky. Darlan ordered Vice Admiral René Godfroy to sail his ships to the French-held North African Bizerte; simultaneously, Admiral Sir Andrew Browne Cunningham ("ABC" to his friends), commander in chief of Royal Navy Mediterranean operations, was ordered to stop him. The two admirals, good friends, settled the issue by a gentleman's agreement: Godfroy discharged his fuel oil and placed the breechblocks of his guns and the warheads of his torpedoes in custody of the French consul ashore, with the British consul as co-trustee. All parties signed a formal agreement, thus achieving Cunningham's objective without violating Godfroy's honor.[132]

It was very different at Mers-el-Kébir, the naval base three miles west of Oran. Much of the French Atlantic squadron was anchored here, including two battleships and two modern battle cruisers, the *Dunkerque* and the *Strasbourg,* built by the French to counter the German battle cruisers *Gneisenau* and *Scharnhorst,* which had proven their deadliness when they mauled the British off Norway. *Dunkerque* and *Strasbourg* could not be allowed to fall into German hands. The French commander, Vice Admiral Marcel Gensoul, had been alerted and told to be wary of the British. Admiral Pound said the only way to destroy them would be "in a surprise attack carried out at dawn and without any form of prior notification." But that was impossible. Catapult was asking a lot of Royal Navy officers as it was; just a week earlier the French had been their comrades. They could not be expected to open fire on them without warning. Thus the task given Vice Admiral Somerville was both difficult and delicate.

He arrived off Mers-el-Kébir shortly after 9:00 A.M. on July 3 with the battleships *Valiant* and *Resolution,* the venerable and feared battle cruiser *Hood,* two cruisers, eleven destroyers, and the aircraft carrier *Ark Royal.* Somerville gave Gensoul four choices. He could sail with the Royal Navy against Nazi Germany and Italy; he could sail to a British port; he could sail to a French colonial port or the United States, where the ships would be disarmed for the duration; or he could sink his vessels within the next six hours. Failing these, Somerville's message ended, "I have orders from His Majesty's Government to use whatever force may be necessary to prevent your ships from falling into German or Italian hands."[133]

Eight hours of palaver followed. Gensoul said that under no circumstances would he permit his crafts to be taken intact by the Nazis, who, until now, had been their common enemies. Faced with an ultimatum, however, he would defend himself by force. Somerville radioed London that the French showed no signs of leaving their harbor. Churchill, speaking through the Admiralty, told him to get on with it, to do his duty, distasteful though it was. Somerville gave Gensoul a series of deadlines, telling the Admiralty that the French were awaiting instructions from their government and that he was having problems with French mines. However, as the afternoon waned, he realized that the French admiral was stalling while he gathered steam, putting his vessels in an advanced state of readiness for sea. Then British intelligence intercepted messages to Mers-el-Kébir from the new French government. Darlan was ordering Gensoul to "answer force with force." He had informed the Germans of what was going on, and he told Gensoul that all French ships in the Mediterranean were on their way. The Admiralty radioed Somerville: "Settle the matter quickly or you may have French reinforcements to deal with."[134]

At 5:55 P.M. the British admiral issued the order to open fire. Within ten minutes one French battleship had blown up, and the other was beached. The *Dunkerque* had run aground—torpedo bombers from the *Ark Royal* finished her off—and 1,250 French sailors were dead. Only the *Strasbourg* had escaped, making smoke and fleeing into the gathering darkness.[135]

Mers-el-Kébir was the culmination of nearly eight weeks of increasing disappointment and distrust between the two former allies. Pétain's government was apoplectic. Darlan vowed revenge. Pierre Laval, the new minister of foreign affairs in the Vichy government, whose tarnished star was rising in the Nazi sun over Vichy, called for a declaration of war on England. Baudouin disparaged Britain's war effort and blamed the war on the English. Pétain broke off diplomatic relations with Britain, and the long, sad epic of his État Français's collaboration with the Germans began. Some French warships, including the battleship *Richelieu,* took refuge at Dakar; the rest—three battleships, seven heavy cruisers, sixteen submarines, eighteen destroyers, and a dozen torpedo boats, almost one-third of the prewar French navy—sailed to the naval base at Toulon. There, for the next twenty-nine months, the fleet rode at anchor.

In England the action at Mers-el-Kébir was wildly cheered. Gallup found that confidence in the prime minister rose to 89 percent—at Chamberlain's peak it had been 69 percent. Francophobia had not been so intense since the Napoleonic years. Even as the guns fell silent off Algeria, Britain learned that Vichy had quashed Reynaud's assurance that the 400 Luftwaffe pilots who had become Allied prisoners would be sent to Britain, and were instead on their way back to Germany. In the House of Commons Churchill said: "I leave the judgment of our action, with confidence, to Parliament. I leave it to the nation, and I leave it to the United States. I leave it to the world and history."[136]

Suddenly every MP was on his feet. Jock Colville noted in his diary: "He told the whole story of Oran and the House listened enthralled and amazed. Gasps of surprise were audible, but it was clear the House unanimously approved." Hugh Dalton wrote: "At the end we gave him a much louder and longer ovation than he, or Chamberlain or anyone else, had yet had during this war." Harold Nicolson noted: "The House is at first saddened by this odious attack but is fortified by Winston's speech. The grand finale ends in an ovation, with Winston sitting there with the tears pouring down his cheeks."[137]

Curiously, the most bitter dissent was heard in the Admiralty. All the flag officers who had participated in Catapult agreed with Cunningham that the attack had been "an act of sheer treachery which was as injudicious as it was unnecessary" and was "almost inept in its unwisdom." What they failed to grasp was that Mers-el-Kébir was not just a military action. Churchill's objective, which he reached, was far greater. Later he tried to explain it to Cordell Hull, who thought it a "tragic blunder." As Hull, an anti-imperialist who harbored a smoldering distrust of Churchill's ultimate motives, set it down, Churchill told him that "since many people throughout the world believed that Britain was about to surrender, he had wanted by this action to show that she still meant to fight."

That was the crux. In little more than two years, the Nazis had seized or conquered Austria, Czechoslovakia, Poland, Denmark, Norway, Belgium, Holland, Luxembourg, and France, and they had done it almost effortlessly. To millions, resistance seemed futile, even suicidal. On May 15, America's ambassador, Joseph P. Kennedy, had informed President Roosevelt that Britain was finished, and that the end would come soon; he expected the Germans in London within a month. The British people didn't think so. In May a Gallup poll found that 3 percent of them thought they might lose the war—by the end of July the percentage was so small it was immeasurable. Their King spoke for them when he wrote Queen Mary: "Personally, I feel happier now that we have no allies to be polite to and to pamper." Though abroad his kingdom seemed doomed, at home Mers-el-Kébir ended talk of a British surrender. The prime minister was particularly anxious about the view in Washington. To his great relief Roosevelt approved, believing, he said, that if there was one chance in a hundred that France's warships might fall into German hands, the attack was justified. Seven months later, Harry Hopkins, arriving in London as the President's emissary, told Colville that "it was Oran which convinced President Roosevelt, in spite of opinions to the contrary, that the British would go on fighting, as Churchill had promised, if necessary for years, if necessary alone."[138]

Most, including Hitler, believed Churchill's declaration to fight on alone applied only to the defense of England. But Churchill intended as well to take the fight to Hitler. He told Britons many times in coming months that Hitler must break the Home Island in order to win the war. Actually, Churchill knew there was another way — in another place — for Hitler to win, one that would negate the need for an all-or-nothing invasion of England. It was also the place that afforded Churchill the best chance to take the fight to Hitler's ally and, if Hitler came to his ally's assistance, to Hitler himself. Where all Britons that summer scanned the seas and the skies overhead, Churchill looked far further, to the place he believed the war would be decided: the Mediterranean Sea.

The Mediterranean lay at the center of Churchill's strategic vision, as it had for the ancient Romans, and as it now did for Mussolini. Churchill later called the Mediterranean "the hinge of fate" upon which the outcome of the war turned. Many in the German navy and Luftwaffe high command understood this. Later in the summer the commander in chief of the German navy, *Grossadmiral* Erich Raeder, told Hitler in private that "the British have always considered the Mediterranean the pivot of their world empire." Raeder believed clearing the British from the Mediterranean would sever England from its Empire and force London to come to terms, if the U-boat blockade did not bring Britain to its knees first. Churchill believed likewise. But Churchill not only saw danger in the Mediterranean, he saw opportunity, the *only* opportunity for Britain to go on the offensive, by sea, air, and on land. This, Churchill intended to do. His war strategy can be summed up thus: defend England; defend and attack in the Mediterranean.[139]

Since the time of the Caesars, dominance of the Mediterranean — *mare nostrum* — had been vital to Italian security. The Mediterranean between Sicily and Tripoli, a distance of about 300 miles, was to Rome what the English Channel and the Northwest Approaches were to London. Malta, a British possession since 1814, and home to a Royal Navy fleet, sits directly astride the sea routes from Italy to its North Africa colonies. The main island of Malta, 95 square miles of Tertiary limestone, rises from the sea 100 miles south of Sicily and about 200 miles northeast of Tripoli. The nearest British naval base, in Alexandria, lay almost 1,000 miles to the east, Gibraltar 1,100 miles to the west. When France fell, the entire British air presence on Malta consisted of three obsolete Gloster Gladiator biplanes, dubbed *Faith, Hope,* and *Charity* by their pilots. A fourth Gladiator was stripped for spare parts. Gibraltar and the Suez Canal are the main portals into the Mediterranean, but Malta since the time of Nelson had been the geographical key to free run of the sea. The harbor at Valletta was the only British deepwater port between the anchorages at Gibraltar and Alexandria, and therefore critical to the Royal Navy, almost as vital as Scapa Flow, the Scottish anchorage and main base of the Home Fleet.

But the British, expecting at least an Italian air attack, if not a full-scale naval assault on Malta, moved their warships (but for submarines) from the naval base at Valletta to Alexandria, to help cover the eastern Mediterranean. Mussolini launched his first air raid on Malta on June 11, and never let up; he understood that only when he controlled the sea could his armies secure the perimeter. His navy of six battleships, nineteen cruisers, one hundred smaller vessels, and more than one hundred submarines was larger than the German navy, and larger than the combined British fleets at Gibraltar and Alexandria. Malta was so central to Churchill's war strategy that he told the War Cabinet later in 1940 that if allocations of concrete for use in building coastal defenses had to be adjusted downward, it must not be done at the expense of three "vital" positions: The Home Island, Gibraltar, and Malta. Mussolini and Churchill (and Grand Admiral Raeder) knew that if the British lost Malta, the Mediterranean would become an Italian lake, and Gibraltar and the Suez Canal would become trapdoors to oblivion for the British. Mussolini, in his navy, had the way; whether he and his naval commanders had the will remained to be seen.[140]

Italy, like Britain, was an imperial sea power. Its most prized colonial possessions, Cyrenaica and Tripolitania, were just two days' sail from Sicily. The Italian merchant fleet, protected by the Italian navy, served as the lifeline to those colonies, which in turn fed Italy. On June 10, 1940, the day Mussolini plunged his dagger into France, the Italian merchant fleet, at 3.5 million tons, was the fifth-largest in the world, behind the U.K. (18 million tons), the U.S. (12 million), Japan (5.5 million), and Norway (4.8 million). More than three-quarters of the Norwegian fleet — 1,000 ships that were at sea when the Germans struck in April — now sailed in alliance with Britain. Mussolini's rush to climb aboard Hitler's war wagon resulted in one of the least noted but most significant shipping defeats of the entire war. On June 11, the day after Mussolini invaded France, his merchant fleet was reduced by 35 percent when 220 Italian freighters and tankers were seized in neutral ports worldwide. Mussolini had failed to call his merchant fleet home before his betrayal of France. He would never make up the loss. Churchill saw opportunity here. He believed the Italians would strike from Libya toward Cairo, but he also believed that Mussolini, with the loss of so much of his merchant shipping, could no longer support his African adventures. Two days after Dunkirk and four days before Mussolini struck, Churchill sent a memo to the Air Ministry: "It is of the highest importance that we should strike at Italy the moment war breaks out." In the early fall Churchill told the House, "Signor Mussolini has some experiences ahead of him which he had not foreseen at the time when he thought it safe and profitable to stab the stricken and prostrate French Republic in the back."[141]

The possibility of a Nazi onslaught against the Home Island had first been raised at a Defence Committee meeting on May 20, when enemy panzers passed Amiens on their way to Abbéville, cutting off the BEF. After a brief discussion, chiefly about the lack of riflemen and rifle ammunition, eight Bren Guns—light machine guns—were manned in Whitehall, including the entrance to No. 10, and two more were placed above Admiralty Arch. They would have been useful only if Germans swarmed out of Buckingham Palace or Trafalgar Square. Three days later graver news from the Channel ports led to more realistic planning; Churchill alerted the Dominion prime ministers to the possibility of an "early heavy attack" on England and told his Chiefs of Staff that "some means of dealing with the enemy's tanks"—he suggested land mines—might be found. By then the issue was judged to be serious. Martin Gilbert writes, "Invasion was now the dominant concern of those at the center of war policy. By the end of June it excluded virtually every thought in Englishmen's heads." In his diary Ironside wrote: "It is the weakness of waiting for an attack that preys upon people's minds." By then the French had surrendered to Italy, too, and RAF scouts were reporting the assembling of barges, lighters, and ferries in the ports of Belgium and northern France, and Whitehall knew that across the Channel, Nazi troops were singing, "We're sailing against England."[142]

In Parliament Churchill first addressed the question of defense against invasion on June 4, as the Dunkirk evacuation was winding down. Yet, even at that early date, with British fortunes approaching their nadir, offense, not defense, underlay his strategic vision:

> The whole question of home defence against invasion is, of course, powerfully affected by the fact that we have for the time being in this Island incomparably more powerful military forces than we have ever had at any moment in this war or the last. But this will not continue. We shall not be content with a defensive war.... We have to reconstitute and build up the British Expeditionary Force once again.... All this is in train; but in the interval we must put our defenses in this Island into such a high state of organization that the fewest possible numbers will be required to give effective security and that the largest possible potential of offensive effort may be realized. On this we are now engaged.[143]

Three weeks later, in a letter to South African prime minister Jan Smuts, a staunch British ally, Churchill made his offense-minded thoughts perfectly clear: "Obviously we have to repulse any attack on Great Britain by invasion." He predicted that Hitler might turn toward Russia and "he may do so without trying invasion." Then: "Our large army now being created for home defence is being formed on the principle of attack and opportunity, for large scale amphibious operations may come in 1940 and 1941."[144]

But for the time being he could attack Hitler only with words. His most eloquent challenge to the Nazis was delivered the day after the French laid down their arms. He spoke for thirty-six minutes, reading from twenty-three pages of typewritten notes. He foresaw a climax:

What General Weygand called the Battle of France is over. I expect the Battle of Britain is about to begin. Upon this battle depends the survival of Christian civilization. Upon it depends our own British life, and the long continuity of our institutions and our Empire. The whole fury and might of the enemy must very soon be turned on us. Hitler knows that he will have to break us in this island or lose the war. If we can stand up to him all Europe may be free, and the life of the world may move forward into broad, sunlit uplands.

But if we fail, then the whole world, including the United States, including all we have known and cared for, will sink into the abyss of a new Dark Age, made more sinister, and perhaps more protracted by the lights of perverted science.

Let us therefore brace ourselves to our duties, and so bear ourselves that, if the British Empire and its Commonwealth last for a thousand years, men will still say, "This was their finest hour."[145]

Later, Edward R. Murrow would say of Churchill: "Now, the hour had come for him to mobilize the English language and send it into battle."

It was as though a great bell had tolled, summoning Englishmen to sacrifice everything save honor in defense of their homeland and western civilization. The world beyond, other than the Empire, was deaf to it. Although listeners then and since took from Churchill's words the impression that he was speaking about the bravery of Englishmen to Englishmen, he was not. He had chosen his words with care. He had not said that a thousand years hence, people would say this was England's finest hour, but that it was the *British Empire*'s finest hour. Hitler had declared that his Reich would last one thousand years; Churchill had now claimed the same for his Empire. Each believed only one empire could survive. Neither considered the possibility that both might perish. Britain fought on that summer, alone in Europe—the Dominions and colonies too distant to offer meaningful help, yet with the Empire comprising one-quarter of the earth's population, sturdy in its support of the Home Island. But the Empire—including India and the outliers of South Africa, Australia, and New Zealand—could not respond fast enough or with enough force to thwart Hitler. Only one Canadian division, withdrawn from France, was in Britain.

Americans were sympathetic but pessimistic, and political leaders there and on the Continent were unimpressed by Churchill's inspired words. Franklin Roosevelt, facing reelection in a country opposed to going to war, was not about to say or do anything that might appear to endorse Churchill and the British Empire. "For those who were not Germans," writes Alan Brooke's biographer, "there seemed that summer only one way of safety—instant and unconditional surrender—and for those who delayed only one fate—certain and imminent destruction." Indeed, Hitler believed that the war was over. He had already staged a victory parade, marching conscripts of the 218th Infantry Division through the Brandenburg Gate. Forty of the Wehrmacht's 160 divisions had been demobilized, and the Führer had drafted a peace treaty he was sure the British would sign, knowing that the alternative was annihilation.[146]

Some Englishmen would sign such a treaty. There existed therefore an alternative to Hitler having to "break us in this Island." In a May 20 telegram to Roosevelt, Churchill had raised the possibility of a peace movement sweeping him from office and his successors having to negotiate with Hitler "in utter despair and helplessness." He mentioned that possibility again in a June 15 cable to the president, suggesting that Hitler in effect need only *bend* Britain, bend it to near the breaking point, and the result would be a new government formed to negotiate a terrible peace in hopes of gaining deliverance for "a shattered or a starving nation." The result would leave Britain "a vassal state of the Hitler empire." Such a settlement would deny the warrior Churchill his battle, the political Churchill his office, and England its sovereignty. All were unacceptable. The Vatican indeed proposed a peaceful settlement of the conflict, and on August 1, King Gustav of Sweden, the doyen of European monarchs (and the source for much of Hitler's iron ore), wrote King George VI, proposing a conference "to examine the possibility of making peace." Some Englishmen—they called themselves "sound" and Winston "unsound"—thought this suggestion merited discussion. The men of Munich were still a force, particularly in the Establishment. Halifax, of course, was one. The United Press quoted him as inviting "Chancellor Hitler to make a new and more generous peace offer." R. A. Butler, Halifax's under secretary, was an energetic supporter of Gustav's peace overtures. According to Björn Prytz, then the Swedish minister in London, on June 7, when the prime minister was commuting to France, attempting to stiffen French resolve, Butler told Prytz that Churchill's inflexibility toward the Third Reich was "not decisive." He saw no reason why the war should not end now in a compromise peace, provided German terms were acceptable, and assured the Swede that British policy would be guided "not by bravado but by common sense."[147]

Hearing of this, the P.M. sent the foreign office a blistering memo scoring the "lukewarmness" in Butler—Butler, whining, protested that he had been misunderstood—and restated the government's determination "to fight to the death."

Churchill told the King that "the intrusion of the ignominious King of Sweden as a peace-maker, after his desertion of Finland and Norway, and while he is absolutely in the German grip...is singularly distasteful." His sovereign agreed. King George had caught the mood of his people; in his diary he wrote: "How can we talk of peace with Germany now after they have overrun and demoralized the peoples of so many countries in Europe? Until Germany is prepared to live peaceably with her neighbors in Europe, she will always be a menace. We have got to get rid of her aggressive spirit, her engines of war & the people who have been taught to use them."[148]

Afterward, Englishmen as skeptical of politicians as Bernard Shaw and Malcolm Muggeridge agreed that had anyone but Churchill been prime minister in the summer of 1940, Britain would have negotiated an armistice with Hitler. In London the tenacious Swedish envoy informed Stockholm that several influential MPs had echoed Butler. Two of His Majesty's ambassadors—Hoare in Madrid, and Lord Lothian in Washington—were seeking contacts with their Nazi counterparts, preparing for diplomatic "conversations."

In Parliament the most prominent defeatist was Lloyd George, England's prime minister in the Great War. Jealous of Churchill, once his colleague, the old Welshman had refused to join his cabinet. Instead he planned to replace him and approach the enemy, asking for terms. "I argue," he told the House in his mellow, persuasive voice, "that the Government should take into consideration any proposals of peace which... review all the subjects that have been the cause of all the troubles of the last few years." He made his position public. In the July 28 *Sunday Pictorial,* he wrote, "I foresaw the catastrophe impending." Had his advice been followed, he continued, it would have led to "a better understanding between the angry nations and to the rebuilding of the temper of peace....I wish to point out that conditions were then more favourable for a discussion on equal terms than they are today, or probably will be a few weeks hence."[149]

In Berlin Lloyd George was being seriously considered as a possible leader of a puppet government. German psychologists told the Führer that Lloyd George reflected Britain's mood. He didn't; neither did Butler nor the Swedish ambassador's informants; they were no longer in step with their countrymen. Every literate Londoner, it seemed, was reading *Guilty Men,** a Labour attack written under the pseudonym Cato on the appeasers that indicted fifteen Tories, among them Baldwin, Chamberlain, Halifax, and Hoare, for neglecting England's defenses. It seemed that Englishmen everywhere were scorning any suggestion of negotiations; in the old British army phrase, they were "bloody-minded." Even Tom Jones, a former deputy secretary to the cabinet, wrote from Cliveden, "Everyone is willing to be conscripted for any duty and the main regret is that we cannot all be used."[150]

Not only had the collapse of the French failed to discourage them; it had actually raised their morale.

Churchill's defiant spirit had set the whole kingdom afire. Dunkirk had been a defeat, yet Englishmen had decked it with the laurels of victory. They had always been braced by the thought that their backs were against the wall, that the odds against them were hopeless. Now they recalled the maxim: "England always loses every battle except the last one." They were, they reminded one another, descendants of Englishmen who, Macaulay wrote, had "lit the bonfires from Eddystone to Berwick-bound, from Lynn to Milford Bay, warning of the Spanish Armada's approach undismayed and had watched, unintimidated, the twinkling of Napoleon's bonfires at Boulogne."[151]

Dorothy L. Sayers wrote:

This is the war that England knows,
When no allies are left, no help
To count upon from alien hands,
No waverers remain to woo,
No more advice to listen to,
And only England stands.[152]

On their display boards, news vendors chalked: "We're in the final—to be played on home ground." Somerset Maugham, reaching Liverpool at last, found no discouragement over the French debacle, only men who said confidently, "It doesn't matter; we can lick the Jerries alone" and "Fear of invasion? Not a shadow of it. We'll smash 'em. It'll take time, of course, but that's all right; we can hang on." "It was," Maugham concluded, "a

---

* Cato was the pseudonym of three journalists, Michael Foot, Frank Owen, and Peter Howard.

very different England from the England I had left a few weeks earlier. It was more determined, more energetic and more angry. Winston Churchill had inspired the nation with his own stern and resolute fortitude."[153]

In *The New Yorker,* Mollie Panter-Downes described the public temper as "grimly sane." On June 22 she wrote: "The individual Englishman seems to be singularly unimpressed by the fact that there is now nothing between him and the undivided attention of a war machine such as the world has never seen before. Possibly it's lack of imagination; possibly again it's the same species of dogged resolution which occasionally produces an epic like Dunkirk." By late summer she herself seemed to have been caught up in the emotional firestorm. "The ordinary individual is magnificent in a moment like this," she wrote, and, two weeks later, "The calm behavior of the average individual continues to be amazing." Like Maugham she finally concluded that the key to the nation's soaring morale was the new prime minister. She quoted the *Times,* which had considered Churchill unsound for ten years, as continuing its suspicions — "Mr. Churchill is still, in some respects, a solitary figure" — and commented: "That solitary figure continues to command the devotion and confidence of all classes which has probably been equaled only by the great William Pitt in 1759, 'the year of victories.' England would seem to have found her man of destiny at a critical juncture, when her well-wishers were beginning to fear that destiny was taking the down, not the up, grade. An extraordinary leader and the determination of an extraordinary people have brought back hope and dignity to a scene that has long and humiliatingly lacked them."[154]

During the summer after France fell, Englishmen awaited, at any moment, the appearance, by sea and by parachute, of the German army. That was the German way. They appeared on the Polish frontier the previous year; they appeared off the coast of Norway that spring; they emerged from the Ardennes in May; they dropped from the sky into Rotterdam. Englishmen, therefore, believed themselves to be in deadly peril, and continued to do so with varying degrees of trepidation until the late summer of 1942, in large part because Churchill told them so. Churchill, in turn, believed the Germans *might* come, and demanded every necessary precaution be taken *should* the Germans come, but he did not believe — that summer or the next — that they *would* come. Soon after the French surrender, he told Colville: "Hitler must invade or fail. If he fails, he is bound to go East [to Russia], and fail he will."[155]

That statement was not the most precise formulation of his beliefs, but it contained the essence: Hitler could try to invade England, and would fail, or Hitler would turn against his partner Joseph Stalin. To that end, Churchill wrote a letter to Stalin in late June in hopes of opening up communications with the Marshal of the sort he had established with Franklin Roosevelt. He entrusted the letter to his new ambassador to Moscow, Sir Stafford Cripps, a socialist whose very appointment as ambassador Churchill intended as a signal to Stalin.

The issue, as Churchill told Stalin (Churchill always pronounced his name *Schtaleen*), was whether Hitler's "bid for hegemony of Europe threatens the interests of the Soviet Union." It certainly threatened England's. Churchill acknowledged that relations between London and Moscow had "been hampered by mutual suspicions" (a marvelous understatement), but said that now only they could contest Hitler's quest for continental hegemony, by virtue of their geographical positions, which were "not in Europe but on her extremities." The idea that Britain was part of Europe but not "in" Europe informed Churchill's political beliefs for his entire life. He would have found nothing parochial or comical in the apocryphal London headline: FOG IN CHANNEL — CONTINENT ISOLATED. Indeed, Hitler had now isolated the Continent. Great Britain's two objectives, Churchill told Stalin, were to "save herself from Nazi domination" and "to free the rest of Europe" from Nazi domination. The message was meant to reassure Stalin. Stalin never replied. Cripps reported that Stalin, after reading the letter, denigrated the possibility of German territorial ambitions and asserted his belief that Germany posed no danger to Russia. After Cripps was dismissed, Stalin ordered his minister of foreign affairs, Vyacheslav Molotov, to pass the minutes of his conversation with Cripps on to Berlin, a gesture intended to remind Hitler of Stalin's abiding friendship.[156]

Churchill had not read Hitler's mind; Hitler had broadcast his intention to crush the Bolshevik Soviet Union in his autobiography, *Mein Kampf*. It was all there. He had written with absolute clarity: "This colossal empire [Russia] in the East is ripe for dissolution. And the end of the Jewish domination of Russia will also be the end of Russia as a state." Hitler, in turn, had no need to try to read Churchill's mind; he was reading his mail. It is not surprising, therefore, that in mid-July, Hitler declared to his military chiefs that "Britain's hope lies in Russia and America." He was correct. He noted that Britain was "back on her feet," sustained in part by their Russian hopes. Therefore, he declared, "if Russia is smashed, Britain's last hope will be shattered.... Decision: In view of these considerations Russia must be liquidated. Spring, 1941."[157]

Churchill arrived at his certainty regarding Germany and Russia through a balance of cold logic and intuition, although some of his colleagues would say it was more of a collision. This was how he approached all problems. Whether parsing geopolitical matters such as continental hegemony, or the Mediterranean theater, or the finer points of the defense of England, Churchill came at every issue with a painter's eye; the whole was larger than the sum of its parts. He saw the beauty and vitality of details, and their effect on larger strategic issues, and demanded that they be scrutinized all the time. The most obvious and simplest of facts portended larger strategic issues. One fact, often neglected in the telling of the tale of that summer, underlay Churchill's planning for a German invasion: A day is divided into daylight hours and nighttime hours. The Battle of Britain is often described as "a battle for air supremacy." In fact, it was a battle for *daytime* air supremacy. Everything changed after dark. Night bombers—British and German—flew without fear of fighters, and with little fear of anti-aircraft fire, but sacrificed targeting accuracy. Fighter planes went aloft at night only when the moon was full, or nearly full, to protect their bombers or search the skies for the enemy's. Armies could maneuver and fight by night or day. But in late June, the German army was in France, while the British army—hobbled but rebuilding—was in England. Churchill of course could not know that the Germans had not yet even contemplated an invasion. But he did know that if the Germans attempted one, they could arrive on English soil in meaningful numbers only by sea. Churchill believed they could not do so. In order to land at dawn, an invasion armada would have to sail at night, but with German fighter planes grounded during darkness, the Royal Navy—its largest ships equipped with radar—owned the night. At night, the Royal Navy could hunt the enemy's invasion barges and ships at will. In a July 7 memo to Ironside, Churchill wrote: "Except in very narrow waters, it would be most hazardous and even suicidal to commit a large army to the accidents of the sea in the teeth of our very numerous armed patrolling forces."[158]

Churchill warned the House that it would be impossible for the Royal Navy "to prevent raids by 5,000 or 10,000 men flung suddenly across and thrown ashore at several points on the coast some dark night or foggy morning." But those raiders would soon find themselves surrounded by units of the British army. If such a force came ashore in northern England or Scotland, it would find itself hundreds of miles from London, and irrelevant. No, the Germans had to come in overwhelming force, and land within one hundred miles of London. Churchill believed that Hitler—if he came—would try to decapitate the British government in London, in order to force a settlement with a new, more malleable government. A military conquest and occupation of all of Britain, from Devon to the Midlands to Scotland, was simply beyond the means of the Wehrmacht, not because the German army lacked the men and tanks, but because Germany lacked the shipping to even *try* to carry such a force to England.[159]

If the Germans tried, Churchill expected to annihilate them. On June 18 he sketched his vision for the House:

> The efficacy of sea power, especially under modern conditions, depends upon the invading force being of large size. It has to be of large size, in view of our military strength, to be of any use. If it is of large size, then the Navy have something they can find and meet and, as it were, bite on. Now, we must remember that even five [German] divisions, however lightly equipped, would require 200 to 250 ships, and with modern air reconnaissance and photography it would not be easy to collect such an armada, marshal it, and conduct it across the sea without any powerful naval forces to escort it; and there would be very great possibilities, to put it mildly, that this armada would be intercepted long before it reached the coast, and all the men drowned in the sea or at the worst blown to pieces with their equipment while they were trying to land.... There should be no difficulty in this, owing to our great superiority at sea.[160]

The previous summer Hitler, unlike Mussolini on June 10, had had the good sense to bring his merchant fleet into the Baltic before striking into Poland. The small size of the German merchant fleet, about 1.2 million tons, was one of four fundamental facts—after the different conditions imposed by daylight and nighttime operations—upon which Churchill based his belief that if the Germans came to England, they would fail. For Churchill, these were the details on which all else turned.

The first: He estimated that to put the first wave of 60,000 to 80,000 German troops ashore would require almost 60 percent of all German merchant shipping. To put a second wave of 160,000 ashore, along with ammunition, tanks, and heavy artillery, would require far more shipping than Germany had at its disposal. As will be seen, those same figures, which boosted Churchill's optimism, dismayed the high command of the German navy.

The second: Germany lacked the specialized landing craft that could put tanks and heavy artillery right on a beach. The Germans would have to capture a port to offload their armor and equipment. If they sailed into a port, they would find the facilities destroyed by the British, the harbor entrance mined behind them such that they could not sail out, and a ring of British artillery pouring fire down on the port.

The third: Churchill later wrote that although the RAF—in both bombers

and fighters—was outnumbered by almost 3 to 1, "I rested upon the conclusion that in our own air, in our own country and its waters, we could
beat the German air force."

The fourth: Sea power. The Royal Navy was overwhelmingly more
powerful than the German navy. Only a "hostile air power could destroy"
the almost one thousand British warships deployed around England,
Churchill wrote, "and then only by degrees." Gaining the upper hand in
only one or two of these categories would gain the Germans nothing; they
had to successfully address all four. "These were the foundations of my
thoughts about invasion in 1940," Churchill wrote. Still, "the possibility of
a cross-Channel invasion, improbable though it was at that time, had to be
most closely examined."[161]

On June 30, General Sir Andrew Thorne, who commanded a corps in the
southeast, told Churchill he thought the Germans would land up to 80,000
men, probably between Thanet and Pevensey on the Kentish coast, and
just sixty miles from London. Churchill, Colville wrote, "is less pessimistic
and thinks the navy will have much to say to this." Still, if the Germans
evaded the Royal Navy and made it to shore, Churchill wanted defenders
on all possible shores in East and West Sussex, Kent, and Surrey. On his
instructions, pillboxes and barbed-wire barricades were built there. Touring them, he asked for a chart of tides and moonrises for the next six
weeks. He saw that once the enemy had committed himself, the outcome
would be determined by mobile brigades stationed inland, and by Royal
Navy destroyers mining and shelling the beaches, at night. Colville noted
that General Thorne, whose men were expected to take the greatest blow,
thought "the German left wing could be held in Ashdown Forest, but he
did not see what could keep the right wing from advancing through Canterbury to London." Mobility and imaginative tactics might prevent that.
Survival would depend on flexibility, intuition, and imagination, traits
(some would say eccentricities) lacking in many of England's generals and
certainly in the previous government. But not in Churchill.[162]

Throughout June, Royal Meteorological Office records show, the Channel was calm; skies were clear, with temperatures in the sixties, and the
British people—including high-ranking military officials—had no doubts
that the invaders would arrive soon. It is all there in their diaries and letters. As early as June 12, Harold Nicolson wrote: "The probability is that
France will surrender and that we shall be bombed and invaded." "The
weather still remains very fine, worse luck," Ironside wrote early in July.
Now that the Germans had "airfields within twenty-five miles of our
shores," Ismay noted, "the possibility of invasion of Britain" seemed

"highly probable... within a matter of weeks." At Cliveden Thomas Jones noted: "Speculation is rife about the 'invasion.' Wherever one goes one sees pillboxes and road barriers and field obstacles." "Speculation" is the operative word, that week and in the weeks that followed.[163]

Most Britons were scared. Yet, Churchill later wrote: "Certainly those that knew the most were the least scared." Those words were written long after the fact, but they reflect his belief during 1940. His private conversations and his memos to his ministers that summer and fall bear out his confidence.

At night primeval darkness descended upon blacked-out Britain. Drivers crept along at twenty miles an hour. The windows of commuter trains were painted black. London lampposts were ringed with white paint to warn oncoming motorists. Still, collisions were common between bicyclists and automobiles, between pedestrians and lampposts. To baffle invading troops, signposts had been removed from the countryside, baffling the locals as well. Late in June, postmen slipped official pamphlets in the mail telling householders what to do when the invasion began. Nearly everyone had some sort of crude weapon, if only a garden tool. German paratroopers would likely arrive by night. In a speech to the Home Guard the prime minister proclaimed that if Nazi paratroopers arrived, "you will make it clear to them that they have not alighted in the poultry-run, or in the rabbit farm, or even in the sheep fold, but in the lion's den at the Zoo!"[164]

Fleet Street had advice, too. "A hand-grenade dump by each village pump," was the slogan of Beaverbrook's *Daily Express*. The *Express* also distressed many who had grown up in a quieter time by pointing out that any boy capable of pitching a cricket ball could throw a grenade. Civilians, even clergymen in their seventies, were armed with whatever was available, often shotguns. Most lacked firearms of any sort. Awaiting rifles from America, members of the Home Guard drilled with pikes, pick handles, and broomsticks. Wives were told to make homemade Molotov cocktails with kitchen kerosene; elderly men were taught how to disable panzers by pouring sugar into their fuel tanks or thrusting crowbars in their track wheels.

People then still thought of war in personal terms. There is no way a twenty-first-century citizen can oppose fleets of modern missiles, but in 1940 one Briton with a weapon, however primitive, could make a difference in the defense of the island. If the Nazis established a beachhead, King

George was prepared to lead a resistance movement. The King ordered a shooting range built in the gardens of Buckingham Palace, and there the Royal Family and royal equerries practiced daily with small arms, including submachine guns and a carbine given to the King by Churchill. The young royal princesses took their target practice with their parents. Clementine later told her daughter that Elizabeth and Margaret "have the most amusing lives, with lots of dogs (although they are those horrid 'corgies') & poneys [sic] & a delightful mother." The delightful mother was a crack shot. On July 10, Harold Nicolson noted that the Queen "told me she is being instructed every day in how to fire a revolver. I expressed surprise. 'Yes,' she said, 'I shall not go down like the others.' I cannot tell you how superb she was.... We shall win. I know that. I have no doubts at all."[165]

In the Nazi invasion the number of deaths would be unfathomable. It was a time when, at every parting, husbands and wives, mothers and children, knew they might be looking their last upon one another. Vita Sackville-West wrote, "It must be in both our minds that we may possibly never meet again." Nicolson replied, "I am not in the least afraid of...sudden and honourable death. What I dread is being tortured and humiliated."[166]

Torture would be the certain fate of those who possessed special knowledge of the island's defenses. Anticipating possible capture, many carried on their persons the means for quick suicide. A week after the French collapse, when the government was preparing to evacuate all civilians from Kent and Sussex, Nicolson, now at the Ministry of Information, wrote Vita, "I think you ought to have a 'bare bodkin' [after Hamlet] so you can take your quietus when necessary. But how can we find a bodkin which will give us our quietus quickly and which is easily portable? I shall ask my doctor friends." Ten days later she wrote him that she had her "bare bodkin." Probably it was poison, not a dagger. Churchill had repeatedly vowed that he would never be taken alive; according to Kathleen Hill, his bodkin was cyanide, which he carried in the cap of his fountain pen.[167]

Britons braced themselves, but against exactly what—gas, invasion, aerial bombardment, parachutists, all of the above?—they did not know. They were quite willing to fight and die, but they lacked the means to fight. Wars are fought by soldiers with weapons. In the first four weeks after Dunkirk, Britain had few of either. Ironside, then commanding Home Forces, including the Home Guard, was attempting to organize the defense of the island. He envisioned "arming of the whole population" with the "existence of the Empire" at stake. On June 22, the day the French signed the armistice at Compiègne, Ironside wrote: "Even the stoutest heart begins to wonder whether he [Churchill] can meet all the eventualities he pictures to himself. I felt it myself as I went round the endless coastline of East Anglia yesterday."[168]

No one had foreseen this. For two centuries His Majesty's Government had sent troops to every corner of the globe while the homeland enjoyed peace. The last battle on English soil had been fought on April 16, 1746, when the army of the Duke of Cumberland, son of King George II, routed the forces of the Stuart pretender, Bonnie Prince Charlie. Now in June 1940 the country seemed defenseless. Harold Macmillan recalled, "Having shipped almost everything we had, we now find ourselves not only alone, but unarmed." He was of course referring to the army; the navy was quite well armed. Still, as Churchill had noted, the success of the Dunkirk evacuation obscured the fact that the men had left their guns, artillery, ammunition, and tanks behind. In England, there were only half as many rifles as needed to defend the island. The evacuation was still in progress when the United States agreed to sell Britain—*sell* is the key word—500,000 World War I rifles, 80,000 virtually obsolete machine guns, 900 howitzers, and 13,000,000 rounds of ammunition. Although British factories were toiling around the clock, they wouldn't make up the losses for at least three months, possibly six. Yet, within two weeks, with great difficulty, equipment for two divisions was scraped together. Churchill ordered that the most battle-ready brigade, languishing for weeks in Northern Ireland, be brought home. As for the Home Guard, realists in the military—including A. J. P. Taylor, who served in the Home Guard—concluded that if the militia somehow managed to assemble at their appointed rendezvous points, they would be massacred.[169]

"I have no scruples," Churchill told Colville, "except not to do anything dishonorable." Exactly where he would draw the line if the Germans came was left unspecified. The question of mustard gas was raised. It was thought the Germans would use it. Churchill wanted to use it first. To Ismay he wrote in a memo: "In my view there would be no need for the enemy to adopt such methods. He will certainly adopt them if he thinks they will pay." Stocks of mustard gas were readied, to be dropped from bombers or shot from artillery. He envisioned "drenching" the beaches with gas, leading Colville to tell his diary: "I suppose he does not consider gassing Germans dishonorable."[170]

Some of his ideas were quaint. He recalled that "a fire ship had been used" by Elizabethan Englishmen against the Spanish Armada. Might something similar be contemplated now? He would scorch England's earth if need be. Oil storage tanks, which had fueled the panzers in France, would be destroyed once the fighting began. The Strait of Dover was already mined. Against the possibility that Germans might wear British uniforms, Tommies would wear a strip of cloth dyed a new shade of yellow. White circles were painted atop British tanks, to warn the RAF off. Army intelligence (incorrectly) believed the Luftwaffe could land as many as twenty thousand troops; therefore, to disrupt gliders, four-hundred-yard-long ditches were plowed across large fields, even those seeded for crops. All bridges over all rivers within one hundred miles of London were rigged for demolition.[171]

For the Home Guard, improvisation was the order of the day. Cans of gasoline were stored near important intersections, the idea being that members of the Home Guard, upon spotting the approaching Germans, would pour the fuel in the road, toss a grenade into the puddle, and make good their escape. British anti-tank mines, so complex and overengineered that they could not be produced in sufficient quantities, were replaced by commercial cake pans stuffed with eight pounds of TNT and fitted with a simple compression trigger. Churchill's imagination turned to his beloved gadgets and scientific schemes. The floating of fuel oil on harbor waters to ignite the invasion barges was one such. Another: Could slender gasoline-filled pipelines be readied behind seaside dunes, to spray flaming fuel upon the invaders? Yes, but what if the invaders came ashore elsewhere, or the winds blew those flames and smoke toward the defenders, which is exactly what happened when the system was tested. That was how things stood in late June and the first days of July, a time when *ad hoc* best describes Britain's defenses. None, including Churchill, knew during those weeks that the Germans had not even drawn up an invasion plan.

The Admiralty told Churchill that the likeliest time for hostile seaborne landings was a moonless night, at high tide, near daybreak. Once the onslaught began, all the church bells in England were to start ringing. Speculation about the German timing continued. On July 11 Harold Nicolson wrote in his diary: "They expect an invasion this weekend." But he also wrote: "I am cocky about this war. Cocky. I really and truly believe Hitler is at the end of his success." On July 20 he noted: "I think Hitler will probably invade us within the next few days. He has 6,000 airplanes for the job.... We know we are faced with a terrific invasion.... Yet there is a sort of exhilaration in the air." Actually, the Luftwaffe force assembled across the Channel was composed of about 2,500 bombers, fighter-bombers, and fighters.[172]

The news was blacked out, beaches and military installations off-limits. Ship arrivals and departures were no longer reported in newspapers. Even weather reports were banned; why tell the enemy what the conditions might be in Sussex next week? Nicolson was still expecting the great attack two months later; on September 13 he wrote: "There is a great concentration of shipping and barges in France, and it is evident that the Cabinet expect invasion at any moment." Ironside had thought it was coming on July 9. On July 12 Sir Alan Brooke told his diary: "This was supposed to be the probable day of invasion!" Colville told his diary on July 14: "There is an ominous calm...and it looks like *der Tag* may be imminent." On that day, Colville noted, even Churchill lacked his usual confidence. On July 22, Sir Alan Brooke, who had only the day before replaced Ironside as commander of Home Forces, went "to the War Cabinet Room where I may have to be near the PM if an invasion starts." That night, while dining alone with Churchill at No. 10, Brooke found Churchill to be "full of the most marvelous courage, considering the burden he is bearing." Brooke added an observation, variations of which would find their way into his diary for the next five years: "He [Churchill] is full of offensive thoughts for the future."[173]

Dining with three of his generals on Friday, July 12, Churchill declared that if the Germans came, he wanted "every citizen to fight desperately and they will do so the more if they know that the alternative is massacre." Colville that night noted that Churchill "is sufficiently ruthless to point out that in war quarter is given, not on grounds of compassion but in order to discourage the enemy from fighting to the bitter end." Contrary to the French experience, no panicked streams of civilian refugees (Churchill preferred the term "fugitives") would clog British roads if the Germans arrived, for there was no escape. Churchill offered that the citizens would fight, even if only with "scythes and brickbats." One of the generals declared that the citizenry should be ordered to stay home; Churchill replied that they would not obey such an order. Then, wrote Colville, Churchill arrived at the root of the matter:

> He emphasized that the great invasion scare (which we only ceased to deride six weeks ago) is serving a most useful purpose: it is well on the way to providing us with the finest offensive army we have ever possessed and it is keeping every man and woman tuned to a high pitch of readiness. He does not wish the scare to abate therefore, and although personally he doubts whether invasion is a serious menace he intends to give that impression, and to talk about long and dangerous vigils, etc., when he broadcasts on Sunday.[174]

On Bastille Day, Sunday, July 14, four days after the first large-scale dogfights between the Luftwaffe and the Royal Air Force, Churchill spoke to the nation over the BBC. Britons believed their plight was desperate, and he did not paint it otherwise, as he had promised Colville he would not. Their losses in France and Flanders had been enormous, "including a very large part of our Air Force." Their enemy was the fiercest in history. Nation after nation had fallen beneath the Nazi juggernaut.

And now it has come to us to stand in the breach, and face the worst that the tyrant can do. Bearing ourselves humbly before God, but conscious that we serve an unfolding purpose, we are ready to defend our native land against the invasion by which it is threatened. We are fighting *by* ourselves alone; but we are not fighting *for* ourselves alone. Here in this strong City of Refuge which enshrines the title deeds of human progress and is of deep consequence to Christian civilization; girt about by the seas and oceans where the Navy reigns; shielded from above by the prowess and devotion of our airmen we await undismayed the impending assault. Perhaps it will come tonight. Perhaps it will come next week.

Then, the caveat, which conveyed his own feelings and offered Britons a speck of hope:

Perhaps it will never come. We must show ourselves equally capable of meeting a sudden violent shock, or what is perhaps a harder test, a prolonged vigil. But be the ordeal sharp or long, or both, we shall seek no terms, we shall tolerate no parley; we may show mercy. We shall ask for none.[175]

He knew the "monstrous force" of the Nazi war machine. But, he added, Britain now had a million and a half soldiers under arms on her own soil, and more than a million volunteers in the Home Guard, and a thousand armed ships sailing under the white ensign, binding them to the United States, "from whom, as the struggle deepens, increasing aide [*sic*] will come." And the Nazis should know the ferocity of British determination: "Hitler has not yet been withstood by a great nation with a will power the equal of his own."

Should the invader come to Britain, there will be no placid lying down of the people in submission before him, as we have seen, alas, in other countries. We shall defend every village, every town, and every city. The vast mass of London itself, fought street by street, could easily devour an entire hostile army; and we would rather see London in ruins and ashes than that it would be tamely and abjectly enslaved.

Nevertheless, he told them, that "while we toil through the dark valley we can see the sunlight on the uplands beyond" provided they remembered who they were: "all depends on the whole life strength of the British race . . . doing their utmost night and day, giving all, daring all, enduring the utmost to the end." This was "a war of the Unknown Warriors; but let all strive without failing in faith or in duty, and the dark curse of Hitler will be lifted from our age."[176]

The Führer had assumed that invasion would be unnecessary. After the fall of France he considered the war over. In the East his pact with Stalin assured continuing peace as long as neither side abrogated it, which Hitler intended to do once the English came to terms. When Hitler ordered the demobilizing of forty divisions, he told *Reichsmarschall* Hermann Göring, commander in chief of the Luftwaffe, that all war plans could be scrapped; he would reach an "understanding" (*Übereinkommen*) with the British. Actually, he expected London to take the initiative; he told Dino Alfieri, the Italian ambassador in Berlin, that he "could not conceive of anyone in England still seriously believing in victory." To Lieutenant General Franz Halder, chief of the Army High Command (OKH), he said that "England's situation is hopeless. A reversal of the prospects of success is an impossibility." His generals agreed; on June 30 Jodl, OKW's chief of operations, wrote: "The final German victory over England is now only a question of time. Enemy offensive operations on a large scale are no longer possible."[177]

The Führer preferred a settlement, freeing the Wehrmacht from the need to defend a Western Front when he attacked his mortal enemy, the Soviet Union. Though he despised Churchill, he admired the British Empire; its existence, he believed, was essential to world order. (All SS officers were required to watch the film *Gunga Din;* that, he told them, was the way a superior race should treat its inferiors.) Therefore he was prepared to offer England a generous treaty. Convinced that they must realize the hopelessness of their situation, he dismissed Churchill's defiance as bluff and expected the British to come to him. After four weeks of waiting, on July 19 he made his move in a Reichstag speech. After insulting Churchill—"I feel a deep disgust for this type of unscrupulous politician who wrecks whole nations"—he said of himself, "I am not the vanquished begging favors, but the victor speaking in the name of reason." He promised Britons that absent a settlement, "great suffering will begin." Speaking directly to Churchill, he said, "Believe me when I prophesy that a great Empire will be destroyed—an empire which it was never my intention to destroy or even to harm." Hinting at liberal terms, he concluded dramatically, "I can see no reason why this war must go on."[178]

The answer came within the hour. Churchill did not deign to comment on the offer—"I do not propose to say anything in reply to Herr Hitler's speech," he said, "not being on speaking terms with him"—but a BBC broadcaster, later supported by the foreign office, addressed the Führer directly: "Let me tell you what we here in Britain think of this appeal to what you are pleased to call our reason and common sense. Herr Führer and Reich Chancellor, we hurl it right back into your evil-smelling teeth!"[179]

In Rome the diarist Count Galeazzo Ciano noted that "a sense of ill-concealed disappointment spreads among the Germans." Actually Berlin was astounded, and Hitler nonplussed. The German General Staff had always assumed that Britain could be defeated only by cutting its sea routes. Although all great powers spend peacetime preparing contingency plans for war against other countries, including their closest allies, the German army did not draft preliminary plans for an offensive against England until June 1937, and the Luftwaffe did not follow through with similar memoranda until 1938.[180]

And these were merely paper exercises. As A. J. P. Taylor has pointed out, Hitler had foreign policy ambitions but no war plans at all; he was, in the words of the historian and novelist Len Deighton, "one of the most successful opportunists of the twentieth century," making it up as he went along. Indeed, it is an astonishing fact—the military historian Basil Liddell Hart calls it "one of the most extraordinary features of history"—that neither the Führer nor his General Staff in Zossen had studied or even contemplated the problems arising from Britain's continued belligerency. They hadn't done it when war broke out; it was still undone nine months later, when the French capitulated. They had worked out elaborate strategies for seizing every European country, including Spain, the Balkans, and their Italian ally; they had drawn up orders of battle for Scandinavia and the Soviet Union; they even knew how, if it became necessary, to overwhelm the Vatican. The German naval war staff, knowing the *Kriegsmarine* would be charged with ferrying German troops to England if the orders came down, had studied the problem in desultory fashion since the previous autumn. The army and Luftwaffe had not. On May 27 the naval war staff had drafted a vague *Studie England,* but in all the banks of steel files in Zossen, there was not so much as a single memorandum on the question of how the greatest army the world had ever known could subjugate Great Britain.[181]

To reach England the Wehrmacht had to cross the Channel or the North Sea. Hitler hated the idea. "On land I am a hero but on water I am a coward," he told *Generalfeldmarschall* Gerd von Rundstedt. Since Nazi Germany had no landing craft and no plans to build any, German troops, if they went to England, would do so aboard river barges. The barges were intended for river traffic; flat-bottomed, 90 feet long, 20 feet wide, with a top speed of 7 miles per hour, they were not built for seagoing excursions. Some operated under their own power, many were towed. Not a single unit in the German army had been trained in the skills of amphibious warfare. The Continent and contiguous lands were the only world the *Generalstab* knew. That world ended at its edge, the western coast of France. Paris had been the objective of the Nazis' great spring offensive, to the exclusion of all else, the last step before the invasion of Russia.[182]

In England the Royal Navy was the Senior Service. The War Office deferred to the Admiralty, the oldest of England's war ministries, founded during the reign of Henry VIII. Officers in the British army were respected and often distinguished, though army commands scattered throughout the empire depended upon the navy for supply and reinforcements. The various far-flung components of the British Empire were tethered together, nurtured, and protected by the Royal Navy. Cruisers and destroyers at Gibraltar protected the western end of the Mediterranean, while the fleet at Alexandria did likewise for the central and eastern Mediterranean. The Home Fleet, from its main anchorage at Scapa Flow, almost five hundred miles north of London, in far northern Scotland, had been charged by the Admiralty with protecting Atlantic merchant shipping and, most important, protecting the Home Island much as escort squadrons protect an aircraft carrier. Destroyers would play a key role in contesting a German invasion. The British began the war with more than eighty destroyers available for deployment in the North Sea and around the Home Island, and a dozen or more for North Atlantic operations. They were fast, could weave and shoot their way through an invasion armada at speeds of thirty-five miles an hour, and were vital to the blockade of Germany and to Britain's survival. But since January, two dozen had been sunk by U-boats, German mines, and the Luftwaffe. The registry of Royal Navy destroyers might have been larger but for the Chamberlain government's decision in 1938 to stop constructing ships, as a means to economize. That was why Churchill sought destroyers from Roosevelt.

By the end of June, the Home Fleet had stationed forty destroyers, several cruisers, and two battle cruisers in ports ranging from Aberdeen and Rosyth in Scotland, to Hull and Yarmouth down the coast, to Dover and Ramsgate in the southeast of England. In the south and southwest, warships were stationed in Portsmouth, Portland, Plymouth, Falmouth, Cardiff, and Swansea. The big ships were supported by more than 900 anti-submarine trawlers, gunboats, minesweepers, motor torpedo boats, minelayers, anti-aircraft ships, and cutters. Almost 200 corvettes — 1,000-ton, 200-foot-long gunboats that carried depth charges — were available to escort Atlantic convoys into home waters or, if need be, to help repel an invasion. Three aircraft carriers were available for island defense; the Germans had no carriers. The Royal Navy would charge into the Channel if the Germans came, and do so under the protective fire of 150 six-inch naval guns sited on bluffs along the Channel coast. Except for submarines, the portion of the Home Fleet that *remained* at Scapa Flow—a "fleet in being"—was larger than the entire German navy. Of Hitler's eighty U-boats, the fifty assigned to the blockade of Britain posed a mortal threat, but only if they kept up the hunt for British merchant shipping on the high seas and the Northwest Approaches to Britain's ports. Churchill expected Hitler to throw a dozen or two of his U-boats into the invasion. Even if they were to inflict pain on British warships, the Royal Navy and any surviving RAF fighters and bombers would hunt them to extinction in the narrow Channel. Hence Churchill's confidence in his navy. Britannia still ruled the waves, and Hitler had to ride them to get to England.

Germany had lost its few colonies in 1918, and with them the imperative for a worldwide navy. Except for U-boat commanders—feared and respected by the British, glorified in Germany—German military glory was reserved for German soldiers, and if Göring had his way, German airmen. German naval officers were considered social inferiors in Germany; they lacked the self-assurance essential to military aggression. Thus, when the Führer issued the first reluctant order to "prepare a landing operation against England and if necessary carry it out," and assigned the task of ferrying the Wehrmacht across the Channel to his admirals on the Bendlerstrasse, the response there was neither confident nor ardent, and for sound reasons. Unless the Luftwaffe hobbled the British Home Fleet along with British fighter planes and British bombers, any success in the daytime skies over southern England would be offset when the Royal Navy sailed forth—at night, as the invaders came on—to thwart the seaborne invasion.[183]

Destroying British ships was critical, and the British had a great many ships. The Germans had no large warships outside the Baltic (and had only four inside the Baltic) to counter the overwhelmingly superior numbers of Royal Navy destroyers and larger capital ships (cruisers, battle cruisers, and battleships). The German navy had begun the war with only twenty-one destroyers and had paid dearly for its April success in Norway, where ten destroyers were sunk or scuttled. Thus, when the subject of supporting an invasion of England was raised, the commander in chief of the German navy, *Grossadmiral* Erich Raeder, submitted a confidential report to the Führer listing his objections to an invasion. Raeder concluded: "The C. in C., Navy cannot for his part advocate an invasion of Britain as he did in the case of Norway."[184]

The other German services were also wary. The Luftwaffe high command concluded that "a combined operation with a landing as its object must be rejected," and Zossen curtly sent a memo that the army "is not concerning itself with the question of England. Considers execution impossible...General Staff rejects the operation." Nevertheless, Hitler persisted, as only he could, and in mid-July *Oberkommando des Heeres* (OKH), the army's high command, drew up plans for an operation encoded *Seelöwe,* or Sea Lion. It was an ambitious strategy, envisioning the landing of 90,000 troops in the first wave. By the third day, 160,000 reinforcements would be landed, to be followed by forty-one divisions, six of them panzers and two airborne. Each force had a specific objective; one would block off Devon and Cornwall, for example, while another cut off Wales. OKH opinion, swayed by Hitler's iron will, reversed itself. The generals now expected the operation to last less than a month. In fact, they thought it would be easy.[185]

But the Führer's naval staff was appalled by *Seelöwe,* for many of the same reasons Churchill was encouraged. Just putting the first wave ashore on so wide a front would require 1,722 barges, 1,161 motorboats, 471 tugs, and 155 transports. Raeder protested that this was self-evidently impossible; naval protection for so vast an armada, even if it could be assembled, would expose every warship and merchant ship the Reich possessed to the gunners of the Royal Navy. He proposed a landing on a much narrower front between Folkestone and Eastbourne with fewer troops, thus minimizing the risk to his fleet. The General Staff rejected that. In such an operation, Zossen argued, the German soldiers might be overwhelmed by defenders.

Actually, there was no need to reconcile differences between the Nazi services. Churchill had been right at Briare. The decisive moment—an air assault on England—was yet to come. The enemy could not try to ferry the Channel until his warplanes were absolute masters of the daytime skies over Britain. OKW realized it. In a paper for the Führer, *"Die Weiterführung des Krieges gegen England"* ("The Continuation of the War Against England"), Jodl noted that administering the deathblow, a landing on British shores, could "only be contemplated after Germany has achieved control of the air."[186]

Before Hitler could invade England, he must first destroy the Royal Air Force and hobble the Royal Navy. Hermann Göring declared that the Luftwaffe had changed its mind; they could do it, he said, and do it easily.

In christening what would come to be known as the Battle of Britain, Churchill envisioned a mighty struggle on the beaches between infantrymen, masterminded by admirals and generals and supported by armor and sea power. Scarcely anyone gave thought to the challenges of aerial warfare. Professional airmen were an exception, of course, but all they knew for certain was that the aerial combat of 1914–1918—the duels between

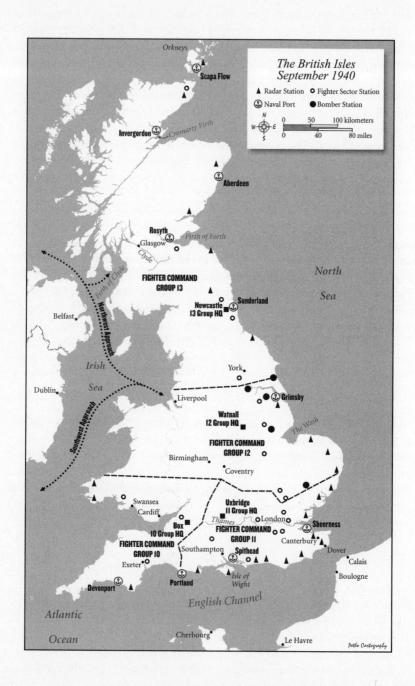

**The British Isles
September 1940**

▲ Radar Station　　○ Fighter Sector Station
⚓ Naval Port　　● Bomber Station

0　　　50　　　100 kilometers
0　　40　　　80 miles

individuals piloting wood and fabric biplanes while listening to the wind in the wires—had been rendered obsolete by advancing technology. Clearly future combat would be far more complex. However, the most influential of their leaders between the wars—Giulio Douhet in Rome, Lord Trenchard in London, Billy Mitchell in Washington, and Hermann Göring in Berlin—had made the wrong assumption. They believed that victory would belong to the air forces which launched the fastest, most powerful bombing offensives. Thus the Luftwaffe had leveled Spanish cities, the Italians Ethiopian villages, the Japanese Chinese cities. There was, air ministries told their governments, no defense against a knockout bombardment from the sky.

Stanley Baldwin was speaking for them in November 1932 when, endorsing unilateral disarmament, he told Parliament that there was no defense against "the terror of the air." In an uncharacteristically emotional speech, he had warned the House of Commons, and hence the country: "I think it well...for the man in the street to realize that there is no power on earth that can prevent him from being bombed. Whatever people tell him, the bomber will always get through. The only defence is offence, which means that you have to kill more women and children more quickly than the enemy if you want to save yourselves."

That dogma still held after the fall of France. Even Churchill believed that victory lay through offensive airpower. On July 8, he told Beaverbrook that the "one sure path" to victory lay in "bombing Germany into submission." It was understood that the targets would be military. Baldwin's terrible thesis of killing women and children aside, the war planners took aim at arms factories, power plants, steel mills, rail yards, and the like, not residential neighborhoods.[187]

Airpower had been crucial in the defeat of Poland, but after the fall of Warsaw, little thought had been given to ways of countering it. During the phony war, RAF strategists, following the dogma Douhet had set forth in his futuristic book, *The War of 19—*, had proposed sending fleets of bombers against industrial targets in the Ruhr. To their chagrin, His Majesty's Government vetoed unprovoked daylight raids. Dropping propaganda leaflets over the Reich that promised destruction to Germans on the ground was approved, but even this went badly; none of the raiders found their targets, and the bombers, unescorted by fighters, suffered such heavy losses that the project was abandoned. On the night of May 16, with General Guderian's panzers beyond Sedan, the British had sent one hundred bombers to pound industrial targets in the Ruhr. The RAF official history acknowledges that the bombardiers "achieved none of their objects." The crews, unable to find a single target, had jettisoned their bomb loads and returned to England having accomplished nothing. That should have given the air marshals pause. It didn't; in the words of A. J. P. Taylor, they continued to believe that "bombing unsupported by land and sea forces could win a war."[188]

Little thought had been given to providing bombers with fighter escorts, and for a valid reason: Both British and German fighter planes lacked the range to escort their bombers on the 1,000-mile round-trip journey to the other's homeland. British and German fighter planes had a maximum range of between 300 and 400 miles—150 miles out, 150 miles home. They could remain in the air for about 90 minutes and could not reach the other side's borders, let alone linger there in support of bombers. Nobody in Bomber Command had considered the possibility that Germany would defeat France and Belgium, capture their airfields—some just 100 miles from London—and park fleets of bombers, dive-bombers, and fighter planes on them. Although the senior ranks of the RAF were convinced in the late 1930s that Bomber Command was the key to victory, and that, by implication, fighter aircraft and other defenses had marginal roles to play, their faith in air offensives was not without heretics. In 1937 a cabinet minister, Sir Thomas Inskip, facing the hard fact that Nazi Germany was winning the bomber race, argued that it really didn't matter. "The object of our Air Force," he said, "is not an early knock-out blow but to prevent the Germans from knocking us out." The RAF, in other words, didn't have to win; it merely had to avoid defeat. For that, the RAF needed fighter planes. The Air Ministry, appalled at this heresy, vehemently disagreed, but HMG accepted Inskip's recommendation, and it was Britain's good luck that the senior member of the Air Council agreed with it.

He was Air Chief Marshal Sir Hugh Dowding. In retrospect, "Stuffy" Dowding—as anointed by his fliers—is seen as the true hero of the Battle of Britain, though his contemporaries were slow to realize it. One reason lay in the nature of the man. He was a difficult man to like. Ever since Trafalgar, Britons had expected their military heroes to be Nelsons, and Dowding was far from that. Tall, frail, and abstemious, he was a bird-watching widower whose career had suffered from tactlessness, unorthodox views, and a remarkable lack of social graces. That he dabbled in spiritualism and was a vegetarian only augmented the perception of his flyboys that he was a strange duck. In the mid-1930s, his seniority—during the first war he had been ten years older than Germany's air ace von Richthofen—entitled him to the RAF's highest post, chief of air staff, but his fellow marshals denied him it. Instead they sidelined him, or so they thought, as head of Fighter Command. If the war was going to be won by aerial bombardment, the only outcome they foresaw, there would be little glory for fighters.[189]

Ignoring them and their strategy, Dowding pursued his own goals with quiet tenacity. In his headquarters in Bentley Priory, an eighteenth-century

Gothic mansion outside London, he organized Britain's anti-aircraft defenses, inspected the balloon barrage that would encircle London when war came, presided over the RAF's change from biplane fighters to metal monoplanes powered by the Rolls-Royce V-12 Merlin engines, pressed for all-weather runways at fighter fields, and took the first, historic steps toward military use of Radio Direction Finding (RDF), or radar, as the Americans later called it.

By July 1940, Dowding had about eight hundred operational Spitfire and Hurricane single-engine fighter planes. He arrayed them in four groups—two frontline and two in reserve. In reserve were No. 10 Group in the southwest of England, and No. 13 in northern England and Scotland. Six hundred Hurricanes and Spitfires went to the frontline groups, No. 12 in the midlands, and No. 11 Group north and south of London, roughly from Ipswich to the Isle of Wright, and most predominantly on the Kent promontory. This was the sector the German invasion barges would most likely target, either north of the Thames estuary, or on the south coast, just west of Dover, or in both places. Therefore, it was the sector Göring targeted. No. 11 Group had to be destroyed before an invasion could be launched, for No. 11 Group served as the shield over southeast England.

But radar was destined to be England's greatest shield in the critical months ahead. Dowding had been one of its champions from the beginning. Before his promotion to Fighter Command, he had commanded RAF research and development, and while there, he had studied the RDF experiments of Robert Watson Watt, a scientist at the National Physical Laboratory. Watson Watt convinced Dowding and those around him that airplanes could reflect radio beams. Yet in his push for radar, conducted with utmost civility and professional aplomb, Dowding had put himself on the wrong side of Churchill's good friend the Prof, Frederick Lindemann. For this, Dowding would later pay. Meanwhile, the Nazis knew something about radar technology but had entrusted development of it to their navy, seeing it as a reconnaissance device, and there it had languished.

Even before the war, Dowding had believed that radar could become a priceless defensive weapon. In 1937 he had ordered work begun along the country's eastern and southern coasts on a chain of coastal RDF stations, a mix of low-level stations, with an effective range of about 50 miles, and high-level, with a range of about 120 miles. By the spring of 1940, Britain possessed a mesh of radio beams comprising, as one Englishmen later called it, an "invisible bastion" against hostile aircraft. Thankfully for the British, Hitler had prohibited spending on any technological research that he believed would not contribute to his objective of a swift victory; radar was one such technology. In July 1940, German technicians were not even sure of the purpose of all those tall towers along the British coast, although many suspected that they were radar towers. Thus, the Luftwaffe began its campaign with an imperfect, at best, understanding of the towers.

Fifty radar stations scanned the skies from northern Scotland on around the Home Island to Wales. Most were located in the east and southeast, facing the North Sea and the English Channel, just twenty-one miles wide at its narrowest point. The outgoing radio signal was sent from wires fixed between two 360-foot towers; the return signal reached twin fixed receivers perched on 240-foot towers. In wooden sheds beneath the towers, technicians studying monitors would phone details on the range, direction, and size of advancing Nazi forces to the central operations room at Bentley Priory, where blue-shirted members of the Women's Auxiliary Air Force (WAAF) plotted their progress on a huge table map, using croupier rakes to move colored counters representing RAF and German aircraft. RAF officers radioed orders to the nine No. 11 Group operations centers — "sector stations" — scattered throughout the southeast and around London. There, orders were radioed to commanders of fighter squadrons, who then led their pilots aloft. German pilots listened in confusion as British pilots received updates by radio, updates that guided them toward the German fighters. How, the Germans wondered, could someone on the ground know where distant German planes were and where they were heading? They did not know that they faced two enemies in the Battle of Britain: RAF airmen in the sky and British radar crews on the ground.[190]

It was now possible for the British to detect enemy aircraft approaching England's shores while they were still as far as 120 miles away — thirty or more miles inside Belgium and France, and more than 70 miles beyond Calais — flying at altitudes of up to 30,000 feet. Although the RAF's long-range radar could peer 30 or so miles into the Low Countries and France, the altitude at which radar could "see" enemy aircraft increased with distance, due to the curvature of the earth. At the extreme range of the radar, that altitude was almost 14,000 feet. Anything flying beneath that altitude, at that range, was "below" the radar. The calculus of time, distance, fighter aircraft climb rate, altitude, and speed became absolutely critical, and would determine the outcome of the air battle over the Channel and the Kent promontory. The controllers at RAF sector stations, once notified by Bentley Priory of a radar fix, needed about five minutes to radio orders to fighter squadrons, during which time the German fighters climbed a further 6,000 to 8,000 feet. A Spitfire needed almost fifteen minutes to reach 20,000 feet. The Germans, therefore, had a head start of around twenty minutes. The "service ceiling" (maximum operational altitude) for both German and British fighter planes was beyond 35,000 feet, for German medium bombers beyond 26,000 feet. Not only could the RDF operators not "see" below certain altitudes, but they were finding that aircraft at tremendous altitudes disappeared from their sight. And all other RAF problems were compounded by the fact that a Luftwaffe squadron could cross the Channel at its narrowest point in five minutes.

Arrayed against the RAF were three German *Luftflotten* (air fleets). *Luftflotte* 3 was stationed in France, *Luftflotte* 2 in Belgium, under the command of Field Marshal Albert Kesselring, and *Luftflotte* 5 in Denmark and Norway. Because of the distances *Luftflotte* 5 had to fly, and the short range of Germany's best fighter, the Messerschmitt Bf 109, the bombers of *Luftflotte* 5 would have to fly without escorts. The burden of carrying out the German attack would therefore fall on *Luftflotten* 2 and 3, with a combined strength of 750 bombers, 250 Stuka dive-bombers, 600 Bf 109 fighters, and 250 twin-engine Bf 110 fighters. Hermann Göring issued his first operational directive for the Battle of Britain on June 30. The first step, code-named *Kanalkampf*, would be a struggle for mastery of the sky over the Channel.

Over the Channel is not where Hugh Dowding thought the fight would take place. He believed the fight, when it came, would take place over southeast England, in No. 11 Group's zone. The Germans kept a fleet of small seaplanes—white and marked with the Red Cross—at the ready, to rescue Luftwaffe pilots shot down over the Channel. British pilots who found themselves in the sea could only hope that a Royal Navy cutter or a local fisherman might happen upon them before they drowned, and many drowned. Göring intended to lure Dowding's Spitfires and Hurricanes out over the Channel by the approach, at high altitude, of his Bf 109s. Then, Stuka dive-bombers, Bf 109s armed with a single 550-pound bomb, and Bf 110s carrying a single 2,200-pound bomb, would scoot far under the fray to attack coastal shipping, Royal Navy warships, and the Channel ports. One million tons of merchant shipping, escorted by the Royal Navy, passed through the Channel each week. Although the Battle of Britain is recalled in the collective consciousness as the first great clash of air forces in history—and it was—the German objective was to attain supremacy over the *seas* by attaining supremacy in the air. This, Göring pledged, was to be accomplished in July, setting the stage for *"Adlerangriff"* ("Eagle Attack"), the weeklong climactic assault on England's military installations, railroad junctions, port facilities, oil depots, and aircraft factories, with the destruction of Fighter Command's coastal airfields the first objective.[191]

Dowding believed England's only hope of survival lay in radar and the RAF's single-engine fighters. He ordered his pilots to avoid direct combat with German fighters whenever possible, diverting them instead to

shooting down enemy bombers stripped of their fighter escorts. Thus the
RAF would keep its Spitfires and Hurricanes in the sky until the autumn's
worsening weather ruled out any possibility of a seaborne Nazi attack
across the Channel.

The *Kanalkampf* began on July 10, when twenty Nazi medium bombers,
escorted by some two dozen twin-engine Bf 110 fighters and forty Messerschmitt Bf 109s, attacked a convoy off Dover. They were challenged by
two squadrons (twenty-four to thirty aircraft) of Hurricanes. That day's
dogfights resulted in thirteen German and seven RAF planes going down,
a ratio that would hold for the next two months. Heavy fighting—and
these first collisions of the RAF and Luftwaffe were deadly—continued
for a full month, most of it over the Channel and the southern coast of
England. It was a testing time for both air forces, a time of feints, of probes,
of changing tactics.

And for the Royal Navy it was a time of terrible losses, from the air,
from mines, from U-boats. Early in the month—before the main air battle
opened on the tenth—the anti-aircraft ship *Foylebank* was sunk off Portland by a swarm of Stukas, with the loss of one hundred seventy of its
three-hundred-man crew. A U-boat sank the destroyer *Whirlwind* south of
Ireland, with forty-seven dead. On the eighteenth, two anti-submarine
trawlers and a minesweeper were mauled; on the nineteenth and twenty-
second, armed patrol trawlers were sunk by the Luftwaffe, with the loss of
eleven men. Two British submarines went down off England's shores that
month, with the loss of seventy-seven crewmen. On the twenty-sixth, the
destroyer *Boreas* was raked by the Luftwaffe, with twenty-one dead. The
next day, the destroyer *Wren* was sunk off Dover and the destroyer
Codrington was sunk off Suffolk, with thirty-six dead. So severe was the
air attack on Dover that the Royal Navy pulled its destroyers from the
port. This was exactly what Göring had set his sights on. On the twenty-
ninth, the destroyer *Delight* was damaged in Portland harbor, with six
dead. The remainder of the crew were rescued, but without a ship they
were effectively out of action. The Royal Navy had more sailors killed in
July than the RAF would lose pilots during the next two months. New
sailors could be trained in a matter of weeks, but even the smallest gunboats took several months to build.

Although the Royal Navy was being hit hard, it had no intention of
withdrawing from the Strait of Dover without a fight. But Dowding took a
hard line against daylight patrols in support of merchantmen and their

naval escorts. Grudgingly, the Admiralty barred the strait to destroyers in daylight. The merchantmen were given a choice: either they reached Dover at dusk, in which case they would be escorted, or they entered the Channel naked.

At dawn on August 8, twenty colliers took the risk. As the colliers formed themselves into a convoy off the Isle of Wight—a daily occurrence—*Kriegsmarine* radio operators at Wissant, opposite Folkestone, listened as the colliers and their Royal Navy escorts exchanged messages in preparation for the run through the Channel. A Luftwaffe strike followed. When the RDF station on the Isle of Wight picked up a strong blip, signaling the approach of a heavy raid, more than thirty Spitfires and Hurricanes went aloft to form an umbrella over the convoy. However, General Johannes Fink, after luring the RAF fighters away with decoys, sent in Stukas, which sank five ships and damaged seven others in less than ten minutes. The survivors scattered, tried to reassemble, and were attacked again, this time by a strong force of Stukas escorted by Bf-109s. The RAF lost sixteen planes, the Germans about twice that number.

The attacks on shipping continued throughout August, with the toll of cargo ships, tankers, armed trawlers, and sailors mounting. Late in the month, the destroyer HMS *Esk* hit a mine and went down off the Dutch coast, taking almost 130 tars with her. The coordinated attacks of the Luftwaffe and *Kriegsmarine* were yielding results, but Göring did not pursue his objectives with alacrity. Rather than trade his replaceable planes for irreplaceable British ships, he preferred the glory that devolved upon the Luftwaffe when his pilots engaged the boys of the RAF head-on, high in the sky, where contrails wrote the story of each day's heroics. German planes flying at 26,000 feet did not sink ships. The German army and navy high command, Churchill later wrote, "regretted the lower priority assigned by Göring to the naval targets, and were irked by the delays."[192]

Britain regretted the *Kanalkampf* sinkings but could spare the ships. On Friday evening, August 9, Churchill dined at Chequers with Pound, Ismay, Eden, Dill, and General Sir Archibald Wavell. Even under the threat of invasion Churchill cherished plans for British offensives. After the women had retired to the drawing room, he spoke at length about de Gaulle's plan for an invasion of French North Africa, supported by the Royal Navy, at Dakar. His view of that day's losses in the strait was philosophical; England, he said, would have to continue using her coastal vessels as bait, though he acknowledged that "the surviving bait are getting a bit fed up." Pound, also undiscouraged, said that they "even had a surplus of coasting vessels."[193]

During July, the RAF lost 70 aircraft and the Luftwaffe more than 180, more than half of them bombers. On neither side was the damage mortal. British spirits were high. All Britain was aroused by the RAF's heroism. The young pilots knew that every Englishman's eye was on them; they were, in Liddell Hart's phrase, "the heroes of the nation."[194]

Each day the German raids grew heavier and more frequent. Afterward, those who fought in the sky were haunted less by memories of fear—their engagements rarely lasted more than ten or fifteen minutes—than by the relentless tension and nerve-sapping fatigue. After a third or fourth sortie, men would fall asleep in their cockpits as soon as they had landed. Two or even three more sorties would lie ahead of them, and although they may have brushed death more than once, their weariness was so great that when dusk fell and darkness gathered, they had no immediate recollection of that day's fighting, not even of their kills. They awoke to the BBC's report of the latest score and, thus rejuvenated by the BBC and the miraculous powers of youth, would head for the village pub.[195]

All of England and all of Germany—indeed, the entire world—anxiously awaited each day's scores, upon which the outcome of the battle, and the likelihood of invasion, seemed to hang. No. 10 echoed with hurrahs after the Air Ministry reported, typically: "The final figures for today's fighting are 85 certain, 34 probable, 33 damaged. We lost 37 aircraft. 12 pilots being killed and 14 wounded." After dinner on Saturday, July 13, Colville wrote in his diary: "Winston said the last four days have been the most glorious in the history of the RAF. Those days have been the test: the enemy had come and had lost five to one. We could now be confident of our superiority."[196]

Churchill believed it. He was citing the figures he had been given, and no one had deliberately deceived him. No one was deliberately misleading the Führer either, but the numbers sent to his Luftwaffe commanders were very different. According to them, those days had been among the most glorious days in Luftwaffe history, and therefore clear evidence of *German* superiority. In retrospect it is clear that the communiqués being issued by both sides were quite worthless.

The RAF accepted their pilots' claims of German trophies without question. However, British accounts of their own losses were always correct. That was not true of Luftwaffe reports. Announcing light casualties for the Luftwaffe and severe British losses was a mighty tonic for Reich morale, and Germans concluded that their airmen were winning the battle.

One problem with deception is that the deceivers deceive themselves. That is what happened to the Luftwaffe's high command. "The Germans," as Churchill told Parliament later in the war, had "become victims of their own lies." The Germans had lost control of the battle's vital statistics, which, by the beginning of August, had become simply incredible. At one point William L. Shirer observed dryly: "German figures of British losses have been rising all evening. First (they) announced 73 British planes shot down against 14 German; then 79 to 14; finally at midnight 89 to 17. Actually, when I counted up the German figures as given out from time to time during the afternoon and evening, they totaled 111 for British losses. The Luftwaffe is lying so fast it isn't consistent even by its own account."[197]

At his country estate Göring studied these bogus figures, counted the number of British ships sunk, and declared that the *Kanalkampf* had been a stunning German victory. After the French capitulation, he had been told that the Royal Air Force had been reduced to fewer than two thousand frontline aircraft, of which between five hundred and six hundred were fighters. That was largely true—then. The *Reichsmarschall* had written the number on a pad of paper and pocketed it. In the fighting that followed, he subtracted the day's losses, as reported to him, at the end of each day. In a Luftwaffe intelligence report dated August 16, he read that the British had lost 574 fighters since July, and that since their factories had provided them with no more than 300, they were left with about 430, of which perhaps 300 were serviceable.

As the remainder on Göring's pad approached zero, he was confident that the invasion could soon begin. But German pilots knew that RAF squadrons were still defending Britain's skies. The *Reichsmarschall* was confused. He would have despaired had he been shown the latest figures from Ministry of Aircraft Production in London. In July alone, British workers had produced 496 fighter planes, four times the monthly rate before Dunkirk. By the end of August, Beaverbrook made 1,081 fighters available, with another 500 undergoing repair. Dowding, it seemed, would end the battle in the skies over England with more fighters than he had at the beginning.[198]

Moreover, the wrecks of aircraft downed over Britain could be recovered by Beaverbrook's Civilian Repair Organization. So efficient was the Beaver's CRO that by the end of summer, one-third of Dowding's fighters comprised parts from crashed Hurricanes and Spitfires. Indeed, through CRO ingenuity, crashed German planes flew again as RAF aircraft. On August 10, Colville noted in his diary: "Beaverbrook, he [Churchill] said, has genius, and, what is more, brutal ruthlessness." Never in his life, "at the Ministry of Munitions or anywhere else," had he seen "such startling results as Beaverbrook has produced." After studying the Aircraft Production charts, General Sir Henry Pownell, who was with them, "agreed that there had never been such an achievement." To be sure, it was a backbreaking job, and one from which the temperamental Canadian was forever resigning. Churchill wouldn't allow it. On September 2, at the end of one memorandum to the prime minister, Beaverbrook lamented, "Nobody knows the troubles I've seen." Beneath it Churchill wrote, "I do."[199]

An elated Göring put his statistics before Hitler, declaring that the RAF was helpless. The Reich, he said, had mastered the sky over *Der Bach* (the

German nickname for the Channel). Now, he proposed preparations for the second phase of the battle: *der Adlerangriff,* the Eagle Attack—Germany's all-out air assault in England. Yet Dowding was noting in his journal that he still believed time was on England's side "if we can only hold on." That day his pilots claimed to have destroyed sixty German planes, and though he may have thought that figure suspect, he was impressed by the skill with which the young Englishwomen at his radar stations had interpreted the direction and ranges of the attackers. In the long run, if the RAF were to prevail, the performance of the WAAF would be crucial.[200]

Luftwaffe airmen were as dangerous as ever. Their superiors were not. Officers of higher ranks committed the blunders and mismanagement within the Luftwaffe. The intelligence that Göring was receiving was appalling. The Germans had only a meager understanding of the British defense system; indeed, at the outset they didn't know where key British airfields were. Operational maps did not distinguish between fields used by Fighter and Bomber Commands. The two factories where Rolls-Royce built the Merlin engines that powered Hurricanes and Spitfires were never bombed, though their location was no secret. Vital orders miscarried. Weather reports were unreliable. Staff work was slow and sloppy. Göring summoned his generals and ordered that under no circumstances should he be disturbed by subordinates in search of guidance. Worst of all, he adopted no coherent strategy, no priority of targets. After the war, Adolph Galland, one of his officers, wrote that "constantly changing orders betraying lack of purpose and obvious misjudgment of the situation by the Command and unjustified accusations had a most demoralizing effect on us fighter pilots."[201]

British RDF (radar) baffled the enemy. Picking up its signals, German airmen reported British radio stations with special installations. Nazi intelligence decided it was a communication system linking RAF pilots with ground controllers, and concluded, on August 7, that "as the British fighters are controlled from the ground by radio-telephone, their forces are tied to their respective ground stations and are therefore restricted in mobility," which, had it been true, would have meant that resistance to mass German attacks was limited to local fighters.[202]

The commander of the Luftwaffe Signals Service, who was among the few Germans who understood the role of radar, urged that an attack on the RDF stations be given priority. A limited attempt on them, made on the day before the first major assault on the British mainland, was ineffective. At Dover, the Germans rocked a radar pylon, but the 360-foot-tall lattice masts were almost impossible to hit; returning after an attempt to destroy four of them, the pilots reported total failure. Göring assumed that the British electronic gear and crews were deep underground and hence safe. (In fact they were in flimsy shacks beneath the towers.) He issued the order: "It is doubtful whether there is any point in continuing the attacks on radar sites, in view of the fact that not one of those attacked has so far been put out of action."[203]

Nevertheless, this was still the mighty Luftwaffe, and its huge fleets of superb aircraft outnumbered the defenders by two to one. After the *Kanalkampf*, they completed plans for *Adlertag* (Eagle Day), the launch of *Adlerangriff* (Eagle Attack). The Führer, unaware that Göring's figures were inflated, authorized him to open *Adlerangriff*. Depending on the weather and other imponderables, the *Führerordnung* (*Führer Directive*) decreed, *Adlertag* could fall as early as August 5. British intelligence officers in Bletchley Park relayed the decision to Churchill, and Dowding issued an Order of the Day to his men: "The Battle of Britain is about to begin. Members of the Royal Air Force, the fate of generations lies in your hands."

On August 6, the *Reichsmarschall* set Eagle Day for August 10, a Saturday. The weather forced him to reschedule it for the following Tuesday, when heavy skies were expected to clear. They did, and that morning, 74 twin-engine Dorniers (which could carry 2,200 pounds of bombs) and 50 Bf 109s took off. The clouds returned; Göring issued a recall order. That afternoon, the clouds rolled away and the offensive was officially on, targeting a 150-mile arc of southern England from the Thames estuary to Southampton. Commanding it was Göring's ablest subordinate, *Feldmarschall* Albert Kesselring, commander of *Luftflotte* 2. Kesselring's men called him "Smiling Albert" (he liked to flash his perfect enamels). He had much to smile about. Soon after daybreak every RAF radar tower in the southeast was sending urgent warnings to Dowding's headquarters.[204]

Among those awaiting the onslaught were a dozen American war correspondents on the cliffs of Dover, including H. R. Knickerbocker, Edward Murrow, Helen Kirkpatrick, Quentin Reynolds, Whitelaw Reid, Virginia Cowles, Eric Sevareid, and Vincent Sheean. Their mood was fatalistic. Among them, Sheean wrote, a "sense of inevitable tragedy had grown heavy." Some had been covering the spread of global conflict since the Japanese seizure of Manchuria in 1931. The Reich seemed invincible. They heard the familiar hum of the desynchronized Messerschmitts, Heinkels—the workhorses of the Luftwaffe, with a range of 1,250 miles and a bomb load capacity of 5,500 pounds—and Dorniers, which grew to a roar as the glittering wings of the great Nazi armada emerged from the dazzling sun-drenched mist over the Channel and approached a coast that had not seen an invader in nine centuries. Experience had taught the newsmen to expect another defeat for democracy.[205]

And then, Sheean wrote, from RAF fields inland, they saw twenty-one squadrons—more than 300 aircraft—of challenging Spitfires rising "like larks, glittering against the sun," maneuvering for position and attack.

They heard the "zoom of one fighter diving over another...the rattle of machine-gun fire, the streak of smoke of a plane plummeting to earth, and the long seesaw descent of the wounded fighter falling from the clouds beneath his shining white parachute." Sheean and his companions no doubt saw a great flotilla of RAF fighters, but they could not have all been Spitfires. On any given day, No. 11 and 12 Groups could count only about 250 operational Spitfires, and around 320 Hurricanes.[206]

The scenes were repeated all that day and all week along the southern coast. Sheean wrote: "In every such battle I saw, the English had the best of it, and in every such battle they were greatly outnumbered." Repeatedly "five or six fighters would engage twenty or thirty Germans....I saw it happen not once but many times." He remembered the Spaniards and the Czechs and wrote: "At Dover the first sharp thrust of hope penetrated our gloom. The battles over the cliffs proved that British could and would fight for their own freedom, if for nothing else, and that they would do so against colossal odds....The flash of the Spitfire's wing, then, through the misty glare of the summer sky, was the first flash of a sharpened sword; they *would* fight, they *would* hold out."[207]

The battle reached its peak between August 24 and September 6, which became known to Fighter Command as the critical period. In the five weeks of fighting between July 10 and August 13, Luftwaffe tactics had been tested by Dowding's strategy. His orders to his pilots to avoid Messerschmitts, to flee from them if necessary and go after the German bombers, had paid off. Nazi fighters flying escort had been at a disadvantage; enemy bomber losses had continued to be high; and, far more important, the RAF continued to be a force in being, warding off the threat of invasion.

With Eagle Day this pattern changed. Kesselring massed a great concentration of Messerschmitts in the Pas de Calais, in northern France. He meant to wipe out the sector airfields of Sir Keith Park's 11 Group—London's air defenses—leaving the capital naked. During this time Churchill repeatedly visited RAF bases at Stanmar, Uxbridge, Dover, and Ramsgate. These were the castle gates, from which its last defenders sallied forth, behind which all England waited. Colville noted that what Churchill saw at the bases "brought the war home to him." The Germans, in fact, had brought the war to his home.[208]

On Thursday, August 15, the Germans decided to test RAF Fighter Command's strength by attacking it from all sides simultaneously. For the first time, *Luftflotte* 5 (Air Fleet 5), in Norway and Denmark, was assigned a major role, to sweep into northern England near Tyneside and seek out industrial targets near Newcastle and Bomber Command airfields. *Luftflotte* 5 sent one hundred bombers escorted by forty twin-engine Bf 110s. The distance from Denmark precluded the possibility of using single-engine Bf 109s to protect the bombers. The Germans paid dearly for their lack of fighter cover. Days earlier, Dowding had moved eighty Spitfire pilots and their planes north, to give both a needed rest. They rose to meet the attackers. The Germans lost sixteen Heinkels and six JU-88s—one-fifth of their bombers—and seven Bf 110s. There were no British losses. Throughout the Luftwaffe, that day became known as *der schwarze Donnerstag:* Black Thursday.[209]

In the south, however, that day's fighting was very different. Here the airfields of No. 11 Group were the targets. In Essex and Kent, airfields at Martlesham, Eastchurch, and Hawkinge were hit; then the enemy attacked two aircraft factories near Rochester and fighter fields at Portland, Middle Wallop, West Malling, and Croydon. Both sides suffered the highest losses for any single day. Before dusk the Germans had flown an unprecedented 1,786 sorties, and the total losses for both sides—109 aircraft—were the highest for any single day of the battle thus far.

Churchill followed the day's fighting from No. 11 Group headquarters at Uxbridge, and he left clearly affected. Climbing into his limousine with Ismay, he said, "Don't speak to me. I'm too moved." His lips were trembling. They rode in silence for a few minutes. Then Churchill turned to Ismay and said something that "burned into" Ismay's mind, so much so that he went home that night and repeated the words to his wife.[210]

Five days later, when the most difficult and dangerous period in the battle was about to begin, Churchill paused during a long address to the House of Commons on the overall war situation, and delivered his tribute to the RAF:

The gratitude of every home in our island, in our Empire, and indeed throughout the world, except in the abodes of the guilty, goes out to the British airmen who, undaunted by odds, unwearied in their constant challenge of mortal danger, are turning the tide of the World War by their prowess and their devotion.

Then, he spoke the words that had so moved Ismay: "Never in the field of human conflict was so much owed by so many to so few." Those words have become immortal, yet they were but a prelude to Churchill's main point, the RAF bombing campaign:

All hearts go out to the fighter pilots, whose brilliant actions we see with our own eyes day after day; but we must never forget that all the time, night after night, month after month, our bomber squadrons travel far into Germany, find their targets in the darkness by the highest navigational skill, aim their attacks, often under the heaviest fire, often with serious loss, with deliberate careful discrimination, and inflict shattering blows upon the whole of the technical and war-making structure of the Nazi power. On no part of the Royal Air Force does the weight of the war fall more heavily than on the daylight bombers, who will play an invaluable part in the case of invasion and whose unflinching zeal it has been necessary in the meanwhile on numerous occasions to restrain.[211]

Bomber Command had more than six hundred medium and light bombers stationed on airfields north of London. Churchill did not intend to restrain them much longer.

On Friday the sixteenth, Kesselring continued to press the attack. *Luftflotte* 5 was grounded — indeed, for the remainder of the battle — but the Germans put up more than 1,700 sorties, raiding airfields almost at will and bombing the hangars at Brize Norton flight-training school. That Sunday the Germans lost seventy-one aircraft, nearly 10 percent of those committed. Nevertheless, after a day's lull the enemy again arrived in force, undiscouraged by the costs of the offensive.[212]

Göring summoned his three *Luftflotten* commanders to Karinhall and ordered them to go after aircraft factories and steel mills as "bottleneck" targets. Four days later he summoned them again to announce: "We have reached the decisive period of the air war against England." As in past conferences he was astonishingly ill-informed. He grossly underestimated the significance of Dowding's radar chain, thus assuring its continued immunity, and his summation of Luftwaffe accomplishments in the battle was wildly unrealistic.[213]

Nevertheless, Fighter Command's situation was critical. Unlike the enemy, Britain had no bottomless reserve of trained pilots. RAF bomber pilots were being retrained to fly Spitfires and Hurricanes. In a single week Dowding had lost 80 percent of his squadron commanders. One of their replacements had never even flown a Hurricane, yet after just three landings and three takeoffs, he led his men into battle. Often pilots had logged no more than ten hours of flight before sighting an enemy fighter. In August, Fighter Command's operational training period was cut from six months to two weeks. Some new pilots had never fired their guns. Some were boys in their teens.[214]

The RAF pilots pushed the limits of human endurance, sleeping in their cockpits between sorties, "undaunted by odds," in Churchill's words, "unwearied in their constant challenge and mortal danger." On the final day of August, accompanied by Clemmie, Pamela, and Colville, he drove to Uxbridge, the frenzied headquarters of Sir Keith Park's No. 11 Group, controlling all the fighter squadrons in southeastern England. The rest of his party took walks in the countryside, but he wanted to talk to the airmen, look into their faces, and hear their stories. That evening Colville wrote: "The P.M. was deeply moved by what he saw this afternoon at Uxbridge."[215]

Park could replace his pilots but not his airfields. If the Germans knocked them out by bombing and strafing, British fighters could neither take off nor land; the Nazis would then command the air over southeast England, and Hitler's invasion could begin. To protect No. 11 Group's fields, Park told his pilots to engage the enemy as far out as possible, but when the Germans greatly increased the proportion of fighters to bombers, the Spitfires and Hurricanes of No. 12 Group had to stay behind to provide No. 11 Group fields with air cover, and there weren't enough of them. The enemy onslaught was too great. Kesselring was putting up over a thousand sorties a day. Charging in from the sea each morning at an altitude too low for British guns, Bf 109s and 110s would sweep the RAF fields in strafing attacks, wrecking repair shops, destroying hangars, ripping apart grounded planes, leveling operations buildings, and leaving airstrips unfit for landing and taking off. The Bf 110s, armed with 2,200-pound bombs, were especially deadly. Once the RAF was shot out of the sky and its airfields smashed, Göring planned on sending his Bf 110s far inland in search of military and industrial targets.

RAF ground crews worked heroically, but before new craters could be filled in, a second flight of raiders would arrive. By dusk all British communications were paralyzed, and when the operations rooms were reduced to ruins, the whole ground-control system failed. One by one the advanced fighting fields were abandoned. And on the tenth day of the new Nazi offensive, a dozen Ju 88s slipped through Britain's fighter protection and hit the Vickers factory near Weybridge, destroying the works and inflicting heavy casualties. The output of Wellington bombers dropped from ninety a week to four.[216]

Minister of Information Duff Cooper told No. 10 that British morale was "extremely high," but the public did not know what its leaders knew. Fighter Command was in crisis. Under Beaverbrook, British factories were producing 115 or more new fighters each week—twice as many as the Germans—but the Nazis were now shooting down more than that. Dowding's aircraft reserve was shrinking. On the last two days of August, the Nazi attacks reached a crescendo with 2,795 sorties. Their primary targets continued to be No. 11 Group's vital sector stations at Biggin Hill and

Kenley. By September 1 both were destroyed. Hangars, aircraft repair shops, operations buildings, communication grids—all were leveled. Of No. 11 Group's seven major airfields, six had been demolished and the five advanced airfields were hors de combat. Still, Churchill and Park conferred on the first and agreed that the Germans had reached their maximum effectiveness and "could not stand the strain much longer as far as an air offensive is concerned."[217]

Incredibly, the German high command didn't grasp the implications of the Luftwaffe's successes. An exception was *Generalfeldmarschall* Fedor von Bock, one of the Wehrmacht's highest-ranking officers. Bock realized that the tide of battle had shifted; while preparing to move his army-group headquarters from France to Poland, he tried to impress upon his commander in chief, Walther von Brauchitsch, the importance of the shift. Finding von Brauchitsch uncommunicative, Bock insisted that for the first time in the battle, the Luftwaffe was making some real headway.

Every day now the Germans were coming in larger numbers and they were threatening Britain's inner defenses. When, after a visit to Fighter Command headquarters at Stanmore, Churchill dined at Chequers with Dowding, Lindemann, and Gort, the enemy bombed Great Missenden, just four miles away.

By the first week in September, the RAF was in desperate straits. Dowding's pilots were no longer permitted to pursue enemy aircraft out over the Channel. Because he lacked rested and refitted squadrons, he could no longer rotate them. In just two weeks he had lost 230 pilots, killed and wounded—25 percent of his pilots. At that rate, in another week Fighter Command would cease to be a disciplined fighting force. The entire air-defense system of southeast England was in danger of destruction. Already the Luftwaffe could very nearly do what it pleased over the area that Sea Lion had targeted for invasion. "If what Göring wanted was air superiority over southeast England for the invasion," Deighton writes, "then by 1 September it was almost his." Air Marshal Park wrote that "an almost complete disorganization made the control of our fighter squadrons completely difficult.... Had the enemy continued his heavy attacks (against fields and the control system) ... the fighter defenses of London would have been in a perilous state." Group captain Peter Townsend believed that "on 6th September victory was in the Luftwaffe's grasp." On September 7, he said, Wehrmacht divisions, panzers, and artillery "could have begun massive landings on British soil."[218]

But the key event determining the outcome of the air battle had taken place on the night of August 23–24. It was a matter of chance. A few of 170 German Heinkels that had been ordered to bomb oil installations at Thames Haven and Rochester became lost. Before turning for home, they jettisoned their bombs. As it happened, the lost raiders were over London. Fleeing homeward, they left behind raging fires in Bethnal Green and East Ham.[219]

This was an error Hitler could not countenance. He had issued a directive to the Luftwaffe: "Attacks against the London area and terror attacks are reserved for the Führer's decision." This was a political rather than a strictly military decree. He was still hoping to bring Churchill to the conference table.[220]

Churchill saw his chance. A month earlier he had sought from the Air Ministry a guarantee that were the Germans to bomb residential areas of London, Bomber Command would be ready "to return the compliment the next day against Berlin." The night following the errant German attack on London—August 25—eighty-one twin-engine Wellingtons and Hampdens carried the war to the heart of the Reich. Berlin was covered with dense cloud; only half the bombers found it. Railroad yards and utilities were the targets. Damage was slight. Ten German men were killed by a bomb that fell near the Görlitzer railroad station, and the Siemens electrical works suffered a temporary loss of production. Unable to locate their targets, many of the British pilots brought their planes home still fully loaded with bombs.[221]

The following morning Churchill sent a memo to the Chiefs of Air Staff: "Now that they have begun to molest the capital, I want you to hit them hard, and Berlin is the place to hit them."[222]

The British had been targeting German military and industrial targets since May—sporadic raids over the Kiel Canal, Rhine River shipping, railroad junctions. But until that Sunday night, no bomb had fallen on the capital of the Reich. William L. Shirer wrote in his diary: "The Berliners are stunned. They did not think it could ever happen. When the war began, Göring had assured them that it couldn't.... They believed him. Their disillusionment today is all the greater. You have to see their faces to believe it.... For the first time the war has been brought home to them."[223]

The club-footed Nazi propaganda minister and former so-called journalist Dr. Paul Joseph Goebbels ordered German newspapers to run the headline FEIGER ENGLISCHER ANGRIFF (Cowardly British Attack). The bombers came again on August 28 and again the following night, and after the third raid, the headlines in the Nazi press screamed, ENGLISCHE LUFTPIRATEN ÜBER BERLIN! (English Air Pirates over Berlin!)[224]

Bombing cities was still an issue in 1940. Both the Hague and the Geneva Conventions—which the Reich was pledged to support—outlawed indiscriminate assaults on peaceful civilians. In May, when a flight of Heinkels had mistakenly killed nearly a hundred German women and children in the old university city of Freiburg im Breisgau, the Germans had blamed it on the RAF. A Nazi communiqué had reported it as an "enemy attack." Goebbels condemned it as the *"Kindermord in Freiburg"* (the "murder of the innocents in Freiburg"), and the British traitor Lord Haw-Haw had denounced it as a "perfectly substantiated atrocity."[225]

Granting London immunity had never been popular in the Luftwaffe. As the autumn of 1940 approached and with no victory in the skies over England, Göring repeatedly asked Hitler to reconsider. Discontent was particularly keen among German fighter pilots. In his postwar memoirs, Adolph Galland—then a Luftwaffe major and fighter pilot, later a general—described London as a target "of exceptional military importance, as the brain and nerve center of the British High Command, as a port, and as a center for armament and distribution." He wrote, "We fighter pilots, discouraged by a task which was beyond our strength, were looking forward impatiently and excitedly to the start of the bomber attacks."[226]

So was Göring, who, unaware of how much damage he had inflicted on the RAF, argued that a strategic shift from fighters over Dover to bombers over London might bring about the hoped-for peace conference, and preserve the Luftwaffe's reputation in the bargain. Göring, Shirer later wrote, made a mistake "comparable in its consequences to Hitler's calling off the armored attack on Dunkirk on May 24." Admiral Raeder, too, championed terror attacks against London, in part as a means to preserve his navy, which he believed would be destroyed in an invasion attempt. If the Luftwaffe and the threat of invasion could not force Churchill to the conference table, perhaps a panicked London citizenry might do so. On August 31 Hitler approved massed raids—by day and night—against the London docks. They were to begin in a week.[227]

On September 4 Hitler delivered a withering attack on the British leadership in Berlin's *Sportpalast,* a winter sports arena and the largest meeting hall in the capital. Addressing an audience of social workers and nurses, he dismissed Minister of Information Duff Cooper as a *"Krampfhenne"* (a Bavarian word for "a nervous old hen"), and said, "The babbling of Mr. Churchill or Mr. Eden—reverence for old age forbids the mention of Mr. Chamberlain—doesn't mean a thing to the German people. At best, it makes them laugh." He then took up the bombings. "Mr. Churchill," he said, "is demonstrating his new brain child, the night air raid." Hitler said he had believed that such madness would be stopped, but "Herr Churchill took that for a sign of weakness." Now he would learn better: "We will *raze* their cities to the ground!" He shouted, "The hour will come when one of us will break, and it will not be National Socialist Germany!" The women leapt to their feet, joyfully shouting, "Never! *Never!*"

Hitler knew that the British were wondering when his invasion would begin. He said, "In England they're filled with curiosity and keep asking 'Why doesn't he come?' Be calm, he's coming! Be calm, he's coming!"[228]

Yet to those who knew the Führer and his byzantine court, there was an air of uncertainty about the Reich's intentions. After listening to Hitler's speech, Count Ciano was baffled. Something about it was not quite right. He wrote in his diary that Hitler seemed "unaccountably nervous."[229]

He was. He had conquered France in six weeks. Now, almost twelve weeks after the French surrender, the English—their army weak but rebuilding, their navy spread thin, their air force down on one knee—had fought him to a standstill. The strategic shift to massed bombings was his last option. If it worked, he would not need to invade England. But on that account, time was not on his side. Churchill understood that there existed one condition among many necessary, though not sufficient, for a successful invasion of England, a circumstance over which nobody had any control and that defied accurate prediction. To launch an invasion, according to the Joint Intelligence Committee, the Germans were dependent upon "a calm sea and restricted visibility." The Channel weather in autumn, when it deteriorated into "equinoctial gales" (as Churchill called them) could prove England's most steadfast ally. The North Sea in autumn was no place for flat-bottomed river barges made top-heavy by troops, artillery, and tanks. In winter it was even worse, and each day that passed brought winter one day closer. That was reassuring; that it was still only early September was not.[230]

On September 6, the Joint Intelligence Committee pored over a sheaf of reports, Enigma decrypts, and aerial photographs. The evidence before them seemed compelling. Enigma decrypts reported that all German army leave had been stopped; maps of English coastal areas had been issued to German officers in Normandy; the transfer of dive-bombers from Norway to France was complete; aerial photographs showed a "large-scale and disciplined" massing of barges (*Sturmboote*) in the Channel ports. Forty-eight hours after that moon and tide, the reports concluded, conditions would be "particularly favorable" for enemy landings. Warning of the "large-scale and disciplined" movement of troop transports toward forward bases on the Channel, the committee concluded that the last enemy preparations were complete. The next afternoon, the seventh, the director of military intelligence told the Chiefs of Staff that the invasion was imminent. At Bletchley Park the Naval Intelligence Section concluded that the landings might begin the following day. The chiefs therefore ordered all defense forces in the United Kingdom to "stand by at immediate notice." The Air Ministry issued an "Invasion Alert No. 1" to all RAF commands, signaling the expectation that the Germans could be expected within the next twenty-four hours.[231]

Late on the cloudless afternoon of Saturday, September 7, Hermann Göring and Albert Kesselring stood with their staffs on the cliffs of Cap Blanc Nez, opposite the White Cliffs of Dover, and watched their huge formation of *Luftflotten,* one thousand aircraft, a third of them bombers, cross the Channel and head for London. It was an awesome spectacle. The enormous armada seemed to shut out the sun and rose nearly two miles high.[232]

The RAF had no warning that London was the target. At 4:00 P.M. Dowding was at his desk in Bentley Priory when he was told British radar had picked up the huge formations approaching from Calais. During previous Luftwaffe raids, including over the past few days, the raiders had split up upon reaching the coast, where British fighters patrolling at 25,000 feet waited for that moment to pounce. On this day that moment never came. *Valhalla* was German slang for an extraordinarily large formation of aircraft. Wave after wave of Valhallas crossed the east coast of Kent, near Deal, and headed straight for London. Eagle Attack was still under way; the targets were industrial centers along the Thames. The Germans hit Woolwich Arsenal first, then the Victoria and Albert Docks, the West India Dock, the Commercial Dock, and the Surrey Docks. Behind them they left a flaming vision of apocalypse. Ships were sunk, catwalks mangled, cranes toppled, and fires set that covered 250 acres and served as a beacon for a second heavy raid. Many German bombs missed their marks and fell into East End neighborhoods—civilian neighborhoods. At dusk that evening, observers in the West End took note of what appeared to be a spectacular sunset. But the glow came from the east. The observers quickly grasped the horrific truth: this was not the tangerine handiwork of the setting sun; the East End was burning.[233]

In the late spring of 1940 it was decreed that the bells of London's churches, which had pealed morning wake-up and evening curfew and called London's faithful to Sunday service for almost three centuries, would ring now only to announce Cromwell, the code word that would alert all Britain to an imminent invasion. When the Chiefs of Staff ordered all troops in Britain to full readiness, that was enough for the Home Guard. At 7:30 they proclaimed Cromwell. Church bells throughout the kingdom rang out their warning. Men deployed. Civilians readied their homemade weapons. The Royal Engineers blew up key bridges, and in the confusion, several civilians were injured stumbling over hastily laid mines.[234]

It was a false alarm. No Germans arrived by sea, but for Londoners, the terror from the skies had begun. Given the hideous glow churning the clouds high above the East End, it would not have been unreasonable had Londoners concluded that their city was soon to be reduced to cinders and ash.[235]

The next day Home Forces commander Sir Alan Brooke told his diary of the night's heavy bombing and fires, and added, "Went to the office in the morning, where I found further indications of impending invasion." He predicted that the next few weeks would prove "the most eventful weeks in the history of the British Empire." The full moon and tides would align the next week. The Germans had not come during the July moon, or the August. They would have to come in the next ten days, or take their chances in October, when the weather, their ally since June, would become their enemy.[236]

To oppose an invasion, reinvigorate the blockade, and hunt U-boats, Churchill needed more destroyers. Help in that regard—very modest help—was on the way at last, but at a price. Franklin Roosevelt's position on sending destroyers to Churchill had shifted (just slightly) between May and late August, a period of twelve weeks during which Churchill fumed to the cabinet that "although the president is our best friend, no practical help has been forthcoming from the United States as yet. We have not expected them to send military aid [troops or pilots], but they have not even sent any worthy contribution in destroyers or planes." At one point, the kingdom's finances looked so bleak that Chancellor of the Exchequer Kingsley Wood suggested requisitioning the nation's gold wedding rings in order to raise twenty million pounds. Churchill approved the plan but suggested it be implemented at a later date, not to retain the twenty million in gold but "for the purpose of shaming the Americans" if for lack of American help England's fortunes should evaporate.[237]

Churchill followed up his original request to Roosevelt for destroyers with another, and another, and another. His missives to Roosevelt became increasingly desperate, the memos to staff more disdainful of the timeliness and quality of American help. To HMG's ambassador in Washington, Lord Lothian, in June: "We really have had no help worth speaking of from the United States so far." That month had been the low point, symbolized perhaps by Henry Ford's refusal to produce engines for British planes for fear his sales of new cars to Americans might be hurt, to say nothing of getting paid were England to lose, as Ford thought likely. In a late July telegram to Roosevelt, Churchill simply begged: "It has now become most urgent for you to give us the destroyers, motor boats and flying boats for which we have asked....Mr. President, with great respect I must tell you that in the long history of the world this is a thing to do now."[238]

Churchill lowered his request to forty ships, and then he raised it to sixty. He cautioned Roosevelt that the Italians, by sending some of their submarines into the Atlantic (Mussolini had more than one hundred, more even than Germany), could help the Germans isolate England. He informed the president that ten British destroyers had been sunk in ten days, and almost one-third of the Royal Navy destroyer fleet had been lost since the start of the war. And he linked the destroyers to his strategic plans for the following year: "Our intention is to have a strong army fighting in France for the campaign of 1941." Finally, he told Roosevelt that "time is all important," for it would not be until February that British production of destroyers and anti-submarine craft could fill the shipping gap, which, however, could be filled by the prompt delivery of U.S. destroyers.[239]

By mid-August, more than three months after Churchill's first plea for older destroyers, Roosevelt began to believe that Britain might, just might, hold on. Ignoring both the isolationists and the Neutrality Acts, the president sent Churchill a message through the State Department in which he proposed a two-pronged deal: a guarantee from England that its Home Fleet would sail to Canada were the Home Island to find itself in extremis, and a straight-up swap of several British naval bases for the American ships. The negotiations for the destroyers imparted a certain sticky relativism to the concept of U.S. neutrality. Germany and Italy, with whom America was not at war after all, would receive no such friendly overtures. Regardless of the sovereign right of nations to trade with any combatant not under legal blockade, a transfer of fifty destroyers to Britain was a clear step in the direction toward war, and that pleased Churchill. But the terms Roosevelt proposed did not. Churchill told Colville that Roosevelt wanted to put a "lien" on the British fleet in return for the destroyers. It was not the deal he expected; in fact, he expected a gift, with no strings attached, and told Roosevelt so: "I had not contemplated anything in the nature of a contract, bargain or sale between us" but rather "a separate spontaneous act." Cadogan found Churchill "rather incensed" over Roosevelt's proposed swap. Churchill, Cadogan jotted in his diary, "says he doesn't mind if we don't get destroyers." But of course he did.[240]

Churchill could not abide Roosevelt's linking the destroyers to a guarantee that were England to fall, its Atlantic fleet would run westward to Canada. He complained in a letter to Canadian prime minister William Lyon Mackenzie King that the Americans sought to "get the British fleet and the guardianship of the British Empire, minus Great Britain." In essence, were the United States to lose a friend, it would gain a fleet. It was the same sort of guarantee the British had wanted from the French. Yet the United States was a noncombatant, not an ally fighting alongside the British as the British had fought alongside the French. Churchill, not pleased, sent a cool response to the president on August 31: "You ask, Mr. President, whether my statement in Parliament on June 4th, 1940, about Great

Britain never surrendering or scuttling her Fleet 'represents the settled policy of His Majesty's Government.' It certainly does. I must, however, observe that those hypothetical contingencies seem more likely to concern the German fleet or what is left of it than our own."[241]

These were bold words, yet Churchill had done his naval calculations: Britain had a fleet of capital ships, including aircraft carriers, and more than nine hundred smaller, but very dangerous, craft. The Germans had nothing of the sort. In the end, no direct linkage between U.S. destroyers and a defeated British fleet made its way into the deal. Rather, the down payment for the destroyers took the form of British naval bases in Newfoundland, Bermuda, and the Caribbean, leased to the Americans for ninety-nine years. Roosevelt, in explaining the transaction to Congress, could not resist the urge to gloat over the killing he had just made in the real-estate market: "The right to bases in Newfoundland and Bermuda are gifts—generously given and gladly received. The other bases mentioned have been acquired in exchange for fifty of our over-age destroyers." The first eight of the over-age destroyers sailed to Britain in early September. Churchill took them. At that point he'd take anything.

Despite the ad hoc nature of England's defenses in June and early July, by September a transformation had taken place. All summer the War Office, under Anthony Eden, had worked around the clock, rebuilding the army. By mid-July Britain had 1,500,000 men under arms; five weeks later Churchill told the House of Commons, "More than 2,000,000 determined men have rifles and bayonets in their hands tonight, and three-quarters of them are in regular military formations. We have never had armies like this in our island in time of war. The whole island bristles against invaders, from the sea or from the air." Those numbers included the Home Guard, but they also included rebuilt regular army infantry and armored units, and the Canadian division. Churchill could not, of course, speak publicly of the specifics of the military transformation, but with each passing week, he grew more sanguine about the fate of any Germans who arrived on British soil. By August the regular army fielded seven divisions between the Thames and the Wash, the great estuary one hundred miles north of London, where the chiefs expected the Germans to come. But by then, invasion barges were streaming through the Channel at night toward the French Channel ports. That meant the Germans might come to the south coast, where only five divisions stood ready, with three in reserve. But by September the situation was even further improved. The troop disposition north of London amounted to four divisions and an armored brigade. In the south, nine divisions were deployed, and two armored brigades. One division was stationed near London, where, if the Germans got that far, Churchill intended to fight street by street. And two divisions and six hundred tanks formed a reserve.[242]

As England's defenses improved, Churchill felt confident enough to send to Egypt almost half of the best tanks in Britain, 48 anti-tank guns, 20 Bofors light anti-aircraft guns (desperately needed in London), and 250 anti-tank rifles. He did so to blunt an anticipated Italian attack, which duly took place on September 13.[243]

In August, having secured his gains in Ethiopia, Il Duce had marched his armies into British Somaliland, where they humiliated the British. Churchill fumed to Eden that "the losses sustained are not compatible with resolute resistance." In particular, Churchill's doubts about his Middle East commander, Archibald Wavell, were growing. Yet, given that Somaliland's entire defense budget for the year was less than £900 ($3,600), how much resistance *could* have been forthcoming? Wavell's casualties during the withdrawal from Somaliland had been light, a fact that the MP for Aberdeenshire, Robert Boothby, recalled infuriated the Old Man, who took it as a sign of a lack of fighting spirit, and so informed Wavell. Wavell replied, "Butchery is not the mark of a good tactician." Churchill was wrong, and he knew it. Generally, those who stood up to him were accorded his respect, but Wavell was the exception to the norm.[244]

On September 13, Mussolini plunged his dagger into Wavell's western flank. On that day, General Rodolfo Graziani, in command of the Italian Tenth Army and 80,000 of Italy's finest troops — infantry, motorized, and led by 300 tanks — lunged eastward out of Libya and into Egypt, driving Wavell's surprised and disordered troops before him. Technically, by crossing the Egyptian frontier, Mussolini had invaded a neutral country, not that such diplomatic niceties were of any concern to Il Duce. Egypt had gained its independence from Britain in 1922 and had been ruled since 1936 by King Farouk I. Farouk despised his British protectors, who were in Egypt by virtue of a 1936 treaty that granted Britain de facto sovereignty were the Suez Canal to be endangered, which, theoretically, it was. Farouk rather admired fascism, especially the Italian variety, as did many of the younger officers in the Egyptian army, including a pair of unknowns named Gamal Abdel Nasser and Anwar Sadat. Egypt's politics were so striated by anti-British, pro-Axis, and nationalist factions that a declaration of war against the invading Italians could not be agreed upon. Thus, HMG kept a watchful eye on Farouk while British diplomats and generals ran the country. Graziani's fight was never with the Egyptian people — many welcomed his presence — but with the British. In Graziani, Mussolini had found his hero. To subvert the Italians' progress Churchill ordered Wavell to poison any wells that "we do not need for ourselves." The Italians pressed on for five days and sixty miles, to Sidi Barrani, where they paused to resupply. Then, inexplicably, given their advantage, rather than strike toward Alexandria and the Suez, they made camp, to the great relief of the outnumbered Tommies to the east. In addition to Graziani's 80,000 men, the Italians had 150,000 more in reserve in Libya. Wavell's Cairo command consisted of fewer than 40,000 men, including cooks, chaplains, and orderlies. His isolation was now total, but Churchill intended to reinforce him.[245]

Brooke had been correct when he told his diary that Churchill was offense-minded. To that end, the prime minister ordered 70,000 troops shipped to Egypt, a journey of almost 14,000 miles and fifty days around the Cape of Good Hope, a trip made necessary because the Mediterranean was, by virtue of the Italian fleet, no longer a British lake. The troops would be followed, Churchill hoped, by more than 50,000 before late December. They were sent not merely to defend Egypt against the Italians but because Churchill intended to take the attack to the Italians in Libya. His private secretary, John Martin, later declared that the dispatch of the troops and armor at a time when Britain herself was vulnerable was an act of courage by Churchill, Eden, and the Chiefs of Staff.[246]

It was also necessary. The security of the British Isles, as it had been since the Napoleonic Wars, was bound to the security of the Mediterranean. The Battle of Britain and the Battle for Egypt were two sides of the same coin. Neither would survive if the other fell. The tanks and men had to be sent.

On the day Graziani struck, September 13, Hitler lunched with the army's Halder and von Brauchitsch, the navy's Raeder, and a Luftwaffe *Jagdfliegerführer* (fighter pilot commander) representing Göring. Luftwaffe intelligence continued to be wildly inaccurate; they were told that although "the prerequisites for *Seelöwe* have not been completely realized," in the past five weeks, their airmen had shot down 1,800 British planes, which would have been double Dowding's total fighter strength. (The actual figure was about 500 RAF fighter planes.) However, the Führer mused, destruction of the RAF might be unnecessary; if their capital was subjected to terror bombing, the British might be seized by "mass hysteria," and the invasion could be canceled. The bombing of London, which had begun on September 7, would continue.[247]

In shifting the German *schwerpunkt* (focus point) from specific military and industrial targets to Greater London, Hitler gave permission, Jodl wrote, "for the use of strong air forces in reprisal attacks against London." It was to mean monumental suffering for British civilians. It also meant defeat for Göring's strategy just as it was about to meet with success.[248]

The fighting in the air reached a climax on Sunday, September 15, which later became known as Battle of Britain Day. Churchill witnessed it; because "the weather on this day seemed suitable to the enemy," he wrote, he and Clementine drove to Park's headquarters at Uxbridge. There they were taken to the bombproof operations room fifty feet belowground, which he compared to "a small theater," adding, "We took our seats in the dress circle." A large-scale map table with rows of lightbulbs above made the chaos in the sky overhead comprehensible. The defenders' commitment was total; when his visitor asked about reserves, Park looked grave and replied, "There are none." In Churchill's words, "The odds were great; our margins small; the stakes infinite." Like the Battle of Waterloo, also fought on a Sunday, this was what Wellington had called "a close-run thing." But it, too, ended in a great British triumph. At the end of the afternoon, Churchill was told that 138 German planes had been shot down at a cost of 26 RAF aircraft, and though the figure for German losses later proved to be higher than it actually was, the significance of the day's fighting could not have been greater. That evening, in a message to Dowding meant for enemy consumption, Churchill declared that the British, "using only a small proportion of their total strength," had "cut to tatters separate waves of murderous assault upon the civil population of their native land." Two days later he told Parliament, "Sunday's action was the most brilliant and fruitful of any fought up to that date by the fighters of the Royal Air Force."[249]

The Germans had been badly stung, and they knew it. The German Supreme Command of the Armed Forces (OKW) reported "large air battles and great losses for the German formations due to lack of fighter protection." The day's operations, involving over three hundred German bombers and one thousand German fighter sorties, were called "unusually disadvantageous," with the heaviest losses when the raiders were homeward bound. In addition, the invasion forces could not be kept at the ready, because the RAF, hitting the Channel ports, was taking a mounting toll of German barges and transports. Churchill and his intelligence chiefs could not know, but it was the death of Sea Lion. On September 17, Hitler postponed the invasion indefinitely on the grounds that winter was approaching and the RAF was "by no means defeated." The Führer had turned his attention to maps of Russia. A German staff officer expressed relief at the prospect of "a real war."[250]

The German high command had been induced to make a momentous strategic shift by a handful of young men in their Hurricanes and Spitfires. More than 400 of those airmen came from overseas: Czechs (80), Poles

(140), New Zealanders (120), Canadians (110), a smattering of Americans, Irishmen, Australians, Belgians, South Africans, and a lone Palestinian from the British Protectorate. Churchill felt profound admiration for the pilots. "But, it is terrible," he told Colville, "terrible, that the British Empire should have gambled on this." That Britain survived to designate September 15 Battle of Britain Day was as much due to Hitler's change of strategy—from destroying the RAF to destroying British cities—as it was to British radar, RAF fighter planes, and their pilots. The German air assault, Churchill later wrote, "was a tale of divided counsels, conflicting purposes and never fully realized plans. Three or four times in these months the enemy abandoned a method of attack which was causing us severe stress, and turned to something new." Thus, that phase of the Battle of Britain did not end with either side in retreat or with Germany mounting a final assault. It did not end with the British knowing that by not losing they had won. Rather, the Battle of Britain overlapped and merged with a new battle, the Battle of London, which, though no one knew it on the fifteenth, had actually begun the previous week. In time, Londoners, looking back, gave the battle a starting date: September 7. They soon gave it a name: the Blitz.[251]

In the East End, the fires of September 7 burned into the morning of the eighth. Not for 274 years—to the week—had London burned so. Seven feet below street level in the ancient precincts once bounded by Roman walls, and later by medieval ramparts, a thin layer of ocher earth testifies to the Great Fire of September 2, 1666. A stiff easterly wind fanned that conflagration for five days, during which it consumed St. Paul's Cathedral, 87 parish churches, and more than 13,000 houses. Yet only twenty unfortunate citizens perished. Within fifteen years Christopher Wren had built fifty-two new parish churches, and by the end of the seventeenth century, he had almost completed his new St. Paul's Cathedral, the dome of which, along with the spires of his churches, had since defined the London skyline. The steeple of St. Mary-le-Bow was one of the most fabulous. In time, Londoners born within earshot of the bells of St. Mary's claimed the right to call themselves Cockneys. They were the first to experience the fury of German bombs. Within days the German bombers no longer made an effort to pinpoint the industrial facilities. London, all of London, became the target, and the entire city was soon hit. It was, said Churchill, "an ordeal for the world's largest city, the results of which no one could measure beforehand."[252]

Several feet beneath the strata of gravel that marks the Great Fire of 1666, another layer of clay, rust-red from oxidized iron, records the first-century story of the warrior queen Boudicca, who torched Roman Londinium. She watched as the Romans came to steal her country, and after she had seen enough, she killed and burned the invader. Plague, smallpox, typhus, and cholera had in the centuries since killed tens of thousands of Londoners, and fire was a constant enemy, but not in the nearly nineteen centuries since Boudicca's revolt had any foe slaughtered Londoners wholesale or reduced the city by fire. By air, here now came Hitler, who had promised to raze English cities, London first.

On the morning of September 8, Churchill and Clementine visited the East End. They noted the "pathetic little Union Jacks" flying from the rubble of what until the previous night had been homes. They stopped outside a shelter that had taken a direct hit, and where forty men, women, and children had died. Churchill, visibly moved, dabbed his eyes with a large white handkerchief. For a moment he and the residents commingled in silence. Then someone yelled: "When are you going to bomb Berlin?" He replied, "You leave that to me." General Ismay recalled the crowd storming Churchill with cries of "We thought you'd come" and "We can take it." An old woman said, "You see, he really cares, he's crying." Some in the crowd begged, "You've got to make them stop." More than one million East Enders had returned to their homes after having been evacuated the previous autumn, when a German bombing campaign was expected at any moment. When the air war did not materialize, they drifted back to familiar neighborhoods, which now collapsed and burned around and atop numbed and terrified residents. Churchill told the gathered what they wanted to hear, that he would hit back, yet a profound grasp of the precariousness of their situation underlay his words: Hitler might reduce their homes, their city, but only by reducing their spirit could he inflict defeat. That test of will had begun. No Europeans had thus far withstood the ordeal. The Luftwaffe, two hundred bombers strong, escorted by four hundred fighters, returned while Churchill was still in the East End. As the raid began, he left through narrow streets blocked by houses that had been blown across them. The warehouses near the docks still burned, spewing forth the merchant wealth of Britain—torrents of flaming whisky, molten sugar, textiles, foodstuffs, and ammunition ablaze and exploding.[253]

More than four hundred East Enders died in the first raid. Thousands more were made homeless. Yet the next day, while the East End burned, Churchill asked Admiral Pound for his help in explaining to Roosevelt the need for merchant ships outfitted with prows and side ports, "to enable tanks to be landed from them on the beaches, or into tank landing craft which could take them to the beaches." The tank transports were not due for delivery until 1942. The beaches Churchill had in mind were those of France. Weeks earlier, with his air forces and country in mortal peril, he told Colville he expected "by 1942 we shall have achieved air superiority and shall be ready for the great offensive operations on land against Germany." Only an optimist could make such a statement. Yet during Britain's darkest hours, when its airborne defenses were being subjected to relentless attack, Churchill plotted his offense.[254]

Defense, however, was London's first order of business against the German aerial armadas. But the world's greatest city could muster virtually none. Many of the city's anti-aircraft guns had been moved to protect outlying airfields and aircraft factories. Only ninety-two AA guns remained to safeguard London. Their previously limited use proved they fired with pathetic effect. For three straight nights, from the seventh to the ninth, they did not fire at all. With the anti-aircraft guns quiet, London's defenses were handed off to night fighters from No. 11 Group. They inflicted few kills. Hundreds of searchlights threw long spears of light into the night sky, a comforting sight to Londoners but of no tactical significance; searchlights could not find targets that flew higher than 12,000 feet. German pilots flew far above the light. Radio-controlled coordination between searchlights and anti-aircraft guns held promise, but the technology—code-named Elsie—had entered the testing stage only weeks earlier. Not until early 1941 would the first AA guns (Churchill always called them "cannons") be outfitted with fire-control radar. Barrage balloons (used to support wires or nets as protection against air attacks) kept enemy planes high, making German targeting more difficult and reducing bomb accuracy, but the Germans were more intent on causing terror than achieving accuracy.[255]

Churchill ordered a doubling of the number of anti-aircraft guns, at the expense of Sheffield, Birmingham, and the tidy West Midlands city of Coventry. Still, the guns remained silent. He then ordered a battery placed in Hyde Park, "where people can hear them blast off." Finally, on the tenth, London's AA guns opened up, pouring thousands of shells into the night sky; the trails of tracer rounds and the beams of searchlights converged and intersected and splayed crazily in the blackness. The guns fired blind, in a box barrage rather than at particular targets. The effect on the German bombers was nil. The guns themselves probably suffered more damage, as their barrels had to be retooled after a few hundred rounds were fired. But the cacophony comforted Londoners. The next day, Harold Nicolson wrote in his diary, "The barrage put up by our A.A. guns cheered people enormously, although people in the East End are still frightened and angry."[256]

For Londoners (except those flush few who could escape to their country houses), the second week of September ushered in a terrible new way of life, and death. German bombers returned most mornings and afternoons for the next month, and for seventy-six consecutive nights, except November 2, when the weather grounded anything with wings. At about eight o'clock each evening, Londoners heard the nervous wailing of the air-raid sirens, which they called "Weeping Willies"; Churchill compared them to "a banshee howling."At the alarm, those with shelters headed there. Within minutes the German bombers were overhead, sowing terror into the night. The first Heinkels marked targets by dropping incendiaries. These were nasty little two-pounders with thermite cores that burned at two thousand degrees, igniting wooden rooftops, which, as they blazed high, became signal fires to guide in more waves of planes bearing high-explosive bombs. Now the blinding flashes of explosions illuminated the vast city, followed by the orchestrated sounds and smells of the raid—the odd *crumping* of the discharged bombs, their whistling as they fell, the stench of cordite and, later, the odor of gas escaping in the shattered buildings—and then the buildings burning in the quenchless flames of hell. Hour after hour it continued until, at dawn, the all-clear sounded and people emerged from homes and shelters into the new day's light: "gray disheveled figures," Malcolm Muggeridge wrote, "like a Brueghel painting of resurrection day—predestined souls rising from their graves."[257]

They rose from the terror bombing that Stanley Baldwin had so feared, against which he said there could be no defense and for which he had planned no defense. They emerged each morning into broken streets covered with smoldering rubble, the dead yellow eye of the sun leering down through a sky smudged by the ashes of their homes, the ashes of their neighbors, their families. They emerged to encounter scenes of monstrous destruction. Smashed pipes swung wildly from skeletal buildings, the facades peeled off, to reveal furnished interiors, like the sectional view of a child's dollhouse. They rose to fires still burning, to stinking raw sewage seeping down gutters. They emerged to unexploded bombs buried up to the fins in marl and mud, just waiting for the clumsy jolt that would start the fuse softly buzzing. They stumbled into lanes so strewn with the glass of shattered windows that Churchill feared a "glass famine." And each morning, hundreds who had sought shelter the night before or rode out the storm in their flats—14,000 Londoners by year's end—did not emerge at all.[258]

On some mornings, folks wandering the wreckage espied a beefy apparition: the prime minister, *their* prime minister. They called him "Winnie," the boyhood nickname he hated but now grew to love. He might be bundled in his Royal Air Force overcoat, his gold-topped walking stick employed to smack rubble out of his path, and he'd likely be gripping a substantial cigar. He might be in the company of Ismay, Clementine, his brother, Jack, or MP and longtime friend Brendan Bracken. But most important, he was there, with them.

Bertrand Russell—logician, pacifist, and Churchill's contemporary—predicted in 1936 that an air attack would turn London "into one vast raving bedlam, the hospitals will be stormed, traffic will cease, the homeless will shriek for help, the city will be a pandemonium," and the government itself "will be swept away by an avalanche of terror." British Fascists and Communists—"those filthy communists," Churchill fumed, were more dangerous than the Fascists—had in turn predicted that an air assault on the East End and London's poor would lead inexorably to either revolution or, at the very least, Churchill's ouster, the formation of a new government, and a negotiated peace. Hitler was counting on very much the same. Britain's Communist newspaper, *The Daily Worker,* remained stridently anti-war, and encouraged workers to take to the streets to display their displeasure with the government. London authorities had predicted the need for regular army troops to maintain order at shelters, but the primary focus of officials was not to control mobs but to tend to the wounded and bury the legions of expected dead. For this they were well prepared. London hospitals had readied beds for 150,000 casualties, but that was thought inadequate; the Imperial Defence Committee estimated that a Luftwaffe bombing of London would leave 600,000 dead and over a million wounded. They had bulldozers dig huge pits outside London; these would become mass graves. Thousands of papier-mâché coffins were readied and a million burial forms were printed, but little consideration had been given to sheltering the obstinate unwounded.[259]

This was more than an assault on bricks and mortar; it was an attack on the spirit of London's eight million citizens. Churchill said as much in a defiant BBC broadcast on September 11: "These cruel wanton, indiscriminate bombings of London are, of course, a part of Hitler's invasion plans. He hopes, by killing large numbers of civilians, and women and children, that he will terrorize and cow the people of this mighty imperial city.... Little does he know the spirit of the British nation, and the tough fibre of Londoners."[260]

During that broadcast he again invoked the "invasion scare," in pursuit of his dual objectives—to build up his armies and air forces in 1941 in order to launch large-scale offensive operations on the Continent in 1942. In a BBC broadcast that day, he prepared the British people for the worst. If the invasion was coming, he told them:

It does not seem that it can be long delayed. The weather may break at any time.... Therefore, we must regard the next week or so as a very important period in our history. It ranks with the days when the

Spanish Armada was approaching the Channel, and Drake was finishing his game of bowls; or when Nelson stood between us and Napoleon's Grand Army at Boulogne. We have read all about this in the history books; but what is happening now is on a far greater scale and of far more consequence to the life and future of the world and its civilization than these brave old days of the past.[261]

He described the assembly of self-propelled barges at Dunkirk, Brest, and Cherbourg; the "tens of dozens" of merchant ship convoys moving through the Strait of Dover into the Channel; the concentration of shipping in German, Dutch, Belgian, and French harbors; and the troop ships in Norwegian harbors. No one, he warned them, "should blind himself to the fact that a heavy, full-scale invasion of this Island with all the usual German thoroughness and method may be launched now upon England, Scotland, or Ireland, or upon all three." Or, as he believed, an invasion may *not* be launched.[262]

His words blazed. So did London. Churchill fully realized that given enough bombs, London, especially the older buildings, would be reduced to rubble. He knew that the mettle and "tough fibre" of Britons had not yet been fully tested, let alone proven. This would be a battle of attrition of unknown duration, and increasing fury. How long—how many weeks, perhaps months, perhaps years—could the Luftwaffe keep up the punishment? He knew Londoners were looking skyward with fearful certainty that the bombardment was the softening up before the final blow—invasion. And if the invasion did not come that year, it might come the next.

But Londoners, though pummeled, did not crack. Scores of tens of thousands had not been killed, as officials had expected. Their ordeal was terrible, but Londoners were taking it. They might have called the bombing raids "The Great Terror" or "The Burning," or any number of monikers that captured the enormity of their predicament, but the word that stuck was *Blitz*. It conjures *blitzkrieg*, with all its ferocity, yet it also diminishes it, cuts it down to size, and manifests a hint of defiance, of spirit.

Even blacked out, London's geography and layout conspired to make it an ideal aerial target. From 15,000 feet overhead, bathed even in modest moonlight, the entire metropolis stretched before German pilots like a well-marked parchment chart. The Thames estuary guided the Germans westward from the North Sea, past refineries and oil tank farms. The great

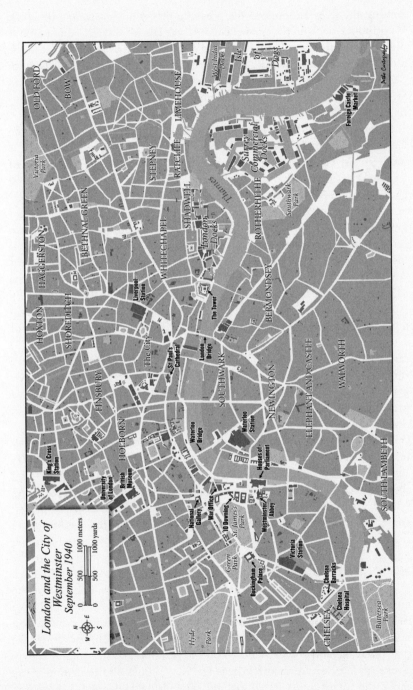

London and the City of
Westminster
September 1940

OLD FORD
BOW
Victoria Park
HOXTON
HAGGERSTON
BETHNAL GREEN
SHOREDITCH
FINSBURY
The City
HOLBORN
King's Cross Station
University of London
British Museum
STEPNEY
WHITECHAPEL
RATCLIFF
LIMEHOUSE
SHADWELL
London Docks
West India Docks
Isle of Dogs
Surrey Commercial Docks
ROTHERHITHE
Thames
Southwark Park
BERMONDSEY
Liverpool Station
St Paul's Cathedral
The Tower
London Bridge
SOUTHWARK
Waterloo Bridge
Waterloo Station
NEWINGTON
ELEPHANT AND CASTLE
WALWORTH
National Gallery
War Office
10 Downing
St James's Park
Houses of Parliament
Westminster Abbey
Green Park
Buckingham Palace
Victoria Station
Chelsea Barracks
Chelsea Hospital
CHELSEA
Hyde Park
Battersea Park
SOUTH LAMBETH
Foreign Cattle Market
Pete Contografty

bend in the river announced the presence below of vast warehouses, the West India Dock and the Victoria and Albert Docks. On clear and moonlit nights, St. Paul's great Latin cross was visible from thousands of feet in the air and from miles away, and marked the center of London as clearly as an "X" on a treasure map. The dark and empty swaths of Hyde Park and St. James's Park served to guide bombardiers to still more targets: Whitehall, Buckingham Palace, and the Houses of Parliament.[263]

In fact, Churchill had known since the first days of summer that the German night bombers were being guided to their targets by something far more precise than landscape features. In late June, the British confirmed long-held suspicions that the Germans were employing a shortwave navigational beam—code-named *Knickebein* ("crooked leg")—to guide their bombers to targets. This was very unwelcome news. Here indeed was an innovation that just might help Hitler make good on his promise to raze English cities. *Knickebein* was based on the Lorenz radio–controlled instrument-flying technology that had been developed in Germany eight years earlier and was used on many U.S. and European commercial flights to guide pilots the final few miles to airfields.

But a Lorenz-like signal was accurate only over short distances; at two hundred miles it could bring an aircraft to within only one or two miles of a target. The Germans had been doing much better than that in night raids, which raised the specter of their having developed a new and very sophisticated radio-beam technology. Bombing accuracy equates to navigational accuracy; if a bomber could be guided at night or in clouds to a precise point over a target, its bombs could accordingly be dropped with precision.

Two of Churchill's science advisers, Sir Henry Tizard and Prof Lindemann, agreed on one generally accepted scientific belief: shortwave radio signals did not bend—that is, follow the curvature of the earth—and therefore could not serve as effective long-range navigational and targeting guides. That attribute of radio waves was why the altitude at which British coastal radar could "see" German aircraft increased as the distance from the transmitter increased. It was to Tizard as much as anyone—including Fighter Command's Hugh Dowding—that the British owed thanks for the Home Island's radar preparedness in 1940. Sir Henry was an old RAF man, chairman of the Aeronautical Defence Committee, and one of the most respected scientists in England. In the late 1930s, Tizard pushed hard to build coastal radar stations and stressed the need for radio coordination between RAF pilots and those radar stations. Tizard believed, correctly, that radar opened a wide window on the position and heading of enemy aircraft. He believed, incorrectly as Dr. R. V. Jones was to demonstrate, that radio waves could not contribute to precision navigation. Tizard was of the old school of RAF celestial navigation by "shooting" the stars. Airmen did so because no better method of navigation had been developed. In Tizard's estimation, the rumored German beam could not improve long-range navigation because it simply would not work due to the earth's curvature.

But in early June, Jones, one of Lindemann's former Oxford students (he was just twenty-eight), demonstrated to Lindemann's satisfaction that the Germans were in fact using long-range radio beams for targeting. A few days later, Jones briefed Tizard. Tizard, who understood radio waves as much as anyone alive (or thought he did), voiced doubts.[264]

Tizard and the Prof had fought an academic feud for almost a decade. They had tangled in 1935 when both served on an Air Defense subcommittee chaired by Tizard. Lindemann's appointment to the committee came via Churchill, who was also a committee member. Tizard had argued for coastal radar, Lindemann for more fighter planes. Both were correct, but Lindemann, frustrated, left the committee. While Tizard continued his work on radar, Lindemann became a Churchill crony and primary science adviser. Tizard retained the respect of the science community, but not of Churchill. The Prof realized that if he and young Dr. Jones solved *Knickebein,* he would not only solidify his position with Churchill but also finally put paid to his old adversary Tizard.

Lindemann prevailed upon Churchill to give young Jones a hearing. Churchill called Tizard, Jones, and Lindemann together on June 21, along with the minister of air, Archie Sinclair, sundry RAF brass, Beaverbrook, and Robert Watson Watt, the father of radar. Dr. Jones held the group spellbound for twenty minutes. He hypothesized that Germans pilots were flying between two radio signals originating at different towers. One beam emitted a series of "dots," the other a series of "dashes." The pilot maneuvered his plane between the beams until the "dots" and "dashes" he received merged into a steady buzz, indicating that he was exactly between the signals and on course. Guided by such a beam, German bombers could put their bombs within an area one mile square, which in 1940 amounted to pinpoint accuracy. Jones asked permission to conduct field tests that he believed would verify his hypothesis. Even Churchill listened without interruption and in awed silence as Jones told the tale, a "chain of circumstantial evidence," Churchill later wrote, "the like of which for its convincing fascination was never surpassed by tales of Sherlock Holmes or Monsieur Lecoq."[265]

When Jones finished, no one spoke. There was in the room, recalled Churchill, "a general air of incredulity." Then Churchill angrily pounded the table and demanded countermeasures to the beams from the Air Ministry, which had up to this point given him only "files, files, files!"[266]

The meeting was finished. So was Tizard. Churchill recalled that "one high authority" in attendance "asked why the Germans should use a beam, assuming that such a thing was possible, when they had at their disposal all the ordinary facilities of navigation." Others at the table, however, "appeared concerned." The insouciant high authority, who clung to the same belief Lindemann had jettisoned just days earlier, went unnamed by Churchill.[267]

It was Tizard. Whether or not Sir Henry had been set up, the result was the same: he had stepped into an open manhole. Having failed to identify the danger of the German beams in his capacity as defender of the air, Tizard offered to resign. Churchill declined, and instead sent Tizard off to the United States—out of sight, out of mind—as head of a small delegation of British scientists. Their mission to explore the exchange of new technologies with the Americans emerged as one of the most critical successes of science and diplomacy during the war. (Yet the mission almost didn't leave home, when Churchill fretted that too much in the way of British technological know-how might be going to the Americans.)

Before he left, Tizard set up a science committee, code-named Maud (for Military Application of Uranium Detonation), to investigate the feasibility of building a nuclear fission bomb using uranium-235. Two expatriate German physicists, Otto Frisch and Rudolf Peierls, thought it could be done; Tizard himself thought the prospects doubtful. Still, Sir Henry appointed six British scientists to the Maud Committee; Frisch and Peierls, by virtue of their alien status, could not serve. With Maud in place, Tizard set off for America. As a direct result of Sir Henry's American mission, Bell Labs began mass-producing for use by the British the cavity magnetron, an English invention and the key to more accurate long-range radar. Tizard's mission resulted, too, in a sense among his American peers that Britain just might survive, or at the least not die just yet. Tizard was astute enough to bring along film footage, shot from Hurricanes and Spitfires, of dogfights and of burning German aircraft spiraling earthward. His contacts in the U.S. military were mightily impressed. Sir Henry converted the unfaithful. Churchill had long warned anyone who listened that science—for good or ill—would win the war, and in the end he was proven correct. But the "Wizard War," as Churchill termed it, was at first fought as desperately between his wizards—Lindemann and Tizard—as between his wizards and those of Hitler's.

Having discovered the German beam (which the RAF code-named Headache), the British needed to defeat it, and soon. Jamming *Knickebein* wouldn't do; the Germans would simply broadcast on another frequency. The British needed a craftier solution to *Knickebein,* and by August had come up with their antidote, which they code-named Aspirin. British transmitters broadcast "dashes" on the same frequency as the German signals, but boosted the power of the decoy "dashes," with the result that German pilots slowly drifted off course while trying to align themselves with the false signal. By late August, Churchill took delight in reports that entire loads of German bombs dropped at night were falling harmlessly into cow pastures, miles from the intended targets. However, those targets were airfields, factories, small ports, and cities, where an error of only a few miles put the enemy over farmland, but no cow pastures dotted the London landscape. A German bomb that missed St. Paul's or the docks by a county mile would detonate not in the countryside but somewhere in Greater London. Still, in his memoir, R. V. Jones claims that "a substantial proportion of bombs went astray" due to the British countermeasures against *Knickebein,* though he does not say how far astray.[268]

Even without the beam, German night bombers could hardly miss London, and German day bombers did not need the beam. Metropolitan London, twenty-eight boroughs comprising more than 750 square miles, and home to almost eight million people, spread outward in all compass points from the center. Yet London's most critical communications centers and supply links were packed together within walking distance of St. Paul's: six railroad stations, the Wood Street Telephone Exchange, General Post Office, London Telephone Exchange, Royal Exchange, and Bank of England. The Guildhall, rebuilt after the 1666 fire, was still the seat of municipal government and the control center for the city's firefighting operations. It would soon burn again. Bombs now dropped into streets of old London lore and nursery rhyme fame, such as Shoe Lane, where Beaverbrook's *Standard* took a direct hit in its rooftop water tower, flooding the building. A David Low cartoon in the next day's edition showed a Cockney lad hawking papers. The headline: BOMB SEVERELY DAMAGED IN SHOE LANE.

Pudding Lane, where the Great Fire had started in a bakery, burned again. Buildings that were standing more than two centuries before Berlin was founded were battered and smashed. Red dust from their ancient bricks drifted through demolished interiors, to settle in old undercrofts, the newest strata in London's soil, someday long hence to tell the story. From the center, narrow and twisting lanes lined with small shops and great nineteenth-century textile warehouses ran east and northeast to the East End, where London's working class lived on narrower streets lined with mean brick tenements, music halls, and old breweries. The workhouses of the East End had come down at the turn of the century, but vast tracts of Dickensian slums remained in some of the poorest areas. These were neighborhoods that still smelled of smoke and sweat, of horses and the effluent from old wood and iron pipes that leeched into the Thames: Silvertown, Poplar, Millwall, Stepney, and West Ham. Neighborhoods whose names rolled musically off Cockney tongues and conjured a locale's medieval origins were blown to dust and burned to ashes: the Minories (after the abbey of the Minoresses [or nuns] of St. Mary), and Elephant and Castle (after a famed eighteenth-century coaching inn), south across the Thames. Clement Attlee was the MP from Limehouse, named for the lime kilns, and as degraded a place in 1940 as it had been in 1919, when D. W. Griffith and Lillian Gish portrayed it in *Broken Blossoms*. And in Wapping, the descendants of Famine Irish, who had fled to London almost a century earlier, lived packed together in vile slums hard by the London docks. And there they died.[269]

The London docks and nearby warehouses accounted for almost one-quarter of the jobs in Metropolitan London, and almost all of the work for East End men. The previous year more than 50,000 ships had tied up to load and unload almost 40 percent of Britain's commerce. By 1942, fewer than 15,000 would steam up the Thames. The docks were the mercantile life of London, and they were dying.

Northwest of central London, the borough of Hampstead was home to 25,000 Jews, and would have been home to far more but for the government's reluctance to allow more Jewish refugees into the country for fear of fostering anti-Semitism. George Orwell thought there was less anti-Semitism abroad in the land than there had been thirty years earlier, but there was still enough dangerous and ugly anti-Jewish sentiment to blind Londoners to Nazi persecutions on the Continent. Orwell told his diary, Jews were "not only conspicuous, but go out of their way to make themselves so," with the result that "you switch off the wireless when the announcer begins talking about the ghettos in Warsaw." Jews monopolized the shelters, so went the canards, and demanded full compensation for bomb-damaged houses, and seemed to be eating pretty well, and never volunteered as fire wardens. These opinions were all lies built on misconceptions and old prejudices. The Home Office conducted a weekly survey of conditions in the shelters and determined that Jews behaved no differently than Gentiles; neither group, they found, "predominates among those who have evacuated themselves voluntarily through fear and hysteria." Jews, along with their Gentile neighbors, were getting by as best they could.[270]

To the north of the city, Islington and Stoke Newington, tidy locales, reached toward the new suburbs growing beyond the metropolitan boundary. Skilled workers, clerks, and factory managers lived there in neat flats, with well-tended gardens in the rear, and room enough among the roses and mums for an air-raid shelter. It was all a long way from the East End, but the bombs came. To the northwest, small factories—aircraft, machine tool, and auto parts—had moved into old textile plants. More than 14,000 such factories were scattered throughout Greater London. One-quarter of Britain's workforce labored there; one-half of all goods produced in England were manufactured within twenty miles of St. Paul's. This was the industrial heart of the empire.[271]

Two miles to the west of St. Paul's, the streets broadened and fed into the West End and the City of Westminster. More than a century earlier, John Nash had widened Regent Street, built the Carlton House terraces, designed St. James's Park, and transformed Piccadilly Circus into a pedestrian mall, thus assuring that the moneyed classes could stroll without care from their grand Regency town houses to their private clubs, to the pastoral precincts of St. James's Park, to the theaters of Piccadilly, and to the shops of New Bond Street.[272]

By mid-September, German bombs had smashed into Regent Street, into a courtyard within Buckingham Palace, and into St. James's Park, Churchill's favorite London venue for a midday stroll, which always included a stop by the lake to feed the ducks, who had by now taken themselves off to safer climes. Members of Parliament doused an incendiary bomb that had dropped into the House of Lords. The West End was hit, but not hard enough for some in the East End. On September 15, about fifty East Enders, outraged by the filthy shelters in their neighborhoods, invaded the West End. The Cockneys, spurred on by their Communist ward bosses and led by six pregnant women with babes in arms, streamed into the Savoy, where management maintained a splendid basement shelter, furnished with bunks, fresh bed linens, and bathing facilities. The constabulary was summoned. Shocked hotel guests and the surly Cockneys faced off in the lobby. In an inspired maneuver, the hotel managing director opened the dining room to the protesters. The staff brewed tea. All ended in calmness. The East Enders departed, without incident.[273]

Every quarter was hit. Chelsea and South Kensington, cityscapes of town houses, their limestone facades blackened by more than a century of London's fuliginous air, marked the far western reaches of Georgian London. Bombs crashed down in Chelsea and onto Victoria Station. South across the Thames and along its banks stretched Southwark, where the Archbishop of Canterbury kept his official residence, Lambeth Palace. When the bombs threatened his cathedral and its treasures, the archbishop expressed his deep concern to Churchill, who assured the prelate that every precaution had been taken to protect it. The archbishop asked what would happen if a bomb were to score a direct hit. Churchill, ever ready with a blasphemous aside, replied, "In that case, my dear Archbishop, you will have to regard it as a divine summons."[274]

Eastward from Southwark, the boroughs of Battersea, Greenwich, and Woolwich spread along the south bank of the Thames. The Woolwich Arsenal, which produced bombs for the RAF, had been the first target hit on September 7.

London's buildings presented stone and brick faces, but their bones were wood—rafters, beams, struts, stairs, flooring, millions of board feet of lumber, old, dry and combustible. The Thames served as London's main source of water for fighting fires. When the moon's phase so conspired, the Thames ran low and narrow. The London Fire Brigade—1,500 spit-and-polish firemen who manned 130 red fire engines and ladder trucks—formed the city's regular fire service. They were backed up by the Auxiliary Fire Service, the mechanical end of which consisted of three thousand small pumpers that had to be towed behind another vehicle, often a black London taxi. Twenty thousand men and five thousand women from all manner of professions—carpenters, cooks, nannies, clerics, and clerks—manned the pumpers, five to a pump. Together, they could clamp 87 miles of hose to the city's 31,439 fire hydrants. A fire's size was measured by how many pumpers were needed to fight it. Prewar, a thirty-pumper was considered a large and dangerous fire. During the Blitz, one-hundred-pumpers were common. December 29 brought the firefighters' most terrible night. They called it the Second Great Fire of London. The regulars and auxiliaries would not so much fight the fire as watch it as it reduced to ash the heart of Wren's London, because the moon was new, and the Thames ran narrow and shallow, and there was scarce water to pump.[275]

On September 17 delayed-action bombs fell into St. James's Park. High explosives dropped near No. 10 and the Foreign Office, which had to be evacuated. Buckingham Palace suffered a hit, and in the ruins of Madame Tussaud's, waxwork arms and legs—including Hitler's—lay scattered about. The Germans, said Nicolson, had "smashed about Bond Street and readjusted the balance." West End, East End, they were all in it together.[276]

It was the night of the harvest moon. By then the Churchill family had been residents of No. 10 for three months, since the week of the French surrender (they had stayed in Admiralty House for the first four weeks of his premiership). No. 10, like the White House, was both a home and the office of the nation's leader. The first floor was all business, dominated by the grand Cabinet Room and the Private Office, as the prime minister's staff and their rooms were known. That was also true of the large state dining room on the second floor, though a white-paneled family dining room adjoined it, and upstairs was all private: large bedrooms with sash windows, cheerful red carpeting, and egg-shell-blue passages. In winter, coal fires glowed in every grate. It was, quite simply, a very pleasant place to live.[277]

Unfortunately it was also combustible and frail. Since June the Churchills had spent more and more time in the basement, either in the air-raid shelter or beside the kitchens, in fortified rooms that had been strengthened with huge beams, and with steel shutters shielding the windows. But the first week of the Blitz brought home the reality that No. 10 Downing Street was a potential death trap. One nearby explosion that Colville described as vast shook the house just as he was entering. He met Churchill, who insisted he had seen, from his bedroom window, a bomb hit Buckingham Palace. A bomb that fell near the Treasury split the east walls of No. 10. Another bomb exploded nearby one evening as Churchill hosted a dinner in the basement dining room. He excused himself and went to the kitchen, located in the rear, on the Treasury side, and ordered the cooks and servers to take shelter. Twenty seconds after they were gone, another large bomb fell between No. 10 and the Treasury. It lifted the entire kitchen floor of No. 10, flattened it against the wall, and crushed everything in between, including the iron cook stoves.[278]

Colville and Bracken agreed that it was "only a matter of days" before No. 10 "fell a victim" to the bombs. Safer quarters were available for the prime minister in Storey's Gate, two blocks away, where a bland stone government building, bearing a dull plaque reading CENTRAL STATISTICAL OFFICE, stood facing St. James's Park. Deep in the earth beneath it lay the Cabinet War Room. The CWR, also known as "The Hole," was actually an underground warren of small rooms, including a bedroom for the prime minister, with a desk, to which was affixed a BBC microphone.[279]

The CWR was for emergencies. For day-to-day living, the building's ground floor had been converted into a concrete-reinforced, steel-shuttered apartment, the No. 10 Annexe. The Annexe was comfortable, though, as Churchill's daughter Mary recalls, his and Clementine's rooms were off a corridor connecting government offices (there were 180 rooms in all, guarded by Royal Marines), "and embarrassed officials would often encounter Winston, robed like a Roman emperor in his bath towel, proceeding dripping across the main highway to his bedroom." Churchill, of course, was never disconcerted. He could appear completely nude without loss of dignity, and sometimes did.[280]

Yet the Annexe, as with No. 10, would be obliterated by a direct hit from a two-thousand-pounder. Churchill's family, friends, and even Chamberlain appealed to him to find more secure sleeping arrangements.

He finally succumbed to the pressure and in mid-October availed himself of the Down Street Underground shelter he called "The Burrow." Located eighty feet below Piccadilly, reinforced by steel and concrete, and closed off to trains, the shelter was the deepest, most secure, and most comfortable haven in London, built as the result of prescient prewar thinking on the part of the directors of the London Transport Executive. The directors had also considered the culinary needs of future shelterees: Caspian Caviar, Perrier-Jouët 1928, and 1865 brandy were always available. The finest cigars were plentiful, thanks to the Cuban consul who, late in the year, delivered five thousand after Churchill's inventory had atrophied. Churchill, when in London, took his rest in Down Street many nights that autumn. Then, for the remainder of the war, he and Clementine resided in the labyrinth of the Annexe (along with almost 270 officials, military planners, and armed soldiers). Clementine hung old pictures on the walls to add a bit of welcoming warmth. Winston protested that the walls should remain bare. She prevailed. He insisted on climbing to the exposed roof to view the raids. Clementine protested. He prevailed.[281]

During the first week of the Blitz, more than 5,000 East Enders, mostly women and children, fled London, some to Greenwich Park, Hampstead Heath, and by railway to points west. The residents of a West Country town compared them to refugees from Bordeaux during the collapse of France. Their possessions and rations fit into kerchiefs and pillowcases. Yet by month's end, fewer than 25,000 residents of the hardest hit neighborhoods had fled. The men stayed behind, to scrape up what work they could find. Many of their women stayed behind to keep an eye on their men. London's middle and upper-middle classes remained at their jobs and in their homes. Unlike Parisians, Londoners did not flee. The general panic and pandemonium predicted by Bertrand Russell was nonexistent. Russell, having renounced his pacifism in May, now safely bicycled between his mistress and his lectures at Harvard University, thousands of miles away in Cambridge, Massachusetts, where the only objects falling from the sky were the crimson maple leaves of autumn.[282]

Discipline, not squads of soldiers, ruled in the London shelters. Eight thousand sheltered each night at a railway goods disposal yard under the Tilbury Arches off the Commercial Road. They segregated themselves: Jews, Irish, Indians, West Indian blacks, Cockneys—each group spent the night in its own enclave, sleeping among horse droppings and standing water on piles of rubbish, folded cartons, and old newsprint. Two buckets served as communal latrines. The prewar planners who had predicted the need for regular army troops to maintain order were wrong. It took only a lone metropolitan policeman to control the long queue that formed each night.[283]

Such was life in the public shelters. The government also produced small, private shelters called Anderson shelters, designed in 1938 by the engineer William Paterson and named for Home Secretary Sir John Anderson. The Anderson shelters had been distributed to 150,000 London residents months earlier. They were flimsy affairs, assembled by bolting together thin sheets of galvanized steel. They lacked floors and were prone to collecting rainwater. They could accommodate six uncomfortably and offered some protection against shrapnel, but not against a direct or nearly direct hit. Their installation called for setting the footings deep in garden soil. Their very design rendered them largely useless for the Cockneys: the East End had been paved over for a century. London's poor held Anderson shelters and their namesake in contempt; if the contraptions had offered any real protection, it's a good bet they would have been called Paterson shelters.[284]

To look at Anderson, humorless and cold, recalled Viscount Antony Head (then a major in War Plans), "You could never possibly conceive that he had ever been a child. He was the opposite of Winston, who retained an awful lot of his childhood with him."[285]

In August 1939 Anderson and Chamberlain crafted the Emergency Powers (Defence) Act, which granted—like similar acts during the Great War—sweeping powers to the executive. But in May of 1940, when the 1939 act came up for renewal, Anderson, in a calculated circumvention of the King's Bench (the division of the English courts system that hears civil and criminal cases), added a new, draconian article (18B, 1A), which allowed for the detainment of people who were suspected of being Nazi sympathizers, thereby stripping Britons of rights they had held close since King John signed Magna Carta. Anderson argued that since detainees under 18B were not charged with a crime but were seized in order to *prevent* a crime, habeas corpus had not been compromised. Sir Oswald Mosley, of impeccable high birth, and for a decade the black-shirted head of England's Fascists, was one of the first detained. That his wife, Diana Mitford Guinness Mosley (one of the Mitford sisters), was also hauled away proved an embarrassment to the Churchill family, as she was Clementine's cousin. By year's end, more than a thousand British citizens (including known Fascists) and hundreds of refugees who had fled Hitler were detained, secretly imprisoned, without arraignment or trial.[286]

Anderson had been one of Chamberlain's most loyal toadies, a Tory's Tory. Churchill kept Anderson on as Home Secretary until October, when he brought him into the War Cabinet as Lord President of the Council. There his duties involved organizing Britain's civilian and economic financial resources, and arresting troublemakers who might impede the war effort. In that capacity Anderson set to work under 18B, rounding up suspected evildoers. Churchill instinctively loathed the idea of keeping "political opponents in prison on *lettres de cachet*," but embracing his emergency powers, he shot off a memo to Anderson: "Let me see a list of prominent persons you have arrested." A few days later he sent along to Anderson a list of "suspected persons" who resided in areas likely to be invaded. He instructed Sir John to "pray let me know in three days what action you find yourself able to take."

Where Churchill was only idly curious about the status of suspected fifth-columnists, he was deeply concerned about the status of London's poor. He ordered Anderson to address the drainage problem in Anderson shelters by instructing residents to place bricks on the edge and cover them with linoleum. The need to introduce some comfort into the shelters soon became moot when steel shortages decreed that England could have ships or shelters but not both. The Andersons were no longer built.[287]

East Enders resented their plight. Harold Nicolson noted the depth of their bitterness in his diary entry of September 17: "It is said even the King and Queen were booed the other day when they visited the destroyed areas. Clem (Davies) says that if only the Germans had the sense not to bomb west of London Bridge there might have been a revolution in the country."[288]

Yet, if fermenting a peasants' revolt was a collateral German hope, that dream died weeks later when a squadron of Stukas targeted Buckingham Palace during a midday raid and put three bombs into the palace court-yards, just one hundred meters from the King and Queen. If not for the good fortune of their windows being swung open at that moment, their majesties would have been cut to pieces by glass shards. The attack indi-cated, Churchill said, that the Germans "meant business." In terms of assault on hearth and home, it meant the royal family was now one with the East Enders. "I'm glad we've been bombed," the Queen said. "It makes me feel I can look the East End in the face." Churchill was furious when he learned that government censors had ordered news of the palace attack squelched. "Dolts, idiots, fools," he fumed. "Spread the news at once. Let the humble people of London know that they are not alone, and that the King and Queen are sharing their perils with them."[289]

Despite the fact that the Empire stood with them, the people of London, including their King and Queen and prime minister, were all of them indeed alone and virtually defenseless against the air attacks. Communist organizers circulated petitions calling for Churchill to initiate peace talks at once. "One cannot expect," Harold Nicolson confided to his diary, "the population of a great city to sit up all night in shelters week after week without losing their spirit." During September thousands of tons of bombs fell on London; more than six thousand Londoners, mostly East Enders, died in the fires. But the morale of Londoners did not crumble with their houses; the peace petitioners got few takers. By the end of September, Edward R. Murrow sensed that spirit. He broadcast from the roof of the BBC, "I have seen many flags flying from staffs. No one told these people to put out the flag. They simply feel like flying the Union Jack above their roof." And, said Murrow, "No flag up there was white."[290]

German parachute bombs, which were actually 2,200-pound naval mines, brought new terrors. These monsters were made more sinister in that they could not be aimed, a condition that necessarily resulted in indiscriminate slaughter. Built to sink battleships, the mines could demolish old brick-and-timber buildings within a five-hundred-meter radius. Churchill demanded that "we should drop two for every one of theirs." At dinner on September 21, he told Lord Gort and Hugh Dowding that although he was averse in principle to retaliation in kind, every German parachute bomb should be answered by an identical British response over an open German city. Gort agreed: "It's the only thing they understand."[291]

The Chief of the Air Staff informed the War Cabinet on September 23 that he had ordered one hundred heavy bombers to attack Berlin. Fifty more medium and heavy bombers were dispatched to bomb German invasion barges in the Channel ports. That evening Churchill told Colville: "Remember this, never maltreat your enemy by halves. Once the battle is joined, let 'em have it."[292]

Although his stated policy in early October remained one of no retaliation, Churchill was, in fact, targeting German civilians. That this was the case was due in part to the abysmal nighttime targeting accuracy of British bombers, less than two-thirds of which actually located their assigned targets, and of those that did, less than one-third placed their bombs within five miles of the target. In the area of the Ruhr, where industrial haze was constant, the figure was a pathetic one in ten. Targeting was so inaccurate, Churchill told Ismay, "If we could make it half and half we should virtually have doubled our bombing power."[293]

The random spray of British bombs meant that even if the targets were industrial or military, German civilians were being hit. Nonretaliation was a polite fiction. On October 16 the War Cabinet instructed Bomber Command to order its pilots to drop their bombs on the nearest German city, including Berlin, if cloud cover obscured industrial targets. The bombers were not to return home with any unused bombs. If Londoners could not take safely to their beds, neither would Berliners.[294]

The fiction of nonretaliation continued when, on October 17, while sipping a glass of port in the smoking room of the Commons, Churchill fielded questions from members who wanted to know when retaliation would begin. As Robert Cary, a Conservative MP from Eccles, gave a long dissertation on the public demand for unrestricted bombardment, Churchill listened. He took a long sip of his port while gazing over the glass at Cary. "My dear sir," he said, "this is a military and not a civilian war. You and others may desire to kill women and children. We desire, and have succeeded in our desire, to destroy German military objectives. I quite appreciate your point. But my motto is, 'Business before pleasure.'"[295]

Churchill took no pleasure in killing women and children. But three days later, in a secret memo to minister for air Archibald Sinclair, he ordered that retaliation with parachute mines be conducted on an experimental basis and that the "use of the heaviest 1,000 pound and 2,000 pound bombs on Berlin is much desired."[296]

Göring's and Goebbels' claim that Berlin airspace was inviolate took on elements of the absurd on the night of September 24, when Goebbels and his dining companions at the Adlon Hotel had to flee to the basement air-raid shelter as British bombs fell. The next night's raid lasted five hours. "The British ought to do this every night," William L. Shirer wrote, "no matter if not much is destroyed. The damage last night was not great. But the psychological effect was tremendous." The Germans had foolishly believed they could bomb Warsaw, Rotterdam, and England without themselves being bombed. Then again, the Germans had believed the war would be finished by autumn.[297]

The Nazi high command considered the raids mere nuisances, and for the most part they were correct. In raids conducted by seventy, eighty, sometimes ninety RAF bombers, little damage was done, in part because the planes had to trade bomb load for fuel in order to make the 1,200-mile round trip, and in part, as usual, targeting at night was a game of guesses. Yet the Soviet high command began to consider the possibility that England was not quite so down and not yet out. In mid-November, Soviet foreign minister Vyacheslav Molotov and his German counterpart, Joachim von Ribbentrop, met in Berlin to hold meetings intended to burnish their agreement on trade and postwar spoils. Churchill, in his memoir (*The Second World War*), writes that the British "though not invited to join in the discussion did not wish to be entirely left out of the proceedings." The ensuing RAF raid forced Molotov and Ribbentrop into a shelter, where, as Stalin later told Churchill, Ribbentrop continued to insist to the Russian that England was finished. "If that is so," replied Molotov, "why are we in this shelter and whose are these bombs which fall?"[298]

By mid-October almost five hundred thousand London children had been evacuated to the countryside. The city they left behind was falling down.

The rail system was in crisis: of six major London stations, only Paddington and King's Cross were in full operation. The main sewage outfall pipe
had been smashed, rendering the Thames an open sewer. Churchill fretted
that a mixing of sewage and drinking water would be disastrous—cholera
had killed thousands a century earlier; it could do so again. Public shelters
remained packed full and filthy, open invitations to outbreaks of diphthe-
ria and influenza. The "glass famine" Churchill feared was far more than a
matter of aesthetics; living conditions would be medieval in a windowless
London at the onset of winter. Driving past a smashed greenhouse,
Churchill commanded that all the glass that was salvageable be carted off
and stored for use during the winter. "The power of enduring suffering in
the ordinary people of every country, when their spirit is roused," Churchill
wrote in his memoirs, "seems to have no bounds."[299]

Humor trumped fear. Golf courses posted new rules. A free drop was
allowed when a ball fell into a bomb crater; members would not be penal-
ized for playing out of turn during a raid. Golf had its hazards, including
British anti-tank mines planted near seaside links. Churchill one evening
told his companions of a golfer who drove his ball onto the shingle. "He
took his niblick down to the beach, played the ball, and all that remained
afterwards was the ball which returned safely to the green."[300]

As civilian deaths far outstripped army casualties, a joke made the
rounds of the East End: Join the army and miss the war. Evelyn Waugh
quipped that if the Germans were really intent on destroying British
morale, they'd parachute in hundreds of marching brass bands. *Gone with
the Wind* was the most popular movie of the year, and it was a good bet
that as patrons departed the cinema, a red glow could be seen somewhere
over some corner of their city. Taxi drivers complained that the glass in the
roads was popping their tires. But they motored onward. Stores without
facades hung signs: "We are *wide* open for business." A newspaper hawker
defiantly chalked his bulletin board: "Berlin claims 1,000 tons of bombs
on London. So what?" Vaudeville and the almost-nude review went on
nonstop at the Windmill, just off Piccadilly, and the showgirls high-kicked
as usual at the Palladium and Prince of Wales. Hotel doormen proudly told
visitors how many air raids had taken place and scoffed at the enemy's
poor aim. A charwoman from the East End showed up at work in the City,
only to find the office building where she had scrubbed floors for years had
vanished the night before. "I guess old Hitler wanted me to have a change,"
she quipped. H. G. Wells—who had predicted such aerial onslaughts
thirty years earlier—was lunching with Somerset Maugham and Lady
Diana Cooper when the bombers appeared. Wells refused to leave the table
until he had finished his cheese: "I'm enjoying a very good lunch," he said.
"Why should I be disturbed by some wretched little barbarian in a

machine?" Agatha Christie came upon a farmer in a lane near her home. He was kicking an unexploded bomb: "Dang it all," he said. "Can't even explode properly." Every Briton had a story.[301]

Londoners went to work in the morning and arrived home by curfew, knowing full well that one or the other, home or work, might not be there by the next morning. The landscape changed nightly. If home and work survived the night, the bus route or rail line might not. And there was always the possibility of arriving home to meet an air-raid warden who bore the news of an "incident"—the death of a wife or husband, son or daughter. Still, Londoners made their way around the bomb craters, over the rubble, on foot, by bicycle when the streets were passable. They queued for their food rations, and listened, attuned to rumblings from over the horizon, not knowing if the disquieting basso profundo carried on the east wind was the arrival home of their flyboys or more of Göring's. In the East End, those with neither home nor work took shelter under railway bridges, in brewery basements and warehouses, and in crypts originally built for coal storage.[302]

Churchill sought them out. They were the only Europeans who had not wilted before Hitler. Bundled into a heavy topcoat, his odd little homburg pulled down low, he hurtled through the city streets in an armored car that somebody described as looking like a huge painted thermos. He detested the cumbersomeness of the vehicle, but his bodyguard pleaded with him to use it. As soon as it delivered him to a scene of destruction, out he'd climb to take off on foot. He might poke at the edge of bomb craters with his walking stick, or scramble up a pile of rubble to get a better view of the damage. He left his aides, literally, in the dust. With a careless slouch and his shoulders hunched, he charged down streets, through puddles and over fallen bricks. Always, he sought out the people. He possessed, said Mollie Panter-Downes, a "great gift for making them forget discomfort, danger, and loss and remember that they were living history."[303]

He told the Commons in early October: "In all my life, I have never been treated with so much kindness as by the people who have suffered most.... On every side there is the cry, 'We can take it,' but, with it, there is also the cry, 'Give it 'em back.'" London, he promised, would be rebuilt, more beautiful than before. But before then:

Long dark months of trials and tribulations lie before us. Not only great danger, but many more misfortunes, many shortcomings, many mistakes, many disappointments will surely be our lot. Death and sorrow will be the companions of our journey; hardship our garment; constancy and valor our only shield.[304]

Before the speech, Churchill had introduced, to much applause, Randolph, who had won a by-election in Preston. Churchill, in his youth, had wished that his father, Lord Randolph, would one day escort him into the Commons, where the son would serve the father "at his side and in his support." That dream was denied by Lord Randolph's calamitous fall from grace and power, scuttled by his mental and physical decay and early death. It would be left to the son, Winston, to escort Lord Randolph's grandson, Randolph, into the chamber. The applause that greeted the pair was for Winston a spontaneous display of support that told him his popularity remained untarnished by the Blitz or by the failure two weeks earlier of his gambit at Dakar, the results of which were just becoming known.[305]

Dakar, before the fall of France, was an obscure French West African port. After France fell, it assumed strategic significance, especially if the Germans were to use it as a base of operations against British convoys sailing for Egypt via the Cape of Good Hope. To scuttle that possibility, Operation Menace was conceived, a straightforward plan that would employ British warships to insert Free French forces led by de Gaulle into Dakar. British intelligence indicated that the Vichy forces at Dakar would not welcome de Gaulle warmly, but this information was ignored. Further, the Free French in London leaked the plans; the scheme might as well have been announced in the *Times*. On September 23 the Free French landed and were met not by a warm welcome but by hot and heavy fire. A British cruiser and battleship were hit by fire from shore batteries and the Vichy battleship *Richelieu*. After two days of desultory firing, Menace was called off. Churchill telegraphed Roosevelt with the unfortunate news. Clementine later called the failure "a classic example of Hope deferred making the Heart sick." Still, after the first sting of regret, Churchill found the positive within the negative: Britain had done *something*. As with Oran, Churchill had shown the world—especially Roosevelt—that Britain was not finished.[306]

Joseph Kennedy thought otherwise. Dakar had been a disaster, he reported to Washington, and Churchill's popularity was falling (it was not). In late October, Kennedy fled to America, the first ambassador to abandon London. Ostensibly, Kennedy departed in order to tender his resignation to Roosevelt in person, but he could have phoned it in while manning his post. His flight earned him the enmity of Londoners and the moniker "Jittery Joe." Once safely home he told the *Boston Globe* in an off-the-record interview that British democracy was finished, that Britain was finished, that Britons were fighting for the preservation of empire rather than for democracy, and that to think otherwise was bunk.[307]

Where Kennedy saw gloom, Churchill saw courage. Of Londoners, he told Colville: "I represent to them something which they wholeheartedly support, the determination to win. For a year or two they will cheer me." In a letter to Chamberlain, who was dying in excruciating pain of bowel cancer, Churchill wrote: "The Germans have made a tremendous mistake in concentrating on London to the relief of our factories, and in trying to intimidate a people whom they have only infuriated." Londoners preferred, he told Colville, "to all be in the front line, taking part in the Battle of London, than to look on helplessly at mass slaughters like Passchendaele."[308]

Throughout October, the War Cabinet pondered the ultimate question: are the Germans coming? All month the Ultra intelligence, the code name for information gleaned from Luftwaffe and Wehrmacht radio traffic, indicated ongoing preparations for the invasion. German logistical units had asked the high command what distance the troops would have to march to reach their port of embarkation. Also: How many "S" days, or Sea Lion days, were to be allotted for vehicle packing and delivery, and how many days for troop embarkation. Aerial intelligence confirmed that the Germans were rehearsing the invasion under cover of synthetic yellow fog. Radio transmissions indicated the invasion date would likely be sometime after October 20. Was it all part of a German disinformation campaign? The Secret Circle had no choice but to carry on its business as if invasion was imminent; to do otherwise would have been a dereliction of duty. The navy patrolled, the RAF patrolled, Bletchley listened. Yet, a sense that the invasion was "off" began to manifest itself more in Churchill's words, private and public. On October 4 he cabled Roosevelt: "The gent has taken off his clothes and put on his bathing suit, but the water is getting colder and there is an autumn nip in the air. We are maintaining the utmost vigilance."[309]

On October 21, while broadcasting to the French, Churchill tossed out a phrase that could only have arisen from his growing optimism: "We are waiting for the long promised invasion. So are the fishes." The words sizzle—defiant, sure to conjure respect from neutral observers. His speeches of June and July had been somber admissions to the probability of invasion and drumbeats to fight on to the end with courage and dignity, and to die likewise. Those speeches had been intended to inspire, but should England fall under the Nazi boot, they were also intended as epitaphs to be read and pondered by future generations. The one-liner built into the October speech was pure Churchillian wit, a wisecrack of the sort he simply could not resist and for which he was so well known. He had not uttered it to cronies in a drawing room over port but broadcast it worldwide and directed it at the most powerful leader and the most awesome military force on the planet. This lone phrase casts Hitler as the fool. It demeans him, tells him, You may yet defeat us, but you will never, not *ever*, beat the spirit out of us.[310]

The address, recorded in French and English, was intended in part to allay French fears that the British had designs on its fleet and West African colonies. "We seek," Churchill said, "to beat the life out of Hitler and Hitlerism. That alone, that all the time, that to the end. We do not covet anything from any nation except their respect." To some Frenchmen, Churchill's claim of not coveting anything rang hollow. The British had tried to sink the French fleet at Oran in July, and had just tried to land a Free French force at Dakar. Churchill added a final pledge:

> Remember we shall never stop, never weary, and never give in, and that our whole people and Empire have vowed themselves to the task of cleansing Europe from the Nazi pestilence and saving the world from the new Dark Ages.... We are on his track, and so are our friends across the Atlantic Ocean, and your friends across the Atlantic Ocean. If he cannot destroy us, we will surely destroy him, and all his gang, and all their works. Therefore, have hope and faith, for all will come right.[311]

Faith that their "friends" across the Atlantic would make their presence known was all Britain and France had. Yet nine days later, Franklin Roosevelt told a Boston audience, "Your boys are not going to be sent into any foreign wars." He did not add his usual qualifier, "except in case of attack." Even had America the will to fight—which it did not—it lacked the way. Churchill ended his address with words that resonated with his own romanticism as well as with the idealized egalitarian spirit of the Republic that Frenchmen so cherished: *"Allons, bonne nuit; dormez bien, reassemblez vos forces pour l'aube* [Good night, then; sleep well to gather strength for the dawn]. For the morning will come. Brightly will it shine on the brave and true, kindly on all who suffer for the cause, glorious upon the tombs of heroes. Thus will shine the dawn. *Vive la France!"*[312]

That night, the painter Paul Maze, who had escaped from Bordeaux in June and was living in Hampshire, wrote Churchill: "Every word you said was like every drop of blood in a transfusion." The inspirational effect of Churchill's words might have been lost had the microphone in the radio studio been turned on when he arrived. Jacques Duchesne (pseudonym of the French actor Michel Saint-Denis), the BBC's French expert and translator, was standing in the room, waiting to perform his duties. "Where is my frog speech?" asked Churchill. Colville, who accompanied Churchill, said Duchesne "looked pained."[313]

Within a week Churchill, thanks to Ultra, became convinced that the invasion was off, or at least postponed until the spring of 1941. On the twenty-eighth, the Combined Intelligence Committee stated that photo reconnaissance indicated a movement of German shipping *eastward,* out of the Channel, a movement that, "if maintained, could reduce the risk of invasion." But the U-boats still posed a mortal threat. And the German bombers were still paying their nightly visits.

More than five hundred RAF fighter pilots had been killed fighting Göring's daylight raids since July, but their sacrifice brought results. By late October, daylight bombings had virtually ceased. Göring ordered them stopped entirely in early November; his daytime losses since July ran almost ten times higher than his night losses. The night skies over Britain promised safety to German aircrew. Göring's switch to night bombing and the dropping of incendiaries randomly throughout London meant the Germans had abandoned any pretense of bombing military targets. The midnight bombs that fell regularly in Berlin meant the British had as well.

By November Chequers had become the regular weekend retreat of the Churchill family. It would be the last autumn of the war that the entire family spent time together. Mary, seventeen, had gone on vacation in July to stay with old family friends, the Montagus, in Norfolk; the Blitz and threatened invasion had prolonged the visit. She wanted to return to London, but her parents were adamant that she not. In September she was packed off to Chequers. Pamela took up residence there in mid-September to await the birth of her first child. Her doctor insisted on accompanying her. He stayed for two weeks, recalled Pamela, to "have some peaceful nights" at the height of the Blitz. Clementine thought the doctor's presence an awkward distraction for Winston, and she expressed her displeasure to Pamela, who replied, "Mama, I can't do anything to make this child appear." Churchill presumed the child would be a boy, to be named Winston, and was therefore not happy when his cousin the Duchess of Marlborough was delivered of a baby boy whom she named Winston just days before Pamela was expected to give birth. Churchill called the duchess and told her, "Pamela and Randolph expect to call their son Winston." The duchess asked, "How do you know it's going to be a boy?" He replied, "If it isn't now, it will be later. I would like to ask you to change the name." The duchess changed the name to Charles. Pamela's son, Winston Spencer Churchill, "Little" Winston, was born in a four-poster bed at Chequers on October 10. Pamela awoke from a chloroform-induced sleep to hear murmurings of "It's a boy, it's a boy." And, she recalled, "Old Winston was right there. It meant a great deal to him."[314]

Randolph, on temporary leave from his army unit and serving in Parliament, took his weekends in the country with Pamela and his parents. Churchill's brother, Jack, a financier six years Winston's junior, always self-effacing and discreet, added his avuncular presence to the scene. His London house bombed out, Jack took to bunking wherever he could, including No. 10 and the Annexe. Jack's wife, Lady Gwendeline "Goonie" Churchill, had long been one of Clementine's most loyal friends, but by late 1940, dying of cancer, Goonie had moved to the country. Her absence on weekends eliminated one of Clementine's connections to social goings-on in the outside world, from which she, too, had of necessity withdrawn. Winston and Clementine's eldest daughter, Diana Sandys, sometimes appeared on weekends to add her own urbanity to the dinner conversation. Her children—Julian, four, and Edwina, two—afforded Churchill the opportunity to behave like a normal grandfather, that is, like a big child, albeit with cigar ashes sprinkled on his vest. He, far more than Clementine, recalled Pamela, knew how to make a child laugh. For Mary, Chequers felt like a great and gloomy house during the week, yet it came alive with the arrival on weekends of her siblings, her parents, and their guests.[315]

Colville, as a private secretary, was often present. He was drawn to Mary's spunk, although he noted that she was often somewhat tense and on occasion peevish. He sometimes arranged to join her and Clementine on their walks about the grounds, strolls that often turned into wild footraces between the two youths. Leaving Clementine behind, Mary and Colville sprinted down forest paths, past the ancient oaks, and dashed to the tops of the low hills. She usually won the race, perhaps because Colville was being gallant, perhaps because he was winded from his cigarette habit. In the presence of her father, Mary's behavior was muted. Such deference to Papa was inculcated early in all the children. Yet during one family luncheon, Mary's spirited nature surfaced. Churchill, expressing surprise and dismay at the speed of the French collapse, announced that the French debacle was so swift it was as if the Germans had simply bypassed France and thrown their full weight against Britain. Mary listened in silence. Then, in a soft and nervous voice, she paraphrased the words her father had spoken months earlier in tribute to the young fighter pilots of the RAF: "Never before has so much been betrayed for so many by so few."[316]

Randolph, not yet thirty, displayed neither his sister's reticence nor her sly humor. He was, recalled Colville, "a most unattractive combination of the bombastic, the cantankerous and the unwise; and yet at times he makes shrewd and penetrating comments and at times can be pleasant. He has none of Winston's reasonableness." He drank heavily, Colville noted, and was not a drinker of good cheer. Randolph, during one dinner, opined at length on how Baldwin had destroyed the fire in politics and deprived the empire of its greatness. World domination, said Randolph, was the greatest ideal and he admired the Germans for desiring it. Randolph's arguments, Colville noted in his diary, "make one shudder." Colville found him to be one of the most "objectionable" people he'd ever met: "Noisy, self-asserting, whining and frankly unpleasant" . . . and "at dinner anything but kind to Winston, who adores him." Randolph's treatment of his father so vexed Clementine that she threatened to ban him from No. 10 lest he give his father a heart attack. Yet Winston's love for Randolph was infinite. At Chequers, Churchill was at his ease with his cronies and his family nearby. And, of course, he loved the food and liquor, spirits of a quality not found in the canteen beneath Storey's Gate. He knew the joys of family life at Chequers might easily be short-lived; the games of croquet on the lawns (he watched), the family strolls and footraces (he avoided all exercise), brandy and reminiscences before the great fireplaces, even Randolph's pathetic tirades. Of Chequers and the Germans, he said: "Probably they don't think I am so foolish as to come here. I stand to lose a lot. Three generations at a swoop."[317]

His family, though in close physical proximity that autumn, was coming apart. Sarah's marriage to the actor and comedian Vic Oliver had dissolved. His music man act had enjoyed a long run of playing the Palladium, the house always packed. But as an Austrian of Jewish ancestry, he had been warned to flee England before it was too late. America seemed the safer place now for an Austrian expatriate and comic actor on the rise. Sarah, if Vic left for the United States, would accompany him out of matrimonial duty, but she harbored no desire to leave England, her parents, and her nascent theatrical career. Vic stayed on in London into 1941, a gesture Sarah found noble given "the sorrow he would have caused me if he asked me to leave Britain at that time." By the following summer the marriage was finished, and Sarah had been commissioned as an RAF section officer. Clementine thoroughly endorsed Sarah's remaining in England because she felt no "Churchill child" should leave the country in its hour of distress. When she learned that one of her nieces was to depart for Canada, she had the child's passport revoked. Churchill disapproved of the entire emigration scheme, calling it a "stampede from the country."[318]

In any case, the program to evacuate children overseas had effectively ended on September 17. That night, the steamship *City of Benares,* bound for Canada, was making poor headway in a gale when it was torpedoed. Seventy-three of ninety children on board perished, as well as more than two hundred of their adult escorts. Many initially made it into the lifeboats. The children began singing *Roll out the Barrel,* but by the time they got to "We'll have a barrel of fun," the ship was gone. The seas then took over, smashing the lifeboats. Four days later Churchill told the Defence Committee that in view of the sinking, the evacuation of children overseas must cease.[319]

Since the days almost two decades earlier when he topped the Irish Republican Army assassination list, Churchill liked to sleep with a gun within reach. He had carried a Colt revolver on his person since the fall of France, but tended to lay it down and forget where, forcing Inspector Thompson to loan him one of his revolvers. Churchill was given to drawing his gun and waving it about while exclaiming, "You see Thompson, they'll never take me alive." In fact, he was a good shot with a rifle and absolutely deadly with his Colt .45. He and Thompson repaired on a regular basis to the outdoor shooting range at Chequers, where Churchill would fire a hundred or so rounds each from his Mannlicher rifle, his .32 Webley & Scott revolver, and his favorite Colt. He was, recalled Thompson, so deadly a shot that anyone who came within range of his gun would stand no chance. Colville recorded one such session: "[Churchill] fired his Mannlicher rifle at targets 100, 200, and 300 yards away. He also fired his revolver, still smoking a cigar, with commendable accuracy. Despite his age, size, and lack of practice, he acquitted himself well.... He always seems to visualize the possibility of having to defend himself against German troops!"[320]

The idea of the prime minister of Great Britain blazing away at the enemy was, with all Britons expecting an invasion, anything but preposterous. Churchill lived daily with the very real possibility of a last stand, a shoot-out between himself and the invaders. Recalled Lord Geoffrey-Lloyd,* "Winston was like an animal in the jungle, his senses attuned to any kind of danger. He had this primitive desire for survival, which was an immense inspiration to the country and the world."[321]

During the ordnance exercise, Churchill opined, "The best way to kill Huns was with snub-nosed bullets." He was referring to hollow-point slugs called dumdums, which pancake upon hitting flesh, crash through internal organs, and leave an exit wound as big as a teapot. They were named after the Dum Dum arsenal near Calcutta, where they were first

---

* Geoffrey-Lloyd (1902–1984) managed the Petroleum Warfare Department within the War Department. In 1945 he was appointed minister of information.

produced in order to give the British an advantage over mutinous locals. Such bullets, Randolph protested to his father, were illegal in warfare. Indeed they were. Churchill in 1906 had declared his opposition to using the slugs against any "civilized foe." The Nazis had forfeited any claims in that regard. To Randolph, Churchill rumbled that since the Germans would "make short shrift" of him if captured, he saw no reason at all why he should have "any mercy on them."[322]

Goebbels tried to parlay Churchill's shooting sessions into a propaganda coup. He procured a photo of Churchill that had run in British newspapers which displayed the prime minister attired in dark pinstripes, immense cigar firmly set in his mouth, a Thompson .45-caliber submachine gun outfitted with a circular magazine (favored by Chicago mobsters) cradled in his arms. The Germans produced a leaflet from the photo with these words: "WANTED, FOR INCITEMENT TO MURDER. THIS GANGSTER, WHO YOU SEE IN HIS ELEMENT IN THE PICTURE, INCITES YOU BY HIS EXAMPLE TO PARTICIPATE IN A FORM OF WARFARE IN WHICH WOMEN, CHILDREN AND ORDINARY CITIZENS SHALL TAKE LEADING PARTS." Goebbels had thousands of the leaflets dropped over Britain. He ceased the program within two weeks, when he realized the image was only boosting Churchill's popularity among Britons.[323]

Plinking with small arms might conceivably address some practical need for self-protection, but whether he was at No. 10, the Annexe, or Chequers, Churchill's behavior during air raids was another matter entirely. With the swagger of Victorian men, he scorned personal danger. Courage, he believed, was the greatest virtue. In October he was sitting in the Cabinet Room when aides told him that an unexploded two-ton bomb in St. James's Park threatened everyone in Downing Street. Churchill glanced up from his papers and said he hoped none of the park's ducks would be hurt. During one raid he summoned Colville to escort him from No. 10 to the Annexe. Colville recalled: "As we emerged from the India Office arch into King Charles Street, we heard the loud whistles of two descending bombs. I dived back under the arch for shelter, and the bomb exploded in Whitehall. Churchill, meanwhile, was striding along the middle of King George Street, his chin stuck out and propelling himself rapidly with his gold-headed walking stick. I had to run to catch him up.... I am sure that in a shipwreck he would have been the last to step into the lifeboat."[324]

He liked to watch the enemy bombers come in, and thoroughly enjoyed the crash and *crump* of the bombs, and the *crack* of the anti-aircraft guns. He relished the entire spectacle. Four decades earlier he had quipped that nothing in life quite so exhilarates as "being shot at without result." When the sirens sounded, Churchill chose between sitting underground watching dust shake out of the rafters and going forth into the raids. Out he went.[325]

His outings sent Clementine, his cabinet, and his bodyguards into fits of angst. Inspector Thompson believed that Churchill's insistence on putting himself in danger was the Marlborough in him. At the first wail of the sirens Churchill donned his tin hat—he called it his "battle bowler"—and, attired in his mauve siren suit or one of his vivid dressing gowns, sometimes both, would depart the underground Annexe for the roof or, if he was at Chequers, for the gardens, there to watch and wait while the enemy approached, or, as he put it, "to walk in the moonlight and watch the fireworks." He did not at all like the fit of the helmet; when it regularly slipped down over his eyes as he gazed skyward, he'd fling it into the bushes for an aide to later retrieve. He might chew on an unlighted cigar, or light one up, in defiance of all rules against smoking during air raids. He ignored any rule he chose to ignore. His Royal Marine valet, in an attempt to impede his mobility, hid his shoes. Churchill demanded they be returned. "I'll have you know," he proclaimed, "that as a child my nurse maid would never prevent me from taking a walk in the park if I wanted to do so. And as a man, Adolf Hitler certainly won't."[326]

His favorite position from which to take in the fireworks was the flat roof of the Annexe. Sited as it was across from St. James's Park, it afforded a splendid view of London, a foolishly dangerous prospect even with an overhanging roof to guard against stray shell fragments. There, gas mask at his side, armed with a glowing cigar and binoculars, he watched for bomb flashes. He counted the seconds until the crunch of the bomb reached him. Five seconds, one mile. Persuading him to leave the roof proved difficult at best.[327]

If he did depart, it was likely because he demanded that his aides locate the exact area bombed, and that they bring the motorcar around in order that he should tour the scene. On one such outing, the blast from a nearby German bomb lifted Churchill's car up off all four tires. The vehicle returned to the ground and rolled along for several yards on two wheels, before finally righting itself. It regained its stability, said Churchill, due to "my beef." On another evening, Churchill, Minister of Labour Ernest Bevin, Pug Ismay, and Jock Colville packed themselves into the armored car. All were well plied with brandy. Their destination was Raynes Park, where they hoped to watch the anti-aircraft guns in action. On the way, a policeman tried to arrest them for driving with too-bright lights. The dutiful bobby was dismissed with a loud, "Go to Hell, man." The phrasing of the outburst excludes Bevin as a suspect in uttering it. Born in a remote West England village and educated in secondary (public) schools, he dropped his "h's" and "g's" in the west country fashion. Bevin would have said *"G' ta 'ell man."* Thus, someone other than Bevin must have told the constable where to go. Colville was too junior, Pug Ismay too polite. Only one suspect remained.

In any event, the group motored onward to the park, where they found the big guns silent. It was raining, and, with no German aircraft overhead, Churchill stopped by the officers' mess, where he sipped a whisky and soda and awaited the fireworks.[328]

Inspector Thompson could do little during air raids to protect the prime minister from the potential folly of his own reckless behavior. On two occasions Thompson had to heave his charge bodily out of exposed doorways in Whitehall as bombs fell nearby. The blast from one wounded some of Thompson's men. Churchill, infuriated at having been shoved, took no notice of the wounded men. Instead he "swore, shook, and stomped about." He bellowed, "Don't *do* that." Thompson could not quite decipher the rest of the "whole gush of ugly sounds" emanating from Churchill. The curses strung together by a perturbed Churchill, Thompson wrote, were "a sin against the language." Such eruptions were well known to everyone who worked for him, from the Chiefs of Staff to his secretaries. But Thompson gave as good as he got, telling Churchill that his behavior was "selfishly stupid." After the tantrum, Churchill voiced a non-apology, after his fashion, for leading Thompson into danger: "I would not do it, only I know how much *you* like it." Yet he could never quite leave it at that. Invariably a glare of long duration followed such scenes, a signal that he considered the entire affair finished, but only on his terms. As for taking to heart Thompson's professional advice, Churchill, with the next keening of the sirens, flew out the door, rooftop bound. His explanation: "When my time is due, it will come."[329]

One early October evening after a late dinner at No. 10, and knowing that on the following day he would be addressing the Commons as well as sponsoring Randolph's entry into Parliament, Churchill, rather than retire, as would most sixty-five-year-old men burdened with great responsibilities, made straightaway for the action. As recalled by anti-aircraft commander Sir Frederick Pile, they first drove to Richmond, where the big guns were banging away and bombs were falling. As usual, Churchill refused his helmet. At about eleven he was told that a demonstration of the new radar-controlled searchlights had been prepared for him at Biggin Hill. He didn't want to leave. "This exhilarates me," he told Pile. "The sound of these cannon gives me a tremendous feeling." Finally, persuaded to move on, they went off in Pile's car, and immediately became lost. Two hours later, after navigating blocked streets in total darkness, the bombs still falling, they found their intended rendezvous point—"the worst two hours of the war for me," Pile wrote. The night was wet and cold. Churchill asked for a whisky and soda. The commander of the searchlight unit replied that there was as much chance of getting a whisky there as in the Sahara, but that he'd send to his mess, ten miles distant. The radar failed to operate, but the whisky was produced, without the dilution of a splash of soda, which was the Old Man's custom. He took one sip, spluttered, and said, "Good God, I have been poisoned. It is neat whisky."[330]

A display of aerial rocket mines was also scrubbed. The rocket experiments off, the party set out for London, bombs still falling. Upon arrival at No. 10—it was now about 4:30 A.M.—Churchill rapped upon the door with his gold-tipped walking stick and announced "Göring and Goebbels coming to report." He invited Pile in for a snack of sardines and Bovril, a foodstuff resembling liquefied beef with the consistency of molasses and rife with the overriding taste of salt. But a spoonful in a tall glass topped off with boiling water and a dash of sherry served as a traditional antidote to London's chills, and in company with tinned sardines, it became a staple of wartime Britain. Churchill and Pile downed their snack, Pile departing as dawn broke. A few hours later, Churchill, looking no worse for his sleepless night, addressed the Commons.[331]

His doctor, Charles Wilson, was among those made exceedingly uncomfortable by his forays into the exploding night. Wilson recalled that during that summer and autumn he visited Churchill regularly, and was begrudged every moment he sought. As the Blitz hardened, Churchill became a source of worry for Wilson: "I used to watch him as he went to his room," he wrote, "the head thrust forward, scowling at the ground, the somber countenance clouded, the features set and resolute, the jowl clamped down as if he had something clamped between his teeth and did not let it go...carrying the weight of the world, and wondered how long he could go on like that and what could be done about it."[332]

His jaunts while the bombs fell seemed to be just the medicine, self-prescribed. Harold Nicolson, in November, noted Churchill's healthy glow: "He seems better in health than he has ever seemed. That pale and globular look about his cheeks is gone. He is more solid about the face, and thinner." His eyes especially moved Nicolson. The lids evidenced no weariness, no pouches or dark lines were to be seen. "But the eyes themselves are glaucous, vigilant, angry, combative, visionary and tragic...the eyes of a man much preoccupied." He *was* preoccupied—with Hitler, the Americans, and the nightly bombings. Yet he was determined that all would end on his terms. In spite of the dangers, the defeats, and the grim prospects for national survival, he was content. Unable to pursue his usual enjoyments—writing, painting, and the laying of row upon row of red Kentish bricks in the gardens of Chartwell—he found a new source of joy. The glow Nicolson noted was due to Churchill's new pastime, the fireworks.[333]

His fondness for late-night outings should not be construed as a fondness for war. He hated the carnage of war. In 1898, at Omdurman in the Sudan, he carried a Mauser pistol into the last great cavalry charge in British his-

tory. At close range, he shot dead at least three Dervishes during two minutes of bloody chaos. He had sent letters home to his mother from the Sudan
condemning the "dirty, shoddy business" of battle. "You can not gild it," he
wrote, "the raw comes through." The glorification of war he saw as a fraud.
Of war, he wrote in 1930, "we now have entire populations, including even
women and children, pitted against one another in brutish mutual extermination, and only a set of blear-eyed clerks left to add up the butcher's bill."
War's utility was altogether another matter. He told Colville that those who
complain that wars settle nothing were speaking nonsense, because "nothing in history was ever settled except by war." War, in spite of its horror,
was the answer when the questions were framed in terms of liberty and the
preservation of the West's most humanistic traditions.[334]

Inspector Thompson couldn't keep his charge from climbing rooftops while
the bombs fell, but the assassination of Churchill was something Thompson
could plan against. Churchill, understanding that the rules of gentlemanly
warfare had changed since his youth, said to Colville, "If you are allowed to
bomb Heads of State, surely you may shoot them?" Thompson's chief concern
centered on two possibilities: an attempt by commandos or a targeted air raid
by fighter-bombers. A pinpoint air raid on Chequers might not get Churchill,
but Thompson wanted to reduce the chances to nil. To thwart an ambush by
suicide parachutists, he posted policemen, some from the local force, some
from London, throughout the grounds, on the roofs, in every outbuilding. The
army was also deployed. Sentries manned the gates and patrolled the grounds.
Passwords were issued and constantly changed. Each sentry maintained an
intersecting field of fire with neighboring positions. Each guard was assigned a
specific sector of the grounds and each, at random times during the night,
flicked on his flashlight to illuminate his area, just for a moment in order to
ascertain who, if anybody, might be lurking. Thompson thought the precautions critical. Churchill loathed the entire routine. It brought the war into his
gardens. It destroyed charm. It introduced suspicion, and nonsense.[335]

German reconnaissance planes made passes overhead, shooting photographs. Incendiary bombs fell nearby on a regular basis, dropped by Heinkels going to or from London. Coincidence could not explain the many
bomb craters that dotted the grounds of Chequers; the house was clearly a
target. The German use of beam navigation gave Churchill pause about the
vulnerability of Chequers to bombing. He told Colville he did not object to
chance but felt it "a mistake to be the victim of design." To preclude the possibility of the prime minister's becoming the victim of design, Thompson
told Churchill he'd have to do what he was told from now on, which was to
sleep in the air-raid shelter. Churchill replied that he would cooperate the

moment he thought it wise to do so. This meant, wrote Thompson, he "would continue to do as he pleased, which was to stay outside and watch." To a Royal Marine who tried to reinforce Thompson's caution Churchill said, "Let me know when they start dropping the bombs."[336]

Chequers was especially vulnerable to attack when the moon was full. To further reduce the chances of Churchill's being consumed by German ordnance, an alternate weekend retreat was proposed, Ditchley Park, the Oxfordshire home of Nancy and Ronnie Tree. Their house stood on forested grounds, thirty miles west of Chequers, away from German glide paths. Both were half American by birth. Ronnie had been brought up in Britain, and Nancy was from Richmond, Virginia, the widow of Henry Field, he of the family of Chicago mercantile fame. As the MP from Leicestershire, Ronnie, though not an intimate friend of the Churchills, had long supported rearmament, and for that he had earned Churchill's respect. Ditchley Park happened to be located just a few miles from Blenheim, a coincidence that appealed to Churchill. His first sojourn to Ditchley took place on Saturday, November 9, as there was a full moon that weekend. Nancy wrote Churchill a short, gracious note in which she bade him to "use the house as your own," whenever convenient and "no matter how short the notice." She may not have realized that Churchill did not travel alone. Ditchley was about to become a full house.[337]

Whether at Ditchley or Chequers, weekends began with the same routine, usually on Friday afternoon, sometimes on Saturday morning. One or two of Churchill's police bodyguards arrived before the rest of the party in order to inspect the house from garret to cellar. The valet and maid then arrived with much luggage. Next, a platoon of thirty-five soldiers arrived by truck, to protect the great man throughout the night. Private secretaries, stenographers, and guests followed, often including the Prof, Bracken, and brother Jack. Finally, in the late afternoon, Clementine and Churchill made their appearance. Churchill's first order of business was a hot bath, to which he might stroll from his dressing room stark naked, to the consternation of newer female typists. On Saturdays and Sundays, he stayed in bed until noon, working and dictating, a supply of Malvern natural spring water at the ready. After dictation came a hearty lunch followed by a short (but certainly not rigorous) walk, then tea, or more likely a whisky. More work until 6:30, at which time he took his nap, always in the company of a hot water bottle. At 8:00, dinner. Although prime cuts of meats were no longer readily available to Britons, some still found their way to Churchill's table. But old favorites such as bushels of fresh oysters, black truffles, or Caspian caviar, even if available, were avoided. All Britons, Churchill included, were on short rations. He kept a somewhat simple table for the duration.

Conversation always flowed at dinner, as did champagne. Pol Roger

(Churchill favored 1928 and 1929) was hauled up from the basements nightly. As always, Churchill dominated at the table. Conversation with him, wrote his doctor, was similar to cricket: he batted and everybody else caught. "Winston talks to amuse himself; he has no thoughts of impressing anybody....He requires no help, least of all from women."[338] After the meal came brandy, port, cigars, and a movie. The first screenings took place at Ditchley. Among his favorites were *The Great Dictator,* released in December, and *Gone with the Wind.* He displayed a schoolboyish love for Vivien Leigh, who played Scarlett O'Hara. He was "pulverized," he said of the characters in the latter film, "by the strength of their feelings and emotions." The film happened also to be one of Hitler's favorites (along with *It Happened One Night*).[339]

The respite afforded by weekends with family and friends at Chequers and Ditchley fed his optimism. Still, somber thoughts swam beneath the surface. A dinner one evening with Clementine and Pamela was had in silence, each alone with his or her own thoughts. Then, cocking his chin and brandishing his knife like a rapier, Churchill told them he expected them to do their duty and take one or two Huns with them when the time came. "But, Papa," Pamela protested, "I neither own nor know how to fire a gun." He nodded toward the kitchen. "There are butcher knives in there," he growled. "Take one out and use it. You can always take a Hun with you." He later said he considered "You can always take one with you" his slogan if the invasion came.[340]

A vicious array of bombs fell upon London throughout the autumn, wicked little incendiaries and two-ton "land mines" delivered by parachute to destroy all and sundry within five hundred meters, and concussive high-explosive bombs and their sinister kin, time-delay bombs that slept soundly until the moment their internal clock went *tick.* On the moonlit night of October 14–15, the Germans mixed in thousands of incendiary bombs with the usual component of high explosives, with catastrophic results. The Balham tube station, where 650 sought shelter, suffered a direct hit: the entrance collapsed; gas, water, and sewer lines in the street above were demolished; the station flooded. At least sixty Londoners drowned in the deluge of sewage and water or were crushed by debris, including a double-decker bus. Leicester Square was rendered a desert. Pall Mall was badly smashed up, the Carlton Club wrecked, the Travellers Club splintered, its members trapped within. No. 10 sustained more damage when the Treasury was hit yet again.

The incendiaries introduced a new and terrifying element. That night almost 400 German medium bombers dropped more than 70,000 incendiaries onto the kindling that was London, starting 900 fires. "To the basements," the civilian rallying cry during raids, was replaced with "To the roofs," where an agile homeowner with a well-placed bucket of sand could erase the danger, if he moved fast enough. The firebombs forced an immediate change in the fire-spotting system. Throughout Britain, almost 1,400 local fire brigades were consolidated into the National Fire Service. Uniforms—dark blue tunics and trousers—were issued, training standardized. Duty consisted of sitting alone on a roof with only a tin hat for protection. In the early going, London seemed to be falling down all around the firewatchers. Churchill foresaw the possibility of the complete destruction of the city, but his faith in Londoners remained undiminished: "Soon, many of the bombs would only fall upon houses already ruined and only make the rubble jump. Over large areas there would be nothing more to burn or destroy. And yet human beings might make their homes here and there and carry on their work with infinite resource and fortitude."[341]

Fortitude was in great demand. A lone civilian wielding a bucket of sand could dispose of an incendiary, but the far more complex and dangerous disposal of unexploded bombs fell to the Royal Engineers. The tools of their trade were simple: a drill, a wrench, and a spool of string. After gaining access to a bomb's fuse *via* wrench and drill, the engineers attached the string to the primer, then uncoiled the spool to a safe distance before giving a firm but measured tug on the line in order to remove the detonator. In the ordinary course of events, the now-impotent ordnance would be trucked far out of the city, to the Hackney Marshes, to be harmlessly detonated. But the laws of physics conspired to render bomb disposal anything but ordinary. Bombs buried nose-down in deep and muddy craters had to be hauled out by rope and pulley. A slip of the rope could start the timing mechanism. Unexploded bombs by the hundreds fell through buildings and into basements; they fell onto rooftops, hung from church steeples, were ensnared by electrical wires, and dropped onto railway lines. One eight-hundred-pounder landed just in front of the steps of St. Paul's and burrowed deep down among gas and water lines. It was hauled out inch by inch over several hours and taken off to the marshes, where, when detonated, it made a crater one hundred feet wide. One bomb parachuted onto the Hungerford railroad bridge, which spanned the Thames. It didn't explode but became welded to the electric rail. Even unexploded, it crippled railroad traffic. Göring was throttling Britain in ways he had not imagined.[342]

Almost 20 percent of German (and British) bombs were duds, but they still closed long stretches of railway lines, important junctions, roads, and airfields as efficiently as time-delay bombs, and both fell at the rate of three thousand per week. They caused such a bottleneck in the transport of food and military supplies that Churchill commanded the ministers of War and Supply to make disposal of unexploded bombs their highest priority. With his usual attention to detail, he told Anthony Eden that he had learned of an American auger that could dig a trench in a matter of hours that otherwise would take several men two or three days to dig manually. "You should, I think, consider ordering a number of these appliances for the use of the bomb disposal squads. The essence of this business is to reach the bomb and deal with it with the least possible delay."[343]

Yet reaching the unexploded bomb was but the first step in a sequence that often proved deadly. German engineers built even more unpredictability and terror into the bomb disposal process. They employed double fuses, one behind the other, so that the removal of the first triggered the unseen second. They installed fuses sensitive to light, in which the detonation sequence began when a UXB squad opened the bomb, exposing the fuse to sunlight. Of all the detonator types, the time-delay fuse was the most terrifying. Because a mechanical time-delay device would likely be damaged in the crash landing of the bomb, the Germans employed an acid drip that burned through a thin metal plate covering a secondary triggering mechanism. It was, said Churchill, "an especially effective agent in warfare, on account of the prolonged uncertainty which it creates." UXB squads knew that if they put an ear to a bomb casing and heard the soft buzzing of the timer, they had fewer than fifteen seconds to find shelter. The largest bombs precluded any chance of success in such a dash. Churchill later wrote: "In writing about our hard times we are apt to overuse the word 'grim.' It should have been reserved for the U.X.B. Disposal Squads."[344]

Despite Clementine's plea to treat his staff more mercifully, Churchill's behavior toward his subordinates continued to be downright ill-tempered, brusque, and often pedantic regarding insignificant details. One night Colville reported to him two unexploded bombs in the Horse Guards Parade. "Will they do us any damage when they explode?" asked Churchill while lying in bed. Colville replied that they would not. "Is that just your opinion," demanded Churchill, "because if so it's worth nothing. You have never seen an unexploded bomb go off. Go and ask for an official report." Trivialities did not escape his attention. Strolling from No. 10, he noticed the flag atop the Admiralty was in tatters. He messaged the First Lord: "Surely you can run a new Admiralty flag. It grieves me to see the present dingy object every morning." He complained of delays when there were none, changed carefully prepared plans at the last minute, and constantly insisted on personal amenities that his overworked staff could not produce. Sounds of hammering during the reinforcement of No. 10 and the CWR brought outbursts of fury. Broad indeed was the spectrum of noises that set him off. The *clang clang* of cowbells drove him to distraction. His secretaries dreaded the possibility on rural outings that a cow or, worse yet, a herd of bell-wearing cows might appear when the Old Man was collecting his thoughts. Whistling in his presence produced a disturbance so immediate and immense that his aides sometimes made whirling motions at their temples to convey their assessment of the wheels in Churchill's head. He issued an order to the entire government against whistling in the corridors. When he heard whistling while walking in St. James's Park or through Whitehall, anywhere, at any time, he confronted the offender—even young boys—and demanded immediate cessation. His horror of whistling, said Churchill, was the only thing he had in common with Hitler.[345]

When workmen resumed their rush to hammer together protective barriers in Whitehall after Churchill had ordered them to cease, he again ordered the hammering stopped, thereby almost bringing to a halt the safeguarding of the very heart of government. His turbulent behavior, Colville wrote, could be explained by a string of disasters from Norway to Dunkirk, to the shipping losses in the Atlantic, and by the threat of invasion. Yet sometimes, when his staff expected an outburst after a particularly bad piece of intelligence had been gleaned, Churchill surprised all by his nonchalance. Ismay recalled a conference convened in August to discuss the role of the Home Fleet in case of invasion. The commander in chief of the Home Fleet, Admiral Charles Forbes, allowed that, in the event of invasion, his heaviest ships would not operate south of Wales. With the fate of England in the balance, it was expected that such a proposal to save the fleet while losing the war would surely drive Churchill to spontaneous combustion. Ismay, somewhat taken aback by Forbes's statement, waited for the inevitable explosion. It never came. Churchill listened in silence. Then, gazing over his spectacles with an indulgent smile, he declared he never took much notice of what the Royal Navy said before an event, because he knew the navy would, once the action began, undertake the apparently impossible without a moment's hesitation if the situation demanded it, as it surely would were the Germans to come across the Channel.[346]

Where he could dismiss out of hand the advice of his valets and bodyguards, the advice of senior officials had at least to be treated with the appearance of sober reflection, although the end result was usually the same: Churchill got his way. An October conversation with General Alan Brooke turned to the whereabouts of General Percy Cleghorn Stanley Hobart, an erratic tank genius whose services were going unused. "Hobo," as Hobart was known in the ranks, had retired and was serving as a corporal in the Home Guard. As Colville recalled the scene, Brooke believed Hobart too wild to recall to duty, but Churchill, citing General Wolfe brandishing his sword while standing on a chair in front of Prime Minister Pitt, declared. "You cannot expect to have the genius type with the conventional copy-book style." Days later, Churchill met with Hobart and formed a favorable impression. He demanded that General Dill, Chief of the Imperial General Staff, give Hobart a tank division that week, if not *that day.* "Remember," Churchill told Dill, "it is not only the good boys that help to win wars; it is the sneaks and stinkers as well." Dill acceded to the order after protesting that Hobart was "impatient, quick-tempered, hotheaded, intolerant, and inclined to see things as he wished them to be instead of as they were." The description fit Churchill. Hobart got his division, two in fact. Three years later Hobart's "Funnies"—flame-throwing "Crocodile tanks" and mine-clearing "Flail" tanks—would be some of the first armored vehicles to come ashore on the beaches of Normandy. By then, the resurrected Hobart had been knighted for services rendered to the Crown.[347]

By late October, Colville wrote, as the invasion threat ebbed, Churchill had regained a quotient of his engaging, if often infuriating and idiosyncratic, self. He followed outbursts—which still came frequently—not with a direct apology, but with generous praise of some disassociated virtue such that the injured party escaped with dignity intact. He reserved his most ferocious epithets for the enemy. "I never hated the Hun in the last war," he told Ismay earlier in the year, "but now I hate them like...well, an earwig." During a luncheon at Chequers, he allowed that, "A Hun alive is a war in prospect." The parachute mines resulted in his "becoming less and less benevolent towards the Germans," noted Colville, "and talks about castrating the whole lot." Still, his loathing of the Hun in general was softened somewhat when it came to the individual soldier, sailor, or airman: When Sir Hugh Dowding advocated shooting at parachuting German pilots, Churchill disagreed, saying that parachuting pilots were "like sailors drowning at sea."[348]

He was easily brought to tears: the sight of an old Londoner poking among the smoking ruins of her home, movies great and silly, the successes—and failures—of his children, a christening, a choir in song. A good politician can harness such sensitivity to effect, and he was a master politician. No other leader on the world's stage then or since dared wring himself dry so often. Churchill could pull it off. Common citizens and peers alike, on the political left as well as on the right, viewed his displays of emotion as proof of Churchill's depth of character, never as weakness.

Partisanship had evaporated under the heat of Hitler's threat; Churchill could do no wrong. His national government, unified and resolute, transcended the politics of the past. His every word, every tear, every scowl that terrible autumn, was seen as pure Churchill to be sure, yet above politics, other than the politics of survival.

Then he accepted the leadership of the Conservative Party. Chamberlain, dying of cancer, resigned from the War Cabinet early in October, leaving the Tories leaderless. Churchill was offered the post. He accepted over the passionate protest of Clementine, who correctly predicted that by taking the leadership, her husband would alienate large numbers of voters who had looked upon him as the "voice of the nation, irrespective of party." Yet his logic in accepting it amounted to: Who else? There was nobody. It was either Churchill or someone of minimum ego, a man of such little substance he could find nourishment in Churchill's wide shadow, because Churchill already *was* the leader—of the party, of Britain, of the Empire. As well, the party chairmanship was an office his father, Lord Randolph, had aspired to but failed to attain. Churchill, by accepting, may have done so more with the vindication of his father in mind than the political consequences. Given his own turbulent relationship with the Tories over the years, accepting the party chairmanship offered him a sweet opportunity for besting his former adversaries. Just a year earlier, in a letter to Clementine, he had lambasted "these dirty Tory hacks who would like to drive me out of the Party" because he had the audacity to oppose the appeasers.[349]

Now, the opportunity presented itself to shepherd the hacks. Mary wrote that her father and mother had "several ding-dong arguments" over the issue. In the end, he took the post. Colville attached no special significance to the decision. He wrote in his diary: "The P.M. went to a meeting of the Conservative Party to accept the leadership." Churchill tried in his acceptance remarks to remove politics from a purely political office, a clever gambit doomed to failure because no outsiders were on hand to appreciate the subtlety of his rhetoric. He accepted the role as leader, he told his fellow Tories, to preserve "the greatness of Britain and her Empire and the historic certainty of our Island life.... The Conservative Party will not allow any party to excel it in the sacrifice of party interests and party feelings." It was his lone domestic political miscalculation that autumn, but it was a whopper, and brought fateful consequences almost five years later.[350]

The North Sea and the English Channel were England's faithful allies. Summer's gentle mists and mild breezes had indeed given way to the "equinoctial gales" that Churchill surmised would, if frequent and ferocious enough, keep the German invasion barges in their French ports. The Old Man was one with British sailors, who for centuries believed that the equinoxes were alone responsible for the particularly powerful seasonal weather they encountered on their worldwide travels. Fortunately for Churchill, the old myths were correct in regard to the Channel weather. But the night skies offered no respite. By late October the nightly toll of London's civilian casualties had fallen somewhat and the incidence of unexploded bombs had dropped considerably. Churchill asked Ismay whether the "easement which we feel is due to the enemy not throwing them, or to our improved methods of handling?" The answer was both. German bombers arrived each night, but the number of sorties was declining. The Luftwaffe was punching itself out. Of Hitler and his air offensive, Churchill declared, "That man's effort is flagging."[351]

London Can Take It, a British propaganda film, gave Americans a visceral look at the courage of Londoners as their city burned. By the end of November the movie had played in 12,000 U.S. theaters. Charles Lindbergh—pro-German, Anglophobe, and isolationist—opined from his Long Island estate that such heroics were no reason to support the British cause, let alone join it. Joe Kennedy was that very month advising Hollywood producers not to make any such films, as they might annoy Hitler. The Luftwaffe in late October and November pounded other British cities—Birmingham, Bristol, Sheffield, Manchester, Coventry three times, Oxford, and Southampton and its port facilities. A November Gallup poll found that only 13 percent of Londoners took shelter when the sirens wailed, although almost 16,000 now lived in the Underground and beneath railroad bridges. Those with homes simply stayed in bed when the alarm sounded, making sure to pull their comforters tight in the event the windows blew in. HMG issued citizens jars of varnish mixed with liquid rubber, with instructions to paint the mixture over windowpanes in order to prevent shards. The stuff was useless.[352]

On October 27 Churchill sent Roosevelt a message that captured Britain's declining fortunes and the growing dangers facing the Empire. It was part boosterism, part desperate appeal. Churchill told the president that the U-boat and air attacks on the Northwest Approaches—"our only remaining lifeline"—could be "repelled only by the strongest concentration of our flotillas." Yet in order to concentrate its destroyers in the approaches, the Home Fleet would have to lessen its presence in the North Sea, or reduce its destroyer presence along the south coast of England, or both. It could not be in all places at once. British food stocks were low and shipping losses were growing very worrisome, for in the last week of October, losses reached almost 160,000 tons, a figure that would have been thought a disastrous *monthly* loss the year before. Churchill told Roosevelt that much in the way of American matériel was needed for Home Island defense, and that the war would probably widen sometime in 1941 to include both Greece and Turkey, further threatening Britain's already precarious position in the eastern Mediterranean. He ended his telegram with: "The world cause is in your hands."[353]

Churchill's prediction regarding Greece proved spot-on, but his timing was off. The next day, October 28, Mussolini—without consulting Hitler—ordered eleven divisions, including the elite Alpini regiment, Italy's finest fighters, across the Albanian border, over the Epirus Mountains and into Greece. The Italians far outnumbered the Greeks, had tanks where the Greeks did not, and fielded superior artillery. But, writes historian John Keegan, Mussolini had window-dressed his army "with expensive new equipment," to the detriment of its fighting integrity. Thus, the Italians were overall weaker in arms, particularly in infantry. Infantry and machine guns made the difference in the mountain passes that tanks could not traverse. Mussolini's troops lacked something else critical to attaining victory, too: motivation. They did not share Il Duce's sense of destiny.[354]

Mussolini's motives were that he didn't much like the Greeks and sought to assert enlightened Italian influence in the Balkans, and that he craved to show Hitler that Germany was not the only great power in Europe. Mussolini's son-in-law Count Ciano had scribbled in his diary the previous November: "For Mussolini, the idea of Hitler waging war, and worse still, winning it, is altogether unbearable." The charge into Greece would show Hitler that he, Il Duce, was no *fantoccini* (puppet). A collateral benefit could be expected to accrue as well from the takeover—the occupation of Greece would provide secure bases in closer proximity to British targets in the eastern Mediterranean. Yet the Italian charge across the doorstep of Egypt had brought Mussolini within reach of the biggest prizes short of London—Alexandria, Cairo, and the Suez. To capture those trophies, he would need to send his navy into full-blown battle against the Royal Navy. With the French fleet neutralized, the Italian and British Mediterranean fleets were fairly evenly matched; the Italians in fact held the edge in submarines and capital ships, the British in aircraft carriers, of which Mussolini had none. But where Mussolini sought to avoid a climactic naval battle, Churchill, in the spirit of Nelson, *invited* a fight. Mussolini's prospects at sea appeared solid. His prospects on land appeared even more solid. In the Western Desert the Italians outnumbered Wavell's forces by almost three to one, with another 180,000 Italian troops bivouacked to the southeast in the Horn of Africa. Even were an attack on Wavell to result in a bloody stalemate, the British would be pushed to the brink.[355]

Yet Mussolini's superior numbers on the ground counted for nothing without control of the sea. The Mediterranean formed the four center squares of Mussolini's chessboard, and Churchill's. By all that was strategically sound, Mussolini should have tried to drive the British out, supported in the air by his own air forces and the Luftwaffe. But in his most disastrous decision of the war (after joining Hitler in the first place), Il Duce chose to safeguard his navy and throw his ground troops into Greece, where the Greeks let the Italians wear themselves out assaulting mountain redoubts. Hitler learned of Mussolini's strike while aboard his armored train en route to meet Il Duce in Florence. Arriving at the station, the Führer stepped from his car onto a red carpet. Mussolini strode forward, saluted, and announced, "Führer, we are on the march! Victorious Italian troops crossed the Greco-Albanian border at dawn today." They repaired to a small room, where Hitler's first words, spoken quietly as they clasped hands, were, "The whole outcome will be a military catastrophe."[356]

Churchill learned of Mussolini's gambit early on the twenty-eighth when Colville interrupted a meeting at the CWR to announce that the Italians were bombing Athens. "Then we must bomb Rome," replied Churchill. Within hours the War Cabinet authorized the bombing, with specific orders to avoid dropping any ordnance on Vatican City. "We must be careful not to bomb the Pope," Churchill told Colville, because "he has a lot of influential friends." Churchill's concern for the safeguarding of His Holiness's person had little to do with the pope's moral presence on the world stage. Churchill's view of the Papacy ran to the traditional Anglican; the pope was largely irrelevant. As British bombers made for Rome, Hugh Dalton, knowing of the woeful inaccuracy of their aim, expressed hope that the pope not be hit. Churchill replied, "I should like to tell the old man to get down into his shelter and stay there for a week." The pope may have had friends in high places, but Churchill was not one of them. Within days the Italian army in Greece learned it had no friends — divine or otherwise. Mussolini threw in reserves that brought his strength up to fifteen divisions, but in just over four weeks, the outnumbered Greeks drove the Italians back through the mountain passes, back into Albania, whence they had come. If Greece were fated to fall to the Axis powers, Germany would have to do the heavy fighting.[357]

The Greeks had a friend: Churchill. And they had a guarantee from Britain: a pledge made by Chamberlain in 1939 to step up with military help if Greek sovereignty was threatened. Given the sorry state of British military affairs, that was now an empty promise. To Churchill, however, a promise was a promise. Greek survival was at stake. That British survival was at stake as well had to be weighed against a very compelling, very English reason for keeping its promise to Greece: honor. Britain had failed the Czechs. It could not fail the Greeks. "We will give you all the help in our power," Churchill told Greek prime minister Ioannis Metaxas, who at first demurred, for fear of invoking Hitler's wrath. Only one military option was available to Churchill to meet his diplomatic obligation, to divide British forces in the Near East and send some to Greece and Crete. The rest would remain in Egypt to face down the Italian armies encamped since September at Sidi Barrani.

It was a solution that defied the most fundamental military maxim: Do not divide forces if the division results in the increased likelihood of the destruction of all forces in detail. To send part of the Egyptian command to Greece was, Eden wrote in his diary, "strategic folly." Eden, in Cairo since mid-October on a mission to assess the offensive possibilities offered there, telegraphed Churchill on November 1: "We cannot from Middle East resources send sufficient air or land reinforcements to have any decisive influence upon course of fighting in Greece." Churchill replied the next day: "Greek situation must be held to dominate other now. We are well aware of our slender resources." All three senior commanders in the Middle East—General Wavell, Admiral Cunningham, and air chief marshal Sir Arthur Longmore—shared Eden's opinion. Churchill did not. Wavell and General Dill expressed their doubts to each other but did not express them forcefully to Churchill, who thought Wavell and Dill pessimistic in any event, and chalked up any hesitancy on their parts to their natural conservatism. Yet their positions called for them to give the boss the bad with the good, regardless of the boss's reaction. They chose—after Churchill made clear his displeasure with their opinions—to hedge their bets.[358]

Churchill retired early on All Hallows Eve, felled by a stomach ailment for which Dr. Wilson prescribed castor oil, but he was out and about on November 1, and in fine fettle. Attired in his RAF uniform, he inspected a Hurricane squadron at Northolt, of which he was honorary commodore. During the ride to the base, he told Colville he was much annoyed at the Italians—several Italian pilots had been captured after being shot down over London—and planned to bomb Rome regularly as soon as he could put Wellingtons on Malta. Colville expressed hope that the Colosseum not be damaged; to which Churchill replied that it wouldn't hurt if the Colosseum had a few more bricks knocked off. He quoted from Byron's *Childe Harold's Pilgrimage:*

> *"While stands the Coliseum Rome shall stand,*
> *When falls the Coliseum Rome shall fall . . ."*

As they drove on, he continued his harangue against the Italians, "whose impertinence in sending bombers to attack us [Britain]," Colville said, "has much annoyed him." He expressed regret at not having studied Greek, lamented the failure of Eton and Harrow to send fighter pilots to the RAF, and predicted a smashing electoral victory for Roosevelt. He also predicted America would enter the war. He punctuated his monologue with bursts of *"Under the Spreading Chestnut Tree."* He mused on the pleasures of the game chemin de fer and the joy he found at the gaming tables of the Riviera. "I should now like," he said, "to have dinner—at Monte Carlo—and then to go and gamble!"[359]

He would soon enough go and gamble in the Mediterranean, with men and arms in the deserts of Libya, in Greece, and in the air above Malta, on Crete, and at the anchorage in Taranto, where the pride of the Italian fleet rode at anchor. Churchill was about to test his luck on several fronts at once. He should have known that to do so with any hope of success requires virtually limitless resources. His were slender; he knew it, and since May had repeatedly cabled that fact to Roosevelt. He had also rued the state of his resources in a memo that went out the day *before* Mussolini invaded Greece. It took the form of a sharp reply to his old Harrow schoolmate Leo Amery, secretary of state for India, who had proposed sending even more reinforcements to Wavell: "I regret very much," Churchill told Amery, "the use of expressions like 'gamble' when applied to the necessary precautions for the life of this country against far superior air forces." He reminded Amery that more than 70,000 troops had already sailed to Egypt; another 53,000 were due there by year's end. "It is very easy to write in a sweeping manner when one does not have to take account of resources, transport, time and distance."[360]

Yet despite his dismissive missive to Amery, and despite his understanding on a strategic level that Egypt—and only Egypt—was the hand to play, he intended to play both the Greek and Egyptian hands. The advantage to be gained in Egypt by offense was the reason that Eden had been dispatched to the Middle East in the first place—to push Wavell into deploying his reinforced army westward in order to forestall an Italian attack before the Germans wandered mightily onto the scene. Wavell had staked out a sound defensive position, but a defensive posture was, for Churchill, no posture at all. He had not sent 70,000 troops from England merely to sit and wait for the Italians. He had sent them to fight Italians, and on British terms. He did not much respect the Italian fighting man. To Colville he allowed, "The Italians are harder to catch than kill." He knew that the North African desert was the place to deal decisively with the Italians, and he had built up his forces accordingly. Then, all the plans changed—within the day—when Il Duce barged into Greece. Churchill justified the decision to help Greece by citing Britain's prewar pledge to Greece, but the decision was borne in large part by his loathing of Mussolini and the Italian soldier. He believed he could lick Il Duce in any fight, anywhere, anytime, so why not two fights at once? Thus, a few days after Il Duce's thrust, Churchill admonished Dill, "Don't forget—the maximum possible for Greece."[361]

Two days *before* the start of Mussolini's Greek crusade, Churchill, intending to take the fight only to the Italians in the desert, telegraphed concise instructions to Eden, then in Cairo, and about to depart for Khartoum: "Before leaving, you should consider searchingly with your Generals possibilities of forestalling [an Italian] offensive.... I thought their existing plans for repelling an attack by a defensive battle and counter-stroke very good, but what happens if the enemy do not venture until the Germans arrive in strength? Do not send any answer to this, but go into it thoroughly and discuss it on return." Churchill, in his memoirs, writes that his memo to Eden of October 26 included the opinion, expressed clearly, "that any forestalling operation on a large scale in the Western Desert would command my keen support." Yet his memoirs fail to note his clear instructions to Eden, also contained within the memo of the twenty-sixth, to keep mum on any big plans until his return to London. Rather, in a nimble rearrangement of the history of those weeks, Churchill writes of Eden: "He was told in extreme secrecy [by Wavell, in Cairo] that a plan was being drawn up to attack the Italians in the Western Desert instead of waiting for them to open their offensive against Mersa Matruh, in Egypt. Neither he nor Wavell imparted these ideas to me or the Chiefs of Staff. General Wavell begged the Secretary of State for War not to send any telegram on this subject, but to tell us verbally about it when he got home. Thus for some weeks we remained without knowledge of the way their minds were working."[362]

Quite so, but the lack of knowledge coming out of Cairo resulted from Churchill's direct orders to Eden, cabled on the twenty-sixth. Churchill, it seems, in writing those pages of his memoirs indulged in what Mark Twain called "stretchers." Then again, he often said that history would be kind to him, because he would write it. In fact, while Eden was in Cairo with Wavell's plan in hand, Churchill, with his political obligations to Greece foremost in mind but lacking the requisite military intelligence to make a fully informed decision, committed critical resources to Greece and Crete. He ordered three squadrons of Blenheim bombers sent to Greece and two battalions of troops to Crete, to be followed by four thousand more as soon as possible in order to free a Greek division on Crete for battle at home against the Italians. Telegrams flew back and forth between London and Cairo. Eden expressed his concerns, as well as those of Wavell,

Cunningham, and Longmore. Cunningham fretted that the lack of anti-submarine protection in Souda Bay made it a dangerous place for his ships to linger. Churchill believed the proper role of warships was to seek out danger. Longmore, for his part, feared that without anti-aircraft protection or revetments, his Blenheims would be exposed while parked on airfields in Greece and Crete. Wavell sought more reinforcements for Egypt (and his planned desert offensive, which Churchill did not yet know of). Ambassador to Egypt Sir Miles Lampson cabled Eden that a diversion of forces to Greece was "completely crazy," a choice of words that brought a rebuke from Churchill. On November 3, Churchill replied to Eden: "Greece, resisting vigorously with reasonable aid from Egypt and England, might check invaders.... Trust you will grasp the situation firmly, abandoning negative and passive policies and seizing opportunity which has come into our hands. 'Safety first' is the road to ruin in war, even if you had the safety, which you have not. Send me your proposals earliest, or say you have." It was then that Eden told his diary, "It seems that Greece is now to dominate the scene. Strategic folly."[363]

Eden, back in London, finally told Churchill of Wavell's plan over dinner of oysters and champagne at the Annexe on November 8. It was an aggressive and quite possibly brilliant plan. In late September, Graziani's Tenth Army, after conducting its virtually unopposed one-week march east out of Libya, stopped at Sidi Barrani. Unmolested by the British, Graziani was unsure of what to do next. Wavell expected him to attempt to press on 75 miles to the vital railhead at Mersa Matruh, and from there the final 145 miles to Alexandria (this was why Wavell balked at sending forces to Crete and Greece). Instead, the Italians set up a line of seven fortified camps that stretched south and slightly southwest for fifty miles from the Mediterranean coast to the great Saharan escarpment. In their camps, Italian officers lived in such comfort that their tactical field guide might as well have been written by Michelin. Orderlies laid out handwoven linen tablecloths and fine porcelain, silk sheets for the officers' nocturnal ease, and cologne to refresh parched skin. Enlisted men were well supplied with canned tomatoes and pasta packaged in cheery blue boxes. Content, they took their ease in their seven forts. Had they reconnoitered the entire line, they would have divined a fifteen-mile-wide gap between their two southernmost camps. They had not. Wavell had. He and General Sir Henry Maitland "Jumbo" Wilson (he was quite a large fellow), Wavell's commander in chief of Egyptian forces, believed that they could insert their troops and tanks unseen between the camps and attack from the rear. Churchill later wrote that he was "delighted" and "purred like six cats" upon hearing the particulars of the plan, code-named Compass. It was due to kick off in early December.[364]

On the night of November 2, but for tethered barrage balloons overhead and searchlight beams stabbing into the blackness, the skies over London were empty. No German bombers came. It was the first quiet night since September 7. Since July 10, 1,300 German aircraft and 2,400 pilots and airmen had been lost over Britain—one highly trained airman lost for every six British civilians killed. These were unacceptable losses for Hitler, not only because the Luftwaffe had not beaten Britain, but because each plane lost over England meant one fewer experienced pilot and crew available for the final, deciding battle he foresaw, a battle not in the west, above London, but in the east. He had made his decision to attack Russia in July; now, on November 4, he told Lieutenant General Halder, "Everything must be done so we are ready for the final showdown." Some in the high command presumed this would be a lunge through the Dardanelles and the Bosporus (the straits) and thence through neutral Turkey to Vichy-controlled Syria, then east to the Iraqi oil fields, or south to the great prize—the Suez, there to join hands with Mussolini, if only he would attack the outnumbered British at his front. Success would eliminate Britain from the Mediterranean and slice the British Empire into isolated halves. It was the strategy demanded if crushing England was Hitler's intent. But he told Halder, "We can only go to the Straits when Russia is defeated."[365]

On the same day as Hitler looked east, Churchill's gaze was fixed westward, on the Atlantic sea-lanes, where the British merchant fleet had lost its five-hundredth ship since the start of the war, bringing shipping losses to more than two million tons, more than 10 percent of the prewar fleet. In November, for the first time in the war, fewer than one million tons of food reached Britain; the Home Office had determined the nation needed to import at least 1.2 million tons of foodstuffs per month to survive. Victory against the Heinkels over London would count for nothing if Britain were starved into submission by the U-boats. Churchill had three months earlier declared in a memo to his military chiefs that the Royal Navy could not win the war, but it could still lose it. Airpower, he had written, could win the war. His two top priorities were to bomb Germany, as heavily and often as possible, while simultaneously securing his sea-lanes. He wanted more bombers dropping more bombs more often on Germany: "The discharge of bombs on Germany is pitifully small," he wrote to Portal and Sinclair. He pulled no punches with Portal: "The first offensive object of the Royal Air Force is the delivery of bombs overseas, and particularly on

Germany.... It is deplorable that so few Bombers are available even on good nights." Yet, realities forced Churchill to attach more importance to the Northwest Approaches than to raining revenge upon Berlin. The supply situation was so critical, he told the Defence Committee, that "the use of naval and air bases in Eire would greatly simplify our problems, but it would be unwise to coerce Ireland until the situation was mortal." Irish neutrality, if Britain's situation became "mortal," wouldn't be worth a half-pence.[366]

All of this he contemplated on November 4, the eve of the American presidential election. Colville predicted a close contest. Churchill predicted a big win for FDR. His hunch proved correct. Roosevelt dispatched his Republican opponent, Wendell Willkie, with almost 55 percent of the popular vote and by a margin of 449–82 in the electoral college. Churchill cabled his congratulations: "I did not think it right for me as a foreigner to express my opinion upon American politics while the Election was on, but now I feel you will not mind my saying that I prayed for your success and that I am truly thankful for it." He predicted a "protracted and broadening war," a struggle "that will be remembered as long as the English language is spoken in any quarter of the globe.... The people of the United States have once again cast these great burdens upon you, I must avow my sure faith that the lights by which we steer will bring us all safely to anchor."[367]

Roosevelt did not reply. Perhaps Churchill's choice of "we" and "us" was presumptuous; perhaps by not replying Roosevelt sought to remind Churchill of his status as supplicant. Maybe he simply forgot. Almost three weeks later Churchill asked Lord Lothian to "find out most discreetly whether President received my personal telegram congratulating him on re-election." Those weeks spent waiting for a signal—any signal—from America brought a mixed bag of news, the most welcome of which arrived on November 12, when Churchill learned that British naval fliers had overnight smashed a good part of the Italian fleet at Taranto.[368]

The raid on Taranto, like a sucker punch, was so unexpected, so awesome in execution and results, that a reprisal in kind was out of the question. The British had done the impossible: they had torpedoed an enemy fleet in the shallowest of waters. Moreover, it was the first attack in history by carrier-based aircraft on capital ships. A Cockney newsboy captured the essence of the raid as only a street urchin can: *Eyetalian fleet done in. No more macaroni.* Taranto, tucked into the heel of Italy, was an ideal port from which to sally forth into the central Mediterranean if, in fact, an admiral's inclination was to sally forth to fight. But Admiral Dominico Cavagnari, Italian naval chief of staff, was not so inclined; he preferred to preserve his fleet rather than fight with it. Thus, six battleships and two cruisers were among the Italian ships riding at anchor at Taranto on the night of November 11. Limited British success against Mussolini's submarines and destroyers notwithstanding, up to that night the central Mediterranean belonged to the Italians.[369]

By the morning of November 12, the sea from Gibraltar to Alexandria was once again a British lake. The Royal Navy Air Arm had carried the day with just twenty-one Fairey Swordfish torpedo bombers—steel-ribbed, canvas-skin biplanes that could summon a top speed of only 138 miles an hour. The planes were virtually obsolete but could still inflict damage if the enemy was asleep, and the Italians had been sound asleep. The Swordfish had lifted off from Britain's newest aircraft carrier, HMS *Illustrious,* at a distance of about 170 miles. They came into the anchorage low, just twenty feet above the water, in two squads, their paths marked by flares dropped from the lead planes. When the Swordfish departed, three of Italy's six battleships had settled into the mud, knocked out of commission for six months. Two cruisers were hit. It was a severe blow, and for Churchill, the best news of the autumn. "We've got some sugar for the birds this time," he quipped while on his way to the House, where he announced, "I felt it my duty to bring this glorious episode to the immediate notice of the House." The result of the raid, "while it affects decisively the balance of naval power in the Mediterranean, also carries with it reactions upon the naval situation in every quarter of the globe." Strictly speaking, he was correct. The lessons learned, or not learned, at Taranto would in just over a year affect the balance of naval power worldwide. Takeshi Naito, Japan's assistant naval attaché to Berlin, thought the raid so significant he flew to Taranto to assess the damage.[370]

Ambassador Joseph Kennedy tendered his resignation on November 6; Neville Chamberlain died on November 9, the war having overtaken and smashed the dreams of both. Kennedy was by then in the United States, infuriating Roosevelt with his public diatribes against England, against the wisdom of U.S. intervention, and even against Eleanor Roosevelt. During a weekend visit by Kennedy to Hyde Park, Roosevelt listened for several uncomfortable moments as Kennedy ranted about the injustices he had been subjected to by Washington bureaucrats. When Kennedy finished, Roosevelt asked him to step from the room for a moment. He called Eleanor in and told her: "I never want to see that son of a bitch again as long as I live." Churchill, in his memoirs, does not accord Kennedy's departure a single word.[371]

Chamberlain's departure was another matter. His bowel cancer had been diagnosed just four months earlier. He remained in the cabinet until early October, when he took to his bed after an excruciating and unsuccessful surgery. He died with sure knowledge that Great Britain, brought to this juncture in large part by himself and his government, might yet win under Churchill's defiant leadership. Churchill, with the permission of King George, had been diligent to the end in sending Chamberlain the latest intelligence reports, a generous gesture and astute, for there simply was no longer any political currency to be gained from pummeling the appeasers. Generosity, or the perception thereof, paid better dividends. Besides, the seismic crunch of every German bomb emphatically rebutted the politics of the old gang. By bringing Chamberlain and Lord Halifax into the cabinet, Churchill signaled an end to the recriminations, if not the divisions. He knew, as Lincoln had known during his great national crisis, that it is far preferable to have naysayers on the payroll—where the need to maintain the appearance of national unity precludes any naysaying—than off, and free to make mischief.

Not that any unreconstructed appeasers could any longer make much mischief. The Duke of Windsor had been shanghaied to Bahamian oblivion. Sir John Reith had been maneuvered into the transportation secretariat, where with the irony Churchill may have intended, he went nowhere. Halifax served at the Foreign Office at Churchill's pleasure. And time had run out for Chamberlain who, to his credit, left his appeasement beliefs behind when he left No. 10.

German bombs denied his parliamentary colleagues the chance to praise him a final time in the chamber where he had served for so long—those in the event who would not damn him. The Parliament buildings, prime targets located as they were alongside the Thames, were taking such a beating from the Luftwaffe that the Commons was forced to convene at Church House, the administrative headquarters of the Anglican Church in Westminster. There, on the twelfth, Churchill eulogized Chamberlain in a powerful and for the most part sincere address. Chamberlain, he told the gathered MPs, "loved peace, toiled for peace, pursued peace...even at great peril and certainly to the utter disdain of popularity or clamour." Chamberlain's reputation, Churchill said, once it was brought into resolution by the "flickering lamp" of history, would be shielded by the "rectitude and sincerity of his actions," but at the end he was "to be contradicted by events, to be disappointed in his hopes, and to be deceived and cheated by a wicked man."[372]

Yet Neville Chamberlain shifted forever the popular meaning of "appease" from "pacify" to "give in," to such an extent that to brand someone an appeaser has since been almost as venomous an accusation in British and American politics as traitor. Churchill, in his eulogy, tried to stave off the inevitable damning. It was a noble public gesture. He had earlier, however, shown the address to Clementine, who pronounced it "very good." Winston replied, "Well of course I could have done it the other way round."

The funeral took place on November 14 in the gloomy precincts of Westminster Abbey, its cold stone walls gripped by the pitchy fingers of the ancient buttresses, the entire edifice smeared by the accumulated soot of seven centuries, the color of dried blood. Inside it was frigid, German bombs having shattered numerous of its windows. Churchill and most of the War Cabinet served as pallbearers. Colville, sitting among the ushers, noted that some in attendance wore looks of disdain and boredom. Churchill was seen to cry. The exact location of the funeral had been kept secret and was divulged to Parliament just two days earlier, out of fear that the exactness of the Luftwaffe's "beam navigation" greatly increased the risk of a calamitous hit on the assembled dignitaries.[373]

That week, Churchill and Lord Lothian (who had come over from Washington) worked together on a proposal to Roosevelt for American aid with no strings attached. Churchill approved a cable from Lothian to Roosevelt that made clear Britain's needs, including help in securing three Irish ports* (if the need arose), help in safeguarding Singapore, and of course more food and more weapons. The telegram, Colville observed, "was intended to make R. feel that if we go down, the responsibility will be America's."[374]

Late on the afternoon of the fourteenth, a Thursday, Churchill and John Martin prepared for a weekend in the country at Ditchley, a safer venue than Chequers on moonlit nights. The Thursday departure—rather than Friday—came about because Churchill was to secretly meet Lothian there, to continue their discussions on securing American goods. As

---

* Churchill, dismayed by Irish intransigence on the use by the British of three Irish naval bases, proposed to the War Cabinet that Britain no longer subsidize Irish agricultural products and no longer risk British ships and sailors to deliver vital food supplies to Ireland. A treaty of 1922, which Churchill helped draft, gave the British the right to use the bases, but the Chamberlain government in 1939, with astounding lack of foresight with war looming, gave control back to the Irish. Churchill telegraphed his tough new stance on Ireland to Roosevelt on December 13. Churchill was ready and willing to take back the Irish ports by force. Britain, he wrote Roosevelt, would no longer help the Irish "while de Valera is quite content to sit happy and see us strangled." (C&R-TCC, 1:112–13)

Churchill was about to depart, Martin was handed a sealed and urgent message for the prime minister, which he passed to Churchill.[375]

The message contained an update on a looming Luftwaffe raid that the War Cabinet had known about for several days based on intelligence gleaned from captured German fliers and verified by Ultra decrypts. The Germans, prone to literalness in their codes, had anointed the operation *"Mondscheinsonate"* ("Moonlight Sonata"). As yet unknown to the British were the exact where and the exact when of the attack, although the interrogations of prisoners seemed to indicate London, Birmingham, or both. The Air Ministry considered the most likely time frame to be sometime between the fifteenth and the twentieth—when the moon was at its most full. The message Martin handed to Churchill contained the latest Air Ministry estimate of the target and date: London, that night.[376]

By then the wizards at the Air Ministry, having solved the problem of the German targeting beam *Knickebein,* had run up against a far more complex German navigation beam, one that ensured a type of night bombing accuracy the RAF could only wish for from its bombers, accuracy that guaranteed more destruction more often for more British cities. The Germans code-named the new beam *X-Gerat* (X-Gadget), another literal encoding, for the system worked by the intersection of radio beacons above the intended target, in the fashion of an "X." Two of *X-Gerat's* four beams were of such high frequency that two hundred miles from transmission they were just one hundred yards wide. The final genius of *X-Gerat* was its use of two clocks that timed—to the second—the release of the bombs. The entire scheme depended upon the pilot's keeping a precise airspeed. The radioman on board the bomber, upon receiving a radio signal that his plane was ten kilometers from the target, started his clocks. At five kilometers from the target one clock stopped, and the other started backwards. Given a steady airspeed, the time taken to travel the final five kilometers would be identical to the previous five kilometers. When the time expired, the bombs were released automatically. It was accurate, and was the most efficient system yet devised to strike industrial targets. If something were to go slightly amiss and the bombs dropped a mile or so off target, houses, hospitals, schools, churches, and shelters would pay the price. *X-Gerat* therefore could hurt British production when it functioned flawlessly, and British morale when it did not.

Because the complexity and expense of the radio equipment precluded rigging the entire German air fleet with receivers, an elite unit, *Kampfgruppe 100,* was outfitted with *X-Gerat* receiving gear. By dropping flares and incendiaries precisely on targets to guide the squadrons that followed,

K-Grup 100 became the eyes of the Luftwaffe. In 1940, the epiphany that
Germany could bomb at night, in almost any weather, moonlight or no,
was chilling. British fighter planes flew blind after sunset. The *crack* of
anti-aircraft guns brought comfort to the citizens but didn't bring down
many Germans—less than 10 percent of Göring's losses to date took place
at night. Britain, after dark, mustered no adequate defense. Churchill later
recalled that he experienced one of the blackest moments of the war when
he grasped the import of the German beam. He called it "an invisible
searchlight." He tried years later to denigrate it: "German pilots followed
the beam as the German people followed the Führer. They had nothing
else to follow." But in 1940, both the beam and Hitler had yet to miss. The
light of perverted science shone upon London, upon all England.[377]

Laymen and leaders alike considered navigation beams used for such
purpose and to such terrific effect to be futuristic dark forces, ethereal con-
duits of death, incredible and wicked beyond all imagination. The British
governing class was largely made up of Victorian gentlemen who were out
of university before Marconi broadcast his first scratchy radio signals
across the sea. Churchill was on the threshold of his middle years when the
Wright brothers took flight. Britons lived lives where electrification was a
relatively new luxury, where central heat was still a dream, and all things
flying were a mystery. The wonder of radio resided not in the programming but in the sheer magic of human voices transported through the air.
"I am still young enough to be amazed at hearing a voice from Washington
as if it were in my own room," Harold Nicolson wrote, after listening to a
speech by Roosevelt. The Luftwaffe had replaced wonder with fear.[378]

Mollie Panter-Downes was told by "experts" that the solution to the
German night raiders would "be found in the air," with anti-aircraft guns,
searchlights, and fighters. One measure proposed by the experts and
looked upon with favor by Churchill was to drop sand from above German
planes in order to foul their engines. It was never tested. Some in the London press chirped that a solution to the night raiders (top secret, *hush-
hush*) had been found. It hadn't. The real solution, when perfected,
Panter-Downes wrote, would dispel "the popular dream of some Wellesian
or Jules Verneish machine that would intercept and cripple raiders by the
pressing of a button."[379]

In fact, the real solution was just that fantastic, was indeed push-button,
and became real when radar-controlled aerial interception (AI) was made
workable the following year and installed on Beaufighter aircraft. Progress
in jamming *X-Gerat* had been made by late autumn. But by November 14,
the antidote, designated Bromide, was not yet fully formulated. That
night, by the light of the hunter's moon, a British city would pay the price,
but it would not be London.[380]

As Churchill neared Hyde Park, he read the message Martin had passed along. Believing the beam was on London, he ordered the car turned around and returned to the CWR. He sent the typists at No. 10 to the deep shelters at Dollis Hill. John Peck and Colville were packed off to the Down Street shelter, where they dined on caviar, old brandy and Havana cigars, and slept soundly. Churchill, pacing the CWR while awaiting the raid, grew impatient. He climbed to the Air Ministry roof, to scan the skies for the raiders.[381]

None appeared. They were on their way to Coventry, where the "Moonlight Sonata" was about to play out. More than four hundred Heinkel bombers made the run to the Midlands, led by thirteen pathfinders of *K-Grup 100*. They came in multiple waves over ten hours to drop more than six hundred tons of high explosives, parachute mines, and incendiaries. Only one German plane was lost, to accident or pilot error, perhaps to a lucky shot by an anti-aircraft battery. Many of Coventry's AA guns had been previously carted off to London. As the German bombers came over Coventry, Fighter Command put one hundred Hurricanes into the air to meet them. They scored not one hit.[382]

Coventry was destroyed by the morning of the fifteenth. The water main had ruptured; firemen stood and watched, helpless, as flames consumed almost one hundred acres in the city center. More than five hundred citizens lay dead in the rubble. Dozens of vital aircraft-component factories had been hit. They had been scattered by Beaverbrook throughout the city and beyond, a wily plan, yet one that failed to account for the new logic of the Luftwaffe, which was to assure a particular target's destruction by destroying everything nearby. The fourteenth-century cathedral was erased, but for its few walls and its spire. Gas, electricity, and water were knocked out. With no water to drink, the stunned survivors quenched their thirst with whisky and beer. Civil authorities surveying the sullen crowds feared a riot and imposed a curfew. Their concern was overwrought; the people of Coventry were too traumatized to riot. When King George arrived, many citizens were too shocked to recognize the tall stranger in their midst.[383]

Berlin declared that Coventry had been knocked out of the war and promised other cities would soon be *"Coventrated."* Yet Coventry's machine-tool production, knocked down by two-thirds, was restored within weeks. In one respect, Churchill got it as wrong as the Germans. He confided to de Gaulle that the carnage of Coventry would surely raise a "wave of indignation" among Americans and bring them nearer to war. In fact, the carnage of Coventry moved Americans to tears, but not to war, or even preparation for war.

Soon after the raid, Air Marshal Sir Philip Joubert felt the need to squelch press accounts that a solution to the German night raiders was nigh, as if the ruins of Coventry had not dissuaded the optimists. Birmingham, Southampton, Oxford, and Canterbury, throughout November and into December, took their turns in the crosshairs of *X-Gerat*. The Luftwaffe pounded the Clyde and the Mersey. Casualties in some of the attacks exceeded those of Coventry, but the government did not publish the figures, for there was no currency in broadcasting the statistics of defeat. Besides, it was not a one-way fight; the British bombed Berlin on the fourteenth and sixteenth, killing more than three hundred civilians. The bombers always got through, as Baldwin had prophesied. Months earlier, Churchill had told Beaverbrook that offensive airpower was the one "sure path to victory." He still believed that. Yet, whatever level of respect was properly due an air offense, few in late 1940 accorded much respect to the current state of *defensive* measures against nighttime raiders. The ease with which vast numbers of German bombers flew unmolested to their targets was due, Churchill said, to the "complete failure of all our methods."[384]

Mollie Panter-Downes saw Coventry as retaliation for the November 8 RAF raid over Munich, strategically not a significant target but dear, so dear, to the Nazis, home as it was of their putsch of November 8, 1923—Hitler's failed attempt to overthrow the government and establish a right-wing government. Colville speculated that the Coventry raid was in retaliation for the November 11 British success at Taranto. Neither was correct. Coventry, Munich, London, Berlin, and Taranto were all part of a murderous slugfest—take a punch, hit back, take another punch.

After Coventry, Churchill told Portal to draw up a plan "for the most destructive possible bombing attack against a selected German town." In early December, Portal outlined his recommendations, which were approved a few days later in a secret session of the War Cabinet, and codenamed Abigail. Among the objectives: "We should rely largely on fires, and should choose a closely built-up town, where bomb craters in the streets would impede the firefighter." And: "Since we aimed at affecting the enemy's morale, we should attempt to destroy the greater part of a particular town. The town chosen should therefore not be too large." Mannheim, Frankfurt, and Hamburg were among the cities considered. The War Cabinet minutes end with a recommendation that no announcement be made "that this attack was being carried out by way of reprisal for the German attacks on Coventry... and no special publicity should be given to it afterwards." Hamburg, Germany's second-largest city, was eliminated from consideration as too large. The War Cabinet selected Mannheim as the target. It was hit on December 16. The results were meager, about thirty civilians killed, but Abigail and Churchill were just getting started. His goal for 1941, he told Colville, was "to bomb every Hun corner of Europe."[385]

On the last day of November, Churchill celebrated his sixty-sixth birthday at Chequers in the company of Clementine, the children, Beaverbrook, Bracken, and the American writer Virginia Cowles. It was a working birthday, the Old Man dictating his usual large volume of memos to sundry ministers, admirals, and generals. How, he asked Admiral Pound, with more American destroyers coming into service, did serviceable vessels "go down from 84 to 77"? He demanded an update on cement production, not only because cement was needed for bunkers but because he fancied the idea of huge, floating concrete gun platforms. He queried a minister as to why soldiers had been forbidden to "purchase cheap vegetables in the districts where they were quartered." And he authorized "the ringing of church bells on Christmas Day, as the imminence of invasion has greatly receded," although he counseled that steps be taken to ensure the people knew the bells were ringing for church services, not invasion.[386]

The next day, Sunday, December 1, the family repaired to the dim confines of the Ellesborough Parish Church, nearby Chequers, where "little Winston" was christened. Local parishioners stayed on after Matins to witness the ceremony, and the tears streaming down Churchill's cheeks. "Poor infant," he whispered within earshot of Virginia Cowles, "to be born into such a world as this."[387]

Harold Nicolson, believing at midsummer that he and his wife, Vita, had only three weeks to live, pledged to each other that they would carry a "bare bodkin." Yet he told his diary at the time: "I think it practically certain that the Americans will enter the war in November, and if we can last till then, all is well." Colville, too, looked toward November for salvation: "If we can hold on until November," he jotted in his diary on June 14, "we shall have won the war."[388]

It was December 1. November was safe away. They had made it that far.

Almost 4,600 more civilians had not. The Blitz had now killed more than 18,000 Britons, including 2,000 children. Yet, for all the ongoing loss, "it was plain," Churchill wrote, "that the Island would persevere to the end" for "winter with its storms had closed upon the scene."[389]

War had always been a seasonal affair. Winter, as long as men had fought wars, was the season to dig in and await spring's rains followed by the heat of summer. Then, when the roads dried, armies could resume the march and get on with the business of killing. The German invasion was surely off until spring, but modern aircraft flying above the weather rendered winter obsolete. Modern war, or at least the high-altitude aerial component, was an all-weather affair, a truth strongly suggested by the German bombs that fell from on high—and killed Britons—regardless of the meteorological conditions below. The sailing was always clear at 26,000 feet.

Any succor England and Churchill derived from foul weather was offset by the mounting disaster in the Atlantic. Britain's Northwest Approaches were in danger of being pinched shut by U-boats, which were sinking British merchant ships faster than new keels could be laid. More than 250,000 tons of British shipping went down in September, more than 300,000 tons in October, almost 376,000 tons in November, and 60,000 tons during the first week of December. One eastbound convoy from North America lost twenty-one of thirty ships. U-boat crews called these months *"Die Glück-liche Zeit"* ("the happy time"). Since June, the only assistance America offered in the Atlantic battle had arrived in the guise of Roosevelt's old destroyers, which were proving more of a burden than a godsend. During a December dinner with Eden, Churchill announced that the few destroyers that had arrived "aren't much good" and were "badly built." Later in the month, he demanded the Admiralty furnish an accounting of the condition of the destroyers, "showing their many defects and the little use we have been able to make of them so far." The destroyers, dating mostly from the early 1920s, had been rendered obsolete by British improvements in destroyer design even before they were launched. The American ships were called "flush-deckers" because they lacked an elevated foredeck—a fore-castle; they could not fire their forward gun in rough seas or at top speed. That did not bode well for convoy escort duty in the wild North Atlantic. They had been designed for coastal defense, Churchill explained to Roosevelt, before the era of dive-bombers. On picket duty in the North Sea, they would make "frightfully vulnerable" targets for Stukas.[390]

In any case, by December the destroyers had not arrived in meaningful numbers; only nine were fully refitted and commissioned by year's end. They dribbled into British ports, their condition deplorable, all of them in need of refitting. One, rechristened HMS *Lewes,* was such a rust bucket that it was still undergoing repairs the following April when a German bomb knocked it out of commission (not out of action, for it had seen none) until 1942. Another was in such sorry shape that it was cannibalized for spare parts. Between May and December 1940, Churchill composed at least thirty-seven memos and letters to his staff and to Roosevelt on the subject of the destroyers and their lamentable condition.[391]

The promised destroyers were not the only American goods not showing up. Modern rifles, B-17 bombers, and ammunition topped Churchill's shopping list. "What is being done," he queried Halifax, "about our 20 motor torpedo-boats, the 5 PBY [patrol bombers], the 150–200 aircraft, and the 250,000 rifles.... I consider we were promised all the above, and more too." Remember, he told Halifax, "Beg while the iron is hot." Sir Alexander Cadogan, on Churchill's orders, rang up Ambassador Lothian with the same question: "What is the status of the 'other desiderata' promised to us?" Lothian told Cadogan that the U.S. attorney general had held up the torpedo boats until at least January 1941, and that only *one* B-17 was ready to wing its way to Britain.[392]

Churchill was fed up. He told Hugh Dalton that he was tempted to simply tell Roosevelt, "If you want to watch us fighting for your liberties, you must pay for the performance." The Prof egged him on: "The fruits of victory which Roosevelt offers seem to be safety for America and virtual starvation for us." Always ready with a statistic, the Prof tossed more fuel onto the fire: "We are putting between 1/3 and one-half of our national effort into fighting Nazidom." The American contribution so far—sold, not given—was "about 1/20 of the annual American national effort." The Americans, Lindemann reminded Churchill, had from an accounting standpoint long ago written off the old destroyers, which were not even carried as assets on the U.S. books. These were hard facts to digest, given that the price England had paid for the fifty rust buckets took the form of British naval bases from Newfoundland to British Guiana, bases that American warships now sailed from in order to protect... America.[393]

Churchill peeled away pieces of the British Empire in exchange for obsolete boats. The Atlantic bases were the first to go, the first installment in the transfer of global supremacy from Britain to America. At the time, nobody, Churchill included, saw it quite that way. Indeed, he tried to frame the deal in terms of British largess when he told Parliament:

> Some months ago we came to the conclusion that the interests of the United States and of the British Empire both required that the United States should have facilities for the naval and air defense of the western hemisphere... [and] had decided spontaneously, and without being asked or offered any inducement... to place such defense facilities at their disposal.... There is of course no question of any transference of sovereignty."[394]

In fact, British sovereignty as measured in pence, shillings, and gold sovereigns was fast disappearing. Since the start of the war, Britain had paid almost $4.5 billion in cash (about $160 billion in modern dollars) for American food and matériel. The United Kingdom's total remaining reserves of gold and dollar-denominated marketable securities was less than $2 billion, a sum accumulated since the start of the war mostly by exporting pottery, Scotch whisky, and South African gold. Yet Britain's immediate needs would cost twice that, a ratio that would not necessarily have proven disastrous in peacetime, but the U.S. terms of sale were cash-and-carry. Britain desperately lacked the cash to buy, and needed more ships in which to carry. "It was a time," Churchill wrote, "marked by an acute stringency in dollars." Lord Lothian summed up the situation when, with decidedly nondiplomatic clarity, he told Washington reporters: "Britain's broke." Roosevelt offered to send a cruiser to Cape Town in order to pick up and deliver to the United States $20 million in British gold bullion as a down payment for services rendered, an offer akin to a noncombatant lifting the boots and pocket watch from a dying trooper.[395]

Churchill's weekend meeting with Lothian in mid-November resulted in the framework of a plan to address the supply and money questions, which Churchill worked into a long letter to Roosevelt. The letter, containing nineteen sections and which Churchill called "one of the most important I ever wrote," went out on December 7. In essence, he told the president, it all came down to two things: control of the seas, a battle Britain was losing; and money, of which Britain had almost none.[396]

Churchill addressed the worldwide strategic situation for 1941 in the first sixteen sections of his letter. Absent is any sign of his previous fawning or pleading; this letter was straightforward and powerful. He was polite, yet firm. On the "mortal danger" of shipping losses, Churchill wrote: "Would this diminution continue at this rate it would be fatal.... In fact we have now only one effective route of entry to the British Isles... against which the enemy is increasingly concentrating." To combat that threat, he asked for "a gift, loan or supply of American vessels of war."[397]

Such was his concern that the Germans might either charm or shoot their way into Irish ports, he dangled before Roosevelt the prospect of a united Ireland. "It is not possible for us to compel the people of Northern Ireland against their will to leave the United Kingdom and join southern Ireland," he wrote, "but I do not doubt that if the Government of Eire would show its solidarity with the democracies of the English-speaking world at this crisis, a Council for the Defense of all Ireland could be set up out of which the unity of the Island could probably in some form or another emerge after the war." Given that a large portion of Roosevelt's voter base consisted of Irish-Americans, this was a rumination that would play well in America, but wreak havoc in Belfast were it revealed. Churchill, more concerned with American sensibilities than those of Ulstermen, sent Minister of Health Malcolm MacDonald to Dublin three times to offer Prime Minister Eamon de Valera a united Ireland, if de Valera joined Britain against Germany. MacDonald, as Chamberlain's Dominions secretary, had negotiated a trade agreement with Ireland in 1938. Churchill despised the treaty but thought MacDonald might be an Englishman the Irish could work with. He was not. Three times de Valera declined MacDonald's approaches, arguing that Churchill could not deliver on the promise even were he so inclined. Later in the year, when MacDonald was made High Commissioner to Canada, the back-channel dialogue ceased.[398]

In his letter to Roosevelt, Churchill moved on to the possibility of Japan's grabbing the oil of the Dutch East Indies. There wasn't much to say on the matter, and he said it quite forthrightly: "We have to-day no forces in the Far East capable of dealing with this situation should it develop." Then, to point number seventeen: money. Churchill let loose. It was clear, he wrote, that the more rapidly the United States fulfilled Britain's needs, the sooner Britain's finances would collapse, until, "we shall no longer be able to pay cash for shipping and other supplies.... It would be wrong in principle...if, at the height of this struggle, Great Britain were divested of all saleable assets, such that after the victory was won with our blood, civilization saved...we should stand stripped to the bone." Reduced to its essence, the letter is more a moral argument than a financial plea. Churchill closed by telling—not asking—Roosevelt to "regard this letter not as an appeal for aid, but as a statement of the minimum action necessary to achieve our common goals."[399]

Roosevelt had a great deal to chew on. He received Churchill's letter while aboard the cruiser *Tuscaloosa* on a two-week vacation in the Caribbean, which included stops at some of America's new (and Britain's former) naval bases. As later related by Churchill, his "great friend" read and re-read the letter, "as he sat alone in his deck chair, and that for two days he did not seem to reach any conclusion. He was plunged in intense thought and brooded silently." The brooding may have been a result of what Churchill made clear in his letter: Britain vanquished would leave the United States alone and unprepared for war, swayed by the isolationists into a mortally dangerous neutrality that could result in a U.S. accommodation with Hitler, a brokered peace both fatal and without honor.[400]

To avoid that outcome, Roosevelt had to find a way to help America's proxy before the proxy went broke, or worse. He had been contemplating a possible solution to the problem for several months, urged on by his interior secretary, Harold Ickes, who had told him in an August letter that it would not reflect well on America if "Britain went down" and America had not sent destroyers to prevent an invasion. Ickes added a homey analogy: "It seems to me that we Americans are like the householder who refuses to lend or sell his fire extinguisher to help out the fire in the home that is next door, although the house is all ablaze and the wind is blowing from that direction." By the time Roosevelt arrived back in Washington from his Caribbean vacation, he thought he had found his legal basis for funneling aid to Britain. It came by way of an obscure federal law that allowed the U.S. military to *lease* property not required for public use. On December 17—without offering any details of what he was pondering—Roosevelt told reporters (for the purpose of publication but without naming the source) of his struggle to find a way to help Britain. He told them, "What I am trying to do is to eliminate the dollar sign." Then he offered a variation on Ickes's parable: "Suppose my neighbor's house is on fire and I have a length of garden hose four or five hundred feet away. If he can take my garden hose and connect it up to his hydrant, I may help him to put out the fire.... I don't say to him...'Neighbor, my garden hose cost me fifteen dollars; you have to pay me fifteen dollars for it.' No!...I want my garden hose back after the fire is over." A reporter asked, "Mr. President, before you loan your hose to your neighbor you have to have the hose." The reporter went on to point out that if British orders for goods could be met only by second and third shifts at American factories, no federal authority was in place to mandate that factories add those shifts. They were fair points; America could not help Britain while running on one shift. Roosevelt avoided mention of the fact that the neighbor in this case needed not only the hose but an army of firemen as well.[401]

On December 12, Lord Lothian, who had been instrumental for more than a year in pleading Britain's case to Americans, died suddenly in Washington. When taken ill, Lothian, a Christian Scientist, refused medical attention. "What a monstrous thing," Churchill exclaimed, "that Lothian should not have allowed a doctor to be called." Lothian's death, coming the very week Roosevelt was pondering Churchill's letter, created a political vacuum in Washington at the worst possible moment. Churchill needed to appoint a new ambassador, and fast. He liked Lloyd George for the job, but only, he told Colville, "if he could trust him." Were Lloyd George to prove disloyal, Churchill added, "he could always sack him." But the ambassadorship would place the former prime minister under Halifax, which Colville argued "would be an obstacle from L.G.'s point of view." On the other hand, if Halifax went to Washington, yet another former appeaser would have been exiled. Churchill drafted Halifax. "His high character was everywhere respected," Churchill later wrote, "yet at the same time his record in the years before the war and the way in which events had moved left him exposed to much disapprobation and even hostility from the Labour side of our National Coalition." Churchill told Colville that if Halifax remained in Britain he "would never live down the reputation for appeasement" and that he "had no future in this country." Without the United States in the war, Churchill told him, the very best

Britain could hope for was an unsatisfactory peace and that he, Halifax, "had a glorious future in America" if he proved successful in getting the United States in.[402]

In the final weeks of the year, while Roosevelt pondered his congressional strategy, Churchill could not do much more than watch as London burned, and ponder two questions: What exactly were the Americans going to do and when? And where was Hitler going to go and when? Spain and Gibraltar had been a source of angst for months. Ultra recently divined a German operation code-named Felix, about which nothing was known beyond the name. Churchill thought Felix might entail a strike into Ireland or Spain. He thought Spain more likely, he told Colville, because that's where he would go if he were Hitler. That is exactly where Hitler sought to go, but Franco, in power largely through the sponsorship of Hitler and Mussolini, demurred. If Gibraltar was to be taken, Franco told Hitler, it would be taken by Spanish troops, not by a coalition of Germans and Spanish.[403]

In fact, the *generalissimo* had no intention of attacking Gibraltar. Spaniards were kept alive by food imports that Britain allowed to arrive only because Spain remained neutral. Franco understood that were he to allow Germans passage to Gibraltar, London would starve Spain by blockade. Thus, despite his debt to Hitler, he thought it best to forestall Hitler's call to arms. In fact, he thought it best to sit this war out. Churchill, in late November, had telegrammed a warning to Roosevelt about the danger of losing Gibraltar and suggested that Roosevelt offer Franco "food month by month so long as they keep out of the war." If Gibraltar were lost, Churchill told Roosevelt, it "would be a grievous addition to our naval strain, already severe."[404]

Gibraltar corked would trap the entire British Mediterranean fleet in the bottle, but only if the Suez Canal was corked as well. Franco, wily and possessed of a sense of global strategy that Hitler lacked, told the Führer that if Germany took the Suez Canal, Spain would then take Gibraltar. The German grand admiral Raeder, who understood very well the centricity of naval power to Britain's status as a world power, had long grasped the importance of the Suez to London, and had tried in September to convince Hitler to pursue the same strategy. Taking Gibraltar *and* the Suez, Raeder argued, would open pathways to the Middle East and make "doubtful whether an advance against Russia from the north will be necessary." Churchill did not know that on the thirteenth of December, Hitler had canceled Felix, or that on December 18, he had signed a directive that began: "The German armed forces must be prepared to crush Soviet Russia in a quick campaign before the end of the war against Britain." Preparations were to be completed by May 15. The operation was code-named Barbarossa.[405]

Churchill later wrote that when the Germans massed on the French and Belgian frontiers in May of 1940, and then cascaded across, he grasped that "we were about to learn what total war means." Indeed, total war had come to France, and was being waged in the Atlantic, and in the skies over England. But in December 1940, the status of life in much of continental Europe—and in Manchuria and the Horn of Africa—was more of a gruesome peace brokered by bayonet than total war.

Stalin, having the previous year partnered with Hitler in the obliteration of Poland, was digesting his Baltic, Finnish, and Romanian territorial takeovers. In December, Stalin's most trusted lieutenant, Soviet foreign minister Molotov, returned from Berlin after negotiations with Ribbentrop over how best to share the spoils, including the carcass of the British Empire. Churchill called Molotov "a man of outstanding ability and cold-blooded ruthlessness" whose very survival within the Bolshevik world of lies, insults, intrigue, and the always present threat of "personal liquidation" fitted him out "to be an agent and instrument" of a leader such as Stalin. Yet in Hitler, Stalin and Molotov encountered a better liar and a more ruthless, more cold-blooded intriguer. Though in December Hitler faced his armies to the west, his vision had already turned to the east.[406]

In the Far East, the Japanese had begun the tenth year of their Manchurian depredations, enslaving the populace in the name of pan-Asian solidarity. "China," Churchill wrote in 1937, "is being eaten by Japan like an artichoke, leaf by leaf." Now, the fourth year of the Sino-Japanese war found a frontline stalemate between Chinese general Chiang Kai-shek's nationalist troops and Japanese general Hideki Tojo's invading armies. Behind the Japanese lines, 400,000 of Mao Zedong's Communist troops were making the emperor pay dearly for Chinese real estate. Japan's moderate prime minister, Prince Fumimaro Konoye, found himself trying to appease Tojo's war party, which believed in purchasing empire by brute force. If Konoye emerged from the political intrigue with more power, the greater Pacific region might yet live in peace. If Tojo proved stronger, a pan-Pacific war was most certainly inevitable, though Churchill stuck to his long-held premise that Japan would think twice before mixing it up with a power as mighty as Great Britain.[407]

Germany, Japan, and Italy had signed the Tripartite Pact in Berlin, on September 27, which pledged support for any signatory who was attacked by a power not already at war with the signatories. By doing so, the Axis arrayed itself against the rest of the world. Churchill later wrote that the agreement "opened wider fields," but the Tripartite Pact posed a conundrum for Churchill concerning the Burma Road. The road wound seven hundred tortuous miles from Lashio, a Burmese railhead four hundred miles north of Rangoon, to Kunming, in Yunnan Province, China, and was absolutely vital to the supply of Chiang Kai-shek's Chinese nationalist army. The British had closed it in August, Alec Cadogan wrote, in an agreement with Japan that "special efforts be made to produce a lasting peace in the Far East." Japan had made no such effort, special or otherwise, because Japan was dealing from strength. The Imperial Japanese army and navy, fueled in large part by the importation of seven million barrels a year of American oil, could go anywhere they pleased in order to make good on their threats. Nearly three months later, in October, the Burma Road was reopened, but the question was, how would Japan react? If Tokyo responded with force, what would Italy and Germany do? Attack England (again)? And what would America do?[408]

With those questions in mind, and with no military means available to dissuade the Japanese from mischief, Churchill cabled Roosevelt and asked for a bit of show-the-flagmanship in the Pacific, a friendly visit by an American naval squadron—"the bigger the better"—to Singapore, to help persuade the Japanese to behave. That such a display of American sea power might provoke the Japanese to a warlike response against the Americans certainly occurred to Churchill, because he understood the true intent of the Tripartite Pact. *Not already at war* was the key concept of the pact, unmasking it as a transparent attempt by the Axis to forestall intervention by the only nation of import not yet at war: the United States. As Churchill saw it, an American fleet cruising menacingly across the Japanese sea routes to Malayan rubber and Indonesian oil might be just the ticket to get the United States into the war. The U.S. fleet made no such foray.[409]

The United States all year had been in no mood for handling any hot potatoes tossed its way by Churchill. Navy chief admiral Harold ("Betty") Stark wanted to keep his ships safe at Pearl Harbor, not send them traipsing about the Singapore Strait in support of Churchill's empire. Even if willing, America wasn't ready. The United States was still struggling out of the Depression, half aware of the coming storm and not half prepared to deal with it. America was willingly isolated in a state of blissful peace, the blush of renewed economic prosperity on the horizon. No mere three-way Axis deal could keep America out of war if that peace was disturbed; nor could Churchill's pleas bring America into it if it was not. America was not entirely oblivious to far-flung events, or at least European events. The most listened-to broadcast of 1940 had been Roosevelt's "dagger in the back" speech. Millions of Italian-Americans still thought Il Duce a stand-up guy. Americans knew old Europe, from where their parents had come, but the

Pacific was another story. Dozens of islands—Guam, Corregidor, Wake, Midway, Guadalcanal—were terra incognita to most Americans. Not until the final weeks of 1941 would they—and most Britons—know just where Pearl Harbor was located.[410]

America was re-arming, after a fashion. With an eye toward strengthening its global presence, the U.S. Navy (at 160,000 officers and men, smaller than both the Italian and German navies) ordered eight new aircraft carriers. Delivery was specified for 1945. The army, an anemic force of 500,000 (if the National Guard was included) field-tested its tough new General Purpose vehicle, GP for short. The GOP's nomination of Wendell Willkie, rather than the isolationist Robert Taft, to run against Roosevelt had sent a subtle message to the world that neither American political party had completely buried its head in the sands of isolation. Roosevelt signed into law America's first peacetime draft bill, a call-up of 800,000 men to serve for one year. Without once using the word "draft" when announcing the law, he termed it the revival of "the three-hundred-year-old American custom of the muster." If his ongoing pledges that American boys would not be fighting in any overseas wars was to be taken at face value, an obvious question arose: Where in the world *would* 800,000 mustered men serve?[411]

Since May, Churchill had wrangled, pestered, and beseeched Roosevelt to join him in his battle for Britain's survival, without success. His missives to Roosevelt were, on the surface, full of facts and figures concerning British air and sea losses, arms production, and finances, yet, with the exception of his long December 7 letter, they are similar in voice to the letters that nine-year-old Winston wrote from St. George's School, seeking the approval of his mother and father. Churchill recalled that, as a boy, his father seemed to him "to own the key to everything or almost everything worth having." Roosevelt held that key in 1940.[412]

Churchill had gained the heights of power only to gaze down upon a nation at its military nadir. He was the defender of a realm that quite possibly would soon prove defenseless. RAF successes against Göring—limited and by no means guaranteed to continue—served up a meager and teasing hope of future victory. These were the months about which Churchill later wrote that it was "equally good to live or die." During those December days, a prediction Churchill made after witnessing the French disaster seemed as likely to be fulfilled as not: in mid-June, on his last flight from France, he had turned to Ismay and asked, "Do you realize we probably have a maximum of three months to live?" Those three months were now coming up on six, but absent an ally, the months gained were simply a stay of execution. Britain's finest hour had given way to its longest nights. The Germans had not arrived by sea, but when the Channel calmed in April and May, when the lilacs announced the coming of spring—and

Hitlerwetter—surely the Germans would come. Yet, as he had since June, Churchill believed that if the Germans came, they would fail.[413]

On December 6, from the North African desert, came news that a British imperial army was on the march, and, unlike the BEF in June, this army was marching forward. Just after midnight, Operation Compass—Wavell's plan to push the Italians out of western Egypt—began when British troops, tanks, and trucks departed Mersa Matruh and headed west, toward the seven Italian camps anchored at Sidi Barrani, seventy-five miles and a two-day march distant. Mersa Matruh, an azure sea to its front, stone cliffs rising around the town on the landward sides, had been an active port and sponge-fishing center since before the Greeks first came to Cyrene (modern Libya) almost twenty-six centuries earlier. It was from here in around 500 BCE that the Persian forces of Cambyses II turned into the desert, in search of the oasis of Siwa, about two hundred miles south, and the first stop on the ancient caravan route to the Sudan. Cambyses and his entire army disappeared somewhere in the desert, perhaps in the great Sand Sea to the southwest, perhaps in the Qattara Depression, an enormous and lifeless bed of salt and sand fifty miles wide, two hundred miles long, and, at more than four hundred feet below sea level, one of the most hellish geographical features on the planet. Alexander the Great, also in search of Siwa, followed the route of Cambyses in 331 BCE. After nearly meeting the Persians' fate, the Macedonian finally made it to the oasis, where the oracle of Zeus Ammon confirmed that the young warrior was indeed of divine ancestry. Alexander departed, sure of his destiny, and conquered the world. Three centuries later, the divine Cleopatra and her lover Anthony favored Mersa Matruh (then named Paraetonium) for frolics in the surf, and elsewhere.

Mersa Matruh was tethered to Alexandria by a small-gauge railroad that snaked 150 miles alongside the same coastal road Alexander had marched on. The British could therefore supply themselves, but the Italian supply lines, though secure, reached back hundreds of miles. That (and the array of their forts) was their weakness. The plan called for the British field commander Lieutenant General Richard O'Connor to move his Western Desert Force—30,000 men supported by six hundred Bren Gun carriers, and scores of light and heavy tanks—undetected from Mersa Matruh to Sidi Barrani. In the tradition of the Saracens, who had learned a millennium earlier the need to live by the desert's rules or die by them, fuel and water had been secreted in cisterns along the route. O'Connor's tanks and men would drink their fill on the two-day journey west. Then, upon reaching the Italian camps, O'Connor's plan called for his armor and troops to insinuate themselves unseen and unheard (not likely in the emptiness of the desert) behind the gap between camp Nibeiwa and camps Sofafi and Rabia. O'Connor then intended to run his tanks and infantry smack into the exposed flanks and rear of the Italians, a most daring maneuver given that O'Connor's forces were outnumbered by almost three to one.

Traditionally, an entrenched defensive force equal in numbers to an attacking force is judged to hold an effective advantage of at least three to one over the attackers. O'Connor's army of 30,000 was, in that sense, at a nine-to-one disadvantage, or would have been had the Italians been facing in the right direction. To the west of Sidi Barrani, almost 150,000 more Italian troops waited in northern Libya. However complete O'Connor's surprise, if a division or two of the Italian forces in Libya drove to the aid of Sidi Barrani, O'Connor's imputed numerical disadvantage could run to nearly twelve to one. He was placing his army in a nutcracker in hopes that the nut would shatter the cracker. With a little overreaching and a bit of bad luck, his army might find a place in military history alongside Custer's 7th Cavalry at Little Bighorn, the Light Brigade at Balaclava, and the Anzacs* at Gallipoli.

Distance was O'Connor's other enemy. Once he motored out of Mersa Matruh, each mile thereafter stretched his supply lines. Were he to find success at Sidi Barrani and thrust westward, he faced nothing but emptiness. Libya spanned one thousand miles of desert except for a narrow strip along the coast where a single road twisted from Bardia in the east to Tripoli in the west. The country was a sea of sand and flaked stone, without roads, devoid of vegetation, bereft of any landscape features that afforded troops protection. The Italians in Libya were linked to Italy by secure seaborne supply lines, and thus the cologne, silk bedsheets, and fine cutlery. O'Connor's force found itself alone in the desert, a true expeditionary unit, fully detached from all that sustained it.

Wavell and O'Connor knew how to fight in the desert, whereas apparently the Italians knew only how to camp there. The British understood that desert warfare was a fluid thing, with mobility the key. Destruction of enemy forces was more important than possession of turf, which could no more be held in the desert than could a patch of water in the open ocean. Wavell's immediate goal was not to sail O'Connor's army across the wide

---

* Although the Australians and New Zealanders ("Anzacs," for Australian New Zealand Army Corps) were not configured as a corps during World War Two, the term "Anzac" stuck, and was used in reference to units of those nations deployed in any theater or operation.

sand seas of Libya, but simply to smash up the Italians at Sidi Barrani and, if things went well, to raid twenty-five miles farther to the west, to Buq Buq. To pull that off, the British would need stealth, great good luck, total surprise, and an enemy with scant fighting will.

They got all four. During the night of December 8 and early hours of the ninth, O'Connor's infantry and supporting Matilda tanks threaded their way between Nibeiwa and the two southernmost Italian forts. To guide their movement, a British advance force had lit a string of beacons crafted from oil drums with one side peeled away, that side facing east, to be seen by O'Connor's troops but not by the Italians. The British had been spotted by an Italian flier, but when he gave his initial (verbal) report, he was told to put it in writing. If he did so, it was either ignored or not read. By 2:00 A.M. on the ninth, O'Connor's force was in place behind Nibeiwa. It was a true imperial army made up of Englishmen, Hindus, Sikhs, Ulstermen, and Highlanders, with New Zealanders manning the troop transports. Two regiments of Matilda tanks were drawn up, ready to support the infantry. This was what the twenty-six-ton monsters had been built for. Virtual castles on steel treads, their two-pound guns could outshoot Italian light tanks while giving cover to the imperial infantry. After a breakfast of bacon, hot tea, and a shot of rum for the road, O'Connor's men moved out. From the Italian camps the breeze carried the aromas of cooking fires and fresh coffee and hot rolls.[414]

The British interrupted breakfast. The pipers of the Cameron Highlanders sounded the charge, the keening of their pipes reaching Nibeiwa as the first rounds from the Matildas smashed into the Italian lines. The tanks came on in ranks, flanked by Bren Gun carriers, their heavy machine guns raking the Italians. Charging pell-mell behind the tanks came the Highlanders, the morning sun bright upon their helmets and bayonets. The Italians fought furiously with machine guns and grenades; General Pietro Maletti burst from his tent, shooting, and was immediately shot dead. Twenty Italian light tanks were reduced to piles of smoking steel by the Matildas, which rolled on, crushing defenders under their treads. It was over in less than three hours, the camp destroyed, more than two thousand prisoners taken. Ten miles north, two more camps waited. The 1st Royal Fusiliers, kicking a soccer ball, led the charge. White flags went up in the Italian camps. The commander of one stood five hundred of his men at attention when the British entered to accept his surrender.

O'Connor's men and tanks rolled onward for two days, north toward Sidi Barrani. By December 12, the entire line of fortifications was swept away, and Sidi Barrani taken, after being shelled to rubble by Matildas and Royal Navy cruisers. The success was so stunning and unexpected that the British found themselves outnumbered by their 39,000 prisoners. One battalion commander radioed that he had captured "five acres of officers, about 200 acres of other ranks." Churchill, delighting in the early reports, referred to the Greek general battling the Italians when he told Colville, "So, we shan't have to make use of General Papagos after all!" He phoned the King: "My humble congratulations to you, Sir, on a great British victory, a great Imperial victory." It was, wrote Colville, "the first time since the war began that we have really been able to make use of the word victory."[415]

O'Connor thrust farther west to Buq Buq, where the original plan called for the raid to end. Wavell, in Cairo, received a message: "We have arrived at the second B in Buq Buq." O'Connor rolled right through, bagging more prisoners. The Italians were on the run, in full flight to Libya. Mussolini was furious. "Five generals are prisoners and one is dead," he told Ciano. "This is the percentage of Italians who have military characteristics and those who have none."[416]

Before Compass kicked off, Churchill had worried to Dill that Wavell might be "playing small" by not "hurling in his full available forces." Within a week of launching his operation, Wavell—shy, tongue-tied Wavell—considered just months earlier by Churchill to be somewhat "dumb," became his hero of the hour. Churchill learned that Wavell had written two books; knowing neither the titles nor the subject matter, he ordered Colville to locate the volumes. It seems the reticent Wavell was a poet, historian, and biographer as well as a fighter. He had penned *The Palestine Campaigns* in 1928 and had just published his latest work, *Allenby,* in which he recounted how Field Marshal Viscount Allenby accomplished in Palestine during the Great War what no other British general in that war could bring off: the total destruction of the enemy at his front with minimum loss to his own men. Wavell had served under Allenby in the Middle East and shared that field marshal's philosophy of leadership: trust subordinates, give them clear orders, and allow them to fill them. Display courage, moral and physical, where called for, not for love of danger but because hard work is to be done. This was the sort of stuff Churchill admired, admitting as it did to a larger view of things, a certain bon ton that would fit in well at his dinner table, as a foil of course for his even larger view of things.[417]

By December 16, O'Connor was across the Libyan border. Churchill cabled Wavell: "Your first objective now must be to maul the Italian Army and rip them off the African shore to the utmost possible extent." His message to Wavell on the eighteenth dispensed with literalness altogether, reading in its entirety, "St. Matthew, Chapter 7, Verse 7." ("Ask, and it shall be given to you; seek, and ye shall find; knock, and it shall be opened unto you.") Churchill had risked all by sending men and tanks from Britain to Egypt when invasion appeared imminent. He had gambled, and so far had won.[418]

The Blitz grew more murderous as the year went out. On December 8 the House of Commons was hit. The next day, Henry "Chips" Channon* wandered upon the scene as Churchill rambled among the rubble. "Suddenly I came upon Winston Churchill wearing a fur-collared coat, and smoking a cigar.... 'It's horrible,' he remarked...and I saw he was much moved, for he loves Westminster." Channon, surveying the smoking ruins of the ancient building, remarked, "They would hit the best bit." Churchill, chewing on his cigar, grunted, "Where Cromwell signed King Charles's death warrant." That night Channon wrote that he had "sensed the historical significance of the scene—Winston surveying the destruction he had long predicted, of a place he loved."[419]

London had seen more than 450 raids between September and late December; the bombs sometimes fell at the rate of one hundred per minute. On December 29 the capital sustained its worst beating. It was Sunday, the preferred day for bombing commercial areas, when warehouses full of combustible goods were locked tight for the weekend, with no employees on duty to snuff out the incendiaries. The new moon promised relief for the raiders, and in tandem with the recent solstice, it made for a low tide that brought the Thames down to the level of a stream. High cloud cover and a heavy mist favored the raiders. *K-Grup 100* leading the way in specially equipped Heinkels lifted off from the squadron's base in Brittany at about 5:30 P.M. local time, an hour later than London time. Once airborne, they picked up the main *X-Gerat* radio beam, broadcast from Cherbourg. The beam was on St. Paul's. Behind the pathfinders came more than two hundred bombers, from bases all over northern France. The raid lasted only two hours, but the incendiaries did their work. The first flight of *K-Grup 100* missed its target by one thousand yards, putting its incendiaries on the south side of the Thames, near Elephant and Castle. Somehow the remainder of the fleet missed the pathfinders' markers and put their bombs square on the designated target, the City (London's financial district), with the result that fires raged along both banks of the river. In fact, even the river burned.[420]

Edward R. Murrow, on the roof of the BBC, opened his broadcast:

---

* Channon (1897–1958), American by birth, was elected the Conservative MP for Southend in 1935. According to Jock Colville, Sir Henry was "a leading light in London café society," a friend of Lady Cunard's and R. A. Butler's. He wrote with elegance and deployed a sharp wit.

"Tonight the bombers of the German Reich hit London where it hurts the most, in her heart. St. Paul's Cathedral, built by Sir Christopher Wren, her great dome towering over the capital of the Empire, is burning to the ground as I talk to you now." But St. Paul's, wrapped in a cowl of filthy black smoke, was not burning. As Murrow spoke, a few fire wardens scrambling among the ancient joists under the lead roof of the cathedral managed to stay ahead of the firebombs.[421]

Other precincts fared worse. The Germans dropped "Molotov bread-baskets," containers that spit out dozens of incendiaries as they fell. The Guildhall went down, and eight of Wren's churches. Paternoster Row disappeared, the publishers and bookbinders done in—as they had been in the Great Fire of 1666—by their stockpiles of glue and paper. Among the lost and irreplaceable treasures: William the Conqueror's eleventh-century parchment charter granting London its freedom. More than a thousand fires started in the East End, always the recipient of ordnance when the Germans released their bombs thirty seconds too soon. Fire wardens, silhouetted by the whipping flames and the glow of exploding incendiaries, scrambled along smashed rooftops, while firemen below scrambled as walls collapsed. The fires burned for two days. Across the river, in South-wark, firemen ran hoses out hundreds of feet onto the mudflats of the Thames, only to watch them melt. "Poor old" London, Harold Nicolson wrote, "is a char woman among capitals, and when her teeth begin to fall out she looks ill indeed." When Churchill and Clementine toured the wreckage the next day, an old woman approached and asked when the war would end. Churchill turned to her and replied, without a smile: "When we have beaten them."[422]

While London burned into the early hours of December 30, Americans gathered around radios as Franklin Roosevelt chatted from his fireside about the state of the world. He stressed the need to safeguard the Atlantic Ocean by supporting Britain, and the need, ultimately, to help Britain defeat the Nazis. Aware that many voters of Irish and Italian ancestry might find aiding Britain an unpalatable prospect, he predicted that both Ireland and Italy—the former neutral, the latter "forced to become accomplices of the Nazis"—would sooner or later be enslaved by Nazi Germany. In Asia the Chinese were putting up a "great defense" against the Japanese. Then, as if to say "enough said," he added a phrase long since forgotten: "In the Pacific is our fleet." The danger as he saw it lay in Europe, where the British fought alone, and to the British must go material support.

The plan went like this: "As planes and ships and guns and shells are produced, your Government, with its defense experts, can then determine
how best to use them to defend this hemisphere.... We must be the great
arsenal of democracy.... There will be no 'bottlenecks' in our determination to aid Great Britain.... Their strength is growing. It is the strength of
men and women who value their freedom more highly than they value
their lives."[423]

The phrase "arsenal of democracy" would long be remembered on both
sides of the sea. These were defiant words, reassuring and full of promise,
but what did they mean in terms of Britain's inability to pay? "No bottlenecks"? Was not Britain's lack of specie a bottleneck? Roosevelt had also
declared his intention to "eliminate the dollar sign" but had offered no specifics on how to do so. On the final day of the year, Churchill telegraphed
his appreciation to Roosevelt for "all you said yesterday...especially the
outline of your plans giving us the aid without which Hitlerism cannot be
extirpated from Europe and Asia." He omitted a line he had written in a
draft: "Remember Mr. President, we do not know what you have in mind,
or exactly what the United States is going to do, and we are fighting for our
lives."[424]

Churchill and Britons had survived to the end of what he called "the
most splendid, as it was the most deadly, year in our long English and British story." It was a year, he later wrote, that surpassed the year of the Spanish Armada, Marlborough's campaigns, Nelson's victories against
Napoleon, even the entirety of the Great War. During 1940, "this small
and ancient Island...had proved itself capable of bearing the whole impact
and weight of world destiny." He added, "Alone, but upborne by every
generous heartbeat of mankind, we had defied the tyrant at the height of
his triumph."[425]

He and his countrymen had indeed, without flinching and without
wavering, defied the tyrant. But they had not yet defeated him.

They fought on, into the New Year of 1941. Alone.

2

The Rapids

Shortly after midnight on January 1, 1941, Churchill telegraphed Franklin Roosevelt: "At this moment when the New Year opens in storm, I feel it is my duty on behalf of the British government, and indeed of the whole British Empire, to tell you, Mr. President, how lively is our sense of gratitude and admiration for the memorable declaration which you made to the American people, and to the lovers of freedom in all the continents on Sunday last." He again resisted the urge to remind the president that he and the British people had no idea whatsoever of just exactly what America was going to do, or how, or when. He had no knowledge of the particulars of the Lend-Lease bill—titled, with no end save symbolism, H. R. 1776—about to be introduced into the U.S. House of Representatives, nor of course could he know the content of the bill when it emerged from the Senate, *if* it emerged from the Senate. When Lend-Lease began its trip through Congress, it would do so on Washington's terms, not Churchill's. If the congressional journey devoured too much time, Britain would go broke, a sorry enough circumstance for the greatest empire in history but now, with the Wehrmacht poised across the Channel, likely fatal as well. It was that close-fought a thing. Still, Jock Colville found Churchill's demeanor "mellow" on the last day of the old year. The telegram to Roosevelt manifested that measured good cheer, taking the form of holiday salutations in which he left unstated an obvious truth, one he could never articulate in public: only if 1940 proved to be America's last year of peace could 1941 prove to be Britain's first year of hope.[1]

Although Churchill claimed he had but one goal, the defeat of Hitler, those who worked for him often had no idea how he proposed to reach it. "His restless mind," wrote Lord Noel Annan, who as a young man in 1941 worked in the War Cabinet office, "bred one military scheme after another." Annan arrived at work each morning "wondering which rabbit had jumped out of the hat during the night." Would it be "Churchill's plan to land at Bordeaux, or at Spitzbergen, or Sardinia, North Africa, the tip of Sumatra? What such expeditions were expected to achieve, and how they would escape annihilation by superior forces, was clear only to Churchill." Maps were blank canvases, the contours of which Churchill filled in and studded with pins and painted with arrows—*his* arrows—pointing hither and yon

toward hoped-for glorious victories in some far-distance place. But, wrote
Annan, he was "oblivious of mountains or logistics" that the maps might
bring to light and in so doing render his arrows pointless.[2]

Vanquished continental statesmen, royals, and the entire Dutch, Belgian,
and Polish governments in exile greeted the New Year in the London clubs,
hotels, and private houses where they had taken up residence. King Zog, of
Albania, lived at the Ritz. King Haakon of Norway dined at Claridge's,
where meats, fishes, and fruits not available to most Londoners appeared
nightly on the menu. Queen Wilhelmina of the Netherlands lived at Claridge's and asked strangers for the latest news while wandering the corridors
in her woolen bathrobe. Czechoslovakia's ousted president, Eduard Beneš,
made the best of his hopeless cause in the capital of the empire that two
years earlier had betrayed him. When in the autumn King Carol II of Romania, a royal playboy, sought asylum, the Foreign Office denied his request
on the grounds that he kept a mistress. Churchill shot off a note to the FO:
"It is true he has a mistress . . . but since when have private morals been a bar
to asylum?" Carol was given permission to flee to Bermuda. His teenage
son, Michael, grabbed the crown, remained in Romania, and waited for the
proper moment to outmaneuver the dictator Ion Antonescu. He would have
a long wait. The kings of Greece and Yugoslavia arrived later in the spring
after disasters by way of the Wehrmacht befell their kingdoms. King George
II of the Hellenes took up residence at Claridge's. Peter, the seventeen-year-
old king of Yugoslavia enjoyed viewing American westerns from the balco-
nies of West End cinemas, where he was often seen, his thumb cocked,
picking off desperadoes with his forefinger, *bang, bang.*[3]

The Polish prime minister in exile Władysław Sikorski spent much of his
time in Scotland, where 20,000 Polish troops trained, and dipped into
mostly empty pockets to raise almost £500 to help repair the London
Guildhall, which the Luftwaffe had toppled. While the Poles trained in
Scotland, the Free French cooled their heels in the south of England.
Charles de Gaulle — referred to by many around Whitehall as "that ass de
Gaulle" — had been ensconced since June 1940 in his shabby office on the
third floor of St. Stephen House, where he fumed as much at Vichy leaders
as at Germans. Although he had in October set up a Free French "state" in
Brazzaville, French Equatorial Africa (modern Chad), in actuality, the
closest he could get to French Dominions in Asia and North Africa were
old maps pinned to his office walls. De Gaulle, Wilhelmina, Beneš, Sikorski — all the beaten leaders — dreamed of someday returning to their
homelands, victorious. Meanwhile, London, command center of the Free
World, would have to do.[4]

The children in British cities, more than 600,000 in all, had been packed
off to the countryside, but they were no longer sent abroad. They would

stay in England to the end. A copy of Magna Carta had been sent to Washington, DC, but Churchill decreed that Britain's works of art stay. "Bury them in caves and cellars," he declared. "None must go. We are going to beat them." London was now the last redoubt, for the Empire's art, for the continental refugees of high birth and low who had poured into the city for two years, the final stop for the lot of them, Churchill included.[5]

T. S. Eliot, a fire warden at the Faber Building, where he was an editor, crafted a phrase that captured the essence of the nation's ordeal in five words:

"History is now and England." ("Little Gidding")

On January 1, Churchill, fuming over Roosevelt's desire to haul off to America the remaining British gold in South Africa, suggested to Colville that America's love of doing good business might overrule its inclination to become a Good Samaritan, with fatal consequences for Britain. He had inserted into and then deleted such accusatory ruminations from his New Year's Eve telegram: "I will gladly give directions for any gold in Capetown to be put on board any warships you may send. . . . I feel however that I should not be discharging my responsibilities to the people of the British Empire if, without the slightest indication of how our fate was to be settled in Washington, I were to part with this last reserve, from which alone we might buy a few month's food." This was an opinion best offered in person, between friends. The ongoing traffic between them in telegrams notwithstanding, Roosevelt and Churchill had yet to formalize a partnership, let alone a friendship.[6]

In the final hours of New Year's Day, Churchill climbed to the Foreign Office roof with his new foreign secretary, Anthony Eden. Eden was "vain and occasionally hysterical" in Colville's opinion, and very protective of his political patch. P. J. Grigg, Eden's successor at the War Office, considered him to be "complete junk." Churchill thought otherwise and had big things in mind for Eden, beginning with the Foreign Office. Eden was content to stay at the War Office following the death of Lord Lothian and Halifax's appointment as ambassador to the United States, but he heeded Churchill's summons to higher office. He later recalled that when Churchill first offered him the Foreign Office, Churchill "reiterated that he was now an old man, that he would not make Lloyd George's mistake of carrying on after the war, that the succession must be mine." That would prove a long time passing.[7]

Eden came from the finest English stock. His lineage on his father's side included Robert Eden, the last colonial governor of Maryland. His mother's side included the Calvert family and Lord Baltimore (whose family crest adorns the Maryland state flag) and reached back to the Greys. Eden's first wife could cite Thomas à Becket as a distant relation. Eden had won the Military Cross during the Great War, and at twenty became the youngest brigade major in the English army. At Oxford he had studied Russian, Persian, and several Arabic and Chinese dialects. When Baldwin in late 1935 made the young war hero and rising Tory his foreign secretary, Churchill opined in a letter to Clementine, "I think you will now see what a light-weight Eden is." But Eden, repulsed by appeasement, resigned in early 1938, thus earning Churchill's respect. Churchill groomed, encouraged, and rewarded the younger man in a generous and protective spirit of a sort he could not possibly have learned from his own father.[8]

Thus it was with his successor-designate that Churchill climbed to the roof of the Foreign Office that night. The air was infused with the aroma of woodsmoke from dozens of still smoldering fires. Broken clouds drifted overhead; a cold, light rain fell. Below spread London, wrapped in darkness blacker even than in Norman times, when the meager light of pitch and tow torches lent to the Thames a zinc hue and cast London Bridge into relief to guide pilgrims home. Gazing skyward, the skies quiet but for sporadic anti-aircraft firing, Churchill and Eden wondered, What would the new year bring? The entire world wondered the same, yet even the mere posing of the question was an act of self-deception, for the answer was inescapable: it would bring a year of storm.

Some in those dark hours heard the knock of opportunity. Newly promoted Lieutenant General Bernard Law Montgomery, fifty-three, a career soldier, Dunkirk evacuee, and son of an Anglican priest, believed his future bright. He commanded V Corps and coastal defense of Britain, having replaced General Claude Auchinleck, a tough Ulsterman who as commander of the Norwegian fiasco asked for and did not receive the tactical air support he needed to press the attack. He came away certain that ill-supported troops cannot give battle. Auchinleck's open disdain for sending men into battle without the tools to finish the job — especially close air support — earned him unjustified enmity in Whitehall and a reputation for undue caution. It also earned him a transfer to India where, early in his career, Auchinleck had studied and become fluent in almost all the dialects of the subcontinent. In his new position of commander in chief, India, it was presumed that Auchinleck's caution would not be exploited by any adversary. Montgomery had never gotten along with Auchinleck and welcomed his departure. "Monty," as Montgomery's troops called him, considered his own chances for promotion splendid, and justifiably so in his estimation, an assessment not shared by some of his superiors who found him pompous and mischievous, a term that, when employed in England, connotes sneakiness, not playfulness. He was four years a widower, his wife having died in his arms of an infection caused by an insect bite. On the day of the funeral, Montgomery appeared late for a staff meeting. "Gentlemen," he told his staff, "I ask you to forgive this display of human weakness." Since then, he had given himself over to the army. Montgomery's "pugnacious attitude" and his willingness to gas the Germans should they arrive impressed Churchill, who kept an eye on the man.[9]

A forty-year-old Royal Navy hero also impressed Churchill. Captain Louis ("Dickie") Mountbatten—great-grandson of Queen Victoria, second cousin of George V, and cousin to the murdered Romanovs—was awarded the Distinguished Service Order for his gallantry in 1940 when he brought his destroyer, HMS *Kelly,* safely to port from the North Sea, where it had been cut almost in half by German torpedoes. Churchill dictated a congratulatory note, and scribbled in the margin of a copy: "I hardly know him." That soon changed, for Churchill had known Mountbatten's father, Prince Louis Battenberg, a naturalized Austrian who in 1914, as first sea lord, worked with Churchill, then at the Admiralty, to bring the British Navy up to a state of war readiness. Battenberg's reward was to be forced into early retirement by the wave of Germanophobia that washed over Britain. Churchill stood by, silent, as Battenberg was banished. Perhaps to atone for his silence then, or because he could not resist a hero, especially one of aristocratic lineage, Churchill took a keen interest in Mountbatten, which much enhanced the captain's prospects of advancement. Mountbatten was charming, fearless, and reckless. And lucky: in just fourteen months Dickie had been torpedoed, bombed, and strafed, had collided with another ship, and had run over a floating mine. At the beginning of the new year, Mountbatten commanded a destroyer squadron in the Mediterranean, where such small warships as *Kelly* were lost with distressing regularity. Mountbatten's command of such a vulnerable ship as well as his wild fighting style much diminished his chances of surviving long enough to gain any further promotion.[10]

The new year found James Joyce in Geneva, dying. F. Scott Fitzgerald soon followed the expatriate Irishman into the night. Virginia Woolf, who had long suffered from depression, followed them both, by her own hand. German bombs had erased her London house. Confiding her thoughts on the war to her diary, Woolf wrote, "I was thinking: we live without a future. That's what's queer, with our noses pressed to a closed door." As she gazed from her window upon the downs and spires and old stone walls of the countryside that she loved, she summoned Walter de la Mare's melancholy words "Look thy last on all things lovely," and in twelve weeks' time filled her pockets with stones and drowned herself in the River Ouse.[11]

Most Britons—Churchill foremost among them—saw a future, and were willing to fight and die for it. That winter, Britons gave way to inexplicable bursts of primitive emotion. *"We want more!"* cried Londoners in defiance as they danced madly though the streets while stomping out incendiaries during one early January raid. Malcolm Muggeridge found himself delighting—disturbingly so—in "the sound, the taste and smell of all this destruction...the faces of bystanders wildly lit in the flames...it seemed as if the Book of Revelation had verily come to pass." Churchill was one with Londoners and Muggeridge. Every night lit by flames was another glorious occasion to either live or die, to stride toward the day when he could deliver unto Germany his version of justice.[12]

For many young American men who wondered if they'd be one of the 800,000 draftees Roosevelt needed for his "muster," revelations arrived via the local draft board as the new year came in. The army got all the draftees; navy and Marine corps recruiting standards were set higher than draft standards, a policy that would leave the bluejackets and leathernecks vastly undermanned should America ever to go to war. All told, almost one million young American men marched off to boot camp, but not yet to war. Those Americans who had already chosen army careers pondered their prospects for advancement. Dwight Eisenhower, a fifty-year-old U.S. Army lieutenant colonel, had until late 1939 served in Manila as chief of staff to Douglas MacArthur, commander of U.S. Army forces in the Philippines. On January 1, Eisenhower served as chief of staff for the 3rd Division. He sought a field command and had told an old friend, George Patton Jr., that he considered himself qualified to command a regiment—perhaps one of Patton's—but that he harbored few hopes of ever attaining higher rank. Eisenhower's name appeared on a list drawn up for General of the Army George Marshall of eighteen career officers who might qualify for division command: Eisenhower was ranked eighteenth.[13]

Although Roosevelt, in 1939, had ordered Army chief of staff George Marshall to build up American armed forces, by early 1941, America fielded only the seventeenth most powerful army in the world, strong enough to lick Canada or Mexico should the situation arise, but no match for the Wehrmacht.

The French in the new year cared little for the latest news from London, or America, or any place in between. The world Frenchmen knew and loved had died the previous June. The Nazi occupiers made sure little news reached Frenchmen in any event. The winter weather was brutal. Gales pushed freezing cold and snow south to the Riviera. Marseille found itself isolated from the rest of southern France by snowdrifts. In Paris, breadlines lengthened, and a shortage of coal for fireplaces spelled doom for the trees of the city's parks. Parisians could only watch as German troops stole food that came by way of America and Morocco and southern France. The French were beaten, and they discerned a future that offered only misery, hunger, and slavery. On New Year's Day, Pétain told his countrymen that for the foreseeable future, "We shall be hungry." The old marshal had to have the coupons clipped from his ration card just like everyone else. He was a beaten man.[14]

Charles de Gaulle, in London, was not. He understood the unbreakable strength of dreams. On New Year's Day, he called on the people of France to remain indoors for an hour, a purely symbolic yet powerful protest that left the streets empty but for the enemy. Most Frenchmen had never heard of de Gaulle until June 18 of the previous year, when, in a BBC address broadcast from London, this minor general declared himself the regent of French honor, its guardian and protector. He told Frenchmen, "Whatever happens, the flame of French resistance must not and shall not die."

He was a Catholic whose politics ran to the right; his oratorical skills were meager, yet they transcended politics. He was not a man of any party; he was a man of France, specifically of the *myth* of France, where given his exile, his presence was, necessarily, a spiritual one. Posters bearing photos of Churchill, Hitler, Mussolini, Stalin, and Roosevelt hung on walls throughout their lands, but Vichy had erased from France all pictorial representations of de Gaulle. Vichy propagandists described him as short, fat, ugly, and a misfit. Frenchmen had no image of the man. Instead, and despite German efforts to jam the BBC, they were guided by only his disembodied voice crackling across the airwaves. By the time Napoleon was de Gaulle's age, his life was nearly finished; the myth surrounding him was complete. De Gaulle was just beginning. Now he called for resistance, and in the dark of night a spark was struck. He wrote in his memoirs: "I felt within myself a life coming to an end.... At the age of forty-nine I was entering upon adventure, like a man thrown by fate outside all terms of reference." Churchill saw the immense importance of imbuing Frenchmen with the will to fight, the *need* to fight. He had done much the same for Britons by leading his listeners back into the mists and myths of English history, where the soul of England resided. There was a critical difference, however: Britons could see and touch their Winnie. Yet, even though Frenchmen could form no image of de Gaulle, he had won over their souls. Churchill recognized this; Franklin Roosevelt did not, with unfortunate results for all concerned.[15]

January 1 arrived in a somber Berlin. The Wehrmacht had months earlier demolished the Maginot Line. Its coal stoves, bunks, and rations enough to feed 250,000 for a year were packed up and shipped off to

German air-raid shelters, where the citizens, based on assurances from their leaders, had presumed the ill-gotten supplies would gather dust from want of use. Instead, dust settled now into Berlin shelters, sifted down from the streets above, where the homes of Berliners burned under RAF bombs.[16]

Berliners crowded shelters on a regular basis, though Jews were forbidden entrance, forbidden in fact to take shelter in any of the basements of Berlin. If they could gain access to a building, Jews were confined to the ground floor; otherwise they took their chances in the streets. Berliners were depressed by the bloody harvest of Hitler's adventures and by their increased awareness that their lives under the Nazis bore no resemblance to the lives they had once lived, or had hoped to live. The Tiergarten was empty, dark, silent, and studded with bomb craters. Such festivities as there were took place behind shuttered windows. In his New Year's Eve address, Hitler excoriated "this criminal" Churchill who for three months has bombed German cities by night "and—as especially the inhabitants of Berlin know—has made special targets of hospitals." The Führer promised he would respond to "the Churchill crimes" and assured Germans that "the war will be waged to the end—until the responsible criminals have been eliminated." He added, "It is the will of the democratic war-inciters and their Jewish-capitalistic wire-pullers that the war must be continued.... We are ready.... The year 1941 will bring completion of the greatest victory in our history." William L. Shirer saw only gloom in Berlin. He had just left Europe after fifteen years on the Continent, leaving behind the "Nazi blight and the hatred and the fraud and the political gangsterism and the murder and the massacre and the incredible intolerance and all the suffering and the starving and the cold and the thud of a bomb blowing the people in a house to pieces, the thud of all the bombs blasting men's hope and decency."[17]

Berliners, as did Londoners, found ways to express their cynicism. The lyrics of the German war song *"Wir fahren, wir fahren, wir fahren gegen Engeland"* ("We are marching, marching, marching against England"), which had played over and over again on state radio the previous summer as the BEF was encircled at Dunkirk, had been revised: *"Wir fahren, wir fahren, wir fahren, schon seit Jahren, mit langen weissen Haaren, gegen Engeland."* ("We are marching, marching, marching; we have for years been marching; with hair turned white by the passage of time we go on marching, against England.") Shirer noted a riddle making the rounds in Berlin: "An airplane carrying Hitler, Goebbels, and Göring crashes; all three are killed. Who is saved? Answer: The German people." Shirer, with insight into the Nazi mind-set that was lacking in Whitehall, predicted that the British blockade of Germany would not succeed in starving Germans, because "Hitler, who is never sentimental about non-Germans, will see to it that every one of the one hundred million people in the occupied lands dies of hunger before one German does. Of that, the world can be sure."[18]

Excepting the myriad peoples who lived within the British Empire, Churchill was not himself overly sentimental about non-Britons and, since their surrender, the French in particular. Pétain, on New Year's Day, told Frenchmen that food shortages in southern France were the result of the British blockade. He did not tell his countrymen that food shipments from the United States to French Morocco, intended for occupied France, were being diverted by the Germans—with Vichy compliance—to Germany. Pétain's obfuscations infuriated Churchill, who in coming months complained bitterly to Roosevelt. When in a few weeks' time the American secretary of state Cordell Hull expressed his opposition to Britain's continued blockade of Vichy, Churchill exploded, telling Halifax, "I cannot believe the United States government would wish us to do simply nothing, and have the war prolonged by having all these cargoes, containing not only food but rubber and other war materials, pass unhindered into Germany." He voiced his cynicism to Roosevelt in typically Churchillian fashion. "For instance, there is a French ship...with 3,000 tons of rubber on board which is certainly not all for the teats of babies' bottles." All kinds of munitions and raw materials, he told Roosevelt, "are going straight to Germany or Italy." From Churchill's perspective, if food shipments to France had to be cut off in order to prevent leakage of matériel to Germany, then so be it. The ships needed to supply Britain could not be spared to supply France, he told Roosevelt, especially as he did not want the British people, "who, apart from heavy bombardment likely to be renewed soon, are having to tighten their belts and restrict their few remaining comforts, to feel that I am not doing my best against the enemy." If the British blockade meant that Frenchmen went hungry so that Englishmen might live, such was war.[19]

In Britain, the U-boat blockade had resulted in all goods but the essential disappearing from pantry shelves. Everyone, including the cabinet, was on half rations (everyone except the swells at Claridge's, the Savoy, the Ritz, and any London dining clubs that remained unbombed). City dwellers with friends in the country might come into a few eggs a month; all others would go eggless. Alec Cadogan was thankful after procuring a few chickens; then they stopped laying. Turkeys were in short supply, and expensive. Meat was parceled out at less than one pound per person per week, bone in, half the ration of a year earlier. To a nation of meat eaters who, for centuries, had begun their day with a mutton chop and ended it with roasts, puddings, and kidney pies, this was *carnivoricide*. Not only were meat and eggs disappearing, but so were the cooks, butlers, and scullery maids of the rich and near rich. A domestic servant crisis developed in the kitchens and laundries of the West End and in the country houses of the gentry when cooks and laundresses marched off to work in the armaments factories. Mollie Panter-Downes observed a marked increase in newspaper help-wanted advertisements taken out by "anguished ladies" in search of servants who would find, it was promised, "enormous wages, happy homes, and safe locales, where a bomb is guaranteed to be unknown." Those servants had less to iron and more to mend: clothing rationing took full effect later in the year, limiting purchases to the value of coupons, no cash allowed, regardless of the shopper's cash flow. Women's Sunday-best dresses would have to do until the end of the war. Suede elbow patches on men's jackets now served a purely functional purpose.[20]

East Enders meanwhile, lower on the social ladder than even those in service to the rich, had no need to fret over the paucity of clothing or beef: they could afford neither in any event. The poor supped on "Blitz soup," a viscous canned concoction foisted upon them by the Ministry of Food. The ministry also supplied dried eggs, which Londoners anointed "dregs." The good citizens of Britain were told that tripe was restricted but chickens for the time being were not. Horsemeat—approved for human consumption—appeared in butcher shops. No coupons were required for its purchase, but sales flagged. Britons avoided horsemeat with the same fervor as Muslims avoid pork.[21]

Fresh meat was not the only item absent from the British retail scene. Silk stockings had gone missing from stores; tobacco was priced beyond the means of most; razor blades were scarce; and pipe cleaners were nonexistent, having been appropriated by women for use as hair curlers. A tea crisis occurred when the Pelton gasworks was hit. It took up to an hour to boil water for tea over small fires stoked from sticks and paper. The problem of how to roast the Sunday joint of beef without gas was rendered moot by the absence of joints of beef. A coal shortage loomed if deliveries from the Welsh mines to London did not increase to 410,000 tons per week from the current 250,000 tons, a situation Churchill found difficult to understand given the slackening in the Blitz and the general good repair of the railroads. Other statistics showed that in spite of German bombs, Britons maintained their humanity after a fashion denied those who lived under Hitler: almost 50,000 British dogs and cats had been rescued from bombed houses.[22]

HMG conducted surveys. The divorce rate was down by half. The birthrate had not declined, and "Winston" as a first or middle name for baby boys more than tripled in popularity.* Surprisingly, in light of dietary restrictions and the lack of central heat, cases of pneumonia and diphthe-

---

* Among those who chose the name were a young, working-class Liverpool couple, "Alf" and Julia Lennon, who honored the Old Man when they named their son—born during an October air raid—John Winston Lennon.

ria were down. The crime rate was also down, curiously, thought Churchill, given the ample opportunities for looting, an "odious" crime in his estimation. Some looting could be excused. He told home secretary Herbert Morrison that a sentence of five years penal servitude given to six auxiliary London firemen caught stealing whisky from a burning pub was "out of proportion when compared with sentences of three or six months for stealing valuables." The firemen, after all, had procured the whisky for "immediate consumption" rather than for personal enrichment. Such bureaucratic blockheadedness riled the Old Man. When a Londoner was fined £100 for disposing of a delayed-action bomb "without authorization," Churchill's fuse ignited. Was this man fined, he asked Morrison, for saving his home? Rather than official opprobrium, he decreed that the heroic citizen should be "awarded the George Medal." And when an obviously "crazy female" was given five years penal servitude for expressing the opinion that "Hitler was a good ruler, a better man than Mr. Churchill," he told Morrison that the sentence was "far too heavy."[23]

On January 2 Harold Nicolson, while strolling through old London—still smoldering from the December 29 raid—noted small groups of sullen civilians standing around in the ruins. He noted their quiet mutterings about the need for revenge, the more revenge the better, and sooner, too. "We are fighting devils," Nicolson wrote that night, "and I don't see why we shouldn't fight like devils in order to let them see what it is like." He noted on his rambles a subtle but definite decline in esprit de corps. When the news of the Taranto raid played across the newspapers in late November—grainy aerial photos of wrecked Italian ships—it was met with skepticism, especially among the lower economic classes, who thought the photos fake. The welcome news that the Greeks were trouncing the Italians in Albania was held up by Cockney newsboys as proof of the sorry state of British arms, for the Italians, trounced by the Greeks, had trounced the English in Somaliland. The string of recent British victories against the Italians in North Africa were seen by East Enders as meaningless. The real enemy, Hitler, still prowled Europe, uncontested and unmolested.[24]

London's poor were skeptical, yet socialist ward bosses in Silvertown, Stepney, and the East End slums had failed to kindle any revolutionary fires among them. East Enders remained faithful to the cause even as their filthy tenements burned and crashed down around them. Most now chose to stay home when the bombs came, and scorned the Anderson shelters, which, carped the ward bosses, "couldn't protect a rooster from rain."

Anderson shelters at least posed no public health menace, unlike the ersatz shelters under railroad overpasses, which were not much more than vectors for disease. A constable visiting one first heard and then smelled it before he saw it: "The first thing I heard was a great hollow hubbub, as if there were animals down there moaning and crying. And then... this terrible stench hit me. It was worse than dead bodies, hot and thick and so fetid that I gagged and then vomited. Ahead of me I could see faces peering towards me lit by lanterns and candles. It was like a painting of Hell." The Cockneys were refused even the satisfaction of reading of their plight in the newspapers; the Ministry of Information, under Duff Cooper, forbade any reporting of where bombs fell or the number of casualties. Those workingmen who took their news from the Communist, alarmist, and decidedly adversarial *Daily Worker* could no longer do so after January 21, 1941, the day HMG took the extraordinary step of shutting it down. Still, newspaper obituaries offered clues; bomb victims were said to have died "very suddenly." If the obituaries contained a grouping of "very sudden" deaths in a particular neighborhood, it was a good bet that the neighborhood in question had been hit hard.[25]

That certain squalid sections of the East End and Southwark, of Manchester, Birmingham, and Britain's other industrial areas, had been destroyed brought forth an ironic response from many of the displaced. The Germans were ridding Britain of slums, a job HMG had avoided for forty years. Londoners who lost their homes to bombs waited an average of five months before being placed in livable abodes. Churchill had outlined to Colville a relief plan to reimburse homeowners up to £1,000 (about $55,000 U.S. in 2012) for their losses, but Parliament had yet to make good on the promise. Soon after John Reith took up his new duties as minister of works (after Churchill eased him out of the Ministry of Transportation), he was instructed by Churchill to "press on" in rebuilding bombed neighborhoods. Yet Churchill told Edward Bridges, secretary to the cabinet, that as far as reconstruction of wrecked cities was concerned, "We must be very careful not to allow these remote post-war problems to absorb energy which is required, maybe for several years, for the prosecution of the war." Cockneys—all Britons—would have to wait a decade for new homes, for reliable supplies of electricity, coal, gas, water, and petrol. The wait for clothing, paper goods, and fresh, plentiful food would last well into the next decade. The only commodities delivered to Britons with any regularity in early 1941 were German bombs.[26]

In his memoirs Churchill equated 1940 with "shooting Niagara" and termed early 1941 a "struggle in the rapids." In January 1941 the lifeline of

Lend-Lease lay coiled on the far shore. Churchill and England fought on, *alone,* a fact he made clear when he articulated the "theme" of his memoirs of 1940:

> HOW THE BRITISH PEOPLE
> HELD THE FORT
> ALONE
> TILL THOSE WHO HITHERTO HAD
> BEEN HALF BLIND WERE
> HALF READY.

In the historical memory of many Americans, the year 1941 does not begin until December 7. For Churchill and Britain, the entire year indeed saw a long and terrible struggle in the rapids. It is true that the Home Island fought with the full support of the Dominions, and given the fact that one-quarter of the world's population lived within the British Empire, it might appear facile to suggest that England stood alone. But in large part it did. Canada would ultimately send 90,000 airmen to Britain; they would play a significant role in the bombing of Germany. But the first Royal Canadian Air Force bomber squadron was not commissioned until mid-1941. Three Royal Canadian infantry divisions and two armored divisions were available for the fight but were widely scattered throughout the Empire, including a division in Britain and a battalion in Hong Kong. Australia offered four infantry divisions. Canberra's enthusiasm for the European war decreased throughout the year as the threat of Japanese attack increased. New Zealand sent 50,000 soldiers and 10,000 airmen overseas during the next two years, but only Lieutenant General Bernard Freyberg's North African corps was operational in early 1941. South Africa offered three divisions, but only for deployment in Africa, where Erwin Rommel mauled them as the year wore on. In early 1941, the forces sent by the Dominions, when combined with British forces, were vastly outnumbered by the Axis. After the fall of France, Hitler had *demobilized* forty divisions, far more than all the armed forces of the Dominions combined. Even late in 1941, after it scrambled for months to put men into uniform, the entirety of the British Empire's armies worldwide—ninety-nine divisions—was dwarfed by the Wehrmacht by a ratio greater than two to one. In early 1941, almost all of Hitler's troops were stationed within six hundred miles of London.[27]

British prospects in the Mediterranean and the Balkans, if the Germans appeared on the scene, looked precarious at best. By the first week of January, the Luftwaffe had stationed more than 150 bombers and fighters in Sicily, just one hundred miles and thirty minutes from Malta. Such a force could menace the Mediterranean from the French Riviera to North Africa. To oppose the German air fleet, the British had but fifteen beat-up Hurricanes parked on Malta, the most critical piece of real estate in the central Mediterranean. Malta was under siege, ringed by Italian minefields and submarines, the Luftwaffe and Italian air force overhead. It was England in miniature—isolated and battered—but with two vital differences: the Germans and Italians, not the RAF, controlled the skies over Malta, and the Italian navy, not the Royal Navy, surrounded the island. Aggressive strategy demanded, as it had since the previous summer, that Mussolini send his fleet and Hitler his paratroopers to take the island.

Menacing German forces had been dispatched to the greater Balkan region. By mid-January almost 500,000 German troops—"tourists," Berlin claimed, who happened to bring along their tanks and artillery—took up positions along the Romanian side of the Danube, again as in Roman times the boundary that separated the barbarian from the civilized world. This sojourn by the Wehrmacht was Romania's reward for joining the Axis in November, a decision born more of necessity than choice. Having succumbed in 1940 to Stalin's demand for the provinces of Bessarabia and Northern Bukovina, and to Hitler's demand that northern Transylvania be ceded to Hungary, the Romanian dictator, General Ion Antonescu, could turn only to Hitler for a guarantee that the rump Romania remain intact. It had not occurred to Stalin that 500,000 German troops were about 480,000 more than needed to guarantee Romania's sovereignty. Yugoslavia and Bulgaria lay south across the Danube. The kingdom of the Bulgars was essentially an eighteenth-century, pre-industrial nation. Its leaders and people lived with the sure knowledge that sooner or later, either Stalin or Hitler—with their mechanized might—would no longer tolerate Bulgarian neutrality. Wherever Hitler intended to go—to Greece in aid of Il Duce seemed a logical destination—he first had to push through Bulgaria. Yet, Bulgarian roads were decrepit and its railroads were in no shape to move a modern army. Bulgaria offered a route south and beyond, but not the best route. Not so Yugoslavia, where the old Hapsburg railroad system connected to the rail lines of Greece, Hungary, Romania, and Austria. Hitler wanted Yugoslavia; Churchill needed Yugoslavia. Hitler could take Bulgaria; Churchill could not protect it. He deduced that the German "tourists" were destined for the Balkans, the threshold to the Mediterranean, the "hinge of fate."

The German naval war staff understood Churchill's thinking, and had prepared a paper in the autumn that warned, "The fight for the African area" is "the foremost strategic objective of German warfare as a whole.... It is of decisive importance for the outcome of the war." The Italians, ill led and inefficient, could not win that fight alone, as their humiliation at the hands of the Greeks and their losses at Taranto and against O'Connor in the desert confirmed. The cagey Franco would not do it, at Gibraltar. Raeder predicted that if the Axis did not occupy Vichy northwest Africa (Morocco, Tunisia, and Algeria), Churchill and the Gaullists would do so in due time, supported by American industrial might. Therefore, the German naval planners concluded, Germany must do it. It was Britain's good fortune that Hitler was a land warrior who rarely (other than in the matter of U-boats) embraced the advice of his very capable admirals. Hitler, looking toward Russia, agreed only to the half measure of sending aircraft to Sicily, and troops to Romania, in anticipation of some future foray into the Balkans, most likely to Greece in support of his hapless ally.[28]

Churchill outlined his Mediterranean strategy on January 6 in a long memo to "Pug" Ismay and the Chiefs of Staff Committee. He saw three critical objectives, reverse images of what the German naval staff saw. The British must hold what they had from the Suez to Gibraltar; engage and defeat the Italian navy and drive the Italian army from Africa (which O'Connor, having taken Bardia the day before, was doing); and keep the Germans out of the Mediterranean. Churchill interwove his immediate goals and his operational wish list, the former concise, the latter detailing the hopes of an impatient man. Yet in contrast to Hitler, who issued Führer Directives that were orders pure and simple and allowed for no interpretation, Churchill probed and examined and sought guidance from his military chiefs. His first priority for early 1941, he wrote, was "the speedy destruction of the Italian armed forces in North-East Africa." Tobruk must be established as a base from which to conduct Libyan operations. In East Africa, the Italians must be swept away. That would secure the Suez and the southeast shore of the Mediterranean.

In the western Mediterranean, there was a chance that Franco would deny Hitler transit to Gibraltar, which raised the happy prospect that Hitler might try to force his way to Spain through unoccupied France in violation of the June surrender terms. In that case, Churchill believed that "the Vichy Government . . . may either proceed to North Africa and resume war from there, or authorize General Weygand to do so." To that end Churchill offered Pétain and Weygand Britain's assistance were they to take the fight to Africa. It was a pipe dream. The Vichy leaders were edging closer to, not away from, willing servitude to their German masters. They believed that Germany would win the war; indeed, they *wanted* Germany to win the war. As well, Weygand, in Morocco, loathed de Gaulle, while de Gaulle loathed Weygand and hated with a fury the Fascist-minded Vichy minister of state, Pierre Laval. The French accorded more importance to their personal grudges than to their national honor. The previous June, Weygand and Pétain had squandered their chance to fight for the honor of France. They had quit, but not before a final act of treachery when they tried to draw in the RAF's last reserves. With each passing month, Churchill's goodwill toward the French had diminished. He allowed to Colville on one occasion and to luncheon guests on another that had Britain "thrown away those planes in France...the war might have been lost."[29]

He would get no help in the western Mediterranean from Vichy France. As Laval's collaboration with the Nazis became ever more apparent, Churchill told Colville he rued the "lamentable lack of Charlotte Cordays."[30]

To secure the eastern Mediterranean he proposed a Balkan bulwark of Yugoslavia, Greece, and Turkey. In essence he hoped to convince the Balkan nations that a bundle of wheat was not as easily broken as individual stalks. With the Italians on the run in Africa, the time had come to divert some of Wavell's desert forces to Greece, not only to support the Greeks but to gird the loins of the Yugoslavs and Turks. "The attitude of Yugoslavia," Churchill wrote, "may well be determined by the support we give to Greece," as would be the attitude of Turkey. He was inviting a showdown with Hitler. But the Greeks understood that the surest way to provoke Hitler was to invite British troops into the fray. As General Alexander Papagos drove the Italians back through mountain passes into Albania, the military situation appeared promising, but Greeks were going hungry. Winter, not the Italian army, was reducing Greek resolve. Mussolini could reinforce his Albanian legions, but Prime Minister Metaxas could not. He desperately needed supplies—tanks, anti-tank guns, rifles, airplanes, ammunition, food, and clothing. He asked the United States for help, but Congress had yet to begin debate on the Lend-Lease bill, and Britain, not Greece, would be the primary beneficiary of any U.S. aid. Metaxas could not crush the Italians without help, yet he continued to decline Churchill's help, a quite reasonable demurral given the half million Germans encamped on the Romanian side of the Danube.[31]

Churchill took a regional view. He predicted that if the Germans came to Il Duce's aid in Greece by way of Romania, Bulgaria, and the Black Sea, "Turkey will come into the war." He followed this hopeful prognostication with a string of first-magnitude "ifs." "If Yugoslavia stands firm and is not molested, if the Greeks take Valona and maintain themselves in Albania, if Turkey becomes an active ally, the attitude of Russia may be affected favorably." That is, Russian fear of an "obnoxious and indeed deadly... German advance to the Black Sea or through Bulgaria to the Aegean" would be lessened by a British presence in the Balkans. Indeed, he wrote, a British presence might persuade Stalin to side with Britain, "but we must not count on this." True. With Hitler's armies poised in Romania, it was highly unlikely that any of Churchill's "ifs" could come to pass. The Yugoslav government was so petrified of provoking Hitler that it refused in March to even meet with Eden, who by then was prowling the region, pleading Churchill's case for solidarity. Metaxas, in Greece, continued to decline with a polite "no" Churchill's offers of military aid right up to his sudden death at the end of January, leaving General Alexander Papagos, the hero of the battle against Italy, to ponder Churchill's proposals, which he finally accepted in early March. The Turks, for their part, wanted nothing whatsoever to do with Churchill's invitation to commit national suicide. They faced Hitler on one side, and their ancient enemy, Russia, on the other. Against these foes, their army contained not a single tank. In fact, Anthony Eden wanted Turkey to remain neutral for the simple reason that Britain could offer no military protection to Ankara if the Turks joined the British cause.[32]

Churchill finished his memo with a confident prediction, which echoed the prediction he had made to Colville and to the House the previous summer: "One cannot doubt that Herr Hitler's need to starve or crush Great Britain is stronger than it has ever been. A great campaign in the East of Europe, the defeat of Russia, the conquest of the Ukraine, and the advance from the Black Sea to the Caspian, would none of them separately or together bring him victorious peace while the British air power grew ever stronger behind him and he had to hold down a whole continent of sullen, starving peoples." But British airpower was not yet strong enough to make a difference, and against a continental enemy it might never prove sufficiently strong. Armies and well-armed allies would make the difference. But Churchill had no armies, and he had no allies. Even if he had, even were he to build his Balkan bulwark, he could not, unlike Hitler, furnish modern weapons to his friends. Churchill, in fact, had no weapons, old or new, to furnish to anyone. Britain, under U-boat blockade, its cash balances evaporating, had but one option, to hold out at home and in the Mediterranean.[33]

Churchill's stream of memos, many dealing with the most mundane of matters, had widened into a river; some of his subordinates would claim a river in flood. The Chief of the Imperial General Staff, Sir John Dill, dining one evening with Sir John Reith, a prewar Chamberlain loyalist, allowed that of Churchill's memos "one...out of ten was perhaps useful—occasionally very good." Important ministers wasted a great amount of time, Dill offered, by having to deal with "silly minutes from the P.M." Some of Churchill's memos indeed treat of subjects not usually associated with Great Men of History, but Churchill would not have been Churchill without his memos. He loved to ponder the finer details of making war, and to then compose the memos that drove Dill to make his intemperate remarks to Reith.[34]

Among Churchill's inquiries, he asked after the progress in developing a four-thousand-pound bomb, for he desired to deliver to the Reich the

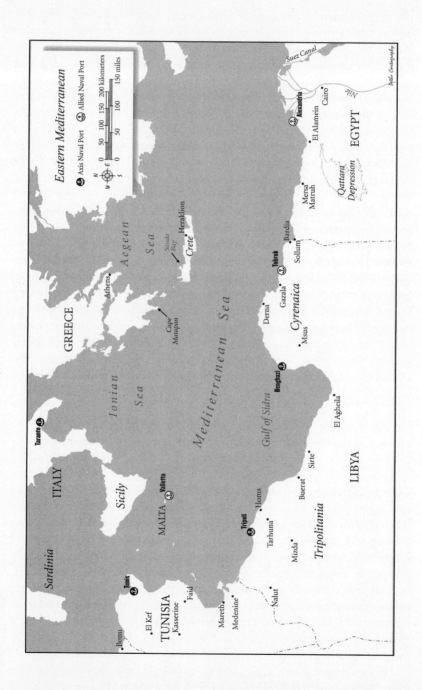

deadliest bomb possible, as soon as possible. Enamored of the idea of dropping incendiaries into the Black Forest with the intention of burning every stick of lumber to the ground, he suggested the RAF test its wares on the French forest of Nieppe, where drought had turned the undergrowth into kindling. Operation Razzle, a scheme to burn German crops, held his interest, although much of Germany's farmland was in the east, beyond the reach of the RAF. He pushed Duff Cooper at the Ministry of Information to take a more honest approach with the news so that Britons might actually believe some of what they read in their newspapers and heard on the BBC. He insisted the press not announce civilian casualty numbers, reasoning that such figures depressed the morale of frontline troops, which he considered Britons to be. Food was always an issue. In one memo he lamented the egg crisis, in another he proposed a solution: "Backyard fowls use up a lot of scrap, and so save cereals." He overlooked no beast: "Have you done justice to rabbit production.... They eat mostly grass... so what is the harm in encouraging their multiplication in captivity?" He tagged the rabbit memo "Action This Day." He believed feeding Britons was more important than buying weapons, and he demanded the import of enough food "to maintain the staying power of the people even if this meant a somewhat slower" buildup of the army. On occasion his coolness bled through. Asked by a minister how best to help the thousands of homeless wandering about London, he suggested they be sent to far-flung places where they would no longer be in the way during air raids.[35]

He launched a classic memo after reading an account of a general who ordered every soldier in his division to run regular seven-mile jogs:

> Is it really true that a 7-mile cross-country run is enforced in this Division from Generals to Privates?...A Colonel or a General ought not to exhaust himself in trying to compete with young boys in running across country 7-miles at a time....Who is the General of this division, and does he run the 7-miles himself? If so, then he may be more useful in football than in war. Could Napoleon have run 7-miles across country at Austerlitz?...In my experience...officers with high athletic qualifications are not usually successful in the higher ranks.[36]

Churchill's memos, Dill told Reith, suggested that he "seemed often unable to appreciate or understand major issues." Actually, both Dill and Reith were unable to appreciate Churchill's grasp of *all* the issues, not only those issues apparent to everybody but also those apparent only to himself. Dill fell silent when Reith asked whether he thought Churchill "did more harm than good—i.e., more nuisance and upset to those running the war." Reith took Dill's silence as a yes. "I am sure," Reith jotted in his diary, "that he [Dill] would have said more harm than good, which is what I feel."[37]

What Dill and Reith failed to recognize was that Churchill saw but one "major issue": victory over Hitlerism. As to his memos having a deleterious effect upon "those running the war," Reith allowed his partisan wrath to unhinge his logic. Churchill was running the war. In doing so he tried to project the image of a ruthless warlord, emitting thunder and lightning, partly in hope of striking fear into the hearts of the Germans—he failed there—but largely to rouse the spirits of his countrymen. There his success was tremendous. Margery Allingham, the mystery novelist, wrote an American friend:

> Mr. Churchill is the unchanging bulldog, the epitome of British aggressiveness and the living incarnation of the true Briton in fighting, not standing any damned nonsense, stoking the boilers with the grand piano and enjoying-it mood. Also he never lets go. He is so designed that he cannot breathe if he does. At the end of the fight he will come crawling in, unrecognizable, covered with blood and delighted, with the enemy's heart between his teeth.

By putting Churchill in the saddle, she wrote, "the British horse gave himself the master whom he knew to be far more ruthless in a British way than anything possible to be produced elsewhere in Europe."[38]

The sailors of the French fleet at Oran had the year before experienced Churchill's "British way" of ruthlessness. Hundreds of thousands of Germans—in Dresden, Hamburg, and Berlin—soon learned the veracity of Allingham's observation. Two years hence, 40,000 Germans would die during three nights of RAF raids on Hamburg—the same number of Britons who had died during the first year of Luftwaffe bombing. Churchill took no pleasure in such methods, but he believed war could be waged only with fury. His upbringing and his worship of the British Constitution guaranteed lifelong deferential relationships with Parliament and the Chiefs of Staff, relationships that precluded, up to a point, any unilateral actions that might smack of the bloodthirsty, the foolhardy, or the dictatorial. Yet as he demonstrated when he pressed ahead with the raid on Oran, at times he behaved like a coalition of one, his options open-ended. He was not a dictator, but even if he had been, in early 1941 he lacked the means to sate any dictatorial inclinations. He expressed to Dill the core truth of the matter: "I feel very doubtful of our ability to fight the Germans anywhere on the mainland of Europe."[39]

Churchill—not knowing with certainty Hitler's planned betrayal of Stalin—could only surmise that the Germans and Soviets had between themselves agreed upon more efficient means for the exchange of critical matériel than had Britain and America. In fact, in the four months since Roosevelt had agreed to send fifty American destroyers, only a few that had arrived were battle ready, and all of them, of course, had been given in exchange for British territory. American matériel was not killing many Germans. And Roosevelt's welcome and inspiring words killed no more Germans than did Churchill's. Britain's financial crisis of the previous summer had not ameliorated; it was worsening, daily. Shipping losses had not been stemmed; they worsened each time a convoy sailed. American factories were now turning out British tank turrets and engines—paid for with Britain's diminishing cash reserves—yet all would be for naught if the cargoes never reached Britain. Just before the new year, Churchill, Eden, Beaverbrook, and Chancellor of the Exchequer Kingsley Wood met to discuss a major problem with supplies—the price demanded by the Americans. Rumor out of the London embassy had it that the Americans were prepared to "wash their hands" unless Britain spent more than $250 million—half of its remaining cash reserves—on "Programme B," arms and munitions enough to outfit ten full divisions, forces not needed until late 1942 at the earliest. The British, on the other hand, sought the matériel proposed in "Programme A"—aircraft engines, tanks, and patrol boats, of which they were in desperate need. The meeting ended with the decision to tell the Americans that if they insisted that "B" must precede "A," the British wanted neither.[40]

Churchill had let loose in a mid-December telegram he drafted to Roosevelt: "If you were to 'wash your hands of us' i.e. give us nothing we cannot pay for...we shall certainly not give in," and though Britain could survive for the time being, it "could not be able to beat the Nazi tyranny and gain you the time you require for your rearmament." Again he held his tongue, and the letter. It was never sent.[41]

Churchill, in the spirit of postwar thankfulness, titled his memoir of 1941 *The Grand Alliance*.* Given the meager, though widening, stream of war matériel arriving from America early that year, a more appropriate title might have been *The Grand Abeyance*. He needed an American in London, a man of high official capacity, a man he could trust, a man who grasped what was truly at stake. Roosevelt needed a fixer in London, someone whose advice he could trust and act upon, a man who could

---

* Churchill's choice of *The Grand Alliance* as the title for the third volume of his war memoirs is pure Winston: he bestows his thanks on the Americans for their wartime help while at the same time, in the fashion of an inside joke, invokes a comparison between his war leadership and that of his glorious ancestor, John Churchill, 1st Duke of Marlborough, whose Grand Alliance defeated the Franco-Bavarian army at Blenheim in 1704 during the War of the Spanish Succession.

debunk or verify Joe Kennedy's claims of poor English morale, a man who could judge if Churchill was a drunk, and if he liked or disliked Roosevelt. Both Churchill and Roosevelt needed a man in London who by virtue of his conductivity would complete the circuit and start the juice flowing between the two leaders. In London, during the first week of January, there was no such American.

But he was on his way. Franklin Roosevelt had dispatched to London a man who appeared about as average an American Joe as ever trod the halls of the White House: Harry Hopkins, son of an Iowa gold prospector and traveling salesman, his mother a schoolteacher. Yet Hopkins was no average guy; he was Roosevelt's most trusted adviser, despised equally by those who hated Roosevelt and those who loved the president but, according to Hopkins's biographer Robert E. Sherwood, considered to be "an Iowan combination of Machiavelli, Svengali and Rasputin." He was due to arrive in Britain via floatplane by way of Lisbon on January 9. His visit was considered so inconsequential by the Foreign Office that its minions failed to pass on to Churchill the telegraph announcing his advent. When Churchill first learned that a certain Harry Hopkins would soon be arriving in London, he asked, "Harry who?" When apprised by Brendan Bracken of Hopkins's special relationship with Roosevelt, Churchill, grasping the importance of the visitor, called for the unrolling of red carpets, if any had survived the Blitz.[42]

While dressing for dinner on January 6, the day he delivered his long memo to Ismay, Churchill delivered to Colville "a discourse on Ladysmith and why he always remembered January 6th." Earlier that day he sent a short note off to General Sir Ian Hamilton, a friend since their India days: "Am thinking of you and Wagon Hill when another January sixth brings news of a feat of arms." In his message to Hamilton he recalled as "one of the most happy memories" the two months spent as a newly recommissioned lieutenant in the South African Light Horse during the British march to lift the Boer siege of Ladysmith. There Hamilton commanded a brigade of mounted infantry that held a vital ridge south of the city, Waggon Hill.* In the early hours of January 6, 1900, the Boers smashed into Hamilton's lines. Inexplicably, he had left his left flank exposed. But Hamilton stood his ground and rallied his troops, and for sixteen hours, until thunderstorms put a finish to things late in the afternoon, defended the hill, which if lost might have spelled a different ending for that war. The

---

* Boer spelling.

besieged British held on until the South African Light Horse appeared on the scene seven weeks later. Churchill, ever in a hurry, was the first of the Light Horse to ride into the relieved city.[43]

Waggon Hill was fought by nineteenth-century men under nineteenth-century conditions. Earthworks snaked along ridgelines, and targeting balloons drifted high overhead. From gun pits came the flash and rumble of rifled cannon. Messages flashed rearward via heliographs; horses sought purchase on muddy slopes as they strained to haul caissons up to the lines. The weapons on the field and all of the slaughter would have been familiar to veterans of Antietam or Cold Harbor, or Balaclava. Yet Waggon Hill qualifies as one of the first battles of the twentieth century, not only temporally but by virtue of the deployment of water-cooled machine guns, sandbagged gun emplacements, and the lethal steel ribbons of rusted barbed wire, upon which hung the bodies of young Englishmen and Boers. The era in which they had grown to manhood died there with them that day. Four decades on, their battle had long since been forgotten, except by those few still alive who had fought alongside them and those, like Winston Churchill, who wished they had.

The feat of arms that Churchill brought to Hamilton's attention—the capture of Bardia—was a minor affair against the Italians on the Libyan coast, and by no means a victory to compare with Ladysmith. As Churchill spun his tale to Colville, Franklin Roosevelt was preparing to deliver his State of the Union address before the U.S. Congress, giving Churchill a new reason to remember the date of January 6. At 2:03 P.M. eastern standard time, Roosevelt steadied himself behind the podium. Then before the assembled senators and representatives, three network microphones, and his wife, Eleanor, who looked down from the gallery, he sketched the general outline of Lend-Lease. During the next fifteen minutes, in terms sure to encourage Churchill and infuriate Hitler and isolationists alike, he pledged American support for those countries fighting against the Axis, and more:

I...ask this Congress for authority and for funds sufficient to manufacture additional munitions and war supplies of many kinds, to be turned over to those nations which are now in actual war with aggressor nations.... They do not need man power, but they do need billions of dollars worth of the weapons of defense.

The time is near when they will not be able to pay for them all in ready cash. We cannot, and we will not, tell them that they must surrender, merely because of present inability to pay for the weapons which we know they must have.

I do not recommend that we make them a loan of dollars with which to pay for these weapons....Let us say to the democracies....

We Americans are vitally concerned in your defense of freedom. We shall send you, in ever-increasing numbers, ships, planes, tanks, guns. This is our purpose and our pledge.[44]

There it was. No American cruisers would be going to Cape Town to haul away Britain's gold. Roosevelt would stand in as Churchill's second in the great duel. To Greece, China, and Britain foremost would go several billions of dollars' worth of tanks, clothing, food, guns, ammunition, and fuel. With crude oil priced at about $1.15 per barrel, a Colt .45 "tommy gun" at about $200, the newly tested half-ton reconnaissance car—the Jeep—at around $800, and new B-17s rolling off the line at $276,000 apiece, several billions of dollars' worth of matériel would go a long way indeed.[45]

The president's words—*if* they translated into congressional action—eased the most acute of Churchill's financial worries, for an infusion of American matériel with costs deferred would buy time. Yet Roosevelt had spoken to matters far beyond merely buying time for Britain. He spoke to America's future, with profound consequences for Churchill and the British Empire. His address has been known since as the "Four Freedoms" speech, in reference to the four moral precepts he attached to the end, a caboose that evolved into a locomotive. The address was a sublime statement of American generosity and American democratic ideals. It contained no mention of Churchill and, but for two offhand references to the British navy, no reference to the British Empire. To those who might reasonably seek a moral basis for aiding nations arrayed against Japan and Germany, to those who asked why this largess, Roosevelt offered his "Four Freedoms":

In the future days, which we seek to make secure, we look forward to a world founded upon four essential human freedoms.

The first is freedom of speech and expression—everywhere in the world.

The second is freedom of every person to worship God in his own way—everywhere in the world.

The third is freedom from want...which will secure to every nation a healthy peacetime life for its inhabitants—everywhere in the world.

The fourth is freedom from fear, which, translated into world terms, means a world-wide reduction of armaments to such a point... that no nation will be in a position to commit an act of physical aggression against any neighbor—anywhere in the world....

Freedom means the supremacy of human rights everywhere. Our support goes to those who struggle to gain those rights or keep them.... To that high concept there can be no end save victory.

Franklin Roosevelt had pushed open an imposing portal that America would never, could never, close. He did not immediately step through. He and America were not prepared. Yet he had announced his intent to remake the world in America's image. *"Our support goes to those who struggle to gain those rights or keep them"* is an absolute statement that admits to no moral relativism and cannot be applied on a sliding scale. Roosevelt usually favored building coalitions, yet he had just made a case for unilateralism in the propagation of freedom.

He had made plain that dictators would not be tolerated in this new world order. He decreed that the Four Freedoms held everywhere. Yet "the democracies" he pledged to support included Greece, run by a dictator, and China, run by the corrupt Chiang Kai-shek. And what of empires of the democratic, liberal, British variety? Here, Roosevelt was silent. In Churchill's world, "empire" and "freedom" were interchangeable, if the empire in question was the British Empire. Not so in Roosevelt's world, as Churchill would learn to his enormous consternation in the coming months and years. Of democratic rights, Roosevelt had not declared, "Our support goes to those who struggle to keep those rights." Rather, he announced his intent to support those who struggle to *gain* or keep those rights. Yet within the British Empire such rights were granted by His Majesty's Government. Within the British Empire, some who struggled to gain those rights—Louis Botha, Michael Collins, Gandhi—were considered terrorists.

Reaction to the address was predictable. The influential German newspaper *Deutsche Allgemeine Zeitung* dismissed it as "Eccentric Arguments for a Lost Cause." The *Chicago Tribune* took much the same position: Lend-Lease would prove "a bill for the destruction of the American Republic."

Churchill's wait was almost over. He would not see the actual wording of the Lend-Lease bill for four days, but, despite his uncertainty as to its specific content, he had heard enough to express his thanks to Roosevelt in a speech January 9, on the occasion of Lord Halifax's imminent departure to Washington as the Crown's new ambassador: "I therefore hail it as a most fortunate occurrence that in this awe-striking climax in world affairs there should stand at the head of the American Republic a famous statesman...in whose heart there burns the fire of resistance to aggression and oppression, and whose sympathies and nature make him the sincere and undoubted champion of justice and freedom, and of the victims of wrongdoing wherever they may dwell."[46]

Halifax's departure was eclipsed by the golden promises from Washington. Still, Churchill found much good to say about the repentant appeaser: "In Edward Halifax we have a man of light and leading, whose company is a treat and whose friendship is an honor to enjoy," a man who has "never swerved from the path of duty as he saw it shining out before him." Halifax did not behold any prospects of luminous paths in his new position. He confided to Alec Cadogan that he felt the prime minister was trying to get rid of him. Cadogan had not the heart to tell Halifax that he was correct, or that he, Cadogan, thought the appointment "a grave mistake." Then there was the matter of Halifax's feelings about Americans. To Stanley Baldwin, Halifax wrote, "I have never liked Americans, except the odd ones. In the mass I have always thought them dreadful!" Yet Halifax embraced his new American duties with alacrity, and conducted them with wisdom and finesse.[47]

Churchill, in his send-off for Halifax, avoided any trip wires. In any case, he wasn't speaking to those millions, nor directly to Roosevelt, but to Roosevelt's good friend and adviser Harry Hopkins, who, just arrived in London, would surely hear of the kind words Churchill had spoken about his boss, sugary words that would no doubt be fresh in Hopkins's mind when he lunched with Churchill the following day. And that was a good thing, for Churchill by now understood that Hopkins was no ordinary visitor.

Before the new partners could get down to the business of financing Britain's war, Churchill had first to win over Hopkins, and Roosevelt had to fight a political battle. Roosevelt knew that no critic could with truth say Lend-Lease committed a single American soldier to the British cause. The president's position, a slippery foothold on the truth, was that Lend-Lease would help guarantee only that Britain get the job done *without* American troops. Roosevelt had talked himself into a Harold Lloyd sort of pickle, out on a ledge with no place to go. He had to nudge America close enough to Churchill's fight to make a difference, yet not so close as to be drawn over the edge. The last war and the sordid peace that followed (both of which looked to many Americans like sops to Old Europe) were fresh in Roosevelt's memory. He was not a European patriot and in fact believed European spheres of influence led inexorably to European wars. If Roosevelt was to join Churchill's cause, he knew that he must articulate new principles—his Four Freedoms—on which to base his proposed policies. Roosevelt truly believed that England defeated meant America threatened, that is, American *interests* threatened. Many in Congress did not. Yet the president and the Congress had plenty of time to work things out. America would not be rushed by anyone.

Churchill was "delighted" by the Lend-Lease bill, Colville told his diary on the eleventh, adding that Churchill considered Lend-Lease to be "a virtual open declaration of war" or "at any rate an open challenge to Germany to declare war if she dares." But the prime minister was well aware, too, of the sentiments of his Chancellor of the Exchequer, Kingsley Wood, who told Colville on the tenth: "In view of this bill [Lend-Lease] it will be more difficult for us to resist the American tendency to strip us of everything we possess as payment for what we are about to receive."[48]

As Lend-Lease was making its way through the U.S. House of Representatives and, if passed there, the U.S. Senate, Churchill knew he must keep his frustrations with American inertia private, and muzzle those of his many colleagues who bitterly protested the lease of the West Indian bases to America as amounting to the same sort of "capitulation" Britain had demanded of Turkey and China in the nineteenth century. Churchill understood that the sorry state of the American destroyers and the injury to national pride over the loss of West Indian bases were ultimately irrelevant. The real significance of Lend-Lease, for which he was effusively grateful, was that it brought America a step closer to war. Lend-Lease took shape not because Churchill had begged so effectively or had outfoxed Franklin Roosevelt—he had not—but because Roosevelt, in spite of tremendous political risk and strong popular dissent, considered it to be in America's interest to aid Britain and, of more immediate political concern, judged his countrymen ready to join him in taking that step.[49]

Roosevelt knew that in defending Lend-Lease he must avoid any statement that bolstered the isolationist case. He had to focus more on the morality of the war than on the weapons Churchill needed, because without a national consensus on the former, the latter would never be manufactured in sufficient quantities to make any difference. In shepherding America to war, or at the least, to preparedness for war, he could not take too long or too heavy a step. He shanghaied Harvard University president James Conant into testifying in support of Lend-Lease before Congress and impressed upon him the need to address only what it authorized, not what it might portend, though failure to pass the bill would, Roosevelt argued, put America at risk of attack should Britain be defeated.

The isolationists did not buy any of it. Although they supported modest aid for Britain, Conant believed they wanted a guarantee that Lend-Lease "would not be a step toward America's involvement in the war." They would get no such guarantee even were Roosevelt in a giving mood, which he told Conant he was not. Yet Roosevelt had preempted the isolationists, who could not afford to appear weak on defense, nor could they criticize the self-evident Four Freedoms. Any attack in that quarter would engender as much support as an attack on motherhood. Still, they knew their countrymen. Vanquishing true and absolute Evil didn't much cut it in 1941 America. Nor among the isolationist America Firsters did the Wilsonian mandate that America "must make the world safe for democracy." America had turned inward during the 1930s, properly so, claimed the isolationists, for danger lurked without.[50]

The isolationist argument was simple, and inflexible. Britain's plight did not much move isolationists, because they saw Britain as everything America strove not to be: imperial, elitist, defined by class distinctions, made wealthy by virtue of taking goods from its colonies rather than by virtue of making goods at home. Could this realm, this distant island, this England, even be properly termed a democracy? Such were the questions Congress would debate. The isolationists prepared massive opposition, much of it centered on Churchill. In the minds of America Firsters, Churchill's pledge to *never* negotiate an end to the war had lured Roosevelt into a cursed web.[51]

For many Americans, and not just the America Firsters, here was Old Europe at it again. Americans had gone over once before and received small thanks, had not even been repaid the money they loaned to defeat the Kaiser. Churchill understood this. He respected Americans enough to stay out of their debate, or at least to not enter it directly. Rather than try to inspire Americans, as he had his countrymen in 1940, he intended to inspire Hopkins.

Churchill knew that his people were willing to take the aerial punishment, but only as long as they believed something greater than aerial revenge upon German cities was forthcoming. Britons craved a real victory in the field against Hitler's armies. A victory of any size would do, obtained in any fashion, and on any front. Still, although he had yet to deliver such a victory, a visit by Churchill to a wrecked neighborhood always brought cheers from the locals. Londoners, when they stuck tattered little Union Jacks into their piles of smashed bricks and snapped timbers, sent a statement of deadly purpose to Churchill. Churchill, in turn, with each appearance, told them that he heard them.

That year he toured every major industrial city and port in England, Scotland, and Wales. He liked to drop into airfields, barracks, AA emplacements, and coastal defenses, and hoist a toast to the defenders, preferably with whisky ("I like my tea cool and *yella*" he told a young officer who offered him a spot of tea during one such visit). If, when he was strolling along St. James's Street on his way to business in Whitehall, a passing workman proffered a hand, he took it. He understood the need to be seen and heard by the people. He grasped the power of photographs to record visits to blasted neighborhoods, such that every citizen who viewed the images felt as if their Winnie had visited their house and theirs alone.[52]

He chose settings with dazzling skill, where the symbolism of the moment could be captured on film, as with his visit later in the spring to the House of Commons after a bomb the night before obliterated the debating chamber. He was seen to have tears in his eyes as he surveyed the wreckage and pledged, in a steady but strained voice, to rebuild the chamber. But when a photographer appeared, his demeanor changed. The resultant photograph captured the scene as choreographed by Churchill. There he stands, in profile, the sharp white northern latitude light diffused by a fine haze of pulverized stone, a scene of utter wreckage, the ancient seat of government smashed. Yet it is Churchill more than the wreckage that the observer notes, his chin thrust forward in defiance, an invitation to Hitler to take another swing. His gaze in such photos is firm, and always directed at a particular shocked or bewildered bomb victim, or skyward, toward some unseen enemy, perhaps toward a higher power, though he put little faith in higher powers. His eyes are never downcast. There is a contemplative quotient to his stare, as if he were regarding a vista he intended to paint. And there is a calmness, too, as if his thoughts were simultaneously with the bomb victim—whether an old Cockney woman or the Commons itself—and in some faraway place. It is the hard, unsettling gaze of a man who has been wronged, and who is intent on righting that wrong.

A visit to a burning street, a few words, a symbolic pose assumed at the instant the photographer triggered his flash, a posture of immutability and imperturbability—this was about all Churchill could offer Britons as the Blitz wore on. He could not of course tell them of naval and troop dispositions; even weather forecasts were censored. He told them he would share with them in the suffering. He told them they must wait for victory. And he told them, "I make no promises and give no guarantees, except that we will do our best." And from them he expected their best. He presumed that not only *could* London take it, but that London *would* take it. Harold Nicolson recorded his appreciation: Churchill "does not try to cheer us up with vain promises." Churchill knew his countrymen. When offered the choice to deliver false good news or the hard truth, he served the bad, for Englishmen, he proclaimed, "seem to like their food cooked that way."[53]

Like Nicolson, so, too, did Churchill hear the murmurings for revenge during his wanderings about town. In Berlin, the Tiergarten, roped off, became increasingly pocked with bomb craters. But British bomb damage, measured by smashed machine tools and fuel depots, was meager, a fact Churchill was acutely aware of. The Germans had dropped far more bombs on Britain since September than the RAF had dropped on Germany, almost four tons of bombs for each ton the British dropped. Even had the British attained tonnage parity, RAF targeting was so terrible that the awful results would not have changed. As well, the price paid in manpower for such inefficiencies could not be maintained. More RAF bomb crews had been killed or captured over Germany than Berliners had been killed on the ground. The most recent testimony to RAF aerial inefficiencies took the form of a message delivered on the last day of 1940 from the British embassy in Budapest. The American naval attaché in Berlin had stated that British air raids on Berlin had done "little damage." Churchill found that intelligence the most troublesome of many such "melancholy reports." The matter of bombing imprecision, he told his staff, "causes me a great deal of anxiety." And yet, although the RAF raids had little effect on German industrial production, they boosted the morale of Englishmen, a trade-off Churchill was forced to accept.[54]

Big four-engine Stirling and Halifax bombers were rolling off assembly lines; they could tote almost seven tons of bombs, nearly triple the capacity of the Luftwaffe's Dorniers and Heinkels. The Avro Lancaster heavy bomber (ready for flight tests) would comprise a horrific weapons system when loaded with a four-thousand-pound bomb (not yet fully developed) and dozens of thirty-pound phosphorous bombs (not yet produced in sufficient quantities) along with hundreds of incendiary bombs. The big bomb was intended to blow away roofs and windows within a wide radius, thus assuring an ample supply of air to fuel the incendiaries and the phosphorous bombs, the former designed to start fires, the latter to melt anything, including people, that came in contact with the phosphorous gel. The Prof believed that German morale would suffer under such an onslaught, a beneficial side effect of the bombing strategy, the primary objective of which was the destruction of Germany's industrial capacity. It was based on the assumption championed by Churchill that even were Hitler to reach the gates of India or the Suez, if Germany itself was destroyed, Hitler must lose his war. Churchill, throughout the year, told his friends and family in the most graphic terms what he planned to do to German cities; in his broadcasts, he told Hitler and the people of Germany. He warned them:

You do your worst and we will do our best. Perhaps it may be our turn soon; perhaps it may be our turn now. We live in a terrible epoch of the human story, but we believe there is a broad and sure justice running through its theme. It is time that the Germans should be made to suffer in their own homeland and cities something of the torment they have twice in our lifetime let loose upon their neighbours and upon the world.[55]

Few in Germany took him seriously. Hitler derided him as "that noted war correspondent." Churchill was well known for his bluster. Yet he yearned for the day when his Lancasters—hundreds of Lancasters flying in great formations—would show them all, Hitler foremost, that his threats had been anything but bluster. He pressed the Ministry of Production for "the largest supply of aircraft gas containers for immediate retaliation" after learning that the army was well supplied with gas artillery shells, an anomalous state of affairs given that "one would hardly expect the army to be engaged in firing gas shells for the next few months. Only invasion would seem to render this necessary." The very quantity—seven thousand—of aircraft gas bombs indicates he envisioned for them a strategic rather than a tactical role.[56]

Hitler considered Churchill the obstacle to peace, and promised "to drop 100 bombs" for each British bomb until Britain gets rid of "this criminal and his methods." The Führer termed Churchill's speeches to Englishmen "symptomatic of a paralytic disease, or the ravings of a drunkard." Such bellicosity delighted Churchill, who listened on a gramophone to translated versions of Hitler's rants. He instructed the technicians to leave intact on the recordings the background cheers of the Führer's adoring hordes. Churchill liked to march around his study in his dressing gown while repeating the parts where Hitler mentioned him by name. Had Hitler better understood the tenacity of Britons and their Parliament, he would have known that Churchill was here to stay. At the height of the Blitz, by a vote of 341–4 the Commons rejected an Independent Labour Party motion to negotiate an armistice. Given the traditional fractiousness of British politics, this was a remarkable declaration of intent to fight on, and to do so behind Churchill.[57]

Yet many, including Jock Colville (who shuddered at the idea of a Nazi victory), thought the prospects afforded by a compromise peace preferable to the prospect of "western Europe racked by warfare and economic hardship; the legacy of centuries, in art and culture, swept away; the health of the nation dangerously impaired by malnutrition, nervous strain and epidemics; Russia and the U.S. profiting from our exhaustion; and at the end of it all compromise or a Pyrrhic victory." Such a scenario had recently been advanced by the military historian and strategist Basil Liddell Hart, who predicted that Hitler, with Napoleon's fate in mind, as well as his outrage over the punishing Versailles peace terms imposed after the Great War, would be emboldened to fight on even were that to ensure the destruction of Germany and all Europe. Of Liddell Hart's thesis, Churchill declared, "It is out of date and he seems more a candidate for a mental home than for serious action." Curiously, Churchill had long adhered to another of Liddell Hart's theories, to always attack the weaker of two military enemies.[58]

As to the immediacy of any German threat to British soil and the climactic battle he so sought, Churchill concluded after a perusal of early January Ultra decrypts that invasion would not come in the winter and likely not in the spring either. It appeared that German troops in the northern coastal areas of France and Belgium were being shipped to the south, thereby reducing the chances of invasion. This opinion he chose not to share with the Americans, for fear that the U.S. supply effort might wane. Some of his military advisers—who read the same Enigma decrypts—disagreed with him and insisted that invasion was still imminent. He encouraged them to prepare for that eventuality—to seek more tanks, more artillery, more gunboats, more infantry divisions. The greater the buildup of military might, the better, he reasoned, for, as he had since the previous June, Churchill intended to use it elsewhere. As his own minister of defence, he told the War Cabinet he wanted to again reinforce Wavell in the Middle East as he had in the autumn, with even more troops and tanks stripped from Britain. He possessed great persuasive skills but not dictatorial powers; the War Cabinet had to approve the reinforcements, and the army, air force, and naval chiefs sought to keep the troops on the Home Island. Churchill demanded that the fight be taken to the Italians in North Africa. He sought, as well, to bait Hitler into reinforcing Mussolini in Africa. He confided to Colville that he "did not see how invasion [of England] could be successful and he now woke up in the mornings...feeling as if he had a bottle of Champagne inside him and glad that another day had come." As the Germans appeared unwilling to put themselves within his reach by descending onto British beaches, Churchill would satisfy himself with battling Italians until such time as Hitler came to their assistance. Then he could fight Germans.[59]

What he could do on the Continent that winter was limited to a few inaccurate bombs and much bombast lobbed in Hitler's direction. He launched pleas to Roosevelt, scribbled numerous memos, attended War Cabinet meetings, kept the King apprised, and waited for American help and better bombing weather to arrive. That was a meteorological knife that cut both ways. The same storms that grounded German night raiders grounded Bomber Command. The first weeks of the new year administered repeated doses of wretched weather. From Moscow, where temperatures fell to below minus twenty-five degrees Fahrenheit, to the Dover coast, which froze, snow, sleet, and bitter cold swept the Continent. Blizzards hit southern France before whipping northwestward across Brittany, and then across the Channel, across Britain, and out into the Atlantic, where Allied convoys pitched and rolled in the furious gales. Central France suffered its worst snowstorm in fifty years, Hungary its coldest winter in more than one hundred. Spaniards, already starving, now froze. Belgians found themselves down to less than two ounces of meat per person per day. Typhus killed the children of Warsaw; bread in that city was not to be had, because Stalin and Hitler had split between themselves the entire Polish wheat harvest.

Although the Luftwaffe in January proved less a strategic presence than a deadly nuisance, almost 1,600 Britons died that month. At the end of the month, the civilian death toll since the start of the Blitz stood at 30,000, fully half of the total British casualties, military and civilian, since the start of the war. Almost 500,000 apartments and houses had been destroyed. The cost to the Germans since late September had been about 600 planes and crews, less than 2 percent of sorties flown. Yet despite their relatively modest losses, the Germans had little to show. British aircraft production had not in the least been hobbled.

The Blitz in 1941, Churchill later wrote, fell into three phases, the first phase being the January lull. Londoners termed the relatively quiet skies the "Lullablitz." The quiet only heightened the uncertainty of where and when the Luftwaffe would next strike and made these weeks a time, Churchill later wrote, "to peer into the future and attempt to measure our ordeal." He asked his RAF chiefs, Beaverbrook, and the intelligence chiefs to determine if the abeyance in raids was due solely to foul weather or to the depletion of German air capabilities, or, the most troubling scenario, if it was purely voluntary, with more sinister plans being readied for the spring. What, Churchill demanded, were German capacities and limitations when it came to airmen, engines, training, planes, and bombs? As the assessments of German strength arrived from various ministries, the Prof weighed the increasingly conflicting statistics while Churchill kept his distance and allowed everyone to have at it. When he convened his chiefs at Chequers to distill the conclusions, the overriding consensus was that nobody knew what the prime minister needed to know.[60]

One certainty stood out among the uncertainties: if things were to be made right in the air, Max Beaverbrook would do so. The Beaver had the face of a gargoyle, a Canadian maritime accent as heavy as a sodden goose-down comforter, and the absolute loyalty of Churchill. He suffered from asthma and continued to threaten to resign when he felt put out, which was often. Churchill refused to consider any such exit. Beaverbrook's mid-1940 crusade at the Ministry of Aircraft Production to expand fighter production had "played havoc with the war policy of the RAF," lamented air chief marshal Joubert, "but he most certainly produced the aircraft that won the Battle of Britain." By early 1941, the strength of RAF bomber and fighter squadrons had increased by almost half over 1940's total, but Britain's three thousand combat-ready planes remained far outnumbered by the Luftwaffe's fleet. That the gap was closing was due to Max.

All Britons wondered about the quiet skies, and worried, for surely this must be the calm before the storm. Had not a disquieting calm settled over all of Hitler's previous targets in the days and weeks before he struck? Mollie Panter-Downes observed that Londoners appeared "to be taking advantage of what may be the last few weeks of comparative sanity to warn everybody else that complete chaos is approaching." Chemical warfare was expected. But what exactly did *chemical* warfare mean? Would pestilence, plague, and other unimaginable vectors of death be delivered by fantastical weapons? Rumor spread that English women would be compelled by the conquerors to bear German babies and that English males would be sterilized. (The truth was more appalling. SS Reichsführer Heinrich Himmler put forth his plans the previous summer in the *Sonderfahndungsliste GB*, or Special Search List for the invasion of Great Britain, which called for all healthy Englishmen of military age to be shipped to Greater Germany as slaves. Six battalions of *Einsatzgruppen*—the hunter-killers of the SS—would be stationed in a half dozen major British cities to facilitate the roundup.)[61]

The paranoia found its way into official circles. Sir John Anderson, now Lord President of the Council, kept up pressure on refugees from the Continent, including Jews who had fled the Nazis without proper paperwork.* Hundreds were rounded up and made to join thousands of other continentals who had been interred in camps since the summer. Arthur Koestler, the repentant former Communist, arrived in Britain without proper paperwork and was packed off to Pentonville Prison, where he resided behind bars for almost two months, during which time *Darkness at Noon* was published. "It was a terrible time," recalled the actor Paul Henreid. "We jumped at every ring of the doorbell...an apprehensive dread took hold of us. How long before it was our turn?" Yet most detainees—excepting hardcase Fascists such as Oswald Mosley—were released in coming months. Henreid's dread would have deepened had he known that Himmler knew who had fled to England; their names were on the *Sonderfahndungsliste GB*. They were to be found and killed. The dread and paranoia spread to Ireland after Luftwaffe raiders overflew their British targets in early January and dropped their payloads onto Irish farms. A one-ton parachute bomb dropped into Dublin's Jewish quarter and hit the city's

---

* Two hundred thousand European Jews had been granted immigration status by HMG since 1933, more than twice the per-capita rate of the U.S., which had accepted 160,000. See Peter Clarke, *The Last Thousand Days of the British Empire* (New York: Bloomsbury Press, 2008), 409.

largest synagogue, an incident that Goebbels claimed the British had per-
petrated in order to sully the good name of Germany among Irishmen.⁶²

For Churchill, Britons' fears begat vigilance, which was good. His most
pressing problem early in the year was not keeping the Germans out of England—he did not believe they were coming, other than by air. His critical
problem was getting food and munitions in. Since October, U-boats in the
Western Approaches had sent more than 150 British ships to the bottom, an
average of 70,000 tons per week. January's miserable weather helped moderate the losses, but in early February, with Göring on vacation enjoying his
toy trains and pilfered art, Admiral Raeder asked Hitler to augment Admiral Karl Dönitz's U-boats with several dozen of Göring's two hundred or so
four-engine Focke-Wulf 200 long-range bombers. The pride of Göring's air
fleet, they cruised at 220 miles per hour, could tote a 4,400-pound bomb-
load, and had enough range to take off from Norway, fly around the British
Isles, and land in occupied France. The bombers, Raeder argued, could perform reconnaissance duty and hit ships threading their way into ports. Hitler approved the request, and the results were immediate. February saw
320,000 tons of British shipping sunk, including 86,000 tons sent down by
German aircraft. So great were British shipping losses and so meager was
British air cover over the ports, especially at night, that a suggestion to put
cats in the cockpits of fighter planes made the rounds in the RAF. The idea
was that RAF pilots (who had been issued extra rations of carrots to augment their night vision) would shoot in the direction in which the cats
looked, cats presumably seeing better than humans at night. If anyone had a
better idea, now was the time to propose it, for between the losses at sea and
the German's smashing up of the ports, Britain found itself more isolated
than ever. "This mortal danger to our lifeline gnaws at my bowels," wrote
Churchill. "The decision for 1941," he predicted, "lies upon the seas."⁶³

He did not know that Dönitz had only twenty-two U-boats in the French
Atlantic ports or that he could send only a dozen or so to sea at any one
time. These months afforded the German navy its best opportunity to
squeeze the life out of Britain, but Dönitz lacked the boats to do so. Still, he
appeared near enough to ruling the waves that when an Admiralty report
of yet another shipping disaster reached Churchill, he fretted to Colville
(who had termed the news "distressing"): "Distressing? It is terrifying. If it
goes on it will be the end of us."⁶⁴

Hyperbolic though Churchill's outburst might now seem, at the time it
was anything but. In the coming months, the battle in the Atlantic would

decide Britain's fate. U-boats hunted British shipping westward to the central Atlantic, far beyond the range of British air patrols. Without enough hulls to carry the food they needed, Churchill faced a terrible choice: food shortages or weapons shortages. Britain could afford neither. Unless Franklin Roosevelt expanded the U.S. patrol zone into the eastern Atlantic, Britain's losses could only worsen. Roosevelt, to Churchill's dismay, declined to expose his navy to any new dangers by doing so.

The steel monsters plying the surface matched the terror of the U-boats. *Bismarck* and *Tirpitz,* undergoing final fitting-out somewhere in the Baltic, loomed as two of the Führer's instruments of springtime destruction. Almost 42,000 tons of displacement each, *Bismarck* and *Tirpitz* were armed with eight fifteen-inch guns, powered by three Blohm & Voss turbines and a dozen Wagner boilers that generated 138,000 horsepower and speed in excess of 31 knots—over thirty-five miles an hour. Their optical equipment for targeting purposes was far superior to anything the British had, and they could outrun and outshoot any British battleship afloat. Yet Churchill, during the first weeks of 1941, did not even know where *Bismarck* was. The very uncertainty as to the two ships' whereabouts was their greatest strength. Churchill later wrote that had Hitler kept "both in full readiness in the Baltic and allow rumors of an impending sortie to leak out from time to time," the Royal Navy "should thus have been compelled to keep concentrated at Scapa Flow...practically every new ship we had," with the result that convoys, already insufficiently guarded, would remain so. Allied (British, Dutch, Norwegian, and Canadian) merchant ships sailed with so little escort and were attacked so regularly that crews kept their lifeboats slung out over the sides for the entire voyage, ready for use.[65]

Such were the generally deplorable conditions upon the seas and in the air during the first two months of 1941. Living conditions on the Continent, from Poland to France, had only worsened since the previous May. Someday, somehow—if Churchill could drag the U.S. into the fight—the final and determining battles would be fought there. Until then, Churchill could only use the occasional broadcast to try to boost the morale of the enslaved Europeans as he had the spirits of Britons in 1940.

It was a hopeless task. Hitler had buried the hopes of all those he had conquered. Hitler held the western half of Europe, Stalin the eastern half. With the release of winter's grip, the dictators planned to tighten theirs. They were partners. Stalin had been a faithful and dependable vendor to the Reich since Hitler struck westward to vanquish the imperialist democracies. He pledged to pour millions more tons of Russian grain and oil into Germany in the coming year. In return, Hitler promised to boost shipments of steel and capital goods to Russia. The target date for the first influx of German steel was mid-1941.

Hitler was most conciliatory regarding Russia in his New Year's greeting to Mussolini: "I do not envision any Russian initiative against us so long as Stalin is alive, and we ourselves are not victims of any serious setbacks.... I should like to add to these general considerations that our present relations with the U.S.S.R. are very good." Those words were a work of pathological obfuscation. German intelligence could detect no hint of any Soviet "initiative" against Germany because none was in any way contemplated. The Soviets sought only increased trade with Germany and increased influence in Eastern Europe, although Soviet foreign minister Vyacheslav Molotov manifested a stubborn greed during his November talks with Ribbentrop. Molotov demanded more leverage in the Balkans. He demanded that German troops leave Finland and that Germany acknowledge Bulgaria to be within the Soviet sphere of influence. As well, he demanded that Hitler divulge any plans he might have pertaining to the Balkans and Greece.[66]

Such impudent requests infuriated Hitler, for he needed free rein in the region, especially in Bulgaria, in order to protect his southern flank from anticipated British adventures in Greece, and for another compelling reason, which he of course did not disclose to Stalin. The previous July he had told his commanders that he intended to attack Russia in the spring. This was why Bulgaria assumed new strategic importance; it not only protected the German southern flank from the British should they land in Greece but also anchored the southern flank of Hitler's line opposite Stalin. In order to deflect Stalin's gaze from central Europe, Hitler dangled the tantalizing prospects of a Russian share in the spoils of the dismembered British Empire were the Soviets to make the Tripartite Pact a four-way deal. So much plunder would there be, and so rich the rewards for the Soviets—in the Far East, the Near East, and in attaining their ancient goal of ready access to the Mediterranean. The idea appealed to Stalin. Yet England fought on, and Hitler could not yet deliver the corpse of the British Empire.

To Stalin, a greater role in the Balkans and Bulgaria appeared the more modest and surer bet and would result in Moscow's geographical buffer edging farther west. In essence, it would result in Germany and Russia sharing hegemony in east-central Europe. Churchill believed Hitler never intended to share power, and he had tried to warn Stalin of that the previous June. Hitler had made clear in *Mein Kampf* that Germany's destiny lay in the east. He had written that modern Germany would pick up where the Teutonic knights had left off six hundred years earlier, in east Prussia. He described the "regents of present-day Russia" as "common blood-stained animals" who belonged to "a nation which combines a rare mixture of bestial horror with an inconceivable gift for lying." Hitler had always believed *Lebensraum* ("living space") lay in the east, that is, in Russia. That was why in mid-1940 he ordered OKW to begin planning for the invasion of Russia, and why, in December, he approved OKW's plan (Barbarossa), which called for the attack to begin in mid-May, with victory expected in five months, before winter.[67]

The logic of a betrayal of Stalin was lost on everybody except Hitler and some—but by no means all—of his inner circle. Churchill, as he had the previous summer, tried to open up a line of communication with Stalin of the sort he had with Roosevelt. He failed. Stalin believed any warnings sent his way by London were ruses, ploys to precipitate trouble between Russia and its good friend Germany. In any case, Churchill had no hard intelligence to confirm his suspicions. Nor, early in the year, did the Americans. The American diplomat George Kennan later wrote that the American legation in Berlin, where Kennan then served, was "slow to recognize that in Hitler's logic the inability to invade Britain would inevitably spell the necessity of invading Russia." William L. Shirer's sources in Berlin hinted at that outcome, but Shirer assumed along with the rest of the world that England must first be conquered. In late 1940, Shirer pondered in his diary the prospects of Hitler going to war with either America or Russia: "I am firmly convinced he does contemplate it and if he wins in Europe and Africa he will in the end launch it unless [because of isolationist appeasement] we are prepared to give up our way of life." Once victorious in Europe, Shirer wrote, Hitler "will attack Russia, probably before he tackles the Americas." Yet, "Hitler's Germany can never dominate the continent of Europe as long as Britain holds out."[68]

Churchill had believed that for a year, too. But he realized that were Hitler to crush the Russians, he could build more sinister heavy bombers at leisure, and perhaps even rocket weapons. He could build ships, U-boats, and modern landing craft. The Führer could then turn his armies westward, toward Britain. Churchill prepared Britons for that eventuality, and prepared his home armies, as well. The next move was Hitler's. If he came to England in the spring, Churchill, his armies growing by the week, would be ready. If Hitler did not come to England, the day would come—perhaps two years hence—when Churchill would go to Europe. That was the plan. But Churchill faced a plethora of unknowns. He sensed the course Hitler would take in the east, but he lacked the counterintuitive instincts and the hard intelligence necessary to parse Hitler's contorted logic. He could only wait.

Other than by air, Churchill could not take the battle directly to Hitler, but he could take it to him indirectly. The previous summer he had approved a proposal to finance and arm those brave enough among the conquered peoples to rise up against their Nazi jailers, to resist by any means and with any weapon. He encouraged those who were too fearful to strike at the enemy; many listened, and in time many fought. During the Battle of Britain he had ordered Ismay to create a force of "specially trained troops of the hunter class" to bring a "reign of terror" to Nazi positions along the European coasts, at first with a strategy of "butcher and bolt," to be followed in time with the storming and reducing of "Hun garrisons" while "leaving a trail of German corpses behind." It was to be a dirty but necessary business.[69]

At the time, Hugh Dalton, minister for economic warfare, which included covert "black" propaganda (lies and misinformation), argued the need "to organize movements in enemy-occupied territory comparable to the Sinn Fein movement in Ireland, to the Chinese Guerillas now operating against Japan...or—one might as well admit it—to the organizations which the Nazis themselves have developed so remarkably in almost every country in the world." A socialist, Dalton called his proposed organization the "democratic international." It would employ tactics such as "industrial and military sabotage, labour agitation and strikes, continuous propaganda, terrorist acts against traitors and German leaders, boycotts and riots." It was clear to Dalton that such an organization must operate "entirely independent" of ordinary departmental or cabinet rules and supervision, including the War Office. In essence, he proposed to Halifax an organizational structure of the sort Americans decades later termed "stand alone and off the shelf." Not only would this special unit function without oversight, but in Dalton's estimation, the success of its future operations depended on "a certain fanatical enthusiasm."[70]

Churchill heartily embraced the scheme. If fanaticism proved necessary in the battle against Hitlerism, then let the mayhem commence. If it did not prove effective, Dalton and his socialist friends could take the blame. In July 1940 Churchill summoned Dalton to join him and the "usual nocturnal visitors"—the Prof and Bracken—to work things up. Over dinner and drinks Churchill asked Dalton to head "a new instrument of war," the Special Operations Executive (SOE). It was exactly the organization Dalton had proposed to Halifax, and it would engage in exactly the sort of murderous raids Churchill had proposed to Ismay. Churchill termed it the "Ministry of Ungentlemanly Warfare." The meeting over, Churchill sent Dalton off with a final command: "And now, set Europe ablaze."[71]

Though that phrase has long been cited as an example of Churchill's determination to smite Hitler, Dalton's biographer, Ben Pimlott, points out the sad irony of the utterance, given the obvious military weakness of Britain at the time. Many within Churchill's circle did not share Dalton's enthusiasm. The Foreign Office was keener on avoiding trouble in Europe than on stirring it up; deceiving friends and neutrals would someday lead to repercussions. And, later in the year, soon after taking over the Ministry of Information, Brendan Bracken, long a political enemy of Dalton, unleashed his own campaign of ungentlemanly rumors directed at the SOE and Dalton. Bracken sought to discredit the SOE in order to merge the "black" propaganda conducted by the SOE into the Ministry of Information, which produced "white" (largely truthful) propaganda. It was a turf war plain and simple. Rumors flourished. Within certain circles the SOE was said to be "infested with crackpots, communists, and homosexuals." T. E. Lawrence, it was whispered around Whitehall, would have given his approval to this "cult of intimate friendship with peasant partisans."[72]

General Auchinleck and Air Marshal Portal had complained to Churchill that the section of SOE that dealt in agitation and subterfuge (versus intelligence) was "a bogus, irresponsible, corrupt show." However unseemly it might appear to refined gentlemen such as Auchinleck and Portal, if assassins could bloody the Nazis, Churchill was all for them. Dalton set up his secret shop in Baker Street.[73]

Whenever they were captured by the Nazis, Dalton's saboteurs and resistance fighters and their families paid a terrible price. Reports of Nazi reprisals against those who defied them arrived daily in Whitehall. When Polish patriots murdered an ethnic German, the Gestapo seized 160 hostages and shot seventeen. Death was the penalty for singing the Polish national anthem. Death was the penalty for two Norwegian trade unionists who had the temerity to speak publicly of fair labor practices. Eighteen Dutch resistance fighters sang their national anthem on the way to their execution. To remind the Dutch that they were not forgotten, British bombers dropped thousands of pounds of tea in two-ounce tea bags with a message: "Greetings from the Free Netherlands Indies. Keep a good heart. Holland will rise again." With the creation of SOE, Churchill came up with something far more lethal than a barrage of tea leaves to help the Dutch—all Europeans—to rise again. To that end, the SOE during the next four years inserted almost five hundred agents, including sixty women (thirteen of whom would be tortured and killed by the Gestapo), behind enemy lines throughout the Continent. If women could spy and if need be kill, Churchill wanted them out there spying and killing. Churchill's SOE agents became—in modern special-forces terminology—force multipliers, sent with his blessing to train the locals, to organize mass mayhem, to spy, and to kill those who needed killing.[74]

HMG could not of course disclose any of this to Britons. Churchill's relationship with Britons was based on the trust he asked them to place in him, and the symbolism he gave in return. During 1941 he had not much else to give but inspiring words, somber poses, and his most inspired gesture of all, the "V" for victory. The "V campaign" began in January when

Victor de Laveleye, a Belgian refugee and head of the BBC Belgian section, made shortwave radio broadcasts from London in which he urged Belgians—who had been scrawling "RAF" on sidewalks and walls—to show their defiance of the Germans by marking the letter "V" in public places. The symbol caught on. In French it stood for *Victorie* (victory); in Flemish (the second major language in Belgium), *Vrijheid* (freedom); in Dutch it stood for *Vryheid* (freedom); in Serbian, *Vitestvo* (heroism); in Czech, *Vitězstoi* (victory). However, with predictable arrogance and astounding stupidity, the Nazis also adopted the symbol. Berlin radio claimed credit for the campaign, noting that the "V"—for *victoria,* the Latin word for "victory"—showed up wherever Germans went in Europe. Indeed it did, but by trying to appropriate the "V" as their own, the Nazis backed themselves into a corner: German soldiers could do nothing but smile and return the salute whenever a Belgian, Dutchman, or Frenchman proffered it. In July, a "Colonel Britton" (the broadcaster Douglas Ritchie) broadcast on the BBC a message from Churchill to occupied Europeans: "It is dark now. Darkness is your chance. Put up your 'V' as a member of this vast army. Do it in the daytime too." They did. In short order, whenever Churchill flashed the "V," flashbulbs popped. The symbol merged with his bulldog snarl into a single defiant entity. For the remainder of his life, he raised it on any occasion of national duress or personal ordeal.[75]

To his staff's amusement and chagrin, Churchill, a cigar gripped between his index and middle fingers, often proffered the "V" with his palm facing inward—the British equivalent of the American raised middle finger—instead of giving the proper, palm-outward salute. Whether the nasty or the patriotic "V," crowds howled with delight, for surely the P.M. was telling Hitler—one way or the other—to bugger off. So powerful was the connection, that had Churchill lost his voice, his two upraised fingers could have done his speaking, without diminution of his message. For the introduction of its nightly overseas programming, the BBC borrowed the first four notes of Beethoven's Fifth Symphony, which corresponded to the Morse code designation for "V"—*dot, dot, dot, dash.* Colonel Britton encouraged the people of occupied Europe to tap the signal on wineglasses and coffee cups whenever Germans entered a room. The Germans were powerless to respond; they claimed to have invented the campaign, after all.[76]

W̲hen touring America in 1940, Duff Cooper found that most of the Americans he met held erroneous opinions about Britain. Americans believed the larger Dominions were still colonies of Britain, something like the thirteen American colonies had been. Virtually every American Cooper met had no idea of the bloodshed that HMG believed would likely result in India between Hindu and Muslim were London to abandon that nation, but Americans were steadfast in their opinion that the British were wrong to be there and should get out. Cooper grew to believe that Britain was losing not only the war in Europe but also the propaganda war in America. Churchill believed he knew Americans. He had written, and Americans had read, numerous magazine pieces, collections of essays, and three great works—his biography of Marlborough, his history of World War One, and his eminently readable account of his youth, *My Early Life.* In 1939 he published a collection of essays, *Step by Step,* that explained how during the 1930s Europe marched toward war. But most Americans did not read books by foreign politicians in order to formulate their political opinions or take a man's measure. On his earlier journeys to America in the late twenties, Churchill attained a minor celebrity status, drawing audiences of three to five thousand to his big city lectures, a sizable number, particularly at a time when most Americans cared little about faraway events. (Granted, his speeches then were not designed to unmask the risks to humanity of totalitarianism but to sell his books and articles.)[77]

Churchill's style, wit, and literary abilities had been well documented in the U.S. press for two decades: *Time* magazine in early 1923 put him on the cover of its seventh issue. By the late 1930s Churchill, an exile within his own party, had been much heard in America, and his words were often prescient. In a 1938 *Saturday Evening Post* article he called for a united states of Europe and the jettisoning of European tariffs. And, of course, he predicted the catastrophic violence that had since overtaken Europe. Yet up until December 1941 most Americans, according to Gallup polls, cared neither about the unsavory events in distant lands nor about whether Winston Churchill was correct in his predictions of a new Dark Age. In 1941, Charles Lindbergh filled sports stadiums with tens of thousands who flocked to his isolationist speeches and hissed whenever Lindy mentioned Churchill's name. Americans grasped a simple truth: If America went to war, their sons would fight, and tens of thousands of them would die.

Churchill might have been half American, but he was all English, and an aristocratic Englishman at that. He put on his pants one leg at a time, but his valet held the pants. He wore a large Breguet pocket watch—the "turnip," he called it—on a heavy gold chain pulled across his waistcoat, which imparted to him a Daddy Warbucks look, this during a decade when most Americans could afford neither a waistcoat, a gold watch, nor a gold chain to hang it on.*

---

* Breguet, Paris made since 1775, the timepiece of choice for Washington, Wellington, Napoleon, and most of Europe's royal swells, including Marie Antoinette.

Churchill's political genius did not extend to the mind-set of working-class Americans, yet it was their support he needed. His greatest weakness as he sought American help was his history. Until 1940, Americans knew of only Churchill the loose cannon, impetuous, often witty, sometimes spot-on in his predictions, but in the end unreliable. "He was all snakes and ladders during much of his earlier career," recalled A. J. P. Taylor, "but on the occasions when he climbed the ladder, he'd seem to find a way to snake right back down." Since becoming prime minister, he had inspired Britain, but Britain teetered still on the edge of the abyss. Given his irregular history, he might prove just the man to administer the final push.[78]

Time, in its first issue of January 1941, named the previously unreliable Churchill 1940 Man of the Year. Churchill, the editors declared, shared with Lenin and Hitler a genius for the spoken word. Through their words, these three giants had changed history, two for ill and one, Churchill, for good, but only should he prevail in the current struggle: "He [Churchill] gave his countrymen exactly what he promised them: blood, toil, sweat, tears, and one more thing—untold courage." Some readers wrote the magazine to express surprise. Churchill as Man of the Year? Why not Hitler? Hitler could lay claim to the prize, not because of the enormity of his misdeeds since 1939 but because Hitler, in the opinion of many Americans, had rebuilt Germany. When the first electric lights in Appalachia were just sputtering into incandescence, the *Reichsführer* was building his autobahns, a system of futuristic roadways Americans would not see for another generation. Now he was busting up the old order pretty smartly. A New Jersey letter writer said: "If England wins...the world will have lost the opportunity to be governed by the smartest master since the days of Moses." Though pairing Hitler with the biblical hero who delivered the Jews from tyranny resounds now with terrible irony, many Americans did not consider Hitler—and certainly not the whole of Germany—an enemy. And, Americans wondered, were Britain and Churchill worthy of American aid, or were they imperialists on the brink of defeat, for whom any help would come too late.[79]

To answer those questions Roosevelt had sent Harry Hopkins to London. He arrived in London on January 9, escorted by Brendan Bracken, who had met him at Poole, on the south coast. Hopkins stopped for the latest news at his embassy on Grosvenor Square and then checked into Claridge's. Churchill had sent Bracken to greet Hopkins for good reason. He had been Churchill's friend and fixer for almost two decades. He, like Churchill, was an optimist, but without the pouts and sulks. When the Old Man went into a funk, Bracken could be depended upon to yank him out. He was also a one-man Ministry of Information, full of knowledge across a broad spectrum. Discussions that took place in Bracken's presence, Colville wrote, "required no books of reference." Within hours of Hopkins's arrival, Bracken pronounced Hopkins the "most important visitor to ever arrive on this island." Given his natural enthusiasm, Bracken's hyperbolic assessment of Hopkins's importance seems predictable, yet when Bracken offered an opinion, people listened, Churchill foremost among them.[80]

To Pamela Churchill, Hopkins appeared a "little shriveled creature with a dead cigarette out of the corner of his mouth," huddled against the winter chill wrapped in his great overcoat. His wardrobe looked as if it had never met a flatiron. His dour, crumpled features were usually topped by an equally crumpled fedora, pulled low. "His was a soul," Churchill wrote, "that flamed out of a frail and failing body." He was a welfare expert, four years a widower, and prone to cynicism. He had served as Roosevelt's commerce secretary from December of 1938 until the previous September when, afflicted with intestinal ailments, he resigned. When Roosevelt learned Hopkins was alone and adrift in Washington, he invited him and his young daughter Diana to live in the White House. Diana took a small room on the third floor, Hopkins, the Lincoln study, just down the hall from the Boss.[81]

On the morning of the tenth, Bracken escorted Hopkins to a basement room at No. 10 Downing St. There, while nursing a glass of sherry and waiting for the prime minister, Hopkins took note of the smashed windows, the scrambling repairmen, and the overall decrepitude of the place. Soon, "a rotund-smiling-red-faced gentleman appeared—extended a fat but none the less convincing hand and wished me welcome to England." They adjourned to a small dining room where over lunch they spent more than three hours in private talks. Churchill made plain his desire to meet the president, the sooner the better, a request Hopkins passed along to Roosevelt. Hopkins probed for any ill will toward Americans on Churchill's part by allowing that in some quarters rumor had it that Churchill disliked Roosevelt. Churchill responded with a "bitter though fairly constrained attack" on Joe Kennedy, who Churchill knew (via a tap on Ambassador Kennedy's phone) was virtually an enemy of Great Britain. To prove his warm feelings for Roosevelt, Churchill sent a secretary to fetch a copy of the telegram he had sent on the occasion of Roosevelt's reelection (which Roosevelt had not responded to).[82]

He told Hopkins that Greece was likely lost, and that Britain would gas Germany if Hitler used gas first. Thus began one of Churchill's bloodthirsty performances: "We, too," he told Hopkins, "have the deadliest gasses in the world," and said that they would use them if up against the wall.

On the humanitarian aid front, Churchill declared that he was opposed to feeding the peoples conquered by Hitler, for that would only make Hitler's job of controlling enslaved populations easier. Finally, he told Hopkins that no secrets would be kept from America. That wasn't true, and Churchill knew it; British interagency telegrams marked "Guard" were not to be shared with the Americans. By the time lunch was cleared, the two had connected; Churchill insisted Hopkins join him for a weekend at Ditchley.[83]

They had Ditchley to themselves, Ronnie Tree having gone off to check conditions in his constituency while his wife took her squadron of mobile canteens to Portsmouth, which had caught the full force of the Blitz the previous night. As Ditchley's midday meal was being readied, Colville recalled that "Mr. Hopkins arrived and his quiet charm and dignity held the table," where small talk and champagne put the diners at ease. Hopkins brought news of the Duke of Windsor, who recently had visited Roosevelt on board his yacht off the Bahamas, where Windsor now served as governor general. Apparently the duke "spoke very charmingly of the King" (a fact that touched Winston), but Hopkins allowed "the Duke's recent entourage was very bad." Windsor—forgotten but, alas, not gone—had been keeping company with a stridently pro-Nazi Swede, a fact that would not play well in America were the press to run with it.[84]

The talk turned to Britain's needs. Colville recorded that Hopkins offered that the proposed Lend-Lease program "would arouse loud controversy, but he felt sure it would succeed." Then the discussion turned—or rather, Churchill turned the discussion—to politics. He told Hopkins, forcibly, that socialism was bad, that jingoism was worse, and that the two combined formed "a kind of debased Italian fascism," the worst creed ever designed by man. Churchill may not have been aware that Hopkins's politics ran beyond the liberal to the fringes of socialism. Roosevelt's conservative enemies hated Hopkins even more than they hated the president. In any event, Hopkins was not there to talk political creeds.[85]

Later in the afternoon, dinner guests began to motor up to the front door. The Marquesa de Casa Maury came at teatime, and also Oliver Lyttelton and the Prof. Bracken, who had chatted with Hopkins, reported to Churchill that Hopkins had told him his mission was to see what Britain needed so that the United States might deliver it—even if it meant transferring to Britain armaments the U.S. Army did not want transferred. Roosevelt, Hopkins had told Bracken, was determined to give Britain everything needed for victory. Hopkins did not inform Bracken that Roosevelt's intentions were conditional on his reporting to the president that Britain was worth the investment. Nor did Hopkins relate that Roosevelt, to placate his generals, would see to it that military equipment shipped in the earliest stages of Lend-Lease was likely obsolete or close to it.[86]

For that night's dinner at Ditchley, the large dining room was lit only by candles aloft in a spreading chandelier and in sconces on the walls. The table was set simply with white linen and four gilt candlesticks with tall yellow tapers in the center. The food, Colville noted, "is in keeping with the surroundings, though I notice some attempt to be less lavish since [Minister of Food] Lord Woolton's recent strictures on over-feeding." Woolton's strictures did not extend to Churchill's champagne.[87]

Later, when the ladies departed after dinner, the men got down to business. Hopkins paid a graceful tribute to Churchill's speeches, which had, he said, "produced the most stirring and revolutionary effect on all classes and districts in America. At an American Cabinet meeting the President had had a wireless-set brought in so that all might listen to Churchill." Upon hearing this, Churchill "was touched and gratified." He said that he hardly knew what he said in his speeches last summer, he had just been imbued with the feeling that "it would be better for us to be destroyed than to see the triumph of such an imposter." When, at the time of Dunkirk, he told Hopkins, he had addressed the cabinet, he had realized that there was only one thing the ministers wanted to hear him say: that whatever happened to their army, they should still go on. He had said it.[88]

Churchill then proceeded on to one of his two favorite topics, the future (the past being the other). He claimed that after the war, he could never lead a party government against the opposition leaders who had co-operated so loyally. He hoped a national government would continue for two or three years so that the country might be undivided in its efforts to put into effect certain measures of reconstruction. He offered that the text of the Lend-Lease bill, which he had read that morning, had made him feel that a new world had come into being. Then he described that future, as he visualized it. He began by predicting that were the socialists of the world to unite, the new world would be one of communism and squalor (he later told the House in 1945: "The inherent virtue of Socialism is the equal sharing of miseries"). But if the Germans built the new world, tyranny and brute force would reign. He pledged that Britain sought no territorial gains, but only the restoration of liberty to those robbed of it by the Nazis. He sought only peace for his English yeomanry, who deserved to feel safe each night within their humble cottages. He had made this speech over numerous dinners for the benefit of numerous guests, some of whom, such as Colville, had heard the talk numerous times. Hopkins wasn't any more interested in the future than in political creeds; still, he listened politely.[89]

Churchill asked Hopkins what he thought. Colville recalled the American's reply as "slow, deliberate, halting...a remarkable contrast to the ceaseless flow of eloquence" to which Churchill had treated the room. In Colville's recollection, Hopkins said that there were two kinds of men: those who talked and those who acted. The president, like the prime minister, was one of the latter. Hopkins claimed Roosevelt was intent only upon one end: the destruction of Hitler. Where Colville paraphrased Hopkins's reply to Churchill, another guest, Oliver Lyttelton, recalled Hopkins's exact words: "Harry Hopkins did not reply for the better part of a minute—and how long that seems—and then, exaggerating his [Midwest] American drawl, he said, 'Well Mr. Prime Minister I don't think the president will give a damn for your cottagers.'" Lyttelton thought: "Heavens alive, it's gone wrong."[90]

Hopkins paused again, and then continued: "You see, we're only interested in seeing that goddamn *sonofabitch* Hitler gets licked."[91]

Colville: Churchill, taken aback, "hastily explained that he had been speaking very freely and was simply anxious to let Hopkins realize that we were not all devoid of thoughts of the future. He would be the first to agree that the destruction of 'those foul swine' was the primary and overriding objective."

As for the future, Hopkins recounted that he had heard Roosevelt sketch out an idea very similar to Churchill's, but that Roosevelt refused to listen to those who talked too much of postwar aims. That was a curious aside, for in his State of the Union address the previous week, Roosevelt—a witness to, but not a participant in, the current ordeal—had linked ongoing aid to Britain to a vision (*his* vision) for the postwar world. Roosevelt had, in essence, declared his intention to win both the war *and* the peace, a bit of hubris given that Churchill and England were doing the fighting, alone. Churchill had earned the right to speculate on the future (although he did not say anything of the sort to Hopkins). Following the speechifying, Churchill, Hopkins, and the other guests—brandy and cigars in hand—adjourned to the projection room to watch some German news films, one of which included a scene of the March 1940 Brenner Pass meeting between Hitler and Mussolini, "which with its salutes and its absurdity," Colville noted, "was funnier than anything Charlie Chaplin produced in *The Great Dictator*." Churchill, always the last to retire, went off to bed sometime after 2:00 A.M. Despite Churchill's relentless monologues, Colville concluded that the boss had sold Hopkins on the idea that some members of the British ruling class were indeed men of action, not words.[92]

The salesmanship continued the following day. *Night Train to Munich* was the night's celluloid feature, followed by more drinks and more robust conversation, less formal and more relaxed than the previous evening. Churchill's mood was upbeat; Enigma decrypts that day revealed that the German invasion forces were moving to southern France to take their target practice, a good sign that the invasion was off at least until spring. This secret he chose not to share with Hopkins. With the fate of his South African gold still in doubt, he asked Hopkins what Americans planned to do with all the gold in the world once they accumulated it? Fill teeth? Hopkins replied they'd put their unemployed to work guarding it. Late in the evening, flush with the news of the German pullback, to say nothing of a brandy or two, and knowing full well the Germans were not coming to England anytime soon, Churchill proclaimed to Hopkins that even though it was wrong to say Britain would welcome invasion, that's just how he and the British people felt. Colville thought the evening a success, telling his diary, "I think Hopkins must have been impressed."[93]

He was. The next day, he wrote to Roosevelt, "The people here are amazing from Churchill down, and if courage alone could win the result will be inevitable. But they need our help desperately, and I am sure you will let nothing stand in the way." He continued: "*Churchill* is the gov't in every sense of the word—he controls the grand strategy, and often the details—labour trusts him, the army, navy, air force are behind him to a man...I cannot emphasize too strongly that he is the one and only person over here with whom we need to have a full meeting of the minds."[94]

Churchill, seeking more than a meeting of the minds, again asked Hopkins about a parley between the leaders. Hopkins advised Roosevelt that a meeting was "essential—and soon—for the battering continues and Hitler does not wait for Congress." But Roosevelt wanted no meeting until his "problem" of Lend-Lease made its way through Congress. As to the rumors rife in Washington (instigated, Roosevelt believed, by Joe Kennedy) that Churchill harbored a personal dislike for Roosevelt, Hopkins declared, "I cannot believe that it is true Churchill dislikes either you or America, it just doesn't make sense." He added, "This island needs our help now, Mr. President, with everything we can give them."[95]

On the fourteenth, Churchill, Clementine, Hopkins, Dr. Wilson, John Martin, Churchill's naval assistant Commander "Tommy" Thompson, and Lord and Lady Halifax entrained at King's Cross for the five-hundred-mile overnight trip to Thurso, the northern terminus of the British rail system and the northernmost town on the British mainland. From there Halifax would sail for America aboard Britain's newest battleship, *King George V*, the pride of the Royal Navy. Martin recalled that they arrived at dawn to the frozen Scottish landscape, the deserted heath covered with snow and "a blizzard howling at the windows." Churchill, fighting a cold, added a morning whisky to his arsenal of medicines. Their final destination was Scapa Flow, reached from Thurso by an overnight run through maniacal seas on board *King George V*. The next morning Halifax and the battleship continued on to America. Churchill, Hopkins, and the rest of the party made their way back south to Edinburgh and on to Glasgow, where on the seventeenth, Churchill told dockyard workers (and Hopkins), "We do not require in 1941 large armies from overseas. What we require are weapons, ships and aeroplanes." Churchill knew 1942 might prove another story altogether, but why peer too far ahead?[96]

That night, after dinner at the Station Hotel, Hopkins lifted his glass in a toast that was to become one of the best remembered of the twentieth century. "I suppose you wish to know," he began, "what I am going to say to President Roosevelt on my return. Well, I'm going to quote you one verse from that Book of Books... 'Wither thou goest, I will go; and where thou lodgeth, I will lodge: thy people shall be my people, and thy God my God.'" Then, he quietly added, "Even to the end." Churchill was in tears. Hopkins's words, Dr. Wilson noted in his diary, "seemed like a rope thrown to a dying man."[97]

The first weeks of 1941 brought Churchill good military news from one quarter only, North Africa. His generally mellow mood noted by Colville at the turn of the year had its genesis in early December with news of the first British victories over the Italians in western Egypt, during Operation Compass. He grew more mellow with each report of a new Italian retreat, first in North Africa, then, within weeks, by the smashup of Mussolini's East Africa empire. By sending men and tanks considered critical to the defense of the Home Island to Africa, he had finally taken the fight to the enemy. In his memoirs Churchill wrote that although Britain's American friends "took a more alarmist view of our position" and considered "the invasion of Britain as probable, we ourselves felt free to send overseas all the troops" the Royal Navy ships could carry in order to "wage offensive war in the Middle East and the Mediterranean. Here was the hinge upon which our ultimate victory turned, and it was in 1941 that the first significant events began."[98]

The events had begun on December 6, 1940, when O'Connor kicked off Operation Compass. By the new year, he had raced fifty miles west from Sidi Barrani and was closing on Bardia, intent on fulfilling Churchill's order "to maul the Italian Army and rip them off the African shore to the utmost possible extent." Bardia, next up on the firing line, was no mere camp in the desert. Sited high above a harbor, it was protected on the landward side by almost twenty miles of trenches and fortifications. Within the lines, General Annibale Bergonzoli, veteran of the Spanish Civil War and a true fighting general, commanded almost 45,000 men. To Mussolini, Bergonzoli radioed: "In Bardia we are, and here we stay." By then, O'Connor's armor had been reduced to just two dozen heavy tanks. He knew that his infantry would have to do the hard work, work that devolved upon the 6th Australian Division, newly arrived from Palestine. On January 3, following an all-night aerial pounding of Bardia and the surrounding trenches, the Sundowners advanced. Waves of them came on, screaming as one, "We're off to see the Wizard, the wonderful wizard of Oz." They went right through the wire and poured into the trenches. Slashing and shooting, they drove a mile-wide wedge to the heart of the city. Three Royal Navy battleships sailed up to the city walls and pummeled the seaside cliff literally into the sea. By dawn on the fourth it was over. Bergonzoli had fled in the night with a few troops, west toward Tobruk. He had, in a manner of speaking, fulfilled his promise to Il Duce. Almost all of his 45,000 troops stayed in Bardia, but as prisoners of the British.[99]

On January 5, following the fall of Bardia, Churchill cabled Wavell: "Hearty congratulations on your second brilliant victory, so profoundly helpful at this turning-point to the whole cause. You knocked and it was opened." He took such delight in the fall of Bardia that he declared January 5 "Bardia Day." Victories of any sort were in such short supply that one would expect such a reaction from such a naturally enthusiastic man as Churchill.[100]

Victory, the word Colville noted had vanished from Britain's vocabulary, had found its way home to Whitehall, to Fleet Street, Chequers, Buckingham Palace, and to the East End. Churchill encouraged Wavell to pursue his foe: "It is at the moment when the victor is most exhausted that the greatest forfeit can be extracted from the vanquished." True enough. This was the same message Lincoln had sent to General George Meade following Meade's victory over Lee at Gettysburg. But Churchill pulled a switch where Lincoln had not. An opportunity had presented itself, as he saw it, of inflicting more damage on the Italians, not in the desert, but in Greece. Churchill's priorities had changed soon after the new year. What he had previously given to Wavell, he now took. He made that clear in a cable on January 11: "Nothing must hamper capture of Tobruk, but thereafter all operations in Libya are subordinated to aiding Greece.... We expect and require prompt and active compliance with our decisions, for which we will bear full responsibility."[101]

The victories over the Italians validated for Churchill his long-held belief that when fighting two enemies it is wise to "consider whether the downfall of your strongest foe cannot be accomplished through the ruin of his weakest ally; and in this connection, a host of political, economic, and geographical advantages may arise and play their part in the argument." In the Great War he applied his strategy to Germany's weakest ally, Turkey, his target the strait between Turkish Asia and Europe—the Dardanelles.

As the Dardanelles campaign took shape, Sir Henry Wilson, former sub-chief of the General Staff, pronounced *his* philosophy of secondary the-aters: "The way to end this war is to kill Germans, not Turks.... All history shows that operations in secondary and ineffectual theater have no bearing on major operations." The veracity of Wilson's maxim was rela-tive to time and place. He was wrong in 1915, because the business of kill-ing Germans had been brought to a bloody standstill by the trench and the machine gun. Churchill's Dardanelles plan offered a strategic alternative to the butchery of Flanders. The strategy made sense, but the execution of it proved wanting and resulted in the debacle of Gallipoli. In fairness to Churchill, the British army's Gallipoli campaign became necessary only when the French and British fleet lost its nerve in the Dardanelles at the very moment the Turks were about to quit their defense of those straits. The fiasco on the peninsula followed.[102]

Now Churchill was again striking the weaker enemy, but killing Italians in Africa inflicted no pain whatsoever on Hitler's Reich. Killing Italians in the desert was not a strategic alternative; it was a sideshow that depleted Churchill's forces against the day when he might have to fight Germans in not one, but two theaters. By his own choice, that day was almost upon him. The strategy of striking the weaker of two enemies contains at least one flaw: the stronger might strike back. Churchill expected Germany to do just that in Greece or North Africa, and he welcomed the prospect.

But on January 10, the blow came in the Mediterranean. On that day, at the height of O'Connor's stunning Libyan push, the aircraft carrier *Illus-trious,* escorting a convoy from Alexandria to Malta and steaming about one hundred miles east of that island, scrambled her Fulmar fighters in pursuit of two lurking Italian torpedo bombers. The Italians were decoys. Almost three dozen German Junkers Ju 88 bombers and Stuka dive-bombers based in Sicily swept down upon *Illustrious* and put six bombs through its flight deck. *Illustrious,* afire and unable to land or sortie its planes, limped to Malta, where it was bombed again, in port. The vital aircraft carrier would be lost to the war effort for more than a year. During the attack, the cruiser *Southampton* was crippled, and scuttled the next day. In less than ten minutes, a handful of German fliers wrenched control of the central Mediterranean from Britain. Wavell in Cairo, along with all of his ships, planes, tanks, and men, had, in just minutes, been cut off from London. Reinforcements would have to again arrive via the 14,000-mile Cape route. Churchill received the news at Ditchley, while delivering a discourse on war to Harry Hopkins.[103]

No such calamities were befalling the British in the Libyan desert. Wavell, despite having fourteen Italian divisions at his front and Churchill with his Balkan plans on his back, ordered O'Connor to drive on. Tobruk,

sixty miles beyond Bardia, fell on January 21, the Australians again leading the charge, this time donning gas masks as they fought through a
vicious sandstorm that gave more fight than did the defenders. So paltry
was the Italian opposition that an Aussie who had served in Palestine proclaimed, "The police in Tel Aviv gave us a better fight than this." Large
groups of Italians tried to surrender to anybody in uniform, including an
Associated Press reporter. One Australian commander told a crowd of
prospective prisoners that he was quite busy and could they please come
back the next day. After hauling down the Italian flag and hoisting one of
their bush hats in its stead, the Australians changed the name of Via Mussolini to Via Ned Kelly. The insult was complete.[104]

Despite Churchill's new Balkan priorities, O'Connor was determined to
hunt down the fleeing Italians. Derna, one hundred miles west of Tobruk,
fell without a fight on the twenty-ninth. The Italian garrison fled, joined
by the Italian farmers who had colonized this green and fertile slice of
coast. A joke made the rounds among the Aussies—the Italians were fleeing Cyrenaica with hopes of getting to Rome and the protection of the Vatican Guard. Churchill could not resist taking a shot at Il Duce. This was
the story, he mused, "of the decline and fall of the Italian Empire...that
will not take a future Gibbon so long to write as the original work."[105]

O'Connor drove farther west, and inland. His 7th Armoured Division
took the fort at Mechili, but the Italians got their tanks out and fled for
Tripoli along the coast road, which curved to the south between Derna
and Benghazi. O'Connor struck out overland in hopes of hooking around
and blocking the Italians at Beda Fomm, south of Benghazi. He intended
to trap Marshal Graziani, General Bergonzoli, and the whole lot. It took
the British thirty hours to navigate the 150 miles of trackless desert. They
arrived at Beda Fomm on February 5 with just a half hour to spare before
the first Italian columns came into view. Many of O'Connor's tanks never
finished the journey; the unforgiving terrain of ravines, jagged boulders,
and spindles of volcanic rock murdered tracks and engines. But the Italians
operated with a greater handicap. In drafting their armored tactics, they
(like the French) allowed for only one in thirty tanks to carry radios. Once
the dance began, they could not choreograph any new moves.[106]

A wild shootout ensued, lasting more than a day, and the Italians got the
worst of it. The scene turned bizarre when Arab traders wandered upon
the battlefield and proceeded to sell fresh eggs to both sides. Italian commanders threw crew after crew into the battle, only to watch them burn in
their tanks. Those who survived were captured, and those few who
escaped disappeared into the emptiness of the desert. O'Connor, victorious, had taken his army farther than any armored force in the brief history
of tank warfare. Churchill had thought his "tremendous swoops and

scoops" through Cyrenaica would take most of February, but it was all over by February 7, all of it finished. Almost the entire Italian army in eastern Libya had been captured or killed, ten divisions obliterated, 130,000 prisoners taken, 400 tanks destroyed. The battle for Cyrenaica was over.[107]

To further humiliate Mussolini, O'Connor radioed the news of Bergonzoli's surrender to Wavell on an open frequency: "Fox killed in the open." Graziani escaped westward with the remnants of his Libyan army, reduced now by half, to 125,000 troops and soon to be bottled up in Tripolitania, a threat to nobody, respected by no one, including the Bedouins who with impunity picked over the charred carcasses of tanks in which rested the incinerated corpses of young Italians. Even Eden, not known as a fount of humor, fired an insult Mussolini's way: "Never have so many lost so much to so few." Mussolini—Churchill called him "the crafty cold-blooded black-hearted Italian"—gazed now from Rome upon the ruins of his North African ambitions.[108]

The road to Tripoli and the heart of Italian North Africa lay open. The first of Churchill's strategic priorities—to sweep the Italians from Africa—was nearly fulfilled. O'Connor, intending to keep up the hunt, sent an aide to Cairo to convince Wavell of the need to pursue the Italians. But Wavell, who had for weeks known of Churchill's Balkan strategy, had already begun planning his new spring campaign. The maps on the walls of his headquarters were no longer of Libya, but of Greece. Almost 60,000 of his best troops under the command of Jumbo Wilson packed their kits and readied for the journey across the sea. When Greek prime minister Metaxas died suddenly in late January, his successor, Alexandros Koryzis, accepted Churchill's offers of assistance. O'Connor was soon replaced by Philip Neame and given command of the Army of the Nile.

When Wavell unveiled his African plans the previous autumn, Churchill had purred like six cats, and more. "He was rapturously happy," recalled Ismay, in his memoirs. "Wars are won by superior willpower," Churchill had declared, "and now we will wrest the initiative from the enemy and impose our will on him." Churchill, Ismay wrote, "was always prone to count his chickens before they hatched." But the results Wavell and O'Connor obtained exceeded even Churchill's grandest predictions.[109]

On February 6, Hitler briefed the man he was sending to North Africa to boost the spirits of the beaten Italians: Lieutenant General Erwin Rommel, who the previous May famously drove his 7th Panzer Division to the English Channel. In Africa, Rommel would command only one smallish armored division and a light mechanized division. His eighty new Panzer Mark III and Mark IV tanks were faster and tougher than anything the British had, but they were vastly outnumbered by Wavell's medium and heavy tanks, and would remain so unless Wavell was ordered to do something inexplicable, such as send his tanks off to Greece, Crete, or some other destination. Rommel called his command the *Afrika Korps*. If the convoying across the Mediterranean of the tanks and men of his 15th Panzer Division went as planned, he'd be fully operational by mid-May. His mission until then was something like O'Connor's, but in reverse—to hold the line in Tripolitania, and to probe eastward if possible. A British push to Tripoli was expected; basic military principles called for exploiting success. Rommel's orders were to blunt the expected advance, and to absolutely avoid committing himself to any general engagement in Cyrenaica against the more numerous British. Although he was the sort of general who followed orders to the letter, he also thought it a general's supreme duty to take the fight to the enemy. He considered nothing finer than waging a well-planned, well-executed battle—offensive, not defensive. His standing orders now conflicted with his love for action, yet the truly innovative soldier always finds a way to have his way, to derange events in his favor, as Churchill liked to put it.[110]

On the same day Hitler briefed Rommel, O'Connor received orders to send his remaining tanks east to Cairo, for maintenance. It was the wrong day to order up repairs, one of those seemingly minor events that in war weigh heavy on the future, though no commander on either side could reasonably predict the consequence at the time. The order seemed to make good sense. The British 7th Armoured Division had atrophied to less than brigade strength, just a few dozen tanks. Any tanks not in need of repairs would be by the time they rolled almost five hundred miles east to where their journey had begun, for prewar British planners had not thought of putting tanks on flatbed trucks in order to transport them to and from the battlefield. Libya had no railroad facilities; British tanks in the desert traveled to where they were going, however great the distance, under their own steam. Thus, as Rommel made for North Africa, Wavell's armor made for Cairo. It was altogether the wrong direction. Churchill months later called the decision an "act of improvidence."[111]

In East Africa that week, a force of British and colonial troops was well on its way to securing another of Churchill's objectives—to flush the Italians from the Horn. Abyssinia (modern Ethiopia), where the Duke of Aosta commanded a flimsy and ill-supplied army of occupation, was Churchill's first target. Eden, during his October visit to the region, met in Khartoum with Wavell, Emperor Haile Selassie, and South African prime minister Jan Smuts, who sent more than 30,000 South African troops to the Sahara to fight for London. Selassie, the first world leader to take refuge in London after the fall of his regime, had returned to Khartoum to tell anyone who listened that the time was right for him to become the first leader to reclaim his capital, and could do so if his men were better armed and better led. Eden and Smuts agreed to help, but each for different reasons. Eden, pushed by Churchill, sought a juncture between the Arabian and African sectors of the Muslim world, a unity of political purpose that would offset the growing anti-British Islamic presence in Jerusalem and Baghdad. Smuts needed a victory to overcome opposition from Boer nationalists, who had no love for England. Smuts had fought on the Boer side forty years earlier but grew to appreciate the British worldview. He believed in the British Empire, yet as one of the architects of the League of Nations, he also believed in a world council dedicated to righting wrongs. Deeply religious—he always carried in his kit a copy of the New Testament—he believed nations (white nations, in any event) had a moral obligation to wage war against nations guilty of self-evident ethical abominations, such as Germany under Hitler. In this interventionism he stood foursquare with Churchill, in part because economic benefits tended to follow intervention. It had been Britain and France, after all, who used their League of Nations mandates to open new imperial pathways in the eastern Mediterranean and Middle East. Selassie's cause was just; Smuts was on board.[112]

The command of Selassie's troops went to an experienced desert fighter, Lieutenant Colonel Orde Wingate, who represented the style of irregular soldiering manifested famously by the likes of General Charles George Gordon in the Sudan, and Lawrence of Arabia, the adventurous sort of soldiering that Kipling lauded and Churchill loved, having done more than a bit of it himself. Wingate showed up in Khartoum in early November bearing a suitcase containing one million pounds sterling. Backed by his start-up money and a firm belief that he was the man who would put the Lion of Judah back upon his throne, Wingate assembled a little army. It was a motley crew: eight hundred men from the Sudan Frontier Battalion and about eight hundred Abyssinian troops, the entire group led by about seventy British commandos. Wingate—a Bible scholar, and a bit beyond eccentric—christened his command "Gideon Force."[113]

Overall command of the expedition went to Lieutenant General Alan Cunningham, brother of Admiral Sir Andrew Browne Cunningham, commander in chief of the Royal Navy in the Mediterranean. Cunningham was a fine infantryman and not afraid of a fight. Sir John Keegan called the East Africa campaign "a *Beau Geste* episode" rife with dashing colonials upon prancing camels, long desert treks, upraised scimitars, oasis gunfights, all in all a series of colonial brawls, fought for the most part between colonial troops for colonial advantage. It was nineteenth-century stuff. Churchill loved it, not least of all the public humiliation inflicted upon Il Duce. Yet, given that Italy's per capita economic output in 1941 was akin to that of Britain's a century *earlier,* it was truly nineteenth-century stuff, and a cakewalk for Churchill.[114]

On January 20, Haile Selassie and Wingate had crossed the frontier where the Blue Nile cascades into the Sudan from Ethiopia. Wingate's column, though almost comically weak, drove up the Ethiopian plateau toward the capital of Addis Ababa, three hundred miles distant. Two Indian divisions marched across the frontier north of the Blue Nile on a bearing for Gondar. The following day, the Sudan Defence Force crossed into Ethiopia south of the Blue Nile. On February 11, Cunningham's army of South Africans, the King's African Rifles, and the Royal West African Frontier Force marched out of Kenya and into southern Ethiopia and Italian Somaliland. The Italians fled from the south of Abyssinia so rapidly that Cunningham's forces could not keep up. The Italians were on the run and British prestige was on the rise.[115]

Events in the desert and East Africa, therefore, made for good news to impart to Hopkins, who stayed on until early February, and to Wendell Willkie, who arrived in late January. Willkie, the Republican loser in the November election, was a big six-foot-one, 220-pound Hoosier who pronounced America "Amurica." He strongly opposed what he called Roosevelt's "alphabet soup" social programs and had campaigned against Roosevelt's relief programs on the slogan "You can't beat Santa Claus." His presence in London as Roosevelt's informal ambassador therefore informed the world that *Amurica* was acting as one. The isolationists might yet dispute that, but Roosevelt was in the process of shoving the American Firsters off the stage. Willkie carried with him a handwritten note from Roosevelt:

Dear Churchill,

Wendell Willkie will give you this. He is truly helping to keep politics out over here. I think this verse applies to you people as it does to us.

> ...*Sail on, O ship of State!*
> *Sail on, O Union strong and great!*
> *Humanity with all its fears,*
> *With all the hopes of future years,*
> *Is hanging breathless on thy fate.*

As ever yours,
Franklin D. Roosevelt

The Henry Wadsworth Longfellow verse was personal, symbolic, perhaps, but it meant a great deal to Churchill. He had the letter framed and toted it about, frame and all, to show visitors, a material manifestation of true friendship.[116]

John "Gil" Winant, Roosevelt's replacement for Joe Kennedy, also arrived in early February. A former governor of New Hampshire, Winant, though a New Yorker by birth, manifested a dour taciturnity often associated with natives of the Granite State. Harold Nicolson found Winant to be "very shy"; he tended to twist his hands while proffering "coy platitudes." Yet Nicolson concluded that Winant was a man of "superb character" who carried himself with "ungainly charm" and manifested a "real if inarticulate force." Winant's credentials were impeccable: St. Paul's School and Princeton. An early supporter of the New Deal, he was rewarded with a post on the new Social Security Board. Roosevelt confided to Harvard's James Conant that Winant would get along well with the Labour faction in Britain, which, Roosevelt told Conant, would almost certainly "be in power when the war is over."[117]

Winant, tall and lanky, considered dark, somber suits to be the only appropriate attire for a gentleman. Photographs of him are reminiscent of Abe Lincoln at his most weary. The resemblance to Lincoln, when noted, pleased Winant no end. Yet the resemblance in large part stemmed from a deep sadness in his eyes, due in no small measure to his being a most unhappily married man. Within weeks of arriving in London he fell in love with Sarah Churchill, an "innocent" affair according to Colville, but one doomed from the start, innocent or not. It simply would not do for the married American ambassador to take up with a married woman who happened also to be the prime minister's daughter. As she had with Vic Oliver, Sarah had fallen for a much older man, a lifelong habit: "Maybe I was looking for a substitute father [she wrote of her marriage to Oliver]; indeed, I have sometimes thought I was trying to marry my father." Winant was Churchill's junior by a decade, yet his dour countenance made him appear a decade older than the Old Man. Within days of arriving, he reinvigorated the American embassy by returning all operations to No. 1 Grosvenor Square from the country estate to which Joe Kennedy had decamped the year before, when the first bombs fell.[118]

Churchill trusted Winant, enough to allow him to vet those of his speeches that might be interpreted by Americans as meddling in U.S. affairs. As with the other Americans who came to call that winter (William Averell Harriman, Colonel William "Wild Bill" Donovan, Hopkins, and Willkie), Churchill opened his weekend houses to Winant. Rare was the weekend in 1941 when Churchill did not host one or more of the Americans. He grew truly fond of their company, and he valued their forthrightness. As well, he knew he must allow them to witness how he managed the war. R. A. Butler wrote that Winant and the other Americans "react well to exhibitions of resolution." This, of course, was exactly how Churchill wanted them to react, and it perhaps led to a third reason he extended weekend invitations: the visiting Americans became an audience for his frequent declamations on resolve and revenge, on war and on peace.[119]

Harry Hopkins departed England on February 8, sold on Churchill's resolution and on the inevitability of invasion. Churchill had portrayed to Hopkins a grim and desperate scene when the Germans would come ashore, which Hopkins reported to the president: "The most important single observation I have to make is that most of the cabinet and all of the military leaders here believe that invasion is imminent. They believe it may come at any moment, but not later than May 1." Indeed, many in the military and the cabinet believed that, but Churchill did not. He believed the surest way for Hitler to lose the war would be to invade England, which would expose his shipping to annihilation, and likewise any Germans who made it ashore. Hopkins, too, came to believe that, telling Roosevelt "her sun would set" were Germany to invade. Yet, that was a premise—an all-or-nothing premise—Churchill did not want to test. But if the test came, Britons were ready. Two weeks after first meeting Churchill, Hopkins cabled Roosevelt: "The spirit of this people and their determination to resist invasion is beyond praise. No matter how fierce the attack may be you can be sure they will resist it, and effectively. The Germans will have to do more than kill a few hundred thousand people here before they can defeat Britain." In fact, as Hopkins grasped after his exposure to Churchill's late-night sessions, Hitler would have to kill them all.[120]

Lend-Lease passed the U.S. House of Representatives on February 8, by a vote of 260–165, thanks in part to a young Texas congressman and rising star in the Democratic Party, Lyndon Baines Johnson. Now the bill would move on to the Senate, where passage was by no means assured. The following night Churchill—his African victories mounting and his meetings with Hopkins and Willkie having concluded with success—addressed Britain and America, his first radio broadcast in five months, and the first since September 1939 in which a British leader could cite any military successes, however modest. He intended to give something of a State of the Empire address. Knowing that America was listening, he served up the good news first, the "series of victories in Libya which have broken irretrievably the Italian military power on the African Continent.... Thus, we have all been entertained, and I trust edified, by the...humiliation of another of what Byron called 'Those Pagod things of saber sway / With fronts of brass and feet of clay.'"

Of Hitler, Churchill asked, "What has that wicked man...been preparing during these winter months? What new devilry is he planning?" Would the coming "phase of greater violence" center on England? "What fresh form of assault will he make upon our Island home and fortress; which let there be no mistake about it is all that stands between him and the dominion of the world?" Churchill then made an astonishing statement, given that he believed through his Ultra decrypts just the opposite of what he now said:

> A Nazi invasion of Great Britain last autumn would have been a more or less improvised affair. Hitler took it for granted that when France gave in we should give in; but we did not give in. And he had to think again. *An invasion now will be supported by a much more carefully prepared tackle and equipment of landing craft and other apparatus, all of which will have been planned and manufactured in the winter months* [italics added]. We must all be prepared to meet gas attacks, parachute attacks, and glider attacks, with constancy, forethought and practiced skill.

He had told his military chiefs since June that the invasion scare begat vigilance on the part of Britons. In his broadcasts and speeches, he chose his words with great care. He never told Britons that Hitler *was* coming, but only that they must be prepared *if* Hitler came. Britons learned little or nothing from their newspapers and the BBC of German troop movements on the Continent or British deployments on the Home Island. They were in the dark. Thus, when they heard their prime minister speak of gas attacks, or the need to fight on the beaches and in the fields, they understandably came away quite concerned, which was Churchill's intent.

Churchill followed the invasion warning with an oft-repeated premise:

> He [Hitler] may carry havoc into the Balkan States; he may tear great provinces out of Russia, he may march to the Caspian; he may march to the gates of India. All this will avail him nothing. It may spread his curse more widely throughout Europe and Asia, but it will not avert his doom.

Here was yet another warning to Stalin, and a signal to Hitler that the British intelligence services were aware of his intentions. Churchill had a message for Bulgarians, as well, advising them not to repeat their mistake of the Great War when they "went in on the losing side." This time around, Churchill said, "I trust the Bulgarians are not going to make the same mistake again." Then he gave voice to his dream of a bulwark in the Balkans: "Of course, if all the Balkan people stood together and acted together, aided by Britain and Turkey, it would be many months before a German army and air force of sufficient strength to overcome them could be assembled." Yet Ultra decrypts had by then shown that the requisite German strength to smash Greece had already been assembled.[121]

Sidestepping his inability to mount any real offense against Germany, he worked in more good news regarding the Italians. At dawn that day Admiral James Somerville had sailed his squadron of three battle cruisers into the harbor at Genoa and proceeded to bombard "in a shattering manner" the naval base there. It appeared Somerville had as easy a go of it with the Italians as Drake had with the basking crocodiles of Cartagena. "It is right," Churchill pronounced, "that the Italian people should be made to feel the sorry plight into which they have been dragged by Dictator Mussolini; and if the cannonade of Genoa, rolling along the coast, reverberating in the mountains, reached the ears of our French comrades in their grief and misery, it might cheer them with the feeling that friends—active friends—are near and that Britannia rules the waves." *Rules the waves?* Britannia, in the Mediterranean and Atlantic, and most distressingly, in the approaches to the Home Island, by no means ruled the waves. Britannia, in fact, for the first time in her history had good reason to fear the sea.[122]

Of Japan, Churchill made no mention. Yet Alec Cadogan had reported to Eden three days earlier that the Foreign Office had listened in on "some very bad-looking Jap telephone conversations from which it appears they have decided to attack us." Such rumors of impending Japanese belligerency abounded throughout the year, but Churchill faced more than enough problems in Europe to preclude his having any meaningful influence in the distant Pacific. Events in the Far East were not only beyond his ability to control by diplomatic carrot, but beyond his means to address with military stick, should the Japanese attack British interests there.[123]

He ended with a reading of the Longfellow verse Roosevelt had sent along with Willkie, which segued into a final slavish expression of thanks to "this great man" Roosevelt. To address the fears of Americans that Lend-Lease would someday result in American boys going abroad, Churchill declared, "We do not need the gallant armies which are forming throughout the American Union. We do not need them this year, nor next year, nor any year that I can foresee." He needed arms, aircraft, and especially shipping, but he did not need armies. This war, he claimed, differed from the Great War, when "America sent two million men across the Atlantic. But this is not a war of vast armies, firing immense masses of shells at one another." "The fate of this war," he declared, "is going to be settled by what happens on the oceans, in the air, and—above all—in this island." And then: "We shall not fail or falter, we shall not weaken or tire. Neither the sudden shock of battle, nor the long-drawn trials of vigilance and exertion will wear us down." The last line of the speech lives on as one of Churchill's best known: "Give us the tools, and we will finish the job."[124]

That statement appears at first pass to be a whopper, given that Germany was a land power, one that only armies could defeat. Yet Churchill—and many of his generals—was informed by his experiences in the Great War, when massed armies faced off for four years along five hundred miles of trenches. Stasis defined the Great War. When the armies did meet—as at the Somme and Passchendaele—unimaginable slaughter resulted. Warfare had since changed, and though Churchill knew intellectually that it had, he did not know it in his gut. Even after the Germans, employing new tactics and new weapons, swept to victory over France in six weeks the previous spring, even as British tanks now swept across Libya, Churchill remained convinced that if great armies met in Europe, the lines would stabilize, and the slaughter commence. This belief would underlie his thinking for the next three years. He believed that if the Germans came to England, they would be obliterated on the seas, on the beaches, and in the fields. Likewise, he believed that if the British returned to Europe too soon and undermanned, they, too, would be obliterated. He therefore sought other means to bring Germany to its knees. He had told his military chiefs the previous summer that airpower was Britain's "one sure path" to victory, but that remained an untested premise, and Britain lacked the aircraft to prove it in any event. Neither the Royal Navy nor the RAF could, alone or together, kill the German army, and killing the German army was the *only* path to British victory. To do so Churchill needed troops, millions more than Britain and the Dominions could muster. Only two nations could supply the manpower: the United States and the Soviet Union, and neither in early 1941 was prepared to do battle with the Wehrmacht. Churchill was correct when he offered that Western Civilization would either be lost or saved in the coming conflagration. Yet he had no strategy in place to meet the challenge.

Jan Smuts, who heard the speech in South Africa, cabled, "Each broadcast is a battle." Everything about Churchill's speeches was extraordinary, not least the speed with which they were scrawled in longhand or dictated straight to the typewriter in odd moments between pressing duties. All his life, critics had called his language florid and overstated. After Dunkirk, overstating England's plight was impossible; after forty years in Parliament, he had finally been provided with a canvas high enough and broad enough to bear his brilliant colors. He gave the lie to Theodore Dreiser's line in *Sister Carrie* "How true it is that words are but vague shadows of the volumes we mean." His words cast their own shadows, and they were long and deep. Certainly he demonstrated that powerful words could alter the course of history. Yet powerful weapons, which Churchill then lacked, and Hitler did not, can alter the course of history more quickly.[125]

One effect of Churchill's warning on invasion was for Dominion ministers worldwide to telegraph their great concern for the fate of the Home Island to Whitehall. Churchill's Dominions minister, Viscount Cranborne, sent Churchill a copy of a telegram he had drafted to the Dominion governments, outlining the pros and cons for German invasion. Churchill responded with vehemence. "What is the point," he asked, "with worrying the Dominions with all this questionable stuff?" He went on to tell Cranborne that if the Germans came, they would be cut off from resupply and communications within a week. RAF bombers would obliterate their landing sites and shipping. Then, "apart from the beaches we have the equivalent of 30 divisions with 1,000 tanks" in reserve, "to be hurled" at the invaders. A million members of the Home Guard stood ready to "deal with sporadic descents of parachutists." All of this information was for Cranborne only; Churchill saw no purpose in it being passed on to the Dominions, where it would likely be leaked. The most telling number in Churchill's reply to Cranborne is the number of divisions under arms in England: thirty. When, in March, Churchill's secretary of state for war, David Margesson, proposed limiting reinforcements to Egypt to two divisions, Churchill shot back: "I do not accept the view that only two divisions can be spared from the immense force now gathered at home. We must not get too 'defense minded.' " Ten months earlier Churchill's regular army in England consisted of the drenched and unarmed survivors of Dunkirk. Now he had an army, a small army relative to Hitler's, but an army.[126]

On February 15, Churchill sent Eden and Dill back to Cairo and Greece. Their mission was not to push Wavell into furthering his Libyan gains, but to push him to prepare for Churchill's planned foray into the Balkans, a strategy Churchill had outlined in a long cable to Wavell. In essence, Churchill wrote, as German intervention in Greece "becomes more certain and imminent," it will be necessary to ship from Egypt to Greece "at least four divisions, including one armoured division." Churchill's hope was that if "Greece, with British aid, can hold up for some months German advance, chances of Turkish intervention will be favoured." If events in Greece didn't work out as planned, "we must, at all costs, keep Crete." It was an ambitious plan, given that Churchill lacked the tools to challenge Hitler not only in Western Europe but anywhere. The prime minister also instructed Wavell to "take all possible precautions for the safety of our two Envoys having regard to nasty habits of Wops and Huns."[127]

Across the Atlantic that month, Franklin Roosevelt was trying to sell Lend-Lease to the U.S. Senate. The isolationists were not buying. Senator Burton Wheeler, a Montana Progressive, crony of Joe Kennedy's, and one of the founders of the America First Committee, proclaimed in a radio address that Roosevelt was going to "plow under every fourth American boy." Roosevelt called the accusation "dastardly." Wheeler, taking his rest at Kennedy's Palm Beach manse, declined to say more. He didn't have to. Dastardly or not, he had a point.

Although the goal of the America Firsters was to create a fortress America immune from foreign attack and insulated from the perils of international intrigue, partisans like Wheeler and Kennedy knew that the most direct route to the hearts of American parents was not to explicate complex geopolitical scenarios but to cite the likelihood of their sons' dying in defense of the old and corrupt imperial order. Wheeler's point was unassailable in its logic: if America was dragged into war, American boys would die. All of them—Churchill, Roosevelt, even the America Firsters—expected the price of Britain's survival to soon be calculated in U.S. dollars. The isolationists, though rankled by that prospect, could, just barely, live with it. But that the price of British survival might soon be calculated in U.S. lives was a calculus the isolationists simply could not abide. Churchill could.

In arguing his case for U.S. assistance, Churchill had to avoid, at all cost, any word or deed that smacked of imperialism, anything that would make Roosevelt's task that much more difficult. To Halifax, he wrote, privately: "It is astonishing how this misleading stuff put out by Kennedy that we should do better with a neutral United States than with her warring at our side should have traveled so far." Publicly, he could voice no such opinion. Hopkins had warned Churchill that Lend-Lease and the isolationists were Roosevelt's battles to fight, that "any move on the part of Great Britain to suggest that the United States would eventually fight on the British side would be fatal" to Lend-Lease and the supplies Churchill so desperately needed.[128]

Churchill told Colville he found it discouraging that Roosevelt was being led by public opinion, but in fact, he understood that Roosevelt was guiding the crowd in a direction of his choosing. This was real leadership, not cheap manipulation, for the herd could only arrive at the desired destination if the shepherd was a masterful shepherd. Churchill could not advise Roosevelt, nor could he interfere in the president's shepherding. Given his personality and the power vested in him in Britain, this frustrated him, and he freely expressed that frustration to the War Cabinet, but never to Roosevelt. Keeping his counsel was not one of Churchill's most dominant traits; the unsent messages to Roosevelt at the turn of the year are cases in point. That those communications remained unsent underscores another of his traits: the wisdom, when occasion demanded, to hold his tongue.[129]

Joe Kennedy and Charles Lindbergh testified against Lend-Lease. Lindbergh declined to draw any moral distinction between Germany and Britain and, in the tradition of Baldwin and Chamberlain, cautioned against provoking Germany. He stated several times he wanted neither Germany nor Britain to win, that "it would be a disaster for Europe" if either side won, a curious line of thought given that one side or the other would have to, someday, win. Of Hitler, he said: "I feel I should maintain a position of absolute neutrality." He favored a negotiated end to the war rather than a British victory, which could only be obtained by invasion of Germany and would result in "prostration, famine, and disease" throughout Europe. America, he said, should not "police the world."[130]

Joe Kennedy, hoping for reinstatement within Roosevelt's inner circle, unleashed a weak and unassertive message that avoided any mention of Hitler and urged America to build up its own defense. Lend-Lease, Kennedy declared, posed some constitutional problems vis-à-vis abdication of congressional oversight in foreign affairs, but all in all, he considered aid to Great Britain a good thing. Then he voiced his true sentiments to newsmen, on background: A certain "anonymous American statesman" (almost certainly Kennedy) told the British writer John de Courcy that many Americans felt "the American people have been bamboozled" and that increased aid to Britain would "lead to inflation and bankruptcy for many of us." The anonymous statesman resented the fact that those Americans who disagreed with Mr. Churchill were tagged as isolationists, "a word that has lost most of its meaning and has become a term of abuse." His congressional appearance and anonymous sniping finished "Jittery Joe" politically.[131]

In early February, James Conant made his interventionist plea before the Senate Foreign Relations Committee, a call against "acquiescing in silence to policies which might lead to the wiping out on this continent of the free way of life." Conant termed the conflict less an imperialistic battle than a "religious war" waged "by picked men fanatically devoted to a philosophy which denies all premises of our American faith." And then Conant, one of Roosevelt's leading science advisers, tossed in a cautionary aside, reminding the nation that the Fascists "are well armed by modern science." Within days of testifying, Conant was on his way to London, sent by Roosevelt to ascertain just how well armed Britain was by modern science.[132]

The *Chicago Tribune* continued to editorialize against Roosevelt and Lend-Lease. Americans listened to the America Firsters, but they began to listen less and were moved by them even less. The isolationists, the writer and political commentator Walter Lippmann wrote, had "forced the United States to make a separate peace and to withdraw from all further association with the other democracies to keep the world safe for democracy." Lend-Lease, he wrote, would ensure that "this country passes from large promises carried out slyly and partially by clever devices to substantial deeds openly and honestly avowed."[133]

Roosevelt had been doing some substantial avowing. His "Arsenal of Democracy" speech had moved America. His "Four Freedoms" speech had moved the world. By late February, Gallup polls showed that 55 percent of Americans thought Britain worth saving and worth supplying. Churchill had sold Roosevelt, and Roosevelt had just about closed his sale with the Congress. Yet, Lend-Lease still lingered in the U.S. Senate, and Gallup polls throughout winter found that almost 80 percent of Americans were against sending an army overseas.

Curiously, in his memoirs Churchill fails to credit an instrumental voice, Edward R. Murrow, in bringing Americans on board his foundering vessel. As much as Churchill and Roosevelt used the new medium of radio to great effect in order to sell their views (it had been just seven years since Roosevelt made his first fireside chat), they knew they could not take to the airwaves too often or try to sell too hard. Fortunately for Churchill, Americans tuned their sets to CBS and Murrow, a newsman who possessed, Eric Sevareid wrote, "a hard core of integrity which the impact of no man however powerful or persuasive ever has chipped." Murrow's reports from London came straight from the heart, and went straight to the heart of the matter, so much so that Ed Murrow was one of the first people Harry Hopkins sought out upon his arrival in London. Murrow spoke of the plight of a people at war. He was, wrote Sevareid, "the greatest broadcaster by far in the English tongue" and "a Boswell-to-a-great-city" in whose broadcasts "one will never find a case of sentiment becoming sentimentality." Murrow's reportage, more so even than Churchill's brilliant rhetoric, served to replace in (some) Americans the image of Britons as appeasers and imperialists with an image of them as courageous lovers of freedom. After a night of bombs, Murrow broadcast that as he "walked home at seven in the morning, the windows in the West End were red with reflected fire, and the raindrops were like blood on the panes." No America Firster could summon such imagery with such power for his cause.[134]

Yet Churchill understood America well enough to know that such imagery, no matter how powerful, was not enough to move America to war. When a luncheon guest at No. 10 suggested that the bombing of Athens by the Germans might prove "a good thing from our point of view as it would shock American opinion," Churchill dismissed the notion. Americans' sentiment, he declared, was not a "classical sentiment" and such raids on ancient and beautiful cities would not horrify Americans any more than other raids on other helpless cities, including London, then the most bombed city in the world. Churchill understood that America would not come in until America itself was the victim of attack.[135]

Much of the intelligence Churchill received (other than Ultra, and some of that was fragmentary) was murky and given to multiple interpretations. Much was rumor. Hints of incomprehensible deeds lurked within the tales. In Romania, rumor had it, Premier General Ion Antonescu—dictator since September and Hitler's ally since November—was "committing sadistic atrocities unsurpassed in horror." In fact, Antonescu was putting down a revolt by his erstwhile allies in the Fascist Iron Guard, still a powerful Romanian force. Colville told his diary that the Iron Guard had rounded up Jews, herded them into slaughterhouses and killed them "according to the Jews' own ritual practices in slaughtering animals." Antonescu's loyalty to Hitler was such that the Führer included a qualified kudos (along with a threat) in his New Year's greeting to Mussolini: "General Antonescu has recognized that the future of his regime, and even of his person, depends on our victory. From this he has drawn clear and direct conclusions which make him go up in my esteem." Churchill drew his own conclusions regarding the Romanian. He instructed Eden to inform Antonescu that "we will hold him and his immediate circle personally responsible in life and limb" were the rumors of mass murder to prove true.[136]

More such stories from occupied nations made the rounds, and more often. Hangings for espionage or treasonous offenses against the Reich were to be expected, as was the hanging of Germans who spied against the British Empire. This was war, after all. The British had hanged two German spies just after the close of the old year. But the Germans were taking retaliation to new and unimaginable heights. Polish priests who had fled

Warsaw told their superiors at the Vatican that they feared the Germans planned to "exterminate" the entire Polish people. Another seemingly preposterous story, this one out of Germany, reached the United States. Doctors in the Reich, so the story went, were transporting tens of thousands of "lunatics and cripples" by buses into the forests and there murdering them. *Time,* under the headline EUTHANASIA? made brief mention of the tale, but prefaced its report with the caveat that the British had admitted to concocting and spreading similar tales during World War One. William L. Shirer stumbled across the same story months earlier and committed it to his diary before departing Berlin. Given German censorship, broadcast of the news was patently impossible. Shirer feared he'd be shot if the Gestapo were to discover his diary.[137]

The world now knows that the rumors which long ago seeped from the Continent augured an unimaginable terror. Between 1935 and 1941, Hitler invited the world to witness as the Reichstag pushed through laws that deprived Jews first of privileges, then of rights, then of citizenship, and then of their status as human beings. But the window went dark in late 1940 and was shuttered tight when many Western journalists departed Berlin in early 1941. Increasingly harsh Nazi excess was expected, but how far into the deepest and blackest regions of human depravity it would go, nobody then knew, or could imagine. Hitler had promised in a January 1939 speech that a new war would mean "the end of the Jews." He repeated the threat in January 1941. Should "the rest of the world be plunged into a general war through Jewry, the whole of Jewry will have played out its role in Europe." He made his intentions clear. But it bears remembering, that even one with so fertile an imagination as Churchill could not imagine at the time the utter evil that the Reich was distilling, and would soon tap.

Churchill tried nonetheless to look beyond the present dangers to the world he envisioned after the war. However wide the range of topics discussed at his dinner table—invasion, the Americans, Charlie Chaplin's latest, the need to bomb every Hun corner of Europe—he often steered the conversation to the postwar world. At Chequers one evening he sketched his concept of a Council of Europe made up of five nations—England, France, Italy, Spain, and Prussia (old Prussia, which had risen a century earlier to unite all the German principalities)—together with four confederations—Northern, Danubian, Mitteleuropean, and Balkan. These nine powers, vested with a supreme judiciary and a supreme economic council to work out currency and trade questions, would manage the affairs of the Continent. There would be no reparations, no war debts, and no demands made on Prussia, although, other than a defensive air arm, Prussia would be limited for one hundred years to fielding only a militia. The English-speaking world would exist apart from the council and yet be connected. And, the English-speaking world would control the seas as a reward for final victory. Russia would somehow (Churchill offered no details) fit into an Eastern reorganization. This was his "Grand Design." Yet he could not make such ideas public, he told Colville, while "every cottager in Europe was calling for German blood and when the English themselves were demanding that all Germans should be massacred or castrated."[138]

Churchill reserved for the dinner table any speculation on the postwar world. In public his only stated goal was victory. Any public discussion of the postwar world would have invited the distractions and divisiveness of partisan politics, of Labourites versus Liberals versus Tories, all touting their respective views on education, "class," jobs, and housing. No good could come of that during wartime. As well, anything short of victory would result in a world not worth living in. When a speech Harold Nicolson gave to the members of a private club on the postwar world was later published, Churchill "absolutely blew up." Nicolson had spoken of a world federation, of the need to grant economic concessions to British colonies, and of the need to offer food to any country that liberated itself. "On what authority," Churchill demanded of Nicolson's boss at the Ministry of Information, "does Mr. Nicolson say we are offering a 'New World government' or a 'Federation'?" That an under secretary should declare his opinions on such matters was improper, Churchill wrote, "especially when I have on several occasions deprecated any attempt to declare [post] war aims." Nicolson feared for his job, but Churchill relented after Nicolson explained that the speech had not been intended for publication. A much-relieved Nicolson scribbled in his diary: "Winston has no capacity for meanness, and that is why we love him so."[139]

Actually, Churchill's penchant for petty and at times outright nasty behavior was quite well known, but Nicolson, having escaped his wrath, can be excused for voicing his relief in such glowing terms. Nicolson made no further speculative public forays into the realm of postwar political affairs. In public, Churchill needed to speak with great care, for many of the words he loved to use had very different connotations across the Atlantic. In America, "class" was a dirty word, and "empire" evoked old men of the old order in the Old World—the very order and world Churchill cherished.[140]

His vision for postwar England was another matter. On that subject, he spoke. During a visit to Harrow late in 1940, he told the young boys of privilege who would someday administer the Empire, "When this war is won, as it surely will be, it must be one of our aims to work to establish a state of society where the advantages and privileges which hitherto have been enjoyed only by the few shall be far more widely shared by the men and the youth of the nation as a whole." He allowed to Colville that since young men of all walks of life were fighting the heroic battles in the air, they should inherit the reins of power at war's end. Churchill knew it could not hurt the cause were those sentiments to reach the American press. Later in 1941, he allowed Eden to speak in public of the postwar world. But Eden sounded more like the vengeful Versailles peacemakers of 1919 than one who might support Churchill's brand of magnanimity in peace. Germany, Eden declared, was the worst master that Europe had ever known: "Five times in the last century she has violated the peace. She must never be in a position to play that role again." Eden's thoughts played well to the vengeful masses, yet Churchill told Colville that he envisioned a "re-united European family in which Germany will have a great place. We must not let our vision be darkened by hatred or obscured by sentiment. A much more fruitful line is to try to separate the Prussians from the south Germans." That line reflects the belief long held by Englishmen that Prussia was the incubator of German militancy. It was true that for almost a century Prussia produced generals, but it was also true that National Socialism was incubated in Bavaria, in the south.[141]

Eden's generalizations on Germany's postwar status—essentially, Germany as POW—were distilled into explicit policy points in an article published by Sir Robert Vansittart, a brilliant thinker and hater of all things German, who as a Conservative MP in the late 1930s had been one of Churchill's allies in the Commons. Vansittart, who served as diplomatic adviser to the foreign secretary, did not differentiate between Germans and Nazis, and desired that after the war, the lot of them be fenced in and left to survive as best they could. "If your policy means anything," Churchill wrote Vansittart, "it means the extermination of 40 or 50 million people." Churchill intended "to talk rather more about the Nazis and rather less about the Germans." When he learned that Vansittart intended to broadcast a speech that presumably would be rife with hatred, Churchill blocked it, that is, until he learned Vansittart intended to speak in French to the French people. This could be allowed, Churchill concluded, because "to the French people...his [Vansittart's] particular views have a real attraction and value."[142]

The French had been crushed. They were too afraid to hate. The resistance leader, Georges Bidault, later wrote that "Paris, in 1941, was paralyzed; it would take a very long time to find men able, or even willing, to risk their lives for the sake of a vague and remote victory." What harm could be done, Churchill decided, if Vansittart stoked Frenchmen's dreams of revenge against Germans? Were the French to replace fear with hatred, they might greet each day sustained by the thought of killing their oppressors.[143]

A luncheon guest at No. 10 wondered aloud how long it would take to sterilize every German. As recalled by another guest, Charles Eade, the editor of *Sunday Dispatch,* "Winston brought the lunch party back to reality by observing that if people like his guests, the product of a very high order of civilization, could be capable of discussing such subjects...it must surely give us some idea of what sort of things that the Germans themselves might be ready and willing to do to us if they ever have the chance." The seepage of Vansittart's brand of hatred into the hearts of decent Englishmen would turn them into the soulless murderers they were now fighting. That, for Churchill, was the same as defeat, and unacceptable.[144]

He kept any hatred he harbored in check in public and usually in private. He told Hopkins that he "hated nobody," and didn't feel he had any enemies—"except Hitler, and that was professional." To dining companions on more than one occasion he offered that "anger is a waste of energy. Steam which is used to blow off a safety valve would be better used to drive an engine." Yet in the heat of the moment following some new and diabolical feat of the Luftwaffe performed at the expense of British civilians, Churchill, in private, often poured forth his loathing of Huns in general and Hitler in particular. He would "castrate the lot" or bomb "every Hun corner" of Europe. It could be fairly asked if his rages were fueled by alcohol, yet in Churchill's case this would amount to a rhetorical question. The rages could come anytime, morning to night, and Churchill drank every day, morning to night. And his rage always and swiftly subsided. He understood the difference between ruthlessness born of the necessity of war, and thuggish cruelty born of pathological hatred. He ended many evenings with a final word to a secretary (or whoever remained awake at that late hour) on the need for Europeans, including Germans, to live together in harmony following the war. Hitlerism was his enemy, not the German people.[145]

Whether behind a microphone or with his cronies in private, Churchill was canny enough to know when a calculated quotient of righteous anger was called for. When Clementine, during a March luncheon held in honor of James Conant, offered that the people of a nation such as Britain, where old ladies served tea and cigarettes to downed German pilots, could never grow to hate Germans, Churchill growled that before the war was over the British would be hating their enemies all right. He said that for Conant's benefit, for the Germans had just dropped their latest bomb—a four-thousand-pounder—on Hendron, killing about eighty civilians. Such a monster bomb, unimaginable just two years earlier, shocked the sensibilities of civilized people. To address such dastardly technologies and tactics with an overly generous heart would undermine Churchill's status as warlord in front of an important luncheon guest. He had to appear resolute yet not bloodthirsty.

Another of his luncheon guests that day, Charles Eade, offered that British bombing was probably accurate enough to avoid killing innocent Germans. Knowing that wasn't so and that German civilians were paying a high price, Churchill ducked the topic. Perhaps for this reason he decided not to inform Conant that the British had just readied for deployment their own four-thousand-pound bomb. When the talk came around to the calls by Britons for retaliation, Churchill fell back on the remark he had made in the Commons smoking room the previous autumn: "Duty before pleasure." Eade recalled that Clementine laughed at this, and said, " 'You are blood-thirsty,' a remark which the Prime Minister did not quite get, and it had to be repeated several times for his benefit."[146]

In his account of the Conant luncheon, Eade hints at another current of conversation at the table, but understandably failed at the time to grasp its import. When the topic of the German four-thousand-pound bomb came up, he asked if it contained "any new form of explosive," which sparked a lively conversation among the well-lubricated guests. Anything new in weaponry, even the rumor of something new, begot terror. Death rays, magnetic mines that floated to the sea surface to seek out targets, huge new bombs—which were fact and which were fiction? Eade notes that at one point during the conversation, the Prof chose to ruminate on the subject of uranium, saying, "Uranium is continually halving itself. Why is there any uranium left on earth?" At the time, uranium was an element most people in Britain and America had never heard of, the physical properties of which very few even in scientific circles understood.[147]

Conant understood. A chemist by education, he served under Vannevar Bush on the National Defense Research Committee, charged by Roosevelt with the task of funding research in order to bring the latest in science and technology to the American military. The NDRC reported directly to Roosevelt and had funded research on uranium. Just weeks earlier, two University of California (Berkeley) physicists had produced minuscule amounts of the hitherto unknown element 94, which they christened plutonium. Conant was familiar with the enormous power inherent in the uranium-235 isotope, though he considered the possibility of unleashing that power to be more science fiction than scientific fact. The Prof thought otherwise, in part because the Maud Committee, formed by Sir Henry Tizard the previous year to determine the feasibility of building an atomic bomb, had kept Lindemann apprised of its progress. The Maud conclusion to date held that with enough money and in about four years' time, a nuclear bomb equal in power to almost two thousand tons of TNT might, just might, prove possible. Two thousand tons equaled the bombing capacity of three hundred Lancaster bombers. This was a terrible power.

During a private lunch with Conant a few days later, Lindemann again brought up the subject of uranium. Conant had recently dined at Oxford with a French physicist who predicted that nuclear power would someday drive electric power plants and possibly even submarines. Thus, when the Prof mentioned uranium, Conant, recalling the Frenchman, replied that some use for uranium might someday be found but that he and his fellow scientists at the NDRC "thought it unwise... to devote the precious time of scientists, with the German threat so critical, to a project which could not affect the outcome of the war."[148]

At that, Lindemann leaned into the table and said portentously, "You have left out of consideration the possibility of the construction of a bomb of enormous power." Lindemann explained that by "arranging for two portions of the element to be brought together suddenly the resulting mass would spontaneously undergo a self-sustaining reaction." This was a startling and provocative statement. Conant had assumed that uranium research in the United States, and most likely in Britain, had as its distant goal a sustained and controlled nuclear reaction, not a catastrophic event. Conant's mission to England consisted largely of setting up a London center where American and British scientists would share secrets, mostly about improvements on proximity fuses, bombsights, and radar. Yet with Lindemann's extraordinary hint at British interest in developing an atomic bomb, Conant realized that he had been made privy to the most secret of information. He knew, too, that proper channels of communication for such information needed to be established, and soon. For his part, Lindemann knew that Conant—directly or through his boss, Vannevar Bush—had the ear of the president, although he did not know, as Conant would learn to his "astonishment," that Roosevelt had little interest in and was rarely briefed on technical matters, including radar and the critical role it had played in the Battle of Britain.[149]

Conant took Lindemann's revelation home to Bush, Roosevelt's point man on atomic research. Within weeks, Bush was made director of a new and top-secret committee, the Office of Scientific Research and Development, in which Conant served as Bush's deputy. In October, the British passed on the Maud report in its entirety to the Americans, and a partnership was soon born.[150]

Lindemann's motive in bringing up the subject went beyond the sharing of science secrets with his American counterpart. The Prof was a truly Strangelovian character, called "Baron Berlin" by those of his many enemies who resented his Teutonic roots. His detractors—including Randolph Churchill—whispered the rumor that he was Jewish, to which Winston Churchill replied that he did not care and could not see why it mattered even if it was true. In fact, Colville wrote, the Prof "looked with contempt on Jews and coloured people" but he reserved his deepest hatred for Germany, not simply Nazis, but all things German. He shared with Churchill the desire to pulverize Germany but did not share Churchill's dream of rebuilding Germany after the war. Lindemann's preferred post-war Germany would be a dead Germany. In uranium he had found an extraordinary means to render it so.[151]

Churchill knew that such a weapon made hatred all the more dangerous and made all the more necessary a vision and plan for the postwar world. However, he also believed that any weapon that could end the war sooner—mustard gas, bacterial warfare, assassinations and sabotage by the SOE, even something as futuristic and dastardly as an atomic fission device—possessed great utility. For the time being, however, conventional bombs would have to suffice. Lindemann, at Churchill's request, commenced work on a scientific and policy paper that addressed how best to deal from the air with German cities. The Prof's conclusions and their implementation by Halifax, Lancaster, and B-17 bombers would within three years go a long way toward fulfilling his dream of destroying Germany.[152]

Churchill tried in his speeches to offer hope to his listeners, whether they were enslaved on the Continent or cowering in British air-raid shelters. As he regularly did for Englishmen, in a spring broadcast he offered the Poles his message:

> All over Europe races and States whose cultures and history made them a part of the general life of Christendom in centuries when the Prussians were no better than a barbarous tribe, and the German empire no more than an agglomeration of pumpernickel principalities, are now prostate under the dark cruel yoke of Hitler and his Nazi gang.
>
> Every week his firing parties are busy in a dozen lands. Monday he shoots Dutchmen: Tuesday Norwegians; Wednesday French or Belgians stand against the wall; Thursday it is the Czechs who must suffer...to fill his repulsive bill of executions. But always, all the days, there are the Poles....A day will dawn, perhaps sooner than we now have a right to hope, when the insane attempt to found a Prussian domination on racial hatred, on the armoured vehicle, on the secret police, on the alien overseer and on still more filthy Quislings, will pass like a monstrous dream.
>
> And in that morning of hope and freedom...all that is noble and fearless in the New World as well as in the Old, will salute the rise of Poland to be a nation again.[153]

His words on this occasion fell short of the mark, for the Poles were suffering depredations not visited upon any of the Western European peoples conquered by Hitler. Poles were starving faster than Himmler could shoot them. Himmler and Hitler as yet ruled no lands farther east on which they could resettle the Polish people, although they had concluded that Siberia would do nicely. Absent a place to send the Poles (and soon enough, to send all Slavs who lived west of the Urals), Reich policy was to put them to work readying the countryside for the millions of German warrior-farmers who would emigrate there to start new lives and make fine German babies. The Poles, at least the Catholics among them, would labor as slaves for the Nazis. But more than three million of Poland's prewar population of thirty-four million were Jews. For them, the most sinister of Himmler's programs had yet to begin, but already Poles, both Christians and Jews, beheld in their future nothing resembling Churchill's "morning of hope and freedom." Rather, they beheld darkness and slavery and unspeakable evil.

No speaker could turn a phrase with Churchill's skill, yet he sometimes turned one too many. Churchill's "real tyrant is the glittering phrase," Australian prime minister Robert Menzies jotted in his diary, "so attractive to his mind that awkward facts have to give way." "Pumpernickel principalities" is just the sort of glittering phrase Churchill could not resist, but perhaps should have on that occasion.[154]

Curiously absent from his broadcast to the Poles was any mention of Stalin, who in partnership with Hitler had chewed off eastern Poland in 1939. Churchill was by now convinced Russia would be Hitler's next victim, and soon. It was inopportune to criticize the Russian Bear for its predations on Poland when at any moment the Bear might himself be mauled, securing for Churchill a new ally and a modicum of respite for Britons. The Poles, for their part, understood with terrible certainty that whether or not Hitler attacked Stalin, their prospects in no way changed for the better. Churchill's words on this occasion were eloquent, the sort that inspired his countrymen, who were further inspired by the sight of captured German airmen, the wreckage of Luftwaffe bombers, searchlight beams stabbing into the night, and the *crack* of AA guns, all of which meant Churchill was giving it back. But Poles could give back nothing. Churchill's words offered them only the modest succor afforded by the knowledge that Winston Churchill was out there, across the miles, and that he had not forgotten them.

Menzies remained in London for much of the year. Though he supported Churchill, he knew that voters back home sought more say in the deployment of Australian troops. His political opposition in Canberra thought him too cozy with London, more British than the British. He pestered Churchill constantly for a greater role within the London government, including a permanent seat in the War Cabinet. Although Menzies, along with Jan Smuts, was frequently invited to sit in on War Cabinet meetings, Churchill was constrained by law—a happy coincidence, given his opposition to the idea—from giving a representative of an autonomous commonwealth nation a permanent seat in the War Cabinet. Still, Churchill found Menzies estimable and entertaining enough to sponsor him for membership in the Other Club, Churchill's private dining society, where a man's company was valued more than his politics. But as the year wore on, Churchill's frustration with Menzies grew. The Australian, recalled Viscount Antony Head (at the time a colonel working in war plans), had taken to "laying down the law to Winston" and telling him where he was wrong on strategy and policy. After a sullen meeting between Churchill and Menzies, held at Chartwell, the Australian made ready to depart. Clementine called out to him, "Oh, Mr. Menzies, you must sign the guest book." Churchill murmured, "Yes, and you know what to write—J. Christ."[155]

The second phase of 1941's Blitz—the "Luftwaffe's tour of the ports"—began in mid-February with four straight nights of raids on Portsmouth, where the quays were smashed and the city center reduced to rubble. The town anointed itself "the smitten city." Then Plymouth came in for it, and the Mayflower stone, which marked the spot from which the Pilgrims had ventured forth to the New World, was blown to smithereens. Göring put Hull, Bristol, Merseyside, Swansea, and Glasgow in his sights, and hit them hard, especially—and worrisomely—just as convoys made port. Göring's uncanny ability to find convoys on the open seas and hit the ports at such opportune times (for Germany) inclined Churchill to believe that a spy had to be forwarding information to the Germans. In fact, the Germans had cracked the British merchantman code years earlier. U-boats and Luftwaffe planners simply followed ships' radio signals. Almost 150,000 tons went to the bottom within sight of land in the last days of February and first days of March, the third worst week of shipping losses since the war began. "The sinkings are bad and the strain is increasing at sea," Churchill cabled Roosevelt.[156]

The president did not reply.

The previous summer, Spitfires and Hurricanes helped keep the Germans out of Britain, but bombers, not fighters, were now Churchill's weapons of choice. Despite Fighter Command's protests, Churchill, in his capacity as minister of defence, demanded more bombers. He understood that British night fighters accounted for few German kills, and would not do so until British airborne radar—the "smeller," he called it—was made far more efficient and lighter. The Germans meanwhile, stung by Fighter Command, had ceased daylight raids the previous October. More RAF fighters, therefore, would not result in more downed German pilots, but more RAF bombers would result in more dead Germans. To accomplish that, Churchill turned to the Aircraft Ministry and Beaverbrook.[157]

Beaverbrook, though not as steadfast a believer as Churchill in bomber warfare, complied. It was the correct decision, made at the correct moment, for by the end of 1940, with growing numbers of RAF bombers lost and in need of repairs (for which there were scarcely any spare parts), Bomber Command was flying only about one-half the sorties flown in the summer. The tonnage of bombs dropped on Germany had fallen to barely a third of the tonnage dropped in September. The RAF was inflicting no pain on the Reich. By January, Beaverbrook's factories began to meet Churchill's demand. The first Lancaster bombers—powered by four Rolls-Royce Merlin engines, and toting up to six tons of bombs—had taken their shakedown flights in mid-January. The Germans had nothing to match the armament, range, and bomb capacity of the Lancasters. These were the instruments of destruction that Churchill needed in order to fulfill his strategic priority, which was, as he stated frequently and with no equivocation, to deliver "an absolutely devastating, exterminating attack by very heavy bombers from this country upon the Nazi homeland."[158]

Beaverbrook took it as his mission to make good on Churchill's oath, and he did so in a manner that pleased no one but the prime minister. The Beaver's staff resented his holding his cards close, and neither the fighter nor bomber wings of the RAF were satisfied with their allotments. But he was not to be denied. He changed production schedules seemingly at random, broke aircraft factories into smaller components, and scattered them in the countryside, where the Luftwaffe could not find them. He unilaterally granted permission to American factories to build Merlin engines under license, and Hurricanes and Spitfires, too, if they desired (the British had to pay cash for the end products). Harold Macmillan thought him "half mad, half genius...who thinks only of his present work, and that all his old fortune, newspapers and women are completely forgotten." Beaverbrook managed by cajoling and by instinct; he operated at full steam ahead, until a crisis arrived, which he would fix before steaming off again at flank speed. Randolph cautioned his wife, Pamela, to avoid at all costs "Beaverbrook's spell, because nothing amuses Beaverbrook more than to have complete control of people's lives, to smash them or put them together as he sees fit." In his dealings with everyone (including Churchill), Beaverbrook was clever to the point of deviousness, yet Churchill, recalled Pamela, "had great respect for Beaverbrook's shrewdness and cunning and ability—tremendous respect." He kept his production schedules and inventory needs on scraps of paper in his pocket and available in case Churchill asked about such matters, which he did often. For this trait alone Churchill respected Beaverbrook, a happy confluence of utility in a friendship of three decades' standing. In Churchill, Beaverbrook found the hero he had sought out since childhood—a great man who appreciated his talents and who welcomed him into his inner circle. In return, Beaverbrook reciprocated with absolute loyalty, although when he and Churchill agreed to disagree—which they did on a regular basis—he was not the sort to back down.[159]

By late February, O'Connor's VIII Corps, now commanded by General Philip Neame, held the Libyan flank, five hundred miles west of Cairo. On the Horn, the Italians still fled before Wingate and Cunningham. All looked well. Harold Nicolson saw the African campaigns as "mere chicken-feed." He told his diary there was no doubt where the real threat lay, "We know that the Great Attack is impending.... When the climate improves they may descend upon us with such force as they have never deployed before. Most of our towns will be destroyed." Expecting the worst, Nicolson closed his diary entry with: "Well, if they try, let them try. We shall win in the end."[160]

On March 1, Hitler secured his right of way to Yugoslavia and Greece when Bulgaria ignored Churchill's warning of February 9 and signed on with Hitler. The Bulgarians had no choice. Since the previous autumn, Hitler had pressed Yugoslavia and Bulgaria to join the Tripartite Pact, as had Hungary and Romania, each in its own turn humiliated and cajoled into becoming Nazi cat's-paws. Bulgaria was the latest to succumb. Its king, Boris, ruled a country that was Russia's only real friend in Europe, a good friend of long standing, by mutual agreement. Czar Nicholas II was Boris's godfather; Russia had backed Bulgaria in its exit from the Ottoman Empire sixty years previously. These were cultural bonds of a sort Hitler could not tolerate, for if Boris and Stalin were to strengthen them, Hitler would be denied his most direct transit to Greece. The Führer made Boris the same offer he had made Antonescu the previous autumn, a guarantee of protection. Of course, the refusal of such protection would result in problematic relations with the Reich. Boris faced a choice between two evils: to make way for the Wehrmacht or to be taken out of the way.

Boris, a peaceful man who liked to collect butterflies and tinker with automobile engines, was made of stern enough stuff to say no to Hitler, but his army could not back him up. No army in Europe could back up any leader who said no to Hitler. Had Bulgaria been protected by an oceanic tank ditch, as was Britain, Boris might have bought more time. Furthermore, Boris's ministers were pro-German, his wife pro-Italian, and his people pro-Russian. His safest move was to put himself under Hitler's protection, which he did on March 1. Hitler now held both banks of the Danube down to the Black Sea, and he had plans for the seven hundred German pontoon bridges sitting on the Romanian bank.[161]

On March 6 Lend-Lease began the third month of its journey through Congress; the U.S. Senate had been debating the bill for almost a month. That day, Churchill displayed his displeasure over the lethargic pace of the legislation when he appeared late, tired, and "grumpy" at No. 10 for a luncheon held for James Conant. The guests dined in awkward silence until Conant voiced his "belligerent" interventionist views. At that, Churchill became animated and turned the talk to Lend-Lease: "This bill has to pass," he snarled. Conant recalled the Old Man's "irritation rising as he spoke." Churchill went on: "What a failure he [Roosevelt] would appear if this bill is not passed. What would happen in the United States if the bill was rejected? Would the president resign" and if so, "who would become president, the vice-president?"[162]

Conant was stunned. He asked himself if Churchill might "really have such a profound ignorance of the American constitutional system." The Harvard man—wary of angering Churchill—gently informed him that an American president, unlike a British prime minister, did not resign after major political setbacks, and that America "did not operate under a parliamentary system," as did the British. Emboldened by "gaining the ascendancy for a moment," Conant tossed out the prospects of American armies coming to the rescue. "We don't want your men," Churchill snarled, "just give us the tools and we shall finish the job." Conant realized at that moment what many of Churchill's dinner companions had long known: "Mr. Churchill had this way of quoting from his own speeches even in casual conversation." Churchill plowed on, insisting to Conant that nobody in England had ever in public asked America to enter the war. Conant took Churchill's words at face value but was skeptical and felt that "Mr. Churchill and his associates were not entirely frank" and tended to say one thing "while thinking quite another," although "no responsible statesman is required to be completely candid." Conant concluded that Churchill had "rather let himself go" during the luncheon, "perhaps unconsciously, perhaps consciously for my benefit."

Conant did not yet understand that Churchill put on a show whenever he had an audience. Ambiguity was alien to the man. Churchill, wrote Sir John Keegan, "had no capacity for sustained dissimulation." His outburst produced the intended results. Conant rushed back to his hotel and—"upset at Churchill's troubled eloquence"—fired off letters to his wife and colleagues in which he asked, "Why don't they pass Lend-Lease? Why doesn't FDR appeal to the country in another radio speech?"[163]

Roosevelt had no need to. Conant, overseas for three weeks, was unaware that during those weeks, Roosevelt's victory in the Senate had gone from a possibility to a certainty. Apparently Churchill's Washington embassy was furnishing him with no better intelligence than Conant was deriving from his friends. In any case, Lend-Lease cleared the U.S. Senate by a vote of 60–31 on March 8. Roosevelt signed it on the eleventh. "The bill," Churchill told Winant, "is a draught of life." But it was not as sweet a draught as he thought. The *New York Times* reported that the president had said the first matériel to be sent to the British and Greeks was not very large in dollars and cents, but, whatever the amount, it would be charged against the limitation of $1.3 billion "placed by the lease-lend bill upon the value of materials that may be transferred from the existing facilities of the Army and Navy. Figures before the President did not necessarily mean the billing price inasmuch as much of the material was considered out of date, or surplus, and *not worth the money paid a good many years ago*"(italics added).[164]

Britain's first shipments of arms, therefore, would consist of junk, long since written off America's books. British pilots were training in America, and American pilots, including women, were ferrying bombers to Britain. Fuel and ammunition arrived at British ports weekly. But as with the obsolete destroyers, Roosevelt told Americans they were getting the best of the deal. No doubt Churchill, too, would get a good deal, *if* Congress passed—and passed rapidly—the pending appropriation of $7 billion. That was a lot of money in 1941. Yet even fully funded, Lend-Lease would only partially address Britain's needs. On the day the bill passed, a dozen oil tankers and refrigerator ships were scheduled to sail for England. In peacetime such a fleet could, by way of round-trip relays, fuel and feed a moderate-size city, indefinitely. Yet, at the rate U-boats were sending British hulls to the bottom in early 1941, Britain would have to spend much of its Lend-Lease windfall on new ships, with little left over to fill their holds.[165]

Churchill put a good face on the matter, as he had with the fifty old destroyers. To the House of Commons, he declared that by taking this action, "the Government and people of the United States have in fact written a new Magna Carta, which not only has regards to the rights and laws upon which a healthy and advancing civilization can alone be erected but also proclaims...the duty of free men and free nations, wherever they may be, to share the burden and responsibility of enforcing them." Later in the year, as tens of thousands of tons of American matériel sailed to Britain, he told the audience at the annual Lord Mayor's Day luncheon, "Never again let us hear the taunt that money is the ruling thought or power in the hearts of the American democracy. The Lend and Lease Bill must be regarded without question as the most unsordid act in the whole of recorded history." Lend-Lease was a start, but enough of a start for Churchill to conclude that Britain no longer would fight with its back to the Atlantic but henceforth with America at its back. That alone would not ensure a British victory, but it would make British defeat almost impossible—almost but not absolutely, because American industrial capacity had yet to reach a level that could guarantee British survival. Harry Hopkins told Churchill he believed America would reach its stride in eighteen months. Churchill estimated America needed at least two years to attain full war production. Hitler's best estimate, which he imparted to the Japanese foreign minister, was four years.[166]

Two years would prove a year too many if Britain's shipping losses continued at February's pace, when almost 320,000 tons went down. March was shaping up as the worst month yet. Losses in the first week approached 150,000 tons, more than twice the average for any *three* weeks of the war, and were easily on a pace to exceed 400,000 tons for the month. Britain's importing capacity—the gross tonnage of material it could handle with its fleet, its docks, and warehouses—had fallen from almost 43 million tons in 1939 to under 29 million, a level not seen since 1917. The Atlantic Ocean, Churchill had predicted early in the year, would be the major battleground of 1941. He anointed the ordeal the Battle of the Atlantic with the same intent as when the previous summer he anointed the pending battle the Battle of Britain, to focus the attention of the government and the people upon the most immediate threat to their existence. But whereas in 1940, the RAF could put into the skies enough Spitfires and Hurricanes to fight the Luftwaffe to a stalemate, the Royal Navy in March of 1941 had not the ships, nor the weapons, nor the advanced radar needed to stop Dönitz's U-boats. As well, the Focke-Wulf 200 bombers that Raeder had snatched from Göring had taken their toll, until Göring returned from his vacation and demanded their return. British shipping losses due to German aircraft began to fall, and continued to do so throughout the spring and summer. By recalling his bombers, Göring had committed a strategic blunder. Still, by March the German navy and the Luftwaffe had just about severed the sea-lanes into Britain.[167]

The continuing success of the Germans against British shipping and the prospect of greater losses to come was, Churchill wrote in his memoirs, "the only thing that really frightened me during the war." U-boats and German bombers had so far sent 15 percent of Britain's prewar merchant fleet of eighteen million tons to the bottom. One million tons had gone down since the American election. Norway had added a thousand ships and almost three million tons to the Allied merchant marine, but Norwegian ships were being hit as hard as British. Were half of the remaining British shipping to go to the bottom, Britain would starve. National survival depended upon convoys bearing wheat getting through. A halving in wheat imports could, in a few months time, result in a Malthusian halving of the British population. It was just that simple. Churchill pleaded with Roosevelt throughout the first seven months of the year to move the American patrol zone into the far eastern Atlantic, to arm American merchantmen (a violation of the Neutrality Act of 1939), and to show the flag in the vicinity of the Azores (where U-boats resupplied and re-armed with impunity). In Churchill's estimation, if Lend-Lease had put America on the path to war, let the journey continue apace.[168]

Roosevelt, though ready to help, was not ready to fight. Restrained by conflicting and strongly held public opinion, he made his way along his chosen path with the same tortured gait he displayed while thrusting himself through the rejuvenating waters of Warm Springs, in the central Georgia foothills of the Appalachians. There, he took his measured and painful steps, with the utmost care, lest his footing be unsure. Heroic as his progress was—in the medicinal springs of Georgia and in the politics of war—Roosevelt's progress when it came to Hitler was not swift enough for Churchill.

With Lend-Lease on the books, Roosevelt dispatched Averell Harriman as his special envoy to London with the extraordinary mandate, to "recommend everything we can do, short of war, to keep the British Isles afloat." Harriman reported directly to Hopkins and the president, a ploy that kept Secretary of State Cordell Hull (to Hull's increasing annoyance) on the sidelines. Harriman also consulted directly with Churchill, thus bypassing the Foreign Office. Lend-Lease was not strictly speaking a matter of foreign affairs but rather one of American national security and, for Britain, national survival. Roosevelt's choice of Harriman was brilliant.

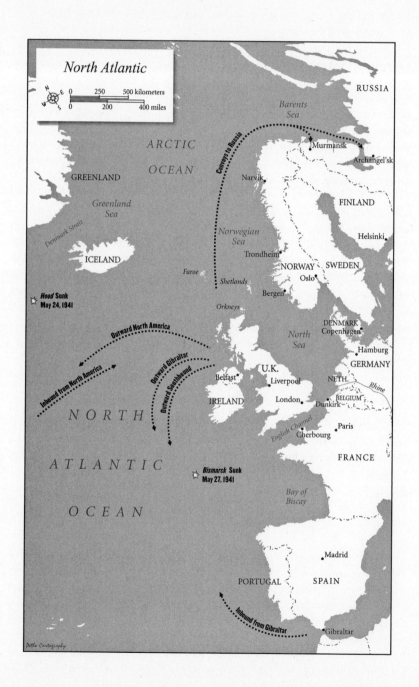

He represented America's capitalist class rather than the Democratic Party's ideological class. He was a product of Groton (the motto of which is *cui severe est regnare,* "to serve is to rule") and Yale. His politics was business. The captains of industry Roosevelt needed on his side listened to Harriman. Almost fifty, he had never lacked that which Churchill always had lacked: money, and not simply money, but *capital.* He dressed the part. If Anthony Eden was the most impeccably attired Englishman in the land, Harriman took the honors for visitors, always smartly attired in trim, custom-made dark suits that accentuated his sharp WASP features. Pamela Churchill was certainly taken with him, and within a few weeks, taken by him.[169]

Young Averell had expanded the railroad holdings of his father, E. H. Harriman, and moved into banking, oil field equipment, and shipbuilding. He was board chairman of the Union Pacific Railroad and of his banking firm, W. A. Harriman & Company, which after a merger became Brown Brothers Harriman. His fellow Yale alumnus, Prescott Bush, son-in-law of W. A. Harriman's president, George Herbert Walker, had recently been made a junior partner. Together, Harriman and Bush sustained a modest loss that year when the U.S. government seized the German accounts maintained by Brown Brothers Harriman. Yet those losses, as well as the Depression itself, were but potholes on Easy Street for Harriman. He had two daughters by his first marriage; one, Kathleen, became fast friends with Pamela Churchill, and they soon shared a London flat, Randolph having been posted to Cairo. Harriman's first marriage had ended in divorce. He was now married to Marie Norton Whitney, the former wife of Cornelius ("Sonny") Vanderbilt Whitney, the son of Gertrude Vanderbilt Whitney, she of the Whitney Museum. Harriman's credentials therefore were as solid as those of Churchill's late cousin, John "Sunny" Spencer Churchill, the ninth Duke of Marlborough, himself the former husband of Consuelo Vanderbilt, who dwelled now mostly in Palm Beach, the Nazis having confiscated her French manse. Sunny's son, "Bert," made do at Blenheim, where the roof leaked and a distinct mustiness permeated the old palace. Harriman and Churchill were connected therefore by marriage, however distantly, like members of one big happy Anglo-American family, but for the distinction that one side was well off and living in peace, while the other was nigh broke and being bombed into oblivion.[170]

Harriman set to work with Beaverbrook to ensure that Churchill received the goods he needed. Since the Beaver spent most weekends with Churchill, Harriman, too, became a regular weekend guest at Ditchley and Chequers, the better to sort things out with Beaverbrook, as well as with Hopkins back in Washington. Harriman and Hopkins had been good friends for almost eight years, having met on a train while both were on their way to Washington during the early days of the New Deal. It was an unlikely relationship—the impeccably dressed tycoon and the scruffy liberal social worker—and for Churchill a fortuitous one.[171]

Churchill sold Harriman, as he had sold Hopkins, on the inevitability of invasion. On Harriman's second visit to Chequers, Churchill offered him a somber assessment. The times called for a "holding action," he said, not "bold new strokes." For his part, Harriman told Churchill that the boldest and most necessary stroke would take the form of a U.S. declaration of war, which he fully supported. That was exactly what Churchill wanted to hear.[172]

Rather than bold strokes, Churchill told Harriman, only two strategic imperatives existed, defense of the Home Island and of the Suez Canal. Loss of one would result in the loss of the other, and of the war. (Yet Churchill was at that moment stripping troops from both the Home Island and Egypt in order to make a very bold stroke in the Balkans.) He played the invasion card not only with his American guests but also continually with Britons, if for no other reason than to impress upon Americans that Britons were not complacent. With both Harriman and renewed Luftwaffe bombing arriving in London at the same time, Churchill set to work imparting to Harriman a concise understanding of Britain's predicament. Peaceful and empty beaches belied the invasion threat, so Churchill found other means of inducing fear of the Hun in Harriman. To that end, he allowed Harriman the great privilege of sitting in on secret Battle of the Atlantic War Cabinet meetings, where the news was all bad all the time. And to give Harriman a taste of fire, Churchill, at the howling of the sirens, escorted him to the roof of the Air Ministry, where after witnessing the horrors, Harriman concluded that Hitler might yet starve or burn Britain into submission. This he soon reported to his boss, as Churchill presumed he would.[173]

To Harriman, as he had to Hopkins, Willkie, and Winant, Churchill expressed his strong desire to meet Roosevelt in person. From Roosevelt, as winter turned to spring, there came no reply.

Early in March, Churchill's team in the Balkans, led by Eden, concluded that they had a good fighting chance in Greece, but only if everything fell perfectly into place by way of getting the troops into position. Four months earlier Eden had thought any such adventure in Greece to be "strategic folly." Now he was putting the best face on it, cabling the War Cabinet from Athens that despite the risks, the operation should go forth. Indeed,

Eden reported that General Papagos and the Greeks now appeared stalwart. To fight and perchance to lose, Eden concluded, was preferable to not fighting at all. Eden, Wavell, and Dill were in agreement that if the British arrived in Greece and got into position before the Germans came, "there was a good chance of holding them." They also concluded, "If the Germans arrived first, it should be possible to withdraw the majority of our forces without great loss." But Dill considered the Greek situation "grimmer than we had thought." He did not express those doubts with absolute precision to Churchill. In any case, the War Cabinet approved the Greek operation on March 7. The cabinet minutes noted Churchill's view "that we should go forward with a good heart." Wavell's troops, who were doing the actual going forward, were taking on more and more of a symbolic role, the embodiment of Churchill's lofty decision to do the right and proper thing. Generals such as Wavell are loath to send men into battle to die for political symbolism. Yet Wavell, like Dill, had not made his concerns clear to Churchill. Thus the War Cabinet made its "bleak decision" (as characterized by Eden) to fight in Greece. Then, with the decision made, Eden, in Athens, related to Churchill that General Papagos, who just a week earlier had seemed stalwart, was now "discouraged." Colville, to his diary, expressed his fear that "our troops will find themselves in a dangerous plight." Churchill was now growing wary of the whole business and felt, Colville wrote, that "it was thrust upon us," partly in order to preserve British prestige in the eyes of the Americans, and partly because Eden, Dill, Wavell, and Cunningham—even after warning of the dangers of stretching resources— "recommended it so strongly." In fact, Eden and company, worn down by Churchill, were only delivering the Balkan front that Churchill had insisted upon for months.[174]

Churchill informed Roosevelt of the decision on March 10:

> Although it is no doubt tempting to try to push on from Benghazi to Tripoli...we have felt it our duty to stand with the Greeks, who have declared to us their resolve, even alone, to resist the German invader. Our Generals Wavell and Dill, who accompanied Mr. Eden to Cairo, after heart searching discussions with us, believe we have a good fighting chance.[175]

Any hope for success in Greece rested in large part not with Wavell or Papagos but with Yugoslavia (and, as Eden had pointed out, with whose ever army arrived in Greece first). To Roosevelt, Churchill declared: "No country ever had such a military chance. If they [the Yugoslavs] fall on the Italian rear in Albania, there is no measure of what might happen in a few weeks." Here he was again with his hypothetical reasoning—*If this, then that, then maybe this.* In fact, the Yugoslavs had no real "military chance" because they lacked the military muscle to take advantage of any so-called opportunity that might present itself. The Yugoslav army stood at more than a million men, but it was a late nineteenth-century army. Its entire armored strength consisted of fewer than one hundred World War One–era tanks. Its air force was minuscule. The Yugoslavs in no way thought that several German armored divisions poised on their borders constituted an opportunity. Churchill knew this, and soon enough so did Roosevelt, after Colonel Bill Donovan, who on the spot and surveying the war situation for the president, reported to Roosevelt that although he, Donovan, respected the fighting spirit of the Yugoslavs, they could no more stop Hitler than had any other small European nation. A fuller and more accurate accounting by Churchill would have informed Roosevelt of Admiral Cunningham's fear that without air cover, his fleet sailed naked in Greek waters, and of Longmore's fear of spreading dangerously thin his meager airpower, and of Jumbo Wilson's fear of spreading his lines too thin. A full accounting would have informed Roosevelt of Wavell's distress at the peeling away from Libya of 60,000 of his best desert troops.[176]

The North African situation was thus: at the very moment Erwin Rommel was about to launch his panzers east toward Egypt, Churchill began moving his best and most battle-hardened troops from Libya to Greece, replacing them with green reinforcements.

March had commenced with the Bulgarians sounding their sour note and Churchill declaring that the Battle of the Atlantic, if not soon won, would spell disaster. After the passage of Lend-Lease, the remainder of the month brought forth a steady stream of encouraging news, and went out with a hurrah of military and political good fortune.

In East Africa, British and colonial armies continued to push through Abyssinia toward the port of Massawa on the Red Sea, where several Italian warships and thirty-five cargo ships rode at anchor. Churchill cabled Eden in Cairo that were the Italians to scuttle the ships, "we shall consider ourselves relieved of feeding the Italian population of Eritrea and Abyssinia." Harold Nicolson had been quite correct when he opined that all of this East African business and much of the Libyan success had been a lot of chicken feed. Yet the African adventures—Sir John Keegan calls them "flights of his [Churchill's] strategic imagination"—boosted morale at home and fed Churchill's resolve to fight the war to a successful conclusion.[177]

The real threats lay in the eastern Mediterranean—in Greece, Crete, and Syria, should the Germans advance along those lines—and in the Western Desert, with Erwin Rommel. As March rolled into its final week, those fronts remained quiet but for a probe by Rommel. Then, good fortune came Churchill's way on March 25, when an Italian battle fleet sailed from the heel of Italy to attack British troop transports bound for Greece. Mussolini, pressed by the Germans to intercept and sink British transports, had taken up the challenge.

The Royal Navy knew of the operation in advance; British code breakers had solved the Italian cipher the previous summer. Admiral Cunningham, from his headquarters in Alexandria, ordered four cruisers and nine destroyers to lie in wait for the Italian fleet. Cunningham himself sailed from Alexandria on March 27 with his main battle squadron and the carrier *Formidable*. The two fleets met off Cape Matapan, the southernmost point of mainland Greece, late on the twenty-eighth. The Italian commander, Admiral Angelo Iachino, on board the battleship *Vittorio Veneto*, had divided his force into three squadrons, one of which, Iachino's, the British found and harassed, damaging the *Vittorio Veneto* and stopping the cruiser *Pola* dead in the water. Admiral Iachino, presuming Cunningham's main force was still in Alexandria, sent two cruisers and two destroyers to the aid of *Pola*. The British saw them coming on radar screens, a technology the Italians fatally lacked. A British searchlight stabbed across the water; gunners found their range, and in minutes the entire Italian squadron was sent to the bottom, along with more than 2,400 sailors and officers. The Italians had been caught so completely unawares that their guns were trained in the wrong direction. Churchill, elated by the news, told Colville that with "the tearing up of the Italian paper fleet" the British could now ferry their troops unmolested to Greece.[178]

The final grand news of the month came out of Yugoslavia. With Bulgaria in Hitler's fold and Turkey resolved to stay out of the war, Yugoslavia was Churchill's last best hope for creating his Balkan front. Colville wrote that week: "The diplomatic battle for the soul of Yugoslavia is reaching its height and sways either way with vertiginous speed." Churchill knew that if diplomacy did not deliver Yugoslavia to Hitler, Hitler would use other means. Yugoslavia's regent, Prince Paul, understood the precariousness of his position. Paul, Churchill had told Colville weeks earlier, was like a man in a cage with a tiger, "hoping not to provoke him while steadily dinner time approaches." Prince Paul had tried to stall for time. But time had run out. Harangued by Hitler at a meeting early in the month, and knowing his position was untenable, Paul (whom Churchill derided as "Prince Palsy") overrode his own sentiments and those of his countrymen. He sent his ministers by secret night train to Vienna, where they signed the Tripartite Pact on the twenty-fifth. Cadogan had predicted the outcome days earlier, when he told his diary, "Yugoslavs seem to have sold their souls to the Devil. *All* these Balkan peoples are trash. Poor dears." Learning that they had finally thrown in with Hitler, he scribbled, "Jugs are signing...silly, feeble, mugs." Within hours of the agreement's being signed, Churchill cabled the British ambassador in Belgrade, Ronald Campbell, and urged him to take whatever action he could to ensure that the pro-British factions in the Yugoslav government knew that London was behind them. "Continue to pester, nag, and bite," Churchill told Campbell, but if the present government "have gone beyond recall," then "we may have to resort" to other measures. He meant a coup d'état.[179]

When the signing of the pact was announced in Belgrade, the city exploded into revolt, a rebellion nurtured into being by the resident RAF attaché, who inspired the Yugoslav air forces to action, having prepared the ground with cash and influence peddled by the SOE. "Good news," Cadogan wrote, "of *coup d'état* in Belgrade." Peter, the seventeen-year-old prince, was declared king and put upon his father's throne. Prince Paul fled to Athens. "A great day," Colville wrote on the twenty-seventh. "Revolution in Belgrade, which puts an entirely different complexion on events in the Balkans and turns darkness into dawn. The P.M. is overjoyed." So much so that he cabled Hopkins with all the good news coming out of East Africa and Belgrade: "Yesterday was a grand day."[180]

It was a false dawn. When the reports from Yugoslavia were confirmed, Churchill concluded, "We must expect bad news." He was correct. Hitler would not abide a double-cross and a revolt within the same week. Churchill's practitioners of ungentlemanly warfare in the SOE had produced the coup; but it would be Hitler who set Yugoslavia ablaze. He greeted the news with fury. The time for pseudodiplomacy had passed. He told his generals his decision, dispensing with his usual verbosity: "I have decided to destroy Yugoslavia."[181]

On March 24, Rommel, fully eight weeks or more before he (and Churchill) expected his desert force to reach full strength, probed tentatively toward the British lines at El Agheila, four hundred miles west of Bardia and five hundred miles east of Tripoli, near the border between Cyrenaica and Tripolitania. Churchill had taken at face value Wavell's prediction sent to London three weeks earlier that "no large scale attack was likely to develop [against Wavell] *before the end of the summer*" (italics added). Wavell had misread his opponent. And Rommel had misread his. He presumed he would find the British at El Agheila in great strength, and preparing to continue their westward attack. Instead, he found them ill prepared to receive even a reconnaissance in force. Rommel was not one to let such an opportunity pass without making mayhem. O'Connor may have weeks earlier telegraphed to the world that he'd "killed the fox in the open," but a new fox had crept right up to the coop, and found the door wide open. Rommel stepped right in. He did so against the expressed orders of his commanders in Berlin, and against the wishes of General Garibaldi, under whom Rommel nominally served. Just the previous week, Berlin had ordered Rommel to avoid any general offensive actions until the early May arrival of his 15th Panzer Division. Churchill, too, had concluded that Rommel's diminutive African army would not grow strong enough to pose any threat until mid-May. Therefore, upon learning of Rommel's probe, Churchill cabled Wavell: "I presume you are only waiting for the tortoise to stick his head out far enough before chopping it off." It was the same message he had sent to French commander in chief Georges in May 1940, when the long thrusts by German panzers appeared to have exposed their flanks.[182]

Rommel probed for six days, but on the thirtieth, he launched a two-pronged blitzkrieg attack toward Benghazi, eighty miles up the coast, and overland toward Derna. Churchill had failed to take into account the character of his enemy. General Philip Neame, commanding the Western Army, had failed to study both his enemy and the terrain. Not until the week before Rommel made his move, and too late, did Neame inform Wavell that the escarpment south of Benghazi failed to protect his flank. He had believed the escarpment could be penetrated only at a certain few choke points; in fact it was porous. Had Neame flown over the terrain, he would have seen this.[183]

In East Africa the news was better; by March 30 the British occupied the whole of Eritrea. The war there was about over, in large part due to Wingate's stunning campaign, which earned him no promotion. He was a little too irregular for the old school generals in Cairo and London. As well, he soon had a breakdown and tried to kill himself by slitting his throat. His reward for his role in conquering Ethiopia was virtual banishment, to Burma. But in less than a year, his nonconformist qualities would serve Churchill well in battling a new enemy far more dangerous than the Italians.[184]

Rommel's mischief aside, the run of good fortune—the victories over Aosta in Ethiopia, the battering of the Italian fleet, and the Yugoslavs' "recapture of their soul"—made for "a wonderful weekend," Colville told his diary, "the culmination of a week of victories." They were at Chequers, where Churchill, attired in his dressing gown, "spent much of the weekend pacing—or rather tripping—up and down the Great Hall to the sound of the gramophones (playing martial airs, waltzes and the most vulgar kind of brass-band songs), deep in thought all the while."[185]

He wandered the halls, deep in thought, because Ultra had revealed on March 26 that following the Yugoslav pact with Hitler (hours before the Yugoslav coup), several divisions of German troops and mechanized infantry had been ordered from the Yugoslav border to southern Poland. Most significantly, so had three out of the five panzer divisions bivouacked in Romania. Thus, when Ultra revealed the orders to move out were canceled following the Belgrade revolt, the import of the reversal in German movements became clear. Russia had been Hitler's next target, until the insolent Yugoslavs defied him. A Joint Intelligence Committee report also included the fact that the Germans had lengthened and reinforced runways at several Polish airfields, and they were not doing so, Cadogan concluded, "for the benefit of Lufthansa."[186]

On March 30, Churchill cabled Eden, in Athens with Dill, that as a result of the Yugoslav coup and "sure information recently received" (the Enigma decrypts), it looked as if "Bear will be kept waiting a bit." The orders and counter orders that Ultra revealed made clear to Churchill Germany's "magnitude of design" directed both southeast toward the Balkans and, eventually, east to Russia: "My reading is that the bad man concentrated very large armoured forces...to overawe Yugoslavia....The moment he was sure Yugoslavia was in the Axis he moved three of the five panthers towards the Bear believing what was left would be enough to finish the Greek affair." He noted that "it looks as if heavy [German] forces will be used in the Balkan Peninsula." On the same day, he cabled William Fadden, acting Prime Minister of Australia (Prime Minister Robert Menzies was in London at the time): "German plans have been upset [by the Belgrade coup] and we may cherish renewed hopes of forming a Balkan front with Turkey....Result unknowable, but prize has increased and risks have somewhat lessened." Turkey, in fact, had nothing to gain by coming in on Britain's side, and did not. Actually, were an enraged Hitler to fling his forces into the Balkans, the foremost risk to Britain—a broad front that would overstretch the already thin lines of the Greek and British forces—would become a reality.[187]

Although Colville did not understand the reason at the time, Churchill's belief that the Bear was soon to be baited was why the Old Man had given "a short lecture on the various invaders of Russia, especially Charles XII." Charles XII, king of Sweden, had in 1700 crushed the Russian army in a battle on the banks of the Narva River. Rather than press his advantage against Czar Peter's beaten army, Charles turned toward Poland, a strategic blunder that devoured four years and much of his army, and allowed Peter to reform his incompetent and corrupt military and regroup his forces. When, late in the decade, Charles again tried his hand in Russia, Peter was ready, and in 1709, earned his moniker "The Great" by smashing Charles's army. Colville leaves unrecorded whether in telling the story

Churchill meant to compare the unprepared Stalin, his army purged of its best officers, to the unprepared early Peter, or the later Charles, impetuous and overconfident, to Hitler.[188]

As horrific had been the fighting on the Western Front in May and June 1940, a clash between Germany and Russia would result in a titanic struggle unlike any the world had ever known. On April 3, Churchill took a calculated risk and sent a personal message to Stalin (as he had the previous summer), through the British ambassador to the Soviets, Sir Stafford Cripps. Churchill made no reference to his highly secret source, but with his usual aversion to obliquity, made his point with clarity and honesty:

> I have sure information from a trusted agent that when the Germans thought they had got Yugoslavia in the net, that is to say, after March 20, they began to move three out of the five Panzer Divisions from Romania to Southern Poland. The moment they heard of the Serbian revolution this movement was countermanded. Your Excellency will readily appreciate the significance of these facts.[189]

Cripps duly received the message. And did nothing with it. Cripps was a devout socialist, and may have been more concerned about Stalin's reaction to the message than the import of the message itself. In an address to Londoners before the war, Churchill had said of Cripps, "Then there is Sir Stafford Cripps, who is in a class by himself. He wishes the British people to be conquered by the Nazis in order to urge them into becoming Bolsheviks. It seems a long way round. And not much enlightenment when they get to the end of their journey." Churchill had sent the socialist Cripps to Moscow as a signal to Stalin that Churchill was willing to let bygones be bygones. The signal was either not received or ignored.[190]

Presuming his first message had been delivered or, given the usual time lost by encoding and decoding, was soon to be delivered, Churchill cabled Cripps again the next day. He advised Cripps on how to develop the argument in person and instructed him to stress to the Soviets that the German move back toward the Balkans could buy time for the Russians to "strengthen their own position." Again Cripps did nothing. He then made one of the most inexplicable and stupid decisions made by any diplomat during the war: he sat on the message for almost two weeks. When Churchill learned of Cripps's lapse, he made plain to Eden his incredulity: "I set special importance on the delivery of this message from me to Stalin. I cannot understand why it should be resisted. The Ambassador is not alive to the military significance of the facts. Pray oblige me." Admonished by Eden, Cripps, the recalcitrant obligee, *again* failed to deliver the message. In coming weeks, Eden warned the Soviet ambassador to the Court of St. James's,

Ivan Maisky, of the probable German attack. Despite Cripps's behavior, Stalin was warned by Maisky. By then Churchill's attention had turned back to the Balkans.[191]

When Churchill first tried to warn Stalin, the impending battle in Greece, not the possible turn of events in Russia, was the most immediate question at hand. Had the Yugoslavs not revolted, Churchill's 60,000 troops in northern Greece might have faced a far smaller German force. Then again, absent the Yugoslav coup, large German troop movement through a compliant Yugoslavia would likely have flanked the British in any event. A plethora of Ultra decrypts pointed to only one certainty during the first days of April—that British and Anzac troops arriving in Greece would soon face attack by an overwhelmingly superior force.[192]

There, Jumbo Wilson's eastern flank, the Aliakmo Line, was anchored near Salonika, on the Aegean, and stretched for almost fifty miles northwest toward Monastir. Northeast of the British line, six Greek divisions of the Greek Second Army formed the Metaxas Line, which also ran west from the Aegean, and faced north toward Bulgaria's Struma Valley, the ancient invasion route into Thrace. To the west, the Greek First Army faced the Italians on the Albanian front. The entire front snaked for more than six hundred miles from the Aegean Sea to the Ionian Sea, through high mountain passes and difficult, trackless countryside. It was the exact sort of front Frederick the Great had in mind when he pronounced, "To defend everything is to defend nothing." Worse, the British lines were not entirely dressed; British battalions still drifted into position. Eden captured the problem in an early March cable to the War Cabinet: "Militarily problem is one of time and space." By early April the troops needed more time to make ready their defense.[193]

They would not get it.

As London and the world waited for news of a German thrust into Greece, Yugoslavia, or even Turkey, Rommel's diminutive forces—short on food, gasoline, and bullets—rolled eastward against Wavell in Cyrenaica. The leagues of Libyan desert so gloriously snatched from Mussolini by O'Connor were again a battleground. But this time the Germans had taken the field. "It seems most desirable," Churchill telegraphed to Wavell on April 2, "to stop the German advance against Cyrenaica." Any "rebuff" to the Germans, he added, would have "far-reaching prestige effects." A rebuff was not a victory, but after Norway and Dunkirk, "rebuff" had about it a certain ring. Ground could be given up for the purposes of "tac-

tical manoeuvre," Churchill instructed Wavell, "but any serious withdrawal from Benghazi would appear most melancholy."[194]

On April 2, the day that Churchill sent his telegram, Rommel's tanks
overran and busted up Neame's front line. Wavell ordered a brigade from
the 7th Australian Division to deploy from Cairo to Libya in order to
stanch the bleeding. It would have made no difference whether the outgunned Tommies and Aussies faced the Germans in Greece or in Libya;
they would have fared the same in either theater. Churchill had forced
Wavell to block two invasion forces, one intent on barging into Egypt, the
other into Greece. With his armies intact and arrayed against one or the
other of the German forces, Wavell might have stood a chance. But with
his armies divided, Wavell stood little chance against either.

Even before he learned of the Australians' redeployment, Churchill saw
the implications, military as well as political, of Rommel's advance. He
cabled Eden, in Athens: "Far more important than the loss of ground [in
North Africa] is the idea that we cannot face the Germans and that their
appearance is enough to drive us back many scores of miles. This may
react most evilly throughout Balkans.... Sooner or later we shall have to
fight the Huns."[195]

They *were* fighting the Huns, in the Libyan desert, and not faring well.
Churchill, having correctly guessed that Rommel had overextended himself, tried to encourage Wavell: "I cannot feel that there is at this moment a
persistent weight behind the German attack....If this blob, which has
come forward against you, could be cut off you might have a prolonged
easement." Of course, were Rommel's forces to "succeed in wandering
onwards they will gradually destroy the effects of your victories."[196]

Rommel wandered powerfully onward. The seasoned Australian 6th
Division had been recalled to Cairo to prepare for deployment to Greece.
Its replacement in the desert—the Australian 9th Division—lacked the
experience to stop Rommel. On April 3 news reached official London that
Wavell had ordered Benghazi evacuated. It was as if a diabolical projec-
tionist were running backward the reel of O'Connor's victories: Mersa
Brega, Beda Fomm, now Benghazi, all taken by the British early in the
year, all now lost to Rommel in just days. Wavell told Churchill that in
view of the situation, withdrawal toward Derna would be necessary.

The withdrawal turned into a rout.

Short on tanks and gasoline, Rommel commanded his supply trucks to
stay close behind the few remaining panzers and to raise as much dust as
possible, to simulate a much larger force. The trick worked. Tommies and
the newly arrived Aussies of the 9th Division, thinking at least two divisions of German and Italian tanks—six hundred in all—were heading
their way, fled eastward, pell-mell toward Derna, 150 miles up the coast.

The Australians, never at a loss for gallows humor, dubbed the race to safety the "Benghazi Handicap." To his wife Rommel wrote that "the British are falling over themselves to get away."[197]

British command had broken down; troops lacked orders, whether to stand and fight or retreat. They ran, covered in yellow dust, their shirts soaked with sweat and stiff as sandpaper. Their faces took on a sickly yellow cast. By the platoon, by the battalion, by the regiment, they fled. Neame tried to restore order. He could not. Wavell flew out from Cairo and saw that Neame had lost control. O'Connor was summoned, too late to turn things around. Derna fell on the night of the sixth. The main British units beat such a hasty exit from the city that the Northumberland Fusiliers realized what was happening only when they saw the 9th Australian division roaring past them out of town. O'Connor and Neame were among the last to flee, in darkness, by car to Timimi, about one hundred miles to the east. Alas, the hero of Operation Compass got turned around somewhere in the desert and ended up rambling down a lost highway, directly toward Derna and the Germans. Within a few minutes, O'Connor and Neame found their car surrounded by men shouting in a foreign tongue. Their driver presumed it was Cypriot, for many of the British truck drivers were Cypriot. When German machine pistols were thrust into his face, O'Connor understood that the Cypriot thesis was terribly wrong. He and Neame spent the next three years as prisoners of war in Italy.[198]

London's citizens were not privy to the debacle in the desert. Nor did they know of the troop buildup in Greece. Of Wavell's prospects, Colville wrote on April 3: "The PM is greatly worried." Churchill's worry stemmed not only from Wavell's ongoing struggle against Rommel in Africa, but because he knew that the British people had been fed only rumors about the Greek deployment. "I must return to the need of telling public," Churchill cabled to Wavell, "that we have sent strong forces to Greece." The American press was running with the story, he explained, while the British press had so far honored HMG's plea for restraint. Even Colonel Donovan had spilled the beans, praising the valor of Britain for sending troops from Egypt to Greece. Such sentiments could only cause Britons to ask, *What* troops have been sent from *where*, and *to where?* It was time for Churchill to come clean with his yeomanry.[199]

He had given to Wavell, then taken, and now would give again. On April 4, Churchill cabled Wavell: "I warned the country a week ago that they must not expect continuance of unbroken successes and take the rough with the smooth." Therefore, he added, "be quite sure that we shall back you up in adversity even better than in good fortune." He was true to his word, taking the great risk of running a convoy (code-named Tiger by Churchill) of six ships carrying almost three hundred new tanks straight through the Mediterranean from Gibraltar to Alexandria, under the guns of the Luftwaffe. He called them his "tigercubs." When one of the ships, approaching Malta, hit a mine and went down, Churchill lamented to Colville, "My tiger has lost a claw." Though he harbored great hopes for his remaining cubs, they would not arrive in Alexandria until early May, at which time it was learned that because their gearboxes tended to jam and they lacked the proper filters to keep the desert sand from mucking up the works, the tanks could not be readied for action until late May at the earliest. Until then, Wavell would have to make do with what he had, which, with Rommel stripping away more each hour, was not enough.[200]

With Derna lost, Churchill concluded that Tobruk, one hundred miles to the east, held the key. From that city the British could swing out to meet Rommel's advanced guard and then swing back north and west to pin the overextended Germans between the escarpment and the sea. "Bravo Tobruk!" Churchill cabled Wavell. "We feel it vital that Tobruk be regarded as sally-port, and not, please, as an 'excrescence.'" The plan looked good on paper. Churchill encouraged Wavell: "Tobruk is your best offensive hook.... All our best information shows they are frightfully short of everything. It would be a fine thing to cop the lot."[201]

Rommel, intending to cop Tobruk at his leisure, drove right past the city. By April 10, he had rolled up almost three hundred miles of British turf as if it were a throw rug.

Ten days earlier, on March 31, Churchill had told Colville that he was quite sure Germany would attack Yugoslavia before either Greece or Turkey. He was partially correct. On April 6 Hitler attacked *both* Yugoslavia and Greece.[202]

Belgrade was hit first, as punishment for its insolence. German bombers flying in relays from Romanian airfields cruised overhead all day on the sixth, unopposed but for ineffectual AA. They came on for the next two days, hundreds of bombers unleashing thousands of pounds of bombs, enough to bury more than 17,000 of the city's residents under the rubble. CBS newsman Cecil Brown reported from the scene: "Belgrade one-quarter destroyed and thousands dead in a few hours...refugees streaming from Belgrade far across the fields for as far as the eye can see." The terrorized animals at the Belgrade zoo escaped. A great bear, dazed and uncomprehending, shuffled past burning buildings, through the smoke, and down to the banks of the Danube. With Stalin in mind, Churchill later wrote, "The bear...was not the only bear who did not understand."[203]

On its march from the Hungarian border to Belgrade, the Wehrmacht lost just 151 men killed to the Yugoslav's untold thousands killed, wounded, missing, or captured. CBS's Brown, arrested briefly by the Germans as a spy, saw firsthand "young murderers bent on wiping out the Serbian people." The Nazis shot down Serbs "the way you would not shoot a dog, not even a mad dog." The Yugoslavs fought on; they sent ammunition to the front on carts drawn by steers "moving at four miles an hour against twenty-two-ton Nazi tanks speeding into battle at forty miles an hour." Brown watched in horror and in awe as the Serbians committed national "suicide by defying Hitler and the New Order." It was not a battle, but a massacre.[204]

Once the Germans crushed Yugoslavia and poured through the Vardar Valley, the British, Anzac, and Greek forces arrayed to the south were doomed. Had the Germans attacked only by way of Bulgaria, the Greek and British lines would have been perfectly arrayed. But as the German attack came from both Bulgaria and Yugoslavia, the Allies found themselves cut off, east from west. For eighteen days, outflanked and outnumbered by more than four to one, the British fought a valiant and well-executed rearguard action, covering almost 250 miles from Salonika to Olympus, then to Larissa, to Thermopylae, and on to Thebes and Athens. All the while, German infantry, German tanks, and German planes ripped at their flanks.[205]

The rearguard action at Thermopylae, fought mostly by the Anzacs, was as heroic and futile a feat as the battle fought there in 480 BCE, when King Leonidas and his bodyguard of three hundred Spartans checked ten thousand Persians. The terrain had changed over the centuries, to the detriment of the British defenders. The pass in ancient times was only about a dozen yards wide, a strip of high ground between the mountains and the sea. The Spercheios River delta had since widened the pass by more than a mile in places. The Germans, as had the Persians, approached from the north. The British and Anzacs, as had the Spartans, dug in at the pass and on the slope of the hillside, which by virtue of its soil content and the oblique angle of the sun's first light, glows bloodred at sunrise. The modern coast road to Athens approaches the pass but turns inland and cuts through a small valley before climbing above and skirting the ancient pass. The Germans came on, the rumble of the three armored divisions audible for miles, the seismic pounding of their approach enough to disturb the water in a canteen, or a man's guts. To bring fire down on the modern road necessitated placing artillery and machine guns all the way up the slope above the ancient pass. This the Anzacs did and, once dug in, for a short while checked the Germans. But the British left flank hung in the air. Wavell asked the Greeks if they could cover the naked flank.[206]

They could not. So rapid was the German advance that by the time Churchill fumed to Wavell that Jumbo Wilson was tardy in getting news out of Greece, the battle was over. On April 20, Churchill cabled Eden in Cairo to ask if Thermopylae might be held for three weeks in order to delay the Germans and allow the "Libyan situation to be stabilized." Such a delay, Churchill wrote, would allow reinforcements to be sent from Egypt to Greece. He asked Ismay for a map of the Thermopylae Line.[207]

He needn't have bothered. Thermopylae fell, not in three weeks, but in three days.

George II, king of the Hellenes, offered that it was now Wavell's "duty to take immediate steps for the re-embarkation of such portion of his army as he could." Wavell and Wilson agreed. So, too, on April 21 did Churchill and the War Cabinet. Churchill wanted it "made clear to the Commanders-in-Chief that the main thing was to get the men away, and we should not worry about saving vehicles." The Anzacs, Churchill told the War Cabinet, "had fought with distinction a rear-guard battle against heavy odds in the most depressing form of action for soldiers." They have "added one more glorious page" to their history. They may have fought a glorious rearguard action, but it was for naught. The Spartans had at least delayed the Persians long enough for the Athenian fleet to ready a trap at Salamis, where it defeated the invaders, who fled for home. This time, the defenders fled. As the Tommies boarded their transports, Greek civilians showered them with flowers, as they had when the Tommies arrived. Then the ships set sail with their cargoes of defeated warriors.[208]

Hitler celebrated his fifty-second birthday on April 20, ensconced in his special train *Amerika,* which had pulled onto a siding just outside a tunnel near Mönichkerchin in the Austrian Alps, lest any unfriendly airplanes appear. None did. The skies remained clear and the Führer enjoyed his latest success amid the splendor of an alpine spring and the accolades of a swarm of OKW big shots, parked in their train at the other end of the tunnel. Hitler, in a gesture both curious and rare for him, ordered that when the Greek army surrendered—as it must, as all his foes must—all prisoners were to be freed. This was his way of paying tribute to the inheritors of the hoplite tradition, brave warriors who happened to meet in battle modern Teutonic warriors more brave and more numerous. Hitler had not sought the battle. He believed Greece was a conflict forced upon him by the mad dog Churchill who had had the bullheaded temerity to send his meager armies to interfere with the Führer's plans for the Balkans.[209]

With the British and Greek forces flushed from the eastern flank, General Thrasyvoulos Tsakalotos, commander of the Greek First Army, saw the hopelessness of his position in the western part of the country. Tsakalotos, in parley with the commander of the SS division at his front, requested that he be allowed to surrender to the Germans, and only the Germans, for even though Tsakalotos knew his war was over, he was determined not to surrender to Mussolini's forces who, he felt, had earned nothing. Mussolini, seeing that he was about to be denied a role in the armistice, dispatched an envoy to Berlin, where Hitler once again sated the needs of his inept ally. While Il Duce waited for the Führer's reply, he kept up the attack against Tsakalotos, who inflicted six thousand *more* casualties on the Italians, this while the war in Greece (or at least the German-Greek-British part of it) had concluded days before. But in the end, Il Duce slipped in on German coattails, and the British skulked out, fleeing by ship to Crete, their baggage once again left behind.[210]

Greece surrendered on April 27. The swastika flag flew that night above the Acropolis. In just three weeks Hitler had destroyed the Yugoslavs, the Greeks, and the British Expeditionary Force. Churchill had divided and re-allocated to Greece his Middle East resources, knowing full well—as he had told Hopkins in January—that Greece was likely lost. Historians have since sniped at him for the military folly of his Greek foray. Yet that is a narrow assessment. It was actually a political decision backed up (insufficiently) by military means. Britain had honored its commitments to Greece, as it had not to Czechoslovakia. In doing so Churchill displayed his bullheaded propensity for doing the right thing with the best of intentions but often in the most wrong of places and at the most wrong of times. He possessed—the Achilles in him—a keen intelligence that was sometimes overridden by improbable notions born of passion disguised as contemplation. Greece was a fitting place for Churchill to have failed so tragically.[211]

Rommel, by roaring right past Tobruk and the Australians holed up within, had cut off Tobruk without a fight, as if it were a lone island fortress upon the sea that, when bypassed, became by virtue of its isolation irrelevant. Thus ended Churchill's plan to hook out of Tobruk in order to bring Rommel to bay. In Tobruk the men of two Australian divisions, the 9th and the 7th, surrounded but for sporadic relief delivered by sea, peered from the trenches from which they had so boisterously driven the Italians just three months earlier. And there—joined by a ragtag mix of Indians, both Muslims and Hindus, free Poles, and British regulars, more than 22,000 in all—they would remain, under siege for almost eight months. Lord Haw-Haw anointed the besieged men "The Rats of Tobruk." Trenches and barbed wire and minefields ran for thirty miles around the city. As in the Great War, any man who showed himself by day would not likely live to nightfall. Remembrances of Gallipoli began to resurface half a world away, in Canberra. Australia had sent its three best divisions for deployment to the Middle East, where it now appeared they would be sacrificed to Churchill's desert strategy. Churchill had cited in his February address the "love for us which has flowed from the Dominions." With their best troops holed up in the desert, and the threat of Japanese hostilities on the horizon, Australians had about run out of love for King and Empire and Churchill. Australia wanted its men home.[212]

One piece of good news emerged from the desert in late April. Rommel appeared to have finally lunged a dune too far. Having pushed almost three hundred miles east from Benghazi, Rommel and his Italian helpmates, as Churchill had predicted, found themselves too far removed from their supply depots. Rommel needed Tobruk and its port in order to resupply and keep up the push to Egypt. He had scarcely any reserves left, except of sheer will and determination. Wavell was coming up short in both will and determination; he was tired, and Churchill knew it. Wavell's forces—especially his tanks—were in worse shape than Rommel's. By sending an army to Greece, the British had, in effect, reinforced Rommel, and had paid the price. Churchill had accepted the risks in Greece and North Africa not only because of the pledges made to Greece and because Alexandria, Cairo, and the Suez were Rommel's ultimate objectives, but because British military prowess was under worldwide scrutiny. Churchill had American public opinion in mind when he told Eden that the fight in the desert must go on, if for no other reason than to debunk the notion "that we cannot face the Germans and that their appearance is enough to drive us back many scores of miles." Actually, their appearance in the desert had been enough to drive the British back many *hundreds* of miles. The battle for Cyrenaica was over, again. And Greece was lost.[213]

In America that week, Charles Lindbergh told audiences in St. Louis, New York, and Chicago that American weapons were killing innocent Europeans, that no amount of arms would gain England parity with Germany, that the British had lost not only Greece but any claim of righteousness, and their prestige, and the war.[214]

In late April, Stafford Cripps finally passed along Churchill's warning of the German troop movements to the Soviet foreign minister Molotov, who passed it along to Stalin. Stalin's response was identical to his response to Churchill's friendly overtures of a year earlier: he never replied. Churchill was furious, more with Cripps than with Stalin. Yet Churchill kept Cripps on as ambassador, for during Churchill's Wilderness Years, Cripps had supported Churchill on the Hitler menace and the need to re-arm.

By late April, Yugoslavia and Greece had been crushed, and Hitler's roads east to the Urals stretched away open and dry through measureless fields of spring wheat greening under cobalt skies. The conquest of the Balkans had forced a postponement of Operation Barbarossa from mid-May to mid-June, a justifiable delay in the Führer's estimation given that the defiance of the Yugoslavs could not go unpunished. The punishment took some time to administer, yes, but Hitler presumed he had all the time he needed to deal with Russia. Yet, wrote William L. Shirer, the Führer's decision to "vent his personal spite against a small country that had dared to defy him was probably the single most catastrophic decision of Hitler's career." This was so because, unless Hitler crushed the Russians by late October, Russia's most fearsome ally would appear on the battlefield: winter.[215]

Yet Hitler had not made his decision in a vacuum; he had been provoked by the British-sponsored coup in Belgrade and by the British troops assembling in Greece. It is worth noting that Royal Navy sea power underlay Britain's ability to put an army into Greece, albeit an ally. Sea power had brought the men across the Mediterranean, and sea power took them back again. When Churchill had declared almost a year earlier that the Royal Navy could not win the war but could still lose it, he was speaking in terms of the navy's role in defeating the U-boats. He also had reflected upon the fact that if more than a quarter million men could be gotten off the beaches of Dunkirk by ships, a quarter million men could be put *on* other beaches by ships. Greece had been a crushing defeat for Churchill, but the Royal Navy had demonstrated the vital role of sea power in putting thousands of men on beaches, friendly or unfriendly. If Churchill could put an army into Greece, he could someday put a larger army into France, Italy, or French North Africa.

But in late April 1941, Churchill's foray into Greece appeared the single most catastrophic decision of his career, a greater disaster than even his 1915 Dardanelles gambit. His Balkan strategy had ended in a complete and devastating rout. The British did not need nearly as many transports to ferry their troops from Greece as had carried them there. Jumbo Wilson made his way back to Egypt; General Sir Bernard Freyberg, commander of the New Zealanders in Greece, was ordered to prepare a defense on Crete. More than 40,000 British, New Zealand, and Australian troops were taken off the beaches between April 24 and 30, but at the cost of several hospital ships lost. Stukas sank the transport *Slamat,* putting seven hundred survivors into the sea. They were picked up by two destroyers, which in turn were sunk by German dive-bombers, killing almost all the survivors.

Evacuees included Palestinian Jews, Yugoslavs, Greeks, and Cypriots. With more than two dozen ships lost, Admiral Cunningham's fleet was ill prepared to defend Hitler's next target, Crete. Greece joined Norway and Dunkirk on the list of inglorious British evacuations, the most inglorious to date, in fact, for where 90 percent of the men were gotten off the French and Norwegian beaches, almost 30 percent remained behind in Greece, killed or captured.[216]

The British press, informed by the Ministry of Information of the impending news, reacted with respectful reticence. Some in the American press tried to put things in a cheery light. According to *Time*, "although the campaign had been lost, there were indications that after details of the Battle of Greece became known, the Greek campaign might possibly go down in history as one of the most brilliant tactical operations of British Empire arms." *Time* also offered, "Although Hitler's men have not yet been stopped, this battle showed that if ever Britons confront Germans on anything like equal terms, Britain stands a good chance of winning." Not only was the British army—the entire British, colonial, and Dominion armies throughout the Empire—outnumbered by more than two to one by the Führer's armies, Hitler had yet to engage any enemy on anything like equal terms.[217]

Churchill had some explaining to do. The "bulwark" of Yugoslavia-Greece-Turkey had failed to materialize, and neutral Turkey now found itself facing two potential enemies—Germany and Russia—without the means to defend itself against either. Churchill, in his memoirs, insists that had Wavell only protested the depletions of his North African forces for deployment to Greece, the War Cabinet would have heeded his advice. He alluded to Wavell's veto power when he explained the Greek debacle to the Commons. Indeed, Wavell had cabled Churchill in mid-March that it had been "very fortunate" that Eden and Dill were in Cairo when "difficult and dangerous decisions had to be taken." Wavell added: "I am sure the decisions were the right ones, though they will bring us new hazards and anxieties." Yet Churchill's telegrams to Wavell leave no doubt that he put his Middle East commander in a box. Wavell could either accede to Churchill's wishes or protest them and face the consequences, which usually took the form of a verbal bludgeoning. A favorite Churchill tactic when faced with a field officer who questioned his military judgment was to stress political goals over strictly military, thus placing the recalcitrant commander—who was not after all a political animal—in a hopeless position. Wavell was about as strong a soldier as there was, but Churchill was the stronger politician.[218]

In the end, and too late, Wavell's predictions of new hazards proved spot on. With Greece overrun, the door was now open for Stalin to swing toward the Dardanelles, or for Hitler to do likewise, or for both to move in concert. Churchill had long been "working on the Turks" to bring them in on Britain's side, but he admitted in a cable to Cripps that the Turks "are unresponsive through fear." Indeed, the Turks were justifiably fearful that either Hitler or Stalin, or both, would soon put an end to their sovereignty. Sound military logic demanded it. After crushing Turkey, Hitler could elect to strike into Iraq, or swing through Syria to the Suez Canal, or both. Were he to sate a modicum of Stalin's appetite for greater influence in Bulgaria and Romania (traditional Russian spheres of influence), Hitler would find himself free to pursue his Mediterranean strategy with an ally on his eastern flank. It was the strategy that his naval planners had stressed was necessary in order to defeat Britain. He was poised to eviscerate the greatest empire in history, to succeed where Napoleon had failed. He prepared to take the next step, to the island he deemed vital to his plan: Crete. But the plan that Crete was vital to was Barbarossa. Crete was home to three RAF airfields, from which long-range British bombers could reach the Ploesti oil fields, in Romania. Hitler needed that oil to fuel his march to Moscow. He was going to Crete to fight the British, but first and foremost, he was going in order to secure his flank.[219]

In early April, Mollie Panter-Downes wrote in *The New Yorker:* "For the past fortnight Londoners had been listening to the unnatural silence at nights and wondering what was brewing." By mid-month they knew. The Blitz, in its third incarnation, had returned. The Luftwaffe again had England's biggest cities dead in its sights. On April 16 more than five hundred German bombers pounded London until dawn. During the raid, Colville dashed to the American embassy in Churchill's armored car to ask Winant's advice on a telegram. He found the ambassador on duty, his wife by his side. The bombs, Colville wrote, "came down like hailstones." By the next morning the city looked as devastated as had been predicted in the late thirties, when the appeasers claimed that the bombers would always get through. The Admiralty wore a new gash. St. James's Palace, where Churchill's parents had moved in 1880, was burning. Austin Thompson, the vicar of St. Peter's, Eaton Square, stepped out onto the steps of his church to call people in to shelter; a bomb erased both the vicar and his church from the cityscape. Chelsea Old Church was demolished, Jermyn Street wrecked, Mayfair badly damaged. Pall Mall, Piccadilly, and lower Regent Street were heavily damaged. Mounds of glass shards lined the edges of roads. Of the more than five hundred German bombers that had made the run, only a dozen had been shot down.[220]

Daylight and fair weather brought out the sightseers, including Pamela Churchill in the company of Averell Harriman, the two of them observed by Colville poking about the devastation in the Horse Guards Parade (in fact, they had just begun their love affair). Churchill made his way through the smoldering rubble in time to chair the 11:30 War Cabinet meeting, where he stunned Cadogan by noting that the damage to the Admiralty improved his view of Nelson's Column—which had emerged undamaged—from his place at the table. Much of the capital did not share Nelson's good fortune. By afternoon a steady, cold rain swept through the city, lending an air of desolation to the scene.[221]

The map of Europe in late April looked as if the sinister octopus of newsreel fame had spewed its black ink into almost every corner of the Continent. Switzerland, Portugal, and Sweden survived only at Hitler's pleasure; each offered him a secure diplomatic conduit to the world beyond. Switzerland also afforded safe haven for his stolen gold, Sweden a steady flow of iron ore. Spain sat in his camp philosophically, but fearing an end to his U.S. food shipments—and sure starvation for his people—the wily Franco was still not about to grant the Wehrmacht free passage to Gibraltar, although Hitler could certainly force his way through Spain were he so inclined. But for these few exceptions to Hitler's rule, the entire map of Europe had gone black. All, that is, but the obstinate Island.

On April 27, Churchill sent Eden to take responsibility in the Commons for the Greek debacle. By virtue of the power traditionally vested in him, a British foreign secretary would be expected to face the Commons after such a disastrous overseas gamble, yet Churchill made sure that the Foreign Office under Eden no longer operated with the smug independence it had enjoyed for more than a century, ever since "Pam" Palmerston made the office a virtual co-equal of the Office of Prime Minister. Churchill "had no love of the foreign office" Colville wrote, and "suspected them of pursuing their own policy" and of being "defeatist and prone toward socialism." He "mistrusted their judgment." Eden labored at Churchill's pleasure, and served with absolute loyalty. Despite that loyalty, Churchill allowed Eden to assume the role of archery target for the MPs, as if Eden actually had initiated the unfortunate course of events in the Balkans. Yet, at the end of the day, by a vote of 477–3, the Commons voiced its support for the government.[222]

Several months later, to Colville's astonishment, Churchill proclaimed that he "had instinctively had doubts" about the Greek venture from the beginning. The Greeks, Churchill told Colville, should have been advised to make the best terms they could with Hitler. He claimed blame for the fiasco lay with the War Cabinet and especially with Dill, whom, Colville noted, Churchill "has now got his knife right into." Colville, incredulous at Churchill's claims, wrote of the incident as if he doubted his own powers of recollection, such were Churchill's powers of persuasion. But on April 27, Churchill would have been hard-pressed to blame the government for the Greek tragedy, for everybody knew quite well that the prime minister *was* the government. That evening, in his first radio address since his "Give us the tools" speech of February 9, he took to the airwaves to explain as best he could this latest in the series of damnable events.[223]

The list of troubles was long and growing longer. As in every speech since the previous May, he offered reassurances to a brave people who needed but did not demand reassurance: "I thought it would be a good thing to go and see for myself...some of our great cities and seaports and which have been most heavily bombed...and to some of the places where the poorest people have had it worst." What he saw "reassured and refreshed." It was like "going out of a hothouse onto the bridge of a fighting ship...a tonic which I should recommend any who are suffering fretfulness to take in strong doses when they have need of it." The morale among the poor and the bombed, he proclaimed, was "splendid." It all added up to the "vindication of the civilized and decent way of living" and "proof of the virtues of free institutions." The cause would be "fought out...to the end. This is the grand heroic period of our history, and the light of glory shines on all." He presumed all Englishmen felt the same.

Many did. When Wendell Willkie, conducting an unscientific survey during his visit, asked a laborer if he supported the war and wanted to go through with it, the man replied, "Hitler ain't dead yet, is he?" and turned back to work. The citizens of Hull were proud of the beatings they took, and informed *The New Yorker* columnist A. J. Liebling that Coventry had nothing on them. Hull, regularly hit hard by virtue of its location on the North Sea, and being the British port nearest to Germany, was but one of Britain's major ports and cities that were taking such beatings. During the Blitz not one mayor of any British city ever asked Whitehall for special protection, not that any could have been arranged. Londoners, of course, never hesitated to tell anyone within earshot that they could take it. Yet Churchill's attachment of glory to mass slaughter rang hyperbolic to many in America, where a clear majority of voters still answered no to the question of going to war for Britain. And no lights of glory shone on the Continent. Enslaved Europeans—who now truly lived dangerously—found scant hope in his words. Yet Poles and Dutchmen, Frenchmen and Norwegians, Czechs, Belgians, Slovenes, Croats, Serbs, and now, too, the Greeks all knew that Churchill was the only European leader who remained to carry on the fight against Hitler. They all knew, as well, that he could not fight alone for much longer.[224]

Churchill had taken to the airwaves not only to thank Britons but to explain the failures in the Balkans. Lowering his voice, he moved on to Greece. He told Britons: "Great disasters have occurred in the Balkans. Yugoslavia has been beaten down.... The Greeks have been overwhelmed. The victorious Albanian army has been cut off and forced to surrender." And then to Africa, where the news was as dreadful: "Our forces in Libya have sustained a vexatious and damaging defeat. The Germans advanced sooner and in greater strength than we or our generals expected." Strictly speaking, this was true. Although Churchill had not *expected* Rommel to attack so soon, in early March Ultra had revealed that Rommel would be ready weeks earlier than the British had predicted. Wavell's hesitancy all along had little to do with the speed or strength of the Germans, either in Greece or North Africa. He assumed German advances on any front would be fast and strong; that was the German way. His overriding concern stemmed from dividing *his* forces. Yet Churchill, in his broadcast, without naming Wavell, rebuked the commander for the decision to send his tanks to Cairo for repair when future events—indeterminate when the decision was made—proved they were best left in Libya. Churchill: "The single armoured brigade which had been judged sufficient to hold the frontier till about the middle of May was worsted and its vehicles largely destroyed by a somewhat stronger German armoured force." Without quite declaring so, Churchill had just told his people that the British had been trounced yet again.[225]

Then, growling, he deflected the audience's attention from HMG's defeats onto Mussolini:

I daresay you may have read in the newspapers that by a special proc- lamation, the Italian Dictator has congratulated the Italian army in Albania on the glorious laurels they have gained by their victory over the Greeks. Here surely is the world's record in the domain of the ridiculous and the contemptible. This whipped jackal, Mussolini, who to save his own skin has made all Italy a vassal state of Hitler's Empire, comes frisking up to the side of the German tiger with yelpings not only of appetite—that can be understood—but even of triumph.[226]

And then he moved on to the guttersnipe. As for Hitler, Churchill repeated his January message to Ismay: "Hitler cannot find safety from avenging justice in the East, in the Middle East, or in the Far East. In order to win this war he must either conquer this Island by invasion, or he must cut the ocean life-line which joins us to the United States." Churchill believed the arithmetic of the situation precluded either possibility: "There are less than seventy million malignant Huns—some of whom are curable and others killable.... The peoples of the British Empire and the United States number more than 200 million in their homelands and the British Dominions alone." This English-speaking alliance possesses "more wealth, more technical resources, and they make more steel than the rest of the world put together."[227]

Churchill failed to cite a third possible path to victory for Hitler besides invasion and blockade. It was the strategy Admiral Raeder and Franz Halder (Chief of the German Army General Staff) had advocated for ten months, albeit meekly, given Hitler's determination to burn Moscow. Halder proposed to dismember the British Empire before the Americans came in, beginning in the Mediterranean, east from Gibraltar to Egypt. Then he advised a strike across Iraq and Persia while enticing the Japanese into smashing Hong Kong and Singapore. The objective was to drive Britain out of Asia. The United States would then reassess the value of supplying Britain with war matériel for an increasingly futile battle. England finding itself cut off from its Dominions, from its Iraqi and Persian oil, and denied use of the Suez Canal, would be ripe for the kill. This was Churchill's fear exactly.[228]

He chose invective over full disclosure. No one objected to his classification of Mussolini as a jackal, but his reference to malignant Huns, *killable* at that, drew protests from Corder Catchpool, a Great War conscientious objector and pacifist who, in an open letter to Churchill, lamented the prime minister's message as "not in accordance with truth, and that the spirit it breathes is a pagan spirit, the opposite of what Jesus taught as to the Christian attitude toward sinful mankind." Catchpool predicted that "if this spirit predominates" in the British people and their leaders, "then the present generation will pass away without any hope of realizing that new and better world for which men are agonizing now." Churchill made no reply to Catchpool.[229]

Churchill ended his address with the final two stanzas of a poem by the Victorian poet Arthur Hugh Clough, words "appropriate to our fortunes to-night, and I believe they will be so judged wherever the English language is spoken or the flag of freedom flies:

For while the tired waves, vainly breaking,
Seem here no painful inch to gain,
Far back, through creeks and inlets making,
Comes silent, flooding in, the main,
And not by eastern windows only,
When daylight comes, comes in the light,
In front the sun climbs slow, how slowly!
But westward, look, the land is bright.[230]

Westward was America, where vast quantities of Lend-Lease wheat, dried milk, powdered eggs, flour, canned pork, and canned fish were being assembled for shipment to Britain. But the first ship would not arrive for a month. Though Churchill proclaimed in public that setbacks stiffened resolve and would somehow in time transform into stepping-stones to victory, when he received bad news in private, he resorted to a behavior associated with children, artists, and geniuses: he sulked. He termed each new defeat the gloomiest, the most troublesome, the most fearful, the blackest. Yet he was never long gloomy, and never afraid. At dinner, among his cronies and family, he could, with a pout, a quiver of the lip, a growl and a scowl, shut down all conversation. Yet Robert Menzies, the Australian prime minister, noted in his diary Churchill's inevitable progress during conversations from doom to effervescence: "The PM in conversation will steep himself (and you) in gloom on some grim aspect of the war…only to proceed to fight himself out while he is pacing the floor with the light of battle in his eyes. In every conversation he reaches a point where he positively enjoys the war: 'Bliss in that age it was to be alive.…Why do we regard history as of the past and forget we are making it?'" Churchill could be moody, petulant, rude, and mercurial, but he never subscribed to the patently obvious logic that given enough setbacks, defeat must necessarily follow. Menzies jotted in his diary, "There is no defeat in his heart."[231]

To Wavell, after Rommel pummeled the British in Libya, Churchill cabled, "We seem to have had rather bad luck." Like a cowboy who gambled away his wages, he added: "I expect we should get this back later." He had a way of seeing gold where others saw dirt. Had Britain not sent troops to Greece, Churchill told his cabinet, "Yugoslavia would not now be an open enemy of Germany." It is true that Yugoslav guerrillas tied up several German divisions for the remainder of the war, but the sacrifice in Greece of more than 16,000 of Britain's finest troops killed and captured in order to bring about that result cannot be construed as a design of strategic magnificence. Luck had not abandoned Wavell; Churchill had.[232]

Since the previous June, when Churchill treated of such calamities in public, even as he promised more dangers to come, he did so with the remarkable result that with each phrase he applied another dash of mortar to the foundation of public trust, until his April 27 speech. For almost a year he had told his ministers that he did not want Britons' tension over possible invasion to abate. It had not. The public's tension was so acute, wrote Panter-Downes, the news from Greece and North Africa so bewildering and so bad, that the morning newspapers "became just about as comfortable as a bomb lying on the breakfast table."[233]

Churchill's speech of April 27 had pushed the dinner hour back to almost
10:00, following which, General Sir Alan Brooke recalled, Churchill "was
in great form...and kept us up till 3:30 A.M." His great form may have
been intended to mask his growing distress, for in the hours following his
broadcast, one of his "golden eggs" had hatched. Enigma decrypts confirmed that the Germans were going to Crete, and that they would arrive
via parachute and glider, with Crete's three airfields as the objectives. This
intelligence was so vital that Churchill suggested to the Chiefs of Staff that
the actual texts be secretly flown to General Freyberg, the commander on
Crete. Churchill assumed that Freyberg, once assured that the intelligence
was valid, would deploy his forces in order to ambush and crush the German
airborne units, so that any German seaborne forces that might appear—if
the Royal Navy did not first sink them—would find themselves cut off on
the beaches. If used to effect, the decrypts could prove a godsend. If not,
and were Crete to fall, Egypt had to be the next target, and as things now
stood, Egypt's defense could not be guaranteed. The loss of Egypt and the
Suez Canal, Churchill told the War Cabinet, "would be a disaster of first
magnitude to Great Britain, second only to successful invasion and final
conquest" of the Home Island.[234]

Should Rommel reach Cairo, an evacuation from North Africa would
have to take place that would make Norway, Dunkirk, and Greece look
like training exercises. A War Cabinet directive of April 28, drafted by
Churchill, called for plans to be drawn up for an evacuation but stipulated
"no whisper of such plans is to be allowed." But before any retreat took
place, "no surrenders by officers or men will be considered tolerable unless
at least 50 percent casualties are sustained by the Unit or force in question.
According to Napoleon's maxim, 'when a man is caught alone and
unarmed, a surrender may be made.' But generals and staff officers surprised by the enemy are to use their pistols in self defence. The honor of a
wounded man is safe." Churchill was fond of the Napoleonic maxim
regarding the surrender of an unarmed man. Had Wavell read Churchill's
autobiography, *My Early Life,* he would have known that Churchill once
applied the maxim to himself when he found himself unarmed and staring
down the barrel of a Boer rifle. In the telling of that tale, Churchill took
pains to inform the reader that his pistol remained some distance away; he
was thus both surrounded *and* unarmed.[235]

The directive continued: "Anyone who can kill a Hun or even an Italian,
has rendered a good service." Then, having already broached the subject of

evacuation, Churchill decreed, "It will be utterly impossible to find the shipping for moving a tithe of the immense masses of men and stores which have been gathered in the Nile Valley." All the ships of the Royal Navy could not get them away, and this time there'd be no heroic fleet of yachts, trawlers, and dories sailing to the rescue. Conceivably, the British could flee south, through the Sudan to Kenya and safety. Those who survived would find themselves out of the war. Given the fact there was no real exit, the battle plan called for—as it did on the Home Island—a last stand.[236]

The language in the directive was the sort Dill had in mind when he told Reith that nine out of ten of Churchill's ideas as expressed in memos were less than brilliant. From Wavell's perspective, the directive was a waste of paper. He needed no man to tell him to do his duty. Churchill envied Wavell his opportunity for glory. To Colville, he admitted that he would "lay down his present office—yes and even renounce cigars and alcohol"—for the chance to lead the resistance in Egypt.[237]

Freyberg, meanwhile, on Crete, received and digested the Enigma intelligence, but the Secret Intelligence Service, in accordance with standard procedures, instructed him not to act on any *single* intelligence source without first verifying the information through a second source. Here was a piece of bureaucratic nonsense, for Ultra came straight from the horse's mouth, and was therefore unimpeachable, as well as unverifiable. Freyberg maintained in later years that the real intent of the SIS directive was to scuttle the defense of Crete's three airfields in order to protect the Ultra secret. Were the airfields to prove too well defended, the Germans might have deduced the leak in their security. Still, Freyberg decided he would man the airfields, and reinforce as best he could whichever airfield came under the heaviest attack. His problem was that the westernmost airfield, at Maleme, near the Royal Navy anchorage at Souda Bay, was seventy miles west of the airfield at Rethymnon, which in turn was eighty miles west of the third airfield, at Heraklion. Still, for the first time in the war, a British commander knew in advance exactly what was coming his way, and when. However, his forces had been so torn up in Greece that he lacked the men and internal lines of communications to mount an effective, coordinated defense of Crete, with or without help from Ultra.

Max Beaverbrook resigned from the Ministry of Aircraft Production on April 30. He had made more enemies in the RAF than he had in the Luftwaffe. Beaverbrook's liability now exceeded his utility, in part because he was willing and eager to gainsay Roosevelt, which could only hurt

Churchill. Max believed the Americans were out to grab everything they could from Britain, including its remaining gold and, when the war was won, its overseas markets—the Empire. He proposed to send a mission to the United States to set the American people straight regarding Roosevelt's canniness and the U.S. government's unwillingness to fulfill promises made to Britain, promises that Max's newspapers had endorsed. "The American government...is asking for the moon," he wrote to Churchill, "and appears unwilling to pay six pence."[238]

Max's mission to the United States could only hurt Churchill and the cause. Max had enough enemies in London; it would not do for him to make new ones in America. Churchill, seeking a way to keep Max in the game and the cabinet, resurrected him on May 1 as minister of state. It was an appointment that carried no specific duties, and invited trouble, for Max might poke his nose into the affairs of other departments, which would beget the enmity of the heads of those departments. Yet the lack of duties freed up time for Max to serve Churchill as friend, foil, and incubator of questionable ideas. Britons, not quite understanding the vagaries of the position, greeted the news with cheers, because they presumed Beaverbrook, given his talents for producing goods, would be overseeing war production. Many Britons considered Britain's war production—and Churchill's management of it—to be pathetic. War production wins wars; yet Britain's factory output was, according to Fleet Street, in a state of slumber. Factory managers and workers shut down their plants on Fridays and took their usual holidays in the country; very few third shifts hummed away in the nation's factories. The *Sunday Express:* "Do we even now understand that we are at a death grips in a fight for our lives?" The taking of holidays, chimed the newspaper, was "a scandalous situation." The *Daily Mail:* "When are we going to get down to the job of winning the war? When are we going to run machines, factories, and shipyards to full capacity?" The solution, according to the press, was a shake-up in government, a radical shake-up. Mollie Panter-Downes wrote that Beaverbrook's new job "carries with it a roving commission to kick inefficiency and departmental dawdling hard wherever it is encountered." Though Britons were suspicious of Beaverbrook's "Canadian accent," his "Fleet Street Methods," his Tory loyalties, and even his "street urchin" face, they knew he was just the man to straighten out the bureaucrats who had mucked up the production of everything from tanks to Blitz soup.[239]

The month of May proved anything but merry. Disaster struck from the air, in the Atlantic, and in the eastern Mediterranean. Shipping losses in the Atlantic were still horrific; a chart tracking them looked "like a fever patient's graph," Mollie Panter-Downes wrote. The Blitz of 1941 had entered its third and most terrible phase, with London taking beatings more vicious than those of 1940. Tarpaulins had disappeared, leaving Londoners to root about inside their roofless houses in dampness and filth. Clocks moved ahead another hour, to double daylight saving, affording Londoners another two hours of fitful sleep before the sounding of the morning all clear and two more hours of daylight in the evening to contemplate the destruction all around. The government could offer them scant aid. When a member of Parliament asked Churchill "not to close his mind" to the question of welfare relief for bombed-out citizens, Churchill replied, "I will keep my mind ajar." Still, Londoners did not complain. Rather, wrote Panter-Downes, they would gladly "lose their homes all over again for the pleasure of hearing that Berliners had just caught as big a packet of hell" from the RAF as they had caught from the Luftwaffe. Londoners could still no doubt take it, Panter-Downes wrote, but had begun to wonder if their government could dish it out. The twelve-month toll of dead Britons approached 47,000.[240]

Gibraltar was the last British toehold on the continent. Tobruk was under siege. Crete was clearly Hitler's next target, its defense problematic at best. The Vichy government was powerless to oppose German troop movements through France to Spain, if Berlin so demanded. Vichy was powerless, too, if Berlin insisted on putting troops into Syria as a prelude to going to Iraq, where an advance guard of German pilots and troops were preparing in consort with the Iraqi prime minister to grab the Mosul oil fields. Franklin Roosevelt, as usual, did not accede to Churchill's pleas for a more belligerent American role. May came in with the usual question hanging fire: Where next would Hitler or one of his surrogates strike, and when?[241]

The answer arrived at sunrise on May 1. The Iraqis had struck the night before. Alec Cadogan jotted in his diary: "Those dirty Iraqis are attacking us at Habbaniya. We have authorized bombing." Cadogan, the Foreign Office mandarin whose duties as permanent under secretary of state for foreign affairs included the articulation of the legal details and niceties of making war, ran into Churchill as the two were entering Parliament. "So you've got another war on your hands tonight," Churchill offered before disappearing down the hallway. Yet, Iraq was another sideshow. The Iraqis were led by Rashid Ali El Gailani, who after staging a coup in March appointed himself prime minister and drove the pro-British regent into exile. Now he had attacked, in violation of a treaty of long standing that granted the British free transit of Iraq and the airbase at Habbaniya, which Rashid's troops had surrounded. The Iraqi port of Basra was the door to Persia. From Basra came the oil that fueled the Royal Navy worldwide.

Churchill could not allow such Iraqi insolence to stand, not only because of the risk of losing the Mosul oil fields, but because he himself, as colonial secretary, had created Iraq one Sunday afternoon in Cairo twenty years earlier, a day, he fondly remembered, spent in the company of T. E. Lawrence and the Hashemite princes he had chosen to rule the newborn nations of Transjordan and Iraq.[242]

Yet to rid Iraq of Rashid and the German threat he needed to peel away more of Wavell's Middle East forces. Wavell, justifiably wary of further diminutions of his troops, suggested instead a parley with Rashid, in hopes of resolving the issue without a fight. Churchill and the War Cabinet overrode the reluctant general. The battle began with the relief of the RAF garrison under siege at Habbaniya, then moved on to a brief fight at Fallujah, west of Baghdad. Then, after a swift march to the capital by a brigade of the 10th Indian Colonial Division, Rashid was put to flight. The 10th was commanded by the profane and savvy Major General William ("Billy") Slim, of whom Churchill said in jest, "I cannot believe that a man with a name like Slim can be much good." Slim was not only good, he had a knack for moving his forces rapidly and over great distances, a talent that he would put to use in Burma in two years. With the 10th Indian Colonial Division on the offensive, Berlin sent a contingent of officers to bolster Rashid's resolve. The German commander, while on final approach to Baghdad's airport, was killed by shots fired by nervous Iraqi gunners. The few German squadrons that Hitler had sent to Iraq left for home, never to return. The British needed just a month to retake Baghdad, and then just three days to set up a new Iraqi government.[243]

Churchill accorded the Iraq campaign a very few pages in his memoirs, calling Iraq a "swift and complete success." Yet he noted that Hitler missed a grand opportunity. "The Germans had, of course, at their disposal an airborne force which would have given them...Syria, Iraq, and Persia, with their precious oil fields." From Persia, where he was held in high regard by the Shah, Hitler could reach "out very far toward India, and beckon to Japan." But Hitler's gaze was fixed upon Russia. Not even the prospect of gaining Iraqi and Persian oil at small cost, nor even the prospect of flying the swastika flag over the Suez Canal, could move him to alter his focus.[244]

Still, although Hitler gazed intensely eastward, he intended to follow through on his Greek and North African successes. For that reason, in Crete, Churchill was about to find himself with another Mediterranean battle on his hands. His "golden eggs" aside, given the sorry state of Freyberg's forces, a successful defense of Crete would prove dicey at best. Yet when logic went against him, Churchill went against logic. When the Ultra decrypts of late April revealed the German plans to attack Crete, he had cabled Wavell: "It seems clear from our information that a heavy airborne attack by German troops and bombers will soon be made on Crete....It ought to be a fine opportunity for killing the parachute troops." The island, he told Wavell, "must be stubbornly defended." Yet Churchill soon jettisoned his fantasy of slaying paratroopers and faced the facts. He confided to the War Cabinet—but not to Freyberg—that he thought the defense of Crete impossible in the long run. Crete lost would result in German control of the air in the eastern Mediterranean. That, Churchill told the cabinet, "is the greatest menace we have to face."[245]

A map of the eastern Mediterranean shows why Hitler was going to Crete. As the largest and southernmost of the Greek islands, it is located in the center of the eastern Mediterranean. The aerial radius from Crete extended to Tobruk, to Alexandria, and north to Athens, and to Romania beyond. British bombers could reach the Romanian oil fields at Ploesti from Crete; German bombers could reach Alexandria. The loss of Crete would place British sea-lanes to Alexandria in mortal danger. Tobruk, already under siege by Rommel, would become vulnerable to massed German air raids. The loss of its naval base at Souda Bay would force the Royal Navy to sail the eastern Mediterranean under the guns of the Luftwaffe. Yet the map also showed Crete to be a most difficult piece of real estate to attack, a long and slender mountainous spine that stretches 200 miles west to east, but is no more than 35 miles wide at its widest. Three mountain ranges from five thousand to eight thousand feet in height run laterally along the island and effectively isolate the north coast from the south. A German invasion by sea was problematic at best; the coastline consists of more cliff than beach. Even had gently sloping beaches awaited the invaders, the Germans had no shallow-draft landing craft in the Mediterranean capable of putting an army on the shore quickly. That left the air, and an air operation of this scope had yet to be attempted in that brief span of warfare since men had first parachuted from aircraft.

General Kurt Student proposed exactly that. Student commanded the Luftwaffe's elite airborne unit, XI Corps. During the 1940 invasion of the Low Countries, Student's first parachute division, 7 *Flieger,* proved the utility of dropping support troops behind enemy lines, to harass and create diversions. On Crete, Student envisioned his men in the lead role. Their targets as Ultra had revealed were the three RAF airfields, which were the keys to Crete. Göring, having been humbled in the air over Britain, embraced Student's plan as a means to recoup his prestige as well as steal yet more territory for Hitler.[246]

Churchill had all winter believed that Crete could be successfully defended from conventional attack, but until the Ultra transcripts, he knew nothing of Student's bold plan. He did know, however, that the loss of Crete would mean the virtual isolation of the Suez Canal and of Wavell's command, a prospect so dangerous to British survival that he cabled Roosevelt: "I feel Hitler may quite easily gain vast advantage very cheaply, and we are so fully engaged that we can do little—nothing to stop him spreading himself."[247]

His gloom would have deepened had Hitler chosen a far more important target. Malta, not Crete, was the correct target to hit first if Hitler's objectives were to secure his North African position and to isolate the British in the eastern Mediterranean and then to kill them via the stepping-stones that led to Cairo: Crete, Syria, and the Libyan desert. Churchill and Mussolini had long known that whoever held Malta would hold hostage the east-west sea-lanes critical to British resupply of Cairo, as well as the north-south Axis supply routes to North Africa. Hitler understood this, too. When Mussolini invaded Albania the previous year, Hitler fumed that Malta and Crete were better targets if Il Duce was intent on securing the Mediterranean. Hitler's closest military advisers at OKW—to a man—pleaded the case for sending Student's force to Malta. When Keitel and Jodl brought Student the plan, he refused on the grounds that Malta was too heavily defended. It was not, but Hitler and Student lacked the intelligence data that might have told them otherwise.[248]

As critical as Malta was to the British, by May 1941, the RAF air fleet on the island—a few squadrons of Hurricanes—had not grown much in a year. The Italian navy had been bitten hard at Taranto and Cape Matapan, but it was still larger than the British fleets at Gibraltar and Alexandria. Mussolini had more submarines in the sea than the British had ships of all classes. But Mussolini's admirals, who operated virtually independent of Il Duce, did not want their ships to fight the decisive battle for the Mediterranean. In effect, they did not want to lose their ships even if by doing so they might win the war. Thus, the Führer chose to let the Luftwaffe pummel Malta, as it had London. Between January 1941 and July 1942, the Luftwaffe and Italian air forces dropped more tons of bombs per person on the island's 270,000 residents than on any other target in Europe. Malta became the most heavily bombed target in the history of warfare. During one stretch, the bombs fell for 179 of 180 days. The Maltese learned to live in caves carved deep into the limestone. Churchill urged the Commons to adopt a relief plan for Malta, similar to the reimbursement scheme he sought for Britons whose homes had been destroyed. In an astounding affront to the people of Malta, the House of Commons did not even respond. Had British civilian casualties during the Blitz been proportional to those on Malta, almost 800,000 Britons would have perished. Yet the Maltese hung on, even as they died under German bombs.

The far western Mediterranean looked poised for disaster as well. On

April 24 Churchill had cabled Roosevelt: "The capacity of Spain and Portugal to resist the increasing German pressure may at any time collapse, and the anchorage at Gibraltar be rendered unusable. To effect this the Germans would not need to move a large army through Spain but merely to get hold of the batteries which molest the anchorage, for which a few thousand artillerists and technicians might be sufficient." Were Gibraltar to be abandoned, the effect on Royal Navy operations in the Mediterranean would be immediate and disastrous, as would the effect in the eastern Atlantic. The Portuguese Azores, 950 miles off the Iberian coast, and the Cape Verde Islands, 350 miles off the western coast of Africa, were perfect staging areas for U-boats. The islands assumed the same strategic significance in the Atlantic as did Malta in the Mediterranean. If Germany controlled the Atlantic islands, her U-boats could patrol far into the South Atlantic, to the west, and, most worrisome for Churchill, station themselves astride his convoy routes around the Cape of Good Hope. For months German submariners had been secretly putting into the islands' coves for minor repairs. Churchill pleaded with Roosevelt to order carrier-based reconnaissance flights to safeguard British convoys in the vicinity of the Azores and Cape Verde Islands.[249]

Time, as always, was not on Churchill's side. He told Roosevelt that a British force was ready to take the Atlantic islands should Hitler take Spain or Portugal but that the force needed more than a week to deploy. He asked the president to "send an American squadron for a friendly cruise in these regions." Harriman, in complete agreement with Churchill as to the immediacy of the danger, had days earlier sent his own desperate cable to Roosevelt: "England's strength is bleeding. In our own interest, I trust that your Navy can be directly employed before it is too late."[250]

Roosevelt declined a show of naval force in the vicinity of the Azores, declined to order reconnaissance flights into the fray, declined all of Churchill's pleas and suggestions. The president's refusal, Colville observed, made Churchill "gravely depressed." On May 3, Churchill—"in worse gloom than I have ever seen him"—dictated to Colville another telegram to the president, this one "drawing a somber picture of what a collapse in the Middle East would entail." Iraq could fall, and Turkey, and the eastern flank of Egypt—Palestine—would be threatened. The Mideast command would collapse. The telegram complete, he indulged in his habit of divining the future. In this instant, the gloom bled through. He sketched for Colville, Ismay, and Harriman—as he had in the cable to Roosevelt—a picture of the world controlled by Hitler, with the United States and Britain isolated and forced to accept a terrible, and in time, fatal peace.[251]

Churchill was just desperate enough to add a remarkable request to his cable apprising Roosevelt of the situation: "Therefore, if you can not take more advanced positions now [in the Atlantic], or very soon, the vast balances may be tilted heavily to our disadvantage. Mr. President...the one decisive counterweight I can see to balance the growing pessimism... *would be if the United States were immediately to arrange herself with us as a belligerent Power*" (italics added). It had come to this: the British prime minister was asking—*begging*—America to declare war.[252]

He had asked Roosevelt much the same question the previous year as France was falling but had framed that request in terms of the "moral effect" an American declaration might have on the French. His new plea was based on a far more fundamental need: survival. Roosevelt, again, declined. He lacked the support to give Churchill what he needed, with the result that Churchill found himself, as usual, desperately short on time and desperately lacking in matériel.

On the moonlit night of May 10, the Luftwaffe smashed London and continued pounding it with high explosives and incendiaries until dawn on the eleventh. The Anglo-Irish poet Louis MacNeice had arranged to spend the night in the dome of St. Paul's Cathedral. He wrote that soon after the raiders appeared, "great tawny clouds of smoke, rolling in sumptuous Baroque exuberance, had hidden the river completely and there we were on the dome, a Classical island in a more than Romantic Inferno. It was far and away the most astonishing spectacle I have ever seen."

Churchill was safe at Ditchley that night, watching a Marx Brothers movie and making inquiries about the damage to London when word came in that the Duke of Hamilton, an old friend of his, had telephoned and sought most urgently to speak to Churchill. Churchill asked Brendan Bracken to take a message from the duke. A few minutes later Bracken returned and informed the P.M.: "Hess has arrived in Scotland." Churchill thought it a joke and told Brendan to inform the duke to "kindly tell that to the Marx Brothers." But a flood of new messages soon confirmed the story. Rudolf Hess, deputy Führer, third in command of the Third Reich, member of Hitler's secret cabinet council, leader of the Nazi Party, Hitler's friend—perhaps his only true friend—for more than a dozen years, had parachuted into Scotland. Either through luck or skill, Hess had actually landed quite near the duke's manor. Thus began an episode of sheer lunacy.[253]

Nobody knew what to make of the news. Pamela Churchill, who was at Ditchley that weekend, recalled that the secretaries, who were vital in connecting Churchill to "whatever was happening" in the outside world, could

garner no intelligence on Hess's adventure. Everybody who was present—
Pamela, the secretaries, Churchill—"had no idea what was happening"
and could only speculate and wonder if "it might be the biggest thing in the
whole war" or if perhaps "Germany was breaking up." History anointed
Hess a sideshow, but when news of his advent first arrived "it was a very
thrilling moment."[254]

Hess's immediate objective was to reach the Duke of Hamilton, who
had met Hess but once, at the 1936 Olympic Games, but who Hess presumed to be a fan of Hitler. Hess's delusional and singularly unilateral
mission was to bring the war to a peaceful conclusion. Knowing of Hitler's
hatred for the Russians (but not being privy to the invasion plans), Hess
believed (in part on being told so by his astrologer) that he and Hamilton
could arrange peace through the large anti-war faction Hess believed
existed in Britain. In interviews with doctors and cabinet officials, Hess
stressed that Hitler was pained deeply over the need to sink British ships
and bomb British cities. The Führer, Hess claimed, found it most difficult
to give the orders necessary to fight such a ruthless war with Britain. Hess,
in what Churchill termed his "keynote," claimed he "thought that if England once knew of this fact it might be possible that England on her part
would be ready for agreement." In other words, once England realized
how kind and considerate a fellow Hitler really was, England would meet
the Führer's wishes.[255]

Churchill in his memoirs writes that he attached no special significance
to Hess's arrival, though in the first hours after learning of Hess's mission,
Churchill was as much in a tizzy as everyone else. In short order it became
clear that Hess was crazy. In fact, Hess's arrant mental condition was so
evident that Churchill considered his subsequent sentence of life in prison
to be unjust. Hess may have once stood close to Hitler, Churchill wrote,
but he "had, in my view, atoned for this by his completely devoted and
frantic deed of lunatic benevolence." He was, wrote Churchill, "a medical
and not a criminal case, and should be so regarded."[256]

The weirdness of the entire episode captured imaginations worldwide,
just as it had captured Churchill's. Days after Hess's arrival, Roosevelt,
dining with Sumner Welles, Harry Hopkins, and Robert E. Sherwood,
asked Welles if he had ever met Hess. Welles had, and described Hess as
fanatically loyal to Hitler and somewhat brutishly stupid. The men discussed Hess's flight. Roosevelt fell silent for a moment. Then he posed the
question everybody was asking: "I wonder what is *really* behind this
story?" Stalin (who never trusted the British) asked both Beaverbrook and
Churchill the same question months later. The whole thing was just too
strange, and the obvious explanation—that Hess was crazy—seemed too
pat. Churchill, or Hitler, or both, *had* to be up to something.[257]

Hess's misadventure handed Churchill a grand opportunity to make mischief at Hitler's expense. With Hess under wraps in the Tower of London and Hitler unsure of just what his protégé was saying to the British, Churchill told Roosevelt that "we think it best to let the press have a good run of it for a bit and keep the Germans guessing." Hitler was not only guessing but sweating, from the moment he was apprised of Hess's errand by two of Hess's adjutants, who had the misfortune to deliver to Hitler a letter of explanation from Hess along with the news that Hess had already departed. They were immediately arrested. Hitler expressed to his personal architect, Albert Speer, his worry that Churchill might use the incident to pretend to Germany's allies that the Reich had extended peace feelers toward Britain. "Who will believe me," the Führer lamented to Speer, "that Hess did not fly there in my name, that the whole thing is not some sort of intrigue behind the backs of my allies?" Japan might change its policy. People would snicker. Hitler regained his buoyancy with the thought that Hess might drop into the North Sea and drown. After the news of Hess's safe landing arrived, Hitler devised his official explanation: he declared that his old friend had gone mad. He also consulted his astrologer, who always divined happy portents from the tea leaves.[258]

Churchill, aware of Hitler's use of astrologers, once summoned one himself. In a what-the-hell moment, he asked the surprised fortune-teller to tell him what *Hitler's* fortune-teller was telling Hitler. Churchill told his friend Kay Halle the story years later with the caveat that "this is just between us."[259]

Hess himself, cursed with good health, given his fate, lived on for another forty-six years, locked away in prison every day and hour and minute of them. His wife sued for divorce in 1944 on the grounds of "desertion and insanity."[260]

Hess's flight was one of two stories from overseas that year—until December 7—that held young American boys spellbound. The other was the hunt for the great German battleship *Bismarck*. The essayist and sportswriter Robert W. Creamer devotes almost as much ink to these two events as he does to Joe DiMaggio's hitting streak in his memoir of that memorable baseball season, *Baseball and Other Matters in 1941*. "Hess and the *Bismarck* served in my innocent mind, and in the minds of other half-thinking Americans," wrote Creamer, "to counterbalance the Nazi victories in the Balkans and North Africa."

The morning after Hess landed, a fine Sunday morning of sun and blue skies, fires still burned in London from the previous evening's air raid. Almost three thousand Londoners lay dead in the rubble, the deadliest one-night toll since the Blitz began nine months earlier. Services were canceled at Westminster Abbey. St. Mary-le-Bow was destroyed, its bells crashing down into the debris. The William Rufus roof of Westminster Hall was gone, the hall itself now a smoldering wreck. Colville watched from Westminster Bridge as fires burned all along the Embankment. Big Ben had been struck, but still tolled out the hours. The debating chamber in the Commons, at the northern end of the Palace of Westminster, had taken a direct hit and, to Churchill's profound sorrow, "was blown to smithereens." (The Lords' chamber was undamaged; the House met there and at Church House for the remainder of the war.) In a letter to Randolph, Churchill mourned the loss of the chamber where he had served for almost forty years. He had once, during the Great War, called it the "the shrine of the world's liberties." Since September, MPs had prowled the darkened halls of Parliament by the light of hurricane lamps; the windows overlooking the Thames had long since been blown out and boarded up; the tapestries had been removed for safe-keeping. Even the smoking room closed early so the attendants could get home to their families before the bombs came. The House chamber was destroyed, but Parliament, Churchill told his son, continued to function "undaunted amid the storms." Days earlier he had ended an address in the old chamber with, "I feel sure we have no need to fear the tempest. Let it roar, and let it rage. We shall come through." They were the last words he spoke there. A decade would pass before the Commons was rebuilt.[261]

As that Sunday evening came on, Colville noted yellow, smoldering bits of burnt paper from some wrecked Fleet Street publishing house raining down like leaves on a breezy autumn day. Hess was by then on his way to the Tower. Londoners waited in homes as dark as Hess's prison cell for the expected nightly onslaught. It appeared obvious that Hitler was softening up Britain for the final attack. They imagined the worst was yet to come.[262]

Within days of Hess's arrival, more critical events overtook Churchill. He had been partially correct when he told Wavell that he thought the invasion of Crete would afford a good opportunity to kill parachutists. When dropped behind, or directly onto, British positions, the German air-borne troops would find themselves outnumbered and cut off from sup-port. If the Royal Navy—protected by Air Marshal Longmore's too-few aircraft—could keep the coast clear of German reinforcements, the para-chutists would be doomed.

That hope was stillborn. Having left so many men and so much equip-ment behind in Greece, the British on Crete found they lacked the troops, anti-aircraft guns, and requisite radio communications between units to stop the Germans. The 30,000 Commonwealth and 10,000 Greek troops on Crete, though outnumbering the expected Germans by more than two to one, were at a disadvantage by having to cover all the airfields and ports along the length of the north shore, whereas the Germans could concentrate their forces at will, and with surprise. The British would have to react, and when they did, they'd face bad terrain and long distances along the single coast road. In essence, at any particular point, the Commonwealth forces would find themselves, as usual, outgunned. The situation in the air was even grimmer. Longmore's air force on Crete consisted of fewer than a dozen Hurricanes and two dozen older planes. The air chief as well did not grasp the need to integrate air support with ground operations, a concept superbly practiced for two years by the Germans. Longmore's few planes therefore did not coordinate with Freyberg's infantry, rendering the former irrelevant and the latter exposed, as was the Royal Navy, which sailed without air protection. Churchill suggested that a dozen Hurricanes be sent from Malta. Such a pittance would have made no difference. The German air fleet assembling in southern Greece, fewer than 150 miles from Crete, was made up of more than 250 bombers, 150 Stuka dive-bombers, 200 fighters, 500 tri-motor Junkers Ju 52 transport planes carrying paratroopers, and 80 gliders carrying 750 airborne troops.[263]

The battle opened on May 19, with Stuka dive-bombers striking at British ships in Souda Bay; then the German fighters destroyed most of the meager British air fleet. Early the next morning, German paratroopers— almost four thousand strong—descended upon the Maleme airfield and the heights above Souda Bay. Sir John Keegan called it "the first great parachute operation in history." Three battalions of New Zealanders, veterans of the desert and Greek campaigns, guarded the Maleme airfield. A New Zealand lieutenant recorded his thoughts as Germans drifted down: "Seen against the blue of the early morning Cretan sky, through a frame of grey-green olive branches, they looked like little jerking dolls" and "those beautiful kicking dolls meant the repetition of all the horror we had known so recently in Greece." An Australian brigade guarded the Rethymnon airfield, seventy miles to the east and a little less than halfway to Heraklion, where just a few British battalions prepared to defend that airfield.[264]

By late afternoon on the twentieth, another wave of almost four thousand paratroopers landed in the vicinity of the Rethymnom and Heraklion airfields. Within hours Churchill telegraphed Roosevelt: "Battle for Crete has opened well." The battle had opened well, but that situation lasted for only a few hours. The Germans, dispersed and confused at first, rallied throughout the night. A New Zealand battalion inexplicably withdrew from a vital hill above Maleme. The Maleme airfield fell to the Germans on the twenty-first. Ju 52 transports began ferrying in the five thousand troops of the 5th Mountain Division, but at great cost: More than half of the Ju 52s sent to Crete never returned. British anti-aircraft guns accounted for only a few of the planes; most were lost while trying to land on beaches, on wrecked airfields, and in plowed fields in order to disgorge their cargoes of troops. The RAF was in far worse shape. By late on the twenty-first, the RAF had no planes on Crete. Freyberg's ground forces were dispersed and unable to coordinate movements. On the night of the twenty-first, the Royal Navy turned away German transports—mostly commandeered Greek fishing boats and small coastal steamers—carrying seven thousand troops. But daylight on the twenty-second brought the Stukas. "A lot of ships lost," noted Colville, "including [cruisers] *Gloucester* and *Fiji*." More than seven hundred of *Gloucester*'s eight hundred crew members went down with the ship. In reply to Colville's expression of grief at the naval losses, Churchill growled, "What do you suppose we build ships for?" The Royal Navy's deflection of the German transports was welcome news, but those losses were not enough to keep the Germans off the island, because the Germans were coming by air. Less than thirty-six hours after telling Roosevelt the battle had opened well, Churchill was forced to inform the president: "Battle in Crete is severe." "Severe" did not do justice to the circumstances. Another last stand was shaping up.[265]

The Germans fought as if Crete were a sacred Teutonic site, pressing the battle, Colville wrote, "with blind courage." They fought with such fury because there would be no escape were they to fail. The British could always evacuate by sea in the event of defeat, and had in fact developed a talent for doing just that. The German paratroopers, on the other hand, were there to stay, one way or another. Their brethren in the Luftwaffe controlled the air, and the parachutists grabbed the airfields. The British had blasted the airstrips to rubble, but the Germans held and repaired the fields. Supplies and reinforcements were flown in during the next seven days, while Stukas riddled any British or Greek troops who tried any heroics. Once in possession of the airfields, the Germans were, in effect, in possession of Crete. But the cost of victory for Student's paratroopers was extraordinary; five thousand out of nine thousand had been killed. Hitler told Student the cost was too high to justify ever staging another operation of that magnitude. The loss of so many of the Ju 52s—the workhorse of supply for the Wehrmacht—was also disturbing. Hitler would need all he could get to feed and arm his armies as they struck deep into Russia.[266]

As of the twenty-eighth, the port of Sphakia, on the island's south side, was still held by the British, but in the end, it would serve as this battle's Dunkirk and Narvik. That day Freyberg's army began the trek over the mountains to Sphakia, with the German mountain troops in pursuit. By battle's end, three days later, the army had lost more than 1,700 killed and 2,000 wounded. Almost 12,000 British and Anzac troops stayed behind as prisoners of the Reich. Just ten days after Churchill told Roosevelt that the battle was "severe," Crete was lost, and the British again were forced to flee the scene of a disastrous defeat by sea. Mountbatten's destroyer HMS *Kelly* was among the Luftwaffe's victims. Captain Dickie survived, but more than half of the crew were lost when *Kelly* capsized and sank while plowing ahead at full speed. Between May 21 and June 2, the Royal Navy, pummeled from the air, lost three cruisers sunk and four damaged, six destroyers sunk and eight damaged, and more than 2,000 officers and seamen killed. The battleships *Warspite* and *Valiant* were damaged, as was the aircraft carrier *Formidable*. It was the Royal Navy's most costly naval battle of the war. German aircraft—in daylight operations—had accounted for all the British ships. Göring had achieved over Crete what he had failed to achieve over Britain: air superiority. He had redeemed himself.[267]

On May 21, the second full day of the battle for Crete, other ominous news arrived at No. 10. It appeared *Bismarck* was preparing to make its run for the high seas. Surface raiders such as *Bismarck* and her sister ship, *Tirpitz,* if free to roam the Atlantic, were as equal a threat to shipping as, or greater than, U-boats. German submarines engendered a primal fear in the crews and passengers aboard their targets; they were the monsters under the bed, lurking unseen beneath the sea, their presence announced by a thunderous eruption of flame from the bowels of some unfortunate merchantman. *Bismarck* was a monster plain and simple. A tanker or freighter captain who espied *Bismarck* setting a course across his bow knew his ship was doomed. Convoy escorts (destroyers and corvettes) proved adequate at hunting and killing submarines, but their small guns and depth charges were useless against capital ships. *Bismarck* amok, undetected by RAF reconnaissance planes, which lacked the range to patrol to the vast reaches of the central Atlantic, could run down any convoy, immune to the minuscule fire of the escorts. *Bismarck,* if she chose, could *ram* her way through a convoy; a thin-skinned five-thousand-ton freighter would perish beneath her bows like a rowboat.

The January German sortie of *Scharnhorst* and *Gneisenau* resulted in the mauling of one convoy—ten ships were sunk in one day—and the loss of more than 115,000 tons of shipping. As a result, the British gained a great deal of respect for the lethality of the *Kriegsmarine*'s surface ships and now had a double-edged problem. Locating the German battleships was difficult enough, but what to do when they were located? Churchill faced two bad choices if Hitler let loose his surface ships. He could chase the Germans and expose the British coast or leave the Germans unmolested and expose the convoys. He lacked the warships to do both. It was an old predicament for the British, which, when Napoleon grasped its significance, led him to contemplate a naval feint in 1804. By sending a French fleet to the British West Indies, he hoped to lure the British Home Fleet into a wild goose chase, thereby allowing his main fleet to land an invasion force on British soil. Had Hitler studied Napoleon's seafaring tactics or only his Russian escapades? Churchill also feared that the mere appearance of German capital ships on the high seas would dissuade America from risking its merchantmen to convoy supplies to Britain, let alone risk its outdated Atlantic fleet to protect those ships. He later wrote that a concentration of surface raiders "in the great spaces of the Atlantic Ocean would subject our naval strength to a trial of the first magnitude." *Scharnhorst* and *Gneisenau* had in January given the trial's opening arguments. *Bismarck* presumed to close the case.[268]

On the evening of May 21, *Bismarck* and the heavy cruiser *Prinz Eugen*, escorted by six destroyers, slipped out of Bergen fjord in Norway under the command of Admiral Günther Lütjens, a stern, humorless veteran of the Great War's coastal gunboat battles, in which his willingness to attack superior forces and his skill at coming away victorious earned him a reputation as a brilliant and courageous tactician. He was Grand Admiral Raeder's first choice to command *Bismarck* on this, her maiden operation, code-named *Rheinübung* (Rhine Exercise). Lütjens, prone to fatalistic premonitions, told fellow officers that *Rheinübung* was to be his "death voyage." The admiral had secured his place on this mission by his superb command of the heavy cruisers *Scharnhorst* and *Gneisenau* during their murderous January spree. The original plan for *Rheinübung* called for these two ships to sail with *Bismarck*, but the British had driven them into French ports, where they were undergoing repairs. *Bismarck* and *Prinz Eugen* (named for Eugene of Savoy, Marlborough's ally at the Battle of Blenheim) would conduct *Rheinübung* alone. Riding at anchor in Bergen fjord, the two ships made tempting targets for the RAF, as dusk lingers in late spring at those latitudes. Were the RAF to appear overhead, Lütjens stood a fair chance of seeing his fatal premonition fulfilled before he even weighed anchor. But high clouds and clinging fog afforded the Germans a perfect opportunity to escape into the North Sea. Not willing to risk an improvement in the weather, Lütjens made his dash for the open sea. In his haste to depart Bergen, he failed to top off *Bismarck*'s fuel tanks.[269]

The British, expecting just such a rapid departure, hoped to shadow the

German ships. If *Bismarck* and *Prinz Eugen* reached the North Sea undetected, the Royal Navy could then only guess which of four routes they would take to break out into the Atlantic. Two of the routes took the ships within British air-patrol range north of the Orkney Islands; the third ran between the Faroe Islands and Iceland, within range of British spotter planes stationed there. Lütjens's fourth choice was the longest—to loop to the north of Iceland and run down the chute of the Denmark Strait, the ice-choked channel between Greenland and Iceland. This was the route he had taken in January. He chose to take it again. Everything was going his way. When the clouds broke over Bergen on May 22, a lone Spitfire, rigged for photo reconnaissance, roared up the fjord just a few feet above the waves and into the teeth of enemy fire. The pilot took a fast look around, turned hard for home, and radioed his message: *Bismarck* is gone.

This news troubled Churchill. Eleven convoys were at that moment on the open seas or preparing to depart British ports. One of them, escorted by two cruisers, both of which *Bismarck* could easily dispatch, was sailing south of Britain, destined for the Middle East with 20,000 reinforcements for Wavell. Were *Bismarck* and the troop transports to cross paths, Churchill's war in Africa would be over. *Bismarck* had to be located, and sunk.

Early on the twenty-second, the escort destroyers dropped away from the far swifter *Bismarck* and *Prinz Eugen*. Alone now, Lütjens steamed north until the early afternoon, when he turned northwest in readiness for the run down the Denmark Strait, fog-bound at this time of year and full of newly calved icebergs. Just before midnight, the German ships turned into the strait. If his luck held, Lütjens would break out into the Atlantic in about thirty hours. This was the most dangerous part of the venture; the navigable part of the channel was at most only thirty miles wide at this time of year, narrow enough that if the British were lucky, their naval radar—limited in range to about twelve miles, and unreliable—could pick up the German ships, that is, if the British had vessels on station. They did. Two cruisers, *Norfolk* and *Suffolk,* positioned themselves in the lower part of the strait. Neither was a match for *Bismarck* or *Prinz Eugen.* Their job was to spot the Germans and shadow them until the battle cruiser *Hood* and Britain's newest battleship, *Prince of Wales,* appeared on the scene. *Prince of Wales* carried ten 14-inch guns and was built to hunt and kill almost anything afloat. *Hood*—the *Mighty Hood* to Britons—was twenty-two years old, armed with eight 15-inch guns, and the pride of Great Britain, feared even by German sailors. When Churchill learned that it was to be *Hood* that would give battle to *Bismarck,* he retired to bed content.[270]

Hood and *Prince of Wales* departed Scapa Flow a few minutes after midnight on the twenty-second, dispatched by Admiral Sir John Cronyn Tovey, commander in chief of the Home Fleet. They made for the Denmark Strait on a course that would take them across the other three exit points into the Atlantic. Had Lütjens elected to make his run through one of them, *Hood* would cross his path. If not, the Germans and British would likely meet and fight at the southern end of the Denmark Strait. When he received the baleful report from the lone Spitfire, Tovey put his flag aboard the new battleship *King George V* and sallied out of Scapa Flow with the aircraft carrier *Victorious,* four cruisers, and seven destroyers. Tovey intended to straddle the three exit routes east of Iceland. Somebody was bound to run into the Germans. Such was the plan.

If *Bismarck* avoided the net, Churchill would need help from Roosevelt. Accordingly, he cabled the president: "Should we not catch them going out, your Navy should surely be able to mark them down for us" and "Give us the news and we will finish the job." That request, to act as Britain's eyes in the Atlantic, created a diplomatic problem for the Americans, for Grand Admiral Raeder had made clear his intentions to shoot any American warship he thought "committed an act of war" by reporting to the British the position of German ships on the high seas. Raeder had a point. International law demanded that neutrals on the high seas mind their own business. But in early April, Roosevelt—in yet another tentative step toward hostilities—declared that American warships would henceforth patrol to twenty-six degrees west longitude, roughly from between Iceland and Greenland south to Brazil. He also declared that if American ships spotted German warships, they would broadcast their location on an open frequency, fully realizing that doing so might trigger an act of war on Germany's part, which presumably (Churchill hoped) would trigger a declaration of war by America. Yet Roosevelt knew that America was not yet prepared in either martial spirit or armaments to carry through on such a declaration. His initiative had been largely bluff, though it had elated Churchill. Colville and Harriman were at Chequers when the news arrived. When Colville asked Harriman if this might mean war, Harriman replied: "That's what I hope."[271]

Churchill would have welcomed a crisis on the seas, and, in fact, he soon tried to engineer just such an incident. Roosevelt's declaration meant that American warships patrolled east almost to the Azores and north to Greenland but not into the hottest battle zones, within one thousand miles of Britain, thereby lessening the chances of running into Germans. Roosevelt had struck a deal with the Danish government in exile to build airbases on Greenland. Had the bases been operational by late May, they might have benefited Churchill in his search for *Bismarck;* but they were not. In any case, the Denmark Strait went unobserved by the U.S. Navy as

Bismarck slipped through. Churchill's ships would have to find *Bismarck* on their own.

Suffolk did just that. She spotted the two German ships in the early evening of May 23 and signaled the contact before running for cover in a fogbank. *Norfolk,* also hiding in the fog, picked up *Suffolk*'s report. Admiral W. F. Wake-Walker, directing the action of both ships from *Norfolk,* and eager to make visual contact, ordered *Norfolk* to the edge of the fogbank, directly under *Bismarck*'s fine optical sights. *Bismarck* loosed its first ever shots in anger, which straddled *Norfolk.* Walker fled back into the fog. It would fall to *Hood,* guided by *Suffolk* and *Norfolk,* to sink the *Bismarck.*

Vice Admiral Lancelot Holland, second in command of the Home Fleet, was on board *Hood,* about three hundred miles away and closing at such high speed that his escort destroyers gave up the chase and dropped back. At about 8:00 P.M. *Hood*'s captain, Ralph Kerr, told his crew that the Germans had been sighted in the strait. All hands were ordered to ready their battle gear—life jackets, flashlights, helmets—and were reminded to change into clean underwear, to prevent infection from shrapnel wounds. The ship was darkened, battle flags run up the masts. Shortly after midnight—it was now the twenty-fourth—the crews of *Hood* and *Prince of Wales* manned their battle stations. *Bismarck* was now about 180 miles to the north, her bottleneck into the Atlantic corked.

Churchill, dining at Chequers, demanded that all news be immediately brought to his attention. The evening's dinner was, as usual, an "entirely male party," Colville noted, consisting of Churchill's brother, Jack, Colville, Harriman, and Ismay. Although the awful news from Crete weighed on Churchill and his guests, the conversation at the table, recalled Ismay, "was confined almost exclusively to the impending clash at sea." They sat up until after 3:00 A.M., late even for Churchill, with hopes of getting some further news from the Admiralty. None arrived. Churchill recalled, "There was nothing for me to do and I went to bed...so well tired with other work that I slept soundly. I had complete confidence in The First Sea Lord, Admiral Pound, and liked the way he was playing the hand. I awoke in peaceful Chequers about 9 A.M. with all that strange thrill which one feels at the beginning of a day in which great news is expected, good or bad."[272]

While Churchill slept, the last great duel of battleships in the Atlantic Ocean began. It was over in less than eight minutes. Just before 6:00 A.M., *Prince of Wales* and *Hood* maneuvered to bring themselves east and south of *Bismarck* and *Prinz Eugen,* such that the rising sun brought the approaching German ships into sharp relief. *Prinz Eugen* came along first in line, which confused the British, for *Bismarck,* the logical leader, was trailing behind and appeared to be the smaller of the two ships. *Prince of Wales,* much of its crew green, and *Hood,* plagued by ineffectual range-finding radar, opened fire on *Prinz Eugen,* to no effect. *Bismarck,* meanwhile, took leisurely aim at *Hood.* One of *Prinz Eugen's* eight-inch shells scored a hit amidships on *Hood,* igniting a fire that popped off ammunition kept at the ready. Captain Kerr ordered his crew to let the fire burn itself out and to take shelter near the superstructure. Kerr, realizing he had shot at the wrong target, ordered a turn to port, in order to reduce *Hood's* profile and to bring its four 15-inch bow guns to bear on *Bismarck.* The turn came too late.

Bismarck's first salvos had straddled *Hood.* Now *Bismarck* had *Hood's* range. She fired another salvo. An officer on *Prinz Eugen* saw the shell splashes and thought that this salvo, too, had missed. But at least one shell had found its mark, possibly beneath the waterline. Within a second or two, a great shaft of flame shot straight up from *Hood's* midsection, high into the morning sky, followed a few seconds later by a catastrophic explosion. *Hood* disappeared for a few moments in the smoke, but large pieces of the ship were seen lofted high into the air. Within a few minutes, the smoke drifted off. *Hood* was gone. Three of her crew of 1,412 bobbed alive in the water. They called out until they found each other amid the oil and debris and dozens of inflatable life rafts, all of which were empty. *Hood,* its stern blown off, its bow broken off, took Admiral Holland and Captain Kerr and every other crewman down with her. Churchill awoke at Chequers to this worst possible news: *Hood* was lost and *Bismarck* was on the loose. He wandered into Harriman's bedroom. Harriman bolted awake to behold an apparition dressed in a yellow sweater over a short nightshirt, his pink legs exposed. "Hell of a battle going on," Churchill mumbled. "The *Hood* is sunk, hell of a battle."[273]

Gloom descended upon Chequers that morning, but Churchill shed no tears at the news of *Hood.* His tears flowed when sentimentality was in the air—a christening, the prospect of casualties among the creatures confined in the London zoo, the recounting over brandy of long-past heroic deeds. The sight of bombed-out civilians brought tears to his eyes; they were innocents. News of the death of soldiers or sailors in battle moved him to resolve, often to anger, sometimes to impetuous decisions, but not to tears. Upon learning of *Hood's* demise, he came downstairs to find Clementine, Sarah, and Vic Oliver in a parlor, Vic at the piano, tapping out on the ivories a few measures of Beethoven, which Churchill took to be a funeral march. "Nobody plays the Dead March in my house," Churchill growled. All in the room but Churchill laughed—a mistake, followed by another. "It's not the Dead March," said Oliver. "It's the Appassionata Sonata." Churchill glowered. "You can say what you like, I know it's the Funeral March." Vic then made a final error, by playing a few more chords from the Appassionata. Churchill erupted. "Stop it! Stop it! I want no

Dead March, I tell you!" Only when Sarah rushed to the piano and advised Vic to play another piece did the moment pass. Vic at least had had the good sense not to whistle the tune.[274]

Churchill learned later that morning that *Prince of Wales* had taken several hits. One shell from *Prinz Eugen* passed without exploding clear through the gunnery plotting station in the superstructure, killing most of the plotters and knocking Captain Leach senseless. Still, *Prince of Wales* let loose four more salvos before withdrawing. Churchill fumed to Colville that the retreat was "the worst thing since Troubridge turned away from *Goeben* in 1914." Churchill berated the Admiralty, the first sea lord, and, when his criticism of the Atlantic action waned, berated Cunningham in the Mediterranean for not risking his ships to block the invasion of Crete. Churchill demanded risk, not caution, from his naval commanders. Yet Cunningham *had* risked his ships, and he had scattered the German invasion fleet. Cunningham had put thousands of British troops on Crete, and by the twenty-fourth, with his ships under constant attack, he was preparing to get them off. His losses were horrific. Cunningham's place in Royal Navy history was secure. Churchill, in his memoirs, finally gave him his due, and he included an anecdote that captures the spirit of the admiral. When an officer protested the risk to the fleet in getting the survivors off Crete, Cunningham responded, "It takes the Navy three years to build a ship; it will take three hundred years to build a new tradition."[275]

It was May 24, Empire Day,* when millions of schoolchildren throughout the Empire were granted a school holiday to celebrate their monarch, salute the Union Jack, and sing patriotic songs. A generation of children had heard inspirational speeches and listened to tales of heroic deeds from the imperial past, tales of Clive of India, Wolfe of Québec, and "Chinese Gordon" of Khartoum, Marlborough, and Nelson. Empire Day 1941 passed without celebration. Churchill would have to impart the news of *Hood* to the Commons the following week, but first a new diversion was to be unveiled that night at Chequers. The Old Man had recently insisted the great house be outfitted with a movie projector. His mood improved somewhat that evening as Marlene Dietrich, starring in *Seven Sinners,* made her Chequers premier.

But he continued to spread his anger between Cunningham and the admirals pursuing *Bismarck*. "The loss of half the Mediterranean fleet," he snapped to Colville, "would be worthwhile to save Crete." In fact, with

---

* In the next decade it would be rechristened Commonwealth Day, and the date moved first to June 10, Queen Elizabeth's birthday, then to the second Monday of March. By the time Churchill celebrated his ninetieth birthday, its original meaning was fast fading from the collective memory.

Cunningham's mounting losses off Crete, about half the Mediterranean fleet *had* been lost since the start of the year. Churchill was incorrect in ascribing hesitancy—cowardice by any other name—to Cunningham, and he was wrong about Admiral Wake-Walker on board *Norfolk* and Captain Leach on board *Prince of Wales*. Leach was correct in withdrawing *Prince of Wales,* damaged, outgunned, her range-finding radar useless. Wake-Walker and Leach ran, not for lack of fighting spirit, but to live to fight another day. It was the correct decision.[276]

Churchill did not at all see things that way. Livid, he wanted to welcome the two commanders home with courts-martial, but Admirals Pound and Tovey insisted the officers on the spot had acted correctly. Years later, his wrath softened by the passage of time, Churchill wrote in his memoirs that Wake-Walker had been "indisputably right" in his decision.

Prince of Wales had put at least three 14-inch shells into *Bismarck,* and as a result the German ship suffered a serious fuel leak and loss of rudder control. The Admiralty did not yet know this. But Lütjens now knew his decision to not refuel at Bergen was fatal. *Bismarck,* wounded and lacking the fuel to make a run for home, had to run for a port in occupied France. *Prinz Eugen,* undamaged, ran for Brest. *Rheinübung* was finished. It remained to be seen whether *Bismarck* was as well. That night, Churchill was told that the Royal Navy would give battle the following morning, but in the early hours of the twenty-fifth, *Bismarck* vanished from *Suffolk*'s radar. Colville recalled that this dashing of Churchill's hopes caused the entirety of the twenty-fifth to be passed as "a day of fearful gloom." Over the next two days and across 1,200 nautical miles, a truly epic naval chase took place on the high seas. Churchill dearly would have loved to be in on the chase and particularly the kill, but he had to satisfy himself with observing from the Admiralty War Room, where he meddled. The "former naval person" had never heard a naval gun fired in battle. His had been an administrative naval career consisting in large part of sticking pins into his wall maps at the Admiralty. On this day, he made a nuisance of himself.[277]

On the morning of Monday, May 26, having vanished for more than thirty hours, *Bismarck*'s position and heading were at last confirmed by an RAF Catalina flying boat, piloted by an American. Tovey, on board *King George V,* gave chase, with *Bismarck* now 130 miles ahead of him. The older battleship *Rodney* joined the hunt. Churchill, ensconced in the Admiralty War Room, oversaw a riotous scene of charts spread across old oak tables, pins marking known positions, admirals demanding information from subordinates, and Churchill needling them all. He pressured Pound to order Tovey to keep up the chase even if it meant *King George V* had to be towed to port for lack of fuel. Pound needed no encouragement; he was an old seadog who believed a captain's place was on the bridge.[278]

Late on the twenty-sixth, Swordfish torpedo bombers from HMS *Ark Royal* scored a crippling hit on *Bismarck*'s rudder. Lütjens radioed the homeland with a last message: "Ship out of control. Will fight to the last shell. Long live the Führer." Early on the twenty-seventh, as Tovey ran in for the kill, he flashed a message to his ships that lives on in Royal Navy lore: "*Get closer. Get closer.*" *Bismarck,* unable to steer, was doomed, but she could still shoot, her final salvos straddling both *Rodney* and *King George V.* The British poured hundreds of shells into the wounded ship, its guns now silent. It burned furiously, the hellish glow of the fires belowdecks visible to British gunners. Slowly, it began to settle by the bows. But it would not go down. Its crew attempted to scuttle her; still the great ship remained afloat. The battle, if it could be called that, had lasted for more than six hours. At around 10:30 A.M. the British cruiser *Dorsetshire,* already having fired 250 shells at a range of just three miles—point blank in naval terms—ran close in and finished *Bismarck* with two torpedoes. Lütjens, his premonition fulfilled, died along with 2,100 of the 2,200 men on board. The sinking of *Bismarck,* ironically, bolstered the old timers' case that battleships still ruled the seas. It had taken a task force of carriers, battleships, destroyers, cruisers, submarines, aircraft, bombs, shells, and innumerable torpedoes to sink the great ship, even as it limped along, crippled.[279]

British destroyers conducted a brief search for survivors, but fearful of lurking U-boats they soon departed, leaving hundreds of Germans behind in the water. Or so went the official explanation. Word had already arrived from Crete that the Luftwaffe had bombed and strafed defenseless British sailors whose ships had been sunk from under them; Dickie Mountbatten soon confirmed the rumors to Churchill. Both sides, it appeared, had jettisoned any pretense to gentlemanly rules of engagement. Late in the day a Spanish cruiser came upon *Bismarck*'s final position and found only hundreds of bodies bobbing on the greasy gray swells.[280]

There would be no sugar for the birds when Churchill addressed Parliament that day. Crete was on the brink; Cairo and the Suez Canal lay exposed. The Vichy government in Syria was thought to be welcoming German military advisers. Rommel appeared unstoppable. The ports and London had taken fierce hits since March. Leslie Hore-Belisha, a Liberal and former member of the Chamberlain government who fancied himself better qualified than Churchill to run the war, had made unflattering comments to the press concerning the "tempo of our war effort." The old Marxist Harold Laski had lauded Churchill as a "war leader." But

Laski—whose bushy eyebrows, plush mustache, long nose, and horn-rimmed eyeglasses qualified him as a double Marxist—cited production bottlenecks and lack of adequate evacuation plans in case of invasion as evidence of Churchill's failings as prime minister and chief administrator. The *Daily Mail* put it bluntly: "When are we going to see an end of masterly retreats? Something is wrong. Britain needs new ideas. She certainly needs a radical shake-up on the home front." Churchill needed a victory, and the sinking of *Bismarck* had given him one, or so he thought.[281]

At noon that day, the twenty-seventh, as he addressed the Commons, Bracken handed him a note. Churchill glanced at it, then told the House, "I have just received news that the *Bismarck* is sunk." He paused to read the mood in the chamber. "They seemed content," he later wrote.[282]

They were anything but. The Germans had lost a battleship; Churchill was losing Crete. Another evacuation—more flight than retreat—was under way. The British press did not, as it had with Greece, extend the benefit of the doubt. Opposition MPs, as they had throughout the month of May, expressed in the strongest possible terms their growing belief that Churchill and his coalition government lacked the ability to win the war. Defeat after defeat testified to Churchill's shortcomings as a strategic war leader. His status as the beloved and brilliant orator who had roused Englishmen was secure, but his reputation as warrior was not. He "is undergoing a slump in his popularity," Chips Channon noted in his diary, "and many of his enemies, long silenced by his personal popularity, are once more vocal."[283]

The leading critic was Leslie Hore-Belisha, who shortly after Churchill announced *Bismarck*'s demise, moved the discussion to the subject of Crete, telling the House that the debacle on Crete was due in large part to the virtual absence of anti-aircrafts guns on the island. He made a fair point. The defense preparation on Crete had been a sorry affair. Churchill, forewarned that Hore-Belisha intended to go after the anti-aircraft guns, was ready with his retort. It took the form of one of his favorite tactics, the bait and switch. Not for nothing had Churchill's dearest friend, F. E. Smith (the late Lord Birkenhead), once said that Churchill spent his entire life rehearsing his *impromptu* remarks. Churchill deflected Hore-Belisha's criticism by declaring that Hore-Belisha, in charge of the armed forces for almost three years under Chamberlain, had left them in "lamentable" shape. Hore-Belisha protested Churchill's slapping him with the appease-ment label; he had in fact advised Chamberlain to modernize the army and introduce a draft. Churchill responded with bare knuckles. "I am not throwing all the blame for this on my right honourable Friend at all—certainly not—but I think it is only fair when he . . . sets himself up as arbi-ter and judge, and speaks so scornfully of the efforts of some others who have inherited his dismal legacy. . . . I think when he speaks this way . . . it is only fair to point out to him that he is one of the last people in this country to take this line." Among the mumbles and murmurs an MP raised his voice: "No recriminations."[284]

Churchill had not finished. "The honourable Gentleman said something about no recriminations, but extremely violent and hostile speeches have been spread about, doing a great deal of harm." He cut to the heart of the matter, as he saw it: "The question arises as to what would happen if you allowed the enemy to advance and overrun, without cost to himself, the most precious and valuable strategic points? Suppose we had never gone to Greece, and had never attempted to defend Crete? Where would the Germans be now? Might they not... already be masters of Syria and Iraq, and preparing themselves for an advance into Persia?... There is... this vitally important principle of stubborn resistance to the will of the enemy." The doctrine implied by some members that battles be chosen "only with a certainty of winning" and that without such certainty "you must clear out" flies against the "whole history of war" and "shows the fatal absurdity of such a doctrine." It was masterful. With an angry rush of rhetorical questions and brass asides, Churchill had transferred the egg from his face to the face of Hore-Belisha, who had played no part whatsoever in the debacle unfolding on Crete. Meanwhile, Churchill avoided the vital questions of why British factories limped along far below capacity. He never got around to explaining why the AA defense on Crete had been so weak, although the answer was self-evident—very few anti-aircraft batteries were available.[285]

Although correct in his admonition to Hore-Belisha that in battle there is no certainty of winning, Churchill, having for more than a year applied his own doctrine of giving aggressive battle when possible, had so far produced defeats. He had lamented to Colville the previous August that in his first three months as prime minister, "everything had gone wrong and he had nothing but disasters to announce." The disasters had only grown in the ensuing ten months. Nothing had worked against the Germans, or against the Americans for that matter. The effort to bring America in proved an ongoing chore and so far as fruitless as the military escapades. Churchill's moods began to take greater swings than usual, and more often. He expressed to Colville his dismay that the rearguard on Crete of 1,200 Royal Marines had been left behind. It was a shameful episode, he told Colville, the responsibility for which rested with all branches of the Middle East command. He began to suspect that his generals, even his cabinet, lacked a fighting spirit. He held them all responsible for the misfortunes.[286]

He was worn out. Three days after *Bismarck* went down, Clementine convinced him to take a few days' holiday at Chartwell. The house had been closed, the staff furloughed. It would be a spartan holiday. After dinner on the first night, Churchill lifted himself up from the table, took a step or two, lay down, and stretched out on the floor next to the table. There, while Clementine and Colville played backgammon, he proceeded to doze, unperturbed by the rattle of dice. The holiday was intended as a much-needed respite for Clementine as well as for Churchill. But the weather was cold, wet, and deplorable and Churchill was, in Colville's words, "restless," "brooding," and "perturbed." He left for London the next day. Always irritable around his staff, his peevishness even extended one morning to Clementine. He became, Colville wrote, "morose at lunch when he discovered Mrs. C had used some of his favorite honey, imported from Queensland, to sweeten the rhubarb." Churchill, who had always mumbled to his ginger cat, goldfish, and ducks, now mumbled to himself. His health was taking the same turn as his moods. The head cold of early March had hung on, come and gone and come again, and at one point had festered into bronchitis, in part because he treated it with snuff,* which only made matters worse.[287]

He displayed no generosity toward his colleagues, especially Eden, who, after months of diplomacy in the Balkans conducted at Churchill's behest, was now soundly criticized by the press and Parliament. Churchill mounted no defense of Eden. Wavell, too, became a favorite Churchillian target, as did the press, the Royal Navy, and the "highly strung and quarrelsome" de Gaulle. The anger extended to Roosevelt's habit (according to Churchill) of following American public opinion rather than leading it. Desperate for America to get in, and frustrated by its inertia, Churchill told Roosevelt, "I hope you forgive me if I say there is anxiety here.... What ever happens you may be sure we will fight on and I am sure we can at least save ourselves. But what good is that?"[288]

With his defeats mounting, he took to interfering in matters best left to others. "John Peck and I agree that the P.M. does not help the government machine to run smoothly," Colville noted in his diary. "He supplies drive and initiative, but he often meddles where he would better leave things alone and the operational side might profit if he gave it a respite." The Admiralty, after the *Bismarck* episode, would have agreed, as would have Wavell. Yet how could Churchill give respite to his subordinates when Hitler gave none to Britain? The Blitz from April into early May had been as bloody as the previous autumn, with Clydeside, Liverpool, Belfast, and London hit. Was the renewed bombing campaign a softening up before

---

* Sixty members of the Other Club had the previous autumn each contributed one pound sterling to buy Winston a solid gold snuffbox known to have been owned by Lord Nelson, one of Churchill's heroes. A dip into the gold box would, for a romantic, invoke an almost spiritual experience. Winston dipped often.

invasion? With their Mediterranean positions tottering, with Hitler still at peace with Stalin, and with the beneficent spring weather upon the Channel, Britons could only wait for the answer.[289]

As if to confirm their worst fears, during the final weeks of May, no bombs fell on London. A hush of suspense—as Churchill had termed the uneasy quiet before September 1939—again spread throughout the land. Other than the occasional German reconnaissance plane droning high overhead, the skies remained empty. The silence was unsettling. Beaverbrook told his fellow press magnate Lord Camrose that the Germans "would launch a very full attack against us...in the next few days." He emphasized "in the next few days" and added, "In my opinion invasion is imminent," and although some people thought otherwise, "I know I am right."[290]

The Luftwaffe did not return to London in late May, nor in early June, nor again in any massed formations for almost three years. Sporadic night raids took place in retaliation for Churchill's ongoing devastation of German cities, but the Luftwaffe was moving east, toward its jump-off points for a far greater, far more dangerous enterprise. Unknown to all the Englishmen who waited each night for the German raiders, the Blitz, part one, had ended on the terrible night of May 10.

On May 28, after pondering for weeks the benefits to Britain of a violent German-American incident on the high seas, Churchill pushed the Admiralty to make such an incident happen. With *Bismarck* sunk but *Prinz Eugen* still on the loose, Churchill informed the first sea lord in a "Most Secret" memo of just how he'd like the cards played. The search for *Prinz Eugen* "raises questions of the highest importance. It is most desirable that the United States play a part in this. It would be far better, for instance, that she [*Prinz Eugen*] should be located by a United States ship, as this might tempt her to fire upon that ship, thus providing the incident for which the United States Government would be so thankful." By orchestrating "a situation where *Prinz Eugen* is being shadowed by an American vessel, we have gone a long way to solve this largest problem."[291]

Although Roosevelt would not have been at all thankful for such an incident, the previous day he had taken a significant step in the direction of war. Moved by the distressing news of *Bismarck*'s raid, he went on the radio to declare an "emergency" in the Atlantic. He ordered the U.S. Navy Atlantic patrol zone pushed as far eastward as the security of American shipping demanded, even if that meant into the hottest war zones near Britain. Since Hitler's U-boats did not operate in the western Atlantic, Roosevelt, by pushing his patrol zones eastward, appeared to be inviting a fight. More than eighty-five million Americans heard their president, at that time the largest radio audience in U.S. history. The speech interrupted the Dodgers game at Ebbets Field, the only instance before or since when an American major league ball game was preempted by a live presidential announcement. "Ladies and gentlemen," intoned the Ebbets announcer, "the president of the United States." Something big was up. Roosevelt was savvy enough to know that the mere interruption of regular broadcasting, more than his actual message, would powerfully convey his point, which was that America was almost but not quite at war: "It is unmistakably apparent to all of us that, unless the advance of Hitlerism is forcibly checked now, the Western Hemisphere will be within range of the Nazi weapons of destruction." He had not volunteered America to do the forceful checking— England was doing that—but he made clear that Hitler must be checked. This was significant. He had moved America a step closer to the battle.[292]

On previous occasions Roosevelt, knowing the effect on Americans of the terrifying newsreels depicting London aflame, tried to instill a sense of urgency in his countrymen by claiming that German bombers had the range to bomb the American east coast. That was a stretch on Roosevelt's part; other than Focke-Wulf 200s, German bombers lacked the range to reach much beyond the halfway point over the Atlantic. Roosevelt knew that no "weapons of destruction" would anytime soon arrive by air. After proffering his terrifying but impossible aerial scenario, Roosevelt turned to the Atlantic. The goal of the Axis powers was world domination, Roosevelt proclaimed; to attain it they must take control of the seas, and to take control of the seas they must defeat Britain. "They could then have the power to dictate to the Western Hemisphere. No spurious argument, no appeal to sentiment, no false pledges like those given by Hitler at Munich, can deceive the American people into believing that he and his Axis partners would not, with Britain defeated, close in relentlessly on this hemisphere of ours." His words packed punch. "Yes, even our right of worship would be threatened. The Nazi world does not recognize any God except Hitler; for the Nazis are as ruthless as the Communists in the denial of God." Roosevelt was prepared to start shooting in defense of international law. The mere threat of attack within the expanded patrol zone would henceforth be considered an attack upon America.[293]

Roosevelt had spoken like a belligerent neutral, and Churchill read too much into the president's words. The problem for Roosevelt was not how to provoke an incident, but how to avoid one. In any case, *Prinz Eugen* sailed home unmolested by the Royal Navy and undetected by the Americans. Churchill would have to wait for another incident to push America into war.

As the troops who had fled Crete regrouped in Egypt, it became clear to Wavell that the entire Middle East command—navy, army, and air force—was so wounded that there really were no further offensive strategic gambles to take. It was time to dig in and await the Germans, from Syria to Tobruk, where the Australians already were dug in—dug in and cut off.[294]

Churchill thought otherwise, and told Wavell "everything must be centered on destroying the German forces in the Western Desert." The attack, code-named Battleaxe, was on for mid-June. Yet by the first of June not a single fully operational unit larger than a battalion remained of the 60,000 men—the best in his army—whom Wavell had ferried to Greece in March. Two entire divisions had vanished. More than 4,000 British and Anzac men had been killed, 8,000 wounded, and 21,000 captured in Greece and Crete, including the Royal Marines left behind on the beaches. Churchill later wrote that North Africa and the Balkans were but two theaters that formed part of a larger theater—the Mediterranean—which in turn was part of the European theater, with the Atlantic theater on one side and the Russian, after June 1941, on the other. Churchill stressed to the Commons that operations undertaken with the best of intentions within limited theaters (Norway, Greece, Crete, North Africa) that resulted in disasters did not necessarily spell the inevitability of defeat in the overall conflict. Yet as he had told Britons a year earlier, victory does not accrue from defeats and evacuations. Since Narvik, Britain had known nothing but defeats and evacuations.[295]

Early June brought one small victory, but at the expense of further denuding Wavell's army. Reports had arrived in Whitehall for weeks that the Vichy government in Syria was allowing Germans transit to Iraq. When in May, Vichy armed forces in Syria disputed the presence of Free French and British troops in Palestine and Transjordan, Churchill suggested to Wavell that he conduct a surprise attack on Vichy warships moored in Syrian ports, "killing without hesitation all who withstand us." In early June, to forestall a large and dangerous German presence in Syria, made all the more easy by the fall of Crete, Wavell's colonial and Free French troops wrenched Syria from Vichy France. Vichy and Free French forces fought their own little civil war for a week, but in the end, the British occupied Damascus. In a letter to Randolph, Churchill chimed that Syria was no longer "in the hands of the Frogs." De Gaulle protested that Churchill had in effect stolen Syria. Churchill ignored de Gaulle; in fact,

he told Colville he was "sick to death" of the Frenchman. This was a sentiment he expressed with increasing regularity over the next four years.[296]

As the events of early June moved inexorably toward a climax in North
Africa, both Rommel and Raeder saw that the supreme opportunity was at
hand to crush the British in the eastern Mediterranean. Raeder drew up a
naval plan to attack Alexandria and the Suez in consort with Rommel, who
would push east from the Western Desert. Conceding to OKW the need to
go ahead with Barbarossa—they could not persuade Hitler to postpone the
Russian gambit, and knew it—they argued that a diversion to Egypt of less
than one-quarter of the forces intended for the Soviet front would deal a
fatal blow to the British in the Middle East. Churchill had been expecting
just such a coordinated attack for more than a month, warning both Roosevelt and the War Cabinet that the loss of Egypt would be tantamount
to the loss of the Home Island. It was a concern he voiced regularly, as his
fortunes turned upon his "hinge of fate"—the Mediterranean.

On June 6, Hitler told his Wehrmacht commanders that during the coming battle in Russia, the commissars of the Soviet Union must all be killed.
He added, "Any German soldier who breaks international law will be par-
doned. Russia did not take part in the Hague convention and therefore has
no rights under it." Hitler's hatred had overruled sound military strategy.
At the very moment when he could kill the British in the Mediterranean,
he rejected Rommel's and Raeder's plan to do so. He believed more important business needed to be conducted—the opening up of the *Ostland* to
German soldier-farmers, and the business of securing that precious farmland by killing the racially impure, the vermin, who stood in his way—
killing if need be all of the Slavs, Bolsheviks, commissars, judges, doctors,
teachers, and especially, and first, all the Jews of Eastern Europe.[297]

Summer was approaching, and shipping losses now far outstripped Britain's capacity to replace them. That Churchill's War Plans staff and their
American counterparts had been meeting and planning in Washington, in
secret, since February was comforting, but it didn't save a single merchant
ship. The Americans sent three battleships and the carrier *Yorktown* from
their Pacific fleet to the Atlantic, which boded well for Churchill's Atlantic
convoys. Unfortunately, Admiral Stark, who opposed these moves, kept
these warships near America's east coast, which rendered them useless to
the British. To the east, were Hitler to attack Russia, as Churchill believed

he would, Britain might find itself better off overnight, but it would be short-lived if Hitler defeated Stalin quickly and decisively—which many in London and Washington thought a good bet. In that case, the Americans might rethink the wisdom of supporting Churchill, and Hitler at that point would have won his war, but for a final stroke against Britain. Always the possibility existed that some unexpected event, somewhere, might alter the American outlook, either to the betterment or detriment of Churchill's European strategy.

Meanwhile, Churchill needed a victory against the Germans, a strategic victory, something bigger than the colonial scuffles of Iraq, Syria, and East Africa. Although always eager to make mischief in Norway—where Hitler now kept seven divisions—Churchill saw his best opportunity in the same theater as Rommel saw his, North Africa. Churchill had shipped new tanks to Egypt at great risk in order that they could fight, and by all that was holy, Wavell had better fight with them. He did, though he knew that the British tanks carried puny cannons and tended to break down. Wavell, his forces depleted by the misadventures in Greece and Crete, launched his counterattack, Battleaxe, on June 15. Rommel, his forces arrayed before Tobruk, expected the attack, and was ready. The attack sputtered from the start. On the morning of June 17, according to Churchill, "everything went wrong." By that evening Battleaxe was seen for what it was, a total failure. The end came near the Halfaya pass, where German 88mm guns, secreted in the brush, held their fire until the British tanks came within spitting range. The tanks advanced no further; all but one were destroyed. The survivors dubbed the place Hellfire Pass. Again the British had to run. They fled eastward, *away* from their objective, Tobruk, sixty miles to the west and still surrounded. Wavell, flying to the front from Cairo, found his army in full retreat. Rommel had by then cut the British forces in two. Wavell had no choice but to concur with his commanders' advice to withdraw. Almost one thousand British troops were left behind, dead and captured. The horizon was speckled with thick black plumes of smoke from more than two hundred British tanks burning like tiny oil refineries. The door to Egypt was open, and Rommel stood astride the threshold.[298]

It was the end for Wavell. As the Army of the Nile fled for home, Churchill saw to it that it did so without Wavell. On June 21 he sent a cable to Wavell in which he lauded the general's "command and conduct of these armies, both in success and adversity," but said, "I feel however after the long strain you have borne, a new eye and a new hand are required in the most seriously menaced theater." Churchill needed a savior of the Nile, a Nelson who, as Nelson had promised his King, would hunt down and annihilate the enemy.[299]

Just six months earlier, Churchill had told his ministers, "In Wavell we have got a winner." Now Churchill needed a new winner, a leader who would take the fight to Rommel. His choice was General Sir Claude Auchinleck, commander in chief in India. He had been criticized by some for his conduct of the Norwegian campaign, but Norway had been an almost impromptu gambit, lacking in air and sea coordination. Churchill was now intent on giving his new commander everything he needed to wage war in the desert. Wavell, in turn, would relieve Auchinleck in India. Colville thought Wavell might go into a sulk and refuse the India posting. Churchill pondered that while they strolled that evening in the gardens. Merely firing Wavell, Churchill allowed, "would excite much comment and criticism." He did not want Wavell "hanging about in London living at his club." Happily, India was about as far from London as any place on the globe. When Dill predicted that Wavell would "use his pen" to write up his side of the story after the war, Churchill replied that "he could use his too, and would bet he sold more copies." Where Dill saw Wavell as the victim of Churchill's strategic folly, Churchill told Colville that he "never really had much confidence" in Wavell, who he had thought played slow for many of the same reasons Lincoln had said of General George McClellan, "He suffers from the slows." Both Lincoln and Churchill harbored grand hopes of victories that never came. Yet where Lincoln generously supplied McClellan (who essentially sat on his hands), Churchill, after reinforcing Wavell in 1940, had since stripped him of his forces.[300]

Dill disapproved of Wavell's dismissal, but he disapproved more of the appointment of Auchinleck. Wavell, he told Colville on the twenty-first, "has got twice Auchinleck's brain." Auchinleck's first significant—and most fateful—decision was to appoint Lieutenant General Alan Cunningham, brother of the admiral, to command the newly renamed and soon-to-be strengthened Eighth Army. Cunningham had led the armies that had swept the Italians from Somaliland. He was a fine infantryman, but he did not know tank warfare. The Chiefs of Staff wrought a final change to the Middle East command when they relieved Air Marshal Longmore and put his deputy, Arthur Tedder, in command. This proved to be one of the more fortuitous promotions of the entire war. Tedder believed in using his aircraft in close ground support of infantry and tanks, a view shared by Dickie Mountbatten who, on June 21, told Churchill, "No naval or military operation should be undertaken without strong air cover." Tedder had developed the tactic—"Tedder's carpet"—of laying down bombs in front of advancing troops. Armies supported by air moved faster and farther, as Rommel had shown at Longmore's expense. Tedder, in fact, allowed the army to direct his planes in tactical operations, something Longmore never countenanced. Still, Tedder shared one burden with Longmore: he did not have enough planes to make a difference, regardless of tactics.[301]

Churchill told Auchinleck that he expected him to attack, and in the next two months at that. Auchinleck replied that his forces would not be ready until the autumn, at the earliest. Churchill fumed but backed off. He had no choice. His Middle East forces were denuded to such an extent that the question was not when to attack, but how best to defend. Such were Churchill's contradictions. Stand up to the Old Man, as Auchinleck did, and he might back down; failure to stand up to him (Wavell) engendered his disrespect. He liked fighters.

The unfortunate business of Wavell having been addressed, a large gathering sat down to dinner at Chequers on the twenty-first: Clementine, Mary, Ambassador Gil Winant and his wife, Constance, Colville, Commander Tommy Thompson, and the Edens. Churchill took the floor—he rarely relinquished it—and mused upon Russia. Days earlier, Stafford Cripps had warned Eden that Russia was weak and could "not hold out against Germany for more than three or four weeks." Dill thought six or seven. Churchill, having perused his Enigma decrypts, announced at dinner "an attack on Russia is certain and Russia will surely be defeated." Still, he claimed he was prepared to go all out to help Stalin. Days earlier he had told his military chiefs that he expected the Germans to very soon bring the war to Russia, with the Baku oil fields and Ukrainian wheat as objectives, and that Britain should "take every advantage which such a conflict offered." The greatest advantage would be gained by giving the Russians the help they needed. Winant agreed, and told Churchill that the United States, too, would send Stalin everything it could. When Colville suggested that support for the Soviets might prove problematic given Churchill's longstanding loathing of all things Bolshevik, Churchill replied that if "Hitler invaded Hell he would at least make favorable reference to the Devil."[302]

After dinner Eden and Colville joined Churchill on his nocturnal prowls in the garden. Colville had noted in his journal a few days earlier the arrival of hot and sunny weather; rhododendrons in full bloom, the heat "tropical and heavy with the scent of flowers." Eden, holding forth on some topic, took a step backward and tumbled "head over heels into the deep ha-ha* and barbed wire fence at the edge of the lawn." The three of them guffawed and traipsed though the moonlit woodlands, on the solstice, like the ancients, and fortified no doubt like the ancients by strong spirits. It was a fine time to be alive, Churchill told Colville, adding, "You will live through many wars but will never have such an interesting time as you are having

---

* Ha-ha: a deep garden trench, one side vertical, the other gently sloping, designed to keep livestock out of gardens. Popular since the seventeenth century, the ha-ha allowed for views uncluttered by walls or fences.

now." The Old Man, who lately had lectured Colville on the various invasions of Russia throughout history, somehow failed to note that this week
marked the anniversary of Napoleon's 1812 invasion of Russia.* The men
did not retire until well into the earliest morning hours, Churchill not to be
seen again until at least 8:00 A.M., for his instructions were clear: he was
not to be awakened before eight for any reason other than the invasion of
Britain.[303]

The skies were silent, empty of German aircraft, as they had been for the
better part of a month. The ports slept unmolested, London untroubled.

One thousand miles to the east, the engines of more than 3,600 German
panzers growled to life. Gunners eased high-explosive shells into the
breeches of more than 7,200 pieces of artillery; officers stood ready, lanyards in hand. More than 600,000 mechanized vehicles, their engines
idling, spewed exhaust that drifted low through fields and woodlands
along a front that stretched almost nine hundred miles, from the Baltic,
through occupied Poland, and south to the Black Sea. The weather held,
pleasant and breezy. The German army of the east, the *Ostheer,* 153 divisions strong, was ready. More than three million assault pioneers and
infantrymen (including fourteen divisions of reluctant Romanian infantry)
crouched behind railway grades and in shallow ditches. Men checked their
Mauser rifles and gave final nervous tugs to chin straps. They smoked a
last ersatz cigarette or gulped down a final mouthful of ersatz coffee, for
real tobacco and coffee had gone missing from their rations months earlier.
If the ordeal before them went as planned, they would enjoy both again by
Christmas, at home with their families, the war over, victory complete.[304]

A few miles to their rear, nearly a million pack horses—almost five
thousand per division—grazed on the infinite sea of grass. They were har-
nessed to wagons full of rations, shells, tents, and clothing. The metallic
ring of bits and buckles carried on the breeze, a familiar morning song to
young country boys and old infantrymen. Farther still to the rear, companies of *Einsatzgruppen,* SS killers, waited near their trucks for the word to
go forth, to carry out their orders and their glorious destiny as codified by

---

* Goebbels, in his diary, cites June 21 as the anniversary. Hitler, to avoid the obvious
comparison, later held June 23 to be the anniversary. Historian Will Durant places
Napoleon at the Russian frontier—the Niemen River—on June 23. It was at the Niemen that Napoleon and Czar Alexander five years earlier had pledged their friendship
for life.

Jodl on Hitler's order: to kill commissars, Jews, intellectuals, Bolsheviks of any age, and nationalists of any persuasion. Farthest to the rear, in the Reich Chancellery, Adolf Hitler paced, and waited.[305]

Seven hundred miles behind the Soviet lines, Joseph Stalin took his rest at the Kremlin. So sanguine was Stalin concerning his relations with Hitler that he had weeks earlier ordered Soviet forces to leave their concrete-reinforced and entrenched defensive positions to take up new positions farther to the east. He did so in order to reassure Hitler that Soviet troop deployments were not meant to be provocative and to show that he trusted Hitler. During those weeks more than eighty German reconnaissance flights took place over Soviet territory. They were dismissed by Berlin as a British ruse intended to create tensions between Germany and its friend Russia. Stalin bought the explanation.

Throughout the spring Stalin had received detailed intelligence reports about Germany's planned treachery from numerous sources, including the Americans in early June and his own chief of intelligence, who months before the invasion proffered the prescient scenario of a German three-pronged attack upon Russia almost exactly like the one that was about to unfold. Nothing if not consistent, Stalin ignored the warnings as he had Churchill's warnings of April and early June. When on June 15, Stalin's best spy in Tokyo, Richard Sorge, informed the Kremlin of the exact date of Barbarossa, Stalin, distrustful of spies, dismissed the intelligence. As for his trade agreements with Germany, the head of the German War Ministry later wrote: "The Russians executed their deliveries up to the eve of the attack." The Soviets had deployed more than thirty-five new divisions near the border during the spring, but again, in order to not provoke Hitler, they were not put on alert. Just after midnight on the twenty-second, a German deserter told his Soviet captors that the invasion was to be launched at 4:00 A.M. The report made its way to the Kremlin, where it was dismissed out of hand. Two hours before dawn, after phone lines were cut, Soviet commanders were finally allowed to place their troops on full alert. Just before 4:00 A.M. more than 2,600 German Messerschmitts, Stukas, and Junkers medium bombers lifted off from airfields in Poland, East Prussia, and Romania, their departures timed such that they would overfly the infantry and artillery exactly at dawn. In the Wilhelmstrasse in Berlin, Ribbentrop was curtly informing Soviet ambassador Vladimir Dekanozov that German troops in Poland and on the Soviet border were at that instant taking "military countermeasures."[306]

Minutes later, as the German aircraft screamed overhead, German artillery opened the greatest cannonade in all history. Along the entire line, almost three million German troops lunged forward. The eruption and flashes of the great guns would have been visible from space, but mankind was twenty years distant from gaining any such heavenly perspective. In those few seconds and within the choking clouds of cordite, the Nazi-Soviet friendship pact disappeared.

The Germans were arrayed in three Army Groups—North, Center, and South—commanded by field marshals Wilhelm Ritter von Leeb, Bock, and Rundstedt, under the overall command of Field Marshal Walther von Brauchitsch. Each group sat astride a historic invasion route into European Russia. Army Group North would ply the Baltic coast, with Leningrad as its ultimate objective. Army Group Center would follow Napoleon's path to Minsk and onward to Moscow. The southern group would strike toward the breadbasket of Russia, the Ukraine; its route demarcated to the north by the impassable Pripet Marshes—about the size of Indiana or Portugal—and to the south by the ridge of the Carpathian Mountains.

Arrayed against the Germans were almost three million Russians, 120 Soviet divisions out of a total national force of 230. The Soviet infantry was backed up by the world's largest, though mostly untested, air force—10,000 fighter aircraft—and almost 24,000 tanks of mixed quality, although the new, fast, and deadly T-34 was scheduled to roll off Russian assembly lines at the rate of 1,700 per month—*if* the factories survived the German onslaught. Sir John Keegan wrote that from the standpoint of matériel, "Stalin the warlord stood on equal, perhaps superior footing to Hitler." Yet almost five hundred of Stalin's generals had been promoted to that rank only the year before in an attempt to replenish the ranks thinned by Stalin's murderous purges. The new generals were all untested. Worse, they and the millions of troops they led were peacefully asleep at their posts when the attack came. Churchill, too, was fast asleep, as was Stalin. Stalin's lack of preparedness, and the immensity of the surprise that overtook him, indicates he had been in hibernation for quite some time. The Bear's somnolence, Churchill later wrote, was astounding, given the intelligence available to him: "So far as strategy, policy, foresight, and competence are arbiters, Stalin and his commissars showed themselves at this moment the most completely outwitted bunglers of the Second World War." Almost ten million Russian soldiers and at least fifteen million Russian civilians would pay with their lives in the next four years for Stalin's bungling.[307]

It was a "marvelous morning," Harold Nicolson told his diary on the twenty-second, "with the smell of roses, hay, and syringa in the air." If the day proved quiet, Jock Colville planned to steal some time to traipse the countryside. It was not to be. Just after dawn, a phone call from the

Foreign Office awoke Colville with the news. Heeding Churchill's standing order, he waited until just past 8:00 to notify the prime minister of the
attack. Churchill greeted the news with a grim smile and instructed
Colville to "tell the B.B.C. I will broadcast at 9 to-night." So great was his
initial joy at the news that he dispatched his valet to Eden's bedroom, bearing a large cigar on a silver platter, and a message: "The Prime Minister's
compliments and the German armies have invaded Russia."[308]

Harold Nicolson, upon hearing the news, told his diary that he was "not
so optimistic.... And if, as is likely, Hitler defeats Russia in three weeks,
then the road to the oil is open, as also the road to Persia and India." Gil
Winant at first thought the news was a "put-up job between Hitler and
Stalin," an opinion Churchill and his secretaries (out of the ambassador's
earshot) "laughed...to scorn." The laughter was born more of pure relief
than real scorn.[309]

Days earlier, burdened by defeats, his sensitivities scuffed by the increasing backbiting of backbenchers, Churchill ruminated over the fate of
Tobruk's garrison and the possible fate of Egypt while moping about his
Chartwell gardens in the company of his yellow cat. He apologized to the cat
during lunch for the absence of cream, the cat being seated in the chair to
Churchill's right. That week he told Eden that he now "wore the medals" of
the Dardanelles, Narvik, Dunkirk, Greece, and Crete. On the automobile
journey to Chartwell, Churchill stopped along the coast to steal a glimpse of
France, but as if to underscore Britain's isolation, haze hid the Continent.[310]

Everything changed with Hitler's betrayal of Stalin. A year to the day
after the French signed their armistice, Churchill looked eastward and,
haze or no, beheld salvation, *if*, that is, the Russians could avoid defeat.
The logic of the situation was compelling. Russia defeated would likely
lead to Britain defeated. But Russia supported by Britain might buy enough
time for the feet-dragging Americans to produce the tools Churchill
needed to keep up the fight. Were America to extend Lend-Lease to Stalin,
so much the better. Russia victorious was altogether another matter. The
ideological enemy of twenty years would not likely change its stripes after
the war, but Hitler's gambit had rendered that question, for the time being,
moot. Thus, without a War Cabinet policy in place to address the morning's turn of events—let alone a strategy to implement such a policy—and
after only a moment's thought, and no hesitation, Churchill made his decision. He would embrace his new fighting partner.

"Ally" seemed an inappropriate moniker given Stalin's brutal history of
pogroms and mass murder. The man, in fact, was a monster. His collectiv-
ization of Ukrainian farms in the early 1930s resulted in the death by starvation of at least five million peasants, and the execution of thousands
more for the crime of hoarding state property—seed for the next year's

grain crop. His Siberian gulags were packed with almost two million prisoners, mostly political, who were worked to death building dams, railroads, and canals. Mass graves lay scattered around Moscow, full of murdered Russian Orthodox priests, university professors, doctors, lawyers, Trotskyites, and other enemies of the state. Churchill, for more than a decade after the Russian Revolution, had considered the Soviet Union to be "the moral foe of civilized freedom"—until Hitler came along. Yet where Hitler was all talk during the mid-1930s, Stalin was all action. By the time he invaded eastern Poland in 1939, he had, in his own provinces and among his own people, established his bona fides as the butcher of the century, perhaps of all time. Churchill, since 1917, had striven to destroy Communist Russia, to "strangle at its birth" this "sullen, sinister state." Now the Soviets and British, Stalin and Churchill, battled a common enemy. Churchill that evening would try to convince Britain—and himself—that old differences must be put aside. The effort would tax even his oratorical skills, for in the eyes of fully half his countrymen, the godless Joseph Stalin was more fundamentally evil than Adolf Hitler.[311]

Stafford Cripps came for lunch that day, June 22, during which Churchill baited the ambassador by calling the Russians "barbarians" and offering that "not even the slightest thread connected communists to the very basest type of humanity." Colville recalled that Cripps took it "in good part and was amused." Churchill was roused. Reversing his prediction of the previous day, that Russia would soon lose, he offered five-hundred-to-one odds that Russia would still be fighting, indeed, "fighting victoriously," two years hence. He adjourned to his study to prepare his speech and remained there for the rest of the afternoon and into the early evening. It was a lengthy speech, an address at once lyrical, poetic, and powerful, promising the free world redemption and Hitler destruction. It was an address that no modern committee of speechwriters could produce, for Churchill painted with his words, creating images that, like all great art, become more real than the scenes depicted, and more evocative than the sum of his grammatical strokes and rhetorical shadings. Colville recalled that, as with his paintings, Churchill made revisions and added final touches to the speech, right up to nine o'clock, the hour of delivery. And as with his paintings, his intent was to challenge his listeners' imaginations and not merely their intellect.[312]

His pace was measured. The invasion of Russia, he declared, was one of the "climacterics of the war," wherein all of Hitler's "usual formalities of perfidy were observed with scrupulous technique." He tagged Hitler "a monster of wickedness, insatiable in his lust for blood and plunder" and "a bloodthirsty guttersnipe" who found satisfaction "grinding up human lives and trampling down the homes and rights of millions of men." The Führer's bloodlust, moreover, "must be fed, not only with flesh but with oil," an oblique way of saying that were Hitler to steal enough Soviet oil, just imagine the places he would go. And although he did not employ the phrase "unconditional surrender," he set out his terms of war, and of peace, which could only be termed unequivocal and unconditional: "We are resolved to destroy Hitler and every vestige of the Nazi regime." And: "We will never parley, we will never negotiate with Hitler or any of his gang." Britain would take the fight to Hitler on the land, in the air, and on the sea until "we have rid the earth of his shadow and liberated its peoples from his yoke." He took a few moments to remind his listeners that "no one has been a more consistent opponent of communism than I have for the last twenty-five years," but said that "all this fades away before the spectacle that is unfolding." Without naming Stalin, he declared that the past "with its crimes, its follies, and its tragedies flashes away." And then he treated of the struggle in the style of a perfectly scored symphony, where the spaces between the notes carry as much weight as the notes themselves:

> I see the ten thousand villages of Russia, where the means of existence was wrung so hardly from the soil, but where there are still primordial human joys, where maidens laugh and children play. I see advancing upon all this in hideous onslaught the Nazi war machine, with its clanking, heel-clicking, dandified Prussian officers....I see also the dull, drilled, docile, brutish masses of the Hun soldiery plodding on like a swarm of crawling locusts....Behind all this glare, behind all this storm, I see that small group of villainous men [who launched] this cataract of horrors upon mankind.

This was not a class war, he offered, but a war to rescue mankind from tyranny, fought "without distinction of race, creed, or party." And lest after such a performance Britons might still hesitate to fight and die for Stalin and his creedless Communists, he brought the Soviet battle home to Britons by declaring it "no more than a prelude to an attempted invasion of the British Isles." He closed with a message to both Britons and Americans: "The Russian danger is therefore our danger, and the danger of the United States."[313]

He had more than put in a kind word for the devil; he had rehabilitated him and outfitted him with wings and a halo. An old Balkan proverb (one of Roosevelt's favorites) proclaimed that it is permissible to walk hand in hand with Satan when crossing a bridge over a chasm. Churchill had just made the transit.[314]

Harold Nicolson thought the address "a masterpiece." Although

Churchill conveyed the sense that Russia might fall—and China, Europe, and India—"he somehow leaves us with the impression that we are going to win this war." Yet Nicolson believed the Russians, "incompetent and selfish...will be bowled over in a touch."[315]

Churchill again had displayed his genius for inspirational rhetoric, but a transformation of sorts was taking place. Sir John Keegan pegs the invasion of Russia as the moment when Churchill's "campaign of bold words" began to give way "to a battle of brute facts." The real killing—in numbers even Stalin could not yet imagine—had begun.[316]

Hitler's astounding betrayal of his partnership with the Russians paralyzed Stalin and many of his senior commanders. Soon after the attack began, a field officer used his radio to inform his superiors that his unit was under fire. He asked, "What shall we do?" He was told, "You must be insane," and reprimanded for making the call on an open frequency. Not until the Germans had advanced twenty miles did Stalin begin to grasp the situation, and not until late in the evening did the Soviet government inform its citizens that Germany had invaded the Motherland. Molotov, not Stalin, made the announcement. No official reaction to Churchill's speech came out of Moscow. Stalin remained in his dacha for a week, stunned, as Hitler's three army groups struck two hundred miles into Soviet territory. When Molotov encouraged him to return to the Kremlin, Stalin replied, "Lenin left us a great legacy, and we, his heirs, have fucked it all up."[317]

Such was his shock that Stalin did not broadcast any message to his nation until July 3. When he spoke, listeners heard the tremulousness in his voice and the clinking of a glass as he refreshed his throat. By then Finland had joined the German ranks and the front extended a further six hundred miles, from the Baltic to Petsamo on the Arctic Ocean. The Finns attacked the northern flank as the Romanians did at the southern, while the Germans mauled the center.

With the Führer's turn eastward, the threat to Britain of invasion vanished—for the time being. In his memoirs Churchill captured his joy at hearing of Hitler's foray with two words: "Eastward ho!" Yet on the morning of the invasion, his grin had been one of grim determination, for he understood that unless the Russians became the first Europeans to keep up the fight against the Wehrmacht, the consequences for Britain would, in the end, prove fatal. The Russians did not have to defeat the Germans (they could not), but they *had* to keep up the fight. As events developed on the Russian front over the next several months, Churchill stood firm on that premise. At an August meeting of the War Cabinet, he offered that were "Germany to beat Russia to a standstill and the United States had made no further advance toward entry into the war, there was a danger that the war might turn against us." "Standstill" meant stasis, which next to an outright Russian defeat was what Churchill most feared. "Standstill" meant breathing room for Hitler, but not for England. Weeks later Churchill telegrammed Roosevelt to share his concern that "as soon as Hitler stabilizes the Russian front, he will begin to gather perhaps fifty or sixty divisions in the west for the invasion of the British Isles." Indeed, Hitler had strong forces in the west, although the Luftwaffe had gone east, and the French ports contained few invasion barges. But that could change.[318]

Churchill, therefore, told his ministers that Britain must remain prepared to repel an invasion. He did so in part because the collateral benefit of preparation was the creation of forces that he could deploy elsewhere. Two memos that Churchill sent to his ministers days after Hitler's betrayal of Stalin capture the workings of his mind. The first reduces his invasion strategy to its essence. In it he told Dill and Ismay that September 1 would be a good date to announce that anti-invasion defenses had been brought to the highest efficiency. He added, "It would be necessary to make it clear...that meanwhile no vigilance is to be relaxed. On the contrary, a note of invasion alarm should be struck, and everybody set to work with redoubled energy." Then, to the real root of the matter: "This however, must not prevent the dispatch of necessary reinforcements to the Middle-East."[319]

The second memo captures the collision of logic, intuition, and imagination that made Churchill who he was (and regularly confused his generals, and was beginning to confuse his American friends). In it, he told Dill and secretary of state for war David Margesson that the success of German parachutists on Crete raised a new and disturbing specter: "We have to contemplate the descent from the air of perhaps a quarter of a million parachutists, glider-borne or crash-landed airplane troops." This was the aeronautical equivalent of his outrageous claim the previous autumn that 500,000 German troops could be carried to England by ship, in a single sailing. Churchill did not know the exact numbers of German parachutists killed on Crete, but he knew that of a force of around nine thousand, about half had been killed; of the five hundred Ju 52s that carried them, about half had been destroyed. This, to capture three airfields. The Ju 52, when configured for civilian duties, carried seventeen passengers. Lufthansa, the German airline, flew Ju 52s; Hitler's private plane had been one, until he switched to a Focke-Wulf 200. Configured for military use, the Ju 52 could carry about a dozen parachutists. Thus, at least 21,000 Ju 52s would be required in order to land 250,000 parachutists on England's scores of airfields in a single drop. Germany had built only about 3,000 of the aircraft since its introduction in 1931. But Churchill could not rest on the assumption that Hitler lacked such a massive air fleet; perhaps the Führer had been building airplanes in some huge, secret underground factory. Churchill's solution was to order that every one of the RAF's 500,000 support personnel, "without exception," should be armed "with a rifle, a tommy gun, a pistol, a pike or a mace" in order to greet the enemy when he came. If the enemy did *not* come, Churchill would be in possession of 500,000 weapons—made in America—that he could someday issue to his armies, when the day came that they ventured back into Europe.[320]

That day, he told Roosevelt in July, would come in 1943, after subjecting Germany and Italy to naval blockade and "ceaseless and ever growing air bombardment. These measures may themselves produce an internal convulsion or collapse." That statement captures the essence of Churchill's war strategy, and his faith in airpower. But plans should be made, Churchill added, to land "armies of liberation when opportunity is ripe." Those landings, in turn, would be spearheaded by thousands of tanks off-loaded from the special tank ships Churchill was asking Roosevelt to build. In coming weeks Churchill made clear where he envisioned those landings would someday take place: in Norway and French North Africa. In the meantime, Churchill told Roosevelt, he intended to bring his tanks to Cyrenaica, to battle Germans and Italians. Churchill's telegrams to Roosevelt in the weeks after the Russian invasion foreshadow a disagreement over strategic priorities that would bedevil the Anglo-American partnership for the next three years. George Marshall and his military advisers did not contest Churchill's call for tanks, especially as Churchill was fighting Hitler, where the Americans were not. "The tools" were Churchill's to use as he saw fit. Marshall and his planning staff had for months been forming a strategy in the event that America's civilian leadership sent the U.S. army into war. Marshall's preferred strategy was simplicity itself: Carry American armies to England, and from there take them to Europe by the shortest and straightest line, across the Channel and into France. This was the direct approach, versus Churchill's indirect approach, which was coming now into focus.[321]

But the invasion of Russia had changed the calculus of tanks and their deployment. Stalin needed tanks, now. For that reason, Churchill demanded that Britain must do for Russia what Roosevelt was doing for Britain—supply the tools, not only because to do so was the best way to help Russia, but because it was the best way to keep the wolf away from Britain. He knew just the man to produce the tools. Within the week, Beaverbrook took over the Ministry of Supply, which together with the ministries of Aircraft Production and Labour formed a three-legged beast that addressed the matériel needs of the armed forces. Immediately the Beaver ordered more factories built, more night shifts, and instilled in the department a sense of urgency he found lacking. The ministry dealt mostly with the army. When Churchill wanted bombers in January, the Beaver had delivered. Now Churchill wanted tanks, for Stalin, who Beaverbrook believed could survive if reinforced rapidly and heavily enough. Beaverbrook produced the tanks and in coming months persuaded the Americans to produce more, thousands more. "Some people take drugs," Churchill told Colville. "I take Max."[322]

By mid-July Stalin had recovered enough of his composure to request that Churchill establish "a front against Hitler in the West [France] and in the North [the Arctic]." By such maneuvers, he argued, "the military situation of the Soviet Union, as well as Great Britain, would be considerably improved." Then, either because he was still in shock or simply ignorant of British public opinion, Stalin proclaimed that such a front "would be popular with the British Army as well as the whole population of southern England."[323]

Thus began Stalin's crusade for a second front. Within weeks he enlarged upon his request by asking Churchill "to create in the present year a second front somewhere in the Balkans or France, capable of drawing away from the Eastern front thirty to forty [German] divisions." Stalin asked for 400 aircraft and 500 tanks *per month*, twice the quantities Britain had available, along with the delivery within three weeks of 30,000 tons of aluminum, enough to build more than 10,000 fighter planes. Then, Stalin offered, "It seems to me that Great Britain could without risk land in Archangel twenty-five to thirty divisions" in order to establish "military collaboration" between the Soviets and British on Russian soil. Churchill not only lacked the transports to dispatch thirty divisions—more than 450,000 men—to Russia, he lacked the divisions. Thanks to Churchill's "invasion scare" re-armament program, thirty just happened to be the number of combat-ready divisions Churchill had in England that summer. Stalin wanted them all.

Stalin's request, Churchill later wrote, was "almost incredible," and indicated "a man thinking in terms of utter unreality." Cripps, always eager to help the Soviets, suggested that Churchill display his solidarity by sending just a few British divisions to fight alongside the Russians. Churchill attached much irony to the pleas of Cripps and Stalin, because just the previous year there had *been* a second front, in France. And just three months before Hitler smashed into Russia, Churchill had pushed into *another* front, the Balkans, thereby buying Stalin several more weeks to take defensive steps. But Stalin, secure in his pact with Hitler, chose to sit on the fence as events played out in France and in the Balkans. Now, he had no fence to sit on; the Wehrmacht had obliterated it. Churchill told Cripps as much after Cripps called for a "super-human effort" to help the Russians: "It is not our fault that Hitler was enabled to destroy Poland before turning his forces against France, and to destroy France before turning them against Russia." As for any "super-human effort" "rising superior to space, time, and geography, unfortunately these attributes are denied us."[324]

When Cripps implied that the Soviets justly distrusted the British given Churchill's refusal to send men to Russia or invade France, Churchill—still fuming over Cripps's failure to deliver his April warning to Stalin—sent a scathing reply: "We have acted with absolute honesty. We have done our very best to help them at the cost of...exposing ourselves...when the spring invasion season comes." To send two or three divisions to Russia "would be silly" and result in those troops being "cut to pieces as a symbolic sacrifice." The Soviets, he told Cripps, had "brought their own fate upon themselves when...they let Hitler loose on Poland, and so started the war." That the Russian government would "accuse us of trying to gain advantage...at their expense...leaves me quite cold. If they harbor suspicions it is only because of the guilt and self-reproach in their own hearts."[325]

There would be no second front anytime soon. Churchill could not comply with Stalin's wishes, and the Chiefs of Staff would not, even had Churchill been so inclined. It was simply unthinkable, Churchill informed Cripps, to contemplate a return to France, where "the bloody repulse... that would be sustained" would result in "the loss of the Battle of the Atlantic and the starvation and ruin of the British Isles." The British Expeditionary Force had been swept from France in 1940 and again just weeks earlier from Greece and Crete. Churchill could do no more. Hitler, Churchill informed both Cripps and Stalin, had "forty divisions in France alone." As well, "the whole coast has been fortified with German diligence...and bristles with cannon, wire, pill-boxes, and beach mines." Any British invasion "would only lead to fiascos" and "would be over without them [the Germans] having to move or before they could move a single unit from your [Russian] front." As for a new Balkan front, it had taken seven *weeks* to land just two unopposed divisions in Greece. The best he could do, he told Stalin, was to send submarines to patrol the Arctic, and dispatch a few fighter squadrons to Murmansk, the vital and northernmost ice-free port in the Soviet Union.[326]

To the Chiefs of Staff he advocated less traditional means of helping the Russians. He told them to "make Hell while the sun shines." Thus Churchill sent his beloved commandos out to ignite Norwegian warehouses and blow up Italian bridges. The results were so paltry—one or two Germans captured for three or four British casualties—that Churchill demanded the cabinet keep all news of commando results away from the press. If the Continent was ablaze, it was at the bidding of Hitler, not Churchill. And Stalin was on his own, alone with his hopes, as had been Churchill while England burned.[327]

By September, Harriman, Beaverbrook, and Hopkins had made their way to Moscow to coordinate a rescue effort. Lend-Lease was Moscow bound. "You can trust him [Hopkins] absolutely," Churchill cabled Stalin. "He is your friend and our friend." Churchill, though disinclined to sacrifice British troops in France, nonetheless was eager to prove himself Stalin's friend. When the service chiefs objected that "not a rowing boat, rifle, or Tiger Moth could be spared [for Stalin] without...grave risk" to England, he told them he expected all branches to give equally, and generously. For the remainder of the year, he made up the middle link in a three-man bucket brigade. He snatched from Roosevelt the munitions he sorely needed, dipped into his own stocks of tanks and guns, and passed everything along to Stalin via Arctic convoys and Iranian railroads. To further encourage Stalin, he promised that a "terrible winter of bombing lies before Germany. No one has yet had what they are going to get."[328]

Stalin was unmoved. He had twice, while pleading for a second front, reminded Churchill that Hitler had already dealt Russian soldiers and civilians more terrible blows than Churchill proposed to inflict on Germany a few months hence. The Red Army, not Churchill's promise of a "terrible winter," was all that stood between Hitler and Moscow. To encourage his armies to fight, Stalin proclaimed his policy regarding surrender. Up to a point, his words echo Churchill's when Egypt appeared threatened: "Those falling into encirclement are to fight to the last and try to reach their own lines." Yet where Churchill declared that to surrender if not surrounded and unarmed would result in dishonor, Stalin declared, "Those who prefer to surrender are to be destroyed by any means, while their families are to be deprived of all state allowances and assistance." Lest anyone doubt him, when Army Group Center overran Minsk just six days into the invasion, Stalin recalled to Moscow the general in charge of the city's defense, Dmitry Pavlov. Pavlov and his top generals dutifully reported to the Kremlin, where they were tried, found guilty of incompetence, and summarily shot. Under Stalin, harshness in defense of the homeland took on new and unimaginable meaning. When he heard that the Germans were using tens of thousands of old men, women, and children as human shields, pushed along in front of the Wehrmacht as it approached Leningrad, and that the Bolshevik defenders of Leningrad held their fire for fear of injuring the civilians, he announced, "I think that if there are such people among the Bolsheviks, then they should be destroyed first, because they're more dangerous than the German Fascists."

The citizens of Minsk might have disagreed; the Germans massacred thousands when the city surrendered in early July. From the Baltic to the Black Sea a war of annihilation had overtaken the dairy farms, granaries, small factories, and mills of Mother Russia. The peoples of White Russia, the Ukraine, and the Baltic states now found themselves crushed between two unforgiving armies—the largest in history—commanded by two unforgiving warlords.

Churchill could not publicly excoriate Stalin for his myopia. He focused his anger on another blunder, one quite minor in the greater scheme of things. He just could not let go of Cripps's bungling of the April telegram in which he had warned Stalin. Cripps's delay roiled the Old Man well into the autumn, when far bigger fish were in need of frying. It was simply too much when he learned in the fall that Stalin had told Beaverbrook that he could not recall "when he was warned." A half year had passed since Cripps's error, and the Germans were by then hurtling toward the outskirts of Leningrad and Moscow. Stalin's lack of concern when given credible warning was frustrating enough, but Cripps's effrontery in sitting on his warning had infuriated Churchill for months. He told Eden, then in Moscow, that Cripps must bear "a great responsibility for his obstinate, obstructive handling of this matter." Had Cripps "obeyed his instructions, it is more than possible that some kind of relationship would have been constructed between me and Stalin."[329]

That was unlikely. Stalin's ongoing suspicion of Britain, not Cripps's blunder, stood in the way of a relationship. In July 1940, Cripps had conveyed to Stalin Churchill's warning of German designs in the East, which Stalin ignored and, incredibly, had actually passed on to Berlin in order to demonstrate his loyalty to Hitler. Cripps's tenure as ambassador was marked by a measured and perceptive approach to the Soviet regime, which he rather admired. This was not a surprise, given his political persuasions, too far left even for his Labour Party. Cripps was a lawyer, considered by many the best in Britain. But Churchill cared little for the man's legal talents; Cripps lacked the conviviality that Churchill desired in his companions. The ambassador came across as austere if not gloomy. He was both deeply religious and a vegetarian, a combination that had earned him around Whitehall the monikers of "Christ and Carrots" and "Stifford Crapps." Years later, espying Cripps walking past (just out of earshot), Churchill offered, "There but for the grace of God goes God." Yet many in Churchill's circle considered Cripps's talents wasted in Moscow and believed he could better serve the government in a post where his great intellect could be brought to bear. Churchill dismissed that notion, calling Cripps "a lunatic in a country of lunatics and it would be a pity to move him."[330]

The war had shifted east on June 22, and in so doing lowered the price

Britons would pay in coming months to preserve their homeland. The price Russians would pay was incalculable, but Stalin let it be known that price was no object. Churchill believed that Stalin intended to fight to the end. To read of his demands on his people, and his threats to those who did not embrace the sacrifice required, is to shudder, in part because his show trials, his pogroms, and his gulags were all manifestations of who he was—a stone-cold killer. He had murdered to gain power, and murdered to keep it. No colleague ever wrote of Uncle Joe, as Churchill's colleagues wrote of him, that he was all bluff and bluster. Stalin possessed none of Churchill's eloquence, nor anything that could be called nobility of character. He saw no need to inspire his people, no need to ask his people to give their blood, toil, sweat, and tears. Yet, whatever their myriad differences in personality, politics, and spirituality, and they were profound, in Stalin Churchill had found an ally who, like himself, was willing to kill as many Germans as it took to defeat Hitler. Over the next three years, many in Washington and London came to believe that Stalin, like the Bolsheviks in the Great War, would quit if he could find a satisfactory way out. Churchill never believed that.

Time magazine had just days before Hitler smashed into Russia noted under the headline of UNMURDEROUS WAR, the "most extraordinary thing about World War Two is not its speed, not its extent, not its tactical scope—but its relative unmurderousness." This proved a colossal mischaracterization when, within four weeks, more soldiers and civilians perished by fire and steel in Russia than had been killed by any manner of weapons in all the previous twenty-two months of war in all of the European, Mediterranean, and African theaters. And it was only the beginning.[331]

Stalin needed British and American help to make up his losses in matériel. Given that during the first seven weeks after the German invasion, only five American bombers were delivered to Russia, his prospects appeared bleak. Yet American bombers did not hold the key to Stalin's survival. Millions of Soviet foot soldiers, armed and clothed and fed by America and Britain, and backed up by thousands of tanks, held the key. Stalin understood attrition. His war would be fought hand to hand and street by street for as long as Soviet soldiers stood. If they could buy enough time, Churchill and Stalin had between them the makings of a lethal one-two punch. Churchill would one day possess enough airpower—supplied by American industrial muscle—to destroy German cities and every person within. "We will make Germany a desert," he had told Colville, "yes, a desert." Stalin, meanwhile, had the manpower to kill German soldiers indefinitely, if, that is, he and Churchill could buy enough time. America seemed to be edging closer to the conflict, yet Churchill had warned Harry Hopkins early in the year that in spite of re-armament plans, America was

at least eighteen months — more likely two years — away from full production. That would put America in fighting trim by mid-1942 at the earliest,
a half year too late were Hitler to finish off Stalin by Christmas 1941.[332]

On July 20 a dinner was held at Chequers in honor of Harry Hopkins,
who had arrived a few days earlier by way of a B-17 bomber. Hopkins
brought smoked hams, cigars, and pledges of support from his boss, but
carried no invitation for the meeting with Roosevelt that Churchill so
craved. That alone would have been enough to put the P.M. in a funk, yet as
frustrated as he was with Roosevelt's inertia regarding a face-to-face meeting, he knew he could voice no such thoughts in front of Harry. He could,
however, safely rail at the usual subjects — Mussolini and Hitler — and the
need for revenge, and he did just that. He and Hopkins sat up chatting until
almost 3:00 A.M. on the twenty-first, Churchill as usual doing most of the
talking. Colville recalled, "When Winston started on what he was going
to do to the Nazi leaders after the war — and the Nazi cities during it —
Hopkins said that he — Winston — only read the bits of the Bible that suited
him and they were drawn from the Old Testament."[333]

On July 24, Churchill received the invitation he had sought for so long.
"Harry Hopkins came into the garden of Downing Street and we sat
together in the sunshine. Presently he said that the president would like very
much to have a meeting with me in some lonely bay or other." Hopkins telephoned the president. Churchill was so enthused that when he got on the
line, he mentioned "a certain rendezvous" before realizing that the line was
not secure. He was mortified, Colville wrote. Mortified, but elated.[334]

The time and place of the meeting — code-named Riviera — were agreed
upon: sometime around August 9 or 10, at Argentia, Newfoundland, a
small fishing village on Placentia Bay. By August 5 newspapers on both
sides of the Atlantic, having noted the disappearance of both Churchill
and Roosevelt from their capitals, concluded a secret meeting was about to
take place, somewhere in the northwest Atlantic. The United Press called
it a "sea tryst." Although Churchill's and Roosevelt's staffs maintained
absolute secrecy, the boys of the press knew better, or thought they did.
American reporters believed they saw their president on the deck of
Potomac on the fifth when the presidential yacht steamed through Buz-
zards Bay, under the Boston & Maine railroad trestle, and north through
the Cape Cod Canal. But the man wrapped in a shawl and waving from his
deck chair was a Secret Service agent. Before dawn that morning, off

Nantucket, Roosevelt had transferred from *Potomac* to the cruiser *Augusta*, which was now pounding north through the Bay of Maine.[335]

Churchill entrained for Scapa Flow on August 3 in the company of Hopkins (just "returned dead-beat from Russia"), Harriman, Cadogan from the Foreign Office, and a bevy of private secretaries (but no female typists, for it was thought the journey too arduous for women). The Prof was on board; elevated to a barony, he had taken the title of Lord Cherwell of Oxford—a two-fingered poke in the eyes of his enemies among Oxford dons—as the River Cherwell runs through Oxford on its way to join the Thames. Inspector Thompson was making the trip, toting his trusty Colt. Churchill left his valet behind; the Old Man's wardrobe and laundry duties—which were prodigious—fell to the gumshoe. The military was duly represented: Dill, Dudley Pound, and sundry colonels and group captains from the Defence Ministry, including Lieutenant Colonel Ian Jacob, who accompanied Churchill on most of his wartime journeys. It was a retinue, Colville recorded, that "Cardinal Wolsey might have envied." Lunch on board the train consisted of sirloin steak followed by fresh raspberry and currant tart. Churchill took his with champagne. Jacob recalled Cherwell calculating on his slide rule (at Churchill's request) the amount of champagne the Old Man had consumed in his lifetime, given that he claimed, "I have drunk fine Champagne with every dinner for the past twenty-years." Cherwell's answer—slightly less champagne than the volume of the railroad car—was a source of mild disappointment for Churchill. He was in fine fettle.[336]

Late on the afternoon of August 4, the entourage departed Scapa Flow aboard *Prince of Wales,* its scars inflicted by *Bismarck* erased by new bulkheads and a fresh layer of gray paint. Captain Leach—the object of Churchill's wrath after the *Bismarck* chase—was in command. The ship ran fast, blacked out, and in complete radio silence. Were Churchill to need any medical attention while on board he would have to see the ship's doctor. Clementine had pleaded with him to take along his physician, Dr. Wilson, but Winston declined, averse as he was to the possibility that the American president might catch sight of a stethoscope following the British prime minister around. Brendan Bracken, newly named head of the Ministry of Information, had suggested Churchill take along cameramen and ministry scribes to record the important, though largely symbolic meeting. Churchill heartily embraced that idea. This being a sea journey, and his every move being filmed, he chose a naval theme from his ample wardrobe, including a dark blue Royal Navy sea coat—the mess dress of the Royal Yacht Squadron—nicely set off by a seaman's cap. Thus attired, he chugged up and down ladders and along the lower decks of *Prince of Wales* (rising seas having rendered the quarterdeck unsafe), looking like a busy little tugboat captain. After dinner on the fifth, the party viewed *Pimpernel Smith,* with Leslie Howard, before turning in around midnight. The seas grew heavier and the great ship heaved. Churchill, finding the voyage a respite from the confines of London, retired to his cabin near the bridge with a C. S. Forester novel, *Captain Hornblower R.N.*[337]

As the ship lurched westward, Churchill brooded over his prospects in the Western Desert, where his tanks had taken a beating at the hands of Rommel. He dictated a memo to the Chiefs of Staff admonishing them to "find a way to restore artillery to its prime importance upon the battlefield, from which it has been ousted by heavily armoured tanks." The father of the tank was harboring doubts about his offspring, yet he should have known after the lessons of France and the Western Desert that the skillful deployment of massed tanks counted for far more than the thickness of their skin. Sheer volumes of tanks, supported by fighter aircraft, could overrun almost any position. The agenda for the coming meeting included tanks, thousands more tanks, made in America. But how many would go to Britain, to be deployed by Churchill where he saw fit, and how many to Russia, where they were most needed?[338]

He therefore decided en route that he needed Beaverbrook at the meeting. The Beaver, asthmatic and claustrophobic, hated the freezing confines of bombers as much as he loathed being stuffed belowdecks on a ship. Still, he made his way to Newfoundland by airplane, arriving after a twelve-hour journey. The plane following, which carried Arthur Purvis, head of the British Supply Council, crashed into a hill shortly after takeoff, killing Purvis and his entire staff. The loss of Purvis (who had overseen British munitions purchases from America during the Great War) was "grievous," Churchill later wrote. When the news broke, Beaverbrook "made no comment. It was wartime." Beaverbrook, exhausted and not as well liked by the Americans as Purvis, would have to bear the burden of resupply alone, a burden made heavier by Churchill's long shopping list, the pages of which he separated with a little red leather strip on which were engraved the words "Ask, and it shall be given. Seek and ye shall find." Inspector Thompson, catching sight of the strip, remarked that the words were a good omen. Churchill agreed: "Yes, Thompson, I hope it is a good omen, for I have much to ask for."[339]

His sought far more than supplies. He planned to ask Roosevelt to take the necessary diplomatic steps—and military, if need be—to garrison U.S. troops, aircraft, and ships in the Azores and Cape Verde Islands. To do so would violate Portuguese sovereignty, but Churchill could no longer afford to abide by diplomatic niceties. And, given Britain's weak position in Asia, he intended to ask Roosevelt to issue an extraordinary warning to Japan: Cease immediately all further territorial expansion or the United

States would go to war. Churchill's motive was transparent. Any explosion in Asia that brought the Americans in against Japan could only strengthen Britain's precarious position in the Far East. He considered the present about as fine a time as any to force Japan's hand. To guarantee that neither Roosevelt nor the State Department diluted the intended message, he set about drafting the threat himself.[340]

On August 6, Roosevelt and Churchill sped toward their rendezvous, their actual whereabouts still unknown to the press. That day the editors of one of America's most widely read newspapers, the *Brooklyn Eagle,* concluded, for no other reason than "the inability of American and British officials to deny" the rumors, that a meeting was indeed about to take place. Two nights later, Churchill took in *That Hamilton Woman,* which crudely plumbed the parallel between Britain's struggles with Napoleon and Hitler. It starred Laurence Olivier as Nelson, grimacing behind his blind eye, and Vivian Leigh (Olivier's wife of one year). Miss Leigh's "dramatic progress," a U.S. critic mused, "has left her only a gender's distance from Mickey Rooney." The film, a romantic hash Churchill much enjoyed (he penned a congratulatory note to the producer, Alexander Korda), treated of Nelson's affair with Emma Hamilton, wife of the British ambassador to the Kingdom of Naples. The movie gave Churchill all of his victories that year; five times he viewed the movie, and five times Nelson emerged victorious. Churchill, Cadogan recalled, was "moved to tears" at the film's climax, when the mortally wounded Admiral Nelson is told the battle is won. When the lights went up, Churchill addressed some of the ship's crew who lingered in the wardroom: "Gentlemen, I thought this film would interest you, showing great events similar to those in which you have been taking part." Cadogan retired for the evening, leaving Churchill and Hopkins at backgammon. Churchill's luck was running strong; he took the American for the equivalent of almost two hundred dollars.[341]

Harry's boss, from whom Churchill sought billions, was known to display more talent as a horse trader than a gambler. Roosevelt was at that hour riding at anchor off Argentia, which as a result of the destroyers-for-territory deal had been transformed in just months from Crown property into one of the U.S. Navy's largest bases. Roosevelt had taken title in fair trade.

As *Prince of Wales* dropped anchor in Placentia Bay at dawn on August 9, Inspector Thompson offered to Churchill that the impending meeting with Roosevelt would surely make history. "Yes," replied Churchill, "and more so if I get what I want from him." Then he made ready to board a launch for the short trip across the water to *Augusta,* where Roosevelt waited. Bracken's insistence on filming the occasion paid off. Footage of the ensuing meeting, released weeks later, had the effect of erasing from the public consciousness the sort of suspicions such secret assignations often engender. Had the sound not failed on the movie camera at the moment of truth, Churchill's and Roosevelt's greetings to each other would have been recorded for posterity.[342]

There stands Roosevelt, near the gangway, his legs made stiff by the steel braces underneath his trousers. He grasps the arm of his son, Elliott, who is attired in his army service uniform. The president wears a light-weight summer business suit. He is smiling broadly, but the cigarette holder is missing; the absence of that jaunty prop means he's all business. And there comes Churchill, scrambling up the ship's gangway, resplendent in his nautical getup. A dark sailor cap is pulled low over his brow. He clutches a pair of gloves in his left hand, which precludes his doffing the cap, which in turn precludes the possibility of any photo being snapped of Churchill arriving hat in hand. He stoops somewhat, and manages an almost subservient slouch as he offers his right hand to the president, who stands almost a head taller than Churchill. Churchill, Colville noted, was keenly aware of the constitutional differences in the roles of prime minister and president: the British prime minister was the King's first minister but was not, unlike the U.S. president, the head of state, or commander in chief. Churchill, therefore, always gave precedence to Roosevelt. In this case, he also gave the president an official letter of introduction from George VI. Unofficially, Churchill and Roosevelt should have needed no introduction because they had met at a dinner at Gray's Inn in 1918, when Roosevelt served as assistant secretary of the navy. Unfortunately, Churchill had forgotten the meeting, a slight to the patrician American and just the type of minor itch that might have festered in a lesser man. But Roosevelt let the oversight go, and over lunch the two men got down to the business of Churchill's wish list.[343]

Roosevelt, however, had also arrived with a wish. He attached no specific conditions to it, yet his intent was implicit in the asking. If Churchill wanted to take home from Argentia news of American guarantees for massive amounts of aid, Roosevelt sought to take home something as significant, if less tangible—a joint statement of postwar aims. Both had for months avoided any public elucidation of their postwar aims, yet within hours of shaking Roosevelt's hand, Churchill set to work on a joint statement, in part to negate "all the tales of my reactionary, Old World outlook, and the pain this is said to have caused the president." Churchill, in his memoirs, took pride in having "cast in my own words" the "substance and spirit of what came to be called the " 'Atlantic Charter.' "[344]

On August 10—Sunday—the two leaders allowed photographers to shoot some pictures for the folks back home. Roosevelt, his staff, and several hundred American sailors crossed over to *Prince of Wales,* where

Churchill had personally choreographed a worship service for his guests, down to the details of seating, the hymns to be sung, and the order in which they would be given voice. He was seen to dab away tears as he and Roosevelt joined the ships' crews in singing, "O God, Our Help in Ages Past." "It was a great hour to live," he wrote in his memoirs, adding, "Nearly half of those who sang were soon to die."[345]

After the ceremonies, Churchill, Harriman, Inspector Thompson, and Alec Cadogan climbed into a whaleboat for a sojourn to the flinty and rain-swept beach, where Thompson observed a change in Churchill's demeanor "as soon as we were on shore." For the first time after "more than a year of some of the most crushing disappointments and reverses ever sustained by a single individual," Churchill seemed to allow all his troubles to "sink into the deep ocean we had traversed." He talked and talked and puffed on his cigar and pointed out sights to the group, and when the rain grew harder, he simply "cupped his hand over his cigar and went on talking and pointing and puffing." Here was a good measure of his buoyant mood, for Thompson knew that when in Churchill's presence "You don't talk if he doesn't." He was talking, and at a clip. Cadogan recalled the party spending several hours wandering along the coastal crags, Churchill "like a schoolboy, taking great pleasure out of rolling boulders down a cliff." He was animated; the meeting with Roosevelt was going quite well. Yet after two lunches, a dinner, and Sunday service with the president, Churchill was waiting for some sign, some confirmation of that which he sought most of all from this meeting: Roosevelt's approval. He soon got it. Later that afternoon Churchill learned from Lieutenant (junior grade) Franklin Roosevelt, USN, that the young man's father "said quite plainly and without reservation that you are the greatest statesman the world has ever known." With that, the granting of Roosevelt's wish for a joint statement became a sure thing.[346]

In its final form, the Atlantic Charter contained eight points, including the pledge that the United States and Great Britain would seek no territorial gains "after the final destruction of the Nazi tyranny." That phrase delighted Churchill, for it meant that America, a neutral power, had made what he called an "astonishing" and "war-like" statement of intent. Point Four had to do with free trade; specifically, it guaranteed that raw materials and trade would be enjoyed by all states "on equal terms." Given America's long history of protectionism versus Britain's history of free trade, Churchill winced at the implication that Britain needed reminding on the subject and gave Under Secretary of State Sumner Welles an earful. Throughout the 1920s and early 1930s, the Americans saw tariffs and protectionism as the best defense against trading blocks, of which the British Empire (with its policy of imperial preference) was the world's largest.

Now, to mollify Churchill and the Dominions, which traded with London on special terms, the president and Welles agreed to modify Point Four by adding the words "with due respect for their existing obligations." The negotiations over the fourth point offered insight into Roosevelt's postwar economic aims. U.S. economic security could only, necessarily, come at the expense of Britain and its special relations.

Point Eight as initially phrased also troubled Churchill. It called for world peace following the war, but recommended no means to keep that peace. He sought inclusion of a declaration of intent to form a world organization—a sort of League of Nations with muscle—led by the English-speaking world in order to guarantee the peace. Many in America wanted nothing whatsoever to do with any such international coalition, given the abject failure of the League. Still, Roosevelt granted Churchill his point (the establishment of a wider and permanent system of general security), which greatly pleased the Old Man because it amounted to "a plain and bold intimation that after the war the United States would join with us in policing the world."[347]

Point Three vexed Churchill most of all, for it contained the seed most likely to grow into bitter fruit. It guaranteed "the right of all peoples to choose the form of government under which they will live" as well as the restoration of "sovereign rights and self-government to those who have been forcibly deprived of them." Churchill saw this as being directed to those nations conquered by the Nazis; but over the course of the next year he began to grasp that the charter lent itself to a "wider interpretation" than he and Roosevelt had intended, or wider than he, at least, intended. The Atlantic Charter, he later warned Roosevelt, could just as easily be interpreted by Arabs as a mandate "to expel the Jews from Palestine." This Churchill could not abide, given that he was, he said, "strongly wedded to the Zionist policy, of which I was one of the authors." Most troubling to Churchill was the prospect that the Atlantic Charter might be cited by rebellious British colonial elements in Africa and India as justification for breaking away from the Empire to gain rights denied them by London. That is exactly how Roosevelt, from the start, intended it to be construed. Yet for the King, the cabinet, and the Foreign Office, that simply would not do. In any event, at Argentia, Churchill, construing the words in a manner to his satisfaction (*restoration* of rights, not the *granting* of), approved the inclusion of Point Three. Oliver Harvey, Anthony Eden's senior private secretary, called the result a "terribly woolly document." Eden, Harvey confided to his diary, felt Roosevelt had "bowled the PM a very quick one." Yet Churchill considered the Atlantic Charter as symbolic and nothing more than a gesture by the two leaders, a nonbinding piece of paper, ratified neither by Congress nor Parliament. "It is silly," he told L. S.

Amery, "to make such heavy weather about these broad affirmations of principle."[348]

Cadogan had attended to the nuances of diplomatic verbiage within the Atlantic Charter, fabulously so in Churchill's estimation. "Thank God I brought you with me," he told Cadogan, who jotted in his diary, "The simplicity of the seven word tribute and his manner of saying it were proof of its sincerity, I was deeply moved and puffed up with great pride." Such sentiments did not come easily to the austere Cadogan, who Inspector Thompson found to be "the coldest" Englishman he knew, and who had "a look that can wither croupiers." It had been fifteen months since Cadogan told his diary on the eve of Churchill's taking the premiership what he thought of Churchill's leadership qualities: "Winston useless....I am not at *all* sure of W.S.C." He was sure now.[349]

Churchill left for home with what he had come for: the promise of far more food, oil, and weapons. Roosevelt also pledged to replace the British forces in Iceland with American troops and to take over air and sea patrols west of Iceland, thus freeing up fifty British warships for patrol of the Northwest Approaches. As well, Roosevelt had agreed to voice Churchill's ultimatum to the Japanese. Churchill, in memos to the cabinet and to acting prime minister Clement Attlee, took delight in pointing out that *he* had drafted the warning. In return, Churchill gave Roosevelt the Atlantic Charter, Point Three and all. The charter was duly announced to the people of both nations, and the world, on August 14.[350]

Prince of Wales was on that day making for home, the seas still rough. The notables spent that evening playing backgammon (Churchill played rashly, but won) and watching a Laurel and Hardy movie and Donald Duck cartoons. When a convoy of more than seventy ships was spotted, *Prince of Wales* threaded its way among the freighters and tankers while Churchill, sweeping his binoculars over the ships, their decks crammed with airplanes and "cannons," declared the sight "delectable." After a stopover in Iceland followed by two more days at sea, Churchill reached Scapa Flow on August 18. The last British prime minister to venture abroad to meet a foreign leader had come home waving a worthless piece of paper. Churchill returned from overseas with something that would prove as valuable as Roosevelt's promise of untold supplies of weapons—a growing fondness for, and trust in, the American president. A friendship had germinated, and would grow, although, as in any friendship, there would be rough spots, in time, very rough. Churchill arrived home content, rested, and enthusiastic, and it showed. Cadogan recalled that on the train journey from Scotland, the Old Man "did himself well, finishing up with a Benedictine, ten minutes later he called for a brandy. The attendant reminded him he had had Benedictine. He [Churchill] said, 'I know, I want some brandy to clean it up.' "[351]

He arrived back at the Annexe on the nineteenth, "smiling broadly," Colville observed, "and still dressed in his nautical clothes." An ebullient Churchill told the cabinet that Argentia "symbolizes...the marshalling of the good forces of the world against the evil forces." He added, "The American Naval Officers had not concealed their keenness to enter the war." Lieutenant Colonel Ian Jacob, who had recorded the sessions between the American and British military chiefs—Churchill did not attend—reached the opposite conclusion. To his diary Jacob confided that "not a single American officer had shown the slightest keenness to be in the war on our side." Rather, the Americans "seem to think that the war can be won by our simply not losing it at sea." Yet Churchill and Roosevelt had hatched a plan for changing the course of the sea war, perhaps the entire war. Roosevelt, Churchill told the cabinet, was all for provoking an "incident" on the high seas and was prepared "to wage war without declaring it." That pledge sustained Churchill throughout the autumn, but in fact, the only thing Churchill had in writing from the president was the Atlantic Charter, which was, if nothing else, an eight-barbed hook on which Roosevelt could reel in empires, evil or benign.[352]

Almost immediately upon his return to London, Churchill learned that Roosevelt had reneged on the promised threat to Japan. Roosevelt's roar of the lion at Argentia, wrote his biographer James MacGregor Burns, "had become a lamb's bleat." Roosevelt instead tried to buy time by keeping up the talks with the Japanese, a process Hugh Dalton called "rather a humbugging negotiation." Several attendees of the Argentia conference told Dalton that "there had been a slide-back in U.S. opinion since May or June" and that Roosevelt's chance to bring America in had gone out with that tide. As for the promise of limitless supplies finding their way from America to Britain, the latest U.S. production figures showed a *decrease* in factory output since the first quarter of 1941, while only two billion of the seven-billion-dollar Lend-Lease program was actually under contract, not enough to make a difference if Russia fell.[353]

Meanwhile, the news from Russia only grew worse. Ultra revealed that the Nazis had engaged in "mass shootings of [almost 40,000] victims described variously by Berlin as 'Jews,' 'Jewish plunderers' [and] 'Jewish Bolsheviks.'" Hitler's armies, seemingly omnipotent, were hell-bent for Leningrad and Moscow. The Führer ordered that Leningrad "be wiped off the face of the earth." He soon decreed that Moscow be likewise erased. The situation in Russia was so dire that Churchill considered asking Stalin to destroy his own oil fields if defeat appeared imminent. He went so far as

to advise the War Cabinet that "we must be ready to bomb the fields ourselves if the Russians did not destroy them."[354]

W e have not yet declared or taken a direct part in a shooting war,"
declared a September 2 *New York Times* editorial. "But we have taken a
position which must force us ultimately to take such a direct part if our
present policy does not prove sufficient to defeat Hitler. It is a position
from which we cannot now retreat...a position from which the overwhelming majority of Americans have no wish to retreat." No one seriously thought that the "present policy" of avoiding conflict with Germany
while supplying Britain food and weapons would bring down Hitler. In
essence, the *New York Times* had proclaimed: We have taken a position
that at some point will lead to war, and we will stick by that position.[355]

    That line of thought held that America was a ship drifting toward war,
and that wasn't good enough for Churchill. To persuade Roosevelt to steer
America into the war remained Churchill's priority for the remainder of
the year. When persuasion failed, the utility of chicanery presented itself.
When his pleas to Roosevelt for more American naval action in the eastern
Atlantic went unheeded, he cooked up schemes. One night earlier in the
year, Churchill, Winant, and Harriman chatted over drinks about the benefit to Britain of an "incident" on the high seas involving a German attack
on an American ship. The U.S. government—at least Congress—would
have been shocked, and anything but thankful, had it learned that Winston Churchill was engaged in a ploy to precipitate a widening of the war,
at America's expense. His request that American ships locate and track
Bismarck had been an attempt to drag the Yanks in. As were his pleas for
American naval patrols in the Azores. Throughout the spring and summer,
Roosevelt refused Churchill's bait, and for good reason. The president had
no solution to the problems that would arise from a U.S. warship running
into the wrong German ship in the wrong place and with disastrous results.
Roosevelt could only hope that nothing unfortunate took place on the high
seas until such time as the U.S. Navy and the American people were prepared, militarily and emotionally, for war.[356]

    Then, at Argentia Roosevelt himself brought up the value of "an inci-
dent" on the high seas, and told Churchill that the United States planned
to put at least one U.S. merchantman, flying the U.S. flag, in every convoy
under escort by U.S. warships. The challenge to Hitler was obvious; were
he to shoot at an American merchant ship guarded by American warships,

he would face the consequences. Again, it seemed as if Roosevelt had given Churchill what he sought.

The incident duly occurred on September 4, when the destroyer USS *Greer*, while making a mail run to Iceland, made sonar contact with a U-boat. *Greer* notified the British of the position and waited for British destroyers to show up. None appeared. *Greer*, meanwhile, dodged two torpedoes fired from the lurking U-boat, while the German sub dodged nineteen depth charges loosed by *Greer*. This potentially incendiary business on the seas ended with *Greer* and its crew steaming unscathed into port. Roosevelt seized the occasion on September 11 to deliver another of his fireside chats, one in which he brought America nearer to outright involvement in the European war. Declaring that Germany was guilty of an "act of piracy" in attacking *Greer*, he unleashed American ships and planes for offensive action. In waters "which we deem necessary for our defense," he declared, "American naval vessels and American planes will no longer wait until Axis submarines lurking under the water, or Axis raiders on the surface of the sea, strike their deadly blow first." They would shoot on sight. By moving the American defense zone even farther east, Roosevelt had, in effect, declared "undeclared war" in the mid-Atlantic. He then proclaimed—as he had to Churchill at Argentia—the right of U.S. ships to escort any nation's ships, anywhere. Still, as he had in late April, he kept his warships out of the hottest battle zones—the Northwest Approaches, the Azores, and along the West African coast—where the dangers to British convoys bound from Britain around the Cape to the Middle East were greatest.[357]

"There has now come a time," Roosevelt told his countrymen, "when you and I must see the cold inexorable necessity of saying to these inhuman, unrestrained seekers of world conquest and permanent world domination by the sword: 'You seek to throw our children and our children's children into your form of terrorism and slavery. You have now attacked our own safety. You shall go no further.'" The United States sought "no shooting war with Hitler," he declared, "but neither do we want peace so much that we are willing to pay for it by permitting him to attack...our ships while they are on legitimate business." To that end, he asked Congress to amend the Neutrality Acts such that merchantmen could be armed (cargo ships were at the time allowed to carry only a handgun and harpoons). He wanted those ships, once armed, to sail under the escort of U.S. warships. Congress acceded to Roosevelt's wishes, in essence claiming sovereignty of the seas in America's name, another virtual declaration of war. Such measures as Roosevelt proposed were costly, but America now spent willingly. The production decline of the first two quarters was reversed. By September, the U.S. government, not even at war, was plowing

$1.8 billion per week into war production, more than was spent at the height of the Great War. With each new motion to Congress, with each new address to Americans, with each new contract let out for planes and tanks, Roosevelt edged closer to war, too close for the America Firsters, yet still not close enough for Churchill.[358]

On October 17 a second and far more serious incident than the *Greer* episode took place. That day, the destroyer USS *Kearny,* escorting a North Atlantic convoy, took a German torpedo in the side; eleven sailors belowdecks were killed. American blood had been spilled, but still Congress remained silent, and America remained at peace.

Then, on October 31, the old four-stack destroyer USS *Reuben James,* escorting a convoy south of Iceland, steamed into the crosshairs of a U-boat, which with two torpedoes sent *Reuben James* and 115 of its crew of 159 to the bottom. Here was the sort of incident that started wars. Churchill telegraphed Roosevelt his regrets: "I am grieved with loss of life you have suffered with *Reuben James.* I salute the land of unending challenge." But the *Reuben James* was not to prove the *Lusitania* of World War Two. Churchill understood now that only an incident far greater than the sinking of a small warship—which had been sailing, after all, in harm's way—would bring America into the war. He admitted as much when he told the War Cabinet the next day that Roosevelt faced "difficulties...as a result of the slow development of American opinion and the peculiarities of the American Constitution. Nobody but Congress could *declare* war. It was however in the president's power to make war without declaring it."[359]

Churchill knew after the *Reuben James* went down that this was a war America would declare on its own terms in its own time for its own reasons, or not declare at all. He thus advised his War Cabinet that "in the last twelve months American opinion had moved under his [Roosevelt's] leadership to an extent nobody could have anticipated." As well, he told the cabinet, the American "Navy was escorting the Atlantic convoys; and finally they were taking a firm line with the Japanese"—though a far less firm line than Roosevelt had promised at Argentia. Churchill said that it would "be a grave error on his part to press President Roosevelt to act in advance of American opinion." Not only would it be a grave error to press Roosevelt, it would be futile. Americans and their president were not to be pressed. On several occasions Churchill voiced his preference to trade six months' worth of supplies for an immediate declaration of war. He'd have to satisfy himself with the supplies, for he'd get no war from America, declared or undeclared, until America was willing.[360]

Roosevelt had injected for effect into his September 11 address a phrase that resonated with beer-and-a-shot Americans: "When you see a rattlesnake poised to strike, you do not wait until he has struck before you crush him." It was just the sort of turn of phrase, brash and dashing, that Churchill relished. Yet by November 1 the rattlesnake had struck repeatedly: USS *Greer, Kearny, Reuben James.* American sailors had drowned. Roosevelt's threat had been cold and clear, but while his actions, in relation to his words, appeared to be ambiguous, they were not: America had been attacked and America had done nothing.[361]

Back in May, a few days after *Bismarck* went down, Churchill cabled his thanks to Roosevelt for declaring a state of emergency in the Atlantic and for his promise of shipping more matériel, on American ships, to the Middle East. Churchill concluded the cable with the arithmetic of battleships in the Atlantic: Britain and Germany had traded great ships, but Germany could not afford the trade. Elated over *Bismarck*'s demise, Churchill ended the telegram with a prediction: "The effect upon the Japanese will be highly beneficial. I expect they're doing all their sums again." In fact, the Japanese had been doing just that for quite some time.[362]

The previous year, Churchill (after the Americans declined his request to rattle their saber on his behalf in the Pacific) planned to send *Hood* and a squadron of cruisers and destroyers to Singapore in order to show the flag and give the Japanese something to think about. That option was now off the table; *Hood* was gone. In late October, to discourage any Japanese incursions westward toward Singapore or India, Churchill dispatched *Prince of Wales* to join the battle cruiser *Repulse*, already on station near Singapore. He informed Roosevelt of *Prince of Wales*'s mission, and outlined his Pacific strategy, such as it was: "This [*Prince of Wales*] ought to serve as a deterrent on Japan. There is nothing like having something that can catch and kill anything."[363]

Churchill's love of the Royal Navy betrayed his judgment. A 35,000-ton fast battleship couldn't catch an airplane, and only with great shooting skill and good luck could it kill an airplane. Even after the British victory at Taranto, even after the disastrous attacks on *Southampton* and *Illustrious,* after the carnage inflicted by the Luftwaffe upon Cunningham's fleet at Crete, Churchill could not concede that an airplane armed with just one torpedo or a single five-hundred-pound bomb might be able to kill his fast battleships. That an Asian race might accomplish such a feat did not square with his belief in the stature of Englishmen and their warships, and the importance of both in the orderly conduct of world affairs. Churchill "attributed to battleships," recalled Ian Jacob, "a power...that they no longer retained."[364]

Churchill was one in his thinking with the old admirals in the navies of the Western world—including the British Admiralty—for whom it was accepted fact that successfully dropping a bomb from several thousand feet onto the deck of a moving battleship was a matter of chance. As for torpedoes, an aerial torpedo attack might prove dangerous on the open ocean, but in the navies of the world and among naval aviators it was accepted fact that in the shallow waters of anchorages, torpedo attacks were not possible. Torpedoes dropped from airplanes hit the water and descended more than one hundred feet before rising to running depth; when dropped into shallow harbors they simply buried themselves in the mud and posed no threat. Yet the British at Taranto the previous November had carried off just such an operation. In Japan, Admiral Isoroku Yamamoto and his naval aviation planners were duly impressed by the raid, and took note especially of the depth of the waters the British torpedoes had run in, just forty feet in places, shallower even than the waters of Pearl Harbor, home of the U.S. Pacific fleet. Some within the U.S. government grasped the turn taken by naval aviation at Taranto. Admiral Harold Stark, chief of naval operations, suggested to Admiral James Richardson, commander in chief of the U.S. fleet in Hawaii, that torpedo nets be strung at Pearl Harbor. Richardson, believing the nets would only get in the way of his ships, did not deploy them.[365]

Churchill, although he hadn't learned the larger strategic lesson of Taranto, remained mindful of remote strategic possibilities—however remote in time, miles, or probability. He had asked Eden early in the year what was planned regarding the 22,000 Japanese-Canadians in British Columbia were Japan to attack the Empire. "The matter is of course for the Canadian government," Churchill wrote, "but it would be interesting to know if adequate forces are available in that part of the Dominion. About thirty years ago, when there were anti-Japanese riots, the Japanese showed themselves so strong and so well organized as to be able to take complete control." The sons and daughters of those immigrants had since grown to be loyal Canadian citizens; a young couple in Victoria, Mr. and Mrs. Hayashi, that very year named their newborn son Winston Churchill Hayashi. In asking what measures were in store for Canada's Japanese, Churchill was a full ten months ahead of Roosevelt, who waited until late November to request from the U.S. Census Bureau the names and addresses of more than 125,000 Japanese-Americans—"Hitler's little yellow friends," *Time* called them—who lived on the American west coast.[366]

In Churchill's estimation, no flank should remain unguarded. Yet when Ismay suggested reinforcing the garrison at Hong Kong, Churchill shot him down: "This is all wrong! If Japan goes to war with us, there is not the slightest chance of holding Hong Kong or relieving it." Any imperial losses in the Pacific would be "dealt with at the Peace Conference after the war," presumably won by Britain. When it came to planning for contingencies in the Pacific, Churchill tended to shoot wide of the mark. Weeks after his inquiry into the Canadian flank, he ordered Ismay to "report on the efficiency of the gunners and personnel managing the 15-inch gun batteries and searchlights at Singapore. Are they fitted with RDF [radar]?" The question implies that he assumed the Japanese would arrive by sea. Some tactical situations demand a creative, counterintuitive approach; this was one. Churchill should have followed up his question about the fifteen-inch guns by asking whether Japanese infantry could negotiate the supposed impenetrable jungle of the Malay Peninsula in order to attack Singapore from the *landward* side. In fact, the new commander in Singapore, Lieutenant General Arthur Ernest Percival, had ordered a study to ascertain whether Singapore could be "burgled by the back door" and concluded that the entire Malay Peninsula, almost three hundred miles in length, needed more airbases, more planes, more tanks, and more men. He was ignored by London; there were no resources to spare in any event. London settled upon a scorched-earth policy for Malaya; if the Japanese came by land, they would find it ravaged. Even were such a policy successfully implemented, the Malay Peninsula stretched like a welcoming gangplank, right up to the gunwales of Singapore island.[367]

On occasion Churchill's strategic vision was distorted by his racial bias. When Harry Hopkins predicted in January that the incident that could spark U.S. involvement would be with Japan, Churchill replied that Tokyo must have been deterred by the demise at Taranto of the Italian fleet, which had appeared so strong on paper. "Fate holds terrible forfeits," he told Hopkins, "for those who gamble on certainties." Churchill believed, correctly, that the highest ranks of the Italian navy preferred to safeguard their fleets rather than fight with them. The Italians had paid for their caution when Churchill's English sailors and fliers struck with the "bold strokes" he championed. He simply could not conceive of the Japanese employing similar bold strokes against American or British fleets. Yet the Japanese had indeed learned a lesson from Taranto, and they intended to apply it. As for the likelihood that Japan would unleash its forces on British interests, Churchill had told Ismay, "Japan will think long before declaring war on the British Empire."[368]

In April, Japanese Foreign Minister Yosuke Matsuoka visited Moscow with hopes of codifying a Russo-Japanese neutrality pact, which by virtue of both Matsuoka's and Stalin's total ignorance of Hitler's looming treachery, it would be Matsuoka's (and Stalin's) good fortune to secure. Weeks earlier, Matsuoka had met with Hitler, who, along with Ribbentrop, planted broad hints that a Japanese adventure against Singapore might pay dividends to both Germany and Japan by virtue of dividing British forces and discouraging the Americans from coming in against either Germany or Japan. Ribbentrop dropped even heavier hints regarding the Führer's designs on Russia, implying that if Japan tied down Stalin's troops in far distant Asia, Germany could dispatch Russia, the traditional enemy of both Germany and modern Japan. But the Reich's foreign minister, a plainspoken thug, failed to articulate his message in terms that a sophisticated diplomat might understand, thus sending Matsuoka to Moscow firm in the mistaken belief that Germany, Japan, and the Soviet Union would for many years to come live together in peace, each pursuing empire after its own fashion.

On July 21, the Vichy government accepted Japanese demands for air and naval bases in the southern part of French Indochina. Four days later, Roosevelt announced an oil embargo against Japan to take effect August 1, together with a freeze of all bank transfers between the United States and Japan. An embargo on American scrap steel sales to Japan had gone into effect months earlier, too late for the Chinese killed over the last decade by Japanese shells and tanks that might as well have been stamped "Made in the USA" (the scrap steel also helped build Japan's new navy). Great Britain followed America with similar measures the next day, and on July 26 the Dutch government in exile in London joined the embargo. Japan, if denied Dutch East Indian oil—some of it so pure it needed no refining—could not exploit its conquests or defend its empire. On Monday, July 28, Dutch authorities in Batavia (modern Jakarta) ordered a cessation of all trade with and payments to Japan. Two Japanese tankers that had just finished taking on oil at Tarakan Island were allowed to leave. An American diplomat offered that the oil gauge and the clock now stood side by side; each drop in the level of Japanese oil brought nearer the hour of decision.[369]

In November 1940, secret and informal talks among the British, Australian, and Dutch had begun in Singapore with the intent of drawing up plans for a response to German raiders in the Pacific or to a Japanese attack. Previous contacts among the parties treated of the usual humdrum issues pertinent to powers in close proximity to one another, mostly how to stay out of one another's way. A second meeting had taken place in Batavia and was followed by a third in Singapore in February 1941, in which U.S. military personnel were present as "observers." At the next conference, in April, the Americans became full participants. Yet by mid-November 1941—after a full year of parleys—the talks had failed utterly to produce any plan to respond to Japanese aggression. The conferees did agree on one point: the need for reconnaissance flights in order to track Japanese naval movements in the South China Sea. The flights yielded nothing. No plan was ever produced to act in unison in the event of a Japanese attack, whether surprise or otherwise.

Dutch East Indian oil, Burmese rice, and Malayan tin and rubber were Japan's ultimate objectives, but to gain them, they had to locate and destroy the American and British Pacific fleets. The location of the former was easy to ascertain; in late November the American fleet rode peacefully at anchor at Pearl Harbor. Locating the British fleet was easy as well, because there was no British fleet to speak of. With ongoing losses in the Mediterranean, the British could not maintain in Asia any concentration of sea power that could fairly be called a fleet.

When it came to the prospect of war in the Pacific, Churchill's thinking throughout 1941, except for the final three weeks of the year, was sometimes contradictory and often naive. He admitted as much in his memoirs when he wrote, "I do not pretend to have studied Japan, ancient or modern, except as presented to me by newspapers and a few books." Yet he was one with Bismarck, who admonished statesmen to imagine themselves in the position of their enemy, "The Other Man." To be effective, such an imaginative leap into the mind and motives of an opponent requires knowledge. Churchill never lacked imagination, but when it came to Japan, he lacked knowledge. As well, as a Victorian gentleman, he thought little of the brown races, the black, and the yellow.[370]

He knew just enough to know that he didn't want a fight with Japan. A year earlier he had told Roosevelt that were the Japanese to thrust toward Singapore or the Dutch East Indies, "We have today no forces in the Far East capable of dealing with this situation should it develop." Months earlier he had told the cabinet that a Japanese attack on the Dutch colonies "would mean war with us." He did not believe they stood a good chance of beating the Japanese, and he told Ismay so. But, as with Greece, they might have to fight over a point of honor. To not contest a Japanese takeover of Dutch possessions would amount to "allowing ourselves to be cut off from Australia and New Zealand, and they would regard our acquiescence as desertion." Yet he didn't see the Japanese precipitating such a crisis. He had told Hopkins early in the year that if faced with the prospects of armed Anglo-American resistance, the Japanese would not come in. He clung to that opinion, despite the fact that Hopkins told him quite clearly that America would very likely *not* go to war with Japan over Dutch interests, or British. During an April War Cabinet meeting, Churchill expressed doubt that Japan would enter the war unless Hitler successfully invaded Britain. In cabinet memos to the Chiefs of Staff and Eden, Churchill claimed the Japanese would be "most unlikely to come in if they thought that by doing so they would bring in the United States." In July he reiterated his April assessment: "I must repeat my conviction that Japan will not declare war upon us

at the present juncture, nor if the United States enters the war on our side."
And, if Japan acted upon Hitler's suggestions and attacked British Asian
possessions, Churchill "felt sure the United States would declare war."³⁷¹

But why? No treaty obligated the United States to do so. And declare
war on whom? Japan, *possibly* but not necessarily, and certainly not on
Germany, where Churchill most needed America. Although Churchill
pledged to Roosevelt in late October to declare war on Japan "within the
hour" if Japan mixed it up with the Americans, Roosevelt had made no
corresponding pledge should Japanese armies pour into Singapore or
Hong Kong. A Japanese move against the Americans—which Churchill
all year made clear he did not expect—would not necessarily bring America into Churchill's war against Hitler. Only two events could bring that
about, the first being an act of war by Hitler against America; yet he had
already attacked the U.S. Navy three times without triggering a declaration of war. The second scenario would find Hitler declaring war on the
United States in support of his Asian ally were Japan to attack America.
The latter possibility, an invitation to ultimate German and Japanese obliteration, was almost too preposterous even for Churchill to contemplate,
for only a fool or a madman would declare war on America where no state
of war existed. And yet, Churchill long held to another maxim regarding
the human condition and warfare: "Madness is however an affliction
which in war carries with it the advantage of surprise."³⁷²

Thanks to the Bletchley crowd, Churchill had known since August that
Josef ("Sepp") Dietrich, a general in the Waffen-SS and one of Hitler's oldest favorite cronies, had assured the Japanese ambassador in Berlin—in
Hitler's name—that "Germany would at once declare hostilities in the
event of a collision between Japan and the United States." Hitler would
prove himself a madman later in the war, but in 1941 he was on top of his
game. Given his craftiness and pathological willingness to lie, his message
to the Japanese, relayed through Dietrich, meant everything, and nothing.
The Führer might join the Japanese if they attacked British or American
interests; then again, he might not.³⁷³

Churchill told the War Cabinet in November that he did not want to be
boxed in by "an automatic declaration of war" against Japan that would
"give the anti-British party [American isolationists] cause for saying that
the United States were again being dragged into a British colonial war." By
then he understood that America had to go in first, and that nothing short
of an attack against America could bring that about.³⁷⁴

Throughout most of 1941, Churchill ascribed to Japan sober enough
judgment to not willingly and with forethought provoke the Americans into
war, an opinion shared by the American isolationists. Robert McCormick's
Tribune declared in late October that Japan "cannot attack us" and that

Pearl Harbor "is beyond the effective striking power of her fleet." Yet Churchill also understood that Roosevelt's ban on oil sales to Japan had been a virtual act of war, one that Japan's war minister, Hedeki Tojo, could not abide, for reasons of both national pride and national survival. Tojo's elevation to prime minister (he remained war minister, as well) in mid-October should have served to close the debate on Japan's immediate inclinations; the war faction in Tokyo had swept away all of the moderates. For Tojo, if the stakes were Japan's survival, which they now were, any distance and any objective, including Pearl Harbor, four thousand miles from Tokyo, must be overcome. McCormick, his head in the sand, can be forgiven his limited vision. But Churchill should have seen Tojo coming. American oil had propelled the Japanese navy for years, until just five months earlier. Only the Dutch East Indies could now supply that oil. And in order to take the Dutch refineries, the Japanese would first have to take Singapore.[375]

Yet Churchill considered the Japanese to be an obedient and compliant race, which, once warned against aggression, as he had done, would heed the warnings. Hugh Dalton, who thought Churchill's demeaning public references to the Japanese "rude," captured the essence of the Old Man's rationale: "The PM does not think the Japs will go to war with us," because he had given the Japanese "very serious warnings" against further aggression in the Pacific.[376]

That Churchill spoke of the Japanese as he might of little children, and to further presume that continued Japanese pursuit of an Asian empire could be forestalled by his "very serious warnings," and to still further presume that Japan's strategic plan was somehow conditional on Hitler's successful invasion of Britain, betrays a dangerous Anglocentric naïveté. Britain was Churchill's Home Island; the British Empire, including the autonomous commonwealths, spanned the globe, which made Britain, in that sense, the world's only global power. Although England's geographical position, within sight of the French coast, was strategically critical to Hitler, it was not to Tojo. Singapore held far more significance than London for the Japanese.

Singapore's six-year-old naval base—twenty-six square miles of protected anchorage, and built to send a clear message to Japan—straddled the sea-lanes to and from the resources Japan most needed, Dutch East Indies oil and Malaya rubber. It had been Hitler's strategic misfortune to knock his head against the unyielding wall of fortress Britain for more than a year. Singapore, for the Japanese, was another matter entirely. It was many things—symbolic of British imperial might, one of the world's great harbors—but given its defenses, it was no fortress. Churchill considered Singapore his Far Eastern jewel. Tojo considered it as nothing more than a target of opportunity.

Throughout November, in a furious flow of telegraphic traffic, Churchill and Roosevelt discussed, and pondered, Japan. The British, having been given access to the American Magic intelligence (which decrypted Japanese diplomatic messages, but not Japanese military communications), could read the tea leaves as well as the Americans could. The Magic decrypts hinted that Japan might take extreme but unspecified measures were its demands—including Japanese hegemony in China—not met. Still, the Americans and Japanese held talks in Washington, with Roosevelt keeping Churchill apprised of the progress or lack thereof. Japanese ambassador Numura and special envoy Saburu Kurusu presented U.S. secretary of state Cordell Hull a modus vivendi that "might give the Japanese government opportunity to develop public sentiment in Japan in support of a... comprehensive program of peace." Roosevelt considered the proposals inadequate and "not in harmony" with America's "fundamental principles" and demands. " I am not very hopeful," he cabled Churchill on November 24, "and we must all be prepared for real trouble, possibly soon."[377]

On Sunday, November 30, Churchill turned sixty-seven. He was now just three years shy of the Bible's allotted three score and ten years, and by any measure, biblical or actuarial, he was indeed an old man. He looked it. His face was deeply creased; his fair skin, which had always exuded a healthy glow, seemed pinched and parched. His stoop was more pronounced. He wore his scowl in public and in the Commons, for the benefit of the press photographers, who that year rarely captured him with any other expression. Before he retired to bed in the early hours of his birthday he cabled Roosevelt—his junior by almost eight years—and again, as he had in May, with full knowledge of Roosevelt's "constitutional difficulties" asked the president—in a roundabout way—to declare war, this time against Japan. The plan, as Churchill outlined it, would have Roosevelt tell the Japanese that any further aggression, anywhere and against anyone, would result in Roosevelt placing "the gravest issues before Congress, or words to that effect." Churchill, as he had in May, apologized to Roosevelt for the temerity of his suggestion, which given the very real constitutional restraints Roosevelt indeed labored under was impossible to execute. "Forgive me, my dear friend," he wrote, "for presuming to press such a course upon you, but I am convinced that it might make all the difference and prevent a melancholy extension of the war."[378]

Birthday salutations arrived from around the world. The King and Queen sent along greetings in a message that would have been a firing offense for a

Hallmark copywriter: "Many happy returns on the day from us both." Churchill dutifully thanked Their Majesties for the "charming message which I received and read with great pleasure." Beaverbrook dispatched a rather more emotional message: "This letter carries Birthday greetings of a difficult colleague & devoted follower.... For those who have served you it will be sufficient glory to be known as Churchill's man." And from Harry Hopkins: "Dear Winston. Happy birthday. How old are you anyway?"[379]

Dill sent greetings, a gentlemanly gesture given that Churchill had just two weeks earlier approved the general's promotion to field marshal and then sacked him. Their relationship had long been unsatisfactory, with Dill unwilling to stand up to Churchill, who was unwilling to appreciate Dill's caution in the face of overwhelming German military superiority in Russia, where Dill foresaw likely defeat for Stalin. That Dill was sixty, the mandatory retirement age for regular army officers, offered Churchill a convenient means of easing him out.* He chose not to consult Eden in the matter. When Eden, who thought Churchill underrated Dill (the P.M. called him "Dilly-Dally"), expressed his chagrin for sacking the CIGS without consulting the Foreign Office, the Old Man replied that he had done so because "I know you will not agree." That was how he conducted his business. When a subordinate objected to a scheme, Churchill badgered the protester. When a subordinate gave in without a fight, Churchill doubted the man's fighting spirit. Colville had noted two months earlier that Churchill's dagger was in Dill's back; in late November he gave it the final twist.[380]

Dill's replacement as CIGS was the commander in chief of Home Forces, General Sir Alan Brooke, a slim fifty-seven-year-old Ulsterman and soon to be the most famous of the Brookes of Colebrooke, a family long known for its military service to the Crown. Twenty-six members of his Ulster clan had fought in the Great War, twenty-seven were fighting in World War Two. The Brookes embodied the spirit of Cuchulain, the mythical Ulster warrior hero; they lived to fight.

Knighted for his heroics at Dunkirk, Sir Alan Brooke was an outdoorsman and avid bird-watcher. In the opinion of Bernard Montgomery, he proved himself "the greatest soldier—soldier, sailor, airman—produced by any country" during the war. Brooke told his diary that he was wary of

---

* Churchill planned to promote Dill to field marshal and ship him to Bombay, a consolation prize for the old soldier, but after Argentia, where Dill displayed an easy ability to get along with the Americans, especially Marshall, Churchill took the new field marshal with him to Washington in late December, there to leave him as liaison to the American chiefs. Dill became, in the estimation of George Marshall and Roosevelt, one of the primary talents of the war, instrumental in creating a genuine working relationship between the Americans and British.

Churchill's "impetuous nature, his gambler's spirit, and his determination
to follow his own selected path at all costs." Brooke ("Brookie" to his
friends) was not a churchgoing man, but upon Churchill's elevating him to
CIGS, the new chief's "first impulse was to kneel down and pray to God
for guidance and support" in working with Churchill. His new boss had
his own reservations about Brooke: "I know these Brookes," Churchill
told Ismay, "stiff necked Ulstermen, and there's no one worse to deal with
than that." Actually, Brooke's older brother Victor had been Churchill's
best friend in India, and Alan Brooke had commanded II Corps in France
with honor and distinction. Like Churchill, he did not countenance woolly
thinking. His usual rejoinder in a debate was brutally straightforward— "I
flatly disagree," often accompanied by the snapping of a pencil. His nickname in the War Office was Colonel Shrapnel. He combined prudence and
rigor; he was both feared and liked by his men. He disliked flamboyance,
and therefore disliked Churchill's cronies, especially Beaverbrook. Brooke
found himself "revolted" one evening at Chequers as Beaverbrook poured
"himself one strong whiskey after another....The more I saw of him
throughout the war, the more I disliked and distrusted him." For Brooke,
self-control was a duty, for Churchill, an impediment to life's joys. Both
men tended to demean lesser minds, and both, having experienced the
slaughter of the Great War (Brooke at the Somme), resisted any strategic
initiatives that might result in static lines and a repetition of that slaughter.
Both were stubborn. In the years to come when Brooke went up against
Churchill, he always gave as good as he got. Brooke, too, sent along birthday greetings.[381]

Jock Colville had not sent a birthday message, busy as he was earning
two shillings a day as a pilot trainee in the RAF. Churchill, over the objections of Eden, had in September finally given his blessings to Colville's aviation ambitions, telling the young secretary that his patriotism was
"gallant." When they said their good-byes in the Cabinet Room, Churchill
offered his hand and parting words: "I have the greatest affection for you;
we all have, Clemmie and I especially. Goodbye and God bless you."
Colville departed with "a lump in my throat such that I had not had for
many years." Within several weeks, somebody with great influence prevailed upon the Treasury to raise Colville's pay to the £400 per year he had
earned while on Churchill's staff.[382]

L. S. Amery, in a birthday tribute voiced during a BBC broadcast, called
Churchill "the spirit of old England incarnate, with its unshakeable self-
confidence, its grim gaiety, its unfailing sense of humour...its unflinching
tenacity. Against that inner unity of spirit between leader and nation the
ill-cemented fabric of Hitler's perversion of the German soul must be shattered in the end."[383]

Tojo's ongoing perversion of the Japanese soul was manifested by his threats that week to cut the Burma Road in order to inflict new terrors upon the Yunnan province of China. Chiang Kai-shek appealed to Churchill for help, specifically to fill the Burma Road with trucks bearing arms. Churchill had to inform Chiang that no help would be forthcoming. As he explained to Roosevelt, Britain was "tied up elsewhere." Tied down, tied up, it was all the same—he lacked the means to further his own cause, let alone Chiang's. Ever optimistic, Churchill was pleased that Emperor Hirohito appeared to be "exercising restraint" even though the Anglo-American embargo was "forcing Japan to decisions of peace and war." He was correct, but Tojo, not the poetically inclined Hirohito, would make the final decision. Churchill, clinging to his belief that the Japanese would pursue a sane course in the Pacific, ended his message to Roosevelt with a prediction: "I think myself that Japan is more likely to drift into war than to plunge in."[384]

On his birthday he told the War Office that war with Japan would "prejudice our chances of defeating Germany." Above all, he advised, "Our policy must . . . be avoidance of war with Japan." But that choice—war or peace in the Pacific—rested entirely with Japan.[385]

Churchill had much to be grateful for; he was in good health, Clementine and the children likewise. Mary, just eighteen, had enlisted in the Auxiliary Territorial Service and was posted to an AA battery near Enfield. Randolph was back behind the lines in Cairo after seeing action in the Western Desert. He had been promoted to major and made a press liaison, a safe posting that afforded him nightly opportunities to drink, gamble (without success), and chase women. To his father Randolph conveyed his "love and deepest admiration." Diana, prone as was her mother to severe bouts of nervous tension, did her duty as an air-raid warden, an unlikely sight, Sarah recalled, dressed in trousers and high heels. She also had been keeping vigil for months at the bedside of her husband, Duncan Sandys, as he recovered after suffering crushed legs in an auto accident. Sandys, wounded in the abortive Norway operation, had harbored hopes of returning to the field, until the car crash. He had since resumed work on his radar and anti-aircraft projects, including rockets, for which he had developed an affinity. Churchill sought to appoint Sandys under secretary for foreign affairs, a critical position, and one for which Sandys possessed no qualifications. Eden objected. Churchill dropped the scheme but brought Sandys into the War Office, an act of such flagrant nepotism that John Peck offered Colville five pounds if he suggested to the Old Man that Vic Oliver be made head of the Ministry of Information.[386]

Vic Oliver sent birthday greetings but had months earlier gone his own way when he and Sarah parted company for good. Clementine had grown fond of Vic, but Churchill had never bothered to get to know him. Sarah, commissioned in the Woman's Auxiliary Air Force, applied herself to learning the skills of photographic interpretation. Her acting career, such as it was, would have to remain on ice for the duration, but she had never possessed either great talent or a great following, and would never do so. She did possess and heavily indulged an affinity for fine wine and good liquor, but unlike her father did not possess the requisite metabolic talent to both drink freely and function flawlessly. She was stubborn, like her father, and Churchill had long ago given her the nickname, "The Mule." It stuck. Churchill expressed his pride at The Mule's secret work, but other than an occasional dinner at Chequers, Sarah—in fact, all of the children—had seen little of their father that year. For that matter, Clementine did not see all that much of her husband.[387]

She found succor in her relief work. She was the driving force behind the Aid to Russia Fund, which by war's end raised more than £8 million for Russian relief, mostly from factory workers, although several well-heeled Tories wrote checks for more than £200,000. Mary found her mother to be "desperately tired, both physically and mentally" from the "strain of her social and domestic life." The reference to the strain of Clemmie's domestic life was Mary's delicate way of implying that her mother suffered from nervous tension and that her parents' relationship bore little resemblance to anything recognizably normal. So "totally preoccupied with events of national importance" was Churchill that year that he left all matters of the children for Clementine to grapple with, including Mary's precipitous (and short-lived) engagement to her young beau, an event Churchill was not even aware of. He had little time for family affairs, and little inclination to find the time. Clementine dressed for dinner every night; most nights her husband did not appear.[388]

His most welcome birthday gift arrived by way of North Africa. Auchinleck had shown Rommel during the preceding week that some British generals could fight. The operation, code-named Crusader, was the largest desert offensive yet undertaken by the British. Under the command of General Alan Cunningham, the hero of Ethiopia, its mission was to swing south around Rommel's lines, which ran fifty miles from his headquarters in Bardia to Sidi Omar. Then, Cunningham planned to swing part of his force northwest in order to draw Rommel into a set-piece battle that, when successfully concluded, would lead to the relief of Tobruk and drive Rommel westward and out of Cyrenaica. Each army fielded about 115,000 men, but Cunningham's seven hundred tanks outnumbered Rommel's by more than two to one, and the British general had surprise on his side. Steady rains had kept German air reconnaissance on the ground; Rommel had no idea the British were about to attack. In fact, Rommel was about to attack Tobruk at the very moment the British emerged from the desert mists on November 17. So complete was the surprise that Rommel's forces were facing the wrong way.

Cunningham made the mistake of thinking Rommel would behave in accordance with his plan and wander into his trap. Rommel did not, because for almost two days he did not believe a British attack was actually taking place, so intent was he on taking Tobruk. When Rommel failed to respond as predicted, Cunningham blundered by spreading his tanks across the desert in a series of isolated columns. Rommel, finally realizing the extent of the British attack, quickly massed his tanks, turned them around, and on November 23, in the largest tank battle thus far fought in the desert, smashed into and through the British lines. The British, in isolated batches and without coordinated command, turned eastward, and fled for home. The Germans also raced east, all the way to the Egyptian border, and then fifteen miles beyond. So confused were the British that entire units of Tommies mingled with Germans, all rushing pell-mell and hell-bent for the Egyptian border. Were Cunningham an aggressive optimist, he might have concluded that he had the Germans surrounded, and that Rommel was ripe for the kill. But he concluded the exact opposite and lost control of the battle.[389]

Auchinleck regained it. On November 25, he relieved Cunningham and ordered the Eighth Army to regroup and attack, presuming, correctly, that Rommel had outrun his supply lines. Within four days Auchinleck drove a corridor through to Tobruk. By the following week, Cunningham was hospitalized in Cairo; the official explanation was that he suffered from "exhaustion." Rommel withdrew into the desert. But then, the best fighters can take a punch or two without sustaining any real damage. Rommel would surely re-arm, and return. On the day before Churchill's birthday, soon after the Eighth Army made contact with the besieged troops in Tobruk, Auchinleck wired the prime minister: "birthday message to you is, Corridor to Tobruk clear and secure. Tobruk is as relieved as I am."[390]

The Home Island was now a fortress. More than a thousand tanks—the equivalent of three fully equipped armored divisions—were deployed within one hundred miles of London, ready to swarm the beaches and strategic ports should the Germans come ashore the following spring. Two days after his birthday Churchill told the Commons:

We have several million men who will fight to the death if this country is invaded, but for whom we have not been able to manufacture the necessary number of rifles, although our rifles are now numbered by a good many millions. Therefore we supplement them with machine-guns, tommy-guns, pistols, grenades and bombs, and, when other things fail, we do not hesitate to place in the citizen's hands a pike or a mace, pending further developments. After all, a man thus armed may easily acquire a rifle for himself.[391]

But Churchill envisioned another use for his ever-growing forces. Believing since June of 1940 that the Germans would not come, he had built up his armies in anticipation of the day they would drive Rommel into the sea, the day they would go to French North Africa, and the day they would cross the Channel to fight on the Continent. Royal Navy engineers had been at work all year designing Churchill's artificial harbors—named "Mulberries" by Churchill. New corvettes and destroyers were sliding down shipyard ways. Tank transport ships had been designed. Lancaster heavy bombers rolled off assembly lines. Europe was Churchill's ultimate objective. When the time was right, he would go there in overwhelming numbers of ships and tanks and men and airplanes, and he'd bring his ports with him.

The Commons and King stood foursquare behind him, although the British army had yet to win a real victory against Hitler. In fact, against the Germans in 1941 Churchill could show nothing but defeats and a few diversions by his commandos and saboteurs. True, *Bismarck* had been dealt with, but that action was more symbolic than strategic as the registry of shipping losses from U-boats confirmed. True, Auchinleck had put Crusader back on track, but Rommel was by no means beaten. Harold Nicolson cringed when Churchill exulted in the House at Auchinleck's good fortune. Libya was a sideshow, Nicolson recorded. "Moscow may fall, Japan may come in against us. France may join the Axis. We may be beaten in Libya." Were any of these eventualities to come to pass, he lamented, "I feel [it] will react very badly on Winston's prestige."[392]

His prestige did not suffer, even as fresh vegetables, sugar, coal, and new clothing grew as scarce as victories. Britons, pummeled since 1940, stood by their Winnie, who, wrote Nicolson, "is the embodiment of the nation's will." Yet his political enemies were of a mind that one or two more disasters on the magnitude of Greece or Crete would spell the end of him. "Christ and Carrots" Cripps, in fact, was aiming to take his rightful place, as he saw it, in the cabinet, perhaps even at the head of a new government, should Churchill lose another battle.[393]

Kathleen Hill compiled a list of more than 120 well-wishers who had sent birthday greetings from around the world—kings, queens, and displaced continental potentates, from the entire ship's company of HMS

Churchill, as well as from all the boys of Harrow. Dominion officials high and low sent messages. Winant jotted a note, Wavell, from India, paid his respects, as did "that ass" de Gaulle. Eden, Attlee, and most of the cabinet sent their regards, as did the maharaja of Nepal. Even Stalin sent a note. No birthday salutations arrived from Franklin Roosevelt.[394]

Churchill lacked only that which he desired most of all, his American cousins fighting at his side. America stood behind him, but not beside him. With just four weeks remaining in 1941, he had no good reason to believe that America would be fighting when 1942 arrived. After almost two years of pleading, cajoling, flattering, prodding, and warning Roosevelt, he had come up short. As with others who brought their cases to Roosevelt, Churchill heard magical words but came away with no answers to his questions. Though the relationship he had with Roosevelt was just ambiguous and promising enough to sustain Churchill's hopes of salvation, it lacked a real strategy. It lacked singleness of purpose. Roosevelt still saw it in terms of "all help short of war." To Churchill, that meant ultimate stalemate, or worse. He sought a relationship with Roosevelt built on his premise "victory or death." The word for such a relationship is "alliance."[395]

During the first days of December, Stalin's most dependable and merciless ally, winter, caught the Germans unprepared. The first snow had fallen on October 6, early even for Moscow, and a harbinger of a winter that would long be remembered for its ferocity. Still, the Germans pressed on. By December 2, a German reconnaissance battalion worked its way through Khimki, a suburb of Moscow. On December 4, the temperature fell to minus thirty-two degrees Fahrenheit; wind-whipped snow slashed at men's skin and eyes like jagged steel filings. The next day, the temperature fell to minus thirty-seven, turning rubber brittle and gasoline into jelly. When their gearboxes froze solid, tanks went nowhere. German soldiers froze to death in their summer uniforms, within sight of Moscow, because Hitler's military chief of staff, General Alfred Jodl, had decreed that the issuance of winter uniforms would cast doubt on the Reich's promise of victory before winter. The Red Army counterattacked on December 5, smashing its way through the German lines in front of Moscow. This was a real counterattack, even though it rolled the Germans back only a few dozen miles. The Germans dug in. For thousands of Germans, clad in their summer gray, their foxholes became their graves. In the first week of December, almost two thousand German soldiers had had frostbitten limbs amputated. The Wehrmacht's ordeal was only beginning.[396]

During the first week of December, Churchill regularly telephoned Bletchley to ask about the disposition of the Japanese Combined Fleet (*Kido Butai*). The Imperial Japanese battle fleet, flying the flag of Vice Admiral Chūichi Nagumo, had disappeared into the vastness of the north Pacific. Another Japanese fleet was rumored to be making for the South China Sea, with designs upon Siam, Malaya, or Java; nobody knew. Each time Churchill asked, the Bletchley reply remained the same: No intelligence was forthcoming. The Japanese navy had vanished.

3

Vortex

By the first days of December 1941, Churchill knew that events in the Far East were moving far ahead of his knowledge of them. Was it to be Peace or War? He had no say in the matter and could do nothing but wait, a state of inactivity he loathed, which demanded a trait he lacked, patience.

These were the longest nights, when the omnipresent bleakness of an English winter seeped into the ancient oak timbers and cold stone floors of Chequers. Churchill's bodyguard, Walter Thompson, recalled that when the winter rains arrived, the ancient house took on a "preternatural and malign" aura. The household staff tried to invest the home with as much Yule warmth as was allowed by the strictures imposed by war and the lack of effective central heat. Churchill spent his weeknights in London, deep within the Annexe, his small room there outfitted with one modest stuffed chair, a small desk, an electric feet warmer, and a twin-size dormitory bed. Naked incandescent bulbs hung on long wires that coiled downward from the concrete ceiling, buttressed by walls of heavy timber, yellowed by eighteen months of cigar smoke. Against the confines of that dank place, Chequers offered succor. The domestic staff bustled about placing sprays of pine boughs and holly branches throughout the great house. Old English country houses display a singular knack for generating more raw cold during winter months than the great outdoors. Chequers being no exception, housemaids piled Welsh coal into the grates, except in the great hall and Churchill's bedchamber, where as was his wont at Chartwell, he demanded log fires, which he liked to prod with an iron poker, in silence and for long periods of time.[1]

Churchill's favorite weeks of the year, the Christmas holidays, were approaching, their start marked at Chequers by servants maneuvering the tall Christmas fir into the great hall, where they adorned it with baked cookies, glass ornaments, and wax candles. Lest the tree ignite, house-keepers tied large sponges onto broomsticks and soaked them in buckets nearby — Churchill's favorite bath sponges, in fact, purloined from the Old Man, who was given to rumbling downstairs, barefoot in a damp silk dressing gown, and demanding his bathing accoutrements of the first servant he encountered.[2]

The wine cellar at Chequers, always well stocked thanks to the generosity of friends, contributed much to a spirit of holiday good cheer. Pol Roger Champagne flowed at each meal. Friends had donated enough Napoleon brandy to pickle a ship's company of would-be Nelsons, "enough to last twenty years of war," Pamela recalled. Churchill's valet, Frank Sawyers, kept a little spirit lamp on hand in order to warm the Old Man's brandy glass, a ritual repeated two or three times each evening. Numerous boxes of cigars arrived, gifts from all over the world. The Cuban government had been generous in that regard, having honored Churchill with a lovely old Queen Anne dresser, the drawers of which were stuffed with hundreds of the finest Havanas. The Exchequer assessed a hefty excise tax on the cigars; Churchill fumed but paid it. The Prof—Lord Cherwell—insisted Churchill forsake the cigars because he feared German agents lurking in Havana might have poisoned the filler. The task of testing the gifts of food and cigars for sinister ingredients fell to young Victor Rothschild, the 3rd Baron Rothschild, a chemist at MI5, and an expert in solving booby-trapped devices. Rothschild concluded that the goods were safe. Still, the Prof cautioned Churchill not to smoke his Romeo y Julietas. He smoked them anyway, whisky in hand, as he wandered the halls of his armed fortress. He had everything he needed to face the dangers beyond the walls—safety for his family, ample food, strong drink, and good company.[3]

The weekend following his birthday, Churchill invited Averell Harriman and his daughter Kathleen to Chequers. Kathleen, a correspondent for *Newsweek,* was a close friend of Pamela's, and as the American woman's twenty-fourth birthday was in a few days, the Churchills proposed a birthday celebration in the country, with Gil Winant and many of the usual gang in attendance, a little something that promised modest respite from the strains of war. Churchill inscribed for Kathleen a copy of his memoir of the Sudan campaign, *The River War.* Though her birthday fell on Sunday, the party was held on Saturday, December 6, the feast of St. Nicholas, the patron saint of sailors (and merchants, archers, and children), celebrated throughout Britain with gifts for the children and with much ceremony in Canterbury Cathedral and in the hundreds of small churches erected in Nicholas's name along the coast, from where Englishmen had sailed to build the Empire and from where they now sailed to defend it. With the gales of winter in mind, British sailors called Nicholas "the saint of cold December," and in chapels ashore and on board ships sought his protection:

> *One there is whom once our fathers*
> *Took their own, their saint, to be*
> *Since his prayers had helped the children*

And the sailors on the sea;
Lord, who dost thine angels send,
Make Saint Nicholas our friend.

On the night of the sixth, Clementine, with a cold coming on, retired early, as did the rest of the household but for Churchill. He drafted several memos addressing the food situation—excepting the armed forces, the average Briton's diet had fallen below the minimum level to sustain good health or the strength to work a full shift in an armaments factory. As Churchill worked away, Brooke telephoned with the news that a Japanese fleet of transports and warships *might* be heading into the Gulf of Siam toward either the Kra Peninsula or Bangkok. Or it might be a bluff, no one knew. Britain lacked the means to stop such a force in any event. Before donning his silk smock, Churchill checked in a final time with the Bletchley analysts, in hopes that they might lay a golden egg with regard to the whereabouts of the Japanese battle fleet.[4]

They could not. The Japanese fleet remained invisible.

Since his birthday Churchill had contemplated more than the location of the Japanese navy. Stalin that week had finessed Britain into declaring war on Finland, Hungary, and Romania. The two latter states had tried and failed to avoid war by appeasing both Germany and Russia. Finland, invaded by Stalin in late 1939 and not surprisingly seeking revenge—and its pre-1939 borders—had joined the Axis days after Hitler strode into Russia. Though Churchill thought Finland's choice of partners "obnoxious" and loathed Romania's Antonescu, he told the War Cabinet that he wanted it to be "on record that in his view this declaration of war on Finland (and also on Hungary and Romania) would not assist either our cause or that of the Russians. The sole justification for it was that it was necessary in order to satisfy the Russian Government." Churchill threw Stalin a bone—three bones—because he could not deliver fast enough the airplanes and tanks Stalin sought. Most important, he could not deliver a second front in Europe. Instead, that week he ordered Eden to Moscow to mollify Stalin.[5]

He continued to ponder the diplomatic conundrum he and Roosevelt might soon face in Asia. Were the Japanese to attack British or Dutch interests but not American, Britain would find itself fighting a new war. But would America come in under such circumstances? For almost six months Churchill had asked Roosevelt for a direct answer. The president had not given one. Accordingly, Churchill informed Harriman that in the event of a Japanese attack, Britain would *not* declare war "within the hour" as he had earlier promised, but would wait until Roosevelt took "such action as, under the circumstances, he considers best." Then, and only then, would Britain—"within the minute"—declare war on Japan.[6]

The two leaders had agreed that week to proceed as partners in an extraordinary venture, the building of an atomic bomb. When American physicists weeks earlier endorsed the Maud Committee's conclusion that a nuclear fission bomb was feasible, Roosevelt diverted several millions of discretionary (and off the books) funds to Vannevar Bush and his atomic scientists. Bush and his cohorts so successfully wrapped a curtain of secrecy around themselves and their work that within months, the American press reported that exploration of the atom at universities had come to a stop, except for the pursuit of "artificial radioactive materials for medical research." Bush, at Roosevelt's request, told Churchill of the American decision to build the bomb, and suggested the joint Anglo-American project be code-named Mayson, in case Maud had been compromised. Churchill replied: "I need not assure you of our readiness to collaborate with the United States Administration in this matter." He appointed Sir John Anderson—"the man without mercy"—as chief administrator on the British side, and put Lord Cherwell in charge of the scientific end of the operation. The atomic project offered Cherwell an opportunity to spite his enemies in academia. It also held promise as a means to annihilate his most hated enemy, Germany.[7]

On the morning of December 7, spurred by the report of Japanese naval forces in the Gulf of Siam, Churchill drafted a proposed threat to Japan, and sent it off to Roosevelt. He sought Roosevelt's approval to inform Tokyo that the British and Dutch would construe any incursion by Japanese forces from Indochina into Thailand as an attack on their interests and "should hostilities unfortunately result the responsibility will rest with Japan." Two days earlier, Halifax had cabled the news that Roosevelt finally agreed to join Britain in such a warning, though no such assurance had yet arrived from the president. Given Britain's state of readiness in the Far East, Churchill's note to the Japanese amounted to his brandishing an empty scabbard.[8]

At Argentia, in August, Roosevelt had told Churchill that he, Roosevelt, could fight a war without declaring war. Such words of defiance (defiance of the U.S. Congress at any rate) offered hope to Churchill, but Roosevelt could not defy Congress, and Churchill knew it. Roosevelt had challenged Hitler by putting American troops into Iceland; he had embargoed the Japanese, and he had overseen the virtual nullification of the Neutrality Acts. The president had irritated many within his military by sending to Churchill America's newest tanks, on the grounds that Britain was fighting a war while America was not. Roosevelt's carefully trod path to war led him even to defy the American labor movement, the very heart of his constituency. Congress in the autumn had threatened to scuttle his quest to arm merchant ships unless he told John L. Lewis and his United Mine

Workers that a contemplated coal strike would be considered virtually treasonous, for without coal, there could be no steel, and without steel, no tanks for Britain, or Buicks and Fords for Americans. Roosevelt strongly advised Lewis to back off; he did. Roosevelt had talked a big game for months, but of America, Field Marshal Dill wrote, "Never have I seen a country so utterly unprepared for war and so soft."[9]

Churchill's luncheon guests on the seventh were Lady Alexandra Mary Cadogan, Duchess of Marlborough, and her teenage son, John George Vanderbilt Henry Spencer Churchill, Marquess of Blandford, grandson of Consuelo Vanderbilt, and the future 11th Duke of Marlborough. Young Lord Blandford was one-quarter American (Churchill, of course, one-half), yet the Vanderbilts and Spencer-Churchills embodied moneyed aristocracy of the sort America Firsters railed against. Fortunately for Britain, the fourth lunch guest, Gil Winant, believed with Churchill that the war was about liberty, not privilege. While making his way to the dining room, Winant encountered Churchill, pacing the hall. He asked Winant if he thought there was going to be war with Japan. "Yes," Winant replied. Then, "with unusual vehemence" Churchill asked if America would declare war on Japan if Japan declared war on Britain. Winant explained that only the American Congress could declare war. Churchill remained silent for a moment, and Winant in that instant grasped the source of his bleak demeanor. If Japan attacked British interests but not American, Churchill might find himself fighting a second war, alone. The fate of Britain, Winant realized, "might be hanging on one turn of pitch and toss."[10]

The evening of December 7 found a somber Churchill taking his dinner at Chequers in the company of Winant and Harriman. Churchill's naval assistant Tommy Thompson and his senior private secretary, John Martin, were also present at the table.* To Harriman, Churchill appeared tired and depressed. "The hunt for the Japanese fleets had turned up nothing. He sat for long moments with his head in his hands." Harriman had learned what the Churchill family long knew: depending on the events of the day—a favorite swan consumed by a badger, news of an old friend's ill

---

* A private secretary almost always dined with Churchill in order to receive, assess, and pass along to him communications deemed vital. The principals at such dinners—Winston, Harriman, Dill, Hopkins, etc.—often neglect to note in their memoirs any lesser aide who might also have attended, referred to as a dogsbody by the British, because they were always around and underfoot, as it were.

health—Churchill at the start of the evening meal regularly sat in cur-mudgeonly silence while his family sat and waited until the somber moment passed, as it inevitably did, often after the first or second glass of champagne, when Churchill began quoting Macaulay or recalled some glorious deed performed by himself long ago and painted the scene in words for those around the table.[11]

This night proved a singular occasion. Shortly after nine, he rose and switched on a small flip-top wireless. A spate of headlines narrated by the BBC's Alvar Liddell rolled in on the static. Something was said of a Japa-nese attack on British ships in the Dutch East Indies, and on American ships at some other location. Churchill and his guests, having missed the first words of the broadcast, sat in confused silence. The butler appeared from the kitchen and announced, "The Japanese have attacked the Ameri-cans." Commander Thompson chimed in, claiming he thought he had heard the announcer say the Americans had been attacked "at Pearl River." That would have put the Japanese at the mouth of China's third-largest river, about 150 miles from Hong Kong. Yet what manner of American shipping would be navigating in those waters? Liddell then repeated his leading headline: American shipping in Hawaii had been attacked. Yet what sort of shipping? And how large an attack? Churchill and his dining companions sat for a moment in silence.[12]

Churchill then leapt to his feet and started for the hall, announcing his intent to make good his pledge to declare war on Japan within the hour if Japan attacked the United States. "Good God," Winant exclaimed, "you can't declare war on a radio announcement." Churchill stopped, looked at Winant quizzically, and asked, "What shall I do?" Churchill then turned to John Martin and barked, "Get me the president on the phone at once." Winant spoke first to Roosevelt, who confirmed the attack but omitted any details as to the extent of the damage, not only because he didn't know the extent, but because the phone line was a regular, unsecured wire, a source of constant worry to Martin because Churchill used it often. Churchill took the phone. "Mr. President, what's this about Japan?" "It's quite true," replied Roosevelt, "They have attacked us at Pearl Harbor. We are all in the same boat now."[13]

Though Churchill did not know exactly where in the broad expanse of the Pacific the Japanese main battle fleet was, he now knew with terrible certainty where it had been hours earlier. He had not yet learned that the Japanese had bombed Hong Kong. And Singapore. And had landed troops near Hong Kong and, an hour before attacking Pearl Harbor, that Lieuten-ant General Tomoyuki Yamashita had put troops ashore at Kota Bharu, four hundred miles north of Singapore. Japanese bombers were at that moment winging their way from Formosa to Manila. In Washington, with the catastrophic news of hundreds, perhaps thousands, of deaths in Hawaii, with the apparent loss of most—perhaps all—of his Pacific battleships, Franklin Roosevelt's need for political subtlety came to an end, and so, too, did his, and America's, long and dreamlike journey to war. The isolationist cause died on the spot. And with the death of almost 2,500 young American sailors, Marines, and soldiers—their war had lasted about as long as it takes to smoke a Lucky Strike or kiss a pretty girl goodbye—Winston Churchill had finally gained his Western ally. Yet only against a new enemy, and in a new war.

Churchill, in his memoirs, titles the chapter devoted to December 1941 "Pearl Harbor!" His use of an exclamation point is not meant to underscore the shock to America of the devastating Japanese attack on its naval base, but to underscore his profound relief. He wrote that late on the seventh, a thought took shape: "So we had won after all." Indeed, he took to his bed happy that night, and "slept the sleep of the saved and thankful." Brooke's diary entry of the seventh stands as a clear measure of the differences between him—a dedicated staff officer—and Churchill, a statesman whose perspective included events and their consequences over the entire globe: "All our work of last 48 hours wasted! The Japs themselves have now assured that the USA are now in the war."[14]

Such was Churchill's joy over the news from Pearl Harbor that he, curiously, chose to share it first with Eamon de Valera. During the early hours of the eighth, Churchill composed a telegram to the Irish prime minister, an odd choice of correspondent, given the twenty-year history of antipathy, if not outright loathing, between the two. To the Irish prime minister, Churchill wrote, "Now is your chance. Now or never. 'A nation once again.' Am very ready to meet you at any time." Yet there was method in Churchill's apparent madness. He had told Roosevelt the previous year that he was prepared to consider a united Ireland if de Valera granted use of three Irish ports to the Royal Navy or, better yet, came in on the Allied side. "A Nation Once Again" happened to be the marching song of Irish republicans two decades earlier. Churchill was offering de Valera a roadmap to Irish unity.[15]

Churchill had long considered Ireland to be the wayward daughter of the Empire for whom a candle always burned in his window. De Valera did not share Churchill's enthusiasm for a family reunion; he never responded to the overture. Rather, he invited both the Japanese consul and German minister to maintain their staffs and embassies in Dublin. Churchill got the message. Though he dispatched subordinates to woo the Irish government into the Allied ranks (without success), and regularly mulled over the option of taking the three Irish ports by force, he made scant official reference to de Valera for almost three years, until late in 1944, when he cabled

Roosevelt concerning the need "to do something for Poland" and the necessity "to do something to de Valera." Many sons of Ireland volunteered for
the RAF, Royal Navy, and British army, but the Irish daughter never
returned home. Yet, as Churchill sifted the implications of the news from
Oahu—victory had in an instant become only a question of time, unheard-
of sums of money, and unfathomable casualties—he looked beyond the
war and beheld there an opportunity to preserve and strengthen the entire
British Empire, even those parts, like Ireland, long lost to London.

By the morning of December 8, events in Asia overshadowed Churchill's
quixotic Irish initiative. He had gone to bed with a clear view of the far
horizon but failed to see the chasm immediately in front of him. North of
Hong Kong, 25,000 Japanese troops had overnight crossed the Sham
Chum River into the British leased territories, where fewer than 2,000
Indian and Scottish troops were strung out along lines that were too
lengthy and too weak. Forced to retreat four miles to the island of Hong
Kong, they joined three battalions of Indians and two of Canadians, the
Winnipeg Grenadiers and the Royal Rifles, sent in late October to reinforce the garrison despite Churchill's warning months earlier that Hong
Kong would fall, reinforced or not. The Canadians in Hong Kong knew
that the Japanese encamped on the mainland were not there to lay siege to
the city but to take it, a result now ordained, for no reinforcements could
be gotten to the outnumbered defenders.

On the Malay Peninsula, the Japanese force under Lieutenant General
Yamashita that had landed to stiff but futile opposition far north of Singapore had by the time Churchill awoke blasted the small RAF contingent
and secured a foothold. Within a day, Japanese infantry and light tanks
crossed the forty-mile-wide Kra Isthmus and reached the Andaman
Sea—that is, the Japanese had reached the Bay of Bengal and the Indian
Ocean. British forces on the isthmus consisted mostly of two undersize
divisions of Indian troops, supported by fewer than 160 older planes, and
no tanks. They were all that stood between the Japanese army and an easy
march down the peninsula to Singapore. Seaward, a few destroyers plus
Prince of Wales and the battle cruiser *Repulse,* recently arrived on station
in the Strait of Johore, were all that stood between the Japanese navy and
Singapore, where Duff Cooper, newly appointed resident minister, was
awakened by sirens and AA guns and exploding Japanese bombs. He
could do nothing but try to compose himself to sleep again.[16]

Yet another Japanese force made its presence known in the Philippines when, about four hours after the raid on Pearl Harbor, carrier-based Japanese fighters and bombers struck Mindanao, six hundred miles south of Manila. From that attack it could be deduced with certainty that further air attacks, and landings, were likely on the Philippines' most vital island, Luzon. General Douglas MacArthur, asleep in his penthouse apartment at the Manila Hotel, was awakened and apprised of the Oahu attack moments after it took place. Events over the next few hours showed that MacArthur, though forewarned by the attack on Pearl Harbor and with full knowledge that the Philippines—the strategic gateway to Malaya— were the real Japanese objective, had been caught napping, disastrously and inexcusably so.[17]

A complete breakdown had occurred between MacArthur, his chief of staff Richard K. Sutherland, and his chief of air operations Lewis Brereton, with the result that virtually the entire U.S. air arm in the Far East was sitting on the ground at Clark Field when more than nine hours after Pearl Harbor, two hundred Japanese bombers and fighters based on Formosa swept in and within the hour destroyed the airfield and everything on it—planes, fuel, and hangars. The *New York Times* reported later in the week that MacArthur claimed little damage had been done. In fact, MacArthur had lost his aerial umbrella. The next day, Japanese bombers obliterated the Cavite Navy Yard, eight miles from Manila. Five hundred American and Filipino men were killed. Admiral Tommy Hart, commander of the anemic U.S. Asiatic Fleet, watched from Manila as his anchorage disappeared under hellish clouds of black smoke. He decided on the spot to take what remained of his little navy, less his submarines, to the Dutch East Indies. On December 10, the Japanese made their first landings on Luzon. MacArthur could oppose them neither by sea nor air. MacArthur's army of 30,000 Americans and three times as many ill-trained Filipinos was effectively surrounded and cut off from reinforcement.[18]

A few days after the attacks on Pearl Harbor and Manila, U.S. Army chief of staff General George Marshall summoned Dwight Eisenhower, recently promoted to brevet brigadier general, to Washington. Eisenhower's first assignment was to come up with a plan to solve MacArthur's supply problem. The new deputy, who displayed a knack for logistics, pondered the challenge for about an hour before concluding that his mission was hopeless. The army had nothing to send MacArthur, and the navy lacked both the ships and the fighting spirit to ferry men or supplies to the Philippines. Eisenhower could do nothing other than recommend that bases be put in Australia from which future forays might originate. No reinforcements would reach MacArthur's stranded army, ever.[19]

On the morning of the eighth, Roosevelt followed up his conversation with Churchill with a cable in which he again offered that they were now in the same boat, adding, "it is a ship which will not and can not be sunk," an ironic choice of words given that the Japanese visitations to Honolulu and Manila had left neither the British nor the Americans enough in the way of ships to harass, let alone destroy, the Japanese navy. Hours later, when Congress declared war by a vote of 382–1, it did so only upon Japan. When Roosevelt spoke to the Congress, he made no mention of Churchill, or Hitler. Japan had plunged America into war but not against Hitler.[20]

Churchill made his way to the House early in the afternoon on the eighth, wielding a rolled-up mass of the morning papers as a battering ram to clear a path through the crowd gathered outside for himself, Clementine, and Pamela. Nicolson, to his diary: "Winston enters the chamber with bowed shoulders and an expression of grim determination on his face." The prime minister told MPs that the War Cabinet had met earlier and had declared war on Japan. He spoke of facing new dangers, pledging, "When we think of the insane ambition and insatiable appetite which have caused this vast and melancholy extension of the war, we can only feel that Hitler's madness has infected the Japanese mind, and that the root of the evil and its branch must be extirpated together." He reminded the House that "some of the finest ships in the Royal Navy have reached their stations in the Far East at a very convenient moment." That was meant for American ears, for with the loss of the fleet at Pearl Harbor, *Prince of Wales* and *Repulse* now formed the Allied naval presence in the western Pacific, perhaps the entire Pacific. The ships signaled to Washington Churchill's intent to contribute to the Far East war. In Tokyo the ships were seen for what they were—targets.[21]

That morning, Churchill sent a personal letter to the Japanese ambassador in which, very politely, he announced that a state of war existed between their two countries. Some of his colleagues thought the note too proper. "But after all," Churchill later wrote, "when you have to kill a man it costs nothing to be polite." He told King George later in the day that he hoped to leave for Washington "without delay, provided such a course is agreeable to President Roosevelt, as I have no doubt it will be," and added that he would defer proposing a visit until the situation with Germany and Italy (neither had yet declared war on America) became "more clear." Then, too impatient to defer, he cabled Washington with a request to meet with Roosevelt in order to "review the whole war plan." Roosevelt did not reply directly; instead, he told Halifax that perhaps sometime around January 7 might work for everybody. For Churchill, that would simply not do. But it would have to. The next move was Roosevelt's alone to make.[22]

Eden, about to depart Scapa Flow for Moscow, thought it unwise that both he and Churchill should leave the country at such a critical time. He also believed that Stalin, who trusted no one, would conclude that Churchill and Roosevelt were up to something. He telephoned his concerns to John Winant, who replied that as far as he knew, no meeting had been arranged. Eden's parliamentary secretary Oliver Harvey told his diary: "Really, the PM is a lunatic; he gets in such a state of excitement that the wildest schemes seem reasonable." Eden set sail later in the day somewhat secure in the belief that the King, Winant, and the War Cabinet would prevail upon Churchill to stay at home. Churchill intended otherwise. Yet, still no invitation had arrived from Roosevelt. And, still, Hitler remained silent.[23]

It was time for Churchill to roll out long-ignored charts of Pacific islands and archipelagos, many of which were unfamiliar even to high-ranking British leaders, including the prime minister. Churchill loved maps, as much for their utility as for their ability to stoke his imagination. Maps and naval charts lifted him away to far-off places and conjured images of heroic adventures long past. This caused problems when he—regularly— meddled with his military planners. Antony Head, a decorated Dunkirk survivor and a junior staff officer in War Plans, recalled Churchill stabbing a finger at a chart of the Philippines while offering that a particular island—which Churchill claimed was actually part of the Dutch East Indies—was "inhabited by dragons." Clementine had supplied much of his knowledge (or lack thereof) of the region in her letters home during a four-month cruise to the East Indies seven years earlier.

Virtually every stop on her tour, from Rangoon to Singapore to Borneo, had now been or soon would be attacked by the Japanese. From Singapore Clementine had suggested to Winston that he procure from the Admiralty a map of the new British naval base, located between Singapore Island and the mainland. Had he done so he would have learned that no fixed defenses were planned for the Malay mainland, an oversight Wavell brought to his attention only weeks before the final battle for Singapore. Clementine had also visited Komodo, where indeed she took part in a "dragon" hunt. Distances across the Pacific and Indian oceans defied imagination, including Churchill's—14,000 miles and fifty-five days sailing from London to Calcutta via Cape Town, 8,000 miles and three weeks from San Francisco to Bombay. Churchill simply referred to "vast expanses" without quite understanding just how vast the expanses were in that watery part of the world. The entire European and North African theaters and much of the eastern

Atlantic war zone fell within a 1,300-mile radius extending from Berlin, within which the newest British and German bombers could depart a base at sunset, cruise halfway across the theater, and arrive home again in time for breakfast. Railroads, which had shuttled troops to the trenches in 1914, could now carry entire armies across the Continent. Modern technology had made Europe a smaller place, but not so the Pacific. All of Europe, the Mediterranean, the Near East, and the entirety of North Africa could disappear into the Pacific Ocean several times over.[24]

In this vastness Churchill expected *Prince of Wales* and *Repulse* to impart to the Japanese a lesson in sea power as practiced by the world's greatest sea power, perfected long before Captain A. T. Mahan, U.S.N., set about putting his thoughts on that subject to paper.* The Japanese understood, as did the British, Mahan's maxim that in distant seas — where colonial fortresses and naval bases were separated by hundreds or even thousands of miles — the destruction of an enemy's fleet must precede any attempt to take a fortress or anchorage. This was in essence a waterborne version of Prussian military philosopher Karl von Clausewitz's dictum that the destruction of enemy armies, not the capture of real estate, should be a commander's first objective. Mahan believed that the destruction of an enemy fleet virtually guaranteed the success of any land-based assault that followed. Churchill wrote of that very circumstance in *History of the English-Speaking Peoples,* where he attributed Cornwallis's surrender at Yorktown to the inability of the Royal Navy to prevent the French fleet from getting between Cornwallis and his seaborne reinforcements: "Seapower had once more decided the issue, and but for the French blockade the British war of attrition might well have succeeded." The rebel American army in the meantime had marched overland four hundred miles to trap Cornwallis, who, encamped and besieged at Yorktown, at the foot of the Virginia Peninsula, realized that he was at the end of his rope. Singapore was now in an identical position. The Japanese forces that had landed four hundred miles to the north were moving smartly down the Malay Peninsula. Unless *Prince of Wales* found and killed the enemy's warships, Yamashita could reinforce at will.[25]

For almost two centuries the security of the British Empire had been guaranteed by great ships, wooden before the late nineteenth century, weighing in at several hundred tons, driven by wind, armed with smoothbore cannons capable of splintering enemy ships, and with a range of a mile or so inland, just far enough to dissuade native troublemakers from harassing British coastal trading posts. In the mid–nineteenth century, James

---

* A. T. Mahan, *The Influence of Sea Power upon History* (Boston: Little, Brown and Co., 1890).

Brooke, a Lord Jim sort of fellow and the self-made Rajah of Sarawak on the northern coast of Borneo, wrote to London that with "a frigate...a slight military force and the English Union Jack," he could "control all the neighboring evildoers." He was correct. Nineteenth-century warships carried all the power necessary to dissuade competing colonial powers and unfriendly natives from harassing the British in their territorial waters.

By 1942 a pair of battleships displaced almost as many tons as Nelson's entire main battle fleet at Trafalgar. Twentieth-century British war wagons were encased by more than a foot of steel, and by 1942 they were equipped with radar and driven by huge motors that could generate enough electricity to light a small city. Most sailed armed with fourteen- and fifteen-inch guns that could loft 1,500-pound projectiles more than twenty miles. *Nelson* and *Rodney* were armed with sixteen-inch guns. These great ships, *Prince of Wales* foremost among them, were the steel needles and iron threads that stitched together the quilt of the Empire, and secured the sea lanes that bound the Empire to London. When Churchill contemplated the Pacific and Indian oceans, he did so only in terms of the sea routes from London to India and, to a lesser extent, British Malaya, Australia, and New Zealand. Churchill and the Admiralty had for two decades paid scant attention to the outlying archipelagos snatched from Germany after World War One—New Britain, northeastern New Guinea, the Bismarck Archipelago, Buka and Bougainville in the Solomon Islands. The remainder of the Solomon Islands, a British protectorate since 1893, had for decades gone largely ignored by London.

But not by Tokyo. The Solomons stretched away into the South Pacific like a fleet of derelict ghost ships, forgotten and undefended. Other than machete-wielding natives and a few remaining British coconut planters, all other Britons had been evacuated to Australia. Other western Pacific archipelagos—the Marshall Islands and the Mariana Islands—had been German territories until they were handed to Japan (then an ally) following the Great War. Japan also ruled the Caroline Islands, which together with the Marshalls and Marianas, formed a buffer midway between Tokyo and New Guinea. These island chains offered jump-off points for further advances in the Pacific. The Japanese had long understood the importance of the Solomons. Their capture would isolate Australia, a scenario now grasped with fear in Canberra but not yet fully appreciated in London. One of these long-ignored Crown possessions, a mostly uncharted mountainous jumble of rivers, malarial swamps, and thick jungle, was virtually unknown to Londoners—Guadalcanal, located at the southern end of the Solomons. Churchill took note of these far-flung places, not because the entire southern Pacific might soon become a furnace in which the antipodal Dominions could perish, but because the sea routes from those regions were vital to transporting reinforcements to the theater of war he most cared about: North Africa. "I wouldn't have thought the Pacific was something which had much troubled Churchill," recalled Mark Bonham Carter, the son of Churchill's old friend Violet Bonham Carter: "He thought in rather continental terms."[26]

That is why Churchill took umbrage at increasing Australian resistance to his demand for more Australian troops. If Londoners had not complained while being slaughtered, he asked his doctor, why should Australians, who had yet to see a single enemy bomb fall? Yet Australia, with just three army divisions stationed at home, feared now for its safety, its survival even. Churchill reassured Australia's new prime minister, John Curtin, that *Prince of Wales* would keep Australia safe from Japanese depredations.

When he first proposed sending *Prince of Wales* to Singapore, the Admiralty, fearing *Tirpitz* might emerge in the Atlantic, "expressed their dissent." Churchill thought likewise, but in reverse, recalled Sir Ian Jacob: "He was thinking in terms of the annoyance caused us by the *Bismarck,* and thought *Prince of Wales* would cause the Japanese a great deal of trouble." Yet "the parallel was not a good one because the Japanese hadn't a vital lifeline, as we had across the Atlantic, which could be threatened and which required constant protection." Churchill was so sure of *Prince of Wales*'s deterrent threat, so enthused at the prospect of his great battleship mixing it up with the Japanese navy, and so positive of the outcome that he instructed the ship's arrival at Cape Town to be "reported to the enemy" *via* radio broadcast. The Japanese duly noted the news. *Repulse* was by then on station at Singapore. With no destroyers available for escort, *Prince of Wales* made the journey to Singapore alone. Too late, having insisted the venture proceed, Churchill told the Admiralty that he regretted the lack of a destroyer escort. "This is a case where I am for 'Safety First.'" The mission itself belied that claim. Churchill discussed the mission in several telegrams, including a message reassuring Curtin, and another to Stalin, which employed the same phrase he had used when he told Roosevelt of *Prince of Wales*'s departure: "It is grand to have something that can catch and kill any Japanese ship."[27]

Admiral Tom S. V. Phillips, in command of *Prince of Wales,* agreed with Churchill's assessment of his battleship's prowess, with one caveat. The Japanese fleet, Phillips told the War Cabinet, consisted of a mix of newer and older ships, as did the British fleet, but Britain's newest and best ships, such as *Prince of Wales,* operating near British Asian possessions "*under cover of shore based aircraft,*" would prove more than a match for the Japanese (italics added). No such land-based air cover was available anywhere near Singapore on December 8. Months earlier Churchill had dissuaded his military chiefs from sending "very great diversions" of aircraft to the Far East. "The political situation in the Far East does not seem to require," he told the chiefs, "and the strength of our Air Force by no means warrants, the maintenance of such large forces in the Far East at this time." Churchill's Far East strategy, recalled Ian Jacob, was based on the premise that "if the Japanese came into the war, it will bring in the Americans and we shall win the war and then, anything we lose we shall get back; that was his simple view of the matter, yet in many ways it was a sensible view." Thus, as the political situation in the Far East wobbled and then collapsed, Churchill chose to keep his aircraft close to home. Had he kept rigidly to his strategy of not reinforcing the Far East with men, planes, or ships, *Prince of Wales* would not have sailed. But he had sent the ship, and now it sailed without air cover. Churchill had suggested to the Admiralty that an aircraft carrier accompany *Prince of Wales* to the Far East. Yet when it became clear that no carrier could be spared, Churchill and the Admiralty sent the battleship anyway, alone.[28]

Foretold by Britain of its coming, the Japanese were waiting for *Prince of Wales* somewhere in the South China Sea, waiting not only with ships, which the powerful British man-of-war might catch and kill, but with airplanes. Late on December 8, *Prince of Wales, Repulse,* and four old destroyers ventured together from Singapore and down the Strait of Johore in search of the Japanese transports that had landed troops far up the Malay Peninsula. Absent air cover, Phillips was sailing into a deluge without an umbrella. He knew this, and although the Admiralty had not *ordered* him to depart Singapore, implicit in the orders that sent him there was the understanding that he behave like an English admiral, that is, that he fight.

Max Beaverbrook and his lieutenant, George Malcolm Thomson,* considered the mission of *Prince of Wales* to be "pure rubbish." The Beaver had begun to think a great many of Churchill's schemes—Greece, Crete, and now the sojourn of the battleships—were rubbish, and had begun to fancy himself a suitable replacement as prime minister should Churchill not survive a vote of confidence or an errant German bomb. Beaverbrook differed with Churchill on North Africa, where Max would abandon the shifty sands in order to establish a second front on the Continent. He differed with just about every Allied military man on the prospects for Russia when he claimed soon after Barbarossa began that with prodigious British and American help, Stalin could last far longer than several weeks, maybe

---

* George Malcolm Thomson, a Scottish-born journalist, served during the war as a deputy to Lord Beaverbrook. By the 1970s, Thomson had earned a reputation as a talented historian and novelist.

even win. By November, Beaverbrook had helped deliver the first install-ments of that aid to Moscow. But Max harbored doubts about Churchill. He "had not so much respect for Winston's intelligence" and strategic acu-men, recalled Thomson, but respected Churchill "as the godsend leader that we had to have." Churchill's dispatch of *Prince of Wales* to the Pacific only reinforced Beaverbrook's uncertainty. Sir Ian Jacob agreed: "Churchill was much too ardent and active a man. He thought something should be going on all the time" and "was so desperately keen for us to have the big-gest part in whatever was going on." He was "not at all a theoretical strate-gist" who "considered the best thing to do and then made quite certain nothing detracted from it, and that the proper forces were concentrated in the proper place."[29]

Admiral Tom Phillips *was* a theoretical strategist, and that was the problem. He was a desk admiral, vice chief of the Admiralty staff, a thinker who was considered by many to be the brains of the Admiralty. He shared four traits with Churchill: he was prone to anger; he was given to meddling in operational plans; he thought Britain's seagoing admirals lacked aggres-siveness; and he worshipped battleships. The Far East venture was to be his first fleet command, and although the previous year he had objected when Churchill divided Wavell's Middle Eastern forces between Greece and Egypt, he embraced the Singapore adventure with alacrity. Knowing of the absence of air cover in Malaya, Phillips might have better served Churchill (and improved his own chances for survival) by pointing out the potential folly in the Singapore gambit. But here was Phillips's chance for glory. Physically, the admiral was a wee man—he had to stand on a box to see from his bridge—who possessed an oversize ego; Admiral James Somerville called him "the Pocket Napoleon." Phillips was well aware of the damage inflicted on capital ships at Taranto and Pearl Harbor, yet those ships had been riding at anchor; *Prince of Wales,* under his com-mand, could zig and zag at speeds of almost thirty-five miles per hour, all the while shredding the sky and everything in it with its vast array of arma-ments. Yet, any gardener who has ever fled a swarm of wasps knows that size and maneuverability do not always carry the day.[30]

The Japanese, like Churchill and Phillips, were not burdened with any doubts whatsoever of their military talents. They had demonstrated at Pearl Harbor the means to deal with the battleships of the world's most powerful navies. When it came to airborne torpedo and bomb attacks against great warships, the Japanese understood what the blasé British and Americans still, incredibly, did not: the Taranto raid and the sinking by aircraft of *Southampton* (a cruiser) had marked late afternoon in the era of battleships. December 7 marked the end of that era.[31]

On the ninth, Churchill outlined to the cabinet his plan for the *Prince of*

Churchill inspects bomb damage during the Blitz. More than 800,000 Lon-doners lost their homes during the bombing raids. (*Getty*)

Between May 26 and June 3, 1940, a flotilla of almost 1,000 British ships, large and small, evacuated more than 330,000 British and French troops from Dunkirk. (*NARA*)

At the height of the Blitz in the autumn of 1940, more than 150,000 Londoners took shelter in the Underground nightly. By war's end, 60,000 British civilians had been killed by German bombs and rockets. (*Getty*)

London, during the Blitz, autumn 1940. St. Paul's Cathedral is wrapped in a cowl of smoke as London burns. (*Associated Newspapers/Rex USA*)

Churchill, Brendan Bracken (middle), and Harry Hopkins, 1941. Bracken had been Churchill's "fixer" for two decades; Hopkins served Franklin Roosevelt in the same capacity. (*Getty*)

NOTRE GLORIEUSE RAF. A PROUVÉ SA PUISSANCE A L'ALLEMAGNE, EN BOMBARDANT ET MITRAILLANT LE TERRITOIRE FRANÇAIS ...

QUANT A NOS BATEAUX !... LES MERS EN SONT PLEINES..!!

A Vichy cartoon takes a jab at Churchill's bombing policy. (*Kenneth Rendell*)

Max Beaverbrook. As minister of aircraft production, he gave Churchill the fighter planes he needed in order to defend England, and the heavy bombers to take the fight to Germany. (*Getty*)

John ("Jock") Colville. But for a stint in the RAF, 1942–1943, Colville served as private secretary to Churchill throughout the war and again during Churchill's premiership from 1951 to 1955. (*Getty*)

Below: Frederick A. Lindemann, Lord Cherwell ("Prof"). Called "Baron Berlin" by his enemies, Cherwell served as Churchill's science adviser for more than three decades. (*Getty*)

Above: Charles Wilson, Lord Moran. Moran served as Churchill's personal physician from 1910 until Churchill's death, in 1965. (*Getty*)

Churchill on board HMS *Prince of Wales*, Argentia, 1941. At his first conference with Roosevelt, Churchill arrived with a long list of needs, aircraft and
tanks at the top. (*Getty*)

Churchill with Franklin Roosevelt, escorted by his son Captain Elliott
Roosevelt, aboard HMS *Prince of Wales* during the Argentia conference,
1941. (*Imperial War Museum, London*)

"Chip off the Old Block" little Winston struts along a London street with his mother, Pamela Churchill, June 1942. (*NARA*)

Clementine greets Winston on the tarmac at an RAF airfield outside London in August 1942 upon his return from Cairo and Moscow. The journey was the first of several he made aboard the B-24 Liberator *Commando*. (*University of South Carolina*)

Churchill and daughter Mary, a sergeant in the Auxiliary Territorial Service, wait for a demonstration of artillery to begin. (*AP*)

Bernard Montgomery, the hero of El Alamein. His victory there, in November 1942, after three years of British defeats and retreats, marked a turning point in the war. (*George Rodger/Life*)

Churchill, Joseph Stalin (center), and Averell Harriman in Moscow, August 1942. (*NARA*)

WELCOME!

"To each American soldier who has left home to join the great forces now gathering in this island, I send a message of greeting and welcome. Wherever you may go in our country you will be among friends. Our fighting men look upon you as comrades and brothers in arms. Welcome to you while you are with us : and when the time comes we will all go forward together and carry the good cause to final victory."

Winston S. Churchill

A 1942 poster greets arriving American troops deployed to Great Britain. By late 1943, more than 300,000 had arrived. (*Kenneth Rendell*)

With victory in North Africa in hand, Churchill in Algiers plans his Mediterranean strategy, June 1943. Seated from left: Anthony Eden, Alan Brooke, Churchill, General Marshall, and General Eisenhower; standing (behind seated men) from left: Air Chief Marshal Tedder, Admiral Sir Andrew Cunningham, General Alexander, and General Montgomery. (*NARA*)

Churchill and Roosevelt at the Casablanca Conference, January 1943. It was here that Roosevelt announced the Allied terms of surrender to Germany, Italy, and Japan: "Unconditional Surrender." (*NARA*)

Churchill arrives at the first Quebec Conference, August 1943. Beside him is Canadian prime minister William Lyon Mackenzie King. Riding shotgun is Churchill's bodyguard, Scotland Yard's Walter Thompson. (*NARA*)

First Lady Eleanor Roosevelt (left) and Clementine Churchill prepare to make an address over the Canadian Broadcasting Company, September 13, 1943. (*AP*)

Churchill addresses the U.S. Congress, 1943. (*NARA*)

Churchill inspects British paratroopers before D-day, June 1944. (*NARA*)

From left: Dwight Eisenhower, Churchill, and General Omar Bradley put new carbines through their paces before D-day, 1944. (*NARA*)

Wales and *Repulse,* already at sea, to "vanish into the ocean wastes and exercise a vague menace" akin to the behavior of "rogue elephants." By then, the *Prince of Wales,* flying Phillips's flag, and captained by John Leach (whom Churchill had wanted to court-martial the previous May), was steaming up the Malay coast escorted by the four old destroyers and the HMS *Repulse. Repulse*'s captain, William Tennant, offered to Cecil Brown, an American reporter who was on board: "We are off to look for trouble. I expect we'll find it."[32]

Near Saigon, more than four hundred miles away, Japanese ground crews were arming two dozen long-range Mitsubishi "Nell" bombers and several dozen "Betty" torpedo-bombers. Churchill and the Admiralty knew that the Japanese were reinforcing the Indochina airfields, but, Churchill later wrote, "sound reasons"—the distance, four hundred miles—implied that *Prince of Wales* "would be outside the effective range of enemy, shore-based torpedo bombers." Here was an astounding case of errant reasoning, given that two days earlier, Japanese airmen had flown almost three hundred miles to Pearl Harbor from aircraft carriers. What was another hundred miles to the best fliers in the world? Churchill—who had once denigrated the Japanese as "the Wops of the Pacific"—later wrote that "the efficiency of the Japanese in air warfare was at this time greatly underestimated both by ourselves and by the Americans."[33]

Tars aboard the two British battlewagons certainly underestimated the Japanese. When late on the ninth word came down to Cecil Brown that a Japanese battleship, three cruisers, and at least four destroyers were thought to be somewhere close ahead, Brown joked that he'd like to get a taxi back to Singapore. "Oh, but they are Japanese," an officer replied, "there's nothing to worry about." Another officer chimed in: "Those Japs can't fly," he said, "they can't see at night, and they're not well trained." Churchill happened to feel the same way: he had told luncheon guests months earlier that as far as Japanese airplanes were concerned, "We are of the opinion that they are not very good." On board the *Repulse,* yet another officer claimed that the Japanese "have rather good ships but they can't shoot straight." The Japanese had in fact been shooting pretty smartly all over the Pacific, while the men on board *Repulse* had yet to fire a single shot in anger during the first twenty-seven months of war.[34]

The next morning, the tenth, at 11:07 in Malaya—3:07 A.M. in London—Brown jotted in his notebook: "Enemy aircraft approaching... action stations." At 11:14 he spied nine Japanese planes at an altitude of around 12,000 feet. "And here they come," he wrote. A wave of torpedo bombers came in low. The *Repulse* dodged nineteen torpedoes "thanks to Providence," the captain signaled to Admiral Phillips. The very next torpedo hit *Repulse* near midships, throwing Brown to the deck. Immediately the ship heeled sharply to one side. Within a minute, from the loudspeakers came the captain's final order: "Prepare to abandon ship." A pause: "God be with you."[35]

A half mile ahead, the *Prince of Wales,* the victim of two torpedo hits, rode low in the water, its steering smashed. Fires burned along its length. On the *Repulse,* Brown slumped to the deck and watched as a dozen Royal Marines dove overboard; all were swept into the still-churning propellers. A sailor leapt from the radio tower and straight down the smokestack. Three dozen tars climbed from belowdecks up the inside of the decoy funnel only to find themselves fatally trapped by a steel grate at the top, locked from the outside. Brown watched, stunned, as hundreds of men scrambled over the sides and into the sea, yet he could not bring himself to join them. Finally, he took a last look at his watch—smashed at 12:35—and jumped. He landed in a mess of debris and heavy oil discharged from the ship, in which he and Captain Tennant and hundreds of sailors struggled to get themselves away from *Repulse* before it went down. Bloodied and soaked by the thick oil, they watched in silence minutes later as the ship, its bow stabbing "straight into the air like a church steeple," heeled over and plunged under the swells with more than half the crew of 1,300 still on board. But the *Repulse* wanted a larger ship's company on its final journey, and Brown, who felt his legs were being pulled from his hips, watched in horror as several nearby sailors were sucked back aboard as the ship went under. *Prince of Wales* followed an hour or so later, with Admiral Phillips and Captain Leach still on the bridge. They were last seen bidding God bless to the crew, of whom more than five hundred joined them at the bottom of the South China Sea. British destroyers arrived later in the day to pluck Brown and the other survivors from the water.[36]

Later, Averell Harriman said of Churchill, "He sent those two battleships to Singapore in order to help. He was very anxious to do his share in the Pacific. He knew it would be mostly the United States, but he wanted Great Britain to do its share." Churchill had tried, and failed.[37]

Before sunrise on December 10, Churchill sent a message to Anthony Eden informing him that the government expected a declaration of war by Hitler within two days. He also told Eden that news had arrived overnight from North Africa by way of Auchinleck that Rommel was "in full retreat" westward. And in Russia, "magnificent Russian successes" had put the Germans on the "defensive and retreat." Still ebullient over the U.S. entry into the Pacific war and its likely entry into the European war, he signed off with, "We are having a jolly time here." The jollifications ended when Churchill, in bed opening his boxes of intelligence briefs, picked up the ringing telephone at his bedside. "It was the First Sea Lord," he recalled. "His voice sounded odd. He gave a sort of cough and gulp, and at first I did not hear quite clearly. 'Prime Minister, I have to report to you that the *Prince of Wales* and the *Repulse* have been sunk by the Japanese—we think by aircraft. Tom Phillips is drowned.'" In all the war, Churchill wrote, "I had never received a more direct shock." As he lay in bed, speechless, he realized that in all of the Indian and Pacific oceans, there were no British or American capital ships, other than the survivors of Pearl Harbor, which he had been told were "hastening back to California." He had no need to consult a map to grasp his position in the Pacific: "Over this vast expanse of water, Japan was supreme, and we everywhere were weak and naked."[38]

Within that expanse the Japanese were rampaging faster and more furiously than any warrior nation in history. Japanese fliers had needed only a few hours on the seventh and eighth to rattle the foundations of three centuries of British, Dutch, and American imperialism. Within days the foundations cracked. Churchill, after the loss of the *Prince of Wales*, told Britons that with the American fleet based at Singapore, the city and naval base could hold out for six months, until offensive Allied operations could be undertaken. But there was no American fleet. Other than a few destroyers and the cruiser *Houston*, no American naval force existed in the western Pacific. Churchill did not grasp that Singapore's fate—in large part due to London's having underestimated the enemy—would likely be determined within weeks. Hong Kong's tenure as a British possession could likely be measured in days. "The Japanese rising sun," wrote Mollie Panter-Downes, was "sending ever more trenchant beams over that empire on which a benign British sun was supposed never to set.[39]

Inspector Thompson kept his counsel as Churchill "moped about, wept, and sat staring off to nowhere for two days after *Prince of Wales* and *Repulse* went down." Thompson had "never seen him take a war shock so hard." Churchill had suffered the sort of devastating loss experienced by Caesar Augustus who, after the slaughter of his finest legions in the Teutoburg Forest, allowed his beard and hair to grow out for months and took to wandering about his palace calling out, "Quinctilius Varas, give me back my legions." Churchill, like the Roman, had sent the pride of his Empire to do battle with an enemy he little understood and vastly underrated, and had paid the price. Thompson recalled Churchill sitting for long moments while mumbling repeatedly to himself, "I don't understand what happened. I don't understand it."[40]

For more than a year he had been shuffling his army and naval forces

about, much as he had once so long ago deployed with enthusiastic abandon his army of 1,500 toy soldiers across the Arabian rugs of his father's
London town house. He recalled in his autobiography, *My Early Life,* that
his decision to embark on a military career was "entirely due" to sending
"infantry divisions with cavalry brigades" into battle as a child. Those
mock campaigns allowed him to study "the noble profession of arms"
(although the young Winston stacked the deck against his "enemy,"
brother Jack, whose army, at Winston's insistence, consisted only of
"coloured" troops, and lacked artillery). The toy soldiers, Churchill later
reminisced, "turned the current of my entire life." Those lead and tin
legions (and every man jack of them a British soldier, no colonials or for-
eigners in Churchill's ranks) were hand-cast and painted in Germany by
Heyde and in Paris by C. B. G. Mignot. They would today be valuable to
collectors for their craftsmanship and priceless for their association with
the young Winston Churchill, but they are long lost. Churchill's daughter,
Lady Soames, attributes the paucity of early Churchill memorabilia to his
parents seeing no reason to preserve for posterity anything of Winston's.
"In those days his [Churchill's] hopes were so unpromising...they
wouldn't have had any idea he was a child prodigy." A military career, at
the time, was the only choice available to an aristocratic lad of meager talent. Had Lord Randolph lived to witness the Greek and Crete fiascoes, the
siege of Tobruk, the loss of *Prince of Wales,* the looming threats to Hong
Kong, Singapore, Burma, and the very essence of the Empire, India, he
would have judged the decision to discard his son's toy lancers and fusiliers
self-evidently correct. The adult Winston had juggled his armies and fleets
like an inept prestidigitator; he slipped his peas under shells, shuffled them
about, and Hitler and Tojo made them all vanish.[41]

Upon learning of the fate of his two warships, Churchill hastened to the
Commons to deliver a brief statement. He returned the following day to
summarize in a long address the news from various fronts and to explain
more precisely the circumstances surrounding the loss of the *Prince of
Wales.* "The House is depressed," Nicolson jotted in his diary, and the loss
of *Prince of Wales* "has numbed us." The House expected Churchill to
explain how the ships were lost; instead, he gave them: "These ships had
reached the right point at the right moment and were in every respect
suited to the task assigned to them." Both ships were sunk, Churchill told
the House, by continuous waves of airborne bomb and torpedo attack
"delivered with skill and determination." Seven Japanese planes were
destroyed, but Churchill did not explain whether by anti-aircraft guns or
by British fighter planes. Following Churchill's remarks, Admiral of the
Fleet Sir Roger Keyes—old, frail, but still sharp—rose and asked
Churchill to assure the Commons that, "erroneous deductions" to the

contrary, "the battleship is still the foundation of sea power and that...the *Prince of Wales* was as well protected against under-water and air attack as the *Bismarck*." The old admiral appeared to have learned nothing from Pearl Harbor. But the latter part of his statement held the key to his query. He asked again, Were the two ships "acting without the support of land-based or seaborne fighters?" The Speaker of the House deemed Keyes's statement inappropriate.[42]

Keyes persisted. Churchill at first ducked, then deflected, the question by asking Keyes if he meant to imply that Admiral Phillips had "acted otherwise than on sound naval grounds." Certainly not, replied Keyes. Another MP asked directly how the seven Japanese planes had been shot down, by British AA or British airplanes? Churchill finally responded: "They were destroyed by anti-aircraft fire." Britain "had only a certain amount of aircraft" to meet its needs, Churchill explained, but had nonetheless sent "as many reinforcement as we could many months ago" to Singapore. In fact, not enough aircraft had been sent to protect the battleships. The fault for that did not reside with the late Admiral Phillips, but with those who had ordered him into hostile waters without air support. That would be the prime minister, with the consent of the War Cabinet and the Admiralty.[43]

Churchill claimed in his memoirs that "chance played so fatal a part" in the tragic loss of the ships. Yet chance was aided and abetted by Churchill adhering too long to his notions of battlewagons and their mythic prowess. The loss of his beloved ships moved him to at last grasp the strategic significance of sending airplanes, whether from airfields or carriers, against heavy ships, though he by no means abandoned his reverence for battlewagons—"gigantic castles of steel" he called them in 1923 (volume 1 of *The World Crisis*). A battleship took five years to build, but an aircraft carrier could be rigged out of a hull in months. Overnight, in keeping with his oft-voiced motto of K.B.O. (keep buggering on), he embraced carriers with enthusiasm. Days after the loss of *Prince of Wales*, he displayed his lifelong ability to learn fast when, on December 13, he approved Admiral Pound's recommendation to send a task force of up to four aircraft carriers to the Indian Ocean, under the command of Admiral James Somerville. "I agree that Admiral Somerville should come home," Churchill told Pound, "to organize this form of warfare." Those words are telling for, although Somerville had been running carriers through the Mediterranean for two years to deliver fighter planes to Malta and Alexandria, large-scale, coordinated carrier operations— *"this form of warfare"*—were new and mysterious to Churchill and the Admiralty. The British proved quick studies, but the Japanese had developed carrier tactics years before, and in the previous week had demonstrated their skill at this form of warfare.[44]

Throughout his life, Churchill's critics—wanting it both ways—claimed on the one hand that he stuck to outdated positions for too long, and on the other hand that he was an opportunist, ever ready to switch positions. He did and he was, and he liked to say, "I would rather be right than consistent." Margot Asquith in 1908 called him a man of "transitory convictions."* But his old colleague Rab Butler attributed Churchill's tendency to switch sides to "the independence of his ideas" and to his "ever testing, courting, and encouraging new ideas." He was as contradictory as the criticisms leveled against him. He had been adjudged a mental case by the military establishment when during the Great War he championed a new and heretical weapon, the tank, which he called his "land ship." Yet in those years, the military establishment had demonstrated—if not mental illness—gross stupidity. The cartoonist David Low chose the army as Colonel Blimp's profession after reading a serving British colonel's letter to *The Evening Standard* that protested the mechanization of the cavalry but insisted that if tanks were to be brought into service, tank crews must be made to wear spurs.[45]

Churchill's vision extended well beyond the known horizon, yet the same man who could envision as revolutionary a change in warfare as the tank, could not, in the face of overwhelming evidence, concede that battleships were dinosaurs. Days after the *Prince of Wales* went down, the old-school Churchill proposed to the War Cabinet the formation of a combined British and American battle fleet consisting of four new, sixteen-inch-gun battleships, along with older American ships in "numbers sufficient to enable a fleet action." He simply did not grasp that fleet actions of that sort were now a thing of the past. Although he could never bring himself to entirely give up the old, when the facts demanded, he embraced the new, in the case of sending carrier task forces to the Indian Ocean, almost literally overnight.[46]

There would be no *Time* Man of the Year honors for Churchill that year. Stalin was in the running for the 1941 prize but failed to take it on the grounds of "grave disqualifications, one moral, the other empiric." Stalin, by virtue of his 1939 pact with Hitler, had opened the floodgates for the Führer; now that coup "had proved a grim joke at the expense of Joseph Stalin." The Indian Confederation of America did, however, vote Stalin "1941's outstanding warrior," and sent him a war bonnet. *Time* named Franklin Roosevelt Man of the Year "because the country he leads stands

---

* She was the wife of Herbert Henry Asquith, who served as prime minister from 1908 to 1916, and the mother of Violet Bonham Carter.

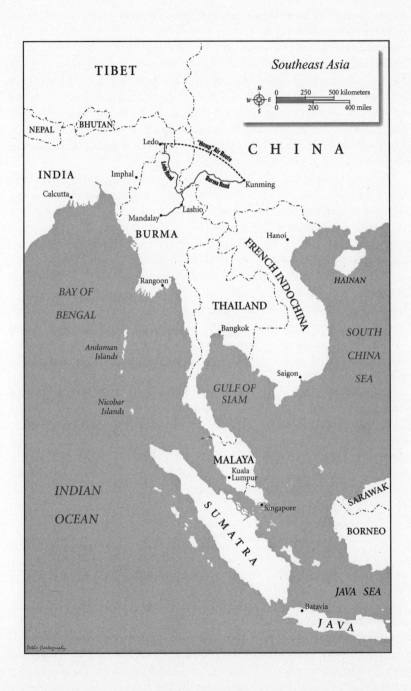

for the hopes of the world." Roosevelt, who "in his own right and on his own record...stood out as a figure for the year and for the age," had led America in mastering its "creeping paralysis" and "had guided the U.S." to its "rendezvous with destiny." He had forced America to grasp "what it can be and therefore will be." Churchill, *Time* recorded, had had "no great moment in 1941." True, Churchill had twice taken Cyrenaica—but only because he "lost it between times." He had "met disaster" in Greece and Crete. British armies "were still losing campaigns" under his leadership. Yet *Time* dabbed salve on the wound: Churchill "was a man of the year, of the decade, and, if his cause is won, of all time."[47]

The news from the Far East did not bode well for his cause. The news from America, specifically from Franklin Roosevelt, was disquieting. There was none. By the early hours of December 11, Churchill still had received no reply from Roosevelt to his request for a meeting. Hitler settled the issue that day when he declared war on the United States. Benito Mussolini goose-stepped right along. From the balcony above the Piazza Venezia in Rome, Il Duce anointed Roosevelt a "supreme fraud" who had led America into war through "diabolical obstinacy." Mussolini pledged that the "powers of the pact of steel" were prepared to inflict more "formidable blows" upon their enemies. "Italians!" he bellowed. "Once more arise and be worthy in this historical hour. We will win!" His lackeys scattered among the crowd cheered. But thousands of other Romans assembled in the piazza below listened in silence. This was a war, and an enemy, they did not want.[48]

And there it was. Hitler and Mussolini with complete disregard for American industrial might had declared war on the United States of America. The U.S. Congress immediately returned the favor. America was in. Roosevelt signed the German declaration at 3:05 P.M. One minute later, he signed the Italian declaration. Only then was Churchill's Grand Alliance finally realized. Harold Nicolson wrote his wife, "We can't be beaten with America in," yet "not an American flag flying in the whole of London. How odd we are."[49]

The previous June, on the eve of the German invasion of Russia, Churchill told Jock Colville that the Russians would likely be quickly defeated. By autumn he had raised his expectations. In late October, after asking his chief of military intelligence to give odds for Moscow falling by winter, Churchill offered his own, "I should be inclined to put it even." Now the Red Army had gone over to the attack. On December 11 Churchill told the Commons that winter's onslaught had not only brought the Germans to a standstill outside

Moscow but had "inflicted upon the German armies and the German nation, a bloody blow, almost unequaled in the history of war." And December, he added, marked "not the end of the winter...but the beginning." Where Russians were "habituated to the severity of their native climate," the German invaders could only scratch meager shelter from the frozen ground, there to conclude, Churchill told the House, that Hitler's Russian gambit was proving to be "one of the outstanding blunders of history."[50]

With Hitler's declaration of war Churchill concluded that it was vital to meet with Roosevelt, immediately. Yet he had *already* asked and been rebuffed. He dispatched another cable to Roosevelt: "Am most anxious" to discuss the Vichy situation in North Africa. Actually, as he had been since the eighth, he was most anxious to discuss everything. This time Roosevelt gave him what he wanted. "Delighted to have you here at the White House," he cabled back.[51]

Overnight, Roosevelt found himself at war in two oceans, and overnight, Churchill's gingerly approach to the Americans changed. When Lord Woolton, minister of food, proposed to increase food rationing, Churchill told him that with the Americans in, "our position is immeasurably improved," and therefore, "we have no longer any need to strike attitudes to win the United States sympathy, we are all in it together, and they are eating better meals than we are." When one of his military chiefs advised a continuation of the careful attitude toward America, Churchill replied, with a leer, "Oh that is the way we talked to her when we were wooing her, now that she's in the harem we talk to her quite differently."[52]

Within twenty-four hours of receiving Roosevelt's invitation, Churchill, Beaverbrook, Harriman, First Sea Lord Dudley Pound, and Air Marshal Charles Portal were rolling north on board the prime minister's private train, bound for the River Clyde, where the battleship *Duke of York*—sister ship of the *Prince of Wales*—waited to carry them to America. Also on board were the newly retired Field Marshal Dill (Alan Brooke stayed behind to man his new headquarters) and Churchill's doctor, Charles Wilson (Clementine insisted Winston take the doctor along). Eighty ancillary staff and two dozen cryptographers also went; all of Churchill's outgoing cables had first to be encoded before being sent to the intended recipient, as did the incoming traffic for the prime minister. His daughter Mary accompanied her Pa-*pa* on the train but would not be making the Atlantic crossing. Late morning on December 13, after bidding "Good-bye, darling" to Mary—who was last off the ship—Churchill and the *Duke of York* made for the Atlantic.[53]

Soon after clearing the Clyde, the ship ran into the worst weather the North Atlantic could throw its way. The escort destroyers, tossed about like rowboats, fell behind. The seas were so roiled that *Duke of York* spent most of the voyage battened down. Dr. Wilson possessed no medicines to combat the nausea and lassitude that overcame almost everyone on board, including the prime minister. Churchill, in his longest letter to Clementine since a forlorn missive sent during a 1936 trip to Marrakech, rued the confinement but allowed that an extra dose of Mothersill's Travel Remedy had staved off any serious bouts of seasickness. The seas were so violent, he wrote, that two of the party suffered broken legs and arms. Paraphrasing Samuel Johnson, he wrote, "Being in a ship in such weather as this is like being in a prison, with the extra chance of being drowned."[54]

He never enjoyed the confinement of long sea voyages; this was the worst ever. Yet aboard the ship he found pleasure in the usual places: his cronies, good food, strong drink, and bad movies. Beaverbrook's lieutenant, George Malcolm Thomson, recalled "there was one movie one night, *The Sea Hawk,* in which there was an attack on a British naval ship by pirates as I remember it. A great deal of countless stuff going on the deck of this sailing ship and I remember Churchill, who was always in his dressing gown. He had dined rather well I think, as usual. I can remember him getting up and shouting 'We're winning, we're winning!' "[55]

Actually, wherever they were fighting, on sea and on land, but for a thin slice of North Africa, they were losing. And so, too, were the Americans. A *New York Times* headline that week screamed: U.S. FLIERS SCORE: BOMBS SEND BATTLESHIP, CRUISER AND DESTROYER TO THE BOTTOM. The *Times* did not say exactly where in the Pacific these alleged heroics took place. In fact, U.S. fliers had not only not hit a Japanese ship, they had not yet even located a Japanese ship.[56]

Still, one item of good news emanated from *Duke of York*'s radio shack: Auchinleck in Libya had accomplished as much in thirty days as Wavell and O'Connor had in sixty the previous year. Axis troops in Bardia, where Rommel had set up his headquarters in anticipation of taking Tobruk, found themselves surrounded. Rommel, outnumbered in tanks by four to one, had fled west with his remaining armor, toward Benghazi, which Auchinleck would claim on Christmas Eve. Days later, Rommel drew up his lines at El Agheila, four hundred miles west of Tobruk. It was an orderly retreat, but it was a retreat, Rommel's first. The Western Desert had changed hands again. Yet this time, the enemy retreating across Cyrenaica was not Italian but German. Given the back-and-forth nature of the battle, and the resourcefulness of Rommel, Churchill resisted any temptation he may have harbored to proclaim in the name of the King, as he had a year earlier, another "Bardia Day."[57]

While aboard ship, Churchill learned from Eden, in Moscow, that Stalin still maintained a healthy appetite for real estate, in spite of having lost much of western Russia to the Wehrmacht. Churchill told Eden that although Britain had declared war on "the cats-paws" of Hungary, Romania, and Finland, the War Cabinet would refuse to satisfy Stalin on this new matter of postwar boundaries. Although Stalin's defeat in the coming summer seemed as likely as, if not more likely than, eventual victory, he had his maps out, and he wanted assurances that Russia's postwar western boundaries would preserve his territorial gains in eastern Poland, Romania, and Finland. As for the three Baltic states, Latvia, Lithuania, and Estonia, which had all bolted the czar's collapsing empire in 1918, Stalin wanted them back. To Attlee, Churchill cabled: "Stalin's demand about Finland, Baltic States, and Roumania [*sic*] are directly contrary to the first, second, and third articles of the Atlantic Charter, to which Stalin has subscribed. There can be no question whatever of our making such an agreement, secret or public, direct or implied without prior agreement with the United States." He told Eden that to "approach President Roosevelt with his [Stalin's] proposals would be to court a blank refusal and might experience lasting trouble on both sides."[58]

He had often during Britain's bleakest hours privately shared with friends and close associates his visions for the postwar world. "After the War" was a phrase heard in popular songs and a turn of phrase used often at the Churchill dinner table, in telegrams to Roosevelt, and in his addresses. It was shorthand for subjects not to be formally considered until Hitler was dead and Europe had reached the "broad, sunlit uplands" of liberty. He had earned the right to muse on the subject of "After the War," yet not once in his first fifteen months as prime minister had he done so in public. Then, curiously given his public reticence on the matter, within a few hours of sitting down with Roosevelt at Argentia, he had set to work drafting the Atlantic Charter, which amounted to a bilateral declaration on international civil rights and the Anglo-American blueprint for the postwar peace (as well as a moral imperative that Americans might fight for). After the two leaders agreed on the text (without consulting Stalin), they announced the Atlantic Charter to the world.[59]

If Churchill and Roosevelt felt it their duty to state their vision of the postwar world, why should not Stalin? Stalin, whose borders after all had been violated, and whose capital was now under siege, believed his claims on the Baltic states to be self-evidently proper. Churchill downplayed Stalin's maneuvers: "No one can foresee where the balance of power will lie . . . at the end of the war," he cabled Eden, yet most probably it would lie with the *bloc* of America and Britain, which would emerge from the war far less "exhausted" than Stalin, who would need Anglo-American help to rebuild more than the Americans and British would need Stalin. Still, Churchill heard enough in Stalin's demands to make him wary, though like a denizen of Plato's cave, he could divine only shadows of things beyond his immediate vision, which was entirely focused on crushing

Hitler. He could not make out exactly what was coming by way of Moscow, or its size, or its speed, but he didn't much care for it. Always remember, he had cautioned Eden, that Bolsheviks are "crocodiles" who understand only force. Years later he told his grandson, Winston Spencer Churchill, that he *knew*—at the first mention by Stalin of postwar boundaries—exactly where the seeds for the next European conflict would germinate, adding that from early 1942 on, he put every strategic decision in the war against Hitler under two lenses: "How will it shorten the war, and how will it prevent the Bear from stealing the peace."[60]

Those may well have been the sentiments of an old man who wanted to reposition himself more favorably in the historical story line. Yet, given the Faustian pact Churchill and Roosevelt made with Stalin, it seems improbable that Stalin's demands suddenly awakened in Churchill the prospect of postwar trouble. This was Joseph Stalin, after all, Hitler's former partner, a gunman who in his youth robbed banks for the Marxist cause and later—also for the cause, his own—resorted to mass murder. Why did Churchill and Roosevelt during the next three years fail, utterly, to hatch any plans between themselves that addressed the possible—probable, even—*consequences* to Europe of their alliance with the Soviet dictator? Both spoke in the starkest terms of the consequences to the world were Hitler to win. From a moral perspective, Stalin was simply the lesser of two evils; he killed his political opponents because they opposed him, not because of their bloodlines. Hitler, victorious, would kill everybody. The death of Hitlerism was therefore the main objective of the Anglo-American-Soviet alliance, but each of the three Allied leaders had a different political agenda, and each envisioned a postwar world different in structure from that envisioned by the other two. Stalin's political objectives were patently at odds with both the Atlantic Charter and Churchill's hopes for democratic European spheres of influence, which he intended first and foremost would serve to keep Prussia (but not all of Germany) down on the farm, quite literally.

The wonder is not that in late 1941 Churchill foresaw future problems with Stalin, but why he ever could have thought otherwise. Churchill was well versed in the history of Russia's relationship with Europe. He had lectured Colville the previous June on the Swedish invasion of 1700 and of Napoleon's 1812 gambit. Now, twice within a generation, the Germans had turned on Russia. Russia was an Asian nation with a foot in Europe, and Western Europeans had regularly stomped on that foot. Protection of Russia's western frontiers had driven Russian foreign policy for two centuries, Czarist, Leninist, and Stalinist. Moscow had always sought a security belt between itself and the West. The West, meanwhile, maintained a cordon sanitaire between itself and the Muscovites. The Poles had historically paid the price for their geographical position in relation to Russia's security needs, and had done so again when Hitler and Stalin signed their 1939 pact. By signing the pact, Stalin believed (incorrectly as he had learned in June) that he had widened his security belt. His war aims were to reclaim it, and to destroy the German threat once and for all. He articulated those aims often during the next three years. He linked all of his war decisions with Russian territorial interests and the German threat to those interests. He never disguised his aim, and held to it, wrote James MacGregor Burns, "with steel-like tenacity." For Stalin, defeating Germany and reclaiming Russian security were two sides of the same coin. Churchill's was a one-sided coin: defeat Hitler. His and Stalin's objectives, therefore, were similar but not identical.[61]

It was a vital distinction. Stalin believed that were Hitler to be assassinated or overthrown, possibly by the Prussian officers whom Hitler despised, the West might reach an agreement with the new Hitler-less Germany and then turn—with Germany—against Russia. It was a paranoid belief, but one strongly held nonetheless. Churchill indeed considered Hitler an interim enemy; he held Germany to be part of the European family, destined to again take its place at the table after Hitler was dealt with. Stalin, however, saw Germany as Russia's perpetual enemy, now more than ever deserving of annihilation. Once Hitler was vanquished, as Stalin saw it, the West would once again consider Moscow and communism to be its supreme enemies, a status cemented with the revolution of 1917. For the duration of the war, Stalin's relationship with his allies was informed by his certainty that Churchill and Roosevelt were not and never would be true friends of Russia.

For their part, Churchill and Roosevelt never entirely trusted Stalin. For the next three years they weighed every decision against the possibility that Russia might quit the war, as the Bolsheviks had done in 1917. They withheld the Ultra secret from Stalin (although they passed along Ultra decrypts as information gained from reliable "agents"), and of course they did not bring Stalin into the atomic bomb project. Yet, where Churchill's trust in Stalin was qualified, his *loyalty* to Stalin was not, and never diminished throughout the war. In Churchill's moral paradigm, loyalty was an absolute, where trust admitted to degrees. Even as Stalin made the extent of his territorial ambitions known in 1943 and 1944, Churchill remained loyal, cabling Roosevelt in April 1944, "I have a feeling that the [Soviet] bark is worse than its bite." Even as victory became certain and Stalin's demands for territory—at the expense of liberty within those territories—hardened, Churchill remained the steadfast partner. After Yalta, in early 1945, Churchill told the Commons that Stalin's "word was [his] bond.... I know of no Government which stands to its obligations...more solidly than the Russian Soviet Government."[62]

Given their distrust of Stalin, why did two such brilliant politicians as Churchill and Roosevelt remain so loyal to an ideological enemy who for almost twenty years had terrorized his own people while declaring capitalism to be his mortal foe? Because, Churchill wrote in his memoirs, they had no decent alternative. "Neither Roosevelt nor Churchill was blind to the continuance of terror and tyranny in the Soviet Union," Harriman later wrote. But they needed Stalin and the millions upon millions of Russian men he could feed into the teeth of Hitler's war machine. Stalin, supported by the West, could buy the time America needed to arm. For England, each day the Russians fought diminished the prospects of a German invasion of the Home Island. As well, Roosevelt and Churchill truly believed that a man's word was his bond; they were gentlemen, after all. As the war progressed, they became quite confident that they could handle Uncle Joe (they often called him "UJ" in their private communications) much as they handled each other—with tenacity (Churchill) and charm (Roosevelt). Yet they never appreciated the fullness of the man. "Let no one think Stalin is a thug...or roughneck," the journalist and author John Gunther wrote three years earlier. Stalin was a reader of Plato, a student of the American Civil War, a man of brains as well as prescient political instinct. He once dismissed a group of Bolshevik writers by telling them to "read Shakespeare, Goethe and other classics, as I do." He had a sense of humor, which Hitler did not. He was perhaps the most politically adroit of all the principals, Allied and Axis. Yet Churchill and Roosevelt believed he was malleable, reachable, and teachable.[63]

Harriman later recalled that Churchill's and Roosevelt's certainty that "they knew how to get along with Stalin" infected the judgment of "lesser lights," including, Harriman admitted, himself. He confessed in his memoirs that he "was not entirely immune to that infectious idea" of getting along with Stalin given the "tough talks" he had held with the marshal in "tough sessions." Beaverbrook tried to prove his loyalty to Stalin by shipping to the Soviets the Lend-Lease matériel Stalin demanded, matériel that Britain desperately needed. Churchill feared Beaverbrook's generosity would result in Britain being "bled white." All of the players, American and British, thought they could handle UJ. In fact, Uncle Joe had never been a man to be handled. Rather, he had proven himself the consummate manhandler.[64]

Eden that month took a pragmatic approach to Stalin's demands, telling the War Cabinet that the Soviets would inevitably, one way or another, get the Baltic states, the implication being now was as good a time as any. For Churchill, this would not do. The time for drawing boundaries, he told Eden, was not yet at hand, and such questions "can only be resolved at the Peace Conference when we have won the war." He then went easy on Eden, whose journey to Moscow was the most important of his career to date.

The Old Man expressed his overall satisfaction with the mission and advised his emissary to "not be rough with Stalin." A discussion of boundaries, however, was out of the question. Such was Churchill's political, and moral, position in regard to Eastern Europe, a position that events and Stalin in time undermined.[65]

Confined by the weather to his cabin aboard the *Duke of York*, Churchill dictated three long memos in which he outlined to the War Cabinet and the COS his plans for Europe and Asia in 1942, and his worldwide plans for 1943, which included the "advantage in declaring now our intention of sending armies of liberation into Europe in 1943." Those words were intended not only for the British chiefs but for Roosevelt and his advisers. Nowhere in the three memos did Churchill refer to the possibility of sending large Allied armies into Europe in 1942; he knew it could not be done. Yet the Americans were already thinking of doing just that—opening a second European front by autumn. Stalin had demanded one since July. Churchill, within months, would find himself under fire from the Americans, Stalin, and British leftists, accused by all of opposing a second front, when in fact, on the advice of his military chiefs, he opposed only a premature second front, a distinction he tried without success to impress upon his allies that year, and upon his critics for the rest of his life.[66]

While Churchill was at sea, Adolf Hitler sated the curiosity of all who had wondered for several days just who would replace Field Marshal Walther von Brauchitsch as commander in chief of the German army and head of *Oberkommando des Heeres* (OKH), the army's high command. Given that Germany was a land-based power, OKH had been, traditionally, the primary military voice within the Wehrmacht, until 1938, when Hitler configured his personal military mouthpiece, *Oberkommando des Wehrmacht* (OKW), which directed all branches of the German military. From then on, the professional staff officers of OKH, loathed by Hitler for their Prussian and aristocratic lineage, exercised less influence. In reality, OKW, sprinkled throughout with Hitler's lackeys, planned and directed operations in all theaters except Russia, where OKH had been left to manage the eastern army (*Ostheer*) under the eye of and at the pleasure of OKW, a relationship that played nicely into Hitler's strategy of pitting his military services against one another. Von Brauchitsch, his heart failing and lacking the stomach to argue with Hitler—who had been outraged by Brauchitsch's strategy of taking Moscow before the Caucasus oil fields—resigned.

It was clear to Hitler that only one German possessed the requisite military genius to replace Brauchitsch, who, he later told Goebbels, was "a coward and a nincompoop." And so on December 19, the Führer appointed himself commander in chief of Germany's army. He was of course already supreme commander of all German armed forces, but C in C was a hands-on job of tactical—not only strategic—decisions. A purge of the ranks had begun; Rundstedt, Guderian, and Erich Hoepner, considered panzer geniuses just a year earlier, were pushed out, and Bock was retired. Field Marshal Wilhelm Keitel stayed on as chief of staff of the supreme command of the German armed forces, an imposing title that belied his status as a rubber stamp for Hitler. Franz Halder stayed on as chief of staff at OKH with hopes of serving as a counterweight to Hitler's increasingly baneful influence over the army. Halder was just the sort of professional soldier Hitler distrusted. The disfavor was returned; more loyal to his army and to Germany than to Hitler, Halder loathed the Führer, yet duty demanded he serve him to his best ability. Colorless and professorial, Halder protected the army's traditions and was one of the very few in the highest ranks who felt it his duty (and was man enough) to apprise Hitler of the Führer's strategic weaknesses. Still, Halder later told a historian that he carried his pistol to staff meetings in the Reich Chancellery with the intent of ridding Germany of the poisonous Austrian, but "as a human being and a Christian" could not bring himself to do so. Yet had he done so, the porcine Göring would have taken Hitler's place, and were Göring to be toppled, Hitler's number three man (and Rudolf Hess's successor), the thuggish yet clever and ambitious Martin Bormann, would assume the leadership, that is, if the more thuggish and more ambitious Heinrich Himmler did not dispute the issue. No lone assassin could dismantle the Nazi apparatus.[67]

Hitler's decision was equivalent to Roosevelt taking over day-to-day operations from Marshall, or Churchill supplanting Brooke. But whereas a peevish Hitler squelched dissent, Churchill (himself often peevish) fostered an often-fractious give-and-take between himself and his generals, with the result that decisions taken were made stronger by having been annealed in the furnace of debate. Hitler's takeover of the army apparatus not only banked the fires of debate, but further fractured his chain of command and set up fiefdoms within the German armed forces, each reporting to Hitler but not to the others, such that Hitler and Hitler alone was privy to *all* information. He thus deprived himself of the unified and coherent counsel of the experts who could best counsel him. But Hitler, suspicious of the lot of them, felt he served his own cause more efficiently by forcing his generals to toil in partial darkness. It later proved a disastrous decision, but at the time it appeared inspired, for as Mollie Panter-Downes wrote that week, "The idea of Hitler as a crazy, Chaplinesque commander who would quickly blunder toward disaster isn't so popular as it was before some of those supposedly crazy notions of his proved pretty sound after all." If anyone was blundering to disaster that week, it was Churchill and Roosevelt, in the Far East.[68]

Late in the afternoon of December 22, after almost ten terrible days at sea, the *Duke of York* sounded Hampton Roads, at the mouth of Chesapeake Bay. The plan had been to cruise right up the Potomac, but Churchill had had enough. He took a military plane to Washington, accompanied by a few of his aides. As the aircraft made its final approach along the Potomac, the group gazed out the windows and "transfixed with delight" took in a sight none had seen in more than two years: "the amazing spectacle of a city all lighted up." When Churchill touched down at the Anacostia naval air station, he saw Franklin Roosevelt sitting in the backseat of a large black sedan that had pulled onto the tarmac. The president had come across the river to welcome his guest in person. It was the sort of generous, seemingly offhand gesture that Roosevelt was master of. Nobody, especially Churchill, was immune to such charm. From Roosevelt's perspective, the arrival by air of a foreign leader was an event not to be missed; no American president had ever flown on an airplane while in office, let alone learned to fly one, as had Churchill more than two decades earlier. Roosevelt watched from his limousine as the prime minister of Great Britain emerged from the aluminum skin of a flying machine into the Washington night as if to proclaim, change is in the air.[69]

Churchill was put up in a suite just down the hall from the president's private rooms and across the hall from the Lincoln study, where Hopkins resided. Rarely was a foreign dignitary accorded such treatment. Late that night the two leaders met in Roosevelt's second-floor study, where Churchill passed on to Roosevelt drafts of the three strategic papers he had composed during his journey. Taken as a whole, the papers were prescient: Churchill saw a maritime war against Japan while Allied ground forces retook islands in a stepping-stone march to Tokyo. He envisioned hitting Germany on the periphery until such time as Russian and Anglo-American armies could squeeze Berlin from the east and west. He saw the need to control the Atlantic as a prerequisite for any European forays. And he saw the strategic value in clearing North Africa and claiming the Mediterranean—knocking Italy out of the war in the bargain—before undertaking an invasion of Europe. Roosevelt was familiar with the gist of Churchill's thoughts, Churchill having worked them into a long letter to the president in late October, to which Roosevelt had made no reply. As well, during the secret meetings of a year earlier between American, British, and Canadian military chiefs (ABC-1 talks), an overall war policy had been worked out in the event of America coming in against both Germany and Japan. The plan called for the defeat of Germany first, beginning with aerial bombing and naval blockade, accomplished in part by shifting some of America's Pacific fleet to the Atlantic. That gentleman's agreement, Churchill hoped, would be codified during the next few days, because with Japan having set America to raging, he feared the American military chiefs might shift to a Japan-first strategy, with disastrous results for Britain if Hitler dispatched the Russians before the Yanks showed up.[70]

Code names for hoped-for operations abounded in Churchill's plans, many chosen by himself. Acrobat was to be the assault that would leave Auchinleck "in possession of Tripoli" within weeks, with his tanks poised "on the French frontier of Tunis." Churchill had no desire to chase Rommel across North Africa; he meant to crush the German's armored forces and then kill Rommel's infantry, pinned down as it would be on the coastal plain. Yet with each passing day it appeared that Auchinleck—low on supplies, his troops exhausted—might come up short. That would imperil Churchill's hopes of getting the Americans into the desert war. When Auchinleck kicked off Crusader, Churchill (taking a naval analogy too far) told the Commons that the outcome of desert battles, like sea battles, could be determined in a matter of hours. The battle had now lasted more than a month, and although Rommel had retreated to the Tripolitania frontier, Auchinleck's Eighth Army, under the command of General Neil M. Ritchie, lacked the tanks to finish him off. Acrobat, therefore, looked to be finished before it started. Still, "the Auk" cabled Churchill with just the news he needed to get Roosevelt on board: the Germans were "hard-pressed," he reported, and he advised that Churchill "press forward with Acrobat." He believed he'd be ready to go on the attack by mid-February.[71]

Auchinleck's optimism also bade well for Whipcord, the most optimistic of Churchill's plans, which was based on the belief that after taking all of Tripoli, the British could jump right to Sicily "while the shock of battle still reigns" in North Africa. With Sicily in the bag, any remaining Germans and Italians in the desert would presumably find themselves isolated, and doomed. That, in turn, would set the stage for Gymnast, the pacification of all of French North Africa, with or without the consent of Vichy, accomplished by landing British—and, hopefully, American—forces commanded by the hero of Dunkirk, Harold Alexander, near Dakar and Casablanca. To bolster Auchinleck, Churchill ordered that several transports carrying the 18th British Division, along with squadrons of fighter planes, anti-tank guns, and one hundred new American tanks, be sent to Cairo via the Cape of Good Hope. Days earlier he had told the Defence

Committee that its "guiding principle" should be that "no resources" required for North African operations "should be diverted elsewhere."[72]

His strategic musings were one with his grand strategies of a year earlier, hopes within hopes. He always saw the European theater in terms of forging a ring around Germany, by naval blockade in the North Sea and eastern Atlantic, and on land from French North Africa, east to Cairo and north through Baghdad to the Caucasus, the eastern perimeter of the ring delineated by the 1,800-mile Soviet front. Churchill meant to probe and test the ring by sea, by air, and on land until he found weaknesses, and then exploit them. He wanted to take the fight everywhere at once, a strategy that frustrated his military advisers (and would frustrate his American allies for the next three years). "Churchill is the greatest military genius in history," Ismay told Averell Harriman. "He can use one division on three fronts at the same time." The editor of Brooke's diaries, Arthur Bryant, writes that "until the end of 1941 Britain had no real strategy for winning the war," and sought only to avoid losing the war by swinging "wildly with all she had, whenever and where ever she was able, and contain her European enemies in a ring of salt water and sand." Yet unlike the previous year, Churchill now had an ally capable of supplying limitless numbers of men and weapons. The Christmas conference where all this would be parsed was code-named Arcadia, an appropriate moniker given Arcadia's literary association with refuge and calm, as well as being home to the temple of Zeus. In Washington, Churchill would find refuge, and in Roosevelt, Zeus, for there was no longer any doubt about who would craft the lightning bolts that would destroy Hitler. The question foremost in Churchill's mind was who would decide where and when to loose them.[73]

Max Beaverbrook considered Churchill's myriad operations to be diversions from the real war, in Russia, where he believed British tanks and troops would serve a greater purpose than in North Africa. General George Marshall also considered Africa a sideshow; he wanted to go ashore in France that year. Dwight Eisenhower, Marshall's deputy for all of a week, held a similar view, though with an eye toward a different theater of war: "I've been insisting that the Far East is critical," he noted in his diary, "and no sideshows should be undertaken until air and ground there is in satisfactory shape. Instead, we are taking on Magnet, Gymnast, etc." Eisenhower, unhappy with his desk job, confided to his diary that he'd "give anything to be back in the field." Averell Harriman, however, agreed with Churchill's ring strategy, and saw the strategic significance of Turkey and the Middle East, where others, especially Beaverbrook, did not.[74]

General Sir Alan Brooke, on the job as CIGS for only three weeks, agreed with Churchill that clearing North Africa and the Mediterranean held the key, but only if overwhelming force could be brought to bear there, an impossibility given the shifting of resources from the Middle East to the Far East, and the ongoing shipping losses in the Atlantic. British generals had for two centuries been trained to think in terms of the naval strategy necessary to sustain land forces in any given theater. Unlike the continental powers, Britain did not have to maintain a standing army of four or five million men to protect its borders; the North Sea and Channel did that. The British army was, by virtue of England's island geography, always an expeditionary force dependent on the Royal Navy. Brooke was such a "salt water" general. He understood that the most significant benefit to be gained by Allied control of the Mediterranean would be an immediate, effective increase in merchant tonnage of one million tons—the equivalent of 200 cargo ships—as a result of cutting the Middle Eastern supply route from almost 14,000 miles around the Cape to less than 4,000 directly through the Mediterranean. Such "new" shipping could then be used to carry more arms and food to Britain, and American troops to Britain or the Far East. Unless and until the Mediterranean was cleared, Allied shipping would descend further into crisis. Another factor contributed to Brooke's enthusiasm for Mediterranean operations. He had come off the beaches at Dunkirk and harbored no desire to return to France until he could do so in overwhelming force.[75]

This brought him into line with Churchill's belief in the need to return to France as well as with Churchill's Mediterranean thinking, but for different, and ultimately conflicting, reasons. As for Churchill's desire to fight in Norway, the Far East, and Africa simultaneously, Brooke knew that Britain—the entire Empire—lacked the men and matériel, especially the shipping, to attempt most, let alone all, of Churchill's multiple and far-flung operations. But Brooke was in London; Churchill was in Washington, where he had the full attention of the president and his military chiefs. Roosevelt, within days of Churchill's arrival, deferred to his advice on the matters of Acrobat, Gymnast, and Magnet, the plan to replace British troops stationed in Northern Ireland by four or more American divisions in order to free up British troops for deployment to North Africa. The details were to be sorted out by the newly created Combined Chiefs of Staff Committee—made up of the American and British army, navy, and air chiefs and their delegates in each capital. The first meetings stunned Dill, who telegraphed to Brooke that the Americans came with no agenda and recorded no minutes. Dill concluded that "at present [the United States] has not—repeat, not—the slightest conception of what the war means, and their armed forces are more unready for war than it is possible to imagine."[76]

To further complicate matters, where Churchill saw opportunities in North Africa, Roosevelt saw them in China. Chiang Kai-shek was dependent on the Burma Road, China's only link to the outside world, over which went fuel and ammunition for Chiang's armies. Were the Japanese to cut the road, Chiang would likely be finished. The entire Allied air defense along the Burma Road consisted of a few squadrons of RAF fighters in Burma and about seventy American mercenaries of the American Volunteer Group, whose few squadrons of fighter planes were divided between Kunming and Burma. The AVG irregulars were paid five hundred dollars for each confirmed Japanese kill. The Americans painted a shark's toothy snout on the noses of their Curtiss-Wright P-40B Tomahawks, and added an evil eye near the radiator intake in hopes of spooking Japanese pilots. They called themselves the Flying Tigers, and they served under a master tactician, Claire Chennault, a retired American army air corps captain who now held the rank of brigadier in Chiang's Chinese air force. Madame Chiang Kai-shek called the Americans her "flying angels." They were few in numbers and lacked spare parts and bullets, but they were the only Allied force since Pearl Harbor to have inflicted any pain whatsoever on the Japanese.[77]

Within days of Churchill's arrival in Washington, Archie Wavell, at Roosevelt's urging, was appointed supreme allied commander in the Far East. His mandate was to hold Malaya, and to coordinate with Chiang in defense of the Burma Road. The latter directive appealed to nobody except the Americans—the Burmese hated the Chinese as much or more than they hated the British. Wavell thought Chiang's forces not up to the task; and Churchill considered all of China a sideshow. Although his father had brought Burma into the Empire in the mid-1880s, Churchill saw value in defending the place in terms of shielding India rather than in saving Burma or defending Chiang and his supply route. Wavell's ABDA (American-British-Dutch-Australian) command was to set up shop in Batavia as soon as possible.

Lacking meaningful air and naval support, his lines of supply already in jeopardy, Wavell was in effect being asked to take one for the home team. Neither Churchill nor his chiefs liked the idea, yet, Churchill later wrote, "it was evident we must meet the American view." With that, he avoided the first spat in the partnership he had sought for so long. Churchill and Roosevelt understood they must accommodate each other much like partners in a three-legged race, where individual mobility and strengths are subordinated to the common cause. Disparate strategic goals, political and military, must not be allowed to undermine the common cause. They understood that for the duration they could not exploit each other's weaknesses, as they might in a friendly rivalry over tariffs. They knew they had to act as one and speak as one, because both their foe in Berlin and their new friend in Moscow were absolute masters of exploiting weakness. The avoidance of a spat in the early days of the alliance did not mean that there would be none down the road, but it meant that the two leaders trusted each other enough to handle the spats as they came along. There would be many.[78]

Shortly after 5:00 P.M. on Christmas Eve, Roosevelt and Churchill made their way to the south portico of the White House. There, the president flipped an electrical switch to illuminate the national Christmas tree, a thirty-foot-tall live Oriental spruce planted far down on the South Lawn and draped with red, white, and blue lights. Roosevelt had ordered the gates opened, and a crowd had gathered behind ropes on the lawn. Following a brief statement by Roosevelt, Churchill delivered a few remarks of his own, which were broadcast back to London by the BBC. As Churchill spoke, soft golden light spilled from the mansion's windows, a sight that would appear strange to most Britons and virtually every European, even the victorious Germans, whose leader had ordered that Germany be blacked out. Churchill, in his Christmas message, simply noted that for at least one night every home "throughout the English-speaking world should be a brightly-lighted island of happiness and peace. Let the children have their night of fun and laughter. Let the gifts of Father Christmas delight their play." And then it was off to drinks, dinner, and a late-to-bed, to prepare the address he would make to Congress in two days. So this was Christmas 1941, another year gone, and a new war just begun. America would not light its national Christmas tree again until 1945.[79]

Adolf Hitler, in Berlin, had forbidden the singing of all Christmas carols except "O Tannenbaum." Fir trees represented the towering strength of the Aryan race. The swastika, not an angel or cross, topped Berliners' Christmas trees, what few there were. Those *Volk* fortunate enough to procure trees likely used them for fuel. Winter had arrived, but coal had not. Food grew scarce, even as it was stolen from the Belgians, French, Poles, and Dutch, who by late 1941 had taken to boiling tulip bulbs for sustenance. Berliners greeted each other with *"Ach, das leben ist schwer"* ("Life is hard"). For German troops in Russia, life was hard, brutish, and short. Soviet propagandists smuggled thousands of Christmas cards into Germany, entitled "Living Space in the East." They depicted "a frozen vista of rows of wooden crosses topped with German helmets."[80]

Soon after Churchill addressed America's children, three hundred Free French sailors descended upon the islands of St-Pierre and Miquelon, France's oldest and smallest colony, located just off the Newfoundland coast. The islands were Vichy property, and Roosevelt, who hoped to lure Vichy into the Western fold through kindness, wanted them to stay that way. But the Vichy government had set up a radio transmitter on St-Pierre for purposes, wrote Churchill, "of spreading Vichy lies and poison" and quite possibly to "signal U-boats now hunting United States ships." Secretary of State Cordell Hull pressured Canada to shut down the station, but Ottawa, not wanting to offend Pétain, declined. De Gaulle, however, saw an opportunity for a symbolic victory over the Vichy lackeys, and before Churchill left for America, he informed him of his plans to capture the islands. Churchill at first approved but then objected after Hull voiced his vigorous disapproval. De Gaulle went ahead anyway. His forces arrived in gunboats and captured the islands without a fight. The victors raised their flag, emblazoned with the Cross of Lorraine. The British were elated. The Canadians were relieved to be off the hook. The Americans were aghast, as was Vichy France. Hull, infuriated (for here was a bald violation of the Monroe Doctrine), referred to de Gaulle and his followers as the "so-called Free French," thus assuring enmity between America and Frenchmen of all political persuasions at the exact moment Churchill saw the looming necessity to court the Vichy in North Africa. For if the Allies were ever to take the fight all the way from Egypt to Morocco, Tunisia, and Algeria, a compliant—better yet, a cooperative—Vichy regime would be far more vital to success than a brigade or two of de Gaulle's troublemakers.[81]

De Gaulle, therefore, had just mucked up the works. Yet he and his cohorts appeared to be the only Frenchmen willing to die in the fight against Hitler, and for that he had earned Churchill's respect and (guarded) support. Cordell Hull, on the other hand, treated de Gaulle with aloofness bordering on contempt. As punishment for his insolence, Hull—the "so-called Secretary of State" according to many in the American press—insisted the Free French be excluded from the roster of Allied countries that were to sign a pledge of allegiance to one another on New Year's Day. Churchill argued for the inclusion of the Free French, but Hull, backed by Roosevelt, carried the day. Churchill sidestepped another spat, and France, free or otherwise, did not officially exist within the alliance, known around Washington as the Associated Powers.

For a century Hong Kong had manifested handsomely the imperial British way of life. It was built on the profits of opium and piracy, ruled in fact from the offices of the towering Hongkong and Shanghai Banking Corporation, and fueled by gin slings and afternoon handicaps at the Happy Valley Racecourse. Hong Kong had been the free-wheeling, free-trade heart of Britain's Far East empire, open for business to any sea captain of any nationality willing and able to journey there, including Franklin Roosevelt's maternal grandfather, Warren Delano Jr., who made and lost several fortunes in the Clipper trade. Delano's daughter Sara, having actually sailed to that city during the American Civil War, inculcated in her son, Franklin, a romantic concept of Hong Kong and China and their roles in the world. Hong Kong was about to assume a new role. Since December 8, fewer than 8,000 Scots, Englishmen, Indians, Canadians, and some local Chinese had been surrounded by more than 30,000 Japanese troops. When the Japanese crossed from the mainland and cut off the water supply, the fight was all but over. Hong Kong's defenders understood that London considered the city a tactical position, to be held as long as possible in order to delay the Japanese and gain time to reinforce the more vital city of Singapore.

Despite Churchill's order to the defenders of Hong Kong to fight "from house to house" if necessary, and his exhortation "to resist to the end," Hong Kong's governor Sir Mark Young, surrounded and outgunned, surrendered on Christmas Day. It was the first colonial possession the British lost in the Pacific, ever. The victors took prisoner thirty Maryknoll missionaries and forced the captive proselytizers to bear witness as Japanese infantrymen bayoneted dozens of hog-tied British and Canadian prisoners. Prisoners spared the sword were beaten with rubber hoses and had water forced "down their throats until they nearly drowned." The rape of Hong Kong's Eurasian, Chinese, and white women began immediately. Three British nurses were raped, then bayoneted, and then burned. Three days later, Japanese troops—*Time* dubbed them "the dwarf-like men"—strutted through the city in triumphal review. By then, their brothers in Yamashita's Twenty-fifth Army had negotiated one-third of the Malay Peninsula, their target, Singapore. That fortress, Churchill told Wavell, "was to be held at all costs."[82]

On the day after Christmas, Churchill addressed the U.S. Congress. Listeners in Britain, where the BBC aired programs without corporate sponsorship, were surprised to learn that their prime minister's message was brought to them by a toothpaste company. Although such cultural divergences between the two nations lent credence to Bernard Shaw's observation that they were two countries separated by the same language, Churchill considered that language the uniting factor and, intending to demonstrate to Americans his mastery of it, had spent more than twelve hours crafting his words. Relieved to be among friends and cousins now (he could trace his American ancestry back five generations, to an officer who served under Washington), he began on a light note and surged ahead without regard to whether the moment was proper for glib pleasantries: "I cannot help reflecting that if my father had been an American, and my mother British, rather than the other way around, I might have got here on my own." With their applause and cheers, the assembled gave him what he came for: approval. Warming to his topic—retribution—he saw no need to inspire the Americans; Japan had done that. He saw no reason to gird Americans against the prospect of firestorms in their cities, of four-thousand-pound bombs obliterating their Parliaments and cathedrals and families, since other than the possibility of nuisance attacks on each coast, massed assaults were far beyond the technological reach of Germany and Japan. Lloyd's of London, in fact, was offering odds of ninety-nine to one against the chance of any property damage occurring on the Atlantic coast.[83]

Churchill worked in this bit of I-told-you-so, which engendered absolute silence from the gallery: "If we had kept together after the last war, if we had taken common measures for our safety, this renewal of the curse need never have fallen upon us. Do we not owe it to ourselves, to our children, to tormented mankind, to make sure that these catastrophes do not engulf us for the third time?" He excoriated the usual suspects with his usual delicious words and phrases: the "wicked men" who spread their "pestilences" and will "stop at nothing that violence and treachery can suggest." Churchill went after the "filthy Quislings" and "the boastful Mussolini... a lackey and serf, the merest utensil of his master's will." Then he gripped his lapels, slowly rocked forward, and delivered the line that brought Congress to its feet, including the isolationists. Of the Japanese he asked, "What kind of a people do they think we are? Is it possible they do not realize that we will never cease to persevere against them until they have been taught a lesson which they and the world will never forget?"[84]

The *New York Times* (under the headline CHURCHILL PREDICTS HUGE ALLIED DRIVE IN 1943) called the speech, which ran for more than thirty minutes, "typical" Churchill, "full of bubbling humor, biting denunciation of totalitarian enemies, stern courage, and hard facts." Yet some of Churchill's so-called hard facts were flabby. Citing Auchinleck's "victory in the Libyan campaign," Churchill declaimed, "Had we diverted and dispersed our gradually growing resources between Libya and Malaya, we would have been found wanting in both places." That was, at best, a lawyerly way of putting things. In spite of his autumn admonition to the British Chiefs of Staff that no diversions detract from Auchinleck's offensive capabilities, Churchill days earlier had ordered the 18th Division, then en route to the Suez, diverted to Singapore. Then, on the day *before* he addressed Congress, he ordered Auchinleck "to spare at once" for Singapore's defense heavy artillery, AA guns, trucks, one hundred new American tanks, and four squadrons (about forty-eight aircraft) of fighter planes, all of which Auchinleck was in need of, soon desperately so. Brooke lamented to his diary that Auchinleck was "struggling along with the forces at his disposal...little knowing his activities must be shortly curtailed" by Churchill's transfer of men and matériel to the Far East. Churchill didn't see things that way. The diminution of his forces, he told Auchinleck, could be accomplished "without compromising Acrobat," the push through Tripoli to Tunisia. And Gymnast, Churchill told his general, was still in good shape because America was now in. He added: "All our success in the West would be nullified by the fall of Singapore." That was true.[85]

That night he was awakened by "oppressive" heat in his bedroom, which was likely caused by a radiator valve stuck in the open position, a familiar nuisance to Americans who lived with central heat but a mystery to Britons, who for the most part did not. He attempted to remedy the situation by lifting a window, which stuck fast. He heaved, and felt a pain in his left arm and chest. In his memoirs he wrote, "I strained my heart slightly." Actually, as Dr. Wilson ascertained the next morning, Churchill had suffered a mild heart attack. Although Moran's memoirs* were considered by Churchill's friends and family to be self-serving and often inaccurate, the doctor's medical sense was sound. In this case he correctly diagnosed Churchill's heart problem, with the result that Churchill found a new detail to dwell on: his pulse. He demanded at all hours that Wilson check his heart rate, yet he also told the doctor not to impart any unsettling news. On several occasions over the next few days, Wilson observed Churchill making quick and furtive checks of his pulse. The doctor told him to ignore his heart rate, which is akin to telling someone not to conjure an image of a polar bear. When his self-diagnosis continued, Wilson took a calculated risk; he persuaded Churchill to slow down a bit but did not tell him what had actually happened, or that what he really needed was several weeks of bed rest. Such a prescription would have terrified Churchill and, more important, Wilson believed, the Americans and Britons.[86]

Two days after his heart episode, Churchill boarded a special train and chugged north to Ottawa in order to thank Prime Minister Mackenzie King and the Canadian people for their support. It seemed to Dr. Wilson that Churchill expected nothing less from the Dominions, and in fact took the Canadians for granted, especially the prudent and plodding Mackenzie King, who was prone to such banal observations as "the great thing in politics is to avoid mistakes."[87]

Canada had paid for its loyalty. Most of its merchant and cruise fleets had been placed at HMG's disposal; many Canadian ships had been lost. The Canadians in Hong Kong were now prisoners, or dead. Churchill was most grateful for Canadian support vis à vis Vichy France. Although Canada, like

---

* First published in Britain as *Churchill: The Struggle for Survival, 1940–1965* (Constable and Company, 1966). Published in the United States as *Churchill: Taken from the Diaries of Lord Moran* (Houghton Mifflin Company, 1966). Knighted in 1942, Sir Charles was made the first Lord Moran in January 1943. The book is part diary and part after-the-fact recollection presented as diary entries. Moran was not present in many of the scenes he paints himself into, and in which he quotes Churchill. Churchill's postwar secretary, Anthony Montague Browne, later declared (author interview, Nov. 15, 1980) that Churchill would no more hold substantive conversations with Moran about politics "than he would discuss the state of his bowels with his chiefs of staff." Browne held suspect much of the "debating, conversations and quotes he [Moran] put into people's mouths."

America, officially recognized Vichy, the vast majority of Canadians shared Churchill's contempt for the puppet government. When he addressed the Canadian Parliament on December 30, with full knowledge that such sentiments would further agitate Cordell Hull, he praised the fighting spirit of Charles de Gaulle. Then he reminded his audience of the prediction made by Weygand before the fall of France: "In three weeks England will have her neck wrung like a chicken." He paused, and directed a hard stare toward the assembly. Then: "Some chicken! Some neck!" That brought every man in the chamber to his feet. It was his most buoyant speech in eighteen months; the Canadians loved it, and Churchill knew it. Before departing Parliament, Churchill posed in the Speaker's Chambers for the photographer Yousuf Karsh. Seeking to capture Churchill at his most leonine, Karsh, without warning and just before he triggered his camera, snatched Churchill's cigar from his mouth. Karsh got the result he sought, a highly perturbed Churchill, looking more the pugilist than the statesman. The artist called his iconic photograph "The Roaring Lion." Moments later, after the storm had passed, Karsh made another photo, this of a benign Churchill, a smile creasing his almost cherubic face. Clementine called it the "happy" picture.[88]

Having regaled and thanked his obligors (though promising many more "dark and weary months of defeat" before victory was theirs), Churchill left Ottawa by train on New Year's Eve. The outside temperature had dropped to minus fifteen degrees Fahrenheit. The mood in the cars was somber. At the stroke of midnight, as the train highballed through the Hudson River Valley, Churchill stepped into the press carriage, a glass of champagne in hand. He raised it: "Here's to 1942. Here's to a year of toil—a year of struggle and peril, and a long step forward towards victory. May we all come through safe and with honor."[89]

One hundred miles to the south, the biggest and gayest crowd in memory gathered in Times Square. Only the military police standing in pairs on street corners and a huge white sign that asked "Remember Pearl Harbor" served notice that this celebration was unique. Just before midnight, as the glowing ball atop the New York Times Building began its descent, Lucy Monroe, the official soloist of the American Legion, began singing "The Star-Spangled Banner." The crowd listened at first in silence, but soon joined in. Radio networks beamed the anthem across the nation. In Washington, the mood was not gay. Troopers of the 3rd Cavalry Regiment, searching for saboteurs, spent New Year's Eve crawling along the aqueduct that carried drinking water to the capital from western Maryland. Infantrymen with fixed bayonets and live ammunition patrolled the Potomac bridges, while others put a cordon around the White House. Not since Confederate general Jubal Early knocked on the city's defenses in the summer of 1864 had so many soldiers swarmed the streets of Washington.[90]

In blacked-out London, a crowd that was gathered around St. Paul's Cathedral sang "Auld Lang Syne" when the clock struck midnight. The bells of London's churches remained silent, as they had for more than a year and a half. Then, inexplicably, the crowd broke into a chorus of "She'll Be Coming 'Round the Mountain," before dispersing and breaking up into ever smaller groups, each to wander home through the dark streets, with the occasional nervous glance jerked skyward. Harold Nicolson had not ventured out, but he listened to his wireless as Big Ben struck midnight. In his diary, Nicolson wrote, "And 1941 is finished.... It has been a sad and horrible year." No fires burned, but London could have served as a model for *Destruction,* the fourth painting in Thomas Cole's five-picture series, *The Course of Empire.* With America in, the odds had improved that London might never resemble Cole's final canvas: *Desolation.*[91]

General Sir Alan Brooke, looking back on the old year, asked for God's help in dealing with the "difficult times with the P.M. I see clearly ahead of me." As for the status of the Dominions, Brooke concluded, "We're not doing too bad. We've only lost about a quarter of the empire." Measured in square miles, his dour estimate was exaggerated. Measured in public confidence, especially among those of the Empire's citizens who dwelled in the Far East, it was not. Given the speed with which the Japanese were building their new empire on the ruins of Britain's old empire, Brooke's calculation seemed destined for fulfillment, and soon. His prediction of the looming difficulties inherent in working with Churchill was of course self-evidently correct.[92]

Churchill now operated in two worlds, one London, where "Action This Day" brought immediate results, the other a new world of action (and inaction) by committees seeking consensus. Churchill, Roosevelt, and Stalin were in overall agreement on the broadest objective, victory, but when they set about drawing up a declaration of solidarity, the devil began insinuating himself into the details. When the Soviet ambassador to the United States, Maxim Maximovich Litvinov, objected, at Stalin's insistence, to the inclusion of the phrase "religious freedom" in the draft declaration of the Associated Powers, Roosevelt (a religious man) lectured the ambassador "about his soul and the dangers of hell-fire." Roosevelt then reminded Litvinov that "freedom of religion" can be also construed to mean freedom *from* religion. Stalin approved the insertion of the clause. The alliance between a Christian republic, a parliamentary democracy, and a murderous Godless dictator could hardly have begun otherwise.[93]

Stalin wanted the declaration to reflect another position dear to him. The first article of the pact called for each signatory to employ all military and economic resources "against those members of the Tripartite Pact and its adherents with which such government is at war." As the Soviet Union was not at war with Japan, the final seven words of article 1 gave Stalin an out should anyone suggest down the road that he declare war on Japan. Roosevelt, meanwhile, happy with the entire document but not happy with the moniker "Associated Powers," came up with a more vivid name: the United Nations. Intent on sharing his suggestion with Churchill, the president wheeled himself down the hallway and into Churchill's room, where the prime minister, preparing for his bath, was wandering about stark naked. Taking no notice of Churchill's nakedness, Roosevelt suggested his proposed name change. Churchill replied, "Good," and added that Byron employed the same choice of words in *Childe Harold's Pilgrimage*. Churchill later told King George that he was the first British prime minister in history to greet a head of state naked. He later wrote he thought Roosevelt's "United Nations" "a great improvement" over the "Associated Powers."[94]

On December 12, the *New York Times* had run a list of the twenty-five* allied combatants. India—whose troops had so far fought in North Africa, Malaya, Iraq, and Persia—was absent from the *Times* roll call. India's exclusion made sense to Churchill; India was, after all, part of the British Empire, its foreign policy dictated by London. Churchill had for months made clear that any change in India's colonial status could only take place after the war, and that he could not, by law, dictate terms to a postwar Parliament in which he and his coalition government might play no role. But Roosevelt sought India's inclusion in the pact, and he instructed Hull to prod the British on the matter, an assignment Hull embraced with alacrity as a staunch anti-imperialist and still fuming over the St-Pierre incident (which he suspected Churchill of encouraging). The War Cabinet objected to India's inclusion, rightly so in Churchill's opinion. Halifax, keen to avoid trouble with the Americans, suggested to Churchill that India's participation in drafting the Versailles Treaty two decades earlier might serve as a precedent for its inclusion in the allied pact, and thus mollify Roosevelt. A compromise was reached: India would be included in the roll call of allies, but without any notation that implied sovereignty. With India, as with the exclusion of the Free French, Churchill deferred to Roosevelt.[95]

He did so again when Roosevelt demanded that the United States be the first signatory to the pact, followed by the other three powers: Great Britain, the Soviet Union, and China. China's emotional importance to Roosevelt was bolstered by strategic considerations. Here was a nation of

---

* The U.S., U.K., U.S.S.R., China; Australia, Belgium, Canada, Costa Rica, Cuba, Czechoslovakia, the Dominican Republic, El Salvador, Greece, Guatemala, Haiti, Honduras, India, Luxembourg, the Netherlands, New Zealand, Nicaragua, Norway, Panama, Poland, South Africa, and Yugoslavia.

almost five hundred million people, he told Churchill, which would emerge from the war armed and eager to fill the vacuum created by the defeat of Japan. Better to court the Chinese now than to have to face them later. China, for Churchill, was an ally, but "not a world power equal to Britain, the United States, or Russia." Yet so firm was Roosevelt regarding China's status that Churchill cabled Wavell: "If I can epitomize in one word the lesson I learned in the United States, it was 'China.'" China took fourth billing.

On one point of language the president failed to prevail; he disliked the designation favored by the press, "World War Two," and called for suggestions for a more poetic name. H. L. Mencken compiled a list of the many proposals that flowed into the White House, including the "War for Survival," the "Necessary War," the "Crazy War," the "War Against Tyrants," the "Devil's War," and "Hell." Any and all of those names applied to the conflict, but the press stuck with World War Two. Churchill, too, offered Roosevelt a name for the war; it summed up in three words the entire legacy of the appeasers and isolationists: "The Unnecessary War."[96]

On January 5, after almost two weeks of discussions, not wanting to further tax Roosevelt's hospitality yet not ready to return home (the American and British military chiefs were just getting down to business), Churchill accepted the offer of Lend-Lease administrator Edward Stettinius to spend a few days at Stettinius's Pompano Beach, Florida, seaside manse. The Old Man needed a break, and Roosevelt and Hopkins needed a break—from Churchill. Eleanor Roosevelt later recalled, "I was solicitous for [Churchill's] comfort, but I was always glad when he departed, for I knew that my husband would need a rest, since he had carried his usual hours of work in addition to the unusual ones Mr. Churchill preferred." The meetings had so drained Harry Hopkins he checked into the Washington Naval Hospital for a week of bed rest.[97]

Churchill and a dozen or so of his party along with a Secret Service detail flew down to the small airfield in West Palm Beach aboard Marshall's plane. From there they motored an hour south to Pompano, where the locals were told that the activity out at the Stettinius house was due to the arrival of an English invalid by the name of Mr. Lobb. Mr. Lobb, upon arrival, headed straightaway for the beach, where he reveled in the warm ocean waters, and swam about, naked, until somebody spotted a large shark. "They said it was only a 'ground shark,'" Churchill later wrote, "but it is as bad to be eaten by a ground shark as any other." Inspector Thompson ordered him out of the water, but Churchill stayed put, pawing happily about. The shark, after describing a long, slow circle, swam off. "My bulk," Churchill shouted to those on shore, "has frightened him into deeper water." Still, from then on he kept to the shallows, where he basked "half submerged in the water, like a hippopotamus in a swamp." Thompson thought Churchill, sunbathing, nude, "looked like a huge, well adjusted, and slightly over-bottled baby boy."

Roosevelt sent along his personal chef and a favorite recipe for clam chowder, but Churchill preferred Bovril washed down with champagne. He smoked his cigars and drank and frolicked in the surf in sunny and isolated South Florida, about as far from the war as he could get. It was his first holiday in three years. Although in early January Americans had no real idea of just what troubles were heading their way, Churchill, bobbing in the Florida surf, knew "without doubt" what lay before them all—"a time of tribulation" and "disappointments and unpleasant surprises." He had told Britons as much for almost two years, and had told Americans the same just days earlier. He knew that upon his arrival in London—"it was to no sunlit prospect that I must return"—he would again have to inform the King, the Parliament, and Britons that the worst was yet to come. After five days of whisky, hot baths, and warm Florida, Churchill telephoned Roosevelt to inform the president that he was about to depart for Washington. Mindful of John Martin's pleas to exercise *some* caution when speaking over nonsecure phone lines, he whispered, "I can't tell you how we are coming, but we are coming by puff-puff, got it? *Puff-puff.*"[98]

Mrs. Roosevelt invited a special guest to dinner on Churchill's penultimate evening in the White House: Louis Adamic. Slovenian by birth, Adamic by 1942 had become one of the most popular and controversial ethnic American writers. His progressive ideas had found favorable conditions in which to sprout at the traditionally anti-imperialist State Department, which had developed on certain desks a list to the left. Having read and enjoyed Adamic's latest book, *Two-Way Passage,* the First Lady must have known Churchill would find no comfort in the author's company. Adamic argued the case for America to take the lead in postwar European political reconstruction by sending "qualified" liberal expatriate thinkers such as himself back to the Old World to inculcate in its citizens a less chauvinistic outlook, such that undesirable elements could not influence events. Chief among these undesirable elements was the "Eagle of Yugoslavia" Draja Mihailovich and his 150,000 mostly Serbian Chetnik guerrillas who had for seven months been fighting a vicious war against Hitler's occupying forces, tying down ten German and Bulgarian divisions in the process. For this Mihailovich was hailed as a hero in the West, and by Churchill.

Adamic, however, supported the partisans led by Josip Broz, a Croat by birth, Socialist by choice, and virtually unknown in America. His followers called him Tito (Churchill, per his habit of getting names wrong, called him Toty). As for other European elements, Adamic saw the Soviets as posing no threat to anyone after the war. Britain was another matter; Britain followed Mihailovich on Adamic's list of undesirable scallywags to be excluded from postwar influence, especially in the Balkans. The Roosevelts, husband and wife, much impressed with Adamic, passed his book along to Churchill. He hated it.[99]

In his memoir of that evening, *Dinner at the White House,* Adamic described Roosevelt as "vivid and agile," the picture of charm. Even Fala, Roosevelt's little Scottie dog, who roamed the room sniffing shoes and performing tricks, came in for Adamic's praise. Adamic portrays Churchill as "a great leader and...also evil" and noted that he was "mostly stomach" with a fat cigar plugged into his "large, round mug." His mouth and eyes "were shrewd, ruthless, unscrupulous." When Adamic asked him how he liked *Two-Way Passage,* Churchill snarled, "I'm r-reading your book and I-I find it—int'r-resting." Adamic's sentence construction seems to ascribe a stutter to Churchill; yet although he experienced difficulty with the sibilant "s" (he had a very slight lisp), he did not stutter. In any case, Adamic correctly concluded before dessert that Churchill would never accept his utopian scheme, or anything like it. His demeanor, Adamic wrote, "was one of complex annoyance....I was a bloody nuisance dragged in by F.D.R. and he had had to put up with me. This was implicit in his manner, integral with his whole personality....He muttered something I did not understand. His half-closed eyes squinted up at me, and he stuck the cigar into his face and pressed his back against the wall." That sounds like Churchill, when perturbed, bored, and, as Adamic implies, running on 80 proof. It was a safe bet that Churchill would not be sponsoring Adamic for membership in the Other Club.[100]

It should be remembered that Churchill during those early weeks of the alliance could not predict with any certainty who among the men he met were destined to go down in history as giants, and who (like Adamic) were destined for the dustbin. George Marshall was still army chief of staff, but if responsibility for Pearl Harbor was to be assigned at the highest link of the command chain, Marshall might be sacked. Churchill would have sacked his top commanders after such a debacle. How much credence, therefore, to give Marshall's opinions? The navy's top man, Admiral Harold ("Betty") Stark, though not officially accused of allowing Pearl Harbor to happen on his watch, was in fact within months kicked upstairs, as commander of the U.S. European Fleet (of which there was none) and naval liaison to London, where, like Field Marshal Dill in Washington, he acquitted himself well. Churchill had yet to hear the names Eisenhower, Patton, or Bradley. He knew of Douglas MacArthur's reputation, yet it appeared during those weeks that MacArthur—the prime candidate to lead American forces, either in Europe or in Asia—was more likely to die a hero's death in the Philippines, and soon. Admiral Ernest King, promoted to chief of naval operations (at Stark's expense, as King saw it), resented Marshall and itched to bring the fight to Japan. Could King—hot-tempered, tough, and no admirer of the British Empire—be made to see the merits of Germany first? Churchill would just have to wait and see. Although Adamic in time faded from the scene, his presence at Roosevelt's table could not be ignored.

Nor could Churchill ignore Mrs. Roosevelt, who "was allowed to sit in at such White House after-dinner conversations." This, recalled one of his secretaries, "so distressed Winston," for in England, following dinner, the women left the men to themselves. Churchill's Chartwell dining table was round (at his insistence, in order to erase any implied hierarchy among guests), but after dinner it rarely included women. Churchill, Colville recalled, "did not in general find the company of women particularly stimulating."[101]

To that rule there existed certain exceptions: Lady Diana Cooper was one, Violet Bonham Carter, the daughter of Prime Minister Asquith another. And above all, there was Clementine. Yet Clementine, for her part, would never think of joining the men for a snifter of old Napoleon, not so much because she considered her place to be elsewhere, or because Churchill forbade her presence—he would not—but because her politics ran just far enough to the left of his that a forceful expression of her opinions in the presence of her husband's circle of cronies would likely result in awkward silence. (Though Churchill was a liberal Tory in the manner of his father, Clementine was at heart an Edwardian Liberal, more comfortable with the traditional Liberal Party.) As well, she did not much care for two of his most favored pals—the Irishman Bracken and the Canadian Beaverbrook, whose aircraft production she respected but who had always annoyed her. So she chose not to participate in the after-dinner sessions, or in politics in general. When she hosted a luncheon or dinner, Clementine, reading her husband's mood, steered the conversation away from any topic that might roil or bore him. If the talk turned to politics, Mrs. Churchill kept her counsel. As for Eleanor Roosevelt's eagerness to socialize with guests such as Adamic and to participate in manly conversations, Churchill was astute enough to grasp that the First Lady was not merely performing wifely social duties, but was a political force, one heard and respected by her husband. Churchill, therefore, as a guest in the president's house, and more beholden to Roosevelt with each tank and plane that rolled off American assembly lines, was willing, if not happy, to put up with the political pronouncements of Adamic and Mrs. Roosevelt.[102]

*   *   *

Franklin Roosevelt, over the course of Arcadia, served up to Churchill every-thing he sought, and more. Roosevelt's deference to Britain on military mat-ters was understandable given that Britain had been fighting a war for more than two years, while the Americans had been losing one for two weeks. There were disagreements: Marshall wanted the Allied effort to begin with a landing on the French coast, in 1942, while Churchill had his sights on Gymnast, the landing in North Africa. To Churchill's surprise and immense relief, as Auchinleck seemed about to stall in the desert, Roosevelt came up with Operation Super-Gymnast—the occupation at the earliest opportune moment of French North Africa by at least 100,000 American and British troops. If Eisenhower thought little of Gymnast, the man tapped by Marshall to lead American troops ashore—Major General Joseph Stilwell—thought even less. Stilwell—"Vinegar Joe" to his men—was chosen after his name topped a list prepared for Marshall of America's most talented generals. Stil-well's diary entries regarding Gymnast illuminate both the validity of his nickname and his loathing of the British. "Gymnast," he wrote, had the potential to become "a rathole," hard to supply and harder to keep. It was "a crazy gamble....The whole goddamned thing is cockeyed." Roosevelt, "a rank amateur in military matters, given to whims, fancies and childish notions," had been "sucked in...by the Limeys."[103]

The lack of shipping and landing craft to undertake Gymnast ensured that it could not be carried out for several months, at best. In fact, within two weeks, with Auchinleck stalled in the desert, the prospects for Gym-nast, super or otherwise, evaporated. Stilwell was told to forget about North Africa and was instead ordered to China, where Chiang—who Stil-well thought "a crazy little bastard"—waited for the help promised by Roosevelt. Yet, other than Stilwell, not much more help was forthcoming for Chiang. As for war matériel, the Americans pegged production of Grant and Sherman tanks at 45,000 for 1942, compared with just 4,200 since May 1940. Roosevelt proposed to build twice as many warplanes in 1942—45,000—than the United States and Britain had built in the previ-ous two years. It was a staggering goal, four times the rate of German and Japanese production combined. Goebbels derided the projections as "insane figures."[104]

When during the meetings the Americans offered that at most they could convert 15 percent of U.S. auto plants to military production, Bea-verbrook replied that 100 percent of British automobile factories had been converted, and encouraged Roosevelt to aim higher. He did, and on Janu-ary 1 he ordered U.S. auto production halted by late February. Within weeks the dearth of new cars became moot when rubber, 90 percent of which came from Malaya and Indonesia, was rationed. The U.S. had no synthetic rubber factories to make up the shortfall. Americans soon learned what Britons had long known; without a spare tire or three stashed in the garage, the family car had a very limited range. Passage by rail—where for fifty years the Pullmans had been Americans' preferred means of conveyance—was soon limited to troops and businessmen on official war business. And then the airlines—their routes and the national fleet of 434 aircraft—were commandeered. By spring, gasoline rationing, as a means to preserve rubber more than oil, dribbled onto the Eastern Seaboard and in the following year spread nationwide, guaranteeing that Americans in the heartland could no longer take their vacations at east or west coast beaches even if their bald tires could carry them there. That proved okay with most because by summer, oil and bilge tar and decomposing bodies—the U-boats' harvest—regularly washed up onto America's eastern beaches.[105]

Roosevelt had agreed to truly power up the American dynamo, yet early in the new year, the steady, relentless hum of infinite American industrial power could only be imagined. America, humiliated in Guam, Wake Island, Pearl Harbor, and Manila, was itching for a fight but was not in the least ready for one. More worrisome from Churchill's standpoint was that Americans including Anglophobes like Admiral Ernest King and Stilwell—and the thousands of volunteers who lined up outside recruiting offices—wanted to take the fight to the Japanese, and the sooner the better.

The damage inflicted at Pearl Harbor precluded any such action. So devastating was the Japanese attack that a small aircraft carrier task force sent to relieve the five hundred U.S. Marines stranded on Wake Island ran for home when its commander, Rear Admiral Frank ("Jack") Fletcher, decided that his need for fuel overrode his mission to relieve the Marines on Wake. When Secretary of the Navy Frank Knox asked Churchill what he would do with such a cautious admiral, Churchill held his tongue in deference to his new allies. Before surrendering, the doomed leathernecks on Wake inflicted the only damage thus far upon the Japanese navy, by damaging a cruiser and sinking a destroyer—with field artillery. So acute was the American navy's embarrassment over the month's events that one of King's first actions as the new navy chief was to change CINCUS—the abbreviation for commander in chief, U.S. Navy—to COMINCH, because CINCUS was pronounced as it looked. Meanwhile, MacArthur and his army were in danger of going the way of Jim Bowie and his Texans at the Alamo. This Americans could not abide, especially if they detected a willingness in Washington to bolster the British Empire at the cost of sacrificing MacArthur. To Secretary of War Henry Stimson, Churchill made clear his fear that an American preoccupation with the Pacific in general and the Philippines in particular would hobble the Europe-first strategy that had been in the works for months, with the result that the war might be lost in both theaters before America entered either. Stimson happened to loathe Admiral King and believed in Europe-first. It was said that Stimson, trying to reassure Churchill, said of MacArthur's army, "There are times when men have to die." So it would be Europe first, after all.[106]

Yet even such a seemingly unambiguous pronouncement as "Europe first" meant different things to different men. The decisions as to where and when and how to attack Germany would have to be hammered out by the newly configured Combined Chiefs of Staff Committee, its first members being George Marshall, U.S. Army chief of staff; Admiral Harold Stark, U.S. Naval Forces Europe; Admiral Ernest J. King, chief of U.S. Naval Operations; and Lieutenant General Henry H. ("Hap") Arnold, U.S. Army Air Forces. For Britain: the aging first sea lord, Sir Dudley Pound; Sir Charles Portal at the RAF; and General Sir Alan Brooke as Chief of the Imperial General Staff. The "imperial" in Brooke's title grated on the political sensibilities of Marshall and King, this before they even met the man. The Combined Chiefs was not formally inaugurated until February, and the principals would not meet until spring, by which time they were in near total disagreement over exactly what "Germany first" or "Europe first" meant. By summer those differences would grow into the first real test of the alliance.

On his final night in Washington, Churchill dined alone with Roosevelt and Hopkins before departing late in the evening for Norfolk, Virginia. The next morning he climbed aboard a Boeing Clipper for a three-hour flight to Bermuda, where the *Duke of York* awaited his arrival. Churchill found the flight much to his liking. The weather was fair, the food and drink plentiful. The big plane cruised at eight thousand feet at a steady 145 miles per hour. Churchill even took the controls for a spell. Recalling the unpleasant shipboard trip westward, he prevailed upon the plane's captain, Kelly Rogers, to take him and a few of his staff all the way to England. The rest of the party followed by ship. The air journey almost proved disastrous when at dawn the next day, after an eighteen-hour flight, Rogers brought his plane out of low clouds, only to realize that he was off course. Where all aboard should have seen the coast of England, they beheld nothing but gray seas. They flew on, and on. Churchill recalled in his memoirs that after several minutes of disconcerting silence, Rogers announced he was turning sharply northward. It was a snap judgment, and a good one, for had they kept on their original course for another few minutes, they would have drifted over Brest, and the hundreds of German AA guns protecting the pride of Germany's surface fleet — the battle cruisers *Prinz Eugen, Scharnhorst,* and *Gneisenau* — moored in the harbor. The turn, however, appeared to RAF radar operators as the track of a lone German bomber heading for England from Brest. Six Hurricanes were scrambled, with orders to shoot down the interloper. Thankfully, Fighter Command's aces failed to locate their target. After five weeks and more than nine thousand miles, Churchill arrived safely home, the first leader of any nation to undertake a transoceanic flight.[107]

Churchill enjoyed travel destinations—Marrakech and the Riviera especially, almost any place warmer than England—far more than he enjoyed the journey, especially if undertaken by way of warship or small plane, where the accoutrements of fine dining and plump mattresses were sadly lacking. When he was confined in a steel or aluminum shell, his restlessness and imagination overtook him. Of his air journey, he later wrote, "I must admit I felt rather frightened," when contemplating the endless ocean spaces below and the distance, more than a thousand miles, from land. "I had always regarded an Atlantic flight with awe." As well he should have. Just two years earlier it was considered sheer folly to attempt an aerial crossing of the North Atlantic in winter, when the weather was at its most unpredictable. The fact that American bomber crews now hopscotched to Britain via Newfoundland and Iceland was due more to their need to refuel rather than to any improvements in weather forecasting or navigation, both of which were still primitive. At night, if the skies were clear, pilots charted their course by the stars. High cloud cover could prove lethal. A plane that lost its way most likely ended up downed, with little chance of rescue for those on board. So perilous was the crossing that the preferred means of getting bombers to Europe was by ship, a means of conveyance Churchill on that occasion found to be unacceptably slow. He was now an old man in a hurry.[108]

Soon after he arrived back in London, the news of his heart problems became known, in large part because he could not keep quiet. He told Eden that he felt "his heart a bit" and had some breathing problems when he tried to dance. Eden passed that news along to his parliamentary secretary, Oliver Harvey, who noted in his diary, "The doctors have told him [Churchill] his heart is not too good and he needs rest." Harvey also told Eden that he had best be ready to assume power if Churchill's health worsened. Harvey also noted that in sickness and in health, Churchill's enjoyment of his Edwardian luncheons was never diminished: "He had beer, three ports, and three brandies for lunch today, and has done it for years." Yet Churchill was down. Hong Kong was gone, Singapore soon to be threatened. And Rommel that day had emerged yet again, viperlike, from under his rock. After drinks with the Old Man, Eden jotted in his diary,

"Winston was tired and depressed, for him....He is inclined to be fatalistic about the House [of Commons], maintained that the bulk of the Tories hated him...and would be only too happy to yield to another." Yet any thoughts of promotion Eden might have entertained were premature (by more than thirteen years, as events turned out). Churchill, his gloomy musings to Eden aside, had no intention of quitting.[109]

On his first day home, while reading the papers on the train to London, he turned to Dr. Wilson and, in a tired voice, said, "There seems to be plenty of snarling." There was. Attlee had warned him by cable that his reception in London would be something less than a triumph. Much mumbling and interruption had occurred in the Commons, Attlee reported, when the first lord of the Admiralty, A. V. Alexander, attempted to give members more details of the circumstances in which the *Prince of Wales* had been caught. The House seemed "fractious," Attlee wrote, and the public and press were "rather disturbed" about the overall situation in the Far East, for which they blamed the government's lack of preparedness. Of more concern to Attlee, the House—and the *Evening Standard* and *Daily Mail*—was "a good deal apprehensive" about India, specifically about the political situation there. Murmurs emanated from the Antipodes as well; the tone in Australia, Attlee reported, was "very negative." Churchill—the entire world—was well aware of that fact. Australian prime minister John Curtin, fearful of a Japanese invasion, had declared in a signed article in the *Melbourne Herald* his nation's intent, taken "free of pangs as to our traditional links with the United Kingdom," to align its foreign policy with and seek the protection of the United States. In effect, Australia had bolted the Empire, an action codified ten months later when the Australian parliament ratified the Statute of Westminster,* retroactive to September 3, 1939, the day London declared war. It was a slight Churchill never forgot. Despite his oft-expressed appreciation for the wartime sacrifice of the Dominions and despite his love of warm, beachy destinations, Churchill would never visit Australia, even when the jet age rendered such a journey no more arduous than a long nap in a garden chair.[110]

A great many MPs of all political stripes and many in the press, Tory and Labour alike, were calling for a cabinet shake-up. Some questioned whether Churchill, as prime minister, could still lead the country; more had concluded that as minister of defence he could no longer lead the war effort. The Commons seemed primed for revolt. Churchill attributed the criticism to the "vast, measureless array of disasters" approaching by way

---

* The Statute of Westminster, passed by Parliament in 1931 over Churchill's violent opposition, granted autonomy to certain Dominions—Canada, Newfoundland, Australia, New Zealand, subject to ratification by their respective parliaments.

of Japan, as well as the belief held by many Britons that the new alliance with America meant that the survival of the Home Island "was no longer at stake." The relief engendered by that conviction allowed "every critic, whether friendly or malevolent, to point out the many errors that had been made." Chief among those errors, according to his critics, was Churchill's creation of the office of minister of defence and appointment of himself the first chief of that department, where he had nothing to show but a plethora of defeats. They wanted him out of that job. Yet a defense "establishment" of the sort the Americans were about to house in their new Pentagon Building did not exist in Britain. Churchill's Ministry of Defence consisted mainly of himself. If replaced, he would be denied his channels of communication with the Chiefs of Staff, and that was unacceptable. His critics acknowledged that he had inspired the nation and procured his Grand Alliance, but at the cost of alienating the Australians, who feared for their lives, and further alienating Indian nationalists who, along with many Americans, including Roosevelt, considered Churchill to be an old school imperialist. He came home to "unhappy, baffled public opinion, albeit superficial, swelling, and mounting about me on every side." He decided to meet the criticism head-on, first by warning the nation that more defeats were on their way, and then by demanding a vote of confidence in the House. It was an astute maneuver, one his critics should have anticipated given Churchill's philosophy in matters both military and political: when attacked, counterattack.[111]

On January 20, as Churchill prepared to address his countrymen, Adolf Hitler spoke to his. By then Goebbels had seen to it that any mention of Churchill in German newsreels or newspapers carried with it some reference to his being a strategic nincompoop, a pawn of the Jews, or a drunkard. Hitler outdid Goebbels:

> That twaddler, that drunkard Churchill, what has he achieved in all his lifetime? That mendacious creature, that sluggard of the first order. Had this war not come, future centuries would have spoken of our age, of all of us and also of myself, as the creators of great works of peace. But had this war not come, who would speak of Churchill?... one of the most abominable characters in world history, incapable of a single creative action, capable only of destruction.

Hitler then repeated a boast made in 1940. Given the fate of the Third Reich, his choice of words have now an oracular and ironic ring to them: "True, one day they will speak of him as the destroyer of an empire he, not we, have ruined."[112]

Also on that day, January 20, Reinhard Heydrich, Himmler's second in

command of the SS, and the ruthless acting protector of Bohemia, convened a conference in the Berlin suburb of Grosser-Wannsee. Göring had
months earlier demanded from the SS a "final solution of the Jewish question." The fifteen Nazi bureaucrats and members of the SS who met at
Wannsee intended to coordinate nothing less than the extermination of the
eleven million Jews who dwelled in Europe and the Soviet Union. "Europe
would be combed of Jews from east to west," Heydrich declared. SS lieutenant colonel Adolf Eichmann, a thirty-six-year-old technocrat, served as
conference secretary. He kept concise minutes, which were subsequently
edited by Heydrich, who inserted coded language of the sort Nazis
employed when referring to lethal actions taken against Jews, partisans,
and Communists. "Eliminated by natural causes" referred to death by a
combination of hard labor and starvation. "Transported to the east"
referred to the mass deportations of Jews to ghettos in occupied Poland,
and then on to the gas chambers planned for Belzec, Treblinka, Sobibor,
and Auschwitz. "Special actions" and "treated accordingly" served as Nazi
code words for summary execution by firing squad or death by gassing in
the specially rigged trucks of the *Einsatzgruppen,* as had been taking place
in the East since Barbarossa began. Tens upon tens of thousands of Ukrainian Jews had already been shot, their bodies dumped into mass graves
that are still being discovered seventy years later. So confident were the
attendees at the Wannsee conference of ultimate success that the nation-
by-nation list they compiled of Jewish populations included Ireland (4,000)
and England (330,000). So efficient was the Nazi killing machine that
Estonia, it was duly noted, was already "free of Jews."

Three weeks before Heydrich convened his conference—Churchill was
just arriving in Ottawa—two Czech commandos were parachuted from a
British Halifax bomber into the Czechoslovakian countryside. They made
for Prague, where Heydrich—hated by all Czechs—had his headquarters.
The two Czechs had been trained by Hugh Dalton's Special Operations
Executive. Their mission, sanctioned by the Czech government in exile,
was to shadow Heydrich until such time as the opportunity presented itself
to assassinate him.[113]

Sir Stafford "Christ and Carrots" Cripps, having been granted his wish
to leave Moscow, arrived home to London on January 23. He was not yet
ready for a retirement dinner and a return to the law courts. The political
left had anointed him as the best successor to Churchill were the prime
minister to be shoved from office, a shake-up that even some on the right

thought overdue. Goebbels, too, thought Cripps was destined for No. 10, from where it was assumed in Berlin that he would Bolshevize England, a feeling shared by many Tories. Cripps was a dour man and an uninspired orator whose only enjoyment seemed to be an occasional cigar, but early in the war he declared he'd given up cigars as a symbolic sacrifice. It was said that Churchill's reaction to that gesture was to mumble, "Too bad, it was his last contact with humanity." Two days after Cripps's return, the prime minister offered him a place in the cabinet as minister of supply, where he would in effect serve under Beaverbrook if Churchill could persuade the Beaver to take the post of minister of production. This would put Cripps in the cabinet but outside the War Cabinet and, worse, under Beaverbrook, whom Cripps despised. Cripps, cautious and adroit politician that he was, deferred his decision on the matter until after the vote of confidence about to take place in the Commons.[114]

Cripps was the most viable of three possible contenders for the premiership in early 1942. Eden and Minister of Labour Ernest Bevin were the others. But Eden and Bevin were Churchill loyalists of high magnitude; their betraying him and the coalition government was out of the question. Attlee, head of the Labour Party and Churchill's natural opponent, had also placed his loyalty to the government above his ambitions. But Cripps was interested, though he was unwilling to make his move until he was sure his support ran deep.

Beaverbrook also saw himself as a possible contender. He had his admirers, himself chief among them. Averell Harriman recalled that Beaverbrook "in the winter of '42 when things were going very badly...thought that Churchill was going to be consumed by the power and he [Beaverbrook] would have a chance at that time to become prime minister." Undoubtedly Beaverbrook possessed some of the qualities of a war leader, foremost his ability to marshal production. But his abrasive personality bled through in public and guaranteed that he could never marshal, as had Churchill, the spirit of Englishmen. This Beaverbrook understood at some level, and he admitted as much in a letter in which he berated Churchill for his North African policy: "On the rock bound coast of New Brunswick the waves beat incessantly. Every now and then comes a particularly dangerous wave that breaks viciously on the rocks. It's called the 'rage.' That's me." His best side, wrote his biographer Kenneth Young, emerged in his service as Churchill's lieutenant and friend, where his agile brain appealed to Churchill, and which the Old Man used "as a whetstone on which to sharpen his own remarkable wits." The Beaver's worst side would be exposed by any shifty attempt to promote himself to captain. In the end, the friendship of three decades trumped ambition; Beaverbrook publicly dismissed the notion of seeking high office and soon after, in a letter to

Churchill, professed his devotion to "the leader of the nation, the savior of our people." Still, he soon began quietly telling Labourites that Churchill was on his way out. He did so behind Churchill's back, knowing full well that such talk could only hurt his old friend. Churchill was not blind to the Beaver's shenanigans. Ernest Bevin said of Churchill's relationship with Beaverbrook, "He's like a man who's married a whore; he knows she's a whore but loves her just the same."[115]

No pretender had earned, as Churchill had since 1940, the wide public respect and popularity needed to assume command in wartime. With criticism coming at him from the Commons and the press, Churchill "resolved to yield nothing to any quarter." He had three unassailable advantages, and he knew it. In 1940 and 1941 he had shown himself the guardian of the national will; unlike Chamberlain, he loved the House of Commons and held sacred that body's place in English life; and though he had critics, he had no rival who could best him in the hearts of Englishmen. Years later, Brian Gardner, Fleet Street veteran and historian, wrote, "Most Britons were prepared to go on waging war with the man they knew, whom many loved, in the siren suit, with the cigar, the V-sign, and the grin. His removal would have been resented. The House of Commons knew this, and most members acted accordingly."[116]

The attack against Churchill was led by the Labour MP Aneurin ("Nye") Bevan, a forty-four-year-old hard-drinking product of the North Wales coalfields, and a speaker whose oratory was as tempestuous and cutting as the gales that raced down the Snowdon Massif. He managed *The Tribune*, a left-wing sheet begun by Stafford Cripps five years earlier, which, on the twenty-third, went after Churchill, and went to the nub of the problem as Bevan saw it: "The question is beginning to arise in the minds of many: is he [Churchill] as good a war maker as he is a speech maker?"[117]

Beaverbrook, who pollinated his newspapers with young, up-and-coming left-wing intellectuals, had mentored Bevan in the 1930s. But for Bevan's lack of ruthlessness, Beaverbrook believed he might have emerged as the Lenin of England, although Beaverbrook also claimed Bevan had become enthralled "with the pleasure of high living," which diverted him from a more pure-Leninist path. Yet, along with Cripps, Bevan had opposed appeasement in the late 1930s and at the time reluctantly saw Churchill as the only alternative (as had Cripps), yet not so much to save the British Empire as to help safeguard the Soviet socialist experiment. This was not patriotism, as Churchill saw it, but the opportunistic championing by the left wing of foreign causes and complex philosophical/political systems of a sort only an intellectual could love. When Colville later wrote that Churchill "hated casuistry," he had Bevan in mind. While Churchill "considered parliamentary opposition to be the lifeblood of British politics, the form in which Aneurin Bevan applied it seemed to contribute nothing toward our principal objective, which was to win." Yet Churchill thought personal animus a waste of time, once telling colleagues in the House, "Such hatred as I have left—and it isn't much—I would rather reserve for the future than the past." He called that "a judicious and thrifty disposal of bile." Churchill enjoyed the company of many of those with whom he disagreed, but he drew the line at Bevan, not because of Bevan's views but because Churchill doubted his patriotism.* That, for Churchill, was an unforgivable sin.[118]

Bevan was the MP for Tredegar, a coal town in the Sirhowy Valley of western Gwent, a place where the local surgeons were kept busy setting the smashed bones of miners and quarrymen, and where the leading causes of death for males were tuberculosis (the Cough) and pneumoconiosis (Black Lung), the disease that killed Bevan's father. Bevan's grandfather had forged the iron fences around a cemetery built far outside town in the mid-nineteenth century, a burial ground where every headstone bears the date 1849, for that was the year cholera swept the valley. The North Wales of Bevan's youth was a place where few over forty had their teeth, where fresh water was so scarce that baths were a rare luxury, and where "cobwebs were used to stop bleeding." There, the cure for coal dust in the eyes was "a comrade's lick." There, in the Ebbw Vale, Bevan early on pledged himself to enlist the government to bring modern medicine to his people. When he spoke to what was in his heart, he did not summon images of distant gathering storms or promise sunlit uplands; he explicated the here and now in words and phrases that crashed down upon listeners like wind-driven hail. Bevan (like Roosevelt and unlike Churchill) spoke to his audiences, not at them. Churchill's listeners basked in his phrases as if at a great distance from some cosmic power source, but Bevan pummeled his audiences with his words. His thick black hair was usually mussed; he was a tad jowly; and his dark eyes telegraphed anger, determination, and inflexibility. Churchill years later called Bevan "as great a curse to this country in time of peace, as he was a squalid nuisance in time of war." Yet Bevan had earned the respect of many of his enemies, for there wasn't a false bone in the man. When he wore a scowl, which he habitually donned in Churchill's presence, he bore a resemblance to John L. Lewis, a grandson of Wales and himself a product of the coal mines of America. Churchill, when peering at Bevan across the House chamber, saw in the Welshman's eyes "the fires of implacable hatred." Indeed, Bevan's goal, for the rest of his life, was nothing less than the extermination of the Conservative Party.[119]

Churchill never asked why Bevan—and Bevan's constituency—so hated

---

* When, in 1960, Churchill was told of Bevan's death, he mumbled a few words of moderate respect, then paused for effect before asking, "Are you *sure* he's dead?"

him and his fellow Tories. "He [Churchill] has no gift for getting into other people's minds," his doctor later wrote, "sometimes he does not even appear to be interested." Churchill had promised Britons only victory over Hitler, nothing more. But now they wanted more; they wanted some sort of explanation from Churchill of Tory peace aims, Churchill's war aims being well known to all. Britons had deduced that with America in, victory was some-day assured, and therefore there was no time like the present to begin a discussion of postwar housing and health and Social Security insurance. Churchill, as he had since 1940, considered any public discussion of the postwar world to be ill conceived, as it could only degenerate into a partisan affair. His stance would prove a costly misjudgment in three years, for although Britons loved their warrior Churchill, he refused to tell them which Churchill they'd get in peace, the old Tory or the old Liberal.[120]

It was the old warrior who showed up in the Commons for three days of debate. The doubters spoke their piece, including John Wardlaw-Milne, Herbert Williams, and Earl Winterton, all Conservatives, and Emanuel ("Manny") Shinwell, an old Glasgow radical and Red Clydesider, a tough, blunt-spoken patriot who shared at least one trait with Churchill, a loathing of pompous intellectualism. On this day, however, Shinwell shared nothing with Churchill. Harold Nicolson thought Shinwell's attack on Churchill "vicious." Randolph, on leave from Cairo, leapt to his father's defense and attacked "most cruelly" those who had abused his father. Nicolson found Randolph to be "amusing and brave," yet along with Bob Boothby, Nicolson "harbored a dreadful feeling that Randolph may go too far." Pamela, in the gallery, "was squirming" as her husband let fly. Yet here was Randolph's chance to do for his father what was denied Winston by his father's early death—mount a display of dynastic solidarity. The result, however, was pure Randolph, pure bombast, and gave new meaning to the concept of bully pulpit. Nicolson noted that Churchill himself looked "embarrassed."

In the end, the father came to the defense of the son after Archibald Southby interrupted Randolph and implied that by virtue of Randolph's being in London rather than in the Western Desert, he was not a fighting soldier. Churchill afterward chased Southby down in the lobby and, shaking his fist in the MP's face, shouted, "You called my son a coward. You are my enemy. Do not speak to me." Randolph, Colville later wrote, was a talented journalist, "a natural orator, an original wit." He made friends easily but lost them more easily. He was "imaginative and original in his ideas," but he became "excessively addicted to drink" and regularly turned "inexcusably abusive." He "squabbled with his father," but remained devoted to him, as the father did to the son. Southby's mistake was not only to attack Randolph but to imply that he was not a brave soldier. Randolph was a brave soldier. His experience in the House that day, the jeers of his peers, and the awakening realization that he would always walk in his father's shadow, moved him within months to volunteer for the newly formed Special Air Service and still later to volunteer for an extremely dangerous mission—to parachute into the mountains of Yugoslavia in order to fight alongside Tito's partisans. Randolph, as did his father before him, chose to earn his country's respect on the battlefield, or die trying.[121]

The following day Churchill wound up the debate with what Nicolson thought a "very genial and self-confident" address wherein he congratulated his opponents on their adroit speechifying. But the engaging and conciliatory Churchill gave way in his peroration to the emphatic: "I make no apologies. I offer no excuses. I make no promises. In no way have I mitigated the...impending misfortunes that hang over us." He ended with an avowal of his certainty in final victory. With that, he said he was finished. Nicolson had already concluded two days earlier that "it is clear there really is no opposition at all." The Old Man insisted on a division—a vote. The bells were rung summoning members into the voting lobbies. The final tally: 423–1 in support of the government, with James Maxton, another old Red Clydesider, the lone dissenter. Bevan abstained. Dozens more could not vote; they were overseas, in uniform.[122]

Though badly misjudging the mood of both the public and the House, Bevan increased his attacks. *The Tribune* let loose on January 30: "It would be an excellent thing for Mr. Churchill to make certain changes in his team, but it would be a profound mistake to suppose that from this alone any fundamental improvement would result.... This is no National Government and Churchill is no National Leader. He struts in that guise but in fact he insists that the war shall be conducted in accordance with the principles of the Tory Party. The British Empire is finished. Nothing can save it. Who wants to? Not the millions who suffered under it. They rejoice to see it go.... We shall need a different spirit than the one which breathed through the speech of the last Imperial spokesman—Winston Spencer Churchill."[123]

As Harold Nicolson exited the vote of confidence debate on the twenty-ninth, he stopped at the electronic ticker in the lobby, where he learned from the uncoiling stream of paper that "the Germans claim to have entered Benghazi." Randolph Churchill was there and told Nicolson that only half of Rommel's reinforcements had reached Africa, a spot of good news among all the bad, had it been true. In fact, all of Rommel's supplies had gotten through, including sixty new panzers.[124]

It had been just over a week since Rommel—his forces newly christened Panzer Army Africa—probed outward from his lines at El Agheila, near the Tripolitania frontier. That Rommel could even contemplate an offensive was due to Churchill's Asian strategy. When Churchill stripped away Auchinleck's men and matériel in hopes of saving Malaya, he dashed all prospects of the Eighth Army crushing Rommel. Of greater significance, in combination with the ongoing ravishing of the Royal Navy in the Mediterranean, the attrition of Auchinleck's forces threw into question his ability to defend against Rommel. In fact, Auchinleck's Operation Crusader had been destined to stall before it began, by events that took place ten weeks earlier, at sea. On November 12 the aircraft carrier HMS *Ark Royal*, returning home from ferrying planes to Malta, was torpedoed twenty-five miles from Gibraltar. Only one crewman perished and more than 1,500 survived, a ready-made crew for another carrier, but no new carriers were on hand. Two weeks later, the battleship HMS *Barham* was torpedoed off Tripoli. *Barham* and more than 800 men of the crew went down so quickly that the U-boat commander who had shot her assumed the battleship had escaped when just moments later he raised his periscope to survey the scene and beheld an empty sea.

Within days, with no jubilant announcement of the sinking coming out of Berlin, the British realized the Germans did not know *Barham* was gone. Churchill of course knew, but he sat on the news until after the vote of confidence. Then, on December 19, Churchill learned that six Italian frogmen riding atop miniature submersibles (he called them "human torpedoes") had penetrated the Royal Navy anchorage at Alexandria and affixed mines to the battleships *Queen Elizabeth* (with Admiral Andrew Cunningham on board) and *Valiant*. The frogmen were captured, but not before the two largest ships in the eastern Mediterranean, their keels ripped apart, settled into the mud, useless hulks. The news was kept from the British people for six months. Churchill and the press had for more than a year denigrated Italian seamanship. *Time* ran a photo taken from astern of several Italian destroyers with the caption: "The British usually see them this way." Yet the Italians, with much help from Stukas based in Sicily, had by late December reduced the entire British eastern Mediterranean fleet to a few destroyers and light cruisers.[125]

In late December, Hitler sent Rommel ten ships bearing gasoline and rations along with an entire air corps transferred from the Russian front. At the time, both Churchill and Hitler considered Rommel to be in "mortal peril." Then, in the last days of the old year, a British task force of three cruisers and four destroyers searching for Rommel's supply ships sailed into a minefield. Within minutes all three cruisers were damaged; one of the destroyers was crippled, while another blew up and sank with the loss of all but one of the ship's company. Thus, a lucky U-boat captain, six Italian swimmers, and an uncharted minefield succeeded in destroying virtually the whole of Britain's eastern Mediterranean battle fleet. The Royal Navy no longer needed the largest anchorage in the eastern Mediterranean to shelter its ships. A cove would have sufficed. And Churchill possessed not nearly enough sea power in the eastern Mediterranean to interdict Rommel's supplies.[126]

By mid-January the supplies Rommel needed had arrived in Tripolitania, as had Rommel, having made good his retreat. Contrary to Randolph's optimistic assessment, not a single German vessel had been lost. On the British side of the equation, Malta was cut off and under constant air attack; its dwindling fleet of aircraft could neither protect the island nor stop Rommel's reinforcements. He had retreated before Auchinleck, but more to the point, he had *escaped* and re-armed. The peril had shifted to the Auk, although the danger was belied by the quietude that had settled over the desert, where the armies dug in and faced each other just beyond field artillery range.

Nights were cool. Intermittent rain showers brought forth blooms to stunted shrubs. Small desert flowers scrabbled from beneath the cracked stones as sunshine as weak as chamomile tea threw indeterminate shadows across the sands. At nine each night both armies tuned their radios to the German news beamed from Belgrade, not for edification but to listen to the melancholy love song played at the end of every broadcast, a tune called *Lili Marlene*. Based on a little-known Great War poem called "The Song of a Young Soldier on Watch," and later set to music and recorded by the Berlin cabaret singer Lale Anderson as "The Girl Under the Lantern," with an understated *omp-pah* rhythm of a march, it told the tale of a young soldier who sought to meet his sweetheart under the lamppost beyond his barracks. Rommel loved the tune, Goebbels loathed it, and Frau Göring crooned it at parties to Nazi big shots. British Tommies, not understanding the German lyrics, made up their own words. The song, once heard, became hard to shake, a haunting presence in the mind. Churchill hated it, given its German genesis.[127]

On January 21, Rommel probed the British lines with a reconnaissance in force, just as he had almost a year earlier. Within hours, the first British troops that Rommel's panzers encountered crumbled before the Germans, just as they had a year earlier. It was now the turn of the British Eighth Army to retreat, again, this time under the command of General Ritchie. A good man and former staff officer under Alan Brooke, Ritchie had never commanded a corps, let alone an army in the field. Auchinleck, meanwhile, had replaced his experienced 7th Armoured Division at Rommel's front with the newly arrived and green 1st Armoured Division, which was now falling back with heavy losses before the oncoming Germans. The Auk, as well, could no longer use the port of Benghazi in order to supply his troops; Rommel had leveled the place on his way out of town in December.

By January 29, as Nicolson learned from the news ticker, Rommel was back. Recalling Churchill's warnings to the House, uttered two days earlier, Nicolson that night jotted in his diary, "Grave disasters indeed." By February 5 the Germans had raced two hundred miles from Benghazi to near Gazala, where they halted. The British dug in behind a defensive line running about forty miles southeast from Gazala before hooking east and partway around Bir Hacheim. Rommel was now approximately forty miles from Tobruk, which Auchinleck told London he intended to abandon if Rommel attacked. There would be no siege this time. Churchill did not object to the plan, but in the days that followed—based in part on incorrect Ultra decrypts—he pushed Auchinleck to execute a counterstroke within weeks. When Churchill learned that Auchinleck's army would not be ready for any such undertaking until June, he termed the situation "intolerable," adding that it would be "judged so by Roosevelt, Stalin, and everybody else."[128]

Auchinleck could fall back in semi-orderly fashion before Rommel, but no such option existed for Arthur Percival, the military commander of Singapore. He was trapped. Percival's enemy, Lieutenant General Tomoyuki Yamashita, had since early December proved his mettle on the Malay Peninsula. Now came Percival's turn to prove his. Yamashita considered his Twenty-fifth Army—charged with capturing Singapore—to be so well prepared for jungle combat in Malaya that it could accomplish its mission with only three of its five divisions. He had fought Chinese guerrillas for three years and noted their tactics of stealth and fast movement, which he trained his troops to emulate. He had spent six months in Germany the previous year, where he became familiar with the genius of blitzkrieg tactics—tanks in the spearhead, close air support, and bold strokes. Hitler had been so impressed with Yamashita that he'd promised him he would stipulate in his will that Germans "bind themselves eternally to the Japanese spirit."[129]

Yamashita had opened his campaign on December 8, when Japanese bombs from a dozen aircraft crashed down outside the Raffles Hotel in Singapore. That morning his troops made two landings four hundred miles north of Singapore, at Singora and Patini, on each side of the Thai-Malay border. The British had long anticipated such a stroke, but their immediate problem was diplomatic. When a British force arrived at the Thai border, Thai border guards refused it entry. Not knowing of the unfolding events at Pearl Harbor, and not wanting to precipitate a political crisis (the Americans would look very much askance at such an incursion), the British turned around and headed south. Yamashita had also made a diversionary landing farther south near Kota Bharu and the nearby airfield with the object of drawing the RAF to the airfield's defense and away from his transports and main forces to the north. Within hours he took the airfield. By afternoon the few squadrons of RAF fighters in the region had been halved in numbers, leaving only mostly inexperienced Indian troops standing between Yamashita and an easy march to Singapore. Light tanks from Yamashita's 5th Division smashed through the Indians, some of whom had never before seen a tank. Implicit in that fact is that the British had no tanks deployed to defend northeast Malaya. The capture of the Kota Bharu airfield rendered the few remaining British aircraft in northern Malaya orphans. Those losses and the loss of the *Prince of Wales* left Singapore hanging like low fruit, and Yamashita was keen to pluck it.[130]

The British Plan B for Malaya had called for a scorched-earth policy similar to the ruin Churchill advised Stalin to inflict on Russian foodstuffs and, especially, Russian oil fields. Rubber and tin were Malaya's most abundant natural resources. More than 40 percent of Britain's rubber came from Malaya; more than half of the world's tin came out of the mountainous spine of the peninsula. It was impossible to chop down the rubber trees, but all equipment having to do with mining and smelting tin should have been destroyed. It was not. The first elements of Yamashita's 5th Division who rode into Kota Bharu not only found ample stocks of rice and gasoline but also discovered that, such was the haste of the British exit, the power plant had not even been turned off, let alone destroyed. Within a week the Japanese crossed the Kra Peninsula to smash the British airfield at Point Victoria, the southernmost point of Burma. With that stroke Yamashita cut off Singapore from airborne reinforcement by way of Europe and India.

Throughout December, Yamashita's 5th and 18th Divisions—the former moving down the eastern shore while the latter scoured the western—found rubber plantations and tin refineries abandoned but intact. They found British lorries topped off with petrol and ready to bring tin and rubber to ports, where docks that should have been demolished were ready to receive Japanese cargo ships. When the Japanese flushed the British from Penang, on the west coast of the peninsula, they found a small fleet of coastal gunboats in perfect running order, which they used to mount raids on British coastal positions. They came upon stores of rice and $250,000 in cash left behind in the British treasury. And they found a radio station, with the microphones on and the generator running, from which on Christmas

Day they broadcast "Merry Christmas and an *Unhappy* New Year" to the residents of Singapore, who did not grasp their terrible position because British censors withheld all information regarding the whereabouts of the Japanese. On the day Penang fell, the British press office told reporters, "There is nothing to report." In fact, all Europeans in Penang had been evacuated, leaving the natives to fend for themselves. The conquerors, wrote Cecil Brown, were "reverting to type . . . that is to say, they are looting food shops and . . . raping the native women." Within a week the Japanese outflanked Kuala Lumpur, the capital of the Malay federation and the railroad center of the country. The railway was intact. In retreat, the British performed exceptionally well—as quartermasters to the Japanese. By New Year's, Yamashita had raced halfway to Singapore.[131]

There, Lieutenant General Arthur Ernest Percival and almost 90,000 men—including 17,000 Australian, 33,000 British, and 40,000 Indian—prepared to destroy the city and naval base if need be, and to fight amid the rubble to the last man, per Churchill's orders. Yet Churchill's initial hope that Singapore might hold out for six months under Percival's command faded overnight when, upon his return to London from Washington, he was "staggered" to learn from Wavell that Singapore's largest, fifteen-inch naval guns faced out to sea. The landward side of the city, which gave out to a gorge, was without heavy defenses. To Ismay, Churchill wrote, "I must confess. . . . It never occurred to me for a moment . . . that the gorge of the fortress was not entirely fortified against an attack from the northward." Why, he asked, had he never been informed? Why, when he had for two years so stressed the defense of Singapore over the Kra Isthmus fallback strategy, had no defenses been erected? "I warn you," he continued, "this will be one of the greatest scandals that could possibly be exposed." In fact, Singapore was no "fortress" in the manner of Gibraltar; it was an island of gentle hills and ridges, twenty-seven miles long by thirteen miles wide. Churchill had formed images of the terrain and of the "fortress," and they were incorrect. The only way to keep the Japanese off the island would have been to bring them to decisive battle on the peninsula; instead, the British fell back, toward the presumed safety of the fortress that wasn't. As for the big guns facing the wrong way, Wavell had sent Churchill incorrect intelligence; several of Singapore's fifteen-inch Vickers guns indeed covered the straits, but they had been supplied with armor-piercing ammunition intended for use against ships. Against men they were useless.[132]

The fault for that lay with Arthur Percival. Percival was a thinker, a planner, and he had displayed great intellect while serving under Dill as a staff officer in the 1930s. Yet, like Admiral Tom Phillips, he lacked field experience. Staff officers fight their battles in map rooms. In ordering Percival to Singapore, Dill broke ranks with those in the British military—and there were many—who traditionally gave more credence to a general's character than his intellect, often with disastrous results. British generals, wrote T. E. Lawrence, "often gave away in stupidity what they had gained in ignorance." But here was an instance where character and courage would have trumped a superior, methodical mind. Following the Great War, Percival served as the intelligence officer for the Essex Regiment in Ireland, where his penchant for torturing suspected Irish rebels resulted in the partisans putting a price on his head. The Irish Republican Army had put prices on a great many heads, including Churchill's, but Percival's case was different; it was personal. The man was despised not only because he had tortured Irish rebels but also because he had enjoyed it. The defense of Singapore would require planning, which Percival had done, and character, of which Percival had none.

But for the British colonial buildings, Englishmen's clubs and polo fields, and Raffles Hotel, Singapore was no paradigm of orderliness or cleanliness. The British called it the city of "Chinks, drinks, and stinks." Most of its 750,000 Malay and Chinese citizens lived in nineteenth-century squalor. Monkeys roasted in open-air markets, where the blood of pig carcasses hanging from meat hooks flowed slowly into shallow gutters. With a blackout on since mid-December, the sounds of the city after sunset consisted in large part of the creaking of oxcarts hauling night soil out of town and the occasional blind firing of anti-aircraft batteries. Yet Singapore's citizens, especially the Chinese among them, got along secure in the knowledge that the British would at the very least protect them. In fact, by mid-January most British officials had left, including Duff Cooper, who Churchill had appointed resident minister after the early December attacks. With the city's fate in the hands of the army, Cooper and his wife, Diana, left for London on January 13. Lady Diana had a final gin sling before leaving for the airport, which helped fortify her when Japanese bombers appeared overhead just as they arrived. Chinese friends hustled the Coopers into the air-raid shelter. It was made entirely of glass. "It seemed a suitable end," Cooper later wrote, "to our mission to Singapore."[133]

By February 1 the Japanese were within twelve miles of the city, but the citizens of Singapore did not know this due to British censorship. For a week the British fought a holding action, but by late on the seventh, the last British troops fled the mainland across the causeway, blowing it up just after they reached the island. The demolition was no more effective than the scorched-earth policy; it took only a few hours for the Japanese to repair the causeway. Soon thereafter, the first of Yamashita's troops, skinny apparitions in tattered uniforms and helmets covered in twigs and banana leaves, crossed over to Singapore. Churchill, trying to inspire the defenders, cabled Wavell in Batavia: "The 18th Division has a chance to make its name in history" (that would be the 18th Division originally destined for Egypt and rerouted by Churchill). He tried to shame the defenders: "The honour of the British Empire and of the British Army is at stake." Attempting, too late, to plan a coherent defense, Churchill drew up for the Combined Chiefs a ten-point plan to convert Singapore into a "citadel," which included the conscription of all able-bodied males to dig anti-tank ditches and build barricades and gun emplacements. He directed again that the city was to be defended to the death and no surrender entertained. "Commanders, Staffs, and principal officers are expected to perish at their posts." The chiefs sent these orders to Wavell—less the order that everyone perish at his post. Not to be denied, Churchill got his message through in a private telegram: "The fight should continue to the bitter end in the ruins of Singapore. Commanders and senior officers should die with their troops."[134]

Then, too late, Churchill and the chiefs ordered as many troops as possible evacuated to Rangoon. But by then Percival and his army (he outnumbered the Japanese by three to one) were fully engaged with the enemy. Percival's air cover had dwindled to just two dozen old fighter planes; the Japanese had more than five hundred modern aircraft available. The 18th Division landed at Singapore just in time to be captured. The Japanese sealed the city's fate when they captured the outlying reservoirs and cut off drinking water. Yet Japanese supply lines were stretched to breaking. An all-out assault by Percival of the sort Churchill demanded might have turned the tide, but Percival, his communications in total disarray, declined the fight. The British still possessed enough anti-tank guns and ammunition to kill every Japanese tank twice over, but the top commanders lacked the resolve to carry the fight to the Japanese. Some of Percival's men—including the war artist Philip Meninsky—wanted to continue the fight but were dismayed to find that the maps they had been issued were of the Isle of Wight. The 8th Australian Division, its four brigades strung along the northern part of the island, briefly pushed the enemy back into the sea, until, that is, the Australians' communication broke down and their commanding general elected to not perish at his post but to flee homeward in a small boat, leaving his troops stranded, and doomed.

Singapore fell on February 15. It was a death foretold—too few defenses, a weak commanding general, a demoralized garrison, and too savvy an enemy. Churchill had known since early January that defeat was inevitable, though he thought the inevitable would arrive in a matter of months, not weeks. Percival and a contingent of six officers met Yamashita at the Ford Motor factory late in the morning. The Japanese general, by then hailed in Tokyo as "The Tiger of Malaya," demanded unconditional surrender by 8:30 that night. It was a bluff; Yamashita knew that *his* forces were outgunned and in the minority. Yet Percival, with no fight in his belly, decided he had no choice; not only had the commander of the Australian 8th Division fled, but the Indian and Malay troops were deserting and the city was almost out of potable water. Thus, for the defenders of Singapore, it was hands up, guns down.

A Japanese newsman reported watching a group of Scottish Highlanders marching off to a POW camp while their bagpipers piped. To the reporter's amazement, the Scots displayed no sadness and, given their surrender, no shame. Such behavior was beyond understanding to the Yamoto people. For a short while after the surrender, Union Jacks still fluttered above Singapore's municipal buildings like artifacts from the distant past. Then the Japanese yanked them down. Intending no irony, the victors renamed the city Shonan—Light of the South. Night fell on a chaotic scene. Two nights earlier, the conquerors had massacred scores of doctors, nurses, and patients in a hospital just outside the city. Now the victors set to massacring Chinese residents, more than five thousand in all, whose severed heads soon adorned pikes throughout the island. Apprised of the debacle, Brooke jotted in his diary: "If the army cannot fight better than it is doing at present we shall deserve to lose our Empire!" Churchill had no need to resort to hyperbole when days later he informed Roosevelt that the fall of Singapore was "the greatest disaster in our history."[135]

So confident were the Japanese that they would keep the city in perpetuity that they rigged the big Vickers naval guns for transport to other Pacific conquests. They already knew the mechanics of the guns; the British and Vickers—the Krupp Works of England—had supplied the Japanese navy with fourteen-inch guns since 1910. Japan had built its latest naval weapons on the Vickers design, and rightly so, for Vickers produced the finest naval gun of the era. The fast and deadly Japanese battle cruiser *Kongo,* which had covered the December landings north of Singapore, was armed with Vickers guns. The British had built *Kongo* for Japan in 1913. The Royal Navy had instructed a generation of Japanese officers in the art of gunnery. "Uncle Sam and Britannia were the godparents of the new Japan," Churchill later wrote, adding that in fewer than two generations the Japanese had gone from the samurai sword to the battleship. The British had taught the Japanese well, as Tommies and tars were now learning from Java to Singapore.[136]

Singapore, which the British over the previous 123 years had nurtured from fishing village to trading post to financial capital of South Asia, had been lost in just seven days. The British and Australian prisoners were soon marched and transported north, to the banks of the River Kwai, in Thailand, where as slave laborers, they began building a 250-mile railroad to Thanbyuzayat, in Burma. More than 13,000 died during the next three years by Japanese bullet and bayonet, as well as from malnutrition and a host of hideous tropical diseases. The survivors dubbed their works project the Death Railroad. Most of the Indian troops, on the other hand, did not share that fate. More than 30,000 mostly Hindu prisoners—they called themselves the Indian National Army—declared their allegiance to the mesmeric Hindu nationalist and Fascist Subhash Chandra Bose, and to Tokyo, which bankrolled Bose. They took up arms against London, and joined the Japanese on the march to the next objective: Burma. Percival survived his captivity. When he returned home after the war, he became a "nonperson," excluded from all victory celebrations and shunned, wrote Sir John Keegan, "for his catastrophic mismanagement of the Malay campaign." Churchill never forgave him.[137]

The Japanese were making Hell while the sun shone, which propelled Joseph Goebbels to flights of celebratory fancy. "If I were an Englishman," he declared to his diary, "I would tremble for the fate of the Empire.... There was a time we considered the existence of the British world empire a necessity for the welfare of Europe. This time is past.... Churchill gambled away the chance we gave England. England will have to pay dearly for this statesman." As for Churchill's political future, both Goebbels and Hitler agreed that "his fall may possibly be expected."[138]

Many in London agreed. Most believed that any further defeats of such magnitude would spell the end for Churchill. Then again, there weren't that many more pieces of the Empire to lose.

Churchill had known since his outward passage to America that Singapore was in serious trouble. The Japanese, he told his Canadian hosts in December, had inflicted upon the British a "cataract of ruin." He had warned of more pain to come, and come it had. Churchill announced the loss of Singapore on February 15 in a broadcast carried around the world. Harold Nicolson wrote that Churchill appealed "for national unity and not criticism, in a manner which recalls Neville Chamberlain." Britons, "too nervous and irritable to be fobbed off with fine phrases," found the speech wanting. Yet, Nicolson asked, "What else could he have said?" Two days later, Churchill took his case to the House and promptly closed it with the announcement that there would be no official investigation into the fall of Singapore (such as had been convened for most of the military disasters since 1939) lest "we were drawn into agitated or excited recriminations at a time when all our minds are oppressed with a sense of tragedy and with the sorrow of so lamentable a misfortune." No such official inquiry ever took place. Recriminations were indeed making the rounds, in the streets and in pubs, and in the Commons, where Churchill that day, in response to questions of the how and why of Singapore, "became irritable and rather reckless." Harold Nicolson feared "a slump in public opinion which will deprive Winston of his legend."[139]

Britons, wrote Mollie Panter-Downes, though openly criticizing Churchill—unthinkable a year earlier—"don't intend to lose Mr. Churchill, but they don't intend to lose the war, either." Britons were fed up with the BBC and the newspapers for having touted successes in the Western Desert and Singapore, when only failures came to pass. They were fed up with increased rationing—two pints of milk per adult per week, strict limitations on cereals and dried fruits. They had been shocked that week when the German battle cruisers *Scharnhorst* and *Gneisenau,* along with *Prinz Eugen,* slipped out of Brest and made a successful daylight dash right up the mine-choked English Channel, past British radar (the Germans had jammed it), and past the big coastal guns (they could not aim in the gathering mist). All three of the ships suffered minor damage from mines, but not enough to keep them from reaching Germany's North Sea ports that afternoon. Torpedo bombers that might have stopped the ships had been sent to Alexandria to prevent further Italian frogman depredations. Six Fairey Swordfish torpedo bombers sent aloft to halt the ships were all lost, along with four Hampden medium bombers. Contrary to rumor, the Admiralty had not been caught entirely flat-footed but had long suspected the German ships might make a break for it. Churchill said he pointed this out to the Commons in order to reassure Britons "that our affairs are not conducted entirely by simpletons and dunderheads." Yet the escape of the German ships and the fall of Singapore led Britons to conclude that a fresh start was needed by way of a cabinet shake-up that, to be effective, must include Sir Stafford Cripps, whose "straight talking," Panter-Downes wrote, was of the sort "people have long and in vain hoped to hear from the Prime Minister."[140]

Cripps had been biding his time for a month, waiting for just such a popular summons, but he was still wary of serving under Beaverbrook.

The January vote of support for Churchill's government may have appeared overwhelming, but the military disasters of February and rising tensions in political circles moved Churchill by mid-February to restructure the cabinet and the War Cabinet. In so doing he reduced the War Cabinet from the supreme nine to the supreme eight, thus further consolidating his power. Secretary of State for War David Margesson was among the first to go. Churchill's treatment of this loyal Tory was less than laudatory, recalled Lord Geoffrey Lloyd: "I must tell you that I could never quite forgive Churchill the way in which he dismissed my old friend Lord Margesson, who was a great friend of his." In fact, Margesson was loyal to

Churchill but no great friend. Margesson, as Chamberlain's imperious chief whip before the war, had been ruthless in suppressing Tory dissent over Chamberlain's appeasement policy, and was instrumental in keeping Churchill out of the government and more or less in exiled opposition. Yet, though Margesson had been a dedicated Chamberlain enforcer, he helped ease both Tory and Labour fears during the transition from Chamberlain to Churchill. He had since served Churchill loyally, and since early 1941, as secretary of state for war, a position he neither sought nor desired but could not refuse when Churchill offered it. The War Office—the name notwithstanding—was administrative, less about strategy and more about updating regulations and keeping records of the whereabouts of men and matériel. With Churchill acting as his own minister of defence, Margesson's job was almost symbolic and consisted more in catching javelins than throwing them, and often Churchill's javelins, as many of his curt, often dismissive memos to Margesson suggest. In one of his last memos to Margesson, written as Singapore tottered, Churchill bemoaned the willingness of British officers in that city to openly discuss—aye, confess to—the collapse of resistance: "They seem to be giving everything away about themselves in the blandest manner," he wrote. "After all, they are defending a fortress and not conducting a Buchmanite* revival."[141]

That was a clever (and petty) way of putting things. Margesson's skills had never been administrative; under Chamberlain he had excelled as a whip in keeping the party in line. For more than a year now he had served Churchill loyally, only to be sacked, Lord Lloyd recalled, when Churchill "needed a scapegoat for all the disasters in the western deserts, but he couldn't face up to doing it personally." Churchill, in his memoirs, simply states that Margesson "ceased to be Secretary of State for War." In fact, Margesson first learned his fate from his own permanent under secretary, Percy James Grigg, who had served as Churchill's private secretary when Churchill was at the Exchequer. Churchill asked Grigg to take Margesson's job, but the career civil servant was hesitant to do so, for the jump from civil service to Crown minister meant a loss of all accrued pension benefits. Churchill pushed. Grigg took the job "as an act of patriotism," recalled Malcolm Muggeridge, even though Grigg suspected that "Winston wanted a Secretary of War who would be a pure stooge." Grigg proved anything but. Brooke later wrote, "Providence was indeed kind to me dur-

---

* A reference to Dr. Frank Buchman, an American evangelical who relocated to England and formed the Oxford Group to preach his creed of reaching God through the practice of frequent and robust confession—"sin and tell," *Time* called it (Jan. 18, 1943). By the late 1930s Buchman's theology formed the underlying creed of Alcoholics Anonymous.

ing the war to have placed P.J. [Grigg] at the helm of the W.O." Grigg
served until the war's end. When Grigg retired, recalled Muggeridge, his
finances were "wiped out...finished," and Churchill "never again communicated with him in any way."[142]

As Churchill shuffled his cabinet, he waited for Beaverbrook's decision
on the Ministry of Production post, which, when it arrived in mid-February
was, to his delight, in the affirmative. But less than two weeks later, Beaverbrook again offered his resignation. He was an ill man. He had long
suffered from asthma; now it had worsened to the point where he contemplated ordering an RAF plane to fly him around at high altitude to clear his
lungs and allow him some sleep. His breathing became so labored that
Churchill, during a meeting, mistook the wheezing for a cat's meow and
ordered, "someone stop that cat mewing." Beaverbrook was on the cusp of
what Churchill later rather unnecessarily termed "a nervous breakdown."
Clementine took the occasion to advise her husband by letter: "My
darling—Try ridding yourself of this microbe which some people fear is in
your blood—Exorcise this bottle imp & see if the air is not clearer &
purer—you will miss his drive & genius, but in Cripps you may have new
accessions of strength." Churchill accepted her advice, and Beaverbrook's
resignation. And with that, Cripps was in, lord privy seal and leader of the
House of Commons.[143]

Yet what appeared to be a political defeat for Churchill can be seen as his
snookering Cripps, whose talents were not in massaging the House but in
coolly arguing legal issues, attributes that serve little purpose in that raucous chamber of partisan free-thinkers. Churchill soon dispatched Cripps
to India on a mission to convince Gandhi to pledge his loyalty to the British
in return for a guarantee of Dominion status after the war. Gandhi and the
National Congress had rejected a similar offer a decade earlier. Now, with
Gandhi preaching that Indians not fight for Britain but rather prostrate
themselves peacefully before the Japanese invader, Cripps's mission could
only end in failure. Thus Cripps, argues historian and parliamentarian Roy
Jenkins, found himself in a nominally high position that was, in fact, "more
shell than kernel." Before departing for India, Cripps, seduced by his
romantic vision of Stalinist Russia, predicted—without the slightest supporting evidence—that the war would be (successfully) concluded in a
year. Britons kept tallies on the predictions of their politicians; the public
man who offered up a promise had better keep it.[144]

Churchill, too, had made promises—that Crete would be defended to
the death, Singapore held, the Germans and Italians swept from North
Africa. Churchill, for almost two years, had been telling his family, his secretaries, little schoolboys at Harrow, that "these are...the greatest days our
country has ever lived." The times were great for Churchill not because his

England was winning—it most decidedly was not—but because England was fighting Germany, and now Japan, to the death. Yet, Mollie Panter-Downes wrote that month, that although Britons trusted Churchill in the past because he had always told them the truth, "there's an uneasy suspicion that fine oratory may carry away the orator as well as the audience." By February Churchill understood that, which is why he now promised only more sacrifice, more defeats, and more hard times, promises he delivered on."[145]

The honorable fight for British survival made the war great for Churchill. His faith in the rightness of his cause and the valor of ordinary Englishmen was unbounded. Calling upon reserves of patriotism that should have been exhausted, he had won the allegiance of almost fifty million Britons gathered around wireless sets in homes and pubs, in West End clubs, and East End warehouses. Even as Singapore tottered, and as Rommel again drove toward Egypt, and despite his unkept promises, polls showed that 79 percent of Britons supported Churchill. These were people who, believing that peace was worth any price, had rejoiced in Britain's betrayal of Czechoslovakia just four years earlier. His words then had failed to move them. Had they listened then, they would not have had to listen now as he told them of one disaster after another, and reminded them that he expected that they all go down fighting in defense of their country.

Now they listened, and Churchill persuaded them that the fate of mankind hung in the balance, and he roused their ardor, stitching the fabric of their resolution with gleaming threads of eloquence and optimism. Thus, from June of 1940 to early 1942, at a time when defeat and enslavement of the Home Island seemed, at first inevitable, then probable, and finally still quite possible, Churchill's star continued to rise, to challenge the dark star of Hitler, whose oratory, though in a different language with contrary rhythms, and to very different ends, had spawned a murderous dystopia. The Führer and Tojo were a pair of Genghis Khans bent upon the destruction of all that civilized men cherished. Churchill was determined to preserve it, and preserve it while wearing a smile and flashing his "V" sign. "It is surprising how he maintains a lighthearted exterior in spite of the vast burdens he is bearing," Alan Brooke observed, himself bearing a heavy burden as Chief of the Imperial General Staff, and charged by Churchill with plotting the strategies to fight their way to final victory.[146]

In a broadcast beamed the previous year to the University of Rochester—located in the upstate New York city where his grandfather Leonard Jerome had practiced law before hitting it big in the New York stock market—Churchill wondered how Hitler had done it, how "nations were pulled down one by one while the others gaped and chattered" until they, too, fell into slavery and darkness. Now "the old lion with her cubs at her side stands alone against hunters who are armed with deadly weapons and are propelled by desperate and destructive rage." Will the lion now fall, the final victim? "Ah no!" declared Churchill, "the stars in their courses proclaim the deliverance of mankind. Not so easily will the onward progress of the peoples be barred. Not so easily will the lights of freedom die."[147]

To the Commons, on the day after Pearl Harbor, he had invoked the same imagery: "In the past we have had a light which flickered, in the present we have a light which flames, and in the future there will be a light which shines over all the land and sea." No matter that Hitler had extinguished the lamps across all of Europe, Churchill generated his own illumination.[148]

Whether it would be enough to light the path to victory grew more doubtful with each mile of desert Rommel stole, with each ship killed by U-boats, and with each new Japanese depredation. On February 12, Alec Cadogan wrote in his diary: "The blackest day, yet, of the war.... We are nothing but failure and inefficiency everywhere and the Japs are murdering our men and raping our women in Hong Kong." The weather was horrid, food in short supply, his chickens had stopped laying. He wrote, "I am running out of whisky and can get no more to drink of any kind. But if things go on as they're going, that won't matter." Cadogan wrote that pessimistic assessment three days *before* Singapore fell.[149]

On February 19, Admiral Chūichi Nagumo's carrier strike force bombed Port Darwin, Australia, inflicting enough damage to force the abandonment of the port as a supply depot. The admiral had sailed his five aircraft carriers unmolested thousands of miles from the northern Pacific to Australia. The raid served to finish off any residual Australian sanguinity. Prime Minister Curtin wanted his troops home, now. The troops in question were the war-hardened 7th Division, then en route by ship to Australia from the Middle East. By that date the Japanese had advanced from Thailand into Burma, with Rangoon the obvious target. Churchill was far less concerned with Australian paranoia than he was with Burma, the final frontier between the Japanese and India. On the nineteenth, Churchill asked Curtin to allow the 7th Division to be diverted to the defense of Burma. Curtin refused, firm in his belief that with Singapore now lost, the 7th Division was needed for the defense of Australia. Both Roosevelt and Churchill had concluded otherwise; they believed that the Japanese would not risk sending tens of thousands of troops four thousand miles by sea from Java to Australia. But for Curtin, the bombardment of Darwin confirmed his worst fears. Roosevelt sent two messages to Curtin in which he stressed the strategic importance of Burma and the need for Australians to help defend it. Curtin stood his ground. The next day Churchill, after repeating his request and before an answer arrived from Curtin, ordered the convoy to Burma. Two days later he informed Curtin, and in so doing verified for Curtin the very arrogance he had ascribed to the war planners in London. Curtin, furious, insisted the convoy turn away from Burma and make for Australia. Churchill backed down. No Australians would defend Rangoon. Instead, the 7th Division went home to join the almost 90,000 American troops Roosevelt had sent to Curtin, an army that by summer would make Australia one of the most secure places on the planet.[150]

By February 24, Wavell had been recalled to Bombay from the Dutch East Indies. Brereton's minuscule air fleet, by then a mere two dozen planes, joined the exodus. A Dutch admiral, C. E. L. Helfrich, replaced Tommy Hart, "a good skipper in a bad storm," not because Hart had failed—he lacked the ships to succeed—but because the Dutch intended to make a last stand off the coast of Java. Helfrich's fleet consisted of five cruisers, including the USS *Houston* (aboard which Roosevelt once enjoyed taking his seafaring holidays), HMS *Exeter,* and ten destroyers. Under certain circumstances it might have proven a formidable force, but with supplies running low at Surabaya, Indonesia, and against the overwhelming Japanese force headed its way, the Allied fleet was sailing on hope, sailing alone, and, like *Prince of Wales,* sailing without air cover.[151]

The torrent of disasters was taking its toll on Churchill. On February 27, Mary Churchill told her diary: "Papa is at a very low ebb. He is not too well physically—and is worn down by the continuous crushing pressure of events." That day, in the Java Sea, events were about to take yet another turn against Britain and her allies. In preparation for the invasion of Java, two Japanese naval task forces, each guarding about fifty troop transports, and each more powerful than the entire Allied fleet, closed on the north Java coast. Admiral Helfrich's little navy, commanded at sea by a fighting Dutchman, Rear Admiral Karel Doorman, was about to refuel at Surabaya when Doorman received word of the Japanese presence. Flying his flag from the light cruiser *HMNS De Ruyter,* Doorman went looking for the Japanese transports in hopes of inflicting some damage before the more numerous and heavily armed Japanese warships of Rear Admiral Take Takagi found the Dutch. Just after 4:00 P.M., the two forces sighted each other and began shooting at a range of about six miles. Churchill was correct when he said that naval battles could be settled in minutes, but this one turned into an eight-hour slugfest. An American newsweekly tallied up the amazing results: "The Jap paid...Japanese heavy cruiser sank. Another Jap cruiser, the *Mogami*...retired in flames. Hits crippled a third

8-inch gun cruiser. Three Jap destroyers blazed up, appeared to be sinking.... Allied bombers reported hits on two more Jap cruisers. At least 17 Jap transports were bombed."[152]

Jolly good news, were any of it true. In fact, not a single Japanese warship was sunk; only one sustained any damage whatsoever. Admiral Doorman drowned inside his doomed ship, followed before midnight by half his fleet. A few nights after the battle, HMS *Perth* and USS *Houston* charged into Banten Bay, near Sunda Strait, and in desperation attacked an overwhelmingly superior Japanese force. Both cruisers were destroyed. Later the same day, HMS *Exeter* (the hero of the December 1939 Battle of the River Plate, where the *Graf Spee* was scuttled) and two destroyers tried to flee Java. All three were sunk. The Japanese had taken the Java Sea without losing a single warship. The annihilation of the Allied fleet was a catastrophic defeat, especially for the Dutch, who had been a major power in the East Indies for three hundred years. The British were on the run, to Burma and India, where they hoped to regroup. But the Japanese were outrunning them. On February 28, Japanese forces landed on Java. Eight days later the island was theirs, as were more than 90,000 Dutch, and thousands of British, Australian, and American prisoners. With the surrender of Java, Wavell's ABDA command simply disappeared.[153]

In Rangoon all order had disappeared a month earlier. The evacuation of Rangoon, ongoing since the Christmas raids, had grown desperate with the first concerted bombings of early February. By February 20, refugees and vehicles of all sorts packed the road north. Thousands took to the Irrawaddy River in small boats. Professional thieves—*dacoits*—fell upon the fleeing citizens, British and Burmese alike, and killed them for what they carried. The fire brigade fled, as did the police and the entire British diplomatic contingent. A British official wrote that city streets were empty except for "criminals, criminal lunatics, and lepers." Somehow, five thousand felons had been released from prison. After sundown they made Rangoon "a city of the damned." Lepers, wild dogs, and lunatics fought over scraps of rotting food at garbage dumps and in back alleys. Business owners and the few remaining Burmese soldiers implemented a scorched-earth policy, burning factories, stores of medicines, and supply depots. The few remaining Flying Tigers—the last defenders of the city—departed the deranged scene that night for Magwe, to the north, where the remnants of the RAF and the main British force, such as it was, had already dug in.[154]

Churchill, in late February, dispatched to Rangoon general Harold Alexander, who had served in France under Brooke and was the last senior officer to get off the beach at Dunkirk. "If we could not send an army," Churchill later wrote, "we could at any rate send a man." "Alex" was an aristocrat, an Ulsterman, a fighter and a man of honor, but two decades earlier, two of his instructors at the staff college, Alan Brooke and Bernard Montgomery, had concluded that he was "an empty vessel." Perhaps Monty and Brooke did not see that Alexander's lack of enthusiasm for planning was due to his greater love of fighting. In France in 1940 he had displayed a knack for which British generals had "always shown a special aptitude...the art of retreat and evacuation." That talent helped save the British army. He also displayed a flair for interservice diplomacy, a trait that would well serve Churchill and the Allied cause. In Burma Churchill needed both a man and an army. In Alexander he had the man, but he lacked an army. British colonial forces in Burma did not number enough to properly be called a corps, let alone an army. An Indian division stationed on the far side of the Sittang River, to the east of Rangoon, had been mauled by the oncoming Japanese Fifteenth Army, itself a force of only two small divisions, about sixteen thousand men. The only Burmese division in the vicinity was suffering attrition through desertion, fueled not by cowardice but by Burmese hatred for the British. A lone British armored brigade held Rangoon. Such was Alexander's "army." He arrived in Rangoon on March 5, just in time to preside over the loss of the city and lead the chaotic breakout from the capital northward to Prome. Rangoon, aflame and abandoned, fell on March 8.[155]

The Japanese used the port to bring in 20,000 more men, and the reinforced Fifteenth Army soon spread outward from Rangoon into the Irrawaddy delta, the most fertile and productive estuary in the British Empire and the source of surplus grains and rice critical to the sustenance of Bengal. The delta had for five decades supplied Bengal enough rice to stave off want; no major famine had occurred in India for more than fifty years, in part because of the relationship between the Burmese rice surpluses and Bengal's needs. The Japanese broke that connection, stealing the Irrawaddy's bounty for Tokyo's consumption and destroying what they couldn't steal. The delta's loss, along with unprecedented cyclones in Bengal later in the year and a worsening drought on the upper Subcontinent, guaranteed rising prices and grain and rice shortages in Bengal, whether or not Japanese troops arrived there anytime soon. The Japanese objective was nothing less than to drive the British out of Burma, starting at Rangoon, six hundred miles south of the Assam frontier. Alexander promptly put Lieutenant General William ("Billy") Slim in charge of the newly formed Burma Corps (Burcorps) in hopes of repelling the invader. Slim was a real fighter, who had subdued the Iraqi and Iranian revolts the previous year. Yet Burcorps was an army on paper only. The British receded before the Japanese tide, Alexander withdrawing north toward Prome while Vinegar Joe Stilwell, commanding six undersize and unenthused Chinese divisions, covered his eastern flank.[156]

The presence of the hated Chinese on Burmese soil—reluctantly agreed to by Wavell—served only to bring more Burmese deserters into the Japanese ranks. A week after the fall of Rangoon, Alexander and Stilwell met for the first time in a pretty little hillside colonial town near Mandalay, a village the British had named May Town—Maymyo. The two generals did not exactly hit it off. Stilwell, with a good ear for upper-class English speech, later declared, *"Extrawdinery!"* Alexander, with a condescending gaze, "looked me over as if I had just crawled from under a rock."* Yet if a joint command was what it took to fight the Japanese, Stilwell was glad to be on board. He wanted not only to hold the city of Toungoo but to attack. But Chiang, to Stilwell's fury, delayed his decision to order Chinese forces south from Mandalay until it was too late, with the result that by the end of the month, the Japanese overran Toungoo. Stilwell and Alexander now had but one decision to make, whether to run to China or to India. Stilwell sent half his Chinese forces back up the Burma Road, the other half north toward Myitkyina, near the Indian frontier, and the only navigable track from India to China. The Japanese commenced chasing Stilwell's troops up the Burma Road and Alexander's emaciated force up the west bank of the Irrawaddy. Burma was doomed.[157]

It took the entire month of April for the Japanese to finish the job, during which time Alexander and Slim skulked off toward Assam, while most of Stilwell's Chinese troops fled to Chungking, joined by hundreds of Burmese deserters. Stilwell, offered a ride out for himself and his immediate staff on an Army Air Force plane, chose instead to walk out with 114 men to Assam, a miserable journey of over two hundred miles along the Irrawaddy and through high mountain passes. His men no longer looked up when an airplane passed over; the Allies had none in the skies. The trek took almost three weeks. As they slogged toward the Assam frontier, Alexander, Slim, and Stilwell raced the Japanese and the coming monsoon rains. When on May 17 Alexander arrived in Kalewa, a border town at the confluence of the Chindwin and Myittha rivers, he had with him just two dozen field guns and as many trucks. It was the longest retreat in British military history. Almost one-third of his original force of thirty thousand stayed behind as casualties and deserters. Stilwell did not lose a man, but his little band arrived in Assam half starved, with the Japanese at their

---

* Churchill wrote of the Englishmen of his generation who either would not or could not pronounce the letter "r." In *My Early Life,* he described an attempt by the commanding officer of the 4th Hussars, Colonel John Brabazon, to catch a train: After waiting for some time on the station platform, Brabazon turned to the stationmaster and asked, "Where is my *twain?*" Told that his train had already gone, the colonel responded, "Gone? *Bwing* me another."

back. The monsoon rains arrived three days later. The Burma Road was lost, along with Burma, Lord Randolph Churchill's imperial legacy, presented by him to Queen Victoria as a New Year's present in 1886.[158]

Blame for Burma's loss and the failure of the first joint Chinese-American-British operation was apportioned along nationalist lines. Chiang, in a letter to Churchill, wrote bitterly, "In all my life of long military experience, I have seen nothing to compare with the deplorable, unprepared state, confusion, and degradation of the war area in Burma." Such words did not endear the generalissimo to Churchill. Stilwell told Washington that he thought the British would rather lose Burma than be indebted to the Chinese for saving it. While Burma tottered, the United States suffered a humiliation of its own when Douglas MacArthur fled Manila for Australia on March 11. Allied thoughts concerning Operation Gymnast (the invasion of French North Africa) went up in the smoke of Rangoon, leading Roosevelt and Churchill to agree that "Gymnast cannot be undertaken." Roosevelt also noted the irony that Stilwell and Alexander, the commanders designate of Gymnast, met instead in Burma, where the Japanese drove them out. Alexander, stranded in Assam and knowing a cul de sac when he saw one, put Billy Slim in charge of the remnants of Burcorps and returned to London. Roosevelt, who never really had a dog in the fight, offered jaunty condolences to Churchill: "I have never liked Burma or the Burmese....I wish you could put the whole bunch of them in a frying pan...and let them stew in their own juices." Churchill, in a note to Roosevelt, offered that the wisest course for the Japanese to now take would be to drive right up the Burma Road to China, and "make a job of that."[159]

This the Japanese did, for a short while, chasing Chiang's tattered army into Yunnan province. Then the Japanese stopped. They had neither orders from Tokyo nor a strategic plan to carry though on their stupendous victories.

Weeks earlier, in early March, Eden and Alec Cadogan suspected the fight might have gone out of Churchill. His most loyal friend, Brendan Bracken, and his most omnipresent political critic, Stafford Cripps, agreed that Eden should be made deputy defence minister. Cadogan and Eden also noted that for several weeks "there has been no direction of the war. War Cabinet doesn't function.... There's no hand on the wheel (probably due to P.M.'s health)." In fact, the alliance itself was drifting, rudderless.

Throughout March and April and into May, Churchill and Roosevelt exchanged telegrams and letters that, taken in the aggregate, underscore Eden's pessimism and show that the two leaders had differing objectives, militarily and politically, and lacked the means to achieve any of them, alone or together. The alliance was looking all hat and no cattle.[160]

These were the weeks when Japanese armies rolled up Burma and Java and the Philippines, where the 75,000 American and Filipino troops trapped on Bataan surrendered on April 9, and marched off to a captivity that would kill almost half of them. Fortress Corregidor fell a month later. In Java, the Japanese had advanced from island to island, up and down the East Indies, until, on March 23, less than a month after landing, they took the Andaman Islands, located three hundred miles off the Thai and Burmese coasts in the Bay of Bengal. Nothing but open ocean separated the islands from Ceylon.

Stalin, meanwhile, began expressing interest in a treaty with his allies that would secure the Soviet Union's prewar borders, a concept entirely unacceptable to Roosevelt and Churchill, both of whom had long believed such matters should be addressed only at the postwar peace conference. Yet Churchill now began to see the practical merit in moderating that stance given that America and Britain had made no plans whatsoever to do anything anytime soon to ease Stalin's burden, other than send small Arctic convoys, which U-boats regularly mauled. Roosevelt considered himself capable of mollifying Stalin, and so notified Churchill. "I think you will not mind me being brutally frank when I tell you that I think I can personally handle Stalin better than either your Foreign Office or my State Department. Stalin hates the guts of all your top people. He thinks he likes me better, and I hope he will continue to do so."[161]

Throughout March, the most pressing question at the Admiralty was, where is Admiral Nagumo's carrier strike force? Churchill thought it only a matter of time, and likely not a great deal of time, before Nagumo launched air and amphibious attacks on Ceylon to gain complete control of the Indian Ocean. That would put the Japanese athwart the sea-lanes to the Persian Gulf and from the Suez to India, and threaten the supply of Stalin by way of Basra as well as the supply of the British in India and Chiang Kai-shek in China. One of Churchill's deepest fears—the loss of access to Persian and Iraqi oil—appeared a distinct possibility. Those two nations, lightly garrisoned by British colonial troops, now lay exposed between the forces of Tojo and Hitler, who was certain to make a spring push into the Caucasus, which, if successful, would bring him that much closer to the Middle East. Rommel, too, appeared poised to strike toward Cairo. Were he to get there, the roads to Baghdad would lie open. The troops Churchill had hoped to array on the Levant-Caspian front were now headed to India. The defense of the northern route into the Mosul oil fields, Churchill cabled Roosevelt, "now depends on the success of the Russian armies." He had summed up the problem to Colville months earlier: "With Hitler in control of Iraqi oil and Ukrainian wheat...not all the staunchness of our Plymouth brethren would shorten the ordeal." The Middle East was the only theater of war exposed to both Germany and Japan, and its defense fell exclusively to the British, who lacked the manpower to repel Rommel and the sea power to repel the Japanese. As March lurched toward April, the question remained, where was Nagumo?[162]

Four months earlier. Louis "Dickey" Mountbatten, a mere captain, and an unlucky one at that—he had lost his ship at Crete—had been promoted to the rank of commodore and shortly thereafter replaced Admiral Keyes as director of Combined Operations. Churchill charged Mountbatten and his small staff with planning raids on the Continent, and coordinating those raids with the Royal Navy, Royal Marines, Army, and RAF. Churchill told him to think of only offense, never defense, and to begin drawing up the matériel and personnel requirements—specialized landing crafts, close air support, waterproof tanks, beach spotters, aerial photography—required for a full-fledged invasion of France. Churchill promoted him over far more senior and experienced Royal Navy officers to vice admiral and sat him down on the Combined Chiefs of Staff Committee, where, Brooke later wrote, Dickie "frequently wasted his own time and ours." Then Churchill—reasoning that the interservice nature of Combined Operations required a grand gesture—insisted that Mountbatten be promoted to the rank of lieutenant general in the army *and* air marshal in the RAF, thus earning Mountbatten the enmity of dozens of more senior offices in those branches of the military. From Churchill he earned the moniker of "triphibian," a word Churchill coined for the occasion, and which soon found its way into *Webster's.*[163]

March closed with Mountbatten's first significant foray as director of Combined Operations, a commando raid on the French port of St-Nazaire, located five miles upstream from the mouth of the Loire. The dry dock at St-Nazaire, built for the French passenger liner *Normandie* (which had burned at its Hudson River pier the previous month), was one of the largest in the world and the only one on the Atlantic coast that offered *Bismarck*'s surviving sister ship, *Tirpitz,* space enough for repairs. *Tirpitz* had for two months been riding at anchor in a fjord at Trondheim, safe from British aircraft. Yet for Germany, the battleship's safety came at a price. *Tirpitz,* at anchor, posed no threat to British convoys. Churchill and Mountbatten were of a mind that the destruction of the St-Nazaire dry dock, which would leave *Tirpitz* no place to run to if damaged, would make a sortie from Trondheim into the Atlantic too dangerous to risk. The British plan was audacious. Escorted by destroyers, gunboats, and 250 commandos, one of the fifty old American destroyers—*Campbeltown*—its bow packed with three tons of TNT, would sail right up the Loire estuary in the dead of night and crash through the gates of the drydock. The plan called for the crew to scuttle the ship while commandos destroyed the port facilities. Then the small gunboats would pick up the sailors and commandos, and everybody would get the hell out of town. Soon thereafter, if all went as planned, the explosives hidden on *Campbeltown*—set on a timer to allow the crew to escape—would blast the drydock to smithereens.

Campbeltown crashed the dock at 1:34 A.M., remarkably just four minutes behind schedule. Everything had gone as planned, with the exception of the most vital component of all—the fuse that triggered the explosives. After *Campbeltown* crashed the gates, nothing. There she sat, a fish out of water. By the time those commandos not killed or captured got away down the Loire or into the countryside, Germans had swarmed aboard *Campbeltown*. A few dozen German technicians, precise as usual, began a methodical inspection of the ship. They worked through the morning while several hundred officers and men toured the vessel and took snapshots for their girls back home. More than four hundred Germans were aboard when, just before noon, the fuse elected to function. The explosion killed them all. For two days, teams of Germans collected bits and pieces of human remains scattered near the wrecked dock. The raid had its intended effect. Hitler treasured *Tirpitz* so much that he allowed it to make only two brief North Sea excursions that year in pursuit of Allied convoys. He thereafter refused to send it into the Atlantic proper. Instead, *Tirpitz* waited for two years in Norwegian fjords for the British invasion that never came. Finally, in November 1944, RAF Lancaster bombers destroyed the ship with six-ton bombs.

The St-Nazaire raid made little strategic difference in the Battle of the Atlantic, other than to keep *Tirpitz* out of the Atlantic, but like the hunt for *Bismarck,* it captured the imaginations of Americans and Britons alike. Churchill, with a nod to the florid, picturesque narrative style of Thomas Macaulay, termed the raid "brilliant and heroic" and "a deed of glory." The commandos, he wrote, had "been eager to enter the fray," and did so "in the teeth of a close and murderous fire." It was the sort of small, sparkling victory he so relished.[164]

In North Africa and Asia, Churchill was getting nothing of the sort. Rommel sat in front of Ritchie's Eighth Army just forty miles west of

Tobruk. The German was reinforcing almost at leisure. That he meant to attack was certain; the only question was when. In Asia and the Pacific the Japanese had conquered everything in their path. In Russia the German spring offensive would surely come, when panzers would pour down Ukraine roads that wound east and south toward Stalingrad, and all the way to the Caucasus, and Iraq and Persia beyond. Almost three months had elapsed since Churchill warned the Commons that multiple disasters would strike; they indeed had. And now, with different motives and different goals, Stalin and Roosevelt prodded Churchill to action. Stalin not only sought to cement his 1939 borders, he insisted upon the opening of a second front. Roosevelt desired a decision on where and when American troops would fight, for it had been four months since Pearl Harbor and American voters were starting to wonder if it might be six more before American fighting men actually went on the attack. Franklin Roosevelt did not want the November midterm elections to come and go without American boys fighting Germans *somewhere*.

As if to deride British arms, on the night when Mountbatten's commandos steamed up the Loire, Admiral Nagumo and his force of five modern aircraft carriers, four battleships, and a bevy of cruisers and destroyers sallied into the Bay of Bengal, steaming for Ceylon. The Admiralty no longer need wonder where the Japanese admiral was. Against Nagumo the Royal Navy arrayed a far less powerful fleet made up of four older battleships, three smaller aircraft carriers, a few cruisers, several destroyers, and a great many inexperienced seamen. Its commander, Admiral James Somerville, a veteran of Mediterranean operations, based his ships in a secret anchorage (code-named Port T) at Addu Atoll rather than in Colombo and Trincomalee, where Nagumo expected to find and destroy the British fleet. Fortunately for Somerville, after four days of cruising south of Ceylon in search of Nagumo, he took most of his fleet back to Port T to refuel. When Nagumo appeared off Ceylon on Easter Sunday, April 5, he didn't find Somerville, but over the next few days he did find 100,000 tons of British merchant shipping, an aircraft carrier, two cruisers, and a destroyer, all of which he sent to the bottom. The British and Japanese traded aircraft casualties, about fifty each, but the net loss for the British was far more severe. Churchill could count only fourteen heavy bombers in all of India. Nagumo, in turn, still had almost nine hundred of his original one thousand pilots and aircraft, more than enough to destroy either the British or the American fleet, whichever he found first. Admiral Somerville, overwhelmingly outgunned, was forced to flee the Indian Ocean and seek refuge on the east coast of Africa, leaving the Bay of Bengal—and India—completely unprotected.[165]

*   *   *

Great Britain had been driven from the Indian Ocean. And yet, incredibly, it appeared that Nagumo had departed as well. Contact was again lost with the admiral. Churchill was sure Nagumo would soon return to finish the job. On April 7, Churchill (who inexplicably presumed that American naval strength was now "decidedly superior to the enemy forces in the Pacific") asked Roosevelt to use those naval forces in order to lure the Japanese back into the Pacific Ocean. Churchill's calculations are difficult to explain unless Roosevelt had failed to apprise him of the facts, which were that the Japanese outnumbered the Americans in battleships eleven to zero, and in aircraft carriers ten to four. A fifth carrier, *Wasp*, and America's newest battleship, *Washington*, which Admiral King wanted to station in the Pacific, had been sent to Britain in order to ferry Spitfires to Malta, a task the depleted Royal Navy could no longer undertake. Symbolic of the plight of the Allied navies, the American admiral who commanded the *Wasp* task force was washed overboard in the mid-Atlantic and lost. And when Admiral Cunningham tried to run a relief convoy from Alexandria to Malta—the island was almost out of oil and food—*every* ship was lost. Brooke confided to his diary, "These are black days."[166]

The Allied naval situation was desperate in all oceans. Churchill's tone reflected that truth when, on April 15, he warned Roosevelt that the British position was "grave" and that unless Admiral Yamamoto's fleets were brought to battle and defeated, there was "no reason why the Japanese should not become the dominating factor in the Western Indian Ocean. This would result in the collapse of our whole position in the Middle East." On April 17 he upped the ante when he cabled Roosevelt: "It is essential that we should prevent a junction of the Japanese and the Germans." The junction Churchill had in mind was one between Rommel and the Japanese, the most likely scenario being a Japanese fleet pounding the port of Basra while Rommel slashed his way to Baghdad. Yet only half a junction could prove as fatal as an actual Axis hookup. Japanese control of the Persian Gulf would as effectively deny Britain oil as an actual Axis junction in the Middle East. A Japanese reduction of Basra and the nearby Iranian port of Abadan—home to the world's largest oil refinery—would guarantee that Abadan oil could not be gotten out of Iran, supplies to Russia could not be gotten in, and, as Churchill warned Roosevelt, the British would be unable to "maintain our position either at sea or on land." Brooke later wrote that from a strategic standpoint, Abadan was more important than Egypt, in that the loss of Egypt did not necessarily mean the loss of Abadan, but the loss of Abadan meant the loss of Egypt. Yet, as Averell Harriman learned later in the year, the British were so stretched worldwide that the only defense Churchill could throw up around Abadan consisted of six obsolete biplanes and a few anti-aircraft guns. If Hitler punched through from North Africa or from the

Caucasus (once he took that region, which he intended to do by late summer), Abadan and all of Persia would be his for the taking.[167]

Roosevelt, in reply to Churchill's pessimistic musings, stated that *his* situation in the Pacific was "very grave" and pointed out that the American navy was supplying and protecting Australia and New Zealand. Left unsaid was the obvious: America was doing so because London could not. Roosevelt also deprecated the possibility of an Axis hookup, calling it a "remote prospect." Yet that conclusion was no more based on fact than was Churchill's presumption that the American navy had been fully reconstituted in the Pacific.[168]

Churchill (and Brooke) had believed since December that any junction between Germany and Japan would either prolong the war for years or lead to a negotiated settlement, and at the least would mean the end of Churchill's government, if not the British Empire. This was the ordeal as Churchill had outlined it to Jock Colville on several occasions.[169]

Yet, as events turned out, Admiral Nagumo himself shortened Churchill's Asian ordeal. Nagumo was one with all Japanese commanders in his absolute belief that imperial orders must be followed to the letter. Creativity in the face of changing battlefield conditions was not a Japanese trait. The Japanese navy liked to divide its forces, which led to highly scripted and complex operations that demanded perfect coordination. The Japanese also favored diversionary tactics intended to lure the enemy into traps or to disrupt the enemy's plans, but tactical inflexibility prevented them from reacting with vigor when their own plans were disrupted. Changes in plans are, necessarily, unscripted, and were therefore studiously avoided by Japanese commanders. The failure of Nagumo's airmen to return a third time to Pearl Harbor on December 7 to destroy the fuel depots and repair shops is the best-known example of a Japanese opportunity lost in rigid adherence to the master plan. Such an attack had been hoped for but not planned to the letter and, more important, not *ordered*.[170]

Admiral Yamamoto planned to dispatch in late April a carrier force to the Coral Sea to cover the planned invasions of Tulagi, in the Solomon Islands, and Port Moresby, on the southeast coast of Papua New Guinea. A Japanese victory in New Guinea would isolate Australia and mark a significant milestone on the road to Yamamoto's main strategic war aim: the erection of an impenetrable ring of air and naval bases around the entire perimeter of the Co-Prosperity Sphere—the bloc of Asian nations led by the Japanese and free of Western powers—before the Americans could re-arm to dispute the issue. With the South Pacific in hand, Yamamoto planned to then take an outer Aleutian island or two in the North Pacific, and to take Midway Island, the outermost link in the Hawaiian chain, 1,100 miles west-northwest of Pearl Harbor. That would close his ring. It was an audacious goal.

The fifty-eight-year-old admiral had studied English at Harvard two decades earlier and had served as naval attaché in Washington in the late 1920s. During his time in Cambridge and Washington, he had grown to respect Americans, and had also learned to play a ruthless game of poker. He was not a gambler, but he knew how to play a hand. Once he took Port Moresby and Tulagi, he intended to shut the door on American designs in the South Pacific by building an airfield on the small British protectorate of Guadalcanal. In support of those objectives, his Port Moresby task forces were to seek out and destroy the meager American fleet that would surely steam into the Coral Sea to dispute the matter. The American response would have to be meager; two of its four aircraft carriers in the Pacific stood off the Hawaiian Islands, which left only two available for duty in the Coral Sea. The odds lay heavily with the Japanese, whose strength and experienced airmen far exceeded the Americans' and Britons' combined. Yamamoto held the cards, a hand made sweeter by virtue of his having dealt it himself.[171]

Then, Franklin Roosevelt launched an audacious—though largely symbolic—strike of his own. In early April, Roosevelt dispatched two of his four carriers to within five hundred miles of Japan in order to carry out a bombing raid on Tokyo. From one of the carriers, USS *Hornet,* sixteen American twin-engine B-25 medium bombers commanded by Colonel Jimmy Doolittle set off for Japan. The damage Doolittle's raiders inflicted was minimal, but Yamamoto, shocked at the affront to his emperor, decided that the time had come for "the annihilation" of the American Pacific fleet. He ordered that the Midway and Coral Sea ventures be carried out virtually simultaneously. Doolittle's raid was just the sort of diversion Churchill had pressed Roosevelt to undertake, and it had had the desired effect on the Japanese. Roosevelt, ebullient over Doolittle's success, telegraphed Churchill, "We have had a good crack at Japan," and added that he hoped it would lead to Japan pulling its "big ships" from the Indian Ocean. This was why the president had played down Churchill's concern over an Axis juncture in the Middle East as a "remote prospect." Yet the prospect would prove to be remote only if the Japanese navy committed an inexplicable error.[172]

This Admiral Nagumo did when, after pummeling the British in the Indian Ocean, he sent three of his aircraft carriers back to Japan for refitting. In trading planes with the British in the Indian Ocean—about fifty each—Nagumo had come out the winner by virtue of the fact that the British were just about out of aircraft, while Nagumo still had almost all of his. Nagumo's fleet emerged, as usual, unscathed. By mid-April, the Royal Navy had virtually nothing left, and what little it had was steaming for East Africa. The Americans had not much more. Churchill's desperation during those weeks was entirely justified. Yet, rather than finish the job, Nagumo, evidencing early symptoms of what the Japanese later called Victory Disease, chose to go home and perform a cosmetic refitting on his ships. Churchill often complained that his generals preferred certainty to hazard. In this case, Nagumo certainly did.

His decision proved disastrous when in early May a diminished Japanese carrier force met the Americans in the Battle of the Coral Sea. It was the first aircraft-carrier battle in history and the first naval battle where combatants could not see the opposing fleet. The Americans lost one carrier sunk and one damaged. The Japanese lost one light carrier sunk — the first such Japanese casualty of the war — and two heavy carriers damaged. The American navy's losses, relative to its overall strength, were far more egregious than the Japanese losses. But Yamamoto folded his hand. By doing so he lost an opportunity and the battle. Churchill later wrote that had the Japanese sailed into the Coral Sea with two or three more carriers, the Americans might well have never sailed out. Yamamoto had long maintained that in order to force a settlement with America, Japan had to destroy the U.S. Pacific fleet within six months of the start of war, or face the consequences of a re-armed United States. Although the Coral Sea affair was an opportunity lost for Yamamoto to do just that, another soon presented itself. He scheduled his decisive battle for dawn on June 6 — one day shy of six months after Pearl Harbor. The place would be Midway Island.[173]

In their exchange of telegrams that winter and spring, Churchill and Roosevelt weighed almost every issue in terms of shipping tonnage, to the point where they became experts on the calculus of hulls and cargo and "manlift," the capacity needed to carry men from one place to another. When Churchill asked for the use of American ships to move 40,000 troops to India, Roosevelt agreed, but he told Churchill that such a shuffling of resources would result in a cascade of disrupted plans: the end of Gymnast; the gutting of the effort to send American troops to Britain for a 1942 invasion of Europe; a halt to shipping munitions to China; and a further reduction in the amount of goods reaching the Russians, who, Roosevelt offered, "are killing more Germans...than you and I put together." He further declared that America's 1942 man-lift capacity was only 90,000 men, a figure he hoped to double in 1943. This shocked Churchill, who in reply proposed that Roosevelt could solve the problem by "giving orders now to double or treble the American man-lift by 1943," as if Roosevelt could somehow conjure ships. Churchill offered that if no improvement could be made to those figures, "there may well be no question of restoring the situation [in Europe] until 1944," which obviously meant that all the inter-Allied talk about a large-scale invasion in 1942 or 1943 was just that, talk. In that case, he wrote, the Allies would reap the "many dangers that would follow from such a prolongation of the war." Shipping was now a zero-sum game. Roosevelt replied with a remarkably detailed calculation of future American "man-lift" that ended with: "Thus, neglecting losses, the total troop-carrying capacity of U.S. vessels by June, 1944, will be 400,000 men." Since these figures were known to the two leaders and their most trusted lieutenants only, the press on both sides of the Atlantic—and Stalin—continued to beat their drums for an immediate second European front, unaware that shipping constraints and the lack of American preparedness, not Churchill, to whom the press ascribed a hesitancy in the matter, were the reasons that there could be none in 1942, and most likely not in 1943 either.[174]

Roosevelt had not pulled his estimate of 400,000 men from a hat; it was the minimum initial number of American combat troops the Combined Chiefs agreed were needed for a successful invasion of Europe. Roosevelt's prediction of when these troops would be ready—June 1944—proved remarkably accurate, and it is largely ignored by those, then and since, who blame Churchill for not busting into Europe earlier. Yet, in the spring of 1942, Churchill and Roosevelt knew that they could not simply wait out Germany for two years. They had to fight, in tandem. But where, and when?

Sir Stafford Cripps arrived in Delhi on March 22. For the next three weeks he conducted lengthy discussions with leaders in Gandhi's National Congress, offering them autonomy down the road. The offer was based on the War Cabinet's promise of postwar Dominion status for India in exchange for absolute loyalty in the war against Japan. Dominion status amounted to de facto independence. The talks went nowhere. If politics is the art of compromise in furtherance of a cause, Gandhi, by not giving an inch, hurt his cause. He persisted in his belief that the British presence in India was bait for the Japanese, who were more likely to invade India if the British did not depart. He demanded either immediate independence or, at the least, a national government. Chiang had just weeks earlier tried to impress upon Gandhi the need to fight the Japanese, for the Japanese despised peacemakers more than war givers, and gave no quarter to either, as the recent slaughters in Singapore and the Nanking massacre in 1937 attested to. The Japanese would spare no one, Chiang warned, whether the British stayed or left. Gandhi listened politely; the generalissimo went home rebuffed. Gandhi understood, George Orwell later wrote, that "if you are not prepared to take life, you must often be prepared for lives to be lost in some other way." Gandhi accepted that a nonviolent opposition to a Japanese invasion might cost millions of lives. Cripps argued the same case as had Chiang, and got no further. Churchill expected as much. He later wrote, "In the intensity of the struggle for life from day to day, and with four hundred million helpless people to defend from the horrors of Japanese conquest, I was able to bear this news, which I had thought probable from the beginning, with philosophy. I knew how bitterly Stafford Cripps would feel the failure of his Mission, and I sought to comfort him." Churchill may have been feeling unusually expansive when writing those words, for upon his return to London, Cripps, not Churchill, found his name associated with the mission and its failure.[175]

It was over India and empire that Churchill and Roosevelt had their first serious political argument. Roosevelt presumed he could speak frankly to Churchill on most matters, including—and mistakenly—India. Churchill, out of politeness, kept Roosevelt abreast of Cripps's progress, or lack thereof. When the talks broke down, Roosevelt blamed Churchill, in the most frank terms. The two men had very different long-term objectives. Beyond the defeat of Hitler, Churchill wanted above all to preserve the British Empire, including of course India, a goal that was anathema to Roosevelt, a devout anti-imperialist. "Preserve," for Churchill, meant "protect." For Roosevelt it meant "keep." On April 11, Roosevelt sent a private letter to Churchill, by way of Harry Hopkins, in which he outlined his position on India in terms of the thirteen colonies and George III. Roosevelt suggested Churchill consider that India might be ripe for the same transformation as the American states had experienced—from colonies to loose federation and finally to nationhood. Churchill in his memoirs offered a benign take on Roosevelt's musings: "The President's mind was back in the American War of Independence.... I, on the other hand, was responsible for preserving the peace and safety of the Indian continent, sheltering nearly a fifth of the population of the globe. Our resources were slender and strained to the full." Had Roosevelt not offered one final incendiary opinion in his missive, the matter might have remained benign. But he added this: "The feeling is almost universally held here that the deadlock has been caused by the unwillingness of the British government to concede to the Indians the right of self-government. I feel I must place this issue before you very frankly, and I know you will understand my reasons for so doing."[176]

Churchill not only did not understand but was enraged by what he saw as Roosevelt's meddling. He had thought that his reaction in December to Roosevelt's verbal lecture had set things straight regarding India, but here was Roosevelt again, and in writing, no less. The note reached Chequers at 3:00 A.M. on Sunday and found Hopkins and Churchill still up and chatting. Upon reading the message Churchill unleashed a barrage of curses that echoed throughout the great house. After regaining (some) of his composure, he voiced his long-held belief that any imposition of political will by the Hindus upon one hundred million Indian Muslims would result in a total breakdown of order, and large-scale bloodshed, and this at the very moment the Japanese were waiting in the wings, with Gandhi and his "Quit India" cohorts ready to accept the enemy peacefully, thereby easing a Japanese passage to the Middle East. Meanwhile, the Muslim League was demanding the creation of a separate Muslim state, Pakistan. To accede to Gandhi's demands would necessitate acceding to the Muslim League. With the war on, Churchill was unwilling to do either. India's defense against Japan required military action, not political. India was poor and life was hard—the average Indian earned less than $15 per year and could expect to live just twenty-seven years. Yet, without its tether to London it would be a far poorer place, and were the Japanese to arrive, Churchill believed it would become a desolate place.[177]

At the end of his tutorial, he told Hopkins that if his resignation would advance the alliance and American opinion, he was willing to do so, but even in that case he was sure the cabinet would continue with its present Indian policy. It was an idle threat, but credible in that the free world looked upon Churchill as the hero of the war. Roosevelt could ill afford to be seen as the man who drove Winston Churchill into political exile. Roosevelt, Harriman later recalled, "was for breaking up the British empire, and Churchill had no intention of doing so. . . . India was a known subject, but not one to discuss with Churchill." Hopkins concluded likewise after Churchill's harangue, and cabled Roosevelt accordingly.[178]

Churchill drafted a sober reply to Roosevelt in which he told the president that a serious disagreement between them "would break my heart, and would surely deeply injure both our countries at the height of this terrible struggle." He also allowed that Roosevelt's letter would remain private, a backhanded yet clear way of telling Roosevelt that the cabinet would erupt if it got wind of his preachifying. Yet, Churchill appears not to have grasped a nuanced element of Roosevelt's thinking: Roosevelt was willing to fight for the survival of Britain, but not for the survival of British *interests*, that is, the British Empire. "The winds of change had begun to blow," Christopher Soames, later Churchill's son-in-law, recalled, "but Churchill had yet to see them."[179]

Within months, Gandhi and the Indian National Congress called for strikes. The "Quit India" movement took to the streets. Ten battalions of British and Indian troops who should have been killing Japanese soldiers became tied down fighting Indian nationalists; more than one thousand Indians were killed. When it was over, the British placed Gandhi under house arrest at a small palace at Poona, and jailed his deputy Jawaharlal Nehru and thousands of "Quit India" partisans for the duration of the war. Gandhi had distanced himself from reality when he advised not only Indians but also Czechs and European Jews to accept their fate: "I can conceive [of] the necessity of the immolation of hundreds, if not thousands, to appease the hunger of the dictators." That proved to be an ironic choice of words given that Hitler's final butcher's bill exceeded six million Jews, and several hundred thousands of Czechs and Dutchmen and Frenchmen, and at least twenty million Polish and Russian civilians. On April 19, Joseph Goebbels dropped an entry into his diary that Churchill himself could have written: "Gandhi gave an interview in which he once again urged non-resistance. He is a fool whose politics seem merely calculated to drag India further and further into misfortune."[180]

Writing years later, Churchill minced no words: The "people of Hindustan...were carried through the struggle on the shoulders of our small island." By 1942 the cost to Britain of defending India was running at almost one million pounds per day, an amount fixed by contracts drawn up in India at exorbitant rates and at the inflated prewar rate of exchange. In essence, the viceroy and India were billing London for India's defense. Churchill informed the viceroy, Lord Linlithgow, that HMG reserved the right to file counterclaims after the war. Yet for Churchill, the fact that more than a million Hindu and Muslim men "*volunteered* to serve" (italics Churchill) in the defense of India, trumped all criticisms of HMG's imperial policy, whether by Roosevelt or Gandhi or anyone else. Loyalty, not British imperial might, kept India bound to London. In return, Churchill wrote, London "effectively protected" India from "the horrors and perils of World War."[181]

In their ongoing correspondence, both Roosevelt and Churchill displayed a knack for knowing when a personal touch was called for—a best wishes to a spouse, or a few generous words about the other fellow's predicaments. Shortly after the India episode, Roosevelt gave Churchill a stamp that had been canceled at Argentia the previous August. This gesture was pure Roosevelt, simple, understated, and symbolic, much like his fireside chats. Churchill reciprocated with a typically Churchillian flourish; he sent Roosevelt specially bound volumes of the complete works of Winston Leonard Spencer Churchill.[182]

Churchill's most cutting response to Roosevelt's position came when, in his memoirs, he took a mighty swipe at his old friend. Of the president's suggestion that the British simply walk away from India, he wrote: "I was thankful that events [the war against Japan] made such an act of madness impossible." Idealism was all well and good, Churchill continued, but not "idealism at other people's expense and without regard to the consequences of ruin and slaughter which fall upon millions of humble homes." Such ruin and slaughter in fact descended upon India in 1946, and led in 1947 to its partition into Pakistan and India, after the murder of thousands of Hindus and Muslims, and the forced migration of millions more.[183]

Hopkins had come to London not to discuss India but to accompany General George Marshall, who was there to brief Churchill and the British chiefs on the proposed American strategy in Europe. Marshall's plan, drawn up by Eisenhower, was straightforward. Operation Sledgehammer would relieve pressure on the Russians—who Eisenhower expected to soon be in dire straits—by putting several divisions ashore in France in the vicinity of Cherbourg on the Cotentin Peninsula. The plan, Roosevelt cabled Churchill, "has my heart and mind in it." It didn't have Churchill's. He told Roosevelt that Sledgehammer should not be undertaken if Russia was losing, but only if Russia was *winning,* for if Russia "is in dire straits, it will not help her or us to come a nasty cropper on our own."[184]

This was Marshall's first introduction to Churchill's late hours and long monologues, in this case on the American Civil War and World War One. Brooke observed that Marshall "was evidently not used to being kept out of his bed till the small hours of the morning, and not enjoying it much!" Marshall told Brooke that he usually left the office at around 6:00 for a short ride on his horse and an early dinner at home, and that he might meet with Roosevelt once every month or six weeks. Brooke replied that he'd be lucky if he did not see Churchill for six hours. Despite the long hours and Churchill's digressions, the talks moved along, the British appearing to agree to an entry into Europe that year. In any case, the lack of shipping and landing craft settled the issue; the Americans could spare only enough ships to transport fewer than three U.S. divisions to Britain. That meant that British troops would be in the van of any invasion, and that meant that the British held veto power over any such proposal. As well, although Royal Navy engineers were designing artificial harbors to supply the troops on the beaches, construction was at least a year off. In addition, no effort had been made to build the specialty tanks that could clear minefields or double as massive flamethrowers. What most disturbed Brooke was that all the landing craft then in Britain could deliver only four thousand men to the beaches in the first wave, a force so paltry that it invited annihilation.

This was the hardest fact that Marshall had not addressed, leaving Brooke to jot in his diary that although Marshall displayed "a great charm and dignity...he did not impress me with his brain." When Brooke expressed his surprise to Marshall that he had given no thought to what the Allies might do after landing—go east, go south, go north—Marshall had no answer, and in fact shocked Brooke by saying that he "had not even studied any of the strategic implications." Still, Marshall left for Washington believing that the British had accepted his proposal to put men ashore that year. In fact, Churchill had agreed only to study the proposal.[185]

Churchill had done to Marshall what Brooke and the British chiefs regularly did to him when he proposed a scheme not to their liking: voiced enthusiasm and then studied the proposal to death. Ismay, seeing through Churchill's maneuver, told the chiefs, "Our American friends went happily homeward under the mistaken impression we had committed ourselves to both Roundup [the larger invasion of France] and Sledgehammer....I think we should have come clean, much cleaner than we did" by reminding the Americans of the horrors of the last war and the debacle of 1940, as well as by telling Marshall that an invasion could be undertaken only when there was "a cast iron certainty" of success.[186]

George Marshall harbored a soldier's natural distrust of politicians. His April meetings with Churchill allayed that distrust; in Churchill, Marshall believed he had found a true statesman, a man he could trust. And in Marshall, Churchill had found a man he could respect, a man who told the truth, whatever the political costs. Thus, Churchill felt regret when Marshall, a few weeks after departing, realized the British had no intention of landing in France, in force, in 1942. The statesman had snookered the soldier. Yet Churchill claimed in his memoirs that he hadn't intended to mislead Marshall, only to bolster his morale and voice British support for their shared, ultimate goal, a second European front. But Marshall, a man who expected to be told the truth, believed what the British had told him. Henceforth, he would prove himself not so easy a mark.[187]

On April 17, the day Marshall and Hopkins left London, Operation Gymnast, the invasion of French North Africa, out of sight and mind for two months, again made its presence known, like a mole in the arcade game. The trigger this time lay with the Vichy government, which that week was hijacked by Pierre Laval, personally despised as much by Hitler as by Roosevelt and Churchill. But Laval was as pro-German a Frenchman as the Führer could wish for. Pétain, old and infirm, had dismissed Laval from the government in the last of 1940 but now recalled him as vice premier. Within days Laval showed who was in charge when he began cooperating with the

Gestapo in its quest to round up and ship east those Jews who had fled central Europe for the safety of France—both occupied and unoccupied France. With Laval in, American policy toward the Vichy regime became obsolete overnight. The American ambassador to Vichy, Admiral William Leahy, was recalled; within weeks Roosevelt made Leahy his chief of staff.[188]

A neutral if not welcoming reception by French North Africans to any Anglo-American invasion had always been of primary importance to Roosevelt. For two years he had resisted the urgings of his liberal colleagues and continued to do business with Vichy. His motive was sound. Knowing that American boys would sooner or later be landing on French soil, or French colonial soil, Roosevelt had hoped to have Vichy as an ally when that day came. Counseled by Leahy, the president believed that French North Africa might not obey Laval's orders and that Pétain, now a figurehead, might fly to Algiers to rally patriotic Frenchmen. The wild card was Admiral Jean Darlan, who remained in the Vichy government as commander of all French armed forces. He had long hated the English, even more so since Churchill had obliterated his beloved ships and hundreds of his sailors at Oran, where Darlan had sent them in order to stay out of German hands. Darlan was also despised by Washington. The Vichy French had at least behaved with consistent poltroonery. Churchill called Darlan a "naval crook," yet even after Oran, Darlan pledged to never allow the French fleet to fall into German hands, a pledge he had so far kept. Still, Churchill considered the admiral's word to be worthless, which is somewhat ironic given that it had been Churchill who had struck Darlan at Oran. From a military standpoint, Darlan, more than Laval, was the riddle in need of a solution. Would the admiral send his fleet to fight the Americans and British if they sailed to Vichy North Africa? From Brooke's standpoint, the whole affair was a mess, a political minefield of the sort military men are keen to sidestep. The CIGS thought nothing would come of the regime change in Vichy, by way of any new opportunities in North Africa. And nothing did. With Gymnast again in play (possibly), Churchill made plans to send Dickie Mountbatten to Washington to whisper its merits in Roosevelt's ear in hopes that Roosevelt—despite the opposition of Marshall and King—would embrace the North African plan a second time.[189]

On May 27, Churchill cabled Roosevelt: "Dickie will explain to you the difficulties of 1942...and outline plans for a landing in the north of Norway." Churchill added that he welcomed Rommel's attack and that South African premier Jan Smuts, on the scene with Auchinleck, "expresses high confidence in the result." He closed with, "We must never let Gymnast pass from our minds." This was not what Roosevelt wanted to hear. Marshall—who had been dragooning as many ships as he could to build up forces in Britain—understood with clarity that Churchill and Brooke had misled him. Now here Churchill came, suggesting a gross diversion from their agreed-upon goal of a landing in France. Churchill's cable was at least straightforward; Mountbatten's mission was to impress upon Roosevelt the "practical difficulties," as Churchill saw it, entailed by Sledgehammer.[190]

The choice of Dickie was inspired. He was staunchly pro-American and, like Roosevelt, charming and high born. Mountbatten was a naval hero, and Roosevelt, a naval animal, greatly admired naval heroes. Within a week, to the great distress of Marshall and King, Mountbatten had almost persuaded the president of the perils of Sledgehammer and had praised the wisdom of Churchill's beloved Jupiter, the proposed invasion of northern Norway, which Brooke had been trying to kill for weeks. Even Churchill by then, with reluctance, sensed that any invasion of Norway was a long shot for that year. Yet Jupiter might well serve as a bargaining chip, to be dropped in favor of something more practical such as Gymnast. By the first week of June, Mountbatten had just about sold Roosevelt, whose choices had been whittled down (as Churchill intended) to Gymnast or nothing. Marshall and King did not see things at all that way; the Pacific, after all, was also a theater of war. They pressed Roosevelt for moves in that direction. Although Marshall and King suspected otherwise, no guile underlay Churchill's dealings with Roosevelt. Unless three criteria were met for Operation Roundup—sufficient troops, sufficient landing craft, and artificial harbor facilities—an invasion of France in 1942, or 1943 for that matter, could only end in disaster. Roosevelt understood this; after all, he had done the calculations as to man-lift. He simply needed a push in the proper direction; Churchill and Dickie gave it.

Hopkins and Marshall's route home from London in April had taken them over the North Atlantic, where fifty-nine American cargo ships destined for Murmansk were idled in Scottish and Icelandic ports. The reasons for the logjam were many and complex—lack of escorts, overburdened port facilities, the long wait to form convoys—but the most obvious explanation was simple: Admiral Dönitz's U-boats were winning the Battle of the Atlantic. Since January, much of the battle had been fought within sight of the American east coast. Dönitz's U-boat strength was up to 250 with more than 90 boats on patrol on any given day—50 or more in the Atlantic, 20 in the Mediterranean, and a dozen or more hunting Russia-bound convoys in the Arctic. On January 12, Dönitz, with American coastal shipping in his sights, had launched Operation *Paukenschlag* (Drumroll) off the east coast of America. U-boat commanders called the next several months their "second happy time," referring to the easy pickings offered by unescorted American ships, which sailed—inexplicably—with running lights ablaze along the well-illuminated east coast of the United States. Resorts from New Jersey to Miami, desperate for business, had kept their seaside lights burning for fear that dousing them would spoil the tourist season, but vacationers, denied planes and trains, could not get there in any event.

The U-boats found their targets starkly silhouetted by the luminous shoreline, a state of affairs that Admiral Samuel Eliot Morison (the official U.S. Navy historian of the war) called "one of the most reprehensible failures" of local governments and the American military during the war. Not until mid-April were the lights ordered turned off. American naval and Coast Guard ships and airborne patrols had begun, but the American navy, failing to grasp the hard-earned lessons of the Royal Navy, had yet to establish coastal convoys to protect ships heading from the Gulf of Mexico to Nova Scotia, where Atlantic convoys began and ended. Getting to Halifax was the responsibility of individual captains. U-boats simply lay in wait for them from New Orleans to the Canadian Maritimes coast. Thirty merchantmen were lost in the Maritimes alone in January, and almost twice as many in February. Churchill had since Pearl Harbor made clear to his subordinates that the war would be won *if* the Allies did not bungle the job. Off their coast, the Americans were bungling it, with the result, Churchill believed, that the U-boats threatened to bring about "the disaster of an indefinite prolongation of the war."[191]

At the Argentia conference, the Americans had pledged to increase annual merchant shipping production by almost sevenfold, to eight million tons. They would need every ton, as residents from Long Island to Florida's east coast who regularly beheld the glow of exploding oil tankers out at sea knew. The flames continued unabated during a seven-month attack that Churchill called a "terrible massacre of shipping along the American coast." The U.S. Navy was so unprepared to meet the challenge that Britain sent some of the fifty formerly American destroyers back across the Atlantic. Not until mid-April did the Americans destroy a U-boat by surface ship. By May the amount of fuel oil reaching New England from the Gulf of Mexico had plummeted by 90 percent. But where New Englanders could don an extra sweater, Russian troops needed guns, munitions, and trucks. Churchill tried to oblige. Stalin was desperate for spare parts to repair the Hurricanes that Britain had sent. Churchill ordered the RAF to dismantle several Hurricanes and ship the needed parts to Russia, a gesture that impressed Harriman, who noted that the American air force would never contemplate such a sacrifice. Stalin needed more than gestures. If the U-boats ravaged the Arctic convoys as they were shipping off the American coast, the Red Army would begin its summer campaigns lacking both a second front in France and the means to hold its own front. Between mid-April and mid-June, twenty-three out of eighty-four ships that left U.S. ports destined for Murmansk were sunk. Seventeen had to take shelter in Scotland, which prompted Stalin to accuse the British of "stealing" goods meant for the Red Army.[192]

And then the situation got worse. When twenty-two of thirty-four ships in one late June convoy went down, Churchill was forced to cancel the Arctic convoys for two months. This infuriated Stalin, embarrassed Churchill, and further fueled the "Second Front Now" crowd in Britain, where the heroic deeds of the Red Army so enthralled the populace that a London publisher used his meager ration of paper to reprint Tolstoy's *War and Peace*, which sold out within days.[193]

The devastation on the seas underscored the importance of the Wizard War. Britain's shipping losses had ameliorated somewhat during the last half of 1941, due to small improvements in radar, the protection offered by Icelandic and Greenland-based air patrols, the American presence across most of the Atlantic, and a decrease in German air attacks on coastal shipping following the invasion of Russia. Still, total losses of British, Allied, and neutral shipping exceeded four million tons in 1941. The losses would have been far greater but for the fortuitous capture on May 9, 1941, of an Enigma machine and code books from U-110 in the North Atlantic. The U-boat's captain, F. J. Lemp, had just lost a running battle with the British escort destroyer HMS *Bulldog*. Lemp, presuming his boat was doomed, ordered it abandoned. But U-110 did not go down. As its crew bobbed in the seas, a boarding party from *Bulldog* stripped her of everything they could carry, including her codes and Enigma machine. The submarine was taken under tow, but soon sank. The *Kriegsmarine* believed her crew and secrets had gone down with her. The British now had in their possession a German naval Enigma machine, not a model but the real deal. Churchill waited more than seven months to tell Roosevelt the good news. By early 1942, already wary of too many "coincidental" interceptions of U-boats—best explained by the British having cracked the German codes, which the army and Luftwaffe dismissed as an impossibility—*Kriegsmarine* cryptologists added a fourth wheel to their Enigma machines, boosting the number of possible letter permutations from the billions into the trillions. The army and Luftwaffe elected to stick with their older, three-wheel models. It was the wrong decision, for Alan Turing and the Bletchley crowd were just now beginning to make calculating machines that possessed the single most critical attribute necessary for breaking a code: computational speed. There are, after all, only so many letters in the alphabet.[194]

The addition of the fourth wheel to Enigma, however, gave the *Kriegsmarine* a hefty advantage in the Atlantic. Compounding that advantage, the German radio intercept and monitoring service (*Beobachtungsdienst*) had broken the British merchant code, allowing the *Kriegsmarine* to listen in on Allied intra-convoy conversations, including Royal Navy situation reports, which tracked the location of U-boats. The accuracy of the British reports greatly distressed Dönitz, but the advantage was his. He knew what the British knew, but the British did not know that he knew. Adding the fourth wheel to the naval Enigma machines resulted in a renewed slaughter of Allied shipping. Between January and June of 1942, U-boats sent six hundred ships, eight thousand crewmen, and three million tons of shipping to the bottom, about one-third of the total tonnage lost since 1939. British, Allied, and neutral losses during the first three months of 1942 increased at a "murderous" rate, Alexander Cadogan told his diary, from 420,000 tons in January to 835,000 in March. The holds of a 7,000-ton freighter such as the American-built Liberty Ships held enough cargo to fill almost one hundred railroad freight cars. Each ship lost, therefore, was the equivalent of a mile-long freight train falling into the sea, taking with it enough supplies to feed, clothe, and fuel a small city or an army division for three weeks. Although American shipyards would launch 2,710 Liberty Ships by 1945, in mid-1942, the Germans were sinking them far faster than they could be launched.[195]

Yet, Hitler, ever fearful of a British invasion of Norway and the disruption of his supply of Swedish iron ore, played small with his U-boats. The Führer "sacrificed the glittering chances in the Atlantic," Churchill later wrote, "and positioned every available surface ship and many a precious U-boat in northern Norwegian waters," the area Hitler considered to be "the zone of destiny" in the war. He also stationed four new infantry divisions in Norway, bringing the total to eleven, more than 120,000 men. There they sat, and waited for the Englishmen who never came. Even though he used it as a bargaining tool, northern Norway truly topped Churchill's list of invasion targets, a fact that Brooke knew only too well. But the three British military chiefs, unlike their German counterparts, could step back from their own interservice rivalries and unite in opposition to their leader's latest questionable scheme. Germany's best chance to secure its perimeter lay in an all-out assault in the Atlantic, but Hitler ignored Dönitz and shepherded his resources, not only in Norway but in the vicinity of the Canary Islands, off the northwest coast of Africa, in hopes of sinking an invasion fleet, which also never came. Had he not done so, had he thrown his boats all in, Allied losses would have been far more horrific. As it was, Churchill termed the U-boat menace "our worst evil." By summer, with Russia in desperate need of supplies, it became Stalin's worst evil as well.[196]

Despite the shipping losses, one statistic above all others offered comfort to Churchill: American oil-refining capacity was twenty times that of Germany. America had more oil underground than it could pump. The war would someday come down to who could afford to bleed the most oil. America's enormous industrial productive capacity came powerfully into play, but only as a function of America's ability to pump—and *deliver*—oil. British factories ceased production without American oil. Tanks went nowhere without gasoline. The United States had enough capacity to pump oil and build factories, tanks, and airplanes far into the future. But with oil, as with food and weapons, delivery was hobbled by the lack of ships to get the oil to Britain and Russia. In May, during the "second happy time," just six U-boats operating in the Gulf of Mexico sank sixty-six ships, of which more than half were oil tankers. The Allies could not afford to lose oil-toting vessels at that rate and expect—or hope—to relieve Russia. Ships, Hopkins now believed, were more important than their cargoes. A few weeks after the Gulf of Mexico massacre, U-boats sent four hundred thousand tons of Allied shipping to the bottom in just seven days, a rate, Churchill informed Roosevelt, "unexampled in either this war or the last, and if maintained evidently beyond all existing replacement plans."[197]

If the Allies could solve the U-boat menace, their oil problem would solve itself. Not so, Hitler's fuel problems. He had to now steal more than Polish and Ukraine wheat in order to move his armies. He needed a great deal more oil. The Ploesti oil fields—Churchill called Romanian oil the taproot of German might—located north of Bucharest supplied as much as 60 percent of Germany's crude oil, enough to sustain a peacetime German economy, but not enough to power the Wehrmacht as well. Because the gasoline consumed by his mechanized forces taxed Germany's modest refining capacity, the solution to Hitler's oil problem lay farther east, in the Caucasus, or even in the Middle East. Each of the almost four thousand Wehrmacht tanks in Soviet territory quaffed enormous quantities of fuel simply standing still—more than twenty-two tons every eight weeks. Hitler's tanks alone would need several hundred thousand tons of fuel to reach and hold the Caucasus. The vast spaces of the Ukraine and the Don Basin contained no petrol stations such as those in Belgium from which German tankers had helped themselves. The panzers were only the first drawdown on Hitler's fuel supplies; his mechanized units, more than six hundred thousand vehicles in all, required thousands of times as much fuel as his tanks.

On Hitler's orders Luftwaffe fighter planes had been designed to fly on synthetic gasoline, which was refined from coal at two large plants in Leipzig and Stettin. But Hitler lacked the capacity to refine the gasoline he needed to move his armies. The Russian Baku oil fields—*if* he conquered them—would contribute to his mobility, but only in two years' time, when new *autobahn*s and railroads of the proper gauge were built in order to connect the Caucasus to Greater Germany. The northern Iraqi oil fields located near Mosul offered the same benefit as the Romanian and Caucasus oil fields, but following Rashid's failed 1941 coup, Hitler had abandoned any thought of forcing his way into Mosul. Likewise, in Iran, the British had barred the door in August 1941 when British and Indian forces invaded Iran from Basra, while the Soviets poured in from the north. That war, if it could be called that, lasted six days, one day longer than a cricket test match. The British lost twenty-two killed. When Reza Shah fled the country, Churchill propped the Shah's twenty-two-year-old son, Mohammad Reza Pahlavi, on the Peacock throne.

But in early 1942, with British and Soviet forces spread so thin, the doors to Iraq and Iran were virtually unguarded. If Hitler smashed through Baku in the north or the Suez in the south, the oil riches of the Middle East would be his for the taking. But he had no plans to do so, and for reasons that appeared to him to be strategically sound. In order to get to Iraq and Iran from the north, he would have to drive through Baku, that is, he would have to *take* Baku. Taking Baku would sate his oil needs and negate the need to proceed farther. But in February, with Rommel cruising toward Cairo, and the Japanese steaming into the Indian Ocean, Admiral Raeder convinced Hitler that the real strategic significance of the Middle East was not its potential source of oil for Germany but its importance to Britain: It was where the British got *their* oil, and where they were most vulnerable. Raeder, in a memo to Hitler, anticipated Churchill's and Brooke's concerns exactly: "Suez and Basra are the western pillars of the British position in the East. Should these positions collapse under the weight of concerted Axis pressure the consequences for the British Empire would be disastrous."[198]

Raeder and Rommel had long proffered a southern plan (*Plan Sud*), wherein Germany and Japan would link up in Basra or Tehran. Britain depended upon Persian* oil to fight its war and Persian railroads to supply Russia. If the Axis took Persia, Britain would lose its primary source of oil. Early in the year Churchill told Ismay, "The oil stringency, which is already serious in Germany and German conquered countries, makes the seizure

---

* Persia had taken the name Iran in 1935. To avoid possible confusion with Iraq in official communications, Churchill ordered that "Persia" be used rather than "Iran" in all wartime memos regarding Iran.

of the Baku and Persian oil fields of vital consequences to Germany, second only to the need of successfully invading the British Isles." Brooke seconded that motion when he told his diary, "All the motive [British] power at sea, on land, and throughout the Middle East was entirely dependent on the oil from Abadan.... If we lost the Persian oil, we inevitably lost Egypt." Egypt lost meant Empire lost, and the war.[199]

Hitler finally grasped that fact in early 1942 and, executing an about-face, approved of Raeder's *Plan Sud,* including that part of the plan that called for securing the Mediterranean flank by either capturing or destroying Malta. To that end, during March and April, the Germans dropped twice the tonnage of bombs on Malta than they had on London during the 1940 Blitz. Bombs formed only part of the peril faced by the Maltese. With London unable to supply the island, the threat of starvation was real, and imminent. "Above all, there was Malta," Ismay later wrote. "To lose her would be almost as painful as to lose part of England itself."[200]

If Malta fell, Rommel could resupply at will and punch past Cairo and into Iraq. But unless Rommel got to Basra, Hitler's oil options came down to Russian oil, or none. Stalin would have to fight the battle for his oil alone. Churchill had no say in the outcome. Yet he pondered a horrific means to deny Hitler the oil: Stalin might be persuaded (if the battle went against him) to destroy his own oil wells. The Baku fields were so saturated with petroleum that Churchill predicted that their destruction would result in "a conflagration on a scale not hitherto witnessed in the world." Rumor in Berlin had it that British commandos were already on the ground, awaiting final orders to blow the Russian oil wells, a prospect that shocked Goebbels, who scribbled in his diary, "That's exactly like them! They [the English] have proven themselves throughout the world as great destroyers of other people's property." Churchill quickly shelved the idea, not because of the insult Stalin might attach to the scheme, but because he and Roosevelt lacked the ships needed to make up the shortfall. In any case, Stalin had no intention of destroying his oil fields. The dictator summoned Nikolai K. Baibakov, deputy to the oil commissar. Cocking his thumb, Stalin pointed two fingers at Baibakov's head and said, "If you fail to stop the Germans getting our oil, you will be shot. And when we have thrown the invader out, if we cannot restart production, we will shoot you again."[201]

Stalin understood that Russia's only hope for salvation lay in the attrition of German men, machines, and fuel. Attrition formed the backbone of Churchill's strategic vision as well. He intended to do his part in constructing a ring of steel around the Reich, a ring he could slowly tighten until nothing remained within it but Hitler's bombed-out Chancellery—preferably with the Führer dead inside. Germany, vulnerable to naval blockade, its navy too small to break out into distant waters to procure needed resources, had to grow geographically in order to sustain itself, a process that in time, if Russia held on, would collapse upon itself. Churchill summed up his philosophy in a memo to the Chiefs of Staff that treated of RAF losses, but his words also applied to tanks, artillery, and men (especially if the men were Russian): "Indeed, like General Grant in his last campaign, we can almost afford to lose two for one, having regard to the immense supplies now coming forward in the future." Churchill had read Ulysses S. Grant's Civil War memoirs when he was thirteen; the utility of attrition as practiced by Grant had been lodged in Churchill's psyche for more than fifty years. Yet Grant at Petersburg had been fighting his last campaign, and he was on the verge of victory; Churchill and Roosevelt had yet to fight their first campaign together as allies. The question that vexed Churchill throughout 1942 was, would American industrial output hit its stride before German armies arrived in the Caucasus?[202]

Yet if Ismay, Dill, and many of the American planners were proven correct in their predictions of a German victory over the Soviets, Hitler's fuel and food problems would solve themselves. The loss of Baku oil would cripple Russian industry and agriculture; further resistance would be futile. Famine, widespread and horrific, would follow. Hitler, victorious, would then turn westward, toward England.

Churchill once told Colville that May was his least favorite month. But at least it ushered in good fighting weather, especially on the Continent, where in 1942 only two options for offensive action presented themselves, "butcher and bolt" raids and RAF bombing. Whenever he summoned Brooke late at night, the CIGS presumed the Old Man had just cooked up another strategic initiative of likely dubious value to Brooke's way of thinking, impossible to pull off, and costly in the execution. This was especially so on weekends when Churchill was at Chequers, recalled Sir Ian Jacob, because the hours and company Churchill kept at Chequers always caused a distressing sense of "anticipation" among the staff officers, especially if Dickie Mountbatten arrived bearing schemes. The staff called these sessions "the midnight follies." During such weekends Churchill put forth ideas like a masting oak spews acorns, some to root but most destined to decay. The invasion of Norway—Operation Jupiter—had been of abiding interest to Churchill, for no other reason Brooke could discern than that Churchill once told him that "Hitler had unrolled the map of Europe starting with Norway, and that he [Churchill] would start rolling it up again from Norway." Archie Wavell, a victim in North Africa of Churchill's strategic misfires, believed

"Winston is always expecting rabbits to come out of empty hats." Churchill now looked to Madagascar, where, were the Japanese to secure a foothold, the entire Indian Ocean would be lost. As well, Madagascar was a French colony, intensely loyal to Vichy ever since Churchill had bombed the French fleet at Oran in July 1940. Here was a grand opportunity to block further Japanese adventures (not that Japan planned to go there) and pluck some real estate from the Vichy portfolio.[203]

This the British did, in a May 5 raid, executed by the 5th Commando at Diego Suarez, on Madagascar's northern tip. It was carried off with total surprise. Vichy forces on the island, however, incited by Admiral Darlan, who told them to never forget Oran, turned the affair into a guerrilla war and fought the British for months. The flash-bang success of the St-Nazaire and Madagascar raids—as they saw them—emboldened both Churchill and Mountbatten who, as chief of Combined Operations, cooked up plans some distance removed from the watchful gaze of the military chiefs, but close enough to Churchill to whet his appetite for action.

By May the Russians had been dug in for six months within artillery range of the German army. The Red Army had the benefit of short supply lines, along which rolled the new and innovative T-34 tanks, steel behemoths armed with 76mm cannons and, most important, built with sloping armored surfaces. No other tank in the world was so designed. The sloped profile effectively doubled the protection offered by the T-34's steel armor; German anti-tank shells simply bounced off. The T-34 tank kept the Russians in the game that year, as did the Soviet conscripts who marched down frozen roads in seemingly infinite numbers, for, as the Germans had learned throughout the autumn, when the Red Army lost an entire division, even an entire army, another appeared almost at once. In late February, with all of Europe clenched in winter's grip, Hitler had told Goebbels that "snow had become physically repulsive to him." By March, Goebbels asked his diary, "Will this winter never end? Is a new glacial age in the offing?" Hitler now grasped that the plight of German troops was "a catastrophe" of the very sort that had befallen Napoleon. Yielding to reality for a change, Goebbels called upon German citizens to donate warm clothing for the troops.[204]

The Führer waited for the "majestic coming of spring," when he intended to preside over a thaw that would flow with fresh blood. He had promised as much when he made his declaration of war upon America: "The beginning of winter only will now check [our] movement; at the beginning of summer it will again no longer be possible to stop the movement." It was a boast typical of Hitler, to be sure, but one taken seriously in Moscow, London, and

Washington. By the late spring of 1942, Roosevelt, Marshall, Ismay, and the man in charge of U.S. war plans, Dwight Eisenhower, all thought it a fair bet that Russia would either be defeated or sue for peace by autumn, as the new Soviet government had done in early 1918. Brooke and Churchill thought otherwise, for a simple yet overriding reason: after almost a year of carnage that left more than a million troops on each side killed or wounded, neither Stalin nor Hitler could call a stop to the battle without risking a loss of prestige in the eyes of their own people, and possible political extinction at the hands of their disillusioned cohorts. No, the business would be settled with finality one day, either in Moscow or Berlin.[205]

Spring brought no relief to Russian civilians, who had so far had the worst of it, especially in Leningrad, where, under siege since late August and lacking coal, food, and oil, more than two hundred thousand perished by early May. Hitler had ordered the complete destruction of the city and its nine million inhabitants, including six million refugees who had fled the countryside for the supposed safety of Leningrad. The Wehrmacht was ordered not to accept a surrender if one was offered. The composer Dmitri Shostakovich managed to escape with his family and a suitcase that contained his almost completed Seventh Symphony, *Leningrad*. He was one of the very few.

The city was surrounded by German armies and three Finnish corps, except for Lake Ladoga to the east, where in winter a rail line had been thrown across the ice in order to keep Leningrad from dying. Still, the people of Leningrad were starving to death at a rate of more than two thousand per day, and would do so for another nine months, until the Soviets punched through a narrow land corridor. With water and sewer lines smashed, epidemics raged. German heavy artillery and bombers pummeled the city day and night. By the time the siege was finally lifted in January 1944, more than a million bodies filled communal graves, more fatalities than British and America casualties, military and civilian, combined, for the entire war. Even Dr. Goebbels flinched at the carnage and the stories of cannibalism, confessing to his diary that a Russian deserter's report that "a great part of the population was feeding on so-called human flesh jelly... is so revolting that it makes one's stomach turn to read it." In their dietary need for fat during the horrific winter of 1942, hundreds of thousands of Russians, from Leningrad to the Black Sea, added a touch of axle grease or crankcase oil to whatever rotten food scraps and bones found their way into cook pots. Even if not one more Russian died as a result of Hitler's eastern designs—and almost twenty million would—Leningrad, by the spring of 1942, served up to Joseph Stalin the requisite justification to smash and burn Germany back into the distant hunter-gatherer past whence it came.[206]

Yet he lacked the means to do so. Churchill could promise Stalin only three convoys every two months made up of twenty-five or thirty-five ships each. And even that promise soon proved impossible to keep. With the Arctic days lengthening to more than twenty hours, German air and sea forces based in Norway simply waited near the Arctic Circle for fat targets to heave into view, with the result, Brooke lamented to his diary, that tanks and munitions Britain desperately needed in North Africa ended up at the bottom of the Arctic Ocean. A bitter Stalin reiterated his demands that Churchill and Roosevelt make good on their promise to draw off German troops from the Russian front by an attack in France. But Churchill and Roosevelt lacked the ships even to carry American troops to Britain. Each ship that sailed for Russia reduced by one the number available for Operation Bolero, the buildup of U.S. forces in Britain in preparation for a cross-Channel foray. Each ship that sailed from America to Britain meant one fewer ship to transport to Cairo the troops and tanks that Churchill needed to build a reserve against Rommel, or for deployment to the rest of the Middle East, or India, should the need arise. The final battles of the European war would someday take place on land. Yet, as Churchill had told Molotov during a tutorial on naval power, the war would be won or lost on the oceans. "Everything," Churchill told Roosevelt, "turns upon shipping."[207]

Hitler's generals had advised him the previous year not to fight a two-front war, the classic nightmare of Prussian military strategists. Yet his gamble had so far paid off handsomely. In fact, his war was a one-front war, the Eastern Front. He had to keep a weather eye on Norway, North Africa, the Atlantic, and the Mediterranean and that obstinate rock, Malta. But in the east he had no enemy at his back. Since December, he had faced two enemies at his front—winter, the destroyer of armies, and the Red Army. Neither, by May, had destroyed the Wehrmacht. The early spring *rasputitsa,* the twice-annual Russian wet season, had halted movement as effectively as the cold of winter, yet warm and dry weather was now spreading northward from the Black Sea in ever widening circles. In early May, the German line in northern Russia was anchored just outside Leningrad, where the swamps were still frozen and snow continued to fall. In the center, the line lunged eastward from Smolensk to encompass Rzhev and Vyazma in a huge salient—a bulge. The roads there remained muddy but would dry within the month. Hitler's Führer Directive No. 41 of April 5 stipulated that the line in central Russia—the Moscow front—be held, while in the north, Leningrad be taken. Farther south, the Ukraine front ran from just east of Orel, Kursk, and Kharkov—where the Red Army had forged its own salient—south to the Sea of Azov. In this sector, General Fedor von Bock (who had been called out of retirement) commanded Hitler's Army Group South, which consisted of six German armies, three of them armored, and two satellite armies. This organization was so massive that within weeks it was divided into two army groups, A and B, each with a different objective. Here in the Ukraine, as famously described by Igor Stravinsky, "the violent Russian spring that seemed to begin in an hour and was like the whole earth cracking" had arrived with all its promise. White birch and oak forests wore thin veils of green, and mushrooms pushed through the still damp soil. Ukraine's rivers and streams ran high from the winter snowmelt and spring rains.[208]

To the south, in the Black Sea sector, three German armies under Erich von Manstein controlled most of the Crimea. The *Ostheer* had yet to take Rostov, the Kerch Peninsula, or Sevastopol. This Manstein intended to do. But the main German thrust would begin in the Ukraine sector, where Army Group South (including Friedrich Paulus's Sixth Army and Fourth Panzer Army) was to smash east into the Donets Basin and make for Voronezh, located on the far side of the Don (and which city Bock was ordered to bypass). The Fourth Panzer Army was then to wheel south, keeping the Don on its left flank until it reached the great bend in the Don, just sixty miles from Stalingrad and the Volga—Stalin's last great natural barrier. Hitler decreed, "We must try to reach Stalingrad," and if they could not take it, smash it with artillery and air attacks until it became useless as an industrial base. Army Group South's final objective, after destroying Stalingrad, was to punch south between the Volga and the Don and drive into the north Caucasus hills. Part of this German force, arrayed in the Black Sea sector, was to wheel sharply south, take Rostov-on-Don, and make for the Baku oil fields and the Caucasus Mountains beyond. Vital to the success of the entire enterprise was that once across the Don, these two massive forces move toward the Caucasus shoulder to shoulder, with the Volga on one flank and the Black Sea on the other, across an eight-hundred-mile-wide front. Once the Caucasus were taken, the war in the east would be over. The result, Hitler told Goebbels, would be that Russia "will then be to us what India is to the British."[209]

Hitler named his offensive Operation Blue. Stalin, as he had a year earlier, had gained reliable intelligence as to Hitler's plans, and, as he had a year earlier, he ignored the information. He presumed any action in the Ukraine sector was meant to be a feint, while the real attack would come against Moscow. As he had been a year earlier, Stalin was soon proven wrong. The preliminaries to Operation Blue opened in the Crimea on May 8 with a German dash down the Kerch Peninsula. It was all over within the week. The Germans captured 170,000 Soviet troops, who had dutifully obeyed Stalin's orders to stand firm. Only Sevastopol, surrounded, remained under Soviet control. Then, on May 12, in a bold stroke that took everyone but the Germans by surprise, the Red Army struck at the Kharkov salient with almost 650,000 men, 1,000 airplanes, 13,000 guns, and 1,200 tanks. The counterstroke, approved by Stalin, was the brain-child of the theater commander Semyon Timoshenko, and the political boss of the Ukraine, Nikita Khrushchev. For three days the Soviets drove the Germans westward, but by doing so they exposed their flanks. Although Hitler's worried generals called for a frontal defense of Kharkov, the Führer termed the Soviet attack "a minor blemish" and refused to change his master plan. He was soon proven correct when Paulus and Erwin von Kleist wheeled their armies into the Soviet flanks and within the week encircled the Soviet army. Stalin had no reserves to throw in. By May 22, the Soviet defeat was total, with almost 240,000 Soviet prisoners taken, and most of the guns and all the tanks lost. Khrushchev, summoned to Moscow by Stalin to explain how it had all gone wrong, presumed he'd be shot. That Khrushchev survived his inquisition was not due to mercy on Stalin's part—the concept was alien to the man—but because Stalin believed in the motivational power of terror.[210]

The Kharhov and Kerch battles had cost Stalin more than 410,000 killed and captured even before the curtain went up on Operation Blue. Given that few of the Red Army prisoners would survive the German slave labor camps, Russian losses that May measured twice the combined Union and Confederate battlefield deaths during the American Civil War, and almost half of British and Dominion battlefield deaths during the four years of the Great War. Hitler, a serious student of Clausewitz, was holding to the Prussian's dictum to annihilate enemy armies rather than try to capture cities. By the end of May, all roads east and south lay open to the Germans.[211]

Months earlier Churchill made a grim prediction to King George, who recorded it in his diary: "If by the spring, Russia was down and out, and Germany was renewing its blitzkrieg here, all our hopes of victory and help from USA would be dashed if America had not by then sent us masses of planes etc." The King seems to have confused "blitzkrieg" and "blitz," but no matter, Hitler would launch both against Britain were Stalin to go down before America tooled up.[212]

On May 31 Roosevelt cabled Churchill: "I have a very strong feeling that the Russian position is precarious, and may grow steadily worse during the coming weeks."[213]

Roosevelt's pessimism stemmed in part from two days of talks with Soviet foreign minister Molotov, who had arrived in Washington from

London on May 29 with demands for an immediate second European front and a doubling in Lend-Lease aid, without both of which the Soviet position loomed dire at best. Regarding the latter demand, Roosevelt explained that each ship that went to Russia meant one fewer ship to build up forces in Britain for the very second front Molotov sought. To placate Molotov on that point, Roosevelt agreed to release an official announcement (which had been dictated by Molotov) after Molotov returned to Moscow: "In the course of the conversations full understanding was reached with regard to the urgent tasks of creating a Second Front in Europe in 1942." Here was Roosevelt at his most politically astute, for he knew that Churchill considered such a front in 1942 a strategic impossibility. The president had served the ball into Churchill's court. Yet, Harriman later wrote, Roosevelt felt that raising Soviet expectations for a second front could only bolster Soviet morale, an end in itself. Soviet morale was about the only thing Roosevelt could boost because, as he told Molotov, the U-boats prevented the boosting of Soviet matériel. Harriman acknowledged that Roosevelt's statement "provided employment for a whole generation of...historians who solemnly argued its merits" in myriad books and journals. Yet the measure of an event has to be taken in the immediate context of the times, and at the time, Roosevelt's pledge helped preserve the alliance, even if it amounted to a Potemkin village of a promise.[214]

Molotov had spent the week before his Washington visit in London, where he and Eden had negotiated a twenty-year treaty of peace in which the Soviets agreed to address the issue of borders only after the war was won. Churchill had been prepared to jettison his long-standing position on that subject and accede to Stalin's demands regarding prewar borders and the Baltic states. Churchill later wrote: "My opinions about the Baltic states were, and are, unaltered, but I felt I could not carry them farther forward at that time." Cordell Hull furiously disagreed, and in a cable to Winant, approved by Roosevelt, threatened to disavow the entire business if Britain appeased Stalin. For Hull, at stake were the tenets of the Atlantic Charter. As well, he insisted that all border issues were to be settled after the war by a new world organization (which he championed mightily). An open break loomed for the alliance. Then Roosevelt suggested to the British that a verbal *promise* of a second front "should take the heat off Russia's diplomatic demands upon England" regarding postwar borders. Eden made the pitch, and to his surprise and relief Molotov went for it. It was a masterful bit of negotiation, one that kept both the Russians and Americans happy, and the alliance intact.[215]

With Roosevelt's promise in hand Molotov returned to London for the formal signing of the friendship treaty. But he arrived bearing a new demand: that the British put *in writing* their own guarantee of a second front. Churchill tried to impress upon Molotov that Britain in Western Europe and North Africa was tying up almost one-half of Luftwaffe fighter strength and one-third of its bombers. Thirty-three Axis divisions sat idle in Western Europe, and eleven more, including two armored divisions, fought on in North Africa. That Britain and America had not launched a second front of the exact sort Stalin sought did not mean they were not forcing Hitler to spread his forces thin. The Allies might not be killing many Germans in the west, Churchill argued, but neither were those Germans killing any Russians. Molotov listened politely, but he still wanted his guarantee. And so to placate both the Americans and the Soviets, Churchill drafted a communiqué for Molotov to take home. It was similar to Roosevelt's promise, and stated "full understanding was reached with regard to the urgent task of creating a second front in Europe in 1942." With that "understanding" in hand, it appeared to Molotov that *both* the Americans and the British had given him what he wanted. In fact, they had given him nothing. Understanding the need to open a second front and doing something about it was not the same thing. To further clarify his (somewhat disingenuous) promise, Churchill composed an aide-mémoire to Stalin in which he reiterated his belief in the need for a second front: "We are making preparations for a landing on the Continent in August or September, 1942." Then Churchill added the caveat that all was conditional and nothing was guaranteed: "We can therefore give no promise to the matter." Molotov left London for Moscow on June 10, and dutifully passed Churchill's letter and his logic on to Stalin, who didn't buy any of it.[216]

Molotov's party had stayed at Chequers during the earlier treaty negotiations, at which time burly Russian bodyguards and two (also burly) Russian chambermaids attended to the needs of Molotov and his two aides. The bodyguards swept the bedrooms for listening devices—"infernal machines"—Churchill called them. Revolvers were dutifully placed on Molotov's bedside table and under the diplomats' pillows. Their beds were made up to leave an opening in the middle of the bedcovers "out of which the occupant could spring" were assassins to appear on the scene. The maids sat without a word on chairs outside their bosses' doors day and night. The entire scene struck Churchill as peculiar. But Churchill, in turn, treated the Russians to an unforgettable experience. They witnessed him at rest, which was a relative concept. Churchill's visits to Chequers afforded him a chance to unwind, and to do so in company of his choosing (although the Russians were an exception to that rule).[217]

The diary entries and letters of visitors to Chequers cast light on a consistent Churchillian pattern of behavior: nobody got as wound up unwinding as Churchill did. The heavier his previous week's burdens, the greater his need for an Alice in Wonderland weekend, as Brooke called them.

Thus, the sense of "anticipation" within the ranks noted by Ian Jacob whenever Churchill appeared at Chequers. Brooke later wrote that he took away no "happy memories" from these long and liquid weekends, each evening "extending well into the morning hours." The Old Man relaxed with a fury, and always with a quotient of wit and good cheer in inverse proportion to what might fairly be expected from a man who had just suffered a terrible week, and most of the weeks since May 1940 had brought terrible news of one sort or another.[218]

The week of Molotov's first visit was no exception. While Eden and the Russian worked out the details of the treaty, Erwin Rommel sent the British Eighth Army packing. On May 26 Rommel swung around General Ritchie's Gazala Line south of Bir Hacheim. Ritchie was not ready. Worse, although he outnumbered Rommel in tanks 700 to 560, he had not massed his tanks in order to strike Rommel's vanguard. Rommel, as usual, *had* massed his tanks. He expected to break Ritchie's lines in a day, but he ran up against General William ("Strafer") Gott and his XIII Corps along with a brigade of Free French. Gott and the French gave Rommel more of a fight than he had yet experienced in North Africa. It took the Desert Fox ten days to clear out the truculent French, who then took to calling themselves the Fighting French. But by then, Ritchie had lost control of the battle.[219]

Once again, the desert winds had turned against Churchill, who often appears in his colleagues' diaries at his most animated after having taken just such a hard military hit. Talking (at length) was Churchill's way, recalled John Martin, "of clearing his head." He talked at the table and he talked on the march. His staff had been delighted when he insisted on the installation of a movie projector at Chequers: "We thought if we had a nice film in the evening he would go to bed," John Martin recalled. "But far from it; he started all over again after the films."[220]

During his weekends of rest he displayed the uncanny ability to work, relax, and rage simultaneously. After telling dinner guests one evening that he hoped victory would bring "an end to bloodshed," he followed with "I must confess I would like to see Mussolini, that bogus mimic of ancient Rome, strangled like Vercingetorix in old Roman fashion." Hitler he would exile to some remote island, "though he would not so desecrate St. Helena." He soon took a harder stand on Hitler's fate, telling the cabinet, "This man is the mainspring of evil. Instrument—electric chair for gangsters no doubt available through Lend Lease." He liked to pepper his dinner-table asides and speeches with the sort of clichés favored by Moscow propagandists in attacks on the bourgeois West (until the alliance): "hyena," "lackey," "dupe," "flunky," "jackal." When used by *Pravda,* such phrases conjured up in Englishmen images of raving Reds, but they worked for Churchill. His often preposterous asides were easily misconstrued as the mirthful musings of a merry old man. They were anything but. Hopkins was more correct than he knew when he quipped that Churchill must have read only the Old Testament.[221]

Along with Molotov, spring had arrived in Britain—the traditional invasion season. Travel by British civilians to the south coastal regions was restricted, as in the previous two years. The word in the pubs was that the Allies were building up armies down on the coast and getting ready to jump a big one across the Channel. The Allies were doing nothing of the sort. In fact, Churchill told Molotov, defenses were fully manned with the expectation that the Germans would arrive if Moscow capitulated. He offered that pessimistic assessment only after Molotov had asked, what will England do if the Red Army collapses? Out came the maps, and Churchill commenced a lesson on the difference between land powers and sea powers. It had become clear to him that neither Stalin nor Molotov understood a fundamental truth: the Allies could not win on land until the seas were cleared of Germans. He told Molotov that he was confident that, backed by American industrial might, the Allies would win, but he stressed, as he had to the King, that if the Red Army collapsed, Hitler would turn toward England.[222]

In that case, he expected Britons to offer themselves up by the scores of thousands. "It would be better," he told Colville the previous July, "to make this island a sea of blood than to surrender." Those were Stalin's sentiments exactly regarding Russians, dictated to his terrorized subordinates from the dacha where he took his weekend rest. His orders to stand firm were dutifully executed by Russians as the mounting slaughter in his country bore out. At Hitler's Berchtesgaden retreat, the *Berghof,* the topic of defending the homeland had not arisen during weekend retreats. The Führer and his cronies consumed tea and pastries while Hitler delivered monologues on the Roman Empire, Jews, and Christianity (and how its "mendacity and hypocrisy" had sapped Nordic development). In the evenings the Führer strolled mountain paths while he opined at length in the company of his Alsatian bitch, Blondi, and his cohorts—Goebbels, Himmler, Bormann, and Göring. They never discussed defeat. And for good reason: they were winning.[223]

On the night of May 30–31—the day Roosevelt cabled to Churchill his deep concern about the Russian front—the RAF threw everything it had against Germany, a demonstration of power and destruction that Churchill hoped would underscore the validity of his claim that the aerial front was indeed a real second front. That night, more than 1,100 British heavy bombers plastered Cologne, ushering in a short-lived era of thousand-bomber raids. The chief of the RAF's Bomber Command, Arthur ("Bomber") Harris, faced with American opposition to the shipment of even more B-17s to Britain (the planes were accumulating on airfields), conceived the idea of massive nighttime raids in order to show the Americans the efficiency of the British strategic air offensive. Harris had to put crews still undergoing training into his bombers in order to assemble a fleet large enough to carry out his plans. He had waited almost two years for the opportunity to punish Germany with such force. In the autumn of 1940, while surveying the destruction the Luftwaffe had inflicted on London, he offered a bit of Old Testament wisdom to his superior, Air Marshal Charles Portal: "Well, they are sowing the wind." Harris now intended that they would reap the whirlwind. Portal believed the RAF could bring Germany to its knees—and the war to an end—sometime in late 1943. Churchill was far less sure. His oft-stated wish to make Germans bleed and burn aside, on the strategic efficacy of bombing Germany, Churchill had offered to Portal, "I have my own opinion about that, namely, that it is not decisive, but is better than doing nothing." In Churchill's estimation, the immediate value of RAF bombing lay in showing the Russians that Britain was doing something. Intending to do much more, Churchill proclaimed the raid "a herald of what Germany will receive city by city from now on."[224]

It had been more than fifteen months since he had asked Lord Cherwell to devise a punishing, retaliatory bombing strategy. It had been less than five months since Bomber Harris was promoted to air marshal and brought to Bomber Command his strategic bombing philosophy, that volume trumps accuracy. It was a strategy born of necessity, since the accuracy of British night raiders was still pathetic; fewer than one-quarter of RAF bombs fell near their targets. Harris would have preferred a scalpel, but he was handed a cudgel. Among the RAF's unintended targets that spring was the ancestral home of Thomas Mann. Better known as the Buddenbrookhaus, the house had stood in the Baltic port city of Lübeck for two hundred years. In fact, 80 percent of the old city of Lübeck was destroyed in what Goebbels called "the British craze for destruction." Mann, safely ensconced in a California bungalow, broadcast a message back to Germany: "I remember Coventry and realize that everything must be paid back." Such were Bomber Harris's sentiments exactly.[225]

Within days of the Cologne raid, the Ministry of Information sent to Russia thousands of propaganda posters: "We lost 44 planes on that [Cologne] raid, but we are prepared to give our lives to destroy Fascism, as you are giving yours. The Fascists will not be able to stand the hell we shall give them together." But from Stalin's perspective, faced as he was with almost two million Germans rolling toward Leningrad, Moscow, Stalingrad, and the Caucasus oil fields, the British were neither giving enough hell nor sacrificing enough men.

Two nights after Harris's heavies smashed Cologne, more than 950 bombers hit Essen, selected as a target specifically because its ancient wood houses and warehouses would fall easy prey to incendiary bombs. A month later, 1,000 of Harris's fleet visited Bremen. The bombers flew in new "streaming" formations, a parade of death that stretched from the target almost all the way back to the North Sea. RAF bombing accuracy, though still dismal, had been improved somewhat by the development of the "shaker" system, whereby planes equipped with the latest electronic navigation systems flew ahead and marked targets with flares and then a next wave of aircraft deposited loads of incendiary bombs on the target, thus providing a concentrated area of fire where the bombers of the main force could drop their high-explosive bombs. The results were devastating. Harris enthused to the press, "Give me a thousand bombers over Germany every night, and I will end the war by October. Give me 20,000 and I will stop it in a single night." The RAF's massed raids impressed the Americans, as Harris intended. Deliveries of B-17s and the American pilots and crews to man them spiked upward. German civilians got the message as well; while Russian and British soldiers as yet posed no threat to Germans, British bombers could get through to burn German cities. Yet Harris took away new and distressing knowledge: his nightly losses, more than 5 percent, were too high, and his resources were too meager to sustain such losses. He needed the Americans to get up to speed, but the American Eighth Air Force had yet to fly a mission.[226]

The Cologne raid was seen by many in Britain and the United States as retaliation for the Luftwaffe's Baedeker raids of April, so named because Göring had targeted several British national treasures that had earned honorifics in the *Baedeker Guide,* including Bath, Canterbury Cathedral, Bury St. Edmunds, and Ipswich. Britons joked that German pilots flew with a copy of *Baedeker* propped next to the bomb sight. It was a time, wrote Mollie Panter-Downes, when owning "a house next door to Anne Hathaway's cottage is...an uncomfortable liability...not a picturesque asset." RAF response to the Baedeker raids was swift. In America, the *New Republic* parsed the question of whether it was retaliatory as well, and concluded that although Cologne had not been an act of revenge, the Allies should continually weigh both sides of the question in order to avoid any action that could "stain our record in the war or drag us down to the Nazi level."[227]

*   *   *

Americans and Britons had not yet fully grasped just how low the Nazi level in fact was. Within days of the Cologne raid, Berlin demonstrated the real nature of cold-blooded retaliation, and it was not about Cologne. Goebbels and his Führer had been mulling over for some time the best and most efficient manner to confiscate the property of those convicted—and executed—for treasonous actions or speech, or for simply being born racially impure. When Goebbels suggested that the confiscation of "terrorists'" bicycles would send a message to would-be troublemakers, Hitler "regarded this proposal as wonderful" and ordered its implementation. For almost three years, far more disproportionate Nazi retaliation against civilians (such as one hundred hostages shot for each German killed) for wrongs against the Reich had been well documented in the West—photos of hanging bodies, firing squads, pushcarts in Warsaw full of emaciated corpses. German vengeance was so swift and terrifying that some of Churchill's advisers in Special Operations cautioned against taking isolated direct action (assassinations and large-scale sabotage) on the Continent until an Allied invasion was imminent, in order to protect civilians from German retribution. Yet Churchill had urged Special Operations to "set Europe ablaze." As usual with implementing any such edict, timing is critical.[228]

That lesson was learned in London after Reinhard ("the Hangman") Heydrich, genius behind the Final Solution and chief of the Gestapo, was assassinated in Prague by the British-trained Czech resistance fighters whom the RAF had parachuted into the country five months earlier. The assassins struck on May 27, lobbing a bomb into Heydrich's Mercedes coupe, shattering the Hangman's spine. He lingered for a week before dying a ghastly death from blood poisoning and infections caused by festering tufts of upholstery that had blown into his gut. Germany's minister of justice—Hitler—moved swiftly to punish the evildoers. More than 1,300 Czechs were immediately executed. The assassins and five cohorts took refuge in a Prague church, where they were found and killed two weeks later. More than 3,000 Jews were transported from the "privileged" concentration camp of Theresienstadt to their deaths in the east. Goebbels, on the day Heydrich was attacked, had 500 of the few remaining Jews in Berlin rounded up; more than 150 were shot the night Heydrich died. But that was only the beginning.[229]

Then the Reich took the blood-letting to levels not anticipated by anyone, including Churchill. On the morning of June 9, a battalion of German security police surrounded the fourteenth-century Czech village of Lidice. Nobody was allowed to leave. The next day the men and boys over age sixteen of the village, 172 in all, were taken behind a barn in groups of ten and shot. Several women were shot, too, and the rest—almost 200—were sent to slave labor camps in Germany. At the local hospital, the Germans found four women who had just given birth. The newborns were murdered, the mothers shipped off to labor camps. The village children, about 90 in all, were sent to Germany, where, if medical professionals established their Aryan purity, they were placed with good Nazi families. Before departing Lidice, the Security Police burned the village, dynamited the ruins, and bulldozed the rubble into a flat, dead landscape, including the cemetery, where the interred had been dug up and bulldozed back into the soil. Berlin ordered the entire operation be photographed. Goebbels called the result his *Gemäldegalerie* (picture gallery). Then, Goebbels announced the details of the Lidice operation to the world, lest anyone else have the temerity to murder another one of Hitler's favorites. It was a tale even Bracken's disinformation wizards could not have conjured in their most macabre moments.[230]

Lidice, Goebbels proclaimed, was justice administered, not retaliation for Cologne. However, he added, if the Allies did not cease the mass bombing of German cities, "he would exterminate Germany's Jews." In fact, he had confessed to his diary almost three months earlier that at least 60 percent of the Jews transported to the east were to be "liquidated," the remaining 40 percent were to become slave laborers, and worked to death. In this regard, the little doctor proved himself a man of his word.[231]

The full extent of the British role in Heydrich's assassination was not revealed for over fifty years. Hugh Dalton, head of SOE and considered a "blabber" who might promise Churchill something he couldn't deliver, was kept in the dark by his subordinates in the Czech section. There is no record of Churchill approving the operation, but SOE had been created as a standalone entity, the better to facilitate plausible deniability. Churchill mentions neither the assassination nor Heydrich in his memoir of the war.[232]

In a broadcast ten months before the Lidice massacre, Churchill proclaimed that "scores of thousands — literally scores of thousands" of Russians had been executed by the Germans. He couched his words in terms of reports from visiting British generals, but his real source was impeccable. German commanders, with their penchant for precise bookkeeping, radioed the death tallies directly to Berlin, and therefore to Bletchley. Thousands of victims were described as "Jewish plunderers" and "Jewish bolshevists." This Churchill chose not to share with the public. He cautioned that the slaughter was "but the beginning" and went on to predict that "famine and pestilence" would "follow in the bloody ruts of Hitler's tanks." The Führer, he declared, was outkilling even his Teutonic ancestors. And not since the Mongols came in the thirteenth century had Europe seen such "methodical, merciless butchery" on such a monstrous scale. "We are in the presence," he concluded, "of a crime without a name." From the Ukraine to the Baltic states, from the Jewish ghetto in Warsaw where four hundred thousand souls existed on rotten flour and foul water, to Holland

and to occupied France and Belgium, the crime grew more monstrous by the day. The previous October, the prison camp for political prisoners at Auschwitz, about forty miles west of Krakow, was enlarged in order to accommodate tens of thousands of prisoners, mostly Jewish. The new camp, Birkenau, was built not as a forced labor camp but as an extermination facility. In late 1941, the SS conducted tests of the gas Zyklon B on Jewish and Russian prisoners in the camp basements. Satisfied with the deadly results, the SS set to work building industrial gas chambers and crematoria that could process two thousand bodies at a time. By mid-1942, a few—very few—escapees from Auschwitz had brought news of the genocide to the West. At the time, the tales could not be verified. The crime Churchill cited still had no name. But Goebbels' *Gemäldegalerie* had given it a face.[233]

By June 12 Churchill felt that a meeting between himself and Roosevelt was past due. They needed to unravel the tangled mess created during Marshall's April visit, to settle on an objective for their armies, and to discuss "Tube Alloys," the atomic bomb project. On that topic, there was not a great deal to discuss; unbeknownst to Churchill, the Americans were about to contract for *all* of Canada's uranium. (It would be almost a year before Churchill learned the extent of America's uranium dealings.) In any case, Britain had no money in its Exchequer to build an atomic bomb, even if it could procure the uranium to do so. The Americans would have to carry the ball on atomic research, and carry it quickly. It was well known in both Washington and London that the Germans were trying to use "heavy water"—available in large quantities as a by-product of ammonia production at a Norwegian hydroelectric plant—to serve as a moderating solution in the creation of element 94 (plutonium) from uranium. Goebbels months earlier had scribbled in his diary one of his more prescient thoughts: "Research in the realm of atomic destruction has now proceeded to a point where its results may possibly be made use of in this war.... Tremendous destruction can be wrought.... It is essential that we be ahead of everybody, for whoever introduces a revolutionary novelty into this war has the greater chance of winning it."[234]

But it was not only the future of atomic research or the timing of the second European front that spurred Churchill's request for a meeting with Roosevelt, but also a naval battle that began in the Pacific on June 4. Churchill had predicted in January that the Americans would regain fleet superiority in the Pacific by May or June, a wildly optimistic assessment based on no empirical evidence. He simply ignored the fact that Admiral

Yamamoto had proven himself the most daring and successful naval strategist of the century, if not of all time. A more realistic line of thought would hold that if the Americans built more capital ships, Yamamoto would sink them.

Yet Churchill's hunch paid off on the morning of June 4 near Midway Island. Yamamoto intended to take Midway that day, and to annihilate the American fleet, which he expected to come in search of his own forces. As usual, his plan was complex, and it depended upon the Americans doing exactly what he expected. Five Japanese naval task forces participated; in aggregate strength at that point, the Japanese force was greater than the Royal Navy's Atlantic and Home fleets combined, and it dwarfed anything the Americans could send to meet it. One Japanese force made for the Aleutian Islands, where it shelled the airbase at Dutch Harbor and occupied the islands of Attu and Kiska, at the western end of the chain. Four Japanese task forces made for Midway, consisting of an advance guard of sixteen submarines and an occupation force of five thousand men in twelve transports protected by two battleships and a bevy of cruisers and destroyers. Then came the big guns: Nagumo's Pearl Harbor Strike Force of four heavy aircraft carriers, well screened by cruisers, and shadowed by seven battleships, on one of which Yamamoto put his flag. In all, more than 160 Japanese warships and support craft were involved. The strike at the Aleutians, intended to draw away Admiral Chester Nimitz's forces, began at sunrise on June 3. By nightfall on the third, with his plan unfolding flawlessly, Yamamoto prepared to execute the final two phases: the occupation of Midway while the Americans presumably sailed north on a wild goose chase, and then the deployment of his fleet to hunt down and annihilate Nimitz's navy. But Nimitz's code breakers had parsed a strand of the Japanese naval code, which told them exactly where Yamamoto and his main force were headed: Midway.[235]

As Yamamoto steamed for Midway, Nimitz prepared an ambush northeast of the island, in an empty swath of the sea that flanked Yamamoto's expected course. Nimitz threw in his lot—the aircraft carriers *Hornet, Yorktown,* and *Enterprise,* along with as many cruisers and destroyers as he could afford. He put in no battleships because he had no battleships. At first things went exceedingly well for the Japanese. Just after daybreak on June 4, they bombed Midway, and then they massacred forty-three misnamed Devastator torpedo bombers from Nimitz's carriers that had the misfortune of locating the Japanese fleet. Sixty American dive-bombers dispatched from Midway along with more planes from U.S. carriers failed to even locate Yamamoto's ships. Shortly after 10:00 A.M., and for about two minutes, Yamamoto thought he had won the battle, and the war. He ordered his bombers re-armed and refueled for another run at

Midway. But the slaughter of the low-flying American torpedo planes had left Yamamoto's shield of Zero Fighters buzzing around his ships almost at sea level when they should have been hovering protectively high overhead. No commander on any Japanese bridge took note of this. Then, a few seconds before 10:26 A.M., three dozen Dauntless dive-bombers from *Enterprise* cruising at 14,000 feet beheld below four Japanese aircraft carriers, the fattest of targets, and the pride of Yamamoto's fleet. The carriers' decks were crammed with refueling aircraft, gasoline lines, bombs, and torpedoes. The U.S. Navy pilots rolled their planes and nosed down. Within six minutes the tide of war in the Pacific was reversed in a maelstrom of exploding fuel and bombs on the blazing flight decks of three of Yamamoto's crippled carriers, including *Akagi,* which had led the attacks on Pearl Harbor, Darwin, Colombo, and Rabaul, the New Britain port that since its capture in January served as the Japanese base of operations in the South Pacific.[236]

Six minutes. Here indeed was a small agate point of the sort Churchill relished and upon which fortunes turned.

Churchill cabled his "heartiest congratulations" to Roosevelt. The battle, he wrote, had "very decidedly altered the balance of the Naval war." Here he fell into characteristic hyperbole, except in this case he was absolutely correct. The balance in the Pacific had shifted so dramatically that he now worried that Admiral King—with the American people fully behind him—might persuade Roosevelt to finish off Japan before taking on Germany. King, who in fact was thinking along those lines, elicited the support of Marshall (still disgruntled over his April mishandling by Churchill), and the two began plotting just such a Pacific-first policy. Roosevelt quashed it. Still, Marshall planned to ship five times as many troops to MacArthur as to Britain, and was already shipping scores of B-17s to the Pacific that had been destined for Britain. The American chiefs appeared ready to abandon Europe-first. This disquieting prospect—in conjunction with Rommel's latest misdeeds—led Churchill, in the same telegram, to call for a meeting with Roosevelt: "I feel it is my duty to come and see you."[237]

Prospects in Africa were troubling. Rommel had paused for a week in early June after bending back Ritchie's southern flank and throwing the Eighth Army into disarray. Initially outnumbered, by mid-June the Germans held a two-to-one edge in tanks. Tobruk, and the 35,000 mostly South African, mostly green troops holed up there, lay exposed just thirty miles to Ritchie's rear. The Tobruk garrison had been told by headquarters that if circumstances developed as they appeared to be developing, the plan called for an evacuation, not a defense. Yet Ritchie failed to order either an evacuation or a buildup of the city's defenses. He had lost control of events, and of the battle. Auchinleck presumed Ritchie would stick to the fall-back-and-evacuate plan; Churchill presumed Auchinleck would hold the city. Auchinleck had infuriated Churchill three months earlier when he claimed he would not be ready to attack until mid-June. When Rommel first struck in late May, the question became, would Auchinleck be ready to *defend* by mid-June? When Rommel lunged out of his positions on June 13 to send Ritchie's army reeling even farther east, the answer became self-evident.[238]

Thus, with American fortunes on the rise in the Pacific while British fortunes again evaporated in the desert, Churchill fretted over a disruption in the Europe-first strategy. Although Roosevelt was firmly disabusing his military men of their Pacific inclinations, no plans existed for a European thrust. Roosevelt wanted something done about that. Years later Marshall told Admiral Samuel Eliot Morison that "the one great lesson he learned in 1942 was that the political leaders must 'do something'; they could not afford the impression of fighting another 'phony war' that year." The U-boat war wasn't phony in the least, and the Allies were losing it. Rommel appeared unstoppable. Russia, again, stood unsteadily at the precipice, and Hitler, again, seemed poised to push the Soviets off. Three days after congratulating Roosevelt on his victory at Midway, Churchill made ready to return to Washington.[239]

The two leaders had to work out the business of where to attack the Germans, of where best to *do something*. Their desperate ally in Moscow wanted to know not only where but when, and more specifically how soon. On June 16, before departing London for Washington, Churchill wrote a letter to King George asking the King's "gracious permission" to propose that the King appoint Eden — "an outstanding minister" — to form a new government should Churchill be killed en route. Then Churchill and his entourage, minuscule compared with his January host, departed the capital. Dr. Wilson, with his supply of sleeping pills, came along, as did Pug Ismay, John Martin, stenographer Patrick Kinna, Frank Sawyers, the valet with Churchill's whisky, and Inspector Thompson with his revolver. Commander Tommy Thompson, Churchill's naval aide, and Brigadier D. G. Stewart, the director of War Plans, also made the trip. Shortly after arriving in Strannraer, Scotland, late on the seventeenth, the group boarded a Boeing flying boat captained by the self-same Captain Kelly Rogers who had flown Churchill home from Bermuda. Churchill, wielding a gold-topped Malacca walking stick and dressed in a siren suit topped off with a black Homburg, was quite animated. But remembering that long and dangerous flight home in January, he was heard by Brooke humming a favorite tune of Tommies during the Great War, "We're here because we're here, because we're here."[240]

They cruised at five thousand feet, high enough to see the red smear of the solstice twilight on the northern horizon. Brooke was entirely enthralled by his first trans-Atlantic flight. Unfamiliar with the jargon of airmen, he noted in his diary that he slept well "after paying a visit to the pilot in his driving compartment on top bridge." All aboard were bemused by the fact that their watches, as they crossed time zones, no longer kept time with the sun. Brooke consulted his watch to determine when in "real time" he might take breakfast. Churchill consulted neither the sun nor his watch but his stomach. For the duration of the war on such journeys Churchill took his meals on "stomach-time" regardless of what his time-piece or the sun told him. Tommy Thompson recalled that on that voyage, as the flying boat neared the American coast, the passengers discussed "the advisability of having lunch or high tea before arrival." The question was put to Churchill, who "settled it with a flat statement that it was time for 'high whisky.'" Sawyers produced the beverages. Captain Rogers took the party over fog-bound Nantucket Shoals and began the run down to Washington. Churchill took his usual seat in the co-pilot's chair. Three hours later, as Rogers ran low up the Potomac, Churchill, spotting the Washington Monument and ever alert to navigational dangers, warned Rogers "that it would be particularly unfortunate if we brought our story to an end by hitting this of all other objects in the world." After almost twenty-seven hours, the big plane skimmed up the Potomac and floated to a stop. On board, it was "stomach-time." The evening meal was served as the party bobbed on the river in the fetid, still air of a Washington summer evening, in the sort of close heat that had driven every president since John Adams to seek relief elsewhere, which is exactly what Roosevelt had done, having decamped to his nine-hundred-acre Hyde Park estate, where cool breezes fanned his forested haven high above the Hudson River.[241]

Churchill and his party spent the night of the eighteenth at the British embassy. Rommel spent that night directing his engineers—"sappers" to the British—toward the British minefields in front of Tobruk. Earlier in the day, his panzers had broken Ritchie's lines, which meandered from Tobruk about thirty miles to the south, where they gave out in a naked flank. Ritchie had chosen to stand firm there when his Gazala Line broke two weeks earlier. A better choice would have been to clear out of Tobruk and fall back nearer to the Egyptian frontier. With his lines broken, that is exactly what Ritchie now attempted. But the day's battle lurched eastward so quickly that Tobruk and its garrison were bypassed. By nightfall the city was surrounded, retreat and resupply impossible. Churchill had told Auchinleck three days earlier that he expected Tobruk to be held. Rommel intended otherwise. On the nineteenth, as Churchill made for Hyde Park, Rommel, his path through the minefields cleared, made straight for Tobruk.[242]

Churchill brought to Hyde Park a memorandum that he had composed for Roosevelt in which he argued that any attempt to invade France that year had no "chance of success unless the Germans became utterly demoralized, of which there is no likelihood." What then to do, he asked Roosevelt, in a manner that answered his own questions: "Have the American staffs a plan? At what points would they strike?" And what of shipping and landing craft? Roosevelt had no answers. Operation Bolero, the buildup of forces in Britain, should continue, Churchill offered, but with an eye to striking somewhere other than France. As Churchill saw things, that left northern Norway (Operation Jupiter) or North Africa (Operation Gymnast) as the only alternatives. During two days of relaxed talks above the Hudson, Roosevelt pondered Churchill's memo but made no commitments. He did agree verbally and informally to exchange information on the atomic bomb project. More important, Roosevelt pledged to fund the entire project. Yet, as Churchill would learn within months, the Americans, for security reasons (or for political reasons couched as security concerns), intended to exchange only information that Britain could use to construct weapons on British soil. Since Britain could in no way build the facilities in which to construct an atomic bomb, the Americans began withholding information.[243]

Churchill and Roosevelt returned to Washington early on the twenty-first. Later that morning, as Roosevelt, Churchill, and Pug Ismay chatted in the president's study, an aide entered and handed Roosevelt a telegram. He glanced at the contents and passed it to Churchill. It read: "Tobruk has surrendered with twenty-five thousand men taken prisoner." Churchill, thinking it must be a mistake, sent Ismay off to get the facts. Presently Ismay returned to not only confirm the fall of Tobruk but advise Churchill that much of the remaining British fleet at Alexandria had been sent south of the Suez Canal to avoid exposure to the Luftwaffe attacks that were expected any minute. Churchill, for a change, was speechless. He later wrote that the shock of the loss was great, but even more shocking was the performance of the army. Singapore, and now Tobruk, had destroyed the reputation of the British army. "Defeat is one thing," he wrote, "disgrace is another." After a moment of respectful silence, Roosevelt leaned forward and asked, "What can we do to help?" Churchill asked the president to ship at once as many new Sherman tanks as he could spare. Roosevelt summoned Marshall, who reported that a few hundred brand-new Shermans were on their way to American armored divisions. He added that it would be a shame to take them away from his men, but if Britain needed them, they'd be on their way. Within days, three hundred new tanks, many so new they lacked engines, were loaded onto five cargo ships. A sixth ship carried the engines. When it was sunk by U-boats, Roosevelt dispatched another. Roosevelt also tossed in one hundred self-propelled 105mm guns. It was a gesture Churchill never forgot. But at the time, given Rommel's genius for tank warfare, and given the decimation of the British desert army in terms of men, machines, and morale, it remained to be seen whether the American tanks would arrive in time to save Cairo.[244]

Over the next four days, Rommel struck deep into Egypt; on June 25 he took Mersa Matruh, just 140 miles from Alexandria. That evening Auchinleck flew out to the front, relieved Ritchie of command, and took personal command of the Eighth Army. The citizens of Cairo and Alexandria were now as distressed as the disintegrating Eighth Army. Panicked Alexandrians caused a run on Barclays Bank. Merchants in Cairo sold out their inventories of luggage within hours. A steady drizzle of ashes fell onto Cairo's streets, the result of the British high command's burning of secret papers. Rommel was expected, and soon. Auchinleck, meanwhile, took his ragged army seventy miles east, to a defensible neck of sand that ran forty miles from El Alamein on the sea to the edge of the great Qattara Depression, a natural obstacle that even Rommel dared not challenge. Rommel paused, too. He intended to wait and hit the British head-on as soon as he was reinforced. Until then, he would bide his time west of El Alamein—just 60 miles west of Alexandria and 140 miles northwest of Cairo—with just a dozen tanks fit for battle.[245]

It was then that Benito Mussolini decided his presence was called for upon the field of battle. Mussolini's motto was *"Il Duce ha sempre ragione"* ("Mussolini is always right"). By the last days of June, he was convinced that Rommel, now poised before El Alamein, would push the final miles to Alexandria, and then to Cairo. The marshal of the Empire—the highest rank in the Italian military, created by Mussolini for himself—journeyed to Derna, where a magnificent pure-white stallion groomed for his triumphant entrance into Cairo waited in its stall for its magnificent rider. Resplendent in his pure-white uniform, Mussolini inspected the troops in Bardia, more than two hundred miles from the action. There he awaited Rommel's invitation. But Rommel had stopped replying to Mussolini's communiqués. Mussolini ended his adventure at Bardia. Rommel, his lines drawn tight at El Alamein, awaited the infusion of tanks and gasoline and men that he had been promised, and that he needed in order to drive to Alexandria and east to Iraq. But RAF cryptologists were reading messages between Berlin and Rommel, with the result that when Berlin radioed the departure date of German supply ships sailing from Italy to Tobruk, RAF pilots started their engines. There was hope yet for the Desert Rats.[246]

Shortly after Churchill learned of the disaster at Tobruk, Harry Hopkins suggested he meet two American generals whom the president and Marshall held in high regard, major generals Mark Clark and Dwight D. Eisenhower. Just two years earlier both had held the rank of lieutenant colonel. Both had since risen high in the ranks due in large part to having earned Marshall's complete loyalty. Eisenhower, fifty-one and Clark's senior by five years, had never held an active field command. He had been promoted to brigadier general less than a year earlier; within days he would arrive in London a major general and gain a third and fourth star within a year. His only field experience was administrative—as chief of staff of the 3rd Division during the Louisiana maneuvers the previous summer, where the audacious tactics of George Patton's 2nd Armored Division had much impressed Eisenhower. Yet Eisenhower had shown Marshall his stuff soon after Pearl Harbor, when given the task of getting relief to his old boss, Douglas MacArthur. Eisenhower failed, but not for want of effort; there simply was no relief to give at the time. He had since labored for Marshall as deputy chief of staff in the War Plans division, or had until the previous week, when Eisenhower—his friends called him Ike—finally got his field command, the biggest of them all: commander of the U.S. Expeditionary Force assembling in Britain. Clark would go along as Eisenhower's deputy.

Churchill, prostrate by the news from Tobruk and the oppressive Washington heat, met the two generals in his "air-cooled room," the same rooms he had occupied in January, just across the hall from Hopkins's suite. It was Hopkins's command center, from where he did the president's bidding. It was no accident that important White House guests were billeted across the hall from Hopkins—Harry could more easily choreograph events, as he did on this day with Churchill and the generals.[247]

Churchill listened as Clark and Eisenhower chatted up the prospects of a cross-Channel invasion in 1943. The two generals had just left their first meeting with Roosevelt, where Operation Roundup, the full-scale invasion of France set for 1943, had been the primary topic of conversation. Churchill let the Americans do most of the talking. The disaster at Tobruk had put North Africa in the forefront of his thoughts, and Laval's coup had brought Gymnast back into the mix. With Eisenhower about to leave for London, it had become clear to all concerned that the American Chiefs of Staff should also depart for Britain for further talks with their British counterparts. The agreement reached by the Combined Chiefs of Staff in Washington amounted to nothing more than an agreement to meet again in London.

Churchill, too, planned to sit in on those meetings—if not guide them—and made ready to depart Washington on the twenty-fifth. As in January, he knew his homecoming would not be a celebratory affair. U.S. newspaper headlines gave him fair warning: ANGER IN ENGLAND; TOBRUK FALL MAY BRING CHANGE OF GOVERNMENT; CHURCHILL TO BE CENSURED.[248]

Rather than make straightaway for London to face the crisis, Churchill, along with Ismay, Marshall, and the dutiful Sawyers, journeyed by train to Fort Jackson, South Carolina, where they watched a newly formed American infantry division conduct a live-fire exercise. As the recruits strutted their stuff, Churchill asked Ismay what he thought of the exercise. Ismay replied, "To put these troops against continental troops would be murder." "You're wrong," Churchill replied. "They are wonderful material and will learn very quickly."[249]

Late on June 25, Churchill and his party, joined by Averell Harriman (who toted some kerchiefs and a Virginia ham for Clementine), boarded a flying boat at Baltimore. At breakfast time the next morning (according to their watches), they landed at Botwood, Newfoundland, for fuel and a sturdy morning meal that most Britons could only dream of: "excellent lobster washed down with Scotch whisky." That week, to placate the vast majority of Londoners who could not afford to pay two or three pounds ($10 to $15) for a meal out, the government placed a cap of five shillings (about one U.S. dollar) on restaurant meals. The plan didn't work; proprietors simply added overhead costs to the bill and trebled the price of wine, on which there was no price limit. Worse, whisky, long rationed at one bottle per month per customer, was in such short supply (alcohol was needed to manufacture smokeless gunpowder) that even regulars could no longer procure their allotted bottle from local merchants. Nobody was starving in Britain, yet very few Britons washed down lobsters with aged Scotch whisky.[250]

Almost seven hundred thousand British homes had been destroyed since 1940. Six million Britons lived without operating sewage systems. In London, more than three hundred thousand houses, one in eight, had been wrecked. Water lines remained smashed. Basements of ruined buildings had been converted (after the bodies of the drowned and burned had been removed) to rainwater catch basins. When the British offered the arriving Americans the use of a barracks for their general headquarters, a Yank who reconnoitered the place learned to his dismay that sewage flowed openly and, given that the newest building was built in 1860, there was no heat. Tens of millions of continental Europeans (and several thousand

Britons who lived in the Underground) would have happily taken up residence in such a place. The American officer wondered how his staff could work there during the winter.[251]

He needn't have asked. A nationwide coal shortage meant cold hearths throughout the land. As Churchill winged his way home, Parliament debated the rationing of coal, which would mean even less coal to heat homes and coal gas to power factories. More than 30,000 coal miners, meanwhile, were in uniform, yet the same citizenry that demanded a second front were demanding that those miners return home to dig the coal. The people demanded their coal; they demanded a second front; they demanded a victory *somewhere*. And they demanded their fish. Fresh salmon and cod had disappeared from fish markets. Britons found themselves chilled in their houses, with no fish in their pots, a ration of two eggs and two thin chops per week, and with little whisky in the cupboard. Starved for sugar, they queued up at candy counters for a penny's worth of gumdrops, "as though," wrote Mollie Panter-Downes, "it was biblical manna." Yet, these were strictures the British could live with, *if* their leaders delivered a victory. "Bewilderment has been the outstanding national emotion," Panter-Downes wrote, ever since Rommel took Tobruk "with the seeming ease of shattering a child's toy." Newspapers told Britons that "everything was going well." It was not. Yet, Panter-Downes noted, Britons remained true to form, "grousing about their leaders in the corner pub while remaining fully determined to fight behind those leaders to the last ditch."[252]

Some in Parliament did not share in that determination. Churchill arrived home to find a motion had been placed in the Commons by a Conservative MP, Sir John Wardlaw-Milne: "That this House, while paying tribute to the heroism and endurance of the Armed Forces of the Crown in circumstances of exceptional difficulty, has no confidence in the central direction of the war." Admiral of the Fleet Sir Roger Keyes, supported by Leslie Hore-Belisha, seconded the motion. By the time Churchill arrived at the Cabinet Room on the twenty-seventh to plan his parliamentary defense, Aneurin Bevan was hard at work honing his parliamentary attack. The mood among conservatives, Churchill noted, was "fairly glum."[253]

He had occupied No. 10 for almost twenty-six months, during which time he had presided over nothing but defeats. He fully expected to survive the vote of censure, telling a Roosevelt aide he thought at most twenty MPs would abandon him. That outcome might under different circumstances be enough to bring down a partisan government but not a national coalition. Yet Churchill understood there could be no more defeats. "Only a few more marches," he later wrote, "one more success, and Mussolini and Rommel would enter Cairo, or its ruins, together. All hung in the balance, and...who would predict how the scales would turn?"[254]

The debate took place during the first two days of July. Churchill remained silent on the first day, but straightaway it became clear to everyone that the opposition was steering toward the rocks. The first rebel, Wardlaw-Milne, a Scottish Conservative, stated his case well enough. The problem, he said, was Churchill serving as both P.M. and minister of defence. The solution was to strip him of the latter office and pass on the leadership of the war to a qualified and dominating commander in chief. Churchill had often told his cronies that he would resign within the hour if any such degradation of his powers took place. Milne had set up the pitch; he then proceeded to throw the ball away. The "dominating" figure he recommended was the Duke of Gloucester, the corpulent and somewhat dimwitted brother of the King, and as unqualified a nominee as could be found in the Isle. As Wardlaw-Milne spoke, mumbles of "why, the man must be an ass" percolated through the House. Harold Nicolson noted in his diary that Wardlaw-Milne had begun well enough, but his mention of the Duke resulted in "a wave of panic-embarrassment" passing through the House. Wardlaw-Milne, Nicolson wrote, "is in fact rather an ass." Mollie Panter-Downes compared Wardlaw-Milne's proposal to the Duke of York of the old nursery rhyme:* "Judging by the reception of the house . . . a nursery rhyme is just now the most likely place for such martial royal excursions." Churchill could not have asked Wardlaw-Milne to do more for his cause.[255]

Churchill's old friend Admiral Keyes—though a dotard now in Churchill's opinion—followed Milne. The old admiral made clear that he objected to the handling of the war effort by the Chiefs of Staff, yet, curiously, not by Churchill, whose loss to Britain were he to be forced out of office, Keyes declared, would be a "deplorable disaster." A member noted that the admiral appeared to be claiming that Churchill both interfered in the war and at the same time didn't interfere enough. Since the entire showdown was, supposedly, about Churchill's performance, Keyes's peroration, by its illogic, served only to bolster Churchill while undermining the opposition.[256]

The next day, Aneurin Bevan demonstrated why he was almost Churchill's equal in parliamentary close combat (Churchill cites the speech in the fourth volume of his war memoirs but fails to name the speaker;

---

* Oh, the grand old Duke of York,
  He had ten thousand men;
  He marched them up to the top of the hill,
  And he marched them down again.

  And when they were up, they were up,
  And when they were down, they were down,
  And when they were only halfway up,
  They were neither up nor down.

such was his antipathy toward Bevan). He began well enough. Of Churchill, he proclaimed: "The Prime Minister wins debate after debate and loses battle after battle." Then, after a pause for effect, he delivered his most memorable criticism of Churchill: "The country is beginning to say that he fights debates like a war and the war like a debate." Unfortunately for the opposition, Bevan, as had Milne, proposed a questionable solution to the lack of military zeal. Bevan's was to put British troops under the command of the many French, Polish, and Czech generals who had fled their homelands to London. This absurd suggestion self-evidently did not lend itself to further scrutiny by the House. Bevan then worked some class-warfare rhetoric into his address, claiming that had Rommel been born British, he would likely not have risen above the rank of sergeant, a prepos-terous assertion given Rommel's upper-middle-class lineage and his long Imperial Army career, which began as an officer candidate and included a stint at the War College in Danzig. Still, Bevan had adroitly exposed the rot in the British class structure, a truth Churchill had acknowledged to Colville almost two years earlier when he declared that the boys from the secondary schools (public schools in America) who had won the Battle of Britain (they made up more than 70 percent of Fighter Command) deserved to run the country after the war. Churchill, an old reformer, was sincere in his sentiments, but by failing to express in public what he felt in private, he allowed Bevan to claim the issue as his own.[257]

Hore-Belisha spoke last, but the old Liberal had learned nothing from his attack of the year before when, attempting to blame Churchill for the fall of Crete, he instead called attention to his own lackluster tenure under Chamberlain as secretary of state for war. Churchill turned that history against Hore-Belisha then, and did so again on this day. Twice within thir-teen months, Hore-Belisha opened the door for Churchill, and twice Churchill burst through. When Hore-Belisha asked about the many mechanical and armament problems of the Churchill tank (designed and produced by the Chamberlain government), Churchill turned the tables by noting that only when the tank's defects became known was it christened the Churchill. These defects had been overcome, he added, laughter now percolating through the chamber, and the tank could be expected to give long, strong, and massive service in the war effort. Churchill's address, Harold Nicolson told his diary, amounted to an explication of the concept of attrition. Britain would soon have more guns and men and tanks in the desert than the Germans, and although Rommel had not yet been brought to bay, numerical superiority must, in time, spell the difference. Toward the end of his address, knowing that the opposition had inflicted fatal wounds upon itself, Churchill sounded "quite fresh and gay."[258]

When the House divided for the vote, the tally was 475 for the government, 25 against. Churchill had survived the strongest parliamentary assault of the war, and by a margin extraordinarily close to the prediction he had made in Washington. Twenty-five votes had been the maximum figure mustered against Pitt the Younger in 1799 when Napoleon appeared poised to rule both the waves and the Continent. Pitt had declared himself the only man in England capable of defeating the little Corsican, and Parliament gave him its vote of confidence. Yet for Churchill, the July vote was more a warning than a victory.

Within days of arriving in Britain, Dwight Eisenhower learned that most Americans in London believed the European war would be lost within weeks unless Stalin parried Hitler's lunges toward the Russian oil fields and the Don. Pug Ismay thought as much, and he told Harriman the Red Army would be finished "in three weeks," although Harriman noted that Ismay had been saying as much for twelve months. This time, however, events seemed to validate Ismay's dismal predictions. By early July, Eisenhower thought the Russian position so desperate that he proposed another look at Operation Sledgehammer, the plan for the cross-Channel invasion of Europe. "Even an unsuccessful attack" in France, he told his public relations aide, Lieutenant Commander Harry Butcher, would be "worthwhile" if it brought relief to the Russians. Churchill and his military chiefs wanted no part of Sledgehammer for the self-evident reason that it was bound to fail and would *not* result in any succor for the Russians. Butcher predicted to his diary: "If Germany rolls up Russia's armies and gains the rich oil fields that seem to be easily in her grasp, will the United States then concentrate on licking Japan first and leaving Germany until later? How much later it is impossible to tell." This was Churchill's fear exactly. But if not Sledgehammer, then what?[259]

Harold Nicolson saw the political implications this way: "If the Russians collapse, they and their friends here will say it was due to Churchill's refusal of a second front. I very much fear that Churchill's own position will not survive a Russian defeat."[260]

Marshall and King arrived in London in mid-July to address the question of a second front. They carried a memorandum from Roosevelt that outlined his priorities and conclusions. The events unfolding in Russia and in the North Atlantic made it perfectly clear to Roosevelt that it was past time to do something. Yet the question of what to do remained, as it had for almost seven months, what exactly? Roosevelt, although seeing the possible merits of Gymnast, still sided with Marshall and Stimson on the need to get into Europe, preferably before the American elections. "Roosevelt was always afraid the American public would get very Pacific minded," recalled Averell Harriman, "and force him to change his Europe first policy." Yet, if Europe proved beyond reach, North Africa—which Marshall considered a sideshow—presented a suitable political alternative. It would remove some of the moral high ground from beneath Stalin. The president made it clear to Marshall that he wanted American boys fighting somewhere before November 3, Election Day. Further, he made clear that if no action was taken by the Allies in 1942, the effect on morale at home and in Great Britain would be disastrous. The Middle East must be held, Roosevelt wrote, in order to prevent a "joining hands between Germany and Japan, and the probable loss of the Indian Ocean" as well as the loss of Egypt, Syria, the Suez, and Iraqi oil. Sledgehammer should be studied, he advised, but if it could not be executed, they should pick another target. One method of protecting the Middle East, he suggested, would be to consider a joint Allied operation "in Morocco and Algiers intended to drive in against the back door of Rommel's armies." And there it was, Gymnast reborn. Secretary of War Stimson called Gymnast Roosevelt's "secret war baby." Churchill, with his barrage of telegrams and personal visits, had brought Roosevelt around. But Churchill had not yet sold Marshall, and Roosevelt, despite his directives to Marshall, left the final decision in the hands of his top general.[261]

As the Combined Chiefs in London prepared to choose a target in order to take pressure off Stalin, the Soviet leader's position only worsened. The previous summer, the Germans had bypassed and cut off Sevastopol, the largest Soviet naval fortress on the Black Sea. During the Crimean War almost a century earlier, Sevastopol withstood a British and French siege for 329 days, time enough for Leo Tolstoy, then a young Russian lieutenant of artillery who happened to be marooned in the city, to write three "sketches" of life under siege. They are fairly short pieces, the first an almost lyrical celebration of the heroics of the brave and patriotic defenders. Yet in the final sketch, written after Sevastopol fell, a deepening despair and intense loathing for the brutality of war permeates the narrative. Tolstoy and much of the czar's army escaped the city. Hitler, when he finally moved fourteen divisions against Sevastopol in early June, took the city in twenty-three days. Boris Voyetekhov, a correspondent for *Pravda*, wrote the epitaph this time—of Soviet naval destroyers unloading shells and leaving port with their decks and holds full of women and children, of the city in flames, and of the last defenders, out of ammunition, swimming out to sea, to certain death. Few in the garrison escaped alive; almost 90,000 were killed and captured. Hitler now owned the Black Sea coast, from Yalta to Kerch, along a two-hundred-mile front. Farther to the north, his armies poured into the Donets Corridor.

By July 7, Army Group B had reached the Don, opposite Voronezh. Hitler's April directive had called for this force to now begin wheeling south down the west bank of the river toward the great bend, where only sixty miles separate the Don and the Volga, and Stalingrad. But Army Group B's commander, Fedor von Bock, feeling a soldier's natural unease at leaving a strategic rail hub such as Voronezh unmolested on his flank, threw his Fourth Panzer Army across the Don and into Voronezh. The operation, he told Hitler, would take only a few days. Paulus's Sixth Army, meanwhile, began its push down the west bank of the Don, alone, and with every mile that much more removed from its panzer screen.

To the British press, Stalin's situation looked dire, at best. Not privy to all the facts, and careless with the few it had, it was full of calls for a second front, sooner rather than later; in fact, a second front now. *The Daily Worker* was again free to join the chorus when HMG lifted the January 1941 ban on its publication, a sop to Stalin. The slogan "Second Front Now" was being scrawled on walls throughout Britain, the handiwork of labor agitators who, in Churchill's estimation, were nothing more than "fools or knaves." Dissatisfaction with Churchill had spread from the Parliament into factories and the armed services. Scottish and Welsh Communists were now one with certain London intellectual elites in believing that Churchill was as much a disaster as the disasters he presided over. Beaverbrook's newspapers, while still supporting Churchill, now framed the moral essence of the fight in terms of helping Russia, as did the British people, who, Mollie Panter-Downes noted, "can't or won't recognize the existence of any substitute for a genuine, slap-up opening of a land offensive on the Continent." Spring was the season, Panter-Downes wrote, when an "Englishman's fancy lightly turns to thoughts of invasion." This summer, however, the question Britons asked was not when the Germans would come to England, but when Englishmen would cross to the Continent. What Britons expected, Panter-Downes wrote, was a demonstration of "the old national talent for the brilliant impromptu, the type of piratical, sea-borne foray which has often studded and sometimes made English history."[262]

Mountbatten had been planning just such a foray for months, the target Dieppe, the strategic port in northwest France. Yet Churchill had also understood for months that a strategically meaningful landing in Europe that summer was out of the question, although throughout the year he harbored hopes for 1943. Yet by July, even 1943 began to look problematic.

Eisenhower, in his memoirs, wrote: "It became increasingly doubtful...
that a full-out frontal attack could be launched in the early spring of 1943,
and because it would be extremely hazardous to begin a major operation
across the English Channel in the fall of the year, we began to realize that a
large-scale invasion might not be possible before the spring of 1944."
Eisenhower reluctantly concluded, as had Roosevelt, that the spring of
1944 might be the earliest the Allies could put an army into France, far too
late to help the Russians. Whether a landing in North Africa—or anywhere, for that matter—would do anything to improve the Soviet situation was now the question du jour among the military planners.
Eisenhower's aide Harry Butcher believed that German and Japanese
"industrialized strength," along with the rubber and oil of Malaya, the
Dutch East Indies, and Burma, would spell the end of the "British Empire,
as we have known it" and leave the United States in "a defensive position,
virtually alone in the world." *Time* reduced the implications to a stark
reality: "Hitler is winning in Russia." If the Red Army does no better than
it has so far, "Russia will be defeated. Germany will win the present phases
of World War II in Europe.... The allies will then have lost their best
chance to defeat Germany and win World War II."[263]

The time had come for the Anglo-Americans to fight; to not fight was to
lose the war in Europe. With that appalling scenario in mind, in early July
Roosevelt instructed King and Marshall to remember three "cardinal principles" when they sat down in London with the British Chiefs of Staff:
"speed of decision on plans; unity of plans; attack combined with defense
but not defense alone." So eager to get to work were the American and
British staffs that they held informal meetings on July 19 in Churchill's
absence. That was a mistake. Churchill, as minister of defence and per the
authority vested in him, had intended to preside at the first meeting. The
chiefs' violation of protocol resulted in a Churchillian detonation at Chequers, where, in front of Hopkins, he paraded up and down the great hall
reading from a book of British war laws. As he finished each page, he
ripped it from the book and threw it down. The chiefs got the message.
Then, within two days of sitting down with the British on the nineteenth,
the Americans reluctantly agreed that Europe was beyond reach in 1942.
Three days later they agreed upon North Africa as the target. On July 24,
Operation Gymnast was rechristened Operation Torch, and a jumping-off
date of late October was settled upon. Torch meant that Roosevelt would
have his men on the beaches before the election; for Churchill and Brooke,

it meant taking the first step in their push to clear the Mediterranean. But Eisenhower—who within a few weeks would be promoted to three-star rank and named commander in chief of Torch—saw things differently from both Roosevelt and Churchill. Like Marshall, Eisenhower looked upon Torch primarily as a sideshow to Roundup, its only merit being that it possibly would "contain" the Germans after the Wehrmacht defeated the Red Army, a defeat that, as the last days of July arrived, Eisenhower believed was imminent. Torch for Ike was a colossal mistake. Its approval by Roosevelt, he told an aide, "is the blackest day in history."[264]

On July 27 Roosevelt cabled Churchill: "I cannot help feeling that the past week represented a turning point in the whole war and that now we are on our way shoulder to shoulder." Actually, they were about to start bumping shoulders. The British and American principals, military and political, had agreed on a target, but for different and possibly conflicting reasons. It became apparent in coming weeks that neither the specific objectives in North Africa nor a follow-through strategy had been addressed. Even the makeup of the invasion force was in doubt. Roosevelt wanted the entire land portion of the venture to be an American operation, based in part on his political need to put American boys into action and in part on his belief that the French North Africans hated the English and would welcome the Americans. He proposed to Churchill that if the British desired to attack Algiers, they do so a week after the Americans landed on the Atlantic coast of Morocco. The British role in Torch, Roosevelt insisted, must be limited to air and sea support. This stunned Churchill. Knowing that Roosevelt heeded the advice of his generals, Churchill tried to persuade Eisenhower to persuade the president to approve a real joint Anglo-American venture. He succeeded a few weeks later, but his influence over Roosevelt was lessening. Churchill understood, Harriman told the president, "that he is to play second fiddle in all scores and then only as you direct."[265]

As for Charles de Gaulle and any role he might play in the invasion, Roosevelt looked upon the Frenchman as a mere soldier and one who manifested Bonapartist ambitions, although nothing in de Gaulle's deeds or words had ever indicated an ambition to become a military dictator. Eisenhower grasped what Roosevelt did not: de Gaulle was hated by the Vichy because he had not surrendered while they had, and because he was everything Vichy loyalists were not—patriotic and courageous. Roosevelt simply did not understand that, with the result that Eisenhower was told by Washington that "under no circumstances" was the Frenchman to be told of the decision on Torch. Churchill, too, had more than his share of problems with de Gaulle, but they came about as a consequence of trying to work with the obstinate Frenchman, not against him.[266]

As Churchill saw it, the major flaw with the original plan for Torch resulted from Marshall's fear that to venture too far into the Mediterranean—specifically to Algiers—might result in his army being cut off. The news of American resistance to attacking Algiers came as a "bombshell," Churchill told the president, and he asked that a British contingency be added in order to strike Algiers, and that American troops be transferred from the Moroccan part of the invasion in order to facilitate a drive east from Algiers, with Tunis the ultimate objective. Roosevelt took his time pondering the concept, but he found Eisenhower in fundamental agreement with Churchill. By mid-September Roosevelt agreed to transfer ten thousand men to the eastern operation, which would now take place simultaneously with the Moroccan landings. This opened up opportunities that Brooke and Churchill had sought all along. For Brooke, a continental second front could not be contemplated as long as Malta lay under siege and Tunis was held by the Axis. Churchill, with his eye on flushing Italy from the war before thrusting northward into Germany's southern flank, strongly believed that if Torch did not include a push from Algiers into Tunisia, with the capture of Tunis as the ultimate objective, it risked becoming a dead end. Churchill prevailed on the matter of Algiers, but the Americans and British continued to debate the details and objectives of Torch into late September, prompting Eisenhower's aide Commander Butcher to complain to his diary, "Trying to follow the evolution of Torch is like trying to follow the pea in a three-shell game."[267]

During the July meetings, the British and American military chiefs had begun to take the measure of one another, and the results were decidedly mixed, and not strictly along national lines: Dudley Pound, the first sea lord, was in Brooke's estimation "an old dodderer" and "beyond retirement." Pound, who was almost sixty-five, was so given to falling asleep at staff meetings that he was replaced by Brooke as chairman of the Chiefs of Staff Committee: "He [Pound] is asleep 90% of the time," Brooke told his diary, "and the remaining 10% is none too sure what he is arguing about." Brooke had no way of knowing that Pound's drowsiness was due to an undetected brain tumor. The CIGS considered Pound's American counterpart, Admiral Ernest King, to be "a shrewd and somewhat swollen headed individual" who was "biased entirely in favor of the Pacific." King (so tough, blue jackets claimed, that he shaved with a blowtorch) had long been known for his hair-trigger temper and heavy drinking. He had sworn off whisky for the duration, but not, as Brooke was to note, champagne or wine, which on more than one occasion resulted in King's becoming quite "nicely lit up" and combative. King joined Eisenhower and Churchill in Brooke's pantheon of those who lacked strategic vision. Marshall, too, in

Brooke's estimation "has got no strategic vision, his thoughts revolve around the creation of forces and not on their employment." Yet Marshall shared Brooke's steadfast belief in "Europe First," although they disagreed on where and when to strike. They both had to keep an eye on Admiral King. As for the strengths of the other major American players, Brooke found Eisenhower "quite incapable of understanding real strategy." The Army Air Force's Hap Arnold "limits his outlook to the air," and General Mark Clark was "very ambitious and unscrupulous." Yet as a group, Brooke later chirped, the Americans were "friendliness itself."[268]

Churchill, for his part, did not think much of his own Chiefs of Staff or high-ranking officers in general. Referring to the COS during a luncheon, he told his guests, "I am obliged to wage modern warfare with ancient weapons."[269]

For their part, the American military chiefs thought as little of their boss's strategic acumen as the British chiefs thought of Churchill's. Marshall was especially wary of politicians. He had pledged to himself never to laugh at Roosevelt's jokes, and he upheld the pledge. Churchill, in April, had displayed his political side to Marshall, who, though completely loyal to Roosevelt and respectful of Churchill as a statesman, remained loyal first and foremost to his troops. He saw no glory in death. He hated to see men die under any circumstances, most of all the transparently political, and that is how he looked upon Torch.[270]

Although Brooke (and Churchill) had sent Marshall home in April with the false impression that they had agreed to a 1942 invasion of France, the two generals got along well professionally, recalled Sir Ian Jacob. This was despite Brooke's "hard, distant, lofty" demeanor, which was manifested by his speaking rapidly and, according to Jacob, with an overbearing air of self-assurance. Brooke also, recalled Jacob, tended to allow his tongue to dart out of his mouth and flit around his lips, lizardlike, an unfortunate quirk that distracted listeners from the merit of his words. If Brooke possessed a sense of humor, it was well concealed.[271]

Compared to Brooke, the dour George Marshall was a cutup. He was also—blessedly for the alliance—unaware of Brooke's contemptuous diary jottings in which he pilloried his American counterpart. Brooke called Marshall a "great man, a great gentleman, a great organizer, but definitely not a strategist." In fact, Brooke termed Marshall's strategic abilities "the poorest." Marshall, in turn, thought much the same of Brooke, and told Hopkins that although Brooke "might be a good fighting man, he lacked Dill's brains." Brooke, though critical to a fault, harbored no ambition other than to win the war. Years later, when he prepared his diaries for publication, he took pains to add italicized explanations for many of his biting pronouncements. Marshall by then was a dying old man whose stature in American and European history could in no way be diminished by Brooke's long-ago scribbling. And Eisenhower by then was president, a shock to Brooke, who wrote: "He certainly made no great impression on me at our first meeting…and if I had been told then of the future that lay in front of him I should refuse to believe it."[272]

Brooke was egalitarian; he criticized everybody, American and British, Mountbatten and Churchill most of all. Churchill, Brooke concluded, "never had the slightest doubt that he had inherited all the military genius of his great ancestor Marlborough!" Yet he could not "understand a large strategic concept and must get down to detail!" As with all who dealt with Churchill, Brooke learned that he was "quite impossible to argue with" and if he did concede a point, tended to later "repudiate everything he had agreed to."[273]

Brooke's worst invective was directed toward Dickie Mountbatten, who the CIGS found to be "the most crashing bore," prone to "always fiddling about with unimportant matters and wasting other people's time." Mountbatten "suffers from the most desperate illogical brain," he told his diary, "always producing red herrings."[274]

The paths of Eisenhower and Bernard Montgomery also crossed during the early summer. Several weeks before the July meetings, Eisenhower paid a courtesy call on Montgomery, who commanded all troops in southeast Britain. Ike made the mistake of lighting one of his daily ration of eighty Chesterfields while waiting for Monty to wind up a staff briefing. The ascetic Montgomery (a devout nonsmoker and nondrinker) detected the aroma of tobacco smoke in the air and barked out that whosoever was the offender should snuff out the fag, immediately. Eisenhower complied, and so learned his first lesson about the diminutive and combative Englishman: Monty liked things his way and only his way. This was true also on the battlefield, where he preferred a set-piece style of combat in which events unfolded in strict accordance with his well-laid plans. Churchill, on the other hand, liked to quote Napoleon's maxim, to wit, that forming a "picture" of a battle was foolish, for conditions could easily be deranged by Providence. Churchill had run up against Montgomery's asceticism the previous year, when after a day of inspecting Montgomery's troops near Brighton, he repaired with Monty to the Royal Albion Hotel, where Churchill anticipated a good whisky and a cigar. Monty declined the libations, declaring that he neither drank nor smoked, and furthermore was 100 percent fit. Churchill rejoined that he both drank and smoked and was 200 percent fit.[275]

The teetotaler Montgomery, with his rumpled corduroy trousers and nonregulation turtleneck sweater, was not the sort who would normally grace Churchill's dinner table, but Montgomery had acquitted himself well in France and at Dunkirk. He was egotistical and brusque, but most of all he was a fighter, and this Churchill respected. In late July, it appeared unlikely, however, that Eisenhower, Montgomery, and Churchill, each possessed of a wildly differing temperament, would anytime soon be conducting vital military business in close proximity with one another, each dependent on the others for common success. The final week of July found Churchill, troubled by events in the Middle East and by personalities in the Kremlin, intent on visiting both venues. Eisenhower had begun planning the North African campaign. Monty, meanwhile, cooled his heels in southeast Britain, awaiting an improbable German invasion or an even more improbable promotion to an active field command in an actual war zone.

By July 14, Hitler's eastern army (*Ostheer*) had established its bridgehead across the Don at Voronezh, but it had taken Army Group B's Fourth Panzer Division a week to take the city. The delay would prove costly as the seasons changed. Meanwhile, Paulus's Sixth Army had kept to the original plan and wheeled south along the Don's west bank. The *Ostheer* had now driven 140 miles farther than in the previous summer, yet the dawdling of the Fourth Panzer Army in Voronezh while Paulus raced south meant that Army Group B was being stretched thin. Stalin by then had rescinded his "stand firm" orders and was now allowing the Red Army to retreat before the *Ostheer*, which lessened the chances of entire Soviet armies being encircled and captured. As a result, although the Germans had captured more than 90,000 Soviet troops within the Donets Corridor since their victory at Kharkov, five times that many Russians had backtracked to fight another day. Still, by the first days of August, the *Ostheer* had driven another 150 miles. Rostov-on-Don, gateway to the Caucasus, fell, and with it the last direct Soviet rail links with the Baku fields. For Stalin, this was a personal affront; in 1908 he had robbed the Rostov–Moscow train in order to help the revolutionary cause. For the same cause he had robbed the Tiflis bank in his native Georgia, leaving three dead at the scene. Rostov and Georgia had been his stomping grounds. They were now Hitler's.

Farther south, elements of Army Group A's First Panzer Army reached Stavropol on August 5, one hundred miles from the foothills of the Caucasus. On the ninth, after racing across the Kuban Steppe, German panzers cruised to within sight of the oil derricks at Maikop. Far to the east-northeast, Army Group B, less Bock, whom Hitler sacked for dawdling at Voronezh, had resumed its offensive and had shot across the Don north of the great bend. Paulus's Sixth Army was now heading full bore for the Volga, and Stalingrad. The question being asked in Moscow, London, and Washington was, would the Germans bypass Stalingrad or try to take it? In fact, on July 23, Hitler had issued Führer Directive No. 45, an order Sir John

Keegan described as the "most disastrous of all issued over his signature." The Führer decreed that while Army Group A made for the Caucasus, Army Group B would take and hold Stalingrad. The city was of high strategic value to the Soviets, which is why Hitler had ordered it smashed in his April directive. Yet destroying a position is not the same as holding it. Stalingrad carried symbolic weight for Hitler, named as it was for his Bolshevik nemesis. In deciding to inflict a symbolic defeat on Stalin, the Führer had forsaken his Clausewitz.[276]

Stalin had allowed his troops to fall back since the Germans crossed the Don, but five days after Hitler issued his directive to take Stalingrad, Stalin issued one of his own; all available forces would be thrown into Stalingrad, and "not a step back" would be tolerated. "Die, but do not retreat" became the Order of the Day on the banks of the Volga.[277]

Western dailies dutifully updated their maps of the Russian front as the German advance pushed ever eastward. A great deal of black ink was required to mark German-held terrain. Yet the maps failed to tell the true story. Army Group A, stretched as it was along a five-hundred-mile front, was rolling though territory, but not holding territory. Panzer spearheads far outran the infantry, which could only slog along at ten or fifteen miles a day. Even farther to the rear, supply trains struggled along roads not made for modern vehicular traffic. The result, wrote Sir John Keegan, was a front so broad that in some places just a few hundred Germans "held" dozen of miles of ground. Western readers who took their news seriously were dismayed at what they read of the Soviet plight. Stalin's generals, however, saw an opportunity.[278]

With the vote of censure behind him and the decision made in favor of Torch, Churchill's attention turned to Egypt, and Stalin. Based on Ultra decrypts, he had prodded Auchinleck for weeks to take the offensive against Rommel, unfairly in Brooke's estimation. Ultra allowed Churchill to peer over his generals' shoulders as if he were with them in the field poring over intelligence reports. Yet Ultra was sometimes wrong. Churchill took Rommel's (decrypted) pleas for reinforcements at face value, while some at Bletchley cautioned that Rommel might be exaggerating his needs in order to force action in Berlin. On one occasion Churchill goaded Auchinleck by citing a decrypted Luftwaffe signal that appeared to reveal the Germans had only half as many tanks in Africa as Auchinleck believed based on his field intelligence. But Bletchley was incorrect; the deciphered message referred only to the German tanks at Auchinleck's immediate front. Rommel, after taking several necessarily desultory and ultimately futile cracks at Auchinleck's El Alamein positions during the first weeks of July, settled into a defensive mode and awaited his promised reinforcements. For his June victory over Ritchie, he was awarded by Hitler a field marshal's baton. He would later say he would have preferred to be given a division. With Rommel dug in before El Alamein and with the fight possibly gone from Auchinleck, Churchill concluded that the situation in the desert called for his presence.[279]

His getting to Egypt involved doing so without contracting any of numerous diseases he would be exposed to along the way. In order for the aircraft to avoid Germans, the outbound leg of the journey would take at least five flying days, going south from Gibraltar to Takoradi, in the Gold Coast, followed by a three-day, three-flight hopscotch across central Africa. This sojourn through "tropical and malarious regions," as Churchill put it, would require a series of inoculations, some of which required ten days to take effect. Dr. Wilson and the War Cabinet sought to put an end to the idea. Just that week, news of a great medical discovery had sifted through the ranks. Two American doctors visiting London from Johns Hopkins University had told Harry Butcher over a few bottles of port of a new drug "called penicillin and derived from bread mold. Takes eleven acres of mold to cure the scorched face of one flyer." Such a drug would have made Churchill's trip safer, but it had yet to be mass-produced. Given the risks posed by African insects and German fighter planes, it appeared that Churchill would not be straying far from London.[280]

Then an American pilot, Captain William Vanderkloot, twenty-six years old and a veteran of ferrying Lend-Lease bombers to Britain, suggested a daring approach: depart England for Gibraltar late in the evening by a four-engine B-24 bomber and refuel in Gibraltar the following morning; then, after departing the Rock at dusk, overfly Spanish Morocco, dodge far south over the desert during the night, and then swing east almost 1,900 miles to the Nile, south of Cairo. A fully gassed-up Liberator could cruise slightly more than seventeen hours at an average speed of 240 miles per hour. It had what it took to make such a journey in two legs.

Churchill liked the spirit of the idea, and he liked the means of transportation—Vanderkloot's modified B-24 Liberator, named *Commando*. The bomb racks had been removed, and eight seats had been bolted down amidships. Toward the rear of the plane, wood slats had been rigged into two berths for the comfort of the highest-ranking passengers, but comfort was a relative concept. The plane was neither heated nor pressurized, necessitating at high altitude the use of oxygen masks, another source of worry to Churchill's doctor, who feared the consequences to his heart of freezing temperatures and thin air. Churchill, not sharing Wilson's concern, asked the RAF ground crew to customize his oxygen mask in order to allow him to smoke his cigars. The request was dutifully carried out. Vanderkloot's proposed route to Cairo could be covered in twenty-three hours compared with five days spent amid "Central African bugs." If they could reach Cairo, there was no reason they could not reach Moscow; Churchill had not yet met Stalin and he felt a face-to-face meeting was the best way to establish a relationship and clear the air. There was much air to clear. Churchill made an executive decision: he would journey to Cairo. When Stalin invited Churchill to Moscow on the thirty-first, the itinerary was expanded to include the Kremlin. The entire journey would prove a daunting undertaking, even for young pilots, and an exhausting slog for an overweight old man with a quirky ticker and seemingly perpetual chest colds that he unwisely chose to treat with snuff and whisky, a generous supply of which Sawyers secreted into *Commando*'s bomb bay.[281]

Brooke left Britain for Cairo by air early on the morning of August 1, intending to swing through Malta on his way. The journey was too dangerous to risk having both Brooke and Churchill on the same airplane. The previous year, Eden and Dill had overshot Malta on their way to Greece and almost flew into the sea. German and Italian fighter planes sought out lone British bombers accompanied by Spitfires on the sound premise that a big shot might be aboard. Brooke arrived at Malta to find scenes of "incomprehensible" destruction, food and gasoline shortages, a harbor full of wrecks, and a population on the brink of starvation. The roads were so full of rubble, and petrol was in such short supply, that Malta's military commander, Field Marshal Gort, had to ride his bicycle around the island. Gort appeared "depressed," as he and his little garrison waited in this "backwater" for the final German assault, which good strategy dictated must be imminent. In fact, a joint German and Italian invasion had been approved in April. But days before Brooke's arrival—and unbeknownst to the British—Hitler, with the cost of the Crete invasion still fresh in his memory, postponed the invasion of Malta because it appeared Rommel might get to Cairo on his own.[282]

Churchill departed London just after midnight on August 1. As he waited on the tarmac, a cable reached him from Dill, in Washington, which concluded: "In the American mind, Roundup in 1943 is excluded by acceptance of Torch." This was not at all what Churchill wanted to hear, given that after Cairo he was going to Moscow to inform Stalin that no second front would materialize in Europe in 1942, a chore he compared to "carrying a large lump of ice to the North Pole." He was not prepared to add 1943 to the equation. The cable, however, served one useful purpose: it would show Stalin that decisions on the second front had not been made by Churchill unilaterally, but had resulted from American and British solidarity. To bolster that argument, Roosevelt, at Churchill's request, instructed Averell Harriman to meet Churchill in Cairo and to continue on with him to Moscow.[283]

With Dill's message in hand, Churchill boarded *Commando*. Box lunches had been stowed in the bomb bay; there was no space for anything resembling a galley, and no meals could be prepared. A little propane camp stove was rigged to heat water for tea or Churchill's hot-water bottle. Tommy Thompson and Churchill's doctor made the trip, along with Inspector Thompson, Sawyers, Ian Jacob, two secretaries, and Alexander Cadogan, who represented the Foreign Office. Eden remained in London to run the store in Churchill's absence. Clementine motored out to the airfield and watched as the "monster bomber, throbbing, roaring & flashing blue lights," lifted off into the night sky. Once aloft, *Commando* swung low over blacked-out southern England, past Land's End and out over the Atlantic, where it climbed to 15,000 feet and ran the 1,500 miles to Gibraltar. Lest any Axis spies prowling that citadel spot him, Churchill told Brooke he intended to disguise his identity with a gray beard. He spent August 2 on the Rock, and lifted off again at dusk. Conversation on board was impossible; the plane had not been soundproofed. Just before sunrise, Churchill climbed from the bomb bay and into the copilot's seat, from where he beheld "in the pale, glimmering dawn the endless winding silver ribbon of the Nile."[284]

He had first seen the river from horseback more than forty years earlier, and although at the time he had yet to dab a canvas with oils, he described it in painterly tones as "a thread of blue silk drawn across an enormous brown drugget; and even the blue thread is brown for half the year...the picture painted in burnt sienna is relieved by a grateful patch of green." Now the whitewashed concrete sprawl of Cairo spilled out of the patch of green, the western edges of the city thrusting toward al Jizah and the pyramids. Rommel, after again testing Auchinleck's lines during the preceding week, sat just 140 miles to the northwest. And here came Churchill, exhilarated to find himself "the man on the spot."[285]

He came not to praise Auchinleck, but neither had he yet decided to bury him. Of two things Churchill was certain: the Eighth Army needed a new commander (Auchinleck had taken over from Ritchie), and Auchinleck should return to Cairo from the front in order to tend to the business of his entire Middle East command, which stretched from Tehran to El Alamein. Brooke arrived firm in his belief that Auchinleck had lost the confidence of the Eighth Army, was a poor judge of character, and should be replaced. Churchill, not yet sure, had invited the general he most respected, Jan Smuts, to Cairo for consultation. Wavell also arrived, from India, in order to brief Churchill and Brooke on events in that theater. It became clear to Churchill that Wavell and especially Auchinleck were so preoccupied with the immediate threats to their fronts that all of Iraq and Iran were essentially without central command, and this with the Germans driving toward Baku and the Caucasus. Churchill proposed setting up a new command in Baghdad, to be called the Middle East command. Brooke had been advocating just such a change for weeks. Auchinleck's old command would be renamed the Near East command, a change Churchill had long championed the self-evident reason, as he later wrote, that Egypt and the Levant "was the Near East...India, Burma, and Malaya, the East...and China and Japan, the Far East." The name changes were fine and well, the sort of housekeeping details Churchill relished, but the obvious and as yet unasked questions were, who would command, and where.[286]

Auchinleck sealed his fate by nominating Lieutenant General Thomas Corbett as the new commander of the Eighth Army. Corbett, in Brooke's estimation, was a "small man" and clearly "totally unsuited" for that command, further proof that Auchinleck could not pick a leader. The Eighth Army was tired. The troops, Churchill told the War Cabinet, were poised to retreat to the Nile delta if an attack came. Late on the third, Churchill kept Brooke up until all hours, lecturing the CIGS on the need for Auchinleck to return to Cairo in order to tend to the business of the Middle East command while someone new took command of the Eighth Army, which led Brooke to exclaim to his diary: "Exactly what I have always told him from the start!" Churchill offered the command to Brooke, a proposal that sorely tempted the CIGS, who in France had "tasted the thrill of commanding a formation in war." Yet he knew he was the wrong man for the job, having no experience in desert warfare, and so told the Old Man.[287]

On August 6, after visiting the front with Auchinleck and meeting Corbett, who Churchill found to be agreeable but without personality, Churchill made the decision to ease the Auk out of Cairo and into the new command in Baghdad. Then the plans collapsed. Churchill offered Auchinleck's job to Brooke, who, like Marshall, was greedy for just such a theater command but was also honest enough to acknowledge (again, as he had three days earlier when offered the Eighth Army) his lack of desert warfare experience. More important, Brooke was selfless enough to not wish the job of working with Churchill on anyone else. The CIGS concluded (but did not inform Churchill in so many words) that the best service he could render England was to stick with Churchill, for better or for worse. Churchill cabled the War Cabinet that Harold Alexander, an obvious choice, be sent at once to replace Auchinleck. Yet Alexander had just been appointed to lead the British forces in Torch, and he had already begun planning that mission with Eisenhower. As for the Eighth Army, Brooke favored Montgomery, whose career he had nurtured for years. Churchill was inclined toward William ("Strafer") Gott, the man

who, along with the Fighting French, had in May delayed Rommel for a
week, thus saving Ritchie's army, and perhaps Cairo. Brooke thought Gott
tired and in need of rest rather than a new command. Churchill, having
spent part of the day with Gott, thought otherwise. The P.M. prevailed.
The command of the Eighth Army went to Strafer Gott. Bernard Montgomery was chosen to replace Alexander in Torch, and Eisenhower was
duly notified of the changes by London.[288]

By lunchtime the next day, Gott was dead, his flying boat shot out of the
sky by a rogue German fighter as the general flew from the front to Cairo
for a hot bath and few days of rest. Churchill and Brooke, stunned by
Gott's loss, shuffled their dwindling deck and produced Bernard Montgomery. Lest Eisenhower conclude that his British allies could not make up
their minds, Churchill sent a cable to London asking that Eisenhower not
be informed of Montgomery's promotion. But Montgomery had already
reported for duty at Eisenhower's headquarters. It fell to Ismay to inform
Eisenhower that Montgomery, too, was being posted to Egypt, and that
yet a third British general would be assigned to Torch. Eisenhower, taking
in the news, told Ismay, "You seem to have a lot of Wellingtons in your
army. Tell me, frankly, are the British serious about Torch?"[289]

Churchill was serious. On August 8 he relieved Auchinleck of command,
offering the general the consolation prize of the new Middle East command
at Baghdad. It was a posting, Churchill admitted, that would be much
smaller than Cairo, given that HMG could spare few troops in Iraq and
Persia, but a theater nonetheless that "may in a few months become the
scene of decisive operations." Given his and Brooke's lack of confidence in
Auchinleck in combination with their fears of Hitler punching through to
Iraq from the Caucasus, it is ironic that Churchill offered Auchinleck the
Iraq command. But after pondering the offer for a few days, the Auk
declined. Brooke thought Auchinleck behaved "like an offended film star"
rather than putting duty first and taking the command, where he might
"restore his reputation as active operations are more than probable." But as
Brooke well knew, the Tenth Army in Iraq was woefully unprepared to
rebut a German attack, and, with Britain's armed forces stretched to the
limit, no reserves could be spared to boost its fighting strength. Were Hitler
to break through to Iraq, the Tenth Army would not so much assume a role
as suffer a fate. Knowing this, Auchinleck instead departed for India and
retirement. Churchill, relieved at having made his decision, took himself off
to the beach, where, as he later related to Harold Nicolson, "I then took off
all of my clothes and rolled in the surf. Never have I had such a bathing."[290]

In a letter to Clementine informing her of the command changes, Churchill
credited Smuts, who "fortified me where I am inclined to be tender hearted,
namely in using severe measure against people I like." He used much the same

language three months later when he told Harold Nicolson that sacking Auchinleck was "a terrible thing to have to do. He took it like a gentleman." Churchill may have truly liked Auchinleck, but he had conducted this unfortunate piece of business with the general not in person, but by letter.[291]

"That was how he did it," recalled Bob Boothby, "in writing, 'You are dismissed,' signed in red ink, WSC typed in red ink under the signature. When he sacked somebody he never thanked them. I don't remember any occasion when he thanked anyone for doing anything." Around Whitehall, a sacking by Churchill was known as "the awarding of the Order of the Boot." Boothby is partially correct, his recollection colored by his own exit from HMG. Early in 1941, he was accused of extorting commissions from Czech citizens who sought his help in reclaiming Czech assets seized by HMG after Munich. Boothby, who in the early 1930s had been touted as a possible future prime minister, had made many Tory enemies for his role as an anti-Chamberlain rebel. In 1941, with the Czech banking irregularities offered as their raison d'être, those enemies maneuvered to bring Boothby down. Boothby defended himself admirably in the House against the kickback charges, and sought Churchill's help on the matter. Returning from the House that day, Churchill told Colville that "if there was one thing in the world he found odious, it was a man-hunt." Yet he let Boothby go it alone, with the result that although Boothby managed to keep his seat in the Commons, he lost his position at the Ministry of Food. "I never forgave Churchill for that," Boothby later recalled. "He ruined my wartime career."[292]

Yet there is an element in Boothby's tale that is common to the recollections of many who ran afoul of Churchill. Boothby never forgave Churchill for that incident, but he understood that Churchill's "ruthlessness and aloofness may have helped to make him a great leader." Churchill had his own awkward way of thanking those who served him. After the war he arranged for Boothby, an ardent European unionist, to go as one of the first five British delegates to the Council of Europe in Strasbourg. Later, Churchill sponsored Boothby for knighthood. The two dined together on occasion for the remainder of Churchill's life.

Auchinleck had joined Boothby, Margesson, Wavell, Dill, Dowding, General Alan Cunningham, Dr. Tizard, and Admiral Dudley North on Churchill's roll call of those he found wanting. Churchill believed that most of his admirals and many of his generals lacked spirit, and he succeeded in sacking several, vested as he was with great powers and an unforgiving temperament when he sensed a lack of aggressiveness. The Royal Navy's admirals, Churchill once told Pound, "seem quite incapable of action." Worse, some—including, Churchill believed, Andrew Cunningham at Crete—displayed a tendency to fear "severe losses" rather than to throw themselves and their ships into the teeth of the enemy. They "shirked" their tasks,

Churchill told Colville. Churchill was said to be so autocratic that Hitler told his own generals that they were fortunate to work for such a reasonable leader as himself rather than for the mercurial Churchill.[293]

Bob Boothby believed that Churchill's ruthlessness toward subordinates was prompted not by any latent, mean-spirited inclination, but solely by the need to defeat Hitler. Churchill himself saw things that way; in his letter to Clementine recounting Auchinleck's downfall, he offered that the changes made in Cairo "were necessary to victory." As for Bernard Montgomery, who by August 10 was hastening to his new command in Egypt, Churchill told Clementine: "In Montgomery... we have a competent daring and energetic soldier" who "if he is disagreeable to those about him he is also disagreeable to the enemy."[294]

While Churchill wrapped up his business with Auchinleck, great events transpired on a South Pacific island that few in London or Washington had heard of. Early on August 7, almost ten thousand U.S. Marines from the 1st and 5th regiments, First Marine Division, slogged ashore on the stinking, hot island of Guadalcanal, where the Japanese had almost completed an airfield from which they intended to sever the American shipping lanes that sustained Australia. Most of the leathernecks carried World War One Springfield bolt-action rifles and wore World War One–era leggings. They secured the beachhead with ease, and the next day they took the airfield. Much of their equipment and almost all of their rations failed to follow them ashore when on August 8, Admiral Frank ("Jack") Fletcher, who had already had two aircraft carriers sunk from under him, turned his ships for home with the meager excuse that he needed to refuel (just as he had when he steamed away from the relief of Wake Island in December), thus earning him the everlasting antipathy of Marines and the moniker Frank "Always Fueling" Fletcher. Still, the Marines meant to hold their ground. America had taken the first step in the journey to Tokyo. For Churchill, the American action on Guadalcanal again raised the concern that had dogged him since January: Would the Americans proceed on that journey at the expense of the European front?[295]

Late on the tenth, Churchill departed Cairo for Tehran, the first leg of his journey to Moscow and "his visit to the Ogre in his den," as Clementine had put it in a letter earlier that week. He later noted the irony of the pilgrimage to "this sullen, sinister, Bolshevik state I had once tried so hard to strangle at birth." Had Hitler kept his bond with Stalin, the Soviets "would have watched us being swept out of existence with indifference and gleefully divided with Hitler our Empire in the East." What, Churchill wondered, did he owe the Soviets? Wavell gave the answer in a poem of many verses, the last line of each being: "No second front in nineteen forty-two." Brooke offered his opinions about Moscow to his diary, and they were not conciliatory: "Personally I feel our policy with the Russians has been wrong from the very start, and as begun by Beaverbrook. We have bowed and scraped to them" without ever asking in return for information on Soviet "production, strength, dispositions, etc. As a result they despise us and have no use for us except what they can get out of us."[296]

Three B-24 Liberators were needed to ferry the entire party to Moscow, including Brooke, Air Marshal Tedder, Cadogan from the Foreign Office, and Archie Wavell, who spoke Russian. It was an unnecessarily large party, Brooke wrote, made so because Churchill felt such a retinue of generals, admirals, and air marshals "increased his dignity."[297]

Harriman had arrived in Tehran two days before Churchill, and he used the time to inspect the British-run Iranian railroad system, which he found to be "the worst mess I have ever seen." He would know; railroading was in his blood. When Churchill arrived on the eleventh, Harriman proposed that the U.S. Army take over the railroad in order to expedite the delivery of Lend-Lease goods to Stalin. Churchill, dubious, agreed to discuss the matter in the autumn. Harriman then joined Churchill on *Commando* for the run to Moscow. The plane was routed east of the Caspian in order to avoid any stray German fighters. The din in the aircraft was such that the two men passed written notes between themselves whenever they had something to say.[298]

Brooke and his party followed in his B-24, but when one of the engines flared out, they had to return to Tehran for the night. The next day the Brooke contingent climbed into an American DC-3, a Lend-Lease offering that the Russians had lavishly outfitted with thick seats and Persian carpets. They flew north by west to Baku to refuel. To Brooke's delight, the plane scared up thousands of water birds as it came in low over the Volga delta. From there they flew north along the Caspian coast, with the Caucasus just twenty miles to the west. The plain below, between the sea and the mountains, was the main line of advance from Russia into Iran. With the Germans driving from the north, Brooke expected to see trenches and anti-tank traps and concrete fortifications in numbers to match the Volga birds. He saw none. "The back door seemed to be wide open for the Germans to walk through for an attack on the Russian southern supply route," he wrote, "and more important still, the vital Middle East Oil supplies of Persia and Iraq!"[299]

On his way to Moscow, Churchill learned that an eleven-ship relief convoy bound from Gibraltar to Malta had lost eight ships and an escorting aircraft carrier to German submarines and aircraft. The three remaining ships brought 12,000 tons of food and petrol to Malta, relief, but at a terrible price. Churchill was not pleased, not only because of the losses, but because he knew that Stalin would demand a resumption of the Arctic convoys, and there were just not enough ships.[300]

After a ten-hour flight from Tehran, Churchill arrived in Moscow late in the afternoon of August 12. Greeted by Molotov, he climbed into a bulletproof car and set off at high speed for a dacha about a dozen miles outside Moscow. There, after availing himself of a hot bath, Churchill found that everything in the guesthouse had been "prepared with totalitarian lavishness." Three hours later he was escorted into the blacked-out Kremlin. Stalin was attired in a gray rough-cloth peasant's blouse and trousers of the same material, tucked into high boots. A handsome handworked leather belt was cinched around his blouse. His eyes had a yellow cast, his face was pocked, his teeth discolored, and his mustache scrawny and streaked. Harriman thought he looked noticeably older and grayer than he had the year before. The marshal and Churchill were close to the same height, around five foot seven, with Churchill an inch or so taller. Where Churchill was given to looking directly into the eyes of his conversation partners, Stalin gazed away into the distance as if he were not listening. But he was. Harriman described the three meetings that took place over the next three days as running "hot and cold"—very hot, and very cold.[301]

The first, which lasted three hours, began on a somber note when Churchill, getting right to the point, announced that there would be no second front in France that year. Any attempt to do so would be so paltry as to offer no help to Russia, and would likely result in the annihilation of the forces on the beaches. But in 1943, Churchill offered, the Allies were prepared to throw twenty-seven divisions ashore, half of them armored.

Stalin, Harriman reported to Roosevelt, "took issue at every point with bluntness." He first lectured Churchill on the need to take risks in order to win wars, and then proclaimed, "You must not be so afraid of the Germans." Churchill, keeping his cool, replied that the British air offensive against Germany was a success, and with American participation would visit ruin on Germany. Here, Stalin expressed some enthusiasm, suggesting that houses as well as factories be targeted. Churchill backed away, saying that any damage inflicted upon "working men's houses" was a by-product of bombs missing industrial targets. He then steered the talk to Torch, which he declared was in fact a second front. Here, he sketched a crocodile and, poking his pen at the crocodile's belly, offered that it was just as sound to strike here, in its soft underbelly, as it was—he now tapped the crocodile's nose—to attack "its snout." At that, Stalin seemed to take interest, asking a great many questions about the operation before pronouncing Torch militarily sound. He added, "May God help this enterprise to succeed," a strange utterance from the leader of an atheist dictatorship (he had been a seminarian before devoting himself to revolution and murder). After more questions from Stalin about the African campaign (including the need to bring de Gaulle in), the meeting adjourned. All in all, it had been a productive start.[302]

The next day's meeting was scheduled for late in the evening to allow Brooke, Tedder, and Cadogan to reach Moscow first. After an eleven-hour flight from Baku they arrived in time for dinner at Churchill's dacha. All recorded similar impressions of the extravagant accoutrements in the villa, including marble walls, wood paneling, rooms too numerous to count, a large aquarium full of tropical fish (which Churchill wanted to feed), and patches of ripe raspberries in the walled gardens. Most of all, they were struck by the food, in variety and abundance unlike anything they had seen in three years. Cadogan thought it all "really rather vulgar." Before dinner Churchill sat down with Tedder to recount the previous day's meeting with Stalin, whom he called "a peasant" and one he could handle at that. Tedder was mortified; all except Churchill knew that the walls likely contained microphones. Tedder scribbled a note and shoved it across the table; it read, "Méfiez-vous" ("Beware"). The Kremlin, too, Tedder assured Churchill, was bugged. At this, Churchill turned and addressed the walls: "The Russians, I have been told, are not human beings at all. They are lower in the scale of nature than the orang-outang [sic]. Now, then, let them take that down and translate it into Russian."[303]

Shortly after ten on the thirteenth, Churchill left for the Kremlin and his second meeting with Stalin. It proved a disaster. Harriman saw it coming. The previous year when he and Beaverbrook brought Lend-Lease to Moscow, their first meeting with Stalin had gone well, but he had arrived at the second in full offensive mode, blunt and insulting. He did so again this day, when he began by reading from a memorandum that Harriman described as "bristling with recriminations," all directed toward Churchill and his "refusal" to open a second front in 1942. He demanded that the front be opened that year. Churchill, shrewdly, promised to respond in writing, thus delaying further recriminations. Stalin came at him verbally, demanding greater sacrifices by the Western powers. Ten thousand* Russians were sacrificed daily, he declared. What were the British doing? Churchill touted the RAF bombing campaign and promised to "shatter

---

* This was not an exaggeration, if both civilians and soldiers are included. Every three months, more Russians died than did Americans in all the wars in American history.

almost every dwelling in every German city" as the war went on. Stalin smiled at that, but claimed a "reluctance" to fight on the part of the British. It was fear, in fact. He accused the British of stealing Lend-Lease material, and snarled that they should try fighting for a change, like the Russians, to which Churchill replied, "I pardon that remark only on account of the bravery of the Russian troops." Harriman, recalling his experience of the previous year, slipped Churchill a note telling him not to take Stalin too seriously. But Churchill hit back, speaking so rapidly that his interpreter fell behind. "Did you tell him this?" Churchill asked his interpreter, and again, "Did you tell him this?" He wanted Stalin to hear each and every point. The British and Americans were *not* cowards, and they would demonstrate that soon. He and Roosevelt were willing to sacrifice 150,000 men in France if they thought it would help Russia, but a foolish enterprise would serve no one. *"Did you tell him this?"* again he asked after each rejoinder. Harriman thought it was Churchill's "most brilliant" performance, during which he not once reminded Stalin of his pact with Hitler. Stalin finally leaned in to the table, and said, "Your words are of no importance, what is important is your spirit." With that, the tension eased. Stalin invited Churchill and Harriman to dine with him the next evening. When the meeting ended at midnight, Churchill, enraged, banged down the corridors of the Kremlin, "looking neither left nor right. He struck a match on the Kremlin wall and without breaking stride lighted a cigar."[304]

He kept Harriman up into the wee hours analyzing Stalin's change in demeanor. Their best guess was that other commissars on the Politburo, holding more power than the West believed, insisted that Stalin take a harder line. Harriman predicted a return to affability at the next meeting.

The next night—later that day, in fact—Stalin hosted a dinner for forty in Catherine the Great's state rooms. Harriman thought the affair more subdued than the feasts he and Beaverbrook had been treated to the previous year. Churchill later wrote, "Silly tales have been told of how these Soviet dinners became drinking bouts. There is no truth whatever in this." Actually there was a great deal of truth. Brooke called the banquet "a complete orgy" of nineteen courses and vodka toast after vodka toast raised by all around the table, a dozen or more in the first hour. The table "groaned" under the weight of hors d'oeuvres and fish and chickens and a suckling pig with a black truffle eye and orange peel mouth. Stalin's aide General Kliment Voroshilov almost drank himself under the table, which he had in fact done at a dinner for Eden in December. When Voroshilov held up his glass to click Stalin's, Brooke was sure the general must have been seeing a half dozen glasses. But the toast came off, as did the banquet. The verbal jousts were friendly, but still pointed. Stalin recounted Lady Astor's comment made during her prewar visit to Moscow: "*Oh,* Churchill, he's finished." The marshal told Churchill he had disagreed. "If a great crisis comes," he recalled saying, "the English people might turn to the old war horse." That pleased Churchill, who asked if Stalin had forgiven him for trying to crush the Bolshevik revolution after the Great War. "All that is in the past," Stalin replied. "It is not for me to forgive. It is for God to forgive." The leg-pulling and toasts went on for four hours. Upon leaving the Kremlin after 1:00 A.M., and still smarting from the talks of the previous day, Churchill told Cadogan he did not really know what he was doing here and he planned to return to London without seeing Stalin again. "He was," Cadogan told Dr. Wilson, "like a bull in the ring maddened by the pricks of the picadors."[305]

But when he again met with Stalin, all went well, as Harriman had predicted. They gathered at seven that evening in Stalin's private rooms in the Kremlin. Bottles were uncorked, food prepared, and the leg-pulling began again, but with good humor. Churchill could not resist chiding Stalin on his pact with Hitler; Stalin, in turn, asked why the British had tried to bomb Molotov when he was in Berlin in 1940. Churchill replied, "In war no advantages can ever be neglected." Stalin, still smarting from the cancelation of Arctic convoys, asked, "Has the British Navy no sense of glory?" Churchill replied that he knew a great deal about navies. Stalin shot back, "Meaning that I know nothing." Churchill then delivered a monologue on the differences between sea powers and land powers, as he had with Molotov in May. The meeting pushed past ten o'clock. Churchill, remembering that he had plans to dine with the Polish general Wyadłsław Anders, who was in Russia searching for thousands of missing Polish army officers, sent off a note canceling their engagement. Stalin and Churchill talked—and drank—past midnight, trading tales and information. Churchill told Stalin that a major British raid would soon take place on the French coast, at Dieppe; Stalin offered to share with the British the blueprints for a new type of rocket (he never did). At 1:00 A.M., a suckling pig was produced, which Stalin fell upon. Churchill finally departed after three with a "splitting headache" (his only reference to the effects of alcohol in his memoirs). By dawn he was bound for Tehran.[306]

He arrived back in Cairo on August 17, having concluded, as he later told the House, that Stalin was "a man of massive outstanding personality...a man of inexhaustible courage and will-power, and a man direct and even blunt in speech....Above all, he is a man with that saving sense of humour which is of high importance to all men and all nations, but particularly to great men and great nations....I believe I made him feel that we were good and faithful comrades in this war but that, after all, is a matter which deeds, not words, will prove."[307]

Early in the morning of August 19, Louis Mountbatten launched his largest military venture of 1942, a triphibious raid on Dieppe by air, sea, and
land of five thousand mostly Canadian infantry supported by thirty
Churchill tanks. This was the operation Churchill had played up to Stalin.
In Cairo, Churchill waited for reports on the results. The results were disastrous—almost one thousand killed and two thousand captured. Churchill
and the Chiefs of Staff, who had approved the Dieppe raid, shared responsibility for the horrific results of Mountbatten's misjudgment.

The first post-battle report from Mountbatten that reached Churchill
proclaimed that the "morale of returning troops is excellent....All I have
seen are in great form." He could not have seen very many, given the numbers of dead and captured. Based in part on that faulty intelligence, Churchill
cabled the War Cabinet, "The results fully justified the heavy costs." Only
weeks later, as the real casualties were tallied, did Churchill see the folly of
the scheme. Yet, the raid served a tangential political purpose, arguing
against any further continental excursions for 1942. Even if the Allies possessed the right type and sufficient quantities of landing craft to mount an
invasion, and they did not, the results at Dieppe spoke directly to the need
for much heavier firepower in such landings, more tanks, specialized tanks
for clearing mines, and paratroop disruption behind enemy lines. It verified
Brooke's (and Eisenhower's) thesis that a beachhead could only be held if
supported by massed aerial bombing of German positions and transportation links leading to the beaches. It verified the need for overwhelming fire
support from the navy right up to the moment when troops hit the beach,
and after, by way of long-distance barrages laid down by battleships, not pot
shots by gunboats. Given that the American Eighth Air Force was just getting off the ground and that the scores of warships needed to support any
large-scale landing were dispersed across the Atlantic on convoy escort duty,
only one conclusion could be drawn from Dieppe as it pertained to a second
European front: no further landings could be contemplated for at least a
year. Any reasonable man could understand that, but, as Churchill had
learned days earlier, Stalin was not that kind of man.[308]

Churchill liked to proclaim that he judged the results, not the man. The
slaughter of Dieppe should have cost Mountbatten his career, and it would
have had he not been a Churchill favorite. Churchill was ruthless in purg-
ing those who displeased him, but his treatment of Mountbatten was an
altogether different matter. By the late summer, Mountbatten's staff at

Command Operations numbered more than 350, including dozens of Americans. Combined Operations had grown from a minuscule unit to Dickie's fiefdom. Although on paper Vice Admiral Lieutenant General Air Marshal Mountbatten answered to the Chiefs of Staff, he in fact had been granted a unique measure of power that he exercised almost unilaterally. Brooke didn't think much of his command qualifications, and he thought even less of many of his schemes. Yet Dickie charmed many, including Franklin Roosevelt, who, as a former naval person himself and the scion of seafarers, liked the cut of Dickie's jib. Lady Emerald Cunard, the queen of London's hostesses, did not, and offered to Jock Colville that Mountbatten "was one of the most tedious men she knew; he thought a mask of superficial charm could compensate for never having read a book." In fact, in the coming months, Churchill was to give Dickie far more significant commands, in Burma, and later in India. He had earned Churchill's confidence and, most important, his absolute loyalty. That's all he needed.[309]

Churchill later wrote that valuable lessons were learned at Dieppe, that the Canadians had not died in vain. But the British chiefs should not have needed a debacle like Dieppe to learn the lessons; they were paid to plan, not to experiment. The maxims of fire support and overwhelming force that Mountbatten violated were well known, including by Churchill, who in this case did not pay his usual attention to the smallest of details. The raid was a complete failure, and the many lives sacrificed in attempting it were lost with no tangible result. Yet Brooke had discussed the plan during at least two staff meetings and had voiced no dissenting opinion at the time. Only when the butcher's bill was tallied did Brooke confide to his diary that "for such an enterprise" the total casualties—three thousand out of five thousand men—were "far too heavy." Usually quick to denigrate Mountbatten, Brooke did not. Nor did Churchill, whose first concern was that his new Eighth Army commander, Bernard Montgomery, might have had a hand in planning the debacle before departing England for Cairo. He had not. In fact, the raid was originally scheduled for early July, but foul weather and German aircraft attacks had forced its postponement. Montgomery, at the time, advised that it be permanently scrubbed. Montgomery bore no responsibility for Dieppe, and Mountbatten escaped taking any. But Beaverbrook took the slaughter of his fellow Canadians hard, and for the remainder of his life loathed Dickie Mountbatten.[310]

After almost thirty-six months of war, the only general Churchill could bring himself to pay tribute to was not British, but Erwin Rommel, who he anointed "a great general" in front of a very surprised House of Commons. The British government that summer conducted a survey in order to gauge the public's opinion of the army, which, Mollie Panter-Downes wrote, had never been accorded the kudos bestowed upon the Royal Navy and Royal Air Force. In one of the questions, homeowners were asked to name the war's "outstanding general." The government presumed respondents would offer the name of a British general. A distressingly high percentage of those surveyed answered "Rommel." England and Churchill liked a "first-class performer." Yet Churchill's respect for Rommel went only so far. Before departing Cairo, he issued orders to Alexander and Montgomery. They were to "take or destroy at the earliest opportunity the German-Italian army commanded by Field Marshal Rommel."[311]

Late on August 23, Churchill, Dr. Wilson, and Harriman boarded *Commando* in Cairo for the run to Gibraltar, with Brooke and his staff following fifteen minutes later in a B-24 Liberator. The fourteen-hour flight took Churchill over the desert and French North Africa and out to sea, where under low clouds they ran just thirty feet above the Mediterranean. According to the captain's reckoning, Gibraltar should have heaved into view, but a heavy mist hung low over the water. The Rock was invisible. Churchill, as was his habit on final approaches, climbed into the cockpit. After a glance out the window, he voiced his fear that they were going to crash into Gibraltar. Vanderkloot, busy at the controls, muttered a few words of encouragement, and flew on. After several anxious minutes, Churchill recalled, the plane "flew into clear air, and up towered the great precipice of Gibraltar." Vanderkloot's reckoning was spot on. Once they were all on dry land, Churchill's military bodyguards, fearing an assassination attempt, confined him to Governor's House. He would have none of it, and proposed disguising himself as an Egyptian demimondain or an American tourist with a toothache (presumably with a knotted bandage around his head) in order to tour the fortress. But in Governor's House he stayed, where over lunch he made clear that he would rather be in Egypt, on the front lines, especially were Rommel to attack within days, which according to Ultra he would do. But he was the prime minister, not a field marshal, and his place was in London, not on the line. Late in the afternoon, angry at having to fly from, not toward, the pending battle, he boarded his plane.[312]

Rommel attacked on August 31. "What I now needed," Montgomery later wrote, "was a battle which would be fought in accordance with my ideas." He got exactly that. Rommel's plans called for turning the Eighth Army's southern flank, above the Qattara Depression, much as he had turned Ritchie's flank on the Gazala Line three months before. Montgomery, anticipating that tactic, fortified the Alam-el Halfa ridge to his rear with an entire infantry division along with dug-in artillery. Then he massed four hundred tanks in front of the ridge, intending to let Rommel flail against his protected left flank. Rommel expected Montgomery to counterattack, at which time he planned to swing past Montgomery's flank and drive through the center of the Eighth Army. When Montgomery refused Rommel's gambit, the German cabled his Mediterranean commander, Field Marshal Albert Kesselring, "The swine will not attack." Actually, Montgomery's command of just two weeks—"brave but baffled" Churchill had called the Eighth Army—was not yet ready to attack, but they were ready to defend their turf. One of Montgomery's first orders to his troops was that if attacked, they would not withdraw. Like the Spartans at Thermopylae, "We would fight on the ground we now held, and if we couldn't stay there alive, we would stay there dead." Rommel learned by September 3 what those who knew Monty had long known: Bernard Montgomery fought battles on his terms and his terms only. By September 4, Rommel had punched himself out against the Alam-el Halfa lines. The two opposing armies settled again into a dusty and belligerent stasis, with two critical differences between this standoff and all the others since 1941. The RAF had established overwhelming air superiority, and the three hundred new Sherman tanks had arrived to add muscle to Montgomery's army. Rommel, in desperate need of the men, gasoline, and tanks that Hitler had promised, would have to make do with what he had.[313]

Churchill, enthused by the Eighth Army's gallant stand, but impatient as always, pestered Brooke for an early *offensive* stroke by Montgomery. Churchill, Brooke told his diary, "started all his worst arguments about generals only thinking about themselves and their reputations and never attacking until matters were a certainty." Monty, not yet prepared to go on the offensive, stood his ground, against both Rommel and Churchill. And so Churchill, too, learned what Rommel had gleaned at Alam-el Halfa.[314]

Early October brought messages from Stalin that worrisomely implied a deteriorating Red Army position. The Luftwaffe had established a two-to-one air superiority in Russia. Stalin requested five hundred fighter planes per month—more than 10 percent of American production—to remedy the situation. Implicit in the Luftwaffe's air superiority was verification of Stalin's argument that RAF bombing of Western Europe had done nothing to take the pressure off Russia. In fact, the Americans had yet to drop a single bomb on Germany, whereas the Luftwaffe by early October had destroyed most of Stalingrad.

Paulus's Sixth Army had been fighting within the city limits for a month and had destroyed the Red October and Tractor factories. All that remained for Hitler to secure his victory was for Paulus to reach the banks of the Volga and hold his ground. The possibility of Stalin negotiating a separate peace with Germany once again dominated Churchill's thoughts. Montgomery, meanwhile, was not yet ready to attack in the desert. The tanks he needed had been sent to Russia, but not enough to placate Stalin, who asked for eight thousand more *per month,* far more than America produced. In the Atlantic, the U-boats were still sending more tonnage to the bottom than the Allies could replace. With the need to deploy all available destroyers out to protect the Torch fleet, which was then readying to sail from America and Britain, no further convoys to Russia could be contemplated. Stalin, in need of 500,000 tons of supplies per month (about seventy shiploads), accused the British again, as he had in the summer, of stealing food, weapons, and matériel that the Red Army needed. As if to validate Stalin's paranoia, the British and Americans canceled the October convoy to Murmansk, this *after* Stalin pleaded for more help. The situation in the Mediterranean was no better. Malta was down to less than two weeks' supply of food, leading Brooke to lament to his diary, "God knows how we shall keep Malta alive." Churchill, meanwhile, prodded Brooke to prod Alexander and Montgomery into launching their attack, well before they were ready, in Brooke's estimation. To his diary, Brooke offered, "It is a regular disease he [Churchill] suffers from, this frightful impatience to get an attack launched."[315]

As Churchill waited for the curtain to go up in Egypt, Eleanor Roosevelt arrived in London for a three-week visit. Like Harriman, she came bearing a Virginia ham. During her stay she and Clementine conducted exhaustive (and exhausting) tours of wrecked neighborhoods, RAF bases, and air-raid shelters. When she met with a contingent of black American troops, she "liked it when their officer, white, insisted that his men were the best in the army." The First Lady, a political activist, was the sort of woman men of Churchill's generation usually beheld from afar, other than when the suffragettes had pushed their way into manly venues where they did not belong. Churchill understood Mrs. Roosevelt to be politically significant, and not merely because she was the wife of the president. A Gallup poll had found that for every two Americans who thought the First Lady talked too much, three "approved of her courage and ability to speak out." Eleanor Roosevelt regularly and with passion advised her husband on matters of policy, including the matter of blacks serving alongside whites in the U.S. military. Her prodding in that regard had brought results. George Marshall pledged to Roosevelt that blacks would make up 10 percent of the troops sent to Britain.[316]

That ratio engendered resentment among many of the 90 percent of American troops who served alongside blacks. Eden tried to persuade Eisenhower to cease the influx of black soldiers, not because HMG or Britons harbored racist beliefs but because white Americans were regularly beating the hell out of black Americans on the streets of London. And the need to find separate quarters for black and white Americans placed a further burden on the atrophied stocks of housing. Eisenhower was only obeying a directive from the Adjutant General's Office that ordered "wherever possible separate sleeping accommodations be provided for Negro soldiers" but in all other regards they be treated as the equals of white soldiers. In fact, they were not. American dining facilities were segregated; black American women were brought over to staff the roving Red Cross canteens that served blacks. The British people, for the most part, accepted blacks in their midst more readily than did the Americans, especially American officers, all of whom were white and many of whom refused to dine in restaurants that served blacks. British villagers were especially welcoming of the blacks. One pub owner, disgusted by the behavior of white Americans, placed a sign in his window: "For the use of the British and coloured Americans only." But in London, to placate white Yanks (who were flush with dollars), many restaurants banned black Americans, and by doing so inadvertently closed the doors on British citizens. When a black official from the Colonial Office was refused service at his favorite restaurant after American officers complained to the proprietor, the repercussions reached all the way to the cabinet, where, after pondering the incident, Churchill commented, "That's all right, if he brings a banjo they'll think he's one of the band."[317]

Something other than precise analysis affected Churchill's opinions of all peoples other than English-speaking. He shared with the Western press and much of the English-speaking world a condescending attitude toward people who were of other than Anglo-Saxon ancestry. Churchill's memos, his dinner-table asides, even his public addresses, are rife with references to Japs, Wops, Frogs, and Huns, often modified with such choice adjectives as "foul," "filthy," "wretched," and "nasty." His friends, family, and colleagues expressed themselves likewise: Sir Alexander Cadogan's diary entries are xenophobic romps, peppered with demeaning references to just about everybody of any nationality other than English—this from the permanent secretary of the Foreign Office, responsible during the war for vetting the legal niceties of Britain's foreign affairs, including the wording of the Atlantic Charter, parent document to the United Nations. Cadogan considered the Slavs to be "poor dears," the Iraqis "filthy," and the Japanese "monkeys." The usually polite and progressive Harold Nicolson referred to "the Japanese" when he contemplated Japan in his diary, until, that is, Japan began trouncing the British in Asia, after which Nicolson wrote of the "monkey men." Lord Cherwell despised Jews. Even Clementine could demean with the best of them. In a late 1941 letter to Winston, who at the time was America-bound on board the *Duke of York*, Clementine wrote words of encouragement: "Well my beloved Winston—May God keep you and inspire you to make good plans with the president. It's a horrible World at present, Europe over-run by the Nazi hogs, & the Far East by yellow Japanese lice.... Tender Love & thoughts, Clemmie." Such were the times.[318]

Churchill called peoples of African ancestry "blackamoors," and he didn't much like them. Once, late in life, he asked his physician, Lord Moran, what happened when blacks got measles; could the rash be spotted? When Moran replied that blacks suffered a high mortality rate from measles, Churchill offered, "Well there are plenty left. They've got a high rate of production." When, during his second premiership, his cabinet debated the adoption of new laws limiting West Indian immigration, Churchill proposed his suggestion for a national motto: "Keep England White."[319]

The First Lady therefore arrived in England during a difficult period for race relations. Normally, she would have spoken her mind. But to the relief of Secretary of War Stimson, her behavior in Britain was "very temperate." She was there to improve morale, not to reform the armed forces. Speaking her mind to Churchill was another matter. When, during a dinner at No. 10, the First Lady took him to task for first backing Franco and then, after Franco showed his Fascist stripes, not backing the Loyalists during the Spanish Civil War, Churchill growled that had the Loyalists won, the first heads to roll would belong to people such as herself and her husband. Mrs. Roosevelt responded by saying she didn't care whether she lost her head. "Well," Churchill snarled, "I don't want to lose mine." Clementine did not help matters when she offered that Mrs. Roosevelt was correct. As Churchill fumed, Clementine separated the combatants, announcing that it was time for the ladies to adjourn to the sitting room and leave the men alone with their brandies and cigars. Of her dining experiences with Churchill, Mrs. Roosevelt later wrote, "I found the P.M. not easy to talk to."[320]

Churchill's behavior could be forgiven given the events unfolding in the Atlantic and in the desert, although in truth he had treated Mrs. Roosevelt no differently than any guest. Of dining with Churchill, Harold Nicolson wrote, "Winston is bad at putting people at ease.... There is a mask of boredom and another mask or film of obstinacy, as if he were saying, 'These people bore me and I shall refuse to be polite.'" Yet, suddenly Churchill would "cease thinking of something else, and the film will part and the sun comes out." The First Lady saw the sun come out at Chequers, when she was treated to the spectacle of Churchill playing with his two-year-old grandson, little Winston. "They sat on the floor," she later wrote, "and played a game and the resemblance was ridiculous." The scene reminded her of the story of the lady who, catching sight of Churchill and little Winston, remarked to Churchill on the resemblance. Churchill looked up and replied, "You are quite wrong, I resemble every baby." He also showed the First Lady a room that he intended to have redecorated in order to accommodate the special needs of her husband, who, Churchill hoped, would soon visit England.[321]

Late on the moonlit night of October 23, almost a thousand pieces of British heavy artillery commenced firing along the El Alamein front. The barrage, which continued into the early hours of the twenty-fourth, served notice to Erwin Rommel that Bernard Montgomery was on his way. At first light, the Highlanders screamed their ancient battle cry, *Caberfeidh*,* as the skirl of their bagpipes rent the silence. They attacked through the blowing grit of a dry desert dawn. By daylight, the Eighth Army—190,000 men, 1,400 anti-tank guns, and almost 1,000 tanks—smashed into Rommel's lines across a six-mile front. The tanks soon stopped while sappers cleared narrow paths—just wide enough to accommodate tank treads—through the half million landmines Rommel had buried at his front. It soon became apparent that the British possessed too few sappers and too few mine detectors. But overall, numbers were with the British. On the northern, coastal end of the German lines (Montgomery's real objective), the XV Panzer Corps was outnumbered at least six to one, in both tanks and men. Panzer Army Africa, more than half of which was made up of Italians, was outmanned and outgunned by almost two to one. To make matters worse for the Germans, Rommel had taken a sick leave weeks earlier and was at that moment resting in a hospital bed in Semmering, a lovely town perched on the pine-forested slopes of the southern Austrian Alps, as far removed from the war as any hamlet in Europe. At about noon, Hitler telephoned Rommel personally with the news from North Africa. "The situation looks very black," the Führer offered. "Would you be willing to go back?"[322]

Rommel's replacement in the field, General Georg Stumme, had assumed the British would attack the southern end of his lines, thirty miles from the sea, in part because the terrain was more favorable and in part

---

* "The antlers of the deer."

because Montgomery had positioned three dummy regiments in the south and had begun construction of a dummy waterline to the dummy forces. Stumme, in turn, lacked the gasoline to move his tanks about at will, north to south and back. He would have to stand and fight where he was. By late morning, under the onslaught of RAF fighters and Montgomery's massed artillery, Stumme found himself completely cut off from almost all of his forces and commanders, north and south. By day's end, Stumme was dead, felled by a massive coronary. Montgomery's field guns raked the German panzer deployments, to horrific effect. Artillery, as Churchill had urged a year earlier, had finally found its place on the desert battlefield. Rommel, returning on October 25 to find a rout in progress, stanched his ruptured lines enough to blunt Montgomery's initial thrusts. Rommel placed his Italian infantry between German mechanized units, in part to protect the Italians, in part to ensure that they remained on the battlefield. Yet unless he was resupplied, his diminishing numbers of men, tanks, aircraft, and artillery could only add up to retreat. He needed gasoline most of all. He radioed his status to Hitler—a message that the Bletchley crowd soon deciphered and Montgomery soon read.[323]

In London, Churchill, desperate for the latest news, badgered his generals without respite. For the first two days, Churchill simply asked Brooke how Montgomery was doing. When Montgomery's progress stalled, Churchill's tone changed. He prepared a stinging telegram for Alexander in which he sought answers to the apparent collapse of the offensive—a conclusion he reached after chatting with Eden over whisky rather than consulting with his military advisers over maps. Brooke recalled the unpleasantness in his memoirs: "What, he [Churchill] asked, is *my* Monty doing now, allowing the battle to peter out. (Monty was always *my* Monty when he was out of favor.)" Why, asked Churchill, had Montgomery "told us he would be through in seven days if all he intended to do was fight a half-hearted battle?" For Churchill, more than a line in the desert was at stake. A by-election weeks earlier had gone against the government by a margin of 66 to 34 percent, a stunning yet symbolic rebuke. Churchill had convinced Cripps, who was threatening resignation, to stay on as Speaker until the battle in the desert was finished, win or lose. A defeat in the desert would very likely result in Churchill being known henceforth as the former prime minister.[324]

For seven days Monty fought, and for seven days he had nothing to show but almost eight thousand wounded and two thousand killed, including the son of Churchill's first true love of almost five decades earlier, Pamela Plowden. The Eighth Army could not punch through the minefield, which had become a no-man's-land. Montgomery threw British and Australian tanks into the minefield with results that evoked the slaughter of the Great

War. His divisional commanders advised he quit the battle and regroup. Having none of it, he threatened to sack those who lacked the appropriate aggressive spirit and replace them with fighters. He understood that if he could not win by fast and bold strokes, he would win though attrition. He could afford to trade tank for tank and man for man until he carried the day. And so he continued to feed his men and tanks into the maw. The next few days would mark a turning point, one way or another, for Churchill, for Britain, for the future conduct of the war.

If Montgomery failed, Torch could not succeed, at least according to plan, not with the British Eighth Army tied down in Egypt, 1,600 miles from the Allied invasion force. In that case, Hitler, on his Russian front, would gain invaluable weeks, if not months, to drive farther into the Caucasus and to pour forces into Stalingrad with no need to watch his back. If Montgomery failed or if Stalingrad fell, Europe-first might become Europe-maybe for the Americans. Stalemate or defeat at El Alamein would exact a heavy political as well as a military price. Churchill informed Brooke that the office of prime minister would go to somebody else if Rommel held his desert position. In that case, Sir Stafford Cripps—who in private regularly deprecated Churchill's war record, but as leader of the House was forced to explain the defeats to Parliament—might start serving vegetarian dinners in a new residence, No. 10 Downing Street. All depended upon Montgomery. Churchill was "finding the suspense almost unbearable," Bracken told Dr. Wilson as the world waited for news from the desert.[325]

On October 30, thanks to Ultra decrypts and on the advice of his lieutenants, Montgomery shifted his main thrust from the coast about ten miles to the south. It was the sort of improvisation Montgomery disliked, but it worked. Rommel, by shifting his armor to the far north, to counter Montgomery's initial strike, had weakened his southern sector. By then, the Desert Fox had fewer than four dozen tanks remaining fit for battle, and they were almost out of fuel. Two ships carrying gasoline to Rommel were sunk as they approached Tobruk, again thanks to Ultra. Montgomery pressed on. His New Zealanders broke Rommel's lines on November 2. Rommel counterattacked in a furious two-hour tank assault, but realizing he was waging a battle of attrition he could only lose, he called off the attack. Early the next day, he left behind a rearguard and turned west. Hopes ran high, Churchill later wrote, that the moment had arrived for the "annihilation" of Rommel's army. Rommel, too, expected as much, as he raced for Tripoli. But the late autumn rains had arrived. Rather than compete with foul weather and washed-out desert tracks, Monty, after a desultory twenty-hour chase, called for a one-day halt. British fighter pilots who were tracking the Germans and calling in the enemy's positions were dumbfounded. Where was the final, fatal strike? Where was the Eighth Army?[326]

Just after he began his retreat, Rommel received a direct order from Hitler: "Stand fast, yield not a yard of room." Sheer will could prevail, the Führer believed, and not for the first time in history, and "as to your troops, you can show them no other road than to victory or death [*Sieg oder Tod*]." Mussolini, completely misreading the situation, sent a telegraph congratulating Rommel on "the successful counter-attack." Rommel's lieutenant, General Ritter von Thoma, called Hitler's directive "a piece of unparalleled madness." Rommel paused for twenty hours in order to adhere to the spirit if not the letter of the order. Then the Desert Fox and his few dozen tanks—soon to be pursued by ten times as many—ran for Libya. Left behind in the flinty scrabble were almost six thousand dead Germans and Italians, their corpses already blackening in the desert heat. British intelligence officers wandered among the bodies and yanked from pockets postcards and love letters from home, written in German and Italian, to sons and lovers and husbands: "We are so glad you are now in beautiful Egypt"; "May Saint Dominic protect you." As night fell the discarded letters scudded across the desert on the breezes, as if following the survivors to sanctuary.[327]

Churchill, elated by the news from Egypt (and a handwritten congratulatory note from the King), told luncheon companions on November 6 that Rommel's army had been cut from its positions, like a limpet is cut from a rock. Slashing the air, as if with a knife, Churchill asked, "And what happens to a limpet when it is cut from its rock. It dies a miserable death." But not for nothing was Rommel called the Desert Fox. He had escaped and would live to fight another day, giving the lie to Machiavelli's maxim that the fox cannot outrun the wolves. The Italian infantry were not as fortunate as their mechanized German brethren. To evacuate their own, the Germans commandeered what little transportation the Italians had. "The Italians," Churchill told the Commons on November 10, "were left to perish in the waterless desert or surrender as they are doing." The Battle of Egypt was won.[328]

On the final day of October, U-559 was depth-charged by the Royal Navy and forced to the surface off Port Said. Its crew was taken aboard British cutters while three tars boarded the submarine and made for the radio room. The scene played out almost exactly as it had aboard U-110 the previous year. U-559 foundered and went down, taking two of the British sailors with her. But the third managed to escape with the boat's codebooks and Enigma machine, complete with the fourth wheel that had stymied

Bletchley for almost a year. The British now held the key to unlocking Dönitz's naval communications. With that month's U-boat codes in hand, Bletchley began reading German radio traffic even as the Torch armada lingered off North Africa. But the advantage vanished when Berlin changed the codes later in the month. Bletchley's wizards found themselves once again stymied. The captured Enigma machine ensured a break-through, sooner or later, but later would not do. Dönitz now had more than two hundred U-boats available for duty in the North Atlantic. He sent one hundred or more on patrol during each of the next six months, more than twice as many as at the start of the year. British losses alone pushed over 710,000 tons in November, the worst of any month of the war; 117 ships went down that month, far more than could be made up by new construction.[329]

On the political front, Cripps, having had his fill as leader of the House, resigned and finally agreed to take the job Churchill had offered early in the year—minister of aircraft production. Cripps's flame had flared in February; El Alamein had snuffed it out, along with any hopes he harbored of leading the nation after the war. Cripps, an American newsweekly offered, had proven himself "politically inept," and had been adroitly kicked by Churchill onto the sidelines. Eden took over the leadership of the House, while keeping the Foreign Office. Beaverbrook, meanwhile, under whom Cripps had refused to serve, returned to London after spending the summer in America, where he had adroitly pushed for a second front while simultaneously defending Churchill against criticism that he wasn't pursuing a second front fast enough. The Beaver was back, and a regular dinner guest at No. 10.[330]

On November 6, as Churchill conjured up images of limpets over lunch, the Torch invasion fleet—more than 650 transports, tankers, hospital ships, and 172 warships, carrying 90,000 men—made for the African coast. It had been at sea for more than two weeks. The ships had sailed from Canada, Hampton Roads, and Britain, and had arranged themselves into three task forces. The Western would land Patton's 34,000 men on the Atlantic coast of Morocco. On the fifth, the Center and Eastern task forces had run past Gibraltar on their way to Oran and Algiers. The armada expected a hot welcome from U-boats, but as the hours passed, not an enemy periscope was seen. The Germans, as the British learned from Ultra decrypts, did not know the fleet was on its way. Bletchley also passed on the astounding (and welcome) news that the Germans had no plan in effect

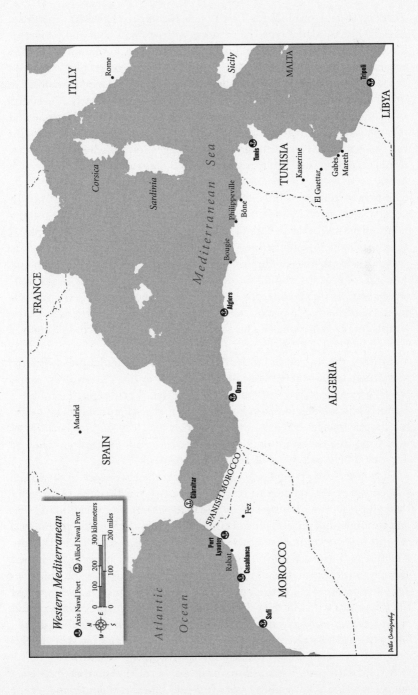

Western Mediterranean

● Axis Naval Port ⊕ Allied Naval Port

N
W E
S

0   100   200   300 kilometers

0   100   200 miles

ITALY

Rome

FRANCE

SPAIN

Madrid

Corsica

Sardinia

Mediterranean Sea

Sicily

MALTA

Tripoli

LIBYA

Tunis ⊕

TUNISIA

Kasserine

El Guettar

Gabès
Mareth

Philippeville

Bône

Bougie

Algiers ●

Oran ●

Gibraltar ⊕

SPANISH MOROCCO

Fez

Port
Lyautey ●

Rabat
Casablanca ●

MOROCCO

ALGERIA

Safi ●

*Atlantic
Ocean*

Dake Cartography

to either destroy or blockade Gibraltar—the key to the entire enterprise, as the Allies needed to run the straits in order to first land and then reinforce the Central and Eastern task forces. But, as Churchill had learned earlier in the year in Egypt, Bletchley was not always correct.

Eisenhower wrote in his memoirs: "British Gibraltar made possible the invasion of northwest Africa." This was so because in early November 1942, the Allies occupied not one other piece of real estate in Europe and the western Mediterranean from which an invasion of North Africa might be launched. The Rock was blessed with a deep harbor where Allied warships could refuel and re-arm, and also was home to a small airfield, which in the weeks before the invasion was crammed full of fighter planes—fourteen fighter squadrons of sixteen craft each—and drums of gasoline. To Eisenhower's dismay, the airstrip was separated from Spain by nothing more substantial than a barbed-wire fence, against which "almost physically...leaned any number of Axis agents." The Spanish government was leaning, as well, toward Hitler. In order to put troops ashore at Oran and Algiers, Allied ships would have to sail through the thirty-mile-long gauntlet between Spain and Spanish Morocco that is the Strait of Gibraltar, less than ten miles wide in places. Were Spanish guns sited on either side of the straits to take those ships under fire, Torch would be doused. Eisenhower could only hope that the Spanish and the French in North Africa remained aloof from the fray and that the Axis presumed the buildup in Gibraltar was a prelude to the relief of Malta (as in fact they did). Regardless, sound strategy called for the Axis to bomb the Rock. Each night, Eisenhower waited for bombings that never came. Each night, Allied soldiers found fitful sleep in the twenty-five miles of tunnels cut deep within the Jurassic limestone, and each morning, they awoke "puzzled, even astonished," to find that no German planes had drubbed the Rock.[331]

During the early planning stages for Torch, the bottleneck of the straits was considered so dangerous by the Americans that they refused to send their ships into the Mediterranean lest they be trapped in that inland sea. Safety first had never been one of Churchill's dictates. Secrecy, not danger, was the first concern of the British. Churchill and Brooke believed that the Americans, inexperienced in such operations, might prove loose-lipped enough to jeopardize the entire plan. American trepidation and ability to keep a secret were but two concerns among many. Churchill also expected the Italians to send out their fleet, still dangerous with six battleships and dozens of supporting warships. Eisenhower—mistakenly—thought the Germans had two aircraft carriers with which to harass the Allied invasion fleet. Darlan and the French fleet were always a wild card.[332]

A vexing question remained up to the eve of the invasion: Did the Germans and Italians have any idea of where the Allies were going, and when?

Brooke, for his part, considered Eisenhower's headquarters to be "conspicuously leaky as regards information and secrets." The unexpected could always be depended upon to happen. In late September, British intelligence had learned that the body of a British officer killed in an airplane crash off the coast of Spain had washed up on a Spanish beach. The dead man carried letters in his tunic that contained enough veiled references to the invasion to clarify for the Germans where the invasion was to take place—if, that is, the Spanish allowed the Germans access to the body. But the Spanish handed the body over to the British, who deduced from beach sand still wedged between the tunic's buttons and buttonholes that the letters had most likely not been extracted from the tunic. The episode troubled London, but it also served to stimulate furtive imaginations within Combined Operations, where the idea took hold of misleading the Germans by planting a body carrying false information on a European beach. The following year the British would do just that with a ploy aptly named Operation Mincemeat.[333]

Eisenhower's main problem as his army neared the African coasts was not compromised intelligence or strictly military, but political. He later wrote that Torch was "a most peculiar venture of armed forces into the field of international politics; we were invading a neutral country to create a friend." Such an action has not, traditionally, been a recipe for friendship. The Americans had known for weeks that the chances for a successful invasion would be greatly increased by having a Frenchman of great stature on their side and on the ground in North Africa when the landings took place, someone who could rally both pro- and anti-Vichy elements and, most important, 230,000 Vichy troops and their officers. But the Allies had done little in the way of addressing the question of who that would be. Pétain or some other authority within the Vichy government would not do; the Americans, having pulled their ambassador in April, no longer recognized Vichy as a legitimate government. America's formerly cozy relationship with Vichy was resented by many in France, and viscerally by the Fighting French, yet de Gaulle, around whom Frenchmen now rallied, was loathed by the Americans and had not even been told of Torch. Representatives of Admiral Jean Darlan had sent messages to the senior American diplomat in Algiers, Robert Murphy, to the effect that the Germans suspected something might soon occur on the Moroccan coast and when it did, they, the Germans, intended to occupy French North Africa. Murphy and Eisenhower concluded that Darlan might be willing to "play ball" and bring the French fleet over to the Allies. Yet Washington and London distrusted Darlan more than all other Frenchmen but Laval. Then, almost on the eve of the invasion, the Americans discovered General Henri Giraud, a brave and decent man. Captured during the fall of France,

Giraud had escaped a German fortress to Vichy France, where he was allowed to live under house arrest only after he promised loyalty to Vichy. He was senior to de Gaulle in rank and beloved by Frenchmen. He looked every inch the gallant soldier—tall, stiff, plainspoken. He was also vain and stupid.[334]

Eisenhower secreted Giraud to Gibraltar by submarine and flying boat on November 7, and that evening as the invasion fleets neared the beaches, he made his pitch to the Frenchman to accompany the Allied forces to North Africa, and there to join the Allies in the first step on the road to the liberation of France. Giraud eagerly embraced the concept, but with two caveats. Honor demanded that he must assume overall command of the entire enterprise, including American and British troops; and the supporting invasion must be launched directly into France. Eisenhower, taken aback, thanked the general for his support but told him his conditions were quite impossible to meet. Giraud was adamant; he must command. They talked well into the evening, but Eisenhower simply could not bring Giraud around to the fact that a Frenchman could not command the Allied armies, in which not a single Frenchman served. The discussion, Eisenhower later wrote, was "one of my most distressing interviews of the war."[335]

That evening in London, the Soviet ambassador to the European governments in exile gave a reception. There, a Czech diplomat took one of de Gaulle's colleagues aside and whispered, "It's for tonight." A telephone call was placed to de Gaulle, who was awakened at home and took the call in his pajamas. Thus, de Gaulle learned that Anglo-American armies were about to land on French soil. His reaction was typical, if understandable: "I hope the Vichy people throw them into the sea! You don't go into France like a pack of burglars."[336]

Churchill was at Chequers that night. Since early October, Ultra decrypts had told him that Field Marshal "Smiling Albert" Kesselring—whose *Luftflotte* 2 had almost brought Fighter Command to bay in 1940—knew that the British were up to something big, but he didn't know when or where and so could not deploy his aircraft to best effect. Many in the German high command were convinced that the Allied destination was northern Norway, which it might have been had Churchill gotten his way with Operation Jupiter. Admiral Raeder, in 1940, had predicted Churchill would strike French North Africa, but he had been ignored by Hitler and the army sycophants at OKW. Most in Berlin thought the attack zone would be the Mediterranean, but not the southern shore. Why land there if the objective was to fight the German army in Europe? Armies fought at close quarters, on land, not from across seas. That had been George Marshall's argument exactly, until Brooke and Churchill—two saltwater strategists—wore him down with relentless argument.

Thus, while the Germans and Italians scanned the sea approaches to Sardinia, Sicily, and Malta, more than three hundred Allied transports and warships, having run the straits, turned southward on their true course. They divided into two streams, the Center force, carrying the American 1st Infantry and 1st Armored Division, on a heading for Oran; and the Eastern, Anglo-American force, bound for Algiers with 23,000 British and 10,000 American troops. Part of the Algerian force—not much greater in size than a division, and wistfully designated British First Army—was ordered to wheel east from Algiers after landing and strike 450 miles to Bizerte and Tunis. Its commander, Lieutenant General Kenneth Anderson, was a blunt, abrasive, and dour Scot given to skepticism that bordered on pessimism. A man of few words, he was nicknamed "Sunshine" by his men. Expecting to be reinforced as he moved east (after all, fully 90 percent of the Torch forces were at his rear), he concluded that he might well reach Tunis in two weeks, before the Germans could reinforce the city and dispute the issue. The first hours of the invasion certainly justified his unusual spate of optimism. Only a single American transport suffered any damage, after being torpedoed far out to sea by a stray U-boat. Undeterred, the battalion of soldiers on board climbed into their landing crafts and headed for shore, a hundred-mile journey. Despite the inexperience of the landing-craft crews, the Algerian landings came off the next morning better than any of the planners had hoped for.[337]

Sarah Churchill, commissioned in the Women's Auxiliary Air Force, was assigned to photographic interpretation and intelligence duties at Medmenham, near enough to Chequers for her to hitchhike there to spend weekends with her parents. She arrived at the house late on November 7, to find her father toweling off in his dressing room as Sawyers assembled his evening attire. As Churchill wielded a pair of ivory hairbrushes to part the few remaining hairs on his dome, he turned to Sarah and said, "Do you know, that at this moment six hundred forty-two ships are approaching the coast of North Africa?" "Six hundred forty-*three*," replied Sarah. "How do you know?" he asked. "I've only been working on it for three months," answered Sarah. "Why didn't you tell me?" Churchill asked, his feelings slightly bruised. "I believe there is such a thing as security," Sarah answered. He chuckled, and retold the story at dinner. Some hours later, as father and daughter sat together before the hearth, the clock in the great hall struck one o'clock. At that moment British troops, including Randolph, began to go ashore on the Algiers beaches.[338]

They met virtually no resistance. This was what the planners had hoped for. Torch was a bold plan, and it was extremely risky. No American involved had ever participated in such an operation, and very few had even seen combat. No such "ship-to-shore" invasion had ever before crossed an ocean to reach the target. Except for the Guadalcanal invasion in August, Torch was the first large-scale amphibious operation conducted by American forces in forty-five years. At Algiers all went well, although two British destroyers were sunk in the harbor while trying to put American Rangers ashore. The fighting was finished by late morning, and the city surrendered early that evening. "Well, here we are," Randolph wrote in a letter to his father, "safe and sound." The trump card in the African deck was in the Allies' hands. It had been secured by Churchill's and Brooke's insistence on attacking Algiers.[339]

Then a message from Algiers reached Eisenhower though Admiral Cunningham: "Darlan wants to negotiate." By a stroke of supreme good luck, Admiral Jean Darlan, commander of all Vichy armed forces, was in Algiers, visiting his son, who had contracted poliomyelitis. Just before Eisenhower left London the previous week, Churchill had told him, "If I could meet Darlan, much as I hate him, I would cheerfully crawl a mile on my hands if by doing so I could get him to bring that fleet of his into the circle of Allied forces." To Cunningham, Churchill made his point more bluntly: "Kiss Darlan's stern if you have to, but get the French Navy."[340]

Vichy loyalists contested the assault at Oran, where the naval forces were British and the landing parties American. Two British cutters trying to land American troops at the harbor docks were raked by ferocious fire from French shore batteries. The docks remained in Vichy hands. The fighting continued throughout that day and the next. The defenders awaited orders; they had not heard from Pétain. In effect, America had gone to war against a people who had been allies since Lafayette helped George Washington secure his Great Republic. Herr Dr. Goebbels believed that the entire North African campaign was a "fight between the City and Wall Street for French colonies." Edward R. Murrow and many of his fellow correspondents in North Africa harbored similar suspicions. American policy, Murrow wrote to a friend, "looks like a sort of amateur imperialism, which aims at making the continent safe for the National City Bank."[341]

The Cross of Lorraine had long suspected as much. During lunch on the eighth, Churchill informed de Gaulle of the landings (about which de Gaulle already knew). Yet Churchill, true to his May pledge to hold Madagascar in trust for the French, also turned over the administration of that island to the Free French, in effect a recognition of de Gaulle's claim to constitutional authority. The Americans, meanwhile, to the chagrin of Churchill—and especially Eden—continued to ignore de Gaulle. In fact, having discovered Darlan in Algiers, they were about to actively court him. Early on November 9, Eisenhower put Mark Clark and General Giraud aboard separate planes bound for Algiers in hopes that Clark could bring Darlan and his fleet into

Allied hands while Giraud persuaded the Vichy forces there to lay down their arms. Darlan could not ignore Clark when the American appeared at his villa. But the Vichy commanders in Oran ignored Giraud; they had taken an oath of loyalty to Pétain. With de Gaulle consigned to irrelevancy by the Americans and hated by Vichy, only Darlan remained as a possible peacemaker. He was the worst of all possible choices.[342]

On the ninth, the Germans volunteered to Pétain to put men and planes into Tunisia in order to "help" Vichy defend its sovereign territory. Pétain had no choice but to agree to this "favor." The first Germans arrived in Tunis by air that evening, followed by squadrons of Stukas and Messerschmitts. Then, by ship, came Mark IV tanks, the twenty-five-ton workhorses of the German army, armed with 75mm cannons, deadlier than any American or British tank and manned by experienced crews who had learned their trade on the Russian front. And by ship came heavy artillery, German 88s, the deadliest field guns ever built.[343]

On the Moroccan coast, where Patton's troops had come ashore at three points—the port of Safi, Fedala, and Mehdia—the weather and landing crafts proved as troublesome and deadly as the enemy. The seas, roiled for a week by storms, calmed somewhat in the last hours before the landings but not enough. The first lesson learned, before a boot hit the beach, was that American landing craft of the era—Higgins Boats—were obsolete. They were made of plywood and without bow ramps, and the troops on board disembarked by jumping over the sides. Dozens of Americans drowned when they jumped into the turbulent waters; Patton himself pulled at least one body from the surf. Tanks and trucks were swept off the flimsy, flat-bottomed barges that carried them. After avoiding the enemy and without the loss of a single ship across the thousands of miles of ocean, Patton's command lost more tanks and trucks in the landings than it did during the day's combat with the defenders.[344]

Patton's troops had the benefit of five hours of darkness to cover their drive to the beaches. The American naval historian Samuel Eliot Morison, who served as an officer aboard one of the covering cruisers, described the night as quiet, with not a light to be seen, the African shore "veiled in clouds and hushed in silence." An offshore breeze carried "the smell of charcoal fires and parched dry grass" out to the ships. An hour passed, and another. Then a beam from a French searchlight shot seaward. Within minutes a dozen French warships—destroyers, a cruiser, and submarines—sailed to engage the Allied fleet. The American admiral Kent Hewitt issued his pre-arranged signal for a general engagement: "Play ball." And then came the bursts of machine guns, "blinding gun flashes," and the "crash of heavy ordnance." For the next several hours, the new French battleship *Jean Bart*, not yet entirely fitted out and incapable of sailing but able to use its fifteen-inch guns, waged a furious gun battle with USS *Massachusetts*. By the end of the day, *Jean Bart* was a burned-out wreck, and seven French warships along with three French submarines and a thousand French sailors lay at the bottom of the Atlantic. George Patton watched the battle unfold from the deck of USS *Augusta;* the landing craft that was to have taken Patton ashore was blown into splinters by the concussion from *Augusta*'s guns. Eisenhower, meanwhile, was unaware of any of the goings-on in Morocco. He had lost all radio contact with both Patton and the navy when the shock waves from *Augusta*'s heavy guns knocked out all of his radio equipment as well.[345]

Once ashore, Patton's 34,000 men received a hot reception from Vichy forces, a resistance spurred in part by Roosevelt's decision to broadcast a message of peace to the Vichy French in Morocco hours *before* Patton came ashore, thereby giving the defenders time to prepare. In Rabat, the resident governor general, Auguste Paul Noguès, his honor at stake, ordered an attack against the invaders. Noguès commanded at least 60,000 men in the protectorate, including several hundred fighter pilots. Fortunately for Patton's men, the French pilots who arrived over the Fedala beaches were not the cream of the Vichy air force and missed the beach entirely on their strafing runs. On the other hand, the American navy had put many of Patton's troops on the wrong beaches, where U.S. Navy planes proceeded to bomb them, as did some elements of Patton's artillery. The scene was utter chaos. While curious Arabs wandered among the wreck-age, green American troops fired at shadows or, having lost their weapons in the surf, crouched behind trees. Some of the troops carried a new weapon. Alan Brooke called it a "rocket-gun" after watching a demonstra-tion in June; the Yanks called it a bazooka. Indicative of the confusion on the beaches, the first bazooka fired in anger at a French tank missed its target and slew a nearby tree. Patton's tanks could not communicate; their radio batteries had drained during the sea voyage. His signal corps was in total disarray. The plan called for Patton to take Casablanca with the con-sent of the citizens, not to have to conquer it, for the simple reason that he might not be able to take the city should the Vichy put up enough of a fight against the untested Americans. With that in mind, Churchill had warned Roosevelt, "The first victory we have to win is to avoid a battle." But by noon on the eighth, Patton was in the thick of a bloody battle, and it was not going his way.[346]

The next day, Eisenhower, desperately trying to bring Darlan around to the Allied side, discovered a fact of French military life long known to Churchill: "the traditional French demand for a cloak of legality over any action they might take." French generals, Eisenhower later wrote, had cast their surrender in 1940 as "merely the act of loyal soldiers obeying the legal orders of their civil superiors." Honor was thus preserved. Churchill, in explaining the Darlan negotiations to the House, offered a less subtle explanation: "The almighty in His infinite wisdom did not see fit to create Frenchmen in the image of Englishmen." The French need for legal justification—"this peculiar form of French mentality"—stemmed from a belief that "an unbroken chain of lawful command" insulates those in the chain from any recriminations, moral or legal. Pétain resided at the top of the chain. So dominant among Frenchmen was this legalistic mind-set, Churchill told the House, that "if Admiral Darlan had to shoot Marshal Pétain he would no doubt do it in Marshal Pétain's name."[347]

On November 10, before Patton took the battle into the streets of Casablanca, Admiral Darlan ordered a cease-fire throughout the theater. As he was senior military commander on the scene, the order was within his authority. Pétain, exercising *his* authority, immediately rescinded the order and dismissed Darlan.[348]

The next day, in violation of the armistice signed in 1940, Hitler invaded unoccupied France. This freed Darlan entirely from the restraints imposed by law and Gallic honor. With Pétain now virtually a German prisoner, Darlan's orders carried the legal weight to deliver both North Africa and the French navy to the Allies. That morning, the commander of Vichy troops in Casablanca approached Patton's lines carrying a white flag. It was a flag not of surrender or capitulation but only of cease-fire. But it ended the hostilities. Thanks to Darlan, Patton, who had promised Roosevelt and Marshall that he would leave the beach "either a conqueror or a corpse," was ashore to stay. Yet, with Darlan, Eisenhower had on his hands a political poison pill. The Frenchman was universally reviled in Washington and London. Although Darlan had issued the orders that secured Casablanca and Oran, he had yet to give the most critical order of all, the order that the French fleets in Toulon and Dakar make for North Africa.

On the night of November 8, the high holy anniversary of his 1923 Beer Hall Putsch, Adolf Hitler made his yearly address to his brown-shirted cronies in Munich. The Führer spoke at the more elegant *Löwenbräukeller,* the old *Bügerbräukeller* having been bombed in a bungled 1939 assassination

attempt on his life. Hitler informed his audience that Stalingrad, but for a
few pockets of resistance, "was firmly in German hands." The job of erasing the city from the banks of the Volga, he promised, would soon be finished, but to avoid another Verdun, it would be done methodically. After
all, he announced, time was now of no consequence. This was an exaggeration but not an outright lie. After losing twenty divisions during five weeks
of murderous fighting in metropolitan Stalingrad, Paulus's Sixth Army had
reached the Volga in the northern part of the city two days earlier. The
Fourth Panzer Army was just two miles away from the south bank, which,
when secured, would complete the encirclement of the inner city. The first
reports from North Africa, meanwhile, were positive—fierce resistance by
the French on all the beaches, German reinforcements about to depart for
Tunis. Hitler did not disclose that Operation Anton, the occupation of
Vichy France, was set to begin in thirty-six hours. From all appearances,
the tide was still rising under the Third Reich. In fact, during the very hours
Hitler spoke, and while his train got up steam for the journey to his East
Prussian headquarters, and while his loyal brown shirts strutted and swayed
under a thick haze of cigarette smoke on the beer-drenched floors of the
Löwenbräukeller, the Third Reich reached flood tide.[349]

A freezing blue haze drifted low over the Volga that night and the next
morning, a harbinger of the hard freezes that very soon would render the
river a land bridge to Stalingrad. Fifty miles to the north and south of Stalingrad, the number two man in the Red Army after Stalin, Marshal Georgy
Konstantinovich Zhukov, had assembled two gigantic forces made up of
eight infantry and four tank armies. Now Zhukov waited. In a sense, Hitler had spoken the truth to his Munich cronies when he offered that time
was of no consequence. Zhukov had it all on his side, while for the Germans in Stalingrad, it was running out.

When the Germans broke into unoccupied France on November 11, they
drove straight for Toulon, where French naval commanders awaited orders
to scuttle the fleet—two battleships, several heavy cruisers, sixteen submarines, eighteen destroyers—and therefore deny the Nazis a naval force
that might have won them the Mediterranean. Only Darlan could give the
order. He had promised in 1940 that he would never allow the French fleet
to fall into German hands; on that day he made good on his promise. He
ordered the French fleet to bolt Toulon and make for Africa, to join the
Allies. The French naval commanders in Toulon, still loyal to Pétain, chose
to stay in Toulon. By then, the Germans had surrounded the port. Even

were the French captains inclined to obey Darlan, any attempt to do so would result in the Germans commandeering the fleet, which they were in fact drawing up plans to do. For almost two weeks, the French warships rode at anchor and in their slips. On November 27 Hitler struck. It took less than an hour for German tanks and troops to smash into the naval base and make for the dockyard, but that was more than enough time for the French commanders, sure now that they had been betrayed, to issue the orders to scuttle. Almost the entire fleet was sent to the bottom. Darlan, whatever his other faults, had kept his promise.

Reaction to the courtship of Darlan and the marriage of convenience came fast and furiously in Britain, and in America, where Roosevelt liberals, Churchill later wrote, were "agog...at what seemed to them a base and squalid deal with one of our most bitter enemies." Millions of Britons, Mollie Panter-Downes wrote, "are convinced that appeasement of a man of Vichy or a man of Munich smells just about the same, no matter what fancy name you want to call it." Churchill, for his part, thought the military gains achieved by Darlan's cease-fire orders outweighed the political risk. Yet, in a cable to Roosevelt he expressed his conviction that the Darlan deal "can only be a temporary expedient." Roosevelt issued a public defense of Eisenhower; Churchill did not. He spoke to Parliament in Secret Session, where he described Pétain—whose name he pronounced as "Peatayne"—"as an antique defeatist." Roosevelt had not consulted HMG on the Darlan matter, Churchill told the House. Yet, from the standpoint of reaching military objectives and saving the lives of his troops, "General Eisenhower was right" to court Darlan. But in public he accorded Eisenhower no such endorsement. Since the Americans, after all, had insisted that Torch was to be an all-American affair, they could stew in their own juices. Stalin, ever pragmatic, offered his thoughts on the subject to both Churchill and Roosevelt. The value of military diplomacy justified not only the relationship with Darlan, Stalin wrote, "but with the Devil himself and his grandma." Stalin also tossed out a phrase that was being much heard around London: the tide has turned.[350]

The Darlan expedient indeed proved temporary when on Christmas Eve, Darlan, who had managed that year to earn the enmity of de Gaulle, Vichy France, Churchill, Eisenhower, and Hitler, was shot dead by a young French royalist named Ferdinand Bonnier de la Chapelle. Although trained by the SOE, Chapelle was not acting under orders from London. He was tried, convicted, and shot, all in less than two days. The mystery around the murder deepened when it was revealed that MI6 chief Stewart Menzies, having left England for the first time during the war, was dining just a few hundred yards away from Darlan's house. Darlan's last words were said to have been "the British have finally done for me." Whether or not the English had a hand in the murder, Darlan's exit freed the Allies from having to further explain their association with the disreputable admiral. Churchill, in his memoirs, acknowledged that Darlan—a Fascist and Anglophobe who had made wrongheaded decisions for two years—had in the end made a decision that allowed the Allies to gain their foothold in North Africa. Had he ordered resistance against the Allies, Torch might have failed. Whether or not Darlan at the time fostered ambitions of ruling over French North African under Allied protection became moot with his death. He had deservedly earned the reputation of an arrogant, conniving turncoat, but his last turn of coat had finally put him on the right side. "Let him rest in peace," Churchill wrote of Darlan, "and let us all be thankful we have never had to face the trials under which he broke."[351]

Darlan's exit left Giraud as head of the French military in North Africa, but it also left a vacuum in French civil affairs. The way was now open for de Gaulle and the Fighting French to assume a place at the table—at the head of the table if de Gaulle was to realize his ambitions. He was loathed in Washington, where Cordell Hull called the Free French "polecats." Roosevelt, in a sarcastic handwritten addition to a cable to Churchill asked, "Why doesn't de Gaulle go to war? Why doesn't he start North by West half West from Brazenville? It would take him a long time to get to the Oasis of Somewhere." The reference was to Brazzaville, located on the Congo River, and the capital of French Equatorial Africa. Yet despite the Frenchman's arrogance, de Gaulle remained for Churchill and Britons the symbol of French valor, the hero who had wanted to fight Germans for three years and deserved the opportunity to do so. Two weeks before Darlan's assassination, Eden had asked de Gaulle whether, if Darlan were to disappear from the scene, de Gaulle could reach some sort of agreement with French North African authorities. De Gaulle answered yes. Darlan had indeed disappeared. In order that the British (and therefore de Gaulle, to whom the British had made commitments) not be excluded from North African politics, Churchill appointed Harold Macmillan (with Roosevelt's approval) as resident minister to Allied Headquarters, where, Churchill hoped, he would serve as a counterweight to Roosevelt's man in Morocco, Robert Murphy. Macmillan, Churchill informed Roosevelt, "is animated by the friendliest feelings towards the United States, and his mother hails from Kentucky." Actually, his mother was a Hoosier, and although Macmillan, like Churchill, was half American, he was British to the bone, and a Tory. Churchill had just dealt himself into the political game in North Africa. Given the stubbornness of Charles de Gaulle, it was to prove a risky and frustrating game of chance.[352]

On November 10, 1942, Churchill delivered two of his most memorable lines while addressing the traditional Lord Mayor's dinner at Mansion House (the Guildhall having been destroyed during the Blitz). Referring to Montgomery's desert victory, Churchill cautioned, "Now this is not the end. It is not even the beginning of the end. But it is, perhaps, the end of the beginning." Then, after calling himself Franklin Roosevelt's "active and ardent lieutenant" in the "mighty undertaking" taking place in French North Africa, Churchill sought to dispel any notion that he had just admitted to a subordinated role within the alliance. "Let me, however, make this clear.... We mean to hold our own. I have not become the King's First Minister in order to preside over the liquidation of the British Empire." In uttering those words Churchill appeared to have confirmed for critics, then and since, his status as an outdated imperialist who either could not see or could not abide a simple truth—the age of European colonialism was just about over, its expiration aided and abetted by Franklin Roosevelt. Yet Churchill's next line, infrequently noted, completed his thought: "For that task, if it were prescribed, someone else would have to be found, and under democracy, I suppose this nation would have to be consulted." Churchill had been asked to form a government for one reason only, to win the war. He was determined that at war's end Britain would regain territories lost to the Axis, much as America expected to recover Guam and Wake Island. If future events demanded a restructuring of the British Empire, the British people would decide the issue. Churchill ended his address with words that encapsulated his belief in both England and the Empire: "Here we are, and here we stand, a veritable rock of stability in this drifting world."[353]

For Churchill, the British Empire was a variation on German philosopher Gottfried Liebniz's best of all possible worlds. Yet that sentiment formed only a part of his worldview. He was a great European patriot as well as a British patriot, and his willingness to stand alone against Hitler was both an expression of that patriotism and the defense of a truth as Churchill saw it: Europe was the birthplace of Western political and aesthetic traditions, the defense of which, since the fall of France, had fallen to Britain. During his Wilderness Years, he had warned of the danger Hitler posed to Europe and by extension to Britain and the Empire. Even after war came, sober men such as Baldwin and Halifax believed they could preserve the Empire by reaching an agreement with—by again appeasing—Hitler. Churchill did not. Britain had gone to war to restore liberty to Europe. Yet he knew that if Britain emerged from the war victorious, it would possibly emerge broken as well.

Churchill, peering backward though history, grasped the ultimate mortality of empires, all save the British Empire, which functioned as a parliamentary democracy, a fact that for Churchill justified—demanded—its continuance. He once told Colville that the one great lesson he had learned from his father was that "the British alone had managed to combine Empire and Liberty." There were inequalities, to be sure, and he wanted them rectified. He told Attlee that the old order was changing and the "pomp and vanity must go." He told Eden that in Egypt "too many fat, insolent and party interests had grown up under our protection" and that in time the rich pashas and landowners would have to pay taxes at the rates paid by the wealthy in Britain, which rates Churchill intended to keep high in order that the financial burden of the war did not fall unfairly on Britain's working class. He pondered as a slogan for postwar reconstruction: "Food, house, and work for everyone." Yet his cousins across the Atlantic considered "empire" and "liberty" to be antonyms. Of Churchill, Eleanor Roosevelt wrote, "He's very human and I like him, tho' I don't want him to control the peace." Churchill understood, wrote Colville, that "republicanism and anti-colonialism were shibboleths in Washington and that no American paused to consider the implications of either."[354]

Churchill believed that the diaspora of English-speaking peoples that had taken place since the sixteenth century had resulted in an empire unique in history, an empire, he wrote, "based on Government by consent and the voluntary association of autonomous states under the Crown." He was one with Aristotle: rule shows the man—to which could be added, rule shows the nation. His was an empire of shared democratic ideals, shared risks, and shared rewards. It was a nation, the mightiest oak in the forest of nations, yet it cast a beneficent shadow in which less civilized peoples might find shelter and grow. On accepting the Tory chairmanship in 1940, he repeated his father's words that he had shared with Colville, that Britain "alone among the nations of the world...found the means to combine Empire and liberty. Alone among the peoples we have reconciled democracy and tradition." He considered the Empire synonymous with democracy, and worthy of long life—even perpetual life—whatever the sacrifice required of himself, of Britons, and of the King's colonial armies.[355]

A year before his Mansion House speech, Churchill addressed the boys of Harrow. He told them: "Never give in. Never give in. *Never, never, never, never*—in nothing, great or small, large or petty—never give in, except to convictions of honour and good sense. Never yield to force. Never yield to the apparently overwhelming might of the enemy."[356]

He had not yielded in 1942, when defeat had been the order of the day.

Even with America in (and for eleven months Clementine regularly reminded Churchill that America was in, yet not *really* in), he lacked the requisite military might to kill his enemies. What remained for Churchill but optimism? The dark days of the previous two years did not justify it, yet he always found the sunny side. He was no man of sorrow. Gloom regularly overtook him after the military disasters that had occurred with depressing regularity, yet it did not linger. It never, his daughter Mary recalls, "un-manned him."[357]

An air of inevitable Allied victory is attached to America's entry into the war; yet 1942 had passed with Britain still on the knife edge. Only in hindsight do we know that El Alamein and Midway Island were turning points; that Hitler erred in his U-boat deployment; and that he erred in not erasing Malta from the map. As 1942 drew to a close, Churchill remained true to his conviction that the rings of steel and concrete that Germany and Japan had thrown up around their respective conquests should be relentlessly probed until weak spots were exposed, and then exploited. By air the RAF had penetrated the German ring, and now, by land, in North Africa, the Allies were testing the tensile strength of the ring, as was Stalin in his namesake city. On Guadalcanal the Americans refused to relinquish their tenuous grip on the southernmost radius of the Japanese ring.

Shortly before Montgomery attacked at El Alamein, Churchill replied to a request by Anthony Eden for his opinion on the "Four Power Paper," a Foreign Office summary of the postwar organization of the Four Great Powers—Britain, China, the Soviet Union, and the United States. Churchill cautioned Eden against jumping to conclusions as to just who would be included in the so-called four great powers. "We cannot, however, tell what sort of a Russia and what kind of Russian demands we shall have to face." He added, "It would be a measureless disaster if Russian barbarism overlaid the culture and independence of the ancient states of Europe." As for China, "I cannot regard the Chungking Government as representing a great world power. Certainly [China] would be a faggot-vote on the side of the United States in any attempt to liquidate the British Empire." In general, Churchill told Eden, he favored a "United States of Europe capable of defending itself against all threats.* Yet, he advised, as enjoyable as it was to

---

* Although he frequently spoke of a "United States of Europe," Churchill did not specify whether that entity would be a loose confederation or a federal system, with member states bound together by a constitution. He continued to speak only in broad and imprecise terms even while championing a "united" Europe after the war.

ponder such questions, "the war has prior claims on your attention and mine." He closed with a piece of homegrown wisdom: "I hope these speculative studies will be entrusted mainly to those on whose hands time hangs heavy, and that we shall not overlook Mrs. Glasse's Cookery Book recipe for the jugged hare—'First catch your hare.' "[358]

In celebration of Montgomery's glorious deeds (and before the Allies landed in North Africa), Churchill ordered that the church bells be rung throughout the land on the following Sunday, November 8. Brooke, Clementine, and daughter Mary were aghast at the suggestion. Clementine became "violent" in her opposition ("quite rightly," thought Mary); Brooke "implored" Churchill to wait until the Torch forces had gained undisputed control of the beaches. Since 1939, too much had gone too wrong too often to risk ringing out false hope. Churchill heeded their advice, but only for a few days. By November 12, the Anglo-American army was safely ashore in North Africa, its eastern elements already pushing toward Tunisia. Montgomery by then had sent Rommel packing and had captured six divisions' worth of Italians.[359]

The church bells rang on Sunday, November 15. After three years of hope, there finally had arrived from El Alamein a dash of glory. Exhilaration was in the air, wrote Mollie Panter-Downes, "a wave of emotion . . . that makes this moment something like those moments in the summer of 1940. There's a big difference, however. Those were grim days in 1940. Today, though sensible Britons think there's certain to be plenty of grimness ahead, for the first time they believe sober reasons for hope are at last in sight."[360]

In an essay he wrote earlier that year, George Orwell observed that Englishmen always remember the military disasters—Mons, Ypres, Gallipoli, Passchendaele. These were the battles "engraved" upon common memory. The battles of the Great War that finally broke the Germans were simply unknown to the general public. "The most stirring battle poem in English," Orwell wrote, "is about a brigade of cavalry which charged in the wrong direction."[361]

El Alamein not only engraved itself upon the common memory, it erased the old memories. Churchill had found his Wellington in Montgomery, a general as ruthless in pursuit of victory as himself. In 1940, Mollie Panter-Downes compared Churchill and his influence on British morale to Pitt's leadership in 1759. In 1942, Churchill lost all of his battles before finally winning in the desert. As the year went out, nobody compared El Alamein

and 1942 with Waterloo and 1815, still less with 1759, "the year of victories," of Pitt, and Wolfe at Quebec, of the Royal Navy smashing French
fleets at Quiberon Bay and Cape Lagos, and of Minden, where English and
Prussian foot soldiers and artillery ended French dreams of continental
hegemony. "Our bells are worn threadbare with ringing for victories,"
Horace Walpole bragged to a friend that year. This was the Empire in
ascendancy. In the summer of 1759, the keel of a 3,500-ton man-of-war
was laid at the Chatham Dockyard, and the next year, in commemoration
of Britain's *"annus mirabilis"* the ship was christened HMS *Victory*. At the
end of 1759, David Garrick composed "Heart of Oak," his paean to the
ships and men of the Royal Navy. As 1942 neared its end, the last stanza of
Garrick's poem applied to all branches of HMG's military:

> *Through oceans and deserts,*
> *For freedom they came,*
> *And dying, bequeathed us*
> *Their freedom and fame.*

Early in 1942, Churchill promised Britons more grave disappointments
and disasters. As the months sloughed off the calendar, he certainly made
good on that pledge, in Singapore, Burma, and the North African desert.
The year had been anything but a year of victories, but it had been a year
with victories. And that was enough.

Churchill alone among the Big Three had journeyed overseas that
year—twice to Washington, once to Moscow—in order to prod the alliance into strategic agreement and in order to preserve the alliance. "The
Big Three" was a phrase that might conjure an image of a mighty war
wagon pulled by three noble steeds; yet, while Churchill and Roosevelt
and the Combined Chiefs of Staff made every awkward effort to ride
together in harness, Stalin rode alone. In fact, for most of 1942, the so-
called Big Three were more a Big Two plus One. The Allied war effort,
George Kennan later wrote, was less one of common, coordinated strategy
than of simultaneous action, the Americans and the British in the west,
Stalin in the east.[362]

Stalin's military chiefs did not consult the British and Americans; they
consulted Stalin. Stalin, in turn, was relentless in pressing his demands
upon his two allies—for more matériel and a second front—which

Roosevelt and Churchill tried in good faith to meet. The Russian front exerted an almost gravitational effect on decisions made by Roosevelt and Churchill, like the moon on the tides. In fact, the Russian front might as well have been on the moon for the lack of intelligence that Stalin allowed to seep out. Roosevelt, sure that he could handle Uncle Joe, had yet to meet the man; Stalin, for his part, refused to leave Russia to meet his allies and did not trust the British. That month, the British ambassador to Moscow, Clark Kerr, reported to Churchill that Stalin not only did not believe the Americans and British would keep their promises to open a second front, but "feared we were building up a vast army which might one day turn around and compound with Germany against Russia." Though sustained by Churchill's letters and telegrams to Roosevelt and Stalin, the "Big Three" largely remained an impersonal linguistic contrivance until Churchill made his pilgrimages to Washington and Moscow. Then, and only then, did the Trinity become personal. The journeys he undertook that year were so hazardous that General Douglas MacArthur proposed Churchill be awarded the Victoria Cross: "No one of those who wear it deserves it more than he," MacArthur told a British officer, if for no other reason than such journeys "through foreign and hostile lands may be the duty of young pilots, but for a Statesman burdened by the world's cares, it is an act of inspiring gallantry and valor."[363]

Churchill had found the path to glory during the year he fought alone after the French surrender, the Last Man Standing. "God knows where we would be without him," Brooke had written in his diary at the close of 1941, "but God knows where we shall go with him." In 1942 Churchill cemented his alliance, though like the foundation of an old country house, it was in need of constant repointing. With his alliance gained, he had found the path to victory. *That* was where they were going.

He liked to "pester, nag, and bite." Speaking in the House shortly after the Torch landings, he anointed himself a "prod." "My difficulties," he admitted, "rather lie in finding the patience and self-restraint to wait through many anxious weeks for the results to be achieved." Actually he pursued neither patience nor self-restraint with any real effort; he was too impatient. He told a member of his Defence Secretariat that action and results were all that mattered: "It was all very well to say that everything had been thought of. The crux of the matter was—has anything been done?" In the Western Desert, something had.[364]

"And now at last," Brooke told his diary, "the tide has begun to turn."[365]

4

Crosscurrents

Within days of the North African landings, Churchill concluded that Torch might wrap up by Christmas. Alan Brooke, too, was confident, telling his diary that Ultra decrypts, if correct, indicated a good chance of "pushing him [the enemy] into the sea before long." Churchill, enthused, began work on a "most secret" memo for the British Chiefs of Staff. His objectives included the "completion of Torch by Christmas"; "bringing Turkey into the war" by March; the buildup of the Anglo-American force in Britain by June; the assembly of landing craft and completion of "preparations for Roundup" by July. Finally, in August or September, "Action." Such was the plan.[1]

On November 12, British paratroopers dropped into Bône, two hundred miles east of Algiers and halfway to Tunis, into which German reinforcements were now pouring. British commandos in small motor launches leap-frogged along the Tunisian coast ahead of General Anderson's diminutive First British Army, which had begun its race to Tunis the day before. Anderson made good progress for a few days, but a lack of locomotives and rolling stock held up his tanks and supplies. The transport situation worsened when the late autumn rains arrived, turning roads into slurries. Anderson, balancing his need for speed against the need to protect his flanks, divided the First Army into three prongs, with the result that he found himself trying to crack a coconut with a fork rather than a bayonet.

Field Marshal Albert Kesselring, commander of German operations in the Mediterranean, had already sent his vanguard to Tunis, and by the end of the month he had put 20,000 Germans there, along with Stukas, panzers, and artillery, forces equal in size to Anderson's and far more experienced. The rest of Eisenhower's troops sat static in Oran and Morocco, the result of a lingering American fear that Hitler would strike into the American rear through Spain with the Luftwaffe and paratroops. Colonel Ian Jacob recorded in his diary that the American chiefs "regarded the Mediterranean as a kind of dark hole, into which one entered at one's peril." Marshall told Roosevelt that week that of three possible Axis options — invading Spain, driving through the Caucasus, and attacking Britain — the invasion of Spain seemed most probable. Accordingly, safety first was Eisenhower's order of the day. On November 23 Brooke complained to his diary of "the very slow rate of progress in North Africa," which he blamed on Eisenhower's inability "to handle the military situation confronting him." By then, the Allies, with 250,000 troops ashore, had doubled the original landing force. Yet only Anderson was making headway, and not much at that. Churchill, unable to prod Eisenhower, unloaded on Brooke. Torch, he told the CIGS, "must be a springboard and not a sofa."[2]

Success in Tunisia depended on two factors—bold initiative (lacking, other than Anderson's drive toward Tunis) and the continued commitment of American resources. Any large-scale diversion of American men, planes, or ships to the Pacific could snuff out Torch. In fact, America that year had sent more troops—460,000 soldiers and Marines—to the Pacific than to Britain and North Africa, where a total of 380,000 Americans served, the vast majority far in the rear. Getting anything, men or machines, to Britain was the problem. U-boats in the Atlantic harvested more than 100 ships and 720,000 tons of Allied shipping that month, the greatest monthly loss of the war to date. Trying to explain the realities of the German naval blockade to Stalin, Churchill wrote, "You who have so much land may find it hard to realize that we [Britain] can only live and fight in proportions to our sea communications." The U-boat successes, Churchill told Stalin, were the "limiting factor" in Anglo-American planning. And every American warship sent to the Pacific made the deadly work of the U-boats that much easier. Then, just days after Torch began, a naval battle in the Pacific whetted the appetites of Americans for more action against Japan, naval action, and this at a time when, as Churchill told Stalin, the Allies lacked the warships to protect both the Torch landings and the Arctic convoys upon which Stalin depended.[3]

On November 12, two days after Churchill's Mansion House address, American and Imperial Japanese naval forces met again in "Ironbottom Sound," hard by the coast of Guadalcanal. Since August, the Japanese had run troops and fast warships—the "Tokyo Express"—from Rabaul to Guadalcanal, four hundred miles down "the Slot," and since August, the American navy had contested the Tokyo Express. In mid-October Tokyo had decided the time had come to obliterate the Americans on Guadalcanal. The Japanese plan called for a task force to shell the Marine airfield into oblivion in support of an invasion force, which would land during daylight sometime on or about November 13. The Americans, meanwhile, were running in their own reinforcements. Forewarned by coast watchers of the Japanese fleet headed their way, the Americans were ready when, at dusk on November 12, the Japanese made for Guadalcanal. The American naval historian Samuel Eliot Morison later wrote that the ensuing battle (two, actually, separated by a day of uneasy quiet) "recalled the Anglo-Dutch battles of the seventeenth century, when each side slugged the other until all but one went down." No quarter was given. By the time it was over, the Americans had taken an awful beating, and had in fact suffered a tactical defeat. But the Japanese admirals, fearing that even larger U.S. forces might be on their way, failed to press on with the destruction of the airfield. Instead, they turned for home and in so doing handed the Americans a strategic victory. The cost to the U.S. Navy was terrible: a battleship, several cruisers and destroyers damaged, two cruisers and six destroyers sunk, and more than sixteen hundred bluejackets killed. It was a price Washington could bear.[4]

Days later, Churchill cabled congratulations on the victory to Roosevelt. Shortly thereafter, Roosevelt announced, "It would seem that the turning-point in this war has at last been reached." Churchill preferred for the time being to stick with his hedged bet of "the end of the beginning." After the war a captured contemporary Imperial Japanese Navy document validated Roosevelt's enthusiasm: "It must be said that the success or failure in recapturing Guadalcanal ... is the fork in the road which leads to victory for them or us."[5]

The Americans had taken the most advantageous fork. But Alan Brooke and Air Marshal Portal feared that if the Americans chose now to strike hell-bent down the road to Tokyo, they would do so at the expense of the European theater. Portal argued that because the Americans considered North Africa an exercise in containment rather than a springboard to the Continent, they saw no contradiction in shifting resources from Britain to the Pacific. For Churchill, this would not do. He had promised Stalin a second front in 1943, and the initial success of Torch had, in his estimation, made that promise a practical possibility.[6]

In Russia later that November week, the Wehrmacht and Red Army reached another fork in another road. At dawn on November 19, Marshal Zhukov threw his armies north of Stalingrad against the German flank. The following day, his armies south of the city struck. Both armies then shot toward the great bend of the Don, thirty miles west of Stalingrad. Zhukov saw the German position around Stalingrad for what it was, more of a "fragile shell" than a steel ring. Supported by an artillery barrage of more than two thousand guns, their movements obscured by a ferocious blizzard, the Soviets—a million strong—smashed through the ill-equipped and none-too-enthusiastic Romanian, Hungarian, and Italian forces guarding Paulus's flanks, killing and capturing more than three hundred thousand of Hitler's allies. By the twenty-first, Paulus and the remainder of his Sixth Army—almost a quarter of a million men—found themselves within the Soviet pincers, which were closing fast. Two days later, the Soviets linked arms at Kalach, on the Don. The Fourth German Panzer Army was forced to flee westward, leaving Paulus's Sixth Army trapped in the ruins of Stalingrad. Paulus's options were reduced to either standing and fighting or attempting a breakout westward from the city to the Don, there to join Field Marshal Erich von Manstein's Army Group Don. But the genius of Zhukov's plan was that it called for a broad encirclement of the Germans rather than a narrow pinch from which Paulus might escape. When Manstein, Germany's greatest strategist, tried to break through to relieve Paulus, he got to within thirty-five miles of Stalingrad before he was stopped. In mid-December, Hitler, who a month earlier had broadcast to the world that the Sixth Army would never leave Stalingrad, reiterated his orders. Paulus, his escape now blocked by Zhukov, obeyed. He had no other choice.[7]

Stalin, as usual, failed to disclose to Churchill or Roosevelt the exact disposition or strength of the Red Army (a habit Churchill and Brooke found infuriating given Stalin's regular belittling of Britain's effort). Only the combatants amid the ruins of Stalingrad knew how the battle was going, and they didn't know much. Their horizons could be measured in yards and feet. Soviet loudspeakers informed Paulus's troops that a German soldier was dying every seven seconds. The most titanic battle in history raged within lines so compact that there were more troops than in all of Tunisia battling each other among a few square miles of rubble, a zone of death not much greater in size than Lower Manhattan or Kensington. The rotting viscera of the dead and the bodily wastes of the living bred typhus and dysentery that killed men as surely—but not as mercifully—as the storm of bombs and bullets. Stalingrad had become like a collapsing star, pulling all in its orbit toward its ever more compressed core, a fiery hell from which nothing escaped. The city was "a vast furnace," a German survivor wrote, a world of "burning, blinding smoke...lit by the reflection of the flames." At night—"scorching, howling, bleeding nights"—terrified dogs plunged into the Volga and paddled madly for the Russian side. Those in London and Washington who waited for news from Stalingrad would have to bide their time until broadcasts announcing the outcome issued forth from Berlin and Moscow. The loser would no doubt accompany an announcement with a somber dirge, the victor with a celebratory march.[8]

During the last week of November, Dwight Eisenhower transferred his headquarters from Gibraltar to Algiers, where he and his second-in-command, Mark Clark, and their retinue took over the St. George Hotel and two villas. That put Eisenhower about three hundred miles west of the Allied front lines, which hooked south from the Mediterranean about fifty miles west of the port of Bizerte to a terminus high in a mountain pass called Kasserine, located in the Western Dorsal of the Atlas Mountains, seventy miles southwest of Tunis. There, drifts of daisies and red poppies spilled over the flinty, wind-swept landscape; the ground was impermeable to entrenching tools, and the terrain offered little defilade.

Near the northern end of the line, Anderson's forward elements had advanced to within just a dozen miles of Tunis. From the heights west of the city, British scouts looked across the plains that had once fed ancient Rome. In the far distance the minarets of Tunis stabbed up into the Mediterranean haze. Beyond Tunis, the ruins of Carthage overlooked the sea. The Romans had come 2,100 years earlier, intent on utterly destroying Carthage, and did so, but only after a long naval siege and house-to-house combat. If Anderson's little army drove into Tunis, this battle could only end in like fashion. The race for Tunis was tightening, but Churchill, still confident that Anderson would take the city by Christmas and that Montgomery would soon run Rommel to ground, began in earnest his campaign for the next Allied effort: Operation Roundup—the invasion of France. Indeed, Montgomery that week pushed Rommel to El Agheila, halfway to Tripoli. Twice before, in 1941 and 1942, Rommel had turned from here and sent the British scrambling back toward Cairo. Short of tanks and gasoline, he could not do so again. After a brief standoff, the Desert Fox fled west, stalked by Montgomery, who now had struck into Tripolitania, the garden of Mussolini's African empire. On December 2, Churchill, enthused by Monty's exploits, told Roosevelt "the chances for Roundup may be greatly improved" by the successes in North Africa and Russian resistance at Stalingrad.[9]

George Marshall, too, was optimistic. He told Roosevelt that Tunis could be occupied within two or three weeks "provided that [Anderson's] two divisions were sufficient to accomplish the task" and the Axis did not do something unexpected. Implicit in that astoundingly qualified assessment are two obvious questions. What plans were in place in the event Anderson's little force proved *insufficient* to take Tunis and, what if the Axis *did* do something unexpected? There was no answer to either question. Meanwhile, more than one hundred thousand American troops served as reserves far in the rear of Anderson, out of action and on guard for an Axis strike through Spain.[10]

Churchill's newfound enthusiasm for Roundup brought him into agreement with Marshall, and into disagreement with Alan Brooke. Churchill had made clear to Brooke that Torch must be a springboard, but a springboard to where? Western France? Southern France? Sardinia, Sicily, Italy, or the Balkans? Both Churchill and Brooke saw opportunities in Sicily and Sardinia to secure air supremacy over the Mediterranean and southernmost

Europe, possibly to bomb Mussolini out of the war. And always in Brooke's calculations was the immediate benefit to Allied shipping gained by opening the Mediterranean, thereby reducing round-trip journeys to Egypt by thousands of miles and effectively adding scores of ships to the fleet. But Churchill had a far more aggressive strategy in mind—he had rediscovered Roundup *and* he wanted to proceed in the Mediterranean. And Operation Jupiter, the invasion of northern Norway, had crept back into his calculations as a means to help safeguard the Arctic convoys and aid Stalin. As for Sicily and Sardinia, Churchill told Brooke, "You must not think you can get off with your 'sardines.'... No, we must establish a western front." In Brooke's judgment any talk of a continental second front was premature. Britain had the troops but lacked the means to feed and fuel them once ashore, and in fact lacked the landing craft to put them ashore. America was not yet prepared to carry the load, not in the air, not at sea, and most assuredly not on the ground in France. Operation Bolero, the buildup of American forces in Britain, had actually slowed, as Churchill knew full well, as did Roosevelt, having been reminded by Churchill that without Bolero, there could be no Roundup.

In wanting to attack everywhere, Churchill manifested two abiding traits: impatience and flexibility in the face of changing fortunes. His belief in an opportunistic strategic approach—attack the weaker of two enemies if the stronger could not be engaged—had not diminished since the 1941 Greek debacle, nor since 1915 and the Dardanelles, for that matter. Now Italy was weak and getting weaker. Once driven from Africa, it would be ripe for the kill. As usual, Churchill was consistent in combining the political and the military in his strategic thinking. In this, he was one with Clausewitz, but increasingly at odds with the Americans, who adhered to other Clausewitz maxims: avoid turning flanks and take the fight directly to the enemy if an opportunity presents itself, and *if*—a critical Clausewitzian caveat—your armies are equal to or greater in strength than the enemy's. Those conditions had clearly not yet presented themselves on the Continent.

But Sicily held promise. The military and political repercussions for Mussolini would be far greater were the Allies to take Sicily rather than Sardinia. Yet from a strictly military standpoint (which the Americans adhered to), Sardinia had much to offer. It was half again closer to southern France and northern Italy than was Sicily. Allied bombers based there would be that much closer to European targets, and an invasion of Tuscany from there would have the effect of cutting off Rome and most of the boot of Italy from Germany, eliminating the need for a three-hundred-mile slog from the toe of Italy to Rome. But Churchill called Sardinia "that piddling option." Only Sicily ("the glittering prize") was worth going after.

On the subject of Sicily, Brooke and Churchill were not far apart. For Brooke, taking Sicily was necessary in order for the British to retake the Mediterranean; Sardinia would not accomplish that. For Churchill, Sicily offered the first step of a campaign north toward Vienna by way of Italy (which would be crushed in the bargain), the Balkans, and the Ljubljana Gap through the Julian Alps and into Austria, but—and this was critical—*only* if Turkey entered the war on the Allied side in order to protect the Balkan flank. Churchill's plan was simplicity itself, to drive Italy from the war in order to induce Turkey to enter it.[11]

Roosevelt, too, grasped the strategic benefits of striking at Germany from the south, and told Churchill so in a November 11 telegram in which the president suggested that he and Churchill and their military chiefs begin planning a follow-up to Torch to include "forward movements directed against Sardinia, Sicily, Italy, Greece and other Balkan areas and including the possibility of obtaining Turkish support for an attack through the Black Sea against Germany's flank." Churchill responded with enthusiasm. He proposed to Roosevelt that after consolidating their North African positions, they "strike at the under-belly of the Axis in effective strength and in the shortest time." Here, exactly, was the strategy he had outlined to Stalin in August. And here came Franklin Roosevelt offering encouragement in the matter.[12]

Churchill needed no convincing. His generals and their American counterparts, however, did. Other than the Italian lack of will to fight (as Churchill believed), there was nothing soft about Europe's underbelly. The Apennine Mountains thrust north through Italy to the Alps, where from France to Slovenia the terrain favored defensive and guerrilla tactics, as several German and Bulgarian divisions were learning in Yugoslavia, and as Mussolini had learned in Greece. Of the Ljubljana Gap, Eisenhower later told his naval aid that he would be damned if he'd put his army into "that gap whose name I can't even pronounce." Admiral King saw the Mediterranean as a dead end, a place where American ships would go to die. The soft underbelly, wrote Samuel Eliot Morison, was "boned with the Apennines, plated with the hard scales of Kesselring's armor, and shadowed by the wings of the Luftwaffe."[13]

Marshall had always advocated a straight-line approach from Britain across the Channel, not only because it was the shortest distance between two points, but because the countryside of northern France and the Low Countries was indeed "soft" and conducive to large-scale armor movement, as the Germans had shown in 1940. Marshall intended to take that straight line in 1943. Yet he lacked the men to do so; Torch had been undertaken at the expense of Bolero, the buildup of American troops in England. Roosevelt backed Marshall, nominally, although just months earlier, the president had concluded with reluctance that the shipping shortage and the final decision on Torch precluded any such venture in France until 1944. Days before he sent his cable to Churchill, Roosevelt assured Marshall that the cross-Channel strategy still had his full support; it did, but Roosevelt had no timetable in mind. His biographer James MacGregor Burns writes that "tactical developments had outrun his [Roosevelt's] strategic decision making" and that Roosevelt "had no definite battle plan." Yet, in his November cable to Churchill, Roosevelt clearly indicated that the under-belly option appeared to be the most promising answer to the question of where next after North Africa.[14]

Thus, Roosevelt proposed a favorite Churchillian scheme to Churchill while Churchill proposed Marshall's favored strategy to Brooke, who was appalled at the prospect of a premature landing *anywhere* on the Continent. Of course, Churchill's newfound enthusiasm for Roundup (even if it had been incubated in the need to placate Stalin) did not in the least diminish his desire to go to Italy. They could do both. Northern Norway, too, was never far from Churchill's thoughts, nor was the Aegean. They could do it all.

Robert Sherwood later wrote that those who accuse Churchill of hesitancy if not outright cowardice in regard to the invasion of France (as had Stalin, quite bluntly, during Churchill's Moscow visit) take a too linear and simplistic approach. Three months before Torch kicked off, Churchill told Roosevelt that the British would willingly accept Marshall as supreme commander of Roundup. Churchill did this knowing full well that Marshall had one and only one strategy in mind, to strike straight into France. Sherwood: "This nomination of the most vehement proponent of the Second Front would hardly indicate that Churchill was attempting to relegate it [Roundup] to the Files of Forgotten Things." He was not trying to do that, yet he had also begun to proclaim a truth as he saw it, that a disastrous defeat on the coast of France "was the only way in which we could lose this war." That conclusion was self-evidently correct. A defeat on the coast of France would lead, if not to immediate defeat, to Marshall and King's shifting the entire American effort to the Pacific. Harry Hopkins, at the time, told an audience at Madison Square Garden that there would be a second front, "and if necessary a third and a fourth front, to pen the German army in a ring of our offensive steel." These were Churchill's sentiments exactly. Roundup was to be one of *several* operations. His multifront thinking was a constant source of worry to Brooke, who wrote in his diary, "He is now swinging away from those [Sardinia and Sicily] for a possible invasion of France in 1943!" Eisenhower, meanwhile, was swinging *toward* Sardinia, where three German divisions were dug in. But to Brooke's astonishment, Eisenhower's "very bad plan . . . never went beyond the landing on the beaches."[15]

On the day Roosevelt sent his underbelly telegram (November 11), Churchill told the Commons that the Allies would in the coming year bring strong force to bear against Hitler in Western Europe. He did not promise a timetable for an actual invasion, nor did he define just what "strong" meant. The invasion, he said, would take place only when "in due course" Germany became demoralized (presumably by the pounding inflicted by the Russians and the RAF). He said, "Moreover, you have first to get sufficient ascendancy even to prepare to strike such a blow." He stressed that planning and preparation for such operations may look like inertia, but were in fact critical. The *New York Times* ran with that story the next day, under the headline: INVASION ACROSS CHANNEL IS PLEDGED BY CHURCHILL. In fact, he had made no such pledge, but the horse was out of the barn. Ever since, the Allied failure to cross the Channel in 1943 has been attributed to Churchill's reluctance, beginning with a pledge he never made, an irony given that by late November 1942, Churchill (next to Marshall) was Roundup's biggest booster.[16]

The American military suspected Churchill liked to engage in "eccentric operations" that depended on bravado, surprise, and speed for success. He did, but that was in part because the British army could not engage the Wehrmacht on anything like equal terms, and the American army had yet to prove its battle worthiness. Cordell Hull and the U.S. military chiefs (and the Free French) also suspected Churchill of harboring imperial designs in the eastern Mediterranean; he did not. He had attacked Vichy "intriguers" in Syria and Madagascar in order to safeguard the Suez Canal and Middle East oil supplies, upon which the British war effort depended. Marshall also suspected, correctly, that Churchill wanted to first clear the entire Mediterranean as a prelude to any contemplated landing in France, thereby, in Marshall's estimation, further delaying his straight-line strategy. And now here was Marshall's boss, the commander in chief, encouraging Churchill on his underbelly strategy. Yet Roosevelt was only approaching the business of war in the same way he approached politics; he liked to allow events to proceed until a choice of action became self-evident. By December no single strategy had become self-evident. Clearly, it was time for Churchill, Roosevelt, and the Combined Chiefs of Staff to sit down and work one out.[17]

The news from North Africa only added to the urgency to do so. On December 1, Kesselring's reinforced troops skirmished with Anderson's forward units and drove the British back. Tanks would occupy a central place in the battle for Tunis, and Anderson's tanks, the American M3 Lee and its modified cousin, the M3 Grant, were obsolete—the main gun was not fitted to a traversing turret, rivets used in construction became lethal projectiles when the tank was hit, and its high profile made it an easy target. They were no match for the German Panzer Mark IV tank and its

75mm gun. A week later, General Dieter von Arnim took command of the Fifth Panzer Army at Tunis, now 25,000 strong, with almost a quarter million Italians and Germans soon to arrive by way of Europe and Rommel's approaching army. The previous year at Kiev, Arnim's masterful tank deployments led to the encirclement of an entire Russian army. He intended, after joining forces with Rommel, to annihilate the Americans and British in Tunisia. Within a week of arriving in Tunisia, he went on the offensive.[18]

To the relief of Churchill and Brooke, Kesselring could not bring himself to undertake the one operation that would most benefit the Germans in North Africa, which was to rub Malta from the map. A convoy of four British ships reached Malta in late November, leading Brooke to exclaim to his diary, "Thank god. This puts the island safe for a bit." It put Torch safe for a bit, too, because holding Malta—from where RAF aircraft and Royal Navy submarines could hunt German troop and supply ships—was critical to the success of Torch. Many of the troops Kesselring was shoving into Tunis had been training for the invasion of Malta. Had Kesselring thought like an admiral rather than a Luftwaffe *Generalfeldmarschall,* and had those troops been dropped into Malta, a swastika would likely have been flying over Valletta, and Rommel, freely resupplied, would have been driving toward Baghdad rather than away from Benghazi. But Kesselring, like Göring during the Battle of Britain (and now at Stalingrad), had placed his hopes in his pilots and bombers. Crete had claimed many of them, and the Russian front called for more. The leaders of the Reich never truly grasped the significance of Malta: "We should frankly tell the German people that we aren't interested in conquering Malta," Goebbels wrote months earlier. "And that's the truth too." Now, as the year neared its end, Goebbels confessed to his diary: "Those in the know see quite clearly that Rommel cannot do anything if he doesn't have gasoline. That is decisive." The British had understood that for two years; it was why they sent convoy after convoy and dozens of warships on suicidal missions to Malta. Now submarines based at Malta ravaged Rommel's supply ships, with the result that, Goebbels lamented, "our supplies are, for the most part, lost" and "the situation in French Africa is not exactly rosy."[19]

Nor was it rosy in Russia, where, Goebbels observed with rare understatement, "we are having some trouble about Stalingrad." He also expressed his feelings on the upcoming Christmas season: "I'll be glad when this whole Christmas racket is over. One can then devote oneself quietly again to real tasks." It would not do, he wrote, for the people to "fall too much for the sentimental magic of these festival days." High on Goebbels' list of real tasks was the "wiping out of the Jewish race in Europe, and possibly in the entire world." The Jewish race, Goebbels wrote, "has prepared this war; it is the spiritual originator of the whole misfortune that has overtaken humanity. Jewry must pay for its crime."[20]

In mid-December, in response to claims by the Polish government in exile that two million Polish Jews had been shipped east to their deaths, Anthony Eden addressed the Commons, where he read from an Allied proclamation that condemned "this bestial policy of cold-blooded extermination" and made a "solemn resolution to ensure that those responsible for these crimes shall not escape retribution." After Eden spoke, a rare moment of silence was observed in the House, in memory of European Jews. "Bestial," a word little used in temperate twenty-first-century political speech, appears to reduce the Nazi barbarities to their most elemental and evil. Yet George Orwell later observed that "bestial" was one of the clichés that by overuse in the 1930s and early 1940s had reduced political discourse to blather. Eden's message went largely unheard outside Britain. The *New York Times* ran a brief story inside the paper (over the course of the war, the *New York Times* ran no page-one lead story on the plight of Polish Jews). In Britain, Sikorski's Free Poles kept the story alive in the British press, which, though having seen its newsprint cut by 20 percent, always made room for the news from Warsaw. Goebbels also recorded his impressions of Eden and the moment of silence: "The English are the Jews among the Aryans" and the Commons "is really a sort of Jewish exchange." As for Eden: "The perfumed British Foreign Minister... cuts a good figure among those characters from the synagogue....His entire bearing can be characterized as thoroughly Jewish."[21]

Thirty plays were running in London's West End in December, twice as many as the year before. Londoners' infatuation with all things Russian was evidenced by the production of Turgenev's *A Month in the Country* at the St. James Theatre, where a second box office had to be opened to accommodate the crowds. A Soviet flag flew above Selfridges; inside, the department store's nearly empty shelves gave the place the feel of Moscow's *Gosudarstvenny Universalny Magazin* (GUM). Such was London's love affair with Russia that the Soviet ambassador, Ivan Maisky, was made an honorary member of the Athenaeum, while at the Windmill Theatre, the nude dancers wore Cossack fur hats and red stars in their navels while performing their special ode to Russia, *Moscow Nights*.

British patriotism found expression in Noël Coward's cinematic directorial debut, *In Which We Serve*. Based on Dickie Mountbatten's exploits in command of HMS *Kelly*, which was sunk from under Mountbatten the previous year, the movie, which Coward also produced and starred in, became an instant hit with Britons, although some wits in the Royal Navy dubbed it *In Which We Sink*. Beaverbrook loathed it, because in an early scene, a copy of his *Daily Express* with a 1939 headline proclaiming No WAR THIS YEAR floats on the waves among the wreckage of a doomed ship and the bodies of dead tars. *Time* called the movie "the first really great picture of World War II." Coward was also a presence in the West End, where his latest play, *Blithe Spirit,* a comedic ghost story, had been pulling crowds into the Savoy Theater for a year and a half, and would keep Londoners laughing for the remainder of the war. Coward, along with his old friends King George VI and Winston Churchill, was one of few Britons as popular in the West End as in the East End, though nobody's popularity topped Churchill's.[22]

On the eve of his birthday, Churchill made his first radio address since May, when he told Britons that conditions would worsen before they got better. Now, with the Allies marching toward Tunis, he used the airwaves to tell Mussolini that Italy would be next to feel Allied wrath: "The fair land of Italy," he promised, would soon suffer "prolonged, scientific and shattering air attack." In fact, the previous night, the RAF had bludgeoned Turin's industrial areas with two-ton bombs. Churchill derided Mussolini as "the hyena" who "broke all bounds of decency" and advised Italians to depose Il Duce (whom Churchill also called "a serf" and "a utensil") if they wanted to save their "fair land" from further withering attacks. He promised to clear Africa of the enemy "before long." Of the future course of the war, he offered, "I promise nothing...I know of nothing which justifies the hope that the war will not be long or that bitter, bloody years do not lie ahead." Britain would fight on, he said, "with a bold heart and a good conscience." He quoted his favorite Kipling:

If you can dream — and not make dreams your master;
If you can think — and not make thoughts your aim;
If you can meet with Triumph and disaster
And treat those two imposters just the same.[23]

He gave Britons fair warning. El Alamein was a battle won, but not a war won.

With Christmas coming, the official view held that only the children should receive presents. Yet, Mollie Panter-Downes wrote in *The New Yorker,* "even the children won't come off so handsomely this Christmas, for toys are scarce, poorly made, and appallingly expensive." The personal columns of newspapers were full of notices from desperate parents in search of secondhand toys and tricycles and doll carriages. None could any longer be bought new. Those Londoners who planned to gift-wrap a bit of their tea or sugar rations for friends or family found themselves on the wrong side of the law when the Food Ministry announced that it was illegal to give away rations, a decision Churchill lamented as "contrary to logic and good sense" and a blow against "neighborliness and friendship." The Board of Trade was set to lower Britons' allotments of clothing coupons from sixty-one to forty per year, which, at about thirteen coupons for a simple dress or man's suit jacket, limited options in the clothing department. To save material, only three-button single-breasted jackets could be made, with no buttons on the sleeves. Waistcoats were limited to two pockets. Still, the news from the desert made up for food, clothing, and toy shortages. Britons were optimistic, although, wrote Mollie Panter-Downes, "several official utterances lately have warned the people that the ramparts they watch are still the White Cliffs of Dover and that an attempt upon them is quite in the cards at some moment when Hitler may believe that popular attention has been diverted elsewhere."[24]

The attention of children playing football in the streets of London's poorer neighborhoods was focused on the automobiles that regularly appeared, not because the car might break up the game, but because automobiles could be used only for official business, and most East End residents neither owned a car nor had any official business to conduct. When a car turned onto an East End street—or the meaner streets of Manchester, York, Glasgow, Liverpool, or Birmingham—it could mean but one thing. The children stopped their games and watched to see whose house received a visit from uniformed officers bearing terrible tidings from North Africa. Bernard Montgomery's victory had resulted in a marked increase in such visitations. The official cars cruised the streets of Mayfair, Chelsea, and Knightsbridge, where the upper classes had embraced their duty. "Britain is class ridden," Pamela Churchill Harriman told a visitor years later, "but it is not class conscious." The gentry had come in for it along with everyone else; their sons had fought and died in the desert beside East Enders.[25]

Pamela remembered that holiday season as being if not the gayest, the least gloomy of the war, in part, she recalled, because of the sense of peace she had attained with the knowledge that her marriage to Randolph was over and, Averell Harriman making a cuckold of Randolph notwithstanding, its end was not her fault, nor was it entirely Randolph's. "I began gradually to realize that there was a deep difficulty between Clemmie and Randolph, and that in fact Churchill worshipped his son and was trying by every possible means to give him any help or advantage he could." Churchill lived for his son—"like all Englishmen, the son, or eldest son, is everything"—while Clemmie lived for Churchill, with the result that soon after her marriage, Pamela "sensed this tremendous antagonism...a deep difficulty between Clemmie and Randolph." Randolph once told her that his mother hated him, and that he had known as much since Clementine went down to Eton and slapped his face in front of the other boys. Pamela, having "come from a normal English family," thought that claim to be "exaggerated and ridiculous." Yet, "gradually through the months and years I began to realize there was a certain truth to what he was saying... that this thing of the eldest son was terribly important to Winston and that the only thing that ever came between Winston and Clemmie was Randolph." Winston, over Clementine's opposition, would call Randolph's commanding officers and say, "I would like my son for three days," and pull Randolph from his military postings in order to accompany Churchill to France, to Cairo, to Tehran. Randolph's absences from his post resulted in him "catching the flak" from his superiors and Churchill catching it from Clementine, whose only concern was that criticism might be directed at her husband.

"It's awfully difficult explaining Clemmie," Pamela recalled, "because I was really fond of her. She was wonderful to me, but she was a very strange woman. She lived totally for Winston." As did Randolph, with the result that Pamela, just twenty-one, found herself a spectator to a battle between Randolph and Clementine for Churchill's love, an unnecessary battle in Pamela's estimation, because his love for his wife and son was unconditional and total, as it was for Pamela and her small son. "I remember going to the Cabinet Room and telling Winston that we wanted to get a divorce. He was wonderful about it. He said, 'Never forget, not only are we devoted to you but you are the mother of my grandson.'" That was "Little Winston," with whom Churchill liked to roll on the floors of Chequers: "Winston was much better with small children than Clemmie was," Pamela recalled. "Clemmie was not good with her grandchildren...she really didn't have any affinity for the young."[26]

In mid-December, with Rommel retreating toward Tunisia, and the Allied drive for Tunis opposed now by a combination of battle-hardened Germans, desert rains, mud, and high mountain passes, Churchill and Roosevelt began planning for what was supposed to be the first meeting of the Big Three. The time had come to make a final decision on the strategic goals for 1943. Topping the agenda, a means had to be found to defeat the U-boats and take command of the Atlantic. The sea war had to be won before any continental European excursions could be contemplated. And how much naval power to assign to the Pacific war? And what to do with

Giraud and de Gaulle? And the vital question, where to go next after clearing North Africa of the Axis.

Churchill suggested that Iceland or North Africa might prove suitable venues for a conference, but Roosevelt vetoed Iceland on account of "the vile climate" and the likelihood of ice forming on aircraft wings (he had last flown before his first election and did not like to fly in any weather, especially in bad weather). The two leaders settled on North Africa. They invited Stalin, who demurred, claiming quite honestly that his focus was entirely on Stalingrad. Stalin, who was also terrified of flying, replied that he need only be apprised of any decisions taken by Churchill and Roosevelt, wherever they chose to meet. He also advised his allies that they take care to ensure that "no time is being wasted" in fulfilling their promise of opening a second front in Europe in 1943.[27]

They settled on Casablanca in the newly liberated French protectorate of Morocco as the conference site, and on Symbol as the code name for the meeting. As it would be a parley to mull over military strategy, Roosevelt told Harriman to inform Churchill that the president wanted "no ringers" at the conference. That is, he wanted to exclude his secretary of state, Cordell Hull. This put Harriman in a delicate spot, for Churchill worked in harness with Anthony Eden. Harriman had to persuade Churchill to exclude Eden, not because Eden had nothing to add, but because Roosevelt sought to distance himself from Hull, who was "forceful, stubborn, and difficult to handle" and would likely prove "a nuisance at the conference." Churchill reluctantly agreed to the decision. Hull, offended, complained to Harriman that the president was not keeping him informed. That was true; Franklin Roosevelt served as his own secretary of state. Yet the exclusion of Eden did not diminish Churchill's enthusiasm for the meeting. He proposed to Roosevelt that they travel under the aliases Don Quixote and Sancho Panza, but British officials thought the aliases were an invitation to the more cynical members of the press to term the venture quixotic. Churchill agreed, and cabled Roosevelt that in order to confuse the enemy, they should travel *incognito* "as Admiral Q and Mr. P.... We must mind our P's and Q's." Although he agreed to leave Eden behind, he informed Harriman that he was bringing along "a couple of private secretaries," his map room staff, and "one or two of the Joint Staff Secretariat."[28]

On Christmas Eve Eisenhower notified Roosevelt and Churchill that the winter rains had forced a shutdown of Tunisian operations for two months. The Germans had driven the British forward elements from the aptly named Longstop Hill, within sight of Tunis. Kesselring and Arnim had won the race. Brooke told his diary: "I am afraid that Eisenhower as a general is hopeless. He submerges himself in politics and neglects his military duties, partly, I am afraid, because he knows little about military matters." The words echo Brooke's sentiments regarding Churchill, of whom he wrote, "Perhaps his most remarkable failing is that he can never see the whole strategical problem at once. His gaze always settles on some definite part of the canvas and the rest of the picture is lost." Yet Brooke, as coolly logical as Stafford Cripps, failed as did Cripps to grasp the essential Churchill. Churchill had not learned his debating skills at an army staff college, where officers are trained to remove the emotional from strategic planning; nor had he learned his skills as a barrister at the bar. His education took place in the House of Commons, where knife fights were fought with words and the objective was to gut an opponent's policy by gutting the opponent. After four decades of honing his skills in the House, Churchill could approach Brooke in no other manner but to cajole, belittle, and berate. In fact, Churchill, more intuitive than logical, possessed the painter's gift for seeing myriad vistas, far and near. He scanned the entire canvas and when he came upon a scene of interest, he paused and pondered before moving on, never fast enough for Brooke. Thankfully for Brooke, Churchill manifested another trait. After arguing his case as if compromise were evil incarnate and the chiefs were too foolish to understand the perfect wisdom of his position, he acceded to their viewpoint if, that is, he had failed to bring them around to his. Brooke did not grasp that when it came to strategic thinking, Churchill could weigh the value of and consequences of several strategic solutions at once, military and political. It fell to Brooke to nudge him toward the most practical.[29]

And that is what Brooke did in the days before the Casablanca parley. He outargued the master arguer, with the result that soon after the new year, the British, in reaching a strategic consensus, accomplished what the Americans did not. Roosevelt warned his generals that the British would arrive at Casablanca with a plan, "and stick to it." They did, but only after Brooke persuaded Churchill to abandon his newfound enthusiasm for Roundup. When Churchill, arguing his case, informed Brooke that "we had promised Stalin we would do so when in Moscow," Brooke replied, "No *we* did not promise!" Brooke, after much difficulty, convinced Churchill that 1943 would afford opportunity in one theater only, the Mediterranean. And that was the case the British prepared to argue at Casablanca. In fact, Churchill prepared so well for the conference that he needed a cruise ship, HMS *Bulolo,* to carry his support staffs, secretaries, and cryptologists to Africa. He had told Harriman he'd be bringing some people along; in fact, he was bringing practically everybody.[30]

Before Churchill made for Casablanca, a messy political affair intruded into the war-making machinery. Late in the year, his old friend Noël Coward, who had worked undercover for Bracken's Ministry of Information, was nominated for knighthood, a reward Coward's good friend King George thought appropriate but that Coward's friend Winston Churchill considered ill advised. Churchill argued against the knighthood based on Coward's having been fined £200 by HMG as a result of spending more than £11,000 during trips to America, which was in violation of the Exchequer's currency laws. This was an extraordinary amount of money, and more than the average British family earned in ten years.[31]

Almost seven decades later, Churchill's resistance to the knighthood was ascribed by some in the press to his "homophobic" mind-set, a charge not supported by any of Churchill's inner circle, who dutifully recorded in their diaries his regular and often acerbic criticisms of men and women, great and small. Did Churchill know who in his circle was a homosexual and who was not? "I wouldn't think he cared," recalled Jock Colville. Churchill was well aware of the homosexual proclivities of certain of the West End theater crowd, sundry university dons, as well as myriad luminaries in HMG and the military, such as his former secretary Eddie Marsh and his bisexual friend Bob Boothby, and T. E. Lawrence, to whom Churchill remained loyal long after Lawrence's death. Winston and Clementine lunched on occasion with W. Somerset Maugham ("Willy" to his friends), who late in life found "great pleasure" in Churchill's presence at his dining table. Evelyn Waugh (who had had a few homosexual affairs at Oxford) was always welcome in the Churchill house, Churchill grateful to Waugh for watching out for Randolph when they served together in Yugoslavia. Churchill, a presiding member of the louche aristocracy (as characterized by the British historian Roy Jenkins) that ruled England, lived a life of valets, gardeners, chauffeurs, champagne, perfumed handkerchiefs, and pink silk underclothes, all the while surrounded by a coterie of the most eccentric Englishmen and -women—including his mother, father, and son—who enjoyed flirtations with debauchery. Homosexuality, illegal in Britain, was considered dangerous but not immoral by Churchill's crowd, and only for the political scandal that might attach to public disclosure. Homosexuals might be a security risk, Churchill once told one of his private secretaries, not only because of the danger of blackmail but because they might feel alien in the mainstream of their own society, "like a black in a white country, or a white in a black one."[32]

Though he cared little about a person's sexual preference, Churchill was often quick with clever barbs about homosexuals. Of the notorious Tom Driberg—Beaverbrook protégé, Labour MP, and serial seducer of young men—Churchill remarked, "That's the man who brought sodomy into disrepute." When he learned from MPs in the smoking room that Driberg had married a somewhat plain woman, Churchill announced, "Buggers can't be choosers." Yet when it came to something as serious as a knighthood for Coward, Churchill stuck to the facts.

Churchill opposed the knighthood because he took HMG's currency laws seriously. He complained about (and paid) heavy excise taxes on the Cuban cigars that found their way to his humidor. He was not a diligent manager of his own money, but he was diligent in paying his taxes (and in taking advantage of any tax loopholes that presented themselves). Despite Coward's secret intelligence work, which could not be divulged in any event during wartime, it simply would not do for news to escape in the midst of fiscal drought, coal shortages, and food rationing that Noël Coward, having been fined for burning through the equivalent of ten years of middle-class wages in a few months while sating his voluptuary appetites in America, had been rewarded with a knighthood.*33

Churchill's personal physician, Sir Charles Wilson (who had been knighted the previous year), was another case altogether. Although Churchill never called Wilson a friend, as he did Coward, the doctor had committed no transgressions that might reflect poorly on Churchill or England. On New Year's Day, Doctor Wilson was made a peer, and became the First Baron Moran.

Churchill had intended to depart London for Casablanca on January 11, but when foul weather pushed his departure back a day, he used the time to fire off a memo to Sir Henry Tizard, who had recommended the RAF follow the lead of the Americans and resort to daytime bombing raids, with the objective of gaining more accuracy. Churchill replied that "since a great proportion of our losses are due to flak, which is more accurate by day than by night, the day bombers will have to fly at a very great height," which would further reduce their accuracy. This was the great tactical conundrum. The Americans, with faith in the protective firepower of their Flying Fortress's eleven .50-caliber machine guns, had embraced the tactic of daylight raids. Yet while conducting a very few such raids over France and the Netherlands, and not one over Germany, they had suffered terrible casualties among their bomber crews. Six months earlier, on July 4, six American bombers—in a statement of American independence—took part in a daylight raid on German airfields in Holland; the planes missed

---

* Coward was finally knighted in 1969.

their targets and two of the six never returned. Churchill believed the best—and safest—way to reduce Germany was by night bombing. Five hundred American bombers were parked in East Anglia, and he wanted them in the air over Germany, at night, even though such a tactical shift would require the retraining of every American airman. Churchill intended to voice his opposition to daytime bombing to the Americans at the upcoming Casablanca meeting. He also meant to ask the Americans just when they might begin dropping bombs on Germany.[34]

The ongoing dispute between Prof Lindemann—Lord Cherwell—and Tizard only served to further muck up the works, and ill serve Churchill. Sir Henry sought to bury the hatchet with Cherwell, but Prof saw no reason to extract it from between Tizard's shoulder blades.* Churchill told Tizard that his bombing suggestion was "all a matter of numbers" and instructed him to prepare a report for his return. But Cherwell, not Tizard, accompanied Churchill to Casablanca, and nobody could assemble numbers like the Prof. Cherwell's objective was to destroy German morale, ergo German houses, which usually contained residents. He and Churchill of course hoped to destroy German industry as well, but poor bombing accuracy—day or night—proscribed inflicting a mortal wound on German industry. But Cherwell knew that as long as bombs fell somewhere within a city, they destroyed houses, and therefore morale. He had advocated that strategy almost a year earlier, in a study that came to be known as the "Dehousing Paper." He had Churchill's full support. Thus, there could be no doubt that Tizard's numbers would never stack up to Cherwell's, or that Sir Henry's suggestion would ever fly.[35]

By this date, after almost forty months of war, the British had poured 70,000 tons of bombs into Germany, the equivalent of 6,000 sorties by Lancaster heavy bombers and more than four times the tonnage the Luftwaffe dropped on Britain during the height of the 1940 Blitz. Within six months, Bomber Command would double that tonnage. But the American Eighth Air Force had yet to get off the ground in any meaningful way. It was headquartered near Bomber Command at the Wycombe Abbey, a girls' school in a former country house tucked into the lovely meadows and crofts of Buckinghamshire. In the months since the school's students and teachers were sent packing, the Eighth had done little more than unpack its charts, sextants, and slide rules. The Eighth Air Force's commander, Major General Carl Spaatz (whose name Churchill mispronounced as "spots"), and much of the Eighth had been siphoned off to North Africa,

---

* In September 1959, Lord Cherwell offered to a colleague that he had finally "buried the hatchet with Tizard. . . . But," the Prof added, "I know where to find the handle." Tizard died the next month (Moran, p. 813).

with the result that the Americans, in a few night raids, dropped fewer tons of bombs on Germany during the final months of 1942 than the Luftwaffe had dropped on London on the first *night* of the Blitz. This was unacceptable to Churchill, who intended to say as much in Casablanca to the overall U.S. air commander, General Ira Eaker, himself a believer in the invincibility of airpower. "The Americans had been in the war for more than a year," Churchill later wrote, "but so far had never thrown a single bomb on Germany by daylight methods."[36]

He never ceased to express to the Chiefs of Staff both his keen desire to bomb Germany and his suspicion that the effects on German industry were neither "decisive" nor up to the "hypothetical and indefinite" objectives cited by Air Marshal Portal and Bomber Harris. "It is very disputable," he wrote in a memo to Portal, "whether bombing by itself will be a decisive factor in the present war." Yet Churchill had also tried to sell Stalin on the idea that the air war was not only a de facto second front but also an effective second front, a claim that Stalin dismissed (but Eisenhower agreed with, as did Goebbels when the bombs took an increasingly greater toll). At the core of Churchill's fluctuating beliefs regarding airpower was the unsettling prospect that if airpower did not reduce Germany to ruin, large Anglo-American armies would have to do so. He had long known that armies would have to go ashore someday, but airpower, as seductively portrayed by Portal and Harris, held up the possibility of sparing the troops (although at terrible cost to the air crews). In one of Churchill's disputatious memos to Portal he argued that even if "all the towns in Germany were rendered largely uninhabitable it does not follow that the military control would be weakened or even that Germany's war industry could not be carried on." In fact, Churchill feared Hitler would scatter war production throughout Eastern Europe such that it became independent of events in the Reich, and untouchable.

In the end, his doubts proved justified. German production of tanks, planes, artillery, and submarines increased during each year of the war, and fell off only during the final twelve weeks (although the rate of increase was assuredly slowed by bombing). Churchill saw the inherent contradictions in the arguments put forth by the strategic bombing advocates. On the one hand, pinpoint accuracy (which was unattainable) was not necessary for a reduction in German morale, but it was absolutely necessary if German industry was to be destroyed. He had no choice but to continue the bombing. It *might* erode morale; it *might* smash industrial targets. Whatever the results, British morale would be boosted. Britons were not to be denied their revenge. By war's end the effort cost Britain almost 11,000 aircraft and 55,000 killed, the Americans more than 8,000 planes and 26,000 killed. As for Spaatz, who later commanded all U.S. air forces in Europe and believed those forces could alone defeat Hitler in 1944, Churchill offered to

Harris that the American was "a man of limited intelligence." Harris's reply to Churchill is ironic, given his bomber mania and the slaughter within his RAF ranks: "You pay him too high a compliment."[37]

Neutral nations also thwarted the destruction of German industry. Sweden, Switzerland, Portugal, and Spain all carried on robust and profitable trade with Germany, to the ongoing frustration of the Allies. Almost 100 percent of Europe's wolframite, a tungsten ore critical to the manufacture of armored steel plate, came from the Iberian Peninsula. Half of Portugal's wolframite went to Germany, a trade policy that resulted in dead Britons. That was one reason Churchill for two years had considered the possibility of taking the Azores by force if Portugal's dictator, Dr. António Salazar, did not agree to grant Allied ships and aircraft refueling rights in those islands. Were Allied aircraft allowed use of the Azores, the air cover over convoys would effectively double. Salazar continued to play both ends against the middle until late 1943, when—after Churchill threatened to take the islands by force—he finally granted refueling and landing rights to the Allies. When Salazar objected to American troops being stationed in the Azores, Churchill again threatened direct action, cabling Eden, "There is no need for us to be apologetic in dealing with any of these neutrals who hope to get out of Armageddon with no trouble and a good profit."[38]

The neutrals profited handsomely from their relations with Berlin. The Swedes supplied the Reich iron ore, canned fish, and ball bearings. The Swiss sold Hitler arms and ammunition, and industrial diamonds used in cutting tools and bomb fuses. Pressed in early 1943 by the British and Americans to curtail their arms trade with Germany, the Swiss promised to look at their trade practices, and then went on that year to increase shipments to Germany by over 50 percent. The Swedes were stubborn when pressed to limit trade with Germany, wrote Dean Acheson, then an assistant secretary in the State Department, but "the Swiss were the cube of stubbornness." The neutrals argued that self-preservation drove their trade policies; it did not pay to say no to Germany. Even Franco, a Fascist and hostile neutral who flirted with outright union with the Axis, had to watch his back. To keep him on the fence the Allies continued to send Franco food to feed his people. There were consequences. The American press attacked Churchill as an appeaser after word leaked out of the State Department that he was pondering an offer to Franco to increase food and oil shipments in return for Spain's making small concessions to Britain, including a reduction in Spain's sale of wolframite to Germany. Lord Cherwell proposed turning the behavior of neutrals against the Germans. He developed a plan to clandestinely introduce botulin into the canned fish Sweden sold to Germany. "A small amount of it [botulin] would be enough to destroy all mankind," he later told one of Churchill's secretaries.[39]

An irony attached itself to dealings with neutral nations. The Allies considered German-occupied countries to be legitimate targets of economic and military warfare. The citizens of those nations were therefore doubly victimized—by the Nazis and by RAF bombs, which were no more accurate when dropped on Holland or Norway or France than when dropped on Germany. But neutrals such as Ireland, Portugal, Sweden, and Spain were immune from RAF bombs, immune from the bloodiest consequences of the war. Neutrals might be persuaded by diplomacy to adopt policies acceptable to the Allies, but they could not be cudgeled into good behavior. Meanwhile, they supplied skilled workers, raw materials, machine tools, and bullets that killed American and British soldiers, and banked the profits. Eamon de Valera (whose term for the war was "the Emergency") was an adroit fence-sitter, dutifully interning both German and British pilots who were forced to land in Ireland (and Americans, too, until an arrangement was made later in the year).

The Swiss allowed Britain to manufacture their deadly efficient Oerlikon 20mm cannon under license but also sold the cannon and ammunition to Berlin. Both Tokyo and Berlin had reached an agreement years earlier with Switzerland to manufacture versions of the gun. Thus, when a Messerschmitt Bf 110 armed with Oerlikon cannons attacked a British frigate, also armed with the anti-aircraft version of the gun, each side found itself shooting at the other with the same Swiss weapon. Only Turkey among the largest neutrals displayed a modicum of moral fortitude, when it risked incurring Hitler's wrath by suspending shipments of chrome to Germany; but it did so only in mid-1944, when Hitler was on a sure path to destruction and only after a threat of economic blockade by the Allies. Neutral nations could not be persuaded to act reasonably by B-17 bombers; nor could they be punished by B-17s when they did not. If Allied bombers blew one of Hitler's munitions factories to smithereens, he could bank on the Swiss making up his loss, and the Swedes for the iron to smelt into new cannons. The ring of steel Churchill envisioned around Germany always admitted to a degree of porosity.[40]

On January 11, the same day that Churchill mulled over Tizard's bombing projections, the *Sunday Dispatch* announced the possibility of "one little bomb that would destroy the whole of Berlin...a bomb that would blast a hole twenty-five miles in diameter and wreck every structure within a hundred miles.... The explosive in this bomb would be the energy contained in the uranium atom." HMG saw no need to comment on such a ludicrous example of sensationalist journalism.[41]

Churchill also used the delay on the eleventh to take a first and perfunctory look at a three-hundred-page paper on postwar domestic policy titled "Social Insurance and Allied Services," produced by Sir William Beveridge, released to Parliament in November and published by the government as a white paper in early December.* The British and American press had been parsing Beveridge's plan for weeks. Churchill had not; the sheer length of the report argued against his reading it.

Beveridge was Britain's leading authority on unemployment insurance, master of University College, Oxford, and an old colleague of Churchill's from his days as a Liberal, when he and Lloyd George had asked Beveridge to prepare the nation's first comprehensive plan for national insurance. The 1942 paper—the Beveridge Report, as it came to be known—amounted to a manifesto of social reform, which the *Manchester Guardian* called "a great and fine thing." It outlined a compulsory, flat-rate national program that would address wage loss, maternity care, pensions, disability insurance, housing, education, widows' benefits, health insurance, funeral expenses—every financial need encountered by Britons from birth to funerary interment. Churchill didn't like what little he read, not because he opposed the idea of HMG restructuring Britain's social security apparatus, but because, as he told the War Cabinet, he did not wish to deceive the people "by false hopes and airy visions of Utopia and El Dorado." Besides, he offered, Britain would be nearly broke after the war, the United States would be a formidable competitor, and Britons would "get very angry if they felt they had been gulled or cheated" by promises made, and then unmade. Yet Beveridge, anticipating Conservative opposition, argued that in a postwar world of reduced tariffs and free markets, a shift of pension and health insurance costs from corporations to the government would make British industry more competitive in world markets.[42]

Beveridge convinced some Conservatives but by no means all. Harold Nicolson thought Beveridge took delight in "upsetting governments and wrecking constitutions" with his radical agenda. "He is a vain man," Nicolson wrote. The usual Conservative strategy in such cases, Nicolson told his diary, would be "to welcome the Report in principle, and then whittle it away with criticism." Many Tory MPs had already concluded that Beveridge's plan was "an incentive to idleness." Nicolson's wife, Vita

---

* In Britain, the publishing of a report such as Beveridge's as a "white paper" signifies HMG's overall intent (without necessarily announcing a time frame) to analyze, debate the merits of, and possibly act upon some or all of the recommendations made.

Sackville-West, expressed her opinion on the matter in tones that would not have surprised anyone who claimed the British upper class lacked empathy for the common man: "I am all for educating the people into being less awful, less limited, less silly, and for spending lots of money on (1) extended education; (2) better paid teachers, but *not* for giving them everything for nothing, which they don't appreciate any how" (italics Sackville-West).[43]

Churchill had so far kept to his self-imposed prohibition of any public rumination on postwar policies. Yet he had known since Pearl Harbor that the war would someday be won. He had told his countrymen in November that the end of the beginning was at hand; now Britons sought some sense of where their government intended to go once victory was attained. They especially sought some sense of where the Conservatives were going, for according to Labour, the party of Baldwin, Chamberlain, and Churchill had brought Britain economic depression, the shame of appeasement, and, finally, war. That Labour could make such a claim with a straight face, having done its best to retard re-armament and having voted against even limited conscription just four months before Hitler invaded Poland, did not among Britons diminish doubts about the Tories.

For more than two years, Britons had merrily sung "The Lambeth Walk" (which Berlin radio called "Jewish mischief and animalistic hopping") as they scrambled down into the Underground when the sirens wailed. Six thousand Londoners scuttled into the shelters every night, a decrease of 10,000 from the previous year and 150,000 from the height of the Blitz. Yet a census of the shelters found that almost 6,000 lived there permanently. Two-year-old children who had never seen the inside of a real house had spent their entire lives beneath the streets. Britons had taken everything the Luftwaffe had thrown their way. They loved Churchill and would recoil against any partisan attempt to change horses in midstream, but someday they would be across the river. They wanted to know what they'd find on the other side, other than Churchill's sunlit uplands. Churchill, after returning from Casablanca, and after a more careful examination of the Beveridge Report, told the War Cabinet that the plan "constitutes an essential part of any postwar scheme of national betterment." This was the old Liberal voicing his belief that government could and should rearrange the social structure, and could do so without degrading into doctrinaire socialism, which he loathed.[44]

Yet, by not telling the British people as much, he missed an opportunity to claim as his cause the postwar rebuilding of Britain. He considered parts of the Beveridge Report worthy, but also a nuisance that interfered with the war effort. Attlee and the Labourites, meanwhile, saw the Beveridge Report as a blueprint for their political future. Many Britons approaching the age of thirty had never voted in a national election, had never had the opportunity to choose their leaders. Their patience was not infinite.

The nation's food supply, as always, occupied Churchill's thoughts as he prepared to leave for Casablanca. Hunger was not killing Britons, but it was diminishing their ability to work, in fields and factories. Churchill dictated a memo on January 12 that reflected the major consequence of the shipping crisis: the food crisis. To the Ministry of Agriculture and Fisheries he wrote, "Please make me a plan to have more eggs." Of the millions of tons of barley and oats grown and imported, he asked, could not some be diverted to "garden hens" in order to increase the egg yield? The memo was similar to many he had sent regularly for almost three years, a combination of desperation and a call for clear thinking. After a visit to Britain months earlier, the Lend-Lease administrator Edward Stettinius reported that forests had been chopped down to harvest the lumber and to make room for farms. Golf courses and parks had been plowed up and converted to crop cultivation. Marshes had been drained. And still, rationing was tightened, and tightened again. Stettinius asked Americans in radio addresses and newspaper interviews to try to imagine that one-third of them lived in New England, rather than one-sixteenth, and that they depended for survival on shipments from thousands of miles away through U-boat-infested waters. Before leaving for Britain, Stettinius asked a colleague what an appropriate gift might be for his hosts.* The answer was "food."[45]

After dispensing his thoughts on eggs, Churchill departed No. 10, pausing for a moment to hug his cat, Smokey, and to instruct Elizabeth Layton to make sure that the feline did not suffer from loneliness in his master's absence. He then set off for an RAF airfield near Oxford, where *Commando,* the B-24 that had ferried him to Cairo and Moscow in August, was being fueled for the nine-hour flight to Casablanca. The trip was of course top secret, but Churchill's exit belied the fact. Harriman and Ismay, who were also making the trip, were already at the blacked-out airfield

---

* As with many of the Americans who visited the Churchills, Stettinius brought them a Virginia ham, from his own farm. When he learned that the maximum weight he could bring on board the Pan American Clipper out of New York was forty pounds, he trimmed the fat off the ham. In London, a colleague told him, "Ed, you should have left your shoes at home if necessary, but not the fat off that ham." Churchill, thanking Stettinius for the diminutive ham, peered into the bag, smiled, and told him *never* again to trim the fat.

when they saw "in the distance a convoy of limousines led by one car with the brightest headlights" in spite of the blackout. The convoy roared up to the aircraft with sirens screaming and lights flashing. Churchill—code-named Air Commodore Frankland—stepped from his car "thinly disguised in the uniform of an air commodore." The real air commodore exclaimed, "Good God, the only mistake they made was they didn't put it in the local newspapers." Churchill's bodyguard tried to hustle him aboard the B-24, but he lingered on the runway and at his leisure reduced his cigar to a stub. Air Commodore Frankland would board when he was ready and not before.[46]

A few minutes later *Commando*'s four big Pratt & Whitney engines growled to life and the plane with its precious cargo lifted into the night. The captain took it up to seven thousand feet. It was midwinter, and frigid inside the metal shell. The aircraft had since August been updated with a heating system of sorts—a kerosene-powered contraption rigged up near the cots. The device almost made an Icarus of Churchill. He awoke in the night with a sharp pain in his foot, caused by the heating element glowing red hot upon his toes. Kerosene fumes permeated the cabin. Afraid the heater would ignite his blankets or the fumes, Churchill jostled Portal awake. The air marshal assessed the situation and reached the same conclusion. They disabled the heater and flew on, chilled and sleepless. All aboard bundled up with their extra layers of clothing, all but Churchill, who wore nothing but his silk nightshirt. "On his hands and knees," recalled Lord Moran, "he cut a quaint figure with his big, bare, white bottom." Before departing for Casablanca, the passengers had been issued parachute harnesses, extra clothing, and currency from all the countries they would overfly, as well as notes written in Arabic promising a reward to whosoever gave the bearer safe passage.[47]

In the early morning, they descended out of high clouds over the Moroccan coast, just west of Casablanca. Below, feluccas drifted on fair seas, and in the harbor dozens of stranded yachts rode at anchor, unable to repatriate to Italy, Greece, or France. Landward, verdant smudges of ancient date palm, orange, and olive groves sketched the outer reaches of the city, in which the minarets of dozens of mosques stabbed skyward and the red-tile roofs of whitewashed limestone houses looked as if a sack of pomegranates had burst and scattered its contents across the landscape. Far to the southeast, the snowcaps of the Atlas Mountains, gilded by morning light, cast their ragged shadows seaward. On the far side of the mountains, Bernard Montgomery was driving Erwin Rommel west, through Tripolitania and toward Tunisia. After landing at the Medouina Airfield, Churchill, to the dismay of his bodyguards, chose to light a cigar and wait on the tarmac for the arrival of Ismay's B-24. The secrecy of the entire mission was going up in smoke. When Ismay stepped from his plane, he was horrified to see Churchill standing in the open, attired in his light blue airman's livery. "Any fool can see," Ismay exclaimed, "that is an air commodore disguised as the Prime Minister."[48]

Casablanca promised an oasis of gay colors after the dead gray of a London winter, a painter's delight. Expecting as much, Churchill had instructed Sawyers to bring along brushes, paints, and palette. The weather, Churchill wrote to Clementine, proved to be very un-English and much to his liking, "bright with occasional showers and like a nice day in May for temperature."[49]

It had been a year since he departed the warmth of south Florida, a year that closed without a second front in Europe. The errant Dieppe raid of August had only underscored his doubts in that regard and had demonstrated to the satisfaction of most of the Combined Chiefs (but not to George Marshall) the futility of trying to establish that front in 1942. Stalin, however, expected that Churchill and Roosevelt would use their time together to deliver that front in 1943. Yet, by the time Churchill landed in Casablanca, he had been convinced by Brooke's arguments and Kesselring's reinforcement of Tunis that Roundup was effectively scotched for 1943. He arrived prepared to argue the case for further action in the Mediterranean. It was the only strategy within reach. However, he was always open to suggestion if the suggestion had to do with taking the fight to Germany. He counseled his military chiefs that if the lessons of Dieppe and the vicissitudes of weather and logistics led the Allies to require a guarantee of success before considering taking offensive action, they would find themselves unable and unwilling to take *any* action. "The maxim 'Nothing avails like perfection,'" he warned, "may be spelt shorter, 'paralysis.'"[50]

Dwight Eisenhower had commandeered the Anfa Hotel and eighteen surrounding villas a few miles outside Casablanca and near enough to the beach that the rumble of the surf carried up to the compound. Churchill enjoyed strolling along the beach and dipping into the surf when the seas allowed. When they did not, noting the fifteen-foot breakers, he came to understand how so many landing craft had foundered during the landings. One villa was reserved for de Gaulle, if he showed up. The *New York Times* later reported, "Many acres of the resort were enclosed in two lines of barbed wire, on which tin cans were hung. If any one had been foolhardy enough to approach these lines he would have been riddled by bullets from machine guns or bayoneted by some of the hundreds of American infantrymen who stood helmeted atop roofs or patrolled the shady walks around the area." Actually, one overweight sixty-eight-year-old former trooper was foolhardy enough to do just that. Returning one evening from a stroll along the beach, Churchill and his bodyguard, Walter Thompson, were dropped off by their driver on the wrong side of the compound, and outside the wire. Unwilling to walk the long perimeter, Churchill, eyeing the wire, saw a solution. "We can climb that, Thompson," he declared, and began to swing a leg over the wire. Thompson heard the *click* of a round being snapped into a rifle, followed by shouts of "Halt!" Four soldiers leveled their rifles at the intruders. "It's *Churchill*," Thompson yelled. The soldiers lowered their weapons, cursing at having almost shot the prime minister, and cursing the prime minister for almost forcing their hand.[51]

Field Marshal John Dill and Roosevelt's military chiefs arrived on January 13. Dill, more than any other Briton, had so far earned Marshall's respect, so much so that Brooke's roster of conference attendees had Dill listed in the American contingent. Yet Dill, in the preceding weeks, had passed on to Brooke the general's strategic goals and plans, gleaned by Dill's close friendship with Marshall. Thus, Brooke went into the meetings doubly armed, with his plans and with Marshall's. That evening, Brooke met with Churchill and stressed that although the Americans and certain members of the British Joint Planning Committee favored an invasion of Sardinia over Sicily, he did not, and intended to make his case to the Americans accordingly. He sought Churchill's assurance that the British delegation would speak with one voice. Churchill concurred.

In all of North Africa, from Cairo to Casablanca, the British had more troops on the ground than the Americans did and more planes in the air, and they were alone in patrolling the Mediterranean Sea, where the Americans feared to go. It rankled within HMG that Franklin Roosevelt did not acknowledge these facts in his addresses to his countrymen. Eden later wrote that he was "concerned about the fact" that Roosevelt's declarations "contained not a single word about the British share in the operations," due in large part to the "legend" that the British "were most unpopular in North Africa." Eisenhower's deputy, Mark Clark—in Brooke's estimation a "very ambitious and unscrupulous" man—was intent on promulgating that legend. He infuriated Brooke by spreading the rumor that the French in North Africa would not fight alongside the British. But Brooke's respect for Eisenhower increased when Eisenhower eased Clark out as his deputy and put him in command of the reserves. Still, Clark's and Roosevelt's political shenanigans aside, until such time as the Americans put more men in the field in the fight against Hitler and conducted that fight with better results than Eisenhower had so far obtained, Churchill possessed leverage. He intended to use it at Casablanca—next target, Sicily, followed by Italy. The proposed Sicilian campaign already had a code name: Husky.[52]

The president arrived late in the afternoon on January 14 after a five-day journey by Boeing flying boat with stops at Miami, Trinidad, and Brazil, and an eighteen-hour flight across the Atlantic to Bathurst, a squalid outpost at the mouth of the Gambia River in West Africa. From there he flew in an army C-54 to Casablanca. His doctor, Admiral Ross McIntire, was as concerned about his patient's health as was Moran for Churchill's. McIntire, worried about Roosevelt's heart, kept digitalis on hand lest the cruising altitude of eight thousand feet trigger an angina episode. Flying was a dangerous business. The American press was not apprised for ten days of the daring journey. When told, the scribblers were agog: "Franklin Roosevelt, with his great sense of historical drama, had again created history with a dramatist's breath-taking stroke. No President of the U.S. since Abraham Lincoln had ever visited a battle theater. No President had ever left the U.S. in wartime. None had ever been to Africa. None had ever traveled in an airplane." Now, *Time* reported weeks later, came Franklin Roosevelt, thirty-second president of the United States, "to shatter all four precedents at once." All true, as was the fact that Roosevelt and his men arrived in Casablanca unprepared for Churchill.[53]

That much became clear during preliminary discussions and at an informal dinner on the fourteenth. Marshall and King stated their desire to wage "all out" war in the Pacific rather than holding actions against Japan. King proposed—to Brooke's amazement—that 70 percent of the war effort be directed toward the Pacific, 30 percent toward Europe. Brooke pointed out that "this was hardly a scientific way of approaching war strategy."

Brooke knew he had a fight on his hands regarding Sicily but presumed he had the full backing of all the British chiefs. Yet some within the British planning staff and one among the contingent had gone off the reservation: Dickie Mountbatten. Mountbatten considered Sardinia the best target, and he crossed the aisle to argue to Harry Hopkins in private the merits of Sardinia. This schism in the British command might have proved problematic had not Mountbatten also argued the case to Hopkins for two other of his favorite schemes—battleships made of ice, and a Rube Goldberg–style weapon Hopkins described as "fantastic." According to Mountbatten, a new type of explosive could be crammed into an old submarine and run right up to the base of a fifty-foot bluff somewhere on the coast of France. The subsequent explosion, Mountbatten proclaimed, would "blow a road right into France." Then, rather than invasion forces having to assault an enfiladed port (as at Dieppe), they could proceed directly through the newly created pass. Mountbatten may not have studied the results of a similar scheme, when Union forces burrowed a huge mine under Confederate lines during the siege of Petersburg in 1864. The mine indeed created an opening, a crater into which Union troops poured—and into which

Confederates poured deadly fire, annihilating the attackers. Hopkins listened, politely, to Dickie's proposal, and judged Mountbatten to be a "courageous, resourceful man" whom the British chiefs "push around." Only time would tell what might become of Mountbatten's indestructible frozen dreadnoughts and exploding submarines.[54]

At dinner that night, King, who had sworn off hard liquor for the duration, consumed enough wine to become "nicely lit up," as recalled by Brooke. Churchill, not realizing King's condition, tried to rebut the admiral each time King — "with a thick voice and many gesticulations" — advised Roosevelt on how best to dismember the French empire and how to fight the war in general, and in the Pacific in particular. The discussion continued well into the early morning hours, the scene lit by candles after an air-raid alert forced the dousing of the electric lights. It was a remarkable scene, the military and political leaders of the English-speaking world chatting by candlelight high on a Moroccan bluff while great armies bivouacked and battled five hundred miles away across the sands.[55]

Over the next week, the Combined Chiefs of Staff met fifteen times to work out a strategy for the coming year. Roosevelt and Churchill dined together daily and spent many hours in private meetings, during one of which Churchill reminded Roosevelt that contrary to their gentleman's agreement of the previous summer on the matter of "Tube Alloys," the British had in fact been excluded from the atomic bomb program. Harry Hopkins assured Churchill that this situation would be "put right" immediately upon Roosevelt's return to Washington. Each evening, the Combined Chiefs briefed the two leaders on the day's discussions, which had not gotten off to a heady start. Brooke called the first few days of discussions "desperate" at one point, concluding, "The USA Joint Planners did not agree with Germany being the primary enemy and were wishing to defeat Japan first!!!" They disagreed, too, on Burma; the Americans wanted a concentrated British and American effort there in order to reopen the Burma Road in support of Chiang, while the British wanted to bide their time until they had the men and matériel to take a solid shot. The air war presented another opportunity for dispute; Churchill conveyed to General Ira Eaker his displeasure over the American Eighth Air Force and its lack of punch, but after spending an hour hearing Eaker out, he withdrew his opposition to daylight raids, in the main because Eaker sold him on the idea of round-the-clock air attacks, Americans by day and the RAF by night. Churchill liked that, later telling a group of American reporters, "There is nothing like a 24-hours service."[56]

Eisenhower flew over from Algiers to outline his plan for taking Tunis. He proposed a strike eastward to the sea with Major General Lloyd Fredendall's II Corps to drive a wedge between Arnim's and Rommel's armies.

Brooke destroyed the idea, pointing out its most obvious defect: with Montgomery and the Eighth Army still five hundred miles to the east, a thrust by II Corps would result in its being trapped *between* Arnim and Rommel. The most likely result would be the defeat in detail of Freden-dall's force in the south and Anderson's forces in the north. The idea went nowhere, and Eisenhower flew back to Algiers. Yet with the need to coor-dinate the British First and Eighth Armies, as well as the French and Amer-ican forces, it was obvious that a Supreme Commander had to be chosen. It was Eisenhower. He "had neither the tactical nor strategical experience" for such a task, Brooke later wrote, but by "being pushed up into the... rarified atmosphere of a Supreme Commander," he could attend to "his political problems." Brooke believed the appointment, while flattering the Americans, would allow British commanders to fight the battles and restore "the necessary drive and co-ordination which has been so seriously lacking." Eisenhower, with just three stars on his shoulders, was outranked by his trio of British lieutenants—Alexander, Tedder, and Cunningham. Marshall, not impressed with Eisenhower's results in Tunisia, told Roo-sevelt that he "would not promote Eisenhower [to four stars] until there was some damn good reason for doing it." He meant a good military rea-son. Roosevelt had in mind a good political reason; Eisenhower's promo-tion would tell the American people that they were taking charge of the war. Two weeks later, Roosevelt submitted Eisenhower's name to the U.S. Senate, and Ike got his fourth star on February 11.[57]

Although Roosevelt remained committed to Marshall's cross-Channel strategy, he was opportunistic enough to see the merit of Churchill's Sicily initiative. After five days of debate, the Combined Chiefs of Staff reached the same conclusion. They also agreed on eight overall strategic priorities. Brooke later wrote that Dill was instrumental in forging the agreement; the alternative, Dill had warned Brooke and Marshall, was to allow Roosevelt and Churchill to make the final decisions, and "what a mess they would make of it!" The final agreement codified the need to defeat Germany first, with wresting control of the Atlantic taking top billing. Second, and closely tied to the first, was the need to get all aid possible to Russia. The plan to take Sicily was third, followed by the continued buildup of American forces in Britain, with the goal of running a small-scale version of Roundup on the Cotentin Peninsula that August. This was a sop to Marshall. Fifth, the Brit-ish agreed on the need to retake southern Burma (Operation Anakim, scheduled for later in the year) in order to open a supply route to Chiang and to draw the Japanese from MacArthur's flank as he moved northward. This was a sop to Roosevelt and King; Churchill believed China would play no role of any importance in defeating Japan. In any event, the British lacked the requisite forces to retake Burma that year even if they believed it would result in an earlier defeat of Japan. The sixth term of the agreement called for a study of Axis oil needs and industrial capacity, for purposes of planning the "heaviest possible air offensive" to destroy German industrial capacity (which both Spaatz and Harris believed might end the war in 1943). Next came the need to establish naval and air control over North Africa and the Mediterranean. The final article stipulated that all matters connected with Turkey would be handled by the British. The entire eight-point plan was "a strategic menu they [the Allies] could not digest," Samuel Eliot Morison later wrote, a case of planners who "had eyes bigger than their stomachs."[58]

Churchill was so eager to get Turkey and its forty-five (underarmed) divisions into the war that he notified the War Cabinet that immediately following the conference he intended to first visit Cairo, to consult with Alexander, who would soon be setting off for Tunisia. Then Churchill intended to set off for Turkey and a meeting with President İsmet İnönü. The War Cabinet objected; the journey was long and dangerous, and Churchill was needed in London. Churchill replied that he was going any-way, and he instructed Eden to arrange with the Turks for an invitation to be sent to Cairo, where Churchill expected to receive and accept it.

Churchill and Roosevelt had one final piece of business to conduct. It centered on Generals Giraud and de Gaulle. Churchill had included in his birthday eve broadcast the battle cry "France will rise again!" Whether de Gaulle would rise with it was the question. Roosevelt's feelings on the sub-ject were well known to Churchill, to wit, the Frenchman was an obdurate obstacle to the advancement of American policy, which held no promise of any meaningful war role (or postwar role for that matter) for France and the French Empire, de Gaulle or no de Gaulle. Roosevelt had for months artfully avoided any official recognition of de Gaulle by arguing that the sovereignty of France rested solely with its people.

But the French, prisoners of Germany, could make no such choice. In contrast to Sikorski and Beneš, who were leaders of governments in exile, de Gaulle was only the leader of certain military units in exile. Churchill had tolerated and supported de Gaulle in that role for thirty months, but on December 10, in secret session, he told the House, "We must not be led to believe that General de Gaulle is an unfaltering friend of Britain." Quite the contrary, de Gaulle possessed the "traditional antagonism engrained in French hearts" toward the English, and had left "a trail of Anglophobia behind him" wherever he went. Churchill's strategy was clear: by sketching de Gaulle in dark shades, he prepared the House for his removal from the political scene were the Americans to demand it. The scathing attack on de Gaulle was symptomatic of Churchill's evolving relationship with Roosevelt and the subtle lessening of Britain's influence over inter-alliance political affairs. Once Darlan was removed from the picture, Roosevelt's man in North Africa, Robert Murphy, lost no time in propping Giraud up as the civil and military leader there. De Gaulle knew the Americans foresaw no role for him, Eden later wrote, and "began to suspect that the British and United States governments were going to make an agreement with Giraud over his head." Eden rode to the Frenchman's rescue when he drew from de Gaulle a promise to meet with Giraud, but Giraud refused on the flimsy pretext that Darlan's assassination created "an unfavorable atmosphere" for such a meeting. The strain imposed by the totality of the political situation in North Africa—Darlan, Giraud, Mark Clark, and Murphy, and their sundry intrigues—led Eden to later observe, "I was not alone in feeling the physical and mental burden. As the months passed we were all to show it, even the Prime Minister."[59]

De Gaulle proved himself the most tiresome Frenchman of the lot. Roosevelt and Churchill had brought Giraud around; he agreed to meet de Gaulle in Casablanca in order to work out a civil and military partnership. But de Gaulle refused, telling Eden that he would agree to meet Giraud alone, perhaps in Chad, but not in Casablanca, where such a meeting could only amplify the subordinated stature of the French. Gallic honor was at stake. Eden tried a different tack; the president, he told de Gaulle, would like to meet with him in Casablanca. De Gaulle again refused, telling Eden that if Roosevelt wanted to meet, they could do so in America. Eden reported de Gaulle's recalcitrance to Churchill, who responded with a warning that de Gaulle's failure to appear would result in his forfeiting any chance of assuming *any* role in Algiers, even the subordinate role envisioned by the Americans. The message was, show up or HMG will be done with you. Roosevelt, who had prevailed upon Giraud to come to terms with de Gaulle, cabled Eden: "I have got the bridegroom, where is the bride?"[60]

After a weeklong sulk, de Gaulle finally agreed to go, arriving in Morocco on January 22. That night, he met with Churchill. "I was pretty rough with him," Churchill told Lord Moran after the meeting, as the two watched de Gaulle make his way down the hill from the residence. Yet, Churchill added, "France without an army is not France. De Gaulle is the spirit of that army...the last survivor of a warrior race." Moran asked Churchill if he had heard Roosevelt's quip that de Gaulle fancied himself a descendant of Joan of Arc. Churchill had and "was not amused." De Gaulle was defiant and arrogant, Churchill told the doctor, but he offered that, with tears now in his eyes, "England's grievous offense in de Gaulle's

eyes is that she has helped France. He cannot bear that she needed help."
The tears appear to be plausibly Churchillian, yet so do the sentiments he
expressed in a letter to Clementine two days later, when he wrote that de
Gaulle brought "comic relief" to the conference. "He thinks he is Clemenceau (having dropped Joan of Arc for the time being)." Of French
leaders, including de Gaulle, Churchill told Clemmie, "They hate each
other far more than they do the Germans" and they "care more for power
and place than for the liberation of their country."[61]

De Gaulle met with Giraud on January 23 and afterward issued a typically enigmatic announcement: "We have met. We have talked." Roosevelt
also met with the two Frenchmen, separately. Giraud and the president chatted with no bodyguards in attendance, but when de Gaulle arrived at Roosevelt's villa, the Secret Service detail—many of the agents armed with
tommy guns—took up concealed positions behind shrubs and draperies.
The union of sorts between the reluctant Frenchmen appeared to be a fait
accompli, although the governing body that was struggling into existence
was so ill defined as to be nonexistent, and was not recognized by London or
Washington as having any official role elsewhere within the French empire,
or in France, where de Gaulle was considered a national hero.[62]

Just after noon on Sunday the twenty-fourth, a fiercely sunny and hot
day, de Gaulle and Giraud's union—a "shotgun wedding," Eden and Roosevelt called it—was consummated with a ceremonial handshake on the
lawn of Roosevelt's villa, with Roosevelt (hatless) and Churchill (under a
gray homburg) looking on. Fifty shocked reporters were also present; they
had been brought over from Algiers not knowing whom they'd be meeting.
One photographer in the group was Sammy Schulman, a short, musta-
chioed, and brassy shooter whom Roosevelt had known for a decade. A
month later, Roosevelt regaled Washington reporters with the story of
what happened next: "I worked it out beforehand with Sammy. After the
pictures of the four of us were taken, Sammy Schulman in the front row
said, 'Oh, Mr. President, can we have a picture of the two Generals shaking hands?' So I translated Sammy to Giraud, and Giraud said, '*Mais, oui,*'
and he got right up and held out his hand. It took Churchill and myself five
minutes to persuade de Gaulle to get on his feet to shake hands. And we
got them to do it. And I think you have all got that picture. If you run into
a copy of the picture, look at the expression on de Gaulle's face!"[63]

The expression of feline contentment Churchill wears betrays the fate of
the canary. Sammy's shots of the four leaders and of de Gaulle and Giraud
are some of the most iconic images of the war. Yet they capture a false
image; de Gaulle, in fact, had agreed to nothing more substantive than a
handshake with Giraud. As much as Roosevelt derided de Gaulle, the
Frenchman had had the last laugh at Casablanca. His Fighting French

forces numbered 50,000, just one-fifth the number of former Vichy troops serving under Giraud, yet de Gaulle and his men supplied the spirit of the French army in North Africa. De Gaulle's army had been formed in reaction to established authority; in a legal sense they were mutineers, first against the defeated Third Republic, then against Vichy, where they were considered freebooters. Charles Maurass, a septuagenarian royalist, Vichy mouthpiece, poet, polemicist, and Pétain counselor, pronounced, "De Gaulle is a traitor who leads the scum of the earth." This the Gaullists took as a compliment. The Fighting French would never serve willingly under former Vichy loyalists, and although Giraud was brave and decent, many in his officer corps were not. Giraud himself served at the pleasure of the Americans, an insult to Gallic pride, and he had so far failed to repeal anti-Jewish Vichy laws or free Gaullist prisoners. The handshake altered nothing, and meant nothing. The marriage lent credence to an old saying in the French cavalry: "Beware of women when they are in front of you, beware of horses when they are behind you, and beware of your leaders wherever they were."[64]

Moments after Sammy snapped his photos, Roosevelt uttered one of the most iconic phrases of the war. Speaking from notes, he outlined in general and necessarily imprecise terms the decisions taken over the previous ten days. Then he nonchalantly added an incendiary line: the Allies demanded "unconditional surrender" from the Axis. Hopkins later recalled the president telling him that the phrase had simply "popped into his mind" as he compared the difficulty of getting Giraud and de Gaulle together to that of arranging a meeting between Robert E. Lee and Ulysses S. "Unconditional Surrender" Grant. "And the next thing I knew," Roosevelt told Hopkins, "I had said it." Roosevelt the multilateralist had just seemingly issued one of the most unilateral declarations in American history, but it was not spur of the moment. In fact, Churchill days earlier advised his War Cabinet that he and Roosevelt had discussed the matter and decided upon terms of "unconditional surrender" for Germany and Japan. The War Cabinet insisted Italy should be included. Churchill understood the matter was to be kept secret. But Roosevelt let it slip. Churchill, in his memoirs, took a mild swipe at Roosevelt when he wrote of Roosevelt's explanation of how he came to utter the words: "I do not feel this frank statement is in any way weakened by the fact that the phrase occurs in the notes from which he spoke."[65]

"Churchill was indignant" at dinner that night, recalled Averell

Harriman, angered not so much by the policy of unconditional surrender but the "unfortunate way Roosevelt announced it." The words "unconditional surrender" sent several messages to several quarters. To the British and American people it signified that there would be no "Darlan deal" with Hitler, Tojo, or Mussolini. It meant that no mere armistice would leave Germany free to refit for purposes of future misdeeds. It meant that no Wilsonian-style Fourteen Points—imprecise, and open to infinite interpretation—would infect the negotiations. In fact, there would be no negotiations. "Unconditional surrender" told Stalin that the Americans and British were in it for the duration. Yet it also told Stalin that his allies expected him to go the distance. The prospect of Stalin making a separate peace with Hitler had worried the Anglo-Americans for more than a year.[66]

Churchill's memory proved fallible when in 1948 he told Roosevelt biographer Robert Sherwood that he had "heard the words 'Unconditional Surrender' for the first time from the president's lips at the conference." Ernest Bevin's memory, too, proved faulty when in 1949, as a cabinet member in Clement Attlee's Labour government, he excoriated Churchill and "unconditional surrender" for the crippling costs associated with rebuilding Germany. Churchill replied to Bevin as he had to Sherwood, that he had heard the words for the first time from the president's lips at Casablanca. Only later did Churchill recall the telegram to the War Cabinet of January 1943. Such errant recollections have muddled the issue ever since.[67]

Criticism and controversy attended the expression from the moment Roosevelt uttered it. Eisenhower didn't like it because it did not define "unconditional," and when the time came for cease-fires and surrenders, Eisenhower would be the man on the spot. "Around headquarters," wrote Eisenhower's press aide, Harry Butcher, such troubles were "attributed to the hard-boiled" insistence of Churchill and Roosevelt on "unconditional surrender.... No surrender has ever been made without some conditions." Eisenhower would later ask his superiors to precisely define the term; they would not. Stalin had said he need not be consulted but only be apprised of decisions taken at Casablanca, and so he was. He did not make a public statement on "unconditional surrender" until his annual May Day speech, where he turned the tables on his two allies by implying that unless they kept their promise to open a second European front that summer, any talk of unconditional surrender was just that, talk. Later in the year, Stalin told Harriman that Roosevelt's remark "was an unfortunate statement." Two years hence, Goebbels employed it as a propaganda tool, extolling Germans on the need to fight to the death because the enemy had left open no other option. "It was a godsend to Goebbels," Harriman later recalled. By the end of the year, Churchill, too, harbored doubts, and told Stalin as much. That conversation remained private until after the war. In public, Churchill never wavered on "unconditional surrender."[68]

Following the news conference, Churchill persuaded Roosevelt to delay his departure to the United States for one day in order to accompany him to Marrakech, "the most lovely spot in the whole world." It is "the Paris of the Sahara," he told the president, where for centuries caravans had arrived from central Africa and where the traders were swindled in the markets and entertained in "the most elaborately organized brothels in the African continent." The two leaders—Macmillan called them the Emperors of the West and the East—sent most of their troop on ahead by air. A small motorcade carried the president, Churchill, and a few aides on the 150-mile trip. The road was lined on both sides by American sentries positioned a few dozen yards apart, an entire division of Patton's infantry, which might better have served the cause by fighting in Tunisia than by performing guard duty in Morocco. In Marrakech the party bivouacked in the Villa Taylor, an oasis of orange and olive groves surrounded by high walls, and home to the American vice consul Kenneth Pendar. A narrow three-story tower rose skyward from the house. Churchill ordered Roosevelt and his wheelchair carried up in order that the president might take in the Atlas Mountains at sundown when, as the sun fell into the Atlantic, the distant snow-covered peaks slowly faded from white to rose to blood red. The two partners enjoyed a "jolly" dinner that night after composing a joint telegram to Stalin in which they congratulated him for his leadership at Stalingrad. The cable also outlined the decisions made during the conference, only one of which held any interest for Stalin, the pledge to put men into France that year.[69]

When Roosevelt left for home the next morning, Churchill accompanied him to the airfield, dressed in velvet slippers and his green-and-red-and-gold-dragon dressing gown. He was thus attired a few hours later, supine in bed under the cover of a light-blue silk bedspread with a six-inch-wide entredeux, the scene lit by numerous candles, when he summoned Brooke and announced that they would "be off" at 6:00 P.M. that evening. Brooke had come to expect that a summons from Churchill might well find him in bed, or emerging from his bath, toweling off his round, white Humpty-Dumpty self, climbing into his silk underclothes, all the while declaiming on some new scheme that he had hatched. On this occasion, Brooke pleaded that he had presumed they'd be staying for two days and that he hoped to get a day of needed rest and do some bird-watching in the foothills. Churchill did not budge. Brooke tried to turn the tables, arguing that a day of painting would be a welcome respite for the P.M. This, too, failed to move the Old Man. "We are off at six," he replied, a cigar plugged into his face. "To where?" asked Brooke. "I have not decided yet," Churchill answered. To either London or Cairo, he added, pending an answer from the Turks.[70]

It was to be Cairo. Churchill spent a few hours before his departure up in the villa's tower, where he painted his only picture of the war, a landscape scene he later gave to Roosevelt. At dusk, *Commando* and an accompanying B-24 carrying Brooke and staff officers lifted off from Marrakech, eastbound for the overnight flight to the Nile. As they climbed to more than 14,000 feet to clear the mountains, the temperature inside the planes fell to below freezing and the clatter of the engines blotted out all conversation. Churchill's craft had been outfitted with windows and a salon with armchairs, such that he at least could peer out in order to track his progress. Brooke and those on board the other Liberator could do nothing but count rivets on the plane's cold aluminum skin. Churchill's party reached Cairo at dawn after an eleven-hour flight. Shortly thereafter they arrived at the home of the British ambassador, Miles Lampson, and his wife, Jacqueline, who asked if they might like breakfast. Brooke suggested they wash up first, but Churchill proclaimed, "No! We shall have breakfast now!" Mrs. Lampson escorted the party into the dining room and asked if the prime minister would like a cup of tea. "I have already had two whiskies and soda and two cigars this morning," Churchill replied, and then asked for a glass of white wine, which, when produced, he emptied in one long gulp. He was in fine fettle and ready for business.[71]

On the morning of Saturday, January 30, Churchill and his party, joined now by Alexander Cadogan from the Foreign Office, boarded their Liberators for the flight to Turkey, their destination, Adana, near the coast just over the Syrian border. Adana had been selected because Ankara was considered too dangerous and too ripe a target for the Luftwaffe, the very situation that underlay Turkish fears of joining the Allies. As Churchill and Brooke flew north along the Mediterranean coast, Hitler promoted General von Paulus to field marshal on the premise that no German field marshal had ever been captured. It was Hitler's way of telling Paulus that he was to fight to the end in Stalingrad, or use his pistol to take his leave with honor. With more than 100,000 of his men killed that month, and with his remaining forces cut in two, Paulus had no army and no fight left. He surrendered his headquarters that night, but the remnants of his army fought on. Churchill by then had boarded a train at Adana and traveled the few miles to where President İnönü waited aboard a train of his own on a rain-drenched plain that had become a sea of mud. The downpour was so

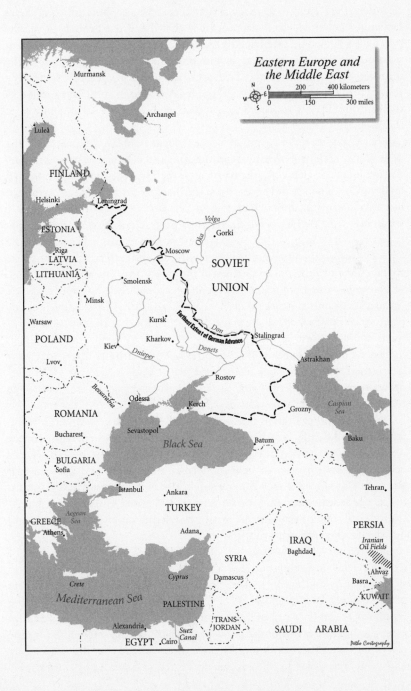

Eastern Europe and the Middle East

0 200 400 kilometers
0 150 300 miles

Murmansk

Archangel

Luleå

FINLAND

Helsinki

Leningrad

ESTONIA

Volga

Gorki

Oka

Riga

Moscow

LATVIA

SOVIET

LITHUANIA

Smolensk

UNION

Minsk

Warsaw

Kursk

Don

Farthest Extent of German Advance

Stalingrad

Kharkov

POLAND

Kiev

Dnieper

Donets

Astrakhan

Lvov

Rostov

Bessarabia

Odessa

Kerch

Caspian Sea

Grozny

ROMANIA

Sevastopol

Baku

Bucharest

Black Sea

Batum

BULGARIA

Sofia

Tehran

Istanbul

Ankara

Athens

TURKEY

GREECE

Aegean Sea

Adana

PERSIA

Iranian Oil Fields

SYRIA

IRAQ

Baghdad

Ahvaz

Cyprus

Damascus

Basra

Crete

KUWAIT

Mediterranean Sea

PALESTINE

TRANS-JORDAN

Alexandria

Suez Canal

SAUDI ARABIA

EGYPT

Cairo

Petho Cartography

relentless that Turkish sentries assigned to protect Churchill took cover beneath blankets, a dereliction of duty that disgusted Brooke. After the two trains "docked," the friendly but reluctant neutral and the confident warlord got down to business, a state of affairs remarkably similar to the meeting between Hitler and Franco at Hendaye in October 1940. The results proved similar as well, although Brooke took some satisfaction in the fact that Turkey appeared to assume "a more biased nature in favor of the Allies."[72]

The Turks feared two possible consequences of an alliance with the Allies: an attack by Germany in retaliation; and behavior of an imperialistic sort by the Soviets once the war was won. The czars had, after all, coveted the Dardanelles and egress from the Black Sea into the Mediterranean for two centuries (İnönü had fought the British at Gallipoli in 1916). Churchill expressed his belief that the Soviets might indeed "become imperialistic," but he argued that Turkey's best protection in that case would be a pact with Britain and America. As well, Churchill offered that a postwar world council would possess sufficient military power—unlike the League of Nations—to reel in states that went astray. He made his case in French (or French as only he spoke it, as noted by Cadogan), "with English words pronounced as French" as he waved his arms about for effect. The argument expressed in English, Cadogan wrote, was excellent, but in French, "I have no idea!" Churchill, wisely, did not pressure the Turks, who, Cadogan wrote, "were resolutely disinclined to be drawn into a war." The Germans knew all of this by virtue of reading Turkish signals traffic. Brooke termed the meeting "a great success."[73]

It was not, other than in the narrow sense that Brooke's Mediterranean strategy could only fare better with Turkey friendly than with Turkey unfriendly. Yet neither was the meeting a complete failure. The Turks accepted a British offer to help modernize their army and allowed vast stores of British war matériel to be stockpiled in southeast Turkey, in case it was needed in Syria, Iraq, or Turkey, should Hitler violate Turkish neutrality. Still, one of the eight priorities decided upon at Casablanca could now be checked off, as unfulfilled.

On February 2, Churchill—back in Cairo—learned that the rest of Paulus's army in Stalingrad had surrendered that day, including twenty-three generals and more than 90,000 troops, who marched off to Soviet prison camps. Only 5,000 of them survived their captivity, the sole living remnants of Paulus's original army of 450,000. The bells of the Kremlin rang the next day. In Berlin, radio programming was interrupted by the roll of muffled drums, followed by the announcement that the Sixth Army had been "overcome by the superiority of the enemy and by unfavorable circumstances confronting our forces." The second movement of Beethoven's Fifth Symphony followed the reading of the communiqué. Regular programming did not resume for three days. Hitler's generals soon witnessed a marked change in the Führer. "His left hand trembled," wrote General Heinz Guderian, "his back was bent, his gaze was fixed, his cheeks were flecked with red. He was more excitable, easily lost his composure, and was prone to angry outbursts and ill-considered decisions." Hitler later told one of his doctors that his sleepless nights were filled with visions of maps marked with the final positions of his armies before they were destroyed.[74]

Stalingrad was the single greatest military defeat in German history and only one of several disasters that had befallen the *Ostheer* since the beginning of the new year. On the Baltic, the Red Army brought relief to Leningrad in mid-January. After 515 days of siege and a yearlong rain of steel from six thousand German guns, the Russians opened a narrow land bridge into the city. In the Caucasus, Hitler's Army Group A, reduced now to just a single army, had been driven back two hundred miles to Rostov, which the Red Army took in mid-February, thereby cutting off the Germans on the southern shore of the Sea of Azov. Two hundred miles to the north, Field Marshal Erich von Manstein's armies had been driven west from the Don and out of Kharkov and Kursk. Since their November lunge across the Volga, the Russians had raced 250 miles across the Don and the Donets rivers. They were now only fifty miles east of the Dnieper. Marshal Zhukov had asked for much from Stalin in the way of men, weapons, tanks, and planes, and Stalin had delivered the goods. Now Zhukov had delivered the results. Stalin—like Churchill, a student of the American Civil War—began telling Western visitors to the Kremlin that Zhukov was his George McClellan except that Zhukov had never lost a battle. (General McClellan had likewise asked President Lincoln for much support, and received it, but he was meek in his approach to the Confederates, and delivered no victories.)[75]

The news from Russia put Churchill in top form. He dined on February 2 at the British embassy, where he watched a film of British troops entering Tripoli and held forth until almost midnight on one of his favorite topics, the 1898 Omdurman campaign in the Sudan. Randolph, on leave, joined the party. Alexander Cadogan, who sat between Randolph and Churchill, found Randolph to be "a dreadful young man. He has been an incubus on our party since Casablanca." The father and son snapped and growled at each other throughout the evening. Had Cadogan been a frequent visitor to Chartwell, he would have known this was how dinner went when father and son shared the table. Accompanying Randolph (and keeping an eye on him) was Churchill's prewar literary assistant, Bill Deakin, now Captain Deakin of the Special Operations Executive. Churchill had just learned from Deakin that while Serbian forces under Mihailovich were keeping Axis troops occupied in Serbia, farther north in Croatia and Slovenia, the peasants, schoolteachers, and intellectuals under Tito were doing likewise, but with no support from the Americans or British. After asking for a report on the matter, which Deakin produced in two days, Churchill shifted British policy in a manner nobody had foreseen.[76]

Tito was a Communist, but he was killing Germans and their Croat Ustasha puppets, and was therefore worthy of assistance. That he was also killing Mihailovich's Chetniks and King Peter's supporters was troublesome, as London backed the return of the king. This was how matters tended to play out in the Balkans, where murderous ethnic feuds had been fought for centuries and where myriad peoples, Churchill once said, produced more history than they could consume. Still, within days of reading Deakin's proposal, Churchill asked Eisenhower for long-range B-24 bombers capable of reaching northern Yugoslavia in order to drop supplies to Tito's partisans. In April, Captain Deakin parachuted into German-occupied Croatia in order to establish relations with Britain's newest and most unlikely ally, Josip Broz — Tito.[77]

On February 3, Churchill prepared for the flight to Tripoli in order to congratulate the general who, like Zhukov, had asked for much, and had delivered: Bernard Montgomery. Late that day Montgomery's forward elements crossed the Tunisian frontier. Tripolitania, the richest Italian colony in Africa, had fallen. A generation of Sicilian and Italian émigrés had paved roads and planted vineyards and olive groves there; they had built irrigation systems worthy of the ancient Roman aqueducts in order to nourish their holdings. It was the last of Italy's African possessions. Il Duce, once emperor of more than 1.2 million square miles in Africa, had lost it all. Now, an American weekly reported, "Italians had only the sands blown across the Mediterranean by the sirocco to remind them" of their lost empire.[78]

Per the agreements made at Casablanca, Alexander and the British now served under Eisenhower. Henry Maitland ("Jumbo") Wilson replaced Alexander as commander in chief, Middle East. Alexander, when he reached Tunisia in two weeks' time, would command all Allied land forces in that theater, a fortuitous circumstance in the estimation of Churchill, because Alex could do no wrong, while Eisenhower had so far done little right. Eisenhower's performance had been so lackluster that George Marshall later expressed to Churchill his surprise that at Casablanca the British had not demanded the lead role in the North African operations. In his memoirs Churchill wrote that the idea never occurred to him. Indeed, Churchill had grown to truly like and admire Eisenhower. Yet with Cunningham directing the efforts at sea, Tedder in the air, and Alexander on the ground, and with the agreement for the invasion of Sicily in hand, Churchill had gained everything he sought while giving Roosevelt what he wanted, an American commander. Harold Macmillan captured the essence of the relationship when he later wrote that the British would run the American show in North Africa like "the Greek slaves ran the operations of the emperor Claudius." Eisenhower, whom Brooke denigrated for never having commanded even a battalion in the field, brought one supremely valuable trait to the task—he brokered no chicanery among and between the Allies. "Everyone is entitled to his own opinion," Eisenhower warned his staff. You can call a fellow officer a son of a bitch, he told them, "but the instant I hear any American officer refer to a brother officer as that *British* son of a bitch, out he goes." He would need every bit of the goodwill engendered by his equable command instincts, for American troops in Tunisia were about to display their complete lack of readiness to fight Germans.[79]

Churchill arrived in Tripoli on the fourth, and after a tour of the harbor by motor launch, he watched as the first British supply ship steamed into the port. With the harbor in British hands, the supply lines for the Eighth Army were reduced by 1,200 miles. Later that day, Brooke and Churchill reviewed the 51st Division, the reincarnation of the old 51st, which had surrendered in France almost three years before. The men of the 51st, who had come to Africa "pink and white" and inexperienced, were now "bronzed warriors of many battles and of a victorious advance." Churchill, standing high on a reviewing stand, watched as the troops paraded past, pipers leading the way. Brooke, a tear running down his cheek, turned to Churchill, who shed tears as well. "One could sense the fathomless depth of relief," Brooke later wrote, "caused by a realization that victory had now become a practical proposition."[80]

The next day, the party was off to Algiers, for what was scheduled to be a brief layover in the company of Eisenhower and Admiral Andrew ("ABC") Cunningham before heading home to London late that night. Cadogan, having now experienced the travails of long-distance travel in an unheated bomber, pledged to his diary never to be "dragged around the world again in these conditions, which are filthy. I don't think P.M. has ever looked into our plane or realizes how beastly it is."[81]

Eisenhower knew from experience exactly what Churchill's visit would entail. Before he left London to command Torch, he and Churchill had instituted regular Tuesday luncheons and frequently took their business to Chequers on weekends, where, given Churchill's work habits and absurdly late hours, Eisenhower often found himself having to stay overnight. Ike knew to expect late nights and long dinners upon Churchill's arrival, and dreaded it. Compounding Eisenhower's discomfort, a rumor had it that German—or Vichy, or Arab—assassins planned on ridding the world of the "Big Cigar Man," whose presence in Algiers could bring nothing but headache to Eisenhower. Ike wanted Churchill out of town as soon as possible. "Safe in London," wrote Eisenhower's aide, Commander Butcher, Churchill "was worth an army, in Algiers he was a target and therefore a heavy responsibility."[82]

But Churchill had come to rest and dine, and this he did, over a long lunch hosted by Eisenhower and attended by Giraud and the resident general of Morocco, Paul Noguès, the former Vichy loyalist who three months earlier had tried to drive Patton's army back into the sea. Cunningham hosted the evening meal at his villa, just across the compound from Eisenhower's. Around the villa Churchill was known as "the man who came to dinner." In fact, he told Brooke his intent was to be the man who came for a day or two, or more. But arrangements were already in place for a midnight departure, which would get Churchill to London without braving the daytime skies. Late in the evening Churchill and his party departed for the Maison Blanche airfield, where, after exchanging farewells with their hosts on the runway, they climbed aboard their two Liberators. Lord Moran swallowed his sleeping pills and took himself off to bed. Brooke donned his pajamas, over which he tugged a fur-lined flight suit and boots. Maps, charts, and beverages were stowed.[83]

But the passengers went nowhere. One of the magnetos had failed on the number one engine of Churchill's Liberator. After a fruitless two-hour attempt to start the engine, the pilot called it a night. The passengers disembarked, and the aircraft was locked down. Moran, by now fast asleep, was left behind. At about 2:00 A.M., residents of the two headquarter villas awakened to knocking upon the doors. Winston was back. Commander Butcher and the Americans believed that Churchill had planned the whole caper in order to grab an extra day in the sun, perchance a dip in the sea. In any event, the man who came to dinner finally left for home late on February 6.[84]

Clemmie had cabled Winston before he arrived in Algiers: "I am following your movements with intense interest.... The door is open and it is hoped that soon Mr. Bullfinch will fly home." Churchill replied, "Keep the cage open for Saturday or Sunday, much love." He returned to the nest on Sunday the seventh.[85]

He had been away from King, wife, and country for twenty-six days. It was to be his last flight on *Commando*. The aircraft, with a different crew, later disappeared with all hands. Cadogan was correct in describing the beastly discomforts and dangers of flight, but he was wrong about Churchill. Churchill had known full well ever since his first flights to Cairo and Moscow six months earlier exactly how beastly such journeys were, and how necessary.

In Burma that week, Brigadier Orde Wingate took his brigade of jungle fighters—he called them his Chindits, the Burmese word for "lion"—across the Chindwin River and proceeded to harass the Japanese behind their lines. The need to reopen the Burma Road had been agreed upon at Casablanca, but Wingate lacked the men, and the RAF lacked the aircraft, to make good on that agreement. General Joe Stilwell, cooling his heels in northern India, the victim of Washington's decision to reinforce MacArthur at his expense, lacked an army. And Churchill lacked the will. China, in his estimation, was not worth the effort. That week, the American press reported that large numbers of Japanese ships were sailing for Guadalcanal, most likely to reinforce the garrison there. But this report soon proved false; the Japanese were sailing to "the Canal" in order to *evacuate* their remaining troops. On February 9 a headline in the *New York Times* declared, FOE QUITS ISLAND. New Guinea was the next Allied target; the Australians would lead the charge. The march to Tokyo had begun.[86]

For thirteen months the Americans, having no real choice in the matter given their lack of preparedness, had deferred to Churchill's strategic judgment. They did so again at Casablanca. It would be the last time. The military tide had turned against Hitler at Stalingrad; now the political tide was turning against Churchill. His vision of the postwar world was drifting into crisper focus, and he was testing the words and phrases he intended to use to articulate that vision when the time was right. Yet, as the months went by, the shapes and forms that the new world would assume increasingly became a matter for Roosevelt and Stalin to determine. Churchill's future, and that of his Empire, was now tied inexorably to the political wishes of his two allies who, Sir John Keegan wrote, "were now supplanting him in importance." The decline in Churchill's influence would be gradual; indeed, in early 1943 Churchill had yet to sense it, but it had begun.[87]

On February 2, a *New York Times* story explicating the decisions made at Casablanca was headlined PRESIDENT IMPLIES 1943 INVASION PLAN. Actually, that decision had not been made in Casablanca. It was more hope than goal, and with each passing week an atrophying hope at that. On February 11, tired and with a head cold coming on, Churchill addressed the Commons. He did not promise a great invasion of Europe but promised that Britain's enemies would "burn and bleed" (a favorite phrase) and that stern justice would be delivered to "the wicked and the guilty." He had sent Roosevelt a draft of the speech for comments. Firm in his belief that the French hated the British and respected Americans, Roosevelt replied that "cooperation by French forces will be best if the American Supreme Command in North Africa is stressed." Churchill duly edited his working notes and placed Eisenhower at the forefront. Within a week he found himself supremely relieved to have done so.[88]

In the days following his address, he could not shake the fatigue and head cold he had brought home from Africa. On the evening of February 16, his temperature shot up. Lord Moran, after listening to his chest, concluded his patient had "a patch" on his left lung. "What do you mean by a patch?" Churchill grumbled. "Have I got pneumonia?" An X-ray taken the next day and a second opinion by Dr. Geoffrey Marshall confirmed Moran's suspicion: Churchill had contracted pneumonia. But given his age, it was the strain on his heart, not his lungs, that worried Moran. The patient took to his bed, with a copy of *Moll Flanders*. He ordered his paperwork reduced to a minimum and jotted notes to Roosevelt, himself taken ill by some African bug, and to Hopkins. To both he lamented his "heavy and long" condition. They responded with get-well notes. Churchill was not a difficult patient, Moran wrote, and did what he was told, "provided, of course, that he is given a good reason." Dr. Marshall did not help matters when he referred to pneumonia as "the old man's friend." "Pray explain," asked Churchill. "Oh, because it takes them off so quickly," Marshall replied. Churchill was thus already in his sickbed when news arrived from the North Atlantic, from Russia, from India, and from Tunisia that might have put him there anyway.[89]

By mid-February, Rommel had barred the back door to Tunisia with his positions along the Mareth Line, a decade-old French defensive network that ran from the Gulf of Gabès inland to a great salt marsh. To Rommel's northwest, on the far slopes of the Eastern Dorsal of the Atlas Mountains, the Allied flank was held against several of Arnim's panzer divisions at Sidi Bouzid and along an eighty-mile front by the green American troops of the II Corps, under the command of Major General Lloyd Fredendall. His job was to keep Arnim in place and to watch and wait for Rommel, who sooner or later, with Montgomery in pursuit, would try to join Arnim. North of

Fredendall, poorly equipped brigades of formerly Vichy French held the ground. In the far north, Anderson's First Army had been stalled for eight weeks on its drive to Bizerte and Tunis, where Kesselring had reinforced Arnim's positions faster than the Allies could harass them. The Eastern Dorsal, thinly held by the Americans and French, defined the German left flank from Gafsa to just west of Tunis.

Eisenhower presumed correctly that Rommel would strike north toward Tunis, but the American was unsure of exactly which route Rommel would choose—the coastal plains or a swing through Gafsa followed by a sharp turn north. And would Arnim attempt a strike in the Faid Pass in the Eastern Dorsal, which would put Sidi Bouzid in his sights and threaten the Allied rear? Allied intelligence thought that scenario unlikely based on the belief that the mountain passes were not conducive to tank warfare. Also, Ultra decrypts gave no indication that Arnim was hatching such a plan. But after visiting Fredendall's Sidi Bouzid deployments on February 13, Eisenhower concluded that the defenses were inadequate, and that this was where the Germans would strike. Eisenhower returned to Fredendall's headquarters at Tebessa (ill placed and more than seventy miles west of Sidi Bouzid), intent on drawing up new plans.

He was too late. Arnim and Rommel attacked the next morning. By nightfall Rommel was through Gafsa, and Arnim's tanks had plowed through the American positions at Sidi Bouzid. Both German panzer forces then made for the Kasserine Pass, in the Western Dorsal, which they overran on February 19 and 20, after overrunning two American battalions that had chosen poor defensive positions. Rommel's panzers then poured north out of Kasserine on the twenty-first, his target Tebessa, where the Allies had stockpiled millions of pounds of food, fuel, and ammunition. Another panzer force swung north toward Thala, which if taken would put the Germans behind Anderson's lines. With Arnim's northern flank anchored at Tunis, Anderson and the French would find themselves in a vise. Alexander arrived from Tripoli on February 20 and, shocked at what he saw, immediately assumed command of all ground forces. He found the Americans at Kasserine totally unprepared for Rommel's push, "too defensive" and too "shell and bomb conscious." They had suffered the consequences of poor command, poor intelligence, and a hardened enemy. When Eisenhower (just that week promoted to four stars) ordered B-17s to bomb Kasserine, the planes became lost and bombed a friendly Arab village within the Allied lines and more than one hundred miles from the intended target. The Americans' first major engagement with Germans ended as it had begun, in complete confusion. Alexander now found himself, as at Dunkirk and in Burma, presiding over a disaster.[90]

Within a week of crashing through Kasserine, Rommel, outrunning his supplies and unable to exploit his success, fell back through the pass to the Mareth Line. So stunning was Rommel's stroke that King George wrote a three-page letter to Churchill stating his dismay over both the political and military situations in North Africa. Churchill dutifully replied that his support of Eisenhower for supreme command had been proven "providential." Had a British general overseen the defeat, he told the King, Britain's enemies in America would have been served up a fine opportunity "to blaspheme." Churchill reminded King George that the Eighth Army, 160,000 strong and "perhaps the best troops in the world," was about to play a key role in Tunisia. Moreover, the great General Alexander would henceforth be in charge of strategy on the ground. This was not meant to disparage the Americans, Churchill offered, for they were brave, "but not seasoned."[91]

Eisenhower sacked Fredendall on March 1 and replaced him with George Patton, who, Ike liked to say, "hates the Hun like the devil hates holy water." The debacle at Kasserine Pass underscored Brooke's doubts about conducting a large-scale invasion of France in 1943, even were the landing craft available. Although the American planners left Casablanca believing that they had been snookered by Brooke and Churchill, the rout at Kasserine proved the British correct. The Americans had to first learn how to conduct a modest campaign before contemplating an invasion of fortress Europe. Tommies in Anderson's army soon came up with a line that captured the essence of Kasserine: *How Green Was My Ally.*[92]

While Rommel undertook his audacious strike, Mohandas Gandhi, half a world away, conducted one of his own. Before Churchill left for North Africa, the War Cabinet endorsed the arrest of Gandhi and hundreds of India National Congress members. On February 9, Gandhi, seventy-two, frail, and under house arrest at Poona, announced that he would fast for three weeks. British and Indian doctors monitored his condition. Churchill, suspecting Indian doctors were slipping glucose into Gandhi's drinking water, informed King George that "the old humbug Gandhi" had remained so healthy "one wonders whether his fast is bona fide." On the sixteenth day of the fast, with somber reports emanating from Gandhi's doctors (which Churchill did not believe), Churchill telegraphed Jan Smuts: "What fools we should have been to flinch before all this bluff and sob-stuff." On the following day, he cabled the viceroy, the Marquess of Linlithgow: "It now seems almost certain that the old rascal will emerge all the better from his so-called fast." Lord Linlithgow replied that he believed that Gandhi ("the world's most successful humbug") was not in dire straits and that his doctors had "cooked" their bulletins to produce the desired effect, all as part of a "wicked system of blackmail." The American press championed the Mahatma's cause; the British press for the most part derided Gandhi's gesture as a ploy, as did Churchill, with sly nonchalance, when he later wrote in his memoirs that Gandhi's taking glucose while on the hunger strike in conjunction with his "intense vitality and lifelong austerity" allowed him to safely ride out the dietary crisis. In fact, Churchill had learned during Gandhi's fast that Indian doctors were not giving him glucose. He did not quite equate Gandhi with the wily main character in Kafka's "A Hunger Artist," but he came close. As for Gandhi's stature in India, he wrote, "Mr. Gandhi's death could have produced a profound impression throughout India, where his saintly qualities commanded intense admiration." In arresting Gandhi, he wrote, the British "had judged the situation rightly."[93]

Roosevelt's special envoy to India, William Phillips, in Delhi since January, asked permission of the viceroy to visit Gandhi and Nehru. Lord Linlithgow refused, and instead invited Phillips on a tiger hunt. Phillips could hardly make a complete report to Roosevelt without seeing Gandhi, but he'd have to try, for Churchill had put Gandhi off-limits. Leo Amery, secretary of state for India and Burma, advised Churchill, "I do hope you will make it quite clear to the president that his people must keep off the grass." Churchill's explosion in front of Hopkins the previous April and the treatment accorded Phillips were clear signals to Roosevelt to stay out of British affairs. The president kept his counsel, despite the pro-Gandhi editorializing of the American press. Roosevelt and Churchill never saw eye to eye on India. In fact, Harriman recalled, "They couldn't see *at all* on India" (italics Harriman).[94]

Gandhi ended his fast on March 3. In newsreels he appeared to be in good health. Churchill, still recuperating from his illness, was not.

By early March, Bernard Montgomery, in position in the town of Medenine, about twenty miles southeast of the Mareth Line, knew with certainty that Rommel would attempt a spoiling attack by hooking out from his Mareth defenses toward Medenine. Air reconnaissance and Ultra decrypts gave Montgomery an advantage he intended to exploit. He prepared for Rommel's attack by massing and concealing his anti-tank artillery. Ultra had been so precise that Montgomery knew which brigades of panzers Rommel intended to deploy, and where he intended to deploy them. On March 6, Rommel struck. Thanks to Ultra, he stood no chance. Montgomery, his anti-tank guns in position, destroyed fifty-two of the oncoming panzers. The Germans and Italians stopped, turned, and retreated to their Mareth defenses. The importance of the British victory at Medenine cannot be overstated; had Rommel sent the Eighth Army sprawling eastward, the Allied timetable in North Africa would have been set back indefinitely. A British defeat would have scotched the invasion of Sicily in 1943, and Italy as well. Stalin, already doubting the ability of his allies to kill Germans, would have had no choice but to at least contemplate a separate peace. But Montgomery held. On March 9, Rommel, hobbled by malaria and festering skin lesions, handed over command of his army to General Giovanni Messe, who now served under Arnim in the newly created Army Group Africa. That night, Rommel departed North Africa for Berlin, never to return.[95]

On the Eastern Front, the victories at Stalingrad and Rostov reinvigorated the Red Army, which struck west throughout January and into February. Yet, as it had the previous spring, it advanced too far and too fast, with the result that its lines thinned. Once across the Donets River, the Russians discovered the Germans had changed the gauge on the railroads, forcing the Red Army to send tens of thousands of trucks and horse carts down muddy and rutted roads. Manstein, sure that Stalin's army had overextended itself again, waited for his moment. He struck in the third week of February with fourteen tank and infantry divisions, and within a fortnight he retook Kharkov, driving the Russians back eighty miles along a two-hundred-mile front. Stalin blamed Churchill and Roosevelt for the setback, claiming the German success "involved a lessening of the German forces in France" due to the lack of Anglo-American aggressiveness. Hence, "renewed Russian complaints about bearing the whole weight of the war." In fact, Stalin *was* bearing almost the entire weight of the war, and Churchill and Roosevelt, to their consternation, were not yet prepared to relieve Stalin of some of that weight. This the Germans knew, and were thankful for. On March 2, Hermann Göring told Goebbels that he was "somewhat worried about our having pretty much stripped the West in order to bring things to a standstill in the East. One dreads to think," Goebbels confessed to his diary, "what would happen if the English and Americans were suddenly to attempt a landing."[96]

The English and the Americans were making no such plans. In fact, during the bleak days of mid-February, when everything everywhere appeared to be unraveling, Eisenhower recommended pushing Operation Husky back from June until July. Churchill received the news in bed, his pneumonia coming on hard. A month's delay would be disastrous, he cabled Eisenhower, and to Harry Hopkins he predicted that if during May and June "not a single American or British soldier" was killing any Germans or Italians "while the Russians are chasing 165 divisions around," the result would be "grievous reproach at the hands of the Russians." Britain, he told his military chiefs, "would become a laughingstock." In fact, the original statement of intent drawn up by the Combined Chiefs at Casablanca called for Husky to begin with "the favorable July moon," those nights of the month when the crescent moon before setting gave paratroopers just enough light to find their targets in advance of the amphibious troops. At Casablanca, Churchill and Roosevelt pushed hard for the June moon, and the Combined Chiefs had since asked Eisenhower to reconsider, but General Ike held firm to his timetable. Nonetheless, Eisenhower only further fueled Churchill's doubts about his aggressiveness when in early April he warned that the presence of two German divisions in Sicily cast doubt on the Allied ability to invade the island. Churchill erupted. How, he asked the Chiefs of Staff Committee, could they reconcile "the confidence the General showed about invading the continent across the Channel" with his discomfort at the prospect of sending one million men now in North Africa to face two German divisions in Sicily? "I don't think we can be content with such doctrines." He added, "What Stalin would think of this when he has 185 German divisions on his front, I cannot imagine."[97]

Actually, he knew exactly what Stalin would think. He had twice promised Stalin a second front in 1943, most recently when he predicted that Tunisia would be cleared by April "if not earlier." By early April, with Eisenhower's armies stuck for three months in the mud and mountains of Tunisia, Churchill's promises to Stalin were self-evidently worthless. Even had Eisenhower taken Tunis by then, the omnipresent shipping shortages guaranteed that no second front could materialize in France that year. Churchill tried to placate Stalin, telling him that Husky was forthcoming, that the RAF was preparing to pummel the industrial heart of Germany, the Ruhr Valley, with heavy raids, including a planned operation to destroy the dams and hydroelectric plants that powered German armaments factories. Dönitz's submarine pens were being bombed; the American Eighth Air Force, with more than six hundred bombers, was now up and flying. Churchill indicated his willingness to embrace more sinister tactics. Told of the German successes in Russia, he instructed Ismay to inform the military chiefs that if Hitler used poison gas in Russia, "we shall retaliate by drenching the German cities with gas on the largest possible scale." That was bluster, but by no means was it bluff. Stalin needed help, and Churchill intended to give what he could. Stalin's armies faced twenty times as many Germans as the Anglo-Americans faced in Tunisia. In only one military classification did the Western allies exceed the Russians in manpower: chaplains.[98]

At Casablanca Roosevelt and Churchill made "control of the seas" their first priority. They meant the Atlantic. In the three months since, as measured by men and ships, they not only failed to control the seas, but had lost control.

On January 30, Karl Dönitz was promoted to *Grossadmiral* and replaced Erich Raeder as commander in chief of the navy (*Oberbefehlshaber der Kriegsmarine*). The appointment of the submariner Dönitz could only mean that the submarine war would intensify. It did, with horrific results for the Allies. Churchill warned Roosevelt that they must assume that Dönitz would be "ready to play a game in which the cards are in [his] hands." Dönitz was as firm a believer in the lethality of his U-boats as Göring was of his airplanes, with the difference that Dönitz's U-boats had hobbled Britain, and might yet cripple her. Britain's convoy escort ships were, Churchill informed Roosevelt, "quite inadequate to deal with the German forces."[99]

The U-boats cruised safely that winter, aided by the worst weather in North Atlantic history. The gales kept escort ships in harbors and Allied long-range bombers battened down on airfields. Such was the fury of the North Atlantic between November and March that ninety-two ships were lost at sea to waves and wind. The U-boats rode out the storms beneath the waves and took their harvest. In March, two convoys bound from New York and sailing on parallel courses with eighty-eight merchant ships were attacked over three nights by fifty U-boats. Twenty-two Allied ships and almost four hundred seamen went to the bottom. German sailors called it the "greatest convoy battle of all time." That massacre brought to almost 21,000 the number of British merchant seamen killed since the start of the war, more than one-fifth of Britain's civilian sailors and, relative to the other services, the highest casualty rate of the war. Ships could be replaced; experienced crews could not.[100]

In mid-March, as the losses mounted, Stewart Menzies informed Churchill that Bletchley had finally broken the German naval code. The Bletchley wizards had also deduced from charting Allied convoy and U-boat positions that the British merchant marine code must have been long compromised, with catastrophic results. Bletchley reworked the British convoy code such that the Germans could no longer listen in on ship-to-ship transmissions and Dönitz could no longer pinpoint convoy locations. Despite that progress, Allied losses in March totaled 108 ships and 627,000 tons, more than half the total British shipping lost during the *ten months* of March to December 1941, when Churchill had given the battle its name.

The British would exploit the Bletchley breakthrough in coming months, but March's horrific losses certainly did not auger a change of Allied fortune, given that they came against the sinking of just fifteen of the more than one hundred U-boats operating in the North Atlantic. The U-boats were so numerous that the Allies could no longer resort to evasive routing for convoys, with the result that the entire convoy program began to disintegrate. March's losses, Churchill cabled Roosevelt, brought Britain near to a "hand-to-mouth" subsistence level. Dönitz had reduced Britain's annual food, fertilizer, and fuel imports from 50 million tons prewar to under 23 million, a figure considered by Churchill to be below the minimum needed to sustain the island. Roosevelt, against the wishes of his military advisers, finally came down on the side of Harriman, who advised that feeding Britain, even at the cost of fighting Germans, was the most pressing issue. Food would go to Britain at the expense of the American armed services, whose demands, Roosevelt believed, were inflated and whose ability in utilizing available ships to meet those demands was notoriously lacking. Churchill, to make more hulls available for transatlantic shipments, reduced sailings to India by half, a measure that, in combination with the Japanese occupation of Burma and an ongoing drought, brought Bengal to the verge of famine.[101]

The Atlantic convoys sailed with little protection, and paid a dear price. Escort ships normally assigned to convoy duty were needed for the run-up to Husky. In mid-March, with losses rising, and on the advice of the Admiralty, Churchill and Roosevelt agreed to cancel that month's convoy to Russia, and to not run any more until September. Roosevelt suggested they not break the news to Stalin for "three or four weeks." He volunteered Churchill for the duty, and asked to see a copy of his message before it was sent. He also offered to send "a supporting message" in tandem with Churchill's, in order to present a unified front. Churchill expressed his thanks for the gesture. On March 30 Churchill cabled the bad news to Stalin. Roosevelt never sent the supporting message.[102]

Stalin's reply was curt, the final line worrisome: "You realize of course that the circumstances cannot fail to affect the position of Soviet troops." What, exactly, did he mean by that? It was well known that German diplomats in Stockholm had expressed interest in a German-Soviet prisoner exchange, brokered by the Swedes. Stalin refused the offer; he tended to prefer that repatriated prisoners be shot or imprisoned in case their experiences in the West had resulted in their embrace of anti-Bolshevik blasphemies. But the mere mention of talks between Germans and Russians could only lead to the worrisome question of what else they might be discussing.

Fear of a separate peace had been omnipresent in the Foreign Office and the State Department for almost two years.[103]

Churchill believed that Stalin would never negotiate with Hitler, but the surest way of discouraging such thoughts on Stalin's part was to win the Battle of the Atlantic. However, the slaughter of March implied that the Allies were not doing so. The Germans had improved U-boat propulsion and radar detection. The *Kriegsmarine* deployed sonar decoys, small radio canisters launched while submerged to confuse listening posts on British escorts. They also deployed buoyant anti-radar decoys that when launched from U-boats mimicked the radar profile of a U-boat on the surface, with the result that Allied bombers took to chasing nonexistent targets. Each *Kriegsmarine* measure and countermeasure was soon countered by British improvements in sonar and especially radar, which was being made more powerful and small enough to fit into the nose of a Sunderland flying boat. It was all part of the naval quotient of Churchill's Wizard War.

The Germans, far ahead in submarine design, had drawn blueprints for bigger, faster boats with six forward torpedo tubes, and that were capable of deep dives to greater than seven hundred feet at high speed. But Dönitz couldn't build them fast enough due to the relentless Allied air attacks on German shipyards. He outfitted his boats with *schnorchels*—telescopic breathing tubes that allowed the U-boats to cruise just beneath the waves on diesel power rather than on batteries. But all the German innovations would prove for naught, for the most effective weapon in the Allied arsenal was the American shipyard, where workers were just beginning to build cargo ships and escort destroyers faster than Dönitz could sink them. And, although Dönitz suspected that Bletchley was now reading *Kriegsmarine* radio traffic, he could not bring himself to accept it as fact. Still, his successes against Allied shipping in March convinced him that more U-boats, better radar, and the most advanced torpedoes could finish the job. Samuel Eliot Morison later wrote: "No enemy ever came so near to disrupting Atlantic communications as Dönitz did that month."[104]

Goebbels, since Casablanca, had been preaching the evils of "unconditional surrender" to the German people. The Hun-hating Lord Vansittart played into Goebbels' hand when he told the House of Lords in March that all Germans were accomplices to Hitler and that Germany should be destroyed "utterly and forever as a military power." It fell to the government's advocate, Lord Chancellor Viscount John Simon, to rebut Vansittart by declaring that the British government (and Premier Stalin) held that, although Nazism must be destroyed, "the whole German people is not, as Dr. Goebbels has been trying to persuade them, thereby doomed to destruction." The *London News Chronicle* welcomed Simon's statement: "It shows that the Government is making a rational and a constructive approach to the problem of Germany's future."[105]

Stalin had made public his thoughts on the subject on February 23 in his Order of the Day, celebrating the twenty-fifth anniversary of the founding of the Red Army. The Red Army, the marshal declared, "was not created for the purpose of conquering" other nations. It was now prepared to drive the Wehrmacht from its borders, Stalin added, and would do so that year, but its strength must be preserved to guarantee the peace. These words raised more questions in London and Washington than they answered. Did Stalin mean to assuage German fears of annihilation as proffered by Goebbels? Did he really intend to stop at his borders after expelling the Nazis? How, if the defeat of Hitler was the first priority of the Allies, could Hitler be beaten if the Red Army halted at its borders after driving out the Germans? Or might Stalin, after driving out the Germans, stop inside Poland's old eastern border, to reclaim the lands he and Hitler had taken in 1939? That would create—at far less cost in Russian lives—a buffer between Russia and a subdued but not yet vanquished Germany. The message within the message was clear, and disturbing. If the Western Allies were not fighting on the Continent by the time the Red Army restored its borders, the Red Army might stop its westward march. Stalin added his favorite gibe: "In view of the absence of a second front in Europe, the Red Army alone is bearing the whole weight of the war."[106]

That was true. Only an Anglo-American victory over Germans would provide an effective response to Stalin. Bernard Montgomery intended to deliver such a victory. He struck on March 20, when 25,000 New Zealanders under General Freyberg, after a long and difficult trek far around the Mareth Lines, delivered a left hook to the enemy flank. Gaullist forces operating just north of Freyberg lent a hand when the New Zealanders encountered Germans dug in on mountain ridges. "Can you clear the Germans?" Freyberg asked a French officer, a viscount whose name was Jacques Philippe de Hautecloque, but who went by the nom de guerre Leclerc. "But of course," Leclerc answered. The French soon began killing Germans and collecting large numbers of prisoners, a modest victory, but their first since June of 1940. To the northwest, George Patton's II Corps had been hammering the German flank at El Guettar since March 16, with the objective of slashing its way east to the Bay of Gabès. It was a battle of American artillery and the 1st Infantry Division—known to its men as the Big Red One—versus German tanks. Patton would not win it, but his troops proved their mettle while drawing two German armored divisions away from Montgomery's immediate front, thereby making Monty's job a great deal more manageable.[107]

Montgomery's main force consisted of Englishmen, Poles, Czechs, Australians, Gurkhas, with their wicked curved kukris, which could take an arm off at the shoulder, and Highlanders, who would happily chase the devil himself—Auld Clootie to a Highlander—straight through Hell if so ordered. At 10:00 P.M. sharp on March 21, they attacked the Mareth fortifications. Eisenhower called the Eighth Army "the most cosmopolitan army to fight in North Africa since Hannibal." It was indeed an imperial army, recalled Sir William Deakin, and the fact that a British *imperial* presence was being brought to bear on the European conflict was a source of abiding pride for Churchill. If the Eighth Army was to be the last truly imperial army, Deakin recalled, Churchill wanted it to play "a decisive part." Montgomery was intent on its doing just that. His tactic of delivering a hook and a jab in tandem, of hitting the Germans in places they didn't anticipate and in ways that disrupted their order of battle, had served him well at El Alamein, and it served him well on the twenty-first.[108]

On the night the Eighth Army threw its left hook—March 20—Churchill broadcast to his countrymen and the world. The topic, for the first time during his premiership, was the postwar world. He outlined in broad strokes his plans for Britons at home, and Britain abroad. He cautioned that 1943 would not see an end to the war, nor perhaps would 1944, but in the end, the Allies would beat "Hitler and his powers of evil unto death, dust, and ashes." And then they would do the same to Japan; it would take time, but victory in the East would be attained. After victory, the three great powers—Britain, America, and Soviet Russia—would form the backbone of a "world organization" that would serve as "safeguard against future war." Within this organization, there would be smaller "councils" in Europe, where the last two great wars had begun. Lesser states could then express themselves through these councils. In Europe, he predicted that the "largest common measure of integrated life" could be achieved without destroying the ancient and individual characteristics of its myriad peoples. Russia must be one of the guarantors of that life; "thus and thus only will the glory of Europe rise again." He had obviously not consulted Roosevelt on the speech. Other than references to China's "long torment" and its need of "rescue," he did not include China as one of the great postwar powers. At best, if Churchill had a say in the matter, China would take its rightful place as a lesser state with friends in high places. Anthony Eden, in Washington that week for talks with Roosevelt (who believed in a *four*-power postwar structure), was told in no uncertain terms by Cordell Hull that "Churchill had made a serious mistake in his speech . . . by not mentioning China."[109]

After sketching his vision of postwar Europe, Churchill moved on to the

Beveridge Report and postwar social changes in Britain. The policies he championed that evening would have appeared radical even to a New Dealer. "You must rank me and my colleagues as strong partisans of national compulsory insurance for all classes, for all purposes, from cradle to grave." On health: "We must establish on broad and solid foundations a national health service." On education: "I hope our education will become broader and more liberal." No one who aspired to higher education would be denied the opportunity, including factory workers, for whom some sort of "part time release" from work must be found. Housing: Entire cities and towns had to be rebuilt, "an immense opportunity not only for improving our housing, but for employment." The taxes to pay for all this would be heavier than before the war, but not so heavy as to "destroy initiative and enterprise." Yet, caveats: "First of all we must beware of attempts to over-persuade or even to coerce His Majesty's Government to bind themselves or their unknown successors, in conditions which no one can foresee and which may be years ahead, to impose great new expenditure on the State without any relation to the circumstances which might prevail at that time.... I am not in any need to go about making promises in order to win political support or to be allowed to continue in office." And, "I tell you around your firesides to-night that I am resolved to not...make all kinds of promises and tell all kinds of fairy tales to you who have trusted me and gone with me so far, and marched through the valley of the shadow, till we have reached the upland regions on which we now stand with firmly planted feet."[110]

It was masterful; he had declared himself for reform and against fairy tales, leaving unanswered the question, was Beveridge's report reform or fairy tale? That question was partially answered by a Tory public relations campaign that began within days of Churchill's call for individual initiative and enterprise. Posters appeared on buildings throughout the land reminding Britons of "Our National Heritage." The centerpiece of each poster was a picture of a national hero—Drake, Elizabeth, Marlborough, Pitt, Nelson, Wellington. Churchill's photo assumed a lesser place on each poster. The message was clear: heroes and individual initiative underlay Britain's greatness. Partisan politics had been dormant for almost three years in the comforting shade of the flag of truce that flew over the coalition government. Churchill wanted things to stay that way, although he looked the other way as Tory posters with his portrait sprouted across Britain. Labour rank and file, meanwhile, feared a loss of their political identity if they continued to serve in a national government that proscribed partisan rhetoric. For weeks many Labourites had advised Attlee and his cabinet cohorts to bolt the coalition, the idea being that Labour would declare absolute loyalty to Churchill on the war effort but simultaneously reclaim its identity and the freedom to oppose the Tories on the domestic front. Harold Nicolson believed such a split was certain to take place within four months.[111]

Nicolson rued the fact that Conservatives were forcing Labour's hand by not coming at the Beveridge Report more honestly, by arguing against the improbable parts while trying to find a way to make the more practical elements work. When the report was brought up for debate in the House, the government paraded out a coalition of cabinet ministers—Tories Sir John Anderson and Kingsley Wood, and Labourite Herbert Morrison—to argue the government's case, which amounted to, as Nicolson feared it would, a transparent attempt to sweep it under the rug. That the dour Anderson did much of the sweeping only hurt the Tory cause. Labour argued for the immediate creation of a Ministry of Social Security; Tories insisted that such decisions await the end of the war. The leftist *Manchester Guardian* called the Tory performance "a lamentable exhibition of how not to handle political dynamite." The *Times* warned Parliament, "The public is in earnest in its determination to secure a new and firmer social foundation...after the war." Still, in a vote that came in at 338 for the government, including 23 Labourites, versus 121 against, the House endorsed the Tory strategy, which was to accept the plan in principle but not in detail. The Conservatives had employed the same strategy of obfuscation that Churchill had himself four decades earlier called "terminological inexactitude"; that is, the Tory response to Beveridge did not exactly add up to lies, but neither did it add up to anything comprehensible.[112]

Churchill believed that the best way to outflank Beveridge without threatening the national government was to stress the absolute necessity of maintaining the coalition, such that when the war ended, Britons would remember who had insisted on solidarity and brought them through the ordeal. To stem the rising tide of Labour unrest and to preserve his status as war leader, Churchill told the Commons that per the agreement made in 1940, a general election would not be permitted. Labour MPs asked why, if the Americans can hold interim elections without harming the war effort, could not Britons? Churchill held firm; there would be no contested elections. Those intent on "seeing the war through to a victorious conclusion," he warned the House, should "avail themselves of every occasion to mark their disapproval of truce breakers." This was less a renewed call for national unity than an adroit maneuver by Churchill, who in effect had just equated parliamentary dissent with disloyalty. Yet beyond the walls of Parliament, Churchill's Tory functionaries felt free to declaim at will on the evils of socialism, because such exhortations were neither disruptive to the war effort nor disloyal to the war leader. Oliver Lyttelton, intent on explicating the perils of Labour collectivism versus Churchill's theme of heroic individualism, told a Conservative meeting: "The great periods in our history were nearly always associated with an outstanding individual and not with a political system.... Nothing could be more ghastly than a uniform cow-like public opinion, which is left willing to browse on artificially fertilized fields, and chew the cud of common pasture."[113]

"Mr. Churchill's historic broadcast dominated the minds and the talk of a majority of Britons last week," Mollie Panter-Downes wrote on March 28. Yet "the general exhilaration was overshadowed by the almost simultaneous setback" in Tunisia when, on the twenty-second, German panzers counterattacked Montgomery's Mareth forces. The German strike kept the Eighth Army off balance and in place for two days. Britons steeled themselves for more bad news, for since 1940, British setbacks had displayed a disconcerting tendency to grow into British defeats. Montgomery responded to the Axis stroke by shifting his main thrust to Freyberg on the left, who, reinforced by the British 1st Armoured Division, and supported by hundreds of RAF fighter and bomber sorties, smashed through the Tebega Gap on March 27. The Germans and Italians directly in front of Montgomery, fearing encirclement, fled north. The next day, Montgomery telegraphed Churchill: "My troops are in possession of whole Mareth defences." An otherwise bleak month—in the North Atlantic, in North Africa, on the Russian steppes—was going out with a victory, and not just a British victory but, with Patton's reinvigorated forces in the thick of it, an Allied victory.[114]

Anthony Eden had been in Washington since mid-March for talks with Roosevelt and Secretary of State Cordell Hull on the makeup and security of postwar Europe and the world. This was the Four Power Plan as Roosevelt saw it, with China as one of the powers, and France excluded. The War Cabinet had approved the plan in principle in November, but the Foreign Office was well aware of Churchill's position on China. Hull held a similar position on France: it was irrelevant. Eden professed a fondness for Hull, but he noted a vindictive streak directed especially toward France and Germany, a mind-set Eden attributed to Hull's having been raised in the hills of Tennessee, where feuds among the hill folk lasted for generations or until everybody was killed off. Hull, over tea with Eden and Roosevelt, suggested the Allies avoid trials after the war by simply shooting Hitler and his cohorts, as the Germans no doubt would shoot the Allied leaders if given the chance. Indeed, Hull had taken Hitler's measure, but such a brutal (yet pragmatic) approach to settling scores offended Eden's gentlemanly sensibilities. He later wrote that he was familiar with the hit song, "The Martins and the Coys," adding, "I felt he [Hull] too could pursue a vendetta to the end."[115]

So could Roosevelt. When it came to France and Germany, he thought little of the French and less of Germans, especially Prussians. During their talks, Roosevelt reiterated to Eden his position on unconditional surrender: Germany would have no rights and East Prussia would disappear within the new Poland. Germany, too, would disappear, dismembered into harmless rump Germanys. Developing his idea a few months later, Roosevelt told Averell Harriman that postwar Germany would be denied airplanes, and German citizens would be forbidden to learn to fly. Germany, Roosevelt proclaimed, would be broken up "into three, four, or five states." Churchill harbored doubts about the wisdom of reducing Germany to an amalgam of impotent agrarian states. His vision for the postwar world included his councils and federations of European nations, with Germany as a participant, but not Prussia. On Prussia he aligned himself with Roosevelt. George Kennan later wrote that both Roosevelt and Churchill failed to see "the true lower-class basis of the Nazi movement; how sure they both were it was still the Prussian Junkers they were fighting." In fact, Hitler and his thugs despised the conservative Prussian class, a hatred that resulted in the degradation first of Prussia, and finally of all of Germany. In Prussia, Kennan wrote, lived courageous and idealistic sons and daughters of the conservative class who despised Hitler for the lower-class criminal he was. Here was a potential source of opposition to Hitler that neither Roosevelt nor Churchill cultivated. Instead, they intended to turn Prussia into a large meadow.[116]

For Churchill (but not Roosevelt) the rest of Germany was another matter entirely. He had told Jock Colville two years earlier that he always included Germany as a member of the "European family." Germany existed before the Gestapo, he told Colville, and it would exist after the Gestapo. "When we abolish Germany, we will certainly establish Poland—and make them a permanent thing in Europe." But what exactly did "abolish" mean? And the Free Poles in London wondered exactly what "establish" meant when it came to Poland. And Stalin had long suspected that Churchill meant to revitalize Germany, which to the Russians amounted to an existential threat. Churchill had not defined his terms. Yet certain beliefs underlay his postwar plans. The future security of Western Europe depended on the strength and cooperation of the nations of Western Europe, and not on the good graces of Russia, or America, for that matter, which indeed had no treaty obligations with Poland or France. Churchill saw the need for an economically healthy Germany as a trading partner for Britain, but first and foremost, he tied Britain's postwar military security to a vibrant France.[117]

Yet for Roosevelt, France occupied the same place in his worldview that China held for Churchill; to wit, no place at all. Over dinner one evening, the president outlined to Eden his concept for postwar power sharing in Europe. It did not include France but rather would be based on the military might of the great powers—Britain, the United States, and the Soviets. The rest of Europe, Roosevelt told a stunned Eden, would be disarmed but for rifles. And France would be partially dismembered, portions of Alsace-Lorraine and northern France lopped off to join a chunk of Belgium in a new state, Wallonia. The president's "ignorance of France was profound," wrote the British historian John Grigg, "yet no impediment to his holding obstinate views on the subject." Noting an unsettling consistency to the president's thinking, Eden asked if France and Germany were to be dismembered, why not the British Empire as well? Roosevelt replied by suggesting that Britain contemplate giving Hong Kong back to China as a "good will" gesture. Eden, amused (and alarmed), asked Roosevelt what territories *he* intended to give up. Roosevelt made no reply. Eden also voiced his opinion that Chiang's regime—corrupt and hated by legions of his countrymen, especially Mao Zedong—did not embody China and that a revolution of some sort would have to take place before China could assume a place among the great powers. Eden found the president's musings to be "alarming in their cheerful fecklessness." Roosevelt made his points with grace, he noted, but "it was too like a conjuror, juggling balls of dynamite, whose nature he failed to understand."[118]

All agreed that the military alliance known as the United Nations should emerge after the war as a world council of some sort. Stalin, in due time, would have to be brought into the discussions. Churchill, Hull, Eden, and Roosevelt each articulated different notions of how the postwar world should be configured, and in particular the Russian role in that world. But together, they lacked a vision of where they were going and how they would get there. Yet as regarded Russia, Roosevelt believed one thing with absolute certainty: if he were only given the chance to sit down alone with Stalin, all would be put right. This belief, George Kennan wrote, was born of F.D.R.'s assumption that although Stalin "was a somewhat difficult customer," he could be brought around "if only he could be exposed to the persuasive charms of someone like F.D.R. himself....For these assumptions, there were no grounds whatsoever; and they were of a puerility that was unworthy of a statesman of F.D.R.'s stature." Churchill (and Eden) hoped for some sort of postwar continuation of the partnership with Russia, but ever since Stalin made known his postwar territorial ambitions, both Churchill and Eden had grown increasingly wary of his intentions. Thus, for London, France represented an insurance policy should Uncle Joe abrogate his agreements. In the coming months, Churchill reminded dinner companions of a truism that formed the heart of Britain's desire to ally itself after the war with a strong France: if nothing stood between Moscow and the English Channel, then the Russians might someday stand on the Channel coast opposite the White Cliffs of Dover.[119]

Roosevelt spoke in general terms of a continued American role in safeguarding the peace, but later in the year he told Harriman that he "had no intention of stationing large American forces in Europe after the war, whether to help keep the peace or occupy Germany." Even were Roosevelt to change his mind, a different president a few years hence might negate the policy and turn America inward, as had happened after the Great War. Eden suspected the U.S. Senate would never ratify any treaty that handcuffed America to the military fortunes of postwar Europe. How then to safeguard the peace? Churchill, on the one hand, sought to tie Britain's postwar security to a special relationship with America. On the other hand, his responsibilities to his King and country demanded that he strive for a final settlement in Europe that did not depend entirely on an active American presence, or on the good graces of Stalin. In late March (over a dinner, Brooke recalled, of "plover's [sic] eggs, chicken broth, chicken pie, chocolate soufflé and with it a bottle of champagne...port and brandy!"), Churchill expressed "his disapproval of Roosevelt's plan to build up China while neglecting France." Vital to Churchill's plan for postwar Europe was a French state that emerged as a power, not a pauper.[120]

With Stalin voicing his disappointment in, if not outright distrust of, the Americans and British, Vice President Henry Wallace publicly framed the postwar stakes in stark terms. "We shall decide sometime in 1943 or 1944," he told reporters, "whether to plant the seeds of World War III." That war will become a certainty, Wallace said, "if we allow Germany to rearm militarily or psychologically." That war will be "probable if we double-cross Russia.... Unless the Western democracies and Russia come to a satisfactory understanding before the war ends, I very much fear that World War III will be inevitable." Wallace's remarks were a clear indication that America had reached no clear understanding with Stalin on postwar policies in Europe, specifically, the fate of Germany. The British press—which with Wallace accorded the Red Army heroic status—praised Wallace. The *Manchester Guardian* declared: "There is one-hundred times more anti-Russian feeling in the United States than there is in this country." The paper also noted that in the United States "there is much more tolerance for fascist systems of government." The *Times* stressed the point in an editorial: "To suppose that Britain and the U.S. with the aid of some lesser European powers could maintain permanent security in Europe through a policy which alienated Russia and induced her to disinterest herself in Continental affairs would be sheer madness." Yet the problem, as

Churchill and Eden increasingly saw it (and as Churchill had told the Turks in January), was that the Soviet Union might prove *too* interested in continental affairs following the war. How far west into postwar Europe Soviet influence extended would depend in large part on how far east Anglo-American armies were when someday they shook hands with the Red Army.[121]

Trust and loyalty do not necessarily march together in lockstep. Churchill saw no need to abridge his loyalty to Stalin even as he sensed trouble over the far horizon. In fact, each of the major Western political players—Churchill, Roosevelt, Harriman, Hopkins, Beaverbrook, Hull, and Eden—was intent on proving that his deep and abiding loyalty to Stalin was equal to if not greater than that of the others. The Anglo-American political theme for 1943 was not really Europe First, but Uncle Joe First. Opening the second front was the *only* action that would demonstrate to Stalin's satisfaction the loyalty of his allies. Within the highest Allied councils Beaverbrook became Stalin's most vocal supporter, so much so that Harriman wrote, "Beaverbrook is for the appeasement policy toward Russia . . . and doesn't give a hoot in hell about small nations. He would turn over Eastern Europe to Russia without regard to future consequences, the Atlantic Charter, etc." For his part, Harriman favored a high-minded relationship with the Soviets that "must be friendly and frank but firm when they behave in a manner which is incompatible with our ideals." Those lofty sentiments presumed that Stalin's endorsement of the Atlantic Charter was sincere and that he actually gave a hoot in hell about Western ideals of democracy.[122]

As he had shown with the Baltic states two years earlier, and with eastern Poland in 1939, Stalin first asked for what he wanted, and if his wishes were not granted, he took it. Roosevelt and Churchill believed that the opening of the second front would give them the leverage they needed to demand that Stalin cease all talk of borders and reconfigured European states until the peace conference following victory. This is what they insisted upon with their lesser allies, the Free Poles and Free French. They also believed they owed Stalin a second front, given the burden he was carrying and their fear that he would "lay this burden down" were they not to open that front. George Kennan ascribes a certain naïveté to this reasoning, given Stalin's history. Would Stalin really contemplate laying his burden down in order to reach another agreement with Hitler, another "pact" that was only as good as Hitler's word, which was no good at all, as Stalin had learned in 1941? Yet, how much, if any, leverage Churchill and Roosevelt gained by opening a second front could only be determined after they opened that front and, after opening that front, how far east they pushed it. Those questions were moot for the remainder of 1943.

The Blitz had ceased in May 1941, but during the first months of 1943, German raids conducted by small groups of Focke-Wulf fighter-bombers took place with frightening irregularity, just often enough and just deadly enough to keep Britons on edge. The Germans flew in beneath the radar to bomb roadways, buses, trains, and. with sinister regularity, schools. A January raid saw a lone Focke-Wulf strafe a school in Woolrich before flying on to the Sandhurst Road School in Catford, Lewisham, where it dropped a 1,100-pound bomb, killing thirty-eight students and four teachers. FIENDISH ONSLAUGHT OF A MURDEROUS FOE read the next day's headline of the *Kentish Mercury*. British rage only grew when the commander of the raid, a Captain Schuman, told reporters in Paris, "The bombs fell just where we wanted them to."[123]

The most deadly incident that year involved no bombs falling at all. It took place in London at the Bethnal Green tube station in the early evening of March 3. Thousands of pedestrians were making their way toward the station when the sirens sounded, followed immediately by the murderous cacophony from anti-aircraft rockets being launched in nearby Victoria Park. The rockets, though developed six years earlier, were newly deployed. What was terrifying about the "rocket guns," the war correspondent Ernie Pyle wrote, was not their actual report, but that "a rocket going up sounds like a bomb coming down." When the rockets went up that evening, the crowd panicked and raced for the entrance to the Underground. A young writer for *Stars and Stripes* named Andy Rooney was among the throng. "I almost turned toward the shelter," Rooney recalled, "but I wasn't that far from my rooms and decided to keep going. I didn't learn what happened until the next day, and then I realized, that's where I almost went down into the station." Rooney made the right decision; almost two hundred Londoners did not. A young woman carrying either a baby or a bundle tripped partway down the steep stairs, causing the people in front of her to fall and the crowd behind her to collapse into one deadly mass. Within fifteen seconds, the shelter had been converted into a charnel house, where 178 men, women, and children were suffocated and crushed. The Ministry of Information kept the details of the tragedy under wraps, with the result that Londoners, not knowing exactly what had happened, concocted their own explanations. One rumor had it that a German agent on the sidewalk had screamed that petroleum bombs were being dropped, thus panicking the crowd. Another, more popular explanation was that it was all the fault of the Jews, who were again accused, as during the Blitz, of losing self-control and rushing the shelter. A poll showed that while 29 percent of Londoners thought favorably of Jews, since the Blitz, those who thought unfavorably had doubled to 26 percent. There was talk in Parliament of proposing a law that forbade anti-Semitism. "A law against hating Jews," Goebbels wrote in his diary, "is usually the beginning of the end for Jews."[124]

Churchill had moved to Chequers the night before the Bethnal Green incident in order to continue his convalescence. Brooke, too, had gone down for two weeks with influenza. The CIGS was so ill that he could not even summon the energy to jot in his diary or undertake his birding. He and Churchill could do nothing but observe from their sickbeds as the situation in the Atlantic worsened, as the alliance drifted toward new shoals, and as Generals Alexander and Montgomery waited for the weather to clear in Tunisia.

In March, Iran declared war on Germany and thus joined the United Nations. Averell Harriman, upon his return to Washington from Tehran the previous August, relayed to Roosevelt the young shah's respect for Churchill and his belief (based on a personal promise from Churchill) that Iran had nothing to fear from the British. But, the shah had told Harriman, "Russia may be difficult!" The shah feared the postwar Soviet government might prove "aggressive" and expressed his desire for stronger ties to Washington. Harriman, the old railroad man, saw an opportunity. The Iranian railroad was in deplorable shape, an opinion he had offered to Churchill the previous summer along with an offer to rebuild and operate the railroad, which Churchill politely declined at the time. Now Harriman prevailed upon friends at the Union Pacific to send surveyors, rolling stock, and modern diesel locomotives to Iran in order to double the capacity of the Iranian railroads, which would double the supplies reaching Stalin and help offset the loss of the Arctic convoys. The British had been running just four or five trains a day from Basra north to Russia, with a capacity of three thousand tons. By late March, teams of American technical advisers, doctors (typhus was rampant; seven of ten Iranian children died before age nine), and railroad men had drifted into Tehran, including the former head of the New Jersey State Police, Colonel H. Norman Schwarzkopf, the man who had hunted the Lindbergh kidnapper and whose new duty involved instilling discipline in the ranks of the Iranian police.[125]

The takeover of the railroad meant that responsibility for the transport of British troops and matériel into Persia, and of British oil out, now rested with the Americans. It was the very erosion of autonomy that had troubled Churchill and Brooke the previous summer. Yet for the sake of their Soviet ally, they had no choice other than to agree. Harriman's management skills paid off; by late 1943, capacity on the Iranian railroad had increased to over six thousand tons per day. Harriman knew railroads, and he knew oil. In 1925 he had been a partner in a consortium to modernize the newly nationalized Soviet Baku oilfields, until the U.S. government barred American companies from doing business with the Reds. By 1943 they were all friends, by virtue of treaties—the Reds, the British, the Americans. The Americans in Iran had come only to help the Allied cause, although Harriman, consummate businessman that he was, had his eye on the future as well. The war would not last forever, but Iranian oil would.

Churchill had tried since Casablanca to keep Stalin abreast of the progress (or lack thereof) in building up sufficient armies in Britain to seriously contemplate a second front on the scale Stalin demanded. The Old Man touted the eight objectives agreed upon at Casablanca, all of which remained unfulfilled by April. He touted British airpower and Montgomery's success at Mareth; Stalin was not impressed. In March (before canceling the Arctic convoys), Churchill informed Stalin that of the twenty-seven divisions America had pledged to send to the United Kingdom to prepare for the invasion of France, seven had gone to Torch, and three more were set to go to Husky. In Britain there is "only one, in addition to the strong air force.... The reason why these performances have fallen so far short...is not that the troops do not exist, but the shipping at our disposal and the means of escorting it do not exist."[126]

This was Churchill's elongated way of telling Stalin that in the spring of 1943, there was one fewer American division in England than when Churchill had visited Stalin the previous August. Despite the pledge made at Casablanca to carry twenty-seven divisions and 938,000 American troops to Britain by December 31, 1943, the Americans had so far come up twenty-six short, although they still had eight months to fulfill their promise. Churchill told Stalin he did not mean to denigrate the American effort, although in effect that was what he was doing. He pointed out that in order to sustain operations in North Africa, the Pacific, and India, and to supply Russia, Britain had to cut its own imports "to the bone." This was true; yet here Churchill in deference to Roosevelt failed to point out the obvious. Had the Americans not dedicated so much shipping to supplying Douglas MacArthur, more would have been available for the "Europe First" strategy. Finally, Churchill told Stalin that were Germany to weaken, Britain would contemplate an assault on the Continent, but if Germany did not weaken, "a premature attack with inferior and insufficient forces would merely lead to a bloody repulse...and a great triumph for the enemy."[127]

Yet any weakening on Germany's part could only be induced by the Red Army. Roosevelt had implied as much in his own message to Stalin: "We hope that the success of your heroic army, which is an inspiration to all of us, will continue." Stalin was not in the least satisfied with the logic of Roosevelt or Churchill. In a telegram on March 15, he repeated his demand that the "blow from the West should...be struck in the spring or early summer." Anglo-American "uncertainty" and delay of cross-Channel operations, he told them, "arouses grave anxiety in me, about which I feel I cannot be silent."[128]

By mid-April, four weeks after Stalin expressed his anxiety, the threat in the North Atlantic appeared to have abated, as had the threat of an Axis counterstroke in Tunisia. Yet everyone from King George to Britain's bakers and candlestick makers had long since learned to put little stock in appearances. The weather in Britain by mid-April showed signs of improvement, but clear skies were always a worrisome invitation to the Luftwaffe. The few unbombed flower beds in parks put on subdued shows, while American soldiers commandeered rugby pitches in Hyde Park, where they played pickup games of baseball (and sometimes faced down British troops who sought to take over the pitch for its intended purpose). The sheep in Hyde Park took to grazing along nearby streets, the iron fences of the park having been torn out and melted down to build tanks and bombs. One Hyde Park battery of AA guns was commanded by Auxiliary Territorial Service sergeant Mary Churchill (who once intervened between two groups of Brits and Yanks about to come to blows over the use of a rugby pitch). Spring, indeed, was nigh. But with HMG still forbidding weather forecasts, Britons never knew what was coming their way.[129]

As always, this included German aircraft. "The London public fears that the German air *blitzkrieg* will suddenly break out again overnight," wrote Goebbels. "Would to God that we were in a position to do it!" Now the RAF regularly bombed the Ruhr Valley and Berlin in increasingly heavy assaults. Churchill kept Stalin apprised throughout April of the massed attacks on Berlin and Hamburg, of tonnage thrown in excess of 700 tons a night, then 800, and then, "the best Berlin has got yet," 1,050 tons. Some Church of England clerics took exception to "the frankly jubilant way in which the press whoops about the tonnage of bombs dropped on German cities." But the average Briton, Mollie Panter-Downes wrote, saw the RAF bombing as "a bad job which has got to be done." Britons, who had "got hell" during the Blitz, allotted little sympathy to German citizens. German propaganda called the raids "terror bombings." They were. And they were necessary; Churchill could give Stalin little else.[130]

In mid-April, the War Cabinet decreed that Britain's church bells could once again call worshippers to Sunday service, beginning on Easter Sunday. And after a superbly nonsensical debate in the Commons, it was agreed that church bells would no longer be reserved for use as a warning in the event of invasion. When an MP asked Churchill what warning system would replace the bells, he replied, "For myself, I cannot help thinking that anything like a serious invasion would be bound to leak out." Austin Hopkinson objected: "How can news possibly leak out," he asked, "when it is an offense to spread alarm and despondency?" "Factual statements," Churchill replied, "especially well intentioned, would fall into that category." That week, St. Paul's regained its voice and Londoners heard the Stedman Cinques flawlessly rendered by Alfred Peck and his thirteen assistants, who had been practicing for three years with muffled clappers. In Coventry, only the cathedral's spire remained, and from it came a bronze tolling. The peal of bells rolling over greening meadows and newly plowed fields augured a return to the splendid isolation from (most) continental calamities that Britons had enjoyed for almost nine hundred years, until the Luftwaffe arrived overhead in 1940. The bells need never have been silenced in the first place; Britons would have known the enemy invasion was at hand by simply turning on their wireless, or by opening their front door and looking up. Yet the bells connected Churchill's yeomanry—and Churchill—to England's past. That they were allowed to ring again only reinforced that connection. All was well.[131]

Then, over the course of the next few days, Churchill was apprised of three developments that raised new and serious questions about the security of Britain, inter-Allied politics and the second front, and the possibility of a new Blitz carried out by new and terrifying weapons. The first shock came on April 13, when Churchill was told for the first time that the Chiefs of Staff had agreed that all available landing craft be sent from Britain to North Africa in order to meet the needs of Husky. Furthermore, the craft were to be kept at the ready in order to exploit any favorable opportunities that developed, presumably by way of a venture onto the Italian mainland. Churchill was a strong backer of exploiting opportunities, but he had not been made aware until this meeting that the paucity of landing craft forced an either/or choice: exploit Sicilian gains, or meet the needs of Sledgehammer, the small-scale strike into France. The shock was more emotional than intellectual; everyone had concluded almost a year earlier that Torch effectively moved Roundup (the large-scale invasion) into mid-1944. In spite of that certainty, Churchill (and Roosevelt) had made promises to Stalin that they could not deliver on. The latest news on the landing craft amounted to the final knell. Over dinner with Brooke that evening—"started being stormy, then improved"—Churchill agreed to the proposal. He informed the War Cabinet that Sledgehammer (and, necessarily, Roundup) were off the table for that year, but he did not inform Stalin.[132]

The second piece of unsettling news arrived two days later, on April 15, when Churchill was informed that RAF intelligence indicated that the Germans were building rockets near Peenemünde, on the Baltic Sea coast. These rockets were not just an advanced version of the small but deadly *Nebelwerfer* rockets shot from tubes mounted on trucks, or the three- and five-inch solid fuel missiles deployed on ships and in anti-aircraft batteries. The German rockets were large, unmanned, and wingless craft propelled by exploding gases and guided by gyroscopes and navigation technology of a sort the British had yet to imagine.

It was the stuff of science fiction. The British had known for four years that the Germans were designing rockets, but nobody in British intelligence knew exactly how far along in the testing and production process German scientists and technicians might be. Nothing was known of propellant, range, guidance system, or payload. At the suggestion of Pug Ismay, Churchill's son-in-law Duncan Sandys was assigned the task of finding out what the Germans were up to, and how to best develop countermeasures. This was nepotism straight up, but Sandys had been involved in the development of anti-aircraft technologies until his 1941 car accident put him out of the air defense planning hierarchy. He saw a future for rockets in warfare, not just for the short-range projectiles fired from tubes, but for futuristic vehicles like the Germans were apparently building, and might soon be testing. Sandys set up a committee code-named Crossbow to recommend countermeasures. Yet Crossbow had first to ascertain just what the Germans were doing. Nobody knew. Days after learning of the German rocket work, Churchill and Brooke motored to the Hatfield Aerodrome to witness a display of the latest British advances in fighter aircraft, described by Brooke as "without propellers, driven by air sucked in in front and squirted out the back! Apparently likely to be the fighter of the future." It had been on the drawing board for more than a decade, and the first British turbo-jet engines had been tested in 1941. But the Exchequer lacked the specie to go into full production. Thus, the jet age arrived along with the rocket age, although neither had yet been christened. Hitler would do that.[133]

The third piece of news that reached Churchill was in some ways the most unsettling of all. That April week, Hitler told the Hungarian regent, Admiral Miklós Horthy, that Jews were "pure parasites" which "like tuberculosis bacilli" infected healthy bodies. "Nations which did not rid themselves of Jews," Hitler told Horthy, "perished." Hungary, a German ally, had not been forced by Berlin to deport its Jewish citizens, and to his credit Horthy did not start now, although he had no objection to forcing Hungary's Jews into slave labor. Other leaders in other capitals had no such choice and no compunction about sending Jews east. Over the next few days, trains carrying more than 2,400 Belgian and French Jews left Brussels and Paris for Auschwitz. On April 19, German authorities in Warsaw decreed that the Jewish ghetto there be combed for Jews to be transported to the death camp at Treblinka. Since early 1940, more than 300,000 Warsaw Jews had died or been sent east. When German trucks and soldiers arrived to collect their cargoes, they encountered something entirely unexpected. More than 1,200 Jews armed with just a few dozen rifles, hand grenades, and homemade bombs fought off 2,100 German troops for almost three weeks, killing 300. The Germans blocked and then flooded underground tunnels and sewers through which Jews tried to flee. They brought in heavy artillery and shelled the ghetto for ten days, and then set the ruins ablaze to smoke out survivors. When they finally retook the ghetto, they shot 7,000 Jews and sent another 7,000 to Treblinka. Several thousand more, who had fled to the Christian part of the city, were hunted down or betrayed. News of the massacres seeped from the Reich and was given much play in the Free Polish and London press. By then, fewer than 50,000 Jews remained alive in Warsaw.[134]

Goebbels and Hitler ignored Allied condemnations of such alleged atrocities. Instead, they hatched a diversion. It took the form of a postwar plan of their own in response to the nebulous federations and world councils being discussed in Washington and London. This was a new "European Charter" that made no mention of *Herrenvolk* (the master race) or *Lebensraum* ("living space," the plan to resettle Germans on conquered lands in the East). Instead, it pledged Germany's intent, as a sort of European attorney, to guarantee the freedoms of every citizen under its care, a pledge the British could not make, said one German newspaper, because Britain lacked a National Socialist Party capable "of guiding the fate of European countries." Goebbels intended to sell Europeans on the wisdom of "European cooperation," a phrase he believed might prove effective in furthering his aims, which had nothing to do with European cooperation but rather with driving a wedge between the Soviets and their Western allies, especially Poland.[135]

The London Poles had in the previous weeks given Goebbels an opening and Churchill a headache. In contravention to Allied policy that discussion of postwar boundaries take place only following the defeat of Hitler, the London Poles published their intent to restore to Poland those portions of the Polish Ukraine grabbed by Stalin in 1939 (and earlier grabbed by Poland after the Russian Revolution). Stalin, for his part, suggested in imprecise terms that the Poles should think of looking to East Prussia for satisfaction. What did that mean? Was Stalin intent on moving his zone of protection against future German aggression farther westward into Polish territory? Complicating matters was the fact that Poland had grabbed the Teschen portion of Czechoslovakia during the Munich crisis, thereby forfeiting some of the moral high ground when it came to talk of restoring boundaries. Eduard Beneš, whose country had been betrayed by the British at Munich, looked now to Moscow for help in restoring the Teschen region to Czechoslovakia. Britain had gone to war over Poland, but which Poland—the Poland that had been violated by Hitler, the Poland that had been violated by Stalin, or the Poland that had, in Churchill's words, "jumped on the back of Czechoslovakia" in 1938? At best, the diplomatic situation was now all bollixed up. Goebbels, gleeful, saw his opportunity, but how best to exploit the suspicions that swam beneath the surface of Allied relations, how best to portray Stalin and the Bolsheviks as the true villains of Europe? For a decade, when the Nazis faced such a challenge, the most reliable arrow in their quiver was also the most crooked: the lie.[136]

On the morning of April 13, Berlin radio triumphantly announced that German troops operating in the Katyn forest, west of Smolensk, discovered mass graves that contained the bodies of more than 8,500 Polish army officers and men, their hands bound behind their backs. It appeared the victims had been shot in the back of the head at close range. Young conifers had been planted over the graves in an apparent attempt to disguise the atrocities. According to Berlin, the Russians had captured the men in 1939 (when Stalin in partnership with Hitler, chewed off his piece of Poland). The Soviets moved the prisoners east to three camps and, Berlin claimed, subsequently marched them out of those camps and murdered them. That the alleged execution methods matched exactly those of Hitler's *Einsatzgruppen* did not perturb Dr. Goebbels, and for good reason. He knew the Russians had indeed murdered the Polish officers (who deserved it, he told his diary, since the Poles "were the real instigators of this war"). He even managed to express his shock over the news to his diary: "Gruesome aberrations of the human soul were thus revealed."[137]

Thus the third troublesome development to come Churchill's way that week. General Anders, who had gone to Moscow the previous year in search of missing Poles, had finally found them. The London Poles, already wary of Britain's resoluteness in restoring Polish borders, now demanded resoluteness in pursuing the truth about Katyn. Two days after the radio bulletin, over lunch at No. 10, Churchill cautioned Władysław Sikorski, who intended to call for a Red Cross investigation, not to pursue the matter. Cadogan was present, and he recorded Churchill as saying, "Alas, the German revelations are probably true. The Bolsheviks can be very cruel."

He advised Sikorski to look to the future, not the past. He was referring to the immediate urgency to preserve the alliance in order to defeat Hitler; only then could Poland emerge as a free member of the European community. As for the Polish officers, Churchill told Sikorski, "If they are dead, nothing you can do will bring them back." But Sikorski, against Churchill's advice, called for the Red Cross investigation. A few days later, Berlin also invited a Red Cross investigation. Goebbels enthused to his diary of the propaganda possibilities. Given that the disputes and hairline fractures within the Anglo-American-Soviet alliance were common knowledge, he saw a chance to help bring about an outright schism, and possibly a negotiated peace. "Our propaganda is suspected everywhere of having blown up the Katyn incident to enable us to make a separate peace either with the English or the Soviets." Although this was not his intention, "such a possibility would naturally be very pleasing."[138]

The Russians had a saying: Poles never learn, and they never forget. Poles, in turn, said of Russians: they are Slavs, but Slavs without hearts. Stalin's reaction to the Polish accusations was swift and final. Within days he broke off relations with Sikorski's government in London, of whom Stalin declared, "They think themselves clever tacticians, but God has given them no brains." Churchill and Roosevelt each advised Stalin to suspend rather than break relations with the London Poles. He would not do so, the Poles having so clearly displayed their "treachery" with their "hideous charges." Roosevelt warned Stalin that the break would have negative repercussions in the American Polish community. Stalin didn't care in the least about Poles living in Buffalo or Chicago. Churchill warned Stalin that Goebbels would make much of the schism, at Allied expense. He assured Stalin that the London Poles were honorable and not "in collusion with the Germans" and added that he was convinced that "German propaganda has produced this story to make a rift" in Allied ranks (the imprecise word "produced" might be taken as either "concocted" or "disclosed"). Stalin did not bend. Churchill contemplated shutting down those Polish newspapers that criticized the Soviets, and told Stalin so. Stalin held firm. In fact, he announced that he would sponsor a new Polish government in exile, in Moscow. When the London Poles pressed the issue, Churchill warned that their "charges of an insulting character against the Soviet Government" would "seem to countenance the atrocious German propaganda." On that front, Goebbels was winning. On April 28, Churchill cabled Roosevelt: "So far this business has been Goebbels' greatest triumph."[139]

In the appendix to *Closing the Ring,* the fifth volume of his war memoirs, Churchill printed part of a January 1944 memo to Eden that implies he was still trying to get to the bottom of the Katyn matter. But he left off the final line: "we should none of us ever speak a word about it." The memo was written at about the time in late autumn when the Soviets gave Kathleen Harriman and American correspondents a tour of Katyn. The correspondents noted many contradictions; if the Germans killed the prisoners in the summer of 1941, why were some wearing winter uniforms? And why were letters written in 1940 but never mailed found in some of the dead men's pockets? On the return trip to Moscow, Kathleen Harriman and her fellow correspondents drank and sang to dull the images of the day. Despite the contradictory evidence, the correspondents came down on the side of the Soviets (considered heroes by most Americans). Cabled *Time* correspondent Richard Lauterbach: "As far as most of us were concerned, the Germans had slaughtered the Poles." Four decades later, Averell Harriman, in defense of his daughter's judgment, said, "She was not a historian, and it wasn't her job to decide whether what she saw was right or wrong."[140]

In fact, within six weeks of Berlin's April announcement, Churchill and Eden knew what had happened at Katyn. Eden had asked for and on May 31 received a report by Sir Owen O'Malley, the Foreign Office liaison with the London Poles. O'Malley was clear in his opinion: "Most of us are convinced that a large number of Polish officers were indeed murdered by the Russian authorities." In his detailed report, seen only by Churchill, the War Cabinet, and King George, O'Malley concluded, "We have, in fact, perforce used the good name of England like the murderers used the little conifers to cover up a massacre; and in view of the immense importance of an appearance of Allied unity and of the heroic resistance of Russia to Germany, few will think that any other course would have been wise or right." O'Malley then plumbed an ethical implication that was not strictly within his diplomatic purview: "What in the international sphere is morally indefensible generally turns out to be in the long run to have been politically inept." London's support of Moscow had come at the expense of the Poles, O'Malley wrote, who have been portrayed as reckless and tactless and who "have been restrained from putting their own case before the public." HMG "have been obliged...to distort the normal and healthy operations of our intellectual and moral judgments." Churchill ordered that O'Malley's report be kept in a locked box and passed only by hand among members of the War Cabinet. Churchill, however, sent Roosevelt a copy in August. They were partners, after all. The report, Churchill told the president, "is grim, a well written story, perhaps too well written."[141]

This was realpolitik in the most Germanic sense of the word. Those who like to debate just when the Cold War began—during the Anglo-Russo struggle for power in Persia and Afghanistan (the Great Game) in the nineteenth century, in Moscow in November 1917, with the 1939 Nazi-Soviet pact—could do worse than look to the Katyn incident, not necessarily at the actual murders, but at the Allied response in the months that followed as Stalin proclaimed his outrage (but never specifically his innocence). Churchill later wrote of the compromises that had to be entertained in the war against Hitler: "terrible and even humbling submissions must at times be made to the general aim." He spoke those words while addressing a tragic affair that took place in 1944, during the Warsaw uprising, when Stalin refused British bombers the right to overfly Poland and land in Soviet territory. Yet his words applied to Katyn as well.[142]

Nancy Astor, during a visit to Moscow in 1931, had with her usual forthrightness asked Stalin when the mass murder of western Slavs would end. "When it is no longer necessary," Stalin replied. Apparently, it was still necessary.[143]

Throughout April, relations between the Allies deteriorated—not only relations between Russia and Poland, but between the Anglo-Americans and Moscow. The need for Roosevelt and Churchill to meet became evident, if only to do (or say) whatever was needed to placate Stalin, and to decide where to go after Sicily, although that decision rested by default with George Marshall, who had yet to make any decision. Yet Brooke, by sending all available landing craft from Britain to North Africa, had effectively settled the question for that year in favor of his Mediterranean strategy. Brooke made his decision, in part, in reaction to Admiral King's sending *his* landing craft to the Pacific, where MacArthur and Admiral Nimitz were preparing to begin their island-hopping march to Tokyo. This was yet another blow against "Europe first" as Brooke saw it. Yet Brooke's shift of the landing craft did not play well at the newly built Pentagon, and underscored the need for Churchill and Roosevelt to meet again relatively soon. Churchill later wrote, "I was conscious of serious divergencies beneath the surface which, if not adjusted, would lead to grave difficulties and feeble action during the rest of the year."[144]

That was a roundabout way of saying the British and the Americans had no strategy in place to fight the war in Europe after the war in Africa was finished. On that front, Allied fortunes had improved. Since busting through the Mareth Line in late March, Montgomery had pushed north, while Patton had punched away at mountain passes and squeezed eastward on the Axis left flank. On April 7, forward units of the Eighth Army and Patton's II Corps awoke to find the enemy had vanished from their front. That morning a British reconnaissance patrol stumbled across a similar patrol from Patton's II Corps. "This is certainly a pleasant surprise," offered Sergeant Bill Brown, from Devon. "Well, it's good to see somebody besides a Nazi," replied Private Perry Pearce of Kentucky. During just six critical weeks—from about the time Rommel went home sick in early March to mid-April—the advantage had shifted in Tunisia from the Germans to the Allies, in the air, on the sea, and on land. By April 20, Montgomery, General Anderson, the French, and George Patton had put Arnim's army in a vise.[145]

The battle for Tunis had entered its most critical phase, a time of "scrunch and punch," Churchill told Harold Nicolson and Duff Cooper on the twentieth over port in the House smoking room.* That night Nicolson wrote of Churchill: "As usual he is very gay." At times during the worst setbacks of the previous three years, his gaiety had been feigned, but Churchill, always determined, was now confident as well. When Nicolson asked about the status of the bey of Tunis, Muhammad VII al-Munsif, whom the Free French accused of being a Vichy sympathizer and German puppet, Churchill replied, "He will have to call himself *Obey* in future." He told Nicolson of a virtual RAF massacre of German transport planes returning to Sicily after landing reinforcements for Arnim. And he revealed that the Vatican had just released a list of prisoners that included Violet Bonham Carter's son Mark. "I only pray," he told Nicolson, that the German planes "were not carrying our prisoners."[146]

No British prisoners had been shot down, but Churchill was correct about the scrunch and punch. By April 22, Arnim had only seventy-six tanks in running order and was so short of gasoline that his men distilled local wines for fuel. The Allies had pushed the Germans into a pocket behind a 130-mile front that looped in a lazy half circle from just south of Cape Bon, where the Eighth Army was dug in, west and northward to Anderson's First Army, hard by the Mediterranean coast about forty miles west of Bizerte. More Axis troops than were captured at Stalingrad were dug in behind the line; every ridge held artillery, every wadi and every road and track was covered by German machine guns and anti-tank guns. Alexander had originally tapped the American II Corps, which held the line between Anderson and the Fighting French, for a supporting role in the final push. Then politics intruded from Washington. Eisenhower, under pressure from home, explained to Alexander that if the American people believed their men "have not played a substantial part they will be even more intent upon prosecuting the war against the Japs" and commensurately less inclined to fight Hitler. To that end, Ike asked Alexander to assign the II Corps a greater role in the end game. Alexander acquiesced,

---

* Cooper had been a minister without portfolio since the fall of Singapore, where he had been resident cabinet minister.

and ordered the II Corps shifted to the north of Anderson's First Army, where it would now form part of the van in the final battle. Patton would not be on hand to lead the charge; he had left for Rabat to plan the Sicilian campaign, where he was to lead the American effort. Eisenhower put his deputy, Major General Omar Bradley, in command of the II Corps. The French held the line between Anderson and Montgomery, at Cape Bon. All was in place. Churchill had Arnim in a vise, and it was closing.[147]

After Bletchley broke the U-boat code in March, convoys were routed away from known wolf pack hunting grounds, with the result that the Allies lost almost two-thirds less tonnage in April (250,000 tons) than in March—a significant improvement, but still terrible, and not worthy of a declaration of victory. And if Dönitz's objective was to fight the battle to a stalemate, thereby preventing an Allied landing on the Continent, he was succeeding. In fact, the American press declared he was winning, period. *Time* wrote that "the hard and hopeful fact—for the Germans" is that "Germany [is] still winning the Battle of the Atlantic....Churchill and Roosevelt both had indicated that the Allies could not hope to launch a major offensive before that margin was beaten in." By early May, the margin had not been. Admiral Ernest King, blunt and incapable of obfuscation, declared, "The submarine menace is being dealt with.... We expect to bring it under control in four to six months." That meant October, the close of the invasion season. Here was the first (and inadvertent) public acknowledgment on the part of the Anglo-Americans that no large-scale invasion of fortress Europe could possibly be undertaken until favorable weather again descended upon the English Channel. And that would be in May or June of 1944, at the earliest.[148]

Patrons of Washington bars and London pubs asked, what will one million American and British soldiers in England and Africa do for a year? Churchill pondered the same question. Secure now in the results soon to be obtained in Tunisia, and quite positive as to how best to exploit them, he proposed to Roosevelt on April 29 that they meet in order to decide where to go after the coming victory and the planned assault on Sicily. Italy appeared to Churchill to be the self-evident target. Another matter had to be addressed. The Americans had failed to exchange information on the atomic bomb, as agreed upon the previous year. Harry Hopkins had promised Churchill at Casablanca that the situation would be "put right." It had not been. The Americans, Lord Cherwell told Churchill, had completely cut off the flow of information. Churchill, furious, asked how soon British scientists could start work on a unilateral basis. Perhaps six to nine months, Cherwell replied, if given the highest priority, and that at the expense of all other war programs. Other issues needed to be discussed as well: the Poles, the Free French, Arctic convoys, the Pacific theater. When Roosevelt did not respond in a timely fashion to the proposal that they meet, Churchill took his case to Hopkins, adding that, as his doctors forbade his flying due to fears of reinvigorating his pneumonia, he could travel by ship in order to arrive in Washington by May 11. Finally, on May 2, as if inviting an old Harvard roommate down for a weekend of bridge, Roosevelt replied, "I am really delighted you are coming. . . . I want you of course to stay here [at the White House] with me."[149]

The meeting, code-named Trident, was on. Stalin would not be there; his presence was required in Moscow for the start of Hitler's summer offensive. In Russia, from Leningrad to Rostov, the spring *rasputitsa* had turned forest floors to marshes, marshes to lakes, and roads to quagmires. A *New York Times* correspondent wrote that along the entire front, "rusting cannon and broken tanks marked the course of old battles." The relative strength of the two opposing armies was about equal. That raised the specter of stalemate. Yet near Kursk, Hitler had assembled the largest tank army in history, and it now awaited orders to attack. With Arctic convoys halted and the Iranian railroad unable to make up the loss, the Red Army would face the Wehrmacht, and soon, with only the men, weapons, and tanks on hand. Stalin's factories and farms contributed 95 percent of the matériel and food his armies needed, but the 5 percent Lend-Lease contributed had proven critical. He needed that boost now, but it was not forthcoming. There was no doubt that the coming battle would be horrific, and quite possibly deciding. In London and Washington, there was growing doubt as to whether Stalin and the Red Army could sustain the effort much longer.[150]

The Soviet leader, as he had for sixteen months, sought from his partners only one answer to only one question: the date of the opening of the second front. Settling that question was high on the Trident agenda. With relations with Stalin at their lowest point since Pearl Harbor, Roosevelt considered his need to meet with Stalin clear and compelling, and to meet without Churchill. As Churchill prepared to sail for Washington, Roosevelt drafted a letter to Stalin wherein he proposed they choose an acceptable place to meet, perhaps Siberia or Alaska, but not Africa—too hot—and not an Atlantic venue such as Iceland, where Churchill, uninvited, might feel excluded. The letter, carried by the former ambassador to the Soviet Union Joseph Davies, was to be hand delivered, and Churchill was under no circumstances to be made aware of its existence. Churchill's claim on Roosevelt's time and attention was lessening in proportion to (as the president saw things) Roosevelt's growing stature within the alliance, a role cemented by virtue of American factory output, and armed forces that now numbered six million strong, and Roosevelt's conviction that he could make things right with Stalin if only they could sit down for an intimate chat.[151]

Early on May 11, RMS *Queen Mary* glided through the Verrazano Narrows and dropped anchor off Staten Island. The grand ship had spent half of the seven years since her maiden voyage in war service, as a troop transport. She was known around the fleet as the "Gray Ghost." Her prewar red-and-black smokestacks had been slathered with gray paint, as well as her black hull and pearl-white superstructure. Anti-aircraft guns rather than deck chairs now spread across the upper decks. Her interior finery—paneled walls, overstuffed settees, China services, acres of carpets, and the world map in the main dining room—had been carted off to New York warehouses at the start of the war, to be stored alongside the innards of *Queen Elizabeth* and *Normandie*. She could carry 16,000 troops, and had ferried almost that many to Australia shortly after the Japanese attacked Pearl Harbor. Her speed—almost thirty knots—made her uncatchable. No U-boat possessed the speed to plot a shot at her unless it found itself fortuitously positioned close abeam as she lunged past.

British and American cruisers had escorted the ship westward while Sunderland flying boats cruised overhead. Aboard the *Queen Mary* for this crossing were more than five thousand Italian and German prisoners of war captured in Tunisia, and destined for a not unpleasant internment in sunny midsouth locales. The prisoners were pleased with their fate; when taunted by Italian-speaking Americans in North Africa, they rejoined, "All right, laugh. But we're going to America. You're going to Italy." The highest-ranking German officers fared the best; they would be billeted at the Greenbrier Hotel in White Sulphur Springs, West Virginia, where they could buy from the Sears catalogue, where vegetable gardens were encouraged and coffee and tobacco were plentiful. Yet the Atlantic passage had not been pleasant for the prisoners, six days locked belowdecks, egress to the upper decks blocked by barbed wire and sandbagged machine gun emplacements manned by Royal Marines. The ship was infested with lice, the result of a previous cargo of kit bags that had been stored in a Cairo warehouse. The prisoners (or any German spies who scouted the ship in Scotland) might have concluded from numerous newly printed signs in Dutch hung throughout the vessel that somebody important—perhaps Queen Wilhelmena—was on board. Ramps that could accommodate a wheelchair had been conspicuously built in certain sections of the ship, as if in preparation for Franklin Roosevelt on the return voyage. That was exactly what British intelligence hoped the Germans would conclude.[152]

The prisoners would be marched off the ship under guard at a Hudson River pier. Another group of passengers would leave the ship here, at anchor in the outer harbor. Among them was Sir William Beveridge, on his way to an international food conference at Hot Springs, Virginia. Beveridge and his wife were not part of the official delegation—anointed "the holy of holies" by Ismay—and therefore had not been quartered in the part of the ship that had been hurriedly deloused for the comfort of the holies. As a result, by the time the *Queen Mary* reached New York, Sir William and Lady Beveridge "bore unmistakable signs of ravage." Max Beaverbrook and Averell Harriman were also on board, as well as Lord Cherwell and Lord Moran. The Chiefs of Staff and Archie Wavell were accompanied by a troop of almost one hundred staff officers. One passenger among the group traveled with a great many crates, boxes, and trunks packed with an odd assortment of habiliments. He was attended to by a platoon of private secretaries and Royal Marine bodyguards. *Queen Mary* had been chosen for the mission to ensure his safe passage. On deck, Air Commodore Spencer, attired incongruously in a navy blue yachting squadron jacket and cap, lit a cigar and gazed toward Manhattan, mostly hidden behind a steady mist and low fog. It had been almost forty-eight years since Winston Churchill first sailed into New York Harbor aboard the Cunard steamship *Etruria;* Victoria was queen and the sun never set on the Union Jack. Now Americans were singing a popular new tune, a syrupy hillbilly number composed by Paul Roberts and Shelby Darnell, "There's a Star-Spangled Banner Waving Somewhere."[153]

For the passengers on the two upper decks, the voyage had had about it a holiday atmosphere, made jollier with each new telegram from Alexander. On May 7, he cabled that the 1st United States Armored Division had entered Bizerte while the British had poured into Tunis. On the eighth, as Germans and Italians tried to flee Tunis by ship, Admiral Cunningham issued the order: "Sink, burn, and destroy. Let nothing pass." On the tenth, Churchill suggested to Attlee and Eden, in London, that England's church bells be rung that night. The date happened to be the third anniversary of his premiership. The bells were rung.[154]

Goebbels found the celebrations in London distasteful: "The capture of Tunis and Biserte is...blown up by the English as a sensational event....All London is drunk with victory." Yet, Goebbels confessed, "We are indeed experiencing a sort of second Stalingrad."[155]

On board the *Queen Mary,* each day's news had been celebrated over long luncheons and longer evening meals followed by hands of bezique and poker. (Beaverbrook and Harriman agreed beforehand that they would not take advantage of Churchill's limited poker skills.) The African victory instilled in the pilgrims a sentiment absent from Allied ranks since Pearl Harbor: confidence.[156]

The principals talked their way across the Atlantic; or rather, they listened as Churchill spoke. Reverting to his opposition to the American Air Force daylight strategy and its paltry destruction of German industrial targets achieved at great cost to the fliers, he told Harriman he intended to voice his displeasure to Roosevelt. Harriman warned that the surest way to provoke the American Chiefs to pack off their B-17s to the Pacific was for Churchill to denigrate the American effort in Europe. Churchill deferred to Harriman on the matter. During one of his shipboard monologues, Churchill put his hand on Beaverbrook's knee and said softly, "You don't talk anymore." Nobody could talk, Beaverbrook later told Harriman, "because the P.M. talks all the time." Yet the Beaver managed to produce "a tirade against the Poles" when informed by Churchill of a telegram from Stalin that excoriated HMG for allowing the London Poles to conduct their "anti-Soviet smear campaign." Beaverbrook—who Harriman considered naive about Stalin—threw his support to Stalin. Churchill threw his support to both Stalin and the Poles, a dual loyalty that could not end well. The subject changed to Burma. Churchill was displeased with Wavell's progress there, yet he and Wavell agreed that Burma was a malarial swamp unsuited for modern warfare. The British spring push in the western Burmese province of Arakan had ended in failure, and would have ended in utter disaster but for the inspired retreat brought off by General William ("Billy") Slim. Churchill held Wavell accountable. Wavell, in turn, fed up with Churchill's long-standing lack of faith in his abilities, threatened to resign. He did not, but only after Brooke told him that if he, Brooke, resigned every time Churchill took an unfair swipe at him, he'd have to do so "at least once a day." Brooke, for his part, told his diary that the upcoming Washington meetings "will entail hours of argument and hard work trying to convince [the Americans] that Germany must be defeated first...they will pretend to understand...and will continue as at present to devote the bulk of their strength to try and defeat Japan!!" Of the pending meetings, Brooke wrote, "I hate the thought of them."[157]

During a lifeboat drill five days out from New York, Churchill disclosed to Harriman that he had ordered a .50 caliber machine gun mounted on the lifeboat which was to carry the highest-ranking personages. "I won't be captured," he told Harriman. "The finest way to die is in the excitement of fighting the enemy." Harriman, distressed at the thought they might actually have to take to the lifeboats, reminded Churchill of his guarantee that a German torpedo could not sink the *Queen Mary*. "Ah," Churchill replied, "but they might put two into us." Here was the bluster of the old warrior who loved a good fight. Of the more than six thousand soldiers on board, Allied and Axis, very few had actually killed an enemy. Churchill had; several, in fact. He loved a fight, but he hated unnecessary fights that cost men their lives. So, too, did Marshall and Roosevelt. But the Americans' sensibilities were informed by politics, decency, reason, and the lessons of Scripture, to which as good Christians they subscribed. Churchill's sensibilities were informed from having witnessed slaughter firsthand on battlefields, in the Sudan and India in the previous century, in Belgium in 1916, and in London in 1940. More so than the American military chiefs, he could see the slaughter that would take place if an inadequate or ill-prepared Allied army landed on French beaches. In coming months, the conflict between his fertile imagination and his fervent desire to kill Germans took its toll on him, and on the alliance.[158]

Churchill loved a parade as much as a good fight. He proposed to Harriman, at Beaverbrook's prodding, to disembark the *Queen Mary* off Battery Park in order to make an unannounced progress by motorcar up Manhattan's avenues, no doubt to great and spontaneous popular acclaim in light of the news from North Africa. Harriman impressed upon the P.M. the dangers inherent in such a venture, the possibility of lurking Italian and Irish radicals, to say nothing of German operatives. With regret, Churchill withdrew his proposal and instead disembarked off Staten Island, where the presidential train, with Roosevelt's private car *Ferdinand Magellan* bringing up the rear, waited on a dockside spur. Harry Hopkins was on board, ready to greet his friend.[159]

Lunch was served during the run down to Washington, "small steak" being one of the menu choices. The entire British contingent went for the "small steak," which turned out to be so generous that none finished his portion. "It resembled a whole week's meat ration," Pug Ismay later wrote. "We were out of practice." By late afternoon on May 11, Churchill and Roosevelt were drinking cocktails in Roosevelt's oval study upstairs at the White House. The following day, Sir John Anderson learned that the supplies of Canadian uranium and heavy water Britain needed in order to produce an atomic bomb had been purchased by the United States—the entire Canadian production capacity. The Americans had frozen Britain out of the Manhattan Project. Indeed, there was much to discuss with the president.[160]

On May 13, Churchill received a message from Alexander: "Sir, it is my duty to report that the Tunisian campaign is over.... We are masters of the

North African shores." Arnim had been captured by the British on Cap Bon along with 150,000 prisoners who included twelve generals and 110,000 Germans. All of this since Churchill set sail. The *New York Times* reported that when a German general approached Bernard Freyberg somewhere north of Enfidaville and asked for peace terms, the New Zealand commander replied: "Unconditional surrender." British tanks, with infantry hanging on their sides, were taking joy rides along the coastal roads of Cap Bon. Every time a tank swung its gun, groups of Germans and Italians rose from the scrub and poppies, hands raised. It was like a grouse shoot; everybody among the Allies took their bag. The French, defeated in 1940, captured 25,000 Axis troops, the Americans almost 38,000, of whom almost 34,000 were Germans. That brought to 400,000 the total of Axis prisoners taken in North Africa since November, at a cost to the British Eighth and First Armies of 35,000 killed, wounded, and missing. The Americans lost about 18,000 killed, wounded, and missing.[161]

The war in North Africa was over. The genesis of the victory, Averell Harriman believed, lay in Churchill's "desperate gamble" in late 1940 to send England's tanks to Egypt at the moment of the Home Island's and the Empire's greatest peril.[162]

A few days after arriving in Washington, Churchill told the U.S. Congress that "the proud German Army has once again proved the truth of the saying, 'The Hun is always either at your throat or at your feet'; and that is a point which may have its bearing upon the future. But for us, arrived at this milestone in the war, we can say 'One Continent redeemed.' "[163]

On the day of the North African surrender, Mussolini took himself off to Rocca delle Caminate, his summer palace near Forlì, where he spent several days clipping articles from newspapers and underlining stories about the African campaign with red and blue crayons. The strut had left his step. His aides noticed that where once his desk was a paradigm of order, it was now cluttered, "like a junk-stall with half opened books, Fascist badges and medals, sheaves of wheat bound in tricolour ribbon." He was embittered, and believed Italians had lost their will to fight, due in part to dozens of Allied air raids on Genoa, Turin, and Naples. The raids had had the effect Churchill intended. Rome's turn came on May 16. The RAF had been hitting Italy in spot raids for almost three years; now hundreds of American B-17s appeared over Rome. Il Duce concluded the bombing was a prologue to the invasion of Sicily (not Corsica or Sardinia, or southern France, or Greece, as was thought in Berlin). And after Sicily, Mussolini believed, the Italian mainland would be the Allies' next target.[164]

Il Duce's instincts were sound, but he no longer had the power to inspire his people to heroic resistance, or to convince Berlin that Sicily was the next target. As he was prone to wild pronouncements, and evidencing the onset of either failing nerves or senility, his opinion was ignored in Berlin.

A *New York Times* headline that week read: INDIA STAFF HERE: WAVELL'S PRESENCE SEEN AS HINT OF EARLY ACTION AGAINST JAPANESE. The *Times* of London ran a similar story, prompting Clementine to write to her husband, "I'm worried at the importance given by the Press... to the presence of Wavell... in your party. I'm so afraid the Americans will think that a Pacific slant is to be given to the next phase of the war.... *Surely* the liberation *must* come first." She had perfectly captured Brooke's fear, and Churchill's, and England's.[165]

To a degree, Wavell's presence at the conference was about taking the war to Japan, but not by way of Burma, where the weak British winter push toward Akyab had been mauled by the troops of Major General Masakazu Kawabe. Churchill and Brooke had decided on their way to Washington to tell Roosevelt that Operation Anakim, the planned invasion of southern Burma, was off the table until 1944. The manpower and resources simply did not exist. Still, two strategies for taking the fight to Japan by way of China were debated in Washington, and Burma played a role in each. Joe Stilwell favored an overland strategy from India, through northern Burma and into China. Yet MacArthur was siphoning off the American troops that had been allotted to Stilwell, and Stilwell's Chinese troops showed no fight. Claire Chennault, who sought to configure his Fourteenth Air Force on Chinese soil as soon as possible, championed an aerial strategy conducted against Japan from bases in China. Wavell saw the obvious flaw in Chennault's plan: China had no gasoline refineries and no means of fueling bomber groups or fighter squadrons. In fact, Allied DC-4 transports flying over the eastern Himalayas—"the Hump"—to deliver fuel and ammunition to China had to make room in their cargo bays for the gasoline needed for the return trip to India. The lack of available troops (especially American troops), tanks, and trucks argued against Stilwell, who concluded that his theater of war was neglected because "Churchill has Roosevelt in his pocket.... The Limeys are not interested in the war in the Pacific, and with the president hypnotized they are sitting pretty." Stilwell, fluent in Mandarin Chinese, respected the Chinese people but thought Chiang corrupt and inept. Although Churchill thought little of Stilwell's plan, he was in complete agreement with Vinegar Joe's assessment of Chiang. Neither Stilwell nor Chennault could put forth any plan to help Chiang that could be seriously considered until Burma was retaken, and for this endeavor there was no plan, only a name. When it came to capturing Burma, Churchill told Brooke, "You might as well eat a porcupine one quill at a time."[166]

Churchill soon shifted his animal analogy from porcupine to shark: "Going into the jungles to fight the Japanese is like going into the water to fight a shark." Instead, he believed the Allies should "set a trap or capture him on a hook." The best place to set such a trap, he concluded, was the northern tip of Sumatra, from where the Royal Navy could harass Japanese supply lines between Tokyo and Singapore. This strategy soon exercised a hold over him, much the same as had Jupiter, the invasion of northern Norway.[167]

Contrary to the *New York Times* headline, Wavell's presence in Washington had more to do with India than with taking the fight to Japan. Churchill thought it time to shuffle the entire command structure in India and Burma, by way of appointing a new viceroy and new commander for Indian military affairs, and creating the position of supreme commander, Southeast Asia. The latter position would not be going to Wavell, about whose aggressiveness Churchill still voiced doubts. No, he had his eye on Wavell for viceroy of India. Eden had politely refused the offer for fear it would end his career; traditionally the viceroy was made a lord, and lords were traditionally denied the premiership. Churchill's choice of Wavell as viceroy, therefore, would signal to Roosevelt that HMG thought that the situation in India demanded a strong military hand rather than a deft political touch.

Churchill favored Auchinleck for commander in chief, India. He liked Air Vice Marshal Sholto Douglas, formerly of Fighter Command, now RAF chief in the Middle East, for the head of the new Southeast Asia Command, or SEAC. Churchill thought the appointment was inspired, in part because Douglas, as an airman, would better appreciate the logistics of supplying Chiang's forces by air. The Americans objected to Douglas. He was as vocal a critic of America as Stilwell was of Britain, and his transparent ambition, as well as his part in the downfall of the hero of the Battle of Britain, Hugh Dowding (who had been kicked upstairs to Washington), were well known on the Potomac. For their part, the Americans began to refer to SEAC as See England Acquire Colonies, so firm was their belief that Churchill wanted to regain his lost Asian domains and had no intention of helping Chiang.[168]

During the two weeks of Trident, Roosevelt gave Churchill what he sought on the atomic bomb project: full cooperation and a promise to share the finished product, which Roosevelt thought might be ready for use in the current war, which he believed might last into 1946 or even 1947. Churchill informed the War Cabinet that a formal agreement would follow. The president also finally acted on Harriman's March suggestion and directed the War Shipping Administration to transfer more ships to the British flag— fifteen to twenty hulls per month. Yet Roosevelt had been singing that tune for months; this latest promise, too, would go unfulfilled. Admiral King and MacArthur needed those hulls. The shadow of King and his Pacific strategy darkened every meeting, from the British standpoint. "The swing toward the Pacific is stronger than ever," Brooke complained to his diary, "and before long they will be urging that we defeat Japan first!"[169]

Brooke believed the Americans felt they had been "led down the garden path" by Torch and Husky, "and now they are not going to be led astray again." France and only France formed the core of George Marshall's strategic plan. Yet there existed one simple and sublime way to satisfy Marshall as well as avoid a full American tilt toward the Pacific, and that was for the British to wait until the Americans insisted upon a date for the invasion of France, which they did, and then agree to it, which the British chiefs did. In doing so, Churchill and Brooke gave Roosevelt and Marshall what they had all along demanded. Acceding to the cross-Channel strategy ensured that the president's and Marshall's attention would be focused at least as much on the European front as on the Pacific. The date agreed upon was May 1, 1944. But whether this was to be the small-scale landing, Sledgehammer, or the larger investment, Roundup, was not decided. So much confusion attached to just what exactly these code names meant that at the State Department and around Eisenhower's headquarters, the newly proposed operation was referred to as Roundhammer. Whatever they chose to call it, it meant that yet another pledge made at Casablanca, and the most important to Stalin—to put men somewhere into France by August 1943—would go begging for another year.[170]

Churchill did, however, have in mind a supreme commander for the invasion, Alan Brooke. That a British general should assume command seemed self-evidently correct to Churchill. After all, Britain had far more men, planes, tanks (albeit many were American built), and ships within the European and North African theaters than did the Americans. As well, at the time of Eisenhower's appointment as commander of Torch, there had been an implied understanding (as Churchill saw it) between himself and Roosevelt that a Briton would command the invasion of France. A committee had been set up to plan that invasion (soon code-named Overlord), headed by an Englishman, Lieutenant General Frederick E. Morgan, whose title was COSSAC—Chief of Staff to the Supreme Allied Commander (designate). Morgan shared with Marshall the belief in a straight-line approach to Germany. He took his assignment seriously and was in no way inclined to put on a show of championing the merits of Overlord simply to placate (or deceive) the Americans.

Churchill and Brooke, too, were believers in Overlord, but only if the operation was undertaken when Germany was on the ropes, put there by the Red Army in the east, the RAF in the west, and Allied armies in Italy and the Balkans (if Churchill had his way). Although they believed it self-evidently true that to go into France prematurely invited calamity, they had agreed to the May 1, 1944, date without proposing the invasion be conditional upon certain objectives having first been met. This lapse in communication invited trouble with Marshall and Roosevelt, which duly arrived in coming months. Meanwhile, from Churchill's perspective, if these conditions were met by the agreed-upon invasion date of May 1, 1944, Brooke should command Overlord. One of Brooke's friends, upon return from Algiers, reported to him that Eisenhower had been quite firm in his belief that only two men were qualified to lead the invasion: George Marshall and Sir Alan Brooke. Brooke was therefore thrilled when, two weeks after Trident, Churchill told him of his likely promotion to supreme commander. The CIGS felt the appointment would be "the perfect climax to all my struggles to guide the strategy of the war" in order to make such an invasion of France possible. Sworn to secrecy by Churchill, Brooke did not tell even his wife.[171]

While the Combined Chiefs of Staff clawed their way toward a consensus on strategy, the president and Churchill shadowboxed over postwar politics. As he had with Eden, Roosevelt outlined to Churchill his vision of postwar Europe, including a diminished France and an utterly destroyed Germany. This was the postwar Germany envisioned by Prof Lindemann and the American secretary of the treasury, Henry Morgenthau Jr., an old Roosevelt friend and fellow gentleman farmer above the Hudson River. Morgenthau, a dour fellow whom Roosevelt called Mr. Morgue, did not hate Germans, but he hated evil, and he especially hated Nazis. His Treasury Department would help determine the fate of Germany, for Lend-Lease was a program with immense foreign policy implications, but at its core it was a banking construct, controlled by the Treasury Department. Treasury, therefore, not State, would take the lead in determining how best to make Germany pay—literally and figuratively—for its transgressions. Morgenthau intended to extract a crushingly heavy price. Such were Morgenthau's sentiments. More significantly, Roosevelt shared them.

Churchill sought something else. During Trident he proposed to Roosevelt a plan for postwar security that consisted of a world council and three regional councils, Asian, North and South American, and European, within which blocs and federated associations would form bulwarks against aggression. The greatest bloc of all would take the form of a "fraternal association" between America and Britain, including a continuation of the Combined Chiefs of Staff. It was all very similar to the ideas he unveiled in his March broadcast, and that Eden conveyed to Roosevelt and Hull during his visit to Washington. Churchill also proposed a "Danubian federation," with Vienna the seat of government, a democratic federation of states, including Bavaria, that would fill the void left by the disappearance of the old Austrian-Hungarian Empire. This new state, in loose alliance with Great Britain (ideally, in partnership with America) and a rejuvenated France, could defend itself against incursions by other powers, including a reinvigorated Germany and the Soviet Union, should Stalin manifest postwar expansionist proclivities. If Stalin proved true to his word and adhered to the twenty-year friendship treaty, France would assume its old role of containing Germany in the west while the Soviets contained it in the east. Germany (demilitarized), however, would emerge as a contributing partner to the economic rejuvenation of Europe. Even Stalin would need German steel after the war. Eden's policy, taking shape at the Foreign Office, was based on three goals: to contain Germany, to resurrect France, and to be prepared to contain the Soviets. "These arrangements," Eden wrote in a memorandum, "will be indispensable for our security whether or not the United States collaborate in the maintenance of peace on this side of the Atlantic." To American ears, all of this had the ring of "spheres of influence" and "alliances," both military and economic, the very structures that had led not only to the current war but to every European conflict since the early Middle Ages.[172]

Where Roosevelt and the State Department saw the greatest threat to postwar Anglo-American relations in Churchill's old order, Churchill increasingly saw it in Stalin's new order. How far west Stalin's influence spread in Europe would initially be determined by where the Soviet and Anglo-American armies met at the end of the war. That was why postwar Anglo-French solidarity meant so much to London despite de Gaulle and his inability to get along with anyone. It meant little to Washington. Roosevelt believed he did not need Frenchmen (especially de Gaulle) to win the war, but Churchill needed a resurgent France to win the peace in Europe. As much as he disliked de Gaulle, he understood that the people of occupied France saw de Gaulle as their savior. Reports circulating in London claimed 80 percent of Frenchmen considered Charles de Gaulle their "symbol of resistance." Roosevelt in turn, and based on Robert Murphy's facile reports from Africa, considered such sentiments nothing more than Gaullist propaganda. He made his thoughts on the subject sneeringly clear in a memorandum he prepared for Churchill during Trident: "He [de Gaulle] may be an honest fellow but he has the Messianic complex." The people of France were behind the Free French movement, Roosevelt believed, but not behind de Gaulle, whose "conduct continues to be more and more aggravated." It was clear to Roosevelt that "when we get into France itself we will have to regard it as a military occupation." He proposed to dump de Gaulle and his French National Committee and oversee the formation of "an entirely new French Committee and subject its membership to the approval of you and me." Churchill later recalled that "not a day went by" in Washington without Roosevelt expressing his "stern" feelings about de Gaulle.[173]

Harangued by Roosevelt, Churchill cabled London on May 21 and advised that HMG break off relations with de Gaulle. Eden replied immediately with a strong dissenting opinion. Giraud and de Gaulle had agreed to meet in Algiers the next week to consummate their marriage by way of creating a new French National Committee. Would it not be wiser, Eden asked, to await the results of that meeting before making such a profound decision? Churchill agreed. A final decision could wait until after Giraud and de Gaulle met. In this decision, Churchill displayed a consistency he held to throughout the war. He deferred (often with great reluctance) to his Chiefs of Staff in military matters, and he deferred (again, often with reluctance) to the War Cabinet in strictly political matters. As a believer in the "Parl" he could not do otherwise. Eden later kidded him about his back-and-forth on de Gaulle, attributing the duality of his opinions to his being half American. But both knew the real reason Churchill inclined to bow to Roosevelt lay with the increasing leverage the Americans had over the British. Here, Eden served the P.M. well, as did Brooke on military affairs, by steering Churchill away from his more incendiary and quixotic inclinations, political or military. In turn, he led them forward, relentless in his quest for their common objective: victory.[174]

Yet, how to fight the war, not how to manage the French or the postwar world, was why Trident had been convened. Left unresolved as the talks neared their end was the strategic question Churchill considered the most critical: where to go after Sicily. What would become of twenty battle-hardened divisions, of Tedder's four thousand aircraft and Cunningham's navy? The momentum of the African victory and the pending Sicily campaign must be maintained. Churchill for his part had Italy and Mussolini in his sights. Only one obstacle stood in his way: George Marshall. Late on May 25, Marshall stopped by Roosevelt's office to say his good-byes to Churchill. He found the two leaders putting the finishing touches on a communiqué to Stalin before setting off to bed. Roosevelt had told Churchill that if he wanted to argue the case for invading Italy, he'd have to stay in Washington for another week. That would not do. Churchill had been gone from London for almost four weeks. He would be off just after sunrise, to visit Alexander and Eisenhower in Algiers. Marshall, having paid his respects, was about to leave, when Roosevelt said, "Why don't you go with Winston?" Coming from the commander in chief, this was more an order than a suggestion. It was now past 2:00 A.M. Churchill was due to depart in six hours. The dutiful Marshall had so little time to pack for the trip that he left his dress slacks behind. But he made the flight.[175]

Churchill and Marshall departed Washington aboard the Boeing Clipper *Bristol,* bound for Newfoundland, the first leg of the journey to Algiers. Accompanying Churchill, along with Marshall, were Ismay and Brooke, as well as Churchill's doctor, Lord Moran, himself the victim of a stomach virus that would force him to leave off at Gibraltar and return to London. Churchill's stenographer Patrick Kinna, was on board, having become in his twenty-two months of service a trusted member of the team. Scotland Yard's Thompson and another detective were also on hand, as was Captain Richard Pim, the caretaker of the maps, all of which were rolled and stowed. Sawyers the valet served, as usual, in his capacity as quartermaster of Churchill's beverages, his Quadrinox sleeping pills, and his hot-water bottle.[176]

The journey much impressed Brooke, who for every leg of every trip that year kept a log of the miles covered and time spent in the air (almost nine hours and 1,300 miles on the leg to Newfoundland). All on board signed one another's "short snorters." These were banknotes carried by those who had made a transatlantic flight, signed by others who had done the same. The "sect," as Brooke called it, was the idea of the first Americans who had undertaken the crossing. Anyone who failed to produce his short snorter upon demand forfeited a dollar or bought a short snort of whisky. In time, as such journeys became more frequent, the participants taped new banknotes to the old in order to accommodate the growing numbers of signatures. Churchill gamely signed his short snorters as the flying boat made its way north through steady mist. After a four-hour stopover at Botwood for dinner, and with foul weather dropping fast upon the coast, *Bristol* lifted off at dusk for the seventeen-hour flight to Gibraltar. The outside temperature was zero, inside not much warmer. Sometime during the night lightning struck the plane, twice. After spending a moonlit night seven thousand feet above the Atlantic, the group reached Gibraltar late in the afternoon of May 27, and stayed the night at the governor's residence. The next afternoon, they climbed into their new Avro York aircraft, a converted Lancaster fitted out with five berths, drawing room, lavatory, and eight windows to take in the views. By nightfall they were drawing warm baths in Algiers, at the villas of Cunningham and Eisenhower.[177]

On the day Churchill and Marshall departed Washington, a British convoy steamed into Alexandria after an uneventful two-thousand-mile run from Gibraltar through waters free of Axis mines and Axis ships. The Mediterranean was open for the first time since 1941. Brooke, always calculating shipping tonnage, concluded that an effective gain of one million tons of shipping was realized by cutting forty-five days and ten thousand miles from the London-to-Egypt voyage via the Cape of Good Hope.[178]

Allied shipping losses in May fell to 200,000 tons—about forty ships. But Dönitz paid with forty U-boats to attain those meager results, twice his losses for March and April when he had sent almost one million tons to the bottom. By June he had pulled his fleets back to the far eastern Atlantic. For the month of June, his U-boats claimed just six ships and 27,000 tons of Allied shipping, a 95 percent reduction from March. British aircraft equipped with microwave radar could now detect surfaced U-boats at night or in fog; coordinates were relayed to surface ships, which then closed in on the targeted submarines. Thirty-eight U-boats were lost to such tactics in the Bay of Biscay during May (called "Black May" in the *Kriegsmarine*) and early June, three fewer than the number of Allied merchantmen sunk in the Atlantic and Arctic oceans, and twelve more than the number of U-boats launched during those weeks. Even as he abandoned the western Atlantic, Dönitz's losses mounted. Since early 1943, British and American merchant ships had been launched faster than the U-boats could sink them, while increased Allied air patrols and the improvements in radar ensured that U-boats were being sunk in far greater numbers than Hitler could replace them. By July American ship construction outpaced losses from all sources—U-boats, mines, surface ships, and aircraft. America had finally hit its stride, building half again as much shipping that year (more than 12 million tons) than Britain produced during the entire war.

Churchill no longer fretted over either the strangulation or the invasion of Britain. Yet final victory was by no means imminent. The American armies had to mature and American shipbuilding had to reach even greater levels, levels that could sustain Britain, Russia, MacArthur, and a second European front all at the same time. "Henceforth," Churchill later wrote, "the danger was not destruction but stalemate."[179]

Beaverbrook agreed. "There seems a real danger," he wrote to Harry Hopkins, "that we shall go on indefinitely sewing the last button on the last gaiter." If the Allies were not prepared to assume the risks and suffer the casualties of a second front, "then let us concentrate at once exclusively on the production of heavy bombers and think in terms of 1950." Churchill had told the U.S. Congress much the same when on May 19 he cautioned, "No one can tell what new complications and perils might arise in four or five more years of war. And it is in the dragging-out of the war at enormous expense, until the democracies are tired or bored or split, that the main hopes of Germany and Japan must now reside. We must destroy this hope."[180]

Every North African port from Alexandria to Casablanca was full of warships, troop transports, landing craft, and cargo ships. Of the one million men holding the North African shore, 160,000 of them would be going to Sicily. Like Lincoln in the months after Grant drove his men across the Rapidan toward Richmond, Churchill now knew his army—British, colonial, French, and American—had gained confidence and strength in the killing fields of North Africa. This army must not be brought to a halt. It had to push on. Such a force had to be led to greater triumphs, to the end.

Churchill told Marshall and Eisenhower that this monstrous machine, once set in motion, could be recalled only with great difficulty. To take this army only as far as Sicily would be to defy momentum, and to defy the strategic maxim to always exploit gains. "Keep on until you get Italy," he told Eisenhower, again and again. Within forty-eight hours of arriving in Algiers, Churchill brought Marshall and Eisenhower around to fundamental agreement. By air and sea the Allies would pound Italy. The rail yards of Rome, just five miles from the Vatican, were the first target. (Churchill, while in Washington, had assured New York archbishop Francis Spellman that precautions had been taken to avoid destroying the Eternal City itself.) Airpower alone might drive Italy out of the war. If it did not, the army could. The final decision to land it on the Italian mainland would rest with Eisenhower. Where on the boot of the mainland the Allies might strike after Sicily would depend on how many Germans poured into Italy, and where they set up their defense. If the Germans drew their line north of the Po River, an Allied thrust toward Tuscany would cut off any Axis forces to the south and avoid a four-hundred-mile slog up the boot. Another strategy entailed stabbing into Naples, followed by a quick run north to Rome. Churchill was so sure that Italy was ripe for the kill that he told Eisenhower that British civilians would gladly halve their rations for a month if it helped flush Italy from the war, an outcome that might, he proposed, come in time for the two of them—himself and Eisenhower—to meet in Rome for Christmas dinner.[181]

Marshall endorsed the Italian gambit, but like Churchill in Washington (who neglected to stipulate the conditions necessary for Overlord to proceed), Marshall failed to articulate a belief that he held to be self-evident: operations in Italy, whatever form they took, would in no way interfere with the planning and execution of Overlord. This oversight, like Churchill's, would lead to trouble within the Anglo-American ranks before the year was out.

Marshall went home and Eisenhower put his staff to work to determine where in Italy to strike. Churchill's demeanor accordingly grew gay. "I have no more pleasant memories of the war than the eight days in Algiers and Tunis," he later wrote. On one morning, an Eisenhower aide found Churchill breakfasting in bed on "one bottle of white wine, one bottle of soda, and a bucket of ice." He was in fine fettle. He had prevailed. On June 1, the party flew to Tunis and motored on to Carthage, where Churchill addressed the troops in the Roman amphitheater. The acoustics were so perfect that no loudspeakers were needed. That night at dinner Churchill offered, "Yes, I was speaking where the cries of Christian virgins rent the air whilst roaring lions devoured them, and yet I am no lion and am certainly not a virgin." At another dinner, the table had been set for thirteen, but "in deference to British superstition," Eisenhower's aide, Harry Butcher, was invited to make it fourteen. When the talk turned to diaries, Churchill proclaimed the practice was foolish because a diary reflected only the daily intuitions and emotions of the writer, which events might later prove incorrect or unsound, thereby making the diarist appear the fool. For his part, Churchill said he'd prefer to wait until the war was over to write his impression, such that "if necessary he could correct or bury his mistakes." All in all, Brooke concluded, Churchill was "in remarkable form." He was, but for de Gaulle.[182]

De Gaulle's presence in Algiers unsettled him. To Clemmie he wrote, "Everyone here expects he [de Gaulle] will do his utmost to make a row and assert his personal ambition." To counter that prospect, the British had secreted out of France General Alphonse Georges (whom Brooke had last seen during the doomed defense of Brittany). It was hoped that the new French Committee would be sufficiently packed with anti-Gaullists such as Georges to keep the tall Frenchman in line. After lunching with Giraud and Georges, Churchill wrote Clementine, "In their company I recaptured some of my vanished illusions about France and her Army." Within two days, the gathered Frenchmen defied Churchill's low expectations and agreed to form the French Committee of National Liberation. It appeared that de Gaulle's influence would be diluted by the presence of Giraud and Georges. Roosevelt believed the agreement would be short-lived and told Churchill that whatever the French agreed to among themselves, they still operated under Anglo-American martial law. "The bride [de Gaulle] evidently forgets there is still a war in progress," Roosevelt wrote. "Good luck in getting rid of our mutual headache." But getting rid of the Frenchman was not that simple. Within weeks, at de Gaulle's insistence, the new French Committee demanded official recognition as the government in exile of France. Roosevelt refused, demanding, as he had during Churchill's visit to Washington, that France when freed was to be "occupied" by Anglo-American forces until such time Frenchmen chose their own government. He offered to "accept" the French Committee but not to recognize it.[183]

And so, on the afternoon of June 4, with no movement on the French question, Churchill boarded his Avro York for the flight to Gibraltar, having brought the Fighting French as close to solidarity as he could, and having brought Marshall around. At the last minute he asked Alexander to accompany him to London to settle some matters known only to himself. Alexander—in the thick of planning the Sicily campaign—could only acquiesce. This meant the York now had one passenger too many. Churchill, in a snap judgment, told Pug Ismay that he must depart the aircraft because "he was very heavy and would overload the airplane." Ismay grabbed his suitcase and hitched a ride on a transport, which subsequently experienced an engine fire on the way to Gibraltar. Neither Alexander nor Ismay "felt in the least aggrieved" by Churchill's "deliciously ingenuous lack of consideration" for their personal safety and convenience because "we knew he would treat himself in exactly the same way—and worse—if he thought it would help the war." Churchill had planned to transfer at Gibraltar to a Boeing flying boat for the final leg of the trip, but hideous weather forced him instead to go by B-24 Liberator. He arrived home the next morning. He had been out of the country for a month.[184]

That day, a German spy at the Lisbon airport reported to his superiors that a thickset man smoking a cigar had been seen boarding a commercial flight, another flying boat, destination London. Phone calls were made, German fighter aircraft scrambled. The hapless aircraft was shot down over the sea, killing all fourteen passengers, including the popular screen actor Leslie Howard. The brutality of the Germans, Churchill later wrote, "was only matched by the stupidity of their agents." Yet, he wrote, his safe arrival home was another example of the "inscrutable workings of fate."[185]

The incident unsettled Britons. The prime minister was out there somewhere in the air, and Britons felt ill at ease about his absence. Upon his safe return, Panter-Downes wrote: "It's not only the conventional clucking old ladies who are hoping to goodness that the Prime Minister won't find it necessary to make any more long and dangerous trips for quite a while." It was the week of the favorable June moon. No invasion forces sailed for Sicily, but they were ready, and waiting, as was Churchill. The lunar cycle put July 9 in the middle of the three most favorable nights for action.[186]

Churchill had long voiced hopes that Stalin would emerge from the war as a guarantor rather than a disturber of the peace. He envisioned Poland and Czechoslovakia—along with Britain and America—standing "together in friendly relations with Russia." Yet in June, Poland's formal relations with Stalin, already suspended, ceased altogether, while Anglo-American relations with Russia reached, in Harriman's estimation, the "low point in the history of the alliance." When apprised of the decisions made during Trident, Stalin scorned them. He briefly pondered Roosevelt's request for a private meeting but declined as soon as he learned of the post-ponement of a second front until 1944. There was no point in meeting and nothing to discuss. He spit out identical and bitter messages to Roosevelt and Churchill wherein he listed their previous promises for a second front in 1943 and warned that the Soviet government "cannot align itself with this decision, which...may gravely affect the subsequent course of the war." He told them, "Your decision creates exceptional difficulties for the Soviet Union...and leaves the Soviet Army...to do the job alone." Churchill tried to mollify him: "I quite understand your disappointment but" the best way to help Russia would be by "winning battles and not by losing them" and certainly not by throwing away 100,000 men in a false start on French beaches. That produced even greater bitterness: "You say you 'quite understand' my disappointment," Stalin replied, pointing out that Churchill could not understand, because he was not in Moscow to witness the fact that "the preservation of Soviet confidence in its Allies... is being subjected to severe stress."[187]

Harriman arrived in London late in the month, sent by Roosevelt on another difficult mission: to inform Churchill that Roosevelt had asked for a one-on-one meeting with Stalin, was rebuked, and was now asking again. Harriman told Churchill over a dinner that lasted into the early morning. After all, Harriman argued, you and Brooke went to Moscow in August to make the relationship personal. Why should the president not do likewise? Churchill voiced disappointment, yet he appeared to under-stand Roosevelt's rationale. But overnight, as the disappointment turned to hurt and then anguish, he changed his mind. The following morning he shot off a cable to Washington in which he argued that his journey to Mos-cow the previous year was intended to get the relationship going, whereas if Roosevelt met with Stalin at this juncture, it would appear to Britons—and the world—to be a slight to Britain. He was correct, yet his opposition was unnecessary. Stalin had no intention of meeting Roosevelt. He ignored a request from Roosevelt to allow American bombers to land in Russia after attacking the Romanian Ploesti oil fields (54 of 178 American bombers were lost on the mission). He had recalled Maisky from London and Litvinov from Washington. There was an atmosphere now "alarmingly reminiscent" of the tensions that preceded the Molotov-Ribbentrop pact of 1939. That is, the question of Stalin making a separate peace, never far below the surface for months, had again bobbed into view. "It was fortunate," Robert Sherwood later wrote, "that Hitler did not know how bad relations were between the Allies at that moment, how close they were to a disruption which was his only hope of survival." Churchill grew so tired of Stalin's diplomatic obduracy that he stopped communicating with him for weeks. There was no more to say.[188]

Late on July 9, the largest armada in history hove to thirty miles off the coast of Sicily, 2,600 troop transports, tankers, and ammunition ships, landing craft, and warships, divided about equally between American and British. The British contingent, carrying Montgomery's Eighth Army, lay off the southeast coast, between Cape Passero and Syracuse. The American ships carrying Patton's Seventh Army aligned themselves roughly between landfalls near Ragusa and Licata, in the west. They had sailed from every North African port, as well as from Canada, Britain, and the United States, from where an entire infantry division was dispatched with all its rations, Jeeps, field guns, trucks, fuel, and ammunition. The men on board the troop ships knew that almost 200,000 Italians and 35,000 Germans waited on shore, although some relief was found in reports that three or four Italian and one German division were deployed in the far northwest corner of the island, having been taken in by false radio messages and an Allied naval feint in that direction. Still, the men knew that the Hermann Göring Division was dug in behind the American beaches. Though torn up in Tunisia, the men and panzers of the Hermann Göring Division were still ready for whatever came their way.

The Allies had no doubts as to Kesselring's willingness to fight. Success depended in large part upon the Italians displaying the same lack of warrior spirit they had shown before the surrender of Pantelleria, an island fortress midway between Tunis and Sicily. Pantelleria—called the Italian Gibraltar—was crisscrossed by tunnels and redoubts and protected by dozens of artillery batteries and squadrons of fighter planes. Mussolini had long

pledged that the garrison would fight to the last man. In early July, an Allied
fleet began shelling the island. After a week of naval and aerial shelling, and
as Allied landing craft circled off the coast, awaiting final orders to make
for Pantelleria's lone beach, the garrison's commander signaled that he was
out of water and ran up the white flag. He had received permission to do so
directly from Mussolini, who was now certain that he alone was the last
Italian willing to fight. Mussolini's doctor had for a long time been dosing
his patient with ever increasing amounts of Bellafolina and Alucol for the
stomach cramps that afflicted Il Duce in times of stress, especially stress
brought on by military defeats. The regimen was now administered on
almost a daily basis. The patient, in fact, was as broken as his people.[189]

Churchill, who thought that three thousand Italians at most garrisoned
Pantelleria, had made a wager with Eisenhower: five centimes (one-twentieth
of a cent) for each Italian captured beyond the three thousand Churchill
predicted. Eleven thousand surrendered. Eisenhower chose not to collect
his four dollars from Churchill.[190]

Now, on July 9, as his fleets battled the seas, Eisenhower pondered
whether the Italians on Sicily would put up more of a fight when the Allied
armies went ashore at dawn. The weather was already proving itself a formidable enemy, a gale out of the west worsened as the flotilla approached
Sicily. On Malta, Eisenhower pondered maps and weather reports in his
headquarters, deep inside a tunnel in the Lascaris Bastion, built by the
Knights of Malta and used since the start of the war as a communications
center by the Royal Navy. Admiral Andrew ("ABC") Cunningham's meteorologists had given Eisenhower hourly updates as the day progressed, and
a tutorial on the Beaufort scale—a measure of wind and waves on a scale
of one to twelve. Each hourly report was worse than the previous. Air
Marshal Tedder, at Eisenhower's side in the tunnels, noted the audacity of
an attempt to invade Italy by sea: "Fancy invading Italy from the south.
Even Hannibal had the sense to come in with his elephants over the Alps."
All day, vast fleets of aircraft passed overhead as even more departed from
Malta's newly reconditioned airfields, all on their way to bomb Sicilian
beaches and two dozen Axis airfields. Late in the evening Eisenhower
stepped outside to watch paratroopers from the American 82nd Airborne
Division and the British 1st Air Landing Brigade sail overhead toward their
drop zones. The British troops were in towed gliders, many of which, cut
loose too soon, lost their way in the winds and the darkness and dropped
into the sea with the loss of all aboard.[191]

As Eisenhower watched the aerial flotilla drift by, a cable arrived from
Marshall: "Is the attack on or off?" Eisenhower had no answer and did not
reply. But the hour was fast approaching when the landings could not be
aborted. Montgomery's forces, on the east side of Sicily, found themselves

in the lee of the wind, Patton's troops, with no protection from the prevailing winds, had a rough ride. If all went well, the three American and four British and Canadian divisions would stake a claim to more than one hundred miles of Sicily by dinnertime on the tenth. As the troop ships marked time, the cruisers, destroyers, and battleships of the fleet ran in along the coast and raked the beaches with high-explosive shells. But orders to go ashore had yet to come down. Then, toward midnight, the winds abated. Eisenhower had already decided that the invasion would go on, storms or no. The word went down to the men on the ships.[192]

That evening, Churchill and Clementine, with "customary instinct for the proper gesture," attended a showing of *Watch on the Rhine*. After the show Clementine, not feeling well, sent one of her handwritten notes to Pamela, requesting that she keep Churchill company as he parsed the news from Eisenhower's headquarters. The two passed the hours playing bezique, the game interrupted regularly by secretaries reporting the delays and deteriorating weather off the Sicilian coast. "I remember thinking," Pamela later recalled, "that if there is anything I can do for the war at least I have to stay awake to keep him company."[193]

Londoners went to bed that night, wrote Mollie Panter-Downes, with a sense of unease, not because of the pending battle in Sicily, about which they knew nothing, but because of the battle on the Russian front. It was clearly the most titanic struggle between armies in the history of the world, and it could go either way.[194]

It was developing along a 190-mile bulge in the lines—a salient—that looped around Kursk, a vital Soviet rail hub located between Orel and Kharkov about five hundred miles southwest of Moscow. Hitler had told his generals to "light a bonfire" there. Stalin, by virtue of Ultra decrypts (couched as the reports of "secret" agents) shared by the British, knew where and when Hitler would attack. The Germans struck on July 5, with 700,000 men, 2,400 tanks and assault guns, and 1,800 aircraft, hitting the salient from the north, west, and south. Opposing them were more than one million Soviet troops, 3,400 tanks and assault guns, and 2,100 planes. Another quarter million Soviet troops were held in reserve, near Kursk, about forty miles within the bulge. Thus, as just seven Anglo-American divisions and six hundred tanks went ashore in Sicily, two million Soviet and German men and almost six thousand tanks were fighting the greatest tank battle of all time. For the next week the world focused its undivided attention on Kursk.

Meanwhile, the aptly named Fighting French were at it again. De Gaulle, unable to fight Germans in Sicily because his North African army (actually

Giraud's army, as he was commander in chief) had been left in Tunisia, picked a fight with the British government over HMG's suppression of the Free French newspaper, *La Marseillaise*. It had been put out of business by the Ministry of Information, which cited war needs as the reason to withhold its newsprint. This was a clever tactic on the part of Brendan Bracken, and one that Londoners readily saw through, especially as anti-Russian Polish newspapers were again free to print as many copies as they liked. De Gaulle regularly was his own worst enemy, yet Londoners remembered that he had been the only Frenchman to back England in June 1940 when it appeared that London would follow Paris into the Nazi maw. For this he had garnered the respect of Britons. Churchill believed with Roosevelt that France was greater than de Gaulle, but he reluctantly disagreed with Roosevelt and Hull, who considered the Cross of Lorraine not worth bearing.

For Roosevelt, the French Empire stood behind only the British Empire on his list of entities he sought to dissolve after the war. "Governing authorities in Washington," Eden wrote in a Foreign Office memo, "have little belief in France's future and indeed do not wish to see France again restored as a great imperial power." If Roosevelt could abet that outcome by ignoring the Fighting French and de Gaulle, so much the better.[195]

"American hatred of him [de Gaulle] is keen," Eden wrote in a memorandum that July week. And now it had come to a head. Roosevelt again, as he had in May, wanted Churchill to break with de Gaulle, leaving Giraud (who, against the advice of the Foreign Office, was visiting Roosevelt that week) in sole control of the French Committee of National Liberation. Churchill was so fed up with de Gaulle that he told Eden the Foreign Office's support of de Gaulle might precipitate a break between Eden and himself. The message to Eden was clear: only one of them would survive such a fissure, and it would not be Anthony. Eden stood fast, based on his belief that "American policies toward France would jeopardize their relations and ours with that country for years to come." Churchill relented on July 20. Eden found him to be "in good form" at dinner that evening, although his mood was darkened somewhat by the death of his black cat, Munich Mouser, who had taken himself off from No. 10 to the Foreign Office to expire. The cat, Churchill told Eden, "died of remorse and chose his death-bed accordingly." The two major obstacles to Roosevelt ridding himself of the troublesome Frenchman lay with Eden's persistence in aligning Churchill with the Foreign Office, and on French public opinion, which Roosevelt ignored. Weeks earlier the Resistance leader Jean Moulin had informed London that the National Council of the Resistance had met and called for the creation of a provisional government in Algiers presided over by de Gaulle, "the sole chief of French Resistance."[196]

De Gaulle's latest stunt over French newspapers played directly into

Roosevelt's hand, and distracted Churchill from the far more pressing events in Sicily and Kursk. Churchill feared that continued financing of the Fighting French (actually American financing, Britain being broke) would lead to a strain in Anglo-American relations, an outcome "that no one would like better than de Gaulle." Brooke told his diary: "A long tirade of abuse of de Gaulle from Winston which I heartily agreed with. Unfortunately his dislike for de Gaulle has come rather late, he should have been cast overboard a year ago." Yet Brooke the military man did not see the politics at the core of Eden's support of de Gaulle. Churchill, sustained by Eden's argument, grudgingly backed de Gaulle because he understood what Roosevelt did not: the Allies needed de Gaulle, and Britain would someday need France.[197]

Like de Gaulle, the Polish prime minister Władysław Sikorski had also brought his defeated soldiers to London when all was lost in the homeland. Unlike de Gaulle, Sikorski was respected *and* revered by Britons. But earlier in the week, as if to foreshadow the troubles that lay ahead for Poland, Sikorski, his daughter Zofia, and several aides were killed when their B-24 spun into the sea just seconds after taking off from Gibraltar. Sikorski's loss disrupted not only the Allied war effort but the postwar world and Poland's place in it. Since 1940 Sikorski had gotten along well with the Russians, who, as much as they now resented the "smear campaign" conducted by the London Poles over Katyn, respected Sikorski. If anyone could have navigated his way to a successful solution of the Polish-Soviet political crisis, it was Sikorski.[198]

The political subtleties and de Gaulle's behavior being parsed by Londoners during the first half of July were shunted to the rear when at midmonth it became clear that the German attack at Kursk was going nowhere. That week the Soviets mounted a counterattack toward Orel, north of the salient; within days the Germans were retreating westward across a three-hundred-mile front. A Soviet attack toward Belgorod, south of the salient, stalled, but Field Marshal Manstein informed Hitler that Army Group South lacked the reserves to hold back the Red Army much longer. The same could be said of Dönitz's ability to hold back Allied shipping in the Atlantic, where Germany was losing one U-boat per day on average. Churchill (who called U-boats "canaries") cabled Roosevelt, "My cat likes canaries . . . we have altogether 18 canaries this month."[199]

The news from Sicily and the Mediterranean was also welcome. After the men had gotten safely ashore on July 10, the Italians had receded from the beaches, and by the fifteenth, it appeared that Sicily might go into the bag within two or three weeks, despite ferocious German resistance. Reports from the Balkans indicated a precipitous fall in the morale of the twenty-four Italian divisions scattered from the Aegean islands to northern Yugoslavia. They would rather surrender to Anglo-American forces than be massacred by the Greeks, or by Tito's partisans. And in Italy, British intelligence concluded that the Italian forces south of Naples would surrender after putting up a token resistance if the Allies landed, but they would not surrender beforehand. The time to strike Italy proper was almost at hand.

By the third week of July, Montgomery's army, halfway to Messina, was meeting heavy resistance from the Hermann Göring Division at Catania, south of Mount Etna. The Eighth Army had the Germans to its front and several rivers and malarial wetlands on its flanks. Malaria began to fell more of Monty's men than did German bullets. But within the week, Montgomery's army resumed its slog toward Messina along the coastal plains. Patton, after a rough start on the beaches—also at the hands of the Hermann Göring Division—had detached a corps, which was now racing toward Palermo. The battle for Sicily was going well.

In June, Eisenhower had told Churchill that a decision on whether or not to invade Italy would depend upon how the Sicily operation turned out. But Eisenhower had made no decision about where in Italy the Allies would go after Sicily, or when. He rejected Naples as too far north. The toe of Italy, just across from Messina and 350 miles south of Rome, appeared as far as Eisenhower was willing to go. He did tell Jan Smuts, then in Algiers, that Rome should be the ultimate target. Eisenhower's German counterpart, Albert Kesselring, was already planning the escape of his forces from Messina, across the narrow straits to the mainland. He could contemplate such a withdrawal only because the Allies had not seen fit to cut off his escape route by invading the toe of Italy when they first went ashore in Sicily, an error Eisenhower grasped weeks later. Meanwhile, on July 19, seven hundred Allied heavy bombers hit the rail yards of Rome. John Martin assured Churchill that "the Pope has a good shelter." By the twenty-second, Patton's detached corps had taken Palermo, cutting Sicily in two.[200]

A visit to London by Secretary of War Henry Stimson during these days threw Churchill's plans for furthering his Italian gains into utter confusion. Stimson, seventy-five, a tough old trooper, had served as secretary of war under William Howard Taft and as a colonel of artillery in France during the Great War. He hated the Hun and was in agreement with Marshall in favor of the cross-Channel strategy. While in London he was told by one of the planners of the French invasion that any prolonged activity in the Mediterranean might threaten the timetable for operations in France.

This deeply troubled Stimson, who saw no future in Italy or the Balkans. When Churchill pointed out to him that Marshall had agreed to a push into Italy proper, Stimson rejoined that Marshall envisioned only temporary action there, perhaps to capture Italian airfields in order to take the bombing to southern Germany. This discussion took place while the Germans at Catania had stopped Montgomery in his tracks.

Churchill used that setback to paint a horrific picture for Stimson of the fate that would befall 50,000 Allied troops on the beaches of France were the Germans to show up in force, which they surely would. The Allies would be driven back into the sea, leaving "the Channel full of corpses" and the entire Western Front in disarray. Churchill added that were he C in C, he would not support Roundhammer (as Stimson mistakenly called the cross-Channel strike), but as prime minister he had pledged his support to whatever the Combined Chiefs decided upon. Stimson pronounced the entire episode a colossal double cross, "like hitting us in the eye." Arriving in Algiers, he told Eisenhower that Churchill "was obsessed with the idea of proving to history" that a Balkan strategy was wise "and would repair the damage history now records for [his] misfortunes at the Dardanelles in the last war." Eisenhower, in turn, feared that if he did not follow up the impending victory in Sicily, he'd be accused of "missing the boat." His aide, Harry Butcher, recorded the frustration at headquarters: "Yet our own government seems to want to slam on the brakes just when the going gets good." These were Churchill's feelings exactly.[201]

Stimson's intuitive reading of Churchill was correct. The secretary's suspicions would have been confirmed had he known that Churchill in mid-July had told the British Chiefs of Staff that the twenty-seven divisions allotted to the cross-Channel thrust "will not be equal to the task of landing and maintaining themselves on land." Instead, he again argued that Jupiter, the invasion of northern Norway, be brought back into play, and that Mountbatten's proposed aircraft carriers made of ice be used there in a supporting role. Stimson might have become unhinged had he been privy to Churchill's line of thought regarding Roundup. That operation, Churchill told the chiefs, should be relegated to the status of a feint. He proposed a similar strategy in Italy, in which he advocated luring German reinforcements into the toe of Italy: "we could contain them there with our right hand and hit out at Naples with our left."[202]

Stimson took himself home to Washington, intent on warning Roosevelt and Marshall of Churchill's wavering before Churchill appeared on the scene to ambush them all. That Churchill was coming to North America had been agreed upon midmonth when he and Roosevelt decided that their need to meet was acute and growing more so. Roosevelt had suggested September 1, but Churchill pushed for mid-August, as he believed events in

Sicily were fast outpacing plans. "I must say," Eden's parliamentary secretary Oliver Harvey told his diary, "the PM doesn't let the grass grow under his feet." The leaders settled upon Quebec City, mid-August, at the Citadel, where in 1759—the year of victories—on the Plains of Abraham, Wolfe and the English snatched Canada from Montcalm and the French. Churchill and Roosevelt invited Stalin, who withheld his response for almost two weeks before declining, although he did acknowledge the need to meet, and suggested a winter rendezvous. Churchill selected the code name for the Quebec meeting, Quadrant, and he put Italy at the top of the agenda. Smuts had sent him a report from Algiers in which he argued, "Rome may mean virtually Italy and its possession may mean this year a transition of transforming the whole war situation and next year finishing it." This was the position Churchill intended to stake out at Quadrant, for he respected Smuts's military judgment above all others', including, on rare occasion, his own. Yet wires had already been crossed; Eisenhower had agreed with Smuts on the need to take Rome at some point, but he had not agreed with Smuts on the timetable to attack Rome. General Ike had his sights set much lower down the leg of Italy.[203]

Churchill, enthused over Smuts's rosy predictions, sent Roosevelt a copy of Smuts's letter. Roosevelt replied, "I like General Smuts's idea and I hope something of that kind can be undertaken." That response would have mortified Stimson, but for Churchill, the president's message was as tasty as one of those Virginia hams the Americans so generously carried to London.[204]

Brooke, too, had reason in late July to allow a smile to crease his usually dour visage; Churchill for the third time in as many months told the CIGS that he was the man to lead the invasion of France, a mere feint was Churchill to have his way, but a vital command none the less. The occasion was a sherry party at No. 10, at which Churchill asked Brooke's wife, Benita, what she thought of her husband becoming the supreme commander of the invasion of France. She was stunned. Brooke had still not told his wife.[205]

On the hideously hot Sunday afternoon of July 25, King Victor Emmanuel III summoned Mussolini to the Villa Ada, where more than four hundred acres of gardens and forest scrubbed Rome's air of grime and heat. Mussolini, like Churchill, lunched with his king each week, on Mondays in Il Duce's case. The Sunday summons was anomalous but not necessarily troubling. Il Duce was well aware of the machinations of many within his Grand Council, including his son-in-law Count Ciano. The previous day, the council passed a motion that gave the King added powers, which amounted to a vote of no confidence in Il Duce. Yet, although his minions had mutinied, Mussolini had no doubts as to who would emerge triumphant; he had fought these political wars for more than two decades. This was, after all, *Anno XXI* of his rule.

The King, wearing a gray marshal's uniform and trousers seamed with red stripes, was at the villa's main door to greet his minister. They moved to a ground-floor salon. Mussolini stood as the King spoke. Things were not going well in Italy, the King offered. Even the Alpine Brigade—one of Italy's more storied units—was rumored to be on the verge of mutiny, and, most insultingly, the troops were singing a nasty little ditty about Il Duce. The council's vote, the King added, accurately reflected the country's feelings toward him. In that case, Mussolini replied, I should tender my resignation. He presumed the King would reject that idea. But Emmanuel did not. "I have to tell you," he replied, "that I unconditionally accept it." Mussolini slumped into a chaise. The King informed his former premier that he intended to appoint the old warrior and head of Mussolini's armies, Marshal Pietro Badoglio, as premier. He then offered to take Mussolini under his personal protection, since he, the King, was his only remaining friend in Italy. A car was waiting outside; it happened to be surrounded by several carabiniera. Il Duce understood: he was under arrest. Emmanuel had undone two decades of fascism in just twenty minutes.[206]

The German ambassador to Rome had the day before reported to Berlin that "Mussolini's position has never been stronger." The ambassador was soon recalled to Berlin. Goebbels lamented Il Duce's downfall to his diary: "It is simply shocking to think that in this manner a revolutionary movement that has been in power for twenty-one years could be liquidated."[207]

Badoglio, Ciano, and the Grand Council presumed that Fascist rule would be preserved, simply without Il Duce. But by nightfall, King Emmanuel, now an absolute monarch, dissolved the Italian Fascist Party. Badoglio, who was to be in charge of only civil authority, took to calling himself the King's executive assistant. The Italian people assumed that Emmanuel would secure peace with honor within days. Nobody in Rome seemed to consider how the Germans might react. The Italian people's renewed faith in royalty was to be short-lived. The new government signaled Berlin that it would continue the fight, but Goebbels and Hitler considered the message nothing more than a delaying tactic to afford Badoglio time to make a separate peace with the Allies. Indeed, within days, Italian diplomats in neutral capitals began to quietly extend peace feelers in the Allied direction.

Churchill learned of Il Duce's downfall at Chequers while watching a movie, *Sous les Toits de Paris,* in the company of Clementine, daughters Mary and Sarah, Alan Brooke, Lord Moran, and John Martin. The projector was stopped, the lights went up, and everyone clapped. London learned of the news during the BBC midnight broadcast, when the Roman decree announcing Mussolini's "resignation" was read. Harold Nicolson noted that the decree did not bear the date of *Anno XXI*. Violet Bonham Carter telephoned Nicolson, overjoyed because this meant the release of her son, Mark, who had been captured in Tunisia. Churchill addressed the Commons on July 27. Peace should be made quickly with Italy, he advised. He condemned the sordid treatment in the British and American press of Italy and its King; the House of Savoy always claimed a special little corner of his heart. He went on: until matters were settled, however, "Italy can stew in its own juice." Nicolson found this phrase to be vulgar, and worse, it defied translation into Italian for BBC rebroadcast to Italy. Nicolson settled on *"L'Italia fara il suo proprio minestrone"*(loosely: "Italy must boil in its mixed-up soup").[208]

"A memorable moment," wrote Brooke of Mussolini's end, "and at least a change from 'the end of the beginning' to 'the beginning of the end.'" As for Churchill's speech, Goebbels recorded, "This old rogue [*dieser alte Gauner*]" was "riding triumphantly on his high horse."[209]

The Mediterranean hinge had turned. Yet Sicily lay more than 1,200 air miles from Berlin, almost four times the distance from Normandy to the Rhine, and with the Alps blocking the way. Allied troops and tanks would not be traversing the Apennines and Julian Alps anytime soon, and if they someday set out on that course, they would find the going far more difficult than a race across the Low Countries. The Americans knew geography and they knew arithmetic. Measured in miles and the difficulty of terrain, attacking Germany from southern Italy was like attacking Washington, DC, from Houston by way of the Appalachian Mountains. Attacking Germany from Normandy, on the other hand, was like going to Washington from the North Carolina coast by way of farmlands, plains, and forests. As Churchill and Brooke prepared for the voyage to Canada, their main concern was that Roosevelt, goaded by Stimson, would scotch any further initiatives in Italy. "Marshall absolutely fails to realize what strategic treasures lie at our feet in the Mediterranean," Brooke complained to his diary, "and always hankers after cross-Channel operations."[210]

Churchill, who hungered for any and all operations that promised success, as Italy surely did, meant to settle the issue once and for all during Quadrant.

Shortly after midnight on August 5, Churchill, accompanied by Clementine, Mary, and a court of 250, departed London by train bound for

Glasgow, and then by launch for the short run to Greenock, where the *Queen Mary,* riding at anchor in the Firth of Clyde, awaited his arrival.[211]

That Mrs. Churchill was among the company was surprising. Her husband's love for her was absolute. He respected her opinions, which she stated with force. But he rarely sought her advice on policy matters. Clementine traveled only as the Great Man's wife, and in that regard, given the immense responsibilities he faced, he tended to ignore her. He had business to conduct on board ship, and did so over lunches and dinners. She was shy and found no joy in sharing her table with eight or ten strangers who sought only her husband's time and energy. She did not manifest a natural or carefree demeanor in such surroundings, her daughter Mary later wrote, and "thus, in a life full of people, she knew much loneliness." She was prone to tension and anxiety. This, Churchill did not understand, given his lack of interest in any "illness which was rooted in nervous or psychological origins." (He once told his doctor he liked neither psychiatrists nor their "queer ideas about what is in people's heads.") The "nervous strain" under which Clementine had lived for four years was "extracting its price," Mary later wrote, and by the time she departed for Quebec, "she was in a state of profound physical and nervous exhaustion." She had no outlets whereby she might find some private joy, did not paint, write books, garden, or gamble. In fact, she hated gambling. Her father had lost much of her legacy at the tables. Churchill did not fare very well himself on the green baize, where, until the war came, he loved to spend an evening while she took to her bed to worry over the probable damage to the family finances. It was hoped the sea voyage might alleviate her stress, yet a voyage such as this, cooped up with strangers, was sure to put her in bed, ill, and soon did.[212]

Averell Harriman, accompanied by his daughter, Kathleen, joined the party. They were heading to their Arden, New York, home for their first vacation in two years. Brigadier Orde Wingate also made the trip, having arrived in London from Burma less than twelve hours earlier, in time to dine with Churchill. Wingate's "brilliant exploits" leading his Chindits in Burma so impressed the Old Man that he decreed the general must go to Quebec. Such was the haste to get Wingate on the train that "Clive of Burma" did not even have time to change out of his rumpled field uniform. Lord Moran was along, as usual. Within minutes of meeting Wingate, about whom he had heard so much from Churchill, Moran concluded that the jungle warrior "is only a gifted eccentric. He is not another Lawrence." After further chats with Wingate, Moran decided that the hero of Burma was "hardly sane—in medical jargon, a borderline case."[213]

Late on the afternoon of August 5, the *Queen Mary,* with the P.M. and his party safe on board, slipped down the Firth of Clyde and past the headlands of Arran. The weather, Brooke noted, was "dirty" and blowing hard. The great ship rolled slightly as it made its way into the North Channel of the Irish Sea and then into the Atlantic proper. She had been repainted and partially refurbished and, like England, appeared fresh, powerful, and confident. Yet Brooke believed the ship was heading for troubled waters. "The nearer I get to this conference the less I like it. I know we shall have hard fighting with our American friends."[214]

The previous November, Churchill had proclaimed the end of the beginning for Hitler's Reich. August of 1943 marked the beginning of the end. Each day at sea, news arrived to bolster that conclusion. The Red Army took Belgorod on August 5, and began pushing west. The lower Dnieper River, Kiev, and the Ukraine were its autumn targets. When Field Marshal Manstein told Hitler that Berlin must send twenty divisions' worth of reinforcements or yield the Donets Basin, Hitler replied that he could spare no forces; they were going to Italy. The previous week, General Heinz Guderian, the architect of blitzkrieg, told Goebbels of his "grave concern" over the status of the war, especially in light of the fact that "we can't afford to be active on all fronts." Also galling to Guderian was the futility of pulling armored units away from the Russian front, where they were desperately needed, for service in Italy and the Balkans, where the geography favored infantry and artillery over tanks. Since early May, sixteen German divisions (including four evacuated from Sicily) had been shifted to Italy, where in April there had been none. Eight more had gone to the Balkans and Romania, and thirteen now stood vigil in Norway. Guderian's observations, taken together with Goebbels' admission that the RAF was now administering ever more punishing blows to Germany, amounted to a complete validation of Churchill's strategy of flexibility and opportunism.[215]

On the sixth, Churchill received word from Eden that an Italian diplomat in Tangier had approached his British counterpart with authorization from Badoglio to open negotiations with the Allies. "Don't miss the bus," Churchill replied, adding that although surrender must be unconditional, "we shall be prepared to accord conditions as acts of grace and not as a bargain." He suggested the term "honorable capitulation" be used in the talks, but Eden reminded him that "unconditional surrender" had been announced publicly at Casablanca. This was a problem. Churchill instructed Eden to convey to the Italians that their surrender would have (possibly favorable) conditions attached, conditional upon their surrendering unconditionally. Roosevelt had concurred in this line of reasoning the previous week, when he cabled Churchill: "Eisenhower should be authorized to state conditions when and if the Italian Government asks him for an armistice." Berlin was well aware of the developing situation; a branch of its intelligence service was intercepting phone calls between Churchill and Roosevelt in which they discussed surrender terms for the Italians. One condition Churchill insisted upon was that 70,000 British prisoners in Italy must be repatriated to England, not transported to "the land of the Huns." The Vatican suggested that by declaring Rome an open city, the Allies might entice the new Italian government to the peace table more quickly; Churchill nixed the idea. Rome was to be bombed relentlessly, he told Eden, until the new government surrendered. A few weeks later, Churchill told reporters, "Of this you can be sure, we will continue to operate on the Italian donkey at both ends, with a carrot, and with a stick." The Italian matter was on the Quebec agenda.[216]

The Battle of the Atlantic was not. The Allies were on the verge of victory. There would be many lost ships and lost sailors over the next twelve months and beyond, but the German blockade was broken.

Elsewhere, the air battles over the Ruhr and Hamburg were reaching monstrous climaxes. Churchill had told the U.S. Congress in May what he had in mind for Japanese cities; his words applied to German cities as well: "It is the duty of those who are charged with the direction of the war to . . . begin the process, so necessary and desirable, of laying the cities and other munitions centres of Japan in ashes, for in ashes they must surely lie before peace comes back to the world." Since May, residents of the Ruhr Valley, who otherwise knew little of the battles in the Atlantic and Russia, were aware from nightly visitations by the RAF that a horrific turn had come in the air war. The RAF had been trimming wicks since 1940; during the early summer of 1943, it set western Germany ablaze. So relentless was the bombing that Churchill, while viewing a British reconnaissance film of the carnage in the Ruhr Valley, turned to his dinner companions and asked, "Are we beasts? Are we taking this too far?" He posed that question in late June over brandy, and it did not mark a philosophical turn on Churchill's part. In the weeks since he posed the question, they had taken it further, and indeed Churchill was intent on taking it much further still. He had his doubts about the effectiveness of the air war, but as he once told the press, "Opinion is divided whether . . . air power could by itself bring about collapse in Germany. There is no harm in finding out."[217]

Many of Goebbels' diary entries between May and late July treat either of the treachery of Jews (he had reconfirmed his thoughts on Jewish treachery after rereading the anti-Semitic screed *The Protocols of the Elders of Zion*), or the increasingly effective RAF bombing in the Ruhr Valley and on Hamburg. The Krupp Works at Essen was hit, completely halting steel production. Three dams in the Ruhr Valley—the Eder, Sorpe, and Moehne—were damaged or destroyed on May 17 when just nineteen Lancasters from the specially trained 617 Squadron, flying only sixty feet above the water, dropped two-ton, barrel-shaped "bouncing" bombs, which skipped upstream to hit the dams just below the waterline. Eight of the Lancasters and their crews were lost, but explosions breached the Moehne dam with catastrophic effect. The resultant flood drowned several dozen factories, and 1,200 residents downstream. "The attacks," Goebbels wrote, "were very successful."[218]

As Goebbels noted the increasing damage inflicted by the RAF, he took some satisfaction in the numbers of British bombers shot down each night. Now, nightly, came flights of five hundred, seven hundred, nine hundred or more Halifax and Lancaster bombers; by day, the American B-17s arrived, in far smaller numbers. The Anglo-American air forces were now administering vicious round-the-clock punishment to the Reich. This was the "24-hours service" that Churchill had promised the American press. Yet the German fighter defense was especially devastating against the American daylight raiders. As a result, in June the Combined Chiefs amended the Casablanca bombing directive, which called for the destruction of German morale (houses), transportation hubs, oil refineries, and armaments industries. Henceforth the air forces were to destroy Germany's aircraft industry. The new directive was code-named Pointblank. In coming months it would serve less as a blueprint for joint Anglo-American strategy than as a source of dispute between RAF and the American planners. Indeed, Bomber Harris simply continued bombing German cities. If aircraft factories were hit in the bargain, so much the better.

With RAF casualties running disturbingly high, often more than 5 percent, approval was given to employ the secret Window program—strips of aluminum foil dropped from incoming bombers that caused German radar screens to dissolve into meaningless static. Window had been kept quarantined in the year since its development for fear that if it was deployed, the Germans would solve it and turn it against Britain. During that year, 2,200 RAF heavy bombers had been lost and almost 18,000 trained airmen killed or captured, including 4,000 airmen captured or killed during the recent offensive. To stanch the bleeding, the War Cabinet allowed Harris to deploy Window. Goebbels, in his diary entry of July 26, noted an unexplained drop-off in RAF casualties, just twelve aircraft shot down of more than seven hundred. This was Window at work.[219]

Hamburg, Germany's second-largest city and largest port, suffered the consequences that week, during what Brooke described as "a new climax of horror." On July 24, the RAF dropped 2,400 tons of bombs on Hamburg, an amount almost exactly equal to the tonnage of bombs the Luftwaffe had deposited on Britain during the previous *twelve months*. The RAF returned two days later, but low clouds and rain forced most of the raiders to turn back. Clear skies and the RAF returned on the night of the twenty-seventh and again on the twenty-ninth. Again Goebbels rued the ease with which the RAF penetrated German defenses. He also rued the death of Hamburg, "A city of a million inhabitants has been destroyed in a manner unparalleled in history." The British in three raids dropped almost ten thousand tons of high explosives and incendiaries on the city. The result, a German official wrote, was "beyond all human imagination." Almost 800,000 citizens were left homeless; the fire storm consumed oil depots and the port, twelve square miles of the city, and more than 40,000 residents.[220]

In one night and in one city and during one firestorm, the RAF had made up for all of London's casualties during the Blitz. A secret German document recounted the disaster: "Trees three feet thick were broken off or uprooted; human beings were...flung alive into the flames by winds which exceeded 150 miles an hour."* Residents who took shelter underground "were suffocated by carbon-monoxide poisoning and their bodies reduced to ashes as though they had been placed in a crematorium." Churchill took along on the *Queen Mary* stereoscopic slides of the damage, along with a small device to view the images. Desiring that Stalin be apprised of RAF results, shortly after arriving in Quebec, Churchill sent the slides and the viewfinder on to Moscow. The images, Churchill wrote Stalin, "give one a much more vivid impression than anything that can be gained from photographs." On August 9, a *Daily Mirror* headline crowed: 50 GERMAN CITIES WILL BE HAMBURGED. The raids were, as Brooke wrote, a climax of sorts. They also marked the beginning of even more deadly raids. With almost 80 percent of Hamburg erased from the map, Bomber Harris now put Berlin—he called it "The Big City"—in his sights.[221]

The Luftwaffe did not turn Window against Britain that year, in part because with much of the Luftwaffe deployed in the east, attacks against Britain had all but ceased; fewer than 2,400 Britons died by German bombs that year. The Germans did, however, invigorate their nighttime fighter defenses, including locating and targeting British bombers by triangulating RAF electronic emissions, and refining their radar to penetrate Window. The RAF soon began paying its previously high price. On average, six hundred RAF airmen were killed or captured each week during the next year. When the *Economist* opined that the air raids were costing the Allies too much, Goebbels lamented to his diary, "Would to god that

---

* The destruction, Bomber Harris later wrote, "must have been even more cataclysmic than the bursting of the two atom bombs over Japanese cities." (Sir Arthur Harris, *Bomber Offensive*, p. 179)

were true." By forcing Germany to defend itself, the raids assured that the Luftwaffe could not attain air superiority over the Russians. And in Italy, where the Allies now held a ten-to-one superiority, the Luftwaffe had all but disappeared. The Germans also had to commit massive ground forces in the west, where more than ninety-five divisions — one-third of German troop strength — were arrayed, including thirteen in Norway, forty-five in the Low Countries and France, and twenty-four in Italy and the Balkans. None were fighting Americans or Britons, but neither were they fighting Russians. They were as effectively tied down as if under attack, but Stalin, who was losing ten thousand Russians — soldiers and civilians — per *day*, did not see things that way. Churchill believed this validated his strategy of hitting Germany from all sides, by all methods, at all times. Goebbels agreed, writing, "It is not a soothing thought to imagine the English attacking us at any point they please with relatively small forces."[222]

That was the very strategy that Henry Stimson was urging Roosevelt to repudiate, even as the *Queen Mary* and Churchill closed on Nova Scotia. "None of these methods of pinprick warfare," Stimson wrote to Roosevelt, "can be counted on" to either lead to the defeat of Germany or "to fool Stalin into the belief" that the West had kept to its pledge to open "a real second front." It was time, Stimson urged the president, to demand Churchill make good on that pledge. Further, it was time that an American was appointed commander of the invasion. He told Roosevelt, "We cannot rationally hope to be able to cross the Channel...under a British commander" because, although the British "have rendered lip service to the operation their hearts are not in it."[223]

Where Stimson saw ineffectual pinpricks, Churchill saw flexibility, the essence of his opportunistic strategic vision. The Americans tended to underestimate the complexity of a cross-Channel operation, while Churchill and the British Chiefs of Staff tended to exaggerate its potential pitfalls, leaving each side in doubt of the other's strategic vision. Marshall stunned Brooke during the conference when he offered that "20 or 30 divisions" landed in France would suffice to rid Europe of Hitler. Brooke knew that such a paltry force would be slaughtered. Stimson and Marshall, for their part, suspected the British did not consider the North African and Italian ventures to be a means to an end — a softening up of Europe as prelude to Overlord — but intended to delay if not undermine the cross-Channel thrust.[224]

Eisenhower believed so as well, and later wrote, "The doctrine of opportunism, so often applicable in tactics, is a dangerous one to pursue in strategy." The Americans suspected the British sought only to nibble away at the edges of the Reich by sea and air and on land in order to drive Germany to the brink, at which time an invasion of France would result in an almost bloodless march from Normandy to Berlin.

That was not true. Churchill and Brooke sought to punch away at Germany until such time as the march to Berlin—and it would be bloody, not bloodless—would have a strong prospect for success. Churchill later reduced the differences in strategic thinking to a few choice phrases. The Americans, he wrote, "feel that once the foundation has been planned on true and comprehensive lines all other stages will follow naturally and almost inevitably.... The British mind does not work quite in this way. We do not think that logic and clear-cut principles are necessarily the sole keys to what ought to be done in swiftly changing and indefinable situations." These ideas informed Churchill's strategic thinking. Its essence was "to assign a larger importance to opportunism and improvisation, seeking rather to live and conquer in accordance with the unfolding event than to aspire to dominate it often by fundamental decisions. There is room for argument about both views. The difference is one of emphasis, but it is deep rooted." Churchill had, since 1940, endorsed a cross-Channel thrust, but as a means of exploiting a collapse in German morale and firepower, not as a means of evoking the collapse. Ismay, writing after the war, confirmed that philosophy when he wrote, "Mr. Churchill and his advisors always recognized that ultimately the *death blow* to Germany must be delivered across the Channel" (italics added).[225]

Onboard the *Queen Mary,* Churchill was receiving his first briefings on Overlord, the proposed invasion of Normandy. He liked what he saw, up to a point. General Frederick Morgan had been ordered by the Combined Chiefs to produce a plan for a "full scaled assault" on Europe. He had been warned that based on Admiral King's needs in the Pacific, he could expect only 3,300 assault and troop ships to carry out his plan. Thus limited, Morgan's plan called for three seaborne and two parachute divisions to land in the general area of Caen. Two dozen British, Canadian, and American divisions would follow in the first weeks after the initial landings. That, Churchill concluded, would not trigger a German collapse if that was the intent; nor was it enough to exploit a German collapse if one was imminent. Churchill suggested that more troops go ashore along a broader front. Five months would pass before the Americans saw the wisdom of his suggestion.

Satisfied with the overall plan, Churchill, as usual, fretted over the details. Given that twenty-foot tides were common along the Normandy coast, he demanded to be briefed on the progress in building the Mulberry artificial harbors he had championed more than two years earlier. Only by building these harbors could enough men, machines, rations, and ammunition be gotten safely ashore in a timely fashion. The target was 12,000 tons daily; success depended on reaching it. Fuel for the trucks and tanks would come by way of another technological marvel, a pipeline under the ocean (Pluto) from southeast Britain to the Normandy town of Port-en-Bessin. The pipeline's deployment would be made more complex because it would probably take place under Luftwaffe attack. A third marvel was intended to protect the artificial harbors from high seas—an artificial breakwater (called a lilo) that consisted of large inflatable rubber bladders that supported underwater concrete screens. A demonstration took place in Churchill's stateroom bathroom. The Great Man watched, perched upon a stool and dressed in his dragon dressing gown, as an admiral and a brigadier splashed away at the overflowing bathtub in which a miniature lilo calmed the waves. A stranger who witnessed the scene, Ismay wrote, "would have found it hard to believe that this was the British high command studying the most stupendous and spectacular amphibious operation in the history of war."[226]

Churchill sought assurance that progress was being made on another concept he held dear: Mountbatten's floating airfields made of ice and code-named Operation Habakkuk. The idea, Churchill stressed, "deserves very keen examination." He had selected the code name, citing the Old Testament text from Habakkuk, "Behold ye among the heathen...for I will work a work in your days...which ye will not believe." Indeed, many among the planning staff were nonbelievers. The idea, which Mountbatten introduced to Churchill during a Chequers weekend, had taken shape in Canada, not surprisingly given the sometimes frigid temperatures there. But Churchill envisioned deploying these million-ton monsters off the coasts of France and in the Indian Ocean, where they would serve as refueling stations for the RAF. No consideration appears to have been given to one critical design flaw: even outfitted with their planned refrigeration systems, the ice crafts would melt. Brooke disparagingly called Habakkuk "one of Dickie Mountbatten's bright ideas," but promised Mountbatten that he would be given an opportunity to present the idea in Quebec. The CIGS really had no choice but to acquiesce, for Dickie, having Churchill's ear, operated on the principle of why talk to the monkey when you have the organ grinder. Thus, the disdain in Brooke's diary entry upon being told by Churchill that he planned to elevate Mountbatten to the Southeast Asia Command: "He [Mountbatten] will need a very efficient Chief of Staff to pull him through."[227]

The Atlantic voyage passed much like the one of May, with nightly games of bezique played with Harriman, who on the previous voyage had cautioned Churchill against deprecating the American daylight bombing strategy. Harriman now cautioned Churchill, who feared Overlord would derail his plans in Italy, against deprecating Overlord. Roosevelt, Harriman warned, was intent that Overlord take place in May 1944, and that was that. Churchill responded that he hoped only to reach the Po River in northern Italy, hold that line, and strike into the Balkans from the Aegean. Given the difficulties of terrain, supply, and the enemy, on any march to the Po, three hundred miles north of Rome, that was far more easily said than done. Eisenhower believed that any plan to reach the Po would necessitate withholding so many men from Overlord "that the cross-Channel operation could not be undertaken in the spring of 1944." That was unacceptable to the Americans.[228]

Meanwhile, Churchill had decided that an invasion of northern Sumatra, which he had first proposed in May, now offered the greatest strategic opportunity in Southeast Asia. On that score, Brooke lamented to his diary: "He [Churchill] has during the sea voyage in a few idle moments become married to the idea that success against Japan can only be secured through the capture of the north tip of Sumatra!" Churchill, Brooke added, "has become like a peevish child asking for a forbidden toy."[229]

On August 9, Queen Mary dropped anchor in Halifax Harbor. Churchill and his party required two Canadian National Railway trains for the trip to Quebec City, which they reached late in the afternoon of the tenth. Churchill left the train just shy of the city in order to complete the journey by car with the Canadian prime minister, Mackenzie King. The principals bunked at the Citadel, on the cliffs above the Old City, while hundreds of staff officers took over the nearby Château Frontenac hotel, whose six hundred rooms had been cleared of guests but for one suite occupied by an elderly woman who was expected to die within days (she, however, lived, and was residing in the same room a year later when the second Quebec conference convened). The Americans were not due for three days.[230]

Prime Minister Mackenzie King and the Canadians found themselves looking in from the outside at their own garden party. Other than being given vague summaries of decisions made by the Combined Chiefs, the Canadians were excluded from the conference. Canada fielded five divisions in Britain and Sicily, including a division under Montgomery. During the Great War, Canada buried 66,000 of her sons, America, 117,000 of hers; adjusted for the difference in populations, America would have needed to plant more than one million crosses in Flanders. Canada had bled for England. Now, again, this nation of just eleven million was suffering several times more casualties on a per capita basis than the United States and almost as many as Britain. When, two weeks earlier, the Canadian commander in chief in London, General Andrew McNaughton, traveled to Malta in expectation of reviewing his troops in Sicily, Montgomery refused. Alexander backed Monty up; Eisenhower did not intercede. It was an appalling slight to Canada, yet since September 3, 1939, HMG's position was that Dominion forces served under British command. The Dominions had neither a permanent seat in the War Cabinet nor any binding say in its deliberations. The logic behind London's arrangement with the Dominions was compelling from a military standpoint. Given that British troops (and British casualties) far outnumbered those of the Dominions, the apogee of the command structure must therefore be British. Franklin Roosevelt also understood that logic and was about to turn it against Churchill.[231]

Within a day of arriving in Quebec, and before Quadrant began, Churchill boarded a train for a journey south to Hyde Park and a private meeting with Roosevelt. He was accompanied by Mary but not by Clementine, brought low by the long sea voyage. Mary had become the darling of the American press as soon as she set foot in North America. Other than being the prime minister's daughter and manning an ack-ack battery in Hyde Park, she lived a normal life, *Time* reported. She did not much frequent London's bare-boned nightclubs, did not smoke cigarettes. She loved to dance. Unlike her sister, Sarah, her father, and her brother, she drank only modestly, although late at night of an evening, she liked to sit before the fire in the company of her father and smoke a cigar. She dated British and U.S. officers. *Time* reported that when one of them, the American cartoonist and creator of G.I. Joe, Sergeant Dave Breger, fifteen years her senior, took her to see prizefights between British and U.S. soldiers, "she saw her first boxing. She asked everyone around her about the rules, cheered, chewed gum." Her nickname was Chip; "she was a member of the jukebox generation" but wise beyond her years and "intelligent without thick lenses.... She has watched too many big minds grapple with too many big problems."[232]

Churchill chose not to take the most direct routes from Quebec to Hyde Park, south through Vermont or along the Hudson. Never one to let the privileges of rank go begging, he instead took his party on a one-day four-hundred-mile detour in order that Mary might behold the majesty of Niagara Falls. While flashing the "V" sign for onlookers at Niagara, Churchill was asked by a reporter what he thought of the falls. He replied that he had been there before, in 1900, and that "the principle seems the same. The water still keeps falling over." Then, after driving across to the American side, he reboarded his train. He loved trains, especially American trains. A decade earlier he had written in *Collier's* of the luxuries of American Pullman cars, the wide and comfortable berths in the deluxe sleepers, the "gargantuan meals" prepared with "skill and delicacy" and served by "the darky attendants with their soft voices and delightful drawl and courteous, docile, agreeable ways" and who were "an unfailing source not only of comfort but of perpetual amusement." Thus ensconced in his favored mode of transportation—and taking delight in flashing his "V" at farmers in their fields as he stood at the window—he made the four-hundred-mile run east on the New York Central main line, past farms and fields alongside the Erie Canal, through the Mohawk Valley, and finally down the Hudson Valley to Hyde Park.[233]

There, the president awaited Churchill with homey meals of hot dogs, hamburgers, and clam chowder (Inspector Thompson thought the hot dogs "abominable"). Roosevelt, jaunty and the picture of civility, was ready to serve up to Churchill a nonnegotiable proposition. Henry Stimson, always wary of Churchill's sway over Roosevelt whenever the two met alone, had delivered his brief to the president. Based on his unsettling conversations with Churchill in London, Stimson advised Roosevelt to repudiate the British "pinprick" strategy and to demand from Churchill a second front in France by May of 1944, and an American commander for that front, George Marshall. During his May visit to Washington, Churchill had told the U.S. Congress: "I was driving the other day not far from the field of Gettysburg, which I know well, like most of your battlefields. It was the decisive battle of the American Civil War. No one after Gettysburg doubted which way the dread balance of war would incline, yet far more blood was shed after the Union victory at Gettysburg than in all the fighting which went before." Now, in mid-August, no one doubted how the war would end, and if the majority of the blood to be shed in France was to be American, Franklin Roosevelt wanted an American in command.[234]

This had not been the case just weeks earlier. Roosevelt and the American military chiefs considered that fair play called for the British to command the French invasion; after all, an American had commanded Torch and Husky. It was now London's turn. Measured by casualties, it certainly seemed only fair that a Briton command Overlord. At the end of operations in North Africa, the U.S. Army and Army Air Force accounted for approximately 18,200 of 70,000 Allied casualties in that theater—2,700 dead, 9,000 wounded, and 6,500 missing. The British and Dominions suffered the vast majority of the remaining 52,000 casualties. By August, more than 100,000 British airmen, soldiers, and sailors had been killed in action since September 1939, along with 45,000 civilians and more than 20,000 merchant seamen. In Sicily, the British army finally surpassed the Home Island civilian casualty count. The final calculations in Sicily showed 13,000 British and Canadians killed, wounded, or missing, along with the equivalent of two infantry divisions laid low by malaria and typhus, versus 10,000 American casualties. Measured by casualties thus far, Churchill had a far stronger case than Roosevelt in the matter of command of Overlord. But Roosevelt's case rested on the assumption that by the time the invasion of France took place, or soon thereafter, American forces would equal the British, and within months would outnumber the British by as many as five to one. Therefore, he concluded, command of Overlord must go to an American.[235]

Shortly arriving at Hyde Park, Churchill acquiesced. Thus, one of the most significant military decisions made at Quadrant wasn't made in Quebec, but on the banks of the Hudson River before the conference even began.

At Quebec, in the days that followed, Churchill and the British chiefs managed to extract four qualifications from the Americans: Overlord would take place only if the invasion forces did not face more than twelve mobile German divisions, including three on the beaches; and only if the Germans could not build up their forces by fifteen divisions within two months. As well, Germany's airpower had to be reduced before the invasion could take place; and artificial harbors had to be operational in order to reinforce and supply the initial force. The British saw these conditions as sound planning, especially as the plan for Overlord called for only three seaborne and two parachute divisions to land on the first day. The Americans saw them as loopholes through which Churchill and the British would try to escape their obligations. Still, Marshall and the Americans signed off, for in spite of the conditions, the Americans had demanded and been granted one of their own: if needed, seven divisions that were now in North Africa and Sicily would be siphoned away for Overlord. Brooke opposed this, telling Marshall that "by giving full priority to the cross-Channel preparation you might well cripple the Italian theater and thus render it unable to contain German forces necessary to render the cross-Channel operation possible." Brooke's logic was sound, but Marshall and the Americans carried the day. In fact, they added a new dimension to the French strategy by proposing an invasion by two divisions on the Mediterranean French coast in support of Overlord. The operation—named Anvil—was intended to draw German troops away from Normandy. Not addressed for the time being was the question of where those two divisions would come from. It soon became clear to Churchill that they would come from the Italian campaign.[236]

Churchill later wrote that his decision to endorse an American commander for Overlord was based on his agreement with Roosevelt's argument that the Americans were likely to put more men on the beaches than the British were; therefore the command should go to an American. Yet

Churchill and the British chiefs also presumed that Eisenhower would replace Marshall, and that Alexander in turn would replace Eisenhower in the Mediterranean. Churchill's logic (and motive) in accepting second billing for Overlord was consistent with his multifaceted strategy. He considered Overlord to be but one of several ventures, critical, to be sure, but not necessarily destined to be more significant than any other. In fact, the success of Overlord, as Churchill saw it, would depend upon the success of all the other operations. Handing over command of Overlord to the Americans placated Washington and opened the way for the British to command most, perhaps all, of Churchill's hoped-for ventures—in the Aegean, the Balkans, Burma, Sumatra, the Middle East, northern Norway, and, most important, Italy, where the Allies had more men in combat than would be going ashore in the early days of Overlord. And, as the Americans already suspected, if the agreed-upon conditions for undertaking the invasion of France were not met, there would be no invasion, leaving the Americans with the command of a nonentity, while Churchill held the rest of the marbles.[237]

But Churchill did not yet grasp that the supreme commander of Overlord would necessarily become de facto supreme commander of all Anglo-American forces in Europe, with veto power over secondary operations and authority to move men and machines throughout the theater in support of Overlord. Churchill thought only in terms of putting men ashore in France, and of holding that position before advancing with caution while other killing strokes were made in Norway, Italy, and the Balkans, and by the Russians in the east and the RAF and American Eighth Air Force over Berlin. Yet, if his Mulberry harbors performed as planned and the port of Cherbourg was captured, tens upon thousands of men and hundreds of thousands of tons of supplies would land in Normandy in the weeks following the invasion. The commander of such a magnificent force—armies within army groups—could only supplant all others. George Marshall understood this. The command of a lifetime within his grasp, he and his wife began quietly sending furniture from their Maryland post to the family home in Leesburg, Virginia, in anticipation of their move to London.[238]

By handing the command over to Marshall, Churchill denied Brooke his dream of a decisive role in the destruction of Hitler's armies (as well as his escape from Churchill's direct influence). On August 15, the CIGS scribbled in his diary: "Winston gave in, in spite of having previously offered me the job!" Churchill explained his reasoning while he and Brooke stood on a terrace of the Citadel high above the Saint Lawrence, and then asked Brooke how he felt about the decision. "Disappointed" was about all Brooke could muster. Years later he wrote, "Not for one moment did he [Churchill] realize what this meant to me. He offered no sympathy, no regrets at having had to change his mind." It took several months for Brooke to recover from this "crashing blow," in part because he suspected Churchill had traded command of Overlord for the appointment of Mountbatten as supreme commander in Southeast Asia. In this, Brooke was partially correct, but Churchill's horse trading with Roosevelt in regard to Asia was more political than military. Roosevelt got on famously with Mountbatten; the American press adored the man. By sending Mountbatten to take charge, Churchill could claim the British were doing their part against Tokyo.[239]

Each night at Quebec, Brooke found a new way to tell his diary what he thought of that day's discussions: "long," "trying," "poisonous," especially as pertained to the Japanese war, and especially as pertained to Churchill's approach to the Pacific theater, which Brooke described as "chasing hares." Where Churchill wanted to nibble at the edges of the Japanese empire, Nimitz and MacArthur wanted to drive from the South Pacific straight to Tokyo, with MacArthur on the left taking aim at the Philippines, and Nimitz on the right island-hopping northward. The Americans therefore demanded more from the British in Burma in support of Chiang, who they believed would prove his worth by holding down Japanese armies in China while the main thrust came from the South Pacific. China, for the Americans, had a vital supporting role in the whole show. But Churchill, Gil Winant reported to Washington, "was quite willing to see China collapse." The Americans suspected the British were fighting in Burma, not for China but for the restoration of British imperial holdings. This, the Americans could not be a party to; the greater the American presence in Southeast Asia, the greater the risk that Roosevelt would be accused of aiding and abetting British imperialism.

Each side was driven by conflicting political strategies, with the result that the strictly military objectives they shared were often made orphans to politics. Wingate's six thousand raiders, Stilwell's Chinese troops in India, and the Fourteenth Army, under General Billy Slim, found themselves the forgotten men in a forgotten theater. Mountbatten's presence would signal a change; Churchill could claim he sent his best man, his "triphibian" warrior, to take up the reins. To placate the Americans, Stilwell would go in as Mountbatten's deputy. Stilwell, caught in the middle and denied a real opportunity to kill his hated Japs, reacted with his usual fury. In a symbolic thumb in the eye to the British, he refused to stand and sing when "God Save the King" was played. After a plea from Marshall, he agreed to stand for the ceremony, but he would not sing. As for his new supreme commander, Stilwell considered Mountbatten to be a "limey mountebank" and "as dumb as that thick-headed cousin of his, the King." Such sentiments lent credence to a saying Churchill liked to toss out over drinks: "There is only one thing worse than fighting with allies, and that is fighting without them."[240]

The same could be said of Brooke's difficulties in fighting a war in harness with Churchill. The meetings of the Combined Chiefs of Staff were contentious, but progress was made. Then, just as Brooke appeared to reach an understanding with the Americans on the need for a general plan for the war against Japan, Churchill insisted again on capturing northern Sumatra, and letting events elsewhere play out on their own. Brooke exploded to his diary, "He [Churchill] refused to accept that any general plan was necessary, recommended a purely opportunistic policy....I feel cooked and unable to face another day of conferences." Pug Ismay, Churchill's liaison with Brooke, found himself caught in the middle of this clash of supremely different personalities. Churchill, well aware of Brooke's disdain of his strategic talents, once dispatched Ismay to ask Brooke why he so hated the prime minister. Ismay returned with Brooke's reply; he in fact loved the prime minister but could not serve him well without disputing that which he disagreed with. Churchill listened, bowed his head, and whispered, "Dear Brookie."[241]

On August 17, Alexander cabled Churchill the news that the last Germans had been flung out of Sicily. The campaign was over; it had lasted just thirty-eight days. But the victory was incomplete: Kesselring's 60,000 men had escaped to Italy. That day, the new Italian government scrambled to meet surrender terms laid down by Eisenhower. The problem, ironic as Churchill saw it, was that the Italian negotiator in Lisbon, General Giuseppe Castellano, wanted to learn from Eisenhower's lieutenant, Bedell ("Beetle") Smith, how best Italy could take the field against the Germans, whom Castellano, a Sicilian, hated. But Smith replied that he could only discuss unconditional surrender. With the invasion of the toe and heel of Italy now scheduled to take place in two weeks, Churchill worried that a quisling government might take power in Rome, or that the Germans would occupy Rome and take direct control. He wanted Eisenhower to convey to the Italians that if, when the Allies landed, they encountered Italian troops fighting Germans, Italy would be welcomed as a co-belligerent in the war against Hitler. But Castellano wanted assurances; the Italian *forze amate* stood no chance in a fight with the Wehrmacht. And Eisenhower could not deliver any such guarantee until the Italians surrendered, unconditionally. Eisenhower also sought reassurance from Castellano that Mussolini would not reappear in the guise of savior. When asked by Smith where Mussolini was being kept, Castellano replied, "Hitler would like to know, too." In fact, Hitler soon learned that Il Duce was being held at Campo Imperatore Hotel, a mountaintop ski resort in Abruzzo, and put plans into place for the very resurrection Churchill feared.[242]

In late June, an RAF reconnaissance flight over Peenemünde, on the Baltic Sea island of Usedom, had photographed a rocket that the Germans had failed to camouflage. With that, Duncan Sandys and Churchill finally knew what manner of vehicle Hitler was building on the Baltic coast, though they lacked any knowledge of weight, speed, propellant, and explosive capacity. On the night of August 17, more than five hundred British heavy bombers hit Peenemünde. The RAF sought to destroy not only the laboratories and test facilities but also the housing where engineers and technicians and thousands of slave laborers lived. Hitler's armaments minister, Albert Speer, had approved the transfer of slave laborers, mostly Poles and Russians, to work at the site after the director of the rocket program, a boyish-looking thirty-one-year-old aeronautics engineer and rocket enthusiast named Wernher von Braun, argued that if the supply of workers could not be maintained, neither could the rocket program (code-named A-4). The RAF raid killed one scientist and several hundred slave laborers. Speer and von Braun soon scattered A-4 research and production facilities throughout Germany, including far under the Hartz mountains. Engineering tests on the A-4 continued at Peenemünde, and on a simpler flying bomb, essentially a small pilotless jet aircraft. This weapon was code-named *Flakzielgert 76* (Anti-Aircraft Target Device 76) to throw British intelligence off the scent. Once the engineering bugs were worked out, they were to be produced at the Volkswagen factory at Fallersleben, near Hamburg. Hitler was so enthused about his new weapons, and so impressed with young von Braun, that he ordered Speer to find a way to make the young scientist a full professor. Meanwhile, at Peenemünde, the Germans did not clear away the rubble from the RAF raid, presuming that RAF reconnaissance flights would conclude from the damage that Peenemünde had been abandoned. The British did exactly that, and did not return for nine months. By then von Braun's rockets were almost ready for deployment.[243]

As Quadrant wound down, Brooke took delight in recording Mountbatten's most inglorious moment, after Dickie finally persuaded the CIGS to allow a demonstration of Habakkuk, the ice aircraft carriers, for the Combined Chiefs. To illustrate the efficacy of the idea, Mountbatten had two large blocks of ice delivered to a conference room, where an emotional discussion had just taken place between the American and British chiefs. Mountbatten explained to the conferees that one block was ordinary ice and the other was called Pykrete, fabricated by strengthening the ice with a specially treated wood pulp mixture. Then Dickie unholstered his revolver and shot the first block, which, as expected, shattered, as did the composure of the men seated at the table. Then Mountbatten proclaimed, "I shall fire at the [other] block to show you the difference." The difference was that the second block was bulletproof. Mountbatten's shot ricocheted off and around the room, barely missing Portal and Ernest King. Outside, a group of junior officers heard the shots. "Good god," one exclaimed, "they've started shooting now." No ice fleet ever sailed.[244]

As the Combined Chiefs scraped their way through the agenda—it was really mostly about Overlord, with a detour to Burma—Churchill and Roosevelt followed Eisenhower's progress on the Italian surrender. This was the first conference attended by the senior diplomatic players—Eden, Cadogan, and Hull arrived on August 18—and the first one that assumed a duality of purpose, military and political. On the diplomatic front, Roosevelt insisted that Eisenhower conduct all negotiations with the Italians, while Churchill argued that politicians handle political matters. There was a further complication: Roosevelt loathed King Victor Emmanuel and Marshal Badoglio for their long and loyal support of Mussolini. Churchill, however, had told Roosevelt two weeks earlier that he'd do business with "anybody who could deliver the goods." Roosevelt had no love for European constitutional monarchies and preferred, as had Woodrow Wilson, to remake Europe in a republican image. Churchill believed that had the victors in the Great War fished a Hohenzollern or Hapsburg heir out of oblivion and put him back on the German or Austrian throne to lead a constitutional monarchy, there would have been no Hitler. Churchill believed in kings, and Victor Emmanuel was a king. He was also the only player in the game; there simply were no republicans in authority in Rome for Roosevelt to deal with. Along with his antipathy toward royalty, Roosevelt harbored a justified distrust of Badoglio. Churchill, too, distrusted the Italian general and expected a double cross, but a double cross of Hitler, he told Roosevelt, not of the Allies.[245]

As Churchill and Roosevelt mulled over the terms of Italian surrender, neither thought to bring either Stalin or the Free French into the discussions. The two leaders kept Stalin informed of developments but assumed he sought no role in furthering them. The French were simply ignored, not surprisingly given Roosevelt's and Hull's disdain for de Gaulle, but ironic given that Roosevelt's most listened-to broadcast of 1940 had been his "dagger in the back" condemnation of the Italian invasion of France. France had vital territorial issues to settle with Italy. Yet Hull—Alec Cadogan called him an "old lady"—refused to even recognize the French Committee of National Liberation. That week the British chose to recognize the FCNL as a legitimate organization in North Africa but not as the presumed provisional government once France was liberated. It was a start. The Americans chose only to "acknowledge" the Gaullists.[246]

The assumption that Stalin sought only updates on events unfolding in Italy was proven wrong in a telegram that arrived on August 22 in which Stalin protested (with his usual bluntness) Soviet exclusion from the Italian surrender: "To date it has been like this," Stalin wrote, "the U.S.A. and Britain reach agreement between themselves, while the U.S.S.R. is informed of the agreement....I must say that this situation cannot be tolerated any longer." Churchill thought the message "rude," and fired off a cable to Stalin that, to Eden's horror, included the line "I am entirely unmoved by your statement." The Old Man and Roosevelt, who was "alarmed" at Stalin's tone, summoned Alec Cadogan, who, after reading the telegram, concluded that Stalin had made a fair point, albeit with his usual rudeness. Anthony Eden solved the problem when he advised that bringing Stalin into the picture now might pay dividends down the road when Stalin wielded the same leverage in Eastern Europe that the Anglo-Americans now wielded in Italy. Welcome Stalin into the Italian negotiations, Eden argued, and a precedent would be set that might prove useful when the Red Army struck out beyond Russian borders and into the Baltics, Romania, and Poland. Churchill agreed with Eden's logic but doubted Stalin would abide by any understanding. He predicted "bloody consequences in the future....Stalin is an unnatural man. There will be grave trouble."[247]

To Harriman, Churchill meant "bloody" in the literal sense. A few weeks later, with such Soviet mischief in mind, Churchill asked the British Chiefs of Staff to draw up a plan to counter a Moscow-backed Communist coup d'état in Greece in the event of a German withdrawal, which Churchill sought to hasten by invading Rhodes and some of the Dodecanese Islands (occupied by Italy since 1912) as soon as Italy surrendered. Churchill saw an impending vacuum in Greece, and he intended to fill it before Moscow nosed onto the scene. His concern stemmed from reports that the two Greek partisan groups—the large and Communist People's National Liberation Army (ELAS), and the small and democratic National Democratic Greek Army (EDES)—were fighting each other with weapons supplied by the Special Operations Executive. Both sides despised King George II of the Hellenes, whom Churchill sought to restore to his throne. Churchill instructed the chiefs to arrange for at least five thousand "troops with armoured cars and Bren guns" to be held ready for a drive into Athens in order to support "the restoration of lawful Greek government." His timing was off by more than a year, but his instinct regarding Stalin's ambitions was prescient. The Soviet leader's bearishness grew with every mile the Red Army gained.[248]

Stalin's inadvertent exclusion from the Italian negotiations drove home the need for the Big Three to meet, not necessarily in Roosevelt's estimation to parse strictly military matters, but to address questions that pertained to the postwar world. Roosevelt, confident that victory against Hitler was not only inevitable but would come within a year (although he thought the Japanese might hold out until 1946 or 1947), had delegated military decisions to his military and turned his attention to winning the peace. Hopkins that month wrote Winant that the Russian offensive, "together with our increased bombing of Germany, is going to make it tough on Hitler and I do not see how he can stand it for more than another eight months." That was the exact amount of time General Carl Spaatz believed it would take for his strategic air forces to put Hitler on the ropes, followed by surrender a few months later. This belief was shared by Bomber Harris. Were Hopkins and Spaatz to be proven correct, the collapse of Germany would take place sometime around May 1944, thereby rendering Overlord unnecessary. An American senator, Sheridan Downey of California, was even more optimistic, predicting that ten big bombing raids per month would finish off Germany by February. Roosevelt and Hopkins hedged their bets in public, but it was time, Roosevelt believed, to find the diplomatic means by which the military alliance known as the United Nations emerged from the war as an international body with muscle, its backbone formed by the Four Powers—America, Britain, China, and Russia. It was time to initiate a dialogue with Stalin on the postwar world, a world that might be only a year distant.[249]

Churchill and Eden believed it premature to bring such an agenda to any meeting with Stalin, but they told Roosevelt that they would bring up the matter of a postwar league with the War Cabinet (including Chinese participation if, Churchill offered over dinner, "they become a nation"). Stalin had only two items on his agenda, Eden argued: "the second front and [Russia's] western frontiers." The question of borders, by implication, also went to the question of Germany's postwar borders, that is, the question of how thoroughly to dismember Germany. Since there would be no second front that year, and since boundaries were not to be addressed until victory was won, a meeting of foreign ministers now, Eden argued, "would almost certainly do more harm than good." Still, the need for the three Big Boys (as anointed by Cadogan) to meet was self-evident, especially as there would be no second front that year. An invitation was dispatched to Moscow. Anchorage, London, and Scapa Flow were suggested as venues for the foreign ministers and, soon thereafter, the Big Three. As Quadrant played out, Stalin agreed to a meeting late in the year, insisting that the foreign ministers meet first in order to set an agenda for the three leaders to follow at their meeting. He suggested the preliminary meeting take place in Moscow, with the Big Three meeting either there or in Tehran. Churchill lobbied for London; he after all had made one trip to Moscow and was now nearing the end of his fourth journey to Washington. The discussion of possible sites dragged on for almost three weeks, until Roosevelt finally agreed to Stalin's proposal of Moscow for the foreign ministers. Churchill, his proposal of London snubbed, could only acquiesce. The diminishment of British influence within the alliance now troubled Eden, who thought Roosevelt was bowling them a fast one: "I am most anxious for good relations with the U.S. but I don't like subservience to them.... We are giving the impression, which they are only too ready by nature to endorse, that militarily all the achievements are theirs."[250]

Eden made that diary entry on September 10, and added, "W., by prolonging his stay in Washington, strengthens [the] assumption" of British subservience. Quadrant had ended on August 24. Most of the staff departed for London and Washington the next day, by train, plane, and ship. The chiefs, Ismay, Eden, Cadogan, Churchill, his secretaries, and his family stayed on for a six-day fishing vacation in the Quebec wilderness. Churchill took his rest on the shores of Lac des Neiges, Eden and his people at Lac Jacques-Cartier, about an hour's drive from Churchill's lodge and three thousand feet up in the Laurentian Mountains. When Eden stopped by Churchill's camp on August 27 to say his good-byes before departing for London, Moran told him the P.M. was tired and unable to shake off troubles known only to himself. Eden found Churchill in his bath, not looking "at all well and was of a bad colour." When Churchill expressed a desire to extend his holiday in the mountains, Eden advised him to do so. Then, splashing about in his bath, Churchill said, "I don't know what I should do if I lost you all. I'd have to cut my throat. It isn't just love, though there is much of that in it, but you are my war machine. Brookie, Portal, you and Dickie, I simply couldn't replace you."[251]

The respite by the lake was just what the doctor ordered, or would have ordered had anyone, including Moran, been able to give orders to Churchill. Log fires burned in the great stone fireplace. Bears and wolves were said to lurk nearby. By day Churchill fished for trout from a canoe, all the while "laying down the law about the fisherman's art" to Moran, who hooked nary a fish. Loons — "divers" to the British — drifted and dunked and cried far out on the lake. Late in the evenings Churchill strolled out to the end of a pier to take in the northern lights. Grilled trout was served up for lunches and dinners; the party accounted for a depletion of the local trout population in excess of three hundred. Clementine, "too overtired for enjoyment," took herself back to Quebec after one day. Her "nervous state," Mary later wrote, resulted in "perplexity and worry" out of all proportion to events. Not so Churchill. The rest worked wonders. By August 29 he was back "in terrific form," Cadogan wrote, "singing Don Leno songs and other favorites of the halls of forty years ago, together with the latest Noel Coward." All the brass but Cadogan, Ismay, and Dudley Pound, who had been troubled by excruciating headaches and was too ill to fly, left by August 29.[252]

Pound, who Brooke for months had criticized in his diary for falling asleep during meetings, in fact was host to an undetected brain tumor and had suffered a minor stroke. His wife of more than three decades had died a month earlier, but he still took himself off to Quebec. When he complained to Churchill of headaches and numbness in his legs, the Old Man insisted he join him aboard *Renown* for the trip to England. On September 1, Churchill, and his now much reduced party, returned to Quebec City. There, joined by Clementine and Mary, he entrained for Washington. His holiday had only just begun. "This quiet life is doing him good," Moran wrote, "but he feels like he is playing truant."[253]

He was. By September 10, Churchill's subordinates agreed with Moran's assessment, including Eden, who told his diary that he found himself depressed and not feeling well, "partly, I think, because of exasperating difficulty of trying to do business with Winston over the Atlantic." Brooke, too, noted Churchill's absence. After attending a cabinet meeting chaired by Attlee, the CIGS wrote that although the meeting was conducted with greater efficiency than Churchill brought to the table, it was a "cabinet without a head." Indeed, Brooke, who was always willing to denigrate Churchill in his diary, took a far softer position during Churchill's long vacation. After delineating Churchill's contradictions and failings—"the most marvelous qualities of superhuman genius mixed with an astonishing lack of vision at times"—Brooke (still smarting from losing command of Overlord) wrote that although Churchill "is quite the most difficult man to work with...I should not have missed the chance of working with him for anything on earth."[254]

Much transpired in the Mediterranean during Churchill's therapeutic truancy. The Italians surrendered (secretly and unconditionally) on

September 3, although thirteen conditions were attached to the "unconditional" surrender, including the transfer of the Italian fleet to the Allies. And that day, two divisions of the Eighth Army crossed the Straits of Messina and landed near Reggio, in Calabria, on the toe of the foot of Italy. It was a tentative foray. Montgomery, denied the landing craft he needed to put more forces on the heel of Italy, or to swing around to the Adriatic coast, could only hold his toehold. Eisenhower hoarded the landing craft for use in Avalanche, the planned seizure of Salerno by the Fifth Army, scheduled for September 8 and 9. In support of that operation, Eisenhower planned to drop the 82nd Airborne Division near Rome to secure the airfields.

This was not the bold strategy of striking into northern Italy favored by Smuts and expressed in his July letter to Churchill. In fact, Mark Clark, in command of the Salerno forces, had argued for a landing north of Naples, but Air Marshal Tedder and Admiral Cunningham were hesitant to send their airships and warships too far afield in support of ground troops, and Eisenhower was loath to send his ground forces beyond his aerial and naval umbrellas. Thus, by caution and default, Salerno became the target. And thus, the Eighth Army, the most seasoned force in the Allied camp, was relegated to a supporting role some two hundred miles south of the main event at Salerno. Montgomery, in his memoirs, wrote with his usual directness of the entire strategy: "If the planning and conduct of the campaign in Sicily were bad, the preparations for the invasion of Italy and the subsequent conduct of the campaign in that country were worse still."[255]

Churchill arrived at the same conclusion the previous week after one of Alexander's staff officers reported that the full complement of twelve Allied divisions would not be ashore in Italy until December 1, and worse, ashore only near Naples. The problem as Churchill saw it was that any delay in getting to Rome would only give Kesselring time to throw in more troops of his own. "The lateness of this forecast," Brooke jotted in his diary, "has sent him [Churchill] quite mad."[256]

The race to Rome was on. But with eight German divisions stationed in northern Italy under Rommel, and eight more to the south under Kesselring, including two near Rome, the Allies stood little chance of grabbing the Eternal City unless they moved with dispatch and landed somewhere near Rome, where five Italian divisions were poised to join the Allies. But Eisenhower's caution gave Kesselring the time he needed to convert south-central Italy into a fortress. Eisenhower now saw his error in not having landed at Calabria in July as part of Operation Husky, thus cutting off Sicily and capturing the troops trapped there. "History would call it [my] mistake," he told Commander Butcher. Had he pursued that strategy, his armies might now be moving north through Italy, but as it was, "a quick collapse of Italy has disappeared into uncertainty." This was due in part, Butcher wrote, to the limitation imposed upon Eisenhower by the insistence of Churchill and Roosevelt on unconditional surrender. Yet, in fairness to the self-critical Eisenhower (who, exhausted, spent three days in the infirmary under his doctor's care), neither the Allied air forces nor navies had wanted anything to do with heavy operations over or within the Messina Straits. All of this came as a great relief to Kesselring, who later wrote, "A secondary attack on Calabria would have enabled the Sicily landing to be developed into an overwhelming Allied victory."[257]

As Eisenhower prepared to hit Salerno (and not with a roundhouse punch), Churchill, still in Washington, proposed to the War Cabinet that the agenda for the agreed-upon tripartite meeting be topped by discussions on the fate of Germany after the war and Russia's role in determining that fate. Russia, and its possible behavior in the future, had become for Churchill a pressing political concern. To Smuts, on September 5, he offered that "Russia will be the greatest land power in the world after this war" and that a continuation of the Anglo-American alliance and its overwhelming airpower would supply the necessary "balance with Russia at least for the period of rebuilding." After that, Churchill wrote, "I cannot see with mortal eye, and I am not yet fully informed about the celestial telescope."[258]

On September 5, President Roosevelt invited Mrs. Ogden Reid to join himself and Churchill for lunch at the White House. She was the publisher of the *New York Herald Tribune* and a strong supporter of Indian independence. She was known for speaking her mind, and Roosevelt had no doubt that she would speak it to Churchill. She did, asking Churchill, "What are you going to do about those wretched Indians?" He replied, "Before we proceed further let us get one thing clear. Are we talking about the brown Indians in India, who have multiplied alarmingly under benevolent British rule? Or are we talking about the Red Indians in America, who, I understand, are almost extinct?" Mrs. Reid was speechless. Roosevelt could not contain his laughter; it was the sort of awkward moment he relished.[259]

Later that day Churchill, who had accepted an invitation from Harvard president James Conant to speak there, took himself off by private train for the overnight run to Boston. On September 6, he addressed a standing-room-only crowd of more than 1,300 students and faculty in Harvard College's Sanders Theatre, tucked into Memorial Hall, a redbrick Victorian Gothic edifice as grand as a cathedral and, with the names of Harvard's Civil War dead embossed on twenty-eight white marble tablets affixed to the walls of the transept, as sacred a place as can be found in that fount of secular wisdom. Teddy and Franklin Roosevelt had walked its corridors, as had Cabots, Lawrences, and Lowells; and Admiral Yamamoto, dead now four months at the hands of American fliers. Inspired by Christopher Wren's Sheldonian Theatre at Oxford, Sanders boasted a semicircular lecture hall with perfect acoustics, high vaulted ceilings, and dark hardwood paneling. But for the statue that stood to the right of the lectern — the Revolutionary War agitator James Otis, depicted speaking out against George III and his Writs of Assistance in 1761 — Sanders offered as English a venue as Churchill could hope for to unveil his remarkable proposal for the postwar world. There he stood, the chancellor of Bristol University, upon a Harvard stage, attired in the cap and gown of an Oxford don borrowed from Princeton for the occasion. He spoke for about four minutes on the cooperation thus far between Britain and America, then:

> The great Bismarck — for there were once great men in Germany — is said to have observed towards the close of his life that the most potent factor in human society at the end of the nineteenth century was the fact that the British and American peoples spoke the same language. That was a pregnant saying. Certainly it has enabled us to wage war together with an intimacy and harmony never before achieved among allies. The gift of a common tongue is a priceless inheritance and it may well some day become the foundation of a common citizenship. I like to think of British and Americans moving about freely over each other's wide estates with hardly a sense of being foreigners to one another.... All these are great possibilities, and I say: "Let us go into this together. Let us have another Boston Tea Party about it.
>
> Let us go forward as with other matters and other measures similar in aim and effect — let us go forward in malice to none and good will to all. Such plans offer far better prizes than taking away other people's provinces or lands or grinding them down in exploitation. The empires of the futures are the empires of the mind."[260]

Churchill was always diligent in seeking Roosevelt's approval for remarks he intended to make on American soil. His extraordinary proposal of common citizenship had certainly been cleared by Roosevelt, who in fact assured him that America was now so far removed from its isolationist past that the idea of dual citizenship would not "outrage public opinion or provide another Boston Tea Party." Eager to measure public reaction to the speech, Churchill ordered the British embassy to sift American newspapers for opinions. The Oxford political philosopher Isaiah Berlin, a Latvian expatriate and staff member at the embassy, was assigned the task. He reported that because the White House had announced the speech would contain little of political significance, it had not been covered. As well, two horrific train crashes that week occupied the front pages of American newspapers. Churchill's great American moment went largely unnoticed. Still, the *New York Times* declared the speech "has opened a vast and hopeful field of discussion.... Down the grim corridors of war light begins to show."[261]

On this day Churchill quite possibly reached the high-water mark of his war leadership. He had nurtured, nagged, and prodded the alliance for almost two years to such a degree that inevitability now attached to the future. First would come victory over Hitler in Italy—I'll soon be meeting Alex in Rome, he told Lord Moran—and then victory over Hitler in Germany. And now here came Roosevelt in apparent agreement on the need to forge a permanent Anglo-American relationship. The potential appeared limitless, including the prospect of the two nations sharing a common military staff system, perhaps even a common currency, the dollar sterling, a Churchillian dream of long standing. Outside Memorial Hall, a battalion of cadets, male and female, stood smartly at attention, while Churchill addressed them briefly from the steps. He had doffed his robes, which had lent him an air of a Cardinal Wolsey, and was attired in a dark blazer, navy bow tie, and light trousers. The cadets listened in respectful silence as Churchill paraphrased his earlier address, punctuating his words by jabbing the granite steps with his walking stick. Then, to cheers, he stepped back and thrust up his "V" for victory. He was ebullient on the return trip to Washington, flashing his "V" to the engineers of passing trains, and darting out to the rear platform of the Pullman in his flowered dressing gown to flash the sign as the train slowed at each station along the way. It was left to Lord Moran to find the poignant irony in Churchill's behavior: "The P.M. stood for some time at the window of his car giving the victory sign to odd workmen in the fields, who could see nothing but a train rushing through the countryside."[262]

On September 7, the Italian naval minister promised Albert Kesselring that the Italian fleet was about to sail "from Spezia to seek battle with the British Mediterranean fleet," and "would conquer or perish" in the ensuing showdown. This pleased Kesselring, although doubting the trustworthiness of the entire Italian government, he had crafted a battle plan to occupy Rome were the Italians to evidence any treachery. He had also concluded that the Allies would play small and invade near Salerno rather than farther north.

Late in the afternoon of the eighth, the BBC announced the Italian surrender. The news came as a complete surprise to Victor Emmanuel and Marshal Badoglio who, not having been informed of Allied plans, thought they had more time to deploy Italian troops in order to make the changeover from enemy to co-belligerent. Later that night and into the morning of the next day, 55,000 men of the British X Corps and the U.S. VI Corps, under overall command of Mark Clark and the Fifth Army, went ashore near Salerno, almost 160 miles south of Rome and 35 miles south of Naples. No aerial or seaborne bombardment preceded the landings in order to keep Kesselring guessing right up to the moment the men went ashore.

But it was exactly as Kesselring expected. He had seen the tentativeness of Eisenhower's campaigns in Tunisia and Sicily and foresaw more of the same in Italy. And he got it, first with Montgomery's landings in Calabria, and now at Salerno. Berlin radio had predicted both operations three weeks earlier. Kesselring had deployed five divisions such that they could rapidly respond to landings from Naples to Salerno. Now they responded. John Steinbeck wrote as a war correspondent from the beaches: "The Germans were waiting for us. His 88s were on the surrounding hills and his machine guns in the sand dunes. His mines were in the surf and he sat there and waited for us." Allied caution had again trumped aggression, and the price paid not only by the troops on the beaches, but by Rome—by all of Italy—was dear. Kesselring, his plans to take Rome in place for weeks, hit the city on September 9 and occupied it the next day after the Italian divisions there drifted off to Tivoli without a fight. "Thus the main problems connected with our security in Italy have been solved," Goebbels chimed to his diary. Life changed overnight for Rome's citizens; they had committed "treachery" in Goebbels' estimation, and deserved the fate that awaited them. Romans joined the citizens of Warsaw, Paris, Rotterdam, and Brussels as prisoners of the Reich.[263]

Churchill believed that Italy's collapse, if it could be capitalized upon quickly, opened up opportunities in the Aegean. On September 8, as the troops were going ashore at Salerno, a British officer parachuted into the Italian lines on Rhodes, just off the Turkish southwest Anatolian coast. The island was the linchpin of Churchill's Balkan strategy; its capture would take pressure off the Turks (who claimed sovereignty over the Dodecanese Islands) and, he hoped, persuade them to come into the war on the Allied side. If the Turks came in, the Black Sea would become an Allied lake and the Danubian Basin would be made ripe for Churchill's ultimate Balkan thrust north into the German flank. The mission of the officer was to persuade the commander of the 30,000 Italian troops on Rhodes to attack the 7,000 Germans across the island. The Italians hesitated; the Germans did not. They attacked preemptively and routed the defenders, executing more than one hundred Italian officers in the aftermath.

Churchill's Aegean initiative was off to a most inauspicious start. He ordered his Middle East commander, Maitland ("Jumbo") Wilson, to dispatch a brigade of four thousand infantrymen to Leros, Kos, five other islands of the Dodecanese, and nearby Samos. The brigade, sliced into battalion-size formations, joined commandos already at work, and the now-friendly Italian troops deployed in the Dodecanese. But until Rhodes was taken, any gains in the Dodecanese would be difficult if not impossible to hold. "This is the time to play high," Churchill cabled Wilson. "Improvise and dare." (Churchill later lamented, "He improvose and dore.") On the thirteenth, Churchill sent off more encouragement to Wilson: "This is the time to think of Clive and Peterborough and of Rooke's taking of Gibraltar." Yet the brigade amounted to less than half the force called for by the original plans drawn up after Casablanca, and the Germans, not the RAF, controlled the airfield on Rhodes. Wilson lacked the troops and planes needed to take Rhodes, but Eisenhower had plenty of both. Churchill presumed that once Eisenhower saw the Aegean treasures to be gained at little cost, he would climb on board. He did not.[264]

While events on Rhodes spiraled into mayhem on September 9, Admiral Cunningham sailed his fleet right up to the Taranto quays in order to put ashore the British 1st Airborne Division, six thousand strong, a gallant operation necessitated by the lack of landing craft to carry the men ashore. The troops landed with only five jeeps, no trucks, no tanks, no artillery, and therefore no means to exploit their audacious arrival. The operation was ironically and aptly named "Slapstick." This unfortunate choice came just a month after Churchill demanded that staff planners not use code names that were boastful or lent themselves to ridicule. It would not do, he wrote, for "some widow or mother to say that her son was killed in an operation called BUNNYHUG or BALLYHOO." Whoever came up with Slapstick had either not read or had ignored the message.[265]

On the way into Taranto, Cunningham's ships passed the Italian fleet coming out. Tense moments ensued; Cunningham had no way of knowing if the Italians would abide by the terms of surrender or fight. The Italian minister of marine, whose fleet now sailed quietly past Cunningham headed for Malta and surrender, had not exactly been straightforward with Kesselring. Hitler had hoped the Italians would at least have the decency to deliver their navy to neutral Spain. Göring had thought otherwise, predicting that Italian treachery would extend to surrendering the fleet to the Allies. He was correct and was prepared for this eventuality. Dornier bombers carrying newly designed radio-guided gliding bombs were ordered aloft to punish the retreating Italians. *Roma*, the flagship, hit by two bombs, broke in half and went down with more than 1,300 of its crew. The rest of the fleet was delivered safely into British hands. Kesselring soon turned the new bombs on the British fleet at Salerno; a cruiser was lost and tars fast learned that aerial bombing had taken a great and dangerous leap forward. The guided bombs portended even more sinister weapons. If an engine was strapped to such a device, and if it was outfitted with even a rudimentary guidance system, it could be flung across the Channel into London. Days later, Duncan Sandys delivered a memo to Churchill that predicted exactly that. After reading it, Churchill told John Anderson that some sort of futuristic German rockets would descend on London by the end of the year.[266]

By the evening of September 10, the entire Mediterranean Sea—but not the airspace over its eastern reaches—belonged to the Allies. Yet by the twelfth, it became distressingly clear that Salerno did not. The men there, pinned down by furious German resistance, hadn't gotten off the beaches. Before going ashore, they had been told by their commanders that they'd be in Naples in three days. Instead, they were still fighting so near the beaches that they could watch their supply ships burn under the new bombs of the Luftwaffe and hear the screams of men in the water. By then, Badoglio and Victor Emmanuel had fled Rome to rendezvous with Allied gunboats, which took them off to Malta. "Surprise, violence, and speed," Churchill wrote, "are the essence of all amphibious landings." At Salerno, Albert Kesselring had turned those criteria against the invaders. It was now obvious to Churchill that the rake of war would have to tear over the length of Italy. Churchill, still in Washington, grumbled to his doctor, "These things always seem to happen when I'm with the president."[267]

There was good reason for that. Churchill went abroad when he saw an acute need to prepare for or react to battlefield climacterics, as after Pearl Harbor and Midway and before Torch and Husky. He liked to conduct business face-to-face, which usually resulted in his getting what he wanted. Now he wanted to get into the Balkans. The Americans believed his motive for doing so was to redress the errors of the Great War, and by comparing the ordeal at Salerno to the mishandled invasion at Gallipoli in 1915, Churchill only reinforced the Americans' belief in that regard. In fact, he wanted to get to Vienna before the Russians. Cadogan told his diary that Churchill, at the White House, spent his days "hurling himself violently in and out of bed, bathing at unsuitable moments and rushing up and down corridors in his dressing gown." He also kept Roosevelt up past 2:00 A.M., and during these long parleys pressed him to keep an open mind on the need for flexibility regarding Overlord. In effect, in spite of the agreements just made in Quebec, he was asking Roosevelt to view Overlord as one of many options, including the developing situation on Rhodes. Roosevelt rebuffed him. Then, in need of respite from Churchill and the hours he kept, the president took himself off to Hyde Park. Before leaving he told Churchill to make himself at home in the White House.[268]

Harriman knew from experience that it was always flexibility with Churchill, whether the battleground was military or diplomatic. Churchill's postwar union with America was a case in point; he told Harriman he "liked the idea of a loose association rather than a formal treaty... an association flexible enough to adjust itself to historical developments." Flexibility had defined since early 1942 the meetings between the British and American chiefs. The discussions were always disputatious, yet so far they had always ended with unified statements of intent. If circumstances later deranged the timely realization of those pledges, that was war and all of its vagaries. The critical point was that the strategies agreed upon admitted to flexibility. Churchill and Roosevelt never flinched from trying to impose design upon chance, which so often rules the business of war, but to date neither had demanded rigidity in strategy. The alliance — a real coalition as Churchill saw it — was functioning. After all, he had been handed the keys to the White House by Franklin Roosevelt, from wherein he conducted high-level meetings, a British prime minister chairing sessions of the American Chiefs of Staff. Here was his dream being made real, a British premier presiding over the crafting of collective policy, in the White House, no less. Of course, the courtesy would be reciprocated when Roosevelt journeyed to London, and especially once some sort of "union" between the English-speaking peoples had been agreed upon in the legislatures of both lands. It need not at first be strictly formal, as he told Harriman, for formal relationships often begin as informal understandings, as had this alliance.[269]

On September 12, their thirty-fifth wedding anniversary, Winston and Clementine journeyed to Hyde Park, their last American stop before leaving for Halifax and the voyage home. The president toasted their health at dinner and tried to dazzle Clementine with "the magnetic quality of his charm" but failed. Clementine, her daughter Mary later wrote, "got along well" with Roosevelt but quickly concluded, "his personal vanity was inordinate." It did not help when Roosevelt called Clementine "Clemmie," a breach of etiquette in Mrs. Churchill's estimation, as she regarded the use of Christian names a "privilege marking close friendship or long association," neither of which described her relationship with Roosevelt.[270]

After dinner that night, Churchill and Roosevelt agreed that an infusion of several divisions of Polish infantry in aid of Tito's partisans might be just the ticket for the Balkans, where Italian troops were already joining the Allied cause. "Any opportunity" that presented itself in the Balkans, Roosevelt told Churchill, should be taken advantage of. This understandably struck Churchill as a validation of his Balkan strategy, although Roosevelt, when announcing the third war bond drive earlier that week, had made no mention of the Balkans, or Tito, or Poles. Roosevelt told Americans that their troops—*your* boys, *our* boys—were on their way to Berlin and Tokyo. Indeed, in the Pacific, the Americans held Port Moresby; their bombers were pounding Rabaul, and a carrier task force was about to strike Wake Island. The invasion of Tarawa Atoll in the Gilbert Islands was planned for November. The advance to Tokyo had begun. Given that the Chinese were incompetent, the Russians were not at war with Japan, and the British were incapable of driving from India to Tokyo, it would be Americans and only the Americans who someday entered Tokyo.

On the European front, it began to look like the Russians and only the Russians would someday reach Berlin. If the Red Army kept rolling west at its current pace, Anglo-American forces would someday enter Berlin only by invitation of Stalin. Churchill had argued for two years that unless agreement was reached with the Soviets to discuss borders only after final victory, whoever in the meantime took territory ruled that territory, which brought the question around, as always, to Poland. What would be the fate of Poland—and Czechoslovakia, the Baltic states, and Austria, Hungary, Bulgaria, and Romania—after the Red Army swept through on its way to Berlin? Roosevelt's suggestion of a move into the Balkans, therefore, helped assuage Churchill's growing uncertainties in regard to Russia.[271]

Happy to have Roosevelt in his court on the Balkans, Churchill returned the favor on the matter of the atomic bomb. The two leaders concluded what amounted to a private treaty. It bypassed both the (written) U.S. Constitution and the (unwritten) British in that neither Congress nor Parliament (nor the full cabinet in either country) knew that an atomic bomb was being produced. They agreed privately that all atomic secrets would be shared, that neither party would ever use the bomb against the other, and that each party would inform the other of intended use against a third party. The fourth clause held that postwar Britain would not pursue commercial use of atomic energy based on knowledge gained in the development of the bomb. This caveat stemmed from American fears that Britain might try to reap commercial rewards from America's wartime financial sacrifice. Churchill's acceptance of the condition shocked R. V. Jones, who had solved the question of how to jam the German targeting beams and now headed the scientific intelligence branch of the Air Staff. Churchill, Jones later wrote, "had signed away our birthright in the postwar development of nuclear energy." Yet Jones understood two truths—the Americans had leverage, and it was typical of Churchill to make such a "magnificent gesture" in order to allay American fears. Churchill had conducted such business throughout Quadrant over dinners with Roosevelt and Hopkins, where men of honor transacted such business. Cadogan's diary entries testified to the good fellowship. Churchill: "This water tastes funny"; Hopkins: "Because there's no whisky in it. Fancy you a judge of water!" And Harry to "Mr. P.M." as Churchill paced the room delivering another monologue: "Your pants is coming down." Yet Churchill, in presuming that the bonhomie he found at the president's table carried weight, failed to grasp a basic tenet of American politics: good cheer is nonbinding. Only the U.S. Congress can bind, and Churchill did not understand just how binding the U.S. Congress can be. Unlike Clementine, Churchill was quite dazzled by Roosevelt's charm.[272]

On September 12, Churchill learned early in the day that Waffen SS parachute commandos had plucked Benito Mussolini from his mountaintop confinement. As Churchill feared, a quisling government was about to be formed in northern Italy, but he had not foreseen that Mussolini, imprisoned for six weeks, would be at its helm. "Italy," Churchill later wrote, "was now to pass through the most tragic time in her history." Goebbels' Italian labor force was growing exponentially. Tens of thousands of Italians were fleeing the developing battles in the south of Italy. Of the flood of "fugitives," Goebbels confided to his diary, "Gigantic columns of Italian prisoners are on their way into the Reich. They are very welcome here as skilled workers." "Slaves" would have been a more accurate description.[273]

That week, German military propaganda celebrated the good news coming out of Italy, especially the drubbing inflicted on Mark Clark at Salerno, which the propagandists compared to Dunkirk and Gallipoli. But Salerno was not yet a battle won, which Goebbels knew well. He had warned the military propagandists to show caution; they had not. He summed up the situation to his diary with a line that happened also to be one of Churchill's favorites: "I have always held...that the skin of the bear must not be distributed until the bear has been killed."[274]

By the time Churchill boarded HMS *Renown* on September 14, the U-boats had all but disappeared from the central and southern Atlantic but for irregular sniping along the South American and African coasts. Since late May, sixty-two convoys comprising 3,246 merchant ships sailed between America and Britain on the northern route; not a single ship was lost. In the southern and mid-Atlantic and Indian Ocean (where Dönitz had sent several U-boats), September's losses from all causes came to about 208,000 tons, not much more than a week's losses earlier in the year. October's losses would come in under 100,000 tons, at a cost to Dönitz of twenty-three U-boats; earlier in the year the British had budgeted a loss of 550,000 tons for October. The Allies were on track to lose less than half the tonnage in 1943 than they had lost in 1942. And Dönitz's losses began to increase exponentially. As summer prepared to give way to autumn, Dönitz pulled his fleet even farther east.[275]

Still, in the Arctic, the threats from U-boats, from *Scharnhorst* and *Tirpitz,* and from long-range German bombers conspired against restarting the Russian convoys. Hitler placed his faith in technological advances, in the air and under the sea. Goebbels enthused to his diary over a new German torpedo (called Gnat by the Allies) that "listened" for and homed in on cavitation noise of around 24.5 kHz, which was equivalent to the "noise" made by propellers on a destroyer cruising at moderate speed. Nine Allied destroyers (and more than a thousand sailors) were lost in September to the new torpedo, but with Dönitz's U-boats leaving the battlefield, the torpedo's deadly efficiencies could not be exploited. With the sea-lanes to Britain secure, the buildup of troops and tanks in Britain in preparation for Overlord proceeded at will. Hitler had long held that control of the Atlantic Ocean was his best defense against the West. His defense had disappeared.[276]

By November, American transports were arriving at British ports after ten-day journeys during which the green troops stuffed belowdecks played poker, wrote letters, and ate hot navy chow. Some of the ships' captains allowed army personnel to set up shipboard radio stations that played records over the PA system for the listening ease of the men below. One recording, however, was often banned: Bing Crosby's new hit, "I'll Be Home for Christmas."[277]

Renown brought Churchill safely into the Clyde on September 19. The voyage had been uneventful but for Mary almost being washed overboard when she accepted a young officer's invitation to stroll the quarterdeck at the moment the ship made a sharp turn in high seas. Had she not snagged herself on a stanchion, she would have been swept away, the event witnessed by Ismay from the bridge but not by Churchill. "We had visions of plunging overboard," Ismay later wrote, "rather than face the Prime Minister."

Churchill received daily briefing on the Salerno landings during the five-day voyage, and the news was worrisome. Little progress was being made, which is to say the men remained trapped on the beaches. For months Hopkins and Stimson had deprecated Churchill's fears of French beaches running red with blood; yet the situation at Salerno was developing in exactly that way. Very worrisome was the fact that more men had gone ashore at Salerno in the first three days than were called for in the Overlord plan for France. Churchill continued to proclaim that the landing was beginning to look like the landings at Suvla Bay during the Gallipoli campaign. Each day of delay at Salerno brought ever increasing concentrations of Germans on the beach perimeter, and increased the chances of the Allies being thrown back into the sea. Churchill proposed to fly there himself to take charge, but Alexander, anticipating such an offer, had already left for the front. Not until Churchill was back on British soil did he receive the news he had been waiting for: "I can say with full confidence," Alexander wrote, "that the whole situation has changed in our favor, and that the initiative has passed to us." Yet it had taken Alexander almost three weeks to establish his armies in the toe and ankle of Italy, and he still had 150 miles to go before reaching Rome.[278]

Shortly after Churchill arrived home, Admiral Dudley Pound submitted his resignation. His brain tumor killed him a month later, on October 21, Trafalgar Day. He was "the smartest sailor in the Royal Navy," Churchill told Jock Colville, "but cautious." Yet Pound's conservative deployment of HMG's fleets had kept England in the chase for four years. Pound lived to see victory in the Atlantic, and the victory was his. Old British sailors will argue that the British Home Fleet at Scapa Flow, by virtue of being a "fleet in being," played as critical a role as the boys in their Hurricanes and Spitfires in keeping Hitler out of England. Hitler tested Fighter Command but could not bring himself to test the Home Fleet. Myth attached to "the few," but the sailors had done their duty, Pound foremost. Andrew ("ABC") Cunningham, hero of the Mediterranean, replaced Pound as first sea lord.

Harry Hopkins checked himself into the hospital in a state of exhaustion as soon as Churchill departed for London. Eisenhower was also worn out and under a doctor's care. Dill, too, was being ground down; he had injured himself while hunting boar in India the previous year and would not live out the next. And Chancellor of the Exchequer Sir Kingsley Wood, whose stewardship of the British purse had kept the Island afloat financially, died suddenly two days after Churchill's return to London. A shake-up in the ranks was taking place of a sort and magnitude no one had foreseen.

The same could be said of the shake-ups Britons experienced at home and at work. On September 23, Churchill addressed six thousand women from all walks of British life in Albert Hall. As with all of his speeches, he had composed it himself. He told the women:

We are engaged in a struggle for life....This war effort could not have been achieved if the women had not marched forward in millions and undertaken all kinds of tasks and work for which any other generation but our own unless you go back to the Stone Age would have considered them unfitted.... Nothing has been grudged, and the bounds of women's activities have been definitely, vastly, and permanently enlarged....It may seem strange that a great advance in the position of women in the world in industry, in controls of all kinds, should be made in time of war and not in time of peace. One would have thought that in the days of peace the progress of women to an ever larger share in the life and work and guidance of the community would have grown, and that, under the violences of war, it would be cast back. The reverse is true. War is the teacher, a hard, stern, efficient teacher. War has taught us to make these vast strides forward towards a far more complete equalisation of the parts to be played by men and women in society.

He had come a long way in the three decades since declaring of the suffragettes, "What a ridiculous tragedy it will be if this strong Government and party which has made its mark in history were to go down on petticoat politics."[279]

Churchill, the Chiefs of Staff, and the cabinet were in need of rest, but none was forthcoming. John Anderson moved over to the Exchequer, Attlee took over as lord president. Max Beaverbrook, who for health reasons had taken himself away from the pressures of producing goods, rejoined the government as lord privy seal. This was an ill-defined position that admitted to elasticity, perfect for Beaverbrook, whose real role in the new command structure was to serve as Churchill's crony, booster, and foil. South Africa's Jan Smuts now sat in on the War Cabinet meetings (informally, at Churchill's invitation) and brought with him a growing distaste for Overlord, which he imparted not only to Churchill, who had his own doubts, but also to King George. The migration of ministers from post to post struck Churchill as both worrisome and comical; when the reorganization was complete, he took a partisan swipe at his Labour colleagues when he told Eden, "Except for me and you, this is the worst government England has ever had."[280]

British troops entered Naples on October 1 to find that the Germans had very efficiently destroyed the port and its facilities before departing. Since coming ashore at Salerno, the Fifth Army had advanced on average just over a mile per day. Still, Churchill cabled Alexander that he looked forward to meeting him in Rome in a month or so. But at Alexander's rate of advance, his armies would not reach Rome, 120 miles to the north, until sometime in February 1944. Churchill's hopes for the swift capture of Rome and a drive to northern Italy had been wrecked on the road to Naples. Albert Kesselring later said of the weakness inherent in the Allied strategy: "An air landing on Rome and sea landing nearby, instead of at Salerno, would have automatically caused us to evacuate all the southern half of Italy." Now the Allies would have to pay in blood for every mile of ground between Naples and Rome, ground they could have purchased at little cost. By early October, the Eighth Army had moved up the Adriatic coast to take the port of Bari and the airfields at Foggia, and had connected with the Fifth Army in a continuous 120-mile line across the Italian peninsula from Naples on the Tyrrhenian Sea to Termoli on the Adriatic. Montgomery's army formed the right flank of the Italian campaign, but in Churchill's mind it also formed the left flank of the Balkan front. A million Allied troops stood idle throughout Eisenhower's command in the western Mediterranean; landing ships and craft were plentiful (although Eisenhower was about to transfer 85 percent of them to Britain). Churchill wanted to put a small percentage of those men and landing craft into the Aegean, where with the capture of Rhodes, the Balkan right flank would be turned, leaving the underbelly of the Balkans exposed. Tito waited with 200,000 well-armed partisans; the Chetniks fielded another 150,000. The Turks, beneficiaries of one hundred million dollars in British and American aide, fielded forty-five divisions, albeit poorly trained, poorly armed, and lacking armored support. Tito held strips of the Dalmatian coast, where supplies could be put ashore. Turkish airfields would allow the RAF to lend air support. The Allied forces Churchill sought would be needed only to prime the pump. Brooke years later wrote that it might have all been accomplished "without committing a single man in the Balkans." Tito, Mihailovic, and the Turks (if they came in) could do most of the rest. Thus began Churchill's newest Aegean adventure.[281]

He climbed onto his new hobbyhorse, Rhodes, which took its place in the stable alongside Norway and Sumatra. On October 3, German troops attacked the Dodecanese island of Kos just three miles off the Turkish coast. British control of the airfield there was vital if the RAF hoped to cover the Royal Navy as it advanced toward the Greek mainland. Holding Kos would also demonstrate British resolve to the Turks. Yet with the airfield and the island virtually undefended, the Germans took Kos in four days, along with more than 1,300 British soldiers and airmen. Now the Germans were within shouting distance of the Turkish mainland. The

Turks, not sanguine and for good reason, decided the time was not yet right to join the Allies.

"Another day of Rhodes madness," Brooke wrote on October 7 after a particularly nasty "battle with the P.M." over the wisdom of the Rhodes strategy. Churchill announced that he was leaving for Algiers in order to bring Eisenhower around. Brooke was beside himself: "This is all to decide whether we should try and take Rhodes....He [the P.M.] is in a very dangerous condition, most unbalanced, and God knows how we shall finish this war if it goes on."[282]

Churchill cabled Roosevelt with a request to send Marshall to Tunisia in order to settle the Aegean strategy. Roosevelt's reply was "cold," Brooke wrote, a flat refusal that left no room for interpretation. The president refused to force any decision on Eisenhower even if he agreed with Churchill's strategy, which he did not. "It is my opinion," Roosevelt wrote, "that no diversion of forces or equipment should prejudice Overlord as planned." Churchill replied the next day, telling Roosevelt that the Aegean plan required only a few weeks' use of nine landing ships, which would not be needed for Overlord for at least six months. He asked for "some elasticity and a reasonable latitude in the handling of our joint affairs." The Mediterranean, he pleaded, was being "stripped bare at a moment when great prizes could be cheaply won." Roosevelt stood firm. "If we get the Aegean Islands," he replied, "I ask myself where do we go from there, and vice versa where would the Germans go if...they retain possession of the islands?" But Churchill didn't care where the Germans might go. He cared about British influence in the eastern Mediterranean. He wanted the Royal Navy there, on station, to send a message to not only Hitler but also Stalin that the Balkans were within the British sphere. It was not to be. The German capture of Kos meant that the British troops on Leros could be neither reinforced nor evacuated. Hitler had no intention of going anywhere after taking the Dodecanese; his goal was to keep the British from grabbing these plums and going someplace themselves, such as the Dardanelles and the Balkans. He succeeded in doing just that. And with Germans now camped just off the Turkish coast, the prospect of Turkey joining the Allies all but disappeared. Churchill instructed Eden "to coerce the Turks into the war." Asked by Brooke how Eden should go about doing that, Churchill replied, "Remind the Turkey that Xmas is coming."[283]

Although Brooke regularly savaged Churchill's strategic priorities, the two were actually in agreement on the Aegean. Yet events had bypassed the Aegean strategy, a fact that Churchill simply could not grasp. Brooke understood what Churchill did not: Rhodes was the correct play, but the timing had gone wrong. Churchill's push for Rhodes could only result in increased American suspicion of his (imperial) motives and a decrease in

American support of operations in Italy, a double disaster. It was a tragedy in Brooke's judgment, the blame for which he put down to his own lack of "sufficient force of character to swing those American Chiefs of Staff and make them see the daylight." Brooke later wrote that he was on the verge of a nervous breakdown that October, not because of Churchill's "Rhodes madness," but because the Americans were stripping the Mediterranean of resources "for a nebulous 2nd front." On November 1, he told his diary what might have been: "We should have been in a position to force the Dardanelles by the capture of Crete and Rhodes, we should have the whole Balkans ablaze by now, and the war might have been finished in 1943." These were Churchill's sentiments exactly. But the Combined Chiefs had agreed at Quebec to strip the Mediterranean of at least six divisions in order to feed Overlord. "It is heartbreaking," Brooke wrote.[284]

Caution, Churchill told one of his stenographers, Marian Holmes, had again prevailed over aggression. Miss Holmes found the P.M. "distressed" by the refusal of Roosevelt to see things his way. Churchill told her he felt "almost like chucking it in" and "the difficulty is not in winning the war; it is in persuading people to let you win it—persuading fools." A few weeks later, on his way to Cairo and Tehran, Churchill offered to HMG's new resident minister to Allied Mediterranean headquarters, Harold Macmillan: "Such caution leads to weak and faltering decisions—or rather, indecisions. Why, you may take the most gallant sailor, the most intrepid airman, or the most audacious soldier, put them at a table together—what do you get? The sum of their fears." Churchill, bitter, never forgave Eisenhower for making the decision. "I was grieved," Churchill wrote in his memoirs, "that my small requests" resulted in Ike's "obdurate" resistance to and ultimate rejection of the Rhodes venture.[285]

Yet it was Eisenhower's decision, not Eisenhower the man, that fueled Churchill's bitterness. In a typically Churchillian display of generosity, the very week Eisenhower scuttled the Rhodes gambit, Churchill received permission from King George to commission a special North African campaign ribbon for Eisenhower and Alexander. The ribbons were embossed with the numerals "1" and "8" in reference to the two Allied armies. Churchill, on his way to Cairo, personally pinned the awards on Ike and Alex. Brooke, for his part, lacked Churchill's ability to maintain numerous (and often conflicting) opinions about a man, with the result that Brooke's criticism of his colleagues' professional judgments, including Churchill's, often took the form of ad hominem assaults. The CIGS blamed Eisenhower and Marshall for the inertia in the Mediterranean, the former for being seduced by Overlord due to its "being easier to understand" than the complexities of the Mediterranean theater, the latter due to the "limitations of Marshall's brain" and his inability to "ever, ever see the end of his nose."[286]

On Overlord there could be no turning back, but not for want of trying on Field Marshal Jan Smuts's part, with the support of King George. Even before Churchill arrived home from Quebec, Smuts whispered the folly of Overlord to the King. Smuts and the King dined together on October 13 and ratified their anti-Overlord alliance. The next day in a letter to Churchill, the King made known his doubts about the cross-Channel plan and expressed his belief that the "underbelly" strategy was correct. He advised Churchill to take the matter up with Roosevelt and Stalin when they met in late November. Churchill swiftly disabused the King of any notion of backing out, writing in return, "There is no question of our going back on what is agreed." Yet there *was* a question, and Churchill raised it at the Chiefs of Staff meeting on the nineteenth when he requested a swing around to the Mediterranean even at the expense of Overlord. "I am in many ways entirely with him," Brooke wrote that night, "but God knows where that may lead us to as regards clashes with Americans." The next week Churchill and Smuts argued to the COS that the Mediterranean theater had more merit than a French landing and that since Britain controlled her own destinies, Britain could choose to fight where she chose. Even Max Beaverbrook, who was in attendance, came around. The Beaver had backed the cross-Channel strategy loudest and longest but, after pondering Churchill's arguments, announced that since they had committed to the Mediterranean, they "should make a job of it." Yet they couldn't go it alone, and they knew it.[287]

On November 1, Churchill wrote a memo to the chiefs in which he lamented Britain's lack of available manpower for expanding operations: "We cannot add to the total; on the contrary, it is already dwindling." All able-bodied men sixteen to sixty-five had been mustered for the services and armaments work, as had all able-bodied women aged eighteen to fifty. The manpower pool had evaporated. Still, Churchill found comfort in the fact that when Marshall took over command of Overlord, and Eisenhower replaced Marshall in Washington, a British commander in the Mediterranean, unfettered by American constraints, could then fulfill British destinies. Yet many in the American press argued that Overlord amounted to a demotion for Marshall and were calling for a bigger role, that of supreme Allied commander in the European theater. In mid-October, Churchill had asked Roosevelt for clarification on the matter, only to receive an indeterminate answer two weeks later. A week later, Churchill instructed Dill, in Washington, to make clear to Hopkins and Admiral Leahy that the British would never accede to a single European supreme commander; to do so would in effect deprive the British Chiefs of Staff of their sovereign authority. Churchill also expressed his doubts about Overlord to Roosevelt, but with not quite the conviction he had displayed to the British chiefs. "I do not doubt our ability ... to get ashore and deploy," he told the president. "I am, however, deeply concerned with the build-up and with the situation that may arise between the 30th and 60th days." Getting ashore would be easy; staying ashore was what worried Churchill. A repulse, he told Roosevelt, could only "give Hitler the chance of a startling comeback."[288]

There was clearly much to thrash out before they met Stalin, and at Roosevelt's suggestion, Churchill agreed to a bilateral conference, code-named Sextant, in Cairo before moving on to meet Stalin, presumably in Tehran, although there were growing doubts both in Moscow and Washington about meeting in such an out-of-the-way place. Roosevelt also suggested that Chiang Kai-shek join the party in Cairo in order that Pacific strategies could be addressed. This should have sounded alarms, but Churchill agreed and, with the Chinese legend of the celestial dragon that protects the holiest places in mind, chose Celestes as Chiang's secret identity.

During the eight weeks between the Allied landing at Salerno and early November, the Red Army struck along a five-hundred-mile front. By October 1 it had taken Smolensk and Katyn, three hundred miles north of Kiev. Stalin intended to fight on through the winter. His factories beyond the Urals were turning out almost 2,000 tanks per month; German factories struggled to produce 350 panzers per month. The Luftwaffe, having been peeled away from the Eastern Front to protect the Reich from the RAF, had lost air superiority. The Iranian rail line was pumping six thousand tons per day of matériel into Russia. The weather was worsening, but winter was not the enemy of the Russian soldier; thirteen million pairs of fleece-lined boots stamped *Made in the USA* ensured that the Red Army marched in relative comfort. One hundred thousand American-made Studebaker trucks assured that the troops' supplies would follow close behind. The Americans offered to ship thousands of armored cars, but Stalin declined; he considered them to be death traps.

The Soviet attack was fashioned on Marshal Foch's broad-front strategy of 1918, whereby gains were exploited until the advancing troops needed replenishment, at which time other strikes were launched elsewhere on the front. As conducted by the Red Army, the strategy resulted in the Germans having to hurry reinforcements to points under attack while simultaneously restricting their ability to reinforce points that might be struck next. It was a strategy, Liddell Hart wrote, that "paralyzed [German] freedom of action." The Red Army command "might be likened to a pianist running his hands up and down the keyboard." On November 6 it took Kiev (just 120 miles from the Polish border) and crossed the Dnieper at several points south of Kiev. The crossing of the Dnieper was a crippling blow to Hitler, for the high west bank of the river offered him the best natural barrier in southern Russia and was expected to form the backbone of the eastern wall, which Hitler had just ordered built. The fortification—the eastern-most bulwark of Hitler's empire—was to run from the Sea of Azov north along the Dnieper to Kiev, and from Kiev north to the Baltic at Narva. But the eastern wall was to remain only a line on paper.[289]

"The more furious the storm," Goebbels told his diary in late September as the southern Russian front deteriorated, "the more determined is the Führer to meet it." Still, he added, "It gives one the creeps to look at the map and compare what we had under our dominion...last year with how far we have now been thrown back." Later that month Goebbels wrote, "We must achieve success somewhere. A kingdom for a victory." Dimly grasping the possibility of national obliteration, he broached the subject of a negotiated peace to Hitler. Their thinking on the matter was in turns precise and delusional. Negotiations with either Britain or Russia would prove problematic, Hitler offered, for "England is not yet groggy enough nor sufficiently tired of war." Any attempt at negotiation would only be seen by London "as a sign of weakness." But in time, "the English would come to their senses." In the east, "Stalin has the advantage," and any peace feelers would only be seen in the Kremlin as dealing from weakness. Thus, in the east, "the present moment is quite unfavorable" for negotia-tions. That was because the Germans were losing in the east. So they pon-dered England again. "The Führer believes it would be easier to make a deal with the English than with the Soviets.... Churchill is absolutely anti-Bolshevik." But the problem with the English *was* Churchill. Goebbels believed Stalin the safer bet as he was a "practical politician," whereas "Churchill is a romantic adventurer, with whom one can't talk sensi-bly.... The Führer does not believe that negotiations with Churchill would lead to any result as he is too deeply wedded to his hostile views, and besides, is guided by hatred and not by reason." In order to better under-stand his English enemies, Goebbels that month read *How Green Was My Valley*. He concluded the English would never "become Bolshevized." This might prove valuable from a negotiation standpoint; the Reich and En-gland shared a common enemy, after all. Both Hitler and Goebbels seemed to have forgotten that Stalin had once been *their* ally.[290]

On September 23 Goebbels displayed a modicum of sense on the matter while dining with Hitler at the Wolf's Lair (*Wolfsschanze*), the Führer's East Prussian headquarters near Rastenburg. "We must come to an arrangement," Goebbels advised, "with one side or the other. The Reich has never yet won a two-front war." England seemed the better choice because "one can always make a better deal with a democratic state." Yet here was Churchill indulging "in orgies of hatred against the Reich" while promising Britons (and Germans) that "the Reich is to face total destruction." Falling under a momentary spell of rationality, Goebbels concluded that "it is quite doubtful whether we can choose between Russia and England." Yet an approach must be made to one or the other. The German people, Goebbels told Hitler, are "yearning for peace." Hitler allowed that he, too, yearned for peace. "The Führer stressed this," Goebbels wrote. "He said he would be happy to have contact with artistic circles again, to go to the theater in the evening and visit the Artist's Club." He had plans for grand art museums in his hometown, Linz, but at the same time was intent on pushing "Vienna back artistically." In the meantime, Hitler told Goebbels, "our big rocket...fourteen tons...is a murderous tool" that would set the English straight. This delighted Goebbels: "I believe that when the first of these missiles descends upon London, a sort of panic will break out among the English people." That night the RAF smashed Hanover.[291]

The Reich's leaders saw their salvation in the planned "great reprisal campaign by rockets" set for February, target: London. Churchill was privy to just enough intelligence to form an incomplete yet increasingly worrisome picture of just what German rocket scientists were up to. He advised Roosevelt, "The Germans are preparing an attack on England, particularly London, by means of very long range rockets which may conceivably weigh 60 tons and carry an explosive charge of 10 to 20 tons." England had no defense against such a weapon. Yet Churchill's most trusted science adviser, Lord Cherwell, was offering "5 to 1 odds against" the Germans developing a rocket. Alexander Cadogan agreed with Cherwell, but confessed his lack of certainty to his diary: "They're preparing *something* there's no doubt" (italics Cadogan).[292]

On October 3 Harriman departed Washington for his new assignment as American ambassador to the Kremlin. He stopped in London for a few days, but only to take his leave. Roosevelt had been pressing him to take the job for months. Since March the Russians had ignored the current ambassador, Admiral William H. Standley, after Standley disagreed publicly with Stalin's declaration that the Red Army alone was bearing the full brunt of the war. Standley, whose remarks had not been cleared by Hull, urged *Izvestia* to publish full and honest accountings of Lend-Lease aid, including 85,000 trucks, 6,100 aircraft, and 8,600 tanks shipped to Russia. The Russian press soon made mention of Lend-Lease, but within weeks came the Katyn incident, the abandonment of Roundup, and the Anglo-American exclusion of Russia from the Italian negotiations. The Moscow post needed new blood; with reluctance Harriman took it. It meant good-bye to London and to Churchill, whose company Harriman thoroughly enjoyed, and to Pamela, whose bed he enjoyed (the lovers' hiatus lasted almost three decades, until 1971, when Pamela Beryl Digby Churchill Hayward became the third Mrs. Harriman). Soon after Harriman left for Moscow, Ed Murrow and his wife, Janet, began frequenting Pamela's salon where, not yet twenty-four, she led England's best and the brightest in discussions that parsed the political mysteries of their age. She spoke French fluently, had dazzling blue eyes, a fabulous figure, and met Henry James's ideal of the English beauty: a complexion "as bright as a sunbeam after rain." She exerted a strong gravitational pull on men, including Murrow. Soon, Murrow and Pamela were conducting their own private salon. Murrow's boss at CBS, William S. Paley, who also fell under Pamela's spell, later called her the greatest courtesan of the twentieth century. It was meant as a compliment. Whatever Churchill knew of all this he kept to himself, for he cared deeply for Pamela, who, by delivering to Winston a fair-haired blue-eyed grandson, could do no wrong in his estimation.[293]

Harriman, accompanied by his daughter Kathleen, arrived in Moscow on the eighteenth. His first duty was to open up the ambassador's residence, Spaso House, to Eden, Molotov, and Hull, who were about to convene the first meeting of the Allied foreign ministers. The talks were intended as a prelude to the first meeting of the Big Three the following month in Tehran, although Stalin still held out for Moscow because, as Molotov explained to Eden, the marshal was "indispensable" to the Red Army's fight. Roosevelt, fearing Tehran would find him so far afield that he'd be unable to meet his constitutional obligations to remain in contact with his government, requested that they meet in Ankara or Basra, but Stalin held firm. Eden, at first skeptical of Molotov's assessment, soon witnessed Stalin in action and concluded that Molotov was not exaggerating. Stalin was in regular contact with his generals on the front lines, and was deeply involved with the planning of an operation in Crimea. Where Roosevelt happily delegated military strategy to his lieutenants and Churchill unhappily did likewise, Stalin was a hands-on commander in chief. Urged by Eden, he finally committed to go as far as Tehran, but no farther. Stalin was not in a giving mood. He wanted guarantees on the second front, and he demanded the Arctic convoys be resumed.[294]

In the spring the Admiralty had proposed, and Churchill accepted, a cessation of Arctic convoys, infuriating Stalin in the process. Now in the autumn, with *Tirpitz* crippled weeks earlier by an audacious attack by three British mini-submarines, and the U-boats having all but disappeared from the Arctic routes, Churchill pushed a reluctant Admiralty to send four large convoys to Murmansk, one per month until February. Presuming that Stalin would welcome the news, Churchill sent a message along to Moscow. Stalin, in a blunt response, claimed Britain had "an obligation" to send the four convoys and virtually demanded they make the run to Murmansk immediately. The Foreign Office found the telegram "outrageous." Churchill refused even to respond, handing it back to the new Soviet ambassador, Feodor Gousev. But to Eden, in Moscow, Churchill cabled that he thought the Soviet "machine," not Stalin, was behind the tone of the cable, in part because it took twelve days to prepare. "The Soviet machine is quite convinced it can get everything by bullying, and I am sure it is a matter of some importance to show that this is not necessarily always true." Stalin shrugged off Churchill's refusal, telling Eden, "I understand Mr. Churchill does not want to correspond with me. Well, let it be so." Then Stalin came at Eden over the only matter that really mattered: the second front. It was exactly as Eden had predicted at Quebec. Unless Stalin got his assurances, and until he believed that the Anglo-Americans were fighting the same war on the same Continent, he was content to let the West stew over the two questions that would not go away: Would the Red Army stop at its borders after expelling the Germans, and would Moscow seek a separate peace with Hitler?[295]

To placate Stalin, Churchill instructed Eden to reassure the marshal that three British divisions had been pulled from the Mediterranean for deployment in Overlord, in accordance with the Quebec agreement. Yet he also informed Eden (but not Stalin) that he objected to this depletion of his forces and that he was gathering four more divisions to "repair the loss." "This is what happens when battles are governed by lawyers' agreements, and persisted in without regard to the ever-changing fortunes of war." It fell to Eden to convince Stalin that Overlord had the full support of the prime minister, when in fact, that very week, Churchill told the Chiefs of Staff he wished to delay Overlord if doing so meant that the battle in Italy (and the Balkans, if he only could get there) would be "nourished and fought until it is won." "We will do our very best for Overlord," he told Eden, but "it is of no use planning defeat in the field in order to give temporary political satisfaction." Three days later, he told Eden, as he had Smuts and the King, "There is of course no question of abandoning Overlord, which will remain our principal operation for 1944." Yet delay amounted to abandonment. Overlord might safely be pushed back to June, or even early July 1944, but any further delay would take it into the spring of 1945. That, Stalin could not abide.[296]

The Anglo-American commitment to Overlord gave Stalin leverage. He used it to effect on Eden and Hull. Eden came to Moscow with hopes of parsing Stalin's intentions as to Russia's postwar borders, but he was hobbled by the refusal of the London Poles and their new leader, Stanisław Mikołajczyk (who had not been invited to Moscow), to allow him to even discuss the matter. Eden acceded to their wishes, yet it was clear that Stalin, too, saw no need to discuss anything. He had already made up his mind. As divulged by *Izvestia*, he intended to preserve his territorial gains of 1939 and to exercise great influence in the "security belt" of the Balkans. *Izvestia* claimed that when the second front was launched, and only then, "will it be easier to decide all other necessary questions." For five hundred years, Western Europe had maintained a cordon sanitaire of small client states as a buffer between itself and the Russians, who Europeans considered an Asiatic race. Stalin intended to turn the tables; the new cordon, under his control, would serve as a buffer against the West, especially Germany. Indeed, a few weeks later Czechoslovak president Eduard Beneš, justifiably wary of France and England, signed a twenty-year treaty of mutual assistance with Stalin.[297]

Together, Hull and Eden might have brought some political will to bear on the question of borders, but to Eden's amazement, Hull dismissed the boundary questions as "a Pandora's box of infinite trouble" and refused to discuss the matter. Harriman offered Eden his full support if he pressed the issue with Stalin, but Eden, respecting the decision of Mikołajczyk, chose not to. Hull proceeded to spend his political capital—all of it—by demanding that Stalin acknowledge China as the fourth power in the nebulous four-power postwar league under discussion. Stalin was only too happy to oblige. He was not at war with Japan. If by signing a four-party declaration of solidarity in fighting "respective enemies" and pledging to participate in a postwar international peacekeeping body he could make the boundary issues disappear, he'd sign, and did. Hull was quite pleased that Stalin had not even raised the question of frontiers, but, Harriman later wrote, Hull failed to grasp the essential truth: Stalin considered the issue settled. The Moscow Accord, though celebrated in Washington and London, was symbolic at best. Stalin might as well have signed it with disappearing ink. But the table had been set for Tehran. An agenda had been worked out for the Big Three to work through. Roosevelt had gained acceptance of his nascent international organization, or at least gained Stalin's willingness to talk about it. Stalin had gained a pledge by the Anglo-Americans to open the second front in the spring of 1944. England and Churchill had gained nothing, and the Polish question had simply been postponed.[298]

By early November both the Italian campaign and the air campaign over Germany were flagging. This was not news Churchill wanted to deliver to Stalin in a few weeks' time. In mid-October, Ultra decrypts had revealed Hitler's decision to strengthen and hold his positions in Italy rather than stage a gradual, fighting retreat. Hitler ordered Kesselring's strength increased from sixteen to twenty-three divisions. That bit of intelligence guaranteed that Eisenhower would not fight in both the Aegean and Italy. News mid-month that Erwin Rommel had been sent to Yugoslavia to command German forces there only reinforced Eisenhower's decision to avoid Rhodes and the Balkans. He considered the mission in Italy fulfilled by the capture of Naples and the Foggia airfields, and the establishment of the 120-mile line that ran from the Tyrrhenian Sea to the Aegean. Eisenhower and Marshall had always seen a secondary and diversionary role for Italian operations—more Germans sent to Italy meant fewer Germans to oppose Overlord. Hitler's decision to reinforce Kesselring, Eisenhower later wrote, "was a great advantage to the Allies elsewhere." He believed that although the Italian campaign was "a distinctly subsidiary operation...the results it attained in the actual defeat of Germany were momentous, almost incalculable." Churchill, too, endorsed the idea of drawing Germans away from France and into Italy, telling Roosevelt so in a telegram on October 26: "The fact that the enemy have diverted such powerful forces to this theater vindicates our strategy." Yet Churchill, seeking to fight far more than a holding action, also told Roosevelt, "At all costs we must win Rome and the airfields north of it." Roosevelt, committed only to Overlord, did not reply. Eisenhower did not have a strategy (or orders) to get to Rome, and the Fifth Army lacked the means. Since taking Naples on October 1, the left flank of the Fifth Army had managed to slog northward about thirty miles; it had maintained its mile-a-day pace for almost two months.[299]

As October went out, Mark Clark's army straddled Highways 6 and 7, about twelve miles south of the town of Cassino and the routes north to Rome. At Cassino, Highway 6 turned north through the Liri Valley. And there, Monte Cassino, a Benedictine monastery called the abbey of abbeys by Benedictines, sat atop the mountain. Its oldest parts dated from the sixth century, when Benedict of Nursia and twelve disciples set to work building their refuge. Clark had to take the monastery in order to get on the road to Rome. But before he could take Cassino, he had to take other hills and towns along Highway 6—Monte Camino, Monte Lungo, Monte Sammucro, and the villages of San Pietro Infine and San Vittore. Although Clark had almost 250,000 men under his command, by late October, ferocious German resistance, freezing rains, and mud had stopped his army. On November 11, Clark called a two-week halt.[300]

The air war over Germany brought its own disappointments. Operation Pointblank, the June decision to target German aircraft factories, was proving more costly than anyone, especially the Americans, had foreseen. American casualties were kept low as long as their B-17s flew missions protected by their P47C Thunderbolt fighters, which when fitted with a reserve fuel tank had an operational radius of five hundred miles, to beyond the Ruhr Valley and back. But when the Thunderbolts peeled away for home, the B-17s suffered horrific losses. During the second week of October, 148 went down with their ten-man crews, including 60 of 291 sent to destroy the ball-bearing factory at Schweinfurt. Pointblank was proving deadly and ineffectual. Bomber Harris continued his night raids against German cities. But his losses also mounted. The efficacy of massed attacks against German cities was in doubt. Churchill, knowing that Stalin approved of the raids, encouraged Harris to pursue his strategy. It was the only help Britain could give Stalin. Harris sent his air fleets to Kassel, where three thousand died and fires burned for a week; four thousand died in Würzburg; six thousand in Darmstadt; nine thousand in Weser; twelve thousand in Magdeburg. In November, Harris threw his bombers at Berlin, which the RAF visited sixteen times between November and March. The aircrews paid dearly. It was a price Churchill accepted because throughout 1943, the RAF, alone among Anglo-American forces, had inflicted pain on the German heartland. Anglo-American soldiers and sailors were fighting, but not well enough or near enough to Germany to satisfy Stalin, with whom Churchill had an appointment in Tehran.[301]

On November 12, Churchill and his usual troupe departed Plymouth aboard HMS *Renown*, final destination Alexandria, with ports of call at Gibraltar, Algiers, and Malta. Sarah accompanied her father as his ADC, and Gil Winant came along, since the agenda in Tehran would treat of both political and military issues. Winant therefore would find himself for several weeks in close proximity to Sarah, and the romantic affections they shared would have to remain unrequited in public. If Churchill learned of the affair, he never mentioned it. After calling on Gibraltar, *Renown* made for Algiers, where during his short layover Churchill did not see fit to meet with de Gaulle, who was in residence. De Gaulle was outraged, doubly so because Churchill *had* thought to invite General Joseph Georges for a chat. De Gaulle considered Georges, unfairly, to be one of the architects of France's defeat in 1940. Duff Cooper, who had just been named minister to the French Committee of National Liberation, later wrote that de Gaulle, "ever on the lookout for an insult," had found one in Churchill's breach of etiquette.[302]

Renown made Malta late in the afternoon of the seventeenth. It is fitting that Churchill spent the next two nights on the little island that had taken such a long and savage beating at the hands of the Luftwaffe, for the next day, the RAF conducted its largest raid yet over Germany. Mannheim, Ludwigshafen, and Berlin came in for it. Two weeks earlier Bomber Harris had briefed Churchill on cumulative RAF and Luftwaffe bomb damage to German and British cities. Whereas Coventry had lost 5 percent of the city center to German bombs, Hamburg had been 75 percent destroyed. As had Malta; its houses, quays, and roads — all constructed of brittle Maltese limestone — had for the most part been blasted back into the fossil particulates whence they came. But the fact that Churchill could take his rest on the island meant that the Maltese had come through the worst of it.[303]

German cities were now getting the worst of it. The next raid over Berlin erased the homes of Goebbels' mother and mother-in-law, blew the windows out of the Goebbels house, and reduced Hitler's favorite hotel, the Kaiserhof, to rubble. Goebbels, the *Gauleiter* (a local political leader) of Berlin, bemoaned to his diary this "time of universal misfortune which has now fallen upon this city of four and a half million.... Hell itself seems to have broken loose over us." A November 24 *New York Times* headline crowed: ZOO ANIMALS ROAM BERLIN STREETS; HEAT OF FIRES FELLS PEDESTRIANS. In fact, in regard to fires, Berliners could count themselves fortunate. The cool autumn weather and Berlin's wide avenues and modern buildings kept firestorms of the Hamburg sort from breeding. Bomber Harris's response to Berlin's structural integrity was to send more bombers from England more often. And from Foggia, from where the Allied air forces could reach targets in southern Germany and Romania, came even more bombers.[304]

The Old Man arrived on Malta with a bit of a sore throat, which within a day had festered into a nasty cold that kept him in bed for most of his short visit. He stayed in the Governor's Palace as the guest of Lord Gort, and as the palace could offer no hot water for his bath, his mood worsened in lockstep with the worsening head cold. His room overlooked a busy promenade up from which drifted the sounds of Maltese making their way through the rubble. It was too much for Churchill, who flung off his bedclothes, threw open the windows, and bawled to the crowd below: "Go away, will you? Please go away and do not make so much noise."[305]

His funk worsened when he learned that Leros had fallen that day; the battle had been a Crete in miniature. The Germans arrived by sea and air; the RAF and Royal Navy did not dispute the issue; British troops on the ground were poorly led. The Royal Navy's lack of aggression grated on Churchill, who christened the new naval commander of the Mediterranean, Admiral Sir John Cunningham (no relation to Andrew), "'Dismal Jimmy'—and not without cause," in Harold Macmillan's estimation. The upcoming meeting of the military chiefs in Cairo also riled Churchill. He and the Americans still held opposing and irreconcilable views. He supported Overlord, but not at the expense of Rhodes, and especially Italy, the only theater where Anglo-American troops were taking pressure off the Russians. He intended to force a showdown. This troubled Brooke, who told his diary: "He [Churchill] is inclined to say to the Americans, all right, you won't play with us in the Mediterranean we won't play with you in the English Channel. And they will say all right then we shall direct our main effort in the Pacific." To Clementine, Churchill cabled: "It is terrible fighting with both hands tied behind one's back."[306]

Alexander and Eisenhower arrived on Malta in order to receive their special North African campaign ribbons. Both men lamented the stasis in Italy but for different reasons. Alexander, as the commander on the spot, had to report that the campaign had stalled. "All roads lead to Rome," he told Lord Moran, "and they are all paved with mines." The entire Mediterranean command believed that an amphibious flanking operation—preferably two, one on each coast—was the best way to get around Kesselring's lines. Earlier in the month, Eisenhower's staff began drawing up plans for such an operation. Code-named Shingle, it called for landing a reinforced division at Anzio, birthplace of Nero and Caligula and since Roman times a holiday resort. Anzio, and its sister city, Nettuno, sat on the Tyrrhenian coast about fifty miles north of, and behind, Kesselring's lines. The towns, about a mile apart, faced narrow beaches. They were built in a basin ringed by woodlands and the Pontine Marshes. Several miles beyond the marshes high hills rose to the west and north. Alexander had sought at least five divisions for the venture, but neither the troops nor the transports were available; they were going to England, for Overlord.

By the time Churchill arrived on Malta, the plan languished in the file of improbable operations. Eisenhower, by the time he arrived on Malta, and presuming he was headed to Washington to replace Marshall as chief of staff, was preparing his exit from the Mediterranean. He considered any new Italian venture a drawdown to the buildup for Overlord. Churchill gave Eisenhower an earful, on both the need to grab Rome and the risks inherent in Overlord. "How often I heard him say," Eisenhower later wrote, "in speaking of Overlord's prospects, 'We must take care that the tides do not run red with the blood of American and British youth, or the beaches be choked with their bodies.'" Eisenhower, like Brooke, departed Malta believing Churchill would press the matters of Italy and Rhodes in Cairo and Tehran. Churchill meant to untie his hands.[307]

During the two-day sail to Alexandria, he drew up a strategic plan. It amounted to Rome first, then Rhodes, by January. Churchill presumed the Sextant talks would be all about settling the Mediterranean issues, with the Pacific theater relegated to a lower slot on the agenda. But Roosevelt had invited Chiang Kai-shek and Madame Chiang to Cairo with the intention of turning the agenda on its head. Brooke made the trip by air, aboard Churchill's Avro York. Upon reaching Cairo, he told his diary: "I wish our conference was over."[308]

It had not even begun. When it did, Churchill saw at once that Roosevelt meant to deny him his showdown. During the first plenary session on November 23, held at Roosevelt's villa a few miles outside Cairo, the president announced that he wanted to talk about the Pacific. Furthermore, Roosevelt pledged to Chiang that large-scale naval operations would soon start in the Bay of Bengal in support of an amphibious operation (code-named Buccaneer) in Burma, all intended not so much to knock Japan back but to get support through to Chiang's forces, whose role in the Pacific war Roosevelt still saw as vital. Thus, Churchill wrote in his memoirs, the Combined Chiefs of Staff "were sadly distracted by the Chinese story, which was lengthy, complicated, and minor...with the result that Chinese business occupied first instead of last place at Cairo." Yet, that week, General Sir Billy Slim (he had been knighted earlier in the year) drove from Assam into central Burma, with one of his corps heading for the Chindwin River, which it crossed on December 3. The Japanese at Slim's front, confused by a British deception campaign, did not even know where Slim was headed. Though Slim was forging opportunities ripe for exploitation, he and Burma were at the bottom of Churchill's agenda.[309]

Roosevelt told Churchill that he had put the Pacific war ahead of the European on the agenda because he did not want Stalin to think they "had ganged up on him on military action." He believed that if they made Japan the primary focus of Sextant, Stalin's suspicions would be allayed. Yet the decision also ensured that the Anglo-American bloc would arrive in Tehran without having reached solid agreement on the second front. Churchill, in his memoirs, could not resist taking a swipe at Roosevelt and Chiang. In spite of vast American aide to China (several millions of dollars of which was stolen by Madame Chiang's family), Chiang "had been beaten by the communists in his own country, which is a bad thing." Brooke, in his memoirs, was more blunt: "Why the Americans attached such significance to Chiang I have never discovered. All he did was lead them down a garden path to communist

China!" As for Stilwell and Chennault, who were feuding over whether Lend-Lease matériel should go to Stilwell's soldiers or Chennault's Chinese air forces, Brooke wrote that Stilwell was "nothing more than a crank," while Chennault, though "a gallant airman" had "a limited brain." During the meetings, Madame Chiang, who spoke perfect English, translated for her husband, leaving Brooke with the impression that Madame "was the leading spirit of the two, and I would not trust her very far.... The more I see of her the less I like her." Not so the other staff officers, whose collective breathing almost stopped when Madame's "closely clinging dress of black satin with yellow chrysanthemums displayed a slit which extended to her hip bone and exposed one of the most shapely of legs."[310]

Churchill warmed to Madame Chiang, telling Clementine by letter that he withdrew "all the unfavourable remarks which I may have made about her." (Madame had voiced strong criticism of British imperial policies during a visit to India the previous year, inciting Churchill to "breathing fire and slaughter against her" to the Foreign Office.) The Chiangs had come out of the shadows to light up the Cairo conference, Madame Chiang by her very presence, but they did so at the expense of Anglo-American cohesion. The meetings with Chiang, Brooke told Marshall, were "a ghastly waste of time," to which Marshall replied, "You're telling me." Still, Roosevelt brought Churchill around on the need for action in Burma, but Churchill's initial support for Buccaneer evaporated when he realized that the landing craft needed for Burmese operations would come from the Mediterranean. Within ten days, as a result of Churchill's counterarguments, Roosevelt overrode his military chiefs and conceded that Buccaneer was dead. Not until April 1945, with American Marines and U.S. soldiers fighting on Okinawa, just 325 miles from the Japanese homeland, would Allied troops finally reopen the India-China road links in northern Burma and retake Rangoon in the south, too late to make a difference in the war against Japan.[311]

After the disagreeable first meetings with Chiang, the conference only went further downhill. The Americans stunned the British by again arguing for an American supreme commander in Europe, an issue Churchill considered settled. The British flatly rejected the proposal. Lest the Americans pursue the question, Churchill pointed out that because of the long-held understanding between the Allies that theater commanders came from the partner with the most forces in the theater, a supreme commander for all of Europe would have to be British because Britain had more men, planes, and ships in Europe than the Americans did. Roosevelt dropped the issue, but he stuck to his Burma plans, which Brooke coldly and methodically dismantled during a meeting of the military chiefs. Admiral Ernie King, enraged by Brooke's demeanor, rose from the table as if to settle the issue with fists. Stilwell, who witnessed the scene, wished King "had socked" Brooke. Pug Ismay thought King's ongoing animosity threatened the cohesion of the Combined Chiefs, and told King so. King replied, "Look here, General, when there's a war they send for the sons of bitches, and that's me." Churchill, meanwhile, argued for his Aegean plans, cautioning Roosevelt that Overlord must not be spelled T-Y-R-A-N-T, a display of rhetoric Brooke thought "masterly." Even the irascible King showed signs of supporting Churchill, but only because if the British navy stayed in the Mediterranean, it couldn't get in his way in the Pacific. Churchill pushed his Aegean strategy with flights of oratory: "His Majesty's government cannot have its troops standing idle; muskets must flame," and Rhodes was the place they must flame. That display led Marshall to smack the table with his fist and exclaim, "Not one American soldier is going to die on that god-damned beach." Marshall's outburst quieted the room, including Churchill, who did not again mention Rhodes in Cairo. But the issue had not been resolved; Churchill carried his Aegean hopes to Tehran.[312]

The British had taken over the grand Mena House hotel in Giza, where Churchill and T. E. Lawrence had stayed two decades earlier when they created new states in the Middle East. The hotel's grandiosity had moved Lawrence to remark that it made him a Bolshevik. Churchill loved it. There, he and Brooke hosted evening dinners as jovial as the afternoon meetings were disputatious. "King was as nice as could be and quite transformed from his afternoon attitude," wrote Brooke after one such meal. Roosevelt's dinner companions included Harry Hopkins and Hopkins's son, Robert, a U.S. Army war photographer who had seen action in Italy. General Edwin M. ("Pa") Watson, Roosevelt's old friend and political adviser, was on hand, as was Roosevelt's son-in-law, Major John Boettiger. Colonel Elliott Roosevelt joined the party, a case of nepotism, but only fair as Alexander Cadogan remarked to his diary, "I suppose we can't talk if we trail Randolph around with us." As always, Roosevelt's squad of Filipino mess men were on hand to produce his meals, including a turkey on Thanksgiving Day, which Roosevelt carved "with masterly, indefatigable skill." A small dance followed, the music supplied by gramophone. All the young men danced with Sarah; Churchill danced with Pa Watson. The gathered sang *Home on the Range*. It was a jolly evening, although tears were visible on his cheeks when Churchill toasted the president. Churchill's cold had abated; the bright Egyptian skies invigorated him, and his spirits brightened, as evidenced the next night when his small party dined and chatted until 1:30 in the morning. "P.M. talked to the whole table from 8:30...to 1:35," recorded Cadogan, "then expressed surprise at having a sore throat." Dickie Mountbatten fell asleep during Churchill's oration, and even Sarah had trouble keeping her eyes open.[313]

The congeniality reached a high point when Churchill and Sarah suggested to Roosevelt that they all take a drive out to the pyramids, which the president had never seen. The idea so enthused Roosevelt, recalled Sarah, that "he leaned forward on the arms of his chair and seemed about to rise," but of course could not, "and sank back again." While the president readied himself, Churchill and Sarah waited outside, where Sarah noted that her father's eyes "were bright with tears." He turned to her and said, "I love that man." Such was Sarah's recollection two decades later. At the time she failed to mention the tears or the affection in a letter to her mother, but she did write, "It really is wonderful how they both get on—they really like and understand each other. The outing, like the evening festivities, had been a smashing success."[314]

The staff meetings were not. Roosevelt, Churchill offered to Anthony Eden, who had arrived on the fourth day of talks, "was a charming country gentleman" but deficient in "business methods." The conference had been planned on short notice, and it showed. Eisenhower had flown in for the second plenary session and confounded Marshall (while pleasing Churchill) by suggesting that the greatest support Alexander's Italian army could give to the European campaign would be to successfully sweep into the Po Valley. Then, as Eisenhower saw it, Alexander could either strike toward southeast France, or turn northeast toward Trieste and Vienna. Given the conditions in Italy, Eisenhower thought one of these thrusts could be undertaken—and accomplished—by the summer of 1944. Inadvertently, Ike had given new life to Churchill's Mediterranean strategy, which Marshall all week had been trying to knock down. After five days of talks, the British and Americans had reached no final agreement on any of their respective strategies, in Europe or the Pacific. That they had agreed upon goals in the Pacific, but not on the means for reaching them, was evidenced by the wording of the Cairo Declaration, issued by the three leaders at the end of the conference. It called for Japan's unconditional surrender and its expulsion from the Asian mainland. It called for an independent Korea and mandated that all Japanese conquests in China, including Taiwan, be restored to China. But the declaration made no mention of how any of this would come to pass.[315]

Just after sunrise on November 27, Roosevelt boarded his Douglas C-54, which Admiral Leahy had anointed *The Sacred Cow*. Churchill climbed into his Avro York. They were heading, unprepared and in fundamental disagreement, to Tehran and the most important meeting to date in the life of the alliance. But Stalin was prepared for them. Harry Hopkins told Moran that if Churchill proved obdurate in Tehran in regard to the second front, Roosevelt would back the Russians. "I am not looking forward to the next few days," Brooke told his diary.[316]

Alec Cadogan thought the weather in Tehran lovely. The skies were Persian blue, the sunshine golden. Tehran, however, came in for a dose of his cynicism: "a squalid town of bad taste. . . . Bazaars quite good—as a sight. Nothing in them." Churchill found Persian security sadly lacking for the advent of three such prestigious personages. A column of mounted Iranian cavalrymen lined the streets, which only showed "any evil people that somebody of consequences was coming, and which way." The cavalry would prove useless if "two or three determined men with pistols or a bomb" attempted to rush the automobiles that carried the distinguished guests. Still, to Inspector Thompson's chagrin, Churchill, who had been warned his life might be threatened, "was very excited, even pleased." As the crowds pressed up against the car, "he looked into everyone's face with the happiest sort of suspicion." Thompson had been told by his army contacts that British agents had rounded up several German evildoers who had parachuted in for the occasion. Meanwhile, the Soviets, who claimed to have uncovered the plot, suggested it might prove beneficial to Roosevelt's health for him to stay at the fortified Soviet legation, next door to the British, rather than at the American legation, two miles removed from the city. Roosevelt made the move on November 28. Ismay thought the Soviet story "a trick" and believed the Soviets had already planted microphones in the walls of Roosevelt's apartments.[317]

Churchill considered it vital that he and the president confer before they met with Stalin. Roosevelt did not think likewise. He was determined that Uncle Joe not feel ganged up on, and equally determined not to be pinned down by Churchill over his Rhodes scheme. Roosevelt meant to see Stalin first, and to see him alone. Shortly after 3:00 P.M. on the twenty-eighth, Stalin paid the president a brief private visit. Forewarned by Ismay that Churchill's exclusion had caused "storm signals" to be run up among the British delegation, Harriman strolled over to "calm the waters." He found Churchill "in a grumbling but whimsical mood." The Old Man told Harriman he would "obey orders" but that he had a right to chair the upcoming meeting because he was the most senior leader, because his name came first alphabetically, and because of the historic importance of the "British Empire, which he represented." He insisted that if nothing else, he host a dinner on the thirtieth, his sixty-ninth birthday, where "he would get thoroughly drunk . . . and leave the next day."[318]

Stalin and Roosevelt meanwhile were getting along famously. The president announced that Russia deserved a warm-water port at the end of the

South Manchurian railroad, and that some of the British and American merchant fleets should be transferred to Russia after the war. "That would be a fine thing," Stalin replied. Roosevelt had not consulted Churchill on either matter. The subjects of France and de Gaulle came up; both leaders agreed that de Gaulle was out of touch "with the real France." The real France, Stalin offered, was busy helping the Germans and would have to be punished after the war. Roosevelt agreed, and added that no Frenchman over the age of forty should be allowed to participate in postwar French affairs. They moved on to Southeast Asia and India, where almost one billion people—Roosevelt often called them "brown people," "of short stature," and "not warlike"—lived under British and French subjugation. Roosevelt proposed that the Allies hold French Indochina in trust after the war, as America had held the Philippines. India, Malaya, and Burma, Roosevelt proclaimed, should be "educated in the arts of self government." He suggested "reform from the bottom" in India "somewhat on the Soviet line." Stalin replied that reform from the bottom would result in revolution. India, he told the president, was "a complicated society." Harriman thought Stalin "showed rather more sophistication than the president." The two leaders agreed that the subject of India should not be brought up with Churchill. Roosevelt's clearest signal to Stalin had to do with Poland. The president made no mention of Poland.[319]

Harriman had earlier in the day offered an impromptu lecture to Eden and Cadogan on the art and science of properly conducting an international conference, leading Cadogan to proclaim to his diary, "I've forgotten a great deal more about that than he [Harriman] ever knew." The waters were anything but calm, and the conference had yet to begin.[320]

As the Big Two broke the ice, Churchill took himself to his villa's garden to shuffle through official papers, including memos to Home Secretary Herbert Morrison. The previous week Morrison had ordered that the Blackshirts Oswald and Diane (Mitford) Mosley be released from prison and placed under house arrest, a decision Morrison made for humanitarian and health reasons. The Mosleys had been held without trial for three years under the special powers granted HMG by section 18B of the legal code. The response to Morrison's decision among workingmen was immediate; ten thousand marched through London's streets to protest what they saw as favoritism. The Commons erupted as well. To Clementine, Churchill wrote, "If I were at home I'd blast the whole [18B] blasted thing out of existence." He offered that Morrison could "sweep it [18B] away" if he followed the "overwhelming arguments I have mentioned to him." Indeed, Churchill made clear to Morrison the constitutional peril of 18B, his loathing of the law, and his desire that 18B be abolished. Yet, he also advised Morrison to argue that although the special powers were deplorable, "the time has not yet come when it [18B] can be fully dispensed with, but we can look forward to that day." In fact, the day *had* come; the peril of invasion had long passed, but Churchill was not yet willing to give up this extraordinary power; 18B stayed on the books. The British electorate took note.[321]

Brooke stopped by the garden to propose that Churchill offer the Americans the Andaman operation in exchange for American guarantees in the Mediterranean. Churchill vetoed the idea, telling Brooke, correctly, that any such promise would prove impossible to keep. Once the large landing ships left the Mediterranean for the Pacific venture, they would never return. By now Churchill's cold had worsened and his voice had almost abandoned him. "He is not fit," Brooke concluded, "and consequently not in the best of moods." That was because his friend Franklin Roosevelt was meeting privately with Uncle Joe. When word reached the British concerning the substance of Roosevelt's meeting with Stalin, Brooke told Moran, "This conference is over when it has only begun. Stalin has got the President in his pocket."[322]

The first plenary session was convened at four o'clock in a large room in the yellow-brick Soviet legation. The principals gathered around a grand round table covered in green baize. Heavy draperies blocked the Persian sunshine. Admiral King and Harry Hopkins were there, but Generals Marshall and Arnold had somehow gotten their wires crossed and were off sightseeing in Tehran, thus leaving Roosevelt to his own devices. Churchill had his full complement of chiefs in attendance. Stalin was accompanied by only an interpreter and Marshal Kliment Voroshilov, a sixty-two-year-old career officer and Stalin toady who had led the (unsuccessful) assault against the Finns in 1939 and had been replaced by Zhukov at Leningrad in 1941 after allowing the Germans to surround that city. Voroshilov, Brooke wrote, would supply Stalin "nothing in the shape of strategic vision." But then, in Brooke's opinion, Stalin had no need of advice: "He [Stalin] had a military brain of the highest caliber," Brooke recalled, and could grasp "all the implications of a situation with a quick and unerring eye.... In this respect he stood out when compared to his two colleagues."[323]

Roosevelt, as the only head of state, was nominated by Stalin to serve as chairman. After the president delivered a long summary of the Pacific war ("a lot of *blah-flum*" according to Brooke), Stalin announced that as soon as Germany was defeated, the Soviet Union would multiply its forces in Siberia and join in the war against Japan. This unexpected turn had the effect Stalin intended. He knew that his Siberian airfields and troops could help the U.S. bring Japan to bay much faster than the Chinese nationalists, who in the seven years since the rape of Nanking had yet to defeat a Japanese army or bomb a Japanese city. And although Churchill had always

pledged to throw all of Britain's resources into the war against Japan upon
the defeat of Germany, Britain was running out of resources. Both Roosevelt and Churchill believed—and continued to believe throughout
1944—that the Pacific war would go on for at least eighteen months,
perhaps two years, after Germany was defeated. Stalin's announcement
was therefore most welcome, but it was clearly conditional upon Anglo-
American armies going to France in May 1944 in order to shoulder their
share of the burden. Then, and only then, would the Red Army march
with them to Tokyo. Left unsaid was the possibility, always present in the
back of Anglo-American minds, that a failure to get into France by May
would place the Soviet Union in untenable military straits, that is, would
foster an atmosphere conducive to a negotiated peace. Stalin had leveraged
that fear for two years, and did so again, in masterly fashion, over the next
three days.[324]

He spoke quietly, as he had done the year before in his first sessions with
Churchill. He doodled on a notepad and smoked hand-rolled cigarettes,
which he kept loose in his breast pocket. His brown eyes gave away nothing. He had changed his wardrobe since they last met, discarding his comrade ensemble of "grey-brown cloth tunic buttoned to the chin and the
trousers of the same material, tucked into knee-boots." He had "blos-
somed out into a multi-coloured uniform" designed, it seemed to Moran,
by a tailor who "has put a shelf on each shoulder. And on it has dumped a
lot of gold with white stars." A fat red stripe ran down the marshal's
creased trousers. When he spoke, he gazed into the distance and looked no
one directly in the eye. "Stalin would have made a fine poker player," Ismay
later wrote. "His expression was as inscrutable as the Sphinx."[325]

He listened as Roosevelt proposed that once Italy was wrapped up, the
Anglo-American armies might swing into the Balkans, link up with Tito's
forces, and drive northeast toward Romania and a conjunction with the
Red Army as it drove west. This suggestion surprised and disturbed Hopkins, who scribbled a message to Admiral King, asking, "Who's promoting
this Balkan business?" King replied that it seemed to be Roosevelt's idea.
But Roosevelt and Churchill had previously discussed this idea, or at least
had discussed Churchill's idea of a thrust through Slovenia toward Vienna.
Churchill followed the president's remarks with a synopsis of his case for
driving from Rhodes through the Dardanelles, if Turkey came in on the
Allied side. If Churchill thought that some version of his Balkan strategy
was on the verge of validation, Stalin quickly disabused him of the notion.
Turkey "was beyond hope" and would not come in, the marshal declared,
and the Dardanelles were not worth the effort. Stalin then proposed that
southern France, not the Balkans, should be the next Anglo-American
objective, the better to coordinate with the Normandy invasion. Churchill

expressed support for the southern France venture but stressed that it must not come at the expense of Italian operations.[326]

Stalin then suggested that it might be best to cease operations in Italy before April, whether or not Rome had been taken, and to then shift six divisions from Italy to the southern France gambit rather than toward some hoped-for conjunction with the Red Army. He proposed that the southern France operation take place on April 1, a month before Overlord. Roosevelt, to Brooke's chagrin, voiced his approval. Operation Anvil, as the southern France plan was then code-named, called for two divisions, with four more to follow. As Brooke saw it, to strip six divisions out of line in Italy, where they were successfully engaging Germans, and throw them ashore in France would allow the Germans to shift their forces to the beachhead, where the defender would have a great advantage. Brooke predicted the "annihilation of these six divisions" if they were thrown into southern France. After dispensing with the Anvil threat, the Germans would then at their leisure shift forces against Overlord. This was the exact scenario Churchill most feared.[327]

Brooke saw that Stalin was pushing a political strategy couched as military strategy. Militarily, any conjunction of Allied armies on the Eastern Front would lead to profound questions of command and control. Who would lead this combined force west to Berlin? Stalin was a unilateralist in military matters. Besides, the tensions within the Anglo-American arm of the alliance testified to the difficulties of joint commands. Stalin's military logic was sound, and Brooke now grasped the politics behind it. The marshal was determined to keep the Anglo-Americans out of any territories he considered to be within his "security belt," which was to say, the Balkans, and perhaps Hungary, Austria, and Czechoslovakia. Stalin did not want the Dardanelles opened; that, too, would bring the British and Americans onto his left flank, in the Black Sea. Thus, as for a thrust through the Balkans, Roosevelt proposed and Stalin disposed. Churchill hadn't even been able to fully develop his argument for Rhodes. Brooke saw the ramifications: "His [Stalin's] political and military requirements could now be best met by the greatest squandering of British and American lives in France." Churchill began to see it as well. After the meeting, Moran found him so dispirited he asked if something had gone wrong. "A bloody lot has gone wrong," Churchill replied. Roosevelt had given Stalin an opening, and the marshal had marched right through.[328]

The dinner that night, hosted by Roosevelt, came to an early end when the president, stricken by a gastrointestinal bug, went green in the face and was wheeled off to his quarters, but not before he and Stalin took turns and delight in excoriating the French and German peoples. The Germans, Stalin proclaimed, understood only authority, and he intended to give them authority, by keeping them firmly underfoot for at least a generation. He also voiced concern about unconditional surrender; the president, Stalin said, should clarify his terms. Otherwise, the resolve of the German people would only be strengthened, and the Red Army would be the primary victim of any such resolve. Harriman agreed with the marshal, but Roosevelt stood firm; he would not make the same mistake Woodrow Wilson made when he announced his Fourteen Points (imprecise and open to wide interpretation). Regarding France, Stalin insisted that the entire French people were helping the Nazis and should be punished accordingly after the war. French colonial possessions should be stripped away and held in trust, as per Roosevelt's suggestion earlier in the day. The demeaning of France continued until Churchill, who had remained silent, protested that he could not envision a civilized world without a strong and vibrant France. Stalin's reply, Harriman recalled, "was contemptuous." France was a charming place, Stalin offered, but it would have no role in postwar international affairs. And no real importance should be attached to de Gaulle, who had little real influence in any affairs. Roosevelt voiced hearty agreement. Churchill was finding himself more the odd man out with each passing hour.[329]

After Roosevelt was wheeled away, Churchill, finding himself alone with Stalin, escorted the marshal to a sofa. There, joined by Eden and Molotov and two interpreters, Churchill and Stalin, in a bilateral conference of their own, settled down to discuss the fate of Poland. But Stalin had not finished his treatise on Germany and Germans. He recounted that when German prisoners of war from the laboring classes (the Communist Party) protested that they were only following orders, he ordered them shot. He was convinced that Germany would re-arm within fifteen or twenty years. Churchill, keen to display his solidarity, replied that Germany had to be kept under wraps for at least fifty years, all the while denied civil and military aviation and an army high command capable of plotting new depredations. Anything less, Churchill offered, would be a betrayal "of our soldiers." When he advised that the three Allies must be willing to take and maintain control over Germany, Stalin answered, "There was control after the last war, but it failed."[330]

Then Churchill wavered on his long-held belief that Germany should emerge after the war a member of the European family—albeit militarily impotent but economically strong. Instead, he threw his lot in with Roosevelt, Morgenthau, Lord Cherwell, and Stalin, all of whom favored a dismemberment of Germany into, as Churchill told Stalin, "a broad, peaceful, cow-like confederation." (Several months later he told Lord Moran, "If the

Ruhr were grassed over our trade would benefit.") This was an about-face from his stance in August 1941, when in announcing the Atlantic Charter, he proclaimed: "Instead of trying to ruin German trade by all kinds of additional trade barriers and hindrances as was the mood of 1917, we have definitely adopted the view that it is not in the interests of the world and of our two countries that any large nation should be unprosperous or shut out from the means of making a decent living for itself and its people by its industry and enterprise."[331]

The Germany of the future that Churchill described to Stalin bore a close resemblance to Roosevelt's postwar Germany, a Carthaginian future, in fact, which is to say, no future. Then Stalin—who had spoken at dinner of punishing Germany—spoke of an economically strong Germany, but denazified and demilitarized, broken into several zones occupied by the victors, but not quite the impoverished pasture envisioned by Roosevelt. Stalin would need German steel and machine tools after the war, but he told Churchill he did not want to wake up one day to find German watchmakers producing rifles and German carmakers building tanks. Only active Allied control applied well into the future would keep Germany in line. Churchill proposed isolating Prussia and folding portions of Bavaria into the Danubian Federation that he had long envisioned. "We are the trustees for the peace of the world," Churchill offered. "If we fail there will be perhaps one hundred years of chaos." So wedded was he to the idea of his Danubian Federation that Churchill seems to have forgotten that the previous "Danubian federation"—the Austro-Hungarian Empire—had been torn asunder by the nationalist tendencies of its component parts, a cascading series of events that led to the Great War.[332]

Then, like two hungry guests at an inn where the kitchen had only one veal chop remaining, they fell upon Poland, specifically its postwar borders. Had Cordell Hull been in the room, he would have argued that any such questions be discussed only at the postwar peace conference, a policy that stemmed in part from Hull's distrust of the British, whom he presumed would try to reclaim all of the Empire's losses, if not more. Every military strategy the British proposed was parsed by Hull and the U.S. State Department (and many in the U.S. military) in terms of, what are the British really up to? Robert Sherwood later wrote, "The State Department was traditionally on the alert against any of its Foreign Service officers who displayed the slightest tendency to become pro-British." But Hull was in Washington. So complete was Hull's isolation that he did not see any transcripts of the Tehran discussions for more than nine months, when Anthony Eden, as a courtesy, briefed him. If Churchill was going to broach the subject of Polish borders with Stalin, now was the moment, with Roosevelt ill in bed and Hull in limbo.[333]

Churchill began by reminding Stalin that Britain had gone to war for Poland. But, he added, Britain was now fighting alongside Russia, and "nothing was more important than the security of the Russian western frontier." Churchill was a pragmatist; the subject had to be addressed before Russian troops overran Poland. Earlier in the day, Hopkins had told Eden that Americans were "terrified of the subject" of Polish borders, which Hopkins called "political dynamite." Large blocs of American voters of Polish, German, Lithuanian, and Ukrainian descent would be voting the following November, and any talk of Polish borders would unsettle them all. Eden stressed to Hopkins that if the matter wasn't addressed now, it would be worse in six months, with Russian armies in Poland and the American elections that much nearer. Those were Churchill's sentiments, but for the part about the American elections. He believed that Poland was "an instrument needed in the orchestra of Europe." It was not a card to be played in American elections.

So, with Stalin, over cigars and coffee, Churchill opened the door: "Are we to try," he asked, "to draw frontier lines?" Stalin replied, "Yes," and asked if it was to be done without Polish participation. "Yes," Churchill replied. Then, using wooden matches, Churchill demonstrated his idea of moving Poland westward, "like soldiers taking two steps 'left close.' If Poland trod on some German toes, that could not be helped." This pleased Stalin.[334]

Churchill was executing a nimble sidestep. Henceforth, the European war would be fought to restore freedoms, but not necessarily borders. The Atlantic Charter stipulated that "sovereign rights and self-government be restored to those who have forcibly been deprived of them" and "all the men in all the lands live out their lives in freedom from want and fear." The charter also contained the fuzzy pledge that after "the final destruction of Nazi tyranny" the subsequent peace must "afford to all nations the means of dwelling in safety within their own boundaries." But boundaries did not draw themselves, nor did they result from elections along strict ethnographic lines; otherwise, Eire would swallow Ulster, and Scotland might opt out of the United Kingdom. Boundaries were drawn by the strong, ideally with due consideration given to ethnographic and geographic realities. Indeed, the eastern Poles were far outnumbered by their Ukraine and Belarus neighbors. That entire swath of Poland, pried from Soviet Russia in the early 1920s, had been part of czarist Russia. Why would the Poles want to maintain dominion over the vast Pripet Marshes and the peoples there when German farmland and industry could be had with the stroke of a pen? Churchill told Stalin that if Germans in the western reaches of the new Poland chose to flee westward into the new Germany, so be it. The Poles could have it all, territory and liberty.

Churchill was setting a new course among numerous shoals. Poland was an ally; two Polish divisions were readying for deployment to Italy. Polish pilots had defended London. Poland was dying, its citizens butchered, its crops plundered to feed the Reich. Yet the Polish government in exile, in London, had not been elected, so, in fact, there was no real Polish government in exile, only Polish democrats biding their time before returning to Poland. Churchill would fight henceforth to restore their freedoms, but not their borders. As allies, the London Poles would of course be consulted in the matter, but they would not be allowed to unilaterally determine the borders of the Poland they might someday return to. German borders would be determined by the victors in order to protect Europe, and especially Poland, from Germany. And in deference to Stalin, Polish borders would be drawn to protect Russia's western frontier, necessarily at the expense of Poland. Before bidding Stalin good night, Churchill suggested that the three leaders—himself, Stalin, and Roosevelt—"form some sort of policy which we could recommend to the Poles, and advise them to accept."[335]

Before adjourning, Churchill offered his most favored caveat: "I have no power from Parliament...to define any border lines." Indeed, Churchill was reverential of his King, his cabinet, and Parliament, but this out afforded him safety and deniability. He knew that the last British prime minister to sit down with a European dictator to draw frontiers had helped precipitate this war.[336]

The next morning, when Churchill again suggested to Roosevelt that they meet for lunch before the plenary session, Roosevelt again refused. The second snub by Roosevelt fully alerted Churchill to the course change Roosevelt was steering in their relations. "The change came about," Sir Ian Jacob later wrote, "when the Americans felt they had developed enough power to conduct their own line of policy."

It showed the President in a new light. He [Roosevelt] was determined to break free from entanglement with Churchill and the British, and to meet Stalin without any prior consultation or agreement on a common line beforehand. Churchill was greatly disturbed by this development.... That the president should deal with Churchill and Stalin as if they were people of equal standing in American eyes shocked Churchill profoundly, and seemed to nullify all the patient work that he had done during the previous three years.

Roosevelt's execution of his strategy could generously be described as petty, mean-spirited, and conducted at his friend's expense. Roosevelt's behavior "shocked Churchill," but underlying his actions, Jacob wrote, was "a superficial" and "dangerous" understanding of Russia's "age-long goals in Eastern Europe."[337]

The image many Americans had of Russia was formed in part by the fawning praise of Russia spewed by Henry Luce and all but the most rabid anti-Roosevelt newspapers. *Time* had named Stalin its 1942 Man of the Year. Luce's saccharine salute to Stalin was purged of any reference to Stalin's purges. No mention was made of the *Holodomor*, the famine that resulted in the slow death by starvation of several million Ukrainians in the early 1930s. Rather, Stalin faced "immense disorderliness" and "the problems of providing enough food for the people," which he solved by "collectivizing the farms" and the introduction of "20th century industrial methods" to his "superstitious, illiterate people." Stalin and the Russians were heroes, and "have fought the best fight so far" against Hitler. No mention was made of England fighting alone for two years while Stalin was in league with Hitler. *Life* displayed acute myopia when it reported that Russians are "one hell of a people" who "think like Americans." The murderous secret police organization NKVD was described as "a national police force similar to the FBI." Americans who didn't read newspapers and magazines could take the measure of Mother Russia in one of the year's most popular films, *Mission to Moscow,* based on the memoirs of Joseph E. Davies, the former American ambassador to the Kremlin. One reviewer wrote that the film's "Russians look like fur-coated Americans, and the Soviet Union is pictured as a land of magnificent food and drink, as it probably was in the circles in which the Davieses moved.... Despite its Hollywood flourishes, *Mission to Moscow* has power.... But Franklin Roosevelt and Joe Davies are the ones mainly glorified. Of President Roosevelt, even the Russians speak in hushed, reverent tones." The movie might have had power, but it was Hollywood fantasy power, though it at least made a passing reference to Stalin's purges.[338]

Roosevelt had arrived in Tehran firm in his belief that his powers of charm and persuasion would carry the day, although his knowledge of European politics was thin and his knowledge of Russia thinner still. Sir Ian Jacob, describing Roosevelt, used almost the same phrases as did Averell Harriman and George Kennan: "He [Roosevelt] had no idea.... He seemed to imagine that he could handle Stalin." That he could not became apparent to Churchill as the three leaders worked their way through three more meetings and two dinners, which Cadogan called "woolly and bibulous." As for Roosevelt's performance, Cadogan wrote, "[The] President, in his amateurish way, has said a lot of indiscreet and awkward things."[339]

During their second private meeting, Roosevelt outlined to Stalin his concept of a postwar international organization that would be charged with keeping global peace. It would consist of a General Assembly composed of members of the alliance. Overseeing this assembly would be an executive committee consisting of the Soviet Union, the United States, the United Kingdom, and China. This committee would deal with nonmilitary matters such as food and health. Stalin (like Churchill) thought China a curious choice as the world's fourth "great" power, but he did not press the issue. Of the executive committee, Stalin asked, would its decisions be binding? Likely not, Roosevelt replied, as the U.S. Congress would never permit America to be bound by decisions made by such a body. The third branch of the organization would take the form of "The Four Policemen"—Russia, the United States, the United Kingdom, and China—and would be charged with keeping the peace, if necessary by bombing and invading aggressor nations. Stalin listened politely, then steered the discussion to the treatment of Germany. As he had told Churchill the previous evening, Germany, once defeated, must be forcibly kept from reinventing itself as a military power. Yet from what he had heard so far, Roosevelt's proposed international organization could not supply the safeguards that he, Stalin, thought necessary.[340]

No discussion took place about the possibility that one of the Four Policemen might be the aggressor of the future. As with all the talks at all the conferences, the press (never in attendance) were given only broad summaries after the fact. Roosevelt did not publicly unveil his blueprint for a world organization until late May of 1944.

After Roosevelt and Stalin finished their chat and before the start of the second formal session, Churchill, with anthems playing and honor guards standing at attention, presented Stalin with the Sword of Stalingrad, a gold and jewel-encrusted dagger offered as a gift from King George VI, "in token of the homage of the British people . . . to the steel-hearted citizens of Stalingrad." Stalin accepted the sword, and passed it on to Voroshilov, who proceeded to drop it out of its scabbard and onto his great toe. Despite Voroshilov's gaffe and the obvious discomfort of all present, Churchill later wrote that as the sword was carried out of the room by an honor guard, he spied Roosevelt sitting off to one side, "obviously stirred by the ceremony." In fact, Roosevelt found such displays of pompous imperial symbolism to be distasteful contrivances. The show meant much to Churchill, little to Roosevelt, and still less to Stalin. British historian Roy Jenkins later noted that Joseph Stalin was not about to accept a jeweled bauble as any sort of substitute for an assault on France.[341]

Stalin, with characteristic bluntness, said as much a few minutes later at the start of the second plenary session, when he came right at Roosevelt much as he had come right at Churchill during their second session in Moscow the previous year. "Who will command Overlord?" the marshal demanded. Roosevelt replied that the decision had not been made. Stalin replied that he could hardly take Overlord seriously until it had a commander, and by the same logic, until it had a commander, it would appear the Anglo-Americans were not taking it seriously. He insisted the commander be named within the week. A brief, uncomfortable silence followed. Roosevelt had no answer ready. Churchill then made a gallant attempt to defend the merits of action in Rhodes and Turkey. As for Overlord, he again stressed the conditions that had to be met in order to undertake the invasion, including that of the Germans having no more than twelve divisions in reserve in France on the day of the invasion. Where Churchill saw sound planning and contingencies, Stalin saw equivocation. He interrupted: "I wish to pose a very discreet question to the Prime Minister about Overlord....Do the Prime Minister and the British Chiefs really believe in Overlord?" Certainly, replied Churchill, given that the conditions as outlined were met. "When the time comes it will be our stern duty to hurl across the channel at the Germans every sinew of our strength." Given that Stalin and Roosevelt had already agreed upon the date, May 1, Churchill had no choice but to accept the inevitable. Hopkins had warned him that Roosevelt would come down on the side of Stalin, and he had.[342]

Brooke was livid. "After listening to the arguments put forward for the last two days," he told his diary, "I feel more like entering a lunatic asylum...than continuing with my present job." And as for the way his boss and Roosevelt had comported themselves in the meeting, "Winston was not good, and Roosevelt even worse." Stalin, alone but for Voroshilov at the table, and surrounded by twenty-six American and British luminaries, including Franklin Roosevelt and Winston Churchill, had taken control of the conference. In what John Keegan called "one of the most brutal contrivances of public embarrassment recorded in diplomatic history," Stalin had shamed Churchill into conceding his total commitment to Overlord, as well as the need to appoint a commander, and soon.[343]

Stalin hosted that night's dinner, due to start in just an hour. Churchill, while changing into his evening dress, had Sawyers summon Moran to treat his sore throat, which had lingered now for more than two weeks. Asked by Moran how the day's business had turned out, Churchill growled, "Nothing more can be done here." But he held out hope that something could be done with President İnönü and the Turks, whom he planned to meet in Cairo in a few days. With Turkey in, he told Moran, he could more reasonably argue the case for his Balkan strategy and perhaps a delay in Overlord. He would have developed the thought further, but Stalin awaited his arrival. Sawyers interposed, "You are late, sir." "Bloody," Churchill growled, and stomped out.[344]

Only the principals and their closest aides attended that night's feast—Hopkins, Molotov, Eden, Harriman, and Ambassador Clark Kerr. Sarah had not been invited, nor had Elliott Roosevelt. But he successfully crashed the affair by lingering just outside the door until Stalin waved him in. Stalin's banquets, as Churchill had learned in Moscow, were fueled by prodigious quantities of vodka and wine, and humor of Stalin's crude variety. The marshal needled Churchill relentlessly throughout the evening, Harriman recalled, and several times implied that Churchill, "nursing some secret affection for the Germans, wanted a soft peace." Roosevelt listened, smiled, but did not rise to Churchill's defense. Rather, the president delighted in Churchill's unease. Roosevelt "always enjoyed other people's discomfort," Harriman recalled. "It never bothered him much when other people were unhappy."[345]

Churchill did not rise to the bait until Stalin proposed to shoot at least 50,000 German officers after the surrender in order to ensure Germany's docility well into the future. "I would rather," Churchill replied, "be taken out to the garden here and now and be shot myself rather than sully my own and my country's honour by such infamy." Roosevelt then chimed in with a compromise; he suggested that only 49,000 officers be shot. Eden, meanwhile, was making desperate gestures in Churchill's direction intended to peg the whole scene as a joke. It might have ended there had not Elliott Roosevelt, by then drunk, wobbled to his feet and endorsed Stalin's plan, adding that he was sure the U.S. Army would support it.

At that Churchill walked out. He found himself alone in a semidarkened room. A few minutes passed; then he felt hands clasping his shoulders from behind. He turned to find Stalin and Molotov, each smiling broadly. They had "been playing," they assured Churchill, adding that "nothing of a serious kind had entered their heads." Stalin had a very captivating way about him when he chose, Churchill recalled, and this was his most captivating moment of all. Still, Churchill later wrote that he "was not then and am not now fully convinced that all was chaff and there was no serious intent lurking behind." He wrote those words long before the official documents regarding the Katyn massacre were released by HMG. The law forbade him to write what he knew, which was that Stalin and the Politburo were guilty of ordering the NKVD to murder the Polish officers in the Katyn forest. The obtuse reference to "no serious intent lurking" in Stalin's remarks was as close as he could get to the root of the matter. And of course, the law kept him from telling the world that Roosevelt, too, knew that Stalin had murdered the Poles. Churchill had sent Roosevelt the very precise and damning Foreign Office report on the matter. Stalin's joke, if he was joking, was crude but in character. Roosevelt's participation, given his knowledge of Katyn, was disgraceful.[346]

In Cairo, Roosevelt had taken to delivering seemingly good-natured jabs at Churchill during the cocktail hour or at dinner. "Winston," the president declared one evening, "you have four hundred years of acquisitive instinct in your English blood, and just don't understand why a country might not want to acquire land somewhere if they can get it." At Tehran, the ribbing took the form of bullying gibes uttered with forethought solely for the pleasure of Stalin, who joined with Roosevelt in the "teasing," as Roosevelt biographer Robert Sherwood termed it. It was a shabby display, perhaps to be expected from the coarse Stalin, but not from Churchill's genteel friend Franklin Roosevelt. As he had after demeaning de Gaulle at Casablanca, Roosevelt took delight in recounting to his cronies back home, including America's first female cabinet secretary, Secretary of Labor Frances Perkins, the humiliations he inflicted upon Churchill. "As soon as I sat down at the conference table, I began to tease Churchill about his Britishness, about John Bull, about his cigars, about his habits. It began to register with Stalin," who smiled, and then laughed aloud, as Roosevelt pressed on. Roosevelt said he had felt enough at ease to call Stalin Uncle Joe, which brought forth another guffaw from the marshal. "The ice was broken," Roosevelt told his cabinet, "and we talked like men and brothers." Alan Brooke termed Roosevelt's display a "betrayal." Years later, Lady Mary Soames offered, "The president's behavior hurt my father," but as with all tribulations that came Churchill's way, "it did not unman him."[347]

The next day, November 30, was Churchill's sixty-ninth birthday. Lord Moran expected to find his patient in "poor fettle" that morning, after the previous evening's sordid events, but Churchill had already dismissed the episode as if it were "only a bad dream." After breakfast he met privately with Stalin, where he argued the case for further actions in the Mediterranean before Overlord. Stalin did not buy it. Instead, he warned that if by May Anglo-American forces had not landed in France, "bad feeling" and an erosion in Russian resolve would result, for Russians were "war weary." Here again was Stalin playing his negotiated peace card.

During the third plenary session, as friendly as the previous night's dinner had not been, Roosevelt and Churchill pledged their absolute allegiance to Overlord. And they pledged their support of a warm-water port for the Soviet Union. The military decision on Overlord having been taken, Churchill could only promise to support and nurture the operation, although he reminded Stalin that landing craft, not British reluctance, would determine the issue. Having gotten what he came for, Stalin stressed secrecy and deception in planning the invasion; were the Germans to learn even the meanest of details, the Allied invasion forces and the Red Army would find themselves in extreme peril. The Germans had proven themselves quite adept at such subterfuge, Stalin admitted, at the expense of the Red Army. Churchill and Stalin agreed on the need for false radio messages, dummy tanks and planes and airfields, and covert cover plans. They stressed the need for covert radio traffic intended to confuse the Germans as to when the Anglo-American invasion and the Soviet summer offensive would be launched—simultaneously or sequentially—thus denying the Germans the option of shifting troops from one front to the other. And of course, disguising the "where" of both Allied offenses was paramount. "The truth is so precious," Churchill told Stalin, "that she should always be protected by a bodyguard of lies."[348]

The formal session adjourned on that note, and the principals and military chiefs wandered off to their lodgings to dress for dinner, which was to take place in the British legation, at Churchill's insistence. The children were invited, Elliott, Randolph, and Sarah, as were the leading diplomats. It was to be quite the affair, and why not, it was his birthday, after all, Churchill later wrote. As well, he was the oldest of the leaders. And in a barely disguised jab at his allies, he wrote, "We were by centuries the longest established of the three Governments; I might have added, but did not, that we had been the longest in the war."[349]

As the dinner hour approached, Stalin made his appearance, escorted by fifty Russian policemen who took up positions at the doors and windows. Roosevelt's Secret Service men shadowed the Russians. Inspector Thompson supplied Churchill's security. Thompson, when among Russians, liked to carry two guns under his jacket. Roosevelt brought along a birthday gift, a lovely Kashan bowl Harriman had purchased from a museum curator earlier that day after Roosevelt, realizing he had not thought to procure a gift for Churchill, had dispatched his ambassador to find something appropriate.[350]

The banqueting room in the British legation was done up in county house elegance—white linens, bone china, numerous candelabra casting a golden light over the scene. Portraits of British royals hung on the walls, which were inlayed with glass mosaics. Thick red draperies covered the windows. Persian waiters in red-and-blue livery and wearing white gloves tended to the needs of the assembled. Brooke noted that the waiters' gloves seemed too large, which resulted in the fingertips flapping when they handled the plates. A cake with sixty-nine candles sat in the middle of the table.[351]

Churchill announced that the meal would be conducted in the Russian style, with toasts encouraged, but with champagne instead of vodka. One of the first salutes raised was to Sarah, by Roosevelt. Churchill then proclaimed that the whole political world was now a matter of tints, and England's was getting pinker. Stalin replied, to much laughter, "A sign of good health." Roosevelt returned to the tint theme later in the evening when he announced that the effect of the war would be to "blend all those multitudinous tints, shades, and colors into one rainbow where their individuality would be lost in the whole." Brooke thought that a "fine idea." He had had a fine day, prevailing upon the Americans that the window for Overlord should be expanded to June 1 to allow for changes in circumstances, which had a habit of changing. By doing so, Brooke bought more time in the Mediterranean. The CIGS that night was, for a change, in a festive mood, a good thing, because the festivities continued into the new day. Churchill raised a glass to "Stalin the Great" and another to Roosevelt, in tribute to the president's "devotion to the cause of the weak and the helpless." And when Stalin raised a toast to Brooke, which in effect accused him of not liking Russians, Brooke responded by referring to Churchill's remarks earlier in the day regarding lies and deception. Then he raised his glass to Stalin, and asked, might "one's outward appearance deceive one's friends?" In fact, Brooke added, he felt only "friendship and comradeship" toward Stalin and the Red Army. Stalin liked that, and told Brooke that "some of the best friendships of this world were founded on misunderstandings."[352]

Toast followed toast; Churchill drank to the proletarian masses, Stalin to the Conservative Party. Then the marshal turned to Roosevelt and lifted his glass to America, without whose production of tanks and planes "the war may have been lost." This facile salute ignored the fact that for almost two deadly years, while America prepared for war and Stalin avoided war, Churchill and Britain alone had fought the war. Still, Churchill later wrote that he "went to bed tired but content, feeling sure that nothing but good had been done. It certainly was a happy birthday for me."[353]

The next afternoon, when Churchill and Stalin sat down to discuss Polish borders, they did so without Roosevelt's direct participation. The president explained at length to Stalin his domestic political difficulties, and announced that he could not take part in any such discussion for at least a year; nor could he be publicly associated with any arrangement arrived at. "This," Eden later wrote, with great understatement, "was hardly calculated to restrain the Russians." When Stalin sensed weakness, he struck.

Pressed by Churchill to outline his frontier demands, Stalin responded with anything but restraint. He "asked for the Curzon Line, with Lvov to go to the Soviet Union." The Curzon Line, proposed as Poland's eastern border by British foreign minister George Curzon in 1919, ran from the Baltic to the Czech border. But when Polish borders were finally established in the early 1920s, the frontier fell 150 miles east of the Curzon Line, in territory that had been part of czarist Russia. Stalin wanted that territory back. In many places the Curzon Line almost exactly overlay the Ribbentrop-Molotov Line of 1939, a happy coincidence for Stalin, who pointed out that the frontiers of 1939 were the most ethnographically correct. Eden and Churchill saw immediately where Stalin was going and asked if he was proposing the Ribbentrop-Molotov Line. "Call it what you will," replied Stalin.[354]

He indeed was proposing that the British in effect ratify the Ribbentrop-Molotov pact, but he couched his argument in terms of the British accepting a Polish frontier of their own invention. Churchill ordered a map produced, and pointed out differences between the two lines in the Baltic north and in the south, where Lvov fell on the Polish side. Stalin waved off the differences. He wanted the Polish border moved such that Lvov would end up on the Russian side. Churchill later wrote, "I was not prepared to make a great squawk about Lvov." In the north, Stalin sought Königsberg, which Churchill had no objection to. Königsberg going to the Russians would solve the problem of a year-round Baltic port. Churchill then suggested the new western Polish border follow the Oder River, which Stalin did not object to. However, the Oder flows from two tributaries, the Western Neisse and the Eastern Neisse. No one in the room thought to clarify which branch of the Neisse would define the new Polish border. Churchill concluded by telling Stalin, "The Poles would be wise to take our advice." But Eden began to doubt they would ever reach a settlement that the Poles would agree to. And he joined Churchill, Brooke, Ismay, and Cadogan in feelings of dismay and perplexity with the "American unwillingness to make ready with us for the conference in advance." "Above all," Eden later wrote, "I began to fear greatly for the Poles."[355]

The final piece of political business conducted in Tehran was an agreement in principle by the Big Three to the Curzon Line and the need to reward Poland with German territory. Roosevelt had sat in on but had not contributed to the discussion, but he joined his partners in endorsing the solution. He did not tell Cordell Hull of this, and indeed told the London Poles months later that he had not agreed to any such arrangement. But whether through a translator's indiscretion or Roosevelt's unwillingness to articulate his position for fear of domestic political repercussions, Stalin believed Roosevelt had agreed. Consequences accrued a year later.[356]

Stalin had come to Tehran seeking assurances on only two matters: Overlord and his western borders. He left Tehran with both. Roosevelt had arrived believing Stalin to be, in his own term, "getatable." The president left believing he had got at Stalin, although he told reporters that Stalin proved "tougher than he had expected." Robert Sherwood called the end of the Tehran Conference the "supreme peak of Roosevelt's career." Perhaps, but Roosevelt had paved his chosen path to Stalin's good graces over his friendship with Churchill. Alec Cadogan concluded that Churchill's lack of guile was as vital to the alliance as was Roosevelt's wit and homespun charm. Churchill was as he appeared; Franklin Roosevelt was not. Cadogan believed Churchill "has very few reticences; U.J. is shrewd enough to spot that, and must, I think, have satisfied himself that he was reading an open book, that there was no concealment or duplicity, and he could have faith."[357]

Stalin indeed thought he was reading an open book, but the conclusions he took from it were not at all those Cadogan had in mind. Four months later, Stalin regaled Milovan Djilas, Tito's third in command, with stories of the Tehran Conference. Djilas, in Moscow as head of a Yugoslavian diplomatic mission, arrived at the Kremlin at about the same time Randolph Churchill and his mission arrived at Tito's headquarters. "Perhaps you think," Stalin told Djilas, "that just because we are allies of the English we have forgotten who they are, and who Churchill is. They find nothing sweeter than to trick their allies.... And Churchill? Churchill is the kind who, if you don't watch him, will slip a kopeck out of your pocket. Yes, a kopeck out of your pocket. By God.... And Roosevelt? Roosevelt is not like that. He dips in his hands only for bigger coins. But Churchill? Churchill—even for a kopeck." At a later meeting, even the wooden Molotov displayed a stunted sense of humor when he recounted a toast Stalin had made to Churchill, a salute to the importance of secrecy in the coming invasion. But the toast, Molotov allowed, was actually a backhanded slap at Churchill's 1915 gambit in the Dardanelles, where the "failure occurred because the British lacked sufficient information." The irony escaped Churchill who, Molotov said, had been "in his cups." Djilas concluded that "Churchill had left a deep impression on the Soviet leaders as a farsighted and dangerous 'bourgeois statesman'—though they did not like him." Nor did they have faith in him. Cadogan had it backwards.[358]

Of Tehran Churchill later wrote: "On my right sat the President of the United States, on my left the master of Russia. Together we controlled practically all the naval and three-quarters of all the air forces in the world, and could direct armies of nearly twenty million men, engaged in the most terrible of wars that had yet occurred in human history." Yet Churchill understood that the United States and the U.S.S.R. accounted for the vast majority of that awesome power. With an American soon to command the largest of the Western armies and Stalin in command of the Eastern, Churchill's influence over the management of the war could only diminish. Churchill had arrived in Persia secure in his nineteenth-century belief in England's imperial destiny; he left having learned a cold lesson. He now had no choice but to regard the status of his small island nation from a mid-twentieth-century vantage point, and it was one of declining geopolitical might. He had always been good at adapting to changing conditions, political or military, but this was different: the sun was setting on an entire era.[359]

The magnitude of the shift in power taking place was captured in an offhand remark made to reporters a few weeks after Tehran by Harold L. Ickes, the American secretary of the interior. It had nothing to do with Polish borders or the autonomy of Greece or France, or the fate of Germany, or the restoration of continental monarchs. It had to do with the resource that powered the great powers, a commodity Britain had monopolized and taken for granted for almost a quarter century. "Tell me the sort of agreement that the United Nations will reach with respect to the world's petroleum reserves when the war is over," Ickes proclaimed, "and I will undertake to analyze the durability of the peace that is to come." This cautionary note stemmed from the fact that America, which produced 95 percent of Allied aviation gas (from its domestic oil supply), was, according to Ickes, "on the verge of becoming a net importer of oil." Of the current oil production in the Middle East, America controlled about 15 percent, Britain 85 percent. That, America could not abide. The war was being fought in Europe and the Pacific, but the spoils would be found in the Middle East. Of the future, *Time* reported, "the oil-conscious British are fearful."[360]

Churchill later told his old friend Violet Bonham Carter, "I realized at Tehran for the first time, what a small nation we are. There I sat with the great Russian bear on one side of me, with paws outstretched, and on the other side the great American buffalo, and between the two sat the poor little English donkey who was the only one, the only one of the three, who knew the right way home."[361]

Despite a growing awareness of his diminishing role within the alliance, Churchill departed Tehran fully intending to find the right way home. As always, the path led through the Mediterranean.

5

Pilot

On December 1, the day they departed Tehran, Churchill, Stalin, and Roosevelt put their signatures to a statement of intent. Issued to the world on December 6, it became known as the Tehran Declaration. In it the three leaders pledged: "No power on earth can prevent our destroying the German armies by land, their U-boats by sea, and their war plants from the air. Our attack will be relentless and increasing." Reuters called it a "death sentence for the Axis." No mention was made of dividing Germany into four, five, six or more demilitarized duchies, or of reparations; no call was made for Germans to throw off their Nazi leaders to avoid annihilation. The Big Three pledged their "determination that our nations shall work together in war and in the peace that will follow." The declaration included the remarkable line, "We look with confidence to the day when all peoples of the world may live free lives, untouched by tyranny.... We leave here, friends in fact, in spirit and in purpose." Harriman later wrote that the declaration "was an astonishing statement for Stalin to have signed.... His ideas of tyranny were quite different from ours. Tyranny, for him, did not exist in the Soviet Union." Rather, tyranny for Stalin "was capitalism exploiting the downtrodden." Churchill, in his memoirs, explained that he and Roosevelt could see no decent alternative: "It would not have been right at Tehran for the Western democracies to found their plans upon suspicions of the Russian attitude in the hour of triumph and when all her dangers were removed."[1]

That is a generous enough sentiment, but after Tehran—and for the duration of the war—Churchill pondered ways to check the Soviets in the event Stalin abrogated agreements made in good faith. Roosevelt, meanwhile, began to voice his intent to avoid postwar European entanglements. Indeed, in an early February telegram, the president told Churchill what he had told Harriman in mid-1943: other than maintaining a zone of occupation in Germany, American troops would be coming home after victory. "I am absolutely unwilling to police France and possibly Italy and the Balkans as well," Roosevelt wrote, adding, "after all France is your baby and will take a lot of nursing in order to bring it to the point of walking alone."[2]

Even before the secret talks in Tehran had finished, Stalin made public his demand that several million German laborers and all German industry be shipped to Russia after victory in lieu of 1.6 billion gold marks in repa-rations, demands that led Goebbels to snort to his diary, "We would rather defend the last remnants of our walls than to accede to such a demand." The English, wrote the little doctor, "would like to use this occasion to sell out the entire German future." Actually, it was Roosevelt and Stalin who led the charge to do so, although Churchill's post-dinner comments to Sta-lin certainly indicate that he now endorsed the harshest possible treatment of Germany.[3]

Then Goebbels expressed a prescient thought: "Nobody in England seems to recognize that once the Soviet Union is in Europe, it will be a much more dangerous opponent of the British Empire." Churchill's pro-posal to cede eastern Germany to the Poles in exchange for Stalin getting eastern Poland had been leaked to and reported by the yellow press in Lon-don. "I can hardly imagine that the leading English statesmen are so stupid and shortsighted," wrote Goebbels, "as to put that sort of an estimate on Bolshevism. Stalin won't think of fulfilling obligations entered upon with England and America." At least one old Englishman was not so stupid and shortsighted.

While the Big Three had been laying plans in Tehran, Jan Smuts deliv-ered a speech in London that Goebbels thought "sensational." Smuts pre-dicted that following the erasure of the Reich from the map ("nothing new," wrote Goebbels), the "Russian colossus would dominate the entire European Continent. England would come out of this war with honor and glory but poor as a beggar. The United States would in large measure be the heir to the British Empire." Why, Goebbels asked himself, would the British pursue such a ruinous policy? He was truly befuddled. Every Allied bomb that fell on Berlin reminded Goebbels and Hitler—indeed, all Ger-mans—that their English and American cousins considered the sins of the Reich to be far more egregious than the sins of Stalin and his Asian Bolshe-vik hordes. Goebbels and Hitler could not understand how this could be and (until their final moments on earth) remained hopeful that England and America would see the light.[4]

On December 2, two tired old men along with their military chiefs and aides arrived back in Cairo to resume their talks. Three days later Roo-sevelt and Churchill signed a statement of purpose. Foremost, nothing would be allowed to interfere with Overlord. Churchill offered that he was committed to the operation "up to the hilt." Likewise, nothing would be allowed to interfere with Anvil, the curtain-raiser for Overlord in southern France. Yet in Tehran, Brooke and Churchill had gained the vital endorse-ment that they should reassess Anvil in the spring, based on the availability of landing craft. Anvil, as Churchill saw it, was not written in stone. Dur-ing their talks, to Churchill's great relief, Roosevelt agreed to kill Buccaneer, the operation in Burma that Roosevelt had promised Chiang. It died in part because Mountbatten had demanded 50,000 troops for the task when Churchill expected a request for 15,000. As well, and as usual, no landing craft could be spared for the adventure. Mountbatten would have to make do with what he had for the foreseeable future. Finally, Churchill and Roosevelt agreed that nothing would interfere with operations in the eastern Mediterranean, *if* Turkey entered the war. In pursuit of that objective, President İnönü and the Turks arrived for three days of talks, during which neither Roosevelt nor Churchill could move them into the Allied camp. İnönü "pleaded his country's unpreparedness" but "expressed his readiness 'in principle' to come into the war." The most the Turks would accede to was use of their airfields by Allied airmen. General Marshall was well satisfied with that; he feared Turkey's entry on the Allied side would "burn up our logistics right down the line." Weeks later Jock Colville found Churchill smoking a Turkish cigarette, the first time Colville had seen the P.M. indulge that habit. Churchill, holding the cigarette aloft, declared, "They were the only thing [I] ever got out of the Turks."[5]

Churchill also took up the problems of Yugoslavia and Greece. In each country a civil war was being fought between Communist and non-Communist partisans. All sides in each conflict were being armed by Britain. In both countries the Communists fielded the more powerful force, Tito in Yugoslavia, and the ELAS in Greece. In late November Tito set up a provisional government in Bosnia; one of its first acts was to forbid King Peter to return to Yugoslavia. Churchill and Eden, concluding that Tito's partisans would rule Yugoslavia once the Germans were expelled, believed King Peter's only hope for a role in future Yugoslavian affairs was to repudiate Draja Mihailovic and his Serbian Chetniks, who were colluding with the Germans in the fight against Tito. But the Chetniks were also working closely with the Americans and harbored dozens of American airmen—hundreds by summer—shot down during raids on Romanian oil fields. It was a dicey situation. Churchill, with his man in Yugoslavia, Bill Deakin, acting as intermediary, began negotiations with Tito. In coming weeks the Old Man offered significant military assistance in return for Tito's keeping an open mind on the subject of a working accommodation between himself and King Peter. Churchill was offering a great deal with no guarantees in return.[6]

The situation in Greece, Cadogan wrote, "bore unpleasant similarities to that of Yugoslavia." All the Greek partisans despised King George of the Hellenes. Here, in obverse of their treatment of Tito, Churchill and Eden decided to cease aiding and arming the Greek Communists. That alone would not help King George, because the non-Communist EDES loathed him as much as did the ELAS. The solution, Churchill concluded, was to persuade the king to agree to not return to Greece until and unless asked to do so by the electoral choice of the Greek people. As with King Peter, compromise was King George's only hope; his best chance for seeing a royal government installed under Prime Minister Georgios Papandreou was to stay out of Greece and above the fray. Eden brought the reluctant king around during two days of long talks. Then to Eden's disbelief, Franklin Roosevelt wandered onto the scene and told King George to stick to his guns and to not make any declaration. The president's intervention, Eden later wrote, was "irresponsible," more so because Eden had briefed Winant and Hopkins on the British policy. But they had failed, in turn, to brief Roosevelt. King George, convinced that "the British now wanted to get rid of him," took Roosevelt's advice to heart and refused to give the public pledges Churchill had demanded. The Greek civil war continued until an uncertain cease-fire was patched up in February.[7]

Jock Colville later wrote, "It would be hard to find two worse advertisements for hereditary monarchy than George of Greece and Peter of Yugoslavia."[8]

On December 4, Roosevelt, in one of the most difficult and most momentous decisions of his presidency, chose Dwight Eisenhower to command Overlord. Roosevelt informed Churchill, who told Brooke over dinner, but Marshall did not learn of the decision until the next day, when Roosevelt summoned his Army Chief of Staff and told him, "I feel like I could not sleep with you out of the country." Marshall, disappointed but as always dutiful, immediately sent a radiogram to Eisenhower, but the wording in the cable was so garbled that Eisenhower "was unable to deduce his [Marshall's] meaning with certainty." Eisenhower knew only that the president would be arriving in Tunis late on the seventh or early on the eighth. In his memoirs he wrote, "There can be little doubt that the President felt that the command only of 'Overlord' was not sufficient to justify General Marshall's departure from Washington." Churchill saw the appointment of Eisenhower as validation of his belief that Overlord was to be but one operation among many, and not necessarily the biggest or most critical. Overlord, so far, was just a name on a piece of paper. In fact, during December, both Churchill and Eisenhower directed their efforts toward Italy, where a real battle with real consequences was being fought.[9]

On December 5, Roosevelt drafted and Churchill initialed a memorandum to Chiang outlining the decisions made in Tehran. There was no mention of Stalin's promise to join the Pacific campaign once Germany was defeated (it was thought security at Chiang's headquarters was far too lax for such news to be divulged). One line in the memo underscores Roosevelt's state of mind: "Conference with Stalin involves us in combined operations on European continent in late spring giving fair prospect of *ter-*

minating war with Germany by the late summer of 1944" (italics added). Throughout the coming year, such optimism infected the thinking of many Allied military and political leaders. Churchill harbored no such illusions.

General Spaatz and Bomber Harris were two of the leading optimists. They believed that if enough bombers were sent often enough, Germany would be reduced to rubble, its people rendered incapable of resistance. They believed that Germany might crack by March, certainly by midyear, because the RAF and Eighth Air Force were erasing German cities and their inhabitants from the landscape. In late November, the *Daily Mirror* crowed: RAF WENT OUT AGAIN; KNOCKOUT ASSAULT STARTS. In December, the *Daily Express* proclaimed that airpower meant "no more Passchendaeles."[10]

The optimism was also fed by the Russian winter offensive, which began the first week of December when the Red Army struck westward in the Kiev sector along a front that stretched from the Pripet Marshes south to the Black Sea. In the southern Ukraine, the Germans fell back toward the Bug River. Just 150 miles beyond lay the Prut River and Bessarabia, a former czarist dominion in eastern Romania. Within weeks an entire German army in the Crimea found itself bypassed by the Russians, and cut off. In mid-January, the Red Army struck in the Leningrad sector, relieving that city on January 27 after almost three years under siege. The Soviets then turned west, and drove the Germans back to the Estonian frontier. The overall length of the Russian front remained the same, close to 1,200 miles, but as German manpower shrank, defense of the front became more difficult. The Russian strategy, wrote Liddell Hart, "provided the clearest possible demonstration of the decisive importance of the ratio between space and force." The Russians "could live where any Western army would have starved." The Red Army "rolled on like a flood, or a nomadic horde." A German officer wrote, "The advance of a Red Army is something Westerners can't imagine. Behind the tank spearheads rolls a vast horde, largely mounted on horses. The soldier carries a sack on his back, with dry crusts of bread and raw vegetables collected on the march.... The Russians are accustomed to carry on for as long as three weeks in this primitive way, when advancing." But in German troops "weakness and wide spaces produced a feeling of helplessness." Stalin intended to exploit those feelings until he reached Berlin.[11]

The Russian army was not the only Allied force on the march in early December. On the second, Mark Clark and the Fifth Army struck out toward Monte Camino, with Monte Cassino its final objective. Clark was on his way to Rome. Some at Eisenhower's headquarters thought he'd be there by New Year's. All, including Eisenhower, were bucked up by Clark's near-term prospects. Two days after Roosevelt told him that his appointment as supreme commander would become effective January 1, the president asked Eisenhower if he'd prefer the official announcement be delayed "until Rome is captured." Eisenhower's press aide, Commander Butcher, thought that a fine idea because "since [Ike's new command] isn't effective until January 1, we might get Rome by then, which would make the transition perfect." But between December 8 and Christmas Day, German reinforcements and terrible weather stalled Clark's advance. He did not get to Rome by January 1. By then, Eisenhower was on his way to a two-week leave in the United States, and the Fifth Army was stalled in mud and freezing rain, within sight of its objective, Monte Cassino. By then, Churchill was plotting a new way of getting to Rome.[12]

A few weeks before the Cairo Conference, Eisenhower and Montgomery had made a five-pound bet (even odds) on whether Germany would fall by Christmas 1944. Ike bet yes, Monty no (Montgomery recorded his bets in a ledger). General Freyberg bet Monty ten pounds that the war against Germany would be over by October 31, 1944. Admiral Bertram Ramsay, who had planned the naval operations for Torch and Husky, bet an even fiver that the war would be over by January 1, 1945. Over dinner in Cairo on December 7 — Roosevelt had flown that day to Tunis — Churchill polled Smuts, Eden, and most of the military chiefs as to their opinions of when the war with Germany would end. Admiral King — "consumed more than a bottle of champagne... and was showing wear" — predicted sometime between March and November 1944. Marshall agreed. Brooke gave six-to-four odds on March. Dill gave even odds. All the military men — Portal, Cunningham, Hap Arnold, Major Leslie Hollis — put their money on sometime between March and November. Churchill, Eden, and Smuts were not so sanguine. Churchill later wrote that he "was struck by the optimism. The idea was rooted that Hitler would not be strong enough to face the spring campaign, and might collapse even before Overlord was launched."[13]

Eisenhower, in his memoir *Crusade in Europe,* wrote that Churchill and the British hoped the Italian campaign "might lead to an unexpected [German] break that would make the Channel operation either unnecessary or nothing more than a mopping-up affair" to be conducted only when "the Allies could go in easily and safely." Yet the votes of the American chiefs at the dinner indicate that it was *they* who thought that way. Churchill had pledged in Tehran that Overlord would take place in May; he knew it would be both a difficult and bloody affair. After seeing the initial plans for the invasion the previous August, he advised that more men go ashore. Otherwise, he feared a repulse on the beach. He never saw it as a mopping-up affair. Eisenhower by December had taken only a cursory look at the plans for Overlord. On his way to Washington, he told reporters, "We will win the European war in 1944."[14]

Other prognosticators had already seen their predictions go belly-up.

Admiral William ("Bull") Halsey, commander in chief of U.S. Navy South Pacific forces, had stated with confidence months earlier that 1943 would bring "complete, absolute defeat for the Axis." Halsey no longer engaged in such speculation, telling reporters, "I refuse to gaze into the crystal ball anymore.... Only God knows."[15]

By December 9, unable to shake the sore throat and cold that had dogged him since he left London, Churchill felt he was on the cusp of a physical breakdown. Smuts thought the Old Man had "exhausted himself, and then had to rely on drink to stimulate [himself] again." The South African began to doubt whether Churchill could stay the course. At lunch that day, Churchill admitted to Brooke that he felt tired, flat, "and had pains in his loins." His degree of fatigue was evidenced by the fact the he had lost his appetite and hardly spoke. Between small spoonfuls of soup he swatted flies with a fly whisk and counted the corpses. He could summon only enough energy to pronounce the soup "*dee*-licious" while sending more flies to the mortuary. Brooke wondered how near Churchill was "to a crash." Churchill wondered the same. He later wrote that he found himself so tired that he no longer dried himself after his bath, but lay on the bed wrapped in a towel.[16]

Shortly after midnight on December 11, Churchill and his party left Cairo in their Avro York, bound for Tunis to pay a courtesy call on Eisenhower. Churchill intended to fly on to Italy from there, to buck up Alexander, whose armies were being ground down by the enemy, by the terrain, by the worst winter weather in years, and by an outbreak of typhus. Lice and malaria were the common enemy for both armies.

At daybreak Churchill's plane landed at an airfield outside Tunis. The place appeared abandoned. No guards were in evidence; no cars waited. Churchill's pilot had brought them down to the wrong field. The prime minister hauled himself and his official boxes out of the York and sat down on the edge of the runway. There he waited, recalled Brooke, "in a very cold morning wind like nothing on earth." A steel-cold mist blew out of the north. Moran pressed Churchill to get himself back inside the heated plane. He refused. He remained perched upon his boxes, a very long way from home. He wore a scowl on his face, which shone now with perspiration. "He seemed to be going from bad to worse," Moran wrote. When the mix-up was sorted out, the party reboarded the York and made for the right airfield. By then Churchill had gone gray in the face, to Moran's professional discomfort. After arriving finally at Eisenhower's headquarters near Carthage, Churchill slumped into a chair, where he remained for the rest of the day, too weak even to read his telegrams.[17]

Moran by then was sick with worry. His patient spiked a temperature of 102; he was exhausted, mentally and physically. His lungs were seriously congested. Here was a combination of blows even the Old Man might not survive. He was indeed an elderly man, having just begun the final year of his biblical three score years and ten. Moran believed with medical certainty that Churchill would probably not make it to the next year. The prime minister needed the best that medicine offered, but other than sulfa drugs and serums, mid-twentieth-century medicine did not offer much hope for an elderly man. Moran lacked the equipment and facilities to make a proper diagnosis. Of particular concern was the possibility that Churchill had contracted a virulent strain of influenza that was making its way around the world. In Germany it was called *Kellergrippe* (cellar flu), and it killed 2,000 Berliners that week. Britain reported 1,148 deaths for the week. When Goebbels learned that King George had taken ill, he gushed to his diary, "How wonderful if the epidemic were to prove fatal!"[18]

Moran had a very sick man on his hands. A standing joke among Churchill's private secretaries held that if the Old Man became suddenly ill, the secretary on duty was to summon Lord Moran, who would then summon a real doctor. Moran proceeded to do just that, requesting that a pathologist, Dr. Robert Pulvertaft, and two nurses be flown out from Cairo, and that an X-ray technician and his machine be sent from Algiers, along with a supply of digitalis, lest Churchill's heart act up. A heart specialist, Dr. D. E. Bedford, was also summoned from Cairo. During the afternoon of December 13, the X-ray was duly taken. It showed a shadow on Churchill's lung. "Do you mean I've got pneumonia again?" he demanded of Moran. Moran prescribed treatment with M&B (so called after the British company that made it, May and Baker), a sulfonamide early antibiotic. The next day, Moran found Churchill "breathless and anxious looking." His pulse was racing and irregular; he was suffering from cardiac fibrillation. "My heart is doing something funny," Churchill said. When it worsened, he pleaded, "Can't you do anything to stop this?" Moran gave him a dose of digitalis and promised it would soon take effect. It did, but not for four hours, during which time Moran, holding Churchill's hand and monitoring his pulse, realized "that we were at last right up against things."[19]

"No signs of improvement yet," Moran wrote in his diary on December 15. That day, Pilot Officer John Colville received an urgent summons to report to No. 10 Downing Street in uniform. There he was told that the prime minister was "seriously, perhaps fatally, ill with pneumonia at Carthage." Colville's orders were to escort Mrs. Churchill to Tunis at once in order for her to be at her husband's bedside. A twin-engine Dakota was waiting for them at Lyneham airfield, but Beaverbrook insisted the party wait until he could procure a four-engine B-24 Liberator. Twenty hours later, Clementine, Colville, and Grace Hamblin, serving as Mrs. Churchill's secretary and orderly, boarded an unheated, blacked-out Liberator, and were soon Africa bound. The overnight flight to Gibraltar lasted nine hours, and from there, after a brief stopover, they continued on to Tunis, another six hours in the air, during which time they were cut off from any news. They could only speculate on the Old Man's condition, and from Clementine's somber demeanor, that was just what she was doing. Colville and Grace passed the hours sipping coffee and quietly chatting, in order to keep an eye on Mrs. Churchill, who "could not sleep and was rather alarmed."[20]

Hustled from the airfield at first light by Eisenhower's staff, the party arrived outside Churchill's villa, where inside Churchill lay in bed, barely stirring and somewhat disoriented, having realized Sarah was absent from the chair where she had been keeping a vigil. A moment later, Sarah escorted Clementine into the room; Churchill had not been told of her arrival and could have been excused if he thought he was delirious at the sight of an apparition. Colville entered a few minutes later, expecting to find a "recumbent invalid." Instead he beheld "a cheerful figure with large cigar and a whisky and soda in his hand." The crisis had passed.[21]

Colville rejoined Churchill's staff that week, and but for a brief interlude that summer when he was granted leave for RAF duty, he remained in the private secretariat until the end of the war.

Eisenhower's appointment as commander of Overlord (not yet made public) resulted in a shake-up of commands throughout Allied ranks. Air Chief Marshal Tedder would serve as Ike's deputy, with authority over all air forces, strategic and tactical. Admiral Bertram Ramsay was given command of Overlord naval operations, including the landings, code-named Neptune. Churchill wanted Eisenhower's chief of staff Bedell ("Beetle") Smith, who got along well with the British, to remain in the Mediterranean, but Ike took Smith to London. Within weeks, Eisenhower insisted upon and was granted complete control of all Allied air forces, tactical and strategic. Air Chief Marshal Trafford Leigh-Mallory, of Fighter Command, went in as Eisenhower's air commander in chief, with control of all tactical air forces. Bernard Montgomery was to leave the Eighth Army at the end of the month to command Twenty-first Army Group, the designation for the Allied troops in Britain dedicated to Overlord. In that capacity Montgomery would command all Overlord ground forces during the initial stage of the invasion. Churchill (and Eisenhower) preferred Alexander in that role, but the War Cabinet insisted upon the hero of El Alamein. Churchill acceded peacefully, in the belief that Alexander would emerge as the hero of Italy, where glory would accrue with the capture of Rome and the pursuit of the enemy all the way to Vienna. Henry Maitland ("Jumbo") Wilson, Middle East commander in chief, was raised to supreme commander Mediterranean. Brooke remained as CIGS and with Churchill's sponsorship was promoted to field marshal. Portal was elevated to air chief marshal. By Christmas, many of the appointees were on their way to London to take up their new posts. Jumbo Wilson, not yet familiar with the central and western Mediterranean, could not immediately bring anything to bear in that theater, where the command shake-up had created a power vacuum. Churchill, alone at Tunis with time on his hands and frustrated by the stasis in Italy, decided to fill it himself.

On Christmas Eve, Franklin Roosevelt announced in a radio broadcast the appointment of Dwight Eisenhower as supreme commander Allied Expeditionary Force. Henceforth, wherever General Ike put his headquarters would be known as SHAEF, Supreme Headquarters Allied Expeditionary Force. The president also asked Americans to pray for Churchill, ill in North Africa. Roosevelt and Eisenhower were religious men. The president told Harriman after Tehran that he believed the Russians "as deeply religious people were bound to stand up against the atheist ideology of Soviet communism and its repressions," a naive sentiment that presumed that whoever stood up against Stalin would not be scythed down. In the spring, Roosevelt would write a prayer for the soldiers going ashore in Normandy; it ran on the front page of the *New York Times* on June 7. Churchill didn't write prayers, and he didn't say prayers. Eisenhower, who believed the God of Justice was on the Allied side, once told Lord Moran, "Freedom itself means nothing unless there is faith." Bernard Montgomery claimed his chaplains were more important than his artillery. General Alexander, too, was a man of abiding faith, as was Jan Smuts, who kept his Greek Testament close at hand and examined every decision under the lens of Christian doctrine. Over dinner one night, Smuts admonished Churchill, "Gandhi... is a man of god. You and I are mundane people. Gandhi has appealed to religious motives. You never have. That is where you have failed."[22]

In fact, Churchill believed that was where he had succeeded. On Christmas Day, the Coldstream Guards hosted a church service in an old corrugated-steel warehouse that the army was using to store ammunition. Although feeling well enough to attend the service, Churchill, per his habit, chose not to. Instead, he prepared to discuss the Italian campaign with Eisenhower, who was due to arrive before noon. Clementine attended the service, along with Sarah, Colville, General Alexander, and Moran. As the padre intoned the Gloria in Excelsis, the bells of a nearby church rang out, and a white dove, which had been roosting in the rafters of the warehouse, "fluttered down in front of the congregation." After the service, when Clementine told Winston of the dove, he dismissed the episode as a conjuring by the minister who, he said, most likely released the bird from under his surplice. When Alexander, who believed the mysteries of this life would be revealed in the next, told Churchill of the message from above delivered on the wings of a dove, Churchill huffed, "There is nothing in such stuff."[23]

The remark surprised no one. He regularly reminded those around him that he had declared for agnosticism early in manhood. He had so informed his mother, Jennie, in letters home from India. He informed the world at large in his autobiography, *My Early Life,* where he wrote that while in India he passed through "a violent and aggressive anti-religious phase," which in turn led to an embrace of good old-fashioned British empiricism. He soon realized under fire in combat that a dash of faith offered some comfort. The result was typical Churchill: "I therefore adapted quite early in life a system of believing whatever I wanted to believe." His meager relationship with God was neither reverential nor deferential, but one that reflected Stanley Baldwin's political philosophy: "Never complain and never explain." He did not begin his speeches with pleas to the Almighty for guidance, nor did he end them with supplications for divine blessing. He did not ask Providence for the strength or wisdom to win the war. He told Britons, "As long as we have faith in our cause and unconquerable will power, salvation will not be denied us."

Late one evening in Tehran, he told Stalin, "I believe God is on our side. At least I have done my best to make Him a faithful ally." Stalin grinned, and replied, "And the devil is on my side. Because, of course, everyone knows the devil is a Communist and God, no doubt, is a good Conservative." That was Churchill playing the straight man to Stalin. He did so again when (as told by Jan Smuts) he suggested the pope might play some role in securing the peace. "The Pope," Stalin replied thoughtfully, "the Pope. How many divisions has he?" Stalin, Churchill noted with irony, seemed to bring up God quite frequently in conversation.[24]

Churchill did not.

Churchill's scant theological leanings tended to incline toward Spinoza's hands-off deity: God helps those who help themselves. Providence may have put him—and Cromwell, Marlborough, Pitt, and Nelson—on earth, but Providence disclosed no plan for success, and offered no guidance or revelation. Churchill guided himself.

Thus, while his wife and daughter and colleagues beheld the white Christmas dove and were moved to quiet contemplation and wonder, Churchill, in bed with his dispatch boxes, cigars, and whisky, found guidance in his maps and plotted the course of his armies. The agreed-upon date for Overlord was just four months away. Eisenhower was due to arrive at any moment to discuss operations in Italy, including putting an invasion force ashore south of Rome, at Anzio, a gambit that Churchill believed would open the road to Rome.

Churchill had awaked from his fever one day at Carthage to find Sarah sitting at the bedside. She had been reading *Pride and Prejudice* aloud to him, even as he slept. "Don't worry," he told her. "It doesn't matter if I die now, the plans of victory have been laid, it is only a matter of time."[25]

Yet by Christmas Day, it had become obvious to Churchill that not enough plans had been laid. The Fifth Army, slogging toward the Liri Valley, had gained less than ten miles in almost three weeks. It would certainly not be in Rome by New Year's. The recollections of Eisenhower and Churchill part company at this point. Eisenhower fails to mention in his memoir the optimism at his headquarters in early December, when he thought a delay until January 1 of the announcement of his elevation to supreme commander was a grand idea, since by then the Allies might be in Rome. Churchill, in his history of the war, writes that the deadlock in Italy "led General Eisenhower to yearn for an amphibious flanking attack." Strictly speaking, if to hope is to yearn, Eisenhower yearned for such an operation. But by Christmas he considered it beyond reach and believed that to attempt it would be overreaching, with possible catastrophic consequences. A plan for such an operation, code-named Shingle, had been on the books for two months. By Christmas, Churchill considered it absolutely critical to Allied success.[26]

Eisenhower described Shingle as an "end run" around Kesselring's flanks. Churchill, unfamiliar with the American football term, asked what the expression meant. In English parlance it was a "cat-claw." In boxing terms, it was a left hook delivered in conjunction with an uppercut by the Fifth Army at the Rapido River near its confluence with the Liri. Then, if all went well, Fifth Army would take Monte Cassino and strike up the Liri Valley to join hands within the week with the Shingle force. Then, with Kesselring's forces presumably in disarray, the Fifth Army would march the final thirty-five miles to Rome, while the Eighth Army, on the Adriatic side of the Apennines, executed a sweeping left turn in the same direction. Eisenhower saw great risk in the Anzio operation, and he warned Churchill. He voiced his fear of "the hazard of annihilation to the landing force if Fifth Army should be unable to reach it by land." He further feared that without resupply by the landing ships soon departing the Mediterranean for Britain and Overlord, the Anzio beachhead would remain exposed. It was one

Churchill in his siren suit with Eisenhower, May 1944. (*NARA*)

Churchill and Brooke on their way to Normandy aboard a Royal Navy destroyer, June 12, 1944. (*NARA*)

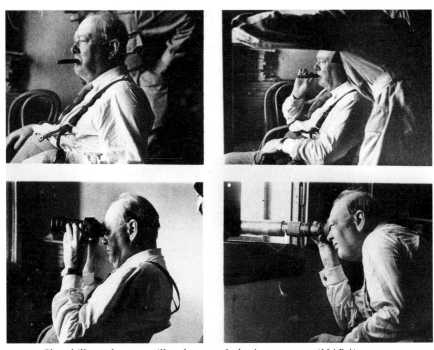

Churchill watches an artillery barrage, Italy, August 1944. (*NARA*)

Churchill receives a bouquet of flowers from a little girl in Italy, August 1944. (*NARA*)

Churchill and de Gaulle lay a wreath at the Tomb of the Unknown Soldier, Paris, November 11, 1944. (*NARA*)

Left to right: Brooke, Churchill, Montgomery, and General William Simpson crossing the Rhine, winter 1945. (*NARA*)

Churchill scribbles a message to Hitler on a British artillery shell at the Rhine, winter 1945. (*NARA*)

Churchill climbs the wreckage of a Rhine bridge, March 1945. He had fulfilled his longstanding promise to make Germany "burn and bleed." (*NARA*)

Churchill exits Hitler's bunker, Berlin, July 1945. (*NARA*)

Churchill prepares to give his radio address announcing the German surrender, May 8, 1945. (*NARA*)

Churchill joins the royal family, from left, Princess Elizabeth, Queen Elizabeth, and King George VI, on the balcony of Buckingham Palace on VE-day, May 8, 1945. (*AP*)

Churchill, with Clementine, campaigns in the general election, June 1945. A victory would give him the electoral mandate he lacked when he formed his 1940 government. (*NARA*)

Churchill, in his rompers, and Clementine, taking a few days' rest before the Potsdam Conference, pose for a photographer on a French beach, July 1945. (*NARA*)

Churchill, Truman, and Stalin at the Potsdam Conference, July 1945. (*AP*)

Churchill, with Harry Truman, arrives at Westminster College, Fulton, Missouri, March 1946, to deliver what became known as the Iron Curtain speech. (*National Churchill Museum, Westminster College, Fulton, Mo.*)

Churchill sits for a portrait by Douglas Chandor, 1946. (*NARA*)

Churchill lights a cigar as he paints a landscape on a hilltop outside Château de Lourmarin, near Aix-en-Provence, 1948. Wherever Churchill went in retirement, his brushes and paints went, too. (*Getty*)

Out of office, Churchill with new friends, Miami, 1946. (*History Miami*)

Churchill in his Order of the Garter regalia with his son, Randolph, and grandson, Winston S., 1953. (*Library of Congress*)

Clementine (left) looks on as Churchill greets Queen Elizabeth II on his last night as prime minister, April 1955. (*Getty*)

Diana and Randolph, holding his ever-present cigarette, on a London street, 1960. (*Corbis*)

Sarah Churchill under arrest for public drunkenness, Southern California,
1958. (*George Lack Estate*)

Sir Winston and daughter Sarah, nicknamed "the mule" in childhood. (*Corbis*)

Sir Winston Churchill greets New York from his chair on the deck of the yacht *Christina*, as she arrives in the Hudson River, April 12, 1961. The owner of the yacht, Aristotle Onassis, stands behind Churchill, glass in hand. (Others unidentified.) (*AP*)

Churchill's casket, draped by a Union Jack, is carried from St. Paul's Cathedral by members of the Grenadier Guards, January 30, 1965. (*Getty*)

thing, in Eisenhower's estimation, to draw German troops away from France to Italy. It was another matter entirely if the Germans sent enough troops to Italy to defeat the Allied armies there. The force Eisenhower considered large enough to hold and exploit the Anzio landings simply was not available. These concerns he expressed to Churchill on Christmas Day, and again during their final meeting a week later, before Eisenhower left for Washington and London. But Shingle would not come on Eisenhower's Mediterranean watch; he had no dog in that fight.[27]

Eisenhower expressed his doubts about Anzio in almost the same terms Churchill used to express his concerns about Overlord. Churchill was not the only commander who feared that an undersize force thrown onto a beach faced "annihilation." The Christmas meeting was attended by most of the military brass in the theater—Eisenhower, Air Marshal Tedder, Jumbo Wilson, and Alexander. Brooke, who never backed down when he disagreed with Churchill, had already left for London. Another man whose opinion might have carried weight, Mark Clark, had not been invited to the meeting. His Fifth Army would supply the men for Shingle. The assembled agreed that the operation should be enlarged to two reinforced divisions, and should go forward. But it could not. With the exodus of landing ships from the Mediterranean to England, the planners came up fifty-six ships short.

Only Roosevelt could approve a change of plans regarding landing craft. Churchill sent a cable to the president: "The landing at Anzio...should decide the battle of Rome." Yet, he told the president, eighty-eight landing ships were required, and that number could only be reached by delaying the scheduled transfer of the fifty-six ships to England for Overlord. It would "seem irrational" not to do so, Churchill wrote. To send the ships to England would result in "stagnation" or worse on the Italian front. He was angry, and he was frustrated. Between them, the Americans and British had pledged to build 1,500 ships and landing craft of all types per *month,* and yet in the only European theater where Anglo-American forces were fighting Germans, the fate of the Allied campaign rested with just fifty-six landing craft. Two days later, Roosevelt approved the use of the landing craft. Operation Shingle was on, and Churchill himself was planning the details, including an increase in the force from 20,000 to more than 70,000.[28]

Splendid news from the polar region arrived on Boxing Day. The Royal Navy had brought the *Scharnhorst* to bay off the Norwegian coast. (This was especially welcome news, as *Scharnhorst*'s escape from Brest in February 1942 had nearly brought down Churchill's government.) When the German battle cruiser had in the previous days attacked a convoy bound for Russia, Admiral Sir Bruce Fraser, aboard the *Duke of York,* gave chase. *Scharnhorst* made for the safety of Norway, but by Christmas night, Fraser and his heavy ships had closed in on the German ship. On the twenty-sixth, surrounded, nearly out of ammunition, aflame, and crippled by torpedoes and shells, the *Scharnhorst* finally went under, taking all but thirty-six of her crew of two thousand to the bottom. *Tirpitz,* wounded in late September by Royal Navy midget submarines, still lived, but the German navy, having already lost the submarine war, now had to face a reality that Churchill had seen in early autumn: the Battle of the Atlantic was over. There had been a time when the mere threat of sorties by the German surface fleet terrorized Allied shipping and kept the Home Fleet near home. Now the German threat—its surface fleet, and much of its U-boat fleet—had vanished. Hitler ordered newer, faster, more heavily armed submarines built, but they were not due for deployment until mid-1945. As 1944 came on, the buildup for Overlord proceeded apace. With the arrival of each fresh American division, Britain was being transformed into the largest military staging area in history.

On December 27, Churchill, under doctor's orders, left Carthage for a two-week convalescence at Marrakech, during which time he took de facto command of the Mediterranean theater. He hinted at his intentions in a medical bulletin he wrote, which was issued from No. 10 Downing that week: "I feel a good deal better than at any time since leaving England, though of course a few weeks in the sunshine are needed to restore my physical strength.... The M and B, which I may also call Moran and Bedford, did the work most effectively.... I have not at any time had to relinquish my part in the direction of affairs, and there has been not the slightest delay in giving the decisions which were required from me. I am now able to transact business fully.... I shall not be idle." In fact, with the British chiefs and War Cabinet in London, Churchill found himself free to plan his own war.[29]

At Marrakech, as after Casablanca, he again took over the Villa Taylor, surrounding himself with a diminished troop of family and friends—Beaverbrook was summoned for companionship—and a skeletal staff of typists, private secretaries, and military advisers. Randolph and Sarah joined their father, the son, as usual, tending toward bellicosity and drunkenness, which inevitably led to "a bickering match" between himself and Winston. Randolph was especially poisonous toward de Gaulle, whom he advised his father to dump, in part because de Gaulle had just arrested five former Vichy leaders for treason. Three of the five had aided the Allies during Torch, and their safety had been spoken for by Roosevelt and Churchill. Henri Giraud opposed the arrests, but de Gaulle was forcing him out as co-president of the FCNL. De Gaulle was now the state, such as it was. To Harold Macmillan's chagrin, Churchill listened to his son, who was feeding Winston numerous reports on de Gaulle that were "mostly invented." "Randolph was the cause of the trouble," Macmillan told his diary. "It is really too bad for the boy to worry his father. But Winston is pathetically devoted to him." After witnessing several such scenes, Colville wrote, "Randolph is causing considerable strife in the family," and when Randolph again went off on de Gaulle, Colville noted, "Winston almost had apoplexy and Lord Moran was seriously perturbed." Randolph's commanding officer, Fitzroy Maclean, assured Colville that Randolph's behavior would change once they joined Tito in Yugoslavia, "owing to the absence of whisky and a diet of cabbage soup." Years later, Evelyn Waugh, who served with Randolph in Yugoslavia, was told that Randolph, a heavy smoker, had undergone a biopsy for a suspected cancerous growth in his lung. To everyone's surprise, including Randolph's, the biopsy came back negative. "A typical triumph of modern science," Waugh offered, "to find the only part of Randolph that was not malignant and remove it."[30]

Yet Randolph, in his own insufferable manner, brought into clearer focus the trouble that was brewing with de Gaulle. De Gaulle, not Randolph, was the real source of the difficulty. To address it, Churchill sent his York aircraft to Algiers in order to retrieve his old friends Alfred Duff Cooper and his wife, Lady Diana Cooper. He was in his new position of HMG's minister to the French Committee of National Liberation, and Lady Diana was a notable in her own right, at fifty-one still one of England's great beauties. Her portrait had graced a *Time* magazine cover in 1926; she was a respected actress and one of England's best-known hostesses. Over men, including Churchill, she exerted a certain power, as Lord Moran witnessed at dinner one evening in Marrakech. "There," Moran whispered to Colville, "you have the historic spectacle of a professional siren vamping an elder statesman." Duff Cooper, who loved France and the French, could only hope that he could exert such sway over de Gaulle. Cooper's new assignment—to make peace with de Gaulle, or at least to avoid more trouble—proved difficult from the start.[31]

When Roosevelt telegraphed orders directly to Eisenhower to not allow the Gaullists to prosecute three of the arrested Vichy luminaries, Macmillan— now resident minister for the entire Mediterranean—feared a complete collapse of relations between the French and the British and Americans. Roosevelt added a handwritten postscript to his cable: "It seems to me that this is the proper time effectively to eliminate the Jeanne d'Arc complex and return to realism." Upon learning of the cable, Macmillan told his diary, "The president hates de Gaulle and the French National Committee....He would seize on any excuse to overthrow them and restore Giraud." De Gaulle delayed a showdown when he announced that the three Vichy leaders would not be tried until a French government was in place. Still, Roosevelt wanted de Gaulle out, and Churchill was leaning that way.[32]

The antics of Randolph and de Gaulle were distractions for Churchill, who wanted to focus his attention on only Italy. He summoned Captain Pim and his entire map room staff to Marrakech in order to better plot his Anzio campaign. Montgomery, on his way to London to assume his new command, flew in for New Year's. Eisenhower, about to leave for a two-week vacation in the States before reporting for duty in London, was summoned by Churchill to discuss Anzio; again Eisenhower expressed his fears about the gambit—too small a force thrown against too powerful an enemy. On New Year's Eve, Churchill asked Montgomery to look over the plans for the Normandy campaign. Montgomery at first protested that since the Combined Chiefs of Staff had approved the plans, it was not his place to second-guess them. Churchill insisted. Montgomery (never a man for celebrations anyway) cut short his New Year's Eve dinner with Churchill and Clementine to take up the task. In deference to Monty, the rest of the party celebrated the New Year before the midnight hour. Punch was served, and orderlies and typists wandered into the room to partake of the festivities. After a brief speech by Churchill, everyone linked arms and formed a circle to sing "Auld Lang Syne."[33]

Montgomery wrote fondly of the evening in his memoirs, noting that it marked the beginning of a friendship between himself and Churchill and Clementine that only deepened over the next two decades. That was true; Montgomery signed the guest book at Chartwell forty-six times, second only to the Prof's eighty-six. Yet the friendship almost sputtered at the start when Clementine invited Monty's aide-de-camp, Noel Chavasse, to the New Year's Eve dinner. "My ADC's don't dine with the Prime Minister," Montgomery replied tartly. "In my house, General Montgomery," said Clementine, "I invite who I wish and I don't require your advice." Chavasse dined.[34]

The next morning, New Year's Day 1944, Churchill marched into Clementine's room and announced, "I am so happy. I feel so much better." Later in the day, the Old Man and his party, including Montgomery, motored to an olive grove in the countryside for a picnic, one of many during his days of recuperation. There, Monty delivered to Churchill his first, unfavorable, impressions of the Overlord plan. "This will not do," Monty declared. "I must have more in the initial punch." He had earlier offered his opinion to Eisenhower, who told him to recommend any and all changes he thought appropriate when they next met in London. But Eisenhower had Italy, not Normandy, on his mind. He departed Marrakech that morning with the unsettling feeling that "the insistence of the P.M. indicated he had practically taken tactical command of the Mediterranean." He had. Eisenhower's staff began referring to Shingle as "the P.M.'s pet project." It was. Marrakech picnics were "sacrificed to stern duty," Moran wrote. "Councils of war" were held in the gardens of the Villa Taylor. When Moran pointed out to Churchill that Hitler not only made war policy but even planned the details, Churchill replied, "Yes, that's just what I do." With all the brass having departed, he found himself alone in Marrakech, happily so, prompting Lord Moran to tell his diary, "As the P.M. grows in strength his appetite for war comes back."[35]

In early January 1944, RAF and American bomber crews sailed off on a series of secret missions over France that their superiors were closemouthed about. Normally, the flyers' commanders briefed flight crews on intended targets—a particular factory, for example, or rail yard in a particular city. But now the flight crews were given only coordinates, and told not to miss. The airmen were not privy to the fact that throughout the late autumn, British reconnaissance flights had snapped photos of dozens of strange-looking wooden and concrete structures scattered from Normandy to the Pas de Calais. The structures looked like Alpine ski jumps—narrow and about five hundred feet long. Some sat upon concrete foundations. Heavy electrical cables and winches implied that the structures might serve as some sort of catapult. When analysts marked the sites on maps, they reached an unsettling conclusion: each was positioned such that its axis pointed toward London. It was left to one sharp-eyed WAAF (Woman's Auxiliary Air Force) analyst to spot a propellerless aircraft near one of the sites. Another analyst recalled similar buildings being photographed at Peenemünde the previous May. The analysts could only conclude that they were looking at German launch sites. Exactly what manner of device was to be launched remained unknown. RAF and American bomb crews now flew in the service of Crossbow, Duncan Sandys's operation to destroy the mysterious sites. But accuracy, as usual, left much to be desired. "The bombing of the launching emplacements," Brooke confided to his diary on January 11, "is not going well." The bombing, in fact, continued to not go well for seven more months.[36]

Not so Churchill's Moroccan holiday. He worked mornings, picnicked in the afternoons, and dined splendidly by candlelight each night. Late in the evening, dressed in his dragon robe, he sang along to Gilbert and Sullivan recordings sent to him for Christmas by Mary, "the best present I ever gave him." Eduard Beneš, on his way home from Moscow, where he had signed a friendship treaty with Stalin, stopped by for dinner, during which Beneš expressed his belief that "we must be ready for a German collapse any day after May 1." Again, as he had in Cairo, Churchill polled his dinner companions as to whether they believed Hitler would still be in power on September 3, 1944. Answering no were Sarah, Commander Tommy Thompson, John Martin, Beneš, and Major General Leslie Hollis. Hollis's pronouncement carried weight; he was Ismay's deputy and attended many of the overseas conferences and most of the military planning sessions throughout the war. Churchill and Beaverbrook answered yes.[37]

On January 12, Charles de Gaulle, after a month of what Duff Cooper termed "boorish" refusals to meet with Churchill, agreed to dine with the prime minister. Still offended by Churchill's not seeing him while en route to Tehran, and furious over Roosevelt's intervention in his plan to try the three Vichy loyalists, the general arrived in Marrakech in a "difficult and unhelpful" mood. Churchill, too, was in a low mood, having been shocked that day to learn that Count Ciano and the other conspirators who had ousted Mussolini had been shot. As Churchill waited for de Gaulle, Duff Cooper later wrote, he pondered ridding the alliance of the Frenchman once and for all, not only because Roosevelt sought to but because, as Churchill told Cooper, "You like the man, I don't." As the hour of the meeting approached, Cooper and Clementine advised Churchill to act with civility toward de Gaulle. "I hope there will be no explosions," Clementine wrote in a letter to Mary. There were not. After a cool start (de Gaulle "talked as if he were Stalin and Roosevelt combined") the two leaders "parted friends" two hours later. Churchill even agreed to attend a review of French troops the following day. The review, where Churchill and de Gaulle stood side by side, "was a great success," Cooper wrote, and Churchill was "much moved by the cries of 'Vive Churchill,' which predominated over the cries of 'Vive de Gaulle' as the Spahis and Zouaves marched past." Years later Cooper wrote of Churchill, "After spending more than a half century in the de-humanising profession of politics, Winston Churchill remains as human as a school-boy." The words were written in appreciation of Churchill's willingness to stick with de Gaulle—despite de Gaulle's misdeeds—for the greater good of France and Europe.[38]

A picnic in the mountains (without de Gaulle) followed the review of troops. Such outings were not simple affairs to bring off. American troops guarded the surrounding area, which included a deep gorge through which

a river ran. Churchill's orderlies laid out long trestle tables, white tablecloths, folding chairs, Berber carpets, and large wicker baskets containing
oranges, olives, grilled lamb, and chilled liquid refreshments, "the whole
caboodle," recalled Lady Diana Cooper. So luscious were the oranges that
Montgomery, who was leaving for London later in the day, ordered that an
aircraft be procured, loaded with oranges, and sent ahead to England. As
with any meal with Churchill, the picnic began on an uncertain note. Lady
Cooper, a friend of three decades, had long known how to best approach
Churchill at the dinner table. "He was always grumpy before dinner," she
recalled, "then after a couple of drinks, became funny and more witty."
After his first glass of brandy Churchill leaned in toward Lady Diana and
whispered, "Lord Moran says I am to have another glass of brandy." Yet
Moran had said no such thing. "Well," Lady Diana recalled, "three times
he had another glass of brandy with the result that I saw it coming." What
she saw coming was an excursion by Churchill and several aides down to
the river in the gorge, where he scrambled about on the boulders in the
streambed. When it came time to ascend from the ravine, the Old Man
found he lacked the mobility. Lady Diana lowered a long white tablecloth,
into which Churchill was wrapped like a baby in a bundle. With two aides
pulling, two pushing, and another carrying the Old Man's cigar, they
regained the high ground.[39]

Churchill's long absence from London had been noted at the highest levels. Brooke told his diary on January 7, "Winston, sitting in Marrakech, is
now full of beans and trying to win the war from there....I wish to god he
would come home and get under control." He was coming home soon, but
with no intention of getting himself under control. Yet he was not fully fit,
was prone to bouts of exhaustion, and experienced occasional trouble on
his feet, as borne out by the expedition into the ravine. One evening in
Marrakech, Clementine confided to Lady Cooper, "I never think of after
the war. You see, I think Winston will die when it's over....You see...
we're putting everything we have into this war, and it will take all we
have."[40]

It was taking all Roosevelt and Harry Hopkins had. In a New Year's Eve
cable to Churchill, the president made casual reference to spending a few
days in bed "with a mild case of the 'flu.'" Five days later, Roosevelt told
Churchill that Harry Hopkins, too, had come down with the flu and would
be spending a few days in the Naval Hospital. The illness wasn't severe,
Roosevelt offered, but "it makes you feel like an Italian soldier looks." In
fact, Roosevelt was a sick man, experiencing abdominal pains, fluid in his
lungs, and heart palpitations. Hopkins was an even sicker man. He did not
in fact spend a few days in hospital, but the better part of seven months,
during which time he underwent surgery for his stomach ailments, all of

which, he would learn within a year, his doctors had misdiagnosed. Hopkins, in great pain, was shuffled between the Mayo Clinic and the Naval Hospital before undertaking a long convalescence at White Sulphur Springs. So sudden and total was his disappearance that Churchill concluded he had had a falling out with the president. In February, Churchill dispatched one of the few letters he sent to Hopkins that year. It was a scroll, actually, hand-lettered with five lines from the final scene of *Macbeth*. It began: "*Your son, my lord, has paid a soldier's debt....*" Stephen Hopkins, Marine Private First Class, eighteen, had been killed in the Marshall Islands. For three years Churchill had found a friend and ready ear in Hopkins, who had championed England's cause more strongly and more effectively than did the president's chief of staff, Admiral Leahy, and his secretary of state, Cordell Hull. Hopkins, not Roosevelt, had been Churchill's best friend in the White House. He had completed the circuit between his boss and Churchill. That connection was now fraying.[41]

By January 3, the Russians had driven one hundred miles beyond the 1939 Polish frontier; that is, the Red Army had struck into Poland for the second time in four years. Churchill saw the political implications of the Red Army's success and telegraphed his concerns to Anthony Eden. The questions of the Baltic States and Bessarabia, Churchill wrote, "have largely settled themselves through the victories of the Russian armies." Churchill reminded Eden that when at Tehran they offered Königsberg in East Prussia to Stalin, they made no mention of the Baltic States, "which clearly would be compromised" by a Russian march through them to East Prussia." In fact, Churchill wrote, once the Russians take "physical possession of these territories...it is absolutely certain that we shall never be able to turn them out."[42]

The implication for Poland was clear. Then Eden cabled with the news that the London Poles insisted "Poland, as a reward for Polish suffering and fighting," must "emerge from this war with...her eastern provinces intact and her western provinces increased." That would not do; Churchill had already proposed to Stalin the ceding of a large swath of eastern Poland to Russia. Were the Poles to refuse the offer, Churchill told Eden, he would consider England's obligations to Poland fully discharged: "I would certainly not take any further responsibility for what will happen in the future." The London Poles, Eden reported, feared that in Poland's war-weakened state, chewing off of large portions of Germany would prove difficult "in digesting." As well, Eden offered, in light of the heroic victories of the Red Army, "there is public impatience with the Poles." Britain may have gone to war for Poland, but Britons, like their American cousins, had put the Russians on a pedestal. Still, Eden was optimistic. But that faith was shaken by a telegram from Stalin to Churchill on January 7 wherein the marshal stated that the declarations of the London Poles left him to conclude that "there is no foundation for reckoning on the possibility of bringing these circles to reason. These people are incorrigible." The London Poles, pressed by Eden, finally agreed to discuss "all outstanding questions" with the Russians, including the Curzon Line. But they would not accept the Curzon Line before any such discussions. Moscow rejected the offer. The London Poles, Stalin informed the British, "did not want neighborly relations with the Soviet Union." That news, Eden later wrote, came "like a blow to the face." With the Red Army now one hundred miles beyond Poland's 1939 border, Churchill grasped the inevitable. To Eden he cabled: "Considering that Russia has lost perhaps thirty millions of citizens...they have the right as well as the power to have their western frontiers secured."[43]

Churchill departed Marrakech on January 14, intent on being in London when the troops went ashore at Anzio. He went by air to Gibraltar, and then by *King George V* to Plymouth, and finally by train to Paddington Station, where late in the morning of the eighteenth he was met by the entire cabinet and Chiefs of Staff. He had been away for sixty-seven days, an extraordinary amount of time for any leader to be absent from his capital, and doubly so for a leader during wartime. He took himself straightaway to the House, which had just reconvened after the Christmas recess. Harold Nicolson recorded Churchill's entrance: "We were dawdling through questions...when I saw (*saw* is the word) a gasp of astonishment pass over the faces of the Labour Party opposite. Suddenly they jumped to their feet and started shouting.... We also jumped up and the whole House broke into cheer after cheer while Winston, very pink, rather shy, beaming with mischief, crept along the front bench and flung himself into his accustomed seat." He rose to take questions, and although Nicolson applauded his effort, he also noted that he "looked pale when the first flush of pleasure had subsided, and his voice was not quite so vigorous as it had been." Concerns about Churchill's health now regularly found their way into the diaries of the Old Man's colleagues.[44]

Following Questions, Churchill chaired a cabinet meeting during which he disabused Brooke of any hopes that he would return to London under control. The P.M. "rambled on till 1:30 P.M.," Brooke told his diary that night. "He was looking well, but I did not like the functioning of his brain much! Too much unconnected rambling from one subject to another." Indeed, at the following day's Chiefs of Staff meeting, Churchill launched into his plans for operations "after Anzio is over." This was three days before Anzio even began. He foresaw putting several thousand commandos supported by tanks on islands off the Dalmatian coast. For Churchill, the Aegean still held its place as a theater of destiny. That night, Brooke unloaded to his diary: "The P.M. is starting off in his usual style!! I don't think I can stand much more of it.... His method is entirely opportunistic, gathering one flower here, another there! My God how tired I am of working for him. I had not fully realized how awful it is until I suddenly found myself thrown into it again after a rest."[45]

Churchill was back.

Eisenhower had arrived in London on January 16, assured by Roosevelt and Marshall that they would not second-guess his decisions, would never try to force commanders on him, and would back him completely. The president had put the "supreme" in supreme commander. Eisenhower had told the president that he intended to deploy his forces in pursuit of one military objective—the destruction of Hitler's armies. All decisions would be taken with that objective in mind. "Geographical points," he later wrote, "were considered only in their relationship" to killing German armies. And politics was not to be considered at all. He made clear to Churchill in coming weeks that were his superiors—Roosevelt and Marshall—to order him to undertake operations based on political priorities, he would of course obey those orders. But he would not otherwise bend his military strategy to politics. Eisenhower noted Churchill's "concern as a political leader for the future of the Balkans... but as a soldier I was particularly careful to exclude such considerations from my own recommendations." Churchill also harbored a deep concern for Poland; in fact, with the Red Army driving west, he increasingly harbored concerns for all of Europe. This divergence in philosophies between Eisenhower the warrior and Churchill the warrior-politician would in coming months have profound consequences.[46]

The Yanks had arrived in Britain, almost one million strong. Another million were due by June, and yet another million by year's end. Dwight Eisenhower's Irish driver (and alleged mistress), Kay Summersby, later wrote that London, "like a discreet matron carried away by one too many cocktails," had become "a playgirl of a city." Since the Battle of Britain, RAF pilots on weekend leave had hastened to London for forty-eight hours of whiskey and women. The GIs' arrival "really blew the lid off." The Americans spent their dollars in any number of stores and pubs and clubs; the locals had little money to spend and, with everything from sweets to eggs to clothes rationed, little to spend it on. Summersby declared her pride at watching the poorest of Londoners slide right past American PXs while casting "not a glance at the American boys emerging with cigarettes and sweets and other treasures." Britons, meanwhile, saw their milk ration reduced to two pints per week. Irving Berlin's all-soldier musical *This Is the Army,* starring its New York cast, was entering its third month of playing to standing room only crowds at the Palladium; every shilling of the proceeds went to the British armed forces.[47]

One evening months earlier, after he had viewed photos of destroyed German cities, Harold Nicolson's thoughts turned to London, which was largely unvisited by the Luftwaffe in 1943. Whereas almost three years earlier, Nicolson and all Londoners had feared for their lives, they now felt free to complain about their sacrifices. Nicolson was pleased that one of his favorite restaurants "retained all its old atmosphere," but "the Travellers, on the other hand, has become a battered *caravanserai,* in which the scum of the lower London clubs are served inadequately by scared Lithuanian waitresses." And when Nicolson came across boozy American troops frolicking in the Underground with their "East End Jewish girls," he went home and told his diary, "I hate it."[48]

England, wrote Mollie Panter-Downes, resembled "a vast combination of an aircraft carrier, a dock jammed with men, and a warehouse stacked to the ceiling with material labeled 'Europe.' "[49]

The legions of soldiers had time on their hands, if not on their side. Arriving GIs joined the uniformed Welshmen, Scotsmen, Norwegians, Poles, Dutch, Indians, Czechs, Belgians, Canadians, Newfoundlanders (until 1949, Newfoundland was a self-governing Dominion), Aussies, and New Zealanders who had turned Piccadilly Circus into the Times Square of England. It was the sort of chaotic commingling that had occurred on the island with regularity since prehistoric times and of which Daniel Defoe wrote:

From this amphibious ill-borne mob began
That vain, ill-natured thing, an Englishman.

At night battalions of tarts strutted down the blacked-out streets, as they had at the height of the Blitz (Ed Murrow had called them "London's bravest"). Now they solicited clients with whispers of *"tovarisch"* ("comrade"). Darkened doorways became love nests and from alleys drifted the sounds of fistfights and catcalls and blasphemies in a babel of languages.

The whores carried small flashlights that they played on their faces for a few seconds when a soldier nodded interest, the narrow beams dancing in the deep shadows with a flickering, strobe effect. Old air-raid wardens in tin hats barked orders to cut the torches. They were ignored. When low-pressure atmospherics wrapped the city in a vile mix of acrid chimney effusions and impenetrable Channel fog, the nighttime became downright bizarre. Automobiles—the top half of their headlights painted black—crept along like purblind beasts of burden, led by passengers or Good Samaritans who placed one hand on the front fender while reaching out with the other in hopes of feeling their way to the proper destination. After much tribulation, many stumbles, and a bit of good luck, the autos and their caretakers might actually find their way home. London, after almost five years under blackout conditions, was still wrapped, Jock Colville wrote, "in Stygian blackness."[50]

On January 21, Eisenhower's senior Overlord staff met for the first time, at Norfolk House, a neo-Georgian building just off St. James's Park, which had been put off limits to civilians in part to mask the comings and goings at the former mansion. Montgomery presented his findings on the initial plans for Overlord. As he had told Churchill, he now told his colleagues, "The initial landing is on too narrow a front and confined to too small an area." As well, the landings—code-named Neptune—called for too few men, just three divisions, which invited congestion on the beaches and possible disaster were the Germans to concentrate their tanks and send in their planes. Monty supported the concept of the Mulberry artificial harbors but stressed the need to capture the port of Cherbourg. That objective necessitated the widening of the landing zone to include a beach on the Cotentin Peninsula, which was separated from the main landing beaches by the four-mile-wide double estuary of the Vire and Douve rivers. To resolve that problem, Montgomery proposed dropping two divisions of American paratroops ten miles inland from the beach and west of the Douve. Finally, he insisted "the air battle must be won before the operation is launched." Eisenhower, who had taken only a cursory look at the plans before he left North Africa, found himself in general agreement with Monty's suggestions, but for one. Montgomery proposed scrapping Anvil, the two-division invasion of southern France, in order to free up the troops and landing craft needed to expand Overlord. Eisenhower acknowledged that Anvil could not now precede Overlord as planned, but he declared that it must follow soon after. He would consider an outright cancellation only as a last resort. All agreed that the time needed to assemble the appropriate force for Overlord—and to destroy German airpower and disrupt French rail lines—would delay the invasion for a month. That was exactly the flexibility Churchill and Brooke had sought, and believed they had gained, in Tehran.[51]

Given the need to make the Normandy landings under a nearly full moon, and on a rising tide within sixty minutes after dawn, the delay effectively pushed Overlord into the first week of June. Secrecy being as critical as logistics to Overlord's success, Operation Bodyguard was soon born, a multifaceted campaign of radio intercepts, double agents, and false intelligence. Its stepchild, Operation Fortitude, entailed the creation of phony armies from Scotland to southeast England. The phantom armies broadcast phony radio messages that the Germans were welcome to intercept and interpret at their own risk. The ranks of the nonexistent units consisted of brigades of inflatable rubber tanks and squadrons of plywood planes, which when photographed from the air by German reconnaissance flights indicated massive troop buildups.

New Allied weapons also contributed to the cause. Major General Percy ("Hobo") Hobart, the erratic tank genius whom Churchill had brought back into service in 1940 (over Brooke's objections), was put in command of building specialty tanks—"swimming" tanks that could come ashore under their own power; tanks that "flailed" minefields with wildly spinning chains; and flame-throwing tanks capable of incinerating large buildings. Montgomery and Eisenhower added dimensions to Overlord not imagined by the original planners. Three days later, Eisenhower briefed the Combined Chiefs of Staff on his new plan. Even though events were now going the way Brooke had argued for, he could not bring himself to write a complimentary word about Eisenhower: "I certainly agree with his [Eisenhower's] proposal, but it is certainly not his idea, and is one of Monty's. Eisenhower has got absolutely no strategical outlook and is totally unfit for the post he holds."[52]

Days after Montgomery argued for the cancellation of Anvil (and Eisenhower agreed to postpone it), Churchill came up with another means to reinforce Overlord. It took the form of landing three armored divisions in Bordeaux a few weeks after the start of the Normandy venture, which, according to plan, by twenty days after D-day would find Allied troops well inland. He code-named the operation Caliph, and proposed that the three divisions be moved from the Mediterranean to Morocco before being shipped around the Iberian Peninsula and into the port of Bordeaux. In Caliph, Churchill beheld a solution to a problem he anticipated: Anvil must necessarily draw down Alexander's landing ships and troops and thereby force a halt in the springtime Italian campaign. In Churchill's estimation, a shift from Anvil to Caliph would both support the Normandy invasion (Eisenhower's first priority) and improve prospects in Italy (Churchill's theater of destiny). It would establish two distinct theaters — France and Italy/Mediterranean — under two supreme commanders (Eisenhower and Jumbo Wilson). This was an alternative far superior to the god-awful muddle that would result from two simultaneous and mutually dependent operations within close proximity, one in southern France and the other in northern Italy, where Churchill presumed Alexander would be by May. Brooke dismissed Caliph as a "wild venture." After the British Chiefs of Staff and Churchill discussed the matter, Brooke wrote, "I think we have ridden him of this for the present." They had, but only for the present.[53]

More than 25,000 Allied troops, British and American, went ashore at Anzio and Nettuno on January 22. Surprise was total. The beaches were undefended; the men came ashore with ease and by noon reached the first day's objective of driving three miles inland. This put the invasion force about forty miles north of Kesselring's rear, and sixty miles north of the Fifth Army. That morning, Brooke enthused to his diary over bagging 172 pheasants on a one-day shooting holiday and, in reference to the surprise attained at Anzio, added, "This was a wonderful relief."

That was the last positive diary entry Brooke would make in regard to Anzio for several months. By the next day, 15,000 more troops came ashore, along with almost four thousand vehicles (far too many, Churchill believed, and he told Alexander to make sure he landed enough men to fill his thousands of trucks). Then, instead of striking inland, the men sat static on the Anzio beaches for two days. And that was the problem. With their backs to the sea and six divisions' worth of German reinforcements rushing from northern Italy to their front, the Allies found themselves ripe targets for the German 88s hastily dug into hillsides above and around the beach. By January 28, Churchill knew the invasion had failed. He famously described the situation a few weeks later when he told Colville and Brooke, "I thought we should fling wildcat ashore and all we got was an old stranded whale on the beach." Churchill liked to repeat his favorite phrases for effect; this one was accurate and it captured exactly the stasis on the beaches. Even the code name, Shingle, took on a terrible irony, for it was on the seashore shingle that the army remained. The fault for that, as Churchill saw it, lay with the American commander, General John P. Lucas. He came, he saw, he consulted, and as a result, his men died. Kesselring, in contrast, deployed his forces with precision. Yet Sir John Keegan sided with Lucas in a critical regard: "Had Lucas risked rushing at Rome the first day, his spearheads would probably have arrived, though they would have soon been crushed."[54]

The idea of Italy having any sort of soft underbelly was being refuted daily sixty miles south of Anzio. The coordinating blow by Mark Clark's Fifth Army in support of the Anzio landings had begun on January 17 when British forces attacked across the lower Garigliano River. On January 20, six thousand Americans from the 36th Texas Division tried to attack across the Rapido, swollen by winter rains, its currents deadly. The surrounding terrain was a quagmire; no roads led in or out of the area. For three days the Texans tried, and for three days they failed to take the far banks, with more than one thousand killed. It was a gruesome defeat for the Texans, the Fifth Army, and Churchill. In order to get to Anzio and the great prize—Rome—the Fifth Army had to get across the Rapido and take Monte Cassino, where the German 1st Parachute Division was now dug in on the slopes. On January 24, Clark threw the American 34th Division onto the mountain; on February 12, after almost three weeks of close combat, the Germans threw it off. The road to Rome had not been shortened by as much as a foot.[55]

The most formidable obstacle the Allies faced in Italy was Albert Kesselring's Gustav Line, which began just north of the mouth of the Garigliano River on the Tyrrhenian coast. Built by the quasi-military German construction company Organization Todt, which was also rushing to complete Hitler's Atlantic Wall, the Gustav Line—a man-made bifurcation of the Italian peninsula that was as formidable as a mountain range—was an extraordinary feat of engineering, a coast-to-coast concrete fortress with interlocking artillery sites, barbed wire, machine guns, and mines, behind which Kesselring deployed the thirteen divisions of his Tenth Army. In the west, the line was anchored by Monte Cassino, which overlooked Highway 6, the road to Rome. From there the line ran east over the spine of the Apennines to the mouth of the Sangro River on the Adriatic coast, where the Eighth Army was engaged in its bloodiest action of the war. Unlike the Maginot Line, the Gustav Line could not be easily outflanked, as the battle for the Liri Valley proved, hourly.

Yet, in a critical regard, Hitler's decision to dig in and stand fast rather than to have his army slowly pull back into northern Italy played into Churchill's hands. Hitler's Italian forces were tied down and therefore not available to reinforce the Atlantic Wall. This result had been the goal of Churchill and Brooke from the start. They had always seen Italy as both an end in itself and a means to restrict Hitler's ability to deploy his forces on his terms only. But Churchill had never sought stalemate; he wanted to lure Hitler's armies to their doom. That strategy was only half fulfilled. Hitler's divisions in Italy would not be going to Normandy, but unless and until Alexander got his armies off the beach at Anzio and around the German flank at Cassino, the Allies would not be going to Rome. Rome was not only a great political prize but a vital military objective, for without control of the airfields near Rome, there could be no Anvil; nor of course could there be a swing by Alexander northwest to France or northeast toward the Balkans and Austria. Thus all roads led to Rome. In early February, Brooke and the British Chiefs of Staff wired Washington with the opinion that "the only thing to do is to go on fighting the war in Italy and give up any idea of a weak landing in southern France." This was just what Churchill had anticipated two weeks earlier when he proposed Caliph, a plan Brooke considered "a wild venture." Yet unless the Combined Chiefs came up with a better way to reinforce Overlord, Anvil would have to go forward sometime after the Normandy invasion, at the probable expense of Italian operations.[56]

In mid-February, Kesselring unleashed an all-out attack upon the Anzio beachhead. Had it not been for the Ultra decrypts that warned the Allies of Kesselring's plans, Lucas and his little army would have been thrown into the sea. Alexander sacked Lucas on February 23. The men on the beachhead moved into underground warrens of muddy trenches, foxholes, and basements—and not just the infantry but the support troops, too, including mechanics, weathermen, medics, and cooks. There was no rear to move back to. Lice infested uniforms and bedrolls; malarial mosquitoes swarmed out of the marshes, which Mussolini had drained years before but the Germans had now flooded. Allied ranks were swelled by hundreds of Italian orphans who, their parents dead and their homes destroyed, wandered into the lines, as did hundreds of stray dogs and cats, which the troops adopted. German artillery and Stukas raked the beach, daily, hourly, constantly. A German bomb fell so close to the stone house where newspaperman Ernie Pyle was sleeping that the concussion tossed him out of bed and blew his cigarettes out of the pack. He gathered them up and smoked them all by lunchtime. Nearly 4,500 Allied troops never made it off the beach alive.[57]

As February went out, Hitler, who had promised retaliation for months, turned the Luftwaffe loose upon London. The Blitz was back and with a fury. The raids came like hammer strokes; smaller fleets of Heinkels came in fast and dropped more powerful bombs than in 1940. They no longer came during the "bomber's moon" but on the darkest of nights, guided by their navigation beams. The raiders knew not to linger over London, due to the improvements the British had made in radio-controlled anti-aircraft targeting. Bell Laboratories manufactured an electronic gun director that measured the speed, course, and altitude of aircraft, along with wind direction and muzzle velocity of the anti-aircraft shells. The final calculation determined the altitude at which the proximity fuses of the anti-aircraft shells were set to burst. All of these calculations, and the automatic aiming and firing of the guns, were performed by a component of the system that Bell called the "computer."[58]

The Germans, in turn, befuddled British radar by turning Window—tinfoil streamers—against Britain, as the British had done over Hamburg. London's children called the foil streamers "flutterers" and danced around trees laden with them, like Maypoles, wrote Mollie Panter-Downes. But other than the children, no one enjoyed the onslaught (with the exception perhaps of one old man, his tin hat always at the ready). When the sirens wailed, Churchill once again took himself off, as he had during the 1940 Blitz, to Hyde Park now, where Mary's AA battery produced the music of the night. Once again Londoners had to shovel glass from gutters; once again crowds lined up at shelters before sundown. The windows were again blown out of No. 10. Londoners demeaned the attacks as the "Baby Blitz." But the bombers were getting through. "The glow of fires in the sky shows the damage was widespread," Colville wrote after one raid. "London seems disturbed by the raids, and less ebullient than in 1940–41."[59]

By mid-February the battle for the Gustav Line was faring no better than that for Anzio. A second attack on Monte Cassino, by the New Zealanders, was planned for February 16. The ferocity of the battle for the town of Cassino and the monastery above it led some in the English clergy to express fears that Rome, too, would be subject to destruction, a worry Mollie Panter-Downes downplayed in a February 13 column in *The New Yorker,* in which she wrote of "anxious concern over the fate of Rome—concern which, judging by the extreme solicitude the Allies were showing for the Monte Cassino Monastery, seemed hardly necessary." The solicitude ended on the night of February 15–16 when the Americans, believing that Germans had taken up positions in the monastery, dropped 1,400 tons of bombs onto it, almost twice the tonnage the Luftwaffe dropped on London during the first night of the 1940 Blitz. The bombing left the monastery in ruins, although its walls remained somewhat intact. The New Zealanders attacked the next morning and were repulsed. The

Germans had not, in fact, been inside the monastery, but they soon occupied the ruins, which afforded them almost perfect protection.[60]

That the Allies could send almost an entire air force to bomb a single church testified to the awesome power of their air fleets. But thousands of planes meant thousands of casualties. On February 19, Colville noted that nine hundred bombers had been sent out to Germany the previous night, and that 5 percent did not return. Actually, as Churchill told the House on February 22, a thousand bombers had been sent to four German cities, nine thousand tons of bombs were loosed, and seventy-nine aircraft—8 percent—did not return. RAF losses were staggering, and mounting. But Churchill remained committed to the bombing campaign. He spoke to the House that day for one hour and eighteen minutes, his first major address in five months. He directed most of his remarks at Germans, telling them that unconditional surrender did not mean they would become slaves.

He also promised Germans that he intended to bomb Germany into ruins. He told MPs (and reminded Americans), "Turning to the air, the honour of bombing Berlin has fallen almost entirely to us. Up to the present we have delivered the main attack upon Germany." Then he spoke of the cost: "Excluding Dominion and Allied squadrons working with the Royal Air Force, the British islands have lost 38,300 pilots and air crews killed and 10,400 missing, and over 10,000 aircraft since the beginning of the war and they have made nearly 900,000 sorties into the North European theatre." But there would be no respite, for air crews or Germans: "Scales and degrees of attack will be reached far beyond the dimensions of anything which has yet been employed or, indeed, imagined." He advised German citizens to flee their cities and take refuge in the countryside. He predicted German retaliation for the air campaign, and not the usual sort of raids that had been taking place. He disclosed for the first time in public what form the retaliation would take: "There is no doubt that the Germans are preparing on the French shore new means of assault on this country, either by pilotless aircraft, or possibly rockets, or both, on a considerable scale."[61]

Mollie Panter-Downes noted that Londoners did not much comment on Churchill's warnings of impending attack "by pilotless planes and rocket shells." Most people, she wrote, "had enough to worry about right now with planes that did have pilots." But she had misheard Churchill. He had not warned of "rocket shells" of the sort batteries in Hyde Park shot skyward in search of German planes. Rather, he had warned of *rockets*.[62]

In his address, Churchill covered every world battlefront, and every political nuance on the international scene and at home. He cautioned that the war in Europe would probably not end in 1944. He gave details of his pledge to Stalin made at Tehran that Soviet borders would be protected and that Polish borders would be moved. He declared the Curzon Line as

HMG's policy, and declared his faith in Stalin's promise that he sought "a strong integral independent Poland as one of the leading Powers in Europe." He added, "He [Stalin] has several times repeated these declarations in public, and I am convinced that they represent the settled policy of the Soviet Union." Then he took a swing at naysayers in Britain and America who denigrated the Grand Alliance:

> My hope is that generous instincts of unity will not depart from us in these times of tremendous exertions and grievous sacrifices, and that we shall not fall apart, abroad or at home, so as to become the prey of the little folk who exist in every country and who frolic alongside the Juggernaut car of war, to see what fun or notoriety they can extract from the proceedings. There is one thing that we agreed at Tehran, above all others, to which we are all bound in solemn compact, and that is to fall upon and smite the Hun by land, sea and air with all the strength that is in us during the coming Spring and Summer.[63]

When earlier that week the former Archbishop of Canterbury decried the bombing of German cities and the prospect of Rome being bombed wholesale, the House of Lords responded with an official declaration that the bombing of German cities must and would go on.

March 1, and the invasion of France, was just three months distant. Churchill insisted it be called a "liberation" and that "invasion" be used only in reference to crossing the enemy—German—frontier. The Combined Chiefs of Staff obeyed the directive, and even Roosevelt agreed to do so. Invasion or liberation, Overlord would be the most critical step yet taken by the Anglo-Americans toward the destruction of Hitler. The Russians could not do it alone; nor, it appeared, could Bomber Command. Brendan Bracken saw Overlord as "the most desperate military venture in history." Alec Cadogan, the permanent under secretary for Foreign Affairs, called it "the most hazardous enterprise ever undertaken." It was that (at least from the Anglo-American standpoint), yet it was just one operation among many, one element on the military landscape.[64]

There were other landscapes—economic, political, social—over which the players had to make their way. For the next three months, Dwight Eisenhower's horizon justifiably extended to Normandy, and not much further. Charles de Gaulle, in Algiers, had his sights set on getting to Paris, the London Poles on getting to Warsaw, Beneš on getting to Prague. The

Allied military chiefs parsed vistas worldwide—in Italy, in the vastness of the Pacific, in Burma. Likewise in the political sphere, Harriman, Halifax, Hull, and Eden shared many problems, and many solutions, but certainly not all. British diplomats around the world tussled with local leaders over local problems; in Bengal the famine was worsening. At home, British authorities clashed with disgruntled Britons over wages, ration cards, food shortages, and a beer shortage. Each participant in the drama operated in a limited sphere, but Churchill's responsibilities encompassed all things military, political, and economic—internationally and in the Home Island. And it was all in flux. His duties were kaleidoscopic in their haphazard variety. Poland and Overlord certainly dominated his thoughts, but there were numerous other worries as well.

It was obvious that Romania, which had been extending peace feelers in Stockholm since late 1943, would soon be overrun by the Red Army. Churchill knew that once the Soviets gained Bucharest, the matter of a separate peace with Romania would become moot. The Hungarians and Bulgarians, too, were getting jittery as the Red Army rolled toward the Carpathians. In mid-March, after Hitler learned that the Hungarians had sent out peace feelers to the West, he sent in the Wehrmacht to occupy the country and installed a pro-Nazi puppet government. The new government soon ordered the deportation of 450,000 Hungarian Jews and Romas to the death camps. The Finns, too, saw the writing on the wall. With Leningrad freed, the Finns knew that the Red Army would soon come their way. It did, in an early June surprise attack. Finland's Marshal Carl Mannerheim concluded a separate peace with the Soviets in August.

Greece was in a state of civil war. When Greek troops in Egypt mutinied in April, Churchill told General Bernard Paget, in Cairo, that HMG was "prepared to use the utmost force if necessary, but let us avoid slaughter, if possible." Paget put down the revolt with the loss of one British officer and no Greeks. Yugoslavia, too, was in a state of civil war; by April Churchill threw his full support to Tito and cut all ties with the Chetniks. Churchill finessed King Peter, a Serb, into sacking his cabinet and appointing Dr. Ivan Šubašić—a Croat, pro-Tito and acceptable to Stalin—as prime minister. Tito did not ask for a seat in the government and agreed to defer a plebiscite on King Peter until after the war.[65]

Italian politics came into play in March, when Roosevelt, citing American "public opinion" (it was an election year), pushed Churchill to sack King Emmanuel and Badoglio, who was, after all, a Fascist holdover. Churchill, preferring the strong hand of Badoglio to the fractious Italian politics that would surely result from his sacking, thought the idea foolish. "Why break the handle of the coffee pot," he told Brooke, "... and burn your fingers trying to hold it, why not wait to get to Rome and let it cool off?"[66]

Roosevelt sifted all questions of Italy, Poland, and Ireland in terms of election year politics—Italian, Irish, and Polish Americans formed the backbone of his constituency. On the one hand, he did not want to lose the Polish bloc; on the other, he did not want Stalin doubting the sincerity of the agreements made at Tehran with regard to Poland. For his part, Churchill examined Poland strictly in terms of Britain's commitment to the Free Poles. He considered other European countries—Romania, Yugoslavia, Greece, Italy, Bulgaria—largely in terms of their susceptibility to Communist takeover. Upon Ireland, where he expected mischief, he kept a wary eye. Indeed, late in the year de Valera proclaimed Ireland's duty and right as a neutral to offer sanctuary to Germans accused of war crimes. Where Roosevelt weighed issues regarding Europe in terms of American politics, Churchill weighed them in terms of Europe, its future, and Britain's role in that future. Stalin, likewise, weighed matters in terms of Russia's role in postwar Europe. His armies were now inside Poland, or as Roosevelt pointed out to Polish Americans throughout the year, inside one of the many configurations of Poland that had come and gone for over a century. He asked, which was the real Poland? His point was, Poland defied geographical definition, which even the American Polish community admitted was true. Yet American Poles and especially the London Poles were repulsed by the idea of ceding even one inch of prewar Poland to the Bolsheviks. Still, ever politically agile, Roosevelt managed to keep the Polish voting bloc in his pocket, as well as Stalin, or so he thought.[67]

In the forgotten war in Burma, the Americans and Chinese under Vinegar Joe Stilwell could only slog though the northern Burmese jungle in their mission to build the Ledo Road from northern India to China, their flanks protected by the guerrilla warfare genius Orde Wingate and his Chindits. Brooke thought the stress of battle "had sent Wingate off his head," but before any consideration was given to relieving him, Wingate, the "Clive of Burma," was killed in an airplane crash in March, thus removing the unique fighter from the scene. General Sir Billy Slim and the Fourteenth Army had captured a major Japanese supply base sixty miles south of Mandalay but had outrun their own supply lines. Further operations were canceled until after the monsoons. Malaria, as it had in Italy, felled more troops than the enemy. But the Allies had a new and secret scientific weapon in the war against mosquitoes and lice. Later in the year the British and American governments lifted censorship from "one of the great scientific discoveries of World War II." It was a discovery, proclaimed *Time,* that would "be to preventive medicine what Lister's discovery of antiseptics was to surgery." Churchill told the Commons, "It is an insecticide called D.D.T. We have discovered many defences against tropical disease, and, above all, against the onslaught of insects of all kinds, from lice to mosquitoes and back again. The excellent D.D.T. powder, which has been fully experimented with and found to yield astonishing results, will hence-forward be used on a great scale by the British forces in Burma and by American and Australian forces in the Pacific and, indeed, in all theatres."[68]

Worldwide, disparate commanders demanded from the planners in Washington and London more men, more ammo, more medicines, and more 120-octane aircraft fuel. There was Overlord, to be sure, but there were also Burma, Norway, the Aegean, Anzio, the Philippines, the Marshall and Gilbert islands, and always, for Churchill, Sumatra. In mid-March he again proposed to his Chiefs of Staff a strike into Sumatra as a stepping-stone to Rangoon, an idea Brooke called "impossible" and "full of false deductions and defective strategy." It was never carried out.[69]

Problems demanding solutions abounded. Palestine presented a singular one, not of any immediate military nature, but one with significant long-term implications. In 1939 the Foreign Office produced a white paper that called for an end to Jewish immigration to Palestine in 1944 and the establishment of a single Palestinian state in which the Arabs, by virtue of holding veto power on any further Jewish immigration, would outnumber Jews three to one. The white paper, produced as a gambit should war come, was intended to placate Arabs throughout the Middle East. Chamberlain believed that if war came, the Arab world would be a far stronger ally against Hitler than five hundred thousand Palestinian Jews. Parliament was to take up the white paper in May 1944. The British military chiefs advocated adoption. Churchill did not, and considered the white paper to be a betrayal of the Balfour Declaration* and a betrayal of Jews. He had opposed the policy in 1939 and still did, because the Arab majority within a single Palestinian state would never allow the Jewish minority to execute a partition into two separate states. If trouble arose over partition, Churchill told Ismay, it will come from the Arabs and that "left to themselves, the Jews would beat the Arabs." He used parliamentary procedures to keep the bill from coming to a vote, thus delaying the debate until after the war. His support for Zionism never flagged, even when later in the year, two young Zionist terrorists assassinated Lord Moyne (Walter Guinness), resident minister in the Middle East. Moyne was an old Churchill family friend and had hosted Clementine onboard his yacht *Rosaura* during their pacific journey a decade earlier. He had long opposed Zionism,

---

* Promulgated in 1917 by Foreign Minister Arthur Balfour, which called for HMG to support "the establishment of a national home for the Jewish people" in Palestine with the guarantee that "nothing shall be done which may prejudice the civil and religious rights of existing non-Jewish communities in Palestine."

but he had moderated his opinions somewhat since his posting to Palestine. When Churchill learned that Zionists worldwide protested the death sentence imposed on Moyne's assassins, he advised Cairo officials, where the murder took place, to hang the killers, and hang them quickly. The sentence was carried out.[70]

Churchill, like many in senior army and Foreign Office positions, was sympathetic to Arab nationalism—the Arabs had helped Britain drive the Turks out of the Levant. As well, Muslims were at least monotheistic, unlike Gandhi and his troublesome Hindus with their grotesque pantheon of hydra-headed gods and multi-appendage goddesses. Yet unlike many of the Arabists in the military and Foreign Office, Churchill never courted Arabs at the expense of Jews. Relations between Anglican and Jewish Englishmen were often based on complete ignorance. At the end of the war and soon after the Nazi atrocities against Jews became known, Harold Nicolson, upon learning that the *Daily Mirror* (which he thought was owned and run by Jews) was encouraging service members to vote Labour in the upcoming election, confessed to his diary, "Although I loathe anti-Semitism, I do dislike Jews."[71]

Churchill was no anti-Semite, although his words had smacked of anti-Semitism in 1920 when he opposed giving economic aid to Soviet Russia, citing "the gravest objections to giving all this help to the tyrannic Government of these Jew commissars." He was at first wary, too, of the Balfour Declaration. Its call for a Jewish "national home" did not necessarily mean "autonomous state," but the door was opened and Chaim Weizmann led his Zionist followers through. When it came to Palestinian Jews, although many of his generals were mostly pro-Arab if not anti-Semitic, Churchill pushed hard for the creation of a Jewish state in Palestine, Arab opposition or no. During a cabinet meeting the previous July, he had reiterated his support: "I'm committed to the creation of a Jewish national home in Palestine ... and at the end of the war we shall have plenty of force with which to compel the Arabs to acquiesce in our designs."[72]

The French always demanded Churchill's time. In Algiers the French were at each other's throats, again, which only reinforced Roosevelt's belief that de Gaulle should have no role whatsoever in Overlord or the civil administration of liberated France. In early March, the Gaullists in Algiers put former Vichy minister of the interior Pierre Pucheu on trial for conspiring with the Germans in the executions of hundreds of French citizens. Harold Macmillan considered Pucheu to be a traitor and "a black criminal," but he feared repercussions for de Gaulle if Pucheu were shot. The trial itself damaged de Gaulle's reputation. The prosecutor, General Pierre Weiss, was "an object of universal contempt," Macmillan wrote, not least because he was "an open and known pederast, surrounded by 'pansy' officers." Although Macmillan thought Pucheu put up a strong defense, he predicted "rough justice will be done." It was. Pucheu was found guilty and shot, an act, Churchill told Colville, that did de Gaulle and the French "very great harm" in London and "above all in the United States." Still, Churchill insisted that the Leclerc Division, heroes of the Tunisian campaign, be brought from North Africa to Yorkshire in order to train for their as yet undefined role in the Battle of France. Duff Cooper would later write that he admired de Gaulle for his "superb intransigence" and admired Churchill for sticking with de Gaulle despite his own misgivings and despite Franklin Roosevelt, whom Cooper called "the stumbling block" to restoring France to its proper place in the European family.[73]

In late March, de Gaulle took his intransigence to new levels when his French Committee of National Liberation declared itself the provisional government of metropolitan France—all unoccupied French territories worldwide. Macmillan saw the decree as a direct rejoinder by de Gaulle to Roosevelt over the president's refusal to recognize the authority of the FCNL. Henri Giraud opposed the gambit, but Giraud no longer cast a shadow in French politics. His greatest sin, in de Gaulle's eyes, had been his willingness to act as America's protégé. Giraud had been America's man in Algiers; de Gaulle considered himself France's man. "Giraud has been an unconscionable time dying," Macmillan wrote an underling in Algiers, adding, "Let him die." Churchill, counseled by Macmillan and Duff Cooper, accepted the fact that de Gaulle—now sole president of the FCNL—was destined to return to France as that nation's leader. He advised Roosevelt to invite de Gaulle to Washington in order that the Frenchman might bask in symbolic recognition. It would have to be symbolic because the Americans still refused to recognize the FCNL.[74]

Anthony Eden violently disagreed with Roosevelt on the matter of de Gaulle, telling his diary, "President's absurd and petty dislike of de Gaulle blinds him. It would be folly for us to follow him in this." Roosevelt made his disdain for de Gaulle clear in a late April telegram in which he told Churchill, "I do not have any information which leads me to believe that de Gaulle and his Committee of National Liberation have as yet given any helpful assistance to our allied war effort." Still, Roosevelt, urged on by Churchill, agreed to meet de Gaulle in Washington at some point down the road, but only if de Gaulle requested the meeting. "I will not ever have it said," Roosevelt told Churchill, "that I invited him to visit me in Washington."[75]

The men of the two Moroccan-French divisions that had suffered 2,500 killed and wounded on the Gustav Line had just cause to dispute Roosevelt's denigration of French help in the war effort. As did the men of Leclerc's 2nd Armored Division. As did the more than one hundred thousand members of the French resistance armed by the Special Operations Executive. Dozens of independent French resistance groups had taken up dozens of disparate duties. Some printed clandestine newspapers—*La Voix du Nord, Libération (sud), Défense de la France.* Some helped downed Allied flyers escape over the Pyrenees into Spain and Portugal. The resistance was populated by Communists, Gaullists, monarchists, Jews, Catholics, Protestants, republicans, socialists. More than 90,000 were killed during the war, and the Germans, in reprisal for resistance activities, murdered several thousand more Frenchmen—including women and children. In the final weeks before D-day, French railroad workers (*cheminots*) sabotaged their own rail lines; other resistance cells blew up German communications centers and electric power stations. They operated even as Allied bombers intent on disrupting German communication and rail hubs dropped ordnance right on top of them.

Forty thousand Maquis (the Corsican name for the brushwood in which fighters took cover), poorly armed and lacking ammunition, were prepared to do their part. They were young men who had fled to the Massif Central and Savoy Alps to avoid slave labor in Germany. By the spring, German soldiers and Vichy police were battling the Maquis in their mountain redoubts. The Maquis, like the rest of the resistance, waited for more guns, bombs, and ammunition. They listened for the secret phrases inserted into BBC broadcasts that warned them and guided them—"The dice are on the table." ... "It is hot in Suez." ... "The tomatoes should be picked." They especially waited to hear two lines from Paul Verlaine's poem *"Chanson d'automne"* ("Autumn Song"). The first, *"Les sanglots longs des violons de l'automne"* ("The long sobs of the violins of autumn"), was to be broadcast on the first two nights of the invasion month. The second, *"Blessent mon coeur d'une langueur monotone"* ("Pierce my heart with a dull languor"), would signify that the invasion was imminent. The French underground awaited those words, and awaited the return to France of the man all of France considered their leader: Charles de Gaulle.[76]

The Anglo-American alliance had from the beginning lumbered along despite political and military differences of opinion over de Gaulle, the Aegean, India, the timing of Overlord (and now Anvil). With victory assured if not yet in sight, differences in American and British postwar economic goals began to seep into the relationship like sand into a well-oiled gearbox. Late in 1943, five senators, including Republican Henry Cabot Lodge Jr. of Massachusetts and Democrat Richard Russell of Georgia, proclaimed that America had become a "global sucker." They called for American aid to be used as a lever—the British saw it as a cudgel—to obtain postwar economic and political advantages. Churchill had had the five in mind when he excoriated "naysayers" in his February speech. By early 1944, Roosevelt was troubled enough by the trade picture (and by congressional pressure) to drop from Lend-Lease all British purchases of discretionary goods that did not directly contribute to the war effort. The cost to Britain to buy these goods stood at about $400 million, or roughly one-third of its $1.5 billion in gold and dollar balances (a balance Roosevelt had kept hidden from the U.S. Congress).

The new policy could only add more debt to the British balance sheet and undercut Britain's ability to compete in world markets after the war, especially against the United States. Treasury Secretary Henry Morgenthau Jr. was then working up the financial and banking parts of that policy in detail. From a strictly financial standpoint, such machinations were journal entries, a way to manage accounts. It was only business. Morgenthau, an abiding friend to Britain during his decade at Treasury, was in fundamental agreement with the demand for Britain to spend down its balances, but he advised taking no action until later in the war to avoid disrupting—possibly obliterating—postwar Anglo-American relations. But the five senators, the press, and the Congress had forced the issue.

There were other issues. Roosevelt asked Churchill—demanded, really—that British and American trade officials sit down in Washington (the meeting to be chaired by Roosevelt) to work out a postwar oil policy. Churchill didn't like that idea at all, and in late February he told Roosevelt that many in Britain saw such a meeting as the first step "to deprive us of our oil assets in the Middle East." Roosevelt replied with a curt rebuff; the talks must proceed, in Washington. "I cannot change my position in this regard." As for British worries over Middle East oil, Roosevelt replied, "I am disturbed by the rumors the British wish to horn in on Saudi Arabian oil reserves." In late February Roosevelt sent two telegrams to London in which the president cited the "manifest need" for all of the United Nations to address the issues of postwar trade and monetary policy, oil, tariffs, commodities, and cartels. Believing the telegrams had been ghostwritten by Roosevelt underlings (as usual, he could not bring himself to denigrate his "friend") and signed by the exhausted president, Churchill sent a memo to Eden and advised they simply ignore the communications: "All this frantic dancing to the American tune is silly.... My recommendation is to let it all rip for a bit."[77]

Britain exported virtually nothing to offset Lend-Lease imports; the ratio in dollar imports and pound exports was near one hundred to one. That would appear to set up an economic disaster in the making, yet the eminent British historian Peter Clarke points out in *The Last Thousand Days of the British Empire* that Britain's problems were more financial than economic. Clarke pegs the spring of 1944 as the start of those one thousand days. The country was running at full employment, with factories humming along on three shifts, but they were producing weapons and munitions, not exportable goods. The question, addressed later in 1944 by 1,200 international bankers at the Bretton Woods Conference in New Hampshire, was how could Britain trade its way out of the financial hole it would find itself in at war's end? The short answer was: on terms set by America. After Bretton Woods, the U.S. dollar served as the world's reserve currency; artificial exchange rates were banished; nations paid their debts at the new — and ultimately burdensome to Britain — rates of exchange. The World Bank was created on the principle that nations could not draw down from their "paper" account surpluses without first making real deposits, at exchange rates set by the markets, with the result that by the end of the war, the British pound — and Britain — was relegated to secondary status. Churchill did not deem Bretton Woods worthy of mention in his memoirs of the war.[78]

Roosevelt convened his preliminary oil summit in the spring, at which time the British had no choice but to abandon their policy of restricting production at their Middle East concessions in order to maintain profit margins. Yet, concluded *Time,* the "big problem" with oil "in the postwar world will not be scarcity but surplus [and price collapse]."[79]

In early March, Churchill received a short letter from Roosevelt that contained an extraordinary proposal in the form of a memorandum on the future of Iran prepared for the president by Major General Patrick Hurley, an Oklahoma oilman, former secretary of war under Herbert Hoover, and now Roosevelt's man in Tehran. In his note, Roosevelt offered that it would take "thirty or forty years to eliminate the graft" in Iran and to properly prepare the people for democracy. In the interim, the country would "need trustees"; Roosevelt nominated America, Russia, and Britain for that role. The trustees' mandate would be the "care and education" of Iranians. For comic relief he tossed in, "From your and my personal observation I think we could add something about cleanliness as well." One line offered a direct challenge to Churchill and the British Empire: "I do not want the United States to acquire a 'zone of influence' — or any other nation for that matter."[80]

Hurley's report had to do with Iran, but his vision went far beyond the Middle East. "This plan," he wrote, "may become the criterion for the relations of the United States toward all the nations which are now suffering

from the evils of greedy minorities, monopolies, aggression, and imperialism." Although Hurley included Germany in his pantheon of evil imperialists, Great Britain was his real target. France, Holland, and Belgium would
no doubt emerge from the war too hobbled to maintain their empires. Italy
had already lost hers. Germany would lose all. That left Britain, which to
be maintained (by America) as a power in the new order "must accept the
principles of liberty and democracy and discard the principles of oppressive imperialism." Hurley did not mince a word: "I must say that if imperialism is dead, it seems very reluctant to lie down." He expressed his belief
that "the ultimate destiny of the English speaking peoples is a single destiny," yet "British imperialism is being defended today by the blood of the
soldiers of the most democratic nation on earth." That relationship had to
change. America was "approaching the irrepressible conflict between
world-wide imperialism and world-wide democracy" and had to assert its
values, specifically the Four Freedoms. Hurley called his policy "nation
building." Roosevelt did not inform Churchill that Hurley held a stake in
the Sinclair Oil Company, which was then in negotiations with Iran for oil
concessions.[81]

Roosevelt sent Hurley's proposal to the State Department for comment.
Dean Acheson, then an assistant secretary of state, thought Hurley "vain
and reckless," and characterized his plan as "messianic globaloney." Upon
hearing that, Hurley charged Acheson with being "for monopoly and
imperialism and against democracy." Roosevelt, by pitting his minions
against each other, avoided direct involvement in the entire unseemly
affair. Although Hurley left government work in 1945 and Acheson later
rose to secretary of state, the philosophical underpinnings of Hurley's
"nation building" intrigued many in Washington, then and since. Likewise, the question of whether Roosevelt's economic agenda was simply
imperialism of a different stripe has been pondered ever since. Churchill's
war was indeed imperial, in the sense he fought to *preserve* the British
Empire by deploying—with the advice and consent of the Dominions—its
imperial troops worldwide. He sought no financial gain; Roosevelt did.
Churchill sought no territorial gain; Stalin did.[82]

Much was in need of discussion. Churchill proposed meeting Roosevelt
in Bermuda at the end of March. Roosevelt, having never fully recovered
from Tehran and in increasingly ill health, declined. The president, in fact,
spent the entire month of April fishing and reading and relaxing at financier Bernard Baruch's 23,000-acre South Carolina plantation, during
which time no one outside of his cabinet knew his whereabouts.[83]

Churchill did not reply to Roosevelt's "nation building" letter for almost
three months. When he did, he told Roosevelt that Hurley's pronouncements "make me rub my eyes." He added, "I make bold, however, to sug-

gest that British imperialism has spread and is spreading democracy more widely than any other system of government since the beginning of time." Churchill thought in terms of postwar nation *rebuilding,* but Roosevelt had in mind something else entirely.[84]

The question of Polish borders above all other political issues commanded Churchill's attention. The Poles were proving themselves as stubborn as Stalin. Colville feared that the effort to persuade the Poles to cede territory would be compared to the betrayal of the Czechs at Munich. Owen O'Malley in the Foreign Office believed so, and he repeated to Colville a line from his report on the Katyn murders: "What is morally indefensible is always politically inept." The Poles, for their part, refused to entertain any notion of ceding territory, this despite pledges by Stalin that Poland would remain free and independent. Then Stalin announced he could no longer communicate with Churchill on the matter because their correspondence was regularly leaked to the press by the British. In fact, the Soviet embassy was the source of the leaks. Stalin further mucked up the works when he permitted *Pravda* to run a story that claimed the British were in secret peace negotiations with Berlin, a charge that prompted Churchill to proclaim to Brooke, "Trying to maintain good relations with a communist is like wooing a crocodile.... When it opens its mouth you cannot tell whether it is trying to smile, or preparing to eat you up." By mid-March, Churchill concluded that his efforts to forge a Polish-Soviet agreement had failed and that he soon would have to "make a cold announcement to Parliament" on the matter. "It all seems to augur ill," Colville told his diary on March 18, "for the future of relations between this country and the U.S.S.R."

The Old Man began telling friends that he would not be around to witness those relations, because he had not long to live. One evening in March he informed the gathered—while *"La Marseillaise"* played on the gramophone—that although he had not much time left, he had a political testament for after the war: "Far more important than India or the Colonies or solvency is *the Air.* We live in a world of wolves—and *bears*" (italics Colville). Three nights later the Old Man lamented to Colville that "this world ('this dusty and lamentable ball') is now too beastly to live in. People act so revoltingly they just don't deserve to live." Yet, as always, he remained cautiously optimistic. On April 1 he wrote to Roosevelt of Stalin's belligerency, "I have a feeling the bark may be worse than its bite."[85]

By then, more than two months after the first assaults on the Gustav

Line and the Anzio landings, no progress whatsoever had been made at either place. The New Zealanders again tried to storm Monte Cassino on March 15, with the same bloody results as in February. On the twenty-fifth they called it off. Clark's army had gained but a few miles in two months. The troops under siege at Anzio had gained nothing.[86]

Events on the Home Island vexed Churchill as well. Three by-elections did not go well for the coalition government and especially for the Tories. In the first one, in January, a hitherto unknown Common Wealth Party (a Socialist party formed in 1942) candidate beat both the Tory and Labour candidates. This was a rebuke to the coalition and foreshadowed events to come. The Tories barely won the second election, held in a traditional Conservative constituency. This was a rebuke to Churchill, who had taken a strong stand against the Independent candidate. The third election proved even more of a disaster. For all but five of the previous 210 years, a member of the Cavendish family, one of England's wealthiest, had represented West Derbyshire. When an Independent challenged the sitting Cavendish MP, twenty-six-year-old William John Robert Cavendish, Marquess of Hartington, Churchill weighed in, calling the election a mandate on the government and telling electors "their votes can prove the heroic temper of our island in these tremendous days." Voters gave Cavendish the boot.[87]

The elections, like the Polish affair, did nothing for Churchill's peace of mind. Colville found him in the Annexe one night, "sitting in his chair," looking "old, tired, and very depressed." He was muttering that any more such defeats might force a general election. "Now," Churchill said, "with great events pending, when national unity was essential: the question of annihilating great states had to be faced." Yet, he added, it was beginning "to look as if democracy had not the persistence to go through with it."[88]

Even his beloved Parliament briefly rebuked him, or so he believed when in late March an amendment was inserted into a groundbreaking education-reform bill, which passed the House by one vote. The amendment, sponsored by Thelma Cazalet, a former suffragette and the Conservative MP from Islington East, called for equal pay for women teachers. The problem, as Churchill saw it, was not with giving women equal pay (this would come to pass in his next premiership) but that the government bill had not included any such clause. The vote, therefore, amounted to a vote of no confidence. Churchill—who championed the reforms—demanded that the offending clause be removed and that the House pass the original government bill in a vote of confidence. Harold Nicolson blamed the episode on "the idiocy of the House" and hoped that Churchill might back down. He did not, telling one MP, "I am not going to tumble around my cage like a wounded canary. You knocked me off my perch. You have now got to put me back on my perch. Otherwise I won't sing."

Cazalet withdrew her amendment. The House put Churchill back on his perch by a vote of 425–23. Roosevelt, who had just had his veto of a tax bill (which he said served the greedy, not the needy) overridden by Congress, thought Churchill's battle with the Commons "splendid," and cabled his congratulations, adding, "Results here would be almost as good if we operated under your system." Colville thought Churchill's forcing the issue was like "cracking a nut with a sledgehammer."[89]

That the House and prime minister had drifted into conflict was due in part to the fact that Anthony Eden was both Leader of the House and foreign secretary. No man could possibly do both jobs, and by late March, Eden was doing neither very well. Eden feared himself on the verge of a breakdown. He broached the subject of quitting the Foreign Office to Churchill, who rejected the notion: "You will have to go on as you are for a few months longer." Then, in early April, with Eden clearly an ill man, Churchill offered some words of sympathy — "You are my right arm; we must take care of you" — and packed Eden off for three weeks of rest. In Eden's absence Churchill took over the Foreign Office.[90]

Thus, in the run-up to the great gambit in Normandy, Churchill served as prime minister, defence minister, and foreign minister. In his multiple roles, he chaired cabinet meetings, and War Cabinet meetings, and Chiefs of Staff meetings, and took his weekly lunches with the King and Eisenhower. Alec Cadogan, at the Foreign Office, now serving temporarily under Churchill, began to pepper his diary entries with many of the same impressions Brooke and Colville confessed to their journals. On April 12, Colville told his diary: "Struck by how very tired and worn out the P.M. looks now." The same day, Cadogan wrote: "[P.M.] kept me from my work for three hours today on matters that shouldn't have taken twenty minutes. How does he get through his work?" Cadogan on April 19, after a late afternoon cabinet meeting: "An awful day....P.M., I fear, is breaking down....I am fussed about the P.M. He is *not* the man he was 12 months ago, and I really don't know if he can carry on." Brooke, the same day, after a Chiefs of Staff meeting that ran to 1:30 A.M.: "P.M. tired, listless, and lacking decision."[91]

The Old Man was tired — from setting a pace others had difficulty keeping up with. He promised Colville he would make his bedtime 1:30, but he regularly stayed up past three o'clock. He had a bed installed in his room adjacent to the House so that he could take short naps between sessions. He carried the greatest burden, and he not once considered laying it down. While Cadogan took himself home to dine at 8:00 P.M. after the "awful" cabinet meeting of the nineteenth, Churchill prepared for the Chiefs of Staff meeting that Brooke found so unproductive. Eden was, of course, on sick leave. "Everyone's exhausted," Alec Cadogan told his diary, "but I suppose we've got to plug along." Even the young, strapping Jock Colville allowed a quotient of pessimism to penetrate his natural optimism. Everyone is "gloomy," he wrote on April 14. "Now in the shadow of an impending struggle which may be history's most fatal, a restless and dissatisfied mood possesses many people in all circles and walks of life. And over everything hangs the uncertainty of Russia's future policy towards Europe and the world."[92]

"Public opinion at the moment is not good," Harold Nicolson told his diary. "They are exhausted by five years of war." Factory workers were sending HMG a message by voting with their feet throughout the land. More than two hundred thousand coal miners had gone out on strike in Wales and Yorkshire. Textile workers went out in Scotland. More than four times as many working days were lost to strikes that year as in 1940. Britons had not gone to the polls in a general election since 1935. They were impatient and exhausted. Brendan Bracken, foreseeing more unrest over the horizon, predicted to Jock Colville (much as Roosevelt had predicted to Harriman in 1941) "a crushing defeat for the Conservative Party at the next election and its possible collapse like the Liberals after the last war." Nicolson, upon stepping into the lavatory at the Blackheath Railway Station, beheld a scrawl on the wall: "Winston Churchill is a bastard." Nicolson, furious at the insult, feared that "Winston has become an electoral liability now rather than an asset. This makes me sick with human nature. Once the open sea is reached, we forget how we clung to the pilot in the storm."[93]

The pilot, as usual, was scrutinizing the seas all around, near and far, with the result that he failed to set a steady course. He became mired in details and his dispatch boxes backed up. He had learned that the Americans were no longer painting their aircraft, which lessened their weight and added twenty miles an hour to their speed; "Pray let me know," he asked the Aircraft Ministry, if the RAF was considering doing likewise. When he noticed an "untidy sack with holes in it and sand leaking out" in St. James's Park, he demanded it be removed. The park had been closed to civilians, and other than military men on their way to secret meetings and a scaup duck that Brooke liked to observe, St. James's Park was empty and neglected. Other details had political overtones. Churchill objected to a proposal by the Home Secretary to hold a national day of prayer for the success of Overlord. Such an event would be a "grave mistake," Churchill wrote. "In my view there is no need for a national day of prayer or thanksgiving at this time." Mollie Panter-Downes noted that Montgomery was making a show of touring the land inviting "God to scatter the Allies' enemies and the public to scatter its cash in war bonds." Churchill took note of and shut down Montgomery's public relations and prayer tour. The prayers being said by Britons that spring were not only for the safety of their sons, but for rain; a severe drought was killing winter crops and did not bode well for the summer harvest. Rural wells ran dry, forcing villagers into long lines to procure buckets of water. Panter-Downes wrote that with millions of troops moving about the country, England was in the position of the hostess of a modest house whose "influx of guests has run the cistern dry."[94]

Churchill's relations with his military chiefs were as arid as the countryside. On the heels of Operation Caliph, his plan to support Overlord by sending three divisions into Bordeaux, came proposals to liberate Norway, and to drive into the Aegean "in the event of Overlord not being successful" or German troops there being "beyond our power to tackle." He saw these ventures as "flanking movements." But the time for flanking movements had passed. He and Britain were committed to Overlord. Yet Churchill was not trying to evade that commitment; he was performing due diligence in the event that the Germans sent enough panzers to France to trigger a cancellation of the invasion, as agreed upon in Tehran. Eisenhower pondered the same question. His grandson and biographer later wrote that Eisenhower was in constant contact with Marshall during February and early March regarding the problem of what to do "should German moves in the next several weeks rule out Overlord as impractical." As Eisenhower saw it, Anvil, the south of France operation, presented the only possible alternative. Churchill and Eisenhower understood that perfect certainty about Overlord could never be achieved, and that "an irrevocable commitment to Overlord was not possible until the troops were ashore in France." And they could not go ashore until the Combined Chiefs of Staff delegated to Eisenhower the absolute authority to do whatever needed to be done in order to not only carry out Overlord but also sustain it. This they did in February when they formally designated him supreme allied commander, giving him authority over all Allied land, sea, and air forces. Churchill could probe and prod Eisenhower, but he could make no demands.[95]

This did not apply to Churchill's British chiefs, from whom he demanded much. Brooke's diary references to Churchill grew more furious. After one particularly difficult February meeting (and most were now difficult), Brooke wrote, "I often doubt whether I am going mad or he is really sane." After another he wrote, "I can not stick any more meetings like this." During a March meeting, Churchill claimed to have discovered a new island off the coast of Sumatra, and proposed sending a fleet there. Admiral Cunningham replied that with the Japanese fleet in Singapore, such a move would be "courting disaster." Of the meeting Brooke wrote, "I began to wonder

whether I was in Alice in Wonderland, or whether I was really fit for a lunatic asylum." And of Churchill: "I...am honestly getting very doubtful about
his balance of mind....I don't know where we are or where we are going as
regards our strategy....It is a ghastly situation." And on March 23, "I feel
like a man chained to the chariot of a lunatic!!" To Dill, in Washington,
Brooke wrote: "I am just about at the end of my tether." Brooke was not
alone in fighting ongoing battles with Churchill. Admiral Sir Andrew Cunningham's autobiography, *A Sailor's Odyssey*, conveys the same frustration.
Air Chief Marshal Portal also expressed his doubts about Churchill, who,
Portal felt, did not appreciate the proper role of airpower. Yet Portal grossly
overrated the effectiveness of strategic bombing. He shocked Brooke that
spring when he claimed that he could have won the war by early 1944 if not
for "the handicap of the other two services!!" Brooke usually reserved his
double exclamation marks for prime-ministerial quotations.[96]

Brooke's diary entries, when cherry-picked, portray a meddlesome and
infuriating prime minister, the strangler fig in Brooke's neatly tilled garden
of military strategy. Yet Brooke's diaries—and those of the other journal
keepers—are informative only when taken as a whole. After a particularly
disputatious afternoon meeting, Brooke was summoned to dinner by
Churchill. The CIGS expected to be sacked. "On the contrary," he wrote,
"we had a *tête-à-tête* dinner at which he [Churchill] was quite charming,
as if he meant to make up for some of the rough passages of the day." They
discussed their children and Churchill's difficulty in controlling Randolph.
They discussed "the President's unpleasant attitude lately." They mused
on Italy, and the latest German air raids. Concerned for Brooke's health,
Churchill told him to take some time off so as not to wear himself out.
Later that night, after a post-dinner meeting of the Chiefs of Staff where
Brooke found Churchill to be "much more reasonable," the CIGS told his
diary, "He has astonishing sides to his character." Equally astonishing is
that it had taken Brooke almost three years of working side by side with
Churchill to reach that conclusion. When thirteen years later Brooke—by
then Lord Alanbrooke—sent a personally inscribed copy of his published
(and abridged) diaries to Churchill, he wrote that his criticisms were his
way of unwinding each night, mere "momentary daily impressions." He
added, "I look upon the privilege of having served you in war as the greatest honour destiny has bestowed on me."[97]

Despite the tumultuousness of the staff meetings, to say nothing of the
tumultuous goings-on in Churchill's mind, the chiefs and Churchill com-
plemented each other. Churchill brought illumination, which his chiefs
brought into focus. Churchill never seriously considered sacking any of
them, and none of them ever seriously considered resigning. In his capacity
as minister of defence he never overrode their policies. Anthony Eden

wrote that attending a meeting with Churchill was "a splendid and unique experience. It might be a monologue. It was never a dictatorship." Colville noted the criticisms leveled at Churchill by the Chiefs of Staff, who, in Colville's opinion, lacked Churchill's "imagination and resolution" and could not see that it was Churchill who provided them "guidance and purpose." The chiefs and Churchill worked together in harness, the black steed of Churchill's passion and the white steeds of the coolly logical Brooke, Cunningham, and Portal.[98]

Clementine Churchill later said of Brooke, "We might have won the war without Alanbrooke; I don't think we would have won it without Winston."[99]

The diarists noted Churchill being in "top form" as regularly as they noted his fatigue or inattention to his boxes or tendency to ramble on. A narrow sampling of "P.M. tired" diary entries yields as incomplete and distorted an image of Churchill as a narrow sampling of "P.M. in top form" entries. He had to be taken whole in order to form an accurate image of the man. Not for nothing did John Martin later say that Churchill had about him "a zigzag streak of lightning on the brain."[100]

When he addressed his countrymen on March 26 the lightning was missing. The subject was the postwar world. He promised Britons that national health insurance would follow victory, along with a complete overhaul of housing, including "a clean sweep of all those areas of which our civilization should be ashamed." The slums would go, but nothing would be done that would interfere with the war effort. Change would come, but only after victory. He proclaimed that "the greatest scheme of improved education that has ever been attempted by a responsible Government...will soon be on the Statute-book." Britons were not impressed. "They feel like they have asked for bread," Mollie Panter-Downes wrote, "but have been given, if not a stone, simply a promise of thousands upon thousands of prefabricated houses, at modest rent." Steel shares rose immediately on the promise of the prefabricated future, "but peoples' spirits noticeably did not." Harold Nicolson was pained by the comments of colleagues who thought Churchill had sounded like "a worn and petulant old man.... The upper classes feel that all this sacrifice and suffering will only mean that the proletariat will deprive them of all their comforts and influence, and then proceed to render this country and Empire a third class state."[101]

On his way to bed in the early hours of April 5, Churchill allowed to Colville that although the prospect of the second front worried him, "I am hardening to it." By "hardening" he meant that his support for Overlord was growing. He had used the same term a month earlier in a cable to Marshall, which he referenced in a March 18 telegram to Roosevelt, where he repeated, "I am hardening for Overlord as the time gets nearer." On April 1, he again cabled Roosevelt, "As you know, I harden for it the nearer I get to it. Eisenhower is a very large man." On April 7, Good Friday, Montgomery unveiled to the Chiefs of Staff and Churchill the final plans for Overlord. Brooke was duly impressed, calling it "a wonderful day." According to Brooke, Churchill—"in a very weepy condition" and lacking "vitality"—addressed barely a few remarks to the assembled.[102]

In fact, Montgomery's presentation had lessened Churchill's anxiety over the invasion, for since the first meetings of January, Montgomery had put meat on the bones of Overlord. Six divisions would now go ashore in the first wave, supported on the flanks by three airborne divisions. By D-day plus two days, a further six divisions would be ashore. Montgomery laid out the particulars. Four natural phenomena had to fall into alignment like plums in a slot machine for the invasion to have any chance for success. Three could be predetermined: the tides, the phase of the moon, and the length of time between morning nautical twilight—dawn—and sunrise. The tides had to be near ebb but rising, such that combat engineers could clear exposed German mines and obstacles from the beaches. Then, three hours of rising tides would serve to carry the men farther up onto the beaches. The moon had to be a bomber's moon—full or near full, in order that the paratroopers could operate in the lunar beam. Finally, the optimum length of time between dawn and sunrise had been calculated to be about sixty minutes, enough time for the navy and air forces to rake the beaches with shell fire but not so long as to allow the Germans to recover and coordinate their defense and counterattack. Three mornings in June fell into nearly perfect alignment on all three counts, the fifth, sixth, and seventh. Montgomery picked June 5 as the most favorable. The fourth natural element was entirely unpredictable: the weather. Ideally, Eisenhower told his press aide, the morning of D-day should be clear, with a light onshore breeze blowing the dust and smoke of battle inland, to confuse and blind the Germans.[103]

A few days after the April 7 meeting, Churchill telegraphed Roosevelt with a brief summary. Again he stressed his support for the enterprise. "I am becoming very hard set on Overlord." He told Roosevelt that he had expressed to Eisenhower and Montgomery his "strong confidence...in this extraordinary but magnificent operation." And he expressed his disagreement with "loose talk" on both sides of the Atlantic that predicted horrific Allied casualties. It would be the Germans who suffered, he told Roosevelt. To Eisenhower, Churchill offered that if by the coming winter, the Allies had taken the Channel ports, Cherbourg, and Paris, he would "assert the victory to be the greatest of modern times." Eisenhower replied that the Overlord timetable called for Allied armies to be on the German borders by winter. Churchill late in the month told Colville that on D-day he intended to be onboard a Royal Navy warship just offshore the beaches, and to be "one of the first on the bridgehead, if he possibly could—and what fun to get there before Monty."[104]

On the day after Montgomery's briefing, the debate over Anvil assumed new and troublesome dimensions. Ten days earlier, George Marshall proposed a halt in Italian operations once the Anzio beachhead was united with Alexander's army, in order that ten divisions could be siphoned away from Italy in support of Anvil, which Marshall insisted must follow Overlord by July 10. The Americans' rigidity on Anvil led Brooke to exclaim to his diary that it was "impossible to accept" Marshall's plan to "go on the defensive in Italy. They fail to realize the forces available do not admit to two fronts in the Mediterranean." Eisenhower told his naval aide, Commander Butcher, that he was "delighted" by Marshall's decision "to forget Rome."[105]

Eisenhower and the British Chiefs of Staff debated the matter, Eisenhower arguing that the German army, not a psychological prize such as Rome, should be the target. Brooke and the British counterargued that Rome was a military target and had to be taken in order for the Allies to continue northward into France or toward Trieste. By April 8, the Anvil question had become an unholy mess. Brooke, seeing Anvil's negative consequences to the Italian campaign, joined Churchill in trying to introduce some flexibility into the debate. Roosevelt and Marshall, for their part, remained inflexible; they had promised Anvil to Stalin at Tehran, and that was that. Ironically, it was the continuing stalemate on the Italian front that had brought the wisdom of Anvil into question. "There was no use in landing in France," Churchill later wrote, "unless we did so at the right time.... All turned on the capture of Rome." Churchill fired off a telegram to Marshall protesting the abandonment of Rome, and was coolly rebuffed. Jumbo Wilson advised scrubbing Anvil altogether because there were simply not enough landing craft in the Mediterranean to undertake the operation. The Americans offered to bring landing craft from the Pacific to the Mediterranean, but only for use in Anvil, thus thwarting any British plans for amphibious operations in the Aegean. Then they withdrew the offer.[106]

Admiral King once again, as he had in 1942, began grumbling about the need to shift the war effort to the Pacific. Eisenhower played that card by reminding Brooke that U.S. Republicans wanted to draft Douglas MacArthur for a presidential run. MacArthur, in correspondence with Nebraska congressman Albert Miller, had disparaged the New Deal and offered that he believed the European war was just about over. The letters, which Miller leaked to the press, gave Britons pause. The implication of Eisenhower's gambit was that as president, MacArthur would shift everything to the Pacific. But Brooke held firm: Italy must be reinforced, and certainly not stripped. Marshall saw Italy as a stalemate and a diversion from striking into Germany through France. Churchill saw Italy as a substitute for Anvil. Eisenhower, whose first and most critical duty was to make Overlord a success, was caught between his American superiors and the British. Finally, on April 19, after General Alexander announced his plan to begin his Italian offensive in mid-May with a hoped-for junction with the Anzio forces by early June, the Americans conceded that Anvil could not take place in July. Eisenhower and Brooke hammered out an "appreciation" for the Combined Chiefs that did not mention Anvil and called for Rome to be Alexander's springtime objective. The Anvil debate, full of twists and turns, lay dormant until mid-June, when it metastasized into crisis.[107]

In the east, Hitler had staked his hopes on the Wehrmacht's resolve and the inability of the Red Army to fight on during a terrible winter, but the Red Army had ignored the winter. In February the Russians encircled 50,000 Germans on the lower Dnieper front. In March, the Red Army swept past Odessa, crossed the Dneister River on a three-hundred-mile front, and closed on Czernowitz, in Bukovina. The Russians bypassed the Crimea, leaving a German army trapped there. The Russian winter offensive had been so powerful that many in London and Washington believed the war would be over before summer. But even the Russians could not ignore the spring rain and mud season—the *rasputitsa*. In April the battle lines began to stabilize from the Baltic to the southern Ukraine.

The stabilization of the Eastern Front, David Eisenhower later wrote, "dashed lingering hopes on both sides of the Atlantic that Germany would be defeated before summer." This is a vital observation, and it relates to several other unsettling lines of thought that percolated through the ranks and led to "a climate of doubt that persisted at all levels." Most obvious, Eisenhower writes, was the realization that if the war did not end before summer, Overlord would have to take place. That truth, in turn, led to doubts over the ability of green American recruits to stand up to the Wehrmacht; the debacle at Kasserine had taken place only a year earlier, and at Anzio—"part of the Kasserine legacy"—the men were still on the beaches. Those doubts commingled with growing doubts about Soviet intentions. Would the Red Army attack as agreed upon or stand by while the Anglo-Americans and Germans punched themselves out in the west? This was a fear Brooke had expressed to his diary at Tehran. On April 8, Eisenhower cabled the Normandy invasion date to Moscow. The Kremlin did not respond for two weeks, during which time the doubts only grew.[108]

The question of unconditional surrender weighed on everyone. Eisenhower sought permission from Roosevelt to "clarify" the terms of surrender in order that he could drop propaganda leaflets over Germany assuring Germans that fundamental rights—religion, assembly, trade unions—would be restored. From Eisenhower's soldierly perspective, Germans willing to surrender were far more desirable than an entire nation fighting to the last man standing. Roosevelt flatly refused, telling his Chiefs of Staff, "I am not willing at this time to say that we do not intend to destroy the German nation." Any "clarification" of surrender terms would be read by Moscow as backtracking on the annihilation of Germany agreed upon in Tehran. Stalin was quite willing to expend millions of Russian lives to gain that end. Churchill, like Eisenhower, saw in unconditional surrender the potential for horrific loss in Allied lives, but he thought better of bringing the subject up with Roosevelt. Churchill's frustration over his diminished role in all matters political and military was evidenced by a remark he made in mid-April to Cadogan: "This battle [Overlord] has been forced upon us by the Russians and by the United States military authorities." That was true, as was the fact that he had "hardened" to the plan.[109]

During April, as the invasion forces conducted field exercises on English beaches and in the countryside, the Allied air forces fully implemented Eisenhower's pre-invasion air strategy known as the Transportation Plan, the object of which was to bomb every French rail hub, bridge, and tunnel that led to Normandy in order to isolate German forces and deny them mobility. Almost one hundred individual targets were marked for destruction, as well as dozens in Calais, to put the Germans off the scent. More than 120 German radar sites were added to the list. Eisenhower later wrote that Churchill feared that up to 80,000 Frenchmen would die in the bombings. Churchill was indeed worried, and told Roosevelt in an April telegram that he and the entire War Cabinet feared the "French slaughters" would result in 80,000 casualties, including 20,000 dead, an estimate that ultimately proved correct. It would be another Oran, a slaughter of Allies by friendly fire, Churchill argued, on a far bloodier scale. It was a strategy that would make enemies of the French. Churchill's fear of French resentment did not in the end prove justified.

The French themselves were divided on the issue, with several resistance leaders telling HMG that the bombings would be resented in France, while

Major General Pierre Koenig, commander of French forces in Britain, told Eisenhower that the French people would accept twice the casualties if the sacrifice helped rid France of the reviled Boche. The War Cabinet asked Eisenhower to restrict targets to those that would yield no more than one hundred French casualties. Eisenhower refused, on the grounds that such restraint would "emasculate" the strategy. He assured Churchill that thousands of warning leaflets were dropped into the French countryside before the bombers came on. Not satisfied, Churchill went over Eisenhower's head, to Roosevelt, and asked the president to overrule his general. Roosevelt flatly refused, telling Churchill, "However regrettable" the loss of French lives, "I am not prepared to impose from this great distance any restrictions on military action by the responsible commanders that in their opinion might mitigate against the success of Overlord or cause more Allied casualties." The president's reply hinted at a fundamental change in their relationship. Although Churchill was the man on the spot, in London and at the center of the planning and the action, his advice no longer carried the weight with Roosevelt that it once had. Roosevelt henceforth and from his great distance would be the final arbitrator in all such matters.[110]

A German radio transmission intercepted in May vindicated Eisenhower's air strategy: "The raids carried out in recent weeks have caused systematic breakdown of all main line; the coastal defences have been cut off from the supply bases of the interior."[111]

May came in, and brought with it the most beautiful weather in years. Alec Cadogan, spending a few days at his Northiam cottage, effused to his diary, "The daffodils are over, except the very late white ones. And the narcissi are still out, and the spiraea arguta, like little snowmen. And the wallflowers a warm cloth of gold and bronze. The old pear tree in full bloom.... Lilac coming out.... Another gorgeous summer day." It was all "heavenly." He also noted the need for rain. Churchill, however, ushered in the new month with "gloomy forebodings" about the future behavior of Russia. "I have always not liked the month of May," he offered to Jock Colville, who recalled that one of the first remarks Churchill had made to him four years earlier was, "If I were the first of May, I should be ashamed of myself." But May 1944 began to prove itself praiseworthy.[112]

On May 11, Alexander made his move against the Gustav Line. In light of Anvil's being postponed, it was hoped that this thrust would draw Germans away from Normandy. It did; twenty-five German divisions were now in Italy, and more had been sent to the Balkans in anticipation of an

Allied thrust north toward Vienna. On May 15, after four days of preparatory strikes, a Canadian corps was thrown into the battle for Monte
Cassino. On the seventeenth, two Polish divisions led the final assault on
the monastery. Along the Gustav Line twenty Allied divisions faced seven
divisions of the German Tenth Army. The preponderance of Allied men,
artillery, and aircraft began to bend the German lines. Kesselring ordered
that reinforcements be rushed south from Anzio to defend his line.

It was too late. The end for the Germans at Monte Cassino came on
May 18 when, after a point-blank artillery barrage and an assault by the
Polish II Corps, the heights were taken. On that beautiful spring morning,
Polish troops — less four thousand killed and wounded — entered the
ruins of the monastery. The Germans had fled overnight. The Allied army
pursuing them was one of the most cosmopolitan in history. In the Imperial Army: Britons, Canadians, New Zealanders, South Africans, Newfoundlanders, Indians, Ceylonese, Swazi, Mauritians, and Caribbeans. In
the American: a black division and a Japanese American regiment. Among
the Allies: Italians, French, Poles, Moroccans, Algerians, Tunisians, and
Senegalese. By May 18, more than 32,000 men — including Germans — lay
dead and buried within sight of St. Benedict's mountain sanctuary. But
Highway 6, the road to Rome, was open. With Kesselring's withdrawal of
troops from Anzio, the time was ripe for an Allied breakout there, which if
successful would cut off the German Tenth Army, now fleeing north from
the Gustav Line. On May 23, the Allies finally broke out from the beachhead, where they had lived under fire for four months. Three days later
they linked up with Clark's Fifth Army. Then they turned toward Rome.[113]

As the Italian campaign came to life, a meeting was held in London that
would have far more repercussions in coming years than the bloody battle
for Monte Cassino. The previous November the London press had reported
that the Nobel Prize–winning Danish physicist Niels Bohr had escaped to
London from German-occupied Denmark by way of Stockholm. In fact,
the RAF secreted him out in the cramped bomb bay of the aptly named
Mosquito bomber, where he passed out for lack of oxygen. In London the
scientist spoke with various luminaries, including Alec Cadogan, who
gushed to his diary: "Bohr. What a man! He talked... for ¾ hour, about
what I haven't the least idea." Soon thereafter Bohr disappeared. In fact, he
had been taken to the United States, to Los Alamos, as an official British
consultant to the Tube Alloys project; that is, he was working on the Manhattan Project. He brought with him German drawings for the design of a

uranium heavy-water pile, which if built, would behave more like a reactor than a bomb, with resultant explosive forces not much more powerful than conventional bombs.[114]

This should have told the Americans that the Germans were heading in the wrong direction if building an atomic bomb was their goal. But General Leslie Groves, head of the Manhattan Project, believing that the drawings had been allowed to fall into Bohr's hands in order to put the Allies off the scent, dismissed that intelligence. Bohr also believed that the results obtained at Los Alamos might prove to be either the biggest disaster to befall mankind—if the bomb was built and deployed down the road by nations now left out of the program—or the biggest boon, if it made war unthinkable. This was a new and unique way of looking at things, a concept Roosevelt and Churchill had not yet considered. An atomic bomb, for Churchill, was simply a bomb bigger than all others, a weapon to be used in pursuit of strategic objectives. That was the purpose of weapons, after all. Bohr saw more transcendent implications.[115]

Such was Bohr's renown that he was invited to meet with Franklin Roosevelt, to whom Bohr advised a policy of sharing atomic research with the Russians in order to maintain the trust between the Allies that had been nurtured for almost three years. The alternative—keeping the Russians out of the picture—would lead, Bohr believed, to a breakdown of trust, possibly of the alliance, and would have potentially disastrous postwar consequences, the most likely being a nuclear arms race, with the Russians making their own bomb sooner or later. Here was the scientist grasping immense political implications while so far the politicians grasped only the immediate military implications. Roosevelt sent Bohr back to London in March after telling him that any such proposal to expand the nuclear family would have to be approved by Churchill per the Quebec agreement of the previous year. This Bohr attempted to do. Sir John Anderson sent Churchill a memo that outlined Bohr's thoughts and proposed a meeting be arranged. On it, Churchill scribbled, "collaborate" and "on no account." Weeks went by. On May 16, after R. V. Jones impressed upon Lord Cherwell, Churchill's science adviser, the importance of the meeting, Bohr was finally summoned to No. 10. Cherwell accompanied him.[116]

The meeting did not go well. Bohr, who often told R. V. Jones that clarity and accuracy of statement are mutually exclusive, elected to err on the side of accuracy, thus delivering such a long and complex monologue that Churchill thought him "a muddled thinker" who wanted to give away British secrets to the Russians. "Indeed," R. V. Jones later wrote, "Churchill did wonder if he was a Russian agent." Churchill reiterated his belief that the atomic bomb was simply a bigger bomb than all others and that he and his friend Franklin Roosevelt had everything under control. Then he dismissed Bohr. R. V. Jones bumped into Bohr after the meeting and asked how it went. "It was terrible!" replied the great scientist. "He scolded us like two schoolboys!"[117]

That week, Cherwell briefed the Chiefs of Staff on N spores—anthrax and bacteriological weapons. This was not the mustard gas of the Great War but something far more deadly. Churchill informed Ismay: "As you know, great progress had been made in bacteriological warfare and we have ordered a half million bombs from America for use should this mode of warfare be employed against us." Cherwell explained in detail the effectiveness of the bacterial agents; victims died suddenly and peacefully a week after exposure. Just six bombers could drop enough "gas" to kill everyone within a square mile. Churchill intended his threat as a "deterrent" lest Hitler gas the troops on the Normandy beaches. The invasion forces would carry no gas masks. Were they gassed, Churchill intended to unleash every poison he had on the population of Germany. He had on many occasions since May 1940 pledged to his nation, to his family, and to the world that Britain would never be the first to use poison gas, but now, with the liberation of the Continent imminent, he pushed the chiefs for a plan to gas Germany if by doing so the war would end sooner. This shocked the Foreign Office, recalled Antony Head, who drafted a planning memo in response to Churchill's query. "A Foreign Office chap wanted to include a paragraph," recalled Head, "saying that such a policy would forfeit moral principle. In other words, it's a bit of a shit streak to use gas, which we were all aware of. We put the paragraph in because he [Churchill] wanted it in such a hurry." As for the Foreign Office scribe who authored the paragraph that raised objections to the use of poison gas, Churchill scribbled on the memo: "Pray tell, who are the uniform psalm-singing defeatists who have written this paper?"[118]

By mid-May every soul in Britain—2.8 million Allied troops and 47 million Britons—knew the big show was close at hand. Almost five hundred American war correspondents reached that conclusion when they were told to sign powers of attorney and wills. The British people knew because Home Guardsmen were posted at just about every crossroads in the country, checking civilians' papers and directing never-ending streams of jeeps and trucks this way and that. Late in the month, civilian travel to Ireland was banned. Military bases were locked down. HMG, at the insistence of Eisenhower, had a month earlier forbidden all diplomatic communications between embassies and their home countries—including those conducted by courier and cipher — except when initiated by the United States, Poland, or the U.S.S.R. No foreign diplomats were allowed to enter or leave the country. A ten-mile-wide coastal strip from the Firth of Forth to Land's End had been made off-limits to civilians. Intra-island commercial shipping was shanghaied in its entirety for the invasion. The ports were jammed with every sort of ship afloat, as well as hundreds of components of the artificial harbors, on which thousands of workers applied final welds, after which the sections were submerged to hide their presence from German reconnaissance flights. Railways had announced that schedules could change without notice and that certain routes and trains would be off-limits to civilians, also without notice. This had now come to pass.

Milk and mail delivery went by the boards because the milkmen and mailmen had been recalled to Home Guard duty. Regular commerce came to a halt; fresh fish disappeared from markets, coal from cellars, and beer from pubs. Mollie Panter-Downes wrote that if the High Command was seeking to confuse the Germans with all the troop movements, they had clearly succeeded in confusing the locals. Residents of villages that were full of Yanks one night awakened to find them gone by dawn, replaced by Canadians, who were in turn replaced by the British. The big London railway stations were full of only soldiers and their wives and girlfriends. "The women who have come to see their men off nearly always walk to the very end of the platform," wrote Panter-Downes, "to wave their elaborately smiling goodbyes as the train pulls out. Sometimes they look to one as if they're standing on the extreme tip of England itself."[120]

And from across the Channel came the regular dull throb of Allied bombs falling in France, similar to the roll of distant thunder, with the unsettling difference that the concussive pulse generated by high explosives moves through bedrock at the speed of sound and can spawn a tremor in a tumbler of water at forty miles, or in a man's belly.

The French knew nothing, but de Gaulle suspected much. On May 15, de Gaulle, in Algiers, unilaterally declared the French Committee of National Liberation the provisional government of France, with himself as president. He proclaimed the Third Republic had not ended but had only been interrupted by the bastard Vichy regime. Roosevelt, driven as Eden saw it "by his absurd and petty dislike of de Gaulle," still wanted to throw de Gaulle overboard. Eden considered that option to be "folly" and advised Churchill in the strongest terms to not do so. Although Churchill heeded Eden's advice, he was one with Roosevelt in telling de Gaulle nothing about Overlord until after it had been launched.[120]

In London on the fifteenth, the very few in the land who knew the exact dates and time of the invasion gathered for a final briefing at Montgomery's headquarters at St. Paul's School. Eisenhower and the SHAEF command attended, as did the entire War Cabinet, King George, the British Chiefs of Staff, dozens of American generals, Jan Smuts, and Winston Churchill. No representative of the Free French attended, even though Eisenhower planned to land the First French Army in Marseilles in the follow-up to Overlord. Churchill again offered a few fighting words after the briefing, as he had on April 7. Butcher called Churchill's address a real "stemwinder," wherein he proclaimed "bravery, ingenuity, and persistence as human qualities of greater value than equipment." One phrase in particular struck Eisenhower: "Gentlemen," Churchill intoned, "I am hardening toward this enterprise." Eisenhower took this to mean that Churchill, who "had long doubted its feasibility and had previously advocated its further postponement in favor of operations elsewhere...had finally, at this late date come to believe with the rest of us" that Overlord was the "true course of action in order to achieve victory." Eisenhower wrote these words just three years after the war, in his memoir *Crusade in Europe*. The passage has dogged Churchill ever since. The British historian Max Hastings cites Eisenhower's recollection when he writes in *Winston's War* that Churchill had all along believed Overlord "represented an option but not an absolute commitment."[121]

In fact, it was both. Churchill had at first considered Overlord a commitment lacking muscle, and he had argued (successfully) that the early, puny version be beefed up. Every plan in war is an option, to be examined, weighed, and adjusted, until it is carried out, or not. Eisenhower later wrote that part of his job was to make alternate plans in case Overlord proved "impractical" to carry off, or if strategic objectives changed in a way that brought that particular option into doubt. In war, several options must be kept open at the same time; if only one option is on the table, it is not an option. By early March, within five weeks of Eisenhower and Montgomery's strengthening of the plan, Churchill began sending his "hardening" telegrams to Marshall and Roosevelt. By May 15 he had long since hardened to the plan, a hardening that had not come about with the speed of quick-set cement, but the end result was the same. On May 8, just a week before the final unveiling of the plan, during a private lunch with Eisenhower, Churchill leaned into the table and announced, with tears in his eyes, "I am in this thing with you to the end." Eisenhower failed to mention the luncheon in his memoir. When David Eisenhower wrote of the May 15 meeting in his 1986 book, *Eisenhower at War*, he did not imbue Churchill with the monolithic resistance to Overlord that his grandfather had in his book. Rather, the younger Eisenhower refers to the evolution over three years of Churchill's position on cross-Channel operations, from Sledgehammer to Roundup and finally to Overlord.[122]

Churchill had not been alone in his concerns about Overlord. Air Chief

Marshal Leigh-Mallory expressed serious doubts to Eisenhower about the wisdom of the American airborne attacks. The terrain was atrocious, unsuitable for both parachutists and gliders. German anti-aircraft batteries would have a field day in targeting the slow-moving transport planes, whose gas tanks were not self-sealing, and were thus flying firetraps. He foresaw a "futile slaughter" of the paratroopers followed by the likely failure of the landing at Utah Beach on the Cotentin Peninsula, which in turn would lead to the ruination of the entire enterprise. Eisenhower heard Leigh-Mallory out before conducting a "soul-racking" examination of the problem, alone. He decided to go ahead with the airborne operations. Yet, Eisenhower instructed Leigh-Mallory to put his concerns in writing, to protect the airman from condemnation in the event his dire predictions came to pass. In that case, Eisenhower expected to bear the responsibility.[123]

Churchill often expressed his concerns through emotion accompanied by tears, thus appearing indeterminate, even weak. Yet all the participants were concerned; they would have been foolish not to be, and they were not foolish men. Montgomery expected the Germans to begin throwing panzer and mechanized infantry divisions at the beachhead within hours of the landings. His logic was simple. The trickery of Bodyguard would expire at H hour, when the troops went ashore, at which time the Germans would finally know the truth and react with force and speed and fury. Eisenhower, concerned that the Germans would mass on the beaches, asked Churchill to extend the ban on diplomatic communications beyond D-day, to lull the Germans into believing the real invasion was yet forthcoming. Again, his logic was simple: if the Germans did not believe D-day was a feint, the invasion was in deep trouble from the start.[124]

Years later, when it was all over, Eisenhower in his memoirs stressed the abominable consequences had Overlord failed. Churchill could have written the words. "The two countries [Britain and the United States] were placing all their hopes, expectations, and assets in one great effort.... Failure... would be almost fatal. Such a catastrophe might mean the complete redeployment" of U.S. forces to the Pacific. The effect on Allied morale would be "so profound that it was beyond calculation." Finally, if Overlord failed, Russia "might consider a separate peace." Churchill had argued that very case ever since he first saw the preliminary—and inadequate— plans for Overlord the previous August.[125]

Since early in the year, Erwin Rommel's command, Army Group B in northwestern France, had been working to batten down the northwest

French coast. Rommel could not know of the delay in Allied plans wrought by Montgomery's proposals of late January, but he knew the Americans and English were coming, if not in May, then in June. His orders were to complete construction of a defensive barrier roughly four hundred miles in length—Hitler called it his Atlantic Wall—from Brittany, east through the Cotentin Peninsula, and on through Normandy, across the Seine estuary to the Pas de Calais. Rommel believed that the Allies were not likely to attempt a landing on the Cotentin, where the Germans would only have to seal the seventy-mile-wide neck of the peninsula to trap the invaders. Brittany, farther south, was also a similar dead end. Even were the Allies to find a way to put men ashore on Brittany's inhospitable beaches, they would find the ports of Brest, Lorient, and St-Nazaire well fortified and bristling with arms. Any landings even farther south would take the Allies beyond the range of their Spitfire fighter support, which was critical to the operation. Brittany would put the Allied armies closer to the Pyrenees than to Paris. The Seine estuary was too irregular; the chalk cliffs of the Pays de Caux were too high; they gave out near Dieppe, which by virtue of the British raid in 1942 had demonstrated the unwisdom of trying to invade a fortified port directly. That left Normandy or Calais.[126]

Rommel's superior in the west, Field Marshal Gerd von Rundstedt, agreed with Rommel's overall assessment but favored the Pas de Calais as the target; it offered the straightest line and shortest distance between England and France. The German Fifteenth Army, nineteen divisions strong, was stationed there, and in Allied headquarters it was assumed that it would be released promptly to deliver a counterstroke in Normandy when the troops came ashore. Hence, the Allied campaign of false radio transmissions. German intelligence was intercepting a great deal of radio traffic between numerous Allied units in the southeast of Britain. The signals were as false as the phony units sending them, all part of Operation Fortitude and intended in part to keep the German Fifteenth Army tied down in Calais. Although in general agreement on the site of the invasion, von Rundstedt and Rommel disagreed on the fundamental question of how best to meet the invader, wherever he arrived. In addition to static defenses manned by artillery and infantry, six panzer divisions were available in northwestern France. Rommel, the apostle of armored war in 1940, was now an apostate. He wanted to dig in on the beaches and fight a defensive battle, yet one that admitted to flexibility and timely deployment of reserves, a battle such as Montgomery successfully fought during Rommel's first assault at El Alamein in 1942.

To that end, Rommel insisted that the six panzer divisions—more than 1,100 tanks and self-propelled guns—be placed under his command in order to bring them to bear on the beaches. Von Rundstedt favored holding the tanks in reserve until he could launch a decisive counterattack once the Allies showed their hand. His logic was simple: the Wehrmacht by brilliant armored maneuver had defeated both the French and the BEF in 1940, and it could do so again. Flexibility underlay von Rundstedt's claim on the panzers. But Rommel wanted the tanks put under his command, because, unlike in 1940, the Allies now controlled the air, as evidenced by the ongoing destruction of the very rail and road routes that von Rundstedt needed to deploy his tanks for counterstrokes. The debate lasted into April.[127]

Thanks to Ultra, the Allies were privy to almost every exchange of views between Rommel, von Rundstedt, and Berlin. Churchill was reading messages soon after they were sent. Hitler, who initially favored Rommel's strategy (and his prediction of Normandy as the target), finally made a decision that effectively hobbled both Rommel and von Rundstedt. Employing the wisdom of Solomon, the Führer divided the panzers between Rommel and OKW — the German army supreme command. Von Rundstedt would have no claim on the tanks. Hitler further ordered that the panzers under OKW could be deployed only on his authority. Only three of the six armored divisions were arrayed south of the Seine, and only one was under Rommel's direct command near the Normandy coast. Hitler's decision served himself, Rommel, and von Rundstedt ill, but it served the Allies well. It was "probably the most important decision of all those affecting the Allies and the Overlord plans," F. W. Winterbotham wrote in *The Ultra Secret*.[128]

Yet Winterbotham failed to note that the British often did not know with certainty if Ultra decrypts were valid or as phony as the Allied Fortitude signals. The intelligence game was a wilderness of mirrors. Almost every SOE agent the British dropped into Belgium and Holland was captured by the Germans and forced to relay false information back to London. Likewise, every German agent dropped or smuggled into Britain during the war was captured, and then offered a choice: become a double agent or hang. Almost all chose to cooperate, and in their roles as part of Bodyguard fed phony intelligence to Berlin, where Hitler upon reading it gradually grew to believe that Calais, not Normandy, would be the target, especially as the Fortitude signals (from phantom Allied units) seemed to verify the intelligence. Or did Hitler falsely appear to favor Calais? Three times in the early spring, the British intercepted messages from Hitler that clearly indicated he favored *Normandy* as the objective. Which was it? The Allies could not know with certainty until after the landings. Then, and only then, would German panzer and troop deployments tell them what Hitler believed.[129]

All spring Rommel pleaded with Berlin for more barbed wire, concrete, and men. Intercepted communications reinforced Churchill's concern that

Rommel would mass his forces on and near the beaches, throwing everything he had against everything the Allies had, in a Great War–style battle.
Another Somme or Passchendaele was what Churchill (and Brooke) most
feared. Montgomery read the tea leaves differently. He believed Rommel
would never simply sit behind his defenses until the opportunity for a "big
push" presented itself, but would constantly assault and harass the Allies
from the start. Yet if Rommel assembled a powerful enough force in short
order, the nature of his counteroffensive would not be "harassment" but
"onslaught." When Ultra verified Rommel's plan to gather his panzer
reserves and throw them upon the beaches, Churchill's fears seemed confirmed. If Rommel could stall the first three or four waves of invaders long
enough for more panzers (and the Fifteenth Army, from Calais) to appear
on the scene, he would win the battle. Hitler had sixty divisions in France
and the Low Countries; sound strategy called for him to hurl as many as
could be spared at the invaders.[130]

Chance would play its usual role in the affair, whether induced by miscommunication, misunderstanding, or the weather. Churchill's strategic
musings and regular proclamations on the roles of chance in warfare put
him in general agreement with Clausewitz, who wrote, "War is the province of chance," a force constantly present on the battlefield, where it
"increases the uncertainty of every circumstance and deranges the course
of events." Clausewitz believed fighting a war demanded finding a balance
between reason and unreason, where success required both intuition and
planning, and where luck always lurked. Most of all, fighting a war
demanded political and military leaders who understood this. Clausewitz
was no Prussian automaton, but a complex man and complex thinker. Liddell Hart, Britain's premier strategic thinker in the years between the wars,
discounted the importance of Clausewitz. Many in the British military
establishment — who presumed a Prussian could teach them little — blamed
Clausewitz for the murderous turn that warfare took in the trenches of
1915, an ironic assessment that implies that the long-dead Prussian had
somehow ordered Britain's often stupid generals to conduct the Great War
as they had. British political leaders traditionally had little interest in the
actual practice of war and for the most part had left the planning and fighting to the admirals and generals. Not Churchill. As a trained soldier who
possessed, Ismay later wrote, "an encyclopedic" knowledge of the history
of warfare, Churchill had arrived at many of the same truths Clausewitz
held dear — confuse the enemy; add creative and idiosyncratic elements to
the conflict; control the deranging of events on the battlefield. When it
came to fighting, Ismay recalled, Churchill "venerated tradition, but ridiculed convention."[131]

Clausewitz also advised simple plans and tactics not prone to easy foul-up. He advised that attacks should be made only on important objectives, with overwhelming force, and that goals should not be overly ambitious. Overlord was anything but simple; its ambitions were great. Whether its forces were overwhelming would be determined on the beaches. And now the day of battle—June 5—was almost at hand.[132]

On June 3, a sunny and breezy day, Eisenhower called a meeting of his commanders and meteorologists at Southwick House, the Royal Navy compound where Eisenhower kept his Portsmouth headquarters. His chief meteorologist, Group Captain John Stagg, who the day before had forecast several days of moderate weather, now predicted gale-force winds, high seas, and low cloud cover for June 4 and 5. A series of low-pressure areas in the North Atlantic were lined up and making for England and Normandy. The Allies could take hourly barometric readings as far afield as Iceland and Greenland, and those readings did not bode well for the fifth. The Germans could not gather weather data in the far reaches of the North Atlantic, an intelligence deficit that would soon blindside them. At the 9:30 P.M. meeting that night, the skies still clear, Stagg reaffirmed his prediction. Eisenhower polled his commanders; they were unanimous in agreeing that the invasion should be pushed back a day, pending a review at the 4:30 A.M. meeting on June 4, just eight hours hence. Parts of the great invasion task force were already at sea; ships that had not yet sailed waited in harbors, packed with troops. At the 4:30 A.M. meeting, Eisenhower asked Stagg if he foresaw any change in his forecast. Stagg replied in the negative. Asked when he thought the front would begin to close on the Channel, he replied, in four or five hours. Eisenhower ordered the postponement.

By ten that morning, the winds had risen and the clouds had closed in. By eleven o'clock, gale warnings had been run up for the Channel. The June 4 storm scrubbed the fifth. That left the sixth, possibly the seventh, but only if the weather cleared. By then the men would have been aboard the transports for almost four days. A cancellation until late in the month would disrupt the entire logistics structure, to say nothing of the morale of the men and the leaders in London, Washington, and especially Moscow, where Stalin might conclude that his allies had never been sincere in their promise of a second front. A two- or three-week delay would give Rommel time to further reinforce his positions. Nothing could be gained by a postponement, but much would be lost. Eisenhower ordered that they reassemble at 9:30 that night to review the situation.[133]

Churchill by then was aboard his private train, parked on a siding out-side Portsmouth near Eisenhower's tented field headquarters. Brooke, as usual, took a dim view, writing in his diary, "Winston...is touring the Portsmouth area and making a thorough pest of himself." The P.M. desig-nated the train his "advance headquarters," a moniker Eden found to be absurd, given that the train was cramped and there was only one telephone and one bath and "Mr. Churchill seemed to be always in the bath and Gen-eral Ismay always on the telephone."[134]

The P.M. had entrained on June 2 with the intention of boarding a Royal Navy cruiser at Portsmouth for a front-row seat as the men went ashore in Normandy. He had asked Admiral Ramsay to make the neces-sary arrangements but had not informed Brooke, knowing full well the CIGS would vehemently oppose such showmanship. Days earlier, Eisen-hower had gotten wind of Churchill's plans and insisted that he cancel them. Churchill refused, citing his position as HMG's minister of defence, and the power vested in him by that office to go wherever he pleased in order to conduct HMG's military business. Eisenhower, who thought Churchill's presence in the fleet would be a distraction, and dangerous, took his case to King George, who, over three days and in three letters, pleaded with Churchill to reconsider. Finally, when the King implied that he, too, would join the battle—he was a former Royal Navy sailor, after all, and veteran of the Battle of Jutland—Churchill relented. He stressed in his memoir that he had deferred to his King, not to Eisenhower.

That squall behind him, Churchill waited aboard his train for another tempest to blow in: Charles de Gaulle. The War Cabinet had insisted the Frenchman be at least informed of the date of the invasion; to not do so would be an insult to France. On June 3, Churchill sent his York to Algiers to retrieve the general, several of his aides, and Duff Cooper. After an overnight flight, they arrived at Northolt Airport just past dawn on the fourth, as the Channel weather deteriorated.[135]

At Portsmouth, Churchill, Ernest Bevin, Jan Smuts, and Ismay waited on the railroad spur for de Gaulle, who soon could be seen walking up the line in the company of Duff Cooper, Anthony Eden, and Pierre Viénot, de Gaulle's ambassador to HMG. Churchill, sensing the historic nature of the proceedings, stepped forward arms outstretched to embrace de Gaulle, who, in his khaki uniform and kepi, two stars on his collar, stood stiffly at attention. Of Churchill's gesture, Eden later wrote, "Unfortunately, de Gaulle did not respond easily to such a mood." The tableau resembled a short man trying to embrace a telephone pole. Smuts was altogether the wrong man to be on hand, having declared in a radio address that France would never regain its former position of authority in Europe, an insult the French could never forgive (although Smuts had also predicted the British

Empire would emerge from the war in extremis). The parley in the railroad car began well enough, with Churchill outlining the particulars of the
military plan while de Gaulle, a military man first and foremost, listened
intently, posed questions, and seemed to be enjoying himself. Then
Churchill strayed to the topic of the civil governance of France, and the
need for de Gaulle to ask Roosevelt's permission to conduct civil affairs.
With cold finality, de Gaulle cut Churchill off. "Why do you seem to
think," he thundered, "I have to submit my candidacy for the government
of France to Roosevelt?" The French government existed as a matter of
fact, de Gaulle stated, with himself at its head, and that was that. Churchill
responded in kind, "I want you to know, General, that every time we must
choose between Europe and the open sea we will choose the sea. . . . Between
you and Roosevelt, I will always choose Roosevelt." Bevin objected, telling
de Gaulle that not all in the British government felt that way. Eden, too,
tried to calm the waters, but to no avail. "The meeting," he later wrote,
"was a failure."[136]

Franklin Roosevelt spent the weekend of June 3 and 4 resting at Edwin
("Pa") Watson's Blue Ridge Mountains home. He read his Book of Common Prayer in order to find the proper words for a blessing to be read on
the night of the invasion. He intended to make a radio address on the fifth,
but of course would make no mention of events in the English Channel.
Rather, his purpose was to congratulate Alexander and Mark Clark on the
liberation of Rome—"the symbol of Christianity"—which took place on
June 4. It was a hollow victory, Sir John Keegan later wrote. Rome had
been declared an open city. Clark should have bypassed it in pursuit of the
retreating Germans, which the Fifth Army could then have encircled and
captured, with General Oliver Leese's Eighth Army driving in from the
right flank to close off the German retreat. That was Alexander's plan,
drafted in accordance with the Clausewitz maxim that he, Eisenhower,
and Churchill held dear: capture armies, not real estate. But Clark, suspicious of British tactics and intent on securing the glory he thought due
him, instead took his army directly into Rome, and thus lost his chance to
encircle the Germans. Kesselring and his armies began a fighting retreat
150 miles to their Gothic Line in the Apennines—the Allies called it the
Pisa-Rimini line—where they successfully thwarted Allied advances into
the Balkans until the final weeks of the war. Within eight weeks of the capture of Rome, at the insistence of Roosevelt and Marshall, and against
Churchill's earnest disapproval, Jumbo Wilson's Mediterranean forces

were reduced by seven divisions, four French and three American, for deployment in Anvil. Clark got his front-page glory, for one day, until events in Normandy on June 6 erased Rome from the collective consciousness of Britons, Canadians, and Americans.[137]

At Eisenhower's Portsmouth headquarters, the rain smacking the windows during the evening meteorological meeting of June 4 testified to Group Captain Stagg's forecasting prowess. Across the Channel the gale was in full blow. An attempt to land on June 5 would have proven disastrous. Prospects for the next day appeared hopeless as well. Then Stagg made what Eisenhower called an "astonishing" forecast: late on June 5 fair weather in the form of a weak high lasting perhaps thirty-six hours would form a break between the low-pressure systems. That sounded promising for the sixth, but opened the unsettling possibility that the first landings might take place under suitable conditions while the follow-up landings would have to be scrubbed as the second storm arrived, leaving the initial forces trapped on the beaches. Eisenhower asked Stagg what exactly the weather would be like in twenty-four hours. "To answer that question," Stagg replied, "would make me a guesser, not a meteorologist." After pondering Stagg's assessment, Eisenhower announced the invasion was on, pending a final review at the 4:00 A.M. meeting on June 5, in seven hours. When they reconvened before dawn on the fifth, Stagg held to his forecast; a break in the weather was imminent. Eisenhower put questions to his commanders: Could the navy gunners spot targets? Could the parachute transports find their drop zones? Could the landing craft reach shore? The answer from each of the commanders was in the affirmative. "Okay," Eisenhower announced, "we'll go."[138]

Later that morning, after paying a visit to British troops who were boarding their landing ships, Eisenhower played a game of checkers with Butcher; the result was a draw. That night, June 5, Dwight Eisenhower wrote by hand a message to be broadcast if the liberators were repulsed. It began: "Our landings...have failed to gain a satisfactory foothold and I have withdrawn the troops."[139]

Churchill, scrubbed from the mission by King George, took his train back to London. As the evening of June 5 came on, Churchill cabled Stalin with the news that the invasion was on for the following morning. Stalin was dining with the Yugoslav writer and Tito's number three man, Milovan Djilas. Handed Churchill's telegram, Stalin turned to Djilas and said, "Yes there will be a landing, if there is no fog. Until now there was always something else that interfered. I suspect tomorrow it will be something else. Maybe they'll meet up with some Germans."[140]

Field Marshal von Rundstedt dined with cronies that night at his headquarters at Château St-Germain. Thanks to the misinformation of Fortitude, he now believed that the invasion in the west would come in the Pas de Calais and in tandem with the Russian summer offensive. Since the Eastern Front showed no signs of activity that week, the west should remain quiet as well. Shortly after nine o'clock he was informed that the second line of the Verlaine couplet—"Pierce my heart with a dull languor"—had just gone out over the BBC. German intelligence had known the meaning of the line for weeks. Von Rundstedt didn't buy it. "Does anyone think the enemy is stupid enough to announce his arrival over the radio?" he exclaimed to a guest. Then, a bit worse for drink, he retired for the evening.[141]

Erwin Rommel had told his superiors that the first day would spell the difference between victory and defeat for the Reich. That day, he said, would be *Der längste Tag* ("the longest day"). The evening of June 5 did not find Rommel in Normandy, because on the morning of the fourth, after studying the latest weather reports, which predicted a continuation of high winds, high seas, and rain, Rommel concluded that the Allied invasion would not come for at least several days. Thus reassured by the gales blowing in the Channel, he took himself off to Bavaria to celebrate his wife's birthday. Because his meteorologists could not peer as far west into the Atlantic as could Eisenhower's, Rommel had no idea that a brief break in the foul weather was on its way.

Brooke that night offered to his diary: "I am very uneasy about the whole operation. At the best it will fall very far short" of expectations, and "at the worst it may well be the most ghastly disaster of the whole war. I wish to God it were safely over."[142]

Churchill dined with Clementine in the Annexe that evening, one of just four dinners alone in each other's company since January. After dinner he made a final trip downstairs to the map room to assess the latest airborne dispositions. Shortly before she went to bed Clementine joined him, a rare foray for her into the domain of the planners and chartists. Churchill told her, "Do you realize that by the time you wake up in the morning twenty thousand men may have been killed?" His calculation did not include Germans. He knew that if his estimate of Allied casualties proved accurate, the invasion had been repulsed on the beach. His declaration—part melodrama, part cold calculation wrapped in sentiment—was in character. And consistent; he had proclaimed for two years that a disastrous defeat on the coast of France "was the only way in which we could lose this war." And now the moment was at hand. He lingered in the map room for a few moments before going to bed at about the time the first of the airborne troops glided and parachuted into the Normandy countryside.[143]

It was shortly after midnight, June 6.

Guided by the near-full moon, Bomber Command spent the first hours of the day dropping more than five thousand tons of bombs on coastal batteries and nearby rail lines, the greatest tonnage of bombs dropped in a single night during the war. To deflect German attention from the goings-on in Normandy, a Montgomery look-alike had days earlier been sent to Gibraltar along with his "staff" with orders to make his presence there known, which would presumably lead the Germans to conclude that with Montgomery (who Berlin knew was to command the invasion) out of the country, no invasion was imminent.* Another deception operation, aerial in nature, took place early on June 6 off the Pas de Calais, where the lead planes in a fleet of British aircraft dropped tinfoil strips just off the English coast, and then turned and took up position in the rear of the little aerial armada. The radar "picture" created by the tinfoil told the Germans that *something* was out there. Then, the next squadron of planes dropped their tinfoil a mile or so in front of the first, before turning for the rear, while the first squadron by then had come around and dropped more tinfoil another mile or so toward Calais—and so on slowly across the Channel, with the effect that the steadily advancing (and confusing) radar "picture" appeared to confirm for the Germans in Calais an oncoming seaborne invasion fleet. Meanwhile, two squadrons of RAF bombers carrying radar-jamming equipment overflew Normandy in order to blind the remaining German radar operators there. By 2:00 A.M. the Germans no longer could "see" what was coming their way.[144]

What was coming their way was an Allied armada divided into two broad streams and subdivided into five lesser streams—one for each target beach. The fleet, under the overall command of Admiral Sir Bertram Ramsay, was made up of almost 7,000 vessels, including 1,200 combat ships (four-fifths of them Royal Navy), 700 tugs and minesweepers, and 800 large transports, many towing sections of the Gooseberry prefabricated breakwaters, which would protect the Mulberry harbors. Ten miles off shore, on board more than 4,200 landing ships and landing craft, more

---

* The operation almost unraveled when the fake Montgomery was seen "swaggering about half-drunk in Gibraltar, smoking mammoth cigars like a chimney." The real Montgomery—a nonsmoker and teetotaler—took great umbrage with his portrayal. (Butcher, *My Three Years with Eisenhower*, pp. 549, 583)

than 132,000 British, Canadian, and American young men of the Twenty-first Army Group under the command of Bernard Montgomery waited to make their run into the beaches. Shortly before dawn, while the troop transports stood off shore, seven battleships, two dozen cruisers, and one hundred destroyers hammered the beaches with thousands of high-explosive rounds. Four years ago that week, Admiral Ramsay had directed the evacuation of 337,000 British and French troops from Dunkirk, a feat performed over nine days under the guns and bombs of the Luftwaffe. The fleeing army of 1940 had left all of its baggage—tanks, guns, trucks—behind in Dunkirk. On this day, Ramsay intended to put his army ashore in nine hours, and they would be bringing their baggage with them, thousands of trucks, armored cars, field guns, tanks, bulldozers, and jeeps.[145]

The Second British Army under Lieutenant General Miles Dempsey would land one Canadian and two British divisions on Sword, Juno, and Gold beaches, which ran westward for sixty miles from just east of Caen and the Orne River, where the 6th British Airborne Division, eight thousand strong, was assigned the task of taking key bridges. Then there was an eleven-mile break marked by cliffs, beyond which lay the two American beaches, where the three divisions of Omar Bradley's First U.S. Army would land. The first beach, Omaha, ran west for almost twenty miles, from just west of Port-en-Bessin, which in ten weeks' time would serve as the terminus of Pluto, the fuel pipeline under the sea. The port, guarded by gun emplacements and German flak boats, had to be taken intact. Finally, across the Vire and Douve estuaries, Utah Beach curved westward for three miles. It was the beach nearest Cherbourg. The early capture of the port facilities of Cherbourg was so great a priority, Eisenhower later wrote, that "rapid and complete success on Utah Beach was...a prerequisite to real success in the whole campaign." Marshes traversed by a few cause-ways stretched behind Utah Beach to the roads that led to Cherbourg. To secure those causeways and crossroads, 15,000 American paratroopers of the 82nd and 101st Airborne divisions arrived by glider and parachute soon after midnight, the parachutists dropped from 850 C-47 transports into the hedgerows and fields near the villages of Ste-Mère-Église, Ste-Marie-du-Mont, and St-Côme-du-Mont. The towns had to be taken in order to secure the neck of the Cotentin Peninsula. Many of the C-47s overshot the landing zones by miles, and dropped their paratroopers into the sea, or into the marshes, where they disappeared forever into the mud under the weight of their packs.[146]

When shortly after dawn the battleships ceased their bombardment, the destroyers ran in to rake the beaches. It was a risky piece of business because German long guns—155mm and 177mm artillery—that could shoot far out to sea were arrayed in bunkers behind the beaches. The largest naval bombardment in history culminated with a barrage by several tank transports that had been converted into rocket platforms, each capable of unleashing salvos of 1,100 three-inch rockets, each salvo the equivalent of one hundred cruisers firing at once. The brilliant flashes of red and yellow that tore the sky, and the shudder of explosions on the beaches felt even aboard the ships, belied the ineffectiveness of the attack, because for all the flashing and banging and booms, very few Germans were killed, because the Germans had taken shelter in reinforced concrete bunkers deep under and behind the bluffs. As the destroyers finished their run and turned seaward, American B-17s came on a final time to hit the beaches and coastal defenses. But in the faint light and haze, most of the pilots overflew their targets and dropped their bombs inland.

A short while later, the first wave of infantry made for shore, about a platoon to each landing craft. The little boats came on in neat formations, stitching the sea with hundreds of long gray wakes. Behind them more landing craft steered in lazy circles, waiting their turn. Stinking blue-gray plumes of diesel exhaust overlay the seas, which were running to three feet, a combination sure to induce retching in the human cargo. As each soldier embarked, he had been issued writing paper, a carton of cigarettes, and a small packet; its contents included seven sticks of chewing gum, one razor blade, chewing tobacco, insecticide, twelve seasickness pills, and two vomit bags. The seasickness pills had the unfortunate side effect of inducing a drugged lethargy. Sailors who knew that refused to take them; soldiers who took them soon wished they hadn't. But the bags were put to use that morning.[147]

The second wave would bring in combat engineers to deal with remaining mines, spotters to direct air and naval fire, and bulldozers to clear paths through the dunes, but all plans hinged on the first wave holding the beaches while sappers cleared the way for the following waves. As the landing craft of the first wave closed on the beaches, the big guns on the Allied ships fell silent; no fighter planes screamed close overhead, no bombers droned far above. In Britain seven thousand heavy bombers and five thousand Spitfires and P-51B Mustangs awaited further orders and targets. The German Third Air Fleet, stationed on the Normandy coast, consisted that morning of just 169 planes and pilots.[148]

German gunners behind the beaches, not knowing if the Allied bombers would return, risked glances from their pillboxes, earthen bunkers, and fire holes strung along the bluffs. Gazing with incredulity through lifting haze and drifting smoke and the dust of pulverized concrete, they beheld the incoming landing craft, and behind that fleet, an armada that stretched to the horizon in all directions—seaward, eastward up the coast, westward down the coast. Thousands of barrage balloons drifted above the ships. For many Germans, the scene could only unfold in silence—their eardrums had been ripped by the concussions of the naval barrage. Though unprepared for what they saw, Erwin Rommel had prepared them well to defend against it. More than 11 million mines lay buried on the beaches, in the dunes, and in the waters around the anti-tank obstacles. Hundreds of miles of concertina wire curled in front of and on top of seawalls, up gullies in the dunes, and crosswise on the sand, where deep ditches had been dug that could swallow tanks. Even had no Germans waited, the mines and the barbed wire would have taken a terrible toll. But the Germans were there, and now they fingered their triggers and held lanyards slack and awaited the command to fire. The difference in the exact set of the tide along the entire front determined that H hour was slightly different on each beach. On Omaha, H hour was now, 6:30 A.M.[149]

A bloodred sun climbed over Normandy's farms and fields. Apple orchards were in full bloom. For a few lingering moments, all was quiet on the Western Front.

Then, as the landing craft steered for the shingle, the warships opened up again, now lobbing their shells far inland. On Omaha Beach, where the Americans expected to encounter one or two battalions numbering perhaps 1,500 men (Ultra was not perfect), 7,000 men of the veteran 352nd Division raked the oncoming Americans with machine guns, mortars, and 88s pre-sighted onto every square meter of beach. Amphibious tanks swam toward the beaches; of twenty-nine going in to Omaha, twenty-two sank with their crews; five were blown up. Now the combat engineers and infantry were wading and swimming and crawling ashore under murderous German fire. Ernie Pyle took it all in from a ship standing off Omaha Beach. A bureaucratic snafu had kept him from going ashore in the first wave. He could only wait his turn, and did so by playing gin rummy while Bing Crosby crooned "Sweet Leilani" over the ship's PA system. Pyle found the scene incongruous. Men sat reading *Life* magazine as the ship shuddered from nearby misses. They listened to BBC reports that told them "how the war before our eyes was going." The ship was dry, warm, the coffee fresh. "But," wrote Pyle, "it wasn't like that ashore. No, it wasn't like that ashore."[150]

Jock Colville, granted two months' fighting leave from No. 10, had rejoined his 168 Squadron of the Second Tactical Air Force two weeks earlier. He flew a Mustang over the Normandy beaches shortly after the first men went ashore. Low cloud cover kept the fliers under two thousand feet, low enough to identify individual Allied ships and "their huge guns belching flame and smoke" as they kept up the barrage. And low enough to prove dangerous. The vagaries of war were brought home to Colville when, "by a million to one chance," a fifteen-inch shell from HMS *War-*

spite struck one of the planes in Colville's squadron. The plane and its pilot simply disappeared.[151]

Shortly after 6:30 A.M. on June 6, Erwin Rommel received an urgent telephone call from OKW. The Allies were ashore, in Normandy. As at El Alamein, Rommel found himself away from his command at the very hour when his presence was most vital. He immediately asked OKW to send two panzer divisions to the beaches. He was told that only Hitler could make that decision, and that the question could be put to Hitler only when he awoke. The Führer had as usual worked well into the early morning hours and had elected to sleep in. No one dared wake him. Not until two in the afternoon did Hitler convene a staff meeting.[152]

Rommel had based his defense on the tactical principles of the Great War—static positions, bunkers, tunnels, trenches, barbed wire, mines, all defended by concentrated fire. But whereas in the Great War the attacking British could always haul themselves back to their own trenches after a failed gambit, today there was no place to run to. Shortly after waking at eight o'clock, Churchill took himself to the underground map room to follow the plotting of Allied positions. The lines on the charts inched inland as the morning wore on, a hundred yards here, a half mile there. The news from the British and Canadian beaches was good, as it was from the westernmost American beach, Utah, where fewer than 200 men of 21,000 were killed going ashore. Tanks had raced across the causeways and established contact with the airborne units. But on Omaha it was a bloody and close-fought affair. There, as if to confirm Brooke's and Churchill's fears, the battle bore far more resemblance to the Somme and Passchendaele than to any action fought thus far in the Second World War.

At noon, satisfied that the landings had not been repulsed out of hand, Churchill was driven to the House. All there knew that Rome had fallen, and presumed he would be speaking on that subject. He did, and at great length, delivering a history of the Italian campaign from Sicily to Rome. Then he paused. "I have also to announce to the House that during the night and the early hours of this morning, the first of the series of landings in force upon the European Continent has taken place." The House erupted. Churchill continued: "So far the commanders who are engaged report that everything is proceeding according to plan. And what a plan! This vast operation is undoubtedly the most complicated and difficult that has ever taken place." He later in the day telegraphed the same message to Stalin. Thus, within a span of just thirty hours, Rome had been taken and the Atlantic Wall breached. And neither bad luck nor the enemy had so far deranged events on the battlefield. Four years after being thrown out of France, the British were back.[153]

By then, on the beaches and in the heavily wooded bocage, almost 2,500 American and 500 British and Canadian men lay dead, and 6,000 more had been wounded. The vast majority of American casualties took place on Omaha Beach, but by early afternoon the beach was theirs. Even as Churchill spoke, a half million more men in two dozen southern English ports and numerous small harbors and coves prepared to embark for Normandy. Patton's 4th Armored Division was conducting war games on the Salisbury plain, awaiting its turn. More than one hundred tugboats readied to tow across the Channel the two Mulberry artificial harbors—made up of four hundred steel and concrete components weighing 1.5 million tons. Churchill first sketched these technological marvels in a 1917 memo to Lloyd George, and again in 1940. Each artificial harbor could handle more than ten thousand tons of supplies per day, enough to feed and arm twenty-five divisions. The men were ashore, and the means to supply them was on its way. Still, Churchill harbored enough doubts to return to the House later that evening, where he warned that the reports from the beaches gave no "indication of what may be the course of the battle in the next days and weeks, because the enemy will now probably endeavour to concentrate on this area, and in that event heavy fighting will soon begin and will continue without end, as we can push troops in and he can bring other troops up. It is, therefore, a most serious time that we enter upon. Thank God we enter upon it with our great Allies all in good heart and all in good friendship."[154]

For weeks English farmers had been hoping for rain for the sake of their crops. The rain had finally arrived, Mollie Panter-Downes was to write, but the farmers now wished for blue skies "for the sake of their sons, fighting in the skies and on the earth across the Channel." By early evening, trains carrying the first of the wounded began running through an English countryside in full springtime bloom, "festooned with dog roses and honeysuckle." Women who had weeks earlier waved good-bye to their men now stood at railroad crossings, shopping baskets on their arms, and watched as the trains sped past. "They don't know whether to wave or cheer or cry," wrote Panter-Downes. "Sometimes they do all three."[155]

The second front was now an irrevocable reality. Germany had never won a two-front war. Indeed, in Italy Hitler faced a third front. If he deployed his reserves properly, or if he robbed from his eastern front to eliminate the threat in the west, he might soon find himself, again, fighting a one-front war. The Bletchley crowd and Churchill—and the men on the beaches—awaited the Führer's next move.

The Overlord plans called for the Americans to put thirteen divisions ashore in the first few weeks, the British and Canadians twelve. By early August, twenty-one of thirty-seven divisions in France were to be American. The disparity in Anglo-American numbers—and casualties—could only widen, and that begat another irrevocable reality. Not only was the slow but relentless transfer from Britain to America of command of the war nearly complete, so, too, was the transfer of global supremacy from London to Washington. Roosevelt, who on numerous occasions had made clear to Churchill his disdain for spheres of influence, was carving out the world's largest. Indeed, America's sphere of influence was expanding far beyond North and South America (claimed by James Monroe) to encompass the entire Pacific once the Japanese were defeated, which assuredly they would be. Australia, in 1942, had chosen America, not London, as the partner it would march beside into the future. The Philippines, when cleared of Japanese, would remain an American interest. Churchill did not begrudge Roosevelt the spread of American might, and could not stop it in any event. The potential for Soviet hegemony in much of Europe was what worried Churchill.

Triumph over Hitler was now—almost—a certainty, as was the prospect for postwar tragedy in Eastern Europe. Churchill and Britons might yet remain captains of their souls, but they were no longer masters of their fate. The European war would be fought on Eisenhower's and Zhukov's terms, the peace conducted on American and Russian terms, if America intended to make its presence known in postwar Europe, but Churchill had known since receiving Roosevelt's February telegram that the president sought to get out of Europe at the first available opportunity. Churchill did not know that in March, Roosevelt had told the State Department he wanted no part in maintaining order in France, Belgium, and Italy, where he foresaw chaos, and the Balkans, which were already in an advanced state of chaos. Further, to keep American troops as far as possible from trouble, he instructed the State Department to insist that northwest Germany form the American zone of occupation, the better to get his boys home from North Sea ports should trouble occur elsewhere in Europe. In a memo to Edward Stettinius, Roosevelt frankly acknowledged that "political considerations in the United States makes [sic] my decision conclusive." In late May, the president telegraphed Churchill with a summation of his directive to the State Department. Then, four days before D-day, Roosevelt reiterated his stance to Churchill. Quoting his February telegram,

Roosevelt said: "I am absolutely unwilling to police France and possibly Italy and the Balkans as well." And, he offered, "The reasons are political, as you well know." It was an election year.[156]

Beyond Europe, the British were no longer masters of the fate of hundreds of millions of subjects throughout the Empire. This was underscored in early June when Churchill received a reply from Roosevelt to his desperate plea for American shipping to relieve the "grievous famine in Bengal." More than seven hundred thousand Bengalis had died since early 1943, in large part because the Japanese controlled Burma and its surplus rice. Churchill informed Roosevelt that although 350,000 tons of surplus Australian wheat was available, the ships to carry it were not. Could the president supply the ships? After waiting more than four weeks, Roosevelt replied in the negative, and with "regret." He cited the effect of such a "diversion" on military operations. Churchill—and King George and London—could do almost nothing for the Bengalis; at least a million more died during the next twelve months.[157]

Edmund Burke wrote that empires die for a number of reasons, including the inability to govern disparate peoples in far-flung lands. Churchill possessed the will to save His Majesty's Empire, and to guarantee the peace in Europe, but he lacked the way. Despite the staggering losses the British had sustained since 1939, despite their sacrifice and their refusal to give in when they fought alone, the peace, when it came, would be Stalin's to violate. With the Americans in their ascendancy, the solution to containing a belligerent Stalin no longer rested with London. For better or worse, it rested with Washington. And Franklin Roosevelt had just made his thoughts clear on that subject.

Sometime in 1944, a new word crept into the lexicon of international politics: "superpower." It was not coined with the British Empire in mind.

6

Anchorage

Few U-boats roamed the Atlantic in early June; their harvest was meager. The sea routes to Britain were secure, the flood of American men and matériel unstoppable. The British, Canadians, and Americans were ashore in Normandy. And with seven thousand American and British heavy bombers based in Britain, with Alexander driving to the Po Valley in northern Italy, and with the Russians poised to strike in the East, Germany had lost the war. But the Allies had yet to win it. Some, including President Roosevelt, believed they all but had.

A week before D-day, Roosevelt dropped a "blockbuster" on Washington reporters. In an almost offhand manner he outlined his "blueprint" for a postwar world organization. This was the first the press heard of the world council Roosevelt had proposed the previous November in Tehran. Roosevelt divulged no particulars, thus leaving both isolationists and internationalists somewhat befuddled. The president did stress that whatever came into being would not impinge on the "integrity" of the U.S. He chose the word carefully. It is synonymous with "sovereignty," *Time* reported, a "wicked, isolationist word" in the minds of internationalists (known then as "one-worlders"), who championed a world government. Yet "sovereignty" formed the essence of isolationism and the national identity as championed by Senator Robert Taft and the anti-one-worlder Republican Party. Roosevelt was sending a message to both the internationalists and Republicans: his world organization would not diminish U.S. autonomy (the Republican fear), but it would move the United States toward a cooperative, multilateral role in world affairs (the one-worlder dream). The "blueprint," Roosevelt told the press, envisioned an organization that would stop aggression, not an organization "which you would have to call on whenever some country wanted to build a bridge over a creek." Roosevelt then permitted "some high authority" to leak more details to the press, including his intent to establish a World Court, and to build his new world council around the Four Powers, with smaller nations sitting in on a rotating basis.[1]

In June, Henry Luce editorialized in *Life* magazine on the coming new world order, and America's role in it: "With the establishment of a firm lodgment on the continent, we are now the most powerful nation on earth." But with that power came responsibilities, wrote Luce, including the moral imperative for America to participate in the postwar recovery of Europe, especially as the Allies' stated military strategy entailed the utter destruction of Germany. Europe would need to be rebuilt, not simply policed. Economic order had to be restored. The military story would end, perhaps soon, but the political story was just beginning. Here came Roosevelt with his vision of a postwar world council, a vision Churchill shared. And here came Luce with his vision for an American role in postwar Europe, which Churchill also shared. But Roosevelt, despite his call for a world organization, had made clear to Churchill that American troops would get out of Europe at the first opportunity. As for rebuilding Germany, Secretary of the Treasury Henry Morgenthau Jr. was working up a plan that amounted to a Carthaginian peace of the very sort St. Augustine decried in his reflections on the obliteration of Carthage by the Romans, a peace that offered no hope to the vanquished, a peace, as St. Augustine saw it, bereft of any moral quotient, a peace that disgraced the victors.[2]

Churchill found this troubling. He envisioned the special relationship between Britain and America as forming the backbone of postwar European stability. Churchill, knowing that postwar Britain would not wield anything like the power of prewar Britain, and knowing that Russia would emerge as the greatest continental power, believed that if America intended to play no role, European salvation lay with the old diplomatic standby: spheres of influence. Roosevelt and Hull loathed any arrangement that smacked of European spheres of influence, believing, as had Woodrow Wilson, that they led ultimately to war. Churchill, with his eye on Greece, had just proposed to Stalin a division of labor in the region: Britain would manage Greek affairs, while Stalin would manage Romanian. It was an understanding between gentlemen. On June 1, Churchill asked Roosevelt for his blessing, and assured the president that Britain and Russia "do not of course wish to carve the Balkans into spheres of influence." Yet that is exactly what Churchill and Stalin were edging toward, on Churchill's part because Greece was an ally, and on Stalin's part because Romania was an enemy. The two leaders indeed had "interests" in the region.[3]

As he had for a decade, and as he would in coming years, Churchill saw Britain as being in Europe, yet not fully "in." It was as he had told Stalin in 1940: Britain lay just off the west coast of Europe (as Asiatic Russia lay just beyond the eastern reaches). As he had for four years, Churchill believed European peace and security could best be guaranteed through regional European councils and federations, including a Danubian federation in central Europe, and a Balkan council in that region. Central to Churchill's vision for Western European security, recalled his son-in-law Lord Soames, was "France taking Germany by the hand and leading her back into the community of nations." But Roosevelt held France, and especially de

Gaulle, in something approaching contempt, while Morgenthau wanted to take Germany by the neck, and wring it.[4]

Later in the summer, delegates from thirty-nine allied nations met at the Dumbarton Oaks conference, held at a Federal-style mansion in Washington, DC, that had once belonged to South Carolina senator John C. Calhoun and since 1940 had housed a Harvard University research center. There Roosevelt's "blueprint" was used to lay the groundwork for the "United Nations Organization," including a General Assembly and Security Council where the Four Powers would sit, joined by three other nations on a rotating basis. The Russians insisted that they be granted sixteen seats in the General Assembly, one for each Soviet republic. The Americans replied that in that case, the United States should have forty-eight seats. The Americans proposed that each permanent member of the Security Council have a veto, but also barred any party with a dispute before the Security Council from voting on it. The Russians objected to the implication that the Security Council might pass judgment on one of its own members. The Americans had no ready reply. The questions were left unresolved. France was excluded from the parley, rightly so, claimed Senator Tom Connally, chairman of the Senate Foreign Relations Committee, because Britain, Russia, China, and the United States had "shed their blood for the rest of the world, while France has played the role of only a minor state in this war." In London the European Advisory Commission had been sitting for over a year, its American, British, and Russian delegates studying questions of how best to deal with a defeated Germany. France—de Gaulle—had been excluded from any role.[5]

The war was not being fought to determine who fielded the strongest armies. Politics—*interests*—underlay the war, in the Clausewitzian sense, as it did all wars. This was why Churchill had reached out to Tito, and why he took in the wayward Romanian king, and insinuated HMG into Greek affairs, and grudgingly tolerated de Gaulle. He was positioning Britain for the future in those areas of Europe that he saw as critical to British interests. Stalin was doing much the same. And that was why Churchill had been trying to draw Roosevelt into a postwar role in Europe. If not America, who? The answer was self-evident: the Soviet Union. The writer and political commentator Walter Lippmann published a slim but important volume that summer, *U.S. War Aims,* in which he foresaw the implications of the power shifts taking place. Spheres of influence were a reality, he argued. After the war, America, splendidly protected by the moats of the Atlantic and Pacific oceans, would need to protect the perimeters of its sphere—in Asia (where the restored European colonies would serve as buffer to China), and especially in the Atlantic. Anticipating NATO by five years, Lippmann argued that the Atlantic now assumed the central role in global politics that the Mediterranean had played for two thousand years. To secure the Atlantic in alliance with Western European democracies would ensure that all of Western Europe formed a cordon sanitaire between the U.S. sphere and the Russian. This, Lippmann argued, would make war between the two powers "a virtual impossibility." This was so, he wrote, because neither side could conceivably put an army into the other's heartland and no other technology existed that might alter the military balance in a war.[6]

Lippmann's "safety-in-distance" reasoning came undone a year later in a sunburst of atomic energy in the New Mexico desert. But his prediction of the Atlantic's centricity in American affairs was prescient. His proposed alliances with Western European nations to safeguard America's interests brought some comfort to Churchill, who sought some form of union with America. Yet Taft Republicans hated the word "alliance" as much as one-worlders hated the word "sovereignty."

Thus, if Hitler was defeated by October, as many in Washington and London believed, no plan whatsoever was in place to safeguard and rebuild Europe. October was just sixteen weeks distant.

Early on June 9, Ultra revealed the unsettling news that Hitler had ordered his Fifteenth Army from the Pas de Calais to Normandy, and also ordered two panzer divisions rushed from Poland to Normandy. This was the hammer blow the Allies most feared. A panzer division and a brigade of SS Hitler Youth were already pounding Montgomery's positions near Caen, with another panzer division on the way. Yet another panzer division was hitting the Americans near Carentan. The arrival of the Fifteenth Army and more panzers could doom the invasion. Then, late on the ninth, Ultra revealed one of the most welcome Führer directives of the war: Hitler, still suspicious that the Pas de Calais might be the real Allied target, rescinded his orders (OKW knew that George Patton and the Third Army were not in Normandy and concluded they might be heading for the Pas de Calais). Dumbfounded by Berlin's change of mind, von Rundstedt and Rommel considered resigning. The next day Montgomery declared the beachhead secure, the eleven-mile gap between the British and American beaches having been closed. For Churchill, Montgomery's assessment amounted to the unofficial opening of the summer travel season. The Old Man called Brooke and proposed they meet Monty at Montgomery's Normandy headquarters on Monday, the twelfth. They were going back to France.[7]

Despite Montgomery's declaration, Churchill feared a "crystallization of a front in France" and the subsequent repetition of the horrors of the

Great War, a concern, recalled Harriman, shared by Roosevelt. In static lines Churchill saw the potential for slaughter. So, too, did Rommel, but the slaughter of the invader, on or near the beaches. A few days after D-day, as the beachhead slowly widened and deepened, General Ian Jacob found Churchill in the map room pondering large charts of Normandy. How soon after all of the Allied divisions are fully ashore, Churchill asked, will the battle lines stabilize? They most likely will not, replied Jacob, until the Allies reach the Rhine. Such large-scale fluidity of entire armies ran counter to the Old Man's Great War experience. He had known all along that many men would die on the beaches, and if not on the beaches, then in the bocage in the following days and weeks. Even if the lines did not stabilize, and the Allies advanced as Jacob predicted, there would be slaughter, and it would only increase as Allied armies neared the German homeland. Churchill knew the veracity of Marlborough's admonition to his cautious Dutch ally during their war against the French: the pursuit of absolute victory without slaughter will, in the long run, result in slaughter without victory.[8]

The maps Churchill gazed at were marked by "phase lines," series of concentric rings running inland from the beaches like ripples on a pond. They marked the timetable for the planned expansion of the beachhead in the days and weeks following D-day. Each line carried a notation of D + and a number. Caen, for example, was to be taken on D-day, and bridgeheads to be thrown east across the Orne River by D + 1. By D + 9, the lodgment was to be more than eighty miles wide and a dozen deep. By D + 17 (June 23), the entire Cotentin Peninsula, including Cherbourg, was to be secure. By then the Allies expected to hold a line stretching from south of Caen near Falaise, west through Vire, and ending at Granville on the Bay of Biscay. At that point, the plan called for a wheeling breakout by D + 20 from the western (American) flank, while the British and Canadians pivoted on the eastern, Caen flank. By D + 40, the Allies hoped to be halfway to the Loire. Somewhere near that date, the Anvil landing would take place, with the objective of driving up the Rhone Valley to Lyon and on to Dijon, there to make contact with the Normandy forces driving east. By D + 90, the British would be across the Seine and facing the Low Countries, with the Americans on the right facing Verdun. Such was the grand plan. Both Eisenhower and Montgomery later wrote that all of the Overlord objectives were met. They were, but the timetable was not. The lines indeed stabilized, slowly and steadily. During the first few days, the delays could be measured in hours, as could be expected for such a supremely complex operation. Yet, as happens to a navigator whose course is off by just a degree, time and distance have a way of turning small variances into very large errors.[9]

Eisenhower knew this. On June 10, meeting with the American Chiefs, who had arrived the day before, he put to them almost the same question Churchill had asked Jacob, what to do if a "stabilization" of the lines took place? Sixteen Allied divisions—four hundred thousand men—were now ashore. But at least six panzer divisions and the Fifteenth Army (if Hitler again changed his mind) presented a real threat. Eisenhower set his SHAEF planning staff to work to find a solution. George Marshall had come to London not to discuss options, but to demand that Anvil, the Marseilles landing conceived as a complement to the hammer of Overlord, be carried out as soon as possible. But after just two meetings between the British and Americans, Marshall conceded that Anvil could take place only when conditions were right. This was fine with Brooke, but only if Anvil did not come at the expense of Italian operations. To throttle Alexander's momentum, Brooke told his diary later in the month, would be "madness."[10]

The fall of Rome and the D-day landings triggered the need for a final decision on Anvil. That, in turn, triggered a crisis in the Allied ranks. Churchill, Roosevelt, and the Combined Chiefs of Staff all agreed that the only military objective was to defeat Germany as quickly as possible. But they disagreed on how best to meet that objective. Eisenhower's overriding concern was to reinforce and supply Overlord. He was open to alternatives to Anvil, including Caliph, the infusion of troops into the Bordeaux ports. He was willing to consider allowing Alexander to exploit his Italian victories in order to draw more Germans away from France. His was a strictly military objective, and yet he possessed the sharp political skills needed to bring it off, for Churchill and Marshall brought both military and political perspectives—and talents—to the table. Marshall had promised Stalin Anvil at Tehran, in part because of Stalin's transparent political discomfort with his Western allies appearing on his flanks (within his sphere of influence) by driving north through Austria, as Churchill advocated. Churchill's strategy was as political as Stalin's; he wanted to get to middle Europe before the Soviets did. Brooke, like Eisenhower, took a strictly military position, but one at odds with Ike's. Anvil formed Churchill's penultimate great strategic debate of the war; the last debate came in the final weeks of the conflict when Eisenhower refused to strike toward Berlin. To be sure, Eisenhower and Montgomery soon differed over a broad-front or narrow-front strategy as the best way to get across the Rhine and to the Elbe, but that was for the two commanders to debate and resolve in coming months.

"*Now*," Brooke told his diary on June 11, Marshall finally saw the wisdom of the Italian operations Brooke had championed for a year. He added, "I do not believe he [Marshall] has any strategic vision whatsoever." Eisenhower's support of Anvil was conditional; if the Normandy beachhead did not expand according to the timetable, a Brittany landing would put reinforcements next to Bradley and the First Army. If the Allies broke out of Normandy, Anvil might be the better choice. Ike, wisely, wanted to wait and see. Marshall, on the other hand, backed Anvil unconditionally. But after five days of talks between June 9 and 13, the Combined Chiefs arrived at a decision satisfactory to all.[11]

It took the form of a directive to Eisenhower and Jumbo Wilson, commander in chief of the Mediterranean theater. The directive held that all Allied forces should be deployed "to assist in the success of Operation Overlord." To that end, three amphibious options in support of Overlord were to be considered, and the best one selected: the choices were Brittany; the south of France; or the head of the Adriatic, with the dual objective there of cutting off Kesselring in Italy and then racing to Vienna. Option three invited trouble, which duly arrived not long after the ink dried. Field Marshal Alexander and Jumbo Wilson endorsed the Adriatic operation, codenamed Armpit, no doubt by the Americans. Anvil, meanwhile, was soon rechristened Dragoon, no doubt by the British. Churchill, who believed that too much miscellaneous equipment was going ashore, argued that wherever the Allies went, they should be filling the landing crafts with fighting men and bayonets rather than "dental chairs and Y.M.C.A. institutions."[12]

By the twelfth, when Churchill and Brooke crossed the Channel on board the destroyer HMS *Kelvin*, the Allies were a few days behind schedule, yet not distressingly so. Men and supplies were pouring in through the Mulberries; the Germans had virtually no presence in the air. Still, progress had been so minimal that Churchill had to take his picnic lunch with the sea at his back, just four miles behind the front lines. There, Montgomery displayed his maps and again stressed his strategy, arrived at in January, to draw the Germans to his front in order that the Americans could swing out from their zone. Brooke was taken not only with Montgomery's expert presentation but by the fact that the French countryside looked remarkably undisturbed after five years of German occupation and five weeks of Allied bombardment. Churchill described the situation thus: "We are surrounded by fat cattle lying in luscious pastures with their paws crossed." He reboarded *Kelvin* late in the afternoon, and after a short cruise up and down the beach during which *Kelvin* fired a few salvos toward the German lines for Churchill's benefit, the ship turned for England. The last time he departed France, five years earlier, he told Ismay that they likely had but three months to live.[13]

Just before midnight that night, as Churchill and Brooke neared London aboard Churchill's train, the first pilotless German bombs lifted off from their ramps in Belgium and northern France. They flew at between three thousand and four thousand feet and at speeds around 350 miles per hour.

Each carried a 1,875-pound high-explosive warhead. They were all targeted on Tower Bridge, but only four of the twenty-seven that were
launched hit Greater London that night and early on the thirteenth. Some
fell into the sea, and others veered off course over the English countryside,
a trend that continued for the next month when out of 2,754 flying bombs
that hit Britain, only 800 hit Greater London. Most were catapulted from
the ramps the RAF had been targeting for months; some were launched
from Heinkel 111s, to little effect.

They were devilish devices, propelled by a pulse-jet engine that worked by
alternately gulping compressed air and jet fuel, which accounted for the
pulsing, throaty *thrump, thrump, thrump, thrump* as they rumbled overhead. Their most sinister feature (aside from the payload) was the terrifying
screech they made as they fell to ground. Their targeting was rudimentary.
A miniature propeller (a vane anemometer) on the nose of each bomb was
preset to spin a certain number of times (based on distance and air speed)
between launch and London. When the preset number of revolutions was
reached, the propeller tripped the diving controls, putting the bomb into a
nosedive. The screech—or buzz—of the falling bomb was a result of
the engine stalling during the dive, an unintended design consequence of the
weapon. Thus, as Londoners fast learned, as long as you could hear the
damnable things passing overhead, you were safe. If you heard the engine
stop, you were in trouble. Berlin called the bombs the vengeance weapon,
V-1 for short. Londoners anointed them doodlebugs and buzz bombs.[14]

On the third night of the attacks, Duff Cooper dined at the Dorchester
with Lady Cunard, who, as she had during the Blitz, refused to leave her
apartment. Told by Cooper that the new attacks were being carried out by
pilotless planes, she claimed that was impossible and that anyone who
believed "such rubbish" was stupid. A hotel servant who overheard the
conversation offered that the pilotless planes were a good sign, "as it
proved how short of men the Germans were, that they were obliged to send
their aeroplanes over empty." During a meeting of the Chiefs of Staff on
June 19, Churchill decreed that henceforth the weapons would no longer
be called "pilotless planes" but "flying bombs." Brooke found Churchill
"in very good form" that night, "quite 10 years younger, all due to the fact
that the flying bombs have again put us into the front line!!"[15]

The arrival of the flying bombs marked the start of a new era, soon
anointed the "rocket age," a concept made all the more horrifying by virtue of the fact that Hitler—and only Hitler—had all the rockets. During
the next four weeks, the 2,754 V-1s that hit Britain killed 2,752 Britons and
destroyed more than eight thousand houses. That ratio continued into
early August, by which time, Churchill told the House, "5,735 of these
robots have been launched upon us, killing 4,735 persons, with 14,000

more or less seriously injured." He told the House that while he was touring a wrecked neighborhood, an old man asked him, " 'What are you going
to do about it?' I replied, we have never failed yet. He seemed contented
with the reply. That is the only promise I can make." The need to bomb the
V-1 launch sites in northern France disrupted operations in Normandy,
and reduced the number of missions over Germany. Still, where Hitler
delivered 4,500 tons of explosives to Britain that summer, the British and
Americans dropped 48,000 tons on Germany, but at a terrible cost of more
than 14,000 flyers killed or missing. The V-1s did not kill many, but coming as they did hourly, day after day, week after week, they set everyone's
nerves on edge. "I am sure of one thing," Churchill told the House, "that
London will never be conquered and will never fail, and that her renown,
triumphing over every ordeal, will long shine among men." But, as Brooke
told his diary, "The danger really lies in the flying rocket with a 5-ton warhead." This was the V-2, which the British high command—but not the
British people—knew was coming, and soon.[16]

As the buzz bombs came on, the battle of the beachhead turned into a
stalemate, and the alliance itself appeared poised to self-destruct. The core
dispute was over Anvil, the secondary invasion of France. After being
guided by Eisenhower and Brooke to a wait-and-see attitude toward Anvil,
Marshall had journeyed to Italy in mid-June, where he learned from Alexander and Wilson that they were keen on the Adriatic operation. His
response, and that of the other American Chiefs, was to harden their
stance. Anvil must go forward, sometime in August at the latest. Now what
had been a debate turned into a crisis. Alexander and Churchill argued to
the British Chiefs of Staff for the Adriatic plan. Brooke dismissed any strike
toward Vienna as "wild hopes," not least because such an operation could
not start until September and they would then "embark on a campaign
through the Alps in winter!" At a June 21 meeting, Churchill, "who had
evidently been lunching very well," Brooke wrote, "meandered for ¾ hours
producing a lot of disconnected thoughts which had no military value."
Over the next few days Churchill and the British chiefs drafted separate but
almost identical memos for Roosevelt and his chiefs that called for no diminution in Alexander's forces; that is, they implicitly called for the cancellation of Anvil. On June 27, the importance the British attached to Italy
appeared to be validated by an Ultra decrypt that revealed Hitler's intent to
defend the northern Apennines, since a breakthrough there would have
"incalculable military and political consequences." Churchill argued in his
long memo that Overlord could be nourished without stripping Alexander's
army. He ended with "Let us not wreck one great campaign for the sake of
winning the other." Roosevelt's reply, Brooke wrote, was "a rude one at
that." The Americans insisted that Anvil be "carried out at once." And the

most unseemly part of Roosevelt's reply in Brooke's estimation was his last paragraph: "Finally for pure political considerations over here I would never survive even a slight setback in Overlord if it were known that fairly large forces had been diverted to the Balkans."[17]

Yet the British had not argued for a diversion but wanted only to press on in Italy. Churchill drafted an angry response, including the line: "The whole campaign in Italy is being ruined, and ruined for what?" For, as he saw it, ten mostly untrained divisions, including seven French made up mostly of black North Africans, to advance "up the Rhone Valley about five months hence." He offered to fly to Washington, Bermuda, Quebec, wherever Roosevelt would meet him, in order to resolve the deadlock. In the end, he did not send the cable. He had no leverage. As Brooke put it to Churchill on June 30, it came down to essentially telling the Americans, "All right, if you insist on being damned fools, sooner than falling out with you, which would be fatal, we should be damned fools with you, and we shall see that we perform the role of damned fools damned well."[18]

By mid-June the war in the east had remained relatively dormant for six weeks. With the Eastern Front stabilized, the Russians faced a strategic dilemma as to how to deal with the three German Army Groups they faced: North, Center, and South. To continue the attack in the southernmost sector held the promise of striking deeper into Romania on a track for Bucharest, Belgrade, and Budapest. Yet by virtue of a huge salient that Army Group Center had forged beyond Minsk, such a course would leave the right flank of the Red Army exposed. Similarly, in the north, if the Red Army struck out westward from Estonia toward Riga with the Baltic on its right, it would find its left threatened by Army Group Center. Neither strategy would result in the Red Army taking a direct bearing on Berlin; the southern strategy would grind to an end in the Balkans, the northern in East Prussia.[19]

Most significant, if Hitler took the strategically correct course and pulled in his northern and southern flanks, as well as the Minsk salient, he could establish a defensive line strong enough to prolong the war indefinitely in both the east and west. If Hitler folded Army Group North three hundred miles back to Königsberg and ran his line due south through Brest-Litovsk to Kovel and the Carpathians, he would cut the length of his front in half and effectively double his strength. He could then contemplate shifting some his 166 divisions in the east to the west, a prospect that troubled Washington and London, and especially Montgomery, who for three weeks after the D-day landings expected a counterattack but did not know when or in what strength. The possible consequences of a German counterattack to the Red Army and the Anglo-American forces were vastly different. Punching holes in the Red Army lines was like digging on a beach; the next wave erases the effort. If Hitler wiped out thirty Soviet divisions, Stalin would replace them. But if he wiped out half of the twenty-five Allied divisions that were in France by late June, he would fling the Allies from the Continent. Sound strategy called for Hitler to do just that, to tighten his eastern line and concentrate his western armies against the invader.

But, like Napoleon, Hitler could not bear to exchange conquered territory for security. To not do so was a faulty strategy, and, as Brooke put it, the Germans "were bound to pay the penalty" for it. The Russian high command had concluded in May that the key to opening the entire Eastern Front was to destroy Army Group Center, which still occupied the most critical sector of historic White Russia and blocked the roads to Warsaw and Berlin. The Russian operation was code-named Bagration, after Pyotr Bagration, a hero of Russia's 1812 repulse of Napoleon. Stalin personally chose the day of attack: June 22, the third anniversary of Hitler's plunge into Russia. To put the Germans off the scent, the Soviets conducted a disinformation campaign consisting of false radio signals that indicated a massive buildup of Soviet artillery and armored units south of the Pripet Marshes, which led the Wehrmacht to conclude that the main attack would come in the southern Ukraine. Then, to further muddle German thinking, on June 11 the Red Army struck out from the Leningrad sector into Finland. This assault was conducted with two objectives in mind: to serve notice to the Finns that their doom was nigh, and to keep Hitler wondering if the Soviets and British might be on the verge of launching dual operations through Finland and Norway for the purposes of cutting off Germany's supply of Swedish iron ore. The Führer now kept seven divisions in Finland and twelve in Norway against that possibility. From the Allied perspective, the more Hitler scattered his forces, the better the chances for success in Normandy and on the Eastern Front.[20]

As the date for Bagration neared, Montgomery found himself in virtually the same place he had been since D-day. He had planned to take Caen on D-day and then drive his armies east, with the Channel on his left and the Americans on his right, destination, the Seine. Failing to do so, he was forced to change his strategy. Rather than strike Caen, he allowed the Germans to punch themselves out at his front. Still, sooner or later (and Churchill was wary of anything that smacked of "later"), Caen would be the hinge upon which the entire plan turned. The American role was to break out from their beaches, take Cherbourg to the west, and swing around south and east to cover Montgomery's right flank. But Rommel and the weather disrupted the plans. On June 19, the worst Channel storm in four decades blew for four days, destroying the Omaha Beach Mulberry harbor and bringing the war in Normandy to a halt. Eisenhower later called the action during June and July "The Battle of the Beachhead." Had the master plan gone as planned, the battle would have been over by the time Churchill made his visit on June 12.

The Channel storm was still raging on June 22, when on the Eastern Front a far more murderous storm broke at dawn as Operation Bagration kicked off. So effective was the Soviet misinformation campaign that only 37 weakly supported German divisions along the five-hundred-mile Minsk salient found themselves facing 166 Red Army divisions supported by 2,700 battle tanks and 1,300 field guns. The results were immediate, and staggering; the Red Army pushed one hundred miles west within days. Three weeks later, on July 11, another entire Soviet army hooked south under the Pripet Marshes on a general heading for Cracow. The Western press proclaimed Germany to be finished but for the formalities. A *Kansas City Star* headline brayed RED SPEED STUNS NAZIS, YANKS STRIKE IN FRANCE. In fact, the Germans had conceded the Cotentin Peninsula to the Americans. The Yanks took Cherbourg on June 25 after the German commander—ordered by Hitler to fight to the last man—asked his American counterpart to fire one artillery round at the main gate in order to preserve German honor. The Americans fired, and honor preserved, the Germans surrendered. Along the rest of the Normandy front the Allies had not advanced much beyond the beaches. Monty finally took Caen on July 9—D + 33—after bombing it almost to powder on July 8. That week George Patton and the first units of his Third Army—whose whereabouts vexed the Germans—landed in Normandy. That night was the last one of favorable moon and tides for an invasion at Calais; given that no Allied army appeared there, the Germans should have concluded that Patton was headed elsewhere, probably to Normandy. They did not.[21]

By then von Rundstedt no longer commanded the armies to Montgomery's front. In late June, with the Cotentin taken, von Rundstedt told his superiors that any counterattack on the British sector was bound to fail. "What should we do?" asked OKW's Keitel. Replied von Rundstedt: "Make peace, you fools, what else can you do?" On July 1, von Rundstedt was forced into an early retirement. His replacement, Field Marshal Hans Günther von Kluge, a hero of the Russian battles and a born fighter, arrived on the scene full of fire in his belly. He castigated Rommel for his lack of initiative, and announced his intention to attack. But after his first visit to the front, he realized how desperate the situation really was. Von Kluge also carried a secret. For almost two years, a group of anti-Hitler conspirators had sought his support in a plot to kill the Führer. It was their understanding that von Kluge had agreed to join the plot, but only after

Hitler was dead. Rommel, too, was aware of the plot. Not reporting that information to authorities was no less treasonous than joining the plot.[22]

The Red Army, in the six weeks between June 22 and the last week of July, smashed more than two hundred miles west—in the center to the east bank of the Vistula and the outskirts of Warsaw, in the north to the borders of East Prussia, and in the south to northern Bukovina and the Hungarian frontier. Operation Bagration occupies little space in the collective memory of the West, where Normandy, the Ardennes Bulge, and Dunkirk have assumed sacred status, yet Bagration, more than any other action that year, served to put Germany down on one knee. Churchill did not even name the battle in the final volume of his war history, where he wrote with stupendous understatement, "The Russian summer offensive brought their armies in late July to the river Vistula." Yet, Churchill was one with many in the West in his inability or unwillingness to grant Bagration its due. During those late June and July weeks when the Red Army swept through an area about the size of Great Britain (north to south and east to west), the Anglo-Americans were still fighting the Battle of the Beachhead on a front only a few miles deep and eighty miles wide, in a swath of Normandy about the size of Cape Cod.[23]

On July 20, Churchill visited Cherbourg and Utah Beach before moving on to visit Montgomery's positions over the next two days. He had notified Montgomery that he'd be coming, which led Monty to ask Eisenhower to keep visitors away at all costs. Montgomery's planned breakout, code-named Cobra—a sweep to the Brittany ports and an envelopment of the Germans at Bradley's front—was set to start within days.

Churchill's reaction to Montgomery's query to Ike was to summon Brooke and fly into "an unholy rage" over Monty's insubordination. "And who is Your Monty that he thinks he can dictate to me? Who does he think he is, trying to stop the Prime Minister from visiting?" It was now D + 44, and the Allied armies were not that much farther away from the beaches than they had been on his first visit of June 12. Churchill, fed up, told Eisenhower that he would support him in any decision having to do with relieving British generals who did not live up to Ike's expectations. Although Eisenhower, too, was losing patience with Monty, he had no intention of relieving Britain's revered hero of Alamein. Still, on July 20, Eisenhower's naval aide, Commander Butcher, told his diary that Ike was "blue as indigo over Monty's slowdown." The problem, as Eisenhower saw it, was that Montgomery's stated strategy of letting Rommel punch himself out against the British and Canadians depended upon Rommel's following the script. He wasn't doing that. "Rommel knew that play by heart," Butcher wrote. He simply kept his panzers out of range of Montgomery's artillery. Butcher did not know that Rommel was no longer in Normandy; he had been injured when an Allied fighter strafed his car on July 17, and he was on his way to a hospital in Germany. In any event, another week of foul weather delayed Montgomery's Operation Cobra. Still, though Eisenhower was not about to relieve Monty, he was so fed up with the general that he asked Churchill "to persuade Monty to get on his bicycle and start moving."[24]

As Churchill toured the American lines on July 20, at Hitler's East Prussian *Wolfsschanze,* Colonel Claus von Stauffenberg, who had lost his left eye, right hand, and two fingers on his left hand during an RAF attack in North Africa, was readying himself to report to the Führer on the state of Germany's homeland defenses. Von Stauffenberg was at the center of a small but dedicated ring of conspirators who believed Germany's only hope of avoiding obliteration lay in the killing of Hitler. Rommel and von Kluge, who had taken over the injured Rommel's command, had agreed to back the mutineers if their plot succeeded.

Von Stauffenberg carried a briefcase, which contained two bombs, into Hitler's East Prussian headquarters. Each had to be armed. When Stauffenberg stepped into a restroom to do so, his damaged hands confounded him. He had armed only one by the time he was called into the conference room. Shortly thereafter he excused himself and left the building. When the subsequent explosion tore through the hut, Stauffenberg, convinced that no one in the room could survive, ordered his driver to take him to a nearby airfield, where he boarded a small plane for Berlin. His assessment of the damage was wrong. Although four people were killed and almost all the survivors were injured, Hitler, shielded from the blast by the heavy, solid-oak conference table, emerged only slightly wounded, his composure and clothes in tatters. Upon his return to Berlin, Stauffenberg urged his co-conspirators to begin the second phase of the coup, the takeover of Nazi offices and radio stations. But after Hitler personally spoke on the state radio, the conspirators realized the coup had failed. They were tracked to their Bendlerstrasse offices and arrested after a brief shoot-out. Stauffenberg was taken outside and shot. Churchill later told the Commons, "When Herr Hitler escaped his bomb on July 20th he described his survival as providential; I think that from a purely military point of view we can all agree with him, for certainly it would be most unfortunate if the Allies were to be deprived, in the closing phases of the struggle, of that form of warlike genius by which Corporal Schicklgruber has so notably contributed to our victory."[25]

Hitler believed Rommel and von Kluge were both involved in the plot, and rather than face the hideous torture Hitler was unleashing on suspects, Kluge bit down on a cyanide capsule on August 18. Rommel, told by Berlin that he could chose between a trial for high treason or suicide, did likewise on October 14.[26]

By July, the stasis in the west and the Soviet advance in the east served to highlight the need for the Big Three to convene. "When are we going to meet, and where?" Churchill cabled Roosevelt on July 16. A week later, when the Red Army took Lublin, Stalin established a Polish Committee of National Liberation there, in effect a puppet government. That made the need to meet critical. Churchill suggested Scotland to Roosevelt and Stalin, but as usual Stalin would not leave Russia, and Roosevelt was not about to travel to Britain during the American election season. He had just been nominated for a fourth term and had eased out Henry Wallace—seen by Democrat party regulars as too pro-Soviet—as vice president and put Missouri senator Harry S. Truman on the ticket. In reply to Churchill, Roosevelt suggested they meet in Bermuda or Quebec. Churchill, as usual, would have to go to Roosevelt. With the Red Army closing on Warsaw—it reached the eastern outskirts days later—Churchill insisted that Stanisław Mikołajczyk, the head of the London Poles, make straightaway for Moscow in order to take part in the formation of a Polish government. Otherwise, the London Poles might find themselves the odd men out when Stalin liberated Warsaw. Seeking a "fusion of some kind" between the Poles backed by Moscow and those backed by America and Britain, Churchill asked the president to send Mikołajczyk and Stalin a message stating his strong support for Mikołajczyk.[27]

Roosevelt's letters to the two, wherein he simply told them he hoped they "could work out the whole matter" between themselves, amounted to the mildest of endorsements of the London Poles, and a signal to Stalin and Mikołajczyk that the United States was not as keen as Britain regarding the fate of Poland.

At the end of July, on orders from the London Poles, 40,000 lightly armed members of the Polish resistance in Warsaw commanded by General Bór Komorowski rose up against their German jailers. The Red Army stood off across the Vistula while for almost six weeks a battle reminiscent of Stalingrad raged in the Polish capital. Komorowski asked Eisenhower to bomb airfields near Warsaw; he declined, explaining honestly that Warsaw was not in his theater. Churchill asked Stalin to send in his troops, but the marshal considered the uprising to be an "adventure" by "a group of criminals" intent on seizing power. Churchill found the Soviet behavior "strange and sinister" but could do nothing to change Stalin's mind. The Soviet refusal to allow Allied planes to land behind Red Army lines after parachuting supplies into the city killed any chance of serious relief. Warsaw was beyond the range of Allied aircraft based in Britain (which would have to overfly the entire Reich in any event) but not beyond the range of Italian-based aircraft. RAF and Polish air force pilots flew almost two hundred relief missions, a round-trip jaunt of 1,400 miles. Stalin held airfields just fifty miles from Warsaw. Roosevelt refused to send American aircraft on any relief missions. Unbeknownst to Churchill, the Americans were negotiating with Stalin for use of Siberian airfields and did not want to upset that applecart by asking to use his Polish fields as well. Stalin changed his mind six weeks later, but by then it was too late. Half the resistance fighters had been killed, and more than two hundred thousand civilians murdered. In early October, after sixty-three days of fighting, Komorowski surrendered his remaining forces to the Germans. The Red Army would not relieve Warsaw until January 1945. "Such was their liberation of Poland...," Churchill later wrote.[28]

Another piece of intelligence found its way out of Poland that July. On July 7, Dr. Chaim Weizmann and the Jewish Agency for Palestine brought the atrocities taking place at Auschwitz to Churchill's attention. Although Weizmann offered no specifics, especially as to the numbers of murders there, Churchill demanded action. The RAF's Portal replied that only pinpoint daylight raids could hit the railroads leading into Auschwitz. That meant the Americans would have to act, because the RAF flew only night missions, which by any measure would likely prove more dangerous to the prisoners at the camp than to the railroad leading to it. Yet for American heavy bombers to reach Auschwitz from Italy or Britain they would have to fly over the heart of the Reich, by day and without fighter support. No raids were undertaken. Three years later, during a debate on setting up a Jewish state in Palestine, Churchill told the House: "I must say that I had no idea, when the war came to an end, of the horrible massacres which had occurred; the millions and millions that have been slaughtered. That dawned on us gradually after the struggle was over." The word "Auschwitz" does not appear in the Churchill-Roosevelt correspondence.[29]

In mid-June Roosevelt, through Eden, had let it be known to de Gaulle that if the Frenchman found himself in Washington in early July, the president would meet him. This was as much of an invitation as de Gaulle would get. He arrived on July 6 on board Roosevelt's personal Skymaster (a four-engine C-54 configured for civilian use), which the president had put at his service. De Gaulle was greeted with a seventeen-gun salute instead of a twenty-one-gun salute, a simple and concise way of telling him that his was not a state visit. When the two leaders met, Roosevelt outlined his four-power plan and indicated that America might station forces around the globe, including in France, in order to safeguard the locals, because other than the Big Four, the rest of the world's nations, including France, would be grouped on a lower tier. De Gaulle came away shocked, he later wrote, that the president—"this artist, this seducer"—by "considering Western Europe as a secondary matter risked endangering the Western World" and civilization itself. "It is the West," de Gaulle told the president, "that must be restored." If the West declined, de Gaulle argued, "barbarism will ultimately sweep everything away." France "above all" must be restored along with its "political vigor" and "self-reliance." Roosevelt claimed he was "open to these considerations," as he felt "a genuine affection for France." The talks ended with de Gaulle concluding that Roosevelt's "idealism...cloaks a will to power." As a parting gift, Roosevelt gave the general a framed photo of himself, signed: "To General de Gaulle, who is my friend."[30]

Meanwhile, in Charlottesville, Virginia, scores of Americans were attending an intensive sixty-day French-language program in preparation for journeying to France to administer civil matters there until Germany was defeated. De Gaulle pledged to not countenance these sixty-day wonders, and in fact did not. Soon after leaving Washington, de Gaulle learned of a letter Roosevelt had written to New York congressman Joseph Clark Baldwin, in which Roosevelt described de Gaulle as "tractable" in regard to future problems, adding, "I suspect he is essentially an egoist." In his memoirs, de Gaulle wrote, "I was never to know if Franklin Roosevelt thought in affairs concerning France whether Charles de Gaulle was an egoist for France or for himself."[31]

In fact, like Churchill, he was an egoist both for his nation and for the West. As disparate as their personalities were and as much as de Gaulle grated on Churchill, they shared the belief that postwar Europe must not be left defenseless and must not depend entirely on the Americans for security. On July 13, de Gaulle, back in Algiers, learned that the American government had issued a statement in which it declared the French Committee of National Liberation "qualified" to oversee the civil administration of France. But "qualified" does not equate with recognition. Two weeks later, de Gaulle, Roosevelt, and Churchill reached agreement on a statement that "only" the provisional government of France could exercise governing authority and issue currency. This statement, too, did not equate with recognition of the FCNL as the provisional government, but it edged closer. Seven French divisions now made ready to land in Marseilles. Leclerc's 2nd Armored Division landed in Normandy on August 1. De Gaulle later wrote, "We returned to France bearing independence, Empire, and a sword." The sword was short, de Gaulle wrote, but it was a sword.[32]

The stasis on the Western Front finally ended on July 25 when, with Montgomery holding the eastern flank, the American First Army, now part of Omar Bradley's Twelfth Army Group, wheeled from its positions around St-Lô. Eisenhower later wrote, "The line we actually held when the breakout began on D + 50 was approximately that planned for D + 5." Five days later, when George Patton and the Third Army poured through the lines, the Germans no longer had need to ponder Patton's whereabouts. The stalemate had actually worked to Allied advantage. Rather than push slowly into France for the previous seven weeks, with the likelihood of horrific casualties and the possibility of decisive German counterattacks on their overextended flanks, the Allies built up their forces almost at leisure until the day arrived—and now it had—when those forces could be unleashed with an awesome fury. Patton's 4th Armored Division entered Avranches on July 29; within the week, Patton was outrunning his communications on his drive toward Le Mans. Von Kluge (not yet unmasked as being sympathetic toward the plot against Hitler) sent off messages to Berlin, decrypted by Bletchley: The front had been "ripped open" and indeed had "collapsed." Churchill was highly enthused; the stalemate he feared, and that had indeed developed, had broken. His enthusiasm was contagious. Ike's naval aide, Harry Butcher, told his diary that Churchill had infected Eisenhower with his optimism. Ike now believed the war would end in 1944. His intelligence chief, Major General K. W. D. Strong, told Butcher that he "thought the war would be over in three months." Butcher told his diary, "I expect we will be home for Christmas."[33]

The breakout should have spelled the absolute end of any further debate over where to go next. Operation Dragoon (formerly Anvil), the south of France gambit, was on for August 15. But Churchill did not go quietly. On August 4, as Brittany was tumbling into Allied hands, he cabled Roosevelt with the suggestion to put troops into the Brittany ports. The next day, during a long lunch with Eisenhower at the supreme commander's forward headquarters at Sharpener Camp near Portsmouth, Churchill pleaded his case—"using phrases that only he can use," Butcher wrote—to shift Anvil/Dragoon to the Brittany ports, in order that Alexander's Italian campaign not be hobbled. "Ike said no," Butcher wrote, "continued saying no all afternoon, and ended up saying no in every form of the English language at his command." At one point Churchill threatened to "lay down the mantle of my high office" if Eisenhower did not come around. Ike said no, again. Butcher found Eisenhower "limp" after the parley and quite sure Churchill would raise the matter again in a few days "and simply regard the issue as unsettled." But it was settled. Two days later, Churchill—with the support of the British Chiefs—went over Eisenhower's head as he had in late June and sent cables off to Hopkins and Roosevelt. Their responses were predictable. Hopkins ventured that the Boss would respond in the negative. He did, telling Churchill that resources for Dragoon could not be diverted for operations in Brittany. On August 8, Churchill replied to Roosevelt, "I pray God that you may be right. We shall, of course, do everything in our power to achieve success."[34]

Earlier that week, Churchill had delivered a long address to the House in which he declared that the future peace in Europe would be guaranteed by four great powers, Britain, Russia, the United States, and France. Churchill's France, unlike Roosevelt's France, would reclaim its glory (and its colonies). "It is one of the main interests of Great Britain that a friendly France shall again be raised," Churchill told the House, "and raise herself, to her rightful place among the great Powers of Europe and of the world." And he acknowledged the leader of that resurgent France: "In these last four years I had many differences with General de Gaulle, but I have never forgotten, and can never forget, that he stood forth as the first eminent Frenchman to face the common foe in what seemed to be the hour of ruin of his country, and possibly, of ours." Duff Cooper, in Algiers, thought the speech marvelous. And with Churchill due to stop in Algiers on the tenth en route to Naples, Cooper believed "an excellent opportunity" was at hand for de Gaulle and Churchill "to make up their quarrel." De Gaulle did not share that belief, and he refused to meet Churchill. He gave no reason, Cooper later wrote. It was simply another example of de Gaulle's "superb intransigence." Churchill, in a letter to Clementine, described de Gaulle's behavior as "insolent."[35]

Denied the chance to meet with de Gaulle, Churchill spent his time in Algiers talking politics with Randolph, who was recuperating at the Duff Coopers' from back and knee injuries he suffered when his aircraft crash-landed in Yugoslavia, killing nine of nineteen on board. Evelyn Waugh had been aboard, and he came away severely burned. Of Randolph, Churchill wrote to Clementine: "He is a lonely figure by no means recovered as far as walking is concerned." He was also a notoriously difficult houseguest, known to fancy the women and the contents of the liquor cabinet, but most of all the telephone, which he'd use for hours at a time to place calls throughout the world, recalled *Country Life* travel writer Graham Norton, who moved in those circles. "And as the phone was infinitely more expensive than liquor they [hostesses] used to say 'unlock your liquor cabinet and disconnect your telephone.'" Norton was using the telephone at Chartwell when he first met Randolph, who strode up to him and uttered the first words Norton heard from the scion of the Churchill family: "Give me my fucking phone." Yet, despite his arrogance, noted by all, Randolph's political instincts were sound. He advised his father to bear with de Gaulle, as he was a man without a country, while Churchill had the Empire behind him.

Family matters were not discussed during the brief stay; to do so was to invite a scene. Randolph's marriage to Pamela was in ruins, and all of London knew it. Harold Nicolson, in a letter to his sons, wrote, "Randolph's marriage is going wonky and Winston is terribly distressed. The old boy is tremendously domestic and adores his family."[36]

For four years the Mediterranean had occupied the center of Churchill's strategic military vision, and rightly so, Harold Macmillan and Jan Smuts believed. Now it occupied the center of his political vision. From Brooke's standpoint, Churchill's vision, both military and political, had often not been acute; now it was failing utterly. "Life has a quiet and peaceful atmosphere about it now that Winston is gone [to Italy]!" he told his diary that week. "Everything gets done twice as quickly." He added: "I feel we have now reached the stage that for the good of the nation and the good of his own reputation it would be a godsend if he [Churchill] could disappear out of public life. He has probably done more for this country than any other human being has ever done," yet "I am filled with apprehension about where he may lead us next." Churchill was tired, and knew it. A few weeks earlier he had told Clementine and Harold Macmillan, "I am an old and weary man. I feel exhausted." Clementine countered with, "But think what Hitler and Mussolini feel like!" Winston replied, "Ah, but at least Mussolini has had the satisfaction of murdering his son-in-law." Macmillan noted that the repartee followed by a short stroll seemed to revive Churchill.[37]

The trip to Italy revived him even more. After arriving in Naples on August 11, Churchill spent the next seventeen days organizing the eastern Mediterranean to his satisfaction. After two days of talks with Tito and Dr. Ivan Šubašić, the Ban of Croatia, he was rewarded with only a vague promise from Tito—who was using half the ammunition supplied by Britain to fight Serbs—to strive for a democratic government following the war. To Clementine, Churchill wrote: "It may well be the case of Tito first, the Ban second, and the king nowhere." Still, Tito was one with Churchill on the need to kill Huns. Churchill was pursuing two strategic goals, one wartime and short-term, the other postwar and long-term. He sought compliant, friendly neutrals in the region postwar, in order that the Mediterranean remain a British lake. Yet to reach that goal he had to arm the very antimonarchist and sometimes pro-Communist partisans who wanted no part of being British stooges in peace. The fires of nationalism—which had torn apart Austria-Hungary—were again burning throughout the region. In Tito's case, the saving grace (for Churchill) was his unwillingness to live under any thumb, be it Moscow's or London's. A well-armed neutral was almost as good as an ally. Greece presented a similar set of problems. Ultra decrypts verified a German withdrawal, which could leave Athens in the hands of the ELAS Communists, and that would surely result in civil war, an outcome that Churchill could not abide. In a cable to Roosevelt, he proposed sending ten thousand British troops to Greece to maintain order until elections took place, and he asked for American logistical support to carry it off. Roosevelt approved.[38]

The readmission of Italy to the regional community of nations also came in for Churchill's scrutiny. He wanted the process to be gradual, and controlled from Washington and London, for the Italians had committed vile deeds. Yet he wanted the process to continue. "He was like a dog on a bone" over the matter, Harold Macmillan told his diary, adding, after listening to a long dissertation on Italy by Churchill, "Winston gave a really remarkable demonstration of his powers." Over dinner with Macmillan he advised, "We should be guided by the precept of Machiavelli that, if one has benefits to confer, they should not be conferred all at once."[39]

It was a working holiday. He took four dips in the sea, including one at the Blue Grotto, and thoroughly enjoyed several outings with Alexander during which he fired a howitzer (missing the target), toured the Cassino battlefields, and witnessed a firefight between German and Allied forces from just five hundred yards away. The firing was "desultory and intermittent," he later wrote, "but this was the nearest I got to the enemy...and heard the most bullets in World War Two." He could not let go of his Viennese ambitions, telling dinner guests one evening that the full-scale assault on the Gothic Line that Alexander planned to launch on August 26 might result in a breakthrough that would allow the Allies to "swing to the right, overcome Austria, and so change history." When days earlier Roosevelt informed him that a conference was on for September in Quebec, Churchill had replied that he sought to put the Adriatic amphibious operation on the agenda. It was not to be. The Balkans and Eastern Europe held no promise—other than the promise of trouble—for Roosevelt and America.[40]

Years later, Malcolm Muggeridge, veteran of MI6, editor of *Punch,* and a frequent and sometimes vicious critic of Churchill, sided with the Old Man on the Aegean/Vienna strategy. "If he [Churchill] had had Roosevelt's support that could have altered the whole war." After the collapse of Italy, "there was nothing to stop them [an Allied thrust north], absolutely nothing.... All those populations [in Austria, Romania, Hungary, Bulgaria] wanted someone to come in there before the Russians came. They didn't give a damn as long as it wasn't the Russians." But it was the Russians, and they were coming.[41]

On August 15, Churchill watched the Dragoon landings from the deck of the Royal Navy destroyer *Kimberly.* Three American divisions went ashore in St. Tropez Bay, near Marseilles, and seven French divisions soon followed. Days earlier, during a short boat trip across Naples Bay, Churchill waved to American soldiers on board their landing ships and sailing for France. He later wrote, "They did not know that if I had had my way they would be sailing in a different direction." The glittering prize of Austria was all but lost. Still, Churchill told Alexander that even if the war came to an early end, he should make "ready for a dash with armoured cars" to Vienna.[42]

In France the breakout phase was over; the pursuit phase had begun. Patton's Third Army took Orleans on August 17. On August 23, the resistance in Paris staged a general uprising. On the twenty-fifth, after two days of gun battles in the streets, the Germans withdrew, a maneuver that spared Paris. Leclerc and his 2nd Armored Division liberated the City of Light that day, while de Gaulle, with a thespian's timing, arrived that afternoon at the Ministry of War. Inspecting the premises, he found nothing missing after four years of occupation "except the state. It was my duty to restore it: I installed my staff at once and got down to work."[43]

By the time Churchill returned to London on August 29, Montgomery had pushed the Germans back across the Belgian border and captured almost all of the V-1 launch sites. On August 31, Patton's spearheads crossed the Meuse River at Verdun. Three days later, elements of the American First Army captured Namur, one hundred miles to the north. During the last week of August, Hitler ordered 20,000 slave laborers to reinforce the *Westwall,* which the Allies referred to by its Great War name, the Siegfried Line, consisting of four hundred miles of bunkers and anti-tank ditches that faced the old Maginot Line and ran along the Belgian and Dutch borders all the way to the Rhine.

In early September, the American First Army probed the Siegfried Line in the Eifel, the low range of mountains that spread from east Belgium into western Germany. Patton, by then, had pushed on another thirty-five miles to the Moselle, just thirty miles from the German frontier and the great industrial area of the Saar, and just one hundred miles from the Rhine. But so rapid had been his charge that Patton's main forces had run out of gasoline. His six strong divisions faced five weak German divisions, but he could not take the fight to them. Meanwhile, the British freed Brussels on September 3 and Antwerp the next day (but not the Scheldt Estuary, the gateway to the port), also less than one hundred miles from the Rhine, and the Ruhr, the heart of German industry. On this flank the British faced a gap almost one hundred miles wide; no Germans were available to fill it. "Rarely in any war," Liddell Hart later wrote, "has there been such an opportunity." To Montgomery, promoted to field marshal on September 1, Churchill cabled: "How wonderful it is to see our people leaping out at last after all their hard struggles." On that day, Eisenhower took over direct command of the battle from Monty. Eisenhower's decision to assume the dual role of supreme commander of air, sea, ground, and air forces "is likely," Brooke wrote, "to add 3 to 6 months on to the war!"[44]

In the east, the Red Army remained halted outside Warsaw but had driven into Finland. There Marshal Mannerheim, who had replaced Risto Ryti as president in mid-August, was negotiating a peace treaty with Moscow, which was signed on September 19. In the south, the Red Army had smashed into Romania, where, after King Michael ousted Antonescu in a coup on August 23, the Romanians quit the Axis. At a stroke Hitler had lost—and Stalin gained—twenty Romanian divisions in front of the Red Army, and thirty more in Romania. When the front collapsed, the roads opened to Bulgaria and Yugoslavia, and Hungary beyond.

Bulgaria was next. The economy was in ruins; food prices had risen 700 percent since 1939. Consumer goods were nonexistent. Berlin had forced Bulgaria, an unenthusiastic partner from the start, to convert its industry to armaments production. But the Bulgarians had served Hitler well by embracing their role in the occupation of Yugoslavia and Greece, where they were known to take pleasure in torturing captured partisans. A story made the rounds that they had tied prisoners to the open tops of corrugated barrels and lit fires under them. To the House, Churchill condemned the Bulgarians and the "wickedness for which they have been responsible both in Greece and Yugoslavia. They have suffered nothing themselves. No foot has been set upon their soil.... The conduct of their troops in harrying and trying to hold down, at Hitler's orders, their two sorely pressed small neighbours, Greece and Yugoslavia, is a shameful page for which full atonement must be exacted." Since April, Moscow had been pressuring the Bulgarians to quit the Axis, but they could not as long as Hitler's armies were closer at hand than the Red Army. On September 8, with the Red Army almost at the border, Bulgaria's new prime minister, Konstantin Muraviev, declared for the

Allies. The Red Army crossed the border the next day and within a week had rolled across the country, putting Stalin's armies just two hundred miles from the Adriatic. By late September, Stalin's bulwark against any future threat from the West was taking shape. Churchill was likewise trying to build his bulwark against Russia on the northern Mediterranean littoral. And Hitler, but for his fanatical Austrian Nazis, was now virtually alone.[45]

On the homeward-bound flight from Naples to Britain, Churchill spiked a temperature of 103 degrees. A large party that included Clementine, Jock Colville, and the Chiefs of Staff awaited his arrival at Northolt airfield. But upon landing, Moran bundled up his charge and rushed him from the aircraft to a waiting car, which sped off to London. The Old Man's temperature hit 104. An X-ray revealed a spot on his lungs; his pneumonia had returned for a third time. Again Moran paraded out the M&B doses and again Churchill took to his sickbed, this time at the Annexe. His recovery was swift; by September 1 his temperature was normal; Colville noted he had cleaned up his box and was "in tearing form." On September 4, Churchill, infuriated by Stalin's treatment of the Warsaw partisans, sent Roosevelt a copy of a telegram that had gone off to Stalin in which Churchill noted the slaughter in Warsaw (the Germans were now murdering doctors, nurses, and patients in the city's hospital), adding that if the Warsaw Poles were overwhelmed, and it appeared they would be, "the shock to public opinion here will be incalculable." When Stalin made no reply, Churchill proposed cutting off convoys to Russia but was persuaded by Eden that to do so would only further hurt the Poles. Stalin's armies were legitimately in need of refit and resupply; to cease the convoys would only delay that effort. Days earlier Moran had told his diary, "Winston never talks of Hitler these days; he is always harping on the dangers of communism. He dreams of the Red Army spreading like a cancer from one country to another. It has become an obsession, and he seems to think of nothing else." Churchill intended to address those concerns, and more, with Roosevelt at the upcoming conference in Quebec.[46]

The skies over Britain had been empty of V-1 flying bombs for four days by the time Churchill boarded the *Queen Mary* at Greenock on September 5, bound for Quebec. Of slightly more than 10,000 V-1s launched toward Britain, 7,488 had crossed the Channel. Of those, more than 3,900 were shot down; 2,419 reached Greater London, killing more than 6,000 and injuring more than 18,000. On September 7, Duncan Sandys told reporters, "Except for a last few shots, the Battle of London is over."

Sandys's pronouncement was about as wrong as wrong can be. Early the next evening, the first two V-2 rockets fell in Greater London. They measured forty-six feet high, weighed fourteen tons at launch, and flew at more than 3,600 miles an hour, propelled by liquid oxygen and a three-to-one alcohol-to-water mixture. Launched from near The Hague, they covered the two hundred miles to London in just under five minutes. Outrunning their own concussive sound, they descended in silence at almost two thousand miles per hour; their roar, like a freight train overhead, arrived only after they detonated. Their 2,200-pound warhead could eradicate a city block. HMG, not wanting to tell the Germans if their targeting was effective, did not announce the assaults and instead told Britons that gas mains had exploded, a story HMG held to for weeks, even as Britons put two and two together when "gas mains" began erupting at the rate of five a day.[47]

By September 8, Churchill and the *Queen Mary,* with four thousand passengers on board, including wounded American soldiers, were more than halfway across the Atlantic. Clementine and Sarah made the trip, as did Jock Colville, Lord Moran, favored science adviser Lord Cherwell, and a vast number of British military representatives. The *Queen* took a southerly route in order to avoid any lurking U-boats, and thus the passengers found themselves sweltering in the Gulf Stream as temperatures reached eighty degrees, which to an Englishman is a heat wave. Churchill, still under the weather as result of his large doses of M&B, passed the time playing bezique and reading *Phineas Finn* and *The Duke's Children.* He did not prepare for the upcoming conference, to Brooke's chagrin. At meals he waxed pessimistic on the postwar world. He would miss none of his Labour colleagues except Bevin—"mediocrities," he called them—if they bolted the coalition. And if he was voted out of office: "What is good enough for the English people is good enough for me." Dark days were ahead, he pronounced over dinner one evening. Peace would find consumer goods in short supply, Britain in dire financial straits. All he wanted to do was get the soldiers home and see to it that they had houses. And, he said, "The idea that you can vote yourself into prosperity is one of the most ludicrous that was ever entertained."[48]

The menu at one dinner included oysters, roast turkey, ice cream, cantaloupe, and Stilton cheese, "all washed down by a remarkable Liebfraumilch, followed by 1870 brandy; all of which," Colville wrote, "made the conversation about the shortage of consumer goods a shade unreal." All noted Churchill's lethargy as the *Queen* drove west. Brooke: "He [Churchill] looked old, unwell, and depressed. Evidently he found it hard to concentrate and kept holding his head between his hands." Lord Moran told Colville he did not give Churchill a long life, and, Colville wrote, "he thinks when he goes it will either be a stroke or the heart trouble" that had first showed itself in the White House in 1941 and then again at Carthage in 1943. "May he at least live to see victory," Colville told his diary, adding, "Perhaps it would be well that he should escape the aftermath."[49]

The Château Frontenac and the Citadel were again taken over by Anglo-American luminaries, both military and civilian. The setting was familiar, but the business at hand was new. The Quebec conference (code-named Octagon) was more about managing the peace than winning the war—how best to keep Germany down once it was defeated, and how best to coordinate Allied forces in the Pacific. It had been nine months since Churchill had said his good-byes to Roosevelt in Cairo, their longest separation since sailing into Placentia Bay three years before. European military strategy was not on the agenda. The European Front was effectively in the hands of Eisenhower, who, although having made clear that he intended to pursue a broad-front strategy, was willing to exploit any German weaknesses, including the apparent gap to Montgomery's immediate front. Churchill, still fixed on the Adriatic, declared to the Chiefs of Staff that "we are coming to Quebec solely to obtain landing ships out of the Americans" to land in Istria and seize Trieste. In the Pacific, the chiefs argued, Britain had to display solidarity with the United States by contributing large Royal Navy forces to the American push in the central Pacific. Churchill disagreed and stuck to his Sumatra and Singapore strategy. All of this led Brooke to tell his diary: "I am feeling *very, very,* depressed at the thought of this meeting, unless Winston changes radically we shall be in hopeless situation."[50]

Brooke's worries did not materialize. Churchill, not wanting to be seen as shirking his duties in the Pacific, agreed to a British naval presence in the central Pacific, where Admiral Nimitz's fleets—and soldiers and Marines—were driving north, with Okinawa their penultimate destination, the Japanese homeland their final objective. MacArthur, meanwhile, was driving toward his objective, the Philippines. Nimitz and Admiral King wanted no part of any plan that included the Royal Navy; in fact, the Americans, so mightily re-armed, believed they had no need of the Royal Navy in order to defeat Japan. As always, they suspected Churchill was only after reclaiming lost British colonies. Churchill did nothing to help matters when he announced at one of the plenary sessions that Vienna and Singapore were the most important objectives in their respective theaters. By doing so, Brooke wrote, "he was not assisting with our discussions with the American Chiefs." Yet, despite Churchill's detours to Austria and Malaya, the military meetings went well, in part because the American Chiefs, flush with victories in the Pacific and confident that the European war could end by Christmas, were in a conciliatory frame of mind.

The Americans agreed to seek no further reductions in Alexander's army. Indeed, Brooke told his diary, "The Americans have shown a wonderful spirit of cooperation." The optimism had spread to many in high office, but not Churchill, who told Colville that "it was even money the Germans would still be fighting at Christmas, and if they did collapse the reasons would be political rather than military."[51]

The Americans proved themselves amenable, as well, on the matter of zones of occupation in a vanquished Germany; they desired to occupy part of western Germany shoulder to shoulder with the British and sought only egress to Essen. Here, guided by Eden, Churchill introduced a new element by proposing that the French, too, be given a zone. This was a wily incremental stroke of the sort Roosevelt was master of. The Americans had yet to recognize de Gaulle's FCNL, which by then was the de facto government of France, if not de jure in the eyes of Roosevelt. By not rejecting outright a French role in postwar Germany, Roosevelt tacitly acknowledged de Gaulle's leadership, for if the time to carve the zones arrived within weeks, as many thought, who else but de Gaulle could accept such a proposal in the name of France? Roosevelt was not on his usual game. Churchill told Colville he feared the president was now "very frail."[52]

On the matter of how to punish postwar Germany, Churchill, who had long proposed an economically reinvigorated but disarmed Germany, displayed his growing subservience to Roosevelt and the Americans. In late July, the Red Army had liberated the Majdanek death camp on the outskirts of Lublin. Unlike the Treblinka and Sobibor camps, which the Germans had destroyed and plowed under before the Red Army arrived, Majdanek was abandoned with such haste that it was functional when the Soviets marched through the gates. Reports reached the West within weeks. A hut lined with asbestos was used to burn inmates alive. Four gas chambers were used to kill up to 250 prisoners at a time, with either carbon monoxide or Zyklon B pellets, which produced cyanide gas when exposed to air. Bodies were carted to a nearby crematorium, where the remains were rendered into ashes; the ashes, in turn, were used to fertilize the cabbage crop. A warehouse contained tens of thousands of shoes. A local woman told a visiting American journalist that when the camp was in operation, loudspeakers continually played Strauss waltzes. " 'The Beautiful Blue Danube,' " she said, "can never be beautiful to us again." Another woman repeated words the Americans had heard many times that day: "I hope you Americans will not be soft with the Germans."[53]

At a dinner on September 13 attended by Churchill, Roosevelt, Lord Moran, Lord Cherwell, and Admiral Leahy, Henry Morgenthau outlined his plan for Germany's future: plowing German industry under, destroying its shipyards and coal mines, and converting the country to a pasture.

Harry Hopkins was not at the table, nor was he even in Quebec, a source of worry for Churchill, who had always counted on Hopkins to explain and champion his thoughts to Roosevelt. Instead, here was Morgenthau, who had attended none of the previous conferences. When Morgenthau finished his presentation, Churchill objected. He was all for disarming Germany, he said, but not for making it a wasteland. "I agree with [Edmund] Burke," he said. "You cannot indict a whole nation." The English people, he warned, will not stand for the enslavement of their fellow working-class Germans. Morgenthau pointed out that destroying the Ruhr could only help British steel exports and Britain's balance of payments. As Stalin had at Tehran, Roosevelt offered that a German factory turning out steel furniture could be easily converted into an armaments plant. Churchill had no counterplan to offer, but he made clear he would not go along with Morgenthau. His reaction had been "instinctive revulsion," Moran noted, adding, "He hates cruelty." But within forty-eight hours Cherwell had brought Churchill around. (It was during these weeks that Churchill told Moran that "if the Ruhr were grassed over it would be good for our trade.") Roosevelt and Churchill signed off on the Morgenthau Plan on September 15.[54]

It was a stillborn concept. Stimson, Hopkins, and Hull thought the plan hideous, and told Roosevelt so. In early October, Hull told Roosevelt it would be inhuman to condemn Germans to starvation, and he read back to the president a transcript from a meeting where Roosevelt had endorsed the severest treatment of Germany: "Looking forward to converting Germany into a country primarily agricultural in character." Roosevelt did not recall the quote, but soon after his talk with Hull he scotched the Morgenthau Plan.

Both Churchill and Roosevelt had come to Quebec, as many of their companions had noted, tired and unfocused. The same could be said of the alliance. Robert Sherwood later wrote, "The Allies were well prepared for war to the death in Europe, but they were ill prepared for the cataclysm of sudden total victory." The meeting in Quebec had really been called in order that the British and Americans could reach agreement on an agenda for the next gathering of the Big Three, which Roosevelt soon proposed to Stalin. It appeared a meeting of the minds had taken place at Quebec, when in fact it had not. Poland—Stalin's first priority, and Churchill's—was not even discussed.[55]

When the conference ended on September 17, Churchill, his family, and a few aides journeyed by train to Hyde Park. There, with the pressures of plenary sessions out of the way, Churchill regained his strength, helped in

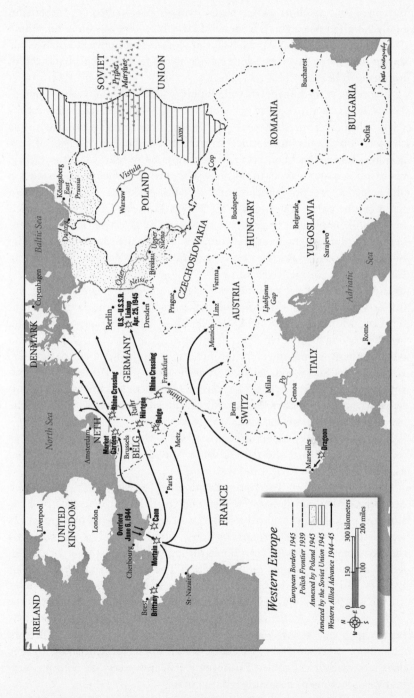

Western Europe

part by a succession of picnics that Clementine described as "rather fun, really," high praise coming from her. Harry Hopkins was on hand, which greatly cheered Churchill, who believed Hopkins's absence in Quebec was due to his having fallen out with Roosevelt. In fact, Hopkins had been ill for most of the year.[56]

The news from Europe was startlingly good, although Colville noted, "From the American papers one would scarcely believe any British troops were fighting." *Time* that week ran a map of the Western Front with the caption "The Yanks are coming." In fact, after stabbing into a slice of German territory at Aachen, the Yanks had stopped to refit. To Patton's fury, his gasoline quota was cut to the bone so that Montgomery could be fueled and armed in order to launch Operation Market Garden. This was to be a strike by the paratroopers of the 1st British Airborne Division, supported by a Polish parachute brigade, on the north bank of the Rhine at Arnhem — the supposed gap at his front. The American 101st and 82nd Airborne Divisions would likewise drop into Holland near the Wilhelmina Canal and the Meuse River, respectively. Once the bridges over these and four other waterways were taken, the plan called for Allied armor and infantry to roar north through Holland to link up with the paratroopers at Arnhem. Monty intended to exploit the gap — which was closing, if it had ever been wide to start with — in front of the Ruhr. It was the British who were coming. Montgomery began his attack on September 17. By then, wrote Robert Sherwood, the highest authorities in the British and American command believed that "German surrender could come within a matter of weeks or even days." Churchill did not share that optimism, but the news from Europe was indisputably good.[57]

As the Churchill party boarded the *Queen Mary* in New York on September 20, Colville found the Old Man "looking far, far better — indeed as John Peck would say, 'in rude health.' "[58]

By the time Churchill arrived in London on the twenty-sixth, Operation Market Garden had failed, terribly. The weather had worsened and the skies over Holland precluded the arrival of reinforcements or supplies, as well as the bombing of German positions. Allied armored columns clogged the two-lane highway that ran north through Holland (sowed with minefields, and with wetlands on either side). The failure to take the Scheldt Estuary had allowed the Germans to evacuate 60,000 men from there to fill the gap Monty was trying to penetrate. The offensive failed utterly, with the result, Colville told his diary, "The First Airborne Division has been wiped out at Arnhem." Nobody on the Western Front — British, Canadian, or American — would be going home for Christmas. Three days later, Churchill cabled Roosevelt: "It seems pretty clear to me Germany is not going to be conquered this year."[59]

Churchill tried to put a good face on the Arnhem disaster when he addressed the House on September 28, but it could not be gilded, even by Churchill. "Full and deeply-moving accounts have already been given to the country and to the world of this glorious and fruitful operation, which will take a lasting place in our military annals, and will, in succeeding generations, inspire our youth with the highest ideals of duty and of daring. 'Not in vain' may be the pride of those who have survived and the epitaph of those who fell." As for the foolhardiness of Hitler's decisions that summer to give up no ground in France and in the east, Churchill offered, "I always hate to compare Napoleon with Hitler, as it seems an insult to the great Emperor and warrior to connect him in any way with a squalid caucus boss and butcher. But there is one respect in which I must draw a parallel. Both these men were temperamentally unable to give up the tiniest scrap of any territory to which the high watermark of their hectic fortunes had carried them."[60]

Since his July 20 visit to Normandy, Churchill had spent more time out of Britain than in. This was a source of worry to deputy prime minister Clement Attlee, who believed the P.M.'s absences were deleterious to getting business done on the home front, including putting into place a plan to rebuild the thousands of houses destroyed since 1940, and by the V-weapons that month. Attlee therefore would have reacted poorly had he known that on the night Churchill arrived back in London, he asked Ismay and Air Chief Marshal Portal to arrange a travel itinerary that would get him to Moscow as soon as possible. With Stalin's armies in Romania and Bulgaria, and poised to strike up the Danube for Belgrade and Budapest, events in and near the Balkans needed to be addressed. As well, with the Red Army standing idle as Warsaw burned, the issue of Polish freedom had to be addressed.

On September 29, Churchill informed Roosevelt of his travel plans, and his agenda in Moscow, which included summing up for Stalin decisions made in Quebec, discussions on the Balkans and Poland, and the Pacific Front. As Roosevelt had already told Churchill that he was about to propose to Stalin another meeting of the Big Three, Churchill framed his visit to Moscow only in terms of laying the groundwork for that meeting. He pledged to keep Roosevelt informed as the talks progressed, asking that Averell Harriman be allowed to sit in on the meetings in order that Stalin would conclude that he was in the presence of both of his allies, not simply his British ally.

Harry Hopkins saw danger—just a little over a month before the presidential election—in the possibility that Stalin and Churchill might make some sort of joint statement that would have the effect of relegating Roosevelt to the sidelines. Roosevelt, persuaded by Hopkins, sent off a message to Stalin in which he made clear that Churchill was not authorized to speak for the United States. Stalin saw that message, Harriman later wrote, as a sign that his allies lacked cohesion and will, especially regarding Poland. Harriman believed Roosevelt erred by not encouraging Churchill to stress the solidarity of America and Britain while pressing questions of Polish borders and the formation of a democratic Polish government. Consequently, Stalin sensed weakness. Before departing for Moscow, Churchill told Colville that he was making the trip in order "to discourage any idea that the U.K. and the U.S.A. are very close to (as exemplified by the Quebec conference) the exclusion of Russia." He intended to show Stalin that he was not being left "in the cold." Yet Roosevelt's message to Stalin had the effect of putting Churchill out in the cold. It allowed Stalin to conclude, Harriman believed, that any decisions he reached with Churchill were nonbinding.[61]

On October 3, Churchill and Clementine attended a performance of Shaw's *Arms and the Man;* the next night they attended a stage production of *Richard III.* It was an astute public relations gambit. As in 1940, Churchill's ventures out in public told Londoners that he was with them, that he, too, accepted the risks. Although Cherwell calculated that the odds were 648,000 to 1 against a rocket falling on Churchill on any given night, it was a time when only optimists bought green bananas.

Late on October 7, Churchill boarded his Avro York for the run to Moscow. Churchill's aircraft was comfortable, but the journey to Moscow was still long and dangerous; Moran, worried about Churchill's heart, wanted assurances that the plane would not fly higher than eight thousand feet. The Old Man tended to become ill on such pilgrimages. He was just eight weeks shy of turning seventy and was not the robust specimen he had been in 1940. The trip took thirty-six hours—twenty-three of them in the air—with stops in Naples and Cairo. Churchill arrived in Moscow on October 9. He was understandably tired; Stalin was not.[62]

Averell Harriman, writing years later, pointed out two errors that Churchill committed when recalling these Moscow days in his war memoirs. The first is insignificant: Churchill wrote that Stalin put him up in a Moscow house, when in fact he stayed in the country again, although a Moscow apartment was made available, and Churchill used it for one night during the next ten days. The second errant recollection was egregious: Churchill wrote that Harriman attended the first session of the talks (code-named Tolstoy). He did not. He thus could not have known (and in fact only learned in bits and pieces over the next three days) of the agreement reached by Stalin and Churchill, a carving up of Eastern Europe into spheres of influence of the very sort Hopkins feared and Roosevelt loathed.

Alone with Stalin, Churchill sketched their agreement on a half sheet of paper. In Romania the Russians would have 90 percent "predominance," while the British would exercise 90 percent influence in Greece. Yugoslavia and Hungary would be managed equally by Russia and Britain, and Bulgaria would be 75 percent Moscow, 25 percent Britain and America (which effectively meant Britain, since the United States wanted no part of any such arrangement, either there or in Greece). Stalin studied the paper briefly, and then with his blue pen checked his agreement. The deed done, Churchill asked Stalin, "Might it not be thought rather cynical if it seemed we have disposed of these issues, so fateful to millions of people, in such an offhand manner? Let us burn the paper?" Stalin replied, "No, you keep it." Before leaving for Moscow, Churchill had told Roosevelt he was glad Harriman would sit in on the meetings, but he had added, "You would not, I am sure, wish this to preclude private *tête-à-têtes* between me and U.J. . . . as it is often under such circumstance the best progress is made. You can rely on me to keep you constantly informed of everything that affects our joint interests." On October 11, Churchill brought Roosevelt up to speed on the talks, cabling "we have considered the best way of reaching an agreed policy about the Balkan countries." In fact, they had already reached a policy, although in Stalin's estimation, it, and anything else they agreed upon, was nonbinding.[63]

Churchill also told Roosevelt that the next phase of the talks was about to begin—a parley over the Curzon Line among Stalin, Churchill, the London Poles, represented by Stanisław Mikołajczyk (whom Churchill had summoned from London), and Bolesław Bierut, a Communist International veteran and head of the Lublin Poles. Harriman, who on the twelfth sat in as an observer at the first meeting between Churchill, Stalin, and the London Poles, realized within minutes that a serious miscommunication had taken place, the responsibility for which lay with Roosevelt. The president had personally assured Mikołajczyk in June that he had not endorsed the Curzon Line at the Tehran Conference. He had indeed not participated in discussions of the Polish eastern border, but apparently he had told Stalin and Molotov that he endorsed moving the western Polish frontier almost 150 miles west to the vicinity of the Oder, and did so in language that was just imprecise enough to be "warped in translation." To Stalin's ears, that implied a shift westward in Poland's eastern border as well, which is exactly what Churchill had proposed to Stalin over after-dinner drinks at Tehran. But with the American election now less than four weeks away, there was no chance that Roosevelt would clarify those remarks for public consumption.[64]

Churchill had for almost a year accepted the Curzon Line or something very close to it as the best demarcation of a new eastern border for Poland. Stalin demanded it, and Lvov as well. When Lord Curzon proposed the line as Poland's eastern border in 1919, he did so after taking into account the ethnicity of the region's citizens. Poles lived west of the line for the most part, Russians to the east.

With that logic in mind, Churchill set to work on Mikołajczyk for the next five days in order to bring him and the London Poles around. In doing so he deployed the same weapons he used in negotiating with his Chiefs of Staff. First he asked; then he pleaded; then he threatened, harangued, and demeaned. In Stalin's presence he told Mikołajczyk that this would be a poor time for HMG and the London Poles to split. The Old Man held out the prospect of Danzig and East Prussia going to Poland, parts of Silesia and its mineral riches as well, and a 125-mile-wide fertile swath of eastern Germany. Mikołajczyk said he could make no decision, that only the Polish nation could do so. Public opinion, he said, would not allow such a unilateral decision on his part, to which Churchill replied, "What is public opinion? The right to be crushed!" When the Lublin Poles joined the discussions on October 14, it became immediately clear that they were pawns of Moscow. They "seemed creepy" to Eden, who, nodding in the direction of Bierut and another, whispered to Churchill, "the rat and the weasel." Churchill cabled a report of the talks to King George, and with a directness he would not have employed had the Polish leader in exile been a constitutional monarch (and perhaps a cousin of the King), wrote: "The day before yesterday was 'All Poles Day.' Our lot from London are, as Your Majesty knows, decent but feeble." The Lublin Poles, Churchill told the King, appeared to be "purely tools." He held out hope of a settlement, but added, "If not we shall have to hush the matter up and spin it out until after the [American] election." He didn't get the settlement. Mikołajczyk insisted on Lvov remaining in the new Poland. Churchill dismissed him with the threat that England might well consider its obligations to Poland to have been met, and at an end.[65]

When Churchill proposed a fifty-fifty power sharing between the London and Lublin Poles within a new Polish government, Stalin and Molotov refused, demanding instead that 80 percent of power be vested in the Lublin party. And, Lvov was nonnegotiable. Eden, to his diary, confessed, "And so at this time, after endless hours of the stiffest negotiations I have ever known, it looks as though Lvov will wreck all our efforts." Mikołajczyk, who Eden thought showed "a calm courage" throughout the meetings, returned to London, promising Churchill he would do his best to bring his colleagues around. He said he hoped to return with an answer within a few days.[66]

Moscow nights were filled with banquets that stretched into early morning. The luminaries attended a performance at the Bolshoi Theater on October 16. It was Stalin's first appearance at the theater since the start of the war, and for him to attend in the presence of a foreigner was even more remarkable. When Stalin and Churchill stood in their box to acknowledge the crowd, the audience erupted with a "sound like a cloudburst on a tin roof," Eden wrote. Between acts, Churchill and Eden hastened to the restroom, where they discussed at length—or Churchill declaimed at length on—a new strategy to deal with the Poles. Eden reminded the prime minister that the show could not continue until they returned, and reminded him again, and again. When they finally returned to the box, their hosts made no mention of their absence, although at dinner the following night in Stalin's Kremlin apartments, Stalin pointed toward a door and said, "That's where you can wash your hands if you want to, the place where I understand you English like to conduct your political discussions." Churchill found himself warming to Stalin, telling Clementine in a cable from Moscow, "I have had vy nice talks with the Old Bear. I like him the more I see him. *Now* they respect us here."[67]

On October 27, five days after returning to London from Moscow, Churchill told the House: "I am very glad to inform the House that our relations with Soviet Russia were never more close, intimate and cordial than they are at the present time." Yet, he warned, "The future of the world depends upon the united action in the next few years of our three countries [America, Great Britain, and Russia]. Other countries may be associated, but the future depends upon the union of the three most powerful Allies. If that fails, all fails; if that succeeds, a broad future for all nations may be assured." He told the House that the three great powers "are all firmly agreed on the re-creation of a strong, free, independent, sovereign Poland loyal to the Allies and friendly to her great neighbour and liberator, Russia." That Churchill anointed Russia Poland's "liberator" is at best an ironic choice of words given Stalin's eagerness to destroy Poland in 1939. Churchill then went on to scold the London Poles, who, had they taken the advice "we tendered them at the beginning of this year, the additional complication produced by the formation of the Polish National Committee of Liberation [sic] at Lublin would not have arisen; and anything like a prolonged delay in the settlement can only have the effect of increasing the division between Poles in Poland, and also of hampering the common action which the Poles, the Russians and the rest of the Allies are taking against Germany." He had not said so in so many words, but in effect he had just told the Poles that they were responsible for whatever came their way.[68]

Mikołajczyk never returned to Moscow in search of an agreement. Instead, unwilling to agree to any settlement before the peace conference (the same stance Churchill had taken early in the war), he resigned from the Polish government in late November, handing over the reins to the moderate voice of Polish socialism, Tomasz Arciszewski. Arciszewski then reconstituted the London Poles, Churchill told the House, "in a form that in some respects I certainly am not able to applaud." Had Mikołajczyk reached a settlement with Stalin, Churchill added, "he would be at this moment at the head of a Polish Government, on Polish soil, recognized by all the United Nations, and awaiting the advance of the Russian Armies moving farther into Poland as the country was delivered from the Germans." He pressed the point—and the rebuke—further: "If the Polish Government had agreed, in the early part of this year, upon the frontier there never would have been any Lublin Committee to which Soviet Russia had committed herself, so I now say that if Mr. Mikolajczyk could swiftly have returned to Moscow early in November...to conclude an agreement on the frontier line, Poland might now have taken her full place in the ranks of the nations contending against Germany, and would have had the full support and friendship of Marshal Stalin and the Soviet Government." Churchill's message was clear: the London Poles had done nothing, and now all of Poland would face the consequences.[69]

Stalin had told Churchill during their meetings that he personally favored recognition of de Gaulle and the FCNL but had not stated so publicly for fear of introducing division into the ranks of the Big Three. Churchill sent a telegram to Roosevelt on October 14 in which he proposed the recognition of de Gaulle's provisional government. France was cleared of Germans, he told the president, and de Gaulle was firmly in charge of civil matters. It had been Eden who brought Churchill along slowly to this day. The foreign secretary later wrote: "No one was wiser than Mr. Churchill in giving weight to arguments which he had resisted at the time if, on later reflection, he judged them sound." Hull had likewise advised Roosevelt that a failure to recognize de Gaulle would reflect badly on the United States if Russia and Britain did so. Roosevelt's turnaround came so fast that when Churchill arrived back in London on October 22, he learned that the Americans had announced their recognition of the FCNL the day before, even before official notification from Roosevelt arrived in London.[70]

This meant that Duff Cooper served now as ambassador to the government of France, not simply as representative to the FCNL. When Churchill visited de Gaulle in Paris on November 10, his host was no longer simply *le général*, but *l'état*. The next day, the twenty-sixth anniversary of the armistice, Churchill and de Gaulle laid a wreath to the Unknown Soldier at the Arc de Triomphe and then, swept along by a crowd of hundreds of thousands of ecstatic Frenchmen, marched side by side down the Champs-Élysées. The crowd, Cadogan recorded in his diary, chanted "Chur-chill, Chur-chill" the entire time, the P.M. grinning and waving wildly all the while. When Churchill laid a bouquet at the foot of Clemenceau's statue, the military band struck up, on de Gaulle's orders, *"Le Père la Victoire"* ("Father Victory"). De Gaulle leaned into Churchill, and said, in English, "For you." "And it was only justice," de Gaulle wrote in his memoirs.[71]

Over dinner at the Hôtel de Ville—the Paris city hall—de Gaulle asked Churchill what had struck him the most during the day's events. Churchill responded, "Your unanimity." Still, despite the amity attached to the occasion, de Gaulle made absolutely clear to Churchill that France sought—and deserved—a role in the occupation of Germany and that although he appreciated an Anglo-American-Soviet invitation to sit on the European Advisory Commission, which would plan Germany's postwar fate, it was only a first step. De Gaulle demanded that France become a "full associate" in managing the peace. Churchill agreed, and told Roosevelt so in a telegram on November 16. Roosevelt's reply was lukewarm at best—Eden called it "snarky to the French, and generally arrogant and aloof." The president proposed putting off any talk of French involvement until the next meeting of the Big Three. He added a familiar refrain that could only disturb Churchill, and did: "You know, of course, that after Germany collapses I must bring American troops home as rapidly as transportation problems permit."[72]

Roosevelt intended to bring the troops home in order to speed them by rail across the country so that they could make ready to embark from the American West Coast for the invasion of Japan, where all within the U.S. military expected American casualties to exceed one million. The president's vision extended to the distant Pacific, to the enemy that drove America into this war. Churchill and Eden gazed across the Channel, as Englishmen had for centuries. They saw that Roosevelt's decision would leave in Europe an undermanned and ill-equipped French army of barely eight divisions, an exhausted British army, and the Red Army.

By late fall, Churchill's attention turned to Greece, where in early December civil war again ignited. Communist ELAS paramilitary forces had taken over half the police stations in Athens and attacked the British embassy; their political arm, the EAM, had walked out of Prime Minister Georgios Papandreou's royal government. At issue, as Eden saw it, was the necessity of bringing the Greeks around to settling their differences "through the ballot box, and not by the bomb." Eden pressed King George of the Hellenes to agree to a regency under the Greek Orthodox archbishop Damaskinos, in order to take the wind out of the EAM sails. Churchill, who knew that the Germans had allowed Damaskinos to perform his duties in the See of Athens, where the late dictator Ioannis Metaxas had not, believed the archbishop was "both a quisling and a Communist." Cadogan quipped that the archbishop was Churchill's "new de Gaulle." Churchill refused to press the Greek king on the matter, telling the cabinet, "I won't install a dictator [Damaskinos]—a dictator of the left." Under no pressure from Churchill to do otherwise, King George persisted in refusing a regency, claiming the appointment of a regent would signal the Greek people that he had abandoned them. At least two dozen civilians were killed when demonstrations erupted in Athens in early December. There, Lieutenant General Ronald Scobie and five thousand British troops found themselves on the verge of going to war against the Greek Communists.[73]

On December 5, Churchill cabled Scobie with orders to open fire if need be to restore order. One sentence in the cable soon brought trouble: "Do not however hesitate to act as if you were in a conquered city where a local rebellion is in progress." "Occupied" would have been a far better word choice, but Churchill was on the warpath, sustained by his belief that the 30,000 British casualties suffered in the defense of Greece in 1941 justified a return to Greece; indeed, he believed that the Greek people had appreciated the British effort then, and desired it now. As well, Churchill had paid a goodly price in Moscow for influence over Greek affairs, and he intended to keep the bargain he had reached with Stalin. He advised Scobie to handle the situation without bloodshed if possible, "but also with bloodshed if necessary." Churchill told Roosevelt that he knew little of Damaskinos, but that British officials in Athens believed the archbishop "might stop a gap or bridge a gully." Had Churchill tended to his boxes—three "hopelessly overcrowded" boxes by then, Colville noted—he would have known that the archbishop was the best choice if the goal was to bring the warring parties in Greece to the conference table. The difficulty with taking a hard—military—stance in Greece, as Eden saw it, lay in the possibility that world opinion would hold that British troops were trying not to restore order, but rather to restore the king at the point of a gun.[74]

American opinion on the matter soon arrived by way of the new U.S. secretary of state, Edward Stettinius, and the American columnist Drew Pearson. Stettinius had taken over on December 1 from a very tired Cordell Hull, who had served in his office for almost twelve years, the longest term of any American secretary of state. Stettinius, upon assuming his post, issued a statement that strongly implied that British actions in Italy and Greece were nothing more than imperial interference in the affairs of allied states. This was insult enough, but someone at either the State Department or the White House leaked to Pearson Churchill's "shoot to kill" cable to Scobie. Pearson ran with it in the *Washington Post,* thus raising again the question of whether American boys were dying for opportunistic British imperialism. Churchill was "incensed," Colville wrote, that his private communication should find its way into the American press. It appears that Pearson came into possession of the cable because a very tired Jock Colville, who composed the telegram to Scobie at 4:00 A.M. on December 5, forgot to mark it "Guard," which would have signified that the cable was not intended for American eyes. Instead, it was routed through American military and diplomatic channels, and finally to Pearson. Colville confessed his omission to the Old Man, who very "kindly" told the young secretary "that it was his [Churchill's] fault for keeping me up so late."[75]

The *Times, New Statesman,* the solidly leftist *Manchester Guardian,* and the Labour Party joined Pearson in fits of indignation, criticism that Cadogan called "swill" and "dishonest and libelous trash." Aneurin Bevan and the more rebellious Labour MPs "see a heaven sent opportunity," Colville wrote. Churchill's intervention in Greece brought on a vote of confidence on December 8. During the House debate, Churchill slashed away at those who faulted his policy, including the U.S. State Department and Franklin Roosevelt. Proclaiming his resolve to proceed in Greece, he announced: "I say we march along an onerous and painful path. Poor old "England! Perhaps I ought to say 'Poor old Britain.'" This was a direct jab at Roosevelt, who insisted—for fear of offending Scots, Welshmen, and the Northern Irish—that U.S. government communications never refer to "England," only "Britain." Churchill pushed on, again with America in mind: "We have to assume the burden of most thankless tasks and in undertaking them to be scoffed at, criticized and opposed from every quarter; but at least we know where we are making for, know the end of the road, know what is our objective." The objective—in Greece, Italy, every place the Nazis had occupied—was democracy. He told the House that British troops in Athens were there not to impose democracy but to safeguard the right of Greeks to make their choice—be it democracy, socialism, constitutional monarchy, even communism—in secret, without fear, at the ballot box. "Democracy," he offered, "is no harlot to be picked up in the street by a man with a tommy gun."[76]

Churchill won the vote of confidence by a margin of 279–30. Two days later, he sent a note to Harry Hopkins in which he wrote, "I hope you can tell our friend" that law and order in Athens is "essential" and a condition for any talks with the warring parties there. Churchill also told Hopkins: "I consider we have a right to the president's support in the policy we are following." He did not get that support, at least not in public. Instead, on December 11, Roosevelt sent a telegram in which he told Churchill, "As anxious as I am to be of the greatest help to you in this trying situation, there are limitations imposed . . . by the mounting adverse reaction of public opinion in this country."[77]

By mid-December, all armies on the Western Front, German and Allied, were refitting in anticipation of an Allied thrust to the Rhine within weeks. Five mostly green American divisions held the heavily wooded and hilly Ardennes sector of the front, where General Omar Bradley considered any German attack "only a remote possibility." On December 15, Field Marshal Montgomery told reporters that the Germans were incapable of staging "any major offensive operation." The following day, ten panzer divisions and fourteen infantry divisions appeared as if by sleight of hand in front of the Americans in the Ardennes sector. The surprise was complete, the German buildup having been conducted under strict radio silence. The skies were threatening, perfect cover for the Germans, and inhospitable for Allied fliers. Within days, the German salient—the bulge in the lines—extended almost to the Meuse at Dinant. The vital port of Antwerp was the German objective. All in the West followed the battle, anointed the Battle of the Bulge. The German successes of December 16–24 "were enormous shocks to the public," Mollie Panter-Downes wrote, adding that most Britons, who had believed this would be the last Christmas of the war, now believed they were in for "at least another year of fighting." One Englishman did not. Churchill, believing the Germans had made a fatal error by attacking the Ardennes rather than girding their defenses on the Rhine, told the cabinet, "I think this battle is more likely to shorten the war than to prolong it."[78]

By Christmas Eve, secure in the ultimate outcome of the Battle of the Bulge, Churchill turned his attention to Greece. Chequers had been prettified for what should have been a peaceful family Christmas. The great fir was up, sent as a gift by the American public for the second year in a row. Little Winston, now four, anticipated much in the way of sweets and cakes. Mary believed she knew what her papa would bestow on her in the way of a Christmas gift. She loved horses. Each Christmas, she recalled, her father gave her "generous cheques towards my post-war wish for a hunter, usually accompanied by a drawing." Her father "was quite difficult to give presents to from a family point of view, as there was so much competition!" On his birthdays, Mary always gave her father a carnation for his buttonhole. Clementine liked to give him velvet slippers with his monogram, or perhaps an "evening" siren suit in velvet. And to his children Churchill always gave copies of his books upon publication.

On this Christmas Eve, Churchill gave his family something entirely unexpected; after pondering the Greek crisis all day, he ordered his new C-54 (a gift of General Arnold) readied and, after informing—but by no means consulting with—his War Cabinet, left Chequers after dinner in order to take charge of events in Athens. To accompany him on the journey, the Old Man shanghaied Jock Colville, two female typists, his doctor, Lord Moran, and Anthony Eden. "Hell," Eden told his diary before departing, "I was looking forward to a quiet family Christmas." So began Churchill's strangest odyssey of the war.[79]

Brooke committed his thoughts on the matter to his diary: "Winston has done a spectacular rush to Greece, to try and disentangle the mess.... And what are we to get out of it all? As far as I can see, absolutely nothing!" The British would have to withdraw sooner or later, Brooke wrote, and Greece "will become as communistic as her close neighbors consider desirable." Brooke had weeks earlier predicted that Churchill would ultimately shift 80,000 men to Greece. That week, when the remainder of the 49th Division was ordered to Greece, British forces there numbered close to 80,000. They were fighting Greeks, who months earlier had been fighting Germans. Brooke needed those troops in Italy, where the campaign had stalled at the Gothic Line just north of Pisa and Florence, and sixty miles south of the Po River. The Po was Alexander's and Clark's objective. Sixty miles, a distance Hitler's panzers once advanced in a day early in the war, a distance Montgomery advanced in the first two days following his victory at El Alamein. It had been almost fifteen months since Anglo-American forces landed in Salerno. Those forces had needed nine months to advance 150 miles to Rome, and in the six months since, had crawled only another 150 miles. Fifteen months, 450 days, three hundred miles, an average advance of less than three-quarters of a mile per day. And now the prime minister was off to Greece. "Meanwhile," the CIGS told his diary, "the campaign in Italy stagnates."[80]

The overnight flight, with a refueling stop in Naples, brought Churchill into Athens early on Christmas afternoon. Machine-gun fire could be heard throughout the city. British Beaufighters circled overhead, in search of ELAS positions to strafe with cannons and rockets. General Alexander had come in from Italy; Harold Macmillan, HMG's resident minister in the Mediterranean, was also on hand. Churchill and Eden met them on board the aircraft for a two-hour discussion, during which Churchill's position on King George of the Hellenes began to shift under the guidance of Macmillan and Eden, who suggested convening a conference of all Greek parties, chaired not by Papandreou but by Archbishop Damaskinos. It was likely that the ELAS would boycott any other arrangement. The British embassy was without heat and often without electricity; the weather had turned bitterly cold, so from the airport the party traveled down to the harbor in armored cars and boarded HMS *Ajax*, which offered relative safety. Sleep for the weary was not to be had, Colville noted, because gun battles continued on the mainland, and depth charges were detonated at random intervals to discourage any underwater assault on *Ajax*. Shortly after dusk, Papandreou and the archbishop boarded *Ajax* to meet—separately—with Churchill. The visitors were greeted by the ship's company singing a robust version of "The First Noel." Events almost took an unfortunate turn. It is a tradition in the Royal Navy for tars to dress up in silly costumes on Christmas Day and then to spring silly pranks on their crewmates. When crew members spied a tall, bearded man walking up the gangway, dressed in ecclesiastical robes and carrying a long black staff, they presumed he was one of their own and made ready. Fortunately, *Ajax*'s commanding officer intervened, and Damaskinos was escorted to a stateroom without incident.[81]

While Churchill took the measure of Papandreou, the archbishop entertained the lesser lights in Churchill's party. Damaskinos had brought a bottle of ouzo as a gift, which the British partook of heartily, thinking the clear liquid was water. After downing a tall glass of the stuff (mixed with whisky), Colville told his diary, "I have never felt closer to death." He also concluded that Damaskinos cut "a magnificent figure and also has a sense of humor." Churchill thought likewise after meeting with Damaskinos. Thus, the holy man whom Churchill had weeks earlier called a quisling and dictator now found himself in the prime minister's good graces, addressed now by Churchill as "Your Beatitude." Colville noted that "we are now in the curious topsy-turvy position of the Prime Minister feeling strongly pro-Damaskinos (he even thinks he would make a good regent)." That was Churchill's way; nothing substituted for a face-to-face meeting. It was agreed that Damaskinos would indeed chair the meeting of all parties scheduled for the next day. Papandreou—who Macmillan thought "a worthy man, but vain, and therefore shifty"—was being marginalized, and that meant King George of the Hellenes was as well.[82]

The meeting with the Greek factions took place on December 26 at the Ministry of Foreign Affairs. Getting from *Ajax* to the ministry proved a dangerous business. Two artillery shells straddled the ship as Churchill prepared to leave. A burst of machine-gun fire peppered a stone wall above his head. Churchill went by armored car, scolding Colville on the way for not carrying a weapon in such perilous circumstances. To placate the Old Man, Colville borrowed a tommy gun from the driver. "What is *he* going to do" in case of attack? asked Churchill. "He will be busy driving," Colville replied.[83]

They found the ministry blacked out and without electricity or heat. Kerosene lamps burned in the bleak conference room. Damaskinos took his place at the head of the table, a signal to the ELAS that movement toward a settlement was under way. The problem was, the ELAS were not in attendance. Then, after Churchill and the archbishop made their opening remarks, "three shabby desperados, who had been searched and almost stripped before being allowed to enter, came into the dimly-lit conference room." The Communists had arrived, ready to talk rather than shoot. Churchill and the British departed, leaving the Greeks to sort things out among themselves. By the next afternoon they had reached an agreement. The Communists accepted Damaskinos as regent. Papandreou drafted a letter of intent to King George of the Hellenes in that regard, a statement Macmillan believed would prove Papandreou's death warrant. (It did not. He served as prime minister twice again from 1963 to 1965.) At Churchill's request, Damaskinos pledged absolutely and without reservation to guarantee Papandreou's safety. King George promised not to return to Greece until the people had spoken in a plebiscite. By late on December 27, it was done. Churchill had not strictly speaking secured a cease-fire, let alone a signed truce, but he had secured the regency. "Greece's troubles were by no means over," Eden later wrote, "but at the least the Greek people would now have a chance to choose their destiny without fear."[84]

On December 29, the day he returned from Greece, Churchill received a cable from Stalin in which the marshal threatened to recognize the Lublin Poles to the complete exclusion of the London Poles. The interests of the entire Polish people, Stalin wrote, cannot be sacrificed "in favor of a handful of Polish emigrants in London." Roosevelt, when informed, cabled Stalin that he was "disturbed and deeply disappointed" by the message. "I am more than ever convinced," the president wrote, "that when the three of us get together we can reach a solution of the Polish problem." Stalin, in reply, promised a "free and democratic Poland" but also reminded Roosevelt,

"The problem of Poland is inseparable from the security of the Soviet Union." As well, Stalin told Roosevelt, he did not want Polish anti-Soviet partisans operating in the rear of the Red Army as it drove into Germany. In fact, the Soviets and their Lublin puppets had been systematically destroying the Polish resistance movement since August. Churchill joined Roosevelt in asking Stalin to delay any irrevocable decision on the Lublin Poles until the three leaders met at the end of January. Since October, when Roosevelt first proposed a Big Three meeting to coordinate the final assault on Germany and its partition into occupied zones, events had outpaced plans.

The Red Army was now poised to overrun western Poland and strike into Germany. The war in Europe could be over in weeks, yet no agreement had been reached on the structure of the United Nations Organization, which would keep the peace, or on the makeup and role of the European Advisory Commission, which would manage German affairs, or on the fundamental question of Polish borders. The president had proposed to Stalin that they all meet in Scotland; Stalin declined and suggested the Crimean seaside resort city of Yalta as an alternative. Roosevelt, an ill man, protested the vast distances he'd have to travel to the Crimea, and proposed Malta, or Athens, or Cyprus. He had lost twenty pounds during the fall campaign, which had ended in his election to a fourth term. He had been hit that year by influenza, angina, and bronchitis. He was weak and could no longer stand behind a podium, supported by his steel braces, to deliver speeches. His lungs crackled with fluid retention, a symptom of congestive heart failure. He allowed to Stalin that his doctors were worried that a journey to Russia would be dangerous.[85]

Stalin gave no ground. He could not leave Russia, he told Roosevelt, on the advice of *his* doctors. The leaders agreed after much back-and-forth to convene in Yalta. The town was a two-day ride by armored train for Stalin, but for Roosevelt it would require a 4,800-mile, ten-day sea journey to a secure Mediterranean port, and a 1,300-mile flight from there to Yalta. Churchill's journey would not be nearly as arduous, but its long air legs would prove tiring for any traveler. The Crimean climate would do nothing to ameliorate the situation. Conditions in Yalta were so bad, Churchill told Hopkins, "we could not have found a worse place for a meeting than if we had spent ten years on research."[86]

On New Year's Eve, Harold Nicolson and his wife, Vita, crouched in front of the dining room fireplace at their ancient Kentish estate, Sissinghurst, and listened to the "gabbles" of Adolf Hitler as he broadcast to his countrymen. The reception was bad, but they heard enough of Hitler's "horrible...voice" to grasp that he was warning Germans of their fate were they to lose their "moral staunchness." He declaimed "on the strength of the *Führung,* on the need for unanimity, on the order of the *sein oder nicht sein* [to be or not to be] theme." Jock Colville also listened, and thought Hitler "seemed in low spirits." His Ardennes gambit had stalled, but it had made for a bleak Christmas in London.[87]

The New Year arrived in a snowbound Europe—"Sunshine and frost," Colville told his diary on January 1. The skies blued that morning, perfect flying weather, as evidenced just after dawn, when eight hundred Luftwaffe fighter planes screamed over Allied airfields in Holland and Belgium "at zero feet" and destroyed 130 RAF planes caught on the ground, including Montgomery's new American-built C-54. With fields and roads covered in drifting snow and with hard frosts coming daily, the countryside looked like "a fairyland," Colville wrote, and added, "The V-2 rockets are falling like autumnal leaves."[88]

Churchill, icebound at Chequers with the roads to London impassable, spent most of New Year's Day dictating memos in bed, far too many, in Brooke's estimation, and "all of a futile nature...due to faulty reading of documents...or concern with details he should not get himself mixed up with." The meeting with Roosevelt and Stalin at Yalta was on, but getting there was proving problematic. When Roosevelt's doctors objected to the president flying over the Alps in his unpressurized Skymaster, Churchill suggested that he and Roosevelt meet in Malta, and then fly at a more friendly altitude on a southern route over the Black Sea: "We shall be delighted if you come to Malta....Everything can be arranged to your convenience. No more let us falter! From Malta to Yalta! Let nobody alter!" Churchill also suggested Argonaut—"which has a local but not deducible association"—as the code name for the conference (it was to the Black Sea that Jason sailed in search of the Golden Fleece). His cables implied a jaunty optimism that Churchill did not in fact feel. John Peck thought that the end of the war "and the problems it will bring with it are depressing the P.M." Churchill's mood can be measured by New Year wishes he sent a colleague: Best wishes "for this new disgusting year."[89]

Montgomery and Patton were preparing to hit the Ardennes salient, the former from the north, the latter from the south. Once the salient was sealed, Eisenhower intended to turn his armies toward the Rhine. Churchill cabled Roosevelt with the opinion he had expressed to the cabinet at the height of the Battle of the Bulge, that the German gambit in the Ardennes "is more likely to shorten than to lengthen the war." Yet Eisenhower had not yet decided upon his strategy for exploiting the German defeat in the Ardennes. He had no plan for the endgame, and was weighing the advantages of encircling—and destroying—the Ruhr Valley before continuing east on the north German plains against an attack on a broad front along the upper and lower Rhine. He could make no decision, he told the chiefs, until he knew what the Russians intended to do, and when. To answer that question Air Marshal Tedder had been dispatched to Moscow, but he was held up in Cairo by foul weather. Churchill, with little faith in Tedder's ability to extract any information from Stalin, told Colville that sending Tedder to Moscow "is like sending a man who has learned to ride a bicycle to paint a picture." The Old Man took matters into his own hands and telegraphed Eisenhower's concerns directly to Stalin.[90]

While awaiting Stalin's reply on military matters, Roosevelt and Churchill heard from the marshal on political matters. On January 4, Stalin informed Roosevelt by cable that given the fact that the London Poles were "aiding the Germans," the presidium of the Supreme Soviet of the U.S.S.R. had no choice but to recognize the Lublin Poles. Roosevelt duly informed Churchill, adding that he was not going to reply to Stalin, "but we may discuss the matter at the meeting." Harriman later wrote that Roosevelt "held fast to his belief that he personally could accomplish more in man-to-man talks with Stalin than Churchill, the State Department or the British Foreign Office." Churchill became less sanguine as the month went on: "Make no mistake," he told Colville. "All the Balkans, except Greece, are going to be Bolshevised; and there is nothing I can do to prevent it. There is nothing I can do for poor Poland."[91]

Roosevelt continued to freeze Churchill out, much as he had before Tehran. "Much to my regret," he cabled, the Yalta trip will force the postponement of "my projected visit to the United Kingdom until a later date." The president had long promised to make such a trip, and had told Eden at Quebec that he would visit London after the election, "win or lose." The London press had run with the rumor of a presidential visit for months. Mollie Panter-Downes wrote that were Roosevelt to come to England, "he will get as big a hand here as Churchill got in Paris." But Roosevelt, Harriman later wrote, "with careful regard for Stalin's suspicions," was approaching Yalta exactly as he had approached Tehran; he avoided Churchill in order to placate Uncle Joe. As well, he was concerned that a visit to England so soon on the heels of Churchill's Greek sojourn might appear to Americans as a presidential endorsement of British imperialism in the eastern Mediterranean. Eleanor Roosevelt, fearful of a domestic backlash, advised her husband not to visit London or Paris. When Churchill suggested to Roosevelt that they spend at least a few days on Malta planning for the conference, Roosevelt declined. He told Churchill he'd be heading straight to Yalta within hours of arriving in Malta. Furthermore, he offered the opinion that the Yalta portion of the trip should last no more than "five or six days." Churchill was "disgusted" by Roosevelt's unwillingness to spend more than a few days at the most important meeting of the war, Colville wrote, "and says even the Almighty required seven to settle the world. (An inaccuracy which was quickly pointed out to him. Viz. Genesis I)."[92]

Late on January 8, Field Marshal Brooke, summoned by the P.M., found Churchill working in bed "sipping coffee, drinking brandy and smoking his big cigar." The Old Man was in fine form because he had received directly from Stalin the information Eisenhower most desired and that Tedder, stuck in Cairo, could not procure. To Churchill's delight, Stalin informed him that the Red Army would soon be on the move, not later than midmonth. The message had been personal. Colville had long noted the ease with which Churchill could be charmed, and Stalin, for all his bluntness, could charm with the best of them.[93]

In the east, eight Soviet armies had been reorganized along the eight-hundred-mile battle line from the Baltic to Belgrade. Each Soviet army was given a designation that identified the portion of the front it occupied; any two of the armies were as large as the Anglo-American forces in the west. The Eastern Front, static in the Warsaw/central sector since August, ran south from just east of the East Prussia frontier to within a few miles of Warsaw, and then along the east bank of the upper Vistula. The remnants of Hitler's Army Group North, twenty-six divisions and almost two hundred thousand men, were trapped behind Soviet lines in Latvia. In the far south, Tito and the Soviets had held Belgrade since late October, but the Germans still held the Yugoslav-Hungary border region. The Red Army had surrounded Budapest, where almost two hundred thousand Germans found themselves trapped within the city. The overall length of the Eastern Front had shrunk by four hundred miles since the summer, which bene-fited both the attackers and the defenders, but Soviet supply lines now stretched rearward more than eight hundred miles. Since August, the Red Army had rebuilt the railroads, and they now brought up millions of tons of supplies by rail and by road, aboard tens of thousands of American-made Studebaker trucks. By January, Soviet armies north of the Carpathi-ans were ready, but until Churchill extracted that fact from Stalin, the Western allies had no idea of just how ready. In fact, Russian complaints about the weather, Russian secrecy in general, and Russian stasis on the front since the Warsaw uprising had led many in Anglo-American circles to doubt Russian intentions, and to underestimate Russian capabilities.[94]

Hitler certainly underestimated the threat in the east. On January 9, he confidently told his generals that the Red Army lacked the threefold superi-ority in men that an attacker traditionally needed to forge a breakthrough.

When first apprised of the Soviet buildup, Hitler scoffed, "It's the greatest bluff since Genghis Khan! Who's responsible for this rubbish?"[95]

The Führer was correct in regard to the entire length of the front, but incorrect regarding that portion Stalin intended to attack. Marshal Zhukov commanded the First Belorussian Front, which was arrayed just east and south of Warsaw. To Zhukov's left, the armies of the First Ukrainian Front under the command of Marshal Ivan Konev were astride the Vistula about thirty miles east of Cracow. Together, Zhukov and Konev commanded 160 divisions, twice as many as the Allies had arrayed west of the Rhine, and 32,000 pieces of artillery. These two massive Soviet armies alone accounted for almost one-third of the Red Army's total strength, and outnumbered the Germans at their front by six to one in men, eight to one in artillery, six to one in tanks, and eighteen to one in aircraft. The Berlin-Dresden axis lay just over three hundred miles due west.[96]

On January 12, Konev struck. His heavy artillery put down a barrage with a density of more than six hundred shells per mile of front, a display Sir John Keegan called "an earthquake concentration of artillery power." Zhukov followed on January 14. The rest of the Soviet armies north of the Carpathians, but for the northernmost on the Baltic, soon followed. The German front collapsed. On the sixteenth, Hitler transferred his headquarters from Ziegenberg, near Frankfurt, to the Chancellery in Berlin. Warsaw fell to Zhukov on January 17. To the south, Konev was driving for Cracow and Breslau. Upper Silesia, Germany's second-most-important industrial area, lay just beyond. Albert Speer had scattered armament factories throughout the region, which had so far escaped damage at the hands of the RAF and the Eighth Air Force. On January 20, Hitler, to the dismay of his commanders east and west, announced to his captains, "I'm going to attack the Russians where they least expect it. The Sixth SS Panzer Army is off to Budapest!" It was a wild diversion born of delusion.[97]

On January 22, Konev's forces crossed the upper Oder, less than two hundred miles from Berlin. South of there, on January 27, the Red Army entered the Nazi extermination camp at Auschwitz. On Himmler's orders (issued months earlier in anticipation of this day), the Germans had blown up the last of the gas chambers and fled, leaving behind almost eight thousand starving Jews and Polish POWs, along with the pilfered luggage, dentures, and eyeglasses of their victims. The pelf included almost one million women's dresses, and 38,000 pairs of men's shoes. By then, another Soviet army had driven deep into East Prussia, where fleeing SS troops blew up Hitler's *Wolfsschanze* on their way out of Rastenburg. All along the front, SS units herded Allied POWs and slave laborers westward toward concentration camps in Germany. Those who straggled or collapsed from hunger were left to die on the roadside or shot.[98]

Two million East Prussians now fled in a human stampede before the Red Army. "It was as if," Sir John Keegan wrote, "the submerged knowledge of what the Wehrmacht had done in the east" seized Germans "with terror and flung them on the snowbound roads in an agony of urgency." Eight centuries of Germanic settlement was undone in days. "Speed, frenzy and savagery characterized the [Soviet] advance," professor John Erickson wrote. "Villages and small towns burned, while Soviet soldiers raped at will and wreaked an atavistic vengeance" on any home or village that displayed any insignia of Nazism. Soviet T-34 battle tanks chased down and crushed German refugees "in a bloody smear of humans and horses.... Raped German women were nailed by their hands to the farmcarts carrying their families." When Tito's number three man, Milovan Djilas, visiting Stalin in Moscow, voiced his disdain for such atrocities, Stalin answered, "Does Djilas, who is himself a writer, not know what human suffering and the human heart are? Can't he understand it if a soldier who has crossed thousands of kilometers through blood and fire and death has fun with a woman or takes some trifle?" Stalin told Djilas, "You have imagined the Red Army to be ideal, and it is not ideal, nor can it be.... We have opened up our penitentiaries and stuck everybody in the army."[99]

On January 27, Zhukov's forward units crossed the Oder, the last natural obstacle between his armies and Berlin, less than one hundred miles distant. Having again outrun his supplies, he paused.

That day, Hitler moved to his new Berlin headquarters—a concrete-and-steel bunker deep beneath the Chancellery. While chairing the first meeting there, Hitler asked Göring and Jodl, "Do you think the English are enthusiastic about all the Russian developments?" Jodl replied, "They [the English] have always regarded the Russians with suspicion." Göring added, "If this goes on we'll get a telegram [from the English] in a few days." No telegram was forthcoming, but the RAF was, and the American air forces, and the Red Army. Three days later, Albert Speer prepared a report for Hitler that summed up the consequences of losing Silesia. The coal supply would last two more weeks; aircraft were plentiful, but supplies of synthetic fuel were exhausted. The report began: "The war is lost." Hitler read the first line and ordered the report placed in his personal safe. By February 3, Zhukov had established secure bridgeheads across the northern Oder.[100]

Churchill, Sarah, Eden, and the chiefs left by air for Malta on January 29, reaching the island the next morning. Churchill arrived chilled, tired, and with a temperature that spiked to 102 degrees. Sarah thought, "Here we go again." Lord Moran told his diary: "He [Churchill] has a bad habit of running a temperature on these journeys." The Old Man, lacking the strength to leave the plane, spent six hours in restless sleep on the tarmac before being whisked off to a cabin on board HMS *Orion*.[101]

While Churchill recuperated, the British and American Chiefs of Staff sat down for talks on the proper strategy Eisenhower should pursue in order to kill the German armies at his front. Eisenhower had finally submitted his "appreciation" for future actions in which he proposed to attack along the length of the Rhine, and cross it at several points. This broad-front strategy displeased the British, who argued that Germany was, in essence, already defeated and that Eisenhower's plan was too methodical and too cautious. Instead, the British argued, Eisenhower should hurl Montgomery's army into the Ruhr basin with Berlin the ultimate objective while the American armies along the upper Rhine guarded that flank. Eisenhower had already expressed his total opposition to this "pencil line thrust on Berlin." Marshall, at times "brutally frank... stood four-square behind Eisenhower," Ismay later wrote, "and the British had no option but to give way." Brooke and Churchill had understood since late summer that through "force of circumstances"—the Allied army "was predominantly American"—they would have to accede to the Americans' wishes. Still, they came away believing that Marshall, although closing the door on any further discussion, did not close it on the prospect of getting as far east into Germany as possible in order to discourage the Russians from pushing west. The British welcomed this prospect, believing it left open the possibility of getting to Berlin, and of denying the Soviets the North Sea and Baltic coasts. But Marshall had not endorsed, let alone championed, a run to Berlin, and he had made it absolutely clear that he would continue to back Eisenhower in his strategy, wherever it took the Allies.[102]

Had Field Marshal Sir John Dill, the British liaison to the American Chiefs, been present, he might have guided Marshall to a more precise statement of intent and mediated Marshall's growing dislike of the supercilious Brooke. But Dill had died in November in Washington. So great was Marshall's respect for Dill that he arranged for the field marshal to be buried in America's Valhalla, Arlington National Cemetery.

With brass bands playing national anthems and with the Stars and Stripes and Union Jacks snapping in the breeze, Roosevelt sailed into Valletta Harbor on February 2 on board the cruiser USS *Quincy*. Wearing a cloth cap, and with a cape hanging off his shoulders, he waved from the bridge as *Quincy* passed alongside *Orion*. All who saw the president were shocked by his gaunt, almost skeletal, appearance. He would ordinarily have emerged refreshed and invigorated after a ten-day sea voyage. Instead, he looked frail and exhausted. After a brief informal meeting with Churchill, Eden, and the Combined Chiefs in the ship's wardroom, Roosevelt kept to his stateroom until the aircraft were readied to ferry the delegation to Yalta late that night. Eden told his diary: "He [Roosevelt] gives me the impression of failing powers."

The president spoke little during the meeting. Again, as before the Tehran Conference, Churchill and Roosevelt failed to forge a united front to present to Stalin. The matter of the framework of the United Nations Organization had been settled in the early autumn at Dumbarton Oaks, but the exact mechanism for Great Power voting had yet to be worked out, and Stalin had stated his belief that any Great Power that was party to a dispute should be able to exercise its veto prerogative; that is, any of the Big Four could effectively override the wishes of the General Assembly. Allied zones of occupation in Germany had been proposed at the second Quebec conference, but the question of whether the French would gain such a zone had not been settled, and nor had the question of German reparations. Stalin had made himself quite clear in that regard; he wanted everything not nailed down in Germany carted off to Russia. Most critically, Roosevelt and Churchill had not agreed on a policy to guarantee Polish borders and Polish liberties. Eden confided to Harry Hopkins that "we were going into a decisive conference and had so far neither agreed what we would discuss nor how to handle matters with a Bear who would certainly know his mind."[103]

Pug Ismay framed the Yalta Conference in Clausewitzian terms: "War is a continuation of policy by other means." Both sides, Ismay later wrote, the potential losers and winners, must give political consideration to the consequences of their military decisions, the loser to preserve what he can from the wreckage, the winner "in order to ensure that the purposes for which he took up arms, will be realized in the post-war." The main German armies had now been compressed to the German frontiers, east and west. They would henceforth fight on German soil for German soil, if not for German honor. The Greater Reich had disappeared. Sixteen Wehrmacht divisions in Norway, and more than twice that many in Croatia and Italy, were effectively cut off from Berlin. German troops in Amsterdam were now trapped behind Allied lines. The end was coming, and it was coming fast. For Poland the end had come; the Red Army now occupied the entire country. While on board *Orion* Churchill wrote a long letter to Clementine, in which he offered: "The misery of the whole world appalls me and I fear increasingly that new struggles may arise out of those we are successfully ending."[104]

At about midnight on February 2, twenty American Skymasters and five British Yorks began lifting off at ten-minute intervals from Luqa airfield on Malta for the seven-hour flight to the Crimea. A sixth York, carrying staff members from the Foreign Office and War Cabinet, had lost its way and crashed in the Mediterranean on the trip to Malta. Most on board were drowned, including aides to Cadogan and Brooke. Seven survivors were picked up, but the plane took vital maps, charts, and papers to the bottom. Churchill had not done much preparation for the Yalta meeting to begin with; now he could not catch up. The loss of the papers, Harold Nicolson wrote, "will cast a gloom over the conference."[105]

The Russians had been told originally that about thirty-five Americans and a like number of British would make up the entourage traveling to Yalta. That figure now stood at close to seven hundred. Yet only two members of it really mattered.[106]

The fate of Poland—of all central and Eastern Europe—rested with a dying man, a tired man, and Joseph Stalin, described by his comrade Milovan Djilas as "an ungainly dwarf of a man" whose "conscience was troubled by nothing, despite the millions who had been destroyed in his name and by his order."[107]

The aerial flotilla arrived at the Laki airfield in the Crimea early on February 3. Yalta was about eighty miles distant, a seven-hour drive on rutted and washed-out coastal roads. Soviet troops, many of them stout women, guarded the entire route. Stalin arranged for Roosevelt and the Americans to take up residence in Yalta itself, at the Livadia Palace, the summer home of Czar Nicholas II, where once a thousand servants tended to the care and feeding of seven royal Romanovs. The plenary sessions would take place there. Churchill and the British were put up at the Vorontsov Palace, about twenty minutes from Yalta. Alec Cadogan found the place to be of "indescribable ugliness," built in 1837 "in what Baedeker so aptly describes as a combination of the Moorish and Gothic styles. You couldn't possibly imagine what it looks like." The furnishings, Cadogan wrote, were "of an almost terrifying hideosity." Sarah Churchill tried her hand at a description: "It looked like a Scottish baronial hall inside, and a cross between a Swiss chalet and a mosque outside." It was perched on a bluff high above the sea. A great stone staircase on the seaward side was set off by three pairs of sculpted lions: one pair slept on their paws, another stared seaward, the third bared their fangs to roar. A pair of stone lions guarded the front gates. Another huge lion sculpture occupied a prominent place in the grounds. This beast had one eye open and one closed. Whether Churchill saw—or Stalin intended—the irony in the menagerie of stone lions remains unrecorded. The British were warned by the Soviets to take care where they strolled; the area had not been fully cleared of land mines.[108]

Stalin arrived on February 4 and took up residence in the Yusupov Palace, more a country estate than a palace, situated between the Churchill and Roosevelt sanctuaries. The Germans had looted all three residences of furniture and fixtures but, remarkably, had not destroyed them on their way out of town. Stalin, in turn, stripped three Moscow hotels of furniture and fixtures, along with cooks, chambermaids, and waiters, which he sent by train to Yalta so that the gathered Allied elites might sleep and dine in relative comfort as they charted the course of the postwar world. Churchill raised a toast in that regard at a small dinner party hosted by Roosevelt the evening of February 4: "The whole world will have its eyes on this conference. If it is successful we will have peace for one hundred years."[109]

Five years later, Churchill wrote in his memoirs, "Poland had indeed been the most urgent reason for the Yalta conference, and was to prove the first of the great causes which led to the breakdown of the Grand Alliance." He had telescoped his memory by the time he wrote those words. Each of the Big Three brought his own most important priority—or two—to Yalta; Churchill's was Poland. Roosevelt came seeking a final determination on the structure of his beloved United Nations Organization. He came, as well, seeking firm commitments from Stalin on the Pacific war. General MacArthur had taken Manila that week, and the war against Japan had entered a new and critical phase. Issues in need of discussion abounded: the Russians, by sending troops into northern Iran, seemed poised to make mischief there. The issue of German reparations had to be addressed, along with the "dismemberment" of Germany (a term Stalin insisted upon) and the organization of Allied zones of occupation in Germany and Austria. Should France have such a zone? Churchill thought it should; Stalin, having months earlier signed a friendship treaty with de Gaulle, thought France should have a role, but limited; Roosevelt, though he loathed de Gaulle, was not about to cast a veto or waste political capital over that issue. A great deal more than Polish borders and the structure of a Polish government was on the Yalta agenda—or, rather, would have been if the Big Three had arrived with an agenda in place. They had not. Instead, during eight days of afternoon meetings and evening feasts, the agenda presented itself as each of the leaders waited for just the right moment to lay claim to the matter that most concerned him.[110]

Stalin certainly held Poland to be a matter of interest, but for reasons different from—and at odds with—Churchill's. Churchill later wrote that Poland was discussed at seven of the eight plenary sessions. Poland indeed was mentioned often, but not until the third session did the Big Three get down to brass tacks on Poland, because, as Averell Harriman later wrote, "the fate of Poland...had been largely decided before Roo-sevelt and Churchill took up the subject with Stalin at Yalta. Events were in the saddle." The dispute, at its core, came down to this: Was Poland (its borders and future government) a clean slate to be filled in (Churchill and Roosevelt), or was the Communist Lublin government (in place in War-saw) to form the basis for the evolution of Polish self-government (Stalin)? Churchill reminded Stalin that Britain had gone to war for Poland on a point of honor. Stalin, as he had for three years, reminded Churchill that Poland was not simply a matter of honor for the Soviet Union, but a ques-tion of both honor and security—honor because the Russians had been in regular conflict with the Poles for centuries, and security because Poland occupied that swath of Eastern Europe that emptied onto the Russian homeland. He also pointed out to Churchill that he thought it ironic that Churchill wanted to dictate terms to Poland, while he, Stalin, who was called a dictator, simply wanted the Poles (guided by his Lublin puppets) to chart their own course. It was a mess that defied solution.[111]

And although Roosevelt composed a handwritten letter to Stalin during the conference that made clear his concerns about Poland, the president displayed an insouciance that regularly took the form of jokes that served only to undercut the importance of the issue. Eager to end one discussion that was going nowhere, Roosevelt offered, "Poland has been a source of trouble for over five hundred years." Toward the end of another meeting, Roosevelt, while perusing a map of Eastern Europe, asked Molotov how long ago certain areas belonged to Poland. When Molotov replied, "a very long time ago," Roosevelt said, "This might lead the English to ask for a return of the United States to Great Britain." On that note, Roosevelt, exhausted, adjourned the meeting. Of Roosevelt's behavior Eden later wrote, "I do not believe that the president's declining health altered his judgment, though his handling of the conference was less sure than it might have been."[112]

During the plenary sessions of February 9 and 10, the Big Three finally reached an agreement on Poland, or, more accurately, an interim agree-ment. Despite his insistence that nothing be dictated to the Poles, Stalin prevailed. The Lublin Poles would be recognized as the Polish provisional government; in turn the Lublin government would pledge to hold elections as soon as possible (Stalin thought within a month), but the validity of the elections was to be guaranteed not by representatives of the three Allies on the spot, but rather by the Big Three foreign ministers, who would meet in Moscow. This barely satisfied Churchill's insistence that Poland be "mis-tress in her own house and captain of her soul." He could return to London and truthfully tell the House that he and Roosevelt had not thrown over the London Poles, had not accepted in toto the Lublin government, but had agreed to a mechanism (free elections) for all Polish factions to take their cases to their countrymen. Yet no Polish leaders of any stripe had been invited to Yalta to air their opinions on the matter. Finally, the Big Three settled the matter of Polish borders, but again, as an interim recommendation to be taken under consideration at the peace conference. The borders east and west would take the general shape discussed a year earlier at Tehran—half of East Prussia to the Poles, half to Russia; the Curzon Line would define the eastern border, and Upper Silesia would go to the Poles, but Lvov to Russia. The new border would shift to the Neisse River in the west, but, as at Tehran, no final decision was made on which branch of the Neisse, the Eastern or Western. In effect, the final decision on Polish borders, like many of the issues discussed at Yalta, had been taken "under consideration." Churchill later wrote, "It was the best I could get."[113]

"For further consideration" became the order of the day. Stalin insisted that German reparations amount to $20 billion and that half go to Russia. Churchill objected. Twenty billion was far more than Germany could pay; it was the oppressive peace of Versailles redux. He insisted that an actual figure not be included in any declaration; Stalin prevailed, though Roosevelt saw the resolution as agreeing to disagree, the matter to be settled later. Likewise, the matter of German "dismemberment" was sidestepped by all agreeing that the first step in that direction must take the form of Allied zones of occupation. There would be four: France was in. On the makeup of the United Nations, the Russians—to Roosevelt's delight—dropped their demand for separate membership for their sixteen republics and said they'd settle for just two. Roosevelt agreed that the offer "deserved sympathetic consideration." Molotov had shot for the stars and was rewarded with the moon. Yet this agreement, too, was only "in principle," to be considered and possibly codified at the first meeting of the United Nations in San Francisco, in April (Belarus and Ukraine were admitted in October). That was Roosevelt's style—move things along but don't press.

On the Pacific front, Roosevelt sought concession from Stalin for airbases on the Asian mainland; Stalin sought the return to Russia of Sakhalin and other territories grabbed by Tokyo in 1905. Manchuria would be a Russian "sphere" (Roosevelt's quest to quell spheres of influence did not extend to Russia). Asia was an area of discussion that Churchill claimed he had no interest in. "To us," he later wrote, "the problem [Pacific deals and agreements] was remote and secondary." Perhaps, but Stalin and Roosevelt had reached agreement on a number of Asian matters in secret and without consulting the British or Chiang. "This [agreement]," Eden wrote, "was, in my judgment, a discreditable by-product of the conference." It also, Eden wrote, undermined the argument of those who attributed Roosevelt's decisions at Yalta to his illness. During a conference that was "strenuous even for a man of Churchill's energy," Roosevelt found time and energy to conduct a parallel conference with Stalin.[114]

It was left to Roosevelt to utter perhaps the most important statement—or at least the statement most full of portent—of the conference. In what Churchill called a "momentous declaration," Roosevelt volunteered during the first plenary session that he did not think American troops would stay on in Europe much longer than two years after Germany's defeat. He had told Harriman much the same two years earlier, and had told Churchill several times in 1944. The statement was meant to diminish Stalin's wariness of the West ganging up on him. It reconfirmed for Churchill his belief in the need for a strong France. To Stalin it also sent a clear message of indecision, if not weakness. It told Stalin that agreements made at Yalta depended on trust for their implementation but might be abrogated through force. To Eden it was another occasion when Roosevelt "mistakenly as I believe, moved out of step with us, influenced by his conviction that he could get better results with Stalin direct than could the three countries negotiating together. This was an illusion."[115]

The illusion was conjured under circumstances that would try the stamina of a young man, let alone three old men. Churchill's day began at midnight, when he took to his bed to read dispatches and newspapers until the early hours. He rose and bathed shortly before noon, and took what he referred to as "brunch," appropriating the American name for the midday meal. Plenary sessions began around 4:30 each afternoon and ran until about nine at night. Each of the Big Three hosted a feast during the conference, Churchill's turn coming on February 10. These liquid affairs were defined by lengthy toasts and "buckets of champagne," as described by Cadogan. "I think we're making some progress," Cadogan told his diary, "but this place is still rather a madhouse." During these affairs, myriad jolly men leapt to their feet to offer, as they thought, toasts of warmth and wisdom. Churchill raised one such to the Soviet army: "The men who have broken the back of the German war machine." They toasted political parties, the King of England, the common man, leaders, women, the alliance, the future. During Stalin's dinner, given at the Yusupov Palace, Cadogan estimated that fifty toasts had been raised; Edward Stettinius pegged the toasts at forty-five and the courses at twenty. Celebrants fell asleep; some slipped beneath the table. Thus, the future of the world was agreed upon. "I have never known the Russians to be so easy and accommodating," Cadogan wrote in a letter to his wife. "In particular, Joe has been very good." He added, "The president in particular is very wooly and wobbly." The president, Churchill confided to his doctor, "is behaving very badly.

He won't take any interest in what we're trying to do." But what were they trying to do? After eight days they had agreed to disagree, agreed to postpone final decisions, and, as Churchill put it, agreed "to consult about a consultation."[116]

On February 11, the Big Three signed their Declaration on Liberated Europe—the Yalta Declaration, as elastic a document as produced during the war. In essence it was a reprise of the Atlantic Charter, that is, not a law but a loose confederation of words upholding the "right of all people to choose the form of government under which they will live" and pledging the "restoration of sovereign rights and self-government to those people who have been forcibly deprived of them by the aggressor nations." Two weeks later, Churchill explained it all to the House. First, he placed blame for the need to even conduct such negotiations squarely at the feet of the London Poles:

> Let me remind the House, and those who have undertaken what I regard as the honourable duty of being very careful that our affairs in Poland are regulated in accordance with the dignity and honour of this country, that there would have been no Lublin Committee or Lublin Provisional Government in Poland if the Polish Government in London had accepted our faithful counsel given to them a year ago.

Then, after posing rhetorical questions on the viability of the Yalta Declaration—will it work, will elections be "free and unfettered"—he gave his answer:

> The impression I brought back from the Crimea, and from all my other contacts, is that Marshal Stalin and the Soviet leaders wish to live in honourable friendship and equality with the Western democracies. I feel also that their word is their bond. I know of no Government which stands to its obligations, even in its own despite, more solidly than the Russian Soviet Government. I decline absolutely to embark here on a discussion about Russian good faith.[117]

Churchill left Yalta early on the evening of February 11. The plan called for him to stay one more night, but upon driving into the grounds of the Vorontsov Palace, he turned to Sarah and said: "Why do we stay here? Why don't we go tonight—I see no reason to stay a minute longer—we're off." He strutted into the private office and announced, "I don't know about you—but I'm off. I leave in fifty minutes." And he did, in ninety minutes, to be exact. The staff packed up everything, including laundry that was still damp, and were off within two hours. Churchill motored forty miles to Sevastopol, where the Cunard liner *Franconia* rode at anchor, his home for the next three nights. Meanwhile, Stalin, Sarah wrote, "like some genie, just disappeared." Roosevelt flew off to Cairo on the morning of the twelfth. On the fourteenth, Churchill boarded his Skymaster at Laki for a flight to Athens, where he checked in on Archbishop Damaskinos, the new regent, and where, although the crowds cheered the old Englishman, the underlying political infections that Churchill had treated seven weeks earlier still festered. From Athens, deeply anxious now about the future, Churchill flew on to Cairo, to say his farewells to Franklin Roosevelt, who was taking his rest on the USS *Quincy* after conducting a parley with King Ibn Saud of Saudi Arabia. The president, Churchill later wrote, seemed "placid and frail. I felt that he had a slender contact with life." They never met again.[118]

Within a few weeks, throughout the European theater, the agreements taken at Yalta strained under their structural flaws and Roosevelt's "momentous statement" that American troops would remain in Europe for only two years after the war. This was an opening Stalin soon seized, and exploited. Churchill and Britain now lacked the political and military means to change the course of events in Poland, Czechoslovakia, and Austria—as well as in Yugoslavia, where Tito was prepared to play the Soviets and Anglo-Americans off against each other. But not in Greece, where Stalin, keeping his word, had not interfered. In Greece, Jock Colville later wrote, Churchill's show of force—to guarantee free elections, not override them, as was Stalin's wont—brought Greeks "twenty or so years of...freedom and democracy." Still, a sense of failure had gripped Churchill for the entire journey. By early spring, Stalin's abjuration of the decisions taken at Yalta would guarantee the veracity of Churchill's intuition. One vital matter was not even addressed by the Big Three in Yalta: just exactly where in Germany would the Allied armies finally stop?[119]

Churchill returned to London on February 19. By then the RAF and American air forces were dropping more bombs on Germany on any given night than the Germans had thrown at Britain during any month of the Blitz. During the first ten months of 1944, 250,000 tons of bombs were dropped on Germany—double the amount that had been dropped during the years between 1939 and 1944. Now, entering the final months of the conflict, the British and American air forces were determined to double that figure; 500,000 tons was the goal. It was reached. Roosevelt and Morgenthau may have backed away from their plan for a desolate Germany, but the Allied air forces were well on their way to producing exactly that result. On January 25, four days before leaving for Yalta, Churchill had asked Arthur ("Bomber") Harris whether Berlin and Dresden, along with Leipzig and Chemnitz, might not be "especially attractive targets" by virtue of their importance to German communication and rail networks. Air Chief Marshal Portal sought to concentrate on German tank factories, which were still rolling out new Tiger tanks. The tanks were no longer intended for massed attacks but for the defense of German towns and cities; just one of them could hold up an infantry company for a day. Harris thought he could hit both the tank factories and the rail centers. The RAF and the Russians believed that such a bombing offensive was critical not only to shortening the war but to winning it. The Red Army could not do it alone. On January 29, the day Churchill had departed for Yalta, Portal agreed to launch attacks on tank factories and on Berlin, Dresden, Leipzig, and Chemnitz.[120]

As long as rail hubs such as Dresden functioned, Hitler could move freely within his interior lines. The Germans had transferred three divisions to the Russian front and were bringing up eight more. Indeed, that prospect so troubled Stalin that he asked Roosevelt and Churchill at Yalta to direct Anglo-American air forces to destroy all such rail hubs, especially Dresden. The Allied air forces did just that over three nights beginning on February 13, when two thousand tons of high explosives and incendiaries were dropped into the center of Dresden. Water fountains boiled away; ancient bricks and stonework exploded into shrapnel. The Elbe burned, ignited by the jelly of incendiaries. At least 20,000 citizens perished, perhaps as many as 30,000; there could be no exact tally, for most of the victims had been reduced to ash. Ten days after the Dresden raid, Churchill took his weekend at Chequers. Colville and the usual retinue, along with Bomber Harris, accompanied the Old Man. While waiting in the great hall for Churchill to appear for dinner, Colville asked Harris what the effect of the Dresden raid had been. Harris replied, "There is no such place as Dresden." Churchill spoke of the raid in rather less sensational terms. In fact, Colville later wrote, Churchill "never mentioned it in my presence, and I am reasonably sure he would have done so if it had been regarded as anything at all special."[121]

Six weeks later, on April 1, Churchill wrote a memo to the Chiefs of Staff: "It seems to me that the moment has come when the question of the so-called area bombing of German cities should be reviewed from the point of view of our own interests." He went on to say that with the war almost won, continued bombing of that magnitude would result only in the Allies inheriting a ruined nation that could supply no matériel for the rebuilding of British houses, let alone German. In a draft of the memo (which he called his "rough" memo) he had used the word "terror" to describe the bombing, and had added, "The destruction of Dresden remains a serious query against the conduct of Allied bombing." He dropped those lines from his final version after the Chiefs of Staff objected. Yet he had made his point: the time had come to cease the airborne onslaught he had championed for four years.[122]

On March 6, on the grounds that they needed stability behind their lines, the Soviets set up a puppet government in Romania. Churchill had ceded to Stalin during their autumn meetings a 90 percent "interest" in Romanian affairs, but he had not intended that to mean the right to unilaterally install new governments. The coup, Colville wrote, "inflamed the P.M. who saw that our honour was at stake.... The P.M. and Eden both fear our willingness to trust our Russian ally may have been vain and they look with despondency to the future." That future was coming fast.[123]

Since June 1941, the premise that Hitler must be defeated was the mortar that bonded together first Churchill and Stalin, and then the alliance, for more than three years, even as cracks appeared in the foundation. With Hitler and Nazi Germany now doomed, that bonding ingredient no longer sustained the Anglo-American-Soviet alliance. The Yalta meeting had been called not to make plans to defeat Hitler but to settle once and for all the matter of the political shape of postwar central and Eastern Europe. Yet whereas the three Allied leaders had fought together for three years with a common aim, each now positioned himself at cross-purposes to the others, even as to how the final act of the war should play out.

On March 7, forward elements of the American First Army made their way across a railroad bridge that crossed the Rhine at Remagen, about a hundred miles south of Montgomery's British and Canadian armies, which faced the Ruhr. The Germans had intended to destroy the Remagen bridge but the Americans secured it with minutes to spare before the explosive charges were set off. By the morning of March 8, the Americans had a foothold on the east bank. A week later, the American Third Army crossed the Moselle, and seven days after that, it crossed the Rhine in force at Oppenheim, south of Mainz and about 150 miles south of Montgomery. It had taken Montgomery a month to slog to his current position; with the Ruhr at stake, von Rundstedt, under orders from Hitler to defend the Ruhr at all costs, had flooded the lowlands at Montgomery's front. Von Rundstedt (called out of retirement months earlier) had slowed the British advance, but by March 21 Montgomery was ready. That night, the first squads of the Black Watch crossed the Rhine. Two nights later, Montgomery began throwing his main forces across, including the American Ninth Army, which was attached to his command. The operation was code-named Plunder, and Winston Churchill had arrived by air in order to see the curtain go up.

Montgomery had asked Brooke to keep Churchill away, but the Old Man was not to be denied. Not since 1813 had British troops fought on German soil. Accompanied by his naval aide, Tommy Thompson, along with Brooke and Jock Colville, Churchill took up residence at Montgomery's forward headquarters. The Old Man was given two caravans (trailers, to a Yank), one for work and one for sleep. Monty had several caravans, Colville noted, of varying nationalities. One had belonged to the Italian general Bergonzoli; another was used for sleeping, a third was filled with caged canaries and served as a map room. Two portraits of Rommel hung on the wall. On the morning of March 24, Colville and some friends repaired to a hillside overlooking the river. They watched and listened as two thousand big guns put down a barrage, and as fighters and bombers streamed overhead. Far overhead, an aerial armada of gliders and paratroop transports drifted past on its way to the drop zone. At one point Colville spied a distant contrail arching high into the sky on a westerly bearing: a V-2 on its way to Antwerp or London. Churchill took all this in from Monty's headquarters. Everyone noted that some of the Allied planes returned in flames, with parachutes popping open high in the sky.[124]

The next day, the prime minister went on a special quest to the river's edge. There, near Wesel, he climbed onto a wrecked bridge to take in the scene. Brooke thought the adventure misguided, especially when German snipers and gunners began pouring fire at British engineers a few hundred yards downstream. With shells falling nearby and raising great columns of mud and spray, Brooke advised Churchill to depart. Instead, Churchill "put both his arms round one of the twisted girders of the bridge and looked over his shoulder... with pouting mouth and angry eyes! Thank heaven he came away quietly, it was a sad wrench for him, he was enjoying himself immensely!" The next day, after driving south to Eisenhower's headquarters, the Old Man asked Montgomery to join him in taking a motor launch across to the German side. "Why not," answered Montgomery. Churchill later wrote: "We landed in brilliant sunshine and perfect peace on the German shore, and walked about for half an hour or so unmolested." Later that day, as recorded by Brooke, Churchill took himself on a long trek down to the river, where "on arrival he solemnly relieved himself in the Rhine." Brooke could only see Churchill's back, but was sure the Old Man wore a "boyish grin of contentment."[125]

Within a week, Montgomery and the American Ninth Army had established a secure beachhead about twenty miles deep and thirty-five miles wide on either side of Wesel. The American Ninth and First Armies encircled a German army in the Ruhr and met at Lippstadt, near Paderborn. By April 4 Montgomery's Second British Army had pushed even farther east to Hamelin, on the Weser River. This put the British and the Americans on their right about 150 miles from Berlin, a straight shot across the northern German plains. The Russian armies on the lower Oder, meanwhile, had been resupplying for eight weeks and had yet to commence their final, fifty-mile drive to Berlin. In fact, the Russians had told Eisenhower that they would likely not begin that assault until mid-May.[126]

In mid-March, Molotov refused entry into Poland to a British diplomatic mission. On the sixteenth Churchill cabled Roosevelt: "At present all entry into Poland is barred to our representatives. An impenetrable veil has been drawn across the scene.... There is no doubt in my mind the Soviets fear very much our seeing what is going on in Poland." Two weeks later, Churchill protested to Stalin "the veil of secrecy" drawn around Poland and warned that if "our efforts to reach an agreement about Poland are doomed to failure, I shall be bound to confess the fact to Parliament." But they *had* reached an agreement on Poland at Yalta, albeit one so imprecisely worded that it was open to wide interpretation. The word "interpretation" appears repeatedly in telegrams between Roosevelt and Churchill during the last weeks of March and the first week of April (by which time most of Roosevelt's communications were written for his signature by Admiral Leahy or the State Department). A less vague and more rigidly legalistic declaration might not have forestalled Stalin's abrogation of it, but it would have at least served as a means to articulate the exact nature of Stalin's abrogation. The vagueness of the declaration underscores Stalin's adroit (and deceitful) negotiating skills. Now, with the Red Army preparing for the final drive down the roads to Berlin and Vienna, Stalin was free to interpret that agreement in terms satisfactory only to himself.[127]

Then, in late March, Eisenhower, without explaining the decision to the satisfaction of the British Chiefs of Staff (and Churchill), swung his main American forces south, on the Leipzig-Dresden axis, and away from Berlin, in an effort to cut Germany in two. To Montgomery's fury, Eisenhower soon detached the American Ninth Army from his command and swung it toward the southeast rather than into the heart of the Ruhr Valley. To the further displeasure of Churchill and the British military chiefs, Eisenhower had cabled his plans directly to Stalin on March 29, thus bypassing his civilian leaders in London and Washington as well as his only military boss, George Marshall. "Eisenhower," Brooke told his diary, "has no business to address Stalin direct...he produced a telegram that was unintelligible, and finally what was implied in it appeared to be entirely adrift and a change in all that had been previously agreed upon." Churchill, Brooke wrote, "was in a hopeless mood." Montgomery, in his memoirs, produced a telegram Eisenhower had sent him six months earlier: "Clearly, Berlin is the main prize. There is no doubt whatsoever, in my mind, that we should concentrate all our resources and energy on a rapid thrust to Berlin." "But now," wrote Montgomery, "he did not agree....It was useless for me to pursue the matter further."[128]

Eisenhower, William L. Shirer wrote, had become "obsessed" by the idea of an Alpine German national redoubt, where, Ike's intelligence chiefs told him, Hitler and the remainder of his armies would take to caves and Alpine passes to fight on for months, perhaps years. Food, weapons, and ammunition had been gathered or manufactured in deep underground chambers, Ike was told. It was a myth; the national redoubt never existed other than in Goebbels' propaganda bleats. "It would seem," Shirer wrote, "that the allied Supreme Commander's intelligence staff had been infiltrated by British and American mystery writers." Eisenhower had long claimed his objective was to kill German armies; now he thought there were German armies where there were none.[129]

Montgomery might not have been willing to pursue the matter of Eisenhower's new strategy, but Churchill was. For Churchill, Berlin had always been both a military objective and a political objective. He believed, he told Roosevelt in an April 1 cable, that "nothing will exert a psychological effect of despair upon all German forces...equal to that of the fall of Berlin." With the probable betrayal of the Poles and the Yalta agreement in mind, he warned Roosevelt: "If they [the Russians] also take Berlin will not their impression that they have been the overwhelming contributor to our common victory be unduly imprinted in their minds....I therefore consider that from a political standpoint we should march as far east into Germany as possible, and that should Berlin be in our grasp we should certainly take it. This also appears sound on military grounds." Roosevelt, having gone down to Warm Springs on March 29 in hopes of regaining some of his waning strength, replied on April 4 in a long and imprecise telegram that said little to address Churchill's concerns but included the line: "I do not get the point." Eisenhower by then was hell-bent for the national redoubt.[130]

As well, unbeknownst to Eisenhower, who had been told by the Soviets in mid-March that their attack from the northern Oder would not begin until mid-May, the Soviets had moved up the date. On April 1 Stalin met in Moscow with his high command, including generals Zhukov and Konev, whose two armies sat near the Oder just fifty miles east of Berlin. Even with Eisenhower's disarmingly honest disclosure of his strategy in hand, Stalin believed the British and Americans were about to launch an operation toward Berlin. It made good military sense for Eisenhower to do so. Therefore, the marshal told Zhukov and Konev to commence a friendly race from the Oder to Berlin as soon as possible. This decision moved up the attack from mid-May to mid-April. Stalin informed the American ambassador of the decision the next day.[131]

At about this time Czechoslovakian president Eduard Beneš made a comment to Churchill over lunch; as paraphrased by Jock Colville, Beneš said that "America might be materially far more powerful than England," but that "England's cultural dominance was supreme and unchallenged." For Churchill, this was no mean consolation, for he agreed mightily with Macaulay that were Englishmen ever to lose their physical empire, they could be justifiably proud of leaving behind "the imperishable empire" of their laws, their morals, their literature, their sense of justice. England, Churchill told Beneš, "was a small lion walking between a huge Russian bear and a great American elephant, but perhaps it would prove to be the lion which knew the way." It was much the same thought he expressed to Violet Bonham Carter, with the Tehran conference in mind. But now, as the war entered its final weeks, it no longer mattered if Churchill knew the way.[132]

The last substantive exchange of views among the Big Three took place during the final days of March and the early days of April. On March 27 Churchill pleaded with Roosevelt to join him in taking a firm stand against Stalin on the Polish question:

> As you know, if we fail altogether to get a satisfactory solution on Poland, and are in fact defrauded by Russia, both Eden and I are pledged to report the fact openly to the House of Commons. There I advised critics of the Yalta settlement to trust Stalin. If I have to make statement of facts to the House, the whole world will draw the deduction that such advice was wrong.... Surely we must not be manoeuvered into becoming parties to imposing on Poland, and on much more of Eastern Europe, the Russian version of democracy?... There seems to be only one possible alternative to confessing our total failure. That alternative is to stand by our interpretation of the Yalta declaration.[133]

In a cable to Stalin on March 29, Roosevelt addressed Stalin's intransigence as well as a threat by Stalin to effectively boycott the San Francisco conference by not sending Molotov:

I MUST MAKE IT PLAIN TO YOU THAT ANY SOLUTION WHICH WOULD
RESULT IN A THINLY DISGUISED CONTINUANCE OF THE PRESENT WARSAW
REGIME [THE LUBLIN GOVERNMENT] WOULD BE UNACCEPTABLE AND
WOULD CAUSE THE PEOPLE OF THE UNITED STATES TO REGARD
THE YALTA AGREEMENT AS HAVING FAILED.... [134]

Stalin had also accused Churchill and Roosevelt of encouraging secret negotiations in Bern, Switzerland, between Allen Dulles, the OSS bureau chief in Bern, and SS General Karl Wolff, who served under the theater commander, Albert Kesselring. Bern, like Stockholm, was a hotbed of intrigue, and Dulles had indeed held preliminary talks with Wolff, but he had not, strictly speaking, conducted surrender talks. Wolff, for his part, had no authority to do so and was only putting out feelers—and seeking terms—in hopes of bringing Kesselring and Field Marshal Alexander to the table. Why, Stalin asked Roosevelt, were Soviet representatives excluded from the Bern talks? Roosevelt replied—without answering Stalin's question—that the entire unfortunate episode "has developed an atmosphere of fear and distrust deserving regrets." Stalin's reply to Roosevelt was scathing; the marshal quoted Roosevelt's fear and distrust line, and wrote: "You are absolutely right." Churchill, upon seeing Stalin's note, wrote to Roosevelt: "I am astounded that Stalin should have addressed to you a message so insulting to the honour of the United States and also Great Britain.... All this makes it the more important that we should join hands with the Russian army as far to the east as possible, and if circumstances allow, enter Berlin." But Roosevelt had already rejected that strategy. Churchill added: "If they [the Russians] are ever convinced that we are afraid of them and can be bullied into submission, then indeed I shall despair of our future relations with them, and much more."[135]

On April 5 Churchill followed his cable to Roosevelt with his own reply to Stalin, in which he categorically rejected the charge that military negotiations had taken place in Bern. He added: "Still less did any political-military plot, as alleged in your telegram to the president, enter into our thoughts, which are not as suggested of so dishonourable a character."[136]

On that subject, as on Poland and Eastern Europe, there was little left to say, and nothing left to do. It was done.

Early in the afternoon of April 12, in his Warm Springs parlor, Roosevelt complained of "a terrible headache" before slumping over in his chair. He had suffered a massive cerebral hemorrhage. At 3:35 P.M., doctors declared the president dead. The news did not reach Churchill until almost midnight. He ordered his plane to be made ready for the trip to the United States in order to attend the funeral on April 14. He sent off three cables, to Harry Hopkins, to the new president, Harry Truman, and to Eleanor Roosevelt, whom he told: "I have lost a dear and cherished friendship which was forged in the fire of war. I trust you may find some consolation in the magnitude of his work and the glory of his name." Churchill did not in the end travel to Hyde Park. With the war nearing its finish—perhaps within days—it was clear that he considered London the most advantageous place to be. Clementine was not there to advise him. She had left for Moscow two weeks earlier, to tour Red Cross installations as the guest of Stalin. On the fourteenth, Churchill wrote to her: "At the last moment I decided not to fly to Roosevelt's funeral on account of much that's going on here."[137]

On the seventeenth, Churchill paid tribute to Roosevelt in the House. Harold Nicolson thought the address uninspired, "nothing like as good as when he [Churchill] made the funeral oration on Neville Chamberlain, which was truly Periclean." Yet, Nicolson offered to his diary, Churchill's speech showed that "when one really does mind deeply about a thing, it is more difficult to write or speak about it than when one is just faintly moved by pity or terror." Churchill ended his remarks with the words "For us, it remains only to say that in Franklin Roosevelt there died the greatest American friend we have ever known, and the greatest champion of freedom who has ever brought help and comfort from the new world to the old."[138]

On April 13, three days before Zhukov and Konev launched their final drive to Berlin, Vienna fell to the Red Army. Stalin's troops then began moving up the Danube while Eisenhower's forces moved down, in the general direction of Linz. On April 16, American troops took Nuremberg, the locus of Nazidom's most holy rallies. It was a symbolic victory; Nuremberg lay almost 240 miles south of Berlin. The Americans, committed to their broad-front strategy, were wandering farther and farther away from the battlefield that Churchill considered most important: Berlin.

On April 20 Churchill dined alone with his first true love of almost a half century earlier, Pamela Plowden, now the Countess Lytton. Her son John had been killed at El Alamein. Churchill had first met her at a polo match in Assam, India, where her father was the police chief. She was both handsome and pretty, the belle of any city she chose to grace with her presence. After two years of polite courtship by Churchill, she had sought more ardor from him, and informed him so by letter. His pride wounded, he responded, "Why do you think I am incapable of affection? Perish the thought. I love one above all others. And I shall be constant." He proposed marriage while rowing a punt on the Avon under the ramparts of Warwick Castle. Pamela declined. In a sense, his declaration that he loved one above all others was true, but his love was for politics, and to politics he had remained constant during all the ensuing decades.[139]

The previous day, Eisenhower told Churchill of the horrors uncovered at the newly liberated concentration camp at Buchenwald. Only then did Churchill and the British people begin to realize that the propaganda stories about unspeakable murders on an unimaginable scale had been true all along. With some satisfaction Colville told his diary that after the mayor of Weimar and his wife were escorted to Buchenwald to survey the carnage, they went home and hanged themselves.[140]

As Churchill and the countess dined on April 20, the RAF bombed Berlin for the last time, not in order to give any respite to Berliners, but to avoid hitting Britain's allies, the Red Army, who were now at the gates. It was Hitler's fifty-sixth birthday.

That day in Hamburg, twenty Jewish children who had been brought there for medical experimentation were hanged by the SS in the basement of a former school at Bullenhuser Damm, a part of the Neuengamme concentration camp. Twenty Soviet prisoners were also hanged. British troops were inside the Hamburg city limits, but the Germans held the port, where ten thousand Russian POWs and Jews were made ready to march to the Bay of Lübeck, forty miles distant on the Baltic, from where the Germans intended to ship them up the coast to Kiel. Eden and Churchill believed that Montgomery should push on and take Lübeck. This would bar the door to Denmark, which would not only keep the Germans in, but keep the Red Army out. A Russian occupation of Denmark, Eden wrote, "would cause us much embarrassment." Churchill and Eden also agreed on the wisdom of the Americans getting to Prague before the Soviets.[141]

On April 20, Soviet artillery of the 1st Belorussian Front, positioned just outside Berlin, began to shell the heart of the city. Other Russian artillery units soon joined in, lofting high explosives from the east, northeast, and southeast into the Tiergarten, a dead landscape now, where no May flowers bloomed. The shells raked the zoo, empty now of zoological exhibits but for the three hundred German artillerymen who occupied a massive concrete pillbox from which they fired their 88s toward the Soviet lines. Soviet Katyusha rockets fired from American Studebaker chassis raked the Unter den Linden boulevard until only long rows of shredded, blackened stumps of linden trees remained. Heavy Red Army artillery lobbed ordnance into the Reich Chancellery, and into the shell of the old, burned-out Reichstag at virtual point-blank range. Russian gunners hurled tons of explosives into the immediate neighborhood around the Brandenburg Gate, which somehow survived the onslaught and where Victory, astride her quadriga, still clutched the Iron Cross, which the Nazis had substituted for her olive branch. The Pariser Platz was in ruins, yet somehow the Academy of Arts remained unscathed, although its next patrons would be drunken Soviet troops. Nearby, the Adlon Hotel, partially aflame, did not lack for patrons, of a sort: the basement, where Nazi swells had once sheltered themselves at leisure from errant British bombs, had been converted into a field hospital. Yet, for the wounded, there was little medicine, and no hope.[142]

Hitler's Olympischer Platz, its columns and walls ripped by shrapnel, resembled the ancient ruins of Carthage. The Russian artillery fire persisted for twelve straight days without a moment's pause, an inundation of tons upon thousands of tons of steel. Hundreds of Berliners were driven mad. Thousands now committed suicide rather than face the murderous wrath of the Red Army. Fathers murdered wives and daughters rather than allow them to fall into the hands of rapacious Soviet troops. The city waited for the end. In his *Führerbunker* thirty feet below the Chancellery — under six feet of compacted earth and a sixteen-foot-thick concrete roof — Adolf Hitler waited, waited for his imaginary armies to appear to crush the invaders and save everything he had striven to create. Yet the *crump* of each Soviet shell exploding in the streets above was heard, *felt* by Hitler and his dwindling band of fellow true believers. Hitler's oldest and most trusted Nazi cohorts were on hand to celebrate the Führer's birthday — Goebbels, Himmler, Göring, Bormann, and Ribbentrop. The last of the military chiefs were there — Dönitz, Jodl, and Keitel. Albert Speer arrived with birthday greetings but departed soon after, his orders from Hitler clear: to destroy any industrial and electrical centers that the Allies had not. Nothing was to remain standing or operational; the German people, having failed their Führer, deserved nothing. Speer departed with no intention of obeying the order. After the subdued birthday ceremony, Hitler made the trip up to the courtyard in order to encourage a platoon of *Hitlerjugend* — adolescent boys — to fight to the end. He patted one or two on the head, then sent them off to die. Late in the day, Hitler's generals advised the warlord to leave the city and set up a new command. He made no decision, but sent Dönitz to Flensburg, near the Danish frontier, to take command there. That night, Göring made good his escape in a caravan of automobiles loaded down with the air marshal's stolen loot. Himmler, too, fled. Ribbentrop also prepared to flee. Each was secure in his knowledge that Hitler would soon be dead, and each presumed he would soon take control.[143]

On April 22, both Dönitz and Himmler telephoned the bunker and urged Hitler to leave, but by then the Führer had decided to stay, to die at a time and place of his choosing. That night, he sent Keitel and Jodl south, toward Bavaria, to prepare for a last stand under the command of Göring in the phantom mountain redoubt (Hitler, like Eisenhower, had come to believe Goebbels' propaganda). Jodl protested that Hitler, cut off in Berlin, could not control the battle, and added that the Wehrmacht would not fight under Göring. Hitler shot back: "What do you mean, fight? There's precious little more fighting to be done!" The moment was a small island of clarity in a sea of delusion. Albert Speer called the surreal world in the bunker "the Isle of the Departed."[144]

On April 23, Himmler and Göring made their respective bids to supplant Hitler. Göring, by then in Berchtesgaden, wrote a letter to Hitler that cited a 1941 decree that should Hitler lose control of the government, the *Reichsmarschall* was to take command. Himmler that night met with Count Bernadotte in the Swedish consulate at Lübeck, on the Baltic. Himmler proposed, in writing, an astoundingly naive yet not unsound concept: he would arrange for the surrender of German armies in the west while continuing the fight against the Red Army until such time as Eisenhower and the Allies appeared on the scene to take over the battle against the Bolsheviks. By that night, only Hitler's SS guards, Ribbentrop, and Bormann remained with Hitler. Bormann, like Himmler and Göring, was plotting his own escape and ascendancy to supreme power. Hitler, learning of Himmler's and Göring's gambits, flew into a rage. He declared the fat *Reichsmarschall* a traitor, and ordered that he be found and shot, an order Bormann was only too happy to send out over the airwaves. Albert Speer that day had made the dangerous journey by air from Mecklenburg to Berlin, where he landed his cub aircraft in front of the Brandenburg Gate. He had come to ask Hitler to grant him his leave, and he fully expected to be hauled outside and shot for failing to obey Hitler's scorched-earth directive. Instead, after Speer confessed his disobedience, the two chatted amiably, if clumsily. For a moment, Hitler's "eyes filled with tears." Then he waved off Speer with a curt *auf Wiedersehen*. They parted without a handshake, and for the last time Speer left the Chancellery, now in ruins, which he had designed and built seven years earlier.[145]

By April 25, Berlin was surrounded, although a narrow corridor to the northwest was still open, along which thousands fled in hopes of reaching the refuge of the Anglo-American lines. That day, recalled one of Hitler's bodyguards, SS staff sergeant Rochus Misch, Hitler stunned those within earshot when he declared the war lost. Yet Hitler, like Himmler, still clung to a final delusion. After a junction between the Germans and the Americans, both armies would then turn to fight the Soviets. "Hitler didn't think a people like the Englanders would bind themselves with the communists to crush Germany, and he still believed...something could happen. He liked the Englanders," recalled Misch, "except for Churchill."[146]

That day, Russian and American advance patrols met at Torgau on the Elbe, just seventy-five miles south of Berlin. Germany was cut in half. Churchill and Truman had their first telephone conversation that day, the topic Himmler's offer to surrender German armies in the west. They pondered the proposal for less than a minute and agreed that Himmler was not a man to deal with and that all German armies must surrender simultaneously to the three powers, on all fronts. Churchill cabled Stalin with the decision. Churchill would remain loyal to Stalin to the end, but in fact he was now one with Himmler on the need to keep the Bolsheviks from reaching the western borders of Germany. "My mind," Churchill later wrote, "was oppressed with the new and even greater peril which was swiftly unfolding itself to my gaze." As he contemplated the consequences to Europe if the Russians kept up their westward march (they had reached Paris in 1814 and could do so again now), he pondered a response, a military response.[147]

On Saturday, April 28, the Russians moved into Potsdamer Platz, a mere block from Hitler's bunker. The seismic footfalls grew closer. By early the next morning, Hitler had heard enough. He put Dönitz in charge of the government, such as it was, and then dictated his last will and testament, in which he blamed "the ruling clique in England" and "International Jewry" for the war and its forty million dead. Sometime before dawn on the twenty-ninth, Hitler and his somewhat dim-witted mistress of twelve years, Eva Braun, were married in a civil ceremony witnessed by Bormann and Goebbels. The bride wore a dark-blue silk dress; a small private reception followed. The guests listened as the Führer rambled on about the old days, the good days. Later that afternoon, Hitler received one of the last reports to reach him from the world outside. Mussolini and his mistress, Clara Petacci, had been murdered the previous day by Italian partisans. By the time Hitler learned of the deaths, their bodies had been brought to Milan and strung up by the heels from lampposts. Garbled communications spared Hitler from learning of the other momentous event that took place that day in Italy: General Heinrich von Vietinghoff agreed to surrender his Italian forces on May 2. Above the Chancellery, the Red Army swept down the avenues of Berlin.[148]

As Hitler toasted his bride, Churchill dispatched a long telegram to Stalin in a final attempt to salvage the agreements on Poland made at Yalta. In effect, it was a final attempt to salvage the peace. The plan for Poland agreed upon at Yalta, Churchill wrote, called for "universal suffrage" and truly democratic elections. "None of this has been allowed to move forward." Britain had gone to war for Poland, Churchill reminded Stalin. "The British people can never feel that this war has ended rightly until Poland has a fair deal in the full sense of sovereignty, independence, and freedom on the basis of friendship with Russia." Rumors were now coming out of Poland that indicated Polish patriots were disappearing (indeed, the Soviet secret police, the NKVD, was orchestrating mass liquidations of Polish officers and men). In late March, sixteen Polish republicans had been granted safe passage from Warsaw to Lublin in order to meet with Soviet generals. They had disappeared. Molotov, attending the San Francisco conference of the United Nations, at first refused to divulge to Eden any information on the goings-on in Poland. The Allies had agreed at Yalta that representatives from each government were to have free access to areas controlled by the others. Yet, Churchill declared to Stalin, "neither I nor the Americans are allowed to send anyone into Poland to find out for themselves the true state of affairs." A horrific crisis was in the making, Churchill warned: "There is not much comfort in looking into a future where you and the countries you dominate . . . are all drawn up on one side, and those who rally to the English-speaking nations and their associates . . . are on the other. It is quite obvious that their quarrel would tear the world to pieces." Colville thought the telegram a "masterly . . . final appeal to resolve the Polish crisis."[149]

Stalin, that week, imparted his philosophy of war to Milovan Djilas, a guest at the Kremlin: "This war is not as in the past; whoever occupies a territory also imposes on it his own social system. Everyone imposes his own system as far as his army can reach. It cannot be otherwise. . . . If now there is not a communist government in Paris, it is because Russia has no army which can reach to Paris in 1945."[150]

Austria's turn to go under the Soviet boot came later, on April 29, when Moscow radio announced the formation of a provisional government in Vienna. American troops occupied the western two-thirds of the country, but in spite of that and in spite of the agreement made at Yalta, the Soviet government refused to allow American or British missions to enter Vienna. In reality, there was not that much left to enter; the Germans had burned St. Stephen's Cathedral and much of the old city on their way out of town.

In Berlin early the next day, Monday, April 30, Hitler was told the city's defenders would run out of ammunition by nightfall. Late that afternoon, after testing the effect of a cyanide capsule on his Alsatian bitch, Blondi, Hitler proffered one to his new wife. Frau Hitler dutifully took the capsule, and bit down. Adolf Hitler had murdered his last German. A moment later, the widower put the barrel of a German pistol into his mouth and pulled the trigger.

The Americans occupied Munich that morning, and in Italy they entered Turin, where Italian partisans had been fighting Germans for three days. The war in Italy was effectively over, although Albert Kesselring, now commanding all German forces in the west and south, sacked von Vieting- hoff, who had proposed to surrender. Two days later, Kesselring saw the futility of his situation, and surrendered the Italian armies to Alexander.

On the thirtieth, Eisenhower guaranteed the Soviet deputy chief of staff that the right wing of Patton's Third Army in Austria would not advance farther than "the general area of Linz," the city where Hitler had spent most of his childhood and where he had intended to build his *Führermu- seum,* to house his stolen art. His tomb, too, was to be in Linz, to which he presumed Nazi pilgrims would journey for centuries. A model of the museum had been brought down into the bunker; the Führer could not have helped seeing it as the Russians closed in. Two hundred miles north of Linz, the left flank of Patton's Third Army was just sixty miles west of Prague, and under orders from Eisenhower to proceed no farther east. To Truman, Churchill pleaded the case for Patton to continue. The president backed Eisenhower, who had told him that he would not contemplate "any move which I deem militarily unwise." Churchill's concerns, as they had been since before Yalta, were not strictly military. He told Truman: "There is little doubt that the liberation of Prague . . . by your forces might make the whole difference to the post-war situation in Czechoslovakia and might well influence that in nearby countries." Truman and Eisenhower held firm. Eisenhower, in fact, assured the Russians that when the surrender came, Allied troops would withdraw 140 miles from those areas within the Russian zone agreed upon at Yalta. The Russians took Prague on May 4. "The [American] failure to take Prague," Eden later wrote, "meant the Red Army was able to put its creatures firmly in command." The was not the sort of "mutual assistance" Eduard Beneš had in mind when he signed the twenty-year treaty of friendship with Stalin eighteen months earlier.[151]

Also on the thirtieth, Tito's partisans entered Trieste, and by nightfall they were fighting Italians within the city limits. Churchill ordered New Zealand troops to occupy the city, advising that no violence should occur, except in self-defense. But Tito had won the race for Trieste, and Istrea. "It's hard to see how he can ever be dislodged," Colville told his diary. Yet Tito's claim on northeast Italy, Colville wrote, "may split the Italian Com- munist party and thus at least save Italy from the Russian imperialist clutches." It did, and Churchill's show of force ended with the Yugoslavs returning home by mid-June. Truman took a strong stand in support of Churchill on the matter, leading Churchill to conclude that the new president would likewise be stern with the Russians if the need arose, which appeared more likely with each passing day. Colville thought the prospect of the Soviets and their Yugoslav proxies dominating Europe "from the North Cape to Trieste" depressing, but for the fact that "the Americans occupy *de facto* great parts of Germany which belong *de jure* to the Russian zone of occupation." He and Churchill were as yet unaware of Eisenhower's pledge to move his armies out of the Russian zone.[152]

It was the night before May 1, *Walpurgisnacht* (a traditional festival in Europe in which witches are said to await the arrival of spring). For centuries on this night, from Romania to the Baltic, peasants lit bonfires intended to keep at bay demons who they believed roamed the landscape. They stoked the flames with hopes of surviving to the morrow, May Day, the ancient pagan day of rebirth. For a dozen years under Adolf Hitler, *Walpurgisnacht* was also a sacred Nazi holiday when good Germans celebrated the fertility of Nazi youth destined to breed glorious Nazi babies. Soon after the Führer had put an end to himself, a small contingent of SS men hauled his corpse and that of Eva Braun into the courtyard of the Chancellery, rolled them into a bomb crater, and with the help of twenty gallons of gasoline, added one more pyre to the inferno that was Berlin. It was twelve years and three months to the day since Hitler became chancellor of Germany. His thousand-year Reich would survive him by a week.[153]

Goebbels survived him by a day. Two years earlier the little doctor had drawn a bittersweet picture of family life in his diary: "In the evening I am able to devote a little time to the children, with whom I'm having much fun.... Once the war is over I shall be able to devote myself more than hitherto to their upbringing. I could not think and wish for any more beautiful task for the coming peace." With the war now over, the peace Goebbels planned for his children would be everlasting. On the evening of May 1, Herr Doktor and Frau Goebbels poisoned their six children. The little bodies were taken aloft to the courtyard, where two SS officers, as ordered by Goebbels, dispatched the doctor and his wife with two shots to the back of the head. Then the Goebbels family was doused with gasoline and set aflame. Not enough gasoline was available to make a decent job of it, and the Red Army soldiers found the smoldering remains the next day.[154]

By the evening of May 1, the abandoned *Führerbunker* had been set ablaze by the Red Army. The Reichstag had been shelled at point-blank range by eighty-nine Red Army field guns, and then taken after a fifteen-hour gunfight between Russians, who occupied the second floor, and a band of Germans, who occupied the third. The civilian population of Berlin took shelter in the city's basements. The streets above contained only

Soviet troops and dead Berliners. The last Nazi holdouts were fighting from the sewers. Bormann and several hundred of Hitler's entourage had taken refuge at the New Chancellery. They attempted a breakout on foot to the River Spree by way of a subway tunnel under the Wilhelmsplatz. Hunched over in their filthy gray greatcoats, they leaned into the walls and crept through the destruction en masse in the dark. Bormann didn't make it, the victim of a shell that crashed into a tank he had hoped would afford him shelter.[155]

Across the Continent, April had brought splendid weather, with temperatures more reminiscent of the dog days of summer than early spring. "Nobody seems to remember such weather in April before," Colville told his diary. "Surely there has never been such a spring.... The cherries are weighed down with blossom, the chestnuts and the lilac are already out, as is the wisteria in Great Court, before the daffodils have faded." Beneath a "China blue sky" tall elms wore their early coats of pale green. In London during the early hours of May 1, after two weeks of such glorious weather, a wet, heavy snow fell. By daybreak, window boxes were encrusted and lilacs bent under the hoary cloak, but their stubborn blooms pushed through the puffs of snow, an odd sight but somehow appropriate for the day of rebirth. Late in the afternoon, as Churchill strolled through the smoking room of the House, he was asked by an MP how the war was going. He replied, "Yes, it is definitely more satisfactory than it was this time five years ago."[156]

That evening Hamburg radio interrupted Hitler's favorite Wagner, *Götterdämmerung,* with the announcement that *"Unser Führer, Adolf Hitler, ist...gefallen."* He had died bravely, according to Hamburg, "fighting with his last breath against Bolshevism." Wagner himself wrote the original program note for *Götterdämmerung:* "The will that wanted to shape an entire world according to its wish can finally attain nothing more satisfactory than...annihilation."[157]

Churchill hosted a political dinner in the Annexe that night; no military marshals sat in. It was nigh time to reposition himself as England's best choice as peacetime leader. The Japanese had yet to be vanquished, but the war in Europe—England's war—was over. A general election would have to be called. Beaverbrook (and Eden, from San Francisco) argued for a June vote, when victory would be fresh in the minds of the people, rather than a later date. Joining Churchill at dinner were the Beaver, Oliver Lyttelton, the chief whip James Stuart, and Ralph Assheton, all of them Tory political operatives, the field marshals of their party. Brendan Bracken did not attend. Tory regulars had begun to "look askance at the

Brendan-Beaver combination," Colville later wrote, in part because these two supreme Churchill loyalists violently opposed the liberal Tory stance on national health care, housing, and education, which Churchill (an old Liberal) supported. His support of reform in those three spheres, he believed, would deliver him and the party a victory in the general election. He was thus forced to preserve party unity by relegating one of his two best friends to the sidelines. It was Bracken, soon awarded first lord of the Admiralty for his services and loyalty. He had desired the Exchequer, an office even his old friend Winston Churchill knew he was unqualified for. For the first time in five years, Adolf Hitler was not a subject of dinner conversation, or wasn't until Jock Colville brought Churchill the news of the Führer's death. The Old Man, believing Hitler had died fighting, said, "Well, I must say I think he was perfectly right to die like that."[158]

And with that, the party caucus resumed, and continued on past 3:00 A.M. A plan took shape, which had been fermenting since late March, to ask Attlee and Labour to continue the national government until the defeat of Japan, at which time a general election would be held. That might take the elections well into 1946, when Churchill would presumably still be basking in the light of victory. Attlee and Labour, for their part, sought an election by October at the latest, regardless of the status of the Pacific war. All believed that an invasion of Japan would be necessary, a bloody business in which Churchill fully intended Britain would meet its obligations.

Hitler's cannonade of June of 1941 had announced his intention to liquidate Russia; Zhukov's twelve-day barrage had reduced Berlin to rubble. Russian Katyusha rockets now raked the rubble, which heaved from underground explosions as Soviet sappers used dynamite and flamethrowers to clear subway tunnels where Nazi holdouts fought on, and from where the stench of burnt flesh drifted up to the streets. The Russians outnumbered the three hundred thousand defenders of Berlin by more than five to one, outnumbered them in artillery by fifteen to one, and in tanks by six to one. When the end came, the Soviets had suffered 350,000 casualties, including almost 80,000 killed. Within the city limits, where barricaded defenders could hold off large numbers of Soviet attackers, five times as many Red Army troops as Germans had been killed. More than 125,000 Berliners died, many by suicide, and as many women were raped, although exact counts were impossible to ascertain given the fury of the final days. To this day, bones of the dead are unearthed. Hitler's bones will not be among them. The Soviets scraped together Hitler's remains by the night of May 1 and sent them east, toward Russia. Immediately a rumor took hold across the Continent: Hitler had escaped, to his mountain redoubt, to the west, to places unknown. Churchill suspected the Russians were behind it. They were. Weeks later, Stalin "speculated" that Hitler and his top aides might have escaped to Japan via giant U-boats. It was a clever way of manipulating popular fears, a twist on *Walpurgisnacht* that held out the terrible possibility that Hitler might emerge from hiding to rekindle the ashes of his Reich. In fact, parts of Hitler's jaws and skull made it to Moscow. The rest of him was buried beneath a military parade ground in Magdeburg, Germany, which the Soviets occupied for more than forty years. Sometime in the 1970s, the Führer's remains were exhumed and incinerated for a second time. The ashes were flushed into the city's sewer system, where they suffered the fate of Mary Shelley's monster, *borne away by the waves and lost in darkness and distance.*[159]

By May 1, Eisenhower had shifted his attention to the Pacific theater. He was sending the First Army as soon as possible, and he was likely to send Patton and the Third Army as well. Half the American air forces in Europe would be going. In Germany, those American units that had overshot the agreed-upon Soviet and Anglo-American lines of demarcation were already retiring westward.

On May 2, Eamon de Valera, prime minister of Ireland, motored to the German legation in Dublin to offer his condolences on the occasion of Hitler's death. The "Dev" and Ireland had pulled it off, the only English-speaking country in the world to win the war by missing it. Days later Churchill excoriated de Valera during a worldwide broadcast. Referring to the U-boat menace of 1940 and 1941, Churchill said, "This was indeed a deadly moment in our life, and if it had not been for the loyalty and friendship of Northern Ireland, we should have been forced to come to close quarters with Mr. de Valera or perish forever from the earth. However, with a restraint and poise to which, I say, history will find few parallels, His Majesty's Government never laid a violent hand upon them, though at times it would have been quite easy and quite natural, and we left the de Valera government to frolic with the Germans and later with the Japanese representatives to their heart's content."[160]

In Flensburg on May 2, *Reichspräsident* Dönitz's newly appointed leading minister, Count Schwerin von Krosigk, made a radio broadcast to Germans in which he told them, "In the East the iron curtain behind which, unseen by the eyes of the world, the work of destruction goes on, is moving steadily forward." The London *Times* ran the story the next day.[161]

Montgomery took Lübeck on May 2, just twelve hours before the Russians got there. That put Monty's army astride the neck of the Danish peninsula. The next morning, shortly before noon, four German officers were escorted to Montgomery's trailer under a flag of truce. Monty, like the neighborhood curmudgeon who neither seeks nor welcomes visitors, threw open the door and demanded of his interpreter, "Who are these men? What do they want?" They were representatives of Field Marshal Keitel, and they wanted to surrender to the British three German armies that faced the Russians. They said they feared for civilians caught between the armies, and they feared savage treatment at the hands of the Red Army were they to surrender in that direction. Montgomery told them they should have thought of that before they started the war. The Germans asked how they could be saved. Essentially they were seeking Montgomery's approval to continue the fight against the Russians without British interference in their rear. Montgomery refused. He told them that their situation was hopeless, and that until they surrendered, he would continue killing German soldiers and civilians. Then he directed them to a tent where he suggested they have lunch and think things over. They ate, they pondered; they agreed to return the next day with an answer. Two of the officers went back to Flensburg with Montgomery's ultimatum. After consulting Dönitz, they returned the next day, May 4, and at 6:30 P.M. signed the instrument of surrender Montgomery had prepared. Expecting the Germans to do just that, Montgomery had ordered his troops to cease fire late on the third.[162]

The British war in Europe was over. And in the Far East, British and colonial troops had freed Rangoon the previous day. That afternoon, Churchill called his military chiefs to No. 10, where Brooke found him "evidently seriously affected by the fact that the war was to all intents and purposes over as far as Germany was concerned. He thanked us all very nicely and with tears in his eyes for all we had done in the war.... He then shook hands with all of us."[163]

In San Francisco that day, May 4, Molotov admitted to Eden that the sixteen Poles who had been granted safe passage from Warsaw to Lublin had been arrested. Stalin, calling the Poles "diverginists," admitted likewise in a cable to Churchill. Fifty of the fifty-one Allied nations had sent representatives to San Francisco. The fifty-first, Poland, had in effect ceased to exist. The Soviets proposed a horse trade to the British: they would approve the British and American nomination of Argentina for admittance to the United Nations in return for the admission of—in Cadogan's words—"[the] beastly sham Polish Government." This was a deft ploy on the part of Stalin and Molotov. Argentina, its government quasi-Fascist, had been a pro-Axis neutral for five years until finally seeing the light in late March, when Colonel Juan Perón took over and declared war on Germany. The Lublin Poles, whatever their Bolshevik leanings, had fought against the Nazis since 1939.

If Argentina was to be granted admittance, Molotov argued, why not the new Polish government? Eden refused.[164]

Eisenhower's turn to accept a German surrender came at 2:41 A.M. British Double Summer Time on Monday, May 7, at his headquarters in Reims. General Alfred Jodl, for Dönitz, and Bedell Smith, for SHAEF, signed the instrument of unconditional surrender, with French and Russian officers as witnesses. Hostilities were to cease at midnight, and the German entourage was to proceed to Berlin to sign the Russian ratification on the ninth. Shortly before dawn, Pug Ismay had received a call from Eisenhower. "What's happened?" Ismay asked. Came the reply: "It's all over." But it wasn't over until Stalin said it was over. His troops were still mopping up in Czechoslovakia and along the Baltic. He sought to postpone any official announcement until the formal ratification by all parties in Berlin on the ninth.[165]

A predawn thunderstorm broke over London with "an imitation of the blitz so realistic," Mollie Panter-Downes wrote, "many Londoners started awake and reached for the bedside torch." The V-2s had ceased coming over in late March, but nerves were still raw. The blackout had been lifted a week earlier, after 2,061 consecutive nights of darkness. But when the switch was thrown, London's streetlights failed to flare, and though most Londoners took down their heavy blackout curtains (which they converted to black clothes and funeral coverings), they pulled their old curtains closed out of habit. A five-year-old girl who had lived her entire life behind the blackout curtains said to her mother, "It's lovely to let out the light, but how shall we keep out the dark?"[166]

On the afternoon of May 7, as crowds began to gather in expectation of an official announcement, Churchill hosted a lunch for his military chiefs at No. 10. It was a "disturbed" affair, Brooke wrote, marked by Churchill taking phone calls from Truman and Eisenhower over the matter of the official announcement, which Churchill sought to make that evening and Stalin wanted postponed for a day. "As usual," Ismay later wrote, "he [Stalin] had his way." Churchill agreed to delay the announcement, but for only twenty-four hours. Tuesday, May 8, was to be V-E day in England and America; the Soviets would celebrate victory on May 9. The lunch party adjourned to the garden for photographs. Champagne and glasses sat ready on a side table, put there by Churchill himself. He raised a toast to the chiefs as "the architects of victory," and thanked them for the years of work that had brought them all to this day. Inexplicably, none returned the toast. Ismay could not bring himself to believe the slight was intentional. "I had hoped," he later wrote, "that they would raise their glasses to the chief who had been the master planner; but perhaps they were too moved to trust their voices."[167]

That night, the BBC announced that the prime minister would address the nation from No. 10 at 3:00 P.M. the following day. In New York, Paris, Brussels, Moscow, and London, crowds had already taken to the streets. By dawn on May 8, more than a million Londoners—men, women, and children—pressed toward the gates of Buckingham Palace from Whitehall and Piccadilly and Trafalgar Square, from Hyde Park, Parliament Square, the Strand, and St. James's Park and Green Park. London's bells began ringing at sunrise, and rang throughout the morning, a tolling that carried away into the countryside and rolled down the Thames to the Channel. Children paraded through the streets wrapped in American flags and British and Russian flags. Thousands of Union Jacks flew from windows, joined by the Stars and Stripes and the Hammer and Sickle. Mothers hoisted children onto their hips, and the children in turn waved little Union Jacks fixed on slim sticks. Housewives in long breadlines (there was a loaf shortage) waved little Union Jacks while keeping a hand on their string bags. A group of sailors and girls formed a conga line in Piccadilly. Owners of bulldogs paraded their charges outfitted in Union Jack sweaters. Eight times that day, the masses called for their King and Queen, and eight times the royal couple stepped from their rooms onto a balcony at Buckingham Palace, King George attired in his Royal Navy uniform.

Churchill lunched at the palace with the King, the man who five years earlier had handed the seals of office to him with great reluctance. When the crowd again called for a royal benediction, the King invited Churchill to join him and the Queen and the royal princesses, Margaret and Elizabeth, on the balcony. Always respectful of the monarchy, Churchill stood a discreet foot or so behind King George, his posture that of a five-foot-eight-inch man under a five-foot-six-inch ceiling. In photos of the scene, Churchill wears the impish smile of a little boy who has just been told, *Behave yourself.* When the crowd caught sight of Churchill, Mollie Panter-Downes wrote, "there was a deep, full-throated, almost reverent roar."[168]

King George delivered a brief radio address later that day. "Today we give thanks to Almighty God for a great deliverance," he began, and asked Britons "to join with me in that act of thanksgiving." He ended by noting that "in the hour of danger we humbly committed our cause into the hand of God, and He has been our strength and shield....Let us thank Him for His mercies in this hour of victory." Across the Atlantic, President Truman, who was celebrating his sixty-first birthday, issued a proclamation that began "The Allies, through sacrifice and devotion and with God's help, have wrung from Germany a final and unconditional surrender." Declaring it "fitting that we as a nation give thanks to Almighty God, who has strengthened us and given us the victory," he appointed "Sunday, May 13, to be day of prayer." Neither the King nor the president made any mention of Winston Churchill.

In Paris, Charles de Gaulle was swept along the Champs-Élysées and under the Arc de Triomphe by a throng of nearly one million Frenchmen. He told his countrymen: "Honor, eternal honor to our armies and their eternal leaders. Honor to our nation, which never faltered....*Vive la France*." Two months later, the provisional French Assembly delivered a vote that serves as a measure of how completely Franklin Roosevelt and the State Department had misread de Gaulle and France. The Assembly, a cantankerous mix of socialists, communists, liberals, conservatives, republicans, and monarchists, offered Charles de Gaulle the presidency of the Council by a unanimous vote. In October, when the United Nations officially opened, France, its soul reclaimed, took its place as the fifth permanent seat on the Security Council. Three months later, in January 1946, de Gaulle, contemptuous of the proposed new constitution that would underlie the Fourth Republic, resigned. He was, one of his ministers once said, "a man equally incapable of monopolizing power and of sharing it." His self-imposed political exile lasted thirteen years, until January 1959, when, after capturing almost 80 percent of the electoral college vote, he was sworn in as president of the Fifth Republic.[169]

In London on May 8, as three o'clock neared, MPs gathered in the palace yard, where loudspeakers had been set up to carry Churchill's speech. "As Big Ben struck three," Harold Nicolson recorded, "there was an extraordinary hush over the assembled multitude. And then came Winston's voice." His statement ran to just over five hundred words, and took only moments to deliver. Clementine listened at the British embassy in Moscow. Mary heard the address while playing bridge in the country with Jock Colville. Randolph was on an airplane over Yugoslavia when he heard his father's words. Diana and Sarah listened in London. Churchill's recitation of the signing of the surrender and the signatories was as droll as a stationmaster announcing departures and arrivals, until he intoned, "The evil-doers now lie prostrate before us." At that the crowds gasped. Churchill ended with, "Advance Britannia!" The BBC played a recording of buglers sounding

Last Post and closed with "God Save the King," which Nicolson and the House sang along with, "very loud indeed."[170]

Lord Moran listened to Churchill's speech in an overflowing House of Lords (where the Commons had met since the bombing of May 10, 1941). When Churchill finished, a peer turned to Moran and expressed his surprise that the prime minister had made no allusion to God. Moran turned to poet laureate John Masefield and asked what he thought. Masefield replied, "I'd rather have the honest utterance of Winston than the false rhetoric of a lesser man." Abraham Lincoln, Moran offered, "would have struck a deeper note." True, replied Masefield, but "he [Lincoln] was a man of deep piety."[171]

After delivering his statement, Churchill made ready to go to the House of Lords in order to read it to the MPs. On any other day, he could have made the short trip from No. 10 to Parliament in minutes to take Questions, which automatically closed at 3:15, but on this day, his car had to thread its way through the raucous crowds. MPs therefore made supplementary questions until Churchill arrived, which he did at 3:23, Harold Nicolson noted, looking "coy and cheerful." "The House rose as a man," Nicolson wrote, "and yelled and yelled and waved their Order Papers." Churchill responded with a jerk of the head and a wide grin. He read his statement, and added two lines. The first was an expression of thanks to the House for its "noble support" throughout the war. Then, recalling the House's response when, on November 11, 1918, it learned of the Armistice, he moved that "this House do now attend at the Church of St. Margaret's, Westminster, to give humble and reverential thanks to Almighty God for our deliverance from the threat of German domination." He added, "This is the identical Motion which was moved in former times." The motion carried, and the sergeant at arms took up the mace (which, with the House cat, Minny, had survived the Blitz), and the MPs all streamed out, through the lobby, though St. Stephen's Chapel, and into the sunshine of Parliament Square, where mounted policemen tried to forge a path through the gathered tens of thousands.[172]

When Churchill appeared, the gathered erupted in a chorus of *"Winnie, Winnie."* "The crowd," Mollie Panter-Downes wrote, "had ears, eyes, and throats for no one but Churchill." Mothers held up babies who would later be told they had seen the Great Man. A Cockney cried out, *"That's 'im. That's 'is little old lovely bald 'ead!"* After the service, Churchill departed in an open car, a fat cigar and the "V" for victory prominently displayed. Later in the afternoon, he stepped out onto a Whitehall balcony and told the crowd gathered, "This is your victory."

The crowd roared back, *"No, it is yours."*[173]

It was a day, Brooke told his diary, "disorganized by Victory! A form of disorganization that I can put up with." He was pleased when Lady Grigg told him that she had seen him get into his car in Whitehall "with a crowd looking at you, and none of them realizing that beside them was the man who had probably done most to win the war against Germany." "It was all wrong," she said, adding, "tell Lady Brookie from me." Brooke could not resist some parting shots at Churchill, including, "The P.M. has never once in all his speeches referred to the Chiefs of Staff" or how the chiefs conducted the war "at the highest level." Churchill, during a broadcast five days later, paused in the middle of delivering what was in essence a history of the war, and said:

> And here is the moment when I pay my personal tribute to the British Chiefs of the Staff, with whom I worked in the closest intimacy throughout these heavy, stormy years.... In Field-Marshal Brooke, in Admiral Pound, succeeded after his death by Admiral Andrew Cunningham, and in Marshal of the Air Portal, a team was formed who deserved the highest honour in the direction of the whole British war strategy and in its relations with that of our Allies.

The irascible Brooke waxed philosophic in his V-E day diary entry, citing God—as Churchill had not—as the source of his strength (in having to deal with Churchill) and his belief that victory was "ordained" by "a God all powerful looking after the destiny of the world." "And yet," Brooke wrote, despite his troubles with Churchill "of almost unbearable proportions.... I would not have missed the last three and one-half years of struggle and endeavor for anything on earth."[174]

Churchill returned to the Annexe as evening came on, and as hundreds of searchlights that had chased German planes and rockets for five years threw their beams upon London's public buildings and the remaining spires of Wren's churches. Buckingham Palace and the Houses of Parliament were bathed in white light; the face of Big Ben, Mollie Panter-Downes wrote, "loomed like a kind moon." A searchlight picked out Nelson's column. From Fleet Street, Harold Nicolson looked toward St. Paul's and beheld "a concentration of lights upon the huge golden cross." He could hear the sound of cheering in the parks, and found the crowds to be happy "but quite sober." As he made his way home, he noted the smell of distant bonfires in the air. "So I went to bed," he wrote. "That was my victory day."[175]

Churchill dined that evening at the Annexe with Sarah, Diana and Duncan Sandys, and Lord Camrose, publisher of the *Daily Telegraph*. Camrose had long financed Churchill's literary efforts, having paid £5,000 for the serial rights to *Marlborough* (the biography of his luminous ancestor) more than a decade earlier. His presence at the table augured a resurrection of his and Churchill's publishing and financial arrangements.

At about 10:30 P.M. Churchill was told the crowd in Whitehall was still calling for him. Wearing his siren suit now, he returned to the balcony where he had spoken in the afternoon. He told the assembled:

> My dear friends, this is your hour.... There we stood, alone. Did anyone want to give in? [The crowd shouted "No."] Were we downhearted? ["No!"] The lights went out and the bombs came down. But every man, woman and child in the country had no thought of quitting the struggle. London can take it. So we came back after long months from the jaws of death, out of the mouth of hell, while all the world wondered. When shall the reputation and faith of this generation of English men and women fail? I say that in the long years to come not only will the people of this island but of the world, wherever the bird of freedom chirps in human hearts, look back to what we've done and they will say 'do not despair, do not yield to violence and tyranny, march straight forward and die if need be — unconquered.'

He told them that Germany "awaits our justice and our mercy." He told them that Japan, "stained with cruelty and greed," would likewise be vanquished. And he told them that Britain would fight the battle "hand in hand" with America.[176]

That night, bonfires burned the length and breadth of the Home Island, on Beacon Hill in Hampshire and on other similarly named hills in Wales and the Lake District. They burned in town squares from Cornwall to Cambridge, from Oxford to Liverpool. They burned in Coventry and Manchester and Bath and Bristol, and from the Scottish Highlands to the windswept northernmost reaches of mainland Scotland. They burned on Guernsey and Jersey, freed that day, and they burned seven hundred miles to the north on the Orkney Islands. The fires glowed on the Isle of Man and the Isle of Arran, from north to south and east to west, from the Scillies to the Shetlands. Englishmen and Welshmen and Scotsmen and Ulstermen young and old, male and female, danced in the withering firelight, their faces glowing with sweat and dusted by soot and creased by wild grins. Since 1939, as in ancient times, they had proven that they were the warrior races. It was a scene that would have been familiar to Iron Age Britons, to Picts, Scots, and Celts, to the Romans, the Angles and Saxons and Danes, to King Harold, Thomas à Becket, and Eleanor of Aquitaine, to Elizabeth I and Raleigh, to Cromwell. And to Marlborough.

Late in the evening a telegram arrived at the Annexe from Clementine in Moscow: "All my thoughts are with you on this supreme day my darling. It could not have happened without you." Eden expressed similar sentiments from San Francisco: "It is you who have led, uplifted and inspired us through the worst days. Without you this day could not have been." As was his wont, Churchill worked past midnight and well into the early hours of May 9. Hundreds of telegrams had to be answered; the box was in dire need of attention. As he worked on, London officials doused the searchlights in hopes of encouraging the crowds to disperse. In the streets, Churchill's Englishmen, victorious, made for their homes.[177]

It was five years to the day since Hitler had ordered his armies into the Low Countries. In those black days, Churchill told Englishmen that to give in was to sink into the abyss of a new Dark Age. But, he told them, if they never gave in—and they had not—they would someday reach the broad sunlit uplands.

At that latitude and at that time of year dawn comes early, a faint blush on the far horizon. Night defeated, retreats. And light is born again.[178]

7

Ebb Tide

After almost six years of total war, Europeans had reached the upland regions. But from Warsaw to Paris, Berlin to Prague, they found themselves not in Winston Churchill's sunlit pastoral, but in a mutilated, desolate, and blood-drenched landscape. The war had left Europe literally a shambles—a slaughterhouse. In triumph, the victors took measure of the appalling tragedy that had overtaken the Continent since 1939. At least 40 million Europeans had been killed, about equally divided between civilians and armed forces. Poland had paid the highest relative price. More than six million Poles, almost 20 percent of Poland's prewar population, were dead, including three million Polish Jews. This is a number that defies comprehension. A modern reader might form some idea of the enormity of the Polish slaughter if he imagined picking up the morning newspaper every day for five years and reading that three thousand of his fellow citizens had perished the previous day in a terrorist attack. In Warsaw alone, seven hundred thousand had died, more than worldwide British, Commonwealth, and American battlefield deaths combined. Almost half of Poland's doctors, dentists, lawyers, and university professors were among the dead. Weeks after the German surrender, Churchill, still furious over the failure of the London Poles to reach some sort of agreement with Stalin in 1944, told the House, "There are few virtues that the Poles do not possess, and there are few mistakes they have ever avoided." Yet Poland's biggest mistake was the accident of geography that had placed it between the Wolf and the Bear, and the Bear had prevailed. The Lublin Poles accounted for thirteen of the twenty ministers in the new Warsaw government. The sixteen Polish democrats arrested in late March were found guilty of crimes against the state and packed off to prison. Poland had, in effect, become the seventeenth Soviet republic.[1]

Meticulous Nazi records soon accounted for another three million murdered Jews, gassed or shot, along with at least one million other "enemies of the state": Communists, gypsies, and homosexuals. Vichy France had been most accommodating in arresting and handing over to the Germans such undesirables. At least 70,000 of France's prewar Jewish population of 350,000 (of whom about one-half were naturalized citizens or refugees) were sent to their deaths in the east. Three-quarters of Holland's 140,000

Jews were likewise trundled east to their deaths. Italy could count almost 350,000 war dead, split about evenly between soldiers and civilians. The French had lost 200,000 men in 1940, but by 1945, the number of civilians who had perished in bombing raids and concentration camps was 400,000. Ongoing civil and guerrilla wars in Greece and Yugoslavia had so far left 150,000 and 1.5 million dead, respectively. Partisans in both countries were still killing each other, a state of affairs that led Churchill, with Tito in mind, to tell Brooke, "When the eagles are silent the parrots begin to jabber."[2]

Meanwhile, Communist movements grabbed their share of power in Italy and France; the Red Army was or soon would be placing Communists in power in Poland, Bulgaria, Hungary, and Romania. Eduard Beneš returned to Czechoslovakia, where he was confirmed as president by a coalition of Democrats and Communists in the National Assembly. The three Baltic states had disappeared within the Soviet empire. Stalin felt that Russia, given its horrific and heroic sacrifice, had earned the right to take what it pleased. Almost eleven million Red Army soldiers were dead or missing; Soviet civilian casualties have never been calculated with exactness; perhaps fifteen million, perhaps as many as twenty million, were killed by bullet, noose, fire, and starvation, fully half of the Continent's casualties. And still Europeans were dying. Millions of German land mines, from the Oder River to Brittany and Normandy (where six million were buried), were killing civilians at a rate of several hundred a week. Churchill proposed to Brooke that "the Germans find all the mines they have buried, and dig them up. Why should they not? Pigs are used to find olives." Brooke shared the prime minister's sentiments but could not resist pointing out to Churchill that pigs were used to find truffles.[3]

On May 11, the third day of European peace, Churchill cabled President Truman with a request that they jointly invite Stalin to a tripartite meeting at "some unshattered town in Germany" not within the Russian zone of occupation, and that Truman first stop off in London in a display of unity. Churchill pointed out that twice the Americans and British had met Stalin on or near his territory, Churchill four times in all. He further stressed his belief that it was critical that "the American front will not recede from the now agreed upon tactical lines." Truman's response was immediate, unsatisfactory, and reminiscent of Roosevelt's wartime hesitancy. Truman proposed that their respective ambassadors try to persuade Stalin to call for a meeting, and that he and Churchill travel to it separately in order to avoid the appearance of "ganging up" on Stalin. Churchill sent off another cable the next day, telling Truman, as he had Roosevelt, that he was "profoundly concerned about the European situation." American armies were "melting" away, the French were virtually defenseless, and the Russians had two to three hundred divisions on active duty. "An iron curtain is drawn down upon their [the Russian] front." Behind it, Poland was isolated, and controlled by Stalin's Lublin puppets. It would be easy for the Russians, Churchill warned, to drive all the way "to the waters of the North Sea and the Atlantic." He again proposed a meeting of the Big Three at the earliest possible opportunity in order to forge "a settlement with Russia before our strength has gone."[4]

To Eden, in San Francisco for the opening of the United Nations, he cabled similar sentiments:

> TODAY THERE ARE ANNOUNCEMENTS IN THE NEWSPAPERS OF THE
> LARGE WITHDRAWALS OF AMERICAN TROOPS NOW TO BEGIN MONTH BY
> MONTH. WHAT ARE WE TO DO? GREAT PRESSURE WILL SOON BE PUT ON US
> [AT HOME] TO DEMOBILIZE PARTIALLY. IN A VERY SHORT TIME OUR ARMIES
> WILL HAVE MELTED, BUT THE RUSSIANS MAY REMAIN WITH HUNDREDS OF
> DIVISIONS IN POSSESSION OF EUROPE FROM LUBECK TO TRIESTE, AND TO
> THE GREEK FRONTIER ON THE ADRIATIC. . . . ALL THESE THINGS ARE FAR
> MORE VITAL THAN THE AMENDMENTS TO A WORLD CONSTITUTION [THE
> UNITED NATIONS] WHICH MAY NEVER WELL COME INTO BEING TILL IT IS
> SUPERSEDED AFTER A PERIOD OF APPEASEMENT BY A THIRD WORLD WAR.[5]

By the end of the month, Stalin and Truman set a tentative date of July 15 for the meeting. Churchill considered that to be a month too late, and he proposed mid-June or early July at the latest. A delay of a month or more, Churchill believed, would allow the Red Army and the Lublin Poles time enough to effectively settle the matter of new Polish borders without Anglo-American input or oversight. But Truman held firm. As well, he sent word to Churchill through former U.S. ambassador to Moscow Joe Davies that he [Truman] wanted to meet with Stalin before the Big Three met. Churchill warned Truman that any such bilateral meeting would be "regrettable" and would raise issues "wounding" to Britain, the Commonwealth, and the British Empire. Truman backed off but held to the mid-July date. The place would be Potsdam, a suburb of Berlin and the Versailles of Prussian princes. The town was heavily damaged but not utterly destroyed.[6]

Throughout Germany, there was little left "unshattered." Every major city and most of the larger towns had been completely destroyed—Berlin, Hamburg, Dresden, and Stuttgart in the south, Breslau in the east. The RAF and American Eighth Air Force had paid a heavy price for these results: 26,000 American and 55,000 British airmen died over Europe. But the air campaign had wiped out twenty-eight major towns of the Ruhr. On the ground, German soldiers paid a far heavier price. More than five million German soldiers, sailors, and airmen had been killed since 1939 in service to Hitler's vision. Almost two million German citizens had died, as many as six hundred thousand under Allied bombs. The end of the war marked only the beginning of more pain for Germans. Near Berlin—a dead city—squads of German civilians overseen by Allied soldiers dug one hundred thousand graves in anticipation of filling them during the coming winter with the bodies of the frozen and the starved and no doubt thousands more suicides. At least half the German civilian war dead had perished at the hands of the Red Army while fleeing westward early in the year. Within twelve months, most of the Germanic population east of the Elbe—in East Prussia, Poland, the Czech Sudetenland—would be forcibly relocated into the Allied occupation zones, some fourteen million in all as a result of the Yalta agreement to redraw German and Polish borders, and Stalin's demands at Potsdam that no Germans remain within the new Poland. At least one million died of starvation in the process.

The Germanic population of the former Greater Reich fell to under three million from more than seventeen million before the war. The survivors had to be fed, along with eight million displaced persons within Germany—former slave laborers, of which four million lived in the Soviet zone. Hundreds of thousands of Dutch, French, and Polish displaced persons had to be sent home. And Stalin demanded that tens of thousands of Russian POWs be sent east, along with thousands of White Russians and Cossacks who had made the fatal error of joining the German side. The Western Allies dutifully delivered these Russians later that summer—some with families brought from the Ukraine—to Red Army checkpoints. Many were gunned down before even boarding the trains east; others committed suicide rather than return to face the noose. In his memoirs, Dwight Eisenhower makes mention of these "persecutees" and the "terror" they felt, and the suicides, but no mention of their nationality.[7]

One million Germans had fled before the Russians and into Montgomery's zone of occupation, where another million wounded Germans wasted away, with little medicine, little food, and little hope. Montgomery also had to tend to the upkeep of almost two million German soldiers who were now his prisoners and feared falling into Russian hands. In his memoirs, Montgomery wrote: "From their behavior it soon became clear that the Russians, though a fine fighting race, were in fact barbarous Asiatics who had never enjoyed a civilization comparable to the rest of Europe." He told his diary, "Out of the impact of the Asiatics on the European culture, a new Europe has been born." Two immediate problems had to be tackled, the feeding of Germans and the containment of the Russians, were they to wander farther westward. Britain could do neither alone. Weeks later, Churchill told the House that it "would be in vain for us in our small Island, which still needs to import half its food, to imagine that we can make any further appreciable contribution in that respect [trying to feed Germans]." And on the mass expulsion of Germans from newly configured Poland, he predicted, "It is not impossible that tragedy on a prodigious scale is unfolding itself behind the Iron Curtain which at the moment divides Europe in twain."[8]

On May 13 Churchill took to the airwaves, warning Britons:

> I wish I could tell you tonight that all our toils and troubles were over. Then indeed I could end my five years' service happily, and if you thought that you had had enough of me and that I ought to be put out to grass, I tell you I would take it with the best of grace.... There would be little use in punishing the Hitlerites for their crimes if law and justice did not rule, and if totalitarian or police governments were to take the place of the German invaders.... I told you hard things at the beginning of these last five years; you did not shrink, and I should be unworthy of your confidence and generosity if I did not still cry: Forward, unflinching, unswerving, indomitable, till the whole task is done and the whole world is safe and clean.

He also warned of the coming battle with Japan, and repeated his pledge of five years: "We seek nothing."[9]

He did not disclose in his broadcast his belief that the Russians were now intent on making Europe unsafe and unclean. Nor could he disclose his favored solution to the Russian threat. That day, May 13, Brooke wrote of Churchill: "He gives me the feeling of already longing for another war! Even if it entailed fighting Russia!" He was. One of the wagers Montgomery recorded in his ledger in 1943 was a £100 bet between himself and George Patton, who gave even odds that "the armed forces of Great Britain will become involved in another war in Europe within ten years of the cessation of hostilities in the current war." Patton's bet was looking pretty good even before London streets were swept clean of streamers and rosettes from the V-E day festivities. Churchill now asked the British joint planners to study the feasibility of war with the Russians, code-named Operation Unthinkable. In fact, eight months earlier, the British chiefs had composed a paper for the Foreign Office on the possibility of Russia's becoming a future adversary. At the time, Brooke wrote, the Foreign Office "could not admit that Russia may one day become unfriendly" and "considered it very remiss" for the chiefs to contemplate war with Britain's current ally. Yet planning for future military contingencies is the responsibility of military planners. Eden accepted the paper. Still, Brooke told his diary later in May, after revisiting Operation Unthinkable, "The idea is of course fantastic, and the chances for success quite impossible. There is no doubt from now onwards Russia is all powerful in Europe."[10]

Of these weeks Churchill later wrote, "I could only feel the vast mani-festation of Soviet and Russian imperialism rolling forward over helpless lands." Almost a decade later, while addressing his Woodford constitu-ency, he let slip that soon after V-E day, he had directed Montgomery "to be careful in collecting the German arms, to stack them so they could eas-ily be issued again to the German soldiers whom we should have to work with if the Soviet advance continued." No such telegram has been found in official records, but Montgomery, in his memoir, wrote that he protested to London an order that "these [German] weapons should be kept intact." He does not name the official who issued the order.[11]

A message Churchill sent to Eisenhower on May 9, however, contains the same sentiment:

I have heard with some concern that the Germans are to destroy all their aircraft in situ. I hope that this policy will not be adopted in regard to weapons and other forms of equipment. We may have great need of these some day. And even now they might be of use, both in France and especially in Italy. I think we ought to keep everything worth keeping. The heavy cannon I preserved from the last war fired constantly from the heights of Dover in this war.[12]

Neither telegram (if the Montgomery message ever existed) makes clear whether Churchill intended German troops to bear those surrendered weapons.

Churchill, while contemplating a response to the Red Army, hoped for a diplomatic solution, but he planned for war. His fears were well founded, but he failed as he had a decade earlier to correctly read the mood of the British public. For four years, while the Red Army fought valiantly, the British and American people gave it its due. Indeed, the people of both nations had elevated the Red Army and Russians to heroic stature. Churchill had, too, for a year or so after June 1941.

But circumstances had changed, dramatically and dangerously. The Red Army now occupied Warsaw, Budapest, Bucharest, Vienna, Prague, and Berlin. In March 1936 Churchill had told the House:

For four hundred years the foreign policy of England has been to oppose the strongest, most aggressive, most dominating Power on the Conti-nent, and particularly to prevent the Low Countries falling into the hands of such a Power. . . . Observe that the policy of England takes no account of which nation it is that seeks the overlordship of Europe. . . . It has nothing to do with rulers or nations; it is concerned solely with who-ever is the strongest or the potentially dominating tyrant.

That policy had never changed. As he had a decade earlier, Churchill identified an existential threat to Europe. And, as he had in the mid-1930s, he arrived at the right conclusion at the wrong time. And the British military, as it had been a decade earlier, was in no state to deter the Soviet threat. The final butcher's bill would include 244,000 British soldiers, airmen, and sailors. Commonwealth nations and other imperial comrades-in-arms suffered another 100,000 dead—Australia, 23,000; Canada, 37,000; India, 24,000; New Zealand, 10,000, and South Africa, 6,000. Militarily, Britain and the Empire were in no shape to fight a new war.[13]

Yet this time Churchill's worries were shared, not dismissed, by Tories and Labour alike. All within HMG knew him to be correct regarding the Russian threat. In any case, Britain in 1945 lacked not only the will to force the issue with the Soviets, it lacked the way: Britain was broke. When in 1940 Lord Lothian told American reporters that Britain was broke, he meant only that London lacked the cash and gold reserves to buy American arms and food. Now, having emerged victorious, London owed $4.3 billion to America and $1.2 billion to Canada. Britain had little to export and faced American tariffs in any event, and, as Churchill repeatedly told his countrymen, half the food consumed on the Home Island had to be imported.

When Foreign Minister Anthony Eden asked Labourite Ernest Bevin what cabinet position he might seek if Bevin's Labour Party won a general election, Bevin replied that he hoped for the Exchequer. Eden was stunned: "Whatever for?" he asked. "There'll be nothing to do there except to account for the money we have not got." Meat was rationed (horsemeat, not rationed, had lost its stigma), as were cheese, eggs, butter, soap, flour, clothing, and paper. Even a decade later, British high school students performed their math lessons on the backs of old grocery receipts. Petrol, coal, oil—all rationed. Whisky was in short supply, fresh fish, too. The Germans had destroyed or heavily damaged more than 750,000 houses. Public services were paralyzed. London's lights would not fully function for three more months. Transportation was in disarray, delivery of water and electricity unreliable. On May 11, President Truman summarily cut back Lend-Lease shipments to France, Russia, and Britain. Weeks later, he ceased shipments of American coal to Britain—five hundred thousand tons per month and every ounce desperately needed. The message was clear: Britain would soon be on its own. In this want, the Labour Party saw opportunity. Aneurin Bevan famously observed, "This island is almost made of coal and surrounded by fish. Only an organizing genius could produce a shortage of coal and fish in Great Britain at the same time." He assigned responsibility for this state of affairs to the Conservatives, to whose complete extermination as a political party he dedicated his political life.[14]

In mid-May, while planning his unthinkable war against Russia, Churchill proposed to Clement Attlee a continuation of the coalition government until Japan was defeated. Attlee agreed, on the condition that Churchill pledge in writing that the interim government would actively pursue reforms in housing, education, and social security. Churchill made the pledge, believing that Attlee would present the document to the annual Labour Party conference under way in Blackpool, where he would carry the day. Instead, the old socialist Harold Laski, that year's chairman of the conference, opposed Churchill's plan, and was joined by Ernest Bevin, Hugh Dalton, and Home Secretary Herbert Morrison. Attlee, always more conciliator than leader (Eden thought him timid), had no choice but to reject Churchill's offer. The coalition was dead. Just nine months earlier, Laski had proposed to Churchill the setting up of a "Churchill Fund" to support the Royal Society and the British Museum. "As I look at the Europe Hitler has devastated," Laski wrote at the time, "I know very intimately that, as an Englishman of Jewish origin, I owe you the gift of life itself." Churchill expressed his gratitude to Laski but affirmed that he'd prefer a park or playground to be built in his name on the south side of the Thames, "where all the houses have been blown down." That included Limehouse, Clement Attlee's constituency. But now, with Hitler dead, Laski and his Labour cohorts had their sights set on nothing less than the remaking of British government and British life. Five years earlier, Labour support had made it possible for Churchill to become prime minister and create the coalition government. Now Labour walked out.[15]

On May 23, Churchill motored to Buckingham Palace to tender his resignation to King George, who asked Churchill to form a caretaker government until elections could be held and the soldiers' vote from overseas tallied. The elections were scheduled for July 5, the final results to be announced some three weeks later. Churchill had kept to his pledge of nonpartisanship for five years. Now he would assume his partisan demeanor, and few in England could be as partisan as Churchill when he set his mind to it. He had gained the office of prime minister twice, in 1940 and again that day, but neither time through the ballot box. He intended to return to office for a third time, with a mandate from the people.

He had forewarned Britons of his keenness to wage a verbal war against Labour when in March he told the annual Tory conference, "We have all abstained from doing or saying anything which would be likely to impair the unity of the British people.... In doing this we have endured patiently and almost silently many provocations from that happily limited class of Left Wing politicians to whom party strife is the breath of their nostrils, and their only means of obtaining influence or notoriety." He pledged to "maintain this patriotic restraint as long as the National Coalition... continues to work together in loyal comrade-ship." That partnership was no more. He had told Britons: "Our Socialist friends have officially committed themselves—much to the disgust of some of their leaders—to a programme for nationalizing all the means of production, distribution, and exchange." Labour's "sweeping proposals," he warned, "imply not only the destruction of the whole of our existing system of society, and of life, and of labour, but the creation and enforcement of another system or other systems borrowed from foreign lands and alien minds." He asked:

> Will the warrior return, will the family be reunited, will the shattered houses be restored...? They do not regard themselves as a slum-bred serf population chased into battle from a land of misery and want. They love their country and the scenes of their youth and manhood, and they have shown themselves ready to die not only in defence of its material satisfactions but for its honour.... Let there be no mistake about it; it is no easy, cheap-jack Utopia of airy phrases that lies before us.... This is no time for windy platitudes and glittering advertisements.... This is no time for humbug and blandishments, but for grim, stark facts and figures, and for action to meet immediate needs."[16]

In reply some months later, the novelist, playwright, and Labour's literary spokesman J. B. Priestley wrote a thirty-four-page pamphlet titled *Letter to a Returning Serviceman*, in which he warned ex-Tommies to beware "the charmed cozy circle" of home life promised by Churchill. Priestley's BBC broadcasts throughout the war were as patriotic as Churchill's, and almost as well known. His audience consisted of those Britons whom Churchill liked to call his yeomanry. They listened to Priestley, and they paid heed when he told them, "Modern man is essentially a communal and cooperating man.... I do not believe in economic liberty.... Economic life is necessarily a communal life."[17]

"After the war" had for almost six years been a teasing dream. Churchill had used the phrase in speeches for more than a decade, during the 1930s in collating the mistakes of HMG after the Great War, and since 1940 in reminding Britons that numerous questions—jobs, housing, education—could be addressed only "after the war." A generation earlier, the soldiers had returned from the Great War to find no plans in place for the peace. They were expected to take up their plows and tools after a four-year absence as if the whole bloody business—where one *million* men of the Empire had died—had not even taken place. Normalcy had been the byword then, on both sides of the Atlantic. In 1943 Churchill told England:

> War cuts down...on forward planning, and everything is subordinated to the struggle for national existence. Thus, when peace came suddenly, as it did last time [1918], there were no long carefully prepared plans for the future....We must not be caught again that way. It is therefore necessary to make sure that we have projects for the future employment of the people and...that private enterprise and State enterprise are both able to play their parts to the utmost.[18]

Now, after six years of living in a tightly controlled society, necessary in order to defeat Hitler, the returning soldiers and indeed many Britons saw the need for more sacrifice and planning in order to defeat poverty, remove slums, and improve education and services. Planning (at Churchill's behest) had since 1941 led to improvements in the high schools, this while under severe wartime stringencies. A Tory, R. A. ("Rab") Butler, had been the driving force behind the 1944 Education Act, which guaranteed free education for all children through high school. Sarah tried to persuade her father that rationing—on which the prime minister himself had written numerous memos concerning chickens, eggs, and rabbits—had been so well planned that it had resulted in better-fed and better-educated children. Wartime controls had led to a more just sharing of the burdens, and therefore a more just society. Why not continue the planning and shared sacrifice in peace, she asked, in order to build houses, schools, and a better society? Churchill saw things entirely differently, and had said so in March, when he told the Tory conference, "If we are to recover from the measureless exertions of the war, it can only be by a large release from the necessary bonds and controls which war conditions have imposed upon us. No restriction upon well-established British liberties that is not proved indispensable to the prosecution of the war and the transition from war to peace can be tolerated." He touted the Tories' Four-Year Plan, a variation of the Beveridge Report, and built on voluntary cooperation between the government and private enterprise. The plan, he claimed, was an undertaking so liberal that even Gladstone and Lloyd George might shrink from it.[19]

For Churchill, state domination of planning and the attendant control the state needed to implement its plans were two sides of the same coin, a coin minted by socialists for socialists. This he made clear in his first campaign broadcast, delivered from Chequers on Monday, June 4—with disastrous results. He had spent the weekend preparing the speech, and had shown a draft to Jock Colville, who called it "fighting and provocative," and to Clementine, who objected vehemently to one phrase in particular that he intended to deploy. He ignored her protests. The BBC allotted him thirty minutes, too little time in Churchill's estimation. Speaking against the clock for the first time since 1940, he rushed his delivery. After telling listeners that he and the Tories and "many of my Labour colleagues would have been glad to carry on [the coalition]... the Socialist Party as a whole had been for some time eager to set out upon the political warpath, and when large numbers of people feel like that it is not good for their health to deny them the fight they want. We will therefore give it to them to the best of our ability." So far, so good—Englishmen expected nothing less than his best from their Winston.[20]

Churchill went on, paraphrasing the economist Friedrich Hayek from *The Road to Serfdom.* "My friends, I must tell you that a Socialist policy is abhorrent to the British ideas of freedom."

> Socialism is inseparably interwoven with Totalitarianism and the abject worship of the State.... Look how even today they [Socialists] hunger for controls of every kind, as if these were delectable foods instead of war-time inflictions and monstrosities. There is to be one State to which all are to be obedient in every act of their lives. This State is to be the arch-employer, the arch-planner, the arch-administrator and ruler, and the arch-caucus-boss.... Socialism is, in its essence, an attack not only upon British enterprise, but upon the right of the ordinary man or woman to breathe freely without having a harsh, clumsy, tyrannical hand clapped across their mouths and nostrils.

He laced into Labour's Herbert Morrison, who had outlined "his plans to curtail Parliamentary procedure and pass laws simply by resolutions of broad principle in the House of Commons." And he excoriated Sir Stafford Cripps for advocating what amounted to a rubber-stamp role for Parliament in the new socialist state. Then he arrived at the passage Clementine thought hideous:

> I declare to you, from the bottom of my heart, that no Socialist system can be established without a political police.... They would have to fall back on some form of Gestapo, no doubt very humanely directed in the first instance. And this would nip opinion in the bud; it would stop criticism as it reared its head, and it would gather all the power to the supreme party and the party leaders, rising like stately pinnacles above their vast bureaucracies of Civil servants, no longer servants and no longer civil.[21]

Churchill thundered and roared, confident that Clement Attlee lacked the oratorical skills to respond in kind. Ed Murrow of CBS believed so, offering that Attlee approached a subject "as if elucidating some obscure, unimportant passage in a Latin translation." The night following Churchill's Gestapo speech, Attlee—whom Colville described as having "no shred of either conceit or vanity"—took to the airwaves and delivered a devastating reply. Churchill's object, Attlee declared, was to make "electors understand how great was the difference between Winston Churchill, the great leader in war of a united nation, and Mr. Churchill, the party Leader of the Conservatives....The voice we heard last night was that of Mr. Churchill, but the mind was that of Lord Beaverbrook." The timid, balding, sometimes fussy Attlee had made himself overnight into a campaign leader. As for Beaverbrook's role in crafting Churchill's speech, he had "no hand" in the matter, Colville wrote. Beaverbrook and his newspapers had been "firing vast salvos" of late, which mostly, Colville believed, "miss their mark." Churchill, trying to cast Attlee as a bogeyman, had also missed his mark, but Attlee, casting Beaverbrook *and* Churchill likewise, had not.[22]

The Beaver put on a relentless, shrill, and clumsy demonstration of loyalty to Churchill in the pages of his *Express,* but Beaverbrook had never really understood Englishmen and, critically, Englishwomen. The tabloid *Daily Mirror,* Britain's largest-selling paper, did. The only large newspaper not controlled by Camrose, Beaverbrook, or Bracken, the *Mirror* went after the service *wives,* telling the women of Britain on the eve of the election, "Vote for them!" [the servicemen] who "for five long years...from Berlin to Burma...have fought and are still fighting for YOU....You know which way your men would march. Vote for them!" Even Churchill loyalists began to doubt their man; Vita Sackville-West wrote to her husband, Harold Nicolson: "You know I have an admiration for Winston amounting to idolatry, so I am dreadfully distressed by the badness of his broadcast election speeches....If I were a wobbler they would tip me over to the other side." Nicolson's friend the literary critic Raymond Mortimer also jotted a note to Nicolson, in which he wrote, "I think that Churchill more than anyone else was responsible for the squalid lies in these elections. He started the rot with his talk of Mr. Attlee's Gestapo."[23]

Churchill's "favorability rating" as measured by Gallup polls had exceeded 90 percent since El Alamein, but for a brief drop during his January 1944 recuperation in Marrakech and his Christmas 1944 foray to Greece. After V-E day, his favorability numbers dipped into the 80 percent range, a mere bag of shells, for he was the most popular leader in living history, the savior of England. Yet, Gallup's newfangled computations were inexact. Asked if they had an "overall" favorable impression of Churchill,

Britons responded, politely, yes. Thus, as Churchill campaigned up and down and across the land by private train and open auto, delivering ten speeches and broadcasts in the process, he was deeply moved, Eden wrote, by the goodwill and cheering crowds he found along all his routes. Yet, Eden later wrote, "He [Churchill] could not be expected to sense that there was also something valedictory in their message. He would not have been Winston Churchill if he had."[24]

Colville was not optimistic about the election, telling his diary, "Without Winston's personal prestige the Tories would not have a chance. Even with him I am not sanguine of their prospects, though most of their leaders are confident of a good majority." That was true; Churchill, Eden, and Beaverbrook all believed they would take the House with a majority of perhaps eighty seats, maybe even as many as one hundred. Even Attlee believed the Tories would win, later telling Colville that "there might, with luck, be a Conservative majority of only some forty seats." Much would depend on the soldiers' vote, four million strong, and almost 20 percent of the total electorate. Over lunch, Churchill asked General Billy Slim, the hero of Burma, how he thought his troops would vote. "Ninety percent Labour," Slim replied. Churchill grunted. "What about the other ten percent?" Slim said, "They won't vote at all."[25]

On July 3, Churchill delivered his final campaign speech at Walthamstow Stadium, a greyhound racing track in East London. After a band warmed up the crowd of 20,000 with "Deep in the Heart of Texas" and "Umbrella Man," Churchill, accompanied by Clementine, took the stage to tremendous cheers. He had no sooner begun speaking when several thousand Labour rowdies scattered throughout the stadium let him have it. "*We want Attlee,*" they shouted over his words. When he tried to engage them on the topic of free speech — "In a free country like ours..." — they shouted him down with a chorus of boos. "Surely that is not a party question," said Churchill. He went on: "I want to congratulate London...upon her wonderful record in the war.... Would you like to boo that?" He went after the socialists and their "absurd utopias," proclaiming that there must be "improvement of human hearts and human heads before we can achieve the glorious Utopia that the Socialist woolgatherers place before us. Now where is the boo party? I shall call them henceforward in my speech the booing party. Everyone have a good boo." Some in the audience jeered at that. He closed with an election prediction: "I give my entire forgiveness to the booers. They have this to take away with them — I am sure they are going to get a thrashing such as their party has never received since it was born."[26]

That day Churchill instructed the cabinet to prepare legislation for a national insurance plan and a national health service. This was not cynical posturing; Churchill had supported both programs since he put Sir

William Beveridge on the case more than three decades earlier. As for the fate of the coal mines, since the General Strike of 1926 he had been much more sympathetic to the miners than to the mine owners. Churchill did not hate Labour programs; he hated the intellectual arrogance of the left—of Bevan, Cripps, and Laski. Churchill, Colville later wrote, was "never anything but hostile to Socialist theory." He had certainly made that clear during the campaign. In any case, voters were unaware of Churchill's instructions to the cabinet when they went to the polls on July 5.[27]

On July 7, Churchill, Mary, Clemmie, Lord Moran, and Colville made for the Basque coast of France near St-Jean-de-Luz for a one-week vacation before Churchill undertook the next order of business: the Big Three conference due to open in Potsdam on the sixteenth. Churchill himself had code-named the conference Terminal, a curious choice given that the final phase of the war against Japan had yet to begin and the atomic bomb, which might hasten the end of the Pacific war, had yet to be tested. Many military men, including Franklin Roosevelt's chief of staff, Admiral Leahy, who gave odds and took bets, believed it would not work.

Churchill's valet, Sawyers, made the journey to France, as keeper of the Old Man's brushes and palettes and paints. It was intended as a beach and painting vacation, and the absence of paperwork and urgent telephone calls ensured an air of quietude. The Old Man spent his mornings swimming about "like a benevolent hippo" off a sandy beach while a squad of French gendarmes dog-paddled around the Great Man to provide a cordon sanitaire between the P.M. and curious locals. So complete was Churchill's rest and relaxation that he utterly failed to prepare for the Potsdam Conference. To make matters worse, neither had Anthony Eden, who had returned from San Francisco with a duodenal ulcer and, under Lord Moran's orders, had spent much of June in bed resting. Churchill—with the election always intruding on his thoughts—had no heart for the upcoming Potsdam parley, telling his doctor, "Nothing will be decided at the conference...I shall only be half a man until the result of the poll. I shall keep in the background at the conference." A report from Max Beaverbrook arrived that lifted Churchill's spirits; the Beaver now predicted a Conservative majority of one hundred. And although Churchill now believed that he might have lost the service vote, he told Clementine he was quite sure the servicewomen were for him. When Clemmie reminded him that early in his career he had opposed giving women the vote, he replied, "Quite true."[28]

On July 15, Churchill, Sawyers, Mary, and Moran flew on to Berlin, while Colville and Clementine returned to London. Attlee and Ernest Bevin also journeyed to Potsdam; it was Churchill's wish that the British present a unified front to the Americans and especially to Stalin. When Churchill told the House of his desire to bring Attlee to Berlin, a Labour MP called out, "Is the right honourable Gentleman going to take the Gestapo with him?" The Old Man thus arrived at his lodgings in Babelsberg, about six miles from Potsdam, with a hostile House waiting in London, a hostile Stalin waiting in Potsdam, and without any guarantee from President Truman that the Americans were prepared to play hardball with Stalin on the matter of free Polish elections.[29]

Truman also arrived in Babelsberg on the fifteenth, and took up residence in a grand town house two blocks from Churchill's residence. Elements of the British, American, and Red armies—out in force—guarded both houses. The next day at dawn—early afternoon in Berlin—the Americans successfully detonated an atomic bomb in the New Mexico desert. On the seventeenth, before the first plenary session with Stalin, Henry Stimson shoved a piece of paper across a table to Churchill. On it Stimson had scribbled, "Babies satisfactorily born." Churchill did not understand, until Stimson made clear just what had taken place in New Mexico. Of this news, Churchill later wrote, "Here then was a speedy end to the Second World War, and perhaps to much else besides." In that moment, Churchill saw no further need to seek Russian help against Japan, and he saw a possible solution to the Soviet tide rolling westward in Europe. The Prof—Lord Cherwell—beheld a way to make this horrific new weapon even more terrible. Knowing that the initial burst of such a bomb would blind anyone who happened to be looking skyward at the moment it detonated, Cherwell advised that preliminary pyrotechnics be set off as the bomb made its descent in order that the optimum number of Japanese were looking skyward at the moment of truth.[30]

Churchill had anticipated the fate of Japan more than three years earlier. Weeks before the fall of Singapore, with the British Empire reeling from the Japanese blows in the Far East but fully appreciating that the home islands of Japan were the key to the Pacific theater, as much as England was to the European, Churchill communicated to the Chiefs of Staff his strategy: "The burning of Japanese cities by incendiary bombs will bring home in a most effective way to the people of Japan the dangers of the course to which they have committed themselves." The word "incendiary" jumps from the memo. He does not propose the use of parachute bombs or four-thousand-pound high explosives. He does not envision bringing Japan to bay with commandos, sabotage, or trickery. He goes straight to the most efficient solution. He would set Japan ablaze, literally,

for Japanese cities were built of paper and wood. That strategy now fell to
Truman to implement.

The first plenary session opened late on July 17 at the Cecilienhof Palace
in Potsdam, originally built for Crown Prince Wilhelm ("Little Willie").
Eden and Alec Cadogan both found Truman to be "quick and business-
like." And both thought Churchill's performance was a disaster. Eden:
"W. was very bad. He had read no brief & was confused & wooly & verbose." Cadogan: "Every mention of a topic started Winston off on a wild
rampage.... So it was a pretty useless meeting, but these conferences
always have their infantile complaints."[31]

Several issues were on the Potsdam agenda—a warm-water port for
Russia, Russian participation in the Pacific war, the withdrawal of Russian
troops from northern Iran, the fate of the German fleet—but only two
items were of abiding concern to Churchill: free elections in Poland, and
the western Polish border. On the former, Stalin, as he had at Yalta, simply
promised free elections—a lie—and Churchill chose to believe him. On
the latter, Stalin (and the Lublin Poles) would not budge; the occupation of
eastern Germany was a fait accompli, and Stalin was of no mind to withdraw from any part of this fertile swath of conquered territory. Churchill
had believed since Tehran that the new Polish frontier should be delineated
by the Eastern Neisse River where it fed into the Oder, in compensation for
the Poles agreeing to the Curzon Line. Stalin claimed the Western Neisse.
More than one million Germans lived between the two rivers, and Stalin
and the Lublin Poles demanded they be packed off to Germany, to make
room for Polish settlers. Had Churchill and Stalin scrutinized a map at
Tehran when they first proposed shifting Poland westward toward the
Oder (and checked off their acceptance as they had with the "naughty"
memo in October 1944, when they divided the Balkans into spheres of
influence), they might have avoided the current predicament. And had
Roosevelt displayed resolve at Yalta rather than, as described by Eden,
"playing it by ear," a more concise accord might have been reached. And,
had Harry Hopkins been on hand in his role as presidential fixer, he might
have guided Truman to more resolve. But Hopkins was an ill man, and he
had severed his connection with the U.S. government early in the month.
In any case, the Lublin Poles in essence had become the fifth occupier of
Germany.

Churchill believed his tête-à-têtes with Stalin would yield results. Eden
did not. After Churchill enjoyed a five-hour dinner with Stalin, Eden told

his diary: "He [Churchill] is again under Stalin's spell. He kept repeating 'I like that man.' I am full of admiration of Stalin's handling of him." Full of foreboding for Poland, Eden wrote a long memo to Churchill, ending it with: "I am deeply concerned at the pattern of Russian policy, which becomes more clear as they become more brazen every day."[32]

During the conference, Churchill attended nine plenary sessions, with detours to the usual nightly banquets and to dispiriting one-on-one talks with the Lublin Poles ("Communist creatures," Eden called them). The Old Man also spent an afternoon in Berlin, where hungry Berliners cheered when he alighted from his automobile in front of Hitler's Chancellery. Churchill strolled into the crowd. "My hate had died with their surrender," he later wrote. "I was much moved . . . by their haggard looks and thread-bare clothes." After a brief tour of Hitler's bunker and the pit where the bodies of Hitler and Eva Braun were disposed of, Churchill looked about and declared, "Hitler must have come up here to get some air, and heard the guns getting nearer and nearer." He also spoke at the opening of the Winston Club, a nightclub and cabaret opened for British servicemen. There he received a cool reception from the gathered troops, who had voted weeks prior in early balloting.[33]

On the matter of the atomic bomb, Churchill enthusiastically endorsed Truman's decision to use it. Churchill and Roosevelt had agreed in 1943 that both the U.S. and Britain must approve the bomb's use. Yet, although a Royal Navy carrier task force was then attached to Admiral Halsey's Third Fleet, and Churchill was determined to do his part in Japan, the decision to drop the bomb was Truman's alone to make, by virtue of the overwhelming role America would play in the planned invasion of Japan. When Churchill suggested that the Japanese be forewarned that their country would be as utterly destroyed as Germany and that their only chance to preserve lives and honor would be to surrender now, Truman replied that the Japanese had lost any claim to honor at Pearl Harbor. Still, the Allies sent an ultimatum—the Potsdam Declaration—to Tokyo in which they guaranteed the Japanese rights of free speech and religious assembly, and promised that they had no intention of enslaving the Japanese or destroying Japan as a nation. The declaration ended with: "We call upon the government of Japan to proclaim now the unconditional surrender of all Japanese armed forces, and to provide proper and adequate assurances of their good faith in such action. The alternative for Japan is prompt and utter destruction." Tokyo ignored the statement.[34]

Eden later recalled that he and Churchill had discussed the delicate matter of telling Stalin of the atomic bomb, and the more delicate matter of refusing Stalin the "know how" of the bomb's technology if he asked for it. They advised Truman to inform Stalin before the bomb was dropped on

Japan. Truman, in his memoir, *Year of Decisions,* recalls that on July 24 he "casually mentioned to Stalin that we had a new weapon of unusual destructive force. The Russian premier showed no special interest." Truman did not tell Stalin of the "atomic" nature of the new weapon. Churchill and Eden stood a few feet away as Truman spoke with Stalin. As recalled by Churchill, in his memoirs, "I was sure that he [Stalin] had no idea of the significance of what he was being told. Evidently in his immense toils and stresses the atomic bomb had played no part. If he had the slightest idea of the revolution in world affairs which was in progress his reactions would have been obvious.... But his face remained gay and genial and the talk between these two potentates soon came to an end." But as recalled by Marshal Zhukov in his memoirs, "Stalin did not betray his feelings and pretended that he saw nothing special in what Truman had imparted to him. Both Churchill and many other Anglo-American authors subsequently assumed that Stalin had really failed to fathom the significance of what he had heard. In actual fact, on returning to his quarters after this meeting Stalin, in my presence, told Molotov about his conversation with Truman. The latter reacted almost immediately. 'Let them. We'll have to talk it over with Kurchatov and get him to speed things up.' I realized that they were talking about research on the atomic bomb."[35]

Churchill, meanwhile, told Brooke that the new bomb made it "no longer necessary for the Russians to come into the Japanese war, the new explosive alone was sufficient to settle the matter." Churchill, Brooke told his diary, "was completely carried away" by the news from New Mexico and believed the bomb could "redress the balance with the Russians!" Churchill, "pushing his chin out and scowling," declared that "now we could say [to Stalin] if you insist on doing this or that, well we can just blot out Moscow, then Stalingrad, then Kiev, then Kuibyshev...Sevastopol etc. etc. And now where are the Russians!!!" Brooke tried to "crush his [Churchill's] over-optimism" and to "dispel his dreams" based on "the half-baked results of one experiment," but Churchill stood firm. Yet Britain did not have an atomic bomb, and Truman would have been as shocked as Brooke if Churchill had proposed dropping one on the ally that had made the largest sacrifice in the war against Hitlerism.[36]

One other matter occupied Churchill at Potsdam—Lend-Lease. He stressed to Truman the British desire—and need—for a continuation of the program; food was in short supply, and London needed assurance that it could parcel out Lend-Lease matériel to European countries on an as-needed basis. "The president said he would do his utmost," Churchill wrote in his memoirs, "but of course I knew the difficulties he might have in his own country." A month later Truman told his closest advisers that "he was dead set against the U.S. adding to its reputation as a Santa Claus;

he wanted Lend-Lease cut to a minimum now, liquidated as soon as possible."[37]

Churchill left Potsdam without an agreement on Poland. The Red Army was in control of central Europe. Not since 1814, when Russian troops entered Paris, had a Russian army thrust so far west into Europe. With SHAEF decommissioned that week, with Truman sending his armies home and his air forces to the Pacific, and with British troops outnumbered by the Red Army by more than three to one, the fate of not only Eastern Europe but Western Europe rested with Joseph Stalin. It was this state of affairs that led Churchill eight years later to title the sixth and final volume of his war memoirs *Triumph and Tragedy*.

Churchill returned to London with Mary late on July 25 in order to learn his electoral fate. If Beaverbrook's optimistic predictions proved correct, Churchill would be going back to Potsdam in a few days. Father, daughter, son, and Clementine dined together that evening in the Storey's Gate Annexe. Churchill's brother, Jack, joined the party; Beaverbrook and Bracken dropped by. Churchill retired early (for him), shortly after 1:00 A.M., sanguine in his belief that he would receive his electoral mandate. He later wrote that he awoke just before dawn "with a sharp stab of almost physical pain. A hitherto subconscious conviction that we were beaten broke forth and entered my mind.... The power to shape the future would be denied me. The knowledge and experience I had gathered, the authority and goodwill I had gained in so many countries would vanish." He slept until nine, late for Churchill, and was in his bath when, shortly after ten, Captain Pim requested he make for the map room, where charts of battle-fronts had been replaced by lists of constituencies. Colville, Bracken, and Beaverbrook joined Churchill there. The P.M., attired in his siren suit, sprawled in his chair, cigar in hand, as had been his habit in 1940 while he waited for the howl of the air-raid alarm to announce the fireworks.[38]

The first results were unfavorable, and the numbers only worsened as the morning wore on. Early reports showed forty-four Labour gains to just one for the Conservatives. Alexander Hancock, a farmer and unknown Independent crackpot who advocated a one-hour workday, had opposed Churchill in Woodford, a new district carved out of Churchill's old Epping district. The new Epping seat went to a Labourite, and Hancock took 35 percent of the vote in Woodford. Churchill kept his seat, as did Eden. But Bracken lost his, as did Duncan Sandys, Harold Macmillan, and Randolph. The only satisfying news to come over the transom was that Sir

William Beveridge and Leslie Hore-Belisha, both Liberals, had lost. Labour took 393 seats in the new Parliament, the Conservatives 213 (down from 585 in 1935). Had not the Liberals, who ran more than three hundred candidates, siphoned away Labour votes, the Tories would have fared even worse. The Liberals in the end won just twelve seats and were reduced to distant third-party irrelevancy. The *New York Times* declared the Tory defeat "one of the most stunning electoral surprises in the history of democracy." The London *Times* held Churchill accountable for his own political demise: "Mr. Churchill himself introduced and insisted upon emphasizing the narrower animosities of the party fight." The *Daily Telegraph* attributed the results to "a revulsion of feeling against the government rather than to an excess of support to the Socialist policy."[39]

Lunch at the Annexe that day, Mary told her diary, took place "in Stygian gloom." Sarah "looked beautiful and distressed." All in the room "looked stunned & miserable." "Papa struggled to accept this terrible blow—this unforeseen landslide." At some point, Clementine said of the defeat, "It may well be a blessing in disguise." To which Churchill replied, "Well, at the moment it's certainly very well disguised." Neither his sense of humor nor his dignity deserted him. When Lord Moran wandered onto the scene, Churchill asked, "Well, you know what has happened?" Moran replied that he knew, and added something about the ingratitude of the people. "Oh, no," Churchill answered, "I wouldn't call it that. They have had a very hard time." Moran had been so sure that Churchill would be given his mandate and that they'd return to Berlin that he had left his luggage there.[40]

At 6:00 P.M. Churchill ordered drinks and cigars to be brought in for the map room staff. Then he departed the Cabinet War Room—never to return—for Buckingham Palace. At 7:00 P.M. King George accepted Churchill's resignation, telling his former first minister that "the people were very ungrateful after the way they had been led in the war." After a brief audience, Churchill left for No. 10, while King George summoned Clement Attlee to form the new government. No crowds gathered outside Buckingham Palace, and the streets of London were as quiet as a country village. A cold light rain fell. The *New York Times:* "Tonight there were fewer persons at Buckingham Palace for the changing of the Government then there usually are for the changing of the guard."[41]

Before the election, a London *Times* editor informed Churchill that the newspaper was about to advocate two points—that Churchill should campaign as a nonpartisan world statesman and then ease himself into retirement sooner rather than later. "Mr. Editor," Churchill said to the first point, "I fight for my corner." And, to the second: "Mr. Editor, I leave when the pub closes."[42]

The pub had just closed.

Dinner at No. 10 that evening was a somewhat muted affair, Mary later wrote, but less gloomy than lunch. Uncle Jack was on hand, and Diana and Sarah, and Sarah's friend Robert Maugham (Somerset's nephew). Bracken attended, as did Anthony Eden, a remarkable gesture of fealty on his part given that he had learned just five days earlier that his son Pilot Officer Simon Eden, RAF, had been killed in Burma. Clementine took herself off to bed before dinner. The others tried "to say and do the right thing" for Churchill's sake, with some success. Maugham told Harold Nicolson a few days later that Churchill had accepted his defeat with good grace. When someone at the dinner table said to Churchill, "But you have won the race, sir," he replied, "Yes, and in consequence I've been warned off the turf."[43]

Sometime earlier that afternoon, Churchill composed a concession statement, which he sent to the BBC to be read during the nine o'clock news. Brian Gardner, writing in *Churchill in Power,* called the statement "perhaps the most gracious acceptance of democratic defeat in the English language." Churchill:

> The decision of the British people has been recorded in the votes counted today. I have therefore laid down the charge which was placed upon me in darker times. I regret that I have not been permitted to finish the work against Japan....It only remains for me to express to the British people, for whom I have acted in these perilous years, my profound gratitude for the unflinching, unswerving support which they have given me during my task, and for the many expressions of kindness which they have shown towards their servant."[44]

Friday, July 27, was a day for farewells at No. 10. As Churchill took his leave from the Chiefs of Staff, Alan Brooke found himself "unable to say very much for fear of breaking down. He [Churchill] was standing the blow wonderfully well." A decade later, when Brooke—by then the 1st Viscount Alanbrooke—edited his diaries for publication, he inserted a line that stands in sharp contrast to his wartime rants against Churchill: "On reading these diaries I have repeatedly felt ashamed of the abuse I had poured on him [Churchill], especially during the latter years." Then, as if he could not let go, Lord Alanbrooke felt compelled to remind readers that during the latter part of the war "Winston had been a very sick man... with repeated attacks of pneumonia....This physical condition together with his mental fatigue accounted for many of the difficulties in dealing with him....I shall always look back on the years I worked with him as some of the most difficult and trying in my life." Only after enunciating his caveats did the viscount finally add the now oft-quoted tribute to Churchill: "For all that I thank God I was given an opportunity of working alongside such a man, and having my eyes opened to the fact that occasionally such supermen exist on this earth."[45]

Eden thought the entire afternoon a "pretty grim affair." He was the last to leave, having been called into the Cabinet Room by Churchill for a final chat. That night, Eden wrote in his diary: "He [Churchill] was pretty wretched, poor old boy....He couldn't help feeling his treatment had been pretty scurvy." Before Eden left, Churchill looked about and said, "Thirty years of my life have been passed in this room. I shall never sit in it again. You will, but I shall not."

Eden assured Churchill that "his place in history could have gained nothing" by a return to No. 10 in the postwar years, adding, "That place was secure anyway." Churchill accepted that, and the two men parted. As Eden left he reflected upon the six war years he had spent in that room, writing that night: "I cannot believe I can ever know anything like it again."[46]

Churchill departed No. 10 for Chequers, which the new prime minister had put at his disposal for the weekend. Chartwell was not yet reopened and staffed, and although the Churchills were interested in purchasing a London town house at 28 Hyde Park Gate, they had not yet finalized the transaction. Under other circumstances, Mary later wrote, the weekend would "have been a very cozy jolly party" but "we were all still rather stunned by the events of the previous week." Ambassador John Winant was on hand, as was Sarah, who had decided to end their long love affair. It had always been more courtly than torrid, but it was doomed in any event by the fact that Winant was a married man and Sarah—aptly nicknamed the Mule—was a very independent woman. She later wrote that it had been an affair "which my father suspected but about which we did not speak."[47]

Colville—who now served Attlee—was on hand that weekend in order to help Churchill gather his personal effects. The Prof—Lord Cherwell—had motored out, as had Brendan Bracken. Churchill's former bodyguards and private secretaries had gone off to Berlin with the new prime minister. No motorcycle dispatch riders roared up the drive; the phones did not ring; the Chiefs of Staff did not report in. Most noticeably, the secret boxes and Ultra decrypts did not appear. "Now there was nothing," Mary wrote. "We saw with near desperation a cloud of black gloom descend." To dispel the cloud, they played records on the gramophone—American and French marches, Gilbert and Sullivan, and the Noel Gay tune "Run Rabbit Run." They ran movies, too—*The Wizard of Oz* was a favorite. They played cards and staged a croquet match, which Churchill watched from the sidelines. The cloud lingered. On Sunday, the twenty-ninth, the clan of fifteen sat down to dinner at the great round table, where they drank a Rehoboam of champagne in a futile attempt to make merry. At some point during dinner, Churchill said "it was fatal to give way to self-pity, that the Government had a mandate" and that "it was the duty of everyone to support them." Before retiring, they all signed the Chequers guestbook, Churchill last. Underneath his signature he wrote: *Finis.*[48]

Churchill and Clementine took up residence at Claridge's the next day. Two weeks later, on August 14, Churchill hosted a dinner in his Claridge's suite for Eden and a few Conservative colleagues. Late in the evening, they learned that the Japanese had surrendered. The Americans had dropped atomic bombs on Hiroshima and Nagasaki on August 6 and 9. Tokyo had been silent in the days since, but now, as Eden put it, "the six years of ordeal was over." The dinner companions adjourned to another room, where a wireless was set up. There, they listened as Clement Attlee "barked out a few short sentences, then gave the terms.... The war was over."

"There was a silence," Eden wrote. "Mr. Churchill had not been asked to say any word to the nation. We went home. Journey's end."

Churchill had by all rights at age seventy reached the sixth and penultimate of Shakespeare's seven stages of life. The fields and orchards and rose gardens at Chartwell, wild and overgrown after five years of neglect, were in need of his attention, as were the fish ponds, and the fish, and the house itself. Little Winston and the other "wollygogs" needed him, as did Sarah, Mary, Diana, Randolph, and Clementine. Yet he had no intention of becoming Shakespeare's "slipper'd pantaloon." He considered his journey by no means over. He was the leader of the opposition, in which role he enthusiastically took his seat in the front row of the opposition bench in the Commons and proceeded to oppose. On his return to the House (still meeting in the Lords' chamber while the bombed-out Commons was being rebuilt), Conservative MPs leapt to their feet and sang "For He's a Jolly Good Fellow." Labourites countered with "The Red Flag."

Though England's greatest leader led the opposition, Churchill could not reverse the Labour mandate, and knew it. Labour had pledged to nationalize the Bank of England, the coal and utility industries, railroads, and the steel industry. As Labour in coming months and years created government control boards to manage each industry, bureaucracy became Britain's fastest-growing industry. Two years after V-E day, Churchill told the House: "A mighty army of 450,000 additional civil servants has been taken from production and added, at a prodigious cost and waste, to the oppressive machinery of government and control. Instead of helping national recovery this is a positive hindrance." That was one of his gentler rebukes of the socialist experiment. Labour's showcase priority was the creation of the National Health Service (which came to pass in 1948, with Aneurin Bevan installed as its first minister). Labour proposed free health care, free false teeth, free eyeglasses. Just four months after the election, Churchill told the House:

> The queues are longer, the shelves are barer, the shops are emptier. The interference of Government Departments with daily life is more severe and more galling. More forms have to be filled up, more officials have to be consulted. Whole spheres of potential activity are frozen, rigid and numb, because this Government has to prove its Socialistic sincerity instead of showing how they can get the country alive and on the move again.

Sir Stafford Cripps, Churchill declared, "is a great advocate of Strength through Misery."[49]

Churchill, sure that the Labour tide would someday ebb, looked beyond England. He intended, with two broad objectives in mind, to transcend British politics and reinvent himself as an international statesman. He sought a special relationship (that he as yet had not explicitly defined) among the English-speaking peoples, including the Americans, and a similar but more crisply defined relationship among Western European countries—his old idea of a United States of Europe. He was, and had always been, a European patriot. Britons had sacked him, but Europeans loved him. This was political capital he began to invest. On November 16, he told an audience in Brussels that in order to prevent another "Unnecessary War" (caused in part, he said, by America's unwillingness to join the League of Nations and confront German re-armament), "we have to revive the prosperity of Europe: and European civilisation must rise again from the chaos and carnage into which it has been plunged: and at the same time we have to devise those measures of world security which will prevent disaster descending upon us again." He proposed a "United States of Europe, which will unify this Continent in a manner never known since the fall of the Roman Empire, and within which all its peoples may dwell together in prosperity, in justice, and in peace."[50]

Not all in the Tory leadership shared his visions for the future of Britain, of Europe, and even of the Tory party. The voters having thrown out the Conservatives, many in the Tory hierarchy felt it was time for Churchill to step down from the party leadership, to take "a long rest," as Lord Moran framed it. Churchill should write a history of the war, as only he could. He should paint, travel, and enjoy life. "Prefaced by elaborate protestations of admiration and respect," some of Churchill's colleagues began to advance the theme of retirement to Moran. They no longer would tolerate Churchill's grudging, sometimes cruel, and usually overbearing style of leadership. "In short," Moran wrote, "with the war behind them the Tory leaders were no longer prepared to stomach [Churchill's] summary methods." Churchill had no intention of abdicating the Tory leadership. "A short time ago I was ready to retire and die gracefully," he told Moran in 1946. Of the new Labour government, Churchill offered to Moran: "Now I'm going to stay and have them out. I'll tear their bleeding entrails out of them. I'm in pretty good fettle." It was "the Jerome blood," Winston said.[51]

During the first week of January 1946, foreign secretaries and diplomats from around the globe convened in London for the opening session of the United Nations General Assembly. Churchill was not among the luminaries. On January 9 he, Clementine, and Sarah boarded the *Queen Elizabeth,* bound for New York and a two-month vacation in Florida, Cuba, and the eastern United States. Not having yet decided to write his memoir of the war, he worked on his unfinished *History of the English-Speaking Peoples* during the voyage. But soon after he arrived in Miami, he read recently published essays by Eisenhower's aide, Captain Harry Butcher, which Butcher had based on his diary entries. Butcher's tales of Churchill's late nights and liquid lunches were incomplete, trivial, and not at all flattering to the Old Man, who, not about to take such "history" lying down, summoned his prewar European literary agent, Emery Reves. Butcher (and Elliott Roosevelt, with *As He Saw It*) helped force the decision; Churchill would write his version of the war.

On January 22, Harry Hopkins, who been hospitalized for more than two months, wrote a short letter to Churchill, in which he signed off with, "Do give my love to Clemmie and Sarah...all of whom I shall hope to see before you go back." Hopkins's doctors had been treating him for cirrhosis of the liver, but their diagnosis was wrong. The terrible pain he had suffered for almost a decade was due to hemochromatosis—a metabolic disorder of the digestive tract. His letter to Churchill was the last he wrote.

He died a week later. He took to the grave two firm political beliefs. The first was that Britain was the best friend America had and any attempt by America to horn in on British trade would only injure that relationship. His second was that Russia in coming years would become more nationalistic and less inclined to spread communism around the globe. But, regardless of Moscow's intentions, Hopkins believed America's "relations with the Soviet Union are going to be seriously handicapped" by differences over "fundamental notions of human liberty—freedom of speech, freedom of the press, and freedom of worship."[52]

In early February, while Churchill took his ease in the sun, Stalin addressed his party congress and, as recollected by Under Secretary of State Dean Acheson, "with brutal clarity outlined the Soviet Union's postwar policy." Russia would re-arm, Stalin declared, at the expense of producing consumer goods, because "capitalist-imperialist" monopolies guaranteed that "no peaceful international order was possible." George Kennan, then chargé d'affaires in Moscow, wrote an eight-thousand-word policy paper for the Truman administration that later became known as the "Long Telegram." In it Kennan predicted that Stalin's "neurotic view of world affairs" and a tyrant's fear of political insecurity would result in a Soviet foreign policy that would use "every means possible to infiltrate, divide and weaken the West."[53]

Kennan advised a policy of stiff resolve in the face of Soviet belligerence, in part because he believed Russians respected strength, and in part because Russia was exhausted from the war and in no position—yet—to assume a more sinister role on the world stage, other than through proxies (as in Greece and Yugoslavia). Kennan later wrote that had he sent his telegram six months earlier, it would have "raised eyebrows," and had he sent it six months later, it would have "sounded redundant." Fundamental to his diplomatic strategy was his belief—held since before Yalta—that Stalin would never grant to the peoples of Soviet-occupied countries such as Poland and Bulgaria democratic rights that were denied Russians. For the West to think otherwise was naive. To "act chummy" with Moscow, or "make fatuous gestures of goodwill" in hopes that Moscow would grant those rights, would gain nothing, partly because "no-one in Moscow believes the Western world" would "stand firm" against Soviet threats. Yet, Kennan also believed the military requirements needed to advance Moscow's cause were "beyond the Russian capacity to meet. Moscow has no naval or air forces capable of challenging the sea or air lanes of the world." Kennan's strategy later became known as "containment" and for more than four decades, it underlay U.S. policy toward the Soviet Union.[54]

Kennan's dismissal of Soviet air and naval capabilities put him in Walter Lippmann's corner in that regard, but neither one saw (as Churchill did soon after the Dresden raid) the coming reality of long-range bombers and rockets. Bernard Montgomery also believed that the Russians were down and out militarily, noting that when "1,700 American and British aircraft" gave "an impressive display of airpower" during a post–V-E day celebration in Frankfurt, the message "was not lost on the Russians" in attendance. Months later, after a visit to Moscow, Montgomery came away believing that "the Russians were worn out" and "quite unfit to take part in a world war against a strong combination of allied nations." But Churchill was concerned by Moscow's threat to *Europe*, not to the entire planet. And although Russia was not a worldwide naval power, neither anymore was Great Britain. Indeed, a naval vacuum existed in the Mediterranean, a vacuum easily filled by Russia if it decided to finally throttle its enemy of two hundred years, Turkey, or extort from Ankara free passage through the Dardanelles. Most worrisome to Churchill was the fact that there was no Western alliance in place to meet a Russian threat. The war was over; America was building new Packards and Chevys and Philco televisions and General Electric washing machines. "Alliance" was still a troublesome if not dirty word to many Americans, especially the Taft Republicans in Washington.[55]

Three months before Churchill's Florida vacation, he received an invitation from the president of Westminster College, in Fulton, Missouri, to deliver a series of lectures at that school. Churchill received many such invitations, but the postscript on this letter was handwritten—by President Truman. In it, Truman reminded Churchill that Missouri was his home state, and he offered to introduce Churchill at the lectures. Truman asked Churchill—whom the president considered to be "the first citizen of the world"—if he'd like to stop off in Washington first and travel to Missouri from there with Truman aboard the presidential train. Churchill accepted the offer with enthusiasm, suggesting one lecture might be more appropriate, as a series would quite tax his speech-writing skills. He had for months sought to articulate his worldview in a speech that would reach the largest possible audience, and here now came the president of the United States with an invitation that, Churchill told Truman, was "a very important act of state." At noon on March 4, after breakfasting with Truman at the White House, Churchill and Truman made for Union Station. A few White House aides went along on the trip, including Admiral Leahy, press secretary Charlie Ross, and General Harry Vaughan, a beefy, profane, a hard-drinking, cigar-smoking political operative and a Truman crony since the Great War. Truman's newly appointed special counsel Clark Clifford, thirty-nine and a product of Missouri's Washington University Law School, also boarded the presidential train for the eighteen-hour run to St. Louis. Drinks were served as soon as the train left the station—scotch for Churchill, which he took with water, telling his hosts that adding ice to liquor was a "barbaric" American custom, as was the American habit of not drinking whisky during meals.[56]

The meetings between Churchill and Truman in Potsdam the previous July had been brief and formal. Churchill, in fact, came away from Potsdam harboring "deep reservations about Truman," Clifford later wrote. Churchill himself years later claimed he "loathed the idea of [Truman] taking the place of Franklin Roosevelt." Yet at Potsdam, Churchill had been preoccupied with the coming election and the Russians. Since then, the Attlee government, not Churchill, had worked with Truman. The president, as Churchill learned during the train journey, was what Americans call a regular guy. He was blunt, honest, and not given in the least to the wily, often facile machinations that Franklin Roosevelt brought to the table. (Some months later, Lord Moran told Churchill he had learned that Roosevelt told his cabinet that if Churchill had one hundred ideas a day, four might be any good. Churchill responded, "It [was] impertinent for Roosevelt to say this. It comes badly from a man who hadn't had any ideas at all.") Truman, like Eisenhower and Hopkins, came from simple Midwestern stock. What you saw was what you got. With Hopkins now gone, Churchill could not have asked for a better American friend than Harry Truman. At Potsdam, Admiral King had leaned over to Lord Moran, and said, "Watch the President. This is all new to him, but he can take it. He is a more typical American than Roosevelt, and he will do a good job, not only for the United States, but for the whole world."[57]

The rail journey offered the two men a chance to get to know each other. Truman insisted Churchill call him Harry; Churchill agreed with delight, insisting that the president call him Winston. Truman at first demurred, telling Churchill that given his importance to England, America, and the world, "I just don't know if I can do that." Churchill: "Yes, you can. You must, or else I will not be able to call you Harry." Truman replied, "Well, if you put it that way, Winston, I *will* call you Winston." Truman told Churchill that he intended to send the battleship USS *Missouri* accompanied by a naval task force to Turkey, ostensibly to return the body of the Turkish ambassador, Münir Ertegün, who had died in 1944. The president's real intent, however, was to signal the Soviets that America was prepared to play a significant role in the eastern Mediterranean, a role Britain could no longer undertake alone. The U.S. Sixth Fleet, though not yet identified as such (and a presence in the Mediterranean ever since), was born on the trip to Westminster College. Yet, although Truman was growing increasingly wary of the Soviets, he had by no means settled on an adversarial policy toward them. He had been briefed on Kennan's long telegram, but he still harbored hopes of working with Stalin. America, its duty done, her boys coming home, was at peace. The Depression was long past. A new era had dawned, later anointed "The Good Times" by journalist Russell Baker. America, with over 400,000 of her boys buried overseas and at home, was in no mood to hear the rattle of sabers.[58]

As the presidential train rolled past a cyclorama of sleeping towns and darkened farms, Churchill excused himself to work on his speech. He had shown a draft to Secretary of State James Byrnes, who expressed no reservations to Truman, who in turn told Churchill he did not intend to read the final text so that he could tell reporters as much if they asked, which they surely would. But when Churchill emerged from his salon with the finished product, Truman could not resist. After reading it, he called it a "brilliant and admirable statement." As the president handed it back to Churchill, he predicted it would "create quite a stir."

During dinner Churchill asked if it was true that Truman enjoyed playing poker. "That's correct, Winston," the president replied. Churchill offered that he had first played poker during the Boer War, and suggested the cards be brought out for an evening game. Truman said that he and his colleagues would be delighted to set up the game. Green baize and chips were produced; drinks poured. When Churchill excused himself for a moment, Truman warned his companions that Churchill had played poker for more than forty years, was "cagey," loved cards, "and is probably an excellent player." The reputation of American poker was at stake, the president said, adding that he expected "every man to do his duty." Soon after the first cards were dealt, it became apparent to the Americans that their distinguished guest was not a poker player of distinction; in fact, Clifford pegged him as "a lamb among wolves." Within an hour Churchill was down almost $300 (£75, more than $3,500 in current dollars), a great deal of money in 1946, more so for an Englishman whose finances, like his country's, were in a regrettable state. When Churchill again excused himself for a few moments, Truman laid down the law to his four colleagues: They were not to exploit their guest's obvious lack of poker skills. "But boss," Harry Vaughan replied, *this guy's a pigeon!*" Thus, during the early morning hours of the day on which he delivered one of the most memorable speeches of the twentieth century, Churchill tried his best to beat his hosts at their own game. He did not fare well.

Spring had come early to Fulton; the day was warm, the windows thrown open in the college gymnasium, where a small stage had been set up. Churchill was to be awarded an honorary doctor of laws degree, and he had dressed for the occasion in his crimson Oxford robes. A television camera was to have been brought in to broadcast the event, but Churchill, fearing that the bright lights would be a distraction, nixed that idea. Instead, a lone Paramount movie camera was set up. Churchill began his address with broad brushstrokes: the United States with its nuclear monopoly now stood at "the pinnacle of power," and with "an awe-inspiring accountability to the future." He advised that the nascent United Nations be endowed with an international air force. He believed all men should live in their "myriad cottages" free and without fear. "To give security to these countless homes, they must be shielded from the two giant marauders, war and tyranny." He spoke in conciliatory terms of the Soviet Union:

A shadow has fallen upon the scenes so lately lighted by the Allied victory. Nobody knows what Soviet Russia and its Communist international organization intends to do in the immediate future, or what are the limits, if any, to their expansive and proselytising tendencies. I have a strong admiration and regard for the valiant Russian people and for my wartime comrade, Marshal Stalin....We welcome Russia to her rightful place among the leading nations of the world. We welcome her flag upon the seas....It is my duty however, for I am sure you would wish me to state the facts as I see them to you, to place before you certain facts about the present position in Europe.

Then:

From Stettin in the Baltic to Trieste in the Adriatic, an iron curtain has descended across the Continent. Behind that line lie all the capitals of the ancient states of Central and Eastern Europe. Warsaw. Berlin. Prague, Vienna, Budapest, Belgrade, Bucharest and Sofia, all these famous cities and the populations around them lie in what I must call the Soviet sphere, and all are subject in one form or another, not only to Soviet influence but to a very high and, in many cases, increasing measure of control from Moscow.

He could not resist telling the audience that although a terrible war had been fought to a successful conclusion, that war need not ever have happened because "no one would listen and one by one we were all sucked into the awful whirlpool." Although he did not believe the Russians wanted another war, he did believe they sought "the fruits of war and the indefinite expansion of their powers and doctrines." Then he arrived at his central message:

If the population of the English-speaking Commonwealths be added to that of the United States with all that such co-operation implies in the air, on the sea, all over the globe and in science and in industry, and in moral force, there will be no quivering, precarious balance of power to offer its temptation to ambition or adventure. On the contrary, there will be an overwhelming assurance of security. If we adhere faithfully to the Charter of the United Nations and walk forward in sedate and sober strength seeking no one's land or treasure, seeking to lay no arbitrary control upon the thoughts of men; if all British moral and material forces and convictions are joined with your own in fraternal association, the high-roads of the future will be clear, not only for us but for all, not only for our time, but for a century to come.[59]

To safeguard the West's liberties, he proposed a fraternal association of America and Britain, calling that idea "the crux of what I traveled here to say." He offered specifics, including "the continuance of the present facilities for mutual security by the joint use of all Naval and Air Force bases in the possession of either country all over the world."[60]

He had titled his speech "The Sinews of Peace." Many heard more of a war chant. The reaction was immediate, and not favorable. *The Nation,* a small, sober, left-wing magazine, said that Churchill had "added a sizeable measure of poison to the already deteriorating relations between Russia and the Western powers," and added that Truman had been "remarkably inept" by giving Churchill the platform from which to administer his poison. The *Wall Street Journal,* echoing the isolationist mantra of earlier in the decade, rejected Churchill's call for an English-speaking alliance, saying that "the United States wants no alliance or anything that resembles an alliance with any other nation." The *New York Times* noted that the speech was "received with marked applause in the passages where it dealt with the responsibility of this country to see that another World War was avoided, but the proposal for 'fraternal association' brought only moderate handclapping." In fact, the Paramount movie camera set up to capture the scene caught Harry Truman applauding with vigor during Churchill's more controversial passages. Churchill had declared himself an Atlanticist, in the Walter Lippmann mode, and Truman liked it.[61]

Stalin did not, and his reaction was also immediate. He granted an "interview" to *Pravda,* wherein he took the shrewd position that Churchill, by calling for an English-speaking union, was no less a racist than Hitler, and no less a "war monger." By arranging the Anglo world against the rest of the world, Stalin claimed, "Mr. Churchill...[is] presenting those nations who do not speak English with a kind of ultimatum—recognize

[Anglo-American] superiority over you, voluntarily, and all will be well—otherwise war is inevitable." The marshal had a point, and one not lost on the French, who had been seeking an understanding with Moscow for two years (de Gaulle had long predicted France and Russia would emerge as the two great postwar European powers). Truman's response to Churchill's address was muted. When asked by reporters in Fulton if he had read the speech beforehand, Truman declared he had not. "Much to our relief," Clifford later wrote, "Churchill...did not contradict" the president. Still, to placate the peanut gallery, Truman forbade Under Secretary of State Dean Acheson to attend a New York reception for Churchill. Yet the arrival of Kennan's "Long Telegram" just two weeks earlier had set the stage for a reevaluation of U.S. foreign policy, a process Dean Acheson believed necessary although slow in coming about. Churchill had spoken with emotion in contrast to Kennan's lawyerly white paper, but their messages were similar. In those weeks a new era came into being.[62]

The Cold War, as it soon came to be known, had had its start before World War Two ended, but soon enough—from Moscow to London to Washington and on around the globe—all agreed that it had been declared on March 5, 1946, by the Citizen of the World Without Portfolio, in Fulton, Missouri. That month, Truman sent Averell Harriman—who just weeks earlier had resigned his Moscow post in hopes of leaving government—to London as ambassador to the Court of St. James's. Stalin had not withdrawn Soviet troops from Azerbaijan, in northern Iran, as promised, a circumstance, Truman believed, that "may lead to war." "I want," Truman told Harriman, "a man in London I can trust." Stalin pulled his troops from Iran weeks later, but within the year the Russians shot down a British aircraft that had strayed from one of the three Western air corridors leading to Berlin. The fires of war remained banked, but a banked fire, in English folklore, holds the most heat. From the day Churchill delivered his Fulton speech until more than four decades later, all knew the Cold War could turn hot at any time, through weakness of will, geopolitical overreach, or a cascading series of diabolically unfortunate events. Churchill left Fulton secure in his belief that peace would be guaranteed as long as America maintained its monopoly on nuclear weapons. It could not be guaranteed by a nuclear-armed Britain because the U.S. Congress that year passed the McMahon Act, which dissolved the gentleman's agreement Churchill and Roosevelt had reached on atomic bombs. Henceforth Washington would share no atomic secrets with London. Harriman thought the law "shameful" given that during the war Britain "had given us everything they had....Now the Congress of the United States had made it illegal even to exchange information with the British."[63]

On September 19, 1946, seven weeks after Truman signed the McMahon Act, Churchill told a Zurich audience, "The atomic bomb is still only in the hands of a State and nation which we know will never use it except in the cause of right and freedom. But it may well be that in a few years this awful agency of destruction will be widespread and the catastrophe following from its use by several warring nations will not only bring to an end all that we call civilization, but may possibly disintegrate the globe itself."[64]

He had gone to Zurich not to expressly wax melancholic about the possible doom of Europe in the atomic age, but rather to propose a defense. He told the Zurich audience that the recent war had been fought to prevent a return of "the Dark Ages" and "all their cruelty and squalor," though he warned, "They may still return." Then:

> Yet all the while there is a remedy which, if it were generally and spontaneously adopted, would as if by a miracle transform the whole scene, and would in a few years make all Europe, or the greater part of it, as free and as happy as Switzerland is today. What is this sovereign remedy?...I am now going to say something that will astonish you. The first step in the re-creation of the European family must be a partnership between France and Germany....There can be no revival of Europe without a spiritually great France and a spiritually great Germany....We must build a kind of United States of Europe.[65]

His Fulton speech had marked the postwar renewal of his long-held vision of a special Anglo-American relationship. The 1946 Zurich address marked the start of his active campaign for a united Europe, one that would include Germany but would not necessarily include Britain. Historians ever since have plumbed the seeming paradox of Churchill's desire for Britain to be in, but not really *in,* a united Europe. Jock Colville had listened to Churchill's pronouncements on a united Europe throughout the war and had come to understand the root of the matter: in essence, the Old Man sought European stability such that the Royal Navy (which he presumed would assume its former role in global politics after the war) might roam over the high seas without having to fret potential troubles back home. United Europe, for Churchill, meant global opportunity for England. He had called for a "Council of Europe" in a March 1943 broadcast, and had made mention of a "United States of Europe" in a November 1945

Brussels speech. He sought such an arrangement not only to create a Franco-German bulwark against Soviet transgressions but also to align the interests of Germany and France such that they would never again have reason to go to war against each other. That would benefit both Europe and England. Churchill believed that a robust France living in harmony with a rebuilt Germany would, someday — if time and the Russians did not derail events — form such a buffer. In late 1946, neither nation, alone or together, was in any shape to form a buffer between Russia and Britain. Germany had been conquered, partitioned, and reduced in size, and the rump occupied. In France the Fourth Republic, just wobbling into existence, was conducting a pogrom against all things Vichy, while overseas it was fighting a war in Indochina against Ho Chi Minh and the Viet Minh, who had declared a breakaway republic in the north of Vietnam the year before. Rapprochement with Germany was not high on the French agenda.

The reaction to Churchill's Zurich address was, as with his Fulton speech, muted at best. Attlee and Labour thought the objectives of European security "would be better achieved through the United Nations." Chancellor of the Exchequer Hugh Dalton believed any such movement should be driven by Europe's Socialists and for Europe's socialists, an attitude Churchill later derided as "squalid" and "a declaration that if Europe is to unite and Britain is to play any part in such a union, it can only be on a one-party basis — and that party the Socialists." Ironically, Attlee, on the very day he belittled Churchill's grand idea, also gave Churchill "Top Secret" reports that showed the Red Army maintained 116 divisions in occupied Europe, enough force, one Ministry of Defence official concluded, to make "a Russian conquest of western Europe" a "practical possibility." When Churchill sent his son-in-law and champion of the united Europe movement, Duncan Sandys, to France to measure the French reaction to his Zurich speech, Sandys had to tell the Old Man that the French people "were violently opposed" to reconstituting a unified German Reich, although de Gaulle (out of office) "believed firmly in the project." Yet de Gaulle's endorsement came with a caveat: although he sought a unity of purpose between Britain and France with a possible role for Germany, the precise part Germany would play in any such arrangement had first to be determined. De Gaulle was not in the least prepared to endorse a resurgent and re-armed Reich.[66]

Over the next eighteen months, the European unity movement gained momentum, with Churchill pushing from the sidelines. In May 1948 he addressed Europeanists at The Hague:

Since I spoke on this subject at Zurich in 1946, and since our British United Europe Movement was launched in January 1947, events have carried our affairs beyond our expectations.... Great governments have banded themselves together with all their executive power.... Sixteen European States are now associated for economic purposes; five have entered into close economic and military relationship.... Mutual aid in the economic field and joint military defence must inevitably be accompanied step by step with a parallel policy of closer political unity.

He moved on to a vital part of his vision, one not shared by many on both sides of the Atlantic—the inclusion of Germany in this new Europe:

Some time ago I stated that it was the proud mission of the victor nations to take the Germans by the hand and lead them back into the European family, and I rejoice that some of the most eminent and powerful Frenchmen have spoken in this sense. To rebuild Europe from its ruins and make its light shine forth again upon the world, we must first of all conquer ourselves.

On May 5, 1949, ten nations signed the Treaty of London, which brought into being the Council of Europe. That August, after having invested much of his political capital on the issue, Churchill was rewarded with an invitation to Strasbourg and the first session of the Council of Europe Assembly. This was a true, though nascent, European parliament, a congress not of parties but of principles—of the rule of law, free speech, and international cooperation. The Germans were not in attendance, but by the following year, they would be.[67]

Full vindication for Fulton duly arrived a year later when on March 12, 1947, President Truman, with Greece and Turkey in mind, declared to a joint session of the U.S. Congress that henceforth it would be "the policy of the United States to support free peoples who are resisting attempted subjugation by armed minorities or by outside pressures." Greece, where a civil war was being fought, and Turkey, Truman argued, needed aid, hundreds of millions of dollars in aid, to prevent their slipping beneath the Communist wave. He did not propose military action, but the threat of force was implicit in his words. The *New York Times*'s James Reston declared the speech as important as the Monroe Doctrine. The tectonic shift in American foreign policy may have taken Truman only twenty-one minutes to announce, but the ground had been shifting for five years, the final jolt arriving on Friday, February 22, when Lord Inverchapel, the British ambassador, tried to deliver a note to George Marshall, secretary of state for all of thirty days. Marshall had already left Foggy Bottom for the weekend, but his deputy, Dean Acheson, persuaded Inverchapel to leave a carbon copy of the message. The British note was blunt and to the point: having "already strained their resources to the utmost," the British wished to inform Marshall that all aid to Greece and Turkey would end on March 31. Britain was broke and could no longer maintain any force—or influence—in the eastern Mediterranean.[68]

The new policy became known as the Truman Doctrine, a bold declaration of America's intent to guarantee not only the sovereignty of Greece and Turkey, but of nations throughout the world. George Marshall at first thought it unwise. He had learned firsthand doing battle with Churchill during the war that the Balkans were a dangerous place. He had undercut Churchill's ambitions then; now his own president had picked up Churchill's mantle. Marshall was not at all convinced that the Russians were the sinister threat their enemies made them out to be, and he was not certain that Moscow posed any threat to Greece or Turkey.

Marshall that week was in Moscow for talks with Molotov on the occupation of Germany and Austria, and the rebuilding of industrial capacity in those conquered states. The war had ended almost two years earlier, yet peace terms regarding the old Reich had yet to be agreed upon between the U.S. and the U.S.S.R. Marshall had left Washington in an optimistic mood, but by the time he returned home in April, his hopes had evaporated. The Russians, who had stripped Germany and Austria of factories and machines, told Marshall that more would be squeezed from them, the horrific plight of their peoples be damned.

That winter was particularly ferocious, and millions of refugees still roamed central Europe. Each morning in cities and towns throughout Germany and Austria, the frozen bodies of the starved were picked up from streets and alleys by their starving fellow citizens and carted off to communal graves. Stalin, his own country in ruins (as Marshall saw firsthand), would not give an inch, and in fact argued for a delay in the reconstruction of Germany. The German pasture that Stalin (and Henry Morgenthau) had envisioned had come to pass, but far too many millions of people lived there to be sustained. Starvation was the only certainty for millions of Germans. And that was fine with Stalin. The Moscow talks ended in utter disagreement. The Americans and Russians would not meet again for fifteen years. Truman and Marshall did not voice in public the concerns they now harbored about Stalin's intentions—the Red Army was still considered heroic in America. But the Truman Doctrine served notice of a course correction. It amounted to the Atlantic Charter with muscle, and vindication as well of Churchill's 1944 Christmas journey to Athens. A week after Truman's address, Dean Acheson declared: "A Communist dominated Government in Greece would be considered dangerous to United States security." Although Churchill was not one to say "I told you so," Lord Moran wrote, "[Churchill's Mediterranean policy] had been taken over lock, stock, and barrel by the United States."[69]

Marshall understood that only the United States possessed the economic might to lift Europe out of the morass. Yet the British and Americans had not helped matters since 1945 by embargoing sales of raw materials to Germany. Without factories, with its steel industry dead, and without raw materials to build new machine tools to outfit new factories, Germany could only descend deeper into ruin. This Marshall now understood. A European economy without a German presence was something akin to an American economy without New York finances and Pennsylvania coal and steel. Yet the British economy, too, was foundering. This deeply troubled Dean Acheson, for Britain was one of just two European countries where citizens believed in their government, where order was maintained, and where old ethnic and wartime scores were not being settled by gun and bomb. The other was Russia, and that, for Acheson, was the problem. It had been a year since Stalin declared his antipathy toward the West; even those Americans who had put Stalin and the Russians on a pedestal now saw the danger. Acheson and a very few others in the State Department believed America had to help Europe, and especially Britain, not only because it was the right thing to do for the nation that had fought alone for almost two years against Hitler, but because a strong Britain and a reinvigorated Europe could only make for a stronger America in the new world order.[70]

Shortly after Marshall returned from Moscow, Acheson persuaded him to take to the airwaves in order to tell Americans of "the suffering of the people of Europe, who are crying for help, for coal, for food, and for the necessities of life." Marshall did, warning Americans that "the patient is sinking while the doctors deliberate." On June 5, while giving the Harvard commencement address, he announced his plan for European recovery, known since as the Marshall Plan. "The initiative," he stressed, "must come from Europe," but the dollars would come from America. At a press conference on June 12—three years to the day since he and Churchill had visited the D-day beaches—Marshall cited Churchill's 1946 Zurich speech calling for a united Europe as one of the influences underlying his belief that Europe would emerge from the ruins a better place. Stalin, always suspecting the Americans of seeking "control" in any transaction, opted out of receiving aid. Soviet satellites, too, opted out on orders from Moscow, including Hungary, where Moscow had engineered a Communist coup in late May. But sixteen nations of free Europe opted in.

Churchill called the Marshall Plan "a turning point in the history of the world." Almost $13 billion—about 5 percent of yearly U.S. gross domestic product, and 16 percent of the federal budget—would find its way to Europe over the next four years, including more than $1 billion a year to Britain. It was the embodiment of Churchill's fourth moral principle, *In Peace: Goodwill*. Churchill had been advocating European solidarity for two years. Marshall's plan addressed the economic way; now it fell to Europeans to find the necessary political will.[71]

By 1947 Churchill's financial status had improved measurably. His daughter Mary later wrote that for the first time in his life, and through the good graces of friends and publishers, "Winston was rich." Churchill's revenue stream flowed from two sources. Late in 1945, his friend Lord Camrose hatched what Churchill called a "princely plan" to make Chartwell a national possession. Camrose formed a trust to which he contributed £15,000 and by August 1946 had raised another £80,000 through sixteen other subscribers, enough to purchase Chartwell for almost £45,000 and make a gift of it to the National Trust with an endowment of £35,000. Churchill was granted a life tenancy at £350 per year. Upon his death Chartwell—and the documents, paintings, furniture, and mementos Churchill promised to leave there—was to be opened to the public.[72]

By late 1946, with the Chartwell transaction complete, Churchill directed his attention and money toward purchasing nearby farms and remodeling his London house at 28 Hyde Park Gate (and the adjoining No. 27, also purchased). A prize Jersey cow arrived at Chartwell, and Landrace pigs, and in 1948 a Land Rover to tour the estates, which during 1947 had grown to almost five hundred acres. German prisoners of war—Churchill called them all "Fritzy"—supplied much of the labor. One of the Germans fell in love with the countryside and a country girl, and chose to marry and make a new life among the Englanders. The prisoners cleared fields and planted legumes; the walled gardens were home to lettuces; the hothouses hosted cucumbers. Peach and nectarine trees were groomed, grapevines trimmed. The apple and pear trees, which Churchill had planted two decades earlier, were tended to. Roses and wisteria were likewise pruned; the pathways through the rose gardens—laid out by Clementine in the 1920s—cleared. The Chartwell tennis court was converted to a croquet lawn; the mistress of the manor no longer had the stamina for tennis, but she enjoyed long croquet matches with visiting friends, including Field Marshal Montgomery, who Colville in coming years described as having become a "mellow, lovable exhibitionist, tamed but lonely and pathetic." Monty and Clementine had gotten off to a rocky start during Churchill's recuperation in Marrakech in 1943, when Montgomery presumed to dictate the guest list for dinner to Clementine. It got even rockier when Montgomery, who then served as Chief of the Imperial Staff under Attlee, declared that soldiering was a more honorable profession than politics, at which point Clementine shot back, "How dare you have the ill-bred impudence to say such a thing in my house." He was soon forgiven. For the next decade, Monty and Clementine passed many afternoons doing battle on the croquet field. The master of the manor did not compete, though he sometimes watched the games.[73]

Churchill stocked the three fishponds with giant goldfish, which he fed by hand with maggots delivered in tins from London. He attempted to protect his fish from marauding birds by means of a device of his own invention—a floating "pinwheel" of sorts cobbled together from a bicycle wheel outfitted with a series of small mirrors. He explained the mechanics of the contraption to the American journalist Stewart Alsop as they strolled the grounds: as the wheel turned in the breeze, the mirrors, catching the sun's rays, would emit bright flashes, which presumably would frighten off the birds. "Unfortunately," Churchill told Alsop, "on this small island the sun hardly ever shines."[74]

Chartwell's fauna continued to multiply. The Australian government sent two red-beaked black swans as a gift; they were joined by three more, the lot of them furiously ill-tempered. The swans coexisted on the lower lake with a pair of Canada Geese (called Lord and Lady Beaverbrook) and two white swans, a female, Mr. Juno, and a male, Mrs. Jupiter, so named, Churchill explained to Lady Diana Cooper, because the sexes were misidentified to begin with. Sundry ducks and "five foolish geese" also made their home on the lower lakes.

Late each morning, Churchill would summon his Scotland Yard protector and announce, "Sergeant, I'm ready for my walk now." He might ask a typist with a stenographer's pad to accompany him, in case a thought in need of recording burst forth. Then, as recalled by one of the new typists, Cecily ("Chips") Gemmell, "he would stomp out wearing this terrible old battered hat with swan feathers sticking out of it" to feed his "poor little birds" from a basket of stale bread that he carried hooked over an arm. By the lakeside "he'd bark, *arf, arf, arf,* and the swans came running." He used wads of bread as ammunition with the aim of inciting the birds to battle among themselves, the foolish geese versus the ferocious swans. He was more conciliatory toward defenseless winged creatures. Fearing a decline in native butterflies, he oversaw the creation of a butterfly garden and the conversion of a garden shed to a butterfly farm. At one point he contemplated nourishing the butterflies with fountains that would flow with honey and water, but he thought better of the idea. More Jersey dairy cows arrived, along with ponies. The purchase of one neighboring farm brought in a herd of Shorthorn cattle. And in 1947, a poodle named Rufus II arrived, replacing Rufus I, killed by an automobile. Rufus took his dinner with the family in the Chartwell dining room, from a bowl placed upon a special cloth on the Persian carpet, and next to his master's chair. The butler always served Rufus before serving their first course to the guests at table.[75]

In February 1947, Mary married Christopher Soames, a captain in the Coldstream Guards, and assistant military attaché in Paris. The newlyweds took up residence on one of the Chartwell farms, while Churchill began work on his war memoirs there and at 27–28 Hyde Park Gate. By then, Mary later wrote, "Winston now had, if not a veritable kingdom, at least a principality." Two years later, when Christopher Soames prevailed on his father-in-law to purchase a French-bred Grey, Churchill took up the sport of kings. The horse—Colonist II—proved a champion, winning the Salisbury and Lime Tree stakes in 1949 under Churchill's colors (his father Randolph's colors, pink and gray), and six more prestigious races by 1951, when he was put out to stud. Clementine, in a letter to their friend journalist Ronnie Tree, expressed her wonderment at "this queer new facet in Winston's variegated life. Before he bought the horse (I can't think why) he had hardly been on a race course in his life. I must say I don't find it madly amusing."[76]

That Churchill could indulge in such extravagances stemmed from the second and ultimately far more powerful financial stream that irrigated his fortunes: the Chartwell Trust, created with Lord Camrose's help to hold title to Churchill's personal papers and to shield him from the punishing taxes of the times. Clementine, Lord Cherwell (Prof Lindemann), and Brendan Bracken would serve as trustees, and would be charged with two paramount duties: to sell Churchill's wartime memoirs, and to make Churchill's earlier papers available to Randolph when the time came for him to write his father's official biography, "but not until five or ten years after his death." The trust, far more than selling Chartwell, made Churchill a rich man. The British film director and producer Alexander Korda (who also donated a full-fledged cinema to Chartwell) paid £50,000 ($200,000) for the film rights to *History of the English-Speaking Peoples,* a four-volume work that would not be published for another decade. The American publisher Henry Luce paid Churchill £12,000 ($50,000) for the American book rights to his wartime secret-sessions speeches to the House of Commons. Odhams Press ponied up £25,000 ($100,000) for the residual value of his pre-1940 book copyrights. *The Second World War,* Churchill's war memoir and history, proved to be a most powerful generator of wealth. Houghton Mifflin agreed to a $250,000 advance for the American book rights; Henry Luce's *Life* magazine agreed to pay $1.15 million for the American serial rights. These were princely sums, the equivalent of a modern $12 million. The memoir was to run to six volumes.[77]

Churchill's intent was not to write a history of the war but to explore the wartime Anglo-American relationship, and to refute the "rubbish" being written about him by Captain Butcher, Elliott Roosevelt, and left-leaning London newspapers. He oversaw the operation with his usual military precision, with himself as minister of war directing his battalions of literary troopers, who anointed themselves The Syndicate. Captain William Deakin DSO ran the tactical side of the campaign, supported by seven secretaries and typists and a host of current and former Churchill advisers, including Pug Ismay, Field Marshal Alexander, Air Marshal Park, Duncan Sandys, the Wizard Warrior R. V. Jones, Mountbatten's former Chief of Staff General Sir Henry Pownell, and Emery Reves as agent, fixer, and arbiter of editorial content. The Prof checked statistics and translated arcane scientific data into plain English. Denis Kelly, a young barrister, was charged with cataloging Churchill's papers, assisted in that task by Chips Gemmell, just eighteen. The volatile Randolph, who his sister Mary later wrote "could pick a quarrel with a chair," was not part of the team. The key to the entire operation was an extraordinary agreement Churchill struck with the cabinet secretary Edward Bridges. Churchill asked for and Bridges approved that all wartime documents written by Churchill, and replies, be removed to Chartwell for Churchill's use in preparing the memoirs. HMG would have final approval before publication. This arrangement meant that Churchill, with exclusive access, could cull the complete record at his leisure, whereas under British law the papers would be put off-limits to other historians for more than three decades. Kelly had much to catalog.[78]

An early Dictaphone was installed at Chartwell to aid the Great Man in the production process. Churchill gave the machine a test run one day after allowing all the typists the day off. But he failed to press the start button. When it failed to record anything, he banished it. Instead, he dictated his work to the typists, a total of almost one and a half million words over seven years. When critics later demeaned the effort as being carried off more by The Syndicate than by Churchill, Denis Kelly replied with words to the effect that a master chef cannot be expected to prepare each course for a grand banquet. The Syndicate indeed furnished Churchill with official documents, letters, telegrams, and the recollections of some of the principals, but Churchill dictated the narrative and assembled the entire work. The first volume, *The Gathering Storm*, was published in mid-1948, and the final volume, *Triumph and Tragedy,* came out the United States in late 1953, and in Britain in April 1954. Though in places factually incorrect—by commission as well as omission—the memoir "is an invaluable record," wrote parliamentarian and Churchill biographer Roy Jenkins, who also called it "the ultimate literary achievement of the outstanding author-politician of the twentieth century." Churchill's attitude toward the work, as recalled by Deakin, was "This is not history, this is my case."[79]

He prepared his case not only at Chartwell and 27–28 Hyde Park Gate, but on the shores of Lake Léman in Switzerland (August 1946); in Marrakech (New Year's 1947 and winter 1950–51); at the Hôtel de Paris in Monte Carlo (December 1948); at Lake Garda and Lake Carezza for a month; at Beaverbrook's villa, La Capponcina, at Cap d'Ail (summer 1949); at Reid's Hotel in Madeira (January 1950); and in Annecy and Venice (1951). He also took time to slip across to America in 1949 in order to promote his book, visit with Bernard Baruch and Harry Truman, and address the students at MIT. With draconian British currency restrictions in place during these years, Churchill and his party often traveled as the guests of his American publishers (who often paid Churchill's expenses with French francs rather than British pounds) in order to avoid a breach of British currency law.

Churchill's easel and paints always went along on these trips, but Clementine often did not, although she and Lord Moran hastened to Marrakech when Churchill came down with bronchitis during his 1947 visit there. He enjoyed his painting and basking and swimming on these jaunts, although in a letter to Clementine written from Marrakech before the onset of the bronchitis, he wrote of bleak weather and his fear of catching a cold, adding: "England and politics seem very distant here. I continue to be depressed about the future. I really do not see how our poor island is going to earn its living when there are so many difficulties around us." He was back in the wilderness, but with two critical distinctions. He now led the opposition, whereas in the 1930s he had been in opposition to his own party. And he believed he would play a vital role as the future played out, if not in Downing Street, then in his beloved House of Commons. Yet, in response to a 1946 birthday toast raised by Bracken, Churchill, after expressing appreciation at having his friends and family by his side, added: "But we are the past."[80]

The bronchitis crisis of early 1947 passed without effect, but the taps on Churchill's shoulders grew more frequent, more varied, and more serious. His brother, Jack, six years his junior and long afflicted with a bad heart, died in February 1947. "As you get older these things seem less tragic," Churchill told Moran. "In any case there is not much time left." Jack was buried next to his parents in the little churchyard at St. Martin's, in Bladon, just a mile south of Blenheim Palace. Later that year, Churchill underwent a hernia operation, in preparation for which and on the advice of his surgeon, who feared a pulmonary crisis might occur while the Old Man was under anesthesia, he promised to quit cigars. He did not. He then promised the surgeon to reduce his alcohol intake by half. This, too, he failed to do, yet apparently to no ill effect. The surgery went well. By 1948, Moran believed Churchill's arteries were hardening, and the Old Man by then complained regularly of feeling tightness in his shoulders. In August 1949, he lost feeling in his right arm and leg. Moran was summoned from London. He diagnosed a minor stroke, telling Churchill that he had not suffered a hemorrhage but that a "very small clot has blocked a very small artery." A year later, Moran detected a "disturbance of cerebral circulation." If hardening of the arteries is a sign of old age, Moran later wrote, "Winston was an old man before he began writing *The Second World War.*" Churchill believed he should not look too far forward; however much of a future he was to have, it could not be long. But he could always look back, to the days of honor. When asked by Moran's wife which year of his life he'd want to live over, he replied, "Nineteen-forty every time. Every time."[81]

As Churchill's financial fortunes improved during the late 1940s, those of Britain continued their descent. "Victory," Churchill told Moran in 1946, "has turned into sack cloth and ashes." When the Attlee government sent John Maynard Keynes to the United States in 1946 to negotiate a $3.75 billion loan to finance reconstruction, the great economist secured his loan, but on hard terms. Interest was pegged at 2 percent over fifty years (with the proviso that London could skip annual payments in times of economic duress, which it did six times in the coming two decades). This was generous on America's part. But Washington also insisted that London leave the gold standard and make the pound fully convertible in accordance with the Bretton Woods agreement.* This proved a calamity when in 1949 the Attlee government—under continuing economic pressure, and despite months of denials that it would do so—devalued the pound by 30 percent, from $4.08 to $2.80.

A devalued currency results in that nation's products becoming cheaper in foreign markets, but Britain had little to export, and very little that Americans wanted. Of Britain's plight, Churchill told the house in 1950:

---

* The British government paid the final £100 million installment on the loan in December 2006.

"Owing to their [the Attlee government's] follies and wrongful action, a great part of all the loans and gifts we have received from abroad has been spent not upon the re-equipment of our industry, nor upon the import of basic foodstuffs: instead much of this precious aid was lavishly frittered away" on socialist programs. He excoriated Attlee for "[raising] our taxation until it is the highest in the world, and even stands higher today than in the worst years of the war." Between the loans "and the unparalleled sacrifices exacted from the taxpayers" there was no reason why Britain should not have attained "solvency, security and utopian independence. This has been denied us not only by the incompetence and maladministration of the Socialist Government and their wild extravagance, but even more by the spirit of class hatred which they have spread throughout the land, and by the costly and wasteful nationalization of a fifth part of our industries."[82]

That U.S. products were made more expensive in Britain by the pound's devaluation was of little concern in America: Americans were buying American—GM, Studebaker, Ford, Packard, and Chrysler automobiles, and electric clothes dryers, radios, and televisions. American children rode bright-red Schwinn bicycles, sales of which—as with all American products—benefited from tariffs slapped on European imports. Now that Parker Pen could make pens instead of bomb fuses, it rolled out the Parker "51" pen—the latest in writing tools—which sold out at Gimbels in New York. Housewives who had been forced through war rationing to buy the Hormel company's Spam—"the taste tickler"—kept buying it. After all, it was easy to prepare as a suitable and delicious main course for breakfast, lunch, and dinner.[83]

In America, consumption was now a way of life; in Britain, consumption was still a disease that took off old people. Other than shipping their best scotch whisky and linen to America, Britons were not exporting much, not producing much, and not buying much, including British-made Fords or even squat and cheap little Morris Minors. Daimler, Austin, Rolls-Royce, and Humber still produced machines that were virtually hand-crafted (Churchill always preferred a Humber), but most Britons could not afford them, and little else for that matter. Ford U.S.A. produced more than 1.1 million motor cars in 1949; Morris Minor produced only 250,000 *between* 1948 and 1953. Londoners did not experience traffic jams because few Londoners owned automobiles, and those who did found petrol to be in short supply and expensive. Britons stayed home and, as they had for decades, found their entertainment via gramophones and little Bakelite wireless sets.

Americans went on a spending spree while Britons banked their sallow coal fires and pulled on another sweater. Most could not even commiserate over the telephone: fewer than 10 percent of British homes contained one.

When Harold Nicolson attended a January 1947 meeting of the Historic Buildings Committee of the National Trust, he did so wrapped in a greatcoat because there was no heat. Lighting, too, was a matter of chance after Attlee's government imposed rolling blackouts between 9:00 P.M. and 12:00 A.M. and 2:00 and 4:00 P.M. That winter was one of the worst in memory. Its "most crushing blows fell on Britain," Dean Acheson later wrote, with blizzards regularly battering the island, with six million out of work, and with rations below wartime levels.[84]

"Gloom reigned in the bomb-devastated streets of London and the provincial cities," Jock Colville later wrote of those winter months. "London was grey; life was grey." By then Colville toiled as private secretary to the Heir Apparent, Princess Elizabeth, just twenty-one. It was a post he accepted with reluctance, spurred on by Churchill, who told Colville, "It is your duty to accept." Britons depended for sustenance upon millions of food parcels that arrived from the United States and the Commonwealth, including several thousand sent to Buckingham Palace. Princess Elizabeth organized a group of more than one hundred women volunteers who wrapped each parcel and dispatched them to shops and homes throughout the land. Even the royal family carried their clothing ration books that year. Elizabeth had to use her coupons to procure the material for her wedding gown in order to walk down the aisle of Westminster Abbey in November with Philip Mountbatten, her second cousin once removed (and Dickie's nephew). The currency stringency grew so severe that year that the Attlee government slashed the importing of foods and essential commodities, even going so far as to slap a 75 percent import duty on Hollywood films. Hollywood responded by ceasing all shipments of movies to Britain. England found itself now a pale moon eclipsed by the blazing sun of the United States. "My God!" Nicolson proclaimed to his diary in late 1947. "What the poor people of this country have had to suffer in the last seven years." Clothing rationing did not end until 1949. Food rationing had fully seven more years to run. Londoners dwelled now in pea-soup fogs—smog, really, a poisonous, stinking by-product of hundreds of thousands of fireplaces burning soft coal and coal gas. Day was almost as dark as night. Britons called it "austerity," but conditions were not much different from what Americans knew during the Great Depression.[85]

On November 30, 1947, Colville, after dining with the Churchill family in celebration of the Old Man's seventy-third birthday, told his diary: "Winston is in a sombre mood, convinced that this country is going to suffer the most agonising economic distress." The Battle of the Atlantic, Churchill had claimed, was but "a mere pup in comparison." Had Franklin Roosevelt lived just a few years more, he would have witnessed the complete fulfillment of his strategic vision for imperial Britain and its role in the world. The United Kingdom had been reduced to debtor status, and the Empire, with the departure of Burma, Ceylon, and India by 1948, was vastly reduced in geographical scope. King George remained King, but he had to scrub "Emperor" from the royal stationery.

"Never in his [Churchill's] life has he felt such despair," Colville wrote, "and he blamed it on the Government whose 'insatiable lust for power is only equalled by their incurable impotence in exercising it.'" Colville took heart from Churchill's "phrases and epigrams [that] rolled out in the old way, but I missed that indomitable hope and conviction which characterized the Prime Minister of 1940–41." For this misery Churchill held Attlee accountable. Over drinks with Chips Channon one evening at Claridge's, the Old Man said of Attlee: "Anyone can respect him, certainly, but admire—no!"[86]

In the House Churchill registered his displeasure with the Attlee government regularly and with increasing vehemence. He told Britons that it was not the government's management of unfolding events within the diminishing empire, but its *mismanagement*. Of the continuing need of rationing, he said: "What the German U-boats could never do to us has been achieved by our own misguided fellow countrymen through their incompetence, their arrogance, their hordes of officials, their thousands of regulations and their gross mismanagement of our affairs, large and small." On at least seventeen occasions between 1945 and 1950, he delivered addresses wherein he spoke (with a snarl) of "socialism" and "utopia" in the same breath, often tossing in a "feeble," "foolish," "squalid," or "fantasy" for good measure. He just as consistently reminded his listeners that he had been Lloyd George's loyal lieutenant when the great Welshman overhauled British social services earlier in the century. Making his case required a nimble performance; here was Winston Churchill—the leader of the Conservative Party—championing the philosophical underpinnings of Labour's social programs. He was up to the task. It was the heavy-handed implementation of programs, not the programs themselves, he objected to. In July 1946, he told Britons (and three years later told MIT students much the same):

> It is 38 years ago since I introduced the first Unemployment Insurance Scheme, and 22 years ago since, as Conservative Chancellor of the Exchequer, I shaped and carried the Widows' Pensions and reduction of the Old Age Pensions from 70 to 65. We are now moving forward into another vast scheme of national insurance, which arose, even in the stress of war, from a Parliament with a great Conservative majority. It is an essential principle of Conservative, Unionist, and Tory policy—call it what you will—to defend the general public against abuses by monopolies and against restraints on trade and enterprise,

whether these evils come from private corporations, from the mischievous plans of doctrinaire Governments, or from the incompetence and arbitrariness of departments of State.[87]

Later that year he recycled a line he had used during a March 1945 memorial service for Lloyd George (who had died that month): "We do not seek to pull down improvidently the structures of society, but to erect balustrades upon the stairway of life, which will prevent helpless or foolish people from falling into the abyss. Both the Conservative and Liberal Parties have made notable contributions to secure minimum standards of life and labour. I too have borne my part in this." Indeed, he had done so, when he had "ratted" to the Liberal Party four decades earlier. By the late 1940s—long after "re-ratting" back to the Tories—he was one of very few Conservatives who could honestly say that he had been in favor of social reforms from the beginning, albeit while sitting on the opposing bench at the time.[88]

"Winston is happy at Chartwell," Moran told his diary in 1946, "as happy as he can be when the world has gone all wrong." Churchill could only bear witness from the opposition bench between 1946 and late 1951 as Britain's knights and castles—India and Burma, its influence in Egypt and Palestine—were swept from the chessboard.[89]

In early May 1946, Attlee announced his government's intent to remove all British forces from Egypt, including the Suez Canal Zone. This was a policy Churchill could not consent to, telling the House on May 24: "I assert that it is impossible to keep it [the canal] open, unless British personnel are permanently stationed in the Canal Zone. There may be doubts about our ability to keep it open in the air age, even if we have garrisons and fighter aircraft in that zone. But at any rate without that personnel there is no chance of keeping it open whatever." Especially galling to Churchill was the fact that Britain owed Egypt £400 million for services rendered during the war when, as Churchill told the House, Egyptian troops did not fight and "the debt which Egypt owes to us is that in two world convulsions she has been effectively defended by Great Britain and not only by this island. The Australians and New Zealanders and South Africans have shed their blood freely to prevent Cairo and Alexandria being looted and ravished, ground down and subjugated, by Italian and German hordes." To safeguard the Suez, Attlee proposed using one hundred thousand British troops then in Palestine, from where they could respond to a crisis in the Suez. But guarding the canal with troops bivouacked three hundred miles away struck Churchill as ludicrous. As well, British troops in Palestine made easy targets for Zionist terrorists.[90]

In the House of Commons on August 1, with the Suez and Palestine debates ongoing and civil war likely in India, Churchill delivered something of a valedictory for the British Empire:

> Take stock round the world at the present moment; after all we are entitled to survey the whole field. We declare ourselves ready to abandon the mighty Empire and Continent of India with all the work we have done in the last 200 years, territory over which we possess unimpeachable sovereignty. The Government are, apparently, ready to leave the 400 million Indians to fall into all the horrors of sanguinary civil war—civil war compared to which anything that could happen in Palestine would be microscopic; wars of elephants compared with wars of mice. Indeed we place the independence of India in hostile and feeble hands, heedless of the dark carnage and confusion which will follow. We scuttle from Egypt which we twice successfully defended from foreign massacre and pillage. We scuttle from it.[91]

The entire world, Churchill believed, not only the British Empire, was poised on the brink of great and deadly trials. A week after his speech, over lunch with Clementine and Lord Moran, Churchill predicted another war. "You mean in eight or ten years?" Moran asked. "Sooner," Churchill replied. "Seven or eight years. I shan't be here." He thought it would take the form of a final battle between England, Belgium, France, and Scandinavia against the Russians. "We ought not to wait until Russia is ready," Churchill offered. "I believe it will be eight years before she has these [atomic] bombs." He smiled. "America knows that fifty-two percent of Russia's motor industry is in Moscow and could be wiped out by a single bomb." He smiled again. "The Russian government is like the Roman Church; their people do not question authority."[92]

By the autumn of 1946, Attlee chose to keep British troops in the Canal Zone, where Egyptians resented their presence much as Palestinian Arabs (and many Zionists) resented the British presence in Palestine. The debate over Palestine continued into 1947, when in March Churchill told the House: "One hundred thousand Englishmen [are] now kept away from their homes and work, for the sake of a senseless squalid war with the Jews in order to give Palestine to the Arabs, or God knows who. 'Scuttle,' everywhere, is the order of the day—Egypt, India, Burma. One thing at all costs we must preserve: the right to get ourselves world-mocked and world-hated over Palestine."[93]

If the British in Palestine could not or would not force a settlement between Arabs and Jews, Churchill advised Attlee to hand over the British Mandate of Palestine—which was costing London eighty million pounds a year—to the United States, which as the world's greatest power had, in Churchill's view, inherited such responsibilities but had yet to spend a dollar or send a battalion to Palestine. If not to the United States, Churchill advised passing the mandate to the United Nations, which had been created for such purposes. Churchill believed doing so would help Britain keep its promise to help create a national homeland for Jews, a pledge it could no longer make good on by itself. He also proposed transferring troops that were then serving in Palestine to India, where the bloodshed he had long predicted had begun. It made no sense, Churchill told the House in January 1947, that British troops should stay in Palestine because the Labour government believed their exit "would lead to a terrible quarrel between Jews and Arabs." Yet in India, "We are told to leave the Indians to settle their own affairs." Churchill titled his speech "Blood and Shame."[94]

On November 29, 1947, the United Nations, which had taken over the British Mandate in May, voted to partition Palestine into two states, Jewish and Arab. Arabs in Palestine rejected the UN solution.* The Jewish state—Israel—proclaimed its independence on May 14, 1948. The next day, three Arab armies—from Transjordan, Syria, and Egypt—attacked. Churchill believed the Arab coalition would "fall to pieces" as soon as it met Israeli forces. It did. Eight months later, on January 26, 1949, with Britain still not having recognized the new Israeli state, Churchill took to the floor of the House to assault the Attlee government's performance in the Middle East since 1946:

> It took another year after I had urged the Government to quit Palestine, if they had no plan, for them to take the decision to go. They took it a year later when everything was more difficult. Great opportunities were cast away. They took it in such a way as to render themselves unable to bring perfectly legitimate pressure to bear upon the United States to leave the sidelines and come into the arena of helpful, and now that it [Israel] has come into being it is England that refuses to recognize it, and, by our actions, we find ourselves regarded as its most bitter enemies.

Like it or not, Churchill told the House, Israel's statehood marked "an event in world history to be viewed in the perspective, not of a generation

---

* Since 1921, both Arab and Jewish citizens of Palestine referred to themselves as Palestinian; the concept of an Arab Palestinian people evolved in the 1960s.

or a century, but in the perspective of a thousand, two thousand or even
three thousand years." Then he launched a shocking accusation at Foreign
Secretary Ernest Bevin, who throughout the war had served Churchill
with absolute loyalty:

> All this is due, not only to mental inertia or lack of grip on the part of
> the Ministers concerned, but also, I am afraid, to the very strong and
> direct streak of bias and prejudice on the part of the Foreign Secre-
> tary. I do not feel any great confidence that he has not got a prejudice
> against the Jews in Palestine. I am sure that he thought the Arab
> League was stronger and that it would win if fighting broke out, but I
> do not suggest for a moment that he wished to provoke war.... but the
> course he took led inevitably and directly to a trial of strength, and
> the result was opposite to what I believe he expected it to be.[95]

It was a grossly unjust remark. As foreign secretary, Bevin had pursued
a foreign policy largely in accordance with Churchill's philosophy of
strength through affiliation with America. There had been setbacks in the
Middle East, but they were uninvited, and they certainly did not derive
from any anti-Semitism on Bevin's part. But Churchill, liberated from the
constraints of the coalition, had embraced his role of leader of the opposition with alacrity, and on occasion with venom. Self-restraint had never
been Churchill's long suit.

In Egypt and Palestine the British had lost prestige. In Asia they were losing everything. In March 1947, Churchill pressed Attlee to clarify the mandate under which the new (and last) viceroy of India, Lord Louis
Mountbatten, was to serve. Mountbatten had been given fourteen months
to work with Jawaharlal Nehru's transitional government with the goal of
getting Britain out of India, but no one had told him exactly how to do so,
or what compromises to make, especially in the matter of splitting Muslim
Pakistan from Hindu India. Churchill told the House:

> This [interim] government of Mr. Nehru has been a complete disas-
> ter.... Thirty or forty thousand people have been slaughtered in the
> warfare between the two principal religions.... I do not think that the
> fourteen months' time limit gives the new Viceroy a fair chance. We
> do not know what directives have been given to him.... We are told
> very little. What is the policy and purpose for which he is to be sent

out, and how is he to employ these fourteen months? Is he to make a new effort to restore the situation, or is it merely Operation Scuttle on which he and other distinguished officers have been despatched?[96]

"Will it not be a terrible disgrace," he asked the House, "to our name and record if, after our fourteen months' time limit, we allow one fifth of the population of the globe, occupying a region nearly as large as Europe, to fall into chaos and into carnage?" On August 15, 1947—a date Nehru called "a tryst with destiny"—India and Pakistan gained their independence. In coming months, more than seven million Hindus fled Pakistan for India, and a like number of Muslims fled India for Pakistan. At least five hundred thousand Hindus and Muslims were slaughtered in the Punjab alone, the responsibility for which, Churchill told the House, rested with the Socialist government. In late October, India and Pakistan went to war over Kashmir. On January 30, 1948, a Hindu extremist murdered Mohandas Gandhi, who shared with Churchill a vision of a united India and the end of the caste system.[97]

Since the war's end, Churchill had also advised Attlee and Bevin to reach an agreement with Burma, before it, too, bolted the Empire, which it duly did on January 4, 1948, when it exited both the Empire and the Commonwealth as an independent republic. Churchill told the House: "In Burma also my solemn warnings have been fulfilled. Burma has been cast away and is now a foreign country. It is already descending rapidly into a welter of murder and anarchy, the outcome of which will probably be a Communist Republic." Matters were no better in Malaya, where the eleven Malayan states were reconfigured as a British protectorate in 1948. There, Churchill told the House, "the long arm of Communism, unchecked by feeble British Administration, has begun a campaign of murdering British planters and their wives as part of the general process of our ejection." Repeatedly Churchill described Attlee's foreign policy as a scuttle from responsibilities—in Egypt, Palestine, India, Malaya, and Burma—with a resultant loss of both honor and innocent lives. "It does not matter where you look in the world," Churchill told the House in June 1948, "you will see how grievously the name and prestige of Britain have suffered since the British Nation fell flat upon its face in the moment of its greatest victory."[98]

By early 1948, the Western allies had ceased dismantling German factories and shipping them to Russia. In late February the Czech Communist Party, on orders from Moscow and protected by the Red Army, seized power. Eduard Beneš resigned three months later rather than protest the takeover and risk civil war. He would have gotten no military assistance from the West, which once again, as in the days of Munich, lacked the political will to influence events in central Europe. On April 17, the new American ambassador to Britain, Lewis "Lew" Douglas, reported to the State Department that Churchill had told him "now is the time, promptly, to tell the Soviets that if they do not retire from Berlin and abandon Eastern Germany, withdrawing to the Polish frontiers, we will raze their cities." A week later, Churchill told the Conservative Women's Conference:[99]

> Their lot [the Czechs] has been indeed hard. No sooner were they freed from the tyranny of Hitler's Gauleiters than, like Poland, they were dragged down into subjugation by the Soviet Quislings. . . . I hear people say of the Soviet aggressions and intrigues, "Thus far and no farther." That is no doubt a widely-held resolve. But we must not delude ourselves. There will never be a settled peace in Europe while Asiatic Imperialism and Communist domination rule over the whole of Central and Eastern Europe.[100]

But how, other than by force, would "Communist domination" be reversed?

Ten weeks later, on June 24, the Soviets threw a road-and-rail blockade around Berlin. Britain and the United States, in order to feed and fuel their occupation zones, sent thousands of C-54s and C-47s—which had once dropped Allied paratroopers into France—along the air corridors to Berlin. Between June 1948 and May 1949, every meal consumed by Berliners in the Allied sectors, every ounce of coal they burned to heat their homes—a daily requirement of food and fuel of more than 4,500 tons—came by way of the U.S. Air Force and the RAF, which flew more than two hundred thousand flights in all. The decision on whether to go to war rested with the Russians. Were they to shoot down a British or American aircraft flying within the air corridors, even by accident, there would be war. Were the Red Army to march on the Allied sectors of Berlin, there would be war. In a display of resolve, the United States flew squadrons of Flying Fortresses into East Anglia. B-29s followed. They carried atomic weapons. The presence of the aircraft in Britain was not lost on Moscow, which responded by announcing that Soviet air forces would conduct war games over Berlin. "The City is getting panicky," Harold Nicolson told his diary. "It seems to be the final conflict for the mastery of the world." He added: "The Barbarians are at the gate."[101]

In the autumn of 1948, Bertrand Russell shocked liberals on both sides of the Atlantic (including Harold Nicolson) when he stated that "we should make war on Russia while we have the atomic bomb and they do not." The "we" of course was America, since Britain had no atomic bomb. Nicolson believed the Russians were preparing "for the final battle for world mastery," which would result in the "destruction of western Europe" and "a final death struggle with the Americas." Yet he thought the idea of a pre-emptive attack "evil," even if it resulted in "centuries of Pax Americana—an admirable thing to establish." He believed there might be a frail chance—"not one in ninety"—that "the danger may pass and peace can be secured by peace." That slimmest of chances, Nicolson told his diary, should be taken. "Better to be wiped out by the crime of others...," he wrote, "than to preserve ourselves by committing a deliberate crime of our own."[102]

On the other side of the globe, another country jointly occupied by the Russians and Americans was stumbling toward civil war: Korea, annexed by Japan in 1910 with the compliance of London and Washington. Koreans had spent thirty-five years as virtual slaves of the Japanese. Under a United Nations trusteeship, the Russians occupied the northern part of Korea, the Americans the southern, below the 38th parallel. In 1948 Stalin pulled out his troops. National elections were scheduled to take place, to be supervised by the United States. The North Koreans refused to participate. Instead, in early September 1948, the Communists in the north, with Stalin's blessing, declared the Democratic People's Republic of Korea. Both North and South Korea claimed sovereignty over the entire peninsula.

The Soviet blockade of Berlin—and the danger of war—entered its tenth month in April 1949. On April 4, President Truman signed the North Atlantic Treaty, an outgrowth and expansion of the 1948 Treaty of Brussels, in which Britain, France, Belgium, the Netherlands, and Luxembourg had arrayed themselves as a bulwark against Stalin's Red Army. But without America in, the Brussels treaty was a bulwark in name only. Truman's pen stroke created NATO, and brought America in, along with Canada, Denmark, Norway, Portugal, Iceland, and Italy. The treaty stipulated that an attack against any one of the member nations was an attack against all, and would be met with "all necessary assistance," including the use of military force. Yet it would be two more years before NATO's first supreme commander was named: Dwight Eisenhower, who set to work building a true command structure. When in 1952 Hastings ("Pug") Ismay—the 1st Baron Ismay—was made NATO's first secretary-general, he declared NATO's purpose was "to keep the Russians out, the Americans in, and the Germans down." That statement—given that containing the Reds had become settled policy in America and Britain—made for good politics, but Churchill believed then, and had believed since late in the war, that Germany must be up and armed in order to help Britain and France keep the Red Army out.[103]

In 1949 Russia, not Germany, was the threat. If a war began, Berlin would be the place. In late March, just days before Truman signed the North Atlantic Treaty, Churchill told guests at a New York dinner hosted by Henry Luce: "It is certain in my opinion that Europe would have been communized and London would have been under bombardment some time ago, but for the deterrent of the atomic bomb in the hands of the United States." The best way to deal with the Soviets, Churchill proclaimed, was "by having superior force on your side on the matter in question and they must also be convinced that you will use—you will not hesitate to use—these forces, if necessary, in the most ruthless manner." On April 1, the *New York Herald Tribune* ran the headline CHURCHILL DECLARES ATOM BOMB ALONE DETERS RUSSIA FROM WAR. Actually a credible deterrent could only arise from a promise to *use* the atomic bomb if Russia started a war. Churchill advised Truman to make such a statement. To Churchill's satisfaction, he learned while on his way home on board *Queen Mary* that Truman had done just that, telling reporters that he "would not hesitate" to use atomic weapons if the peace and security of the democracies—anywhere—were at stake.[104]

The nuclear consequences to Moscow of provoking war overrode any inclination—if there was any inclination—within the Politburo to head in that direction. Moscow could blockade Berlin, but it could not take it without suffering annihilation. On May 12, six weeks after Truman brought NATO onto the world stage, Stalin and the Politburo lifted the blockade and climbed down. Jock Colville believed an old saying still applied:

> Whatever happens, we have got
> The Maxim gun, and they have not.

It did not apply for long. When the Soviet Union exploded its first atomic bomb three months later, on August 29, 1949, the world became a far more dangerous place.[105]

It became even more dangerous in early October when the Communist Party in Russian-occupied eastern Germany—sponsored and sustained by Stalin and the Red Army—declared the formation of the German Democratic Republic, known in the West for the next forty years as East Germany. It was a puppet police state, neither democratic nor a republic.

And in the Far East, the Communist menace gathered strength in inverse proportion to the decline of the French, Dutch, and British empires. When in April 1949 Communist artillery fired on British gunboats in the Yangtze River, even anti-Communists throughout Asia hung photos of the wounded ships on their walls. On October 1, Mao Zedong declared the People's Republic of China after driving Chiang Kai-shek and two million Kuomintang followers literally into the sea, and to Taiwan. The bloodiest civil war in modern history—more than three million military casualties and at least twelve million civilian—had lasted twenty-two years, interrupted only by the Sino-Japanese War and World War Two, which proved even more deadly to Chinese civilians. Earlier in the year, as the Chinese Communists pressed their advantage, Churchill could not resist working a deft criticism of Franklin Roosevelt into a speech he gave in New York City:

> I was very much astonished when I came over here after Pearl Harbor to find the estimate of values which seemed to prevail in high American quarters, even in the highest, about China. Some of them thought that China would make as great a contribution to victory in the war as the whole British Empire together. Well, that astonished me very much. Nothing that I picked up afterwards led me to think that my astonishment was ill founded.[106]

Now the two old allies, China and Russia, were declared enemies of the capitalist West. "Are we winning the Cold War?" Churchill asked the New York audience. He had no answer. He saw danger in Europe, and in the Far East. All was uncertain. Yet for Churchill, at least one certainty remained—his belief that he was the man to lead Britain in these dangerous times, and would sooner or later have the chance to do so.

Churchill saw Britain's security tied to three interlocking geopolitical circles, each separate from but overlapping the others, and each forming an association in which Britain might again flourish. Taken together, they promised safety and an honorable peace, one worthy of the sacrifice of Britons and Europeans in the late war. In June 1950 Churchill told the House: "First, there is the Empire and Commonwealth; secondly, the fraternal association of the English-speaking world; and thirdly, not in rank or status but in order, the revival of united Europe as a vast factor in the preserving of what is left of the civilization and culture of the free world." To address the concerns of many Bevan Labourites—and Anthony Eden—who did not share his sentiments of a unified Europe, Churchill offered, "With our position as the centre of the British Empire and Commonwealth and with our fraternal association with the United States in the English-speaking world, we could not accept full membership of a federal system of Europe." Much later, in the House, he needed only eight words to state his position on continental Europeans and their drift toward unity: "We are with them, but not of them."[107]

To stake out such a seemingly contradictory position took political adroitness: Britain would in some ways (not yet articulated with exactness by Churchill) be in a united Europe, but not *completely* in, which amounted to saying that Britain would in some ways be "out" of a united Europe. Indeed, from that time to this day, British governments have held to that policy. Although Churchill had voiced his belief in a united Europe for years, he had never addressed the details of the form and authority a European parliament might assume. This was a strategy more in line with Franklin Roosevelt's approach to complex issues—offer few details—than Churchill's usual blunt and clearly stated approach to all matters great and small. As Tories and Labourites debated the role of Britain, if any, in a European union, Harold Macmillan told his diary the question came down to "'United Europe' *with Britain,* on a loose basis of cooperation; 'United Europe' *without Britain*" (italics Macmillan). The extent of Britain's participation in a European parliament would depend on whether that entity took the form of a "functional" body, having broad powers within strictly defined areas (coal and steel production, and tariffs, for example), or a federal model, with its authority vested in a European constitution. As Macmillan saw it, the former structure would not necessarily result in an erosion of sovereignty on the part of member nations, but the latter might, depending upon the political, economic, and military authority vested in the central government by the constitution.[108]

For two decades Churchill approached European union much as he had played polo—first, slash and dash and drive the ball up the field to get in range, then let the details take care of themselves. Likewise, although for two decades he had championed a union of some sorts with the United States, he had not offered details of just what form that union would take. Despite the linguistic and historical bonds between London and Washington, despite Churchill's dream of a shared currency (the dollar-sterling), and his hopes for political and economic ties that were more than "agreements," Churchill knew that Britain would never find itself "inside" the United States. But NATO brought the United States "inside" Europe and promised security, although in 1950 its command structure—both political and military—had yet to be determined. Strengthening Britain's relationship with the United States and developing a closer relationship with continental Europe were Churchill's paramount objectives. "The fact that there is a grave Soviet and Communist menace," he told the House in 1950, "only adds to its [European unity's] value and urgency. Here surely we can find agreement on all sides of the House. No one can say with justice that we are acting and feeling in this way in prejudice to the interests of the British Empire and Commonwealth. Everyone knows that that stands first in all our thoughts."[109]

To the security offered by his three interlocking rings could be added the security provided by the United Nations, but, although Churchill claimed for the United Nations a central role in world affairs, he harbored doubts about its efficacy. During a Brussels conference on European unity in 1949 he declared:

> But there are also fundamental defects in the structure of the United Nations Organization which must be corrected if any progress is to be made. I had always felt during the war that the structure of world security could only be founded on regional organizations.... In consequence, the supreme body has been cumbered and confused by a mass of questions, great and small, about which only a babel of harsh voices can be heard.... It is vain to build the dome of the temple of peace without the pillars on which alone it can stand.

For Churchill, Europe—led by Britain, France, and someday Germany—would form the strongest pillar and the greatest regional organization on the planet. Pointing out that numerous Eastern European nations could not send representatives to the conference, Churchill added, "The yoke of the Kremlin oligarchy has descended upon them and they are the victims of a tyranny more subtle and merciless than any hitherto known to history."[110]

Churchill's sole domestic political objective from 1946 well into 1951 was to push, prod, and excoriate the Attlee government on its economic performance. In 1948 he told the House, "We are oppressed by a deadly fallacy. Socialism is the philosophy of failure, the creed of ignorance and the gospel of envy. Unless we free our country while time remains from the perverse doctrines of Socialism, there can be no hope for recovery." He delivered a variation on that theme again and again, in the House, at constituent meetings, and at Conservative rallies. During one such rally at Blenheim Palace he summed up his position on Labour thus: "Since [1939] two disasters have come upon us: the Second World War and the first Socialist Government with a majority. By supreme exertions we surmounted the first disaster. The question which glares upon us today is: 'How shall we free ourselves from the second?'" Labour had "squandered" first the American loan of almost four billion dollars and then the generous allotments of the Marshall Plan, with the result that "we are now dependent upon further American generosity and also eating up from hand to mouth the remaining overseas investments and assets accumulated under the capitalist system of former years." Out of loyalty to King and country, he muted his criticism when he spoke abroad, but at home, he pressed the attack.[111]

He reserved his most scathing and personal criticism for his old political nemesis, Aneurin Bevan. In July 1948, on the occasion of the launch of the National Health Service, Churchill told his Woodford constituents:

> One would have thought that a man who had been only a burden to our war effort in the years of storm and who had received high office in the days of victory would have tried to turn over a new leaf and redeem his past.... We speak of the Minister of Health, but ought we not rather to say the Minister of Disease, for is not morbid hatred a form of mental disease, moral disease, and indeed a highly infectious form? Indeed, I can think of no better step to signalize the inauguration of the National Health Service than that a person who so obviously needs psychiatrical attention should be among the first of its patients. And I have no doubt that the highest exponents of the medical profession would concur that a period of prolonged seclusion and relief from any responsible duties would be an equal benefit to Mr. Bevan and to the National Health Service.[112]

Here was Churchill in top form, and whether he was in gentlemanly form was not of any concern to him. That sort of harangue sold newspapers and would be quoted in pubs throughout the land. In times of austerity, comic relief is a balm. Churchill delivered regular doses of that relief. Attlee's Labour colleagues spoke in bureaucratese. Churchill did not. He spoke to the common man and, more important, could speak *like* the common man when the situation demanded.

Between mid-1945 and early 1950 Churchill delivered more than two hundred speeches, many quite lengthy. He dictated, polished, and delivered every one of the four hundred thousand words of his addresses — enough to fill a thousand-page volume — that he sent into battle against socialism, in defense of the Empire, and for European unity. It is an extraordinary achievement given that during these years, he was also writing his memoirs and fulfilling his duties as the leader of the Shadow Cabinet.

That he could produce so much was due to the remarkable way he structured his waking hours, which allowed him to squeeze almost two days of work into each day. He spent his weekends at Chartwell, arriving on Thursday night and leaving for London Tuesday morning. At Chartwell, if breakfast was the start of his day, it began sometime after nine in the morning, later if he had dictated into the early morning hours, which he regularly did. Then, as he bid them good night—or good morning—the typists collected the day's work and sent it off by taxi to the printers in London in order that galleys could be delivered to the Great Man by midday. He breakfasted alone, in bed. He once told a Chartwell visitor that he and Clementine had "tried two or three times in the last forty years to have breakfast together, but it didn't work." His bath and a tour of Chartwell's grounds followed breakfast. Early afternoon found the typists on the day shift drifting into the library from their rooms in the village and Chartwell's orchard cottage. There they waited while Churchill, attired now in a dark blue suit, waistcoat, and gold watch and chain, perused galleys and ordered his thoughts in his second-floor study. When he was ready to dictate, he depressed a switch on an intercom connected to the library, and announced, "Come."[113]

For the typists, the terror began as soon as they sat down at the—not so silent—silent typewriters. This was the routine of a quarter century, during which the lion had not lost his roar. He dictated three, four, sometimes five drafts of his addresses. Bill Deakin and Denis Kelly fed him statistics, and transcripts of Labour speeches, and budget and banking data, and military dispositions. All was bustle. Misspellings on the part of typists were met with sighs and sharp rebukes. The omnipresent intrusion of the gramophone did not help matters. "You just typed away and handed it in and sometimes it was dreadful and he'd just scowl," recalled Chips Gemmell. Foreign names especially tripped up the typists. Once, upon glancing at Miss Gemmell's handiwork, the Old Man barked: "You have not got one word in *fifty* right." He used a special code, known only to himself, to delineate sections of a speech—P-1 for housing, or H-3 for foreign affairs, for example. At his command, the typists scribbled the codes in at the appropriate places. At the end came "the great moment" when Churchill announced, "Now I am going to clop." The "clop" was his paper punch; he had no use for paper clips. The pages were arranged, numbered, punched, and finally bound by a thin strip of cloth. Jane Portal*—whom Churchill always called "the Portal"—committed a mortal sin one day when she assembled the pages in the wrong order, which Churchill only discovered while delivering the speech. She was

---

* Later Lady Jane Williams, she was the niece of both R. A. ("Rab") Butler and Air Marshal Sir Charles Portal, later Viscount Portal of Hungerford.

sure she would never again be entrusted with that duty. When a few days later another speech reached the binding-together moment, Miss Portal was duly surprised—and moved almost to tears—when Churchill said, "Let the Portal do it." "You see," she recalled years later, "he was saying 'I've forgiven you, I trust you.' It was a small, personal instant, but it meant a great deal to me. He would do that often with people."[114]

His humor, as with his impatience, was never far beneath the surface. George Christ (rhymes with "whist") joined the team in 1949 and was assigned the duty of procuring official government documents from which Churchill culled salient points for inclusion in his addresses and memoirs. Churchill pronounced Christ's name as one would the Savior's, and delighted in ordering his typists to "get me Christ on the phone" or "get Christ down here at once." Upon such occasions of levity, a pause and a raised eyebrow were Churchill's signals to the typists that they were free to laugh. They were just as free to weep, as he often did while dictating passages that moved him: "I mean I would be weeping and he would be weeping," Jane Portal recalled, "and all the while he was dictating in his marvelous voice and I'd be tap-tapping away, the both of us weeping."[115]

His generosity was as much in evidence as his temper, his humor, and his tears. He ordered that the Chartwell gates remain open as a sign of welcome to any neighbors who might be inclined to stop by. Many did. A supply of old jackets, heavy coats, gloves, and old boots was kept near the front hall during the first bitter winters of victory, to be given to those in need. There were many. He was always willing to pay Randolph's debts, although he would not disclose to his son the exact terms of the Chartwell Trust. He provided for Pamela after her divorce. Lord Moran had never been well off. Churchill insisted on helping him out and executed a seven-year deed of covenant for Moran's wife, which brought her the modern equivalent of $20,000 a year tax free. Chips Gemmell recalled a trip to the races (a typist always accompanied Churchill wherever he went) during which Churchill told her he would not need her services for several hours. He sent her and the driver off with orders to enjoy themselves however they pleased and to meet him at the car after the day's events. When Miss Gemmell climbed into the car late in the day, the Old Man passed her a racing form, on which he had circled various horses. He announced they were winners and that he had wagered one pound on each of them for her. "Well, count up what you won," he ordered. But Chips, confused by the mathematics of odds and payouts, could not. "He was very mad that I couldn't read the numbers," she recalled, "and told me I had won twenty pounds, which was a great deal." It dawned on Miss Gemmell that the Old Man hadn't really placed any bets but had "suddenly thought in the car, poor girl, I'll say I put money on the horses and I'll say to her, work out how much and collect your money; it was a lovely gesture." When his scheme derailed, Churchill pressed a twenty-pound note into her hand.[116]

One Churchillian gesture stood out above all others for Miss Gemmell. "I was the paint lady," she recalled. "On Tuesdays, before returning to London he'd call me upstairs. 'Miss, you'll clean the palettes up and the paintbrushes, and see if I need paints.' And I'd say 'Yes sir.'" She found cleaning the brushes in turpentine a "ghastly business" but attended to her duties, ordered new paints, and tidied up Churchill's studio in preparation for his return. She was thus much moved when one day he called her into the studio and presented her with one of his paintings, "a very flattering portrait." It was a portrait of her.[117]

As he waded ahead on his memoirs and speeches, he faced a daily mountain of letters from persons great and small throughout the world. Replies to such missives did not always flow directly from the Old Man, although his tears often flowed upon reading them. Chips Gemmell was assigned the duty of composing responses on her own, for his signature. One such letter she wrote was to go off to the Massey Ferguson Company, which had sent Churchill an automated bread-making machine. Miss Gemmell composed a long and flowery thank-you note that moved Churchill to observe, "Jesus Christ, Miss, you've really over-egged the omelet this time. It was only a piece of farm machinery." Such moments of silliness were inevitably followed, usually sooner rather than later, by sinister eruptions due to secretarial misfeasance of one sort or another. And so it went each day until early evening, when the staff wandered into the village for dinner and Churchill took his evening meal in the company of any family or friends who happened to be present in the house. Lord Moran was a regular guest. Jane Portal noticed that he used a pencil to scribble notes on his pure-white shirt cuffs, the better to capture the Old Man's wisdom in the book Moran intended to write. Then, sometime after nine or ten, having returned from their meal in the village, the typists reassembled in the library and, as in the morning, awaited the summons from the Great Man: "Come." After he took himself off to bed near midnight, with brandy and a cigar in hand, yet another summons was issued, and the early morning dictation began. Thus, he effectively squeezed almost two working days into each twenty-four hours and left himself time to feed his goldfish and provoke battles between the swans and the geese on the lower lakes.[118]

Churchill turned seventy-five on November 30, 1949. "I am ready to meet my Maker," he told friends that day. "Whether my Maker is prepared for the ordeal of meeting me is another matter." Actually, neither was ready to meet the other. In 1874, the year of Churchill's birth, the great Conservative leader Benjamin Disraeli anointed the great Liberal leader William Gladstone—whom Disraeli had just replaced as prime minister—an "exhausted volcano." But Gladstone, sixty-four at the time, was not exhausted and returned to that high office three more times before resigning at age eighty-four in 1894. Lord Randolph Churchill had derided Gladstone as "an old man in a hurry." But Randolph died young, at forty-five, and therefore did not live long enough to grasp a truism known to old men. As the new decade came in—and with it the second half of the twentieth century—Winston Churchill understood that an old man had best hurry if he is to get someplace in the time remaining to him. *Time,* in early January, named him the *Man of the Half-Century.* The first half of the century had brought Europe and the world a succession of shocks and calamities, the editors wrote, with Churchill offering solutions—and suffering defeats—from within and without the British government. "That a free world survived in 1950, with a hope of more progress and less calamity, was due in large measure to his [Churchill's] exertions." Knowing that a British general election might soon be called, *Time* predicted that "[Churchill] would fight it—as he had fought all his other great battles—on the issue of freedom. Churchill likes freedom."[119]

Not all on the western shores of the Atlantic shared Luce's sentiments. James Reston, one of the premier political reporters at the *New York Times,* later wrote of a dinner party Churchill attended at the *Times* during his 1949 trip to America. "He [Churchill] looked considerably more rounded fore and aft.... There was a curious sort of grayness to his flesh.... He asked for a glass of tomato juice, which I thought was newsworthy, but corrected this impression when the brandy was passed around, and he complained that everybody kept him talking so much that he didn't have time to drink." Reston thought that Churchill "snorted and lisped more than usual, but this may have been induced by sobriety." As Churchill left, "a little shuffly and a little bent, Dr. Howard Rush, the *Times*'s favorite doctor, remarked, 'Jesus, prop him up.' I thought his [Churchill's] political days were over." Reston—Scotty to his friends—had been born in Scotland and grew up with a Scots Presbyterian's natural and ancient distrust of Englishmen. As for Churchill's political days being over, the often-prescient Reston got it wrong this time.[120]

Churchill planned to spend the first few weeks of 1950 at Reid's Hotel in Madeira. Clementine made the trip, as did Diana. Two secretaries and Bill Deakin accompanied Churchill; it was to be a working holiday. But in early January, Attlee called for a general election on February 23. Churchill packed his kit and returned to Chartwell to chart the Conservative campaign. Clementine stayed on in Madeira for a few days before returning to 28 Hyde Park Gate, where on January 19 she received a letter from her husband: "I have not thought of anything since I returned except politics." He and the Tory hierarchy had spent long days at Chartwell planning their manifesto. The problem, he told Clementine, was "not what to *do*" but "what to *say* to our poor and puzzled people." He noted that Gallup polls showed the Tory lead over Labour had fallen from nine to three points, but that four hundred Liberal candidates (running as spoilers and not expected to win many seats) would invariably skewer the final results. "How many seats the Liberal 'splits' will cause us cannot be measured." He thought that "at the outside" the Liberals might win seven seats. He closed with "I am much depressed about the country because for whoever wins there will be nothing but bitterness and strife, like men fighting savagely on a small raft which is breaking up. 'May God save you all' is my prayer."[121]

By the arrival of the new decade, his arteries had further hardened and he was going deaf. His ear, nose, and throat specialist told him he'd soon not be able to hear "the twittering of birds and children's piping voices." Churchill's walking stick no longer served as a fashion statement but served a practical purpose. Before the election campaign even got under way, Churchill summoned his doctor, Lord Moran. Everything had suddenly "gone misty," Churchill told Moran, and he asked, "Am I going to have another stroke?" Moran tried to reassure him by offering that he was likely experiencing "arterial spasms" when very tired. The patient looked up sharply and said, "You mustn't frighten me." It was Moran who was frightened, telling his diary, "This is a grim start to the racket of a General Election."[122]

Roy Jenkins, at the time the youngest MP—the Baby of the House—later wrote that Churchill conducted a more restrained campaign than in 1945. Churchill had the good sense to make no mention of a socialist Gestapo. And although he harangued the Labour Party and its cabal of intellectuals on their nationalization schemes, such topics as coal, steel, and railroads do not lend themselves to flights of oratorical fancy. On the foreign policy front, Churchill was more or less in agreement with Attlee and Bevin, who championed closer ties to the United States, the re-armament of Germany, and a containment policy toward the Soviets. Ignoring his doctor's advice to not stump the country, Churchill delivered eleven campaign speeches in cities and towns throughout the island, including Cardiff, Manchester, Edinburgh, Leeds, and three in his constituency of Woodford. The election was a family affair: Duncan Sandys, Christopher Soames, and Randolph were standing for office as well, and the Old Man campaigned for them. He kept bile out of his message, and instead reverted to humor and metaphor to skewer Labour. It was during this campaign that he coined the term

"Queuetopia." In Cardiff on February 8 he reduced Labour's stultifying jargon to silliness:

> I hope you have all mastered the official Socialist jargon which our masters, as they call themselves, wish us to learn. You must not use the word "poor"; they are described as the "lower income group." When it comes to a question of freezing a workman's wages the Chancellor of the Exchequer speaks of "arresting increases in personal income." ... There is a lovely one about houses and homes. They are in future to be called "accommodation units." I don't know how we are to sing our old song "Home Sweet Home." *"Accommodation Unit, Sweet Accommodation Unit, there's no place like our Accommodation Unit."* I hope to live to see the British democracy spit all this rubbish from their lips.[123]

In Edinburgh on February 14, he told the audience that "by one broad heave of the British national shoulders the whole gimcrack structure of Socialist jargon and malice may be cast in splinters to the ground." In his second campaign broadcast, delivered in London on the seventeenth, he again advised his countrymen to free themselves with one heave of their shoulders, and warned that they might not get a second chance to do so. Then he offered the parable of the Spanish prisoner who, after years of bondage, "pushed the door of his cell—and it was open. It had always been open. He walked out free into the broad light of day."[124]

In Leeds he warned:

> Remember also that, as a Socialist Prime Minister working for the establishment of a Socialist State, Mr. Attlee and his party are alone in the English-speaking world. The United States at the head of the world today vehemently repudiate the Socialist doctrine. Canada repudiates it.... Remember also there is no Socialist Government in Europe outside the Iron Curtain and Scandinavia. It seems to me a very perilous path that we are asked to tread, and to tread alone among the free democracies of the West.[125]

It was during the Edinburgh address that Churchill made his most important foreign policy statement of the campaign, and in so doing not only coined the term "summit meeting" but outlined a belief that would underlie his relations with both America and Russia for the remainder of his political life. First came a warning: "The Soviet Communist world has by far the greatest military force, but the United States have the atom bomb; and now, we are told that they have a thousand fold more terrible manifestation of this awful power." Although the United States had lost its monopoly on atomic bombs, it had a great many in its arsenal. "When all is said and done it is my belief that the superiority [in numbers] in the atom bomb...in American hands is the surest guarantee of world peace tonight." Then:

> Still I cannot help coming back to this idea of another talk with Soviet Russia upon the highest level. The idea appeals to me of a supreme effort to bridge the gulf between the two worlds, so that each can live their life, if not in friendship at least without the hatreds of the cold war. You must be careful to mark my words in these matters because I have not always been proved wrong. It is not easy to see how things could be worsened by a parley at the summit, if such a thing were possible. But that I cannot tell.[126]

He repeated the theme a few days later during his London broadcast: "It is only by the agreement of the greatest Powers that security can be given to ordinary folk against an annihilating war with atomic or hydrogen bombs or bacteriological horrors. I cannot find it in my heart and conscience to close the door upon that hope." This was his first mention of "hydrogen bombs." In Edinburgh he had referred only to weapons a "thousand fold" more powerful than atomic bombs. Indeed, the power of thermonuclear weapons (hydrogen bombs, or H-bombs) is reckoned in megatons versus kilotons for atomic bombs, and in this new calculus Churchill beheld the horrifying difference between the two weapons. One could destroy cities, the other civilization. Five years earlier he had seen the A-bomb as merely the biggest bomb in the arsenal. No more. The Americans were yet two years away from exploding an H-bomb, but in early 1950 Churchill saw—the first world leader to do so—that the enormity of that weapon must preclude its use. Churchill's vivid imagination, not cold logic, drove his thinking on the matter. He had seen London burn once; he could now shut his eyes and behold the entire nation in flames, the entire world. The conclusion was obvious: world wars could still be fought, but could no longer be won.[127]

On Election Day, February 23, Churchill told some Tory cronies that he'd drop into the Savoy later that evening to stand a round of drinks if the early returns showed promise. He never appeared, but rather closeted himself at Hyde Park Gate to listen as the BBC reported the early returns from the larger cities. Labour was holding its own. By late in the morning of the twenty-fourth, town and country returns evidenced a shift to the Tories. But it wasn't enough. Labour saw its great majority of 1945 all but erased, a stunning turnaround and a defeat by any other name, but Attlee and his government survived, barely. The final results showed Labour held 315 seats (13,331,000 votes); the Conservatives 298 seats (12,415,000 votes); and the Liberals 9 seats (mostly in Wales, 2,679,000 votes). That gave Labour an overall majority of six. Churchill, Christopher Soames, and Duncan Sandys fared well, but not Randolph, who for the fourth time in four contested elections was rejected by voters. In a sense, Labour had lost the election—certainly it had lost its mandate—but the Conservatives and Churchill had not won it.

Churchill was seventy-five. He complained to his doctor of tightness in his shoulders and he feared another stroke. Time was now the enemy. But in one regard time was also his ally. Turmoil among the leadership of the Labour party, any internal Labour dissent on matters of budgets, banking, or defense, would lead to a vote of no confidence. In America Churchill would have had to wait four years before another shot at the top, but in Britain—especially in Attlee's Britain, that year—another general election might be called within months. Although Anthony Eden, Rab Butler, and Harold Macmillan each aspired to higher status within the party leadership (and ultimately the leadership itself), Churchill's position as leader was secure. Under his command, the Conservatives had retrieved 85 of the seats they had lost in 1945, and Labour had lost 78. Those Tories who had wanted Churchill to take a long rest in 1945 would have to wait their turn. They could not throw over the man who had brought them this far, in war and in peace. Churchill, therefore, though disappointed by the election results, was not shattered. He believed that his day would yet come. He returned to Chartwell to continue work on his memoirs—only two volumes remained. He prepared, too, for the new Parliament and the battles sure to be fought there. Late one night not long after the election, while dictating a section of his memoir, he turned to Jane Portal and announced, "I know I'm going to be Prime Minister again. I know it."[128]

One among the family was not shattered in the least by the election results: Clementine. Chartwell was her safe haven; the guest list included children and grandchildren and old friends. In 1945 she believed Winston should have retired, and she believed so still. Increasingly afflicted with neuritis, streptococcal infections, and by a bout of lumbago later in the year, she was ready for a pacific retirement at Chartwell. It was not to be.

On March 6, the new Parliament opened with the traditional Gracious Speech, the King's message to the Houses of Lords and Commons. The next day, March 7, the first day of debate, Churchill made clear his intent to press his attacks on the socialist experiment: "The basic fact before us is that the electors by a majority of 1,750,000 have voted against the advance to a Socialist State, and, in particular, against the nationalization of steel and other industries which were threatened. The Government, therefore, have no mandate." He moved that a full debate of all issues "be accorded us in the next fortnight or so." Hansard transcripts record the following exchange:

Mr. H. Morrison [Speaker of the House] indicated dissent.

Mr. Churchill: It will take more than the oscillation of the Lord President's head in this Parliament necessarily to convince us that our desires must be put aside; I ask for a full Debate.[129]

He pressed his attacks for the next twenty months. Debates (and Questions) in the House of Commons are far livelier affairs than business conducted in either the Senate or House of the United States, where long and often boring statements are read into the Congressional Record by members (often to an empty chamber), and where oral interruptions are considered breaches of decorum. In the British House of Commons "Rubbish" and "Nonsense" are oft-heard rejoinders. Laughter—and its cousin the snicker—is a weapon. Members mumble and rustle papers in shows of displeasure at an opponent's words (or mumble and rustle papers in agreement with their party colleagues). Churchill came to do battle. His political nemesis Aneurin Bevan described Churchill's approach to the House thus: "He had to wheel himself up to battle like an enormous gun." When Churchill fired a salvo, his opponents knew it.[130]

Labour MPs once jeered Churchill as he was leaving the chamber; he turned and blew them kisses. No barb could go unanswered. When Churchill castigated Labour for the fiscal hardships Britons lived with, a Labour MP called out, "Why don't you sell your *horse?*" Churchill looked up, and replied, "I was strongly tempted to sell the horse, but I am doing my best *to fight against the profit motive.*" A nod of dissent, a derisive grunt, were gauntlets thrown down. When a member mumbled, "Rubbish," to one Churchill pronouncement, the Old Man replied, "That may be what the right honourable and learned Gentleman has in his head, but it does not carry conviction." When a member called out, "Rubbish," after Churchill claimed Czechoslovakia had become a pawn of Moscow, the Old Man replied: "The right honourable Gentleman seems to have nothing in his head but rubbish." Interrupted during one debate on Moscow's geopolitical intentions, Churchill shot back, "I think the Communist Members and fellow travelers have a pretty good run in this House." Here was an incendiary claim that even the junior senator from Wisconsin,

Joseph McCarthy, would not make on the U.S. Senate floor. But Churchill could toss out such a retort without causing an uproar, because all knew he was without guile. As well, wrote Tory MP Earl Winterton (who in 1950 was the Father of the House, its longest-serving member), Churchill could read the mood of the House: "Winston Churchill is steeped in its atmosphere and traditions; he is familiar with all its varying moods ... he has an instinctive understanding of what it will accept and what it will not accept." The British House of Commons was populated by agile minds and quick wits, and after almost fifty years, Winston Churchill was still one of the most agile and quick-witted. Indeed, at about that time, Winterton called him "the greatest living parliamentarian."[131]

Another colleague, Sir Alan Herbert, the Independent MP for Oxford University, called Churchill "the greatest living British humorist." When giving lectures on the topic of humor, Herbert cited the usual suspects: P. G. Wodehouse, Noël Coward, Nat Gubbins, even Aneurin Bevan. But Herbert's top choice was "Winston Churchill, who, at any time, in any conditions, in any company, on any subject, with never a fault of taste or tact, can make laughter when he wills."[132]

Not all agreed. Roy Jenkins believed Churchill's humor was sometimes "not ... wise ... or gracious" as a result of "one of Churchill's narrownesses"—his hostility to left-wing intellectuals. Churchill believed incorrectly that Labour's leading lights were all products of Winchester College, which he considered a breeding ground of the casuistry he saw and detested in certain intellectuals. Indeed, Hugh Gaitskell and Stafford Cripps, among several other Labour leaders, had come out of Winchester. As a result, Jenkins wrote, Churchill made "constant not very funny anti-Wykehamical [anti-Winchester] jokes in the House." He did, but one man's humor is another man's poison. Churchill, responding to a Labour claim: "We suffer from the fallacy, *deus ex machina*, which, for the benefit of any Wykehamists who may be present, is 'A god out of the machine.'" On another occasion: "I do not know whether they learn French at Winchester." And during a June 27, 1950, debate on British participation in a European coal and steel community, Churchill tossed out: "In this Debate we have had the usual jargon about 'the infrastructure of a supra-national authority.' The original authorship is obscure; but it may well be that these words 'infra' and 'supra' have been introduced into our current political parlance by the band of intellectual highbrows who are naturally anxious to impress British labour with the fact that they learned Latin at Winchester." In fact, the word "infrastructure," a perfectly good Latin-derived word, had come out of France, but Churchill never missed a chance to ridicule his political enemies.[133]

The "supranational authority" under discussion was known as the

Schuman Plan, proposed on May 9 by French foreign minister Robert Schuman, who called on European nations to join together in a community dedicated to shedding tariffs and sharing resources—coal and steel, to start with—in order to regain a competitive edge in the international marketplace and, most significant, to eliminate the resource monopolization that inevitably ended in European wars. Schuman called for talks in Paris. The Attlee government refused to participate, a decision Churchill denounced as "a squalid attitude at a time of present stress." He was not advising a blanket acceptance of the Schuman Plan, but merely a willingness to discuss it. He added that if asked, would he "agree to a supranational authority which has the power to tell Great Britain not to cut any more coal or make any more steel, but to grow tomatoes instead?' I should say, without hesitation, the answer is 'No.' " What he opposed, he said, "is State ownership and management—or mismanagement as it has proved so far—of the industry." He pointed out that under Schuman's proposal, private ownership of industry remained unaffected, adding, "We see no reason why the problems of the British steel industry should not be discussed in common with the problems of the other European steel industries."

And he pointed out the ultimate beauty of the plan: it would bring France and Germany together in mutually beneficial enterprises. It would be "an effective step," Churchill told a meeting of Scottish Unionists, "in preventing another war between France and Germany and lay at last to rest that quarrel of 1,000 years between Gaul and Teuton. Now France has taken the initiative in a manner beyond my hopes." He told the House during the debate of June 27 that to reach this day was why Britain had refused to quit in 1940:

> We fought alone against tyranny for a whole year, not purely from national motives. . . . It was not only our own cause but a world cause for which the Union Jack was kept flying in 1940. . . . The Conservative and Liberal parties declare that national sovereignty is not inviolable, and that it may be resolutely diminished for the sake of all the men in all the lands finding their way home together.

He predicted the consequences if Attlee refused participation in the talks about the Schuman Plan:

> The absence of Britain deranges the balance of Europe. I am all for a reconciliation between France and Germany, and for receiving Germany back into the European family, but this implies, as I have always insisted, that Britain and France should in the main act together so as

to be able to deal on even terms with Germany, which is so much stronger than France alone. Without Britain, the coal and steel pool in western Europe must naturally tend to be dominated by Germany, who will be the most powerful member.[134]

Attlee stood firm; he would not send any ministers to Paris.

Schuman held his meetings without the British. Almost a year later, in April 1951, France, Italy, West Germany, Belgium, Luxembourg, and the Netherlands signed the Treaty of Paris and by so doing created the European Coal and Steel Community. The six states pledged to create a "common market" for steel and coal. Here, then, was the first step on the road to the European Economic Community and, ultimately, the European Union. May 9—the date Schuman first read his proposal in the French National Assembly—is now celebrated by European Union member nations as Europe Day. (The Council of Europe, which Churchill championed, is not part of the European Union; its member states do not transfer any national legislative or executive sovereignty to the body, which acts through international legal conventions.) The evolution of Schuman's concept into the European Union is a long and fascinating story, but it is not Churchill's story. Events on the other side of the globe that June week in 1950 changed the trajectory of Churchill's thinking, and the final years of his career.

On June 25, the Cold War turned hot. On that day, 230,000 North Korean soldiers, supported by more than 250 Russian-made T-34 battle tanks (the best tank on the planet) and as many pieces of heavy artillery, drove south across the 38th parallel and into South Korea. South Korean forces were outnumbered by more than two to one in men. They had no tanks. On the twenty-seventh, the day the Commons debated the Schuman Plan, the United Nations passed Security Council Resolution 83, calling on member states to offer military support to South Korea. Moscow did not vote, having boycotted the Security Council for six months. The next day, the South Korean government fled Seoul. Within four weeks, the North Koreans had bottled up the South's army and the American Eighth Army in the southeast corner of the Korean peninsula, near Pusan. Given that the North Koreans were clients—proxies—of Moscow, Churchill and the West had to entertain the very real possibility that with the attention of the United States drawn to Korea, Moscow might strike in Europe. If that came to pass, Europe west of the Iron Curtain was virtually defenseless.

Overnight, Churchill's Europeanism became far more narrowly focused. Coal and steel matters could wait. There was now only one priority: the creation of a unified European defense force. By the same token, Churchill's Atlanticist vision, too, became more narrowly focused: America, which had all but abandoned Europe in 1945, had to be brought back into the European picture, in force.

In June 1950, the NATO treaty of 1949 was backed up by nothing more than the paper it was printed on. In 1945, more than 2.8 million American soldiers and almost 300,000 airmen served in Europe. By 1946, 90 percent of both had gone home. By mid-1950, only 80,000 American troops and 20,000 airmen remained, and many of those were support troops.

In late July, based on figures supplied by the Attlee government, Churchill outlined to the House the situation in Europe. The Russians fielded 40,000 tanks; how many were deployed in Europe was unknown, but Stalin had little reason to deploy tanks east of the Urals. The Americans and British each possessed about 6,000 tanks; America's were sitting in America but for a couple of hundred in Europe. Soviet troop strength stood at least at 175 divisions, including 25 or more armored divisions, versus a total of a dozen French, American, and British divisions, of which only two were armored. The East Germans had been allowed by Moscow to create a defense force of 50,000, even though the Red Army provided more than enough men to defend East Germany. That was the status on the ground.[135]

When it came to the air, nobody in HMG seemed to know how many aircraft the Soviets had, perhaps as many as 19,000. And how many of them were stationed within range of Britain? Again, nobody knew. Churchill hammered away at the Attlee government's decision to sell one hundred jet fighters to Argentina, which claimed sovereignty over the Falkland Islands, and another 110 to Egypt, which was blocking Israeli ship traffic in the Suez Canal. What British air forces were available, he asked, to protect those American bombers in East Anglia? If the Soviets had only fifty atomic bombs, he told the House, and if Moscow dropped some of them on Britain, "It would not be pleasant." The Soviets had captured the German rocket works at Peenemünde, he reminded the House, and had learned enough to launch devastating guided missile attacks (armed with conventional warheads) against Britain. And on the seas—or under them—the Soviet U-boat menace appeared to be "far more severe than was the German U-boat force in 1939 and 1940." The European situation was beginning to look like the mid-1930s again, with an existential threat in the East, and Britain unprepared to defend itself. Churchill began again to sound like the voice from the 1930s wilderness. He warned the

House that if the Soviets threw only half their strength against the West, the West would be outnumbered by at least eight to one. He added: "If the facts that I have stated cannot be contradicted by His Majesty's Government, the preparations of the Western Union to defend itself certainly stand on a far lower level than those of the South Koreans."[136]

Ever since Fulton, Churchill's hopes for world peace had rested with the deterrent of the atomic bomb. The Americans now stationed 180 "atomic bombers" in East Anglia. Moscow was aware of that figure because Attlee had announced it in the Commons. But Churchill sought—demanded—a British atomic deterrent. For four years he had pressed the Attlee government to reveal its progress, if any, in building a British atomic bomb, and for four years Attlee had disclosed nothing. His government was, in fact, hard at work building a bomb, for the same reason Churchill would have pursued the matter: to guarantee British sovereignty. Attlee was as determined as Churchill that British foreign policy and defense not be held hostage to the whims and wishes of the U.S. State Department or White House. Attlee's refusal to discuss his atomic plans was proper; Churchill led the opposition, not HMG. Some in Britain concluded that the fourteen inscrutable men in the Kremlin had no design on Western Europe for the simple reason that Moscow could take it with impunity if it so desired, and since it had not, ergo, it had no desire to do so. This was the sort of convoluted logic—peace through trust—that infuriated Churchill. His position was clear, and he had stated it repeatedly since 1945, including to his New York hosts months earlier: "It is certain in my opinion that Europe would have been communized and London would have been under bombardment some time ago, but for the deterrent of the atomic bomb in the hands of the United States. That is my firm belief and that governs the situation today." As for trusting to the goodwill of Stalin after the experience of trusting Hitler, who had claimed too many times that his appetite for geography was satisfied, Churchill added: "Well, once bit, twice shy."[137]

In July, shortly after the North Koreans invaded the south, and with his stances on the need to re-arm and build a British atomic bomb in mind, he told a Plymouth audience, "The fourteen men in the Kremlin are not drifting with events. They work on calculation and design. They have a policy the aim of which we can see; but the execution and timing of their ambition for Communist world government we cannot predict." He told a London audience: "We have always to be very careful nowadays—we politicians, if we take an interest in military matters, or are held to have accumulated some knowledge and experience about them—lest we should be described for electioneering purposes as warmongers." In fact, Labour and many in the press slapped that label on him now on a regular basis. Yet, if the state of Western arms (other than the atomic bomb) was the measure, he was correct. France, which in 1940 sent 140 divisions against Hitler, now fielded fewer than ten. Britain had difficulty assembling a token force of one brigade to send to Korea in support of the Americans. Harold Macmillan told his diary: "It seems that to scrape together 3000 men and their equipment for Korea will take two months!...What have they done to the war equipment? It would appear that they have thrown it into the seas."[138]

On July 27 Churchill moved that the House go into secret session—"I spy strangers"—in order to address the status of the British atomic bomb. His motion lost by a single vote, 295 to 296. But if Churchill continued to push for divisions—votes—the day would come when Labour would lose one, and then another. The day would arrive when Attlee would have to call a general election. "Mismanagement" was the word Churchill now introduced into almost every critique of the Attlee government: "the mismanagement of the housing problem"; "the mismanagement in civil and domestic affairs"; "the mismanagement of our defence forces." And this, directed at Attlee in the House: "The Prime Minister has appealed to us for national unity on Defence. That does not mean national unity on mismanagement of Defence."[139]

His message—and the phrases he used to deliver it—recalled the previous decade: "We must never despair. We must never give in," he told the House. "Our scientific and technical ability is unsurpassed. We may well have time to reorganize and develop the mighty latent strength of Britain surrounded by her Commonwealth. But I warn the House that we have as great dangers to face in 1950 and 1951 as we had ten years ago." The next day Harold Nicolson told his diary that the "state of public opinion after Winston's grim speech...is one of paralyzed shock....We are in a position of blind and dumb dread."[140]

The next week, in early August, the Consultative Assembly of the Council of Europe met for the second time in Strasbourg. "Consultative" was the operative word: motions passed by the Assembly were nonbinding on the governments of member nations. Schuman was there to present his plan. Paul Reynaud, now France's defense minister, was on hand. The Germans sent two contingents, one of Socialists and one made up of members of the conservative Christian Democratic Union, whose leader, Konrad Adenauer, had been elected in 1949 the first chancellor of the Federal Democratic Republic of Germany—West Germany. British socialists led by Hugh Dalton were in attendance, as were Duncan Sandys, Harold Macmillan, and Winston Churchill for the Conservatives. On August 11, Churchill addressed the Assembly. He welcomed the Germans, and called for "a real defensive front in Europe" formed by a continental army made up of "large forces" of Americans, Britons, the French, Greeks, Italians, the Scandinavian countries, and the Low Countries. He forgot to mention the Germans, but his intent was clear. It would take compromise and sacrifice, he warned, and then he added words that anticipated the inaugural address of a young American president a decade later: "Those who serve supreme causes must not consider what they can get but what they can give." He ended by offering a motion calling for "the immediate creation of a unified European Army subject to proper European democratic control and acting in full co-operation with the United States and Canada."[141]

Macmillan thought the speech masterful, delivered with power and touches of humor that found their mark. "It is really more like a broadcast than a speech," he told his diary. "But then the trouble is that WSC's broadcasts *are* speeches." Churchill staked his reputation on his motion; defeat could end his long crusade for some sort of federal European structure, and certainly would mean the end of the idea of collective European security. He had addressed no details of command and control of such a European army, knowing that offering details might undermine the whole edifice. The French were wary of the Germans. The Germans were afraid of re-arming, believing that any German army would be large enough to provoke the Russians but not strong enough to repel them. The German General Staff had been abolished; Germans who served in a European army would therefore serve under the command of other nationalities. Macmillan, fearing that German volunteers would likely be former Nazis, preferred an army of conscripts—that is, if the Germans agreed to an army of any sort. The members of the Assembly pondered all of this and more before taking their vote. "No one is quite sure what turn the debate will take," Macmillan wrote.

The vote came in at 89 for the motion, 5 against, with 27 abstentions (including most of the British socialists). "It is strange," Macmillan wrote that week, "how, abroad as well as at home, what Churchill puts forward one year as a daring paradox, becomes an accepted truism a year later." Macmillan dined with Churchill the night of the vote, and found the Old Man "to be *very* pleased and *very* excited." Given that the object of the Europeanists was to bring about reconciliation between Germany and France, Churchill had "a right to be pleased. Without his immense personal prestige, which he has thrown quite recklessly into this campaign, it might not have been achieved."[142]

In mid-September two divisions of U.S. forces under the overall command of General Douglas MacArthur staged an amphibious assault at Inchon, in northwest South Korea. The invasion was a stunning success; within two weeks the Inchon forces and the Pusan armies met and then drove the North Koreans back across the 38th parallel. Pyongyang, the North Korean capital, was liberated, "the first Communist capital to be liberated by the forces of the free world," crowed *Time*. By late October, UN forces were chasing the North Korean army up the peninsula toward the Yalu River, the border with China. MacArthur declared that the boys might well be home by Christmas. In mid-November MacArthur informed George Marshall—the new secretary of defense—that he was launching a general offensive by the U.S. Eighth Army northward to the Yalu, to detect how many, if any, Chinese might be in North Korea, and to secure the peninsula once and for all. In defiance of the most basic military doctrine, MacArthur divided the Eighth Army into four separate columns. MacArthur had earlier told President Truman that at most three hundred thousand Chinese might get into the fray but that he did not believe the Chinese would send in any forces. But they did. The Eighth Army had almost reached the Chinese border in northwest North Korea when, on November 25, one million Chinese troops smashed into the American lines, into the flanks, even into the rear of some forces. The Chinese armies, hidden on both sides of the Yalu in deep mountain passes, had gone completely undetected by the Allies. By the end of the year, UN forces—mostly American—had been driven back over the 38th parallel, and in the weeks that followed, driven eighty miles south of Seoul, which again was lost. It was the longest retreat in American history.[143]

On November 30, Churchill's seventy-sixth birthday, President Truman told reporters that the UN would not abandon its mission in Korea. He followed that with a promise to "take whatever steps are necessary" to meet military objectives. A reporter asked if the atomic bomb might be one such step. Truman replied that use of the atomic bomb was under "active consideration." That statement, Dean Acheson later wrote, and a false news report that MacArthur might be given authority to use the bomb, threw the Attlee government into a panic, and resulted in Attlee's "scurrying across the ocean" to meet with Truman. Macmillan saw Truman's remark as a typically "diplomatic" response, "a cliché as a synonym for doing nothing." Attlee saw it as a step toward atomic war. The prime minister, in Macmillan's words, "bolted, like a rabbit, from his hole, and is off to Washington (what a picture and what a contrast to the great Churchill days)."[144]

Macmillan and Churchill did not know—and would not learn for another year—that Attlee had good reason to fret about the American position. The previous year Attlee had agreed to abolish the Anglo-American Combined Chiefs of Staff organization. That body had been critical to

Churchill's plans for continued Anglo-American military cooperation. Attlee shared Churchill's desire for a continuation of the Anglo-American partnership, but whereas Churchill had always badgered the Americans for a real role in that relationship—even in 1944, when Britain was clearly the junior partner—Attlee had willingly assumed the subservient role. He had twice in 1950—in secret—assured Washington that if American air forces commenced bombing operations in China, Britain would commit her air forces to the cause. In doing so, he had written Washington a blank check. Now, with Truman mumbling about the possibility of using the atomic bomb in Korea or China, Attlee had to either stop payment or secure guarantees from Truman that Britain would be consulted if any such measure was taken under consideration. Thus, Attlee went to Washington in early December with hopes of resurrecting the gentleman's agreement on the use of the atomic bomb that Churchill and Roosevelt had forged in 1943, which stipulated that neither country would use the bomb without the approval of the other, but which the McMahon Act of 1946 had effectively quashed. In this, Attlee failed utterly. Truman flatly refused to "consult" with the British, or anyone, on how America would defend itself. Truman offered to keep Attlee "informed" as a courtesy, but there'd be no "consultation."

Dean Acheson, by then secretary of state, let Attlee down gently by explaining that any agreement made between the president and another leader was considered by the U.S. Senate to be a treaty, and therefore subject to Senate approval. As the talks progressed, Acheson realized Attlee had arrived with other items on his agenda, including the need to negotiate with—and mollify—China. More than 60,000 British and Commonwealth troops served in Korea during that war, including legendary regiments such as the Black Watch, the Royal Canadian Regiment, the King's Own Scottish Borderers, and the Royal Irish Fusiliers. But the Americans sent 450,000 men, and the prospects of those now on the ground appeared bleak. Presuming more defeats were imminent, Attlee proposed that Truman offer a cease-fire in order to pull out the troops. Acheson told Attlee that to negotiate with the Chinese after taking "a licking" was the absolute wrong policy. State Department policy was based on George Kennan's belief (shared by Churchill) that to negotiate with Communists from a position of weakness was to invite disaster. "To cut and run," Acheson later wrote, "was not acceptable conduct." Attlee also proposed that the time was right to give the Communist Chinese government a seat in the UN. He was hoping, as Tories saw it, to detach China from Moscow through kindness. Nothing, he told Truman, was more important than relations with China, to which Acheson replied "acidly" that "the security of the United States was more important." Attlee was in an appeasement frame of mind. "Clement Attlee," Acheson later wrote, "was a far abler man than Winston Churchill's description of him as 'a sheep in sheep's clothing' would imply, but persistently depressing."[145]

When the House of Commons adjourned in December for the winter holidays, it did so from its rebuilt chamber, where it first met in late October. It had been almost ten years since a German bomb had obliterated the old chamber. Clement Attlee generously named a surviving stone arch the Churchill Arch. The new chamber was built to hold only two-thirds of the members, a design Churchill had suggested, such that if only half the members showed up, the room would appear almost full. The decision to build the chamber so, Churchill told the House, confused many around the world who "cannot easily be made to understand why we consider that the intensity, passion, intimacy, informality and spontaneity of our Debates constitute the personality of the House of Commons and endow it at once with its focus and its strength." He offered, "I am a child of the House of Commons and have been here I believe longer than anyone. I was much upset when I was violently thrown out of my collective cradle. I certainly wanted to get back to it as soon as possible." Five years after V-E day, the House of Commons had been restored to its prewar splendor, but Britain had not been, and the Empire never would be.[146]

In London that December, the weather turned depressing, and snow and ice and low temperatures persisted through the New Year. This was Churchill's travel season. He left mid-month for five weeks in Marrakech, where Clementine was to join him in early January. On Christmas Day he wrote his wife a short note from the Hotel La Mamounia, where he spent his days painting and his evenings dining on champagne and Marennes oysters. He asked after all the animals at Chartwell—the golden orfes, the Black Mollies, the black swans, and Rufus. He had no distractions, and was hard at work on the sixth and final volume of his memoirs. Of Korea, he wrote: "Much depends on the coming battle."[147]

In London, there was talk of an Eastern Munich. Harold Nicolson now regretted his switch to the Labour Party and its failing socialist experiment. On New Year's Eve Nicolson told his diary: "So ends a horrible year with worse to come.... We are all oppressed by a terrible sense of weakness and foreboding.... The year closes in a mist of anxiety. We shall be lucky if we get through 1951 without a war.... It is sad to become old amid such darkness."[148]

Harold Macmillan began expressing similar sentiments to his diary and continued to do so well into the late summer. In January: "The British Govt has almost ceased to function. The P.M. doodles or talks platitudes; the Foreign Secretary has pneumonia; there are no rearmament plans, no economic plan, and now—no coal!" As in 1947, Britons stoked their fires and pulled on another sweater in anticipation of a long, cold, lonely winter. On January 22 Macmillan wrote: "It is tragic that at such a moment we should have Attlee and Bevin....Churchill is still painting in Marrakesh!"[149]

He was. But if he was to fight his final battle against Attlee and for the premiership, he needed his rest and his strength, which he nourished over eight days with numerous picnics, long evening meals on his veranda, and painting. Still, he managed to proof eight chapters of volume 6 of his war memoirs as well as work on the final draft of the U.S. Book-of-the-Month Club edition of volume 5. He daubed, dictated, and dined until January 20. He returned to London by way of Paris, where on the twenty-second he dined with Madame Odette Pol-Roger, the beautiful socialite whose company and champagne he thoroughly enjoyed (he later named one of his racehorses for her). Churchill arrived in London on the twenty-third, and set to work to bring down the Attlee government.

Britain by then was losing prestige along with the Empire. It could not mediate the Kashmir border dispute. It could not protect Malayan rubber plantations from roving bands of Communist guerrillas. The news from Korea only worsened. In April, the 1st battalion of the Gloucestershire Regiment was surrounded by Chinese forces and annihilated—704 of 750 men were killed or captured. The news from the Middle East became increasingly worrisome. The Egyptian government denied passage through the Suez Canal to British oil tankers bound for the refinery at Haifa, this in abrogation of international agreements.

Then, in late April, the Iranian parliament elected Mohammad Mosaddegh—Churchill called him Mousy Duck—prime minister. The Shah, whom the British and Americans had put on the Peacock Throne a decade earlier, appointed Mosaddegh premier. On May 1, Mosaddegh nationalized the British Anglo-Iranian Oil Company, including its refineries at Abadan. The Attlee government pledged to not abandon the Abadan complex, but failed to explain whether it would meet that pledge through force or negotiation. It resorted to neither.

In February, Labour won a no-confidence vote by a majority of 9. A vote on steel nationalization went to Labour by 10 votes. Remarkably, almost the entire House showed up for these sessions, and divided strictly along party lines, with the Liberals sometimes splitting their few votes. The *Times* speculated that if an influenza outbreak that was then spreading through the land kept enough Labourites from appearing in the Commons, the government might fall. Macmillan told his diary he hadn't seen such attendance—and such partisanship—since the General Strike of 1926. On the day following the steel vote, Labour won a referendum on meat rationing by eight votes. Macmillan scribbled in his diary: "The people do not go into little shops every weekend to buy a piece of steel. But they do grumble every weekend about their minute portion of meat."[150]

The Attlee government hung on, but just. When Labour came to power in 1945, the party was led by the Big Five: Attlee, Ernest Bevin (Foreign Office), Herbert Morrison (leader of the House), Sir Stafford Cripps (Board of Trade), and Hugh Dalton (Exchequer). By the end of 1947, Dalton was out, having been driven from the Exchequer for the egregious offense of leaking vital parts of HMG's budget to a reporter, before the House saw the budget and while the stock market was still open. Cripps took over at the Exchequer, where he raised taxes and forced a reduction in consumer spending, in order, he hoped, to raise exports. He failed. Morrison, who according to Colville "was not short of ambition," sought to maneuver Attlee out of the party chairmanship and himself in. Bevin, a bitter enemy of Morrison, refused to accede to that notion. After five years of marshaling nationalization schemes through the House, Morrison took over the Foreign Office when Bevin finally resigned due to ill health in March 1951. He was dead a month later. Bevin had always been on the opposite side of the House from Churchill, but like Churchill he was a great English patriot. Attlee, who was in the hospital with a duodenal ulcer, could not even pay tribute to Bevin in the House.

Cripps, too, had departed the scene. Plagued by severe digestive distress that his vegetarian diet failed to ameliorate, he resigned from Parliament and the cabinet in 1950, and took himself off to a Swiss sanatorium. He died two years later. Hugh Gaitskell, who also had his eye on the party leadership, succeeded him at the Exchequer in October 1950. When in early April 1951 Gaitskell announced plans to reel in costs associated with Aneurin Bevan's National Health Service by forcing Britons to pay half of their of eye care and dental expenses, and to contribute one shilling (about twenty-five cents) to their prescription costs, Bevan resigned in protest. Two days later, the head of the Board of Trade resigned. When Harold Macmillan heard the news, he told his diary, "If this is true, the Government must fall, and a general election follow."[151]

By the summer of 1951, in contrast to the fractious and disputatious Labour leadership, the Conservatives, led by Churchill, in harness with

Eden, Lord Woolton, Oliver Lyttelton, Rab Butler, Duncan Sandys, and
Harold Macmillan, presented a unified opposition front, with Churchill
firmly in the role of party leader.

By then, House debates, sometimes lasting all night, regularly descended
into bitter shouting matches, with Churchill often being the object of the
invective. But he gave as good as he got. When the minister of defence,
Emanuel Shinwell, muttered his disagreement over re-arming Germany,
Churchill shot back, "Oh shut up. Go and talk to the Italians; that's all
you're fit for." That outburst resulted in one hundred Labour MPs signing
and sending an apology to the Italian government, which in turn demanded
an apology from Churchill, who gave one. During a May debate on the
matter of the Attlee government continuing to sell Malay rubber and other
raw materials to China over the strident objection of the United States
(Churchill opposed the sales), a member shouted, "Do not write down
[criticize] your country all the time." Churchill replied: "Will the honourable Member yell it out again?" The member did just that. *"Sit down!"*
"Untrue!" *"Get out!"* and *"Give way!"* were regularly yelled from both
benches. When Churchill once averred that he only wanted to do what was
best for Britain, a member called out, *"Resign!"* An extraordinary
exchange took place during a July debate on the handling of the Suez and
Iranian crises, when Herbert Morrison, recently elevated to foreign secretary, interrupted Churchill with "They are laughing at the right honourable Gentleman behind him." Churchill replied, "I expect that the right
honourable Gentleman wishes that he had such cordial relations with his
own back-benchers." But Churchill could not leave it there, for Morrison
had recently told an audience of coal miners that Churchill and the Tories
sought war in both Egypt and Iran. Morrison, Churchill declared, "shows
to all the world that his main thought in life is to be a caucus boss and a
bitter party electioneer." Churchill added, "It is tragic indeed that at this
time his distorted, twisted and malevolent mind should be the one to which
our Foreign Affairs are confided."[152]

That night Macmillan told his diary that Churchill's performance was
"one of his most devastating and polished efforts." Under a mass of Labour
"chaff and invective," Churchill "thus established a complete ascendancy
over the party and indeed over the House." He had, but although he had
recovered from his hernia operation and had experienced no minor strokes
for two years, such exertions took an increasing toll on his health. House
debates were trying, and sessions sometimes lasted until morning, an
ordeal even for a younger man. Lord Moran told his diary that if Churchill
"goes back to No. 10, I doubt whether he is up to the job...he has lost
ground and has no longer the same grip on things and events." And Moran,
worried about Churchill's mental health if he did not go back to No. 10,

told his diary, "When the struggle for power is at an end, and his political life is over, Winston will feel there is no purpose in his existence. I dread what may happen then."[153]

All now expected Attlee to call for a general election, with polling likely to take place in October, after the late summer vacation season.

Although Clementine wanted nothing more than to retire from political life, she did not discourage Winston in his quest for No. 10. Yet neither did she encourage him. She believed that his reputation could not be enhanced by another term at the top, and would most likely be damaged. She preferred that husband and wife live out their days at Chartwell, where she had finally found happiness. Their neighbors accepted the family now, whereas in the past they had considered Churchill something of an enfant terrible, and local merchants had considered the family a poor credit risk. All had changed, Mary later wrote. Neighbors were proud of having the Churchills in their midst, and the Churchills for their part became more outgoing and welcoming. Winston and Clementine now opened the Chartwell gardens four times each summer, admission was charged, and the proceeds donated to local charities.

Clementine, though ten years her husband's junior, lacked his energy and was easily exhausted—mentally and physically—by the strains of the political life. In May she had undergone a hysterectomy; in July she continued her convalescence near Biarritz, on the Bay of Biscay, in the company of Mary. In mid-August, with Parliament in summer recess, Churchill (and two secretaries, his valet, and Christopher Soames) set off for Paris to rendezvous with Clementine and Mary. From Paris the party traveled to the Rhone Alps region, where they planned to spend two weeks in the sun at Lake Annecy, near the Swiss border. But the sun failed to shine. Instead, a cold rain fell for a week, at which time Clementine and the Soameses returned to London, while Churchill prepared to take himself and his retinue off to Geneva by train, and from there to Venice, where he expected the bathing on the Lido would be more enjoyable. Told that the French train to Geneva did not stop at the Annecy station, Churchill instructed one of his secretaries to inform the stationmaster that Winston Churchill wishes that the train be stopped in order for Winston Churchill to board. The train was stopped. Churchill and party boarded, along with fifty-five suitcases and trunks and sixty-five smaller articles.[154]

On September 20, a week after Churchill returned to London, Attlee sent him a short note: "My dear Churchill," it read. "I have decided to have a general election in October." He added that he would issue a formal declaration after that night's nine o'clock news. The elections were set for October 25.[155]

Churchill, at seventy-six, knew that this was his final chance to attain his lifelong goal of being sent to No. 10 Downing Street by a vote of the English people. Defeat would mean retirement to the Weald. In a Tory defeat he'd likely retain his Woodford seat, but he would very likely lose the party leadership to a younger man, most likely Anthony Eden. But Eden, at fifty-four, was no longer a young man, nor with his recurring stomach ailments was he a healthy man. The results of a Gallup poll had reached Churchill in Venice: a majority of Conservatives and Liberals favored Eden over Churchill for party leadership. This general election would be Churchill's last as the Tory leader, win or lose. He had formed two governments, in 1940 and 1945, neither with a public mandate. Now, he would stake the reputation he had earned over fifty years on the final campaign. He had the nerve and sinew for the fight. Most of all he had the lion heart. All who knew him knew also that a loss would leave Churchill with little to hold on to.

The general election campaign of 1951 was a Hobbesian affair—not brutish, but nasty and short. Churchill began his campaign in early October, delivering eight speeches and two broadcasts in the three weeks up to polling day, October 25. Churchill's overall theme was the "melancholy story of inadvertence, incompetence, indecision and final collapse, which has... marked the policy of our Socialist rulers."

Foreign affairs offered him rich fields to plow. In late September, after Iranian prime minister Mosaddegh demanded that all British employees in Abadan leave Iran, Britain pulled its personnel out. Churchill, having negotiated the Persian oil concessions in 1914, once again, as during the war, saw events in the Middle East as not only threats to British national security but also personal affronts. During one House debate on the Iranian crisis, he managed to denigrate both the Attlee and the Iranian governments in the same sentence:

> If I may digress for a moment, it would seem that the Government have an advantage in their task in Persia in having so much in common with the Persian Government. They, like them, are holding on to office by the skin of their teeth and, like them, they are persevering in a policy of nationalization without the slightest regard for national interests.[156]

Thus, the campaign's first week found Attlee acceding to Mosaddegh's demand that the British leave Abadan. Mosaddegh, known for fits of public weeping and the occasional swoon, had actually rattled his saber. And Attlee had stood down, leading Churchill to tell a Liverpool audience that Britain had "fled the field" and had "been ejected" from Iran after "fifty years of British enterprise and management." He added a charge of appeasement: "Mr. Morrison, the Foreign Secretary, and his party associates no doubt hope to cover up their failure by saying that the Tories want war, while they are for peace at any price."[157]

Indeed, painting the Tories as warmongers, Churchill foremost among them, formed the core of Labour's strategy. Labour did not fight the election on the merits of socialism, Macmillan told his diary, but on fear — fear of unemployment, reduced wages, fewer social benefits, and, the greatest fear of all, war. During the first week of the campaign, the socialist *Daily Mirror,* with a circulation of four million, introduced a slogan that encapsulated the message: "Whose finger do you want on the trigger, Churchill's or Attlee's?" Churchill pointed out that the finger might be American, or Russian, but it could not be British, as Britain had no atomic bomb because its "influence in the world is not what it was in bygone days." All knew that to be true; and all asked, how does Churchill intend to reclaim that influence? By war, answered Labour.[158]

On the domestic front, Churchill let the Labour record speak for itself. He had stated his case for months, with feeling, but with little exaggeration. Britain's plight would have been hard to exaggerate. The country was stumbling toward financial disaster. Labour had imposed the highest tax rates in the free world. During that fourth quarter of 1951, Britain was hemorrhaging from its gold and dollar reserves at a pace never before seen in its history. At the current rate, the reserves would disappear sometime around mid-1952. The Iranian crisis meant that future oil purchases might have to be made in American dollars, a further drain of three hundred million on Britain's dollar balances. The pound had lost one-third of its value since the war ended. Internal inflation had been creeping up for six years, and was now accelerating as the Attlee government undertook to re-arm, a policy Churchill agreed with. Now, with America beginning its second year on a re-armament spending binge, worldwide commodity prices were spiraling upward, and Britain's finances were out of control. Britain was still the world's second-wealthiest country, a distant second behind the United States, but it clung to that status only because the economies of France, Germany, and Japan were just climbing out of the ruins of war. Churchill could not know it then, but that year's inflationary spike (12.5 percent) would reverse itself within months as the world's largest economies settled into the new order of the consumer society. America's new economic model, based on ever-increasing defense and consumer spending, soon begin to lift Britain from its economic mire, as a rising tide lifts all boats. It was a process that neither Attlee nor Churchill had much control over.[159]

On domestic issues, Churchill chose to tread a mostly metaphorical path during the election campaign. He gave Britons few precise details of Tory economic plans, as he told Moran: "We propose to give the people a lighthouse not a shop window." During one broadcast he averred: "The difference between our outlook and the Socialist outlook on life is the difference between the ladder and the queue. We are for the ladder. Let all try their best to climb. They are for the queue. Let each wait in his place till his turn comes." He nebulously pledged to slow the nationalization of steel and coal. Yet he did make two specific promises, which at his insistence were included in that year's Conservative manifesto. He pledged to build three hundred thousand houses, and in an adroit reading of the public mood, he proposed an excess profits tax be levied on corporations. Britain was re-arming, and would re-arm even more were he to win. Profits were being made on the stock exchanges and in boardrooms, the type of profits the common man did not partake in. Churchill, too, knew how to play the fear card. Ever unable to resist a shot at Bevan, he told an audience at Woodford: "It is certain that a vote for Bevanite Socialism is in fact, whatever its intention, a vote which increases the hazard of a world catastrophe." A return to power of the socialists, he said, would deal "a real blow to our hopes of escaping a Third World War."[160]

Several Tory and Liberal candidates volunteered not to run against each other in constituencies where a divided vote might throw the seat to Labour. One such was at Huddersfield, where Lady Violet Bonham Carter—daughter of the great prime minister H. H. Asquith—ran as a Liberal. She and Churchill had been best of friends since first meeting at a dinner party in 1906, when he was thirty-two and she nineteen. She later wrote that Churchill "seemed to me to be quite different from any other young man I had ever met." Churchill did not appear to notice her at first. When he did, he abruptly asked her age. She gave it. "'And I,' he said almost despairingly, 'am thirty-two already, younger than anyone else who *counts*, though.' Then savagely: 'Curse ruthless time. Curse our mortality. How cruelly short is the allotted span for all we must cram in.'" He then proceeded on a long discourse on the shortness of human life and the vast potential for human accomplishment, at the end of which he announced, "We are all worms, but I do believe that I am a glow worm." By the end of the dinner Bonham Carter was convinced he indeed was, "and my conviction remained unshaken throughout the years that followed." Now, speaking on her behalf at Huddersfield, Churchill reminded the crowd of his two decades as a Liberal, his service to Asquith, and his role in bringing unemployment insurance and old age pensions to Britons. He told the audience:

" 'All men are created equal,' says the American Declaration of Independence, 'All men shall be kept equal,' say the British Socialist Party." He added, "Now is the time to break with these follies."[161]

Speaking in Plymouth on Randolph's behalf two days before polling day, he denounced Labour and Communist charges of warmongering as "a cruel and ungrateful accusation."

> It is the opposite of the truth. If I remain in public life at this juncture it is because, rightly or wrongly, but sincerely, I believe that I may be able to make an important contribution to the prevention of a Third World War and to bringing nearer that lasting peace settlement which the masses of the people of every race and in every land fervently desire. I pray indeed that I may have this opportunity. It is the last prize I seek to win.[162]

Max Beaverbrook predicted a Tory majority of at least one hundred. Max was well informed, but not always accurately informed, as borne out by the margin of error of his predictions in the last two elections. Moran advised Churchill not to put too much stock in Max's rosy prognostications. Churchill replied that since Max's papers were read by millions, "he must know what he's talking about." Max may be right, Moran told his diary, but on all sides Tories were worried, not only about the election results but by Churchill's age and his penchant for neither asking for nor taking advice. Churchill told Macmillan that he hoped for a majority of ninety but would settle for fifty. Macmillan also learned from Brendan Bracken that the Old Man, if victorious, planned to hold office for just one year, perhaps eighteen months at most. Churchill alluded to his planned retirement during a campaign address when he told the audience, "Mr. Eden will carry on the torch of Tory democracy when other and older hands have let it fall." Eden, though ill, was eager, his arms outstretched, to catch the torch.[163]

But Churchill was not prepared to let the torch pass until he claimed his prize—a summit at the top. That was what he sought; it was almost all he sought. Truman was still in the White House, Stalin still in the Kremlin. An election victory would turn the clock back to July 1945, to Potsdam, where the last meeting of the Big Three had been interrupted by the election.

On polling day, Thursday, October 25, the *Daily Mirror* accompanied its slogan—Whose finger on the trigger?—with a large photograph of a chubby man in half silhouette, holding a cigar. The man in the photo was not Churchill. By staging the shot, the *Daily Mirror* crossed the line. Churchill soon filed a lawsuit, and was rewarded with a full, if insincere, apology wherein the editors expressed regret if their words and photos implied in any way that Churchill did not dislike war. But the question asked by Tories on polling day was, how effective had the *Daily Mirror* been in its underhanded campaign? The answer to that question arrived overnight as the votes were counted. The Tories won, but just. Churchill did not get his hoped-for majority of 100, or even 50, but only 18, over all parties. The Conservatives finished with 321 seats, Labour with 295, the Liberals only 6. In fact, Labour, with 13,866,000 votes, outpolled the Conservatives by 229,000 votes. The results did not in any way resemble a mandate for Churchill. By noon on October 26, Attlee knew he was beaten. Early that evening he motored to Buckingham Palace to hand King George the seals of office. An hour or so later Churchill made his journey to the palace, where for the third time since 1940 he was asked by King George to form a government. Once again, as in 1939, when he was called back to the Admiralty, the signal went out worldwide: Winston is back.

The King was a very ill man, recuperating from lung surgery to remove a cancer. Weeks earlier, Churchill, shocked by the King's appearance and always anxious about all things medical, pressed Moran for details of the King's ailment and his chances for recovery. It was then that Moran understood that Churchill's anxiety had to do with his own decline, about which he received regular reminders by way of spells of dizziness, bouts of forgetfulness, numbness in his shoulders, and increasing deafness. And it was then that Moran concluded that Churchill had lost much ground along with his grip on things, and if he returned to No. 10 would not be up to the job. Clementine braced herself for the pending ordeal. Shortly after the election, she wrote a short note to Ronald Tree: "I do hope Winston will be able to help the country. It will be up-hill work, but he has a willing eager heart."[164]

Pug Ismay, happily retired from public affairs, had gone to bed early on the night of October 26. Late that night the telephone on his bedside table jangled to life. The familiar ring had heralded the invasion of the Low Countries, the death of Roosevelt, and the surrender of the German armies. Ismay lifted the receiver; a voice on the other end of the line asked him to stand by for the prime minister. A moment later: "Is that you Pug?...I want to see you at once. You aren't asleep are you?" Ismay explained that in fact he had been. "Well," said Churchill, "I only want to see you for five minutes." Ismay put his head under a cold tap, dressed hurriedly, and within fifteen minutes arrived at 28 Hyde Park Gate. There Churchill told Ismay, a career soldier, that he wanted him to take the office of secretary of state for Commonwealth relations, a political post for which Ismay considered himself totally unqualified. "I thought the cold tap had failed to do its job," Ismay later wrote, "and I was still dreaming." He accepted the position, "overjoyed at the prospect of serving under Churchill again."[165]

Jock Colville's summons arrived the next morning, as he and his wife were enjoying themselves at the Newmarket races. A steward of the Jockey Club found Colville in the crowd and told him that the prime minister was on the line and wished to speak to him. "Whatever he asks you to do," warned Colville's wife, "say no." Colville had returned to the Foreign Office after his two years in service to Princess Elizabeth and was content to finish his career there. But it was not to be. When Colville picked up the phone in the Jockey Club, the prime minister apologized for any inconvenience, and asked if Colville might be willing to meet in person. "Tomorrow?" Colville asked. "No," replied Churchill, "this afternoon." When they met, Colville asked Churchill how long he thought he'd stay on at Downing Street. The question stemmed from Colville's concern that another prolonged absence from the Foreign Office would derail his career. One year, Churchill replied. Colville signed on.[166]

At Chartwell over the next four days, the Old Man reassembled his old team. Eden would again lead the House and head the Foreign Office, the very same dual role that had exhausted him during the war. Colville came aboard as joint principal private secretary, sharing those duties with David Pitblado, an Attlee appointee. Rab Butler would go to the Exchequer, Oliver Lyttelton as colonial secretary, and Lord Woolton as lord president of the council. The Prof—Lord Cherwell—was to be paymaster general. Harry Crookshank, a party lesser light, was to take on the Ministry of Health. Harold Macmillan was to be minister of housing, with a mandate from Churchill to build the three hundred thousand houses he had promised during the campaign. When Macmillan asked Churchill what that might entail and how to go about it, the Old Man answered, "I haven't an idea." Churchill's sons-in-law were brought in, Duncan Sandys as minister of supply, Christopher Soames as parliamentary private secretary. But the nepotism did not extend to Randolph. Randolph, who had served his father during the war as adviser without portfolio and minister of provocation, no longer even served in those capacities. Churchill had grown weary of the knockdown political arguments that Randolph precipitated with regularity. Such verbal jousts had on occasion stimulated the Old Man during the war; now they tired him. One appointment raised eyebrows on both sides of the Atlantic. As he had in 1940, Churchill named himself minister of defence. "It is just folly for Churchill to become Minister of Defence," Macmillan told his diary. "It almost justifies the *Daily Mirror*.... This is a major blunder."[167]

During those autumn weeks, Dwight Eisenhower, supreme commander of NATO, set about organizing his NATO headquarters in Paris. Eisenhower sought something along the lines of his World War Two SHAEF arrangement, that is, allied countries would put their armies under NATO command in the event of war, but they would otherwise maintain sovereign control over their forces. The French Assembly and Robert Schuman, however, advocated the creation of a European Defense Community, something of a supranational military version of Schuman's Coal and Steel Community. The European army, as outlined by then–French premier René Pleven in 1950, would exist separately from the armies of the nations that contributed soldiers to it. De Gaulle, still in self-imposed exile from French politics, saw the EDC as an abdication of French sovereignty. The Scandinavian countries feared Franco-German domination if the EDC succeeded, and a German threat if it did not. Political cartoonists throughout Western Europe panned the plan, citing the absurd problems of command and control inherent in trying to guide brigades and divisions—let alone an entire army—made up of a dozen or more nationalities, all speaking different languages and carrying different weapons. The Bevan wing of the Labour Party opposed the EDC on the grounds that a European army, especially one containing Germans, would provoke Moscow. Eisenhower, too, was wary of bringing German forces into the mix, and remained so for three years. Britons were largely apathetic toward Europe, Dean Acheson later wrote, and, like the French, feared a re-armed Germany. America and NATO were where Britons beheld their salvation. For many Britons, including Churchill, the Atlantic was narrower than the English Channel.[168]

On December 6, Churchill imparted to the House his thoughts on the matter in an address that marked another milestone in the European journey toward unity, and Britain's role in that journey. Churchill told the House he foresaw "a European Army, containing a German contribution of agreed size and strength, [that] will stand alongside the British and United States Armies in a common defensive front. That, after all, is what really matters to the life or death of the free world." Then came the seeming paradox from the man who had argued for almost two decades for a united Europe: "As far as Britain is concerned, we do not propose to merge in the European Army but we are already joined to it. Our troops are on the spot." As with any future European economic union, Britain would be *in* and *out* simultaneously. But it wasn't a paradox. Unlike de Gaulle, whose loyalty was to France *alone,* Churchill was loyal to Britain *first.* It had always been so. He ended his address by declaring that the progress toward a European Defense Community (discussions Attlee had refused to join) amounted to "an enlightened if not an inspiring tale." Noting that the EDC had not yet taken its final shape, he announced that he would not make a final decision on Britain's role until it did.[169]

But the EDC never took its final shape. Churchill mocked the EDC weeks later in the private company of Truman and Acheson. The EDC talks dragged on until 1954, when France, by then losing a war in Indochina, pulled out. But by then Germany had re-armed, and NATO—including Greece and Turkey—had assumed the command structure that Eisenhower had envisioned, and had formed the defensive cordon for Western Europe, largely funded and manned by Churchill's American cousins, which was exactly what Churchill had sought since 1945.

By late 1951, Churchill had reached his goals also regarding the political and economic elements of European union. In February 1949, he had told a council of European ministers meeting in Brussels that their duty, and his, was to return to their respective countries and impress upon the leaders of their governments the wisdom of European unity: "We may even, in the form of an active, enlightened and ever more dominant public opinion, give them the fuel they need for their journey and the electric spark to set all in motion." It was now in motion.[170]

So, too, was the British atomic deterrent, another lynchpin of Churchill's European defense strategy. During the December 6 address, Churchill outlined the essence of that strategy. Having learned upon taking office that the Attlee government had been in the process of building an atomic bomb, Churchill pledged to bring it to fruition. Doing so, he warned the House, "adds to the deterrents against war, but it may throw the brunt on to us should war come." The Russians, upon learning of the American atomic bombers in East Anglia, had called Britain an "aircraft carrier." Britain, therefore, was a prime target. Yet, Churchill added, "We shall not flinch from the duty Britain has accepted."[171]

With the atomic deterrent in hand, he could then proceed to the prize he now saw as the culmination of his career; world peace brought about by a summit meeting between the American president, himself, and Joseph Stalin. He believed still that men of honor keep their word. He shocked one of his private secretaries when he declared that Stalin had never broken his word. Of course Stalin had broken his word, leading to the current state of world affairs. Churchill the romantic was overruling Churchill the statesman and ignoring Churchill the historian.

In early November, while reiterating the dangers posed by a nuclear world, he told the House: "But our great hope in foreign affairs is, of course, to bring about an abatement of what is called 'the cold war' by negotiation at the highest level from strength and not from weakness." He then read to the House the letter he had sent Stalin in 1945, in which he had warned of a dangerous world with Communists drawn up on one side against the English-speaking nations and their allies. "It is quite obvious," he had told Stalin, that such a "quarrel would tear the world to pieces and that all of us leading men on either side who had anything to do with that would be shamed before history." It had all come to pass, he told the House, "with horrible exactitude." Thus, a summit at the top, Churchill believed, was the only way to avert the ultimate catastrophe of World War Three. He also believed that only absolute Anglo-American solidarity could bring the Soviets to the table. As he put it to President Truman, the Kremlin feared a strong Anglo-American friendship, and would try to drive a wedge between Americans and Britons. But if the Soviets grew to fear the unshakable Western alliance enough, they might then see friendship with the West as more advantageous than enmity. In 1942 he told Americans, "If we are together, nothing is impossible, if we are divided, all will fail." He believed that yet.[172]

To that end, on the final day of 1951, Churchill and his retinue—including Colville, Lord Moran, Pug Ismay, Dickie Mountbatten, and the Prof—once again, as during the late war, embarked for the United States on board the *Queen Mary*. At midnight they convened in Churchill's cabin for a champagne toast and a rendition of "Auld Lang Syne." Churchill had turned seventy-seven a month earlier. Bob Boothby, who had been drummed from office in 1940 over alleged financial improprieties, had dined with him that month after the Old Man asked Boothby to lead the British delegation in talks on a united Europe, an act of magnanimity that resurrected Boothby's career. Boothby was an old, but false, friend of Churchill's, and he never forgave the Old Man for not coming to his defense in 1940. Yet on one matter Boothby shared the opinion of many of Churchill's colleagues. Boothby reported to Harold Nicolson that Churchill was getting "very, very old, tragically old." Secretary of State Dean Acheson later wrote that during the Washington meetings, he found Churchill to be "still formidable and quite magnificent," but noted, "the old lion seemed to be weakening."[173]

Acheson later wrote that the French seemed always to arrive in Washington bearing demands, while the American press believed the British did likewise, and in fact ran roughshod over American leaders. But Acheson understood that the British and Churchill had come only in search of friendship. In his third address before the U.S. Congress, an unprecedented honor for a foreign leader, Churchill made clear he had not come "to ask you for money to make life more comfortable or easier for us in Britain." Rather, he came to pledge his support for American policies in Asia, the Middle East, and in Europe. Speaking in a sense to the Kremlin, he declared, as he had many times since 1945, that Britain sought nothing from Russia. Although he regularly called Communists and communism sinister and malignant, he did not do so now. Nor did he refer to the Communists as "godless" or "atheists," as was the wont of many Americans in high office. The words, in fact, do not appear in any of his public addresses delivered between 1940 and 1961. His battle was fought not over Christian dogma, but over liberty. He ended with his favorite Bismarck quote: "Bismarck once said that the supreme fact of the nineteenth century was that Britain and the United States spoke the same language. Let us make sure that the supreme fact of the twentieth century is that they tread the same path."[174]

Harry Truman, who was not running for reelection in 1952, deferred to his successor any decision on a possible summit. That turned out to be Dwight Eisenhower. Churchill's New Year's 1952 Atlantic crossing was the first of four journeys to Washington and Bermuda that he undertook over the next three years, each one a quest for his summit prize. Implicit in that is the fact that Churchill did not leave office in a year or so as he had told his colleagues he would. Instead, he stayed on for almost four more years, in pursuit of his prize, which in the end eluded him. He never flagged in that pursuit, even as pneumonia and then a terrible stroke hobbled him, even as his colleagues, driven in part by their concern for his health, and in part by their own ambitions, sought to ease him out of Downing Street, even as Stalin and his successors rebuffed him after the ogre's death in 1953. President Eisenhower did likewise.

Truman often told Dean Acheson that Churchill was the greatest public figure of their age. Acheson thought that an understatement. Churchill's greatness, Acheson wrote, "flowed not only from great qualities of heart and brain, indomitable courage, energy, magnanimity, and good sense, but from supreme art and deliberate policy." These elements, Acheson believed, fused into a style of leadership "that alone can call forth from a free people what cannot be commanded." One would have to go back almost four hundred years, to Queen Elizabeth I, Acheson believed, to find Churchill's equal. Churchill's final battle, to bring the Americans, Soviets, and British to the conference table, fought into his eighties, was as dogged as any he ever fought. And yet, tragedy is the wasting shadow always cast, sooner or later, by towering heroism.

Jock Colville later wrote that Churchill's "return to power seemed to many to presage the recovery of hopes tarnished by the dismal aftermath of the war." Those hopes fell short of complete fulfillment during the three and one-half years of Churchill's last administration, but during those years, the austerity programs and rationing disappeared, the standard of living rose, if modestly, and Europe remained at peace, albeit an uneasy peace. The first year under Churchill remained bleak: rationing was severe, and coal still scarce. Then King George VI died on February 6, 1952. Colville found Churchill in tears that morning, staring straight ahead, reading neither his official papers nor the newspapers. The Old Man feared he could not work with the new Queen, as he did not know her and "she was only a child." But he pledged to stay on as prime minister until her coronation in mid-1953.

Here was the first delay in his promised departure; there would be more. It was much the same tactic he had used when he delayed the second front during the war: pledge support for an outcome but keep moving the time-table back. Had he announced in early 1952 that he might stay on until 1955, he'd have sparked a palace revolt by Eden, Butler, Macmillan, and most certainly by Clementine, who wanted him out of Downing Street and home in Kent.[175]

On April 24, 1953, the Queen summoned Churchill to Windsor Castle, where she conferred on him the Order of the Garter. He had declined her father's offer of the Garter in 1945. At that time, the law held that the prime minister must approve the monarch's nomination. Churchill, as prime minister, refused his own knighthood. But the law had been changed; the decision was now the Queen's alone to make. And so Churchill became Sir Winston Churchill, K.G.

The young Queen heralded a new era of youthful optimism as the old order and the old wars receded into Britain's collective memory. In early June 1953, twenty million Britons watched Queen Elizabeth's coronation on live television, mostly in pubs, but the new TV experience led to a dou-bling of television sales in Britain. America watched, too. For the young, a golden future beckoned, rich with promise.

But not for the old. For some weeks before the Queen's coronation, Churchill had once again, as during the war, been acting foreign minister after Anthony Eden was forced to undergo a third operation for his debili-tating stomach ulcers. In his role as acting foreign minister, the P.M. con-cluded that the Soviets had changed their stripes following the death of Stalin in March, felled by a stroke, although rumors coming out of Mos-cow had it that he had been poisoned by the murderous head of the NKVD, Lavrentiy Beria, the man responsible for the Katyn forest massacres. Indeed, Beria was arrested in June. Churchill had sent friendly greetings to Stalin's apparent successor, Georgy Malenkov, who responded in kind. It was all simply diplomatic dancing in the dark, but Churchill believed the moment had arrived to "grasp the paw of the Russian bear." He had told Britons since 1950 that the goal of sitting down with the Russians was to work toward a nuclear disarmament treaty, always stressing that any such treaty must include provisions for international inspections and enforcement. Now, believing the moment had arrived, he sent preliminary feelers to Eisenhower, suggesting that they meet in order to plan the big summit. Eisenhower tentatively agreed; Bermuda was to be the place, the date not yet confirmed.

Then, on June 23, just two weeks after the Queen's coronation, Churchill went to rise from the dinner table at No. 10 and instead collapsed into his chair, unable to walk, his words slurred. Colville at first thought the Old Man had had too much to drink. Colville, Christopher Soames, and Clementine managed to get Churchill to bed. They summoned Lord Moran, who took only a few minutes to conclude that his patient had suffered a stroke. When Churchill, pale but mobile, chaired a cabinet meeting the next morning, no one present thought anything amiss. Moran moved him to Chartwell that afternoon. The next day the symptoms grew more severe, so severe that by the following day, his doctors believed the end might come within days. He lost feeling on his left side and then the ability to make a fist. Moran concluded that the "thrombosis is obviously spreading," but did not tell Churchill in so many words. The doctor ordered bed rest—no cabinet meetings, no Questions in the House, and no Bermuda. Moran drew up a medical bulletin that referenced a "disturbance of cerebral circulation." That phrase was axed by Rab Butler and Churchill. The edited bulletin simply stated the P.M. needed respite from his arduous duties. So began an almost two-month news blackout of a sort that would be impossible to pull off in this age of total media. Churchill's health improved slowly during those months. During one low point, he told Colville that he'd resign in October, as he no longer had "the zest" for the work and thought the world was in "an abominable state." He was depressed, he said, by thoughts of the hydrogen bomb.[176]

Then he changed his mind on the matter of resigning. With logic only Churchill could conjure, he told all those who believed he should resign due to his ill health—Clementine, his cabinet colleagues, and Lord Moran—that the time to leave office was not when he was weak but when he recovered. To speed that process, he informed Moran that he had given up brandy, substituting Cointreau instead, and that he had switched to milder cigars. He read a great deal: *Jane Eyre,* Trollope, *Candide, Wuthering Heights, 1984, Phineas Finn,* C. S. Forester. He edited his *History of the English-Speaking Peoples.* He banged croquet balls about on the lawn, more from frustration over his condition than from any love of the game.[177]

Churchill's spirits were boosted in early July by the prospect of Eisenhower's visiting Britain, an idea that apparently had germinated in Churchill's imagination. In fact, Eisenhower followed in the footsteps of presidents Truman and Roosevelt, footsteps that never led to London. Bitterness was Churchill's response as it dawned on him later in the month that Eisenhower was not coming to Britain and did not see eye to eye with him on a thaw in relations with Russia. The Democrats should have won the election, the Old Man told Colville, adding that Eisenhower was "both weak and stupid."[178]

Slowly, he regained his gait and powers of speech. He was cheered by the news on July 27 that the armistice was signed that day ending the Korean conflict. But there would be no V-K day celebrations; the West had not won, and the Chinese or North Koreans might at any time violate the treaty. That night he told Moran that the opportunity for peace had been within reach before the stroke, "if only, Charles, I had the strength. I'm a sort of survival. Roosevelt and Stalin are both dead. I only am left."[179]

Eden, himself frail, paid a visit to Churchill in August. By then Rab Butler was exhausting himself filling in for both Eden and Churchill. Colville noted that Eden seemed to come with one burning thought in mind: "When do I take over?" Yet it dawned on Eden that he would not be moving up to No. 10 until and unless his health improved considerably. Eden's was a family visit, in that the previous year he had married Jack Churchill's daughter, Clarissa, which made him Churchill's nephew-in-law. But the familial bonds did not guarantee a warm relationship. Churchill was growing increasingly resentful of Eden's transparent ambition. The Old Man told Colville that the more Eden tried to hustle him out, the longer he'd stay.[180]

Churchill ran only three cabinet meetings over three months, and kept his visits to No. 10 at a minimum. By late August he was on his way back. Still, one consulting physician, the aptly named neurologist Sir Russell Brain, told Lord Moran that he doubted Churchill could ever again give speeches or answer Questions in the House.[181]

Churchill proved Sir Russell's diagnosis dead wrong in early November, when, on the third, he made his first parliamentary speech since the stroke. Other than members of Churchill's cabinet, no one in the chamber knew he had been ill. Yet rumors of a stroke had percolated through the press. The *Daily Mirror* had repeated the rumor running in the American press that he had been struck down, was expected to recover, and then resign. The eyes of the world were therefore upon him that day. He covered a plethora of domestic and international matters before arriving at the root of the matter: defense. He declared that two dominant events had taken place since 1951—the shift of hostilities in Korea from the battlefield to the conference table, and the death of Stalin. He wondered aloud if the death of Stalin had ushered in a new era in Soviet policy conducive to détente, a "new look." He had no ready answer but told the House he believed all nations act in their best interest and that the Soviets might have "turned to internal betterment rather than external aggression." How could the West encourage such behavior? His proposed solution was to be found in the third dominant event of the last two years:

> I mean the rapid and ceaseless developments of atomic warfare and the hydrogen bomb. These fearful scientific discoveries cast their shadow on every thoughtful mind, but nevertheless I believe that we are justified in feeling that there has been a diminution of tension and that the probabilities of another world war have diminished, or at least have become more remote. I say this in spite of the continual growth of weapons of destruction such as have never fallen before into the hands of human beings. Indeed, I have sometimes the odd thought that the annihilating character of these agencies may bring an utterly unforeseeable security to mankind.

Churchill was unaware at the time that the United States had exploded an H-bomb on the Pacific atoll of Eniwetok in November 1952. The device was far too large—seventy tons—to fit inside an airplane. The Americans were now at work perfecting a smaller though far more powerful version. The Russians had followed in August 1953 with their own H-bomb test in Kazakhstan. Both tests had so far remained state secrets. But Churchill and the world were well aware that a hydrogen bomb would soon be exploded, somewhere, by someone, most likely the Americans.

He developed his remarkable "odd thought" further, and in doing so became the first world leader to articulate what later became known as the policy of MAD: mutually assured destruction.

> It may be that...when the advance of destructive weapons enables everyone to kill everybody else nobody will want to kill anyone at all. At any rate, it seems pretty safe to say that a war which begins by both sides suffering what they dread most—and that is undoubtedly the case at present—is less likely to occur than one which dangles the lurid prizes of former ages before ambitious eyes.[182]

Churchill left the House under his own power, strolling to the smoking room, where he drank brandy for two hours (having abandoned his experiment with Cointreau). The speech was the final hurdle, he told Moran, to restarting the Bermuda talks. Churchill fully expected to soon be meeting with Malenkov, after gaining Eisenhower's approval. He was ebullient, telling Moran, "I'm thinking of substituting port for brandy." That night, Moran said this of Churchill in his diary: "I love his guts. I think he's invincible." Macmillan committed similar thoughts to his diary: "Indeed, he [Churchill] was complete master of himself and the House. It seems incredible that this man was struck down by a second stroke at the beginning of July."[183]

Within the week, Eisenhower agreed to an early December meeting with Churchill in Bermuda, with the purpose of discussing a unified approach to the Russians, preparatory to an Anglo-American-Soviet summit. The French would attend the Bermuda meeting as well, in their role as the third Western power. Indeed, the conference had been postponed not only because of Churchill's summertime hiatus, but because the turnover in French ministers had been so great for so long that the French government at times had no one to send to conferences. Neither the P.M. nor Eden believed the French would add anything of value to the discussion. The Bermuda talks would be fly-by-the-seat-of-the-pants, always a concern to foreign ministers when their heads of state are doing the flying. Churchill's belief that Russia was ready to talk was a result, Moran believed, of Churchill existing "in an imaginary world of his own making." On December 2, Churchill, Eden, Moran, and Colville boarded the pressurized Stratocruiser *Canopus* for the seventeen-hour flight to Bermuda by way of Gander, Newfoundland. For much of the journey—a far cry from the days of rattling and unheated B-24s—Churchill read C. S. Forester's *Death to the French,* an unfortunate choice if he was seen carrying it into the conference.[184]

Clementine did not accompany Winston to Bermuda. She was in Stockholm that week to accept on Churchill's behalf the Nobel Prize for Literature, awarded for Churchill's lifetime writings. The prize was £12,500, tax free, a sum that Churchill in a note to his wife declared was "not so bad!" She likely would not have made the trip to Bermuda in any event. "Her heart had never been in this second term of office," her daughter Mary later wrote. She was tired, and prone to agitation, especially around her husband, to whom she made clear that his soldiering on as P.M. imposed great burdens upon her. She was mistress of Chartwell and the Hyde Park Gate house, as well as hostess at No. 10 and Chequers, where the constant entertaining and steady streams of visitors were a strain. For Clementine, the present held no joy and the future promised only more worries.[185]

Britain had tested its first atomic bomb a year earlier. It deployed its first atomic weapons days after Churchill's November 3 address. Yet the hydrogen weapon, not the A-bomb, obsolete now in Churchill's opinion, lay at the core of Churchill's strategy to bring the Russians into disarmament talks. Soon after the Bermuda meetings began, he learned that Eisenhower did not believe likewise. As if to prove the risks inherent when heads of state sit down to talk, Churchill supported Eisenhower—in turn seconded by his secretary of state, John Foster Dulles—without hesitation when the president declared he felt "free to use," indeed was prepared to use, atomic bombs in North Korea if the Chinese violated the armistice. Eisenhower added that he intended to say just that in an upcoming speech at the United Nations, a copy of which he gave Churchill to look over. Eden was shocked, and told Churchill so in private. Churchill began to grasp Eden's point: any such declaration by Eisenhower would not help to bring the Russians to the conference table. Churchill dispatched Colville to Eisenhower's quarters at the Mid-Ocean Club with a brief note in which he suggested the president temper his language by changing "free to" to "reserved the right to" use atomic weapons. Eisenhower agreed to do so, and offered as well to call for the creation of an international atomic regulatory agency.

The president then told Colville that "whereas Winston looked upon the [hydrogen bomb] as something new and terrible," he believed it to be simply the latest "improvement in military weapons." The president implied, Colville told his diary, that "there was in fact no distinction between 'conventional weapons' and atomic weapons." Churchill had once believed likewise, in 1945, but no longer did. After Churchill at one of the plenary sessions outlined at length his "double dealing" approach to the Soviets—an atomic bomb in one hand, the other extended in friendship—Eisenhower responded with a harangue of a sort none around the table had ever heard at an international conference. As for the Soviets' "new look," Eisenhower compared Russia to a whore wearing a new dress but "it was surely the same whore underneath." The French, predictably, leaked all of this to the press.[186]

Yet Eisenhower had to step with care. Wisconsin senator Joseph McCarthy, chairman of the Senate Permanent Subcommittee on Investigations, was riding high that year, and riding roughshod over the State Department, which for three years McCarthy had alleged was rife with Communists. When, during a private lunch in Bermuda, Churchill asked Eisenhower about McCarthy's influence in America, the president suggested he pay no attention to McCarthy, just as Americans paid no attention to Aneurin Bevan. It was not an apt comparison; Bevan might be a socialist gadfly, but he was not a dangerous presence in British politics. Many Americans presumed the British Foreign Office and the British intelligence services were likewise infested with Reds, a conclusion drawn in part by the defections to Moscow by Donald Maclean and Guy Burgess in

1951, although their exact whereabouts were not ascertained until 1956. It would not do for Eisenhower to encourage the notion that the British and Churchill had bullied him into glad-handing with the godless Communists in the Kremlin. Churchill could not bring himself to condemn his old wartime colleague for bowing to anti-Communist fury. Instead, he shifted blame onto John Foster Dulles, to whom he had taken an immediate and visceral dislike the previous year. "It seems that everything is left to Dulles," Churchill told Moran. "It appears that the president is no more than a ventriloquist's doll." In any case, Churchill went home to London without his prize. There would be no Anglo-American-Soviet summit anytime soon.[187]

Soon after Churchill's return from Bermuda, the *Daily Mirror* began calling for his resignation. One *Mirror* piece, under the headline SHADOW OF A GIANT, quoted the *New York Times:* Churchill "was only the shadow of the great figure of 1940." The *Daily Mirror*'s attacks got under Churchill's skin, Moran told his diary, but an article and cartoon in *Punch* hit the Old Man harder. The article, titled "A Story Without an Ending," was written by Malcolm Muggeridge, then the editor of *Punch*. It was an allegorical tale of a fictitious Byzantine ruler who had served his nation well but had lost his once-splendid faculties to old age and decrepitude. Accompanying the piece was a cartoon that depicted Churchill with a slack jaw, the left side of his face flaccid, as if from his stroke. Churchill's hands as depicted in the cartoon — "podgy, shapeless," in Moran's description — peered out from white cuffs. Churchill held his hands up to Moran. "Look at my hands," he said, "I have beautiful hands." Then he offered that, as *Punch* goes everywhere, he must resign. Years later Muggeridge declared that statement showed that Churchill "was totally out of touch with the contemporary situation," because by 1954 *Punch* did not go everywhere. It once did, Muggeridge declared, "but only in the 19th century."[188]

On March 1, 1954, the Americans detonated a hydrogen bomb over Bikini Atoll in the South Pacific. Three months later, on June 16, Churchill convened a secret session of the Defence Policy Committee at which he and his defence ministers agreed to a dramatic new atomic policy: Britain would build its own hydrogen bomb. The decision was so secret that not even the cabinet was informed. A week later, on June 24, Churchill departed by air for Washington.[189]

It was his last official trip to the United States, his final chance to garner Eisenhower's support for a summit. The usual group attended to his needs—Eden, Moran, Colville, and Christopher Soames. His mood aboard the Stratocruiser was at first somber. To Moran he lamented the changes wrought by the Wright brothers. The world had grown smaller: "It was an evil hour for poor England." But the mood passed, and at ten in the morning British time, he told the steward to remove his whisky and bring on the champagne and caviar. Knowing that Eisenhower, guided by John Foster Dulles, would not agree to a three-party or four-party summit, Churchill arrived in Washington with a new proposal—to conduct a two-party summit, himself and Malenkov.[190]

Thus his mood improved exponentially when on Friday, June 25, shortly after arriving at the White House, Eisenhower voiced no objection to Churchill's holding bilateral talks with the Russians, and did so before Churchill had even presented his case, which he had thought would be a long and complicated process. The objective of talks with the Russians, as Churchill saw it, was to buy ten years of "easement" in relations with Moscow, such that America, Russia, and Britain could divert their monies and scientific research away from catastrophic atomic bombs and into fruitful, peaceful endeavors. Eisenhower agreed, and even suggested that he and Churchill, along with the French and Germans, hold preliminary talks in London before Churchill went off to engage the Russians. Colville noted that Dulles tried to squelch the Russian initiative, without success. Eisenhower hosted a small dinner on Sunday, described by Colville as "very gay," with Churchill and Eisenhower agreeing that Germany must re-arm, even if over French objections. The French, Eisenhower declared, "were a hopeless, helpless mass of protoplasm." In fact, within weeks, the EDC died in the French Assembly and the tri-party occupation of West Germany was lifted, and within ten months, Germany was welcomed into NATO. Another cause for cheer had been Eisenhower's reaction when Churchill told him of the British decision to build a hydrogen bomb: Eisenhower had made no objection. Churchill could return to London a victor. As well, with a summit in mind, if not in hand, he now had another reason to stay on at No. 10.[191]

This he imparted to Eden on the return voyage to Britain, aboard the Cunarder *Queen Elizabeth*, named for the queen's mother, consort of George VI. When asked by Eden when he might resign, he set September 21 as a tentative date. This was important, because British law called for a general election to be held at least every five years. That meant October 1956 at the latest. If Churchill stayed on well into 1955, Eden would have precious little time to chart the course of his new government before the election. Churchill understood that well. Yet he would not go before he met with the Russians.

On that front, while on board the *Queen Elizabeth*, Churchill dictated a telegram to Soviet foreign minister Molotov in which he proposed direct talks between himself and the Soviet leaders, talks in which the United States would not participate. When Eden objected, pointing out correctly that such a message could not be sent without cabinet approval, Churchill dismissed his rationale as "nonsense," telling Colville that if the cabinet objected, he'd resign. That, Colville told the P.M., would split the Tories and the country "top to bottom." Churchill was practicing blackmail of a sort, and it worked. Eden backed off. Churchill's approach to Eden, Colville noted, had been "ruthless and unscrupulous." Eden finally agreed under Churchill's relentless pressure to inform the cabinet that he approved of the message. The telegram to Molotov was duly sent. The Russians waited three weeks to reply, and when they did, their proposal, by its absurd demands, effectively killed any chances of bilateral talks. They demanded a thirty-two-party all-European conference, with NATO withdrawal from Germany topping the agenda. Eden had been correct: by shooting off the message, Churchill had confused the Russians, angered Eisenhower, and alienated his cabinet. They all now questioned his wisdom. Of Churchill's crusade for a summit, Macmillan told his diary: "It was his last passionate wish—an old man's dream—an old man's folly, perhaps, but it might have saved the world."[192]

Churchill admitted defeat during the cabinet meeting following the arrival of the Soviet message. There would be no talks. Churchill's official biographer, Martin Gilbert, needed only a few words to close this chapter of the Great Man's life: "Churchill's last great foreign policy initiative was at an end."[193]

By all rights, so, too, should have been his premiership. But he held on, in part to secure cabinet approval on making a hydrogen bomb, which he duly gained on July 8; four days later he told the House that decisions had been made regarding atomic weapons, but he gave no details. Earlier in the year, he had proposed to leave in June, then July, then September. In August he decided against September. As summer gave out to fall, Eden and Harold Macmillan increased their efforts to move him out, to no avail.

In late July, Macmillan approached Clementine on the matter, a tactical mistake. He should have gone directly to Churchill, but perhaps did not, knowing well the Old Man's blunt style of debate. Churchill summoned Macmillan in order to discuss the matter. Colville feared an eruption. Macmillan was ushered into Churchill's study to find the Old Man engaged with Colville in a game of bezique. Churchill offered Macmillan a whisky and cigar, and continued his game. Then he insisted the score be tallied and that he pay Colville the monies owed. They disputed the exact amount. Churchill's checkbook was sent for and a pen. The pen arrived, the wrong pen. Macmillan meanwhile was allowed to fidget for the better part of a half hour. Finally, Churchill asked if Colville would be so good as to leave the room, because it appeared Mr. Macmillan "wanted to talk about some matter of political importance." The meeting did not last long; it took Churchill only a minute to make his point, which was that he was staying, although he told Macmillan that the party leaders had the authority to replace him as leader. Macmillan knew full well that given Churchill's popularity, a coup by the Tory leadership would spell their doom, not Churchill's. "I cannot understand what all the fuss was about," Churchill told Colville after Macmillan's departure. "He [Macmillan] really had nothing to say at all. He was very mild."[194]

In early August, Macmillan told his diary: "His [Churchill's] present mood is so self-centered as to amount almost to mania. It is, no doubt, the result of his disease [his stroke]." Were Churchill a king, Macmillan wrote, he'd be deposed. When pressed by Butler, Macmillan, and Eden, Churchill replied, "You cannot ask me to sign my own death warrant." Yet by not going he was signing theirs. "All of us, who really have loved as well as admired him," wrote Macmillan, "are being slowly driven into something like hatred."[195]

Churchill's treatment of Eden became shabby. During one luncheon, he told Eden that it would all be his by the time he was sixty. For Eden, that birthday was three years away. Colville wrote that Churchill had begun "to form a cold hatred of Eden, who, he repeatedly said, had done more to thwart him...than anybody else." That was a cruel and untrue assessment. Of Churchill during these final months in office, Colville wrote: "And yet on some days the old gleam would be there, wit and good humour would bubble and sparkle, wisdom would roll out in telling sentences and still, occasionally, the sparkle of genius could be seen in a decision, a letter or a phrase." But Colville asked himself, was Churchill still the man to negotiate with the Soviets and nudge the Americans to a less militant attitude toward Russia? "The Foreign Office thought not; the British public would, I am sure, have said yes. And I, who have been as intimate with him as anybody during these last years, simply do not know."[196]

Churchill turned eighty on November 30, 1954, the first prime minister since Gladstone to hold that office at that age. He was now the Father of the House and the only MP then sitting who had been elected during Queen Victoria's reign. Parliament, to mark his birthday, presented him with the portrait painted by Graham Sutherland, for which Churchill had sat throughout the autumn. He loathed it. In public he declared that it "certainly combines force with candor." In private he called it "malignant."

Clementine thought it hideous, and soon banished it to the attic, and sometime later had it burned. It portrayed him as old, which he was, and his face as coarse and cruel, which it was not. The royal family sent a birthday gift of four silver wine coasters engraved with the signatures of those who joined in giving it. On Churchill's birthday, Clement Attlee, who now led the opposition, delivered a long and generous tribute on the floor of the House, during which he declared that Churchill's wartime speeches reflected both the will of Parliament and of the nation.[197]

Churchill replied to Attlee's address the next day:

I was very glad that Mr. Attlee described my speeches in the war as expressing the will not only of Parliament but of the whole nation. Their will was resolute and remorseless and, as it proved, unconquerable. It fell to me to express it, and if I found the right words you must remember that I have always earned my living by my pen and by my tongue. It was a nation and race dwelling all round the globe that had the lion heart. I had the luck to be called upon to give the roar. I also hope that I sometimes suggested to the lion the right places to use his claws. I am now nearing the end of my journey. I hope I still have some services to render.[198]

His nine grandchildren and four children were on hand for the holiday season. During a family celebration that season, his daughter Diana expressed wonderment of all that he had seen and done in his life. He listened and said, "I have achieved a great deal to achieve nothing in the end."[199]

Churchill pondered his exit during the Christmas holidays and into the winter. Colville later wrote that during the long winter months, "alone with him at the bezique table or in the dining-room, I listened to many disquisitions of which the burden was: 'I have lost interest; I'm tired of it all.'" During a mid-March dinner with Rab Butler, he proclaimed: "I feel like an aeroplane at the end of its flight, in the dusk, with the petrol running out, in search of a safe landing." Finally, in late March, he told Colville that he'd leave just before the Easter recess. Easter fell on April 10 that year.[200]

Churchill made his last major address to the House of Commons on March 1, 1955, on the subject of that year's defence white paper, wherein his government announced for the first time the decision to build a hydrogen bomb. Churchill understood that Britain was indefensible against such weapons, yet he was determined that other countries—Russia—be made indefensible as well. The bomb could not help England regain its former glory but it might just offer England the means to survive. He titled his speech "The Deterrent—Nuclear Warfare." "There is no absolute defence against the hydrogen bomb," he told the House, "nor is any method in sight by which any nation, or any country, can be completely guaranteed against the devastating injury which even a score of them might inflict on wide regions." He went on to ask, "What ought we to do?"

> Which way shall we turn to save our lives and the future of the world? It does not matter so much to old people; they are going soon anyway; but I find it poignant to look at youth in all its activity and ardour and, most of all, to watch little children playing their merry games, and wonder what would lie before them if God wearied of mankind. The best defence would of course be bona fide disarmament all round. This is in all our hearts.[201]

He took care to speak of the "Soviets" and "Soviet communism," telling the House that he was avoiding the term "Russian" because he greatly admired the Russian people "for their bravery, their many gifts and their kindly nature." It was the Communist dictators who posed the threat to human survival, not the Russian people. He declared, "There is only one sane policy for the free world in the next few years."

> That is what we call defence through deterrents.... These deterrents may at any time become the parents of disarmament, provided that they deter. To make our contribution to the deterrent we must ourselves possess the most up-to-date nuclear weapons, and the means of delivering them.

Entire continents, not simply small islands such as Britain, were now vulnerable and would become more vulnerable as the Soviets developed new means to deliver atomic bombs:

> There is no reason why, however, they should not develop some time within the next four, three, or even two years more advanced weapons and full means to deliver them on North American targets. Indeed, there is every reason to believe that within that period they will.

A "curious paradox has emerged," he declared. "Let me put it simply. After a certain point has been passed it may be said: The worse things get, the better." He still believed that, as he told the House, "mercifully, there is time and hope if we combine patience and courage. . . . All deterrents will improve and gain authority during the next ten years. By that time, the deterrent may well reach its acme and reap its final reward." After forty-five minutes, his voice still strong, he came to the end, and his valediction to the House and to his countrymen:

> The day may dawn when fair play, love for one's fellow-men, respect for justice and freedom, will enable tormented generations to march forth serene and triumphant from the hideous epoch in which we have to dwell. Meanwhile, never flinch, never weary, never despair.[202]

Churchill's powers, declared that week's *Sunday Times,* "as he has so brilliantly demonstrated, are still of the highest order." The next day, as the defence debate continued, Aneurin Bevan accused Churchill of allowing America to dictate Britain's foreign policy, declaring that Churchill had canceled his 1953 Bermuda trip because he knew Eisenhower would not accede to a request to hold talks with the Russians. Churchill's reply stunned the House, for he revealed for the first time in public that he had not gone to Bermuda because "I was struck down by a very sudden illness which paralysed me completely. That is why I had to put it off."[203]

Moments later he tucked his reading glasses into a jacket pocket, gathered up his notes, and departed. He delivered two minor speeches in the House during his final month in office, the last a tribute to Lloyd George on March 28. Though he remained the member of Parliament from Woodford for nine more years, Churchill never again spoke in the House of Commons.

On April 4, Winston and Clementine hosted their last dinner at No. 10. Some fifty guests attended, including Queen Elizabeth and Prince Philip. The other grandees present, Colville wrote, included high government officials, members of Churchill's family, and several dukes and duchesses, including the sixteenth Duke of Norfolk, soon to chair a special top-secret government committee code-named Hope Not and vested with the task of planning Churchill's state funeral. Randolph Churchill attended, and predictably got drunk, at one point haranguing his cousin and Anthony Eden's wife, Clarissa, over a nasty article he had written about Eden for *Punch.* Sir Winston presided over all, attired in his Garter, Order of Merit, and knee breeches. His after-dinner speech took the form of a long toast to the Queen: "I used to enjoy drinking during the years when I was a cavalry subaltern in the reign of your Majesty's great-great-grandmother, Queen Victoria." At the end, he raised his glass "*to the Queen.*" Later that night, after the last guests had left, Jock Colville escorted Churchill up to his bedroom. The Old Man sat on his bed, and for several minutes did not speak. Colville imagined Churchill was "contemplating that this was his last night [as P.M.] at Downing Street. Then suddenly he stared at me and said with vehemence, 'I don't believe Anthony can do it.' "[204]

The next evening, Churchill donned his top hat and the frock coat he reserved for such formal occasions and went to Buckingham Palace to resign. Ever since the nineteenth century, an earldom had been the traditional path to the peerage for retired prime ministers who aspired to such titles. But Churchill had no peers, and deserved something more. Thus, the idea of offering him a dukedom was floated, although the Queen was not enthused at creating the first nonroyal duke in eighty years. The most satisfactory outcome for the Palace would be for the offer to be made and for Churchill to decline it. Days earlier, in fact, Churchill had told Colville that if the Queen offered him a dukedom, he would not accept it. Colville passed this information along to the Palace. The Queen indeed made the offer, and Churchill, after a moment's temptation, indeed declined. The Commons was his home, not the House of Lords. He later that night told Colville that he had declined the dukedom because to accept it would have ruined Randolph's political career, for as a Lord, Randolph could not sit in the Commons, from where the sovereign chose the prime minister. In fact, after his 1951 defeat, Randolph Churchill never again stood for office. Of his father, Randolph once said, "Nothing grows under the shadow of a great tree." To the end, the father did what he could to help the son, although Churchill once told one of his private secretaries, "I love Randolph, but I do not like him."[205]

On Wednesday, April 6, Winston and Clementine hosted a tea party at No. 10 for about one hundred of the staff. Late in the afternoon, Churchill left for Chartwell. Clementine, with much to arrange at their London house, stayed behind. Churchill arrived at Chartwell in the gloaming, Mary later wrote, but appeared "in quite good form." A small crowd of neighbors and reporters had gathered outside the house. As Churchill made for the front steps, a reporter called out: How does it feel not to be prime minister?[206]

Churchill replied, "It's always nice to come home."

8

Postscript

1955–1965

Although a general election was not required until 1956, soon after Churchill departed No. 10, Anthony Eden, who wanted to take his case to the people, dissolved Parliament and scheduled elections for late May. Churchill stood for the Commons for the nineteenth time, and was returned to the House in a sweeping Conservative victory on May 27. Eden picked up forty more seats, and the Conservatives this time won a plurality of the popular vote. During the campaign, Churchill was not asked by Eden to make any of the three BBC broadcasts allotted the Tories. The torch had passed.

In mid-May, Soviet foreign minister Molotov informed Harold Macmillan, the new foreign secretary, that Molotov and Soviet premier Nikolai Bulganin, who had succeeded Malenkov, were willing to join in a four-power summit meeting in Geneva. Nikita Khrushchev, too, would attend. Khrushchev, the Ukrainian political boss who had bungled the Kharkov battle in 1942, was now effectively co-leader in the Kremlin and leader of the de-Stalinization effort — the attempt to erase Stalin from Soviet history. President Eisenhower, well aware of Churchill's feelings on the matter, wrote a letter to Churchill in which he expressed wariness of the chances of success in Geneva, adding, "Foster and I know — as does the world — that your courage and vision will be missed at the meeting." The prize Churchill had sought for so long had gone to Eden.[1]

A new man had joined Churchill's private secretariat three years earlier, Anthony Montague Browne. He was not yet thirty at the time, had flown Beaufighters in Burma late in the war, and after coming home had forged a friendship with Jock Colville. Montague Browne, who, like Colville, was officially attached to the Foreign Office, was asked by Harold Macmillan upon Churchill's retirement to stay on with Churchill in order to vet the Old Man's communications with the many foreign leaders who were sure to ask his opinions on myriad matters. The posting, Macmillan assured Montague Browne, shouldn't last more than a year or two. It lasted almost a decade, until the end of Churchill's life. Though the Foreign Office paid Montague Browne's salary, Churchill insisted on repaying the money. Recalled Montague Browne, "Churchill did not want to feel that he was indebted to the government for anything."

Montague Browne titled his memoirs of these years *Long Sunset,* a turn of phrase that applied to both Churchill and the British Empire. He called the portion of the book—about one half—that had to do with Churchill's retirement "Late Afternoon." Yet even as the shadows lengthened, Churchill could not bring himself to fully retire from politics. Montague Browne wrote, "It is undoubtedly true that WSC loved his family deeply. It is also undoubtedly true that they came second to his purposes and his political work. How could it be otherwise?" There were consequences to his wife and children, unintended of course, and it is a perverse irony that Churchill's late afternoon lasted long enough for him to witness them.[2]

After his 1951 election defeat, Randolph never again stood for public office. Instead, he followed in his father's footsteps in the family traditions of the lecture circuit, essay writing, freelance jounalism, and biography. His accomplished biography, *Lord Derby: King of Lancashire,* was published in 1959, and met with critical acclaim. The son, Montague Browne wrote, displayed the same knack for reportage and writing as the father. By then Randolph had begun assembling the papers of his grandfather, Lord Randolph Churchill, in preparation for writing Sir Winston's official biography. Although Churchill had long been inclined to allow Randolph the privilege, he had specifically instructed the trustees of the literary trust to undertake the work only after his death. Randolph, as stubborn as his father, pushed for an early start. Finally, in 1960, Churchill relented. Randolph set to work with the same military precision his father had brought to the task of writing *The Second World War,* and with much the same staff. Yet, recalled the military historian A. J. P. Taylor, Randolph "treated the researchers abominably in his usual arrogant way. He regarded them as quite indistinguishable from the domestic servants." Thus, Randolph's team of researchers underwent frequent turnovers. "They never stayed very long."[3]

The son had inherited the father's cutting wit, but Randolph's came with a serrated edge and did him little good politically, wrote Montague Browne. On one occasion, Montague Browne dissuaded Randolph from following Anthony Eden (whom he despised) to a Washington conference in order to write a no doubt negative magazine story. Randolph: "Oh well, I suppose you're right. I would be the last camel to break the straw's back." Randolph's tastes (as did his sister Sarah's) ran to the extravagant, leading to his asking regularly for financial help from his parents, which meant the Chartwell Trust. The trust purchased him a London house and a three-story redbrick Georgian country house at East Bergholt, Suffolk. Churchill had set up the trust in order to benefit his children, but Clementine resented the children's repeated trips to the well. She believed, Mary later wrote, that "the fruit of Winston's genius and generosity" was being "poured...down the drain" in service to the "fecklessness" of their children. Randolph had married June Osborne in 1948. In 1949, a baby girl arrived—Arabella, named for the First Duke of Marlborough's sister, mistress to James II. But Randolph, wrote Mary with great understatement, "does not seem to have possessed the aptitude for marriage." He and June divorced in 1962. She later committed suicide. Randolph completed two volumes of his father's biography before dying of a heart attack on June 6, 1968, aged fifty-seven. His death, like his life, took place in the shadows: Robert F. Kennedy was murdered on that day. Randolph's passing went little noted.[4]

None of the children but Mary displayed the aptitude for marriage. She remained married to Christopher Soames—made Baron Soames in 1978—for forty years, until his death in 1987. Together they had five children; the oldest, Nicholas, followed his father into government, as the Conservative MP for Bedford.

Sarah and Diana charted the course of their marriages and lives under dark stars. Asked by Montague Browne why the family called Sarah "the Mule," Churchill replied, "Because she's bloody obstinate and she won't breed." During the six years before Churchill retired, Sarah had spent a great deal of her time in the United States pursuing her stage and screen career, with success. She toured the country in a Theatre Guild production of *The Philadelphia Story,* and then appeared in the 1951 Broadway version with Jeffrey Lynn. That same year, she signed on with MGM and starred with Jane Powell, Peter Lawford, and Fred Astaire in *Royal Wedding.* Early in 1952 she made the first of several appearances on NBC's *Hallmark Hall of Fame,* the creation of Joyce Hall, founder of Hallmark Cards, and an admirer of Sir Winston Churchill, with whom Hall struck a financial deal to reproduce Winston's paintings on Hallmark cards. This was the era of live television, and Sarah excelled—in *Amahl and the Night Visitors, Joan of Arc,* and as Ophelia in Hallmark's 1953 two-hour production of *Hamlet.* She had remarried in 1949. As with her first marriage, it was an elopement in the United States, this time at Sea Island, Georgia. The new groom was Anthony Beauchamp, who had served as a war artist and photographer in Burma during the war. Upon first meeting Beauchamp in early 1949, Churchill had taken an immediate dislike to him, for reasons unknown, which may explain Sarah's decision to have the wedding ceremony performed in Georgia. Her sister Mary—Lady Soames—called Sarah the "sunshine" in her parents' lives; Anthony Montague Browne anointed her "the brightest star."[5]

But by the late 1950s, Sarah's star was dimming and her marriage to Anthony Beauchamp failing. It ended utterly in July 1957 when Beauchamp committed suicide by swallowing a fistful of sleeping pills. Beauchamp's death came almost exactly a decade after Gil Winant, hopelessly in love with Sarah, went home to America and killed himself with a gunshot to the head. Never able to control her drinking, Sarah began a long descent into alcoholism. The next year she was arrested in Malibu and fined fifty dollars for public drunkenness. Her father lived long enough to read the newspaper accounts of three more arrests for drunkenness in Britain and a ten-day stay in jail for violating her probation. In a 1959 letter to Clementine written while he was on the Riviera, he attributed Sarah's decline to "the difficulties which are common to women at the change of life." Finally, in 1962, it appeared Sarah might have found happiness when she met and married Henry Touchet-Jesson, the twenty-third Baron Audley. Fifteen months later, Audley died of a massive coronary. Sarah's film and stage career was at an end. In 1967 she wrote a short and lyrical tribute to her father: *A Thread in the Tapestry.* In 1981 she published her autobiography, *Keep on Dancing,* in which she discussed her battles with alcohol in poignant and honest terms. She died an alcoholic in 1982, aged sixty-seven.[6]

Diana suffered the same bouts of depression, fatigue, and nervous tension as her mother, yet Clementine, rather than find common cause with her daughter, had always maintained a discreet emotional distance. Diana had had a nervous breakdown in 1953 and was on the verge of another at about the time her father retired. Unlike Randolph and Sarah, she did not find release from her pain in the bottle. It was Diana who comforted Randolph and Sarah during their regular crises; it was Diana alone who attended Henry Audley's funeral. She was a steady daughter and wife, married since 1935 to Duncan Sandys, who was made minister of defence in 1957 and secretary of state for Commonwealth relations in 1960. They separated in 1956; in 1960, Sandys divorced Diana and soon remarried. Sympathetic to those in severe emotional distress, Diana joined the Samaritans in 1962, an organization dedicated to round-the-clock help for anyone contemplating suicide.

Sometime during the night of October 19–20, 1963, Diana swallowed a massive overdose of sleeping pills and died. Her sister Mary delivered the news to Clementine, herself hospitalized and under sedation that month, on the verge of a nervous breakdown. And it fell to Mary to deliver the news to her father, who, dulled now by old age, only took it in slowly and "then withdrew into a great and distant silence." Both father and mother were too weak to attend Diana's funeral, held in the little churchyard at Bladon, where Churchill's parents were buried.[7]

The theme of the latter portion of Lord Moran's memoirs, *Churchill: The Struggle for Survival, 1940–1965,* is one of Churchill brought low in his retirement years by the relentless onslaught of the Black Dog of depression. It is a tale—exaggerated and incomplete—of Churchill's journey to decrepitude and the slow wasting away of his physical and mental powers. Among the chapter headings are "Swan-song," "Depression," "The Flesh Was Weak," and "The Dying Gladiator." Moran chronicles Churchill's battle with carbuncles in 1955 (which Churchill believed were "malignant"), pneumonia in 1958, and two minor strokes in 1959. Churchill was not afraid of death, yet minor illnesses provoked bouts of anxiety. Moran, Montague Browne later wrote, was always ready and willing to treat his most important—his only—patient.

Although Moran claimed that Churchill had approved his publishing his medical memoirs, he had not secured the approval in writing. The family, then and since, has held that against Moran. His narrative of Churchill's first five years of retirement is rife with scenes depicting Churchill's loneliness and despondency. Moran called the decade of 1954–1964 "a long chronicle of despair." These were years, he wrote, that found Churchill giving up reading; he had not and in fact polished off *War and Peace, Tom Jones,* Scott's *Rob Roy,* and Macaulay's essay on Milton, among many other works. A stack of books borrowed from the local library always occupied Churchill's night table, and the turnover was swift.

Churchill loved his days outside, painting and feeding his menagerie, including Toby, a budgerigar Churchill had received on his eightieth birthday. Where Churchill went, Toby went, including the Riviera. Moran suggested that Churchill teach Toby the Chartwell phone number in case the bird escaped. Churchill replied that he did not know his own phone number. Alas, Toby gained his freedom in 1960 after finding an open window at the Hôtel de Paris. At the end of a Chartwell day, the Old Man enjoyed the movies regularly screened at 9:15 P.M. sharp: *The Bridge on the River Kwai, The Longest Day, The Guns of Navarone,* the 1958 musical *Gigi,* and all the Disney films. Moran wrote that these were the years that found the Old Man spending his days "staring into the fire, giving it a prod with his stick when the room got cold" as the Black Dog of depression hovered nearby. These were "sad years of mounting decrepitude" when Churchill became "the chief mourner at his own protracted funeral."[8]

That was largely untrue during Churchill's first five or six years of retirement, and only partially true during Churchill's last two years. Montague Browne writes that in his thirteen years of service to Churchill, he never once heard the Old Man refer to the "Black Dog." Churchill mourned the passing of the British Empire, recalled Montague Browne, and was profoundly saddened by the dangerous state of world affairs. He expressed his worries in that regard to Montague Browne as only Churchill could: "I always feared that mass pressure in the United States might force them to use their H-bombs while the Russians still had not got any. It's always been a tendency of the masses to drop their Hs." Churchill's melancholy, Montague Browne wrote, was "objective, detached, and sadly logical"; it did not stem from any sort of "subjective mood of deep depression."[9]

Retirement found Churchill busy publishing his four-volume *History of the English-Speaking Peoples*. He regularly attended dinners at his private dining society, the Other Club, and visited Harrow at least once each year. In 1956 he was invited by Eden to lunch at No. 10 in order to meet Bulganin and Khrushchev, co-leaders in the Kremlin, although Churchill told Moran that week that he thought Khrushchev would soon emerge as the real power. Meals, as always, were splendid affairs, and Churchill's intake of roast beef, brandy, whisky, and cigars remained undiminished. He painted dozens of landscapes that met with critical acclaim. The eminent British art critic and historian Ernst H. Gombrich wrote in the *Atlantic Monthly* that Churchill's essay *Painting as a Pastime* contained ideas "so acute and so profound...I could do no better than to build them into the fabric of my book, *Art and Illusion*."[10]

His wanderlust, too, remained undiminished. Churchill's post–No. 10 travels took him to Sicily, Morocco, the French Riviera numerous times, the Italian Riviera, Rome and Paris and New York. In 1959 he journeyed by jet to New York and on to Washington for another stay at the White House, and then to the Gettysburg battlefield in the company of President Eisenhower, who made his home nearby in the shadow of the Alleghenies. On that excursion, Churchill offered a running narrative of the Battle of Gettysburg as Eisenhower's helicopter hovered over the battlefield—the Old Man recounting Union and Confederate troop deployments, the names of the divisions and corps commanders, the time of day and outcome of each skirmish fought. His gait was slower, his hearing almost gone, but the great mind remained strong.

Later that year he stood for election in Woodford, and was returned to the House. And late in 1959, he went to Cambridge, where he planted two oak trees and laid the foundation stone of Churchill College. At his behest, the Prof and Jock Colville had been raising subscriptions for the college since 1955, when Churchill, with MIT in mind, proposed that a similar institution for science and technology be built in Britain. Churchill contributed the first £25,000, and by the end of the decade, more than three million pounds had been raised. Churchill College opened in 1964. The charter contained a clause—suggested by Clementine and endorsed by Churchill—calling for the admission of women on the same basis as men. In 1972 Churchill College became the first of the Oxford and Cambridge colleges to admit women on an equal basis, and allow them to take up residence at the schools.[11]

In January 1957, Queen Elizabeth summoned Churchill to Buckingham Palace to help guide her in the selection of a new prime minister—either Harold Macmillan or Rab Butler. The need to decide arose because of the resignation of Anthony Eden, whose health had collapsed, a condition brought about by the disaster that had befallen Britain during the Suez crisis of late 1956.

It began during the summer, when Egypt's President Nasser nationalized the Suez Canal in retaliation for the United States' and Britain's pulling their financial backing from the great Aswan Dam project in protest of Nasser's increasingly friendly relations with the U.S.S.R. and Egypt's recognition of the People's Republic of China in July. The nationalization of the canal was in violation of an agreement Egypt had signed with France and Britain in 1954. On October 29, the Israeli army launched a preemptive strike into the Sinai; the British and French knew and approved it in advance. Thus, with Israel and Egypt at war and the integrity of the canal zone threatened, Britain and France intervened. In fact, Eden's real objective was to depose Nasser, whom Eden hated for his pan-Arabic nationalism and the French despised for the aid he was rendering to the Algerian rebels. Forty-eight hours after the Israelis attacked, the RAF struck Nasser's forces, followed three days later by a French and British landing at Port Said, on the north end of the canal, which they quickly took. America had not been notified in advance of the operation, and President Eisenhower was furious. Within days, the United States joined the Soviet Union in voting for UN resolutions condemning the British and French. Most Britons questioned the morality of the strike, Colville later wrote, but all believed success was assured. It was not. On November 6, Eden, his cabinet cowed by the American threat to gut the value of the pound by flooding financial markets with sterling bonds, ordered a cease-fire (without informing the French).[12]

Thus Churchill's audience with the Queen. He advised her to choose Macmillan, later telling friends he did so because Macmillan was the older and more experienced man. But all knew that Butler, though loyal in his service to Churchill since 1940, had been a man of Chamberlain, and Munich, and at the time had told Colville that Churchill's criticism of Chamberlain was "vulgar." In the years since, Butler, in private conversations, had made clear his belief that Churchill was a political opportunist and that he, Butler, would be a suitable choice as prime minister. The Queen chose Macmillan. Eden retired to his country house, Rose Bower, in Wiltshire, to write his memoirs. He remained a close friend of Churchill's, and Churchill remained loyal to Eden, who, he told Moran, had "been bitched" by the cabinet when it refused to carry through on the Suez affair. Over dinner Churchill told Colville he considered the Suez operation "the most-ill-conceived and ill-executed imaginable." Asked by Colville what he would have done, the Old Man replied, "I would never have dared; and if I had dared, I would certainly never have dared stop."[13]

Nine months later, on October 4, 1957, Soviet scientists bolted a 184-pound metal sphere that had been polished to a high sheen atop a two-stage R-7 Semyorka rocket and launched it out of the stratosphere and into space, where it dutifully began to tumble around the earth, one pass each ninety or so minutes. The launch was a complete surprise; nobody in the West had seen it coming. They could see it now, overhead. The Soviets called it *Sputnik 1;* it was about the size of a soccer ball. The Western press termed the device "an earth satellite." *Sputnik* was outfitted with a radio beacon, which broadcast back to earth a steady signal. American scientists claimed it was transmitting secret messages. It wasn't. The signal was gibberish, but its message was clear: we can reach you. Several times a day *Sputnik* passed over the United States and Western Europe, just visible with binoculars at dawn and dusk (which is why the Soviets had polished it). Clementine, having returned to England from Max Beaverbrook's Riviera villa, La Capponcina, scribbled a quick note to Winston, now ensconced on the French Riviera at La Pausa, the villa of his European literary agent, Emery Reves. "What do you think of the earth satellite? I heard it on the wireless—it sounded ominous."[14]

It was. The temperature of the Cold War was approaching absolute zero. The Soviet rocket that had launched *Sputnik* had a range of five thousand miles, quite sufficient to reach London. Worse, as the Soviets demonstrated a month later with a second launch, it could carry a payload of more than one thousand pounds, the weight of a small hydrogen bomb, although the payload for this launch consisted only of a dog named Laika, whom the American press dubbed Muttnik. Harold Nicolson believed Britons cared more for the dog than for the implications—men in rockets carrying atomic bombs orbiting the earth in search of targets. Indeed, members of the Dumb Friends League proposed gathering outside the Soviet embassy and observing two minutes of silence. Such was the West's paranoia that the *New York Times* ran a story in which Dr. Fred L. Whipple, director of the Smithsonian Astrophysical Observatory in Cambridge, Massachusetts, claimed that it was "entirely possible the Russians already have a rocket on the way to the moon," where it might detonate an H-bomb during a lunar eclipse later in the week, perhaps in celebration of the fortieth anniversary of Lenin's November 1917 revolution. The Semyorka rocket's accuracy was thought to be wobbly, perhaps within three or four miles of a target at best. Yet accuracy no longer mattered. H-bombs had joined horseshoes and hand grenades, where close counts. Months earlier, President Eisenhower had asked Horace Rowan Gaither, of the Ford Foundation, to form a commission to study America's missile capabilities. One month after *Sputnik* went aloft, Gaither's recommendations were leaked to the press: build more missiles, quickly, and build fallout shelters.[15]

With *Sputnik* speeding along through the heavens, the rocket age and the atomic age had merged, as Churchill in his last major address in the House predicted would happen. But Sir Winston Churchill was no longer a participant in the unfolding of the story. In his reply to Clementine he wrote that *Sputnik* itself did not trouble him but the Soviet gains in science and technology did. "We must struggle on," he wrote, "and [look] to the union with America."

The world press did not think to ask Churchill for his opinion on the earth satellite. The press by then was interested only in news that pertained to Churchill's health. Churchill had spent his entire life creating an identity from his own audacious imagination, which, as Oscar Wilde observed, was the best way to get through life without suffering through it all. Churchill had made his dream a reality; he had imagined himself into Sir Winston Leonard Spencer Churchill, the greatest statesman of the twentieth century. He had fought the monster—Hitler—without himself becoming a monster. He had prevailed on his countrymen during his final year at No. 10 to build the hydrogen bomb, in order to keep the Soviet dictators behind their Iron Curtain. Yet by 1958, new ages and new generations—the atomic, the space, the beat, the rock and roll, the television—had overtaken and bypassed Sir Winston. With no further role to play in history's unfolding, he became a spectator.

On September 12, 1958, Winston and Clementine celebrated their fiftieth wedding anniversary at La Capponcina. Clementine had finally come to accept Max, but she despised the Riviera, especially when her husband did not fare well at the Monte Carlo casino. On September 22, Churchill and Clementine embarked on a Mediterranean cruise as the guests of Aristotle Onassis on board Onassis's yacht *Christina*, a 325-foot, 1,850-ton converted Canadian frigate—a destroyer in American parlance. Onassis, Churchill told Colville after first meeting the shipping magnate in 1956, "was a man of mark." Onassis believed likewise of Churchill. The September voyage was the first of eight cruises Churchill made aboard the *Christina* over the next five years, in the Aegean, the Mediterranean, and to the West Indies in 1960 and 1961, when Onassis set a course from the Caribbean up the U.S. east coast to New York City in order that Churchill could pay one more visit to his other country.[16]

Onassis joined the small circle of family, friends, and staff who tended to Churchill's care and comfort. Any given day might find Bernard Montgomery stopping by Chartwell for tea, Randolph and Evelyn Waugh for dinner, the "wollygogs" for a tour of the Chartwell farms. Requests for interviews, and there were many in the first years, were all screened by Montague Browne, who in the final years composed Churchill's few brief addresses and wrote letters for the Great Man's signature. Two nurses attended to Churchill's needs after 1958; two typists stood by for dictation, cleaned his brushes and palettes, and helped manage his and Clementine's social calendar. A Mr. Shaw — "a Labour man but quite a nice fellow," Churchill told a nurse — ran the Chartwell movie projector. Churchill never dined alone; if no family or friends were on hand, Montague Browne took a seat at the table, and did so for fifteen straight nights during one stretch. In the bargain he listened in awe as Churchill delivered fifteen dissertations on British history. Dinner conversation with Churchill, Montague Browne wrote, "was a wonder and a delight" and "never, ever dull." All who surrounded the Great Man were, in effect, "in service" to Sir Winston. Churchill's bodyguard, Detective Sergeant Edmund Murray, remained nearby at all times, never more than a room away. Lord Moran was expected to appear at once if summoned by Churchill, who did so frequently, often to complain of imaginary ailments. On one occasion Churchill phoned the doctor with the worrisome news that he had taken his temperature only to find it read sixty-six degrees. Montague Browne overheard Churchill's end of the conversation: "What the hell do you mean, in that case I'm dead." A long pause ensued, then, "Well, that is to say, ninety-six, but I would still like you to come around."[17]

His last charge in defense of the Empire came in November 1958, in Paris, when Charles de Gaulle (French premier at the time and elected President of the Fifth Republic in December) awarded him the Croix de la Libération. Churchill made a brief speech, telling the assembled in English that he would not "subject you to the ordeals of darker days" by making his remarks in French. He anointed de Gaulle "the symbol of the soul of France and of the unbreakable integrity of her spirit in adversity." He closed with: "The future is uncertain, but we can be sure that if Britain and France, who for so long have been the vanguard of the Western civilization, stand together, with our Empires, our American friends...then we have grounds for sober confidence and high hope. I thank you all for the honour you have done me. *Vive la France!*"[18]

His mention of "our Empires" was ironic. By 1958, the French had lost Indochina: Cambodia had gained independence in 1953; in South Vietnam the corrupt premier, Ngo Dinh Diem, was desperately trying to prop up his regime with the help of newly arrived American military advisers. Algeria, too, was violently departing the French fold. There, diverse revolutionary armies—united only by their desire to drive out the French—fought the French army from 1954 until final victory in 1962, a war that claimed the lives of at least three hundred thousand Algerians and sent at least one million descendants of French settlers into exile.

The British, meanwhile, were losing lesser jewels in their crown: in July, Iraqi army officers overthrew and murdered King Faisal II, the Hashemite king whose father the British had put on the throne in 1932. The new regime, backed by Nasser and manifesting a pro-Moscow bent, ordered the RAF out of its airbase near Baghdad. The Gold Coast had bolted the empire in 1957, and it became the independent nation of Ghana. Kenya did likewise in 1963, after the decade-long Mau Mau uprising that had claimed at least 20,000 Kenyan lives, and the lives of scores of white European settlers. Among the Mau Mau victims were thirty-two British settlers, including small children, whose deaths at the hands of the Mau Mau had inflamed Britain, and Churchill. The British response was brutal. At one point Churchill wanted to read the Mau Mau initiation oath—he called it "incredibly filthy"—in the House. It called for eating the flesh of disinterred bodies and the eyeballs of enemies, fornicating with sheep, and drinking the "Kaberichia cocktail," a mixture of semen and menstrual blood. He settled for giving MPs a printed version. In Kenya, the British made administering the oath a capital offense; more than one thousand suspected Mau Maus were hanged.[19]

Churchill remained an unrepentant champion of the British Empire to the end. Months before he retired, President Eisenhower suggested—with some nerve—that "a fitting climax" to Churchill's career would be to deliver a valedictory speech proclaiming that colonialism was "on the way out as a relationship between peoples." Churchill's reply was immediate and caustic: "I read with great interest all you have written me about what is called colonialism; namely, bringing forth backward races and opening up the jungles." He declared that in India, "with all its history, religion, and ancient forms of despotic rule, Britain has a story to tell which will look quite well against the background of the coming hundred years." He added that the sentiments and policies Eisenhower advocated "are in full accord with the policy now being pursued in all the Colonies of the British Empire." Yet: "In this I must say that I am a laggard. I am a bit skeptical about universal suffrage for the Hottentots even if refined by proportional representation."

The final few years of retirement formed "a desultory tale," wrote Montague Browne, speaking as much for himself as for Churchill. By the early 1960s, Montague Browne found that he needed only an hour or two each day to address his official, diplomatic duties in service to Churchill. As the months and years passed by, Montague Browne—and sometimes his wife and daughter, or the Colvilles—drifted with Churchill, from one Riviera villa to the next, from one port of call to the next aboard *Christina*. Onassis invited luminous muses aboard for Churchill's entertainment, including Onassis's mistress Maria Callas, Gracie Fields, and Greta Garbo. "There is no doubt," recalled Churchill's grandson and namesake, "that my grandfather enjoyed the company of beautiful women." Near the end of the previous century, Churchill had written his mother after his first Atlantic crossing: "I do not contemplate ever taking a sea voyage for pleasure." He had been especially put off on that voyage by the complete lack of any "nice people" on board. Now nearing the end of his life, he found great pleasure roaming the high seas on *Christina* in the company of his merry companions. On one voyage, Churchill proposed that all the men grow mustaches; they did. Montague Browne thought Churchill's "did not become him." On another, Montague Browne overheard Churchill address a dolphin that was swimming alongside the ship: "I do wish I could communicate with you." It was a good life.[20]

The 1961 voyage to the Caribbean on *Christina* marked Churchill's sixteenth—and last—journey to the United States. A wild storm blew off Cape Hatteras as *Christina* made for New York along the Carolina coast. Churchill, now eighty-six, insisted on sitting atop a piano in the lounge in order to witness the fury outside. He did so supported by four strong Greek seamen. He was Churchill; it could not be otherwise. When high seas struck on these voyages and made dining at a table impossible, Churchill took his meals in bed, propped up by numerous pillows, his bottle of Pol Roger held firmly between his thighs. Onassis and Montague Browne would join him, sitting cross-legged on the floor, with their bottles of Pol Roger held between their thighs. On board *Christina* Churchill could indulge in his love of long games of bezique, cigars, and postprandial brandies. Yet by 1961, Churchill's fire had dimmed enough that Montague Browne, upon *Christina*'s docking in New York City, had to politely decline when President John F. Kennedy telephoned with an invitation for Churchill to spend a few days at the White House. It was time to go home.[21]

When, in early November 1895, twenty-year-old subaltern Winston Churchill disembarked the Cunard steamship *Etruria* at a Hudson River pier and set foot for the first time in his mother's native land, horse-drawn omnibuses plied the dusty macadam roads of New York City. The Ninth Avenue and Third Avenue elevated railroads ran up the island (and spewed glowing embers upon hapless pedestrians below), but the first New York subway would not be operating for almost a decade. London was then ushering in its third decade of underground rail service between Paddington and King's Cross, but young Churchill had not availed himself of this form of public transport and would do so only once during the remainder of his life.

When Churchill first came to American shores, Henry Ford had yet to successfully propel his quadricycle by means of a gasoline engine, and the Dodge brothers were still building bicycles in Ontario, Canada. So, too, in Sheffield, England, was Thomas Humber, whose armored motorcars Churchill relied on during the Blitz, though he would rarely actually operate one in his lifetime—not because he was an aging Victorian man who did not understand the mechanics of automobiles but because he was a Victorian man who believed it only proper that liveried drivers drove carriages, including motorized carriages. Churchill was approaching early middle age when Orville Wright, at Kitty Hawk, took aloft the spruce-and-wire flying machine that he and his brother Wilbur had built. By then the earliest infernal contraptions built by Thomas Humber and Henry Ford were petrifying cows and horses and old women on both sides of the Atlantic. In the motorcar Churchill saw the genesis of the tank; in the airplane, the fighter plane and the bomber. In the early decades of the twentieth century, he mused in magazine articles on the nature of rockets, atomic power, and television. He analyzed the moral and political implications of every new technology brought forth in the first half of the twentieth century. The *Etruria* had carried sail on the 1895 voyage lest its steam engines fail during the ten-day Atlantic crossing. Churchill departed his other country for the final time on April 14, 1961, on board a Pan American World Airways Boeing 707 that, pushed along by the jet stream seven miles high, carried him home across the Atlantic at more than five hundred miles per hour.

Moran's memoir is correct in one regard; after Churchill suffered a serious bout of pneumonia in 1958, his ailments became more frequent and more serious—the 1959 strokes followed in 1960 by a hairline spinal fracture from a fall in his bedroom. Moran ordered bed rest on that occasion. Churchill refused. Caring for Churchill resulted in "open warfare" between the nurses and the patient, nurse Roy Howells recalled. A big blow came in June 1962, when Churchill slipped and fell in his suite at the Hôtel de Paris. While drifting in and out of consciousness, Churchill told Montague Brown that he wanted to die in England. Prime Minister Harold Macmillan dispatched an RAF Comet to bring the Great Man home. The press expected the worst. Montague Browne believed he would have to instruct the Duke of Norfolk to set Operation Hope Not—Churchill's state funeral—in motion. On the flight to London, Churchill, heavily sedated, awoke, and muttered to Montague Browne: "I don't think I'll go back to that place, it's unlucky. First Toby, and then this." Montague Browne had forgotten Toby, the budgerigar, but Churchill had not. The body was frail, but not the wit. On his arrival in London, he flashed the "V" sign from his stretcher. He underwent surgery to insert a pin in his hip. After three weeks in the hospital, he left for 28 Hyde Park Gate, where within three months he could stroll unaided to the little gardens behind the house.[22]

He told Moran he felt he was "lingering," and by 1962 he was. Prof—Lord Cherwell—had died in 1957, at seventy-one. He had served Churchill as science adviser and loyal friend since 1920. Brendan Bracken, fifty-seven, followed Cherwell in 1958 after suffering the horrific effects of throat cancer and botched cobalt radiation therapy. During his 1959 trip to America, Churchill visited Foster Dulles and George Marshall in the hospital, the former dying of cancer, the latter of the effects of two strokes and kidney failure. Two weeks later, Dulles—whom Churchill once described as "the only case of a bull I know who carries his china closet with him"—was dead. Marshall went in October. Alanbrooke went in 1963, but not before publishing his wartime diaries, which hurt Churchill deeply. Another, though lesser, link to the past was broken in 1964 when Montague Phippen Porch, three years Churchill's junior, died. Porch had been Jennie Churchill's third and last husband, and therefore Sir Winston's stepfather. The hardest blow—after Diana's death—came on June 9, 1964, when his friend of nearly six decades, Max Beaverbrook, died of cancer, at eighty-five. Montague Browne began his narrative of these final years: "This is a story of decline." The decline came in 1963 and 1964 in fits and starts, relapses and recoveries, but it came, relentless and unyielding.[23]

Churchill would much prefer to have someone put an old dance hall tune or martial march on the gramophone than turn on the television. He did enjoy an occasional episode of *Sea Hunt,* starring Lloyd Bridges, but otherwise believed, as he told Moran, that "this bloody invention will do harm to the society and to the race." But on April 9, 1963, he watched with satisfaction as a live satellite feed from the Rose Garden of the White House brought him images of President Kennedy bestowing upon him, by Act of Congress, honorary U.S. citizenship. Churchill became the first person to be accorded the honor. The Old Man, too ill to attend the ceremony, was represented by Randolph and young Winston. Seven weeks later, he embarked on his eighth and final voyage aboard *Christina,* a tour of the Aegean. On July 4 he left Athens for London by air; *Christina* was then made ready for its next guest, First Lady Jacqueline Kennedy, who sought a peaceful autumn interlude after the death that summer of her infant son, Patrick. She also sought rest and relaxation in order to prepare herself for the fall campaign season in the United States, which would include a trip to Texas in November. And so it came to pass that Churchill's television again saw use late in the evening of Friday, November 22. That night Churchill sat in silence for a long time before the fire. Yet, as with Diana's death a month earlier, the full impact of the president's murder was dulled by Churchill's advanced age.[24]

As 1964 came on, Churchill still served as the member of Parliament from Woodford, but only infrequently took his place on the front bench, below the gangway, where he had sat during the Wilderness Years of the 1930s. He visited the House of Commons for the last time on July 27, and soon thereafter announced that he would not stand for Woodford in that October's general election. He left Chartwell for the last time in October, taking up residence at 27–28 Hyde Park Gate, where a ground-floor bedroom had been prepared for him. On November 30, he celebrated his ninetieth birthday in the company of his family, the Colvilles, and the Montague Brownes. Champagne flowed all day; a basket of Whitstable oysters was hauled in. Cakes arrived all day from well-wishers, and 70,000 cards and telegrams from around the world. By midafternoon, hundreds of Londoners crowded the street in front of the house. A news photographer snapped a shot of a smiling Sir Winston, attired in a siren suit, peering from behind a parted curtain. Dinner—and brandy and cigars—carried into the early hours of December 1. Ten days later Churchill made an appearance at the Other Club; it was to be his last.

Christmas was a subdued affair. Churchill's gift to Montague Browne was his six-volume war memoir. A few days later, Montague Browne asked the Old Man to sign the books. Churchill managed to sign his full name in the first volume; by the sixth he could only scrawl "W." They were the last papers he signed. Now the Great Man did indeed spend long hours staring into the fireplace. Yet he still took lunch with Clementine, and he still took his cigar and brandy after dinner.[25]

But on January 9 he refused both.

His nurses helped him to bed that night. He was not to leave it again.

On the twelfth—Churchill was by then unconscious—doctors Moran and Brain diagnosed a stroke, and informed the family to prepare for the worst, which the doctors believed would likely come very soon. But they underestimated the strength of their patient. Days passed, and then a week. Old friends and colleagues came by to pay their respects. Violet Bonham Carter stopped in, but only for the briefest of moments: "Good-bye, Winston," she said, standing at the foot of his bed. Then she turned and walked out.

Early on a January day about a dozen years earlier, Jock Colville brought a minor matter of state to Churchill's attention, as the Old Man shaved. Churchill turned to Colville, and said: "Today is the twenty-fourth of January. It is the day my father died. It is the day that I shall die too."

And on January 24, 1965, he did.[26]

Churchill's coffin lay in state at Westminster Hall for three days and three nights. More than 320,000 people filed past the catafalque, the silent queue of men and women and children threading through Parliament Square and on across Westminster Bridge. On the bleak, cold morning of Sunday, January 30, the coffin, covered by the Union Jack, was borne from the hall on the shoulders of eight Grenadier Guards. It was placed on a gun carriage drawn by one hundred Royal Navy seamen and flanked by the guard of honor nearly one hundred strong, in bearskins and greatcoats. Randolph and eight young Churchill men took their places behind the gun carriage. Before and behind, companies of troops from storied regiments—from the Hussars, from the RAF, from the army, in khaki, and the Royal Marines, in blue—stood at attention awaiting the order to march. The Horse Guard in their red jackets waited on their impatient steeds. Hundreds of thousands of Britons lined the Strand and Fleet Street and the roads to Ludgate Hill and to St. Paul's, where the Archbishop of Canterbury, in his purple robes, stood atop the steps and awaited the procession. Shortly after 9:45 the first of ninety cannons in Hyde Park fired its salute. The Earl Marshal of England, in greatcoat and cocked hat, raised his baton.

Then, to the haunting beat of a single drum, the procession began the journey to St Paul's. Only twice in the past 112 years had a nonroyal personage been so honored with a state funeral: the Duke of Wellington in 1852 and Gladstone in 1898. Queen Victoria attended neither funeral, but Queen Elizabeth II honored Churchill by her presence in St. Paul's. She was joined by representatives from more than 110 nations, including four kings, a queen, five heads of state, and sixteen prime ministers. Charles de Gaulle, wearing a plain kepi and simple uniform, unadorned with insignia, medals, or ribbons, stood a head taller than all present as the great imperial ceremony began.[27]

From St. Paul's, the coffin was taken by motor launch up the Thames to Waterloo Station. There it was put aboard one of five Pullman coaches hauled by the Battle of Britain–class locomotive *Winston S. Churchill* for the sixty-mile journey to the Oxfordshire village of Bladon and the little churchyard of St. Martin's, within sight of the spires of Blenheim Palace, where the story had begun. Lord Moran, finding in the end his literary voice, wrote:

> And at Bladon, in a country churchyard, in the stillness of a winter evening, in the presence of his family and a few friends, Winston Churchill was committed to the English earth, which in his finest hour, he had held inviolate.[28]

Eight months later, on the twenty-fifth anniversary of the Battle of Britain, the Dean and Chapter of Westminster Abbey, at the request of the Queen and Parliament, placed a sixty-by-seventy-six-inch polished greenmarble slab in the floor of that thousand-year-old monument to English history. All who enter cannot help but to see it there, in the nave, just a few feet inside the great west doors. Engraved upon it are the words:

REMEMBER
WINSTON
CHURCHILL

SOURCE NOTES

ABBREVIATIONS AND SHORT TITLES USED IN THESE NOTES

C&R-TCC
: *Churchill and Roosevelt: The Complete Correspondence,* 3 vols., edited by Warren F. Kimball. Princeton, 1984.

CAB
: British Cabinet Documents, Public Record Office, Kew.

ChP
: Churchill Papers, Churchill College, Cambridge, U.K.

Hansard
: *Record of Parliamentary Debates* (Hansard).

NYT
: *New York Times.*

Times
: *The Times* of London.

TWY
: *Harold Nicolson: The War Years 1939–1945,* vol. 2 of *Diaries and Letters,* edited by Nigel Nicolson. New York, 1967.

W&C-TPL
: *Winston and Clementine: The Personal Letters of the Churchills,* edited by Mary Soames. New York, 2001.

WM/[name]; PFR/ [name]
: Author interviews.

WSCHCS
: *Winston S. Churchill: His Complete Speeches,* edited by Robert Rhodes James, vols. VI (1935–1942), VII (1943–1949), and VIII (1950–1963). London, 1974.

The Official Biography of Winston Spencer Churchill, by Martin Gilbert (Boston, 1966–1988), is cited as follows:

GILBERT 6
: Volume 6. *Finest Hour 1939–1941*

GILBERT 7
: Volume 7. *Road to Victory 1941–1945*

GILBERT 8
: Volume 8. *Never Despair 1945–1965*

Cv/2
: Companion volume to Gilbert 6 (May–December 1940)

Cv/3
: Companion volume to Gilbert 6 and Gilbert 7 (1941)

The Second World War, by Winston S. Churchill (Boston, 1983), is cited as follows:

WSC 1
: Volume 1. *Gathering Storm*

WSC 2
: Volume 2. *Their Finest Hour*

WSC 3
: Volume 3. *The Grand Alliance*

WSC 4
: Volume 4. *The Hinge of Fate*

WSC 5
: Volume 5. *Closing the Ring*

WSC 6
: Volume 6. *Triumph and Tragedy*

Preamble

1. WM/Sir Ian Jacob, 11/12/80.

2. John Wheeler-Bennett, *Action This Day: Working with Churchill* (London, 1968), 140; Cv/3, 267, 387; Kay Halle, *Irrepressible Churchill: Stories, Sayings and Impressions of Sir Winston Churchill* (London, 1985), 171.

3. Wheeler-Bennett, *Action*, 53–56; PFR/Winston S. Churchill, 5/04 ("summer sunshine"); GILBERT 6, 1214–15 (recollection of Elizabeth Layton).

4. John Colville, *The Fringes of Power: 10 Downing Street Diaries 1939–1955* (New York, 1985), 406; Lord Moran, *Churchill: Taken from the Diaries of Lord Moran* (Boston, 1966), 451; Halle, *Irrepressible Churchill*, 133; Cv/3, 1309, 1471 (Baldwin family); TWY, 307.

5. Mary Soames, *Clementine Churchill: The Biography of a Marriage* (New York, 2003), 383.

6. Wheeler-Bennett, *Action*, 79, 140.

7. WM/Jock Colville, 10/14/80; Colville, *Fringes*, 434; WSCHCS, 7912; Winston Churchill, *My Early Life: 1874–1904* (New York, 1996), 112.

8. Colville, *Fringes*, 170–71; Wheeler-Bennett, *Action*, 93.

9. Moran, *Diaries*, 265.

10. Anthony Montague Browne, *Long Sunset* (London, 1996), 118; Walter H. Thompson, *Assignment: Churchill* (New York, 1953), 84.

11. Thompson, *Assignment: Churchill*, 84; WM/Sir Robert Boothby, 10/16/80.

12. WM/G. M. Thompson, 10/24/80; Colville, *Fringes*, 217; WSC 6, 752.

13. WM/G. M. Thompson, 10/24/80.

14. WM/G. M. Thompson, 10/24/80; Colville, *Fringes*, 136, 142–43, 231; E. L. Spears, *Assignment to Catastrophe*, 2 vols. (New York, 1955), 1:154; WM/Kathleen Hill, 11/4/80; WM/Jock Colville, 10/14/80.

15. Wheeler-Bennett, *Action*, 153; Colville, *Fringes*, 195–96; WSC 6, 733 ("foreign names were made for Englishmen...").

16. Robert E. Sherwood, *Roosevelt and Hopkins: An Intimate History* (New York, 1948), 688.

17. Wheeler-Bennett, *Action*, 182–83; WM/Cecily ("Chips") Gemmell, 7/10/80 (Johnnie Walker Red and daily routine); PFR/Winston S. Churchill, 3/04.

18. Colville, *Fringes*, 417; Sherwood, *Roosevelt and Hopkins*, 24; WM/Sir Ian Jacob, 11/12/80.

19. Colville, *Fringes*, 319; Alex Danchev and Daniel Todman, eds., *Field Marshal Lord Alanbrooke: War Diaries 1939–1945* (Berkeley, 2003), 637.

20. Martin Gilbert, *Winston Churchill: The Wilderness Years* (New York, 1984), 42–44; WM/Cecily ("Chips") Gemmell, 7/10/80; *NYT*, 5/5/09; Warren Kimball, *Finest Hour*, spring 2007, 31–33.

21. WM/Oscar Nemon, 1980.

22. WM/Kathleen Hill, 11/4/80; Colville, *Fringes*, 163–65.

23. WM/Kathleen Hill, 11/4/80; WM/John Martin, 10/23/80; Thompson, *Assignment: Churchill*, 179; WM/Cecily ("Chips") Gemmell, 7/10/80; Moran, *Diaries*, 360.

24. John H. Peck, "The Working Day," *Atlantic Monthly*, 3/65.

25. F. H. Hinsley et al., *British Intelligence in the Second World War*, 5 vols. (London, 1979).

26. Wheeler-Bennett, *Action*, 20, 23.

27. Colville, *Fringes*, 130.

28. Tom Hickman, *Churchill's Bodyguard* (London, 2005), 130; Colville, *Fringes*, 223.

29. WM/Jock Colville, 10/14/80; WM/John Martin, 10/23/80.

30. WM/Sir Ian Jacob, 11/12/80; Wheeler-Bennett, *Action*, 185.

31. PFR/Lady Mary Soames, letter of 9/3/07; Moran, *Diaries*, 100; Colville, *Fringes*, 416.

32. WM/William Deakin, 1980; Thompson, *Assignment: Churchill*, 178.

33. Colville, *Fringes*, 416; Halle, *Irrepressible Churchill*, 263.

34. Colville, *Fringes*, 481; Moran, *Diaries*, 111, 604; WM/Pamela Harriman ("wollygogs"), 8/22/80; Browne, *Long Sunset*, 220–21 (Sinatra).

35. WSCHCS, 6307.

36. Moran, *Diaries*, 604; Winston Churchill, *Thoughts and Adventures* (New York, 1991), 204.

37. R. V. Jones, *The Wizard War* (New York, 1978), 106.

38. Halle, *Irrepressible Churchill*, 345, 346; Moran, *Diaries*, 444.

39. H. Chartres Biron, ed., *"Sir," Said Dr. Johnson* (London, 1911), 112, 213.

40. Biron, *"Sir,"* 216; Colville, *Fringes*, 341; W&C-TPL, 111, 213.

41. WSC 5, 704; Anthony Montague Browne, speech to Churchill Society; Roy Jenkins, *Churchill: A Biography* (London, 2011), 702n; Colville, *Fringes*, 239, 578; Moran, *Diaries*, 781.

42. Colville, *Fringes*, 482; Richard Langworth, ed., *Churchill by Himself: The Definitive Collection of Quotations* (London, 2008), 463.

43. Randolph S. Churchill, *Winston S. Churchill: Youth, 1874–1900* (Boston, 1996), 208.

44. GILBERT 7, 348; Colville, *Fringes*, 526; Danchev and Todman, *War Diaries*, 690–91.

45. WSCHCS, 5818.

46. WM/Viscount Antony Head, 1980.

47. H. H. Asquith, *Letters to Venetia Stanley*, edited by Michael Brock and Eleanor Brock (Oxford, 1982), 267; WM/John Martin, 10/23/80.

48. Violet Bonham Carter, *Winston Churchill: An Intimate Portrait* (New York, 1965), 4; WSCHCS, 6250, 6264.

49. Sherwood, *Roosevelt and Hopkins*, 729; WSC 4, 796–97.

50. Sherwood, *Roosevelt and Hopkins*, 241.

51. Colville, *Fringes*, 158; WM/Jock Colville, 10/14/80; WM/John Martin, 10/23/80.

52. Moran, *Diaries*, 158; WSC 6, 115; Halle, *Irrepressible Churchill*, 257.

53. WM/Jock Colville, 10/14/80; WM/John Martin, 10/23/80; Browne, *Long Sunset*, 114.

54. GILBERT 7, 1322 ("This wicked man..."); WSCHCS, 6277; Langworth, *Churchill by Himself*, 137.

55. WM/William Deakin, 1980; WM/Jane (Portal) Williams, 1980.

56. WM/William Deakin, 1980; WM/Jane (Portal) Williams, 1980.

57. WM/Jane (Portal) Williams, 1980; GILBERT 6, 1156; Thompson, *Assignment: Churchill*, 183; *Daily Telegraph*, 3/18/09.

58. WM/Jane (Portal) Williams, 1980; WM/Jock Colville, 10/14/80; Colville, *Fringes*, 285.

59. WM/Cecily ("Chips") Gemmell, 7/10/80.

60. Vincent Sheean, *Between the Thunder and the Sun* (New York, 1943), 260; Wheeler-Bennett, *Action*, 146–47.

61. WM/John Martin, 10/23/80.

62. Wheeler-Bennett, *Action,* 139.

63. Anthony Storr, *Churchill's Black Dog, Kafka's Mice, and Other Phenomena of the Human Mind* (New York, 1973), 5, 27, 49–50.

64. W&C-TPL, 53; Moran, *Diaries,* 179.

65. Moran, *Diaries,* 112; PFR/Dr. Ron Pies (clinical psychiatrist, professor, Tufts University School of Medicine), 2007; PFR/Dr. David Armitage (Col. U.S. Army, ret.), 2007; Dr. Michael First (editor, *Diagnostic and Statistical Manual of Mental Disorders,* 4th ed., text rev. [DSM-IV-TR], lead author, *Structured Clinical Interview for DSM-IV-TR* [SCID], electronic and telephone communications, 3/07, 10/08; Browne, *Long Sunset,* 119.

66. Hastings Lionel Ismay, *The Memoirs of General Lord Ismay* (London, 1960), 155; Colville, *Fringes,* 215.

67. WM/Jock Colville, 10/14/80; Colville, *Fringes,* 578; Moran, *Diaries,* 827; Langworth, *Churchill by Himself,* 58.

68. John Keegan, *The Mask of Command* (New York, 1987), 236–38.

69. David Rising, "Hitler's Final Days Described by Bodyguard," AP, 4/24/05.

70. Hugh Dalton, *Memoirs 1931–1945: The Fateful Years* (London, 1957), 335–36.

71. David Dilks, ed., *The Diaries of Sir Alexander Cadogan, 1938–1945* (New York, 1972), 267.

72. Mollie Panter-Downes, *London War Notes, 1939–1945* (London, 1972), 62.

73. Dilks, *Diaries,* 267, 272, 283; WM/Jock Colville, 10/14/80.

74. Clare Boothe, *Europe in the Spring* (New York, 1941), 127.

75. WSC 1, 558–59.

76. Vincent Sheean, *Thunder,* 83.

77. Général André Beaufre, *Le Drame de 1940* (Paris, 1965).

78. Charles de Gaulle, *Lettres, Notes et Carnets,* vol. 2: *1942–May 1958* (Paris, 1980), 486.

79. BBC broadcast, 3/30/40; WSCHCS, 6201.

80. Colville, *Fringes,* 25–26.

81. William L. Shirer, *Berlin Diary (The Journal of a Foreign Correspondent 1934–1941)* (New York, 1941), 329–30.

82. Adolf Hitler, *Mein Kampf,* edited by John Chamberlain et al. (New York, 1939), 766.

83. René de Chambrun, *I Saw France Fall* (New York, 1940), 54–55.

84. De Chambrun, *France,* 54–55.

85. Alphonse Goutard, *1940: La Guerre des Occasions Perdues* (Paris, 1956), 131; Boothe, *Europe,* 1941.

86. William Bullitt, *Foreign Relations of the United States,* vol. 1: *1945–1950, Emergence of the Intelligence Establishment* (Washington, DC, n.d.), 469.

87. WSC 1, 454.

88. F. W. Winterbotham, *The Ultra Secret* (New York, 1974), 50.

89. GILBERT 6, 305.

90. Len Deighton, *Blitzkrieg: From the Rise of Hitler to the Fall of Dunkirk* (New York, 1979), 191.

91. Général Maurice Gustav Gamelin, *Servir,* 3 vols. (Paris, 1947), 3:389.

92. Boothe, *Europe,* 241–42.

93. Adolf Heusinger, *Befehl im Widerstreit: Schicksalsstunden der deutschen Armee 1923–1945* (Tübingen, 1950), 88.

94. Panter-Downes, *War Notes,* 56–57.

95. Dilks, *Diaries,* 277.

Cyclone

1. GILBERT 6, 313; John Colville, *The Fringes of Power: 10 Downing Street Diaries 1939–1955* (New York, 1985), 121–22.
2. John W. Wheeler-Bennett, *King George VI: His Life and Reign, 1865–1936* (New York, 1958), 443; GILBERT 6, 307, 317.
3. WM/Lady Mary Soames, 10/27/80.
4. W&C-TPL, 412; Ernst Hanfstaengl, *Hitler: The Missing Years* (London, 1957), 193–96.
5. WM/Lady Mary Soames, 10/27/80; Brian Roberts, *Randolph: A Study of Churchill's Son* (London, 1984), 181.
6. Colville, *Fringes*, 256.
7. Lord Moran, *Churchill: Taken from the Diaries of Lord Moran* (Boston, 1966), 5.
8. Mollie Panter-Downes, *London War Notes, 1939–1945* (London, 1972), 61.
9. Colville, *Fringes*, 736.
10. WSC 1, 475.
11. Brian Gardner, *Churchill in Power: As Seen by His Contemporaries* (Boston, 1970), 6; Colville, *Fringes*, 121–22; Max Plowman, *Bridge into the Future: Letters of Max Plowman* (London, 1944), 710.
12. John Wheeler-Bennett, *Action This Day: Working with Churchill* (London, 1968), 48; WM/Jock Colville, 10/14/80.
13. Wheeler-Bennett, *Action,* 51–53; WM/Jock Colville, 10/14/80; WM/John Martin, 10/23/80; WSC 2, 17.
14. Wheeler-Bennett, *Action,* 161, 195–97; Colville, *Fringes*, 289, 436.
15. Wheeler-Bennett, *Action,* 193–96; WM/Sir Ian Jacob, 11/12/80.
16. John Rupert Colville, *Footprints in Time* (London, 1976), 75–76; Wheeler-Bennett, *Action,* 147; Ian Jacob, "His Finest Hour," *Atlantic Monthly*, 3/65.
17. WSC 2, 28; GILBERT 6, 325; WM/Sir Ian Jacob, 11/12/80; Virginia Cowles, *Winston Churchill: The Era and the Man* (New York, 1953), 317.
18. TWY, 85, 99; Hansard 5/13/40 (WSC statement to House).
19. Arthur Bryant, *The Turn of the Tide: A History of the War Years Based on the Diaries of Field-Marshal Lord Alanbrooke, 1939–1943* (New York, 1957), 21.
20. WSCHCS, 6232; Henry Pelling, *Winston Churchill* (Conshohocken, PA, 1999), 437; WSC 2, 10–11; Wheeler-Bennett, *Action,* 49.
21. Colville, *Fringes*, 196.
22. GILBERT 6, 328–29; WSC 2, 13.
23. Laurence Thompson, *1940* (New York, 1966), 94.
24. GILBERT 6, 342; C&R-TCC, 1:38.
25. Thompson, *1940*, 118.
26. CAB 65/7.
27. Général C. Gransard, *Le 10e Corps d'armée dans la bataille* (Paris, 1949), 141.
28. William L. Shirer, *The Collapse of the Third Republic* (New York, 1969), 664; Charles de Gaulle, *The Complete War Memoirs of Charles de Gaulle* (New York, 1964), 39.
29. Alistair Horne, *Seven Ages of Paris* (New York, 2002), 381–402.
30. WSC 2, 42.
31. Antoine de Saint-Exupéry, *Flight from Arras* (New York, 1942), 116–33 *passim*.
32. WSC 2, 43; de Saint-Exupéry, *Flight*, 120.

33. Hastings Lionel Ismay, *The Memoirs of General Lord Ismay* (London, 1960), 127; Horne, *Seven Ages,* 381; Vincent Sheean, *Between the Thunder and the Sun* (New York, 1943), 142.

34. Ismay, *Memoirs,* 128.

35. WSC 2, 47.

36. Paul Reynaud, *In the Thick of the Fight* (New York, 1940), 323–24.

37. WSC 2, 42–43; de Saint-Exupéry, *Flight,* 120.

38. Len Deighton, *Fighter* (New York, 1977), 58; Ismay, *Memoirs,* 128.

39. Ismay, *Memoirs,* 128–29.

40. GILBERT 6, 334, 358; Colville, *Fringes,* 135.

41. John Rupert Colville, *Man of Valour: The Life of Field Marshal the Viscount Gort* (London, 1972), 204; Anthony Eden, Earl of Avon, *The Reckoning: The Memoirs of Anthony Eden* (New York, 1965), 106.

42. WSCHCS, 6222–23.

43. Jones, *Diary,* 460; W. M. James, *The Portsmouth Letters* (London, 1946), 15.

44. Panter-Downes, *War Notes,* 67.

45. William L. Shirer, *Berlin Diary (The Journal of a Foreign Correspondent 1934–1941)* (New York, 1941), 437–38.

46. WSC 2, 56; Général Maurice Gustav Gamelin, *Servir,* 3 vols. (Paris, 1947), 3:417.

47. WSCHCS, 6232.

48. Roderick Macleod, ed., *Time Unguarded: The Ironside Diaries, 1937–1940* (London, 1974), 327; Premier (Prime Minister) Papers, Public Record Office, Kew, 3/188/3, folio 18; WSC 1, 375.

49. Ismay, *Memoirs,* 131; Colville, *Fringes,* 137–38.

50. WSC 2, 64–65; Macleod, *Time Unguarded,* 328.

51. William L. Shirer, *The Rise and Fall of the Third Reich: A History of Nazi Germany* (New York, 1960), 728.

52. Colville, *Fringes,*139; GILBERT 6, 385.

53. Colville, *Fringes,* 139; GILBERT 6, 385; WSC 2, 69–70.

54. E. L. Spears, *Assignment to Catastrophe,* 2 vols. (New York, 1955), 2:120–21.

55. L. F. Ellis, *The War in France and Flanders 1939–1940* (London, 1953), 368; Macleod, *Time Unguarded,* 331–32.

56. Ellis, *France and Flanders,* 208, 389.

57. Len Deighton, *Blitzkrieg: From the Rise of Hitler to the Fall of Dunkirk* (New York, 1979), 265.

58. B. H. Liddell Hart, *History of the Second World War* (New York, 1971), 77; David Dilks, ed., *The Diaries of Sir Alexander Cadogan, 1938–1945* (New York, 1972), 289–90; CAB 65/7; Macleod, *Time Unguarded,* 332; WSC 1, 393.

59. Spears, *Assignment,* 2: 202, 236–37; WSC 1, 389; Bryant, *Tide,* 90; Macleod, *Time Unguarded,* 321.

60. *Time,* 1/23/41, 23; Roger Keyes, *Outrageous Fortune: The Tragedy of King Leopold of the Belgians 1901–1941* (London, 1984), 308–10, 396.

61. CAB 65/13.

62. Dilks, *Diaries,* 290; ChP 80/11.

63. Dilks, *Diaries,* 291.

64. WSC 2, 99.

65. Thompson, 1940, 137–38.

66. NYT, 5/30/40; TWY, 91; Thompson, 1940, 133–34, 139.

67. Ellis, *France and Flanders,* 368.

68. Ellis, *France and Flanders*, 162–69; Macleod, *Time Unguarded;* WSC 2, 82; Ismay, *Memoirs*, 133.
69. Bryant, *Tide*, 101–2 *passim.*
70. Ellis, *France and Flanders*, 326.
71. Ellis, *France and Flanders*, 182; Macleod, *Time Unguarded*, 340; WSCHCS, 6225.
72. Macleod, *Time Unguarded*, 333ff.; Ismay, *Memoirs*, 134.
73. WSC 2, 100; Hugh Dalton, *Memoirs 1931–1945: The Fateful Years* (London, 1957), 335–36.
74. WSC 2, 101.
75. Thompson, *1940*, 133–36.
76. Alex Danchev and Daniel Todman, eds., *Field Marshal Lord Alanbrooke: War Diaries 1939–1945* (Berkeley, 2003), 72.
77. WSC 2, 428; War Office papers 106/1708; John Spencer Churchill, *Crowded Canvas* (London, 1961), 162–63; WM/Sir Ian Jacob, 11/12/80; Jacob, "Finest," 3/65.
78. Macleod, *Time Unguarded*, 354; Harold Macmillan, *The Blast of War: 1939–1945* (New York, 1967), 81.
79. Panter-Downes, *War Notes*, 63–66.
80. WSCHCS, 6230.
81. Colville, *Fringes*, 147–48; *News Chronicle* 6/5/40; TWY, 93; Gardner, *Churchill in Power*, 55.
82. WSCHCS, 6228.
83. George Bilainkin, *Diary of a Diplomatic Correspondent* (London, 1942), 102.
84. Chief sources for the last three meetings of the council (Paris, Briare, Tours): Spears, *Assignment;* de Gaulle, *War Memoirs;* Ismay, *Memoirs;* S. Petrie et al., *The Private Diaries of Paul Baudouin* (London, 1948).
85. Spears, *Assignment*, 1:293–94.
86. Ismay, *Memoirs*, 134.
87. Spears, *Assignment*, 1:295.
88. Spears, *Assignment*, 1:295.
89. Spears, *Assignment*, 1:295; Petrie, *Diaries*, 53–54.
90. Spears, *Assignment*, 1:314–15.
91. Spears, *Assignment*, 1:316, 2:113.
92. Panter-Downes, *War Notes*, 68; Colville, *Fringes*, 151–53.
93. Spears, *Assignment*, 2:138–39; Ismay, *Memoirs*, 139.
94. Spears, *Assignment*, 2:141–44; Eden, *Reckoning*, 133. The French minutes of the Briare meeting are given textually in Paul Reynaud, *Au Coeur de la mêlée, 1939–1945* (Paris, 1951), 823–24.
95. Spears, *Assignment*, 2:145–47; Eden, *Reckoning*, 115.
96. Spears, *Assignment*, 2:149ff.
97. Reynaud, *Au Coeur.*
98. Ismay, *Memoirs*, 140.
99. Ismay, *Memoirs*, 140–41.
100. Ismay, *Memoirs*, 140–41.
101. *Les Événements survenus en France de 1933 à 1945*, 2:343; Horne, *Seven Ages*, 546n; Shirer, *Collapse*, 618; *Histoire de l'Aviation Militaire Française* (Paris, 1980), 379–80; Deighton, *Blitzkrieg*, 269–70.
102. WSC 2, 156–57; Ismay, *Memoirs*, 142–43.
103. Spears, *Assignment*, 2:163.

104. Ismay, *Memoirs*, 141.
105. WSC 2, 158; Walter H. Thompson, *Assignment: Churchill* (New York, 1953), 194.
106. CAB 99/3; Colville, *Fringes*, 152–54.
107. Earl of Birkenhead, *Life of Lord Halifax* (London, 1965), 459; Dilks, *Diaries*, 297; Ismay, *Memoirs*, 143–44.
108. Eleanor M. Gates, *End of the Affair: The Collapse of the Anglo-French Alliance, 1939–40* (Berkeley, 1981), 250; Gordon Wright, "Ambassador Bullitt and the Fall of France," *World Politics* 10, no. 1, 87.
109. Horne, *Seven Ages*, 573.
110. Spears, *Assignment*, 2:210–13.
111. James Leasor, *War at the Top* (London, 1959), 91; Colville, *Fringes*, 152.
112. Spears, *Assignment*, 2:218–20.
113. Colville, *Fringes*, 155; C&R-TCC, 1:48.
114. Spears, *Assignment*, 2:292–93; WM/Kathleen Hill, 11/4/80; Colville, *Fringes*, 161.
115. Spears, *Assignment*, 2:292–93; WM/Kathleen Hill, 11/4/80; Colville, *Fringes*, 161.
116. L. B. Namier, *Europe in Decay* (London, 1950), 93; Spears, *Assignment*, 2:304, 310–11.
117. Spears, *Assignment*, 2:319–23; WSC 2, 218.
118. J. A. Cross, *Sir Samuel Hoare: A Political Biography* (London, 1977), 339–40.
119. Michael Bloch, *The Duke of Windsor's War: From Europe to the Bahamas, 1939–1945* (New York, 1983).
120. Colville, *Fringes*, 184.
121. ChP 20/9; C&R-TCC, 1:53.
122. ChP 20/49; WSC 1, 1091.
123. Colville, *Fringes*, 166.
124. Panter-Downes, *War Notes*, 72.
125. De Gaulle, *War Memoirs*, 76.
126. WSC 2, 230; Eden, *Reckoning*, 155.
127. William Bullitt, *Foreign Relations of the United States*, vol. 2: *The Intelligence Community 1950–1955* (Washington, DC, n.d.), 465–66.
128. WSCHCS, 6241.
129. WSC 2, 231.
130. Colville, *Fringes*, 171–72; WSC 2, 233; Warren Tute, *The Deadly Stroke*, introduction by John Colville (New York, 1973), 21–28.
131. Tute, *Deadly Stroke*, 73–87.
132. Tute, *Deadly Stroke*, 112–14; WSC 2, 234.
133. For a thorough discussion of the British attack on the French fleet at Mers-el-Kébir, see chap. 5 of Arthur Marder's *From the Dardanelles to Oran* (London, 1974).
134. Tute, *Deadly Stroke*, 148.
135. Tute, *Deadly Stroke*, 152–62.
136. Thompson, *1940;* WSCHCS, 6246.
137. Tute, *Deadly Stroke*, 17; Ben Pimlott, *Hugh Dalton* (London, 1985), 348; TWY, 100.
138. Tute, *Deadly Stroke*, 17.
139. Shirer, *Rise and Fall*, 813.
140. CAB 65/9.
141. Cv/2, 259; WSCHCS, 6287.
142. GILBERT 6, 372, 392; Macleod, *Time Unguarded*, 369; Hermann Löns, *Ein Soldatisches Vermächtnis* (1939), 85; Richard Gerlach, *Das Beste von Hermann Löns* (Hanover, 1980), 16.

143. WSCHCS, 6230.

144. Cv/2, 429.

145. Hansard 6/18/40; WSCHCS, 6238.

146. Deighton, *Fighter,* 8.

147. C&R-TCC, 1:40, 49; Cv/2, 261; Bryant, *Tide,* 151.

148. Thompson, *1940,* 149; WSC 1, 598–99, 695; Premier (Prime Minister) Papers, Public Record Office, Kew, 4/100/3; Birkenhead, *Halifax,* 458, and Llewellyn Woodward, *British Foreign Policy in the Second World War* (London, 1962), 53; Williamson Murray, *Luftwaffe* (Baltimore, 1985), 43.

149. Duff Cooper, *Old Men Forget* (London, 1954), 267; Jones, *Diary,* 465; Lloyd George, *Sunday Pictorial,* 7/28/40; Wheeler-Bennett, *King George VI,* 456.

150. Panter-Downes, *War Notes,* 83–86; Jones, *Diary,* 465–66.

151. Wheeler-Bennett, *King George VI,* 456.

152. Wheeler-Bennett, *King George VI,* 456.

153. Gardner, *Churchill in Power,* 65–66.

154. Panter-Downes, *War Notes,* 71, 91, 97, 110–11.

155. Colville, *Fringes,* 195.

156. Cv/2, 417–18.

157. Shirer, *Rise and Fall,* 798.

158. WSC 2, 286.

159. WSCHCS, 6495.

160. WSCHCS, 6234.

161. WSC 2, 282–84.

162. Colville, *Fringes,* 178–81, 182.

163. TWY, 97; Ismay, *Memoirs,* 153; Jones, *Diary,* 467–68.

164. WSCHCS, 6775.

165. Mary Soames, *Clementine Churchill: The Biography of a Marriage* (New York, 2003), 408; TWY, 100.

166. TWY, 90.

167. TWY, 89, 90, 93; WM/Kathleen Hill, 11/4/80.

168. Macleod, *Time Unguarded,* 369.

169. GILBERT 6, 478; Gardner, *Churchill in Power,* 68; Panter-Downes, *War Notes,* 66; Hansard 6/4/40; A. J. P. Taylor, *English History, 1914–45* (Oxford, 1978).

170. Colville, *Fringes,* 182; Cv/3, 445 (mustard gas).

171. Thompson, *1940,*145.

172. TWY, 101, 103.

173. WSC 2, 298; Macleod, *Time Unguarded,* 383; Danchev and Todman, *War Diaries,* 94.

174. Colville, *Fringes,* 102–3.

175. WSCHCS, 6248.

176. WSCHCS, 6250.

177. *Documents on German Foreign Policy 1918–1945,* vol. 10: *The War Years, June 23–August 23, 1940* (Washington, DC, 1957), 81; Charles Burdick and Hans-Adolf Jacobsen, eds., *The Halder War Diary, 1939–1942* (New York, 1988), 7/22/40; Führer's Conferences on Naval Affairs, 71–73; *Die Weiterführung des Krieges gegen England,* IMT, TWMC, vol. 28, 301–3.

178. Shirer, *Rise and Fall,* 754.

179. Colville, *Fringes,* 200; Leonard Mosley, *Battle of Britain* (New York, 1980), 26; WSC 2, 260.

180. Hugh Gibson, ed., *The Ciano Diaries, 1939–1943* (New York, 1946), 277–78.
181. Deighton, *Fighter,* 272; Liddell Hart, *History,* 87.
182. Klaus A. Maier et al., *Das Deutsche Reich und der Zweite Weltkrieg,* 2 vols. (Stuttgart, 1988), 2:3, 78–79.
183. Shirer, *Rise and Fall,* 752.
184. Shirer, *Rise and Fall,* 752.
185. Shirer, *Rise and Fall,* 762–63.
186. William L. Shirer, *Aufstieg und Fall des Dritten Reiches* (Cologne, 2000), 815.
187. Deighton, *Fighter,* xiv–xv; Hansard 11/10/32; WM/Sir Ian Jacob, 11/12/80.
188. Deighton, *Fighter,* xviii, 57.
189. Mosley, *Battle of Britain,* 50.
190. Mosley, *Battle of Britain,* 54; Telford Taylor, *The Breaking Wave: The Second World War in the Summer of 1940* (New York, 1967), 87; John Keegan, ed., *Collins Atlas of World War II* (New York, 2006), 38–39.
191. BA/MA RL 211/27, *Allgemeine Weisung für den Kampf der Luftwaffe gegen England,* OBDL, Führungsstab, Ia Nr 5835/40, 30.6.40; Murray Williamson, "The Battle of Britain: How Did 'The Few' Win?" *Military History Quarterly* 2, no. 2 (summer 1990).
192. WSC 2, 323.
193. Colville, *Fringes,* 213.
194. Liddell Hart, *History,* 93.
195. Liddell Hart, *History,* 93.
196. Colville, *Fringes,* 194.
197. Hansard 11/11/42; WSCHCS, 6707; Shirer, *Berlin Diary,* 467–68.
198. Deighton, *Fighter,* xvii, 218; Mosley, *Battle of Britain,* 91; A. J. P. Taylor, *Beaverbrook* (London, 1972), 422–30.
199. Colville, *Fringes,* 217; Taylor, *Beaverbrook,* 430.
200. Murray, *Luftwaffe.*
201. Deighton, *Fighter,* 217.
202. Deighton, *Fighter,* 187.
203. Len Deighton, *Unternehmen Adler. Die Luftschlacht um England,* 264–65.
204. R. V. Jones, *The Wizard War* (New York, 1978); F. H. Hinsley et al., *British Intelligence in the Second World War,* 5 vols. (London, 1979), 1:176–77; Ronald Lewin, *Ultra Goes to War* (New York, 1978); Brian Johnson, *The Secret War* (London, 1978); Harold Deutsch, "Ultra and the Air War in Europe and Africa," in *Air Power and Warfare, Proceedings of the Eighth Military History Symposium,* USAF Academy, edited by Colonel Alfred F. Hurley and Major Robert C. Ehrhart (Washington, DC, 1979), 165–66; Maier, *Das Deutsche Reich,* 2:384; Aileen Clayton, *The Enemy Is Listening* (New York, 1978).
205. Sheean, *Thunder,* 201.
206. Sheean, *Thunder,* 199.
207. Sheean, *Thunder,* 201–2.
208. Colville, *Fringes,* 236.
209. Collier, *Defence of the United Kingdom* (London, 2009), 189–90, 450; Helmuth Greiner, *Kriegstagebuch des Oberkommandos der Wehrmacht* (the OKW war diary) 8/15/40; Denis Richards, *Royal Air Force, 1939–1945,* vol. 1: *The Fight at Odds* (London, 1953), chaps. 6 and 7.
210. Helmuth Greiner, *Die Oberste Wehrmacht/Weltkrieg 1939–1945* (Stuttgart, 1954); Ismay, *Memoirs,* 188.

211. WSCHCS, 6265–66.

212. Edward Bishop, *The Battle of Britain* (London, 1960), 142, 149; Helmuth Greiner, *OKW*, 8/19/40.

213. Richards, *Royal Air Force*, 1:178.

214. Deighton, *Fighter*, 219.

215. Colville, *Fringes*, 234–36.

216. Collier, *Defence*, 206–7, 210; Bishop, *Battle of Britain*, 166–69; Alexander McKee, *Strike from the Sky: The Battle of Britain Story* (Boston, 1960), 197–209; Derek Wood and Derek Dempster, *The Narrow Margin: The Battle of Britain and the Rise of Air Power 1930–1949* (London, 1961), 316–25.

217. Colville, *Fringes*, 236–37.

218. Deighton, *Fighter*, 248; Collier, *Defence*, 205; Wood and Dempster, *Narrow Margin*, 332–33; WSC 2, 331–32.

219. Wood and Dempster, *Narrow Margin*, 304.

220. Taylor, *Breaking Wave*, 151; H. R. Trevor-Roper, ed., *Hitler's War Directives 1939–1945* (London, 1964), 38.

221. Helmuth Greiner, *Die Oberste Wehrmachtführung, 1939–1943* (Wiesbaden, 1951), 8/29/40, 8/31/40; Cv/2, 555.

222. Colville, *Fringes*, 230.

223. Shirer, *Berlin Diary*, 8/26/40.

224. *Frankfurter Zeitung*, 8/29/40 and 8/30/40.

225. *OKW*, 8/24/40; *Facts in Review* 2, no. 22 (5/27/40): 217.

226. Adolph Galland, *The First and the Last* (New York, 1954), 40–41.

227. Shirer, *Rise and Fall*, 777.

228. *Frankfurter Zeitung*, 9/5/40.

229. Gibson, *Ciano Diaries*, 290.

230. WSC 2, 229.

231. CAB, 79/6. The chiefs signing the order were Ismay, Pound, Dill, and Peirse, vice chief of the Air Staff.

232. McKee, *Strike*, 125.

233. Collier, *Defence*, 135–40; Wood and Dempster, *Narrow Margin*, 334–39; Mosley, *Battle of Britain*, 120.

234. GILBERT 6, 773–74; WSC 2, 312.

235. GILBERT 6, 774.

236. Danchev and Todman, *War Diaries*, 105.

237. Cv/2, 703.

238. C&R-TCC, 1:56–67; GILBERT 6, 25.

239. C&R-TCC, 1:56–67.

240. Robert E. Sherwood, *Roosevelt and Hopkins: An Intimate History* (New York, 1948), 1980; Cv/2, 255; Dilks, *Diaries*, 322–23.

241. Cv/2, 255 (letter to Mackenzie King); C&R-TCC, 1:69.

242. WSCHCS, 6266.

243. GILBERT 6, 756; WSC 2, 297.

244. WM/Sir Robert Boothby, 10/16/80.

245. Cv/2, 655; Cv/2, 748; Collier, *War in the Desert*, 18–19.

246. GILBERT 6, 756.

247. Greiner, *OKW*, 9/13/40.

248. Greiner, *OKW*, 8/30/40.

249. WSC 2, 337; Deighton, *Fighter*, 262.

250. Taylor, *Breaking Wave,* 165; *Seekriegsleitung Kriegstagebuch,* War Diary of the German Naval War Staff, Part D, Lufttage, for September 16 and 18, 1940.
251. WSC 2, 240.
252. F. H. W. Sheppard, *London: A History* (Oxford, 1998); David Johnson, *The London Blitz* (New York, 1981), 33; WSC 2, 342.
253. Cv/2, 788–89 (Ismay recollection); Thompson, *1940,* 211; Cv/2, 789.
254. Colville, *Fringes,* 192.
255. WSC 2, 343; Mosley, *Battle of Britain,* 143.
256. TWY, 111; Mosley, *Battle of Britain,* 145.
257. William K. Klingaman, *1941: Our Lives in a World on the Edge* (New York, 1989), 3, 7, 12.
258. Klingaman, *1941,* 6–7; WSC 2, 360.
259. Bertrand Russell, *Which Way to Peace?* (London, 1936), quoted in Sheppard, *London,* 262; Colville, *Fringes,* 263.
260. WSCHCS, 6277.
261. WSCHCS, 6276.
262. BBC address, 9/11/40.
263. Johnson, *London Blitz,* 39.
264. Jones, *Wizard War,* 96–97.
265. WSC 2, 384–85; Jones, *Wizard War,* 101–2.
266. Jones, *Wizard War,* 102.
267. WSC 2, 385; Tom Shachtman, *Terrors and Marvels: How Science and Technology Changed the Character and Outcome of World War II* (New York, 2002); see chap. 5 ("Battles Above Britain") for overview.
268. WSC 2, 383–84; Jones, *Wizard War,* 102.
269. Sheppard, *London,* 333.
270. Philip Ziegler, *London at War* (New York, 1995), 175.
271. WSC 2, 343.
272. WSC 2, 343.
273. Mosley, *Battle of Britain,* 138.
274. Kay Halle, *Irrepressible Churchill: Stories, Sayings and Impressions of Sir Winston Churchill* (London, 1985), 168.
275. Klingaman, *1941,* 16.
276. TWY, 115–16.
277. WM/Lady Mary Soames, 10/27/80; Soames, *Clementine,* 379.
278. Colville, *Fringes,* 240–41; Thompson, *Assignment: Churchill,* 206.
279. WM/Jock Colville, 10/14/80.
280. WM/Lady Mary Soames, 10/27/80; Soames, *Clementine,* 384–86.
281. WSC 2, 375.
282. Thompson, *1940,* 213.
283. Thompson, *1940,* 222.
284. Mosley, *Battle of Britain,* 36–37.
285. WM/Viscount Antony Head, 8/6/80.
286. *Time,* 10/3/43; *Time,* 2/1/43; Mark Mayo Boatner, *The Biographical Dictionary of World War II* (New York, 1999), 8. See also *Modern Law Review* 5, no. 3/4 (July 1942):162–73; Tim Pat Coogan, *The IRA* (London, 1971), 58.
287. *Time,* 9/23/40; Cv/2, 440, 446, 764; Colville, *Fringes,* 173; WSC 5, 680.
288. TWY, 114.
289. Mosley, *Battle of Britain,* 139.

290. TWY, 115–16.
291. WM/Jock Colville, 10/14/80; Colville, *Fringes*, 245.
292. Colville, *Fringes*, 249.
293. *Oxford Companion to World War II*, edited by I. C. B. Dear (Oxford, 1995), 179, 331.
294. Martin Gilbert, *The Second World War: A Complete History* (London, 1989), 132.
295. TWY, 121.
296. CAB 120/300.
297. Shirer, *Rise and Fall*, 778; Gilbert, *Second World War*, 128.
298. WSC 2, 584, 586.
299. WSC 2, 581.
300. Colville, *Fringes*, 214.
301. Panter-Downes, *War Notes*, 110; Klingaman, *1941*, 9.
302. Thompson, *1940*, 220; Sheean, *Thunder*, 224–25.
303. Sheean, *Thunder*, 224–25; Panter-Downes, *War Notes*, 137.
304. WSCHCS, 6287.
305. Winston Churchill, *My Early Life: 1874–1904* (New York, 1996), 62.
306. GILBERT 6, 808–10.
307. Joseph P. Kennedy, *Boston Globe* interview, 11/10/40; Victor Lasky, *JFK: The Man and the Myth* (New York, 1963), 58.
308. Colville, *Fringes*, 262, 275.
309. GILBERT 6, 816; C&R-TCC, 1:74.
310. WSCHCS, 6297.
311. WSCHCS, 6297.
312. WSCHCS, 6298; Conrad Black, *Franklin Delano Roosevelt: Champion of Freedom* (Washington, DC, 2003), 595.
313. Cv/2, 979, 985; Colville, *Fringes*, 272.
314. WM/Pamela Harriman, 8/22/80.
315. PFR/Lady Mary Soames, 6/07; WM/Pamela Harriman, 8/22/80.
316. Colville, *Fringes*, 216, 219, 248; WM/Jock Colville, 10/14/80.
317. Colville, *Fringes*, 265; Thompson, *1940*; WM/Pamela Harriman, 8/22/80.
318. Soames, *Clementine*, 387.
319. Soames, *Clementine*, 387; GILBERT 6, 793; Sarah Churchill, *A Thread in the Tapestry* (London, 1967), 56–57; *Time*, 9/30/40.
320. Thompson, *Assignment: Churchill*, 129; WM/Jock Colville, 10/14/80.
321. WM/Lord Geoffrey Lloyd, 11/27/80.
322. WM/Jock Colville, 10/14/80.
323. Mosley, *Battle of Britain*, 121.
324. WM/Jock Colville, 10/14/80; Wheeler-Bennett, *Action*, 118.
325. Churchill, *Early Life* ("being shot at without result").
326. Thompson, *Assignment: Churchill*, 211.
327. Thompson, *Assignment: Churchill*, 210–11.
328. Colville, *Fringes*, 278; Dean Acheson, *Sketches from Life of Men I Have Known* (New York, 1959), 3, 17.
329. Thompson, *Assignment: Churchill*, 211.
330. Cv/2, 907–8.
331. Cv/2, 907–8.
332. Moran, *Diaries*, 9.

333. TWY, 127.

334. Randolph S. Churchill, *Winston S. Churchill: Youth, 1874–1900* (Boston, 1996), 400, 410; Colville, *Fringes,* 273.

335. Colville, *Fringes,* 291; Thompson, *Assignment: Churchill,* 170–75.

336. WM/John Colville, 10/14/80; Thompson, *Assignment: Churchill,* 174.

337. Soames, *Clementine,* 386; Danchev and Todman, *War Diaries,* 123; Cv/2, 1069.

338. Colville, *Fringes,* 319; Moran, *Diaries,* 336; WM/Lord Soames (Pol Roger), 1980.

339. Colville, *Fringes,* 319; Shirer, *Berlin Diary,* 468.

340. PFR/Winston S. Churchill, 3/04.

341. Colville, *Fringes,* 267; Sheppard, *London,* 336; WSC 2, 370–72; Gilbert, *Second World War,* 132.

342. Ziegler, *London at War,* 119–20.

343. WSC 2, 360–61.

344. WSC 2, 360–61.

345. WM/Cecily ("Chips") Gemmell, 7/10/80; Thompson, *Assignment: Churchill,* 183; Colville, *Fringes,* 243; WM/John Colville, 10/14/80.

346. Ismay, *Memoirs,* 188–89.

347. Colville, *Fringes,* 262, 275; GILBERT 6, 862; ChP 20/13.

348. Colville, *Fringes,* 264, 280–81.

349. GILBERT 6, 835.

350. Soames, *Clementine,* 394; Colville, *Fringes,* 259; GILBERT 6, 837.

351. WCS 2, 299, 355; GILBERT 6, 886.

352. Thompson, *1940,* 221–24; Ziegler, *London at War,* 240.

353. C&R-TCC, 1:81.

354. John Keegan, *The Second World War* (London, 1989), 144–46.

355. GILBERT 6, 874–75, 877; Keegan, *Second World War,* 144–46; Cv/2, 1016.

356. Richard Collier, *Duce!* (New York, 1971), 179–80.

357. Colville, *Fringes,* 276; Keegan, *Second World War,* 145.

358. Collier, *War in the Desert;* GILBERT 6, 883–85.

359. Colville, *Fringes,* 283–84.

360. ChP 20/13.

361. Colville, *Fringes,* 224.

362. Cv/2, 1001.

363. GILBERT 6, 885, 905; WSC 2, 536–43; Eden, *Reckoning,* 195.

364. Collier, *War in the Desert,* 21–22; WSC 2, 543.

365. Gilbert, *Second World War,* 137.

366. Cv/2, 1022–23.

367. C&R-TCC, 1:81.

368. Cv/2, 1147.

369. Panter-Downes, *War Notes,* 116 (*"Eyetalian fleet..."*).

370. Panter-Downes, *War Notes,* 114; Cv/2, 1089 ("sugar for the birds"); WSCHCC, 6309.

371. Ronald Kessler, *The Sins of the Father* (New York, 1996), 230.

372. WSCHCS, 6307.

373. Colville, *Fringes,* 294–95.

374. Colville, *Fringes,* 292.

375. WM/John Martin, 10/23/80.

376. Cv/2, 1096; WM/John Martin, 10/23/80.

377. WSC 2, 383–85.

378. TWY, 139; Panter-Downes, *War Notes,* 117.

379. Panter-Downes, *War Notes,* 117.

380. WSC 2, 384–85; Winston Churchill, *Thoughts and Adventures* (New York, 1991), 198–99.

381. WM/John Martin, 10/23/80; Colville, *Fringes,* 295; John Colville, *The Churchillians* (London, 1981), 635.

382. Thompson, *1940,* 227.

383. Public Record Office documents AIR2/5238 and AIR20/2419 indicate that Churchill and the War Cabinet did not know which city would be the target on November 15.

384. Colville, *Fringes,* 297.

385. Cv/2, 1186, 1217–18; WM/Jock Colville, 10/14/80.

386. Cv/3, 1163.

387. Soames, *Clementine,* 395.

388. Colville, *Fringes,* 167; TWY, 96–97.

389. WSC 2, 576; GILBERT 6, 939.

390. David Miller, *U-Boats* (New York, 2000), 126; C&R-TCC, 1:112; Premier (Prime Minister) Papers, Public Record Office, Kew, 3/462/2; Cv/2, 1233.

391. Roger Chesneau, *Conway's All the World's Fighting Ships, 1922–1946* (London, 1980) (HMS *Lewes*).

392. Cv/2, 780, 844–45.

393. Cv/2, 1246.

394. Shirer, *Rise and Fall,* 810–11; WCSHCS, 6269.

395. WSC 2, 556–58; C&R-TCC, 1:102–9.

396. WSC 2, 558.

397. C&R-TCC, 1:107–8.

398. C&R-TCC, 1:107–8; WM/Malcolm MacDonald, 1980.

399. C&R-TCC, 1:107–8.

400. WSC 2, 567–69.

401. GILBERT 6, 694.

402. Colville, *Fringes,* 309, 321; WSC 2, 570.

403. Colville, *Fringes,* 314.

404. C&R-TCC, 1:86.

405. WSC 2, 530.

406. WSC 3, 568–69.

407. Winston S. Churchill, *Step by Step, 1936–1939* (New York, 1959), 137.

408. WSC 2, 497, 523; Dilks, *Diaries,* 329.

409. C&R-TCC, 1:74.

410. *Time Capsule 1940: A History of the Year Condensed from the Pages of* Time, edited by Henry R. Luce (New York, 1968).

411. *Time Capsule 1940.*

412. C&R-TCC, 1:65–66; Churchill, *Early Life,* 33 (from Manchester, *The Last Lion,* vol. 1, and Cowles, *Churchill*).

413. Celia Sandys, *Chasing Churchill* (New York, 2005), 138; Shirer, *Rise and Fall,* 782–83.

414. Collier, *War in the Desert,* 26–33.

415. Collier, *War in the Desert,* 27–28; Colville, *Fringes,* 308–9.

416. Collier, *War in the Desert,* 29.

417. GILBERT 6, 935; Colville, *Fringes,* 309; Mark Mayo Boatner, *The Biographical Dictionary of World War II* (New York, 1999), 602.

418. GILBERT 6, 935; Collier, *War in the Desert*, 29.
419. Cv/2, 1204.
420. Mosley, *Battle of Britain*, 149.
421. Leonard Mosley, *Marshall: Hero for Our Times* (New York, 1982), 150–51.
422. *NYT*, 12/30/41; TWY, 132; Klingaman, *1941*, 16.
423. FDR broadcast, 12/29/40, Franklin D. Roosevelt Presidential Library and Museum.
424. FDR broadcast, 12/29/40, Franklin D. Roosevelt Presidential Library and Museum; Colville, *Fringes*, 321; C&R-TCC, 1:122–23.
425. WSC 2, 628–29.

The Rapids

1. C&R-TCC, 1:120; John Colville, *The Fringes of Power: 10 Downing Street Diaries 1939–1955* (New York, 1985), 326–27.
2. WSC 3, 540; Noel Annan, "How Wrong Was Churchill?" *New York Review of Books*, 4/8/93.
3. William K. Klingaman, *1941: Our Lives in a World on the Edge* (New York, 1989), 24, 92–93; ChP 20/36; ChP 20/21.
4. Klingaman, *1941*, 24–25; ChP 20/36; ChP 20/21.
5. Colville, *Fringes*, 145.
6. C&R-TCC, 1:121–22; Colville, *Fringes*, 327.
7. John Colville, *The Churchillians* (London, 1981), 162; Colville, *Fringes*, 653; Anthony Eden, Earl of Avon, *The Reckoning: The Memoirs of Anthony Eden* (New York, 1965), 168, 215.
8. Lewis Broad, *Anthony Eden, The Chronicle of a Career* (New York, 1955), 4–8; Eden, *The Reckoning*, 435; W&C-TPL, 408.
9. Martin Gilbert, *Churchill's War Leadership* (New York, 2004), 72; Mark Mayo Boatner, *The Biographical Dictionary of World War II* (New York, 1999), 18–19, 372–73; Colville, *Churchillians*, 156–57.
10. ChP 2/416; Colville, *Fringes*, 326; Boatner, *Biographical Dictionary*, 380.
11. Klingaman, *1941*, 90–91.
12. Klingaman, *1941*, 92; WM/Malcolm Muggeridge, 11/25/80.
13. Dwight D. Eisenhower, *Crusade in Europe* (New York, 1948), 9; Carlos D'Este, *Patton: A Genius for War* (New York, 1995), 390–91.
14. Klingaman, *1941*, 43.
15. Charles de Gaulle, *The Complete War Memoirs of Charles de Gaulle* (New York, 1964), 84.
16. Klingaman, *1941*, 44.
17. Klingaman, *1941*, 48; Brian Gardner, *Churchill in Power: As Seen by His Contemporaries* (Boston, 1970), 96; Charles Eade, ed., *Churchill by His Contemporaries* (New York, 1954), 140; William L. Shirer, *Berlin Diary (The Journal of a Foreign Correspondent 1934–1941)* (New York, 1941), 481.
18. George F. Kennan, *Memoirs: 1925–1950* (New York, 1967), 130; Klingaman, *1941*, 18; Shirer, *Berlin Diary*, 448–49, 459.
19. C&R-TCC, 1:147; CAB 65/18 (to Halifax).
20. Mollie Panter-Downes, *London War Notes, 1939–1945* (London, 1972), 122–23, 139–40; Klingaman, *1941*, 14.

21. Klingaman, *1941*, 89–90.

22. Klingaman, *1941*, 89–90.

23. Klingaman, *1941*, 90; GILBERT 6, 895; ChP 20/36.

24. TWY, 136–37.

25. Leonard Mosley, *Battle of Britain* (New York, 1980), 136–37.

26. TWY, 136–37; ChP 20/36.

27. WSC 3, 4.

28. William L. Shirer, *The Rise and Fall of the Third Reich: A History of Nazi Germany* (New York, 1960), 813, 816.

29. WM/Jock Colville, 10/14/80; Cv/3, 39, 973.

30. Colville, *Fringes*, 419.

31. Cv/3, 43.

32. Cv/3, 44; Eden, *The Reckoning*, 270–72.

33. Kennan, *Memoirs*; Cv/3, 44.

34. Cv/3, 165.

35. Cv/3, 430; Colville, *Fringes*, 209 (Operation Razzle); Cv/3, 430.

36. Cv/3, 173.

37. Cv/3, 165.

38. Margery Allingham, *The Oaken Heart* (London, 1991), 169–89.

39. ChP 20/36; WM/Lord Butler, 1980; WM/Viscount Antony Head, 1980.

40. Eden, *The Reckoning*, 203–4.

41. C&R-TCC, 1:115.

42. Robert E. Sherwood, *Roosevelt and Hopkins: An Intimate History* (New York, 1948), l, 14, 15, 234.

43. Arthur Conan Doyle, *The Great Boer War* (Charlestown, SC, 2006); Colville, *Fringes*, 330; Cv/3, 29.

44. Franklin D. Roosevelt Presidential Library and Museum, 1/6/41.

45. H. L. Mencken, *The American Language, Supplement Two* (New York, 1962), 784–85 (derivation of "Jeep").

46. WSCHCS, 6328.

47. WSCHCS, 6328; *Times*, 1/10/41; David Dilks, ed., *The Diaries of Sir Alexander Cadogan, 1938–1945* (New York, 1972), 342; Cv/2, 1268.

48. Colville, *Fringes*, 332.

49. John Rupert Colville, *Footprints in Time* (London, 1976), 153.

50. James Conant, *My Several Lives: Memoirs of a Social Inventor* (Boston, 1970), 229–31.

51. Conant, *My Several Lives*, 231.

52. WM/Sir Robert Boothby, 10/16/80 ("cool and *yella*").

53. TWY, 114; WSCHCS, 6529.

54. TWY, 136–37; Mosley, *Battle of Britain*; Cv/3, 825; Cv/2, 1314.

55. WSCHCC, 6451.

56. Shirer, *Rise and Fall*, 779; Cv/2, 1243.

57. Eade, *Churchill*, 141.

58. Colville, *Fringes*, 305.

59. Walter H. Thompson, *Assignment: Churchill* (New York, 1953), 220; WSC 3, 5; Colville, *Fringes*, 341.

60. WSC 3, 38.

61. Panter-Downes, *War Notes*, 134.

62. Klingaman, *1941*, 88.

63. Klingaman, *1941*, 127; *Time*, 3/14/41, 25; WSC 3, 112, 122.

64. Colville, *Fringes*, 358.

65. Roger Chesneau, *Conway's All the World's Fighting Ships, 1922–1946* (London, 1980), 244; WSC 3, 122.

66. Laurence Thompson, *1940* (New York, 1966), 234–35; Ian Kershaw, *Hitler: 1936–1945 Nemesis* (New York, 2000), 334; WSC 3, 12–13.

67. Shirer, *Rise and Fall*, 806; Kershaw, *Hitler*, 342–44; Adolf Hitler, *Mein Kampf,* edited by John Chamberlain et al. (New York, 1939), 959–61.

68. Shirer, *Berlin Diary*, 459–65.

69. Colville, *Fringes*, 148–49.

70. Ben Pimlott, *Hugh Dalton* (London, 1985), 296.

71. Colville, *Fringes*, 196; Hugh Dalton, *Memoirs 1931–1945: The Fateful Years* (London, 1957), 365–67.

72. Pimlott, *Hugh Dalton*, 301.

73. Pimlott, *Hugh Dalton*, 312.

74. Martin Gilbert, *The Second World War: A Complete History* (London, 1989), 161.

75. Klingaman, *1941*, 47; *NYT*, 7/21/41.

76. Colville, *Fringes*, 441.

77. Duff Cooper, *Old Men Forget* (London, 1954), 270–71.

78. WM/A. J. P. Taylor, 1980.

79. Gardner, *Churchill in Power*, 108; *Time*, 1/6/41.

80. Colville, *Fringes*, 331–33.

81. WM/Pamela Harriman, 8/22/80; WM/Averell Harriman, 8/22/80; Sherwood, *Roosevelt and Hopkins*, 203.

82. Robert E. Sherwood, *The White House Papers of Harry L. Hopkins: An Intimate History* (London, 1948).

83. Sherwood, *White House Papers*.

84. Colville, *Fringes*, 334–35; WM/Jock Colville, 10/14/80.

85. Colville, *Fringes*, 334–35; WM/Jock Colville, 10/14/80.

86. Colville, *Fringes*, 334–35; WM/Jock Colville, 10/14/80.

87. Colville, *Fringes*, 334–35; WM/Jock Colville, 10/14/80.

88. Colville, *Fringes*, 334–35; WM/Jock Colville, 10/14/80.

89. GILBERT 6, 986; WSCHCS, 7235.

90. Colville, *Fringes*, 333–34.

91. GILBERT 6, 986–87 (Lyttelton recollection).

92. Colville, *Fringes*, 331–34.

93. Colville, *Fringes*, 334–35; GILBERT 6, 987.

94. GILBERT 6, 988–89; Sherwood, *White House Papers*, 1:239–40.

95. GILBERT 6, 988–89; Sherwood, *White House Papers*, 1:239–40.

96. GILBERT 5, 990; Lord Moran, *Churchill: Taken from the Diaries of Lord Moran* (Boston, 1966), 6–7; WSCHCS, 6329.

97. Moran, *Diaries*, 6–7.

98. WSC 3, 5.

99. Richard Collier, *The War in the Desert* (New York, 1980), 26–33; John Keegan, *The Second World War* (London, 1989); ChP 20/14.

100. ChP 20/49 (cable to Wavell); Colville, *Fringes*, 329.

101. WSC to Wavell, 1/11/41, ChP 20/49.

102. William Manchester, *The Last Lion* (Boston, 1983), 1:522.

103. GILBERT 6, 988–89.
104. Collier, *War in the Desert*, 30–33.
105. WSCHCS, 6346.
106. Keegan, *Second World War*, 328; Collier, *War in the Desert*, 32–33.
107. Hastings Lionel Ismay, *The Memoirs of General Lord Ismay* (London, 1960), 190; Keegan, *Second World War*, 328; Collier, *War in the Desert*, 33.
108. Keegan, *Second World War*, 147–48, 328.
109. Ismay, *Memoirs*, 195.
110. B. H. Liddell Hart, *History of the Second World War* (New York, 1971), 118.
111. WSC 3, 757; Ismay, *Memoirs*, 270.
112. Boatner, *Biographical Dictionary*, 513–14.
113. Keegan, *Second World War*, 322–24.
114. Keegan, *Second World War*, 322–24.
115. Keegan, *Second World War*, 323.
116. WSC 3, 26–27; *Time*, 10/16/44.
117. TWY, 198; Conant, *My Several Lives*, 231.
118. Colville, *Fringes*, 773; Sarah Churchill, *Keep On Dancing* (London, 1981), 96.
119. Colville, *Footprints*, 153–55; WM/Averell Harriman and Pamela Harriman, 8/22/80; GILBERT 6, 1019.
120. Sherwood, *Roosevelt and Hopkins*, 157.
121. WSCHCS, 6347; F. W. Winterbotham, *The Ultra Secret* (New York, 1974), 99–100.
122. WSCHCS, 6346–51.
123. Dilks, *Diaries*, 353.
124. WSCHCS, 6346.
125. WSCHCS, 6346.
126. Cv/3, 395–97.
127. ChP 69/2; ChP 20/49.
128. Conant, *My Several Lives*, 254.
129. ChP 20/13.
130. Scott Berg, *Lindbergh* (New York, 1999), 414–15.
131. Gardner, *Churchill in Power*, 108.
132. Conant, *My Several Lives*, 232.
133. Steel, *Walter Lippmann*, 389.
134. Eric Sevareid, *Not So Wild a Dream*, 177, 193.
135. Cv/3, 321.
136. Colville, *Fringes*, 350; PFR/Alexander Balas (Iron Guard), 12/08.
137. *Time*, 2/3/41.
138. Colville, *Fringes*, 312–13, 403.
139. Cv/3, 204; TWY, 144–45, 186–87.
140. WM/John Martin, 10/23/80.
141. *Time*, 6/9/41 (Eden address on war aims), 26; Colville, *Fringes*, 329.
142. Colville, *Fringes*, 329; ChP 20/36; ChP 20/30.
143. Cv/3, 974.
144. Cv/3, 974.
145. Cv/3, 977.
146. Cv/3, 320–21.
147. Cv/3, 320–21.

148. Conant, *My Several Lives,* 276.
149. Conant, *My Several Lives,* 274, 277–78.
150. Conant, *My Several Lives,* 274, 277–78.
151. Colville, *Fringes,* 736.
152. Cv/3, 320–21.
153. WSCHCS, 6386.
154. Cv/3, 302.
155. WM/Viscount Antony Head, 1980; Colville, *Churchillians,* 136.
156. C&R-TCC, 1:145; Klingaman, *1941,* 127–30.
157. WM/George Thomson, 1980.
158. Klingaman, *1941,* 98–99; WM/Jock Colville, 10/14/80.
159. WM/Pamela Harriman, 8/22/80; TWY, 189.
160. TWY, 140–41.
161. *Time,* 1/20/41.
162. Conant, *My Several Lives,* 254–55.
163. Conant, *My Several Lives,* 254–55; Keegan, *Second World War,* 538.
164. NYT, 3/12/41.
165. NYT, 3/12/41.
166. NYT, 3/12/41; WSCHCS, 6360, 6505; CAB 115/436; Colville, *Fringes,* 343.
167. ChP 23/9; Keegan, *Second World War,* 104–6.
168. WSC 3, 111–14; Keegan, *Second World War,* 104–6.
169. Harriman and Abel, *Special Envoy,* v–vi; Sherwood, *Roosevelt and Hopkins,* 269.
170. Boatner, *Biographical Dictionary,* 206.
171. WM/Averell Harriman, 8/22/80.
172. WM/Averell Harriman, 8/22/80.
173. WM/Averell Harriman, 8/22/80.
174. Eden, *The Reckoning,* 248, 251, 253; Colville, *Fringes,* 360–61.
175. C&R–TCC, 1:144–45 (3/10/41 cable to FDR).
176. C&R–TCC, 1:144–45 (3/10/41 cable to FDR); Cv/3, 329.
177. Cv/3 (cable to Eden re Italians), 432; John Keegan, *Winston Churchill* (New York, 2002), 138–39.
178. Colville, *Fringes,* 369; Klingaman, *1941,* 194–95.
179. Dilks, *Diaries,* 365; Colville, *Fringes,* 337, 366; GILBERT 6, 1042–43.
180. Colville, *Fringes,* 367; Pimlott, *Hugh Dalton,* 309; Dilks, *Diaries,* 366.
181. Colville, *Fringes,* 367.
182. Keegan, *Second World War,* 328–29; ChP 20/49; Ismay, *Memoirs,* 201; Colville, *Fringes,* 135.
183. ChP 20/37.
184. John Keegan, *Who's Who in World War II* (London, 1995), 175.
185. Colville, *Fringes,* 369–70.
186. Dilks, *Diaries,* 367–68.
187. Cv/3, 426–28.
188. Colville, *Fringes,* 368; Cv/3, 427–28.
189. Cv/3, 447.
190. WSCHCS, 5818.
191. GILBERT 6, 1050–51; Cv/3, 447–48.
192. Winterbotham, *Ultra Secret,* 100–101.
193. Keegan, *Second World War,* 152–54; Eden, *The Reckoning,* 247.

194. Cv/3, 439.
195. Cv/3, 445.
196. Cv/3, 439.
197. Collier, *War in the Desert,* 65–67.
198. Keegan, *Second World War,* 328–29; Collier, *War in the Desert,* 65–67.
199. Colville, *Fringes,* 371; Cv/3, 448–49.
200. Cv/3, 448–49; Colville, *Fringes,* 371.
201. WSC 3, 211.
202. Colville, *Fringes,* 369–70.
203. Brown, *Suez to Singapore,* 4–5; WSC 3, 175.
204. Brown, *Suez to Singapore,* 4–6.
205. Keegan, *Second World War,* 157–59.
206. CAB 65/22.
207. Cv/3, 517–18.
208. Cv/3, 521.
209. David Irving, *Hitler's War* (New York, 1977), 1:246–47.
210. Keegan, *Second World War,* 157.
211. Sherwood, *Roosevelt and Hopkins,* 239.
212. Collier, *War in the Desert,* 67–68.
213. ChP 69/2; Cv/3, 445.
214. Berg, *Lindbergh,* 418–19.
215. Shirer, *Rise and Fall,* 824.
216. Basil Collier, *The Second World War: A Military History from Munich to Hiroshima* (New York, 1967), 186–87.
217. *Time,* 5/5/41.
218. WM/Jock Colville, 10/14/80.
219. Cv/3, 360.
220. Panter-Downes, *War Notes,* 141; Colville, *Fringes,* 374–75.
221. Dilks, *Diaries,* 372; Colville, *Fringes,* 375; WM/Jock Colville, 10/14/80.
222. Broad, *Anthony Eden,* 170; John Wheeler-Bennett, *Action This Day: Working with Churchill* (London, 1968), 77; Colville, *Fringes,* 128.
223. Colville, *Fringes,* 443–45.
224. Eden, *The Reckoning,* 295; WSCHCS, 6378.
225. Eden, *The Reckoning,* 295; WSCHCS, 6378; Winterbotham, *Ultra Secret,* 101.
226. WSCHCS, 6378.
227. WSCHCS, 6378.
228. C&R-TCC, 1:322.
229. George Orwell, "Reflections on Gandhi" (1949), in *The Orwell Reader* (New York, 1984); WSCHCS, 6378.
230. Orwell, "Reflections"; WSCHCS, 6378.
231. Harriman and Abel, *Special Envoy,* 16–17; GILBERT 6, 1018.
232. Cv/3, 560 (Wavell cable).
233. GILBERT 6, 1072; Panter-Downes, *War Notes,* 140.
234. Danchev and Todman, *War Diaries,* 154; ChP 120/10.
235. ChP 120/10.
236. ChP 120/10.
237. Colville, *Fringes,* 391.
238. Kenneth Young, *Churchill and Beaverbrook* (London, 1966), 178–79.
239. Panter-Downes, *War Notes,* 145.

240. Panter-Downes, *War Notes*, 123.
241. Panter-Downes, *War Notes*, 123, 138; Hansard 5/29/41 Oral answers (Cv/3, 735).
242. Dilks, *Diaries*, 375.
243. WSC 3, 254, 255, 265; John Keegan, ed., *Churchill's Generals* (New York, 1991).
244. *Time*, 6/2/41, 24; WSC 3, 264–66.
245. Cv/3, 560.
246. Keegan, *Second World War*, 161.
247. C&R-TCC, 1:176.
248. Keegan, *Second World War*, 161.
249. C&R-TCC, 1:172–74.
250. C&R-TCC, 1:172–74; Harriman and Abel, *Special Envoy*, 31.
251. Colville, *Fringes*, 381–82.
252. C&R-TCC, 1:181–82.
253. WSC 3, 53–55; Sherwood, *Roosevelt and Hopkins*, 293–94; *Time*, 12/27/43, 73; *Time*, 12/27/43, 73 (MacNeice).
254. WM/Pamela Harriman, 8/22/80.
255. WSC 3, 53–55.
256. WSC 3, 53–55.
257. Sherwood, *Roosevelt and Hopkins*, 294.
258. Albert Speer, *Inside the Third Reich: Memoirs by Albert Speer* (Macmillan, 1970), 174–75.
259. WM/Kay Halle, 8/6/80.
260. *Time*, 6/12/44.
261. Colville, *Fringes*, 385–86; Cv/3, 767; WSCHCS, 6399.
262. Colville, *Fringes*, 385–86.
263. Boatner, *Biographical Dictionary*, 596.
264. Keegan, *Second World War*, 166–69.
265. C&R-TCC, 1:191, 192; Colville, *Fringes*, 389.
266. Colville, *Fringes*, 389.
267. Colville, *Fringes*, 389.
268. WSC 3, 305.
269. Boatner, *Biographical Dictionary*, 328.
270. Chesneau, *Conway's*; WSC 3, 305–20.
271. C&R-TCC, 1:192; Colville, *Fringes*, 374.
272. Colville, *Fringes*, 390; Ismay, *Memoirs*, 219; ChP 4/219.
273. WM/Averell Harriman, 8/22/80.
274. WCS 6, 1094.
275. Colville, *Fringes*, 391; WSC 3, 299.
276. Colville, *Fringes*, 391.
277. Colville, *Fringes*, 391.
278. Colville, *Footprints*, 188–89.
279. WSC 3, 316–17.
280. WSC 3, 317–20; Colville, *Fringes*, 403.
281. *Time*, 6/16/41; WM/Averell Harriman, 8/22/80.
282. WSC 3, 317–20.
283. Cv/3, 761; *Time*, 6/16/41, 30; WSC 3, 304.
284. WSCHCS, 6412–15; Hansard 6/10/41.
285. WSCHCS, 6415; Hansard 6/10/41.
286. Colville, *Fringes*, 383, 393.

287. Colville, *Fringes,* 396.
288. Colville, *Fringes,* 396; C&R-TCC, 1:191.
289. Colville, *Fringes,* 382, 402; GILBERT 6, 846.
290. GILBERT 6, 1074 n1.
291. ChP 20/36.
292. Robert W. Creamer, *Baseball and Other Matters in 1941* (Lincoln, NE, 1991), 169–70.
293. Franklin D. Roosevelt Presidential Library and Museum, 5/27/41.
294. WSCHCS, 6490.
295. Cv/3, 731 (to Wavell).
296. Cv/3, 1132 (letter to Randolph); Colville, *Fringes,* 432.
297. WSC 3, 368.
298. WSC 3, 342.
299. Cv/3, 807, 830; *Time,* 3/31/41.
300. Cv/2, 1246; Colville, *Fringes,* 403–4.
301. Colville, *Fringes,* 403; Boatner, *Biographical Dictionary,* 556.
302. Colville, *Fringes,* 403.
303. Eden, *The Reckoning,* 312; Colville, *Fringes,* 403.
304. Keegan, *Second World War,* 181.
305. Keegan, *Second World War,* 181; Shirer, *Rise and Fall,* 849.
306. Keegan, *Second World War,* 180–81.
307. Keegan, *Second World War,* 178–79; WSC 3, 353.
308. Colville, *Fringes,* 403–4; TWY, 174.
309. TWY, 174.
310. Colville, *Fringes,* 402–3.
311. Colville, *Fringes,* 405.
312. Colville, *Fringes,* 405.
313. WSCHCS, 6427.
314. WSCHCS, 6427; C&R-TCC, 2:22 (Balkan proverb).
315. TWY, 174.
316. PFR/Sir John Keegan, 6/04.
317. J. Erikson, *The Soviet High Command* (London, 1962); William Taubman, *Khrushchev: The Man and His Era* (New York, 2003), 162.
318. ChP 65/19; Cv/3, 1107; C&R-TCC, 1:253.
319. Cv/3, 842.
320. Cv/ 3, 870–71.
321. C&R-TCC, 1:224.
322. Young, *Churchill and Beaverbrook,* 200; WSC 2, 577; Richard Langworth, ed., *Churchill by Himself: The Definitive Collection of Quotations* (London, 2008), 324.
323. Cv/3, 956; Cv/3, 1161.
324. WSC 3, 462–63; Cv/3, 1171–72.
325. ChP 20/44.
326. Cv/3, 1171 (to Cripps); Cv/3, 964–65 (to Stalin).
327. Cv/3, 841 (to Chiefs).
328. Cv/3, 991; Cv/3, 1236.
329. GILBERT 6, 1050–51.
330. James C. Humes, *The Wit and Wisdom of Winston Churchill* (New York, 1995), 151; Colville, *Fringes,* 309; Anthony Montague Browne, *Long Sunset* (London, 1996), 76.

331. *Time,* 6/9/41.
332. Colville, *Fringes,* 194; Colville, *Churchillians,* 144.
333. Colville, *Fringes,* 416–17.
334. Colville, *Fringes,* 419; Cv/3, 978.
335. *Brooklyn Eagle,* 8/6/41.
336. Cv/3, 1031; Colville, *Fringes,* 424; WM/Sir Ian Jacob, 11/12/80.
337. WSC 3, 429.
338. WSC 3, 425–27; *Brooklyn Eagle,* 8/6/41; GILBERT 6, 1155–56.
339. WSC 3, 445–46.
340. Cv/3, 111 (draft of threat to Japan).
341. Dilks, *Diaries,* 396–97; *Brooklyn Eagle,* 8/6/41; *Time,* 5/31/41.
342. Thompson, *Assignment: Churchill,* 230.
343. Wheeler-Bennett, *Action This Day,* 207.
344. WSC 3, 434.
345. WSC 3, 432.
346. Thompson, *Assignment: Churchill,* 234, 236, 239; ChP 4/225; Dilks, *Diaries,* 398.
347. WSC 3, 443–44.
348. WSC 4, 890; Cv/3, 1059.
349. Thompson, *Assignment: Churchill,* 271; Dilks, *Diaries,* 277, 280, 401.
350. CAB 65/19; Cv/3, 1079, 1084.
351. Dilks, *Diaries,* 402; Cv/3, 1068; Cv/3, 1079.
352. Colville, *Fringes,* 428; Cv/3, 1111; Cv/3, 1079–81; Keegan, *Second World War,* 538–39.
353. Colville, *Fringes,* 428; James MacGregor Burns, *Roosevelt: The Soldier of Freedom, 1940–1945* (New York, 1970), 118, 134.
354. Shirer, *Rise and Fall,* 854.
355. *NYT,* 9/2/41; Sherwood, *Roosevelt and Hopkins,* 369.
356. T. R. Fehrenbach, *FDR's Undeclared War 1939–1941* (New York, 1967).
357. Franklin D. Roosevelt Presidential Library and Museum, Fireside Chat, 9/11/41.
358. Klingaman, *1941,* 370.
359. War Cabinet No. 112 of 1941; C&R-TCC, 1:265.
360. War Cabinet No. 112 of 1941.
361. Franklin D. Roosevelt Presidential Library and Museum, 9/11/41.
362. C&R-TCC, 1:198.
363. C&R-TCC, 1:265.
364. Wheeler-Bennett, *Action This Day,* 202.
365. Gordon Prange, *At Dawn We Slept: The Untold Story of Pearl Harbor* (London, 1983), 37–39, 320; Liddell Hart, *History,* 227.
366. Cv/3, 236; *Time,* 1/19/42, 9.
367. WSC 3 (memo to Ismay), 177.
368. Colville, *Footprints,* 150; Cv/3, 44; Premier (Prime Minister) Papers, Public Record Office, Kew, 3/156/6.
369. Klingaman, *1941,* 346.
370. WSC 3, 580–81.
371. C&R-TCC, 1:108; ChP 20/13 (Ismay Minute, 7/25/40); Colville, *Fringes,* 335; Cv/3, 575.
372. C&R-TCC, 1:257; WSC 3, 603.
373. Cv/3, 1094.
374. Cv/3, 1555.
375. *Chicago Tribune,* 10/27/41.

376. Cv/3, 1111.
377. C&R-TCC, 1:276.
378. Cv/3, 1530–31.
379. ChP 2/416.
380. Eden, *The Reckoning*, 325.
381. Boatner, *Biographical Dictionary* 63 (Brooke); Danchev and Todman, *War Diaries*, 89–90.
382. Colville, *Fringes*, 446.
383. Cv/3, 1534; Cv/3, 1530–36.
384. C&R-TCC, 1:266.
385. Cv/3, 1530.
386. Colville, *Fringes*, 414–15; Churchill, *Keep On Dancing*, 95.
387. WM/Lady Mary Soames, 10/27/80; Mary Soames, *Clementine Churchill: The Biography of a Marriage* (New York, 2003), 403; Churchill, *Keep On Dancing*, 160.
388. Soames, *Clementine*, 404.
389. Collier, *War in the Desert*, 83–86.
390. Cv/3, 1531 (Auchinleck greetings).
391. WSCHCS, 6519.
392. TWY, 190.
393. TWY, 205.
394. Cv/3, 1534–36.
395. Keegan, *Second World War*, 538.
396. Keegan, *Second World War*, 203, 206.

Vortex

1. Walter H. Thompson, *Assignment: Churchill* (New York, 1953), 3.
2. PFR/Winston S. Churchill, 4/04 (Christmas at Chequers); WM/Pamela Harriman, 8/22/80; Martin Gilbert, *Churchill and the Jews* (New York, 2007), 2; John Colville, *The Fringes of Power: 10 Downing Street Diaries 1939–1955* (New York, 1985), 392.
3. PFR/Winston S. Churchill (Christmas at Chequers), 4/04.
4. Alex Danchev and Daniel Todman, eds., *Field Marshal Lord Alanbrooke: War Diaries 1939–1945* (Berkeley, 2003), 209.
5. Cv/3, 1553; Cv/3, 1235.
6. W. Averell Harriman and Elie Abel, *Special Envoy to Churchill and Stalin: 1941–1946* (New York, 1975), 111.
7. *Time*, 5/11/42, 90; C&R-TCC, 1:279.
8. C&R-TCC, 1:280–81; *Time*, 1/19/42, 9.
9. Arthur Bryant, *The Turn of the Tide: A History of the War Years Based on the Diaries of Field-Marshal Lord Alanbrooke, 1939–1943* (New York, 1957), 233.
10. Cv/3, 1574.
11. WM/Averell Harriman, 8/22/80.
12. Cv/3, 1576–77; WM/Pamela Harriman, 8/22/80; WM/Averell Harriman, 8/22/80.
13. Cv/3, 1576–77; WM/Pamela Harriman, 8/22/80; WM/Averell Harriman, 8/22/80; WM/John Martin, 10/23/80.
14. WSC 3, 604; Danchev and Todman, *War Diaries*, 209.

15. Cv/3, 1579.

16. ChP 20/36; Bryant, *Tide*, 226; Duff Cooper, *Old Men Forget* (London, 1954), 301.

17. William Manchester, *American Caesar: Douglas MacArthur 1880–1964* (Boston, 1978), 209–11; Samuel Eliot Morison, *The Two-Ocean War* (Boston, 1963), 82; Clay Blair Jr., *Silent Victory* (Annapolis, MD, 1975), 134, 171.

18. *NYT*, 12/12/41; Manchester, *American Caesar*, 209–11; Morison, *Two-Ocean War*, 82.

19. Eisenhower, *Crusade*, 21; Leonard Mosley, *Marshall: Hero for Our Times* (New York, 1982), 189–91.

20. C&R-TCC, 1:283.

21. WSCHCS, 6525; TWY, 194.

22. WSC 3, 611; ChP 20/46; ChP 20/20.

23. Cv/3, 1586; Anthony Eden, Earl of Avon, *The Reckoning: The Memoirs of Anthony Eden* (New York, 1965), 330–31.

24. Mary Soames, *Clementine Churchill: The Biography of a Marriage* (New York, 2003), 349–50 (Komodo); WM/Viscount Antony Head, 1980.

25. Winston S. Churchill, *A History of the English-Speaking Peoples*, 4 vols. (New York, 1993), 3:212.

26. WM/Mark Bonham Carter, 10/20/80.

27. Cv/3, 1435; Cv/3, 1455; WM/Sir Ian Jacob, 11/12/80.

28. Cv/3, 1083; WM/Sir Ian Jacob, 11/12/80.

29. WM/G. M. Thompson, 1980; WSC 3, 854; WM/Sir Ian Jacob, 11/12/80.

30. Mark Mayo Boatner, *The Biographical Dictionary of World War II* (New York, 1999), 428; Stephen Roskill, *Churchill and the Admirals* (New York, 1978), 199; Hastings Lionel Ismay, *The Memoirs of General Lord Ismay* (London, 1960), 240.

31. WM/G. M. Thompson, 1980.

32. Cv/3, 1592; Cecil Brown, *Suez to Singapore* (New York, 1942), 298.

33. WSC 3, 619; David Reynolds, *Britannia Overruled* (London, 2000), 141.

34. Brown, *Suez to Singapore*, 311–23; Cv/3, 1474.

35. Brown, *Suez to Singapore*, 311–23; Cv/3, 1474.

36. Brown, *Suez to Singapore*, 328.

37. WM/Averell Harriman, 8/22/80.

38. Cv/3, 1593; WSC 3, 620.

39. Mollie Panter-Downes, *London War Notes, 1939–1945* (London, 1972), 198.

40. Thompson, *Assignment: Churchill*, 245–46.

41. Winston Churchill, *My Early Life: 1874–1904* (New York, 1996), 19; WM/Lady Mary Soames, 10/27/80.

42. Churchill, *Early Life*, 19; WM/Lady Mary Soames, 10/27/80.

43. Hansard 12/11/41; TWY, 196–97.

44. WSC 3, 616; CAB 69/4 (Cv/3, 1651); Winston S. Churchill, *The World Crisis*, 5 vols. (New York, 1923–31), 1:212 ("gigantic castles of steel").

45. The Editors of the Viking Press, *The Churchill Years 1874–1965, with Foreword by Lord Butler of Saffron Walden* (London, 1965), 21; WM/R. A. B. Butler, 12/5/80.

46. Cv/3, 1627.

47. *Time*, 1/5/42, 13–14; *Time*, 3/2/42, 57.

48. *NYT*, 12/12/42.

49. WSCHCS, 6530; TWY, 196–97.

50. Colville, *Fringes*, 404; WSCHCC, 6531.

51. C&R-TCC, 1:286.
52. Cv/3, 1612; Danchev and Todman, *War Diaries*, 209.
53. GILBERT 7, 6–7; PFR/Lady Mary Soames, 6/07.
54. W&C-TPL, 459–61.
55. WM/G. M. Thompson, 1980.
56. *NYT*, 12/12/41.
57. Richard Collier, *The War in the Desert* (New York, 1980), 84–85.
58. Cv/3, 1657; David Dilks, ed., *The Diaries of Sir Alexander Cadogan, 1938–1945* (New York, 1972), 439.
59. PFR/Winston S. Churchill, 5/04; Soames, *Clementine*, 499.
60. WSC 3, 696; PFR/Winston S. Churchill, 4/04.
61. James MacGregor Burns, *Roosevelt: The Soldier of Freedom, 1940–1945* (New York, 1970), 551.
62. WSC 6, 400–401; C&R-TCC, 3:68–69; WSCHCS, 7117.
63. John Gunther, *Inside Europe* (New York, 1938), 464–65; WM/Averell Harriman, 8/22/80; Harriman and Abel, *Special Envoy*, 283.
64. Harriman and Abel, *Special Envoy*, 77, 220.
65. Elisabeth Barker, *Churchill and Eden at War* (New York, 1978), 233–35; ChP 20/50.
66. Cv/3, 1644.
67. Louis P. Lochner, *The Goebbels Diaries 1942–1943* (New York, 1948), 136; Charles Burdick and Hans-Adolf Jacobsen, eds., *The Halder War Diary, 1939–1942* (New York, 1988); Boatner, *Biographical Dictionary*, 200–201.
68. Panter-Downes, *War Notes*, 191.
69. Thompson, *Assignment: Churchill*, 246; WSC 3, 682.
70. Cv/3, 1344–45.
71. John Keegan, ed., *Churchill's Generals* (New York, 1991), 86; Cv/3, 1341; WSC 4, 24.
72. CAB 69/2; ChP 20/20.
73. Harriman and Abel, *Special Envoy*, 216; Bryant, *Tide*, 15.
74. Dwight D. Eisenhower, *Crusade in Europe* (New York, 1948), 22.
75. Bryant, *Tide*, 16 ("salt water" general).
76. Danchev and Todman, *War Diaries*, 281; Bryant, *Tide*, 234.
77. Edward Jablonski, *Airwar: Tragic Victories* (Garden City, NY, 1971), "American Renegades," 26–42.
78. WSC 3, 674; Bryant, *Tide*, 231.
79. WSCHCS, 6535; Written Archives Center, U.S. National Park Service.
80. William K. Klingaman, *1941: Our Lives in a World on the Edge* (New York, 1989), 449.
81. WSC 3, 666.
82. ChP 20/50; *Time*, 1/5/42, 22–23; *Time*, 8/3/42, 15.
83. *Time*, 1/5/42, 16; Moran, *Diaries*, 11; WSCHCS, 6536.
84. WSCHCS, 6537–39.
85. *NYT*, 12/27/41; ChP 20/49; Bryant, *Tide*, 229; GILBERT 7, 28–29.
86. WSC 3, 691; Lord Moran, *Churchill: Taken from the Diaries of Lord Moran* (Boston, 1966), 17–18.
87. Moran, *Diaries*, 20.
88. WSC 3, 679; Martin Gilbert, *In Search of Churchill: A Historian's Journey* (New York, 1994), 295–96.

89. Thompson, *Bodyguard,* 257; WSC 3, 680–81.

90. PFR/Brig. General Albin Irzyk (U.S. Army ret.), 12/11.

91. TWY, 199; WSC 3, 681.

92. Danchev and Todman, *War Diaries,* 217; Klingaman, *1941,* 450–51.

93. Boatner, *Biographical Dictionary,* 324; WSC 3, 682–83.

94. Boatner, *Biographical Dictionary,* 324; WSC 3, 682–83; GILBERT 7, 35; WM/ Pamela Harriman, 8/22/80. This was her secondhand recollection of what Churchill said to Roosevelt when the president encountered WSC naked. Afterward Churchill disputed the recollection of his bodyguard, Inspector Walter Thompson (*Assignment: Churchill,* 248), and his secretary, Patrick Kinna, who both claimed Churchill said to the president, "You see Mr. President, I have nothing to conceal [or "hide"] from you." (GILBERT 7, 28). Churchill later told Robert E. Sherwood (*Roosevelt and Hopkins: An Intimate History* [New York, 1948], 442– 43) that he in fact had secrets to keep from the Americans, and did so.

95. *NYT,* 12/12/41.

96. Mencken, *American Language,* 785–86.

97. *Atlantic Monthly,* 3/65, 79.

98. Tom Hickman, *Churchill's Bodyguard* (London, 2005), 261; WSC 3, 691, 706; Celia Sandys, *Chasing Churchill* (New York, 2005), 148; WM/John Martin, 10/23/80.

99. *Time,* 5/25/42, 22–23; The Adamic Louis Papers, Slovene American Collection, Immigration History Research Center, University of Minnesota; WM/Sir Fitzroy Maclean, 10/15/80.

100. GILBERT 6, 1215 (lisp); *Time,* 9/2/46; *Time,* 11/4/46.

101. WM/Cecily ("Chips") Gemmell, 7/10/80; WM/Jock Colville, 10/14/80.

102. WM/Cecily ("Chips") Gemmell, 7/10/80; WM/Jock Colville, 10/14/80; WM/ Sir David Hunt, 1980.

103. Barbara Tuchman, *Stilwell and the American Experience in China* (New York, 1971), 296, 308–9.

104. Tuchman, *Stilwell,* 625; WSC 3, 705; WSC 4, 123.

105. WSC 3, 689–90; *Time,* 5/5/43.

106. WSC 2, 115; Morison, *Two-Ocean War,* 138.

107. WSC 3, 710–11.

108. WSC 3, 708.

109. GILBERT 7, 53–54; Eden, *The Reckoning,* 369.

110. ChP 20/23; WSC 4, 8.

111. Moran, *Diaries,* 28; WSC 4, 60–61.

112. Brian Gardner, *Churchill in Power: As Seen by His Contemporaries* (Boston, 1970), 150.

113. David Stafford, *Churchill and Secret Service* (London, 2000), 280.

114. *Time,* 3/2/42, 27 ("Christ and Carrots" Cripps); Lochner, *Goebbels Diaries,* 137.

115. Kenneth Young, *Churchill and Beaverbrook* (London, 1966), 230, 232; WSC 4, 75; Cv/3, 1373–74; Gardner, *Churchill in Power,* 183.

116. WSC 4, 61; Gardner, *Churchill in Power,* 157.

117. Gardner, *Churchill in Power,* 147.

118. John Colville, *The Churchillians* (London, 1981), 69; John Wheeler-Bennett, *Action This Day: Working with Churchill* (London, 1968), 79; Charles Eade, ed., *Churchill by His Contemporaries* (New York, 1954), 298; WM/Jock Colville, 10/14/80.

119. Brian Gardner, *Churchill in Power: As Seen by His Contemporaries* (Boston, 1970), 152; Moran, *Diaries,* 80; WSCHCS, 7269.
120. Jan Morris, *The Matter of Wales* (New York, 1984), 404, 405; Gardner, *Churchill in Power,* 152; Moran, *Diaries,* 649.
121. WM/Pamela Harriman, 8/22/80; WSC 4, 61; Gardner, *Churchill in Power,* 157; TWY, 207, 208, 209; Colville, *Fringes,* 737.
122. WM/Averell Harriman, 8/22/80; WSC 4, 61; Gardner, *Churchill in Power,* 157; TWY, 207, 208, 209.
123. Gardner, *Churchill in Power,* 158.
124. TWY, 209.
125. *Time,* 10/24/1941.
126. WSC 3, 576–77.
127. WSC 3, 576–77; W&C-TPL, 558; *Time,* 5/3/43, 40.
128. Collier, *War in the Desert,* 89; WSC 4, 21; TWY, 209.
129. *Time,* 3/2/42, 20.
130. Basil Collier, *The Second World War: A Military History from Munich to Hiroshima* (New York, 1967), 268; *Time,* 3/2/42, 20.
131. Brown, *Suez to Singapore,* 370, 392.
132. WSC 4, 50–51; Collier, *Second World War,* 273.
133. Brown, *Suez to Singapore,* 373; Cooper, *Old Men,* 305; PFR/Michael Browning, 7/04.
134. GILBERT 7, 47, 57; ChP 20/67.
135. John Toland, *The Rising Sun: The Decline and Fall of the Japanese Empire, 1936–1945* (London, 2003), 336–37; *Time,* 3/2/42, 21; C&R-TCC, 1:381; Danchev and Todman, *War Diaries,* 231.
136. WSC 3, 581.
137. John Keegan, *The Second World War* (London, 1989), 261.
138. Lochner, *Goebbels Diaries,* 81, 83.
139. WSC 3, 680; TWY, 212; Hansard 2/17/42.
140. WSC 4, 72, 113; Panter-Downes, *War Notes,* 206–7; WSCHCS, 6615 ("simpletons and dunderheads").
141. WSC 4, 81; WM/Lord Geoffrey Lloyd, 1980.
142. WM/Malcolm Muggeridge, 11/25/80; WM/Lord Geoffrey Lloyd, 1980; WSC 4, 81; Danchev and Todman, *War Diaries,* 713.
143. WSC 4, 75; W&C-TPL, 464.
144. Roy Jenkins, *Churchill: A Biography* (London, 2011), 685.
145. Panter-Downes, *War Notes,* 205.
146. Klingaman, *1941,* 215.
147. WSCHCS, 6427.
148. WSCHCS, 6527.
149. Dilks, *Diaries,* 433.
150. WSC 4, 155–56.
151. Morison, *Two-Ocean War,* 93–97.
152. Soames, *Clementine,* 415; Morison, *Two-Ocean War,* 93–97; *Time,* 3/9/42.
153. Morison, *Two-Ocean War,* 98, 100.
154. Jablonski, *Airwar,* 41–42.
155. WSC 4, 160; Keegan, *Churchill's Generals,* 108–9.
156. For a study of the Bengal famine, see Amartya Sen, *Poverty and Famines: An Essay on Entitlements and Deprivation* (New York, 1982).

157. Tuchman, *Stilwell*, 347; WSC 4, 170.

158. Tuchman, *Stilwell*, 361, 371.

159. Tuchman, *Stilwell*, 361, 371; C&R-TCC, 1:391, 423, 438, 458.

160. TWY, 221; Dilks, *Diaries*, 438.

161. C&R-TCC, 1:421–22.

162. Colville, *Fringes*, 382.

163. Danchev and Todman, *War Diaries*, 438.

164. WSC 4, 121–22.

165. WSC 4, 184.

166. C&R-TCC, 1:382–83, 443; Samuel Eliot Morison, *The Battle of the Atlantic: September 1939–May 1943* (Edison, NJ, 2001), 168; Bryant, *Tide*, 244.

167. C&R-TCC, 1:382–83, 453, 459; Harriman and Abel, *Special Envoy*, 167; Danchev and Todman, *War Diaries*, 290.

168. C&R-TCC, 1:390, 452–54.

169. WM/Jock Colville, 10/14/80.

170. Morison, *Two-Ocean War*, 142.

171. Morison, *Two-Ocean War*, 141; Hiroyuki Agawa, *The Reluctant Admiral* (Tokyo, 1979), 73, 177.

172. Morison, *Two-Ocean War*, 141; Agawa, *Reluctant Admiral*, 140–41; C&R-TCC, 1:466.

173. WSC 4, 188.

174. C&R-TCC, 1:383, 391, 392, 441.

175. WSC 4, 217; George Orwell, "Reflections on Gandhi" (1949), in *The Orwell Reader* (New York, 1984).

176. C&R-TCC, 1:446–47; Harriman and Abel, *Special Envoy*, 131.

177. Sherwood, *Roosevelt and Hopkins*, 530–31.

178. Harriman and Abel, *Special Envoy*, 131; WM/Averell Harriman, 8/22/80; WSC 4, 209; *Time*, 9/14/42, 29.

179. C&R-TCC, 2:449; WM/Lord Christopher Soames, 1980.

180. Lochner, *Goebbels Diaries*, 177.

181. WSC 4, 204–5.

182. C&R-TCC, 1:484, 491.

183. WSC 4, 219.

184. C&R-TCC, 1:441; GILBERT 7, 117.

185. Danchev and Todman, *War Diaries*, 247, 249.

186. C&R-TCC, 1:458.

187. Mosley, *Marshall*, 204–5.

188. Boatner, *Biographical Dictionary*, 1999, 305.

189. C&R-TCC, 1:460.

190. C&R-TCC, 1:494.

191. David Miller, *U-Boats* (New York, 2000), 127; WSC 4, 109; Morison, *Two-Ocean War*, 108.

192. WSC 4, 112, 118, 123; Sherwood, *Roosevelt and Hopkins*, 544; Harriman and Abel, *Special Envoy*, 169.

193. Panter-Downes, *War Notes*, 264.

194. Miller, *U-Boats*, 117–18, 134, 174–75.

195. Miller, *U-Boats*, 117–18, 134, 174–75; Dilks, *Diaries*, 433.

196. WSC 4, 112, 118, 125.

197. C&R-TCC, 1:528.

198. WSC 4, 296.
199. WSC 3, 702–3; Bryant, *Tide*, 357.
200. Ismay, *Memoirs*, 273.
201. Cv/3, 160; Lochner, *Goebbels Diaries*, 189–90; *NYT*, 4/2/08.
202. WSC 3, 702.
203. WM/Sir Ian Jacob, 11/12/80; Danchev and Todman, *War Diaries*, 187.
204. Lochner, *Goebbels Diaries*, 130, 135
205. Lochner, *Goebbels Diaries*, 189; Harold Lee Hitchens, *America Goes to War* (Chicago, 1942), 66; Danchev and Todman, *War Diaries*, 348.
206. Lochner, *Goebbels Diaries*, 179; PFR/Alexander Balas, 12/06; *Time*, 2/1/43, 33.
207. C&R-TCC, 1:382.
208. *Time*, 5/11/42, 17.
209. Collier, *Second World War*, 296; John Keegan, *The Second World War* (London, 1989), 221–22; WSC 4, 343.
210. Keegan, *Second World War*, 222–23.
211. John Keegan, *The Mask of Command* (New York, 1987), 255, 286.
212. Gardner, *Churchill in Power*, 131.
213. C&R-TCC, 1:503.
214. Harriman and Abel, *Special Envoy*, 138.
215. Harriman and Abel, *Special Envoy*, 136.
216. C&R-TCC, 1:441; WSC 4, 314, 327, 341–42; Harriman and Abel, *Special Envoy*, 136.
217. WSC 4, 336–37.
218. Danchev and Todman, *War Diaries*, 100.
219. Collier, *War in the Desert*, 90–91.
220. Danchev and Todman, *War Diaries*, 154; WM/John Martin, 10/23/80.
221. Colville, *Fringes*, 412; Kew, British Archives, Cabinet Minutes (electric chair); see George Orwell, "Politics and the English Language" (1946) in *A Collection of Essays by George Orwell* (Orlando, FL, 1970).
222. WSC 4, 334–35.
223. Colville, *Fringes*, 412; Keegan, *Mask*, 282–283.
224. *Time*, 8/17/42, 24; GILBERT 7, 75; GILBERT 6, 1205; *NYT*, 6/1/42.
225. *Time*, 7/13/42, 92; Lochner, *Goebbels Diaries*, 155.
226. Arthur Harris, *Bomber Offensive* (London, 1947), 52, 310; *Time*, 6/8/42.
227. Panter-Downes, *War Notes*, 226; *Time*, 6/12/42, 32.
228. Lochner, *Goebbels Diaries*, 229.
229. David Stafford, *Churchill and Secret Service* (London, 2000), 280; William L. Shirer, *The Rise and Fall of the Third Reich: A History of Nazi Germany* (New York, 1960), 991.
230. Shirer, *Rise and Fall*, 991–92.
231. *Time*, 6/12/42; Lochner, *Goebbels Diaries*, 147–48.
232. Stafford, *Secret Service*, 281.
233. WSCHCS, 6475.
234. Lochner, *Goebbels Diaries*, 140.
235. Morison, *Two-Ocean War*, 150–51.
236. Morison, *Two-Ocean War*, 155–61.
237. C&R-TCC, 1:510.
238. Keegan, *Atlas*, 64–65.
239. C&R-TCC, 2:510.

240. Danchev and Todman, *War Diaries*, 266; WSC 4, 375.
241. Harry C. Butcher, *My Three Years with Eisenhower* (New York, 1946), 24; Danchev and Todman, *War Diaries*, 266; WSC 4, 376.
242. Collier, *War in the Desert*, 92.
243. WSC 4, 381, 382; GILBERT 7, 426.
244. WSC 4, 383–84.
245. Collier, *War in the Desert*, 92–93.
246. Richard Collier, *Duce!* (New York, 1971), 184–85.
247. WSC 4, 386.
248. WSC 4, 386.
249. WSC 4, 386; Bryant, *Tide*, 333.
250. Harriman and Abel, *Special Envoy*, 144; Panter-Downes, *War Notes*, 232.
251. Butcher, *Eisenhower*, 13, 24.
252. Panter-Downes, *War Notes*, 233, 234, 235, 238.
253. WSC 4, 392.
254. WSC 4, 386.
255. TWY, 231; Panter-Downes, *War Notes*, 234.
256. WSC 4, 398.
257. WSC 4, 400; Boatner, *Biographical Dictionary*, 462.
258. TWY, 232.
259. Butcher, *Eisenhower*, 5, 12, 22, 28.
260. TWY, 235.
261. WSC 4, 447; Eisenhower, *Crusade*, 69; WM/Averell Harriman, 8/22/80.
262. WSC 5, 72; Panter-Downes, *War Notes*, 224.
263. Eisenhower, *Crusade*, 68; *Time*, 7/13/42, 20–21; Butcher, *Eisenhower*, 23.
264. WSC 4, 444 (Roosevelt memo to American Chiefs); Butcher, *Eisenhower*, 51; Sherwood, *Roosevelt and Hopkins*, 648.
265. C&R-TCC, 1:545; Harriman and Abel, *Special Envoy*, 171–72.
266. John Grigg, *1943: The Victory That Never Was* (New York, 1980), 156; Eisenhower, *Crusade*, 83, 85.
267. WSC 4, 529–33; Butcher, *Eisenhower*, 52.
268. Danchev and Todman, *War Diaries*, 272, 357, 358, 359, 364, 634.
269. Colville, *Fringes*, 289.
270. Mosley, *Marshall*, 202, 211; Burns, *Roosevelt*, 286.
271. WM/Sir Ian Jacob, 11/12/80.
272. Danchev and Todman, *War Diaries*, 249, 276; Sherwood, *Roosevelt and Hopkins*, 523.
273. Danchev and Todman, *War Diaries*, 588, 634.
274. Danchev and Todman, *War Diaries*, 716.
275. ChP 20/67; Viscount Montgomery of Alamein, *The Memoirs of Field Marshal Montgomery* (London, 1958), 69–70.
276. Keegan, *Mask*, 288; Keegan, *Second World War*, 226–28.
277. Keegan, *Second World War*, 228; *Time*, 1/4/43, 21.
278. Keegan, *Mask*, 265.
279. F. W. Winterbotham, *The Ultra Secret* (New York, 1974), 109; Stafford, *Secret Service*, 283–84.
280. WSC 4, 452–53; Butcher, *Eisenhower*, 12.
281. Bruce West, *The Man Who Flew Churchill* (New York, 1965), 31, 32; Sandys, *Chasing Churchill*, 152; Moran, *Diaries*, 56; WSC 4, 452–53.
282. Bryant, *Tide*, 353; Danchev and Todman, *War Diaries*, 288.

283. WSC 4, 475.

284. West, *Man Who Flew Churchill*, 104–5; W&C-TPL, 405; WSC 4, 456.

285. WSC 4, 456; Winston S. Churchill, *The River War,* edited by John Muller (London, 2003).

286. WSC 4, 456–57.

287. Danchev and Todman, *War Diaries,* 289.

288. Danchev and Todman, *War Diaries,* 293.

289. WSC 4, 465; Ladislas Farago, *Patton: Ordeal and Triumph* (New York, 1963), 179.

290. WSC 4, 467; TWY, 259; Danchev and Todman, *War Diaries,* 296.

291. TWY, 259; W&C-TPL, 467–68.

292. Colville, *Fringes,* 256; WM/Sir Robert Boothby, 10/16/80.

293. Colville, *Fringes,* 391.

294. W&C-TPL, 467.

295. Joseph M. Mueller, *Guadalcanal 1942* (Oxford, 1992), 29, 34, 35; Morison, *Two-Ocean War,* 172.

296. W&C-TPL, 466; WSC 4, 475; Danchev and Todman, *War Diaries,* 300.

297. Danchev and Todman, *War Diaries,* 297.

298. Harriman and Abel, *Special Envoy,* 165–66.

299. Harriman and Abel, *Special Envoy,* 165–66; Danchev and Todman, *War Diaries,* 300; Dilks, *Diaries,* 470.

300. Bryant, *Tide,* 375.

301. Thompson, *Assignment: Churchill,* 268–69; WSC 4, 466; Harriman and Abel, *Special Envoy,* 159; George F. Kennan, *Memoirs: 1925–1950* (New York, 1967), 279 (Stalin's yellow eyes).

302. Harriman and Abel, *Special Envoy,* 152–53.

303. Dilks, *Diaries,* 471–72.

304. Harriman and Abel, *Special Envoy,* 157–59; Thompson, *Assignment: Churchill,* 268; Martin Gilbert, *Churchill: A Life* (New York, 1992), 727–30.

305. Harriman and Abel, *Special Envoy,* 161; WSC 4, 492; Dilks, *Diaries,* 472; Danchev and Todman, *War Diaries,* 301–3.

306. Harriman and Abel, *Special Envoy,* 163; WSC 4, 499.

307. WSCHCS, 6675.

308. GILBERT 7, 211–12.

309. Boatner, *Biographical Dictionary,* 380; Danchev and Todman, *War Diaries,* 438; WM/Averell Harriman, 8/22/80; Colville, *Fringes,* 622.

310. Danchev and Todman, *War Diaries,* 317; WSC 4, 509.

311. WSC 4, 63, 471; Panter-Downes, *War Notes,* 235–36.

312. WSC 4, 523; Danchev and Todman, *War Diaries,* 313.

313. Montgomery, *Memoirs,* 100, 107; Ronald Walker, *Alam Halfa and Alamein* (Wellington, NZ, 1966), 180 ("The swine will not attack").

314. Bryant, *Tide,* 412.

315. Danchev and Todman, *War Diaries,* 326; Bryant, *Tide,* 407.

316. Joesph P. Lash, *Eleanor and Franklin* (New York, 1971), 664, 666.

317. Butcher, *Eisenhower,* 20; Philip Ziegler, *London at War* (New York, 1995), 219; *Time,* 10/19/42, 33–34.

318. W&C-TPL, 459; TWY, 198.

319. Peter Catterall, ed., *The Macmillan Diaries: The Cabinet Years, 1950–57* (London, 2003), 383; Moran, *Diaries,* 692.

320. Joseph P. Lash, *Eleanor and Franklin* (New York, 1971), 600–64, 667.

321. TWY, 258; *Atlantic Monthly*, 3/65, 79–80.

322. Desmond Young, *Rommel: The Desert Fox* (New York, 1967), 147.

323. Collier, *War in the Desert*, 109–10; Danchev and Todman, *War Diaries*, 338.

324. Bryant, *Tide*, 417, 421.

325. Moran, *Diaries*, 83–84; Bryant, *Tide*, 412, 421.

326. Collier, *War in the Desert*, 115; Montgomery, *Memoirs*, 137–40.

327. Collier, *War in the Desert*, 115; William L. Shirer, *The Rise and Fall of the Third Reich: A History of Nazi Germany* (New York, 1960), 920; Young, *Rommel*, 251; TWY, 349.

328. WSC 4, 601; TWY, 257; WSCHCS, 6694.

329. Miller, *U-Boats*, 188.

330. Kenneth Young, *Churchill and Beaverbrook* (London, 1966), 248–50; *Time*, 11/30/42, 38.

331. Eisenhower, *Crusade*, 95.

332. WSC 4, 529

333. Bryant, *Tide*, 415; Winterbotham, *Ultra Secret*, 140; Danchev and Todman, *War Diaries*, 332.

334. Eisenhower, *Crusade*, 88; Grigg, *1943*, 41; Butcher, *Eisenhower*, 145.

335. Eisenhower, *Crusade*, 99–100.

336. Jean Lacouture, *De Gaulle* (New York, 1965), 121–22.

337. Winterbotham, *Ultra Secret*, 307; Bryant, *Tide*, 423; Boatner, *Biographical Dictionary*, 9.

338. Sarah Churchill, *Keep On Dancing* (London, 1981), 111; WM/Pamela Harriman, 8/22/80.

339. GILBERT 7, 251–52; Bryant, *Tide*, 423, 424; Morison, *Two-Ocean War*, 220–24.

340. Eisenhower, *Crusade*, 105; Butcher, *Eisenhower*, 178.

341. WSC 4, 616; Lochner, *Goebbels Diaries*, 235 (Dec. 7, 1941); A. M. Sperber, *Murrow: His Life and Times* (New York, 1986), 217.

342. Butcher, *Eisenhower*, 179.

343. Collier, *War in the Desert*, 149–50.

344. Morison, *Two-Ocean War*, 82.

345. Eisenhower, *Crusade*, 104; Farago, *Patton*, 202; Morison, *Two-Ocean War*, 225, 228.

346. Carlos D'Este, *Patton: A Genius for War* (New York, 1995), 431, 435; Bryant, *Tide*, 333.

347. Eisenhower, *Crusade*, 104–5; WSCHCS, 6729 (Darlan).

348. Farago, *Patton*, 200–201.

349. Shirer, *Rise and Fall*, 922–23.

350. Panter-Downes, *War Notes*, 253; WSC 4, 632; 651; C&R-TCC, 2:7; TWY, 266.

351. WSC 4, 647; Eden, *The Reckoning*, 414.

352. C&R-TCC, 2:90, 103, 104.

353. WSCHCS, 6695.

354. Joseph P. Lash, *Eleanor and Franklin* (New York, 1971), 664; Wheeler-Bennett, *Action This Day*, 74, 75; Danchev and Todman, *War Diaries*, 474; Colville, *Fringes*, 340.

355. Wheeler-Bennett, *Action This Day*, 74; Churchill, *English-Speaking Peoples*, 1: preface; Cv/2, 925–26.

356. WSCHCS, 6499.

357. Lady Mary Soames letter to PFR, 11/07 ("un-manned him").
358. GILBERT 7, 239–40; Dilks, *Diaries,* 488.
359. Soames, *Clementine,* 419; Danchev and Todman, *War Diaries,* 338.
360. Panter-Downes, *War Notes,* 251.
361. George Orwell, "England, Your England" (1941), in *A Collection of Essays by George Orwell* (Orlando, FL, 1970).
362. George F. Kennan, *Russia and the West Under Lenin and Stalin* (Boston, 1960), 349.
363. GILBERT 7, 217.
364. GILBERT 7, 255; Martin Gilbert, *Churchill's War Leadership* (New York, 2004), 50; Danchev and Todman, *War Diaries,* 207.
365. Danchev and Todman, *War Diaries,* 345.

Crosscurrents

1. Alex Danchev and Daniel Todman, eds., *Field Marshal Lord Alanbrooke: War Diaries 1939–1945* (Berkeley, 2003), 344; GILBERT 7, 270–71.
2. Richard Collier, *The War in the Desert* (New York, 1980), 159; Robert E. Sherwood, *Roosevelt and Hopkins: An Intimate History* (New York, 1948), 659; Danchev and Todman, *War Diaries,* 342, 346.
3. John Keegan, *The Second World War* (London, 1989), 297, 312, 317; GILBERT 7, 265.
4. Samuel Eliot Morison, *The Two-Ocean War* (Boston, 1963), 199–205.
5. Sherwood, *Roosevelt and Hopkins,* 656; Morison, *Two-Ocean War,* 208.
6. GILBERT 7, 271.
7. Keegan, *Second World War,* 234, 235.
8. Keegan, *Second World War,* 231, 234.
9. Harry C. Butcher, *My Three Years with Eisenhower* (New York, 1946), 198; Arthur Bryant, *The Turn of the Tide: A History of the War Years Based on the Diaries of Field-Marshal Lord Alanbrooke, 1939–1943* (New York, 1957), 428; C&R-TCC 2:48–49.
10. Sherwood, *Roosevelt and Hopkins,* 658.
11. Danchev and Todman, *War Diaries,* 346, 347; GILBERT 7, 298.
12. C&R-TCC, 1:669, 2:11.
13. Morison, *Two-Ocean War,* 238; Butcher, *Eisenhower,* 644.
14. James MacGregor Burns, *Roosevelt: The Soldier of Freedom, 1940–1945* (New York, 1970), 314.
15. Danchev and Todman, *War Diaries,* 346, 350; C&R-TCC, 1:552; Sherwood, *Roosevelt and Hopkins,* 588, 615; Butcher, *Eisenhower,* 644.
16. *NYT,* 11/12/42; GILBERT 7, 255; Bryant, *Tide,* 428; WSCHCS, 6698.
17. Sherwood, *Roosevelt and Hopkins,* 591; WSCHCS, 7160 ("intriguers").
18. Mark Mayo Boatner, *The Biographical Dictionary of World War II* (New York, 1999), 13–14; Bryant, *Tide,* 442.
19. Danchev and Todman, *War Diaries,* 342; Louis P. Lochner, *The Goebbels Diaries 1942–1943* (New York, 1948), 160, 352.
20. Lochner, *Goebbels Diaries,* 243, 245, 250.
21. Lochner, *Goebbels Diaries,* 251, 252.
22. Leonard Mosley, *Battle of Britain* (New York, 1980), 191; Philip Ziegler, *London at War* (New York, 1995), 224; *Time,* 12/28/42.
23. WSCHCS, 6714; *Time,* 12/7/42, 40.

24. Mollie Panter-Downes, *London War Notes, 1939–1945* (London, 1972), 254, 255, 257; GILBERT 7, 264.

25. WM/Pamela Harriman, 8/22/80.

26. WM/Pamela Harriman, 8/22/80.

27. Burns, *Roosevelt*, 315; C&R-TCC, 2:73.

28. C&R-TCC, 2:109; WSC 4, 667–70; W. Averell Harriman and Elie Abel, *Special Envoy to Churchill and Stalin: 1941–1946* (New York, 1975), 177–78.

29. Danchev and Todman, *War Diaries*, 351, 451.

30. Danchev and Todman, *War Diaries*, 346; Bryant, *Tide*, 443.

31. *Time*, 12/28/42.

32. *Daily Telegraph*, 5/11/07; WM/Jock Colville, 10/14/80; Mary Soames, *Clementine Churchill: The Biography of a Marriage* (New York, 2003), 69 (pink silk underclothes); Anthony Montague Browne, *Long Sunset* (London, 1996), 219–20.

33. Tom Hickman, *Churchill's Bodyguard* (London, 2005), 219–20.

34. Tizard memo, Imperial War Museum archives; WSC 4, 679–80.

35. John Colville, *The Churchillians* (London, 1981), 35.

36. Dwight D. Eisenhower, *Crusade in Europe* (New York, 1948), 61; WSC 4, 679.

37. GILBERT 6, 1205–6; John Colville, *The Fringes of Power: 10 Downing Street Diaries 1939–1955* (New York, 1985), 563.

38. GILBERT 7, 647.

39. Dean Acheson, *Present at the Creation: My Years in the State Department* (New York, 1969), 48, 49; Browne, *Long Sunset*, 127.

40. Acheson, *Present*, 48, 49, 52.

41. Brian Gardner, *Churchill in Power: As Seen by His Contemporaries* (Boston, 1970), 211.

42. GILBERT 7, 292–93.

43. TWY, 286, 264–65.

44. *Chambers Biographical Encyclopedia* (London, 1984), 135; GILBERT 7, 367; *NYT*, 1/8/39.

45. WSC 4, 930; Edward Stettinius Jr., *Lend Lease: Weapon for Victory* (New York, 1944), 254–55.

46. Harriman and Abel, *Special Envoy*, 180; Hastings Lionel Ismay, *The Memoirs of General Lord Ismay* (London, 1960), 284–85.

47. Lord Moran, *Churchill: Taken from the Diaries of Lord Moran* (Boston, 1966), 85–86; WSC 4, 674–75.

48. Harriman and Abel, *Special Envoy*, 180.

49. W&C-TPL, 471.

50. GILBERT 7, 273.

51. *NYT*, 1/25/43; Walter H. Thompson, *Assignment: Churchill* (New York, 1953), 276.

52. Anthony Eden, Earl of Avon, *The Reckoning: The Memoirs of Anthony Eden* (New York, 1965), 398; Danchev and Todman, *War Diaries*, 338, 356.

53. Sherwood, *Roosevelt and Hopkins*, 671–73; *Time*, 2/1/42, 11.

54. Danchev and Todman, *War Diaries*, 359; Sherwood, *Roosevelt and Hopkins*, 688–89.

55. Danchev and Todman, *War Diaries*, 359.

56. GILBERT 7, 417; WSCHCS, 6785.

57. Danchev and Todman, *War Diaries*, 361; Sherwood, *Roosevelt and Hopkins*, 689; Bryant, *Tide*, 454–55.

58. Danchev and Todman, *War Diaries*, 362; Morison, *Two-Ocean War*, 239; WSC 4, 692.

59. GILBERT 7, 277; Eden, *The Reckoning*, 416–17.

60. Eden, *The Reckoning*, 420, 421.

61. Moran, *Diaries*, 88; W&C-TPL, 475.

62. Sherwood, *Roosevelt and Hopkins*, 685.

63. The American Presidency Project, 17: Excerpts from the Press Conference for the American Society of Newspaper Editors, 2/12/43.

64. *Time*, 2/5/45; Rene De Chambrun, *I Saw France Fall* (New York, 1940), 100.

65. Sherwood, *Roosevelt and Hopkins*, 695–97; WSC 4, 687.

66. WM/Averell Harriman, 8/22/80.

67. Sherwood, *Roosevelt and Hopkins*, 695–97; WSC 4, 687–88.

68. Butcher, *Eisenhower*, 386; *Time*, 5/10/43; GILBERT 7, 581; WM/Averell Harriman, 8/22/80.

69. Moran, *Diaries*, 89–90, WSC 4, 94–95; GILBERT 7, 31.

70. Danchev and Todman, *War Diaries*, 368–69.

71. Danchev and Todman, *War Diaries*, 368–69; David Dilks, ed., *The Diaries of Sir Alexander Cadogan, 1938–1945* (New York, 1972), 508, 510–11.

72. Danchev and Todman, *War Diaries*, 375.

73. Danchev and Todman, *War Diaries*, 375; WSC 4, 710–11.

74. *Time Capsule 1943: A History of the Year Condensed from the Pages of* Time, edited by Henry R. Luce (New York, 1968), 121; *NYT*, 2/9/43; Keegan, *Second World War*, 236, 237, 458; William L. Shirer, *The Rise and Fall of the Third Reich: A History of Nazi Germany* (New York, 1960), 933.

75. *Time*, 2/1/43, 33–34.

76. Dilks, *Diaries*, 511; GILBERT 7, 318–19.

77. GILBERT 7, 318–19.

78. *Time Capsule 1943*, 121.

79. Butcher, *Eisenhower*, 691; Sherwood, 677; *Sunday Telegraph*, 2/9/64, 4.

80. Danchev and Todman, *War Diaries*, 378–79.

81. Dilks, *Diaries*, 513.

82. Butcher, *Eisenhower*, 255.

83. Danchev and Todman, *War Diaries*, 380.

84. Bryant, *Tide*, 474–75.

85. W&C-TPL, 477.

86. *NYT*, 2/3/43; *NYT*, 2/9/43.

87. John Keegan, *Winston Churchill* (New York, 2002), 161.

88. C&R-TCC, 2:138; GILBERT 7, 337.

89. Moran, *Diaries*, 95–96.

90. Collier, *War in the Desert*, 162–63; John Keegan, ed., *Churchill's Generals* (New York, 1991), 114; Eisenhower, *Crusade*, 145; Thomas E. Griess, ed., *The West Point Atlas for the Second World War, Europe and the Mediterranean* (New York, 2002), 41; Butcher, *Eisenhower*, 267.

91. WSC 4, 734; GILBERT 7, 348.

92. Butcher, *Eisenhower*, 273.

93. GILBERT 7, 348, 350; WSC 4, 736–37.

94. *Time*, 5/3/43; GILBERT 7, 343; WM/Averell Harriman, 8/22/80.

95. Collier, *War in the Desert*, 168; Keegan, *Second World War*, 342.

96. *Time*, 3/22/42, 26; Lochner, *Goebbels Diaries*, 262.

97. GILBERT 7, 338, 379.

98. GILBERT 7, 352.

99. C&R-TCC, 2:161.

100. Morison, *Two-Ocean War*, 242; Harriman and Abel, *Special Envoy*, 212.

101. Morison, *Two-Ocean War*, 242–44.

102. C&R-TCC, 2:177.

103. C&R-TCC, 2:180.

104. David Miller, *U-Boats* (New York, 2000), 123–24; Morison, *Two-Ocean War*, 242.

105. *Time*, 3/22/43.

106. *Time*, 3/22/43.

107. Collier, *War in the Desert*, 171–73; Eisenhower, *Crusade*, 151.

108. WM/Sir William Deakin, 1980.

109. WSCHCS, 6755; *Time*, 4/16/43, 18–19; Sherwood, *Roosevelt and Hopkins*, 716.

110. WSCHCS, 6756.

111. TWY, 286.

112. *Time*, 3/1/43, 30.

113. *Time*, 4/16/43; WSCHCS, 6771.

114. WSC 4, 769; Panter-Downes, *War Notes*, 274.

115. Eden, *The Reckoning*, 440.

116. Eden, *The Reckoning*, 438–39; Sherwood, *Roosevelt and Hopkins*, 714–15; Harriman and Abel, *Special Envoy*, 227.

117. Colville, *Fringes*, 245, 312.

118. Eden, *The Reckoning*, 432–33; George F. Kennan, *Russia and the West Under Lenin and Stalin* (Boston, 1960), 368; John Grigg, *1943: The Victory That Never Was* (New York, 1980), 156.

119. Kennan, *Russia and the West*, 355.

120. Harriman and Abel, *Special Envoy*, 227; Danchev and Todman, *War Diaries*, 390.

121. *Time*, 3/22/43, 15.

122. Kennan, *Russia and the West*, 359–63; Harriman and Abel, *Special Envoy*, 206–7.

123. Ziegler, *London at War*, 237.

124. Ziegler, *London at War*, 238; Ernie Pyle, *Brave Men* (New York, 1944), 324; PFR/Andy Rooney, 5/08.

125. *Time*, 3/15/43, 28–29; WM/Averell Harriman, 8/22/80; Harriman and Abel, *Special Envoy*, 165–66.

126. NYT, 3/11/25; WSC 4, 749.

127. WSC 4, 749.

128. WSC 4, 747, 751.

129. GILBERT 7, 370; Panter-Downes, *War Notes*, 279.

130. Lochner, *Goebbels Diaries*, 387–88; Panter-Downes, *War Notes*, 282.

131. Charles Eade, ed., *Churchill by His Contemporaries* (New York, 1954), 300–301; *Time*, 5/3/43.

132. Danchev and Todman, *War Diaries*, 393.

133. GILBERT 7, 383; Danchev and Todman, *War Diaries*, 394.

134. Martin Gilbert, *The Second World War: A Complete History* (London, 1989), 421.

135. *Time*, 3/29/43, 25; Lochner, *Goebbels Diaries*, 325.

136. *Time*, 3/15/43; GILBERT 7, 676.

137. Lochner, *Goebbels Diaries*, 318, 332.

138. Dilks, *Diaries*, 520; Lochner, *Goebbels Diaries*, 348; WSC 4, 759.
139. Dilks, *Diaries*, 526; C&R-TCC, 2:194, 199; WSC 4, 759–61.
140. *Time*, 2/7/44; *Time*, 7/17/72; WM/Averell Harriman, 8/22/80.
141. C&R-TCC, 2:389, 398–99; GILBERT 7, 665.
142. Burns, *Roosevelt*, 373–74; WSC 6, 141.
143. *Time*, 2/5/43.
144. WSC 4, 783.
145. Collier, *War in the Desert*, 173.
146. TWY, 291.
147. Keegan, *Second World War*, 343; Butcher, *Eisenhower*, 285.
148. *Time*, 4/17/42, 31; *Time*, 5/10/43, 30.
149. GILBERT 7, 417–18; C&R-TCC, 2:206.
150. *Time*, 4/19/43, 32.
151. Burns, *Roosevelt*, 367–68.
152. *Time*, 5/10/43, 25; Harriman and Abel, *Special Envoy*, 201; Ismay, *Memoirs*, 294.
153. Ismay, *Memoirs*, 294.
154. GILBERT 7, 397–98.
155. Lochner, *Goebbels Diaries*, 360.
156. Harriman and Abel, *Special Envoy*, 209.
157. Harriman and Abel, *Special Envoy*, 206, 209, 211; GILBERT 7, 397–98; Danchev and Todman, *War Diaries*, 400–401.
158. Harriman and Abel, *Special Envoy*, 205; WM/Averell Harriman, 8/22/80.
159. Harriman and Abel, *Special Envoy*, 202.
160. GILBERT 7, 418; Ismay, *Memoirs*, 295.
161. NYT, 5/13/43, 5/14/43.
162. Harriman and Abel, *Special Envoy*, 210.
163. WSCHCS, 6782.
164. Richard Collier, *Duce!* (New York, 1971), 195.
165. W&C-TPL, 479–80.
166. Danchev and Todman, *War Diaries*, 394; GILBERT 7, 399.
167. WSC 4, 786.
168. WSC 4, 786–87.
169. Danchev and Todman, *War Diaries*, 405; Morison, *Two-Ocean War*, 244.
170. Danchev and Todman, *War Diaries*, 405; Harriman and Abel, *Special Envoy*, 210–11; Bryant, *Tide*, 540–41.
171. Danchev and Todman, *War Diaries*, 420.
172. WSC 4, 803; Eden, *The Reckoning*, 439, 461.
173. WSC 4, 801; C&R-TCC, 2:210–11.
174. Eden, *The Reckoning*, 448–49.
175. WSC 4, 811.
176. GILBERT 7, 335.
177. Danchev and Todman, *War Diaries*, 412–13; WM/Sir Ian Jacob, 11/12/80.
178. Bryant, *Tide*, 528.
179. WSC 4, 831.
180. WSCHCS, 6784; Harriman and Abel, *Special Envoy*, 215.
181. Butcher, *Eisenhower*, 318, 322–23.
182. WSC 4, 816; Danchev and Todman, *War Diaries*, 415; Butcher, *Eisenhower*, 319, 325.
183. W&C-TPL, 484; C&R-TCC, 2:230–31.

184. Ismay, *Memoirs,* 301.
185. WSC 4, 830.
186. Panter-Downes, *War Notes,* 284.
187. WSC 4, 803; Harriman and Abel, *Special Envoy,* 212–13.
188. Harriman and Abel, *Special Envoy,* 212–13.
189. Collier, *Duce!,* 195–96.
190. Eisenhower, *Crusade,* 164–65.
191. Vincent Orange, *Tedder: Quietly in Command* (London, 2004), 225.
192. Eisenhower, *Crusade,* 171–72.
193. Panter-Downes, *War Notes,* 284.
194. Panter-Downes, *War Notes,* 285.
195. Eden, *The Reckoning,* 461.
196. Eden, *The Reckoning,* 452–53, 463; Jean Lacouture, *De Gaulle* (New York, 1965), 130.
197. Danchev and Todman, *War Diaries,* 427; WSC 4, 801; C&R-TCC, 2:208.
198. Panter-Downes, *War Notes,* 285.
199. C&R-TCC, 2:328, 341.
200. GILBERT 7, 443–44.
201. Bryant, *Tide,* 552; Butcher, *Eisenhower,* 373–74.
202. GILBERT 7, 444–45.
203. C&R-TCC, 2:331, 336, 345; GILBERT 7, 443–44.
204. C&R-TCC, 2:331–32.
205. Danchev and Todman, *War Diaries,* 429.
206. Collier, *Duce!,* 226–31.
207. Lochner, *Goebbels Diaries,* 407.
208. TWY, 308–9.
209. Danchev and Todman, *War Diaries,* 433; Lochner, *Goebbels Diaries,* 417.
210. Danchev and Todman, *War Diaries,* 433.
211. GILBERT 7, 463.
212. Soames, *Clementine,* 333, 334, 338, 446; Sherwood, *Roosevelt and Hopkins,* 831; Moran, *Diaries,* 112.
213. WSC 5, 67; Moran, *Diaries,* 114.
214. Danchev and Todman, *War Diaries,* 436–37.
215. Keegan, *Second World War,* 472; Lochner, *Goebbels Diaries,* 415.
216. GILBERT 7, 464–65; C&R-TCC, 2:357; WSCHCS, 6784.
217. WSCHCS, 6778; GILBERT 7, 437, 468; Dilks, *Diaries,* 551; *Time,* 12/13/43, 36.
218. Lochner, *Goebbels Diaries,* 383.
219. Lochner, *Goebbels Diaries,* 407; Bryant, *Tide,* 555–56; WSC 5, 520–21.
220. Lochner, *Goebbels Diaries,* 419.
221. Bryant, *Tide,* 556; GILBERT 6, 468; *Daily Mirror,* 8/9/43.
222. Lochner, *Goebbels Diaries,* 429, 442; Keegan, *Second World War,* 429.
223. Trumbull Higgins, *Winston Churchill and the Second Front* (New York, 1957), 205.
224. Danchev and Todman, *War Diaries,* 405.
225. Trumbull Higgins, *Winston Churchill and the Second Front* (New York, 1957), 203; Eisenhower, *Crusade,* 160; Robert E. Sherwood, *The White House Papers of Harry L. Hopkins* (London, 1949), 2:763; WSC 3, 673.
226. WSC 5, 74–75; Ismay, *Memoirs,* 309; Basil Collier, *The Second World War: A Military History from Munich to Hiroshima* (New York, 1967), 387.

227. Danchev and Todman, *War Diaries*, 437, 439; WSC 5, 75–76.
228. Eisenhower, *Crusade*, 199.
229. Danchev and Todman, *War Diaries*, 447.
230. Ismay, *Memoirs*, 310.
231. Danchev and Todman, *War Diaries*, 431–32.
232. *Time*, 8/30/43; *Time*, 11/8/43, 8.
233. WSC 5, 82; Kay Halle, ed., *Winston Churchill on America and Britain* (New York, 1970), 263.
234. WSCHCS, 6782; Thompson, *Assignment: Churchill*, 280.
235. GILBERT 7, 397; Ismay, *Memoirs*, 310–11.
236. Sherwood, *Roosevelt and Hopkins*, 758–59; Ismay, *Memoirs*, 311; Danchev and Todman, *War Diaries*, 442; Bryant, *Tide*, 587.
237. WSC 5, 85; Ismay, *Memoirs*, 311.
238. Sherwood, *Roosevelt and Hopkins*, 759.
239. Danchev and Todman, *War Diaries*, 441–42.
240. Barbara Tuchman, *Stilwell and the American Experience in China* (New York, 1971), 489–90; Leonard Mosley, *Marshall: Hero for Our Times* (New York, 1982), 301; Danchev and Todman, *War Diaries*, 445.
241. Danchev and Todman, *War Diaries*, 444–45; Noel Annan, "How Wrong Was Churchill?" *New York Review of Books*, 4/8/93.
242. WSC 5, 106–7; Butcher, *Eisenhower*, 394–95.
243. Albert Speer, *Inside the Third Reich: Memoirs by Albert Speer* (Macmillan, 1970), 368–69; GILBERT 7, 474; David Johnson, *V-1, V-2* (London, 1981), 26.
244. Danchev and Todman, *War Diaries*, 444–45.
245. C&R-TCC, 2:369, 370.
246. Eden, *The Reckoning*, 467–68.
247. Harriman and Abel, *Special Envoy*, 225–26.
248. Harriman and Abel, *Special Envoy*, 234–35; Ismay, *Memoirs*, 367; Dilks, *Diaries*, 584–85.
249. *Time*, 10/25/43, 21; Sherwood, *Roosevelt and Hopkins*, 755.
250. Eden, *The Reckoning*, 466, 470; Harriman and Abel, *Special Envoy*, 222; Dilks, *Diaries*, 560.
251. Eden, *The Reckoning*, 468–69.
252. Dilks, *Diaries*, 556; Soames, *Clementine*, 447.
253. Eden, *The Reckoning*, 468–69; Moran, *Diaries*, 122–23.
254. Eden, *The Reckoning*, 470; Danchev and Todman, *War Diaries*, 451, 452.
255. B. H. Liddell Hart, *History of the Second World War* (New York, 1971), 456; Viscount Montgomery of Alamein, *The Memoirs of Field Marshal Montgomery* (London, 1958), 190.
256. Danchev and Todman, *War Diaries*, 448.
257. Butcher, *Eisenhower*, 386–87; Liddell Hart, *History*, 446.
258. WSC 5, 128–29.
259. WM/Averell Harriman, 8/22/80; Richard Langworth, ed., *Churchill by Himself: The Definitive Collection of Quotations* (London, 2008), 553.
260. WSCHCS, 6824.
261. Sherwood, *Roosevelt and Hopkins*, 750; GILBERT 7, 494; *NYT*, 9/8/43.
262. Dilks, *Diaries*, 560; Moran, *Diaries*, 123, 126.
263. Lochner, *Goebbels Diaries*, 444, 460; Liddell Hart, *History*, 455, 458; Gardner, *Churchill in Power*, 224–25.

264. Keegan, *Second World War*, 351; WSC 5, 114; Kay Halle, *Irrepressible Churchill: Stories, Sayings and Impressions of Sir Winston Churchill* (London, 1985), 227; WSC 5, 224–25.
265. Liddell Hart, *History*, 467; WSC 5, 662.
266. WSC 5, 141–42.
267. Moran, *Diaries*, 127.
268. Gardner, *Churchill in Power*, 225; Dilks, *Diaries*, 559.
269. GILBERT 7, 494; Martin Gilbert, *Churchill: A Life* (New York, 1992), 753.
270. Soames, *Clementine*, 448.
271. GILBERT 7, 487.
272. Dilks, *Diaries*, 554–55; Jones, *Wizard War*, 474.
273. WSC 5, 117; Lochner, *Goebbels Diaries*, 460.
274. Lochner, *Goebbels Diaries*, 457.
275. WSC 5, 10, 12, 13; Morison, *Two-Ocean War*, 376.
276. Lochner, *Goebbels Diaries*, 466; Morison, *Two-Ocean War*, 244–46.
277. PFR/Dr. Porter Crowe (private, U.S. Army, 1942–1945), 6/06.
278. Ismay, *Memoirs*, 320.
279. WSCHCS, 6855; Langworth, *Churchill by Himself*, 427.
280. WM/Jock Colville, 10/14/80; Dilks, *Diaries*, 562.
281. Liddell Hart, *History*, 455; Danchev and Todman, *War Diaries*, 466.
282. Danchev and Todman, *War Diaries*, 458–59.
283. C&R-TCC, 2:501, 504, 506; Danchev and Todman, *War Diaries*, 467.
284. Danchev and Todman, *War Diaries*, 465–66.
285. Gilbert, *Churchill: A Life*, 755; Harold Macmillan, *War Diaries: Politics and War in the Mediterranean, January 1943–May 1945* (New York, 1984), 295; WSC 5, 224–25, 326.
286. Danchev and Todman, *War Diaries*, 463, 465.
287. GILBERT 7, 530–31; Danchev and Todman, *War Diaries*, 463, 465–66.
288. Keegan, *Second World War*, 319; C&R-TCC, 2:556–57.
289. Keegan, *Second World War*, 472–74; Keegan, *Atlas*, 106–7; Liddell Hart, *History*, 481, 492.
290. Lochner, *Goebbels Diaries*, 435, 461.
291. Lochner, *Goebbels Diaries*, 464, 468, 477–79, 483.
292. Lochner, *Goebbels Diaries*, 467; C&R-TCC, 2:559–60; Dilks, *Diaries*, 573.
293. *Time*, 3/15/42, 24; Harriman and Abel, *Special Envoy*, 234–35; Joseph E. Persico, *Edward R. Murrow: An American Original* (New York, 1988), 217–18.
294. Eden, *The Reckoning*, 481; C&R-TCC, 2:545–46.
295. WSC 5, 270; GILBERT 7, 571.
296. WSC 5, 242–43, 290.
297. Harriman and Abel, *Special Envoy*, 244; *Time*, 10/25/43, 29.
298. Harriman and Abel, *Special Envoy*, 244.
299. C&R-TCC, 2:562–63; Eisenhower, *Crusade*, 190, 199, 200, 213.
300. *Time*, 2/28/44.
301. Liddell Hart, *History*, 602–3; Keegan, *Second World War*, 426–27.
302. Duff Cooper, *Old Men Forget* (London, 1954), 317.
303. GILBERT 7, 557.
304. Lochner, *Goebbels Diaries*, 522–23.
305. Moran, *Diaries*, 138–39.

306. Macmillan, *War Diaries*, 401; Danchev and Todman, *War Diaries*, 472; W&C-TPL, 485.

307. Eisenhower, *Crusade*, 195, 198–99; Butcher, *Eisenhower*, 465.

308. Danchev and Todman, *War Diaries*, 475.

309. WSC 5, 328–29; Boatner, *Biographical Dictionary*, 509.

310. C&R-TCC, 2:597; WSC 5, 328–29; Danchev and Todman, *War Diaries*, 477–81.

311. W&C-TPL, 487; Danchev and Todman, *War Diaries*, 480; Sherwood, *Roosevelt and Hopkins*, 782.

312. Ismay, *Memoirs*, 312; Mosley, *Marshall*, 262; Tuchman, *Stilwell*, 516; WM/Viscount Antony Head, 8/6/80; Danchev and Todman, *War Diaries*, 480.

313. WSC 5, 341; Danchev and Todman, *War Diaries*, 478; Dilks, *Diaries*, 578, 580, 587; Sarah Churchill, *A Thread in the Tapestry* (London, 1967), 63.

314. Churchill, *Thread*, 62–63; Sarah Churchill, *Keep On Dancing* (London, 1981), 117.

315. Eden, *The Reckoning*, 491; Moran, *Diaries*, 141; Danchev and Todman, *War Diaries*, 482; Eisenhower, *Crusade*, 199.

316. Danchev and Todman, *War Diaries*, 482.

317. Dilks, *Diaries*, 580; WSC 5, 342; Thompson, *Assignment: Churchill*, 283; Danchev and Todman, *War Diaries*, 482; Ismay, *Memoirs*, 377.

318. Harriman and Abel, *Special Envoy*, 265–66.

319. Moran, *Diaries*, 144; Harriman and Abel, *Special Envoy*, 165–66; David Halberstam, *The Best and the Brightest* (New York, 1969), 81.

320. Dilks, *Diaries*, 579.

321. W&C-TPL, 487; WSC 5, 679–80.

322. Danchev and Todman, *War Diaries*, 483; Moran, *Diaries*, 143.

323. Danchev and Todman, *War Diaries*, 483.

324. Moran, *Diaries*, 145.

325. Moran, *Diaries*, 145–46; Ismay, *Memoirs*, 338.

326. Sherwood, *Roosevelt and Hopkins*, 781.

327. Arthur Bryant, *Triumph in the West, 1943–1946* (London, 1959), 89–91.

328. Harriman and Abel, *Special Envoy*, 266–67; Bryant, *Triumph*, 89–91; Moran, *Diaries*, 145.

329. Harriman and Abel, *Special Envoy*, 268–69.

330. WSC 5, 360.

331. Gilbert, *Churchill: A Life*, 761; Moran, *Diaries*, 208; WSCHCS, 6475.

332. WSC 5, 360.

333. Sherwood, *Roosevelt and Hopkins*, 796.

334. Eden, *The Reckoning*, 494–98; WSC 5, 361–62.

335. Dilks, *Diaries*, 400; WSC 5, 362.

336. WSC 5, 362.

337. John Wheeler-Bennett, *Action This Day: Working with Churchill* (London, 1968), 209–10; WM/Sir Ian Jacob, 11/12/80.

338. *Time*, 5/10/43; *Time*, 1/4/42; *Life*, 3/29/43.

339. Wheeler-Bennett, *Action This Day*, 209–10; WM/Sir Ian Jacob, 11/12/80; Dilks, *Diaries*, 580.

340. Sherwood, *Roosevelt and Hopkins*, 785–86.

341. WSC 5, 364; Jenkins, *Churchill*, 722.

342. WSC 5, 372–73.
343. Danchev and Todman, *War Diaries*, 485; Keegan, *Second World War*, 378.
344. Moran, *Diaries*, 148.
345. WSC 5, 373–74; Harriman and Abel, *Special Envoy*, 191.
346. Harriman and Abel, *Special Envoy*, 273–74; WSC 5, 374.
347. Dilks, *Diaries*, 578; Frances Perkins, *The Roosevelt I Knew* (New York, 1946), 84; PFR/Lady Mary Soames, telephone conversation, 4/07.
348. Moran, *Diaries*, 151; GILBERT 7, 583–84; WSC 5, 383–85.
349. WSC 3, 384.
350. WSC 5, 383–85; Harriman and Abel, *Special Envoy*, 176.
351. Danchev and Todman, *War Diaries*, 486–88.
352. Danchev and Todman, *War Diaries*, 486–88; Harriman and Abel, *Special Envoy*, 276–78; Sherwood, *Roosevelt and Hopkins*, 793.
353. WSC 5, 388.
354. WSC 5, 396–97; Eden, *The Reckoning*, 496–97.
355. WSC 5, 396–97; Eden, *The Reckoning*, 496–97.
356. Sherwood, *Roosevelt and Hopkins*, 797.
357. Sherwood, *Roosevelt and Hopkins*, 799; Dilks, *Diaries*, 586.
358. Milovan Djilas, *Conversations with Stalin* (Orlando, FL, 1962), 73, 115.
359. WSC 5, 384.
360. Martin Gilbert, *In Search of Churchill: A Historian's Journey* (New York, 1994), 5; *Time*, 12/27/43.
361. WM/Jock Colville, 10/14/80; Wheeler-Bennett, *Action This Day*, 96.

Pilot

1. W. Averell Harriman and Elie Abel, *Special Envoy to Churchill and Stalin: 1941–1946* (New York, 1975), 283; WSC 5, 405.
2. C&R-TCC, 2:709.
3. Louis P. Lochner, *The Goebbels Diaries, 1942–1943* (New York, 1948), 536.
4. Lochner, *Goebbels Diaries*, 536, 540–42.
5. Robert E. Sherwood, *Roosevelt and Hopkins: An Intimate History* (New York, 1948), 802.
6. Anthony Eden, Earl of Avon, *The Reckoning: The Memoirs of Anthony Eden* (New York, 1965), 499–500; WSC 5, 467–68, 473.
7. Eden, *The Reckoning*, 498–99; David Dilks, ed., *The Diaries of Sir Alexander Cadogan, 1938–1945* (New York, 1972), 584–85.
8. John Colville, *The Fringes of Power: 10 Downing Street Diaries 1939–1955* (New York, 1985), 550.
9. Dwight D. Eisenhower, *Crusade in Europe* (New York, 1948), 206; Sherwood, *Roosevelt and Hopkins*, 803; WSC 5, 419.
10. *Daily Mirror*, 12/29/43; *Daily Express*, 11/20/43.
11. B. H. Liddell Hart, *History of the Second World War* (New York, 1971), 569, 571.
12. Harry C. Butcher, *My Three Years with Eisenhower* (New York, 1946), 456.
13. Basil Collier, *The Second World War: A Military History from Munich to Hiroshima* (New York, 1967), 386; Alex Danchev and Daniel Todman, eds., *Field Marshal Lord Alanbrooke: War Diaries 1939–1945* (Berkeley, 2003), 492;

WSC 5, 419; Viscount Montgomery of Alamein, *The Memoirs of Field Marshal Montgomery* (London, 1958), 214–15.

14. Eisenhower, *Crusade,* 199.

15. *Time,* 1/3/44.

16. Danchev and Todman, *War Diaries,* 493–94; WSC 5, 420.

17. Danchev and Todman, *War Diaries,* 496; Lord Moran, *Churchill: Taken from the Diaries of Lord Moran* (Boston, 1966), 159.

18. *Time,* 12/27/43, 86; Lochner, *Goebbels Diaries,* 546.

19. Danchev and Todman, *War Diaries,* 497; Moran, *Diaries,* 161–62; Anthony Montague Browne, *Long Sunset* (London, 1996), 142; WM/Jock Colville, 10/14/80.

20. Colville, *Fringes,* 455–56.

21. Colville, *Fringes,* 455–56.

22. Harriman and Abel, *Special Envoy,* 283; Moran, *Diaries,* 57.

23. Mary Soames, *Clementine Churchill: The Biography of a Marriage* (New York, 2003), 456.

24. Eden, *The Reckoning,* 495; *Time,* 12/27/43, 46 (Smuts); John Wheeler-Bennett, *Action This Day: Working with Churchill* (London, 1968), 104.

25. Sarah Churchill, *A Thread in the Tapestry* (London, 1967), 69.

26. WSC 6, 427.

27. Butcher, *Eisenhower,* 465; Eisenhower, *Crusade,* 212–13; WSC 6, 427, 434.

28. C&R-TCC, 2:632–33; Collier, *Second World War,* 377.

29. WSCHCS, 6880.

30. Colville, *Fringes,* 456, 464; Harold Macmillan, *War Diaries: Politics and War in the Mediterranean, January 1943–May 1945* (New York, 1984), 331–32, 335; John Pearson, *The Private Lives of Winston Churchill* (New York, 1991), 415.

31. Colville, *Fringes,* 465; WM/Lady Diana Cooper, 10/20/80.

32. Macmillan, *War Diaries,* 335; C&R-TCC, 3:626.

33. Colville, *Fringes,* 459; Montgomery, *Memoirs,* 211.

34. Colville, *Fringes,* 459.

35. Martin Gilbert, *Churchill: A Life* (New York, 1992), 765; Butcher, *Eisenhower,* 65, 473; Moran, *Diaries,* 169–70; WSC 5, 444.

36. David Johnson, *V-1, V-2* (London, 1981), 32; Butcher, *Eisenhower,* 462.

37. PFR/Lady Mary Soames, letter of 9/3/07; Colville, *Fringes,* 463.

38. Duff Cooper, *Old Men Forget* (London, 1954), 315, 319.

39. Moran, *Diaries,* 169; WM/Lady Diana Cooper, 10/20/80.

40. Danchev and Todman, *War Diaries,* 510; Soames, *Clementine,* 461.

41. C&R-TCC, 3:641, 649; Sherwood, *Roosevelt and Hopkins,* 805–6.

42. GILBERT 7, 652.

43. Eden, *The Reckoning,* 503–6; GILBERT 7, 648.

44. TWY, 344.

45. Danchev and Todman, *War Diaries,* 514–15.

46. Eisenhower, *Crusade,* 194, 225.

47. Kay Summersby, *Eisenhower Was My Boss* (2008), 125–28; Mollie Panter-Downes, *London War Notes, 1939–1945* (London, 1972), 300.

48. TWY, 292, 353.

49. Panter-Downes, *War Notes,* 322.

50. Summersby, *Eisenhower,* 125–28; Butcher, *Eisenhower,* 14 (Edward Murrow quote); John Steinbeck, *Steinbeck: A Life in Letters* (New York, 1975), 264; Colville, *Fringes,* 517.

51. Montgomery, *Memoirs*, 219–20.

52. Montgomery, *Memoirs*, 211–12; David Eisenhower, *Eisenhower at War 1943–1945* (New York, 1991), 121; Danchev and Todman, *War Diaries*, 516, 518.

53. Danchev and Todman, *War Diaries*, 519; WSC 5, 692–93.

54. Danchev and Todman, *War Diaries*, 515; Colville, *Fringes*, 476; John Keegan, *The Second World War* (London, 1989), 357.

55. Keegan, *Second World War*, 356; John Keegan, ed., *Collins Atlas of World War II* (New York, 2006), 114–15; Thomas E. Griess, ed., *The West Point Atlas for the Second World War: Europe and the Mediterranean* (New York, 2002), 49.

56. Danchev and Todman, *War Diaries*, 518.

57. Ernie Pyle, *Brave Men* (New York, 1944), 258–65.

58. *Time*, 6/12/44, 10.

59. Panter-Downes, *War Notes*, 314; Colville, *Fringes*, 475, 479.

60. Panter-Downes, *War Notes*, 312; Keegan, *Atlas*, 114–15.

61. Colville, *Fringes*, 474; WSCHCS, 6883.

62. WSCHCS, 6883; Panter-Downes, *War Notes*, 314.

63. WSCHCS, 6893.

64. Colville, *Fringes*, 473; Dilks, *Diaries*, 592.

65. WSC 5, 549.

66. C&R-TCC, 2:649–50; Danchev and Todman, *War Diaries*, 518.

67. James MacGregor Burns, *Roosevelt: The Soldier of Freedom, 1940–1945* (New York, 1970), 483.

68. *Time*, 6/12/44; WSCHCS, 6996; Danchev and Todman, *War Diaries*, 534.

69. Danchev and Todman, *War Diaries*, 534.

70. WSC 5, 689.

71. TWY, 469.

72. Cv/3, 1087; Cv/2, 1120.

73. Macmillan, *War Diaries*, 335, 382; Colville, *Fringes*, 482; Duff Cooper, *Old Men Forget* (London, 1954), 324, 336.

74. Macmillan, *War Diaries*, 409.

75. Eden, *The Reckoning*, 520; C&R-TCC, 3:109.

76. Eisenhower, *Eisenhower at War*, 260.

77. C&R-TCC, 2:527, 744, 745, 749; GILBERT 7, 700.

78. Peter Clarke, *The Last Thousand Days of the British Empire* (New York, 2008), 27–29.

79. *Time*, 5/15/44, 85.

80. C&R-TCC, 3:3.

81. C&R-TCC, 3:3.

82. Dean Acheson, *Present at the Creation: My Years in the State Department* (New York, 1969), 133–34.

83. *Time*, 5/15/44.

84. C&R-TCC, 3:140.

85. Danchev and Todman, *War Diaries*, 516; Colville, *Fringes*, 473, 476, 478, 479; C&R-TCC, 3:69.

86. Collier, *Second World War*, 376; Keegan, *Second World War*, 354–56; GILBERT 7, 526.

87. *Time*, 1/24/44; *Time*, 2/28/44.

88. Colville, *Fringes*, 474.

89. TWY, 357–58; C&R-TCC, 3:78; Colville, *Fringes*, 480.

90. Eden, *The Reckoning*, 521, 523.

91. Dilks, *Diaries,* 612, 618, 621; Colville, *Fringes,* 484; Danchev and Todman, *War Diaries,* 541.

92. Dilks, *Diaries,* 612; Colville, *Fringes,* 484.

93. Colville, *Fringes,* 477; TWY, 347, 355.

94. WSC 5, 695–97; Panter-Downes, *War Notes,* 317–18.

95. WSC 5, 694; Eisenhower, *Eisenhower at War,* 134.

96. Danchev and Todman, *War Diaries,* 519, 521, 532, 533, 534, 547; Arthur Bryant, *The Turn of the Tide: A History of the War Years Based on the Diaries of Field-Marshal Lord Alanbrooke, 1939–1943* (New York, 1957), 171.

97. Danchev and Todman, *War Diaries,* xvii, 525.

98. Eden, *The Reckoning,* 575: Colville, *Fringes,* 489.

99. Moran, *Diaries,* 763.

100. WM/John Martin, 10/23/80.

101. WSCHCS, 6913; Panter-Downes, *War Notes,* 317; TWY, 356–57.

102. Colville, *Fringes,* 483; C&R-TCC, 3:54, 74.

103. Montgomery, *Memoirs,* 247; Butcher, *Eisenhower,* 545.

104. Colville, *Fringes,* 485; C&R-TCC, 3:87; Eisenhower, *Crusade,* 243.

105. Danchev and Todman, *War Diaries,* 536; Butcher, *Eisenhower,* 509.

106. Bryant, *Tide,* 180, 183.

107. Eisenhower, *Eisenhower at War,* 190–91; *Time,* 4/24/44.

108. Eisenhower, *Eisenhower at War,* 196, 206, 207, 209.

109. Eisenhower, *Eisenhower at War,* 206; C&R-TCC, 3:133; Dilks, *Diaries,* 621.

110. Eden, *The Reckoning,* 523–24; Eisenhower, *Crusade,* 232; C&R-TCC, 3:127.

111. Eden, *The Reckoning,* 524–25.

112. Dilks, *Diaries,* 624–25; Colville, *Fringes,* 487.

113. Liddell Hart, *History,* 535; Bryant, *Tide,* 181n.

114. Dilks, *Diaries,* 566.

115. Richard Rhodes, *The Making of the Atomic Bomb* (New York, 1986), 523–24; GILBERT 7, 715; R. V. Jones, *The Wizard War* (New York, 1978), 474.

116. Rhodes, *Atomic Bomb,* 528–30; Jones, *Wizard War,* 476.

117. Jones, *Wizard War,* 477.

118. GILBERT 7, 776; WM/Viscount Antony Head, 1980.

119. Panter-Downes, *War Notes,* 319, 323–24; Pyle, *Brave Men,* 375.

120. Eden, *The Reckoning,* 520.

121. Eisenhower, *Crusade,* 134, 245; Butcher, *Eisenhower,* 539; Max Hastings, *Winston's War: Churchill 1940–1945* (New York, 2010), 361.

122. Butcher, *Eisenhower,* 535; Hastings, *Winston's War,* 361.

123. Eisenhower, *Crusade,* 246; Butcher, *Eisenhower,* 552.

124. Butcher, *Eisenhower,* 552.

125. Eisenhower, *Crusade,* 222.

126. Collier, *Second World War,* 393–94.

127. Keegan, *Second World War,* 375; Collier, *Second World War,* 394; Eisenhower, *Eisenhower at War,* 218.

128. F. W. Winterbotham, *The Ultra Secret* (New York, 1974), 185.

129. Keegan, *Second World War,* 373, 379.

130. Eisenhower, *Crusade,* 257; Winterbotham, *Ultra Secret,* 193.

131. Trumbull Higgins, *Winston Churchill and the Second Front* (New York, 1957), 199–201 (on Clausewitz); Hastings Lionel Ismay, *The Memoirs of General Lord Ismay* (London, 1960), 269–70.

132. WSC 3, 659; for an examination of Churchill and Clausewitz, see Carl von Clausewitz, *On War* (London, 1982).

133. Eisenhower, *Eisenhower at War*, 245–48.

134. Danchev and Todman, *War Diaries*, 553; Eden, *The Reckoning*, 526.

135. Cooper, *Old Men*, 329.

136. Danchev and Todman, *War Diaries*, 553; Eden, *The Reckoning*, 526; Cooper, *Old Men*, 330; de Gaulle, *War Memoirs*, 556–57.

137. Burns, *Roosevelt*, 476; Keegan, *Second World War*, 361.

138. Eisenhower, *Crusade*, 250; Butcher, *Eisenhower*, 562; Eisenhower, *Eisenhower at War*, 250–51.

139. Eisenhower, *Eisenhower at War*, 252.

140. Milovan Djilas, *Conversations with Stalin* (Orlando, FL, 1962), 81.

141. Eisenhower, *Eisenhower at War*, 260–61.

142. Danchev and Todman, *War Diaries*, 554.

143. GILBERT 7, 794; WSC 5, 631; Soames, *Clementine*, 463.

144. Collier, *Second World War*, 398.

145. Keegan, *Second World War*, 378.

146. Keegan, *Second World War*, 382; Eisenhower, *Crusade*, 240.

147. Keegan, *Second World War*, 378–79; Pyle, *Brave Men*, 381.

148. Keegan, *Second World War*, 378–79; *Time*, 6/12/44, 19.

149. Sir John Keegan, *Six Armies in Normandy* (Penguin, 1983), 132–33.

150. Pyle, *Brave Men*, 382–83.

151. Colville, *Fringes*, 492.

152. W. G. F. Jackson, *"Overlord" Normandy 1944* (Newark, DE, 1979), 179.

153. WSCHCS, 6947–48.

154. GILBERT 7, 795; WSCHCS, 6947–48.

155. Panter-Downes, *War Notes*, 329.

156. C&R-TCC, 3:147, 160–61.

157. C&R-TCC, 3:116, 155.

Anchorage

1. *Time*, 6/12/45.

2. *Life*, 6/19/44.

3. C&R-TCC, 3:153.

4. WM/Lord Soames, 11/8/80.

5. Charles de Gaulle, *The Complete War Memoirs of Charles de Gaulle* (New York, 1964), 722.

6. Walter Lippmann, *U.S. War Aims* (Boston, 1944), 134–35; Ronald Steel, *Walter Lippmann and the American Century* (Boston, 1980), 404, 408–10; *Time*, 7/17/44, 99–100.

7. David Eisenhower, *Eisenhower at War 1943–1945* (New York, 1991), 286; Alex Danchev and Daniel Todman, eds., *Field Marshal Lord Alanbrooke: War Diaries 1939–1945* (Berkeley, 2003), 556; F. W. Winterbotham, *The Ultra Secret* (New York, 1974), 196–97.

8. WM/Averell Harriman, 8/22/80; Winston Churchill, *Marlborough: His Life and Times* (London, 1947), 2:259; John Wheeler-Bennett, *Action This Day: Working with Churchill* (London, 1968), 200–202.

9. Dwight D. Eisenhower, *Crusade in Europe* (New York, 1948), 267; Eisenhower, *Eisenhower at War*, 214; John Keegan, *The Second World War* (London, 1989), 392.

10. Danchev and Todman, *War Diaries*, 556, 563.

11. Danchev and Todman, *War Diaries*, 556, 563.

12. Arthur Bryant, *Triumph in the West, 1943–1946* (London, 1959), 216–17.

13. Danchev and Todman, *War Diaries*, 557.

14. David Johnson, *V-1, V-2* (London, 1981), 40–41.

15. Duff Cooper, *Old Men Forget* (London, 1954), 333; Danchev and Todman, *War Diaries*, 560.

16. WSCHCS, 6958, 6961, 6978, 6980; Danchev and Todman, *War Diaries*, 563.

17. Danchev and Todman, *War Diaries*, 561, 563; C&R-TCC, 3:219, 223.

18. Danchev and Todman, *War Diaries*, 565; C&R-TCC, 3:226.

19. Basil Collier, *The Second World War: A Military History from Munich to Hiroshima* (New York, 1967), 386; Keegan, *Second World War*, 479.

20. Keegan, *Second World War*, 479–80; Eisenhower, *Eisenhower at War*, 325, 336; Danchev and Todman, *War Diaries*, 532.

21. *Time*, 7/17/44, 17; Keegan, *Second World War*, 390; Eisenhower, *Eisenhower at War*, 330.

22. Eisenhower, *Eisenhower at War*, 351.

23. Keegan, *Second World War*, 480; WSC 6, 128.

24. Danchev and Todman, *War Diaries*, 572–73; Harry C. Butcher, *My Three Years with Eisenhower* (New York, 1946), 618; Bryant, *Triumph*, 241.

25. William L. Shirer, *The Rise and Fall of the Third Reich: A History of Nazi Germany* (New York, 1960), 1035–36; WSCHCS, 6997.

26. Mark Mayo Boatner, *The Biographical Dictionary of World War II* (New York, 1999), 284, 467.

27. C&R-TCC, 3:254, 266.

28. C&R-TCC, 3:258–59; WSC 3, 136, 139, 145.

29. Martin Gilbert, *Churchill and the Jews* (New York, 2007), 211–13; WSCHCS, 7376.

30. *Time*, 7/17/44, 18; Charles de Gaulle, *The Complete War Memoirs of Charles de Gaulle* (New York, 1964), 574–76.

31. De Gaulle, *War Memoirs*, 574–76; Jean Lacouture, *De Gaulle* (New York, 1965), 136.

32. Lacouture, *de Gaulle*, 144; de Gaulle, *War Memoirs*, 579.

33. Eisenhower, *Crusade*, 267; Butcher, *Eisenhower*, 620–21.

34. Butcher, *Eisenhower*, 634–35, 638; C&R-TCC, 3:267.

35. WSCHCS, 6980; Cooper, *Old Men*, 335–36.

36. WM/Graham Norton, 10/8/80; TWY, 397; W&C-TPL, 498, 501.

37. Danchev and Todman, *War Diaries*, 520–21; Harold Macmillan, *War Diaries: Politics and War in the Mediterranean, January 1943–May 1945* (New York, 1984), 474.

38. W&C-TPL, 501; C&R-TCC, 3:274, 279; GILBERT 7, 910.

39. GILBERT 7, 908–9; Macmillan, *War Diaries*, 507–9.

40. GILBERT 7, 910; WSC 6, 94, 122.

41. WM/Malcolm Muggeridge, 11/25/80.

42. WSC 6, 101.

43. De Gaulle, *War Memoirs*, 648.

44. B. H. Liddell Hart, *History of the Second World War* (New York, 1971), 558; Danchev and Todman, *War Diaries*, 585; Charles B. MacDonald, *The Siegfried Line Campaign* (Washington, DC, 1990), chaps. 36–42.

45. WSCHCS, 7001.
46. C&R-TCC, 3:310–11; Lord Moran, *Churchill: Taken from the Diaries of Lord Moran* (Boston, 1966), 185; John Colville, *The Fringes of Power: 10 Downing Street Diaries 1939–1955* (New York, 1985), 507.
47. Johnson, *V-1, V-2,* 115.
48. Colville, *Fringes,* 509–11.
49. Danchev and Todman, *War Diaries,* 589; Colville, *Fringes,* 509–11.
50. Danchev and Todman, *War Diaries,* 589.
51. Danchev and Todman, *War Diaries,* 593; Colville, *Fringes,* 511.
52. Colville, *Fringes,* 513.
53. *Time,* 9/11/44.
54. Moran, *Diaries,* 190–91, 193, 208.
55. Robert E. Sherwood, *Roosevelt and Hopkins: An Intimate History* (New York, 1948), 818.
56. Mary Soames, *Clementine Churchill: The Biography of a Marriage* (New York, 2003), 475.
57. *Time,* 9/25/44, 19; Sherwood, *Roosevelt and Hopkins,* 818; Colville, *Fringes,* 517–18.
58. Colville, *Fringes,* 517.
59. Colville, *Fringes,* 520; C&R-TCC, 3:341.
60. WSCHCS, 6991, 6996.
61. C&R-TCC, 3:341, 345; W. Averell Harriman and Elie Abel, *Special Envoy to Churchill and Stalin: 1941–1946* (New York, 1975), 354–55; Colville, *Fringes,* 523.
62. David Dilks, ed., *The Diaries of Sir Alexander Cadogan, 1938–1945* (New York, 1972), 682.
63. C&R-TCC, 3:345; WSC 6, 227–28; Harriman and Abel, *Special Envoy,* 356–58.
64. Harriman and Abel, *Special Envoy,* 360.
65. WSC 6, 239.
66. Anthony Eden, Earl of Avon, *The Reckoning: The Memoirs of Anthony Eden* (New York, 1965), 563.
67. Eden, *The Reckoning,* 564; W&C-TPL, 506.
68. WSCHCS, 7015–17.
69. WSCHCS, 7067.
70. Eden, *The Reckoning,* 562.
71. Dilks, *Diaries,* 679; de Gaulle, *War Memoirs,* 723.
72. De Gaulle, *War Memoirs,* 723–24; C&R-TCC, 3:391, 395; Eden, *The Reckoning,* 574.
73. CAD 689; Eden, *The Reckoning,* 577–78.
74. WSC 6, 289; C&R-TCC, 3:458; Colville, *Fringes,* 529; Eden, *The Reckoning,* 577–78.
75. Dilks, *Diaries,* 686; Colville, *Fringes,* 533, 535.
76. WSCHCS, 7052.
77. C&R-TCC, 3:451, 456.
78. Mollie Panter-Downes, *London War Notes, 1939–1945* (London, 1972), 353, 354; Dilks, *Diaries,* 689.
79. PFR/Lady Mary Soames, letter of 9/3/07; PFR/Winston S. Churchill, 5/04; Eden, *The Reckoning,* 580.

80. Danchev and Todman, *War Diaries*, 638.
81. Colville, *Fringes*, 540, 545; Eden, *The Reckoning*, 580–81.
82. Colville, *Fringes*, 540.
83. Colville, *Fringes*, 541; WSC 5, 315.
84. Macmillan, *War Diaries*, 620; Eden, *The Reckoning*, 582.
85. Harriman and Abel, *Special Envoy*, 390; C&R-TCC, 3:476–77.
86. Sherwood, *Roosevelt and Hopkins*, 847.
87. TWY, 428; Colville, *Fringes*, 547.
88. Colville, *Fringes*, 548–50.
89. Collier, *Second World War*, 454; Danchev and Todman, *War Diaries*, 641; Colville, *Fringes*, 548–50; C&R-TCC, 3:486, 488.
90. Colville, *Fringes*, 549; C&R-TCC, 3:488.
91. Colville, *Fringes*, 555; C&R-TCC, 3:492; Harriman and Abel, *Special Envoy*, 390.
92. Eden, *The Reckoning*, 554; Panter-Downes, *War Notes*, 349; Harriman and Abel, *Special Envoy*, 390; C&R-TCC, 3:593; Colville, *Fringes*, 551.
93. Danchev and Todman, *War Diaries*, 644.
94. Danchev and Todman, *War Diaries*, 644; Collier, *Second World War*, 457; Liddell Hart, *History*, 663.
95. Collier, *Second World War*, 457–58; Shirer, *Rise and Fall*, 1091.
96. Collier, *Second World War*, 457–58.
97. Keegan, *Second World War*, 511; Shirer, *Rise and Fall*, 1097.
98. Martin Gilbert, *The Second World War: A Complete History* (London, 1989), 634.
99. Keegan, *Second World War*, 510–12; Milovan Djilas, *Conversations with Stalin* (Orlando, FL, 1962), 95, 110.
100. Keegan, *Second World War*, 510–12; Shirer, *Rise and Fall*, 1098.
101. Moran, *Diaries*, 216; Hastings Lionel Ismay, *The Memoirs of General Lord Ismay* (London, 1960), 385.
102. Ismay, *Memoirs*, 384–85.
103. Harriman and Abel, *Special Envoy*, 390; Eden, *The Reckoning*, 592.
104. Ismay, *Memoirs*, 383; Collier, *Second World War*, 454; Soames, *Clementine*, 480.
105. TWY, 433.
106. Eden, *The Reckoning*, 592.
107. Djilas, *Conversations*, 106.
108. Dilks, *Diaries*, 702; Sarah Churchill, *Keep On Dancing* (London, 1981), 128; Jim Bishop, *FDR'S Last Year* (New York, 1974), 364.
109. Bishop, *FDR'S Last Year*, 320; Harriman and Abel, *Special Envoy*, 104.
110. WSC 6, 366.
111. WSC 6, 369, 372; Harriman and Abel, *Special Envoy*, 405.
112. WSC 6, 372; Bishop, *FDR'S Last Year*, 346; Eden, *The Reckoning*, 593.
113. Harriman and Abel, *Special Envoy*, 406; WSC 6, 385.
114. WSC 6, 390; Bishop, *FDR'S Last Year*, 364; Eden, *The Reckoning*, 594.
115. WSC 6, 354; Eden, *The Reckoning*, 390.
116. Bishop, *FDR'S Last Year*, 384, 412; Dilks, *Diaries*, 707–9; Moran, *Diaries*, 247.
117. WSCHCS, 7116–18.
118. WSC 6, 353, 397; Churchill, *Keep On Dancing*, 134.
119. John Rupert Colville, *Footprints in Time* (London, 1979), 179.
120. GILBERT 6, 1161, 1165.
121. Colville, *Fringes*, 562–63.
122. GILBERT 7, 1257.

123. Colville, *Fringes,* 570.
124. Colville, *Fringes,* 576.
125. Danchev and Todman, *War Diaries,* 677, 679; WSC 6, 416.
126. Collier, *Second World War,* 465–66; Viscount Montgomery of Alamein, *The Memoirs of Field Marshal Montgomery* (London, 1958), 330.
127. C&R-TCC, 3:572, 600.
128. Danchev and Todman, *War Diaries,* 679; Montgomery, *Memoirs,* 331.
129. Shirer, *Rise and Fall,* 1105–6.
130. C&R-TCC, 3:603, 605, 608.
131. Keegan, *Second World War,* 166–67; Collier, *Second World War,* 469.
132. Colville, *Fringes,* 564.
133. C&R-TCC, 3:588.
134. C&R-TCC, 3:596.
135. C&R-TCC, 3:610, 613.
136. C&R-TCC, 3:614.
137. GILBERT 7, 1291–1293; W&C-TPL, 526.
138. TWY, 449; WSCHCS, 7140.
139. Colville, *Fringes,* 591; Randolph S. Churchill, *Winston S. Churchill: Youth, 1874–1900* (Boston, 1996), 411.
140. Colville, *Fringes,* 591.
141. Gilbert, *Second World War,* 669; WSC 6, 516.
142. Keegan, *Second World War,* 521–22.
143. Shirer, *Rise and Fall,* 1112, 1117; Albert Speer, *Inside the Third Reich: Memoirs by Albert Speer* (Macmillan, 1970), 480.
144. Shirer, *Rise and Fall,* 1114; Speer, *Memoirs,* 473.
145. Speer, *Memoirs,* 480, 485.
146. David Rising, "Hitler's Final Days Described by Bodyguard," AP, 4/24/05.
147. WSC 6, 502–3; Harry S. Truman, *Year of Decisions* (Garden City, NY, 1955), 106–7.
148. Shirer, *Rise and Fall,* 1131, 1138; Danchev and Todman, *War Diaries,* 686.
149. GILBERT 7, 1318–22; Eden, *The Reckoning,* 615–16; Colville, *Fringes,* 592.
150. Djilas, *Conversations,* 114.
151. WSC 6, 506–7; Eden, *The Reckoning,* 616.
152. Colville, *Fringes,* 596–97.
153. Shirer, *Rise and Fall,* 1133.
154. Louis P. Lochner, *The Goebbels Diaries, 1942–1943* (New York, 1948), 254.
155. Shirer, *Rise and Fall,* 1136–37; Keegan, *Second World War,* 528.
156. Colville, *Fringes,* 588, 590; TWY, 453.
157. TWY, 453; *Time,* 5/14/45, 70.
158. Colville, *Fringes,* 596.
159. Rising, "Hitler's Final Days"; Keegan, *Second World War,* 532; Mary Shelley, the final line of *Frankenstein; Time,* 5/7/45, 45.
160. WSCHCS, 7150.
161. *Times,* 5/3/45.
162. Montgomery, *Memoirs,* 335–36.
163. Danchev and Todman, *War Diaries,* 687.
164. Dilks, *Diaries,* 736, 738.
165. Ismay, *Memoirs,* 394.
166. *Time,* 5/7/45, 37; Panter-Downes, *War Notes,* 373.
167. Ismay, *Memoirs,* 395; Danchev and Todman, *War Diaries,* 687–88.

168. *The Daily Telegraph,* 5/8/45; Panter-Downes, *War Notes,* 376.
169. Cooper, *Old Men,* 325.
170. TWY, 457.
171. Moran, *Diaries,* 269.
172. WSCHCS, 7154; TWY, 457.
173. WSCHCS, 7155; Panter-Downes, *War Notes,* 377–78.
174. WSCHCS, 7161; Danchev and Todman, *War Diaries,* 689.
175. Panter-Downes, *War Notes,* 378; TWY, 459.
176. WSCHCS, 7155.
177. Soames, *Clementine,* 375; GILBERT 7, 1351.
178. My wording recalls the translation by Emily Wilson (*Six Tragedies,* Oxford, 2010).

Ebb Tide

1. WSCHCS, 7214.
2. Alex Danchev and Daniel Todman, eds., *Field Marshal Lord Alanbrooke: War Diaries 1939–1945* (Berkeley, 2003), 691; John Keegan, *The Second World War* (London, 1989), 590–91.
3. Danchev and Todman, *War Diaries,* 691.
4. WSC 6, 571, 573.
5. WSC 6, 575.
6. WSC 6, 578.
7. Keegan, *Second World War,* 592–93; Dwight D. Eisenhower, *Crusade in Europe* (New York, 1948), 439.
8. Viscount Montgomery of Alamein, *The Memoirs of Field Marshal Montgomery* (London, 1958), 356; WSCHCS, 7214.
9. WSCHCS, 7163.
10. Danchev and Todman, *War Diaries,* 598, 690, 693, 695; Montgomery, *Memoirs,* 214–15.
11. Montgomery, *Memoirs,* 336; WSC 6, 570; GILBERT 8, 1070.
12. WSCHCS, 8612.
13. WSCHCS, 5694.
14. Anthony Eden, Earl of Avon, *The Reckoning: The Memoirs of Anthony Eden* (New York, 1965), 637.
15. GILBERT 7, 972.
16. WSCHCS, 7130–33.
17. J. B. Priestley, *Letter to a Returning Serviceman* (London, 1945); *Time,* 12/31/45, 92.
18. WSCHCS, 6764.
19. WSCHCS, 7133.
20. John Colville, *The Fringes of Power: 10 Downing Street Diaries 1939–1955* (New York, 1985), 606; WSCHCS, 7170.
21. WSCHCS, 7172–73.
22. Roy Jenkins, *Churchill: A Biography* (London, 2011), 793; Colville, *Fringes,* 606–7.
23. Brian Gardner, *Churchill in Power: As Seen by His Contemporaries* (Boston, 1970), 299; TWY, 472, 475.
24. Henry Pelling, *Winston Churchill* (Conshohocken, PA, 1999), 560; Eden, *The Reckoning,* 638.
25. Colville, *Fringes,* 611; Gardner, *Churchill in Power,* 301.

26. WSCHCS, 7201–3.

27. John Wheeler-Bennett, *Action This Day: Working with Churchill* (London, 1968), 72–73.

28. Colville, *Fringes*, 610; Lord Moran, *Churchill: Taken from the Diaries of Lord Moran* (Boston, 1966), 276, 279; W. Averell Harriman and Elie Abel, *Special Envoy to Churchill and Stalin: 1941–1946* (New York, 1975), 397 (Leahy offers odds).

29. Hansard 6/14/45; Colville, *Fringes*, 611.

30. WSC 6, 637–38; Anthony Montague Browne, *Long Sunset* (London, 1996), 127.

31. Eden, *The Reckoning*, 632, 634; David Dilks, ed., *The Diaries of Sir Alexander Cadogan, 1938–1945* (New York, 1972), 765.

32. Eden, *The Reckoning*, 634.

33. Moran, *Diaries*, 291.

34. WSC 6, 642.

35. Harry S. Truman, *Year of Decisions* (Garden City, NY, 1955), 416; WSC 6, 669–70; Georgii Konstantinovich Zhukov, *The Memoirs of Marshal Zhukov* (New York, 1971), 674–75.

36. Danchev and Todman, *War Diaries*, 709.

37. WSC 6, 632; *Time*, 8/27/45; *Herald Tribune Europe*, 12/29/06.

38. WSC 6, 674–75.

39. *Time*, 7/9/45; Mary Soames, *Clementine Churchill: The Biography of a Marriage* (New York, 2003), 508–9; WSC 6, 674–75; Gardner, *Churchill in Power*, 307.

40. Soames, *Clementine*, 509; Moran, *Diaries*, 307.

41. Gardner, *Churchill in Power*, 307–9.

42. NYT, 1/25/65.

43. Soames, *Clementine*, 509; TWY, 479.

44. Gardner, *Churchill in Power*, 308; WSCHCS, 7204.

45. Danchev and Todman, *War Diaries*, 713.

46. Eden, *The Reckoning*, 639.

47. Soames, *Clementine*, 511.

48. Soames, *Clementine*, 511; Colville, *Fringes*, 612.

49. WSCHCS, 7505, 7257.

50. WSCHCS, 7252–53.

51. Moran, *Diaries*, 335.

52. Robert E. Sherwood, *Roosevelt and Hopkins: An Intimate History* (New York, 1948), 922, 931.

53. Dean Acheson, *Present at the Creation: My Years in the State Department* (New York, 1969), 150–51.

54. George F. Kennan, *Memoirs: 1925–1950* (New York, 1967), 290–91, 546.

55. Montgomery, *Memoirs*, 362, 454.

56. Clark Clifford, *Counsel to the President* (New York, 1991), 100–2.

57. Clifford, *Counsel*, 100; Moran, *Diaries*, 303, 350.

58. Clifford, *Counsel*, 101.

59. WSCHCS, 7286.

60. WSCHCS, 7289.

61. WSCHCS, 7286; NYT, 3/6/46.

62. GILBERT 8, 204–6, 211.

63. Harriman and Abel, *Special Envoy*, 550–51.

64. WSCHCS, 7382.

65. WSCHCS, 7380–82.

66. GILBERT 8, 286–88; WSCHCS, 8016.

67. WSCHCS, 7367.

68. Clifford, *Counsel*, 131; Acheson, *Present*, 217–18.

69. Clifford, *Counsel*, 138; Moran, *Diaries*, 231; Leonard Mosley, *Marshall: Hero for Our Times* (New York, 1982), 396–98.

70. Acheson, *Present*, 212.

71. Mosley, *Marshall*, 402; Acheson, *Present*, 217–18; Clifford, *Counsel*, 145.

72. Soames, *Clementine*, 522.

73. Colville, *Fringes*, 648; John Colville, *The Churchillians* (London, 1981), 156.

74. Stewart Alsop, *Stay of Execution: A Sort of Memoir* (New York, 1973); WM/ Cecily ("Chips") Gemmell (German prisoners), 7/10/80.

75. WM/Cecily ("Chips") Gemmell, 7/10/80; Roy Howells, *Churchill's Last Years* (Philadelphia, 1965), 163–64; Diana Cooper, *The Light of Common Day* (London, 1959), 109.

76. GILBERT 8, 563n2; Soames, *Clementine*, 522, 564.

77. GILBERT 8, 244–45.

78. Soames, *Clementine*, 543.

79. Jenkins, *Churchill*, 824; GILBERT 8, 315.

80. W&C-TPL, 545; Moran, *Diaries*, 339.

81. Moran, *Diaries*, 341, 344, 356, 838.

82. Moran, *Diaries*, 336; *Herald Tribune Europe*, 12/29/06; WSCHCS, 7909.

83. *Time*, 6/13/45; *Time*, 9/3/45, back cover.

84. Nigel Nicolson, ed., *The Harold Nicolson Diaries: 1907–1963* (London, 2004), 346.

85. Nigel Nicolson, *Diaries*, 346; Colville, *Fringes*, 618–21.

86. Colville, *Fringes*, 620–21; GILBERT 8, 422.

87. WSCHCS, 7387–88, 7525.

88. WSCHCS, 7387.

89. Moran, *Diaries*, 336.

90. WSCHCS, 7314, 7328.

91. WSCHCS, 7376.

92. Moran, *Diaries*, 337–38.

93. WSCHCS, 7458.

94. WSCHCS, 7458.

95. WSCHCS, 7774–77.

96. WSCHCS, 7444.

97. WSCHCS, 7447, 7655 (Punjab massacres).

98. WSCHCS, 7673.

99. Martin Gilbert, *Churchill: A Life* (New York, 1992), 879.

100. WSCHCS, 7627.

101. Nigel Nicolson, *Diaries*, 361.

102. Nigel Nicolson, *Diaries*, 363.

103. David Reynolds, ed., *The Origins of the Cold War in Europe* (New Haven, CT, 1994), 13.

104. GILBERT 8, 467.

105. Colville, *Fringes*, 626.

106. *Time*, 1/5/50; WSCHCS, 7797.

107. WSCHCS, 8023.

108. Peter Catterall, ed., *The Macmillan Diaries: The Cabinet Years, 1950–57* (London, 2003), 17.

109. WSCHCS, 8023.
110. WSCHCS, 7793.
111. WSCHCS, 7653; WSCHCS, 7501.
112. WSCHCS, 7680.
113. GILBERT 8, 226; WM/Cecily ("Chips") Gemmell, 7/10/80.
114. WM/Cecily ("Chips") Gemmell, 7/10/80; WM/Jane (Portal) Williams, 1980.
115. WM/Jane (Portal) Williams, 1980.
116. Gilbert, *Churchill: A Life*, 887; WM/Jane (Portal) Williams, 1980; WM/Cecily ("Chips") Gemmell, 7/10/80.
117. WM/Cecily ("Chips") Gemmell, 7/10/80.
118. WM/Cecily ("Chips") Gemmell 7/10/80; WM/Jane (Portal) Williams, 1980.
119. Richard Langworth, ed., *Churchill by Himself: The Definitive Collection of Quotations* (London, 2008), 330; *Time*, 1/5/50.
120. James Reston, *Deadline: A Memoir* (New York, 1991).
121. W&C-TPL, 553.
122. Moran, *Diaries*, 358, 360.
123. Jenkins, *Churchill*, 829; WSCHCS, 7927.
124. WSCHCS, 7938, 7948.
125. WSCHCS, 7915.
126. WSCHCS, 7943.
127. WSCHCS, 7951.
128. Moran, *Diaries*, 359; GILBERT 8, 514.
129. WSCHCS, 7966.
130. Pelling, *Winston Churchill*, 642.
131. WSCHCS, 8236, 7897; Charles Eade, ed., *Churchill by His Contemporaries* (New York, 1954), 58, 301.
132. Eade, *Churchill*, 295.
133. WSCHCS, 8017, 8023, 8191; Jenkins, *Churchill*, 837.
134. WSCHCS, 8005, 8016, 8018, 8021, 8023, 8025, 8027.
135. WSCHCS, 8059.
136. WSCHCS, 8062.
137. WSCHCS, 7800.
138. WSCHCS, 8028, 8048; Catterall, *Macmillan Diaries*, 4.
139. WSCHCS, 8119, 8075.
140. WSCHCS, 8065; Nigel Nicolson, *Diaries*, 372.
141. WSCHCS, 8068–69.
142. Catterall, *Macmillan Diaries*, 6, 7, 10.
143. *Time*, 10/16/50, 10/30/50.
144. Acheson, *Present*, 467–69, 478; Catterall, *Macmillan Diaries*, 33.
145. Acheson, *Present*, 478, 481–82.
146. WSCHCS, 8109.
147. W&C-TPL, 558.
148. Nigel Nicolson, *Diaries*, 374.
149. Catterall, *Macmillan Diaries*, 33, 47, 49.
150. Catterall, *Macmillan Diaries*, 52.
151. Colville, *Fringes*, 759; Catterall, *Macmillan Diaries*, 63.
152. Catterall, *Macmillan Diaries*, 53–54, 90; WSCHCS, 8203, 8238, 8240.
153. Catterall, *Macmillan Diaries*, 90–91; Moran, *Diaries*, 360.
154. Soames, *Clementine*, 562; GILBERT 8, 631.

155. GILBERT 8, 638; WSCHCS, 7214.
156. WSCHCS, 8243.
157. WSCHCS, 8246.
158. WSCHCS, 8253.
159. Alec Cairncross, *The British Economy Since 1945*, 2nd ed. (Boston, 1995), 55–57, 102–3.
160. Moran, *Diaries*, 384; WSCHCS, 8256, 8261.
161. Violet Bonham Carter, *Winston Churchill: An Intimate Portrait* (New York, 1965), 4–5; WSCHCS, 8268.
162. WSCHCS, 8283.
163. Moran, *Diaries*, 366; Catterall, *Macmillan Diaries*, 105; WSCHCS, 8283.
164. Soames, *Clementine*, 429.
165. Hastings Lionel Ismay, *The Memoirs of General Lord Ismay* (London, 1960), 453.
166. Colville, *Fringes*, 631.
167. Catterall, *Macmillan Diaries*, 111, 114–15.
168. Acheson, *Present*, 608.
169. WSCHCS, 8307.
170. WSCHCS, 7793.
171. WSCHCS, 8307.
172. WSCHCS, 8297.
173. Nigel Nicolson, *Diaries*, 378; Acheson, *Present*, 595.
174. WSCHCS, 8329.
175. Colville, *Fringes*, 634, 641.
176. Moran, *Diaries*, 433, 436–37; Colville, *Fringes*, 675.
177. Moran, *Diaries*, 473.
178. Colville, *Fringes*, 672.
179. Moran, *Diaries*, 475.
180. Colville, *Fringes*, 673.
181. Moran, *Diaries*, 489.
182. WSCHCS, 8504–5.
183. Moran, *Diaries*, 527; Catterall, *Macmillan Diaries*, 272.
184. Moran, *Diaries*, 535–36; W&C-TPL, 575.
185. Soames, *Clementine*, 581.
186. Colville, *Fringes*, 683–85.
187. Moran, *Diaries*, 540.
188. Moran, *Diaries*, 557; WM/Malcolm Muggeridge, 11/25/80.
189. GILBERT 8, 593.
190. Moran, *Diaries*, 595.
191. Colville, *Fringes*, 692–93.
192. Colville, *Fringes*, 698; Catterall, *Macmillan Diaries*, 325.
193. GILBERT 8, 1036.
194. GILBERT 8, 1039.
195. Catterall, *Macmillan Diaries*, 343.
196. Colville, *Fringes*, 706–7.
197. Soames, *Clementine*, 446; GILBERT 8, 1073.
198. WSCHCS, 8609.
199. Sarah Churchill, *A Thread in the Tapestry* (London, 1967), 17.
200. GILBERT 8, 958; Colville, *Fringes*, 705.
201. WSCHCS, 8627.

202. WSCHCS, 8633.
203. *Sunday Times*, 3/6/55; GILBERT 8, 1101.
204. Colville, *Fringes*, 708.
205. Colville, *Fringes*, 708; Browne, *Long Sunset*, 148.
206. Soames, *Clementine*, 597.

Postscript

1. GILBERT 8, 1151.
2. Anthony Montague Browne, *Long Sunset* (London, 1996), 158; WM/Anthony Montague Browne, 11/15/80.
3. WM/A. J. P. Taylor, 12/1/80.
4. Browne, *Long Sunset,* 150; Mary Soames, *Clementine Churchill: The Biography of a Marriage* (New York, 2003), 545, 552.
5. Browne, *Long Sunset,* 152.
6. W&C-TPL, 628; Soames, *Clementine*, 633.
7. Soames, *Clementine*, 634–35.
8. Lord Moran, *Churchill: Taken from the Diaries of Lord Moran* (Boston, 1966), 840; Roy Howells, *Churchill's Last Years* (Philadelphia, 1965), 65.
9. Browne, *Long Sunset*, 302, 310.
10. *Atlantic Monthly*, 3/65.
11. Soames, *Clementine*, 619.
12. John Colville, *The Fringes of Power: 10 Downing Street Diaries 1939–1955* (New York, 1985), 720–21.
13. Moran, *Diaries*, 756; Colville, *Fringes*, 51, 721.
14. W&C-TPL, 621.
15. Nigel Nicolson, ed., *The Harold Nicolson Diaries: 1907–1963* (London, 2004), 412; *NYT*, 11/5/57.
16. John Colville, *The Churchillians* (London, 1981), 214.
17. Howells, *Churchill's Last Years*, 64; Browne, *Long Sunset,* 142; WM/Anthony Montague Browne, 11/15/80.
18. WSCHCS, 8687.
19. Moran, *Diaries*, 562; *Time*, 6/13/60.
20. Randolph S. Churchill, *Winston S. Churchill: Youth, 1874–1900* (Boston, 1996), 257; Winston S. Churchill, *Memories and Adventures* (London, 1989), 115.
21. Browne, *Long Sunset*, 278, 288–89.
22. Browne, *Long Sunset*, 312.
23. Kay Halle, *Irrepressible Churchill: Stories, Sayings and Impressions of Sir Winston Churchill* (London, 1985), 325; Browne, *Long Sunset*, 312.
24. Moran, *Diaries*, 566; Howells, *Churchill's Last Years*, 128, 140.
25. Howells, *Churchill's Last Years*, 194–95.
26. Moran, *Diaries*, 840–41; Colville, *Churchillians*, 19.
27. The Editors of the Viking Press, *The Churchill Years 1874-1965, with foreword by Lord Butler of Saffron Walden* (London, 1965), 240–42.
28. Moran, *Diaries*, 842.

COPYRIGHT ACKNOWLEDGMENTS

INDEX

The abbreviation WSC in subheadings refers to Winston Churchill. Italic page numbers refer to figures.

376, 382, 570; and Holland, 51, 60; and London immunity, 152; loss of air superiority, 739; and Malta, 248, 285, 348; and Mediterranean Sea, 111; mismanagement of, 144; and possible German invasion of Britain, 125–26, 130, 132–33, 137; and radar, 138; reconnaissance planes, 194, 376, 797, 828; reports of air superiority over Britain, 142–43, 159; and Royal Navy, 131, 132, 140, 141; and Russian front, 706; and second front in Europe, 603; and shortwave navigational beam, 168, 169, 170–71, 194, 213, 214, 801; Signals Service, 144; transfer of prisoners to Britain, 98, 109; WSC's reports on, 12; and X-Gerat beam, 214–17, 232

Lütjens, Günther, 357–59, 363, 364
Luxembourg: German threat to, 41, 44; and NATO, 983; and spring of 1940, 37; Wehrmacht's attack on, 48, 61
Lyttelton, Oliver, 279, 281, 654–55, 920, 1010, 1017

MacArthur, Douglas: drawing Japanese to, 627; Eisenhower as chief of staff, 240, 540; and Korean War, 1004–05; and march to Tokyo, 714; and Pearl Harbor attack, 425; and Philippines, 240, 425, 465, 496, 714, 872, 899; and presidential politics, 821–22; reinforcements for, 535, 662, 670, 679, 681, 686; reputation of, 465; safety of, 467; on WSC, 596
Macaulay, Thomas, 16, 24–25, 117, 422, 499, 910, 1041
MacDonald, Malcolm, 59, 221–22
Mack, Henry, 102–03
Mackenzie King, William Lyon, 156, 458, 709
Maclean, Donald, 1027
Maclean, Fitzroy, 33, 787
Macmillan, Harold: and Attlee, 1007–08; and Beaverbrook, 310; on Churchill-Roosevelt relationship, 633, 639; and Conservative Party, 996, 1009, 1010; and Council of Europe, 1003, 1004; on John Cunningham, 748; and de Gaulle, 787–88, 808; and

election of 1945, 949; and election of 1951, 1013; as foreign secretary, 1037; and Greece, 888, 889; and Italy, 867; and Mediterranean Sea, 737, 866; as minister of housing, 1017; and North Africa, 590; and possible German invasion of Britain, 125; on Pucheu, 807–08; and united Europe, 986; on WSC, 1026, 1030; WSC's recommendation for prime minister, 1043; WSC's relationship with, 866; and WSC's resignation as prime minister, 1030–31
MacNeice, Louis, 350
Madagascar, 520, 584, 605
Maeterlinck, Maurice, 6
Maginot, André, 44
Maginot Line: German threat to, 42, 44–45, 46, 61; and Wehrmacht, 241; and Weygand, 90
Magna Carta, 177, 237
Mahan, A. T., 428, 428n
Maisky, Ivan, 326, 607, 691
Majdanek, 873
Malaya: independence of, 981; and Roosevelt, 754; and rubber, 466, 481, 548, 1008, 1010; and tin, 481; and Wavell, 453; and WSC's strategy, 478, 481. See also Singapore
Malay Peninsula: and Japanese strategy, 405, 407, 424, 456, 481; and Singapore, 403, 427, 428, 482
Malenkov, Georgy, 1022, 1026, 1029
Maletti, Pietro, 230
Malta: as British possession, 111–12; and Alan Brooke, 550, 556, 606; civilian casualties, 348; and Eisenhower, 692; food supplies of, 518, 556, 571; and Hitler's strategy, 518, 522, 556, 593, 606; and Italian navy, 248; and Kesselring, 606; and Luftwaffe, 248, 285, 348, 479, 518, 747; Mussolini's air raids on, 112, 248, 348; relief efforts for, 562–63, 580, 606; and Royal Air Force, 348, 354, 606; submarines based at, 606; and U.S. Navy, 501; and WSC's strategy, 112, 206, 247, 248, 348, 349, 606; WSC's visit to, 747, 748
Malthus, Thomas, 6
Manchester Guardian, 619, 654, 658, 885

ABOUT THE AUTHORS

WILLIAM MANCHESTER was a hugely successful popular historian and renowned biographer. In addition to the first two volumes of *The Last Lion,* his books include *Goodbye, Darkness, A World Lit Only by Fire, The Glory and the Dream, The Arms of Krupp, American Caesar,* and *The Death of a President,* as well as assorted works of journalism. He was awarded the National Humanities Medal and the Abraham Lincoln Literary Award. He passed away in 2004.

PAUL REID is an award-winning journalist. In late 2003, Manchester, in failing health, asked him to complete *The Last Lion: Defender of the Realm.* He lives in North Carolina.

"Masterful . . . The collaboration completes the Churchill portrait in a seamless manner, combining the detailed research, sharp analysis and sparkling prose that readers of the first two volumes have come to expect."
—**Associated Press**

Spanning the years 1940 to 1965, *The Last Lion: Defender of the Realm* begins shortly after Winston Churchill became prime minister—when Great Britain stood alone against the overwhelming might of Nazi Germany. In brilliant prose and informed by decades of research, William Manchester and Paul Reid recount how Churchill organized his nation's military response and defense, convinced FDR to support the cause, and personified the "never surrender" ethos that helped win the war. We witness Churchill, driven from office, warning the world of the coming Soviet menace. And after his triumphant return to 10 Downing Street, we follow him as he pursues his final policy goal: a summit with President Dwight Eisenhower and Soviet leaders. In conclusion, we experience Churchill's last years, when he faces the end of his life with the same courage he brought to every battle he ever fought.

"Matches the outstanding quality of biographers such as Robert Caro and Edmund Morris, joining this elite bank of writers who devote their lives to one subject."
—*Publishers Weekly* (starred review)

"Brilliant and beautiful, evocative." —*The Boston Globe*

"A must-read finale for those who loved Manchester's first two books."
—*USA Today*

"The final volume is . . . majestic and inspiring." —*People*

"One of the most thorough treatments of Churchill so far produced."
—*Library Journal* (starred review)

**NAMED ONE OF THE BEST BOOKS OF THE YEAR BY
THE WALL STREET JOURNAL • THE DAILY BEAST
ST. LOUIS POST-DISPATCH • THE DAYTONA BEACH
NEWS-JOURNAL • KIRKUS REVIEWS • BOOKLIST**

A BANTAM BOOKS TRADE PAPERBACK

Cover design: Matt Tanner
Cover photo: © Central Press/Getty Images

For exclusive content from our authors and books, sign up for the Random Reads newsletter. BantamDell.com

U.S.A. $20.00 CANADA $23.00

ISBN 978-0-345-54863-4

BIOGRAPHY

52000

EAN

9 780345 548634